T0407144

THE OXFORD HANDBOOK OF

NINETEENTH-CENTURY WOMEN PHILOSOPHERS IN THE GERMAN TRADITION

THE OXFORD HANDBOOK OF

NINETEENTH-CENTURY WOMEN PHILOSOPHERS IN THE GERMAN TRADITION

Edited by
KRISTIN GJESDAL
and
DALIA NASSAR

OXFORD
UNIVERSITY PRESS

OXFORD
UNIVERSITY PRESS

Oxford University Press is a department of the University of Oxford. It furthers
the University's objective of excellence in research, scholarship, and education
by publishing worldwide. Oxford is a registered trade mark of Oxford University
Press in the UK and certain other countries.

Published in the United States of America by Oxford University Press
198 Madison Avenue, New York, NY 10016, United States of America.

Library of Congress Cataloging-in-Publication Data
Names: Gjesdal, Kristin, author. | Nassar, Dalia, author.
Title: The Oxford handbook of nineteenth-century women philosophers in the
German tradition / Kristin Gjesdal and Dalia Nassar.
Description: New York, NY : Oxford University Press, [2024] |
Series: Oxford handbooks series | Includes bibliographical references and index. |
Identifiers: LCCN 2023017636 (print) | LCCN 2023017637 (ebook) |
ISBN 9780190066239 (hardback) | ISBN 9780190066253 (epub) |
ISBN 9780190066260
Subjects: LCSH: Women philosophers—Germany—History—19th century. | Women
philosophers—Germany—Biography | Philosophy, German—19th century.
Classification: LCC B2743 .G54 2024 (print) | LCC B2743 (ebook) |
DDC 193.082—dc23/eng/20231113
LC record available at https://lccn.loc.gov/2023017636
LC ebook record available at https://lccn.loc.gov/2023017637

DOI: 10.1093/oxfordhb/9780190066239.001.0001

Printed by Sheridan Books, Inc., United States of America

Contents

PART II MOVEMENTS

PART III TOPICS

Contributors

Frederick C. Beiser was born and raised in the US and studied in the UK at Oriel and Wolfson Colleges, Oxford. He lived in Berlin for many years, receiving stipends from the Fritz Thyssen Stiftung and Humboldt Stiftung. He has taught at many universities in the US—Penn, Yale, Harvard, Colorado, and Wisconsin—and is currently Professor of Philosophy at Syracuse University, New York. Beiser is the author of many books on German philosophy. In November 2015 he was awarded the Bundesverdienstkreuz by the then president of Germany, Joachim Gauck.

Karen de Bruin is Professor of French and Director of the Honors Program at the University of Rhode Island. Her scholarly work focuses primarily on the writings of Germaine de Staël. She has also published on French Huguenot culture in the Cape Colony, memorialization theory and practice, and the professional practice of running a successful languages department. Finally, she has actively engaged in the public humanities through projects such as a radio show dedicated to "all things aesthetic in the state of Rhode Island," and art exhibitions and public memorials on the history of slavery in Rhode Island. She has been awarded the Honor of Chevalier des Palmes académiques by the French government.

Andrew Cooper is Associate Professor of Philosophy at the University of Warwick. His research interests include modern European philosophy, philosophy of science, and aesthetics. He is author of *The Tragedy of Philosophy: Kant's Critique of Judgment and the Project of Aesthetics* (State University of New York Press, 2016) and *Kant and the Transformation of Natural History* (Oxford University Press, 2023), and has recently completed an English edition of Amalia Holst's major work, *On the Vocation of Woman to Higher Intellectual Education* (Oxford University Press, 2023).

Daniel O. Dahlstrom is John R. Silber Professor of Philosophy at Boston University. He is the author of numerous essays and monographs on the work of German philosophers from the eighteenth through the twentieth centuries, including *The Heidegger Dictionary* (2013; expanded 2nd edition: 2023) and *Identity, Authenticity, and Humility* (2017). In addition to editing *Philosophy of Mind and Phenomenology: Conceptual and Empirical Approaches* (2015) and *Kant and His German Contemporaries* (2018) and coediting *Heidegger on Logic* (2023), he has also translated major works and lectures of Mendelssohn, Hamann, Schiller, Hegel, Husserl, and Heidegger.

Adrian Daub is professor of German Studies and Comparative Literature at Stanford University, where he directs the Michelle R. Clayman Institute for Gender Research. He has published widely on German intellectual history and questions of gender and sexuality. His books include *Uncivil Unions* (University of Chicago Press, 2012), *Tristan's Shadow* (University of Chicago Press, 2013), *Four-Handed Monsters* (Oxford University Press, 2014), and *The Dynastic Imagination* (University of Chicago Press, 2020). His book *What the Ballad Knows,* on ballad aesthetics, memorial culture, and German nationalism, came out with Oxford University Press in 2022.

Corey W. Dyck is Professor of Philosophy at Western University. He is the author of *Kant and Rational Psychology* (Oxford University Press, 2014), the translator and editor of *Early Modern German Philosophy: 1690–1750* (Oxford University Press, 2019), and editor of the collection *Women and Philosophy in Eighteenth-Century Germany* (Oxford University Press, 2021). Among his current projects is a monograph, *The First Fifty Years of German Metaphysics*, which considers the history of German philosophy in the first half of the eighteenth century. He has held visiting positions at the University of Oxford, the Johannes Gutenberg University of Mainz, and the Martin Luther University of Halle-Wittenberg, where he was also recently an Alexander von Humboldt research fellow.

Anna Ezekiel received her PhD in philosophy from McGill University in 2013. Since then, she has worked as an independent historian of philosophy and translator focused on post-Kantian German philosophy and the work of historical women philosophers. Her main research project is the rediscovery and interpretation of the philosophical thought of Romantic writer Karoline von Günderrode (1780–1806). Anna's translations of Günderrode's writings appear in *Poetic Fragments* (State University of New York Press, 2016), *Philosophical Fragments* (Oxford University Press, forthcoming), and *Women Philosophers in the Long 19th Century: The German Tradition*, edited by Dalia Nassar and Kristin Gjesdal (Oxford University Press, 2021). For the latter volume, she also translated philosophical writings by Bettina Brentano-von Arnim, Hedwig Dohm, Lou Salomé, Edith Stein, Gerda Walther, Clara Zetkin, and Rosa Luxemburg.

Renata Fuchs is an instructor of German in the Department of Modern Languages and Classics at the University of Alabama. She received her PhD from the University of Illinois at Urbana Champaign in 2014. Her research areas include the Romantic era, contemporary German literature, German-Jewish literature, Holocaust studies, women's writing, visual arts, and translation studies. Her recent translation project focuses on memoirs and diaries by Leon Najberg, the last survivor of the Warsaw Ghetto Uprising. Her latest article contributes to the critical interest of intermediality between literature, art, and religion and its relationshop to the new digital technologies in the context of Rahel Levin Varnhagen's letters and Caspar David Friedrich's paitings.

Kristin Gjesdal is professor of philosophy at Temple University. Her scholarship covers philosophy of interpretation (hermeneutics), philosophy of art, phenomenology, and modern European philosophy. With Dalia Nassar, she is the editor of the recently published *Women Philosophers in the Long Nineteenth Century: The German Tradition* and this volume. She is the editor and coeditor of seven further volumes in her areas of research. Her monographs include *Gadamer and the Legacy of German Idealism* (Cambridge University Press, 2009); *Herder's Hermeneutics* (Cambridge University Press, 2017/2019), and *The Drama of History: Ibsen, Hegel, Nietzsche* (Oxford University Press, 2021).

Daniela Katharina Helbig is senior lecturer in history and philosophy of science at the University of Sydney. Her research is primarily concerned with the history of technology and its implications for the theory of history. She mainly works in the context of modern European intellectual history and science, but also has a long-standing interest in science and technology in the Middle East.

Paula Keller is a Junior Research Fellow at Jesus College in the University of Cambridge. Prior to coming to Cambridge, she did graduate work at Humboldt University in Berlin, where she became fascinated by Rahel Varnhagen's writings. Paula has worked on the history of philosophy, with a particular interest in women in philosophy and the idea of formation in Classical German Philosophy. She also has an interest in contemporary feminist philosophy and epistemology, having published on feminist understandings of objectification and the philosophy of testimony. In her PhD dissertation, on the possibility of epistemic emancipation in an unjust world, she linked her systematic and historical interests.

Katherina Kinzel is Assistant Professor in the History of Modern Philosophy at Utrecht University. She did her PhD at the University of Vienna and has been a Fulbright Scholar at Temple University. She works on German philosophy in the nineteenth and early twentieth centuries, focusing in particular on the history of "scientific philosophy" from Kant to the Vienna Circle. She has published on neo-Kantianism, hermeneutics, and historicism.

Katharina Teresa Kraus is Miller Associate Professor of Philosophy at Johns Hopkins University, Baltimore, USA. She is the author of *Kant on Self-Knowledge and Self-Formation* (Cambridge University Press, 2020) as well as numerous articles on Kant's theoretical philosophy in journals such as *Studies in History and Philosophy of Science*, *European Journal of Philosophy*, and *Noûs*.

Samantha Matherne is the Gardner Cowles Associate Professor of Humanities in the Philosophy Department at Harvard University. She is the author of *Seeing More: Kant's Theory of Imagination* (Oxford University Press, forthcoming), *Cassirer* (2021) for the Routledge Philosophers series, a coauthor (with Dominic McIver Lopes, Mohan Matthen, and Bence Nanay) of *The Geography of Taste* (Oxford University Press, forthcoming), and the editor of the first English translation of Edith Landmann-Kalischer's philosophy, *Edith Landmann-Kalischer: Essays on Art, Aesthetics, and Value* (translated by Daniel O. Dahlstrom, Oxford University Press, forthcoming).

Ronny Miron is Professor of Philosophy at Bar Ilan University, Israel. Her research is focused on post-Kantian idealism, existentialism, phenomenology, and hermeneutics, as well as current Jewish thought. She employs an interdisciplinary perspective combining the aforementioned traditions. She is the author of *Karl Jaspers: From Selfhood to Being* (2012), *The Desire for Metaphysics: Selected Papers on Karl Jaspers* (2014), *The Angel of Jewish History: The Image of the Jewish Past in the Twentieth Century* (2014), *Husserl and Other Phenomenologists* (2018, edited book), and *Hedwig Conrad-Martius, The Phenomenological Gateway to Reality* (Springer, 2021).

Cat Moir Wolfe is Honorary Senior Lecturer in German at the University of Sydney where she was Department Chair until 2020. She is the author of *Ernst Bloch's Speculative Materialism: Ontology, Epistemology, Politics* (Haymarket Books, 2019), and has published widely on critical theory, Marxism, and German intellectual history. In 2020, she left academic and is currently retraining as a psychologist at the University of Toulouse Jean-Jaurès, France.

Lydia Moland is John D. and Catherine T. MacArthur Professor of Philosophy at Colby College in Waterville, Maine. She has published extensively on Hegel and German Idealism, including *Hegel's Aesthetics: The Art of Idealism* (Oxford University Press, 2019). Her biography of the American abolitionist Lydia Maria Child was published in 2022 by University of Chicago Press. Together with Alison Stone, she is editing the *Oxford Handbook of American and British Women Philosophers in the Nineteenth Century*. She is the recipient of awards from the National Endowment for the Humanities, the American Council of Learned Societies, the Deutscher Akademischer Austauschdienst, and the American Academy in Berlin.

Dermot Moran is the Inaugural Holder of the Joseph Chair in Catholic Philosophy, Boston College. He was previously Professor of Philosophy (Logic and Metaphysics) at University College Dublin. He is a Member of the Royal Irish Academy and Institut International de Philosophie. Publications include: *Introduction to Phenomenology* (2000), *Edmund Husserl: Founder of Phenomenology* (2005), *Husserl's Crisis of the European Sciences and Transcendental Phenomenology* (2012), and, coauthored with Joseph Cohen, *Husserl Dictionary* (2012). Edited works include: Husserl's *Logical Investigations*, 2 vols. (Routledge, 2001), *The Shorter Logical Investigations*, *The Phenomenology Reader*, coedited with Tim Mooney (Routledge, 2002), *Phenomenology. Critical Concepts in Philosophy*, 5 vols., coedited with Lester E. Embree (Routledge, 2004), *The Routledge Companion to Twentieth Century Philosophy* (Routledge, 2008); *The Phenomenology of Embodied Subjectivity* (Springer 2014), coedited with Rasmus Thybo Jensen; *Empathy, Sociality, and Personhood. Essays on Edith Stein's Phenomenological Investigations*, coedited with Elisa Magrì (Springer, 2017); *Conscious Thinking and Cognitive Phenomenology*, coedited with Marta Jorba (Routledge, 2018); and, with Anya Daly, Fred Cummins, and James Jardine, *Perception and the Inhuman Gaze. Perspectives from Philosophy, Phenomenology, and the Sciences* (Routledge, 2020).

Dalia Nassar is Associate Professor of Philosophy at the University of Sydney. Her research sits at the intersection of the history of philosophy (especially nineteenth-century German philosophy), environmental philosophy, ethics, and aesthetics. She is the author of two monographs, most recently, *Romantic Empiricism: Nature, Art, and Ecology* *from Herder to Humboldt* (Oxford University Press, 2022) and is coeditor with Kristin Gjesdal of *Women Philosophers in the Long Nineteenth Century: The German Tradition*.

Karen Ng is Associate Professor of Philosophy at Vanderbilt University. She specializes in nineteenth- and twentieth-century German philosophy, with particular emphases on Hegel, German idealism, and Frankfurt School Critical Theory. She is the author of *Hegel's Concept of Life: Self-Consciousness, Freedom, Logic* (Oxford University Press, 2020).

Rodney K. B. Parker is an historian of phenomenology at King's University College at Western University. Prior to this he was an assistant professor at Dominican University College, postdoctoral researcher at the Center for the History of Women Philosophers and Scientists, University of Paderborn, adjunct professor at Western University, and visiting scholar at the Husserl Archives, KU Leuven. He is the editor of *The Idealism-Realism Debate Among Edmund Husserl's Early Followers and Critics* (Springer, 2021).

Lydia Patton is a philosopher of science and historian of philosophy, whose research has appeared in journals including *Studies in History and Philosophy of Modern Physics*, *Synthese*, *Monist*, *History and Philosophy of Logic*, and *Historia Mathematica*, and in dozens of edited collections. Recent work focuses on gravitational wave astronomy, scientific method, Kantian philosophy of science, and the history of philosophy of science. Patton is the editor of *HOPOS* and coeditor with Walter Ott of the collection *Laws of Nature*.

Anne Pollok is a historian of philosophy (eighteenth- to twentieth-century aesthetics and philosophy of culture). She was teaching assistant at Stanford University (2008–2013) and Associate Professor of Philosophy at the University of South Carolina, Columbia (2013–2020). In 2020 she joined the faculty at Gutenberg University Mainz, Germany, as research assistant. Numerous essays on Moses Mendelssohn, Ernst Cassirer, and women philosophers of the eighteenth and nineteenth centuries and her book *Facets of Humankind: On Moses Mendelssohn's Anthropology* (Felix Meiner, 2010) attest to her research interests.

Dorothy Rogers is a professor at Montclair State University, where she teaches courses on philosophy, pedagogy, and feminism in the Department of Educational Foundations and serves on the advisory board of the Gender Studies Program. Her primary research interest is in feminist social and political thought and women in the history of philosophy, particularly in the Americas in the nineteenth and early twentieth centuries. She has authored and edited a number of books and articles on women in the early idealist movement in the US. In her most recent volumes, *Women Philosophers: Education and Activism in Nineteenth-Century America* and *Women Philosophers: Entering Academia (1880–1920)* (Bloomsbury, 2020 and 2021), she made intentional efforts to explore women's philosophy and activism across lines of race and culture in North America. She is currently working with Joel Katzav and Krist Vaesen on a project to recover the writings of American women philosophers in the early twentieth century in a collection titled *Knowledge, Mind and Reality* (Springer, forthcoming). She is a member of the Society for the Advancement of American Philosophy, the Society for the Study of Women Philosophers, the Society of Women in Philosophy, and the Society for US Intellectual History.

Joe Saunders is Associate Professor of Philosophy at Durham University. His research focuses on ethics and agency in Kant and the post-Kantian tradition, but he also has interests in media ethics and the philosophy of love. His article "Kant and the Problem of Recognition" won the 2015 Robert Papazian Prize.

Sandra Shapshay is Professor of Philosophy at Hunter College and the Graduate Center, City University of New York. Her research areas are ethics and aesthetics in nineteenth-century philosophy, with focus on Schopenhauer and Kant, as well as contemporary environmental aesthetics and philosophy of art. She is the author of numerous publications on Schopenhauer, including *Reconstructing Schopenhauer's Ethics: Hope, Compassion, and Animal Welfare* (Oxford University Press, 2019), and is the editor of the *Palgrave Schopenhauer Handbook* (2018). Recent publications in aesthetics include "A Two-Tiered Theory of the Sublime" (*British Journal of Aesthetics*, 2021), "What Is the Monumental?" (*Journal of Aesthetics and Art Criticism*, 2021), and "Contemporary Environmental Aesthetics and the Neglect of the Sublime" (*British Journal of Aesthetics*, 2013).

Alison Stone is Professor of Philosophy at Lancaster University. She has published widely on German idealism, feminist philosophy, and related topics. Her most recent books are *Nature, Ethics and Gender in German Romanticism and Idealism* (Rowman & Littlefield, 2018) and *Being Born: Birth and Philosophy* (Oxford University Press, 2019). She is currently working on women's contributions to nineteenth-century British philosophy. As part of this she is editing *Frances Power Cobbe: Essential Writings* for the Oxford New Histories of Philosophy series and coediting with Lydia Moland the *Oxford Handbook of American and British Women Philosophers in the Nineteenth Century*.

Clinton Tolley is Professor of Philosophy at the University of California, San Diego. He is the author of numerous essays on modern German philosophy, including work on Kant, Hegel, and Husserl. He is also the coeditor and cotranslator (with Sandra Lapointe) of *The New Anti-Kant* (Palgrave, 2014).

Giulia Valpione is a postdoctoral researcher at the University of Padua, having previously studied at the University of Jena. She has conducted research in Italy, Germany, France, and Brazil. She has published articles in several languages on the political philosophy of German Romanticism, Kant, and Hume. She has also written on Salomon Maimon's philosophy. She is the editor of *L'Homme et la nature dans le romantisme allemand. Politique, critique et esthétique* (LIT Verlag, 2021). She is also Editor-in-Chief, together with Laure Cahen-Maurel, of the online, open-access, peer-reviewed international journal of philosophical Romanticism *Symphilosophie*. She is writing a monograph on the influence of the natural sciences on the political thought of German Romanticism.

Íngrid Vendrell Ferran is Heisenberg Fellow at the Goethe University Frankfurt. She received her PhD from the Free University in Berlin and her Habilitation from the Friedrich Schiller University of Jena. Her research interests are phenomenology, philosophy of mind, epistemology, and aesthetics. She is the author of two books: *Die Emotionen. Gefühle in der realistischen Phänomenologie* (Akademie, 2008) and *Die Vielfalt der Erkenntnis. Eine Analyse des kognitiven Werts der Literatur* (Mentis, 2018).

Ulrike Wagner is an Assistant Professor (*wissenschaftliche Mitarbeiterin*) at Bard College Berlin and director of the German Studies Program. She received her PhD in German and Comparative Literature from Columbia University and an MA in North American Studies and German Literature from the Free University of Berlin. Her current research interests concern the global history of the humanities and practices of philology; relations between German Romanticism and American Transcendentalism in the context of religious debates, historicism, classicism, and aesthetics; German-Jewish women writers; and feminist theory and practice. She is co-editor of *Herder and Religion* and has published, among others, in *Literature and Theology*, the *Hegel Bulletin*, *Herder Jahrbuch/Herder Yearbook*, and *Amerikastudien/American Studies*. She is currently completing a monograph, titled *Transatlantic Philology: Emerson, Germaine de Staël, Fuller, Herder, and the Critical Practices of Reordering Religion and Antiquity*.

Jason Maurice Yonover is Desai Family Postdoctoral Research Associate at Princeton University. He has research interests in the German-language legacy of Spinoza's philosophy and in political thought broadly. His work has been funded by the German Academic Exchange Service (DAAD), the US Department of Education, the American Philosophical Association, and other institutions. It has most recently been published in the *British Journal for the History of Philosophy*, the *European Journal of Philosophy*, and the Blackwell *Companion to Spinoza*.

EDITORS' INTRODUCTION

FROM Plato and Aristotle, via Descartes and Hume, to Kant, Schiller, Hegel, Schopenhauer, Kierkegaard, Nietzsche, and beyond—more often than not, the canon we read in standard philosophy classes is a list of one male after the other. It is as if—until very recently—only men have the capacity for philosophical thinking. But is this really the case? Is it really the case that a wider range of thinkers only began to contribute to philosophy in the last few decades? And if this is *not* the case, why have we only heard about the men?

These are questions that students often ask when they first discover philosophy. By the time of their graduation, however, the questions are usually forgotten. Explicit or implicit, the assumption is that philosophers are male, and that women philosophers did not exist before Simone de Beauvoir and Hannah Arendt. Hence, the study of the philosophical tradition has become largely equated with the study of works by and on European male philosophers. Handbooks, companions, and readers reflect this image and, intentionally or not, serve to bolster it. Indeed, to some extent the endorsement of this assumption has been a hallmark of the fully socialized philosopher.

Over the last decade, however, this story has begun to fall apart. As part of a wider effort to recover marginalized and overlooked figures in philosophy, this volume is dedicated to retrieving the works of women philosophers in the long nineteenth century—from the French Revolution to World War I. Its focus is on women writing in explicit relation to the rich and formative German-language tradition and the movements that emerged within it, including the late Enlightenment, romanticism, idealism, socialism, neo-Kantianism, and phenomenology.

It is crucial to note, right from the beginning, that our focus on the German tradition is not meant to be culturally, linguistically, or historically essentialist. Instead, it is chosen because it captures many of the great movements of modern philosophy and also because the focus on the German-language context (as well as its interlocutors and reception) keeps the door open for future handbooks and readers dedicated to the works of women and other marginalized groups in philosophy in other language-areas, cultures, and time periods.

Pursuing such a focus, this volume builds on previous research in the history of philosophy, in particular, early modern philosophy. Over the last two decades, research in the area of early modern philosophy has uncovered women's vast contributions to philosophical discourses and schools from Cartesianism and Newtonianism in France to the reemergence of Platonism in Britain, and the rise of rationalism in Germany.[1] Early modern women published in a number of subfields, including metaphysics, epistemology, and aesthetics, and contributed to debates surrounding education, gender equality, and suffrage.[2] Moreover, in their time, works by early modern women were read, discussed, and often played a key role in shaping the movements of which they were part. Today we can safely say that it would be impossible to fully appreciate the philosophical transformations of the sixteenth and seventeenth centuries without a proper grasp of the interventions of women philosophers. In other words, a history of early modern philosophy that fails to consider the contributions of women would be historically and systematically incomplete.

The same, we believe, holds for the long nineteenth century. This is the century of Kant and Hegel, of Marx, Schopenhauer, and Nietzsche: figures whose works often trigger a lifelong interest in philosophy. But it is also a century in which women developed new and pathbreaking positions in philosophy—making the period even more fascinating. Who were these women? What kinds of questions did they ask? And how did they philosophize? It is the goal of this *Handbook* to begin to answer these questions and thus further advance a more inclusive and richer understanding of the period and the philosophical resources it offers.

Women in nineteenth-century philosophy have received considerably less attention than women in earlier and later periods.[3] This might lead us to think that there are few or no women philosophers in this period. But women did not cease to think, write, and publish philosophy after the early modern period. The opposite is in fact the case. Over the long nineteenth century, women within the German-speaking context were deeply

---

[1] Excellent introductions to early modern women philosophers, especially those within the French and British contexts, can be found in Eileen O'Neill, "Early Modern Women Philosophers and the History of Philosophy," *Hypatia* 20, no. 3 (2015): 185–197, and Jacqueline Broad, *Women Philosophers of the Seventeenth Century* (Cambridge: Cambridge University Press, 2002). There are, in addition, several edited volumes which include essays by contemporary scholars on women philosophers of the period. See, for instance, *Early Modern Women on Metaphysics*, ed. Emily Thomas (Cambridge: Cambridge University Press, 2018), and *Routledge Handbook of Women and Early Modern Philosophy*, ed. Karen Detlefsen and Lisa Shapiro (New York: Routledge, 2023). On the German context, see *Women and Philosophy in Eighteenth-Century Germany*, ed. Corey W. Dyck (Oxford: Oxford University Press, 2021). For an overview of women's contributions to the history of western philosophy more generally, see *A History of Women Philosophers*, 4 vols, ed. Mary Ellen Waithe (Dordrecht: Springer, 1988–93).

[2] See, for instance, Karen Green, *A History of Women's Political Thought in Europe, 1700–1800* (Cambridge: Cambridge University Press, 2014), and *Women and Liberty, 1600–1800: Philosophical Essays*, ed. Jacqueline Broad and Karen Green (Cambridge: Cambridge University Press, 2017).

[3] This position is explicitly articulated or conveyed in the form of editorial choices. For example: under the title *Feminist History of Philosophy*, a recent volume edited by Eileen O'Neill and Marcy P. Lascano includes contributions on Wollstonecraft and Beauvoir, but does not cover the rich legacy of women philosophers in the German tradition in the period between Wollstonecraft and existentialism. See *Feminist History of Philosophy: The Recovery and Evaluation of Women's Philosophical Thought*, ed. Eileen O'Neill and Marcy P. Lascano (Cham, Switzerland: Springer, 2019).

and directly engaged in philosophical debates, often shaping discussions in innovative and radical ways. A few examples can illustrate our point and at the same time offer a first introduction to the figures and movements covered in this volume.

In the transition from the eighteenth to the nineteenth century, philosophers focused on the question of the "human vocation"—of what a human being is "for," what we, as free yet finite beings, should aspire to achieve and what we can hope for. Kant, Fichte, and Schleiermacher (among others) contributed to this debate, as did a number of women. After all, the category of potentially free but finite beings is not limited to male subjects.[4] However, many male philosophers argued that women do not possess the acumen for intellectual achievement and have no role to play in public life, the university included.[5] In short, they derided the very idea of women having a "vocation" outside the home and family. Women philosophers begged to differ.

Amalia Holst, for instance, focused on the relationship between women's vocation and education. In her book *On the Vocation of Women to Higher Intellectual Education* (1802), Holst argues that women cannot be excluded from seeking to achieve their vocations on account of gendered "duties." Specifically, Holst contends that the widespread view regarding women's place within society is in fact not rationally justified. This is because, she argues, power relations play a significant role in determining social roles. In other words, already in the first decade of the nineteenth century, Holst put forward the view, later associated with twentieth-century critics of the Enlightenment, that we cannot isolate the pursuit of reason from social and political questions. Nor can we determine the human vocation independently of gender, history, and power relations.

Holst was not the only woman who participated in the discussion of the human vocation. Sophie Mereau takes up the question through a critical examination of Fichte's contribution. She analyzes Fichte's conception of autonomy and its relation to marriage, situating it in the social and political reality in which she (and Fichte) lived. Mereau finds significant potential in Fichte's philosophy but also recognizes its limitations—it applies only to those members of humanity who can concretely realize their freedom. Mereau thus argues that unless both members of a marriage are recognized as free, we cannot

---

[4] For the purpose of this volume, we mostly follow nineteenth-century binary gender descriptions, though the category of "women" sometimes included what we today would speak of as women, trans, and nonbinary people.

[5] The fact that many women were publishing philosophical texts of high quality did, however, require some male philosophers to alter their argumentative strategies. Thus rather than blandly claiming that women simply did not possess certain capacities, they relied on the argument that women have the duty to subordinate these capacities to their roles as wives and mothers. In a review of Amalia Holst's *On the Vocation of Women to Higher Intellectual Education* (1802), for instance, the author writes, "even if one grants the capacity for higher intellectual development to the female sex, as soon as one considerts its calling as wife, housewife, and mother, it is impossible to concede that it is destined to rise to the scientific culture of men." Unsigned review of *On the Vocation of Woman to Higher Intellectual Education* (by Amalia Holst), *Kaiserlich-Priviligirte hamburgische Neue Zeitung* 34, February 1802, no. 27, reprinted in Amalia Holst, *On the Vocation of Woman to Higher Intellectual Education*, ed. Andrew Cooper (Oxford: Oxford University Press, 2023), 140–141. We thank Andrew Cooper for bringing this to our attention.

speak of the ideal marriage that Fichte (some years after Mereau) goes on to describe as "a union [that] is necessarily and completely determined by nature and reason."[6]

Another woman philosopher who criticizes Fichte is Karoline von Günderrode. Like Mereau, Günderrode points out that Fichte's focus on subjective freedom presupposes a world in which everyone—men and women—can realize their freedom. But while Mereau remains focused on human relations, Günderrode extends her discussion of the human vocation to include our moral obligations to the larger natural world. Her distinctive moral position—which departs from the mainstream idealist position—prefigures twentieth-century environmental ethics.[7]

In these varying ways, Holst, Mereau, and Günderrode furnished some of the most original and relevant arguments about the human vocation. But they were certainly not alone. Women supplied key premises, arguments, and perspectives to other debates and areas within nineteenth-century philosophy.

Germaine de Staël, also in the early part of the period, offers a penetrating account of passions and politics, and analyzes, with sharpness and originality, the phenomenon of political fanaticism.[8] She also discusses tolerance, liberalism, cosmopolitanism, and republicanism. In addition to political philosophy, she contributes to metaphysics, philosophy of art, and ethics. Staël was a pioneer in situating philosophy within a larger historical, political, and natural context.

Later in the century, women continued to question the premises and presuppositions of their male contemporaries. This is particularly evident in socialism, where we find women challenging allegedly neutral ideas or assumptions, such as the category of the "worker." Furthermore, while Friedrich Engels and August Bebel had begun to think about women's rights within a Marxist framework,[9] it was Clara Zetkin who most coherently argued for women's emancipation from a socialist perspective. Zetkin demonstrates the intersectionality of women's struggles with those of the worker. She also analyzes systemic racism and its place within a larger socioeconomical model of exploitation (global capitalism) and criticizes child labor. For Zetkin, the category of

---

[6] J. G. Fichte, *Foundations of Natural Right According to the Principles of the Wissenschaftslehre*, ed. Frederick Neuhouser, trans. Michael Baur (Cambridge: Cambridge University Press, 2000), 274–275. Mereau develops her critique in her novel *Das Blüthenalter der Empfindung* (Gotha: Justus Perthes, 1794).

[7] For Günderrode's philosophy of nature, see Dalia Nassar, "The Human Vocation and the Question of the Earth: Karoline von Günderrode's Philosophy of Nature," *Archiv für Geschichte der Philosophie* 104, no. 1 (2022): 108–130.

[8] See Kristin Gjesdal, "Passion and Politics: Staël on Fanaticism, Philosophy, and Moral Psychology," in Paul Katsafanas, ed., *The History and Philosophy of Fanaticism* (Routledge: London, 2023), 143–160.

[9] In his 1879 book *Woman and Socialism*, Bebel argued that "there can be no emancipation of humanity without the social independence and equality of the sexes." August Bebel, *Woman under Socialism*, trans. Daniel De Leon (New York: Schocken, 1971), 5–6. Engels wrote in his 1884 *The Origins of the Family, Private Property and the State* that "the first condition for the liberation of the wife is to bring the whole female sex back into public industry." Friedrich Engels, *Origin of the Family, Private Property and the State: In light of the Researches of Lewis H. Morgan*, ed. Eleanor Burke Leacock and trans. Alec West (New York: International, 1972), 138.

"worker" is not abstract, but refers to an individual human being, with a specific age, gender, history, and ethnic identity. In her late work, Zetkin takes a clear stance against fascism, anchoring her criticism in a sophisticated analysis of what she sees as the intrinsic relationship between capitalism and fascism.

Rosa Luxemburg extends Marxist thought by systematically investigating the connection between capitalism and imperialism. From Luxemburg's perspective, imperialism is a necessary outcrop of capitalism. In making this argument, Luxemburg seeks to refine Marx's claim that capitalism requires unending growth. In addition, Luxemburg argues that imperialism on its own cannot achieve the goals of capitalism. The capitalist-imperialist project must "develop" the economies of the colonized so as to make them part of capitalist economy. Luxemburg, moreover, insists on the fundamental democratic nature of the worker's movement. She does not follow Lenin and others in their emphasis on the need for a governing party elite. For Luxemburg, socialism is and remains a movement of the people—and by "people" she did not mean only men from the global North, but also women, as well as men and women from the global South.

Around the same time, women played a key role in the early discussions of Nietzsche's work. It is a well-known fact that Nietzsche himself is far from progressive in his views on gender. This does not escape the attention of women philosophers. They debate the extent to which Nietzsche's views on gender limited the relevance of his critical philosophy. In this discussion, we find contributions by Hedwig Dohm, Lou Salomé, Helene Lange, Ellen Key, Laura Marholm, Gabriele Reuter, and Helene Stöcker. All of these philosophers critically engage with Nietzsche and with one another.[10] Dohm, for example, takes Nietzsche to task for abandoning his critical attitude as soon as he turns to the subject of women. Here he becomes an essentialist and falls short of the critical ethos he usually defends. But Dohm also reproaches Salomé for passively accepting Nietzsche's essentialism. In an essay published in 1899, she criticizes Salomé's statement that women *should* become mothers. Any such claim, Dohm argues, denies women's freedom. Furthermore, Dohm notes, in a rather mean ad hominem attack, that Salomé herself never became a mother and thus failed to live up to her own theory. (Needless to say, Dohm would not have known if Salomé could have had children in the first place.)[11] Yet Dohm also speaks respectfully about Salomé's larger philosophical contribution, which spans important discussions of embodiment and eroticism (widely conceived), and develops the philosophical potential of psychoanalysis.[12]

Edith Landmann-Kalischer indirectly engages in the Nietzsche debate. One of the most significant philosophers of art in the late nineteenth century, Landmann-Kalischer

---

[10] For a discussion of women philosophers' interest in, appropriation of, and response to Nietzsche, see Carol Diethe, *Nietzsche's Women: Beyond the Whip* (Berlin: de Gruyter, 1996). Diethe does not consider Key.

[11] Hedwig Dohm, "Reaktion in der Frauenbewegung," *Die Zukunft*, November 18, 1899.

[12] Dohm characterizes Salomé as "one of the most profound authors" she knows. See Hedwig Dohm, "Nietzsche and Women" (1898), in *Women Philosophers in the Nineteenth Century: The German Tradition*, ed. Dalia Nassar and Kristin Gjesdal, trans. Anna Ezekiel (Oxford: Oxford University Press, 2021), 134.

comes to Nietzsche via her connection to the poet Stefan George. In contrast to subject-oriented theories of taste (e.g., Kant's), she argues in her early work that aesthetic experience contributes to our understanding of an object (and thus aesthetic judgment is an objective form of judgment). She goes on to articulate a detailed account of the nature of artistic truth. Taking cues from Nietzsche, but also from the romantics, Landmann-Kalischer contends that art has the unique capacity to make visible what is only otherwise accessible to the "eye of the mind."[13]

The topic of embodiment is taken up again by women phenomenologists. In the lead-up to World War I—but still within the long nineteenth century—Edith Stein's focus on embodiment and empathy both builds on and extends the dominant forms of phenomenology. For her, empathy is grounded in the bodily subject. Moreover, empathy is an entirely fundamental (enabling) condition for intersubjectivity. Anchoring the capacity for empathy in our embodied being, Stein argues that we can have empathy with nonhuman beings. Empathy is intended toward *living* bodies. As such, empathy extends to the larger nature of which human beings are a part, including animals and plants.

Stein is perhaps the best-known woman in the phenomenological movement. She was not, however, the only one. In her dissertation on the ontology of social community (1923), Gerda Walther, Stein's erstwhile student, challenges both Stein's and Husserl's prioritization of empathy, and argues that our connection to one another is founded on a "feeling of oneness" that, in turn, enables empathy. This insight is also at the heart of her 1918 keynote address to the Freiburg Phenomenology Circle, in which she criticizes Husserl's transcendental phenomenology. Walther's position influenced Heidegger's later critique of Husserl.[14]

Hedwig Conrad-Martius is one of the few phenomenologists who directly engages the life sciences. She articulates her own philosophy of biology, and develops an ontology in light of that. She also writes popular works that offer philosophically sophisticated critiques of the latest trends in biology. Else Voigtländer, in turn, defends a novel account of self-feeling in her early work. According to Voigtländer, self-feeling is connected to and influences bodily and mental well-being, and vice versa. It also influences our relation to others. While Voigtländer's research and analysis draw on examples from literature, her understanding of philosophy intersects with empirical psychology.

In each of these cases, we witness not only a deep understanding of philosophical questions and premises, but also a willingness to develop them in new directions. These philosophers deliberately position themselves within the most important discussions of their times, expand these discussions with a set of original arguments and objections, *and* influence their contemporaries. If we fail to acknowledge their works—and the works of other women philosophers—we are left with an impoverished pool of arguments, a far more limited understanding of the intellectual context in which

---

[13] Edith Landmann-Kalischer, "Über künstlerische Wahrheit," *Zeitschrift für Ästhetik und allgemeine Kunstwissenschaft* 1 (1906): 457–505.

[14] See Rodney Parker, "Gerda Walther and the Phenomenological Community," *Acta Mexicana de Fenomenología* 2 (2017): 45–66; here: 50.

nineteenth-century philosophers were working, and the voices to whom they were responding, and also, inevitably, with an incomplete picture of the movements to which they contributed: their complexity, nuance, and philosophical significance. In addition, if we overlook the voices of these women (and other groups that have been marginalized in the discipline and its canon) we may end up with the impression that the canonical figures were self-created geniuses operating in a vacuum, rather than in constellations with a wider range of thinkers, some of whom are lesser known today, but whose importance should not, for that reason, be underemphasized.

We need, at this point, to ask why these original and important thinkers have been ignored. In trying to understand the particular context of women philosophers in the long nineteenth century, scholars have pointed out that philosophy, in this period, becomes increasingly rooted in academic institutions and that women, due to their exclusion from higher education and academic posts, become more marginalized from the central philosophical debates.[15]

In Germany, women were not formally admitted to universities until 1900.[16] And even after they were able to study at universities, women faced challenging conditions. Many were not able to receive supervision or support for continuing their studies, including the habilitation that was required for women to pursue an academic career.[17] It was not until 1947 that a woman philosopher held a professorship in Germany. Liselotte Richter, who was the first woman to habilitate in philosophy in Germany in 1946, became a professor at the University of Berlin in the winter semester of 1947–48. (Katharina Kanthack had submitted her habilitation at the Free University of Berlin in 1933, but was not able to defend it until 1950 on account of the war.) Some forty years earlier, in 1909, Anna Tumarkin was made extraordinary professor of philosophy at the University of Bern in Switzerland. While Tumarkin had the right to advise graduate students, she was not a

---

[15] Eileen O'Neill argues that the nineteenth century was not a particularly friendly century for women philosophers, in part because of what she describes as the "purification" of philosophy—i.e., the discipline taking on a very specific and narrow conception of what constitutes a philosophical work. O'Neill, "Early Modern Women Philosophers and the History of Philosophy."

[16] The first European university to formally admit women students was the University of Zurich. While women had been permitted to audit from 1847, in the winter semester of 1866/67, the Russian Nadeshda Suslowa, who was admitted to study medicine as an auditing student in 1865, was retrospectively enrolled and, at the end of the year, became the first woman in the German-speaking world to be awarded a doctorate. It would be another thirty years before German universities officially admitted women, with the state of Baden leading the way in 1900. Saxon universities opened their doors to women in 1906, while Prussian universities admitted women in 1908. For an overview of the admission of women to German universities, see Patricia M. Mazón, *Gender and the Modern Research University: The Admission of Women to German Higher Education, 1865–1914* (Stanford: Stanford University Press, 2003).

[17] This was the case, for example, with Husserl and Stein. Husserl supported Stein's work up to the dissertation, but he would not recommend her for habilitation, the degree required for an academic position in Germany. See Mary Catharine Baseheart and Linda Lopez McAlister, with Waltraut Stein, "Edith Stein (1891–1942)," in *A History of Women Philosophers*, vol. 4, *Contemporary Women Philosophers: 1900–Today*, ed. Mary Ellen Waithe (Dordrecht: Kluwer, 1995), 157–189, 158–159 in particular.

regular professor and did not fully share professorial privileges. In this way, many highly qualified women were barred or held back from academic positions that offered prestige and recognition.

However, women's exclusion from or marginalization within academia can at best offer a partial explanation of their absence in the history of philosophy. For even though the barriers between academic insiders and outsiders were strengthened as formal, academic credentials became increasingly important, we need to remember that not all the well-known male philosophers of the nineteenth century held academic positions in philosophy or even composed academic-style writing. Hence a focus on academic credentials and prestige cannot, per se, explain why women have been ignored in philosophy.

Moreover, even though women's access to formal education in the nineteenth century was—as it had been in earlier periods—severely limited, secondary schools now became an option for women. While these schools were not on par with the male-only *Gymnasien*—they did not, for instance, offer ancient languages, the mastery of which was a requirement for university entry—they still improved women's access to education.[18] Furthermore, in the mid-century, tertiary education became accessible to women in the form of vocational institutes. Feminists Louise Otto-Peters and Auguste Schmidt established the Von Steyber Institute, a teachers' college, which offered women the opportunity to study literature and history while preparing them for their (teaching) vocation. In addition, although women were not permitted to enroll at a German university until the early twentieth century, particularly resourceful women audited seminars and lectures. Mereau, for instance, attended Fichte's private seminars and debated his ideas concerning autonomy and marriage directly with him.[19]

Many women made the best out of their exclusion from the academic system. Rather than addressing a narrow group of academic peers, they often wrote for a more general public. Furthermore, their philosophizing was not limited by the academic topics du jour, but motivated by broader experiences and urgent contemporary issues. In many cases, this meant that the women philosophers were well known in their time: their works were published in large quantities, distributed, read, and translated into a number of languages. In other words, women's exclusion from academic philosophy did not prevent them from obtaining extraordinarily solid positions within philosophy more widely conceived.

Again, a few examples can illustrate this point. Originally, Staël's *Germany* was published in a staggering 10,000 copies, though these copies were destroyed by Napoleon's troops before they left the printers. The book was republished three years later and quickly sold out. Regarded as the first systematic engagement with the (German) romantic spirit, *Germany* became immensely popular. In the United States, it inspired thinkers from Ralph Waldo Emerson and Margaret Fuller to the abolitionist

---

[18] James C. Albisetti, "The Rise of the Higher Girls' Schools," chap. 2 in *Schooling German Girls and Women* (Princeton: Princeton University Press, 1988).

[19] See Adrian Daub, *Uncivil Unions: The Metaphysics of Marriage in German Idealism and Romanticism* (Chicago: University of Chicago Press, 2012).

philosopher Lydia Maria Child. Both Fuller and Child wrote popular biographies of Staël.[20] Staël's other works were equally popular. In England, Mary Wollstonecraft honed her arguments through a critical discussion of Staël's early study of Rousseau.[21] Wollstonecraft's daughter, Mary Shelley (the author of *Frankenstein*), wrote a study of French thinkers that includes an essay on Staël's life and work.[22] In Germany, Staël's essay on fiction was translated by none other than Goethe. Malwida von Meysenbug, a member of the circles around Nietzsche and Salomé, also took an interest in Staël.[23] Staël's work reached eager readers in Italy, Russia, Sweden, and beyond.[24]

Another example is Günderrode. While Günderrode did not gain widespread attention before her death in 1806, she became a household name following the publication of Bettina Brentano von Arnim's *Günderode* (1840). *Günderode*, which bears the stamp of its author (i.e., Brentano von Arnim), is based on the letters the two women exchanged between 1804 and 1806. The text also includes many of Günderrode's essays. A bestseller in Germany, *Günderode* was partially translated into English by Fuller (at first anonymously). In 1842 Fuller wrote an essay on the book for the *Dial*, the journal she coedited with Emerson, extolling the work's presentation of Platonic friendship.[25]

Women in the latter half of the nineteenth century were similarly influential, with large audiences and significant print runs. Some even won major prizes in philosophy. *Die Gleichheit,* the journal which Zetkin edited from 1891 to 1917, went from having a distribution of 4,000 in 1892 to more than 124,000 in 1914.[26] Luxemburg, in turn, played a critical role in the German Socialist Democratic Party School, which was modeled on the university, but with a special focus on educating workers in political theory, history, and economics. Although Luxemburg was hesitant to join the school at first, she quickly became one of its most influential faculty members, and many of her students, who often praised her lectures and teaching style, went on to lead socialist and communist

[20] For an account of Staël's influence on Child, see Lydia L. Moland, "Is She Not an Unusual Woman? Say More: Germaine de Staël and Lydia Maria Child on Progress, Art, and Abolition," in *Women and Philosophy in Eighteenth-Century Germany*, ed. Corey W. Dyck, 213–231 (Oxford: Oxford University Press, 2021).

[21] See Mary Wollstoneraft, review of *Letters on the Works and Character of J. J. Rousseau*, by Germaine de Staël, *Analytical Review* 4 (August 1789): 360–362. See also Mary Seidman Trouille, *Sexual Politics in the Enlightenment: Women Writers Read Rousseau* (Albany: State University of New York Press, 1997), 221–235.

[22] Mary Shelley, "Madame de Staël (1766–1817)," in *Lives of the Most Eminent Literary and Scientific Men of France*, vol. 2 (London: A. Spottiswoode, 1839), 295–344.

[23] Malwida von Meysenbug, *Individualitäten* (Berlin: Schuster and Loeffler, 1901).

[24] John Clairborne Isbell, *The Birth of European Romanticism: Truth and Propaganda in Staël's "De l'Allemagne"* (Cambridge: Cambridge University Press, 1994), 2–3.

[25] As a writer for the American magazine the *Atlantic Monthly* put it in 1873: *Günderode* "had great popularity, and the young German 'girls of the period,' the young and sentimental wives, the flaxen-haired, blue-eyed 'femmes incomprises,' of all Germany, wept over it as their grandmothers had wept sixty years before over the 'Sorrows of Werther.'" M. E. W. S., "A Curiosity of Literature," *Atlantic Monthly: A Magazine of Literature, Art and Politics*, February 1873, 211.

[26] Daniel Gaido and Cintia Frencia, "'A Clean Break': Clara Zetkin, the Socialist Women's Movement, and Feminism," *International Critical Thought* 8, no. 2 (2018): 277–303.

movements across Europe.[27] When Luxemburg was released from Barnim Street women's prison in 1916, more than a thousand women gathered to celebrate her work and condemn the fact that many party leaders would, apparently, be happier seeing her go to prison than come out of it.[28] In 1912, Hedwig Conrad-Martius was awarded one of Germany's most prestigious philosophy prizes—a fact that was widely reported, including in the *San Francisco Examiner*, which published it under the headline "German Fraulein Is a Clever Thinker."[29]

The point is not so much that women philosophers were not read, heard, or acknowledged in their own time. They were widely read, even celebrated, and often highly influential. In fact, it seems clear that it is primarily over the last century that philosophers and historians of philosophy have ignored their works.

Importantly, not everyone has failed to value the significant contributions that women made to German philosophy in the nineteenth century. There are indeed scholars who have done important work on women philosophers. Mary Ellen Waithe, Dorothy Rogers, and Carole Diethe are just a few examples.[30] And beyond philosophy, in fields such as German studies, history, political science, and international relations, feminist scholars have been paying attention to the works of women philosophers, including Rahel Levin Varnhagen, Dorothea Mendelssohn Schlegel, Germaine de Staël, Karoline von Günderrode, Bettina Brentano von Arnim, Fanny Lewald, Clara Zetkin, Rosa Luxemburg, and others.[31] As historians of nineteenth-century philosophy, we therefore

---

[27] See J. P. Nettle, *Rosa Luxemburg* (Oxford: Oxford University Press, 1966), vol. 1, chap. 9. Luxemburg's students include Paul Fröhlich, Rosi Wolfstein-Fröhlich, and Wilhelm Pieck.

[28] See Jacqueline Rose, *Women in Dark Times* (London: Bloomsbury, 2014), 63.

[29] The prize, awarded by the University of Göttingen, was judged entirely blindly. Two hundred essays were entered, and Martius's essay on positivism was the winner—to the great astonishment of the judges. The *San Francisco Examiner* reported the award on September 22, 1912.

[30] See Waithe, *A History of Women Philosophers*; Dorothy G. Rogers, *America's First Women Philosophers: Transplanting Hegel, 1860–1925* (New York: Continuum, 2005); Diethe, *Nietzsche's Women*.

[31] See for example Trouille, *Sexual Politics in the Enlightenment*; Janet Besserer Holmgren, *The Women Writers in Schiller's "Horen": Patrons, Petticoats, and the Promotion of Weimar Classicism* (Newark: University of Delaware Press, 2007); Katherine R. Goodman and Edith Waldstein, *In the Shadow of Olympus: German Women Writers around 1800* (Albany: State University of New York Press, 1992); *Salons der Romantik. Beiträge eines Wiepersdorfer Kolloquiums zu Theorie und Geschichte des Salons*, ed. Hartwig Schultz (Berlin: de Gruyter, 1997); *Revolution und Emanzipation. Geschlechterordnungen in Europa um 1800*, ed. Katharina Rennhak and Virginia Richter (Köln: Böhlau Verlag, 2004); Barbara Becker-Cantarino, *Schriftstellerinnen der Romantik. Epoche—Werke—Wirkung* (Munich: Verlag C. H. Beck, 2000); Jean H. Quataert, *Reluctant Feminists in German Social Democracy, 1885–1917* (Princeton: Princeton University Press, 1979; reprint, 2015); Mazón, *Gender and the Modern Research University*; Birgit Mikus, *The Political Woman in Print: German Women's Writing 1845–1919* (Oxford: Peter Lang, 2014); *Tugend, Vernunft und Gefühl. Geschlechterdiskurse der Aufklärung und weibliche Lebenswelten*, ed. Claudia Opiz, Ulrike Weckel, and Elke Kleinan (Münster: Waxmann, 2000); *Women's International Thought: A New History*, ed. Patricia Owens and Katharina Rietzler (Cambridge: Cambridge University Press, 2021). From within philosophy, important work on nineteenth-century women includes, in addition to Waithe's contribution, Rogers, *America's First Women Philosophers*, and some of the contributions in *Women and Philosophy in Eighteenth-Century Germany*, ed. Corey W. Dyck (Oxford: Oxford University Press, 2021). Needless to say, many of the contributors to this volume have also published pathbreaking scholarship on women philosophers in the nineteenth century.

need to ask ourselves why we, as a group, did not follow the individuals who did pioneering work in rescuing the works of women philosophers and take the lead from colleagues in other disciplines.

There are no simple answers to this question—and any attempt at an answer will have to consider a complex web of explanations, some of which would have to draw on the sociology of science and discussions of disciplinary power structures. This, however, applies to the entire history of philosophy. The question, though, is why it is the case that in nineteenth-century philosophy and its historicization there seems to be a particularly eager and efficient forgetfulness of women's contribution.

Eileen O'Neill, Christia Mercer, and Sabrina Ebbersmeyer have all aired the possibility that women's works did not gradually and accidentally slip out of focus, but were intentionally forgotten and that this forgetfulness happened around the nineteenth century.[32] For as Ebbersmeyer convincingly demonstrates, significant attention was paid to women's writings throughout the eighteenth century as well as in earlier periods.[33]

Moreover, even at the beginning of the nineteenth century, there were men who both defended women's right to study and publish and praised their historical achievements. Theodor von Hippel, Kant's friend and the mayor of Königsberg, is one example. Hippel wrote about women's rights, arguing that women were not only as capable as men, but also that their education had been stymied by men. "Women," Hippel writes in 1792, "are without question capable of enjoying that inner freedom of the soul. . . . But we have too often denied the existence of this latter faculty in the opposite sex and affirmed the heart, reckoning only with that organ. As if the one were of use without the other!"[34] Hippel evidences his point with historical examples: Laura Bassi taught physics in Bologna, while Signora Agnes of Milan taught mathematics. He also notes how Germany, with Dorothea von Rodde-Schlözer, has finally had its first woman to receive a doctoral degree (this was, however, achieved in exceptional circumstances).[35] There is a remarkable contrast between Hippel's acknowledgment of Dr. Schlözer and, say, Schiller's sour comment, in a letter to his friend Körner, about August Ludwig Schlözer's "farce with his daughter, who is quite pathetic."[36]

---

[32] Eileen O'Neill, "Disappearing Ink: Early Modern Women Philosophers and Their Fate in History," in *Philosophy in a Feminist Voice: Critiques and Reconstructions*, ed. Janet A. Kourany (Princeton: Princeton University Press, 1997), 17–62; Christia Mercer, "Descartes Is Not Our Father," *New York Times*, September 25, 2017, https://www.nytimes.com/2017/09/25/opinion/descartes-is-not-our-father.html; Sabrina Ebbersmeyer, "From a 'Memorable Place' to 'Drops in the Ocean': On the Marginalization of Women Philosophers in German Historiography of Philosophy," *British Journal for the History of Philosophy* 28, no. 3 (2020): 442–462.

[33] A 1631 work, written under the authorial pseudonym of Johann Frauenlob (literally: Johann Women's-praise), lists more than two hundred women philosophers across history. Public catalogues of women philosophers could also be found in the eighteenth century. Ebbersmeyer, "From a 'Memorable Place' to 'Drops in the Ocean,'" 442–462.

[34] Theodor Gottlieb von Hippel, *The Status of Women: Collected Writings*, ed. and trans. Timothy F. Sellner (Middletown, DE: Xlibris, 2009), 251.

[35] Hippel, *The Status of Women*, 252.

[36] See Harald Sack, "Baroness Dorothea von Rodde-Schlözer – Philosopher and Salonnière," *SciHi Blog* August 10, 2020. Retrieved September 12, 2023. http://scihi.org/dorothea-von-rodde-schlozer/.

In a recent article, Mercer has suggested that women were ejected from the history of philosophy thanks to Hegel's influence.[37] Mercer is certainly onto something. Hegel is evidently no supporter of women philosophers. In his *Philosophy of Right* (1821) he makes it clear that "women may well be educated, but they are not made for the higher sciences, for philosophy and certain artistic productions, which require a universal element."[38] Hegel, moreover, is a philosopher who connects systematic philosophy with the history of philosophy, such that the history of philosophy plays a decisive role in philosophy as a discipline (determining, for instance, the questions posed or considered to be relevant, or the assumptions that are regarded as indubitable or self-evident).

Nonetheless, the emphasis on Hegel risks covering over the larger and even more unpleasant fact, indicated by Schiller's previously mentioned comment: many, perhaps *most*, of the philosophers we study as part of the nineteenth-century canon—the gateway figures to the field—took an active stance against the inclusion of women in philosophy. In other words, a good majority of the philosophers we study today did not only passively underappreciate the women among them, but actively and systematically rejected women's intellectual potential. And this is despite having amazing women philosophers around them.

In Kant's *Anthropology from a Pragmatic Point of View* (1798), for instance, we find the following observation: "as concerns scholarly women: they use their *books* somewhat like their *watch*, that is, they carry one so that it will be seen that they have one; though it is usually not running or set by the sun."[39] The obvious paradox seems to have escaped him. If other male philosophers react to erudite women in the same way he did, little is gained by carrying around a book. Hence, it is reasonable to assume—as Hippel had already done—that the book was indeed carried for the purpose of reading.

In his 1797 *Foundations of Natural Right*, Fichte offers a similar line of reasoning.[40] Against Hippel's call for equality, he maintains that once a woman is married to a man,

---

[37] Mercer, "Descartes Is Not Our Father."

[38] Hegel's reflections continue: "the difference between man and woman is the difference between animal and plant: the animal is closer in character to man, the plant to woman, for the latter is a more peaceful [process of] unfolding whose principle is the more indeterminate unity of feeling. When women are in charge of government, the state is in danger, for their actions are based not on the demands of universality but on contingent inclination and opinion." G. W. F. Hegel, *Elements of the Philosophy of Right*, ed. Allen Wood, trans. H. B. Nisbet (Cambridge: Cambridge University Press, 1991), 207. For a broader discussion, see also Alison Stone, "Hegel on Law, Women and Contract," in *Feminist Encounters with Legal Philosophy*, ed. Maria Drakopolou (London: Routledge, 2013), 104–122.

[39] Immanuel Kant, *Anthropology from a Pragmatic Point of View*, ed. and trans. Robert B. Louden (Cambridge: Cambridge University Press, 2010), 209.

[40] Fichte, *Foundations of Natural Right*, e.g., 266–270, 298–307. In a different mode, Amalia Holst thanks Hippel for his support of women in her *On the Vocation of Woman to Higher Intellectual Education*, 8. Importantly, Holst is not willing to go as far as Hippel when it came to granting women full access not only to education, but also to public offices and politics. See Ulrike Weckel, "Gleichheit auf dem Prüfstand. Zur zeitgenössischen Rezeption der Streitschriften von Theodor Gottlieb von Hippel und Mary Wollstonecraft in Deutschland," in *Tugend, Vernunft und Gefühl. Geschlechterdiskurse der Aufklärung und weibliche Lebenswelten*, ed. Claudia Opiz, Ulrike Weckel, and Elke Kleinan (Münster: Waxmann, 2000), 209–249; here: 222–223.

"the husband is the administrator of all her rights; she wills her rights to be asserted and exercised only insofar as *he* wills them to be. He is her natural representative in the state and in society as a whole."[41] Fichte goes on to deny women the ability to pursue science, philosophy, and universal arguments. In his view, women have nothing to teach men, and their writings should be limited to special women's literature.[42]

It is perhaps Schopenhauer's "On Women" (1851) that takes the prize for nineteenth-century misogyny (and the competition, as we have shown, is fierce). Leaning on Rousseau, Byron, Schiller, and an entire catalogue of misogynists, Schopenhauer observes that one need only look at a woman to see that she "is destined neither for great mental nor for physical work."[43] Not even in the area of arts, which the idealists had considered to be a field where women could possibly leave a mark, is there a place for women.[44] If women think they are valuable, Schopenhauer adds, they are best compared to the monkeys at the holy temples of Benares.[45] In a similar vein, Nietzsche claims that women can be neither friends nor lovers—in fact, it is debatable whether they are human beings at all: "in the love of a woman are injustices and blindness toward everything that she does not love. . . . Woman is not yet capable of friendship: women are still cats and birds. Or at best cows."[46]

Women are vain, silly, and irresponsible; they are compared to apes, cats, and cows. It is easy, at this point, to lose the voice of a distanced academic and ask, very plainly: Should we laugh or cry? At least in the most extreme cases, the comments are probably intended to be funny. But how funny, after all, are they? And, moreover, such jokes only work if they play on or even confirm, rather than challenge, an already established consensus. In this way, they point to both psychological and sociopolitical factors that likely played into the exclusion of women philosophers.

Psychologically, one may note that the need for comic relief of this kind often occurs precisely when a dominant group feels threatened by newcomers—in this case, the philosophy ladies and their books. Politically, it is worthwhile to remember that in the nineteenth century, feminism and discussions of women's rights and suffrage were, to an increasing extent, part of the general discourse. From the late eighteenth century onward, women like Holst, Lewald, Dohm, and Zetkin—they were a fair few and they were vocal—demanded the right to education, equal work conditions, and suffrage. Many saw significant changes coming, including, presumably, the male philosophers discussed earlier. And it seems that for them, this was a frightful prospect.[47]

---

[41] Fichte, *Foundations of Natural Right*, 299.

[42] Fichte, *Foundations of Natural Right*, 304–305.

[43] Arthur Schopenhauer, "On Women," in *Parerga and Paralipomena*, trans. Adrian del Caro and Christopher Janaway, vol. 2 (Cambridge: Cambridge University Press, 2014), 550

[44] Schopenhauer, "On Women," 555.

[45] Schopenhauer, "On Women," 557.

[46] Friedrich Nietzsche, *Thus Spoke Zarathustra*, ed. Adrian Del Caro and Robert Pippin, trans. Adrian Del Caro (Cambridge: Cambridge University Press, 2006), 41.

[47] If so, this would not be a phenomenon relevant only to the nineteenth century. As Mary Midgley put it in her discussion of the situation at Oxford after World War II, her male colleagues, returning from the war, might have felt insecurity "at the thought of finding themselves in competition with those

Highly intelligent men such as Kant, Fichte, Hegel, Schopenhauer, and Nietzsche must have known about the women who read and published philosophy. And they must have known about the women's rights movements—both early in the century and in their later configurations. Accordingly, it would be incorrect to suggest that the views these thinkers defended simply reflect the *Zeitgeist*. Instead, their positions were deliberately chosen among a roster of available approaches. (One need only recall Hippel, or even Friedrich Schlegel, to recognize the various positions available at the time.) Furthermore, they defended their views with vigor and systematicity. It would be plausible to assume that attitudes shared by the most celebrated male philosophers also filtered into the history of philosophy. That is, the very moment women philosophers demanded access to academia, they were, at one and the same time, systematically chided for their efforts and their achievements *and* erased from history.

It is no longer enough to shrug our shoulders and ignore nineteenth-century philosophers' discussions of women's abilities and rights. Nor does it suffice to actively point to the more productive aspects of their works (such as the points highlighted when we consider Hegel's influence on Simone de Beauvoir). As Dohm clearly argues, these philosophers' choices demonstrate blind spots, possibly even a breakdown of rationality, and the philosophers in question must be held responsible for them.[48]

It is high time we follow Dohm's example and ask to what extent misogynist comments—like the ones mentioned here—point to larger, systemic issues in the positions at stake. While we do not wish rashly to dismiss philosophers because of their misogynistic views, we believe it is necessary to engage critically with these views, and, when relevant, hold the philosophers in question accountable for choosing what today appears to be a reactionary position among a whole host of possible positions to defend. Moreover, we need to examine the way we do (and have been doing) the history of philosophy, ask questions about how historical figures like Hegel, Schopenhauer, and Nietzsche still influence our understanding of philosophy itself—of what is worthy of our attention and what is not—and investigate whether the methods, assumptions, and goals of the history of philosophy are themselves part of the problem.

The works of the women philosophers discussed in this volume offer crucial systematic resources and examples for how such a discussion can be conducted.

Just as we want to hold the male philosophers accountable for their philosophical choices, the works of women philosophers must be measured in a similarly critical way. In the excitement of discovering new philosophical works, we cannot simply assume that the works of women philosophers represent philosophically promising or politically progressive perspectives. Some of their views emerge as philosophically sound and

sinister representatives of the modern world, qualified women." Mary Midgley, *The Owl of Minerva* (London: Routledge, 2005), 138.

[48] Hedwig Dohm, "Nietzsche and Women," in *Women Philosophers in the Long Nineteenth Century*, ed. Dalia Nassar and Kristin Gjesdal, 128.

even avant-garde. But in many cases, we encounter a combination of arguments that are illuminating and arguments that leave us puzzled, or even appalled.

At the beginning of the century, Staël's abolitionist views—expressed, for instance, in her bidding Jefferson to end slavery in the US South—are bold and clearly stated.[49] However, while her novella *Mirza* (1795, though written nine years earlier) may be full of good intentions, it reproduces clichés about women's sacrifice, and the agency of Staël's African protagonist is hampered by the fact that her story is told by her male lover, then retold by a European traveler. Similarly, in her focus on women who seek honor and glory, Staël is often unaware of her own class privileges. A bit later in the century, we find the same lack of awareness in Dohm, who emphasizes the need for (middle-class) women to employ maids in order to work, without, however, paying any attention to the needs of the maids themselves. Defending the idea that women's rights are workers' rights (and vice versa), Zetkin at times airs condescending views about the need to educate working-class women to socialism. And, alongside Luxemburg, she opposed birth control and emphasized the need for working-class women to prioritize childbirth.[50] Laura Marholm, Lily Braun, Lou Salomé, and Helene Stöcker all sanctioned Nietzsche's elitism and his views on women in ways that many today will deem unacceptable. Along with Braun and Key, Stöcker and others defended eugenics in the name of the women's (people's) cause.[51] Salomé leaned toward a biological understanding of women that has, since her time, been heavily criticized. In her essay "The Human Being as Woman" (1899), she associates female creativity with the woman's less differentiated and more physical being and speaks about the "eternally virginal and eternally maternal."[52] From a religious point of view, Stein, in a series of essays that discuss education with respect to embodiment, writes that "girls' education should lead to the development and affirmation of their unique feminine nature. Relevant to this is her God-willed place by man's side: she is not to be in his place but also not in a degrading role unsuitable to the dignity of the person."[53]

Among the figures covered in this volume, Else Voigtländer is perhaps the most difficult case. Failing to gain an academic position, Voigtländer worked as an assistant for Adalbert Gregor, a psychopathologist who turned to eugenics. She later managed a women's prison, a post she held through World War II. She was a member of the National Socialist Party.[54]

[49] Staël to Thomas Jefferson, January 6, 1816, in *Madame de Staël: Selected Correspondence*, ed. Georges Solovieff and Kathleen Jameson-Cemper, trans. Kathleen Jameson-Cemper (Dordrecht: Springer, 2000), 367–369.

[50] Quataert, *Reluctant Feminists*, 95–99. See also R. P. Neuman, "Working Class Birth Control in Wilhelmine Germany," *Comparative Studies in Society and History* 20, no. 3 (1978): 408–428.

[51] See Ann Taylor Allen, "German Radical Feminism and Eugenics, 1900–1908," *German Studies Review* 11, no. 1 (1988): 31–56.

[52] Lou Andreas Salomé, *Der Mensch als Weib*, ed. Hans-Rüdiger Schwab (Taching: Medienedition Welsch, 2014), Kindle. The translation is ours.

[53] Edith Stein, "Problems of Women's Education," in *Essays on Woman*, ed. Lucy Gelber and Romeus Leuven, trans. Freda Mary Oben (Washington, DC: ICS, 1996), 196. See also "The Separate Vocation of Man and Woman According to Nature and Grace," in *Essays on Woman*, esp. 70–73.

[54] For a thorough overview of her position and what is known about her political background, see George Heffernan, "Phenomenology, Psychology, and Ideology: A New Look at the Life and Work of Else Voigtländer," *Phenomenological Investigations* 1 (2021): 1–49.

In her work, discussions of self-worth and self-feeling are interspersed with anti-Semitic views of the kind currently discussed in the context of Martin Heidegger.[55]

To take seriously the position of women philosophers includes—as is the case with male philosophers—an effort to hold them philosophically accountable: to situate them within their historical context, study their arguments, retrieve what is valuable, point out what is unacceptable or problematic, and discuss to what extent their problematic arguments damage their overall perspectives. This is definitely work in progress—and will continue to be so, as more voices, texts, and figures are uncovered.

In taking on the hard work of assessing the works of historical figures, it is inspiring to see the enthusiasm and joy with which women turned to philosophy in the long nineteenth century. In their works, women philosophers reflect on the challenges of entering the field as women. But they also voice an overwhelming feeling of freedom when reading, writing, and publishing philosophy.

A clear illustration of this point is Lewald. In her 1871 autobiography, Lewald recalls her excitement upon reading Kant's *Anthropology*. (She suggests her entire upbringing had prepared her for [Kantian] philosophy!) But contra her Enlightenment hero, she makes it clear that "it is the emancipation of women that I demand for us, that emancipation for which I have striven and have gained for myself, the emancipation to work seriously."[56] Similarly, Rosa Luxemburg expresses her eagerness to engage in serious philosophical-critical discussions surrounding *The Accumulation of Capital*: "I was well aware that the book would run into resistance in the short term; unfortunately, our prevailing 'Marxism,' like some gout-ridden old uncle, is afraid of any fresh breeze of thought. . . . Should I start firing away right now? Or should I wait and take up the defense of the whole question later on, doing it all in one wash—in something like a political pamphlet?"[57] Toward the end of the long nineteenth century, Stein recalls how learning about Hedwig Conrad-Martius's award helped her reach the decision to study philosophy. "One day," she writes, "an illustrated journal carried a picture of a woman student from Göttingen, who had won a prize for a philosophical thesis. She was Husserl's highly talented student, Hedwig Martius." A few days and some practical considerations later, the young Stein informs her astounded family of her decision to leave for Göttingen: "it was as though lighting had struck out of the blue. My mother said, 'If you need to go there to study, I certainly won't bar your way.' "[58] The courage we find in these women philosophers—the way they persisted in the face of challenges— and the joy they took in entering the field are both admirable and inspirational.

---

[55] See for example Else Voigtländer, "Zur Psychologie der politischen Stellungnahme: Eine massenpsychologische Studie," *Deutsche Psychologie* 3 (1920): 184–206, esp. 203.

[56] Fanny Lewald, *The Education of Fanny Lewald*, trans. Hanna Balerin Lewis (Albany: State University of New York Press, 1992), 156–157; 104 for the reference to Kant.

[57] Letter to Franz Mehring, Feb. 10, 1913, quoted from Rosa Luxemburg, *The Letters of Rosa Luxemburg*, ed. Georg Adler, Peter Hudis, and Annelies Laschitza (London: Verso, 2011), 324–325.

[58] Edith Stein, *Life in a Jewish Family 1891–1916*, trans. Josephine Koeppel (Washington, DC: ICS, 1986), 218.

The canon of nineteenth-century philosophy is in a certain sense fairly new and has benefited from a host of recent additions. Thinkers such as Herder, the Schlegel brothers, Novalis, Schelling, and the Humboldt brothers were—just a decade or so ago—rarely regarded as philosophically relevant. Indeed, even Hegel and Nietzsche were largely ignored within Anglophone philosophy departments until the last few decades of the twentieth century. This belies the porous and shifting character of the canon. And it offers evidence that significant additions to the canon are possible and can take place over a relatively short period of time.

This *Handbook* does not seek to offer a fixed, alternative canon. It does not aspire to provide an exclusionary list of nineteenth-century women philosophers in the German tradition. Nor, however, does it seek to simply add a few more names to the canon that has dominated the discipline. Instead, it seeks, through individual chapters and sections, to shed light on the work, influence, and legacy of a number of understudied and overlooked philosophers—thus contributing to the ongoing effort to revise our knowledge of the history of philosophy, deepen our understanding of the philosophical potential of various arguments, positions, and movements, *and* critically rethink the narratives by which the discipline understands itself.

Focusing on the lineage of German-language thought and culture, this *Handbook* presents thirty-one newly commissioned chapters on the work of women philosophers in the long nineteenth century.

The chapters are divided into three main parts: authors, movements, and topics. In our approach, we have sought to be encompassing and inclusive. However, as is often the case with volumes of this kind, some figures had to be left out and some commissioned chapters did not materialize.

In putting together this volume, we have sought to present the thinkers, movements, and topics of the nineteenth century in a multidimensional and multilayered way, hoping each dimension and layer will shed light on the others. Part I focuses on individual figures; it is composed of fifteen chapters that cover thinkers from the Enlightenment to phenomenology. It begins with Holst, contines to consider romantic and idealist philosophers (Staël, Mereau, Günderrode, Brentano von Arnim), before turning to women from later in the century, including Lewald, Dohm and Salomé, as well as Marxist and socialist thinkers (Zetkin and Luxemburg). This first part concludes with chapters on women phenomenologists, from the very early (or proto-) phenomenologist Landmann-Kalischer to Voigtländer, Conrad-Martius, Walther, and Stein.

Some figures who are not covered in Part I receive attention in Parts II and III, which investigate philosophical movements and topics, respectively. Part II includes chapters on responses to the Enlightenment, romanticism and idealism, socialism and Marxism, pessimism, neo-Kantianism, and phenomenology. Part III covers aesthetics, ethics, philosophy of nature, philosophy of science, philosophy of life and ecology, the philosophical letter, social and political philosophy, and the American reception of German philosophy. It is our hope that this and similar volumes (e.g., the forthcoming *Oxford Handbook of American and British Women Philosophers in the Nineteenth Century,* edited by Lydia Moland and Alison Stone) will instigate further scholarship and debate, thus adding more figures, movements, and topics to ongoing research.

With this outline in mind, we return, finally, to the initial claim with which we began. There were indeed women philosophers in the nineteenth century. *Who* they were, *what* positions and arguments they presented, and *how* they philosophized—all these questions are yet to be answered. Similarly, the question as to why their works, often important in their own time, have since been forgotten, remains to be answered in a more conclusive way.

This *Handbook* offers preliminary answers to these questions. It is our hope, as editors of this and other volumes,[59] that the works of the philosophers discussed here will help us to think through the more systemic challenges that the discipline faces. The rediscovery of women philosophers has now reached a stage where those of us who care about the nineteenth century are starting to see the vast potential of this field of research. We still need to provide more comprehensive responses to the question of why these women have been left out of philosophy. But we can, at this point, take on this work with the optimism, confidence, and assurance that an increasing number of works by women philosophers are becoming available to students and scholars and that their works articulate new insights and challenges, thereby adding yet another reason to return to this fertile period in the history of philosophy.

On completing this edited volume, we would like to acknowledge the contributors who enthusiastically welcomed our invitations to do pathbreaking work on women philosophers, often presenting these philosophers for the first time in English. Clearing new ground in philosophy is never an easy task: it requires historical and interdisciplinary research, sometimes plain detective work, and always a combination of philological patience and analytic clarity. The contributors to this volume generously gave their time and energy: Thank you!

We would like to thank Raciel Cuevas and Darcy Forster for their editorial assistance. Andrew Cooper offered helpful comments to an early version of the introduction. We thank the Department of Philosophy at Temple University and the SSHRC Major Award, "Extending New Narratives in the History of Philosophy," for their financial support. Finally, we would like to thank our editor at Oxford University Press, Lucy Randall, who believed in this project from day one and whose efficiency, competence, and unfailing sense of humor made it a sheer joy to bring the volume to its final stage.

BIBLIOGRAPHY

Albisetti, James C. *Schooling German Girls and Women.* Princeton: Princeton University Press, 1988.

---

[59] Of particular relevance is *Women Philosophers in the Long Nineteenth Century: The German Tradition*, ed. Dalia Nassar and Kristin Gjesdal.

Allen, Ann Taylor. "German Radical Feminism and Eugenics, 1900–1908." *German Studies Review* 11, no. 1 (1988): 31–56.

Anonymous. Review of *On the Vocation of Woman to Higher Intellectual Development*. In *Kaiserlich-Priviligirte hamburgische Neue Zeitung* 34, Stück, 27. Berlin: Heinrich Frölich, February 1802. Reprinted in Amalia Holst, *Über die Bestimmung des Weibes zur höhern Geistesbildung*. Edited by Berta Rahm. Zurich: Ala Verlag, 1984.

Bebel, August. *Woman under Socialism*. Translated by Daniel De Leon. New York: Schocken, 1971.

Becker-Cantarino, Barbara. *Schriftstellerinnen der Romantik. Epoche—Werke—Wirkung*. Munich: Verlag C. H. Beck, 2000.

Broad, Jacqueline. *Women Philosophers of the Seventeenth Century*. Cambridge: Cambridge University Press, 2002.

Broad, Jacqueline, and Karen Green, eds. *Women and Liberty, 1600–1800: Philosophical Essays*. Cambridge: Cambridge University Press, 2017.

Daub, Adrian. *Uncivil Unions: The Metaphysics of Marriage in German Idealism and Romanticism*. Chicago: University of Chicago Press, 2012.

Detlefsen, Karen, and Lisa Shapiro, eds. *The Routledge Handbook of Early Modern European Women Philosophers*. New York: Routledge, 2023.

Diethe, Carol. *Nietzsche's Women: Beyond the Whip*. Berlin: de Gruyter, 1996.

Dohm, Hedwig. "Nietzsche and Women (1898)." In *Women Philosophers in the Long Nineteenth Century: The German Tradition*, edited by Dalia Nassar and Kristin Gjesdal, translated by Anna Ezekiel, 128–138. Oxford: Oxford University Press, 2021.

Dohm, Hedwig. "Reaktion in der Frauenbewegung." *Die Zukunft*, November 18, 1899.

Dyck, Corey W., ed. *Women and Philosophy in Eighteenth-Century Germany*. Oxford: Oxford University Press, 2021.

Ebbersmeyer, Sabrina. "From a 'Memorable Place' to 'Drops in the Ocean': On the Marginalization of Women Philosophers in German Historiography of Philosophy." *British Journal for the History of Philosophy* 28, no. 3 (2020): 442–462.

Engels, Friedrich. *Origin of the Family, Private Property and the State: In Light of the Researches of Lewis H. Morgan*. Edited by Eleanor Burke Leacock. Translated by Alec West. New York: International, 1972.

Fichte, J. G. *Foundations of Natural Right According to the Principles of the Wissenschaftslehre*. Edited by Frederick Neuhouser. Translated by Michael Baur. Cambridge: Cambridge University Press, 2000.

Gjesdal, Kristin. "Passion and Politics: Staël on Fanaticism, Philosophy, and Moral Psychology." In *The History and Philosophy of Fanaticism*, edited by Paul Katsafanas, 143–160. Routledge: London, 2023.

Goodman, Katherine R., and Edith Waldstein, eds. *In the Shadow of Olympus: German Women Writers around 1800*. Albany: State University of New York Press, 1992.

Green, Karen. *A History of Women's Political Thought in Europe, 1700–1800*. Cambridge: Cambridge University Press, 2014.

Heffernan, George. "Phenomenology, Psychology, and Ideology: A New Look at the Life and Work of Else Voigtländer." *Phenomenological Investigations* 1 (2021): 1–49.

Hegel, G. W. F. *Elements of the Philosophy of Right*. Edited by Allen Wood. Translated by H. B. Nisbet. Cambridge: Cambridge University Press, 1991.

Hippel, Theodor Gottlieb von. *The Status of Women: Collected Writings*. Edited and translated by Timothy F. Sellner. Middletown, DE: Xlibris, 2009.

Holmgren, Janet Besserer. *The Women Writers in Schiller's "Horen": Patrons, Petticoats, and the Promotion of Weimar Classicism*. Newark: University of Delaware Press, 2007.

Holst, Amalia. *On the Vocation of Woman to Higher Intellectual Education*. Edited and translated by Andrew Cooper. Oxford: Oxford University Press, 2023.

Kant, Immanuel. *Anthropology from a Pragmatic Point of View*. Edited and translated by Robert B. Louden. Cambridge: Cambridge University Press, 2010.

Landmann-Kalischer, Edith. "Über künstlerische Wahrheit." *Zeitschrift für Ästhetik und allgemeine Kunstwissenschaft* 1 (1906): 457–505.

Lewald, Fanny. *The Education of Fanny Lewald*. Translated by Hanna Balerin Lewis. Albany: State University of New York Press, 1992.

Luxemburg, Rosa. *The Letters of Rosa Luxemburg*. Edited by Georg Adler, Peter Hudis, and Annelies Laschitza. London: Verso, 2011.

Mazón, Patricia M. *Gender and the Modern Research University: The Admission of Women to German Higher Education, 1865–1914*. Stanford: Stanford University Press, 2003.

Mercer, Christia. "Descartes Is Not Our Father." *New York Times*, September 25, 2017. https://www.nytimes.com/2017/09/25/opinion/descartes-is-not-our-father.html.

Mereau, Sophie. *Das Blüthenalter der Empfindung*. Gotha: Justus Perthes, 1794.

M. E. W. S. "A Curiosity of Literature." *Atlantic Monthly: A Magazine of Literature, Art and Politics*, February 1873.

Meysenbug, Malwida von. *Individualitäten*. Berlin: Schuster and Loeffler, 1901.

Midgley, Mary. *The Owl of Minerva: A Memoir*. London: Routledge, 2005.

Mikus, Birgit. *The Political Woman in Print: German Women's Writing 1845–1919*. Oxford: Peter Lang, 2014.

Moland, Lydia L. "Is She Not an Unusual Woman? Say More: Germaine de Staël and Lydia Maria Child on Progress, Art, and Abolition." In *Women and Philosophy in Eighteenth-Century Germany*, edited by Corey W. Dyck, 213–231. Oxford: Oxford University Press, 2021.

Nassar, Dalia. "The Human Vocation and the Question of the Earth: Karoline von Günderrode's Philosophy of Nature." *Archiv für Geschichte der Philosophie* 104, no. 1 (2022): 108–130.

Nassar, Dalia, and Kristin Gjesdal, eds. *Women Philosophers in the Long Nineteenth Century: The German Tradition*. Oxford: Oxford University Press, 2021.

Nettl, J. P. *Rosa Luxemburg*. 2 vols. Oxford: Oxford University Press, 1966.

Neuman, R.P. "Working Class Birth Control in Wilhelmine Germany." *Comparative Studies in Society and History* 20, no. 3 (1978): 408–428.

Nietzsche, Friedrich. *Thus Spoke Zarathustra*. Edited by Adrian Del Caro and Robert Pippin. Translated by Adrian Del Caro. Cambridge: Cambridge University Press, 2006.

O'Neill, Eileen. "Disappearing Ink: Early Modern Women Philosophers and Their Fate in History." In *Philosophy in a Feminist Voice: Critiques and Reconstructions*, edited by Janet A. Kourany, 17–62. Princeton: Princeton University Press, 1997.

O'Neill, Eileen. "Early Modern Women Philosophers and the History of Philosophy." *Hypatia* 20, no. 3 (2015): 185–197.

O'Neill, Eileen, and Marcy P. Lascano, eds. *Feminist History of Philosophy: The Recovery and Evaluation of Women's Philosophical Thought*. Cham, Switzerland: Springer, 2019.

Opiz, Claudia, Ulrike Weckel, and Elke Kleinan, eds. *Tugend, Vernunft und Gefühl. Geschlechterdiskurse der Aufklärung und weibliche Lebenswelten*. Münster: Waxmann, 2000.

Owens, Patricia, and Katharina Rietzler, eds. *Women's International Thought: A New History*. Cambridge: Cambridge University Press, 2021.

Parker, Rodney. "Gerda Walther and the Phenomenological Community." *Acta Mexicana de Fenomenología* 2 (2017): 45–66.

Quataert, Jean H. *Reluctant Feminists in German Social Democracy, 1885–1917.* Princeton: Princeton University Press, 1979.

Rennhak, Katharina, and Virginia Richter, eds. *Revolution und Emanzipation. Geschlechterordnungen in Europa um 1800.* Köln: Böhlau Verlag, 2004.

Rogers, Dorothy G. *America's First Women Philosophers: Transplanting Hegel, 1860–1925.* New York: Continuum, 2005.

Rose, Jacqueline. *Women in Dark Times.* London: Bloomsbury, 2014.

Sack, Harald. "Baroness Dorothea von Rodde-Schlözer – Philosopher and Salonnière." *SciHi Blog* August 10, 2020. Retrieved September 12, 2023. http://scihi.org/dorothea-von-rodde-schlozer/.

Salomé, Lou. *Der Mensch als Weib.* Edited by Hans-Rüdiger Schwab. Taching: Medienedition Welsch, 2014. Kindle.

Schopenhauer, Arthur. "On Women." In *Parerga and Paralipomena: Short Philosophical Essays*, translated by Adrian del Caro and Christopher Janaway, 550–561. Vol. 2. Cambridge: Cambridge University Press, 2014.

Schultz, Hartwig, ed. *Salons der Romantik. Beiträge eines Wiepersdorfer Kolloquiums zu Theorie und Geschichte des Salons.* Berlin: de Gruyter, 1997.

Shelley, Mary. "Madame de Staël (1766–1817)." In *Lives of the Most Eminent Literary and Scientific Men of France*, vol. 2, 295–344. London: A. Spottiswoode, 1839.

Staël, Germaine de. Germaine de Staël to Thomas Jefferson, January 6, 1816. In *Madame de Staël: Selected Correspondence*, edited by Georges Solovieff and Kathleen Jameson-Cemper, translated by Kathleen Jameson-Cemper, 367–369. Dordrecht: Springer, 2000.

Stein, Edith. *Essays on Woman.* Edited by Lucy Gelber and Romeus Leuven. Translated by Freda Mary Oben, PGS. Washington, DC: ICS, 1996.

Stein, Edith. *Life in a Jewish Family 1891–1916.* Translated by Josephine Koeppel. Washington, DC: ICS, 1986.

Stone, Alison. "Hegel on Law, Women and Contract." In *Feminist Encounters with Legal Philosophy*, edited by Maria Drakopolou, 104–122. London: Routledge, 2013.

Thomas, Emily, ed. *Early Modern Women on Metaphysics.* Cambridge: Cambridge University Press, 2018.

Trouille, Mary Seidman. *Sexual Politics in the Enlightenment: Women Writers Read Rousseau.* Albany: State University of New York Press, 1997.

Voigtländer, Else. "Zur Psychologie der politischen Stellungnahme. Eine massenpsychologische Studie." *Deutsche Psychologie* 3 (1920): 184–206.

Waithe, Mary Ellen, ed. *A History of Women Philosophers.* 4 vols. Dordrecht: Springer, 1988–93.

Weckel, Ulrike. "Gleichheit auf dem Prüfstand. Zur zeitgenössischen Rezeption der Streitschriften von Theodor Gottlieb von Hippel und Mary Wollstonecraft in Deutschland." In *Tugend, Vernunft und Gefühl. Geschlechterdiskurse der Aufklärung und weibliche Lebenswelten*, edited by Claudia Opiz, Ulrike Weckel, and Elke Kleinan, 209–249. Münster: Waxmann, 2000.

Wollstonecraft, Mary. Review of *Letters on the Works and Character of J. J. Rousseau*, by Germain de Staël. *Analytical Review* 4 (August 1789): 360–362.

PART I

FIGURES

CHAPTER 1

··

AMALIA HOLST (1758–1829)

··

ANDREW COOPER

THE neglect of Amalia Holst's (1758–1829) contribution to nineteenth-century German philosophy is striking. In recent years, scholars have attempted to reclaim Holst as Germany's Mary Wollstonecraft.[1] While this portrayal sheds light on the weight and orientation of her arguments, it dramatically misrepresents her historical influence. Following its original publication, Holst's major work, *On the Vocation of Woman to Higher Intellectual Education* (*Über die Bestimmung des Weibes zur höhern Geistesbildung*, 1802), received just a handful of reviews, none of which acknowledges the merits of her project or takes her arguments seriously.[2] In contrast to Wollstonecraft's work *A Vindication of the Rights of Woman* (1792), which reached a third edition just four years after publication, Holst's *On the Vocation of Woman* did not outstrip its original print run. Indeed, it was not recognized as a significant feminist text until the twentieth century,[3] nor was it republished until Berta Rahm's revised edition in 1983. As we become increasingly aware of the exclusion of women in the historiography of German philosophy, Holst's writings provide further evidence that the absence of female voices has little to do with the availability of philosophical works by women. To use Sabrina Ebbersmeyer's arresting words, it has far more to do with a deliberate "attempt to keep women out of academia in general and out of philosophy in particular."[4]

---

[1] Berta Rahm, editor's introduction to *Über die Bestimmung des Weibes zur höhern Geistesbildung*, by Amalia Holst (Zurich: ALA Verlag, 1983), 153; Carol Strauss Sotiropoulos, "Scandal Writ Large in the Wake of the French Revolution: The Case of Amalia Holst," *Women in German Yearbook* 20 (2004): 107–108; Andrea Gerhardt, *Wenn die Frau Mensch Wird. Campe, Holst und Hippel im Vergleich* (Norderstedt: Books on Demand, 2017), 84.

[2] See the reviews in *Kaiserlich-Priviligirte* and *Hamburg und Altona* considered in section 4.

[3] Gertrud Bäumer was the first to acknowledge Holst as an important figure in the history of German feminism, in vol. 1 of *Handbuch der Frauenbewegung* (Berlin: Moeser, 1901).

[4] Sabrina Ebbersmeyer, "From a 'Memorable Place' to 'Drops in the Ocean': On the Marginalization of Women Philosophers in German Historiography of Philosophy," *British Journal for the History of Philosophy* 28, no. 3 (2020): 444. See also Eileen O'Neill, "Early Modern Women Philosophers and the History of Philosophy," *Hypatia* 20, no. 3 (2005): 186.

This chapter has two aims. The first is to reconstruct Holst's arguments within debates concerning the human vocation in the German Enlightenment at the turn of the nineteenth century. The second is to discern how Holst's argument in *On the Vocation of Woman* responds to the challenges facing women philosophers in nineteenth-century Germany. Holst's writings, I argue, expose a paradox at the heart of the German Enlightenment. While philosophers made significant gains in unearthing the social conditions of human freedom, they mostly failed to advance either the political status or the education of women.[5] Indeed, the terrors of the French Revolution prompted a conservative backlash across the German-speaking states, widening the gap between the egalitarian rhetoric of the Enlightenment and substantive gains for women. This backlash was partly staged through a proliferation of works—exclusively by men—on the vocation of woman (*die Bestimmung des Weibes*). Wollstonecraft's *Vindication* was dubbed a prorevolutionary text that undermined the natural complementarity of the sexes and the hereditary succession of royal authority.[6] Recognizing that the Enlightenment project, when left in the hands of one sex, leads to an imbalance of power, Holst took it upon herself to consider the vocation of woman from a woman's standpoint. The difficulties facing her attempt, however, reveal the gendered nature of public reason. In contrast to Wollstonecraft, whose arguments were aligned with the theories of right advocated by British reformers such as Edmund Burke, Holst was forced to adopt a range of rhetorical strategies simply to establish the legitimacy of her standpoint as a woman.

The chapter is divided into five sections. In section 1, I begin with a brief sketch of Holst's background in Hamburg in the late eighteenth century. In section 2, I survey the extensive body of literature on the human vocation, highlighting a growing anxiety among the male scholars of the German Enlightenment in regard to the learnedness of women. In section 3, I locate Holst's *On the Vocation of Woman* within the proliferation of texts in the 1780s and 1790s that aimed to define a distinctively female vocation. In section 4, I examine her notion of the sexless mind as an attempt to vindicate woman's equal share in the human vocation while accommodating socially defined norms. I conclude in section 5 with some remarks on the reception of Holst's work in the historiography of German philosophy. To grasp the philosophical importance of Holst's arguments, I argue, we must not simply unearth her striking critique of the Enlightenment but also

---

[5] Sotiropoulos, "Scandal Writ Large," 98. An exception is Theodor von Hippel, who anonymously published two radical works in which he defended an egalitarian conception of marriage and argued that women should be able to hold public offices and even pursue careers. See [Theodor Gottlieb von Hippel], *Über die Ehe*, 3rd ed. (Berlin: Voss, 1792); *Über die bürgerliche Verbesserung der Weiber* (Berlin: Voßischen Buchhandlung, 1792).

[6] For instance, the Philanthropinist Christoph Meiners described Wollstonecraft as an "obstinate enemy to princes and nobility." Christoph Meiners, *Geschichte des weiblichen Geschlechts*, 4 vols. (Hannover: Helwingschen Hofbuchhandlung, 1788–1800), vol. 4, 243. For further discussion of Wollstonecraft's reception in Germany, see Eileen Hunt Botting, "Nineteenth-Century Critical Reception," in *Mary Wollstonecraft in Context*, ed. Nancy E. Johnson (Cambridge: Cambridge University Press, 2020), 51; "Wollstonecraft in Europe, 1792–1904," *History of European Ideas* 39, no. 4 (2013): 514–515.

situate her response within the challenges facing women philosophers in Germany at the turn of the nineteenth century.

1 A PRACTICAL TEACHER

Little is known about Holst's biography beyond the bare details found in several obituaries and bibliographical entries. She was born in Altona on February 10, 1758, to Johann Heinrich Gottlob von Justi and Johanna Maria Magdalena Merchand.[7] Justi was a chief mining inspector for the Prussian states and a financial expert in the management of state property. In addition to his formal role in public service, he was a progressive thinker and restless activist; he campaigned for women's academies and civil courts administered and elected by women officials, and ensured that his daughters received a learned education.[8] Berta Rahm describes Justi as "an extraordinarily versatile and indefatigably active author, translator, editor, cameralist, professor, and promoter of technology and science."[9] Yet a difficult chapter unfolded for the family when Justi was accused of embezzling state funds. While the accusations were never substantiated, he died as a prisoner in Küstrin when Amalia was thirteen. All that is known of Amalia's adult life is that she moved to Hamburg in 1791, married Dr. Johann Ludolf Holst in 1792 at the age of thirty-three, and had three children: Emilie, Mariane, and Eduard.[10] Johann Holst was a lawyer, and directed a pedagogical institute in Hamburg-St Georg. From 1792 to 1802, Amalia was headmistress of the preschool her husband directed, and went on to establish three schools for girls (*Erziehungsinstitute*) in Boizenburg, Hamburg, and Parchim. She left Hamburg for Parchim in 1813, and her husband died in 1825. Holst spent her final years with her son Eduard on the river Elbe in Greater Timkenberg, where she died "quietly and gently" in 1829, seventy-one years old.[11]

Holst clearly imbibed her father's freethinking and his tenacious drive for reform. She dedicated her life to the education of young women and wrote several reactionary texts against a progressive group of Enlighteners known as the Philanthropinists (*Menschenfreunde*). Philanthropinism was a movement for pedagogical reform pioneered by Johann Bernhard Basedow, whose influential text *Elementarwerk* (1774) and model school in Dessau (the Philanthropin) advanced a method of education that sought to foster the natural order of a child's cognitive development. Basedow chastised

---

[7] Dr. Brüssow, "Amalie Holst, née von Justi," *Neuer Nekrolog der Deutschen* (Ilmenau: Voigt, 1831), 63.

[8] One of Holst's obiturists notes that while little is known about her upbringing, her work as a teacher demonstrates a learned education. 'Amalie Holst', in *Freimütiges Abendblatt* (Rostock, 1829), no. 557, col. 741.

[9] Rahm, Editor's Afterword to *Über die Bestimmung des Weibes zur höhern Geistesbildung*, by Amalia Holst, 160.

[10] Dr. Brüssow, "Amalie Holst, née von Justi," 64.

[11] *Das Lexikon der hamburgischen Schriftsteller*, ed. Hans Schröder (Hamburg: Perthes-Besser u. Mauke, 1857), 331.

the "astonishing abundance of disgusting verbal cognition [Verbalerkenntnis]" promoted in the schools, for forcing the student's natural faculties into an arcane mold "without reality."[12] He drew instead from John Locke and Jean-Jacques Rousseau to argue that education must begin with "the natural order of cognition," which begins with sense perception, extends to the rational ordering of ideas, and culminates in the public use of words to express those ideas.[13] Joachim Heinrich Campe, who worked briefly with Basedow at Dessau before starting his own experimental school in Hamburg, argued that a school's curriculum should not be grounded on an abstract, logical system of words but on the concrete human vocation "to make oneself and others happy through the proper training and application of all one's powers and abilities in the circle in which and for which Providence has caused him to be born."[14] The teacher must have a firm understanding of those powers and abilities to construct a classroom conducive to their growth.

Holst's first published work was an anonymous essay titled *Observations on the Errors of Our Modern Education* (*Bemerkungen über die Fehler unserer Modernen Erziehung von einer Praktischen Erzieherin*, 1791), in which she presents the first critique of Philanthropinism by a woman.[15] In her direct and combative style, she introduces herself as a "practical teacher [praktische Erzieherin]" who, while supporting the pedagogical shift toward a focus on the student's natural capacities, finds the Philanthropinists incapable of applying their theory in practice.[16] Holst contends that Basedow and Campe inherit an error from Rousseau, who provided an incisive vision of a child's capacity for learning only to claim that education should be limited, so as not to tarnish the child's natural dispositions, and gendered, for physiology determines a distinct sphere of influence for members of each sex.[17] While she affirms Rousseau's claim that the student's natural capacities should determine his or her educational needs, Holst argues that a practical teacher knows that she must not anticipate the student's needs in advance, for she is aware that it takes several years to allow the student's genius to emerge on its own particular course.[18] The gendered "elementary books" composed by Basedow and Campe purport to offer everything a boy or girl needs in regard to "morality, religion, political science, psychology, criticism and the fine arts."[19] Yet they are poor substitutes for an attentive teacher who herself has a mastery of the sciences, and

---

[12] Johann Bernhard Basedow, *Ausgewählte pädagogische Schriften*, ed. A. Reble (Paderborn: Ferdinand Schöningh, 1965), 26.

[13] Basedow, *Ausgewählte pädagogische Schriften*, 18.

[14] Johann Heinrich Campe, *Väterlicher Rath für meine Tochter*, 5th ed. (Braunschweig: Schulbuchhandlung, 1796), 8.

[15] Helen Fronius, *Women and Literature in the Goethe Era, 1770–1820* (Oxford: Oxford University Press, 2007), 206.

[16] All translations of Holst's writings are my own.

[17] [Amalia Holst], *Bemerkungen über die Fehler unserer modernen Erziehung von einer praktischen Erzieherin. Herausgegeben vom Verfasser des Siegfried von Lindenberg [Johann Gottwerth Müller]* (Leipzig: Carl Friedrich Schneider, 1791), 32.

[18] [Holst], *Bemerkungen über die Fehler unserer Modernen Erziehung*, 35.

[19] [Holst], *Bemerkungen über die Fehler unserer Modernen Erziehung*, 38–39.

is able to introduce their fundamental principles at the right moment and in a manner fitting with a student's particular needs. Holst claims that such books gloss over the sources of scientific knowledge, leaving students with no feeling for the meaning and significance of the sciences as they "rush to the next stream without ever bothering to return."[20]

The editor of *Observations*, Johann Gottwerth Müller, recognized the explosive nature of Holst's argument. He included a preface in which he defends her position while distancing himself from the content of the text: "if she is right, then the public owes her a debt of gratitude, that she has so candidly shared her observations and doubts. If she is wrong, then the builders and guardians of the new system of education gain all the more strength from it, if they can make her errors evident. In both cases she deserves to be heard, and all the more so, for, as a practical teacher [als praktische Erzieherinn], she is entitled to a voice."[21] Müller saw that Holst's observations of child development and her extensive experience in applying pedagogical methodologies led her to emphasize common human capacities before the physiological considerations of sex. On such grounds, the classroom should be coeducational and organized in a manner that does not follow a prescribed curriculum but that cultivates the particular capabilities of each student.

In 1799 and 1800, Holst published a series of letters in August Lindemann's *Musarion: A Monthly Journal for Ladies* (*Musarion: Eine Monatsschrift für Damen*) in which she criticizes Karoline von Wobeser popular novel *Elisa, or the Woman as She Ought to Be* (*Elisa, oder das Weib wie es seyn sollte*, 1795). Wobeser was a champion of women's education, and wrote publicly about the lack of social opportunities afforded to women. In the preface to the second edition of *Elisa* (published in 1798), she contends that "half-enlightenment is always harmful" and demands to know "why should women always be half-enlightened?"[22] While Holst affirms Wobeser's bold demand, she argues that the novel itself fails to challenge the social status of women, for it endorses a passive resignation to present conditions. The story explores the way that Elisa's thorough education enables her to remain steadfast in her duties despite significant setbacks. After falling in love with the worthy gentleman Hermann von Birkenstein, her mother demands that she renounces her love to ensure her sister's happiness. Following a brief inner struggle, Elisa concedes and agrees to marry the unloved Graf von Wallenheim. Despite his unjust whims and unfaithful conduct, she devotes herself to him unswervingly. By relinquishing all hope of material happiness, she dies in the consciousness of her absolute virtue as a dutiful daughter, a faithful wife, and a loving mother. Holst praises Wobeser's depiction of Elisa's impassioned sense of duty in the face of domestic

---

[20] [Holst], *Bemerkungen über die Fehler unserer Modernen Erziehung*, 90.

[21] Johann Gottwerth Müller, editor's preface to *Bemerkungen über die Fehler unserer modernen Erziehung von einer praktischen Erzieherin*, by [Amalia Holst] (Leipzig: Carl Friedrich Schneider, 1791), 4–5.

[22] [Wilhelmine Caroline von Wobeser], *Elisa, oder das Weib, wie es seyn sollte*. 3rd ed. (Leipzig: Heinrich Gräff, 1798), xi.

unhappiness as a moving fable. Yet as "a contribution to morality," she contends, "it is misguided."[23] Wobeser presents feminine virtue as an angelic form of self-sacrifice, such that "the vocation of woman is a superhuman ideal."[24] Not only does she overlook the immanent grounding of human happiness, which begins with "rational self-love," she leaves the institution of marriage completely unchallenged. Holst praises Rousseau's depiction of Julie in *Julie, or The New Heloise* (*Julie, ou la Nouvelle Héloïse*, 1761) as an alternative portrait of feminine virtue, in which the protagonist undergoes a long struggle with her divided love and yet ultimately chooses a worthy husband who respects her as an equal.[25] A woman's self-realization, Holst contends, should not diminish but rather increase her sphere of activity, and, when required, confront social norms that inhibit mutual respect between husband and wife.

Holst's rhetorical creativity, and her frustration with the barriers confronting women's education, culminates in *On the Vocation of Woman to Higher Intellectual Education* (*Über die Bestimmung des Weibes zur höhern Geistesbildung*, 1802). This is a landmark text in the history of German philosophy, not simply because it was one of the first works of philosophy published under a woman's name, but also because it was the first to advocate that women's education should not be grounded in the particular circumstances of her sex but in her perfectibility as a human being. Before I turn to Holst's argument, however, it is important to situate the text within a broader debate concerning the human vocation.

2 EDUCATION AND THE VOCATION OF WOMAN

The *Bestimmung* debate was a defining event of the German Enlightenment.[26] The celebrated philosophers of the movement—including Mendelssohn, Kant, Herder, and Fichte—called on the concept of vocation to redefine the rights of humanity according to what can be vindicated by reason. The debate originated in Johann Spalding's *Consideration of the Vocation of the Human Being* (*Betrachtung über die Bestimmung des*

[23] Holst, "Erster Brief über *Elisa, oder das Weib wie es seyn sollte*," in *Musarion: Eine Monatsschrift für Damen*, ed. August Lindemann (Altona: Hammerich, 1799), Vol. 1, Bk. 4, 352.

[24] Holst, "Zweiter Brief über *Elisa, oder das Weib wie es seyn sollte*," in *Musarion: Eine Monatsschrift für Damen*, ed. August Lindemann (Altona: Hammerich, 1799), Vol. 1, Bk. 4, 32.

[25] "Dritter Brief über *Elisa, oder das Weib wie es seyn sollte*," in *Musarion: Eine Monatsschrift für Damen*, ed. August Lindemann (Altona: Hammerich, 1800), Vol. 2, Bk. 7, 214–216.

[26] Peter Preuss, translator's introduction to *The Vocation of Man*, by J. G. Fichte (Indianapolis: Hackett, 1987), vii–xiv; John Zammito, *Kant, Herder, and the Birth of Anthropology* (Chicago: University of Chicago Press, 2002), 165–171; David James, "Fichte on the Vocation of the Scholar and the (Mis)use of History," *Review of Metaphysics* 63, no. 3 (2010): 539–566; Michael Printy, "The Determination of Man: Johann Joachim Spalding and the Protestant Enlightenment," *Journal of the History of Ideas* 74, no. 2 (2014): 189–212.

Menschen, 1748), which was reprinted eleven times during his lifetime. Spalding defends the rational faith of the Enlightenment, claiming that what one should do with one's life ought to be determined as an instance of thinking for onself (*Selbstdenken*). His aim is to couch the project of autonomy in shared anthropological conditions, such that the highest good of a human life involves the perfection of the capacities (*Fähigkeiten*) given by nature.[27] The task of the philosopher is to identify the stages of formation (*Bildung*) through which one must progress on the way to maturity, including a shift from morality to religion and reason.

Spalding's *Consideration* placed the question of education at the center of the German Enlightenment. For the Philanthropinists, the project of Enlightenment demands a radically new pedagogy capable of realizing the project of independent thinking as a social and political reality. Rousseau's *Emile, or On Education* (*Émile, ou De l'éducation*, 1762), which was immediately translated into German (*Emile oder Über die Erzeihung*, 1762), provided the backdrop against which their case was staged.[28] In the first four books of *Emile*, Rousseau examines the proper education of Emile to illustrate the pedagogical implications of his philosophy. His famous opening lines indicate that nature provides the authoritative grounds for education: "everything is good as it leaves the hands of the Author of things; everything degenerates in the hands of man."[29] While the goodness of nature entails that education should not be entirely mediated by books and scholarship, Rousseau accepts that Emile, as natural man, must nevertheless learn to live in society. The normative foundation of his rationality is rooted in nature, and yet the cultural sphere serves to realize and direct his natural capacities. In book 5, Rousseau turns to the education of Sophie, Emile's future wife. "In everything not connected with sex," he states, "woman is man."[30] To the extent that they share the same organs and bodily needs, men and women are equal. Yet he then asserts that nature has fixed a complementarity between the sexes: "in everything connected with sex, woman and man are in every respect related and in every respect different."[31] The difficulty of comparing men and women thus "comes from the difficulty of determining what in their constitution is due to sex and what is not." Rousseau draws the line according to physiology, claiming that Sophie's education must be oriented toward the duties determined by her reproductive capacities, which is her "proper purpose"; or, in the 1762 German translation, her "ureigene Bestimmung [very own vocation]."[32]

[27] Johann Joachim Spalding, *Die Bestimmung des Menschen, die Erstausgabe von 1748 und die letzte Aufklage von 1794* (Waltrop: Hartmut Spenner, 1997), 82.

[28] Ulrich Hermann, *Aufklärung und Erziehung: Studien zur Funktion der Erziehung im Konstitutionsprozeß der bürgerlichen Gesellschaft im 18. und frühen 19. Jahrhundert in Deutschland* (Weinheim: Deutscher Studien Verlag, 1993), 99.

[29] Jean-Jacques Rousseau, *Emile, or On Education*, trans. Allan Bloom (New York: Basic Books, 1979), 37.

[30] Rousseau, *Emile, or On Education*, 357.

[31] Rousseau, *Emile, or On Education*, 357.

[32] Jean-Jacques Rousseau, *Emile oder über die Erzeihung* (Berlin, 1762), 417–418.

While the *Bestimmung* debate has gained extensive attention in the literature, scholars seldom note that the rights afforded to the human being were not extended to women. Rousseau's natural determination of woman's own vocation appealed to philosophers in Germany who were concerned by the revolutionary social change occurring in France. The final decade of the eighteenth century saw an explosion of texts by scholars associated with the Philanthropin on the particular vocation of woman, including Ernst Brandes's *On Women* (*Ueber die Weiber*, 1787), Christoph Meiners's *History of the Female Sex* (*Geschichte der weiblischen Geschlecht*, 1788–1802), Campe's *Fatherly Advice for My Daughter* (*Väterlicher Rath für meine Tochter*, 1789), Johann Ludwig Ewald's *The Art of Becoming a Good Girl, Wife, Mother and Housewife* (*Die Kunst, ein gutes Mädchen, eine gute Gattin, Mutter und Hausfrau zu werden*, 1802), and Karl Friedrich Pockels's *Characteristics of the Female Sex* (*Versuch einer Charakteristik des weiblichen Geschlechts*, 1797–1802). These texts staged what Carol Sotiropoulos terms a "conservative reaction" against the social upheaval of the late eighteenth century, for they sought to ground the subordinate status of women in naturally determined characteristics.[33] Thus, despite rejecting Wobeser's claim that women should be equal participants in the Enlightenment, the Philanthropinists ultimately agreed with her depiction of Elisa: education must enable women to bear their particular duties with grace and self-composure. Neither Wobeser nor the Philanthropinists advocate for an actual change in social conditions.

While the texts on the vocation of woman exhibit a shift toward an essentialist account of sex, they simultaneously betray a growing anxiety about the changing conditions of citizen society. In *Fatherly Advice*, Campe's concern for the instability of sexual roles is evident in his claim that physiology should form a pillar of female education, for it reminds women that their "sickly constitution" renders them unfit for strenuous study or public office. Physiology demonstrates that men not only have larger muscles and stronger nerves but "also the unmistakable predispositions to a larger, more far-sighted and more comprehensive mind."[34] In *On Women*, Brandes's discomfort with the social change unfolding in the German states is evident in his critique of the "false culture" that has rendered women unsatisfied with their dependent status. He attempts to restore the wayward direction of culture back to nature's path via "a detailed and rational account of the vocation and capacities of the female sex."[35] Education must take the role of correcting the misguided social habits of women, for "in vain one resists recognizing the truth that woman exists for the sake of man."[36] In *Characteristics of the Female Sex*, Pockels's repeated scorn for learned women, and his attempt to constrain the extent on women's education, betrays a distaste for the new social opportunities opening for women. "It is just as absurd to imagine a woman philosopher," Pockels declares, "as it is

[33] Sotiropoulos, "Scandal Writ Large," 113.

[34] Campe, *Väterlicher Rath*, 26.

[35] Ernst Brandes, *Ueber die Weiber* (Leipzig: Weidmanns Erben und Reich, 1787), 17–18.

[36] Brandes, *Ueber die Weiber*, 83.

to imagine a woman standing in rank as a soldier. The vocation of a woman is to become a wife, a mother, and a housewife, in fact, a *pure wife*, a *perfect mother*, and a *prudent housewife*. It is to this end that girls must study. Everything that does not contribute to her vocation leads away from it, and makes her an unnatural sight."[37]

The writings of Campe, Brandes, and Pockels affirm Michel Foucault's observation that the power of discourse is established through performative repetition.[38] While this power was exercised in multivolume books written exclusively by men, the growing popularity of journals in the late eighteenth century provided women with a forum from which to expose the fragility of that discourse. A striking example can be found in a two-part essay published anonymously in the *Teutscher Merkur* in 1791, titled "Some Characteristics and Principles Necessary for Happiness in Marriage" ("Ueber einige zum Glück der Ehre notwendige Eigenschaften und Grundsätze"). The essay consists of a letter from a married woman to her sister, soon to be married. While much of the advice is conventional, its author (now known to be the poet and travel writer Emilie von Berlepsch) includes an attack on the Philanthropinists' pernicious influence on gender relations. Berlepsch cites recent texts on the vocation of woman, particularly Brandes's *On Women*, to present society's low esteem for women as a form of "misogyny [misogynie]."[39] She contends that the "negative consequences of this misogynist tone on society and morals in general cannot be doubted . . . but their influence on the happiness of marriage, as unerring as it is, will perhaps be recognized by many." Misogyny contaminates the minds of husbands, making it impossible for women to take personal satisfaction in their traditional duties. To resist the growing constraints on the happiness of women in marriage, Berlepsch redeploys the prevailing Enlightenment discourse by calling for women's "independence [Selbstständigkeit]."[40] She urges women to "stand alone" and develop a critical "way of thinking."[41] While her solution is one of mitigation rather than social reform, Berlepsch's argument nevertheless reveals the instability of gender relations at the close of the eighteenth century. If the present state of marriage is not a necessity of nature but is constructed through the prevailing tone of society, then it could be otherwise than what it is. The power for change lies in the hands of woman, who is no longer a mere housekeeper and mother but "also a teacher [Erzieherin]," and thus capable of shaping the future generation of citizens.[42]

---

[37] Karl Friedrich Pockels, *Versuch einer Charakteristik des weiblichen Geschlechts. Ein Sittengemählde des Menschen, des Zeitalters und des geselligen Lebens*, 5 Vols (Hannover: Christian Ritscher, 1797–1802), vol. 2, 332.

[38] Michel Foucault, *The Order of Things* (London: Routledge, 2002), 111.

[39] [Emilie von Berlepsch], "Ueber einige zum Glück der Ehe nothwendige Eigenschaften und Grundsätze," *Neuer Teutscher Merkur*, pt. 1 (April 1791): 83.

[40] [Berlepsch], "Ueber einige zum Glück," 89.

[41] [Berlepsch], "Ueber einige zum Glück," 90.

[42] [Emilie von Berlepsch], "Ueber einige zum Glück der Ehe nothwendige Eigenschaften und Grundsätze," *Neuer Teutscher Merkur*, pt. 2 (June 1791): 100–101.

3 On the Vocation of Woman

Read in the context of the *Bestimmung* debate, Holst's book *On the Vocation of Woman* is not simply an exercise in philosophical dispute. It is a public act of confrontation, designed to expose the dynamics of power that have hitherto permitted men to elevate their claims about women's education above the level of critique, and to redefine the vocation of woman from a woman's standpoint. Holst's awareness of her position is evident in the opening lines of the text. "So much has been written about the female vocation [die weibliche Bestimmung] in recent years," she begins. "Men have dared to set a limit that our minds may not transgress in the field of knowledge. They deem that the higher education of our understanding stands in contradiction with our individual duties" (*BW* 1/17).[43] Holst focuses her attack on the claim that sexually defined duties qualify the extent to which one participates in the human vocation. While women are constantly forced to accept the limits of their standpoint, men have proved unable to acknowledge the partiality that comes with the imbalance of power. It is therefore "a need of our times that a member of the other party—a woman—should take up this important matter about which men have, almost exclusively, already written so much. Men, when they judge our sex, are constantly partial to their own and rarely allow justice to be done to ours. Or, if they want to be generous, they go too far indeed. Only a woman can properly assess the individual situation of women in all its aspects and degrees" (*BW* ix–x/15). Holst contends that the unique standpoint available to women sheds light on the partiality of men when it comes to determining the scope of women's education. While she is reluctant to put herself forward as a representative of the female sex, she accepts that an incomplete attempt is better than ongoing silence. She thus calls on men to justify the higher social position they assume as their own: "In the name of our sex, I challenge men to justify the right they have presumed for themselves, which holds back an entire half of humankind, barring them from the source of the sciences and allowing them at most to skim their surface" (*BW* 3/18).

Despite the force of her opening demand, Holst does not launch into a full-blown defense of women's rights in the vein of Wollstonecraft's *Vindication*. She remains committed to women's threefold calling and attempts to demonstrate that "the fulfilment of these vocational duties [Berufspflichten] to the highest degree is not hindered but indeed only dignified and perfected by higher education [die höhere Ausbildung]" (*BW* 2/17). The constraints upon her as a woman writer force Holst to adopt a range of strategies simply to carve out a legitimate position from which to make her claims. She points to influential women in history and cites letters by contemporary women

---

[43] Citations to *On the Vocation of Woman* (*BW*) are in text and provide the pagination from the original version (1802) and Berta Rahm's reprint (1983), separated by a forward slash. Amalia Holst, *Über die Bestimmung des Weibes zur höhern Geistesbildung* (Berlin: Heinrich Frölich, 1802); Amalia Holst, *Über die Bestimmung des Weibes zur höhern Geistesbildung*, ed. Berta Rahm (Zurich: ALA Verlag, 1983).

to refute the sweeping generalizations made by men about the female intellect. She satirizes the arguments of her interlocuters to reveal the anxiety that lies beneath their self-appointed position. She calls on the ideal of Enlightenment to establish a standard in which arguments stand or fall before the judgment seat of reason. And she appeals to her women readers (*meine Leserinnen*) to *be* a refutation by taking up the human vocation to perfect their natural capacities.

4 THE SEXLESS MIND

Despite the diverse range of strategies employed in the text, Host's argument is centered on the claim that women are first and foremost members of humanity, and thus hold an equal share in the human vocation to perfect the rational capacities given by nature. This argument does not deny a meaningful difference between the sexes, but rather redefines how sexual difference bears on the human vocation. Affirming the fundamental tenet of the *Bestimmung* debate, Holst presents woman as "a perfectible being fit for developing its faculties, both physical and moral" (*BW* 2/17). The vocation of woman qua human being is to develop those faculties "in beautiful harmony to an ever-higher perfection." Yet Holst acknowledges that woman also carries a "gentle, amiable, and often unrewarded . . . threefold calling" (*BW* 2/17). The aim of her argument is "to prove that the higher education of woman does not contradict her threefold calling but rather elevates and ennobles it" (*BW* 96/56).

The first step in this task is to expose an error made by the male writers, which permits them to deny women an equal share in the human vocation. Extending the argument she began in *Observations*, Holst contends that this error is to claim that "physical strength is proportionate to mental strength" (*BW* 8/20). The only thing that physiology has shown about sexual difference, she claims, "is that our nerves are finer and more irritable, and our tendons are less taut than those of men" (*BW* 7/19). The salient question is whether finer nerves and looser tendons "have a negative impact on the operation of our thinking, by which I mean, on the power of thought itself" (*BW* 7/19). Holst notes that no physiologist has ever made such a claim, nor is there any empirical evidence to suggest such a connection. It is only Rousseau who conflates mental and physical strength, infecting the Philanthropinists with a false anthropology that obliterates "the line that separates the state of nature from civil society" (*BW* 17/24). By doing so, Rousseau "proposed to drive humanity back into the state of nature, without understanding that remaining in this state was against nature's intention" (*BW* 14/22). This proposal halts the achievements of culture that have been won in reason's progress, and reveals a failure of acknowledgment on the part of men: "if Rousseau and several other writers talk so much about the physical weakness of women, and attempt to deduce from it her subordinate status, if they claim that nature has granted to her a lower position, they misinterpret this kind mother of all beings. They carry over the natural right of raw, uncultured human beings to the social contract of those who are morally cultured. Thus they fall into error, upheld by a failure to acknowledge the possibility of the same constitution of thinking in the female sex" (*BW* 21/25). Holst contends that by prioritizing the state of nature, Rousseau enabled the male writers to take physical strength as a normative foundation of right. These writers grossly miscalculate the advantages afforded by culture, which "outweigh, by an indescribably great measure, everything we could say in favor of the state of nature" (*BW* 14/22). The proportionality of physical and mental strength is a baffling assumption for anyone who claims to be learned, Holst observes, for physical strength should lose its value "as soon as humanity passes from the state of nature to the state of culture" (*BW* 9/20). Through this transition we forfeit the right of violence and receive the immeasurably higher right of justice. To counter Rousseau's influence on her contemporaries, Holst presents an alternative account of the social contract in which the transition from the state of nature to the state of culture entails a new conception of right wherein physical strength is replaced by "the judgment seat of sound reason [der Richterstuhl der gesunden Vernuft]" (*BW* 99/57). She argues that this transition was ordained by nature all along, which intended that human beings should not remain locked in violent contagion but rather "develop all of their powers" (*BW* 18/24). Once human beings have made the transition from nature to culture, rights are no longer determined by physical strength but by reason alone. The Enlightenment project can thus only be completed when members of both sexes acknowledge the same constitution of thinking in each other.

Having exposed the blatant error perpetuated by her male peers, Holst then considers *why* it has been so readily made. Her answer delivers a penetrating insight into the dynamics of power: the error lies in "the human inclination that makes one unwilling to share rights that have been enjoyed exclusively for so long" (*BW* 21/25). Holst's standpoint as a woman anticipates the critical insights soon to be made by Hegel and Marx (and later by Freud and de Beauvoir), who are often celebrated as the first to unearth the ideological structure of Enlightenment self-fashioning. She explains that those who continue to claim that women are naturally unsuited to play an equal role in civic life have received their positional power due to the contingency of strength rather than the necessity of reason, "and men would not like to admit this" (*BW* 26/27). The pleasure men take in their happy social position entraps them in a state of self-deception, rendering them unable to realize the immeasurable advantages of culture.

Holst then seeks to counter this failure of acknowledgment by cataloging the influence of women on the good and ill of society throughout history. Ebbersmeyer notes that the practice of listing notable women from history became an established genre in German literature during the seventeenth and eighteenth centuries.[44] Works such as Peter Paul Finauer's *General Historical Inventory of Learned Women* (*Allgemeines historisches Verzeichnis gelehrter Frauenzimmer*, 1761) and Christian August Wichmann's *History of Famous Women* (*Geschichte berühmter Frauenzimmer*, 1772) present catalogs of learned women—including women philosophers—to show that dedication to study

---

[44] Ebbersmeyer, "From a 'Memorable Place' to 'Drops in the Ocean,'" 445–448.

does not disqualify a woman from fulfilling her threefold duty. After the publication of Wichmann's *History of Famous Women*, however, there is a conspicuous absence of texts celebrating *gelehrte Frauen*, coinciding with the explosion of works that define the vocation of woman such that learnedness contradicts femininity. Holst's catalog redeploys the suppressed genre to deconstruct the physiological determination of sex and reestablish the mutal dependency of the sexes in all matters of civic life. In contrast to the male writers, who define gender roles according to a clean break between public and private, Holst draws from history to show that "both [sexes] have too powerful an influence on the other" for the spheres of society to remain seperate (*BW* 41/33).

Holst then targets Pockels as an exemplar of the mistaken claim that learnedness contradicts femininity, punctuating a series of unsavory passages from *Characteristics of the Female Sex* with sardonic commentary. Her selection unearths a slide from descriptive claims about the actual discrepancy between men's and women's education to normative claims about women's natural capacities. For instance, Pockels observes that "by reading ancient poetry, by nurturing our capacity for thought, and by studying nature and art in depth, we [men] get to know nature in itself and in its sublimity earlier than women" (*BW* 73/46). He then generalizes from this observation to assert that "as a rule, every feeling is greater and more vivid in men than in women" (*BW* 73/46). It thus seems obvious to Pockels to view the conjunction of *learned* and *woman* as a violation of nature: "a so-called learned woman is and remains either a laughable or an adverse creature. Either her learnedness is not right, or, even if it were, then she is not right as a *woman*. If the latter, then as a woman she is a nonwoman, something monstrous, and if this is how she is found in her natural state, she deserves merely to be *gaped at* and certainly never *admired*."[45] Holst does not seek to refute Pockels's caricature of a learned woman. Instead, she presents a counter-sketch of a learned man, who is so absorbed in his profession that he neglects his family, his civic duties, and his own soul. What good will it do to a dutiful wife, she demands, if "her husband is praised in all the learned journals as a wonder of learnedness if he lacks genuine humanity, if he is always grumpy and glum in his home, if he forgets all the duties of a husband, father, and housefather?" (*BW* 138–39/73). Her point is that "if we draw such spiteful conclusions from the learnedness of women, they must also follow for men" (*BW* 143/75).

Holst's parody draws attention to the male obsession with an imaginary learned woman rather than the many frivolous women who genuinely overlook their duties due to sloth and vanity. Pockels's caricature, she contends, betrays a particular male fear that learned women lack femininity. No one complains when a man is educated beyond his particular calling. Indeed, an excess in learnedness is praised among men. Yet as soon as a woman gains knowledge that extends beyond the requirements of her threefold duty,

---

[45] Pockels, *Versuch einer Charakteristik des weiblichen Geschlechts*, vol. 2, 343–344. Cited by Holst at *BW* 131/70. Pockels is in fact citing a letter by Christian Friedrich Sintenis titled "On Learned Women." See Christian Friedrich Sintenis, *Briefe über die wichtigsten Gegenstände der Menschheit*, 4 vols. (Leipzig: Bahrdt, 1794–1798), vol. 3, 281–282.

men feel compelled to write long tracts to implore to the public that learned women will be less pleasing, affectionate, and yielding. "From this kind of language," Holst infers, "one could easily conclude that these men were afraid that in the course of their higher education women may think of calling to account the many injustices they have had to endure. For a creature who knows its duties according to their source and in their entirety will of course also acquire knowledge of its rights along the way, for the two cannot be separated from each other" (*BW* 149–150/77–78).

Holst does not press a radical agenda of mutual acknowledgment. Her focus remains locked on the advancement of women's education. Any argument that restricts women's higher intellectual education must fail, she contends, for the level of education appropriate to her threefold calling is without limit. Here Holst turns the discourse of the Philanthropinists on its head, advocating women's study of physiology, anthropology, natural history, geography, the arts, and philosophy for their own sakes. To provide instruction to their children that does not simply skim the surface but produces "deep knowledge [tiefe Kenntnisse]" (*BW* 76/48), women require far more than a surface understanding of these fields. This is especially true for philosophy, which ties the disciplines together: "but as far as practical philosophy is concerned, which reassures and strengthens one's convictions through the investigations of important truths about *how*, *where*, and *why*, I maintain that these investigations, as the highest duty of all thinking beings, cannot collide with their individual duties. Nature would have to contradict itself" (*BW* 96/55–56). A collision of the highest duty of thinking beings with the individual duties of a particular sex would require nature to contradict itself, Holst claims, for *both* are given by nature. Of course, the objection might arise that, if a woman "were to become a speculative philosopher," she might fail to "fulfill her duties as a wife, mother, and housewife" (*BW* 94/55). Holst concedes that a calling to professional philosophy would likely interfere with a woman's duties, yet only if she were to "rise so high as to create her own philosophical system" (*BW* 95/55). As we see in a Leibniz or a Kant, the creation of a philosophical system takes the labor of a life. Yet even here Holst refuses to concede a limit to the learnedness of women. How much would society actually lose if a woman were to dedicate her life to philosophy? "No more than they lost through the celibacy of Kant or Leibniz, who enriched the world merely through the immortal works they birthed as children of their minds" (*BW* 95/55). Even professional philosophy should not fall outside the remit of a woman's possibilities, for if we accept the learned dedication of Leibniz and Kant as a legitimate expression of the human vocation, it follows that the particular calling of one's sex can be suspended for alternative social ends.

Exceptional circumstances aside, Holst lays down three general principles for the higher intellectual education of women. The first is that "the education of women must be entirely free" (*BW* 63/43). Here Holst builds on the theory of education she developed in *Observations*, in which there can be no predetermined restriction on where a student's natural capacities may lead them. This principle rejects the idea of elementary books written for girls. Even the ancient texts must be available to women, which requires extensive learning of languages. And philosophy, "the science that teaches us our true conditions in regards to the highest being, ourselves and the external world," must be the source from which a woman's learning springs (*BW* 64/43).

The second principle is that the higher intellectual education of women "must flow from the only true source: humankind's duty to develop all its powers and to contribute to the well-being of the whole as an active member" (*BW* 65/43). Holst is well aware that she will be criticized by the male writers for possessing an inordinate desire to transcend her station. Once more she overturns this criticism by pointing to the present social conditions, which make it impossible for women to acquire a legitimate desire for higher learning. Inordinate desires arise when women are denied the true source of knowledge. If education does not spring "from the duty of humankind, nothing could encourage us to develop our intellect other than the wretched desire to shine, and what a miserable purpose that would be!" (*BW* 67/44). Echoing Wobeser's lament in the preface to *Elisa*, Holst claims that it is true that "knowledge makes us humble and self-effacing; half-baked and superficial knowledge makes us vain and proud" (*BW* 65/43).

The third principle places a constraint on women's higher intellectual education: it "cannot be extended to all individuals of the female sex" (*BW* 68/44). Holst concedes that the higher intellectual education of women "extends only to the upper and middle classes." Here we encounter a tension in the text, for Holst does not extend her appeal for mutual acknowledgment to class relations.[46] It would be ridiculous to require the higher intellectual education of the wife of a day laborer or tradesman, she notes, for the sphere of learned knowledge is beyond the practical remit of the lower classes. While she accepts that "the gifts of nature are and must be unequally distributed," Holst's defense of woman's access to higher education clearly undermines any notion that women from the lower classes are less able. "How many philosophical minds," she muses, "which lacked the opportunity for education but could have competed with a Kant or a Leibniz, slumber unnoticed and unused behind the plow!" (*BW* 90–91/53). Her argument is rather that, given the hidden providence of nature, the working class "must satisfy themselves with subordinate purposes" (*BW* 68/44).

The tension between Holst's defense of woman's full participation in the human vocation and her desire to appear as a reformer rather than a revolutionary leaves the public status of women unresolved. She does not explicitly advocate a radical change in civic relations ("I do not want to be a preacher of revolution [Revolutionspredigerin]," *BW* 6/19). Yet she redefines the normative definition of a woman such that she might become an equal partner in marriage, pursue a career as a professional teacher, and even, in exceptional cases, abandon her threefold calling for the life of a scholar. Consider Holst's determination of the sexes, which typifies this ambiguity: "as human beings, both are

---

[46] One of Holst's reviewers notes this tension and uses it against her. He argues that if humanity is conflated with learnedness, such that the vocation of *all* human beings is to perfect their powers through higher intellectual education, then higher education must be offered to every German. Such would be absurd, argues the reviewer, for humanity is perfected through taking up *one* calling. Review of *Über die Bestimmung des Weibes zur höhern Geistesbildung*, in *Hamburg und Altona: Eine Zeitschrift zur Geschichte der Zeit, der Sitten und des Geschmacks* 3, no. 7–9 (Hamburg: Nestler, 1802), 357.

in completely equal relationship to humanity, even if as a consequence of our civic relations, as citizens of the state [Staatsbürger], the same cannot be said of both sexes" (*BW*
143/75). Does Holst accept civic inequality and yet affirm equality qua human being? Or
does she implicitly critique the inequality of men and women as *Staatsbürger*, revealing
such inequality to be unjustified when placed before the judgment seat of reason? Given
her constant allusions to the fact that higher education will inevitably lead women to
become conscious of their subordinate social status, it would seem that Holst's position
falls closer to the latter. Yet her refusal to attack the civic inequality of the sexes, and her
appeal to the providential inequality of the classes, suggests that Holst was unaware or
even uninterested in the full implications of her critique. The task she sets for herself is
to transform the vocation of woman *within* the constraints of her particular threefold
calling. When she boldly declares that the higher intellectual education of women "will
refine, establish a principle for, and extend women's sphere of influence" (*BW* 96/56), it
is a redefinition rather than a deconstruction of women's duties that she has in mind.

5 CONCLUSION

The *Bestimmung* debate was not simply a philosophical dispute concerning the rights
afforded by reason. It was also a constitutive feature of nation building.[47] As the advent
of citizen society in the eighteenth century unsettled the social fabric of the German
states, the proliferation of texts on the vocation of woman reflects a conservative reaction, materialized through the performative repetition of a conception of sexual difference based on physiology.[48] Holst unearths the fragility of this discourse by exposing
the male preoccupation with learnedness in women as a failure to acknowledge the
same condition of thinking in another human being, thereby inhibiting the progress of
reason and placing the Enlightenment project in jeopardy.

The reception of *On the Vocation of Woman* provides a stark insight into the obstacles
facing women philosophers in Germany at the turn of the nineteenth century. An anonymous reviewer for the *Kaiserlich-Priviligirte* dismissed Holst's arguments and instead
launched an attack on her character. He notes that while Holst *thinks* that her higher
education places her among the great pedagogues of her time (Meiners, Pockels, Ewald,
etc.), her "scornful remarks" about the arguments of learned men reveals that "it is impossible to consider that [the female sex] is destined to rise to the scientific culture of
men."[49] Even if one were to concede that women have the capacity for higher intellectual

---

[47] Nira Yuval-Davis, *Gender and Nation* (London: Sage, 1997), chap. 1.

[48] Heide von Felden, "Geschlechterkonstruktion und Frauenbildung im 18. Jahrhundert: Jean Jacques
Rousseau und die zeitgenössische Rezeption in Deutschland," in *Handbuch zur Frauenbildung*, ed.
Wiltrud Geiseke (Wiesbaden: Springer, 2001), 25.

[49] Review of *Über die Bestimmung des Weibes zur höhern Geistesbildung*, in *Kaiserlich-Priviligirte
hamburgische Neue Zeitung*, 34, no. 27 (February 1802): 12.

education, it is "obvious that the author was prevented by her domestic duties from acquiring the necessary instruction on the subjects of which she speaks." For good measure, the reviewer concludes with some unsolicited advice: "the author is to be advised that she continues the praiseworthy business of developing her mind in such a way that her actual female vocation does not suffer from it; but that she guards herself, through her desire to charm gallant men by showing off her immature intellect, from seeking flattery at the expense of pure truth."[50]

A lengthy review in *Hamburg und Altona* criticized Holst's connection between humanity and learnedness. Because she "confuses the concepts of learnedness and humanity," the reviewer declares, "her entire project is, for the most part, cast in shadow."[51] The reviewer retreats to the Philanthropinist trope that "a *learned* woman, in the true sense of the word, is neither human, nor wise, nor charming."[52] Learnedness is not essential to realizing the human vocation but is rather "a trade [Gewerbe] which nature seems to have ordained [bestimmt] to man."[53] In contrast, "woman, with the duties that nature and *femininity* have imposed upon her, is permitted no time for it. If the woman wants to be a scholar by profession, she must renounce the name of wife and mother, and even more of housewife. No one but Nature can do this for her."[54] The reviewer concludes that because a woman's charm lies in her humanity, "the author must concede to me that true learnedness, which is often diametrically opposed to charm and grace, cannot be present in charming women, if she properly separates both concepts from one another."[55] The gendered constraint placed on learnedness returns Holst to the very bind she went to such lengths to undermine: she must accept either that she is not learned, and is playing at a game beyond her station, or that she no longer represents women, for she has departed from the calling given to her by nature. Clearly the reviewer felt no need to deal with Holst's argument that particular duties can be affirmed while transforming the normative definition of woman within them.

On the Vocation of Woman raises an important insight for the reexamination of women's voices in the historiography of German philosophy. Throughout the text Holst retrieves the significant influence that women have exerted in philosophy, statecraft, and the arts despite lacking the opportunities afforded to men. Yet she also argues that the silence of women illuminates the workings of power. The gaps in the history of philosophy bear witness to a profound loss incurred by the failure of those in power to acknowledge the possibility of the same constitution of thinking in subordinate members of society. Anticipating the failure of her reviewers to take her arguments seriously, Holst concludes by calling directly on her "women friends [Freundinnen]" to "refute the writers who

---

[50] Review of *Uber die Bestimmung des Weibes zur höhern Geistesbildung, Kaiserlich-Priviligirte*, 12.
[51] Review of *Uber die Bestimmung des Weibes zur höhern Geistesbildung, Hamburg und Altona*, 208.
[52] Review of *Uber die Bestimmung des Weibes zur höhern Geistesbildung, Hamburg und Altona*, 206.
[53] Review of *Uber die Bestimmung des Weibes zur höhern Geistesbildung, Hamburg und Altona*, 207.
[54] Review of *Uber die Bestimmung des Weibes zur höhern Geistesbildung, Hamburg und Altona*, 207.
[55] Review of *Uber die Bestimmung des Weibes zur höhern Geistesbildung, Hamburg und Altona*, 359–360.

falsely suppose that the higher intellectual education of our minds and the fulfillment of our individual duties cannot exist together" (*BW* 280/130). "Be restless in the training of your mind," she exhorts them, for such is "the best way to silence those prejudices."

BIBLIOGRAPHY

'Amalie Holst', in *Freimütiges Abendblatt* (Rostock), 1829, no. 557, cols. 741–742.

Basedow, Johann Bernhard. *Ausgewählte pädagogische Schriften*. Edited by A. Reble. Paderborn: Ferdinand Schöningh, 1965.

Bäumer, Gertrud. *Handbuch der Frauenbewegung*. Vol. 1. Berlin: Moeser, 1901.

[Berlepsch, Emilie von]. "Ueber einige zum Glück der Ehe nothwendige Eigenschaften und Grundsätze." *Neuer Teutscher Merkur*, pt. 1: April, 63–102; pt. 2: June, 113–134, 1791.

Botting, Eileen Hunt. "Nineteenth-Century Critical Reception." In *Mary Wollstonecraft in Context*, edited by Nancy E. Johnson, 50–56. Cambridge: Cambridge University Press, 2020.

Botting, Eileen Hunt. "Wollstonecraft in Europe, 1792–1904: A Revisionist Reception History." *History of European Ideas* 39, no. 4 (2013): 503–527.

Brandes, Ernst. *Ueber die Weiber*. Leipzig: Weidmanns Erben und Reich, 1787.

Brüssow. "Amalie Holst, née von Justi." In *Neuer Nekrolog der Deutschen*, 63–64. Ilmenau: Voigt, 1831.

Campe, Johann Heinrich. *Väterlicher Rath für meine Tochter*. 5th ed. Braunschweig: Schulbuchhandlung, 1796.

Das Lexikon der hamburgischen Schriftsteller. Edited by Hans Schröder. Hamburg: Perthes-Besser u. Mauke, 1857.

Ebbersmeyer, Sabrina. "From a 'Memorable Place' to 'Drops in the Ocean': On the Marginalization of Women Philosophers in German Historiography of Philosophy." *British Journal for the History of Philosophy* 28, no. 3 (2020): 442–462.

Ewald, Johann Ludwig. *Die Kunst, ein gutes Mädchen, eine gute Gattin, Mutter und Hausfrau zu werden*. Frankfurt: Friedrich Wilmans, 1802.

Felden, Heide von. "Geschlechterkonstruktion und Frauenbildung im 18. Jahrhundert: Jean Jacques Rousseau und die zeitgenössische Rezeption in Deutschland." In *Handbuch zur Frauenbildung*, edited by Wiltrud Geiseke, 25–34. Wiesbaden: Springer, 2001.

Foucault, Michel. *The Order of Things*. London: Routledge, 2002.

Fronius, Helen. *Women and Literature in the Goethe Era, 1770–1820*. Oxford: Oxford University Press, 2007.

Gerhardt, Andrea. *Wenn die Frau Mensch Wird. Campe, Holst und Hippel im Vergleich*. Norderstedt: Books on Demand, 2017.

Hermann, Ulrich. *Aufklärung und Erziehung: Studien zur Funktion der Erziehung im Konstitutionsprozeß der bürgerlichen Gesellschaft im 18. und frühen 19. Jahrhundert in Deutschland*. Weinheim: Deutscher Studien Verlag, 1993.

[Hippel, Theodor Gottlieb von]. *Über die bürgerliche Verbesserung der Weiber*. Berlin: Voßischen Buchhandlung, 1792.

[Hippel, Theodor Gottlieb von]. *Über die Ehe*. 3rd ed. Berlin: Voss, 1792.

[Holst, Amalia]. *Bemerkungen über die Fehler unserer modernen Erziehung von einer praktischen Erzieherin. Herausgegeben vom Verfasser des Siegfried von Lindenberg [Johann Gottwerth Müller]*. Leipzig: Carl Friedrich Schneider, 1791.

Holst, Amalia. "Erster Brief über *Elisa, oder das Weib wie es seyn sollte*." In *Musarion: Eine Monatsschrift für Damen*, edited by August Lindemann, vol. 1, Bk. 4, 345–361. Altona: Hammerich, 1799.

Holst, Amalia. "Zweiter Brief über *Elisa, oder das Weib wie es seyn sollte*." In *Musarion: eine Monatsschrift für Damen*, edited by August Lindemann, vol. 1, Bk. 5, 30–52. Altona: Hammerich, 1799.

Holst, Amalia. "Dritter Brief über *Elisa, oder das Weib wie es seyn sollte*." In *Musarion: eine Monatsschrift für Damen*, edited by August Lindemann, vol. 2, Bk. 7, 213–227. Altona: Hammerich, 1800.

Holst, Amalia. "Vierter Brief über *Elisa, oder das Weib wie es seyn sollte*." In *Musarion: eine Monatsschrift für Damen*, edited by August Lindemann, vol. 2, Bk. 8, 326–334. Altona: Hammerich, 1800.

Holst, Amalia. *Über die Bestimmung des Weibes zur höhern Geistesbildung*. Berlin: Heinrich Frölich, 1802.

Holst, Amalia. *Über die Bestimmung des Weibes zur höhern Geistesbildung*. Edited by Berta Rahm. Zurich: ALA Verlag, 1983.

James, David. "Fichte on the Vocation of the Scholar and the (Mis)use of History." *Review of Metaphysics* 63, no. 3 (2010): 539–566.

Meiners, Christoph. *Geschichte des weiblichen Geschlechts*. 4 vols. Hannover: Helwingschen Hofbuchhandlung, 1788–1800.

Müller, Johann Gottwerth. Editor's Preface to *Bemerkungen über die Fehler unserer modernen Erziehung von einer praktischen Erzieherin*, by [Amalia Holst], 3–8. Leipzig: Carl Friedrich Schneider, 1791.

O'Neill, Eileen. "Early Modern Women Philosophers and the History of Philosophy." *Hypatia* 20, no. 3 (2005): 185–197.

Pockels, Karl Friedrich. *Versuch einer Charakteristik des weiblichen Geschlechts. Ein Sittengemählde des Menschen, des Zeitalters und des geselligen Lebens*. 5 vols. Hannover: Christian Ritscher, 1797–1802.

Preuss, Peter. Translator's introduction to *The Vocation of Man*, by J. G. Fichte, vii–xiv. Indianapolis: Hackett, 1987.

Printy, Michael. "The Determination of Man: Johann Joachim Spalding and the Protestant Enlightenment." *Journal of the History of Ideas* 74, no. 2 (2014): 189–212.

Rahm, Berta. Editor's Afterword to *Über die Bestimmung des Weibes zur höhern Geistesbildung*, by Amalia Holst, 153–161. Zurich: ALA Verlag, 1983.

Review of *Über die Bestimmung des Weibes zur höhern Geistesbildung*, in *Hamburg und Altona: Eine Zeitschrift zur Geschichte der Zeit, der Sitten und des Geschmacks* 3 (7–9). Hamburg: Nestler, 1802.

Review of *Über die Bestimmung des Weibes zur höhern Geistesbildung*, in *Kaiserlich-Priviligirte hamburgische Neue Zeitung*. vol. 34, 27 February 1802. Berlin: Heinrich Frölich.

Rousseau, Jean-Jacques. *Emile oder über die Erziehung*. Berlin, 1762.

Rousseau, Jean-Jacques. *Emile, or On Education*. Translated by Allan Bloom. New York: Basic Books, 1979.

Sintenis, Christian Friedrich. *Briefe über die wichtigsten Gegenstände der Menschheit*. 4 vols. Leipzig: Bahrdt, 1794–98.

Sotiropoulos, Carol Strauss. "Scandal Writ Large in the Wake of the French Revolution: The Case of Amalia Holst." *Women in German Yearbook* 20 (2004): 98–121.

Spalding, Johann Joachim. *Die Bestimmung des Menschen, die Erstausgabe von 1748 und die letzte Aufklage von 1794*. Waltrop: Hartmut Spenner, 1997.

[Wobeser, Wilhelmine Caroline von]. *Elisa, oder das Weib, wie es seyn sollte*. 3rd ed. Leipzig: Heinrich Gräff, 1798.

Yuval-Davis, Nira. *Gender and Nation*. London: Sage, 1997.

Zammito, John. *Kant, Herder, and the Birth of Anthropology*. Chicago: University of Chicago Press, 2002.

CHAPTER 2

....

GERMAINE DE STAËL
(1766–1817)

....

KAREN DE BRUIN

ON July 14, 1817, one of the most courageous writers in France passed away. Escorted to the Chateau of Coppet in a funeral procession led by her dear friends August Wilhelm and Friedrich Schlegel, friends and family from across Europe lamented the demise of this exceptional woman.[1] Germaine de Staël stood up to Napoleon while others cowered; she dared wield her pen against slavery and the slave trade; she fought vociferously against arranged marriages and female servitude; and, despite having been forced into exile by Revolutionary and Napoleonic regimes, she never gave up on writing to promote a modern liberal republic, the only form of government she saw as suitable to France after the Reign of Terror.[2] If there was one common thread among all the battles that she waged, it was that they were for a more just society rooted in freedom, a possibility to which the French Revolution opened the door. Staël's resistance against prevailing thought in the name of freedom and justice not only characterized her actions but also her moral philosophy, a philosophy that she developed largely in response to the events of the French Revolution.

Steeped in Enlightenment political thought, Staël was jubilant when the French Revolution erupted. Then twenty-three years old, Staël saw a path forward for a nation that would honor the sovereignty of the people, the protection of individual freedom, and political equality before the law. In the span of four turbulent subsequent years, Staël bore witness to the disastrous constitutional debates, the storming of the Tuileries, the flight of the king to Varennes, the vote on the death of the king, the abolition of the monarchy, the rise of the National Convention, the creation of exceptional judiciary institutions that sought to prosecute royalists and *constitutionnels* like herself, and,

---

[1] Michel Winock, *Madame de Staël* (Paris: Fayard, 2010), 489; Benjamin Constant, "Nécrologie," *Mercure de France*, July 1817, 175–180.

[2] At least, she thought that the liberal republic was the only possibility of government for France until the Restoration and the renewed possibility of a constitutional monarchy.

most tragically, the ensuing Reign of Terror.[3] Her optimism upended, she was forced to admit that a revolution that had begun in the name of philosophical values—the pursuit of liberty, truth, and justice—had devolved into violent partisan conflict. In her mind, leaders and followers from the royalist right to the Jacobin left had lost their moral compass. In a letter to Louis-Adolphe de Ribbing, she even admitted her own moral disorientation: "what is odious to me about the French revolution is the chaos in which it has thrown all feelings and ideas . . . I no longer know where the beautiful is, the true is, the just is."[4]

Having witnessed firsthand the popular violence of the events leading up to the Reign of Terror and fearing for her own life, Staël went into political exile, which allowed her to gain perspective and clairvoyance: moral philosophy needed to catch up with the events of the French Revolution. The Revolution had veered into the Reign of Terror in large part because of self-interested leaders and the rise of party spirit (*esprit de parti*), synonymous in her lexicon with fanaticism. Party spirit had allowed Revolutionary leaders to degrade language and purge it of truth. Furthermore, it had pushed followers to sacrifice their moral judgment to national interest and more dubiously, to "public salvation."[5] Finally, party spirit, the most dangerous of passions, largely anchored in self-interest and self-love, absolved its leaders and followers of any personal responsibility and moral duty to freedom.[6] For Staël, the root problem in terms of morality during the Revolution was that French moral philosophy had not progressed beyond the seventeenth-century idealist writings of Descartes.[7] Worse, in her view: largely influenced by Locke, who believed that ideas derived from sensations and experience, and not innate feeling, eighteenth-century French moral philosophy had actually regressed while

[3] *Constitutionnels* were for constitutional monarchy. After the fall of monarchy on August 10, 1792, the *constitutionnels* were proclaimed enemies of the Republic. Staël managed to flee France, but she spent much time, money, and energy saving her friends who were also *constitutionnels*. See Winock, *Madame de Staël*, 69.

[4] Germaine de Staël, *Lettres diverses, 1794*, vol. 2 of *Correspondance générale*, ed. Béatrice W. Jasinski (Paris: Pauvert, 1965), 514. Henceforth, translations from all volumes of Staël's *Correspondance générale* will be mine.

[5] The Committee for Public Salvation, the executive power during the Reign of Terror, put in place numerous decrees in the name of "public salvation": the disarming of all "suspects"; the arming of all nonaristocratic "republican" citizens with pikes; the declaration of the civil death of emigrants and the confiscation of all their properties; the declaration of death by guillotine for all those who composed or wrote works that could be suspected of provoking the dissolution of the national assembly, the reestablishment of the royalty, or any other harm to the sovereignty of the people; etc.

[6] Germaine de Staël, *De l'influence des passions suivi de Réflexions sur le suicide (On the Influence of Passions Followed by Reflections on Suicide)*, ed. Chantal Thomas (Paris: Editions Payot et Rivages, 2000), 143–161. Staël describes party spirit in detail in her chapter entitled "De l'esprit de parti" ("On Party Spirit").

[7] Germaine de Staël, *De l'Allemagne (On Germany)*, vol. 2, ed. Simone Balayé (Paris: GF Flammarion, 1968), 107. Henceforth, all nonquoted references will come from this French edition. All French quotes will also be taken from this edition. All English quotes will be taken from the English translation: Germaine de Staël, *Germany*, vol. 2 (New York: Eastburn Kirk and Company, 1814), which appeared in the United States one year after it appeared in print in London. I use the French text as the principal text since there is no scholarly translation of the full *De l'Allemagne*.

political philosophy had progressed.[8] For Staël, Jean-Jacques Rousseau's moral thinking represented a notable exception to the corrupting moral philosophy of the eighteenth century. She appreciated the centrality that he gave to both conscience and the perfectibility of the human species; yet in her view, Rousseau's fanciful reconstruction of the state of nature, his social contract as a moralizing force, and the natural inferiority that he ascribed to women undermined his thinking as a corrective doctrine in France that could give primacy to individual responsibility and duty to freedom.[9] She did see in his novels, though, a possible model for the moral education of the nation.

As France came out of the Reign of Terror and into the Thermidorian period, between 1794 and 1798, not only was Staël one of the first French thinkers to articulate a moderate republican liberalism, but she had also begun to elaborate an informal poetics of a new literary genre—the "philosophical novel"—that she thought could serve to morally reform the nation.[10] This new genre, she reasoned, would seek to implement individual responsibility and duty to freedom as the new public morality of a liberal republic. While Staël sketched the contours of her moral thought and poetics of the philosophical novel during this Thermidorian period, it was shortly thereafter that she discovered German idealism, what she, in line with Kant, referred to as the "new school" of German thought.[11] In this school of thought, she found a metaphysical doctrine that she likened to a Copernican revolution in philosophy and that could ground her notions of personal responsibility and duty to freedom.[12] This "new school" of German idealism also helped Staël refine an aesthetic pathway that could be incorporated into her poetics of the philosophical novel so that it would be able to morally inspire and educate the masses. This aesthetic pathway, though, would depend on a specific type of genius—with a natural proximity to conscience and the capacity to resist injustice—found predominantly in exceptional women writers, whom she was now elevating to the status of moral educators of the nation.

---

[8] Germaine de Staël, *De la littérature* (*On Literature*), ed. Gérard Gengembre and Jean Goldzink (Paris: GF Flammarion, 1991), 370. Henceforth, all nonquoted references will come from this French edition. All French quotes will also be taken from this edition. All English quotes will be taken from the English translation: Germaine de Staël, *The Influence of Literature upon Society Translated from the French of Madame de Staël-Holstein*, 2 vols. (London: Henry Colburn, 1812). I use the French text as the principal text since there is no scholarly translation of the full *De la Littérature*. Presumed to be translated by D. Boileau.

[9] See Germaine de Staël, "Lettres sur les ouvrages et le caractère de J.-J. Rousseau" ("Letters on the Works and Character of J.-J. Rousseau"), in *Oeuvres de jeunesse*, ed. Simone Balayé and John Isbell (Paris: Editions Desjonquères, 1997), 33–99. See also Germaine de Staël, *Letters on the Works and Character of J. J. Rousseau* (London: G. G. J. and J. Robinson, 1789). I use the French text as the principal text since there is no scholarly translation of the full *Letters*.

[10] What I term "informal poetics" is a group of aesthetic principles that recur throughout her writings but that are not regrouped formally. For her use of the term "roman philosophique" see Staël, *Oeuvres de jeunesse*, 145.

[11] Staël, *De l'Allemagne*, vol. 2, 45. In the 1814 English translation, even though Staël writes "la nouvelle école allemande" in the French original text, the translator omits "new." I have chosen to preserve the spirit of the original language used by Staël.

[12] Staël, *De l'Allemagne*, vol. 2, 95.

This chapter brings together, through an examination of Staël's moral philosophy, three fields of study: Staël's political thought, her aesthetic thought, and her literary thought. Through this examination, I show the conjoined nature of Staël's moral philosophy and the impossibility of fully understanding her moral education project without passing through the French Revolution, her commitment to the philosophical novel, and her engagement with German idealism. In the first part of the essay, dedicated to the years 1794–1798, I use the works of three political scientists—Andrew Jainchill, Biancamaria Fontana, and Aurelian Craiutu—to show how the question of moral regeneration became central to Staël's groundbreaking political sketches of a moderate liberal republic. Next, I highlight the year 1795 as an inflection point for Staël, when her literary and political thought becomes conjoined in her project to morally educate the nation through the philosophical novel. Then, I underscore how Staël incorporated the "new German school" into her poetics of the philosophical novel to reinfuse language with truth, cultivate individual moral judgment, and catalyze the moral regeneration of the nation. The result of Staël's ambitious aesthetic project to morally educate the nation in order to buttress political freedom was larger than she perhaps could have ever imagined: along with Chateaubriand, she is widely credited with inaugurating French romanticism, not to speak of moderate republican liberalism.[13]

1 MORAL REGENERATION IN A LIBERAL REPUBLIC

It is not surprising that Germaine de Staël was one of the first thinkers to articulate a resolutely modern conception of a liberal republic. As Alphonse de Lamartine once famously commented, she had been "breathing politics since the moment she was born."[14] From a very early age, she conversed regularly with her father, Jacques Necker, minister of finance under Louis XVI, and saw it as her mission to defend his political and economic thinking. For example, as Biancamaria Fontana relates, after Necker resigned from his position as director general of finance and published his famous *Report to the King* (*Compte rendu au Roy*, 1781), Staël, at age fifteen, wrote to him an anonymous letter praising him for the publication and for having rendered transparent the state of the French budget.[15] From the age of five, regular attendees of her mother's weekly salon, the most intellectual and influential in Paris, also nourished Staël's thinking. As a result of her extensive education and privileged upbringing, by the time that Louis XVI

---

[13] See David Simpson, "The French Revolution," in *The Cambridge History of Literary Criticism,* vol. 5, *Romanticism,* ed. Marshall Brown (Cambridge: Cambridge University Press, 2000), 52.

[14] Biancamaria Fontana, *Germaine de Staël: A Political Portrait* (Princeton: Princeton University Press, 2016), 5.

[15] Fontana, *Germaine de Staël,* 5.

convened the Estates General, Staël's first work, *Letters on the Works and Character of Jean-Jacques Rousseau*, a treatise on moral education and freedom, had already been widely circulated and published, even if against her will, as she writes in her 1814 preface to the reedited work.[16]

Staël continued to "breathe politics" during the first years of the French Revolution. As the daughter of Jacques Necker and the wife of a Swedish diplomat, the baron Erik-Magnus de Staël-Holstein, Staël was permitted to attend the majority of events and deliberations that unfolded between the opening ceremony of the Estates General, at which she took a front seat, and the ensuing ratification of the Constitution of 1791, which she chronicled in great detail in her work *Considerations on the Principal Events of the French Revolution*, published posthumously in 1817.[17] During these events, as Fontana highlights, Staël felt "in her element" and was able to witness for herself the fast-changing politics of the Constituent Assembly.[18]

It was during the sessions of the Constituent Assembly (1789–1791) that Staël immediately recognized a worrying phenomenon, which would quickly become, in her view, the moral bane of the Revolution. The assembly was remarkably coalesced behind the idea of freedom and a constitutional monarchy; however, what began as divisions taking hold within parties, whether on the side of the aristocrats or on the side of the popular party (*parti populaire*), quickly devolved into intolerant partisan thinking, accentuated by passions related to self-interest such as ambition and vanity.[19] According to her assessment, a culture of party spirit—"extreme self-love which does not allow men to tolerate any other ideas than their own"—engulfed the Assembly on both sides, thereby deafening the moderate voices who were in favor of a bicameral legislative body and an executive power with absolute veto, moderate voices among which she counted herself by association.[20] In the end, the increasingly radical voices on the left prevailed and a constitution rooted in the sovereignty of a one-chamber general assembly and a weak executive power with only suspensive veto power predominated. Staël presciently saw the beginning of the end of this first constitution when she wrote: "a constitution of which one of the elements is the humiliation of either sovereign or people must necessarily be overturned by the one or the other."[21]

Indeed, the flight of Louis XVI to Varennes in 1791 effectively overturned both the monarchy and the 1791 constitution, thereby granting both administrative and legislative

[16] Staël, *Oeuvres de jeunesse*, 37. See also Simone Balayé, *Ecrire, lutter, vivre* (Geneva: Librairie Droz, 1994), 15.

[17] Germaine de Staël, *Considerations on the Principal Events of the French Revolution*, ed. Aurelian Craiutu (Indianapolis: Liberty Fund, 2008). Since this is a scholarly edition of Staël's *Considérations sur la Révolution française*, I will only use this English version for all quotes and references.

[18] Fontana, *Germaine de Staël*, 6.

[19] Staël, *Considerations*, 199. See an analysis of Staël's writing on the radicalization of the right and the left in Fontana, *Germaine de Staël*, 25–28. Staël writes about the negative passions of ambition and vanity in *De l'influence des passions*, 74–111.

[20] Staël, *Considerations*, 199–206.

[21] Staël, *Considerations*, 212–213.

authority to the Legislative Assembly (formerly the Constituent Assembly), which would subsequently become the National Convention after the beheading of Louis XVI. The Reign of Terror, a period of mass beheadings and forced exile of dissidents—in the name of "public salvation"—would follow. The advent of the Reign of Terror represented a turning point in both Staël's political and moral thinking. It was the moment when, realizing the impossibility of constitutional monarchy as a future form of government, she shifted immediately to sketching the contours of a liberal republic.[22] It was also the moment when the moral regeneration of the nation became central to her sketch of a liberal republic. Duty to the universal values of freedom, justice, and truth needed to supplant spirit of party, self-interest, and self-love in order for republican institutions of freedom to take root and be respected.

Three relatively recent works in English by Andrew Jainchill, Biancamaria Fontana, and Aurelian Craiutu examine in detail Staël's formulations of liberal republicanism and the central position that moral regeneration occupied in Staël's political thinking.[23] While, by design, these studies do not bridge to her literary and aesthetic texts, they nevertheless serve as a starting point for understanding how moral regeneration became central to Staël's sketch of a moderate liberal republic.

In a chapter titled "The Post-Terror Discourse of Moeurs," Jainchill paints the state of Thermidorian thought on morality in post-Terror France, arguing that, critical of the violent passions unleashed by the Reign of Terror, this group of thinkers fought for the moral regeneration of the nation.[24] These Thermidorian thinkers coalesced around the idea that a republic could only exist if it was buttressed by republican *moeurs*. In a quest to give a future to the republic, they attempted to think through what would constitute an appropriate republican moral education; what institutions could promote this appropriate education; and how this education could be inculcated in both contemporary and future generations. In terms of what would constitute an appropriate moral education, Jainchill shows that these thinkers promoted the study of classical republican virtues and the importance of domestic patriarchal virtues as the pillars of modern public morality.[25] The inculcation of these virtues should happen in public schools, public festivals, and, at home, through the father as moral educator of the family. Furthermore, this multipronged approach to the inculcation of moral values should be supported by public censors, some argued, and also by a civil religion such as *théophilantropie* (theophilanthropy) that promoted love of one's country as the most important civic virtue and that, organizationally, would be overseen by a Committee of Moral Direction made up of a small group of fathers.[26]

---

[22] In contrast with Bettina Brentano von Arnim, Staël did not view the "enlightened monarch" as possible model for a free republic. See chapter 6 here.

[23] Andrew Jainchill, *Reimagining Politics after the Terror* (Ithaca: Cornell University Press, 2008); Fontana, *Germaine de Staël*; Aurelian Craiutu, *A Virtue for Courageous Minds* (Princeton: Princeton University Press, 2012).

[24] Jainchill, *Reimagining*, 62–107.

[25] Jainchill, *Reimagining*, 98.

[26] Jainchill, *Reimagining*, 98.

A participant in these Thermidorian debates and discussions on how to define and promote a republican morality, Staël agreed with the need for virtues such as the love of freedom, but she could not have diverged more widely from these male perspectives in terms of how to inculcate these virtues. However, this is not the focus in Jainchill's following chapter, in which he presents Staël's version of a liberal republic. Instead, he narrowly focuses on an important and unpublished post-Terror political text written by Staël, *Of Present Circumstances That Can End the Revolution and Principles That Must Found the Republic* (1798), and highlights that, for Staël, political equality and civil liberty had to constitute the two foundations of modern republicanism.[27] When he arrives at the central question of morality in her political thinking, he concludes that Staël, like her Thermidorian counterparts, believed in the need for harmony between the population's *moeurs* and republican forms of government but that her solution to the contemporary disharmony was for Protestantism to become the religion of the republic.

While, indeed, if one does not take into account Staël's aesthetic thinking, the primary manuscript studied by Jainchill could lead one to conclude that Staël might be advocating for a national change in religion to buttress a liberal republic. This would be a mistake, though. Indeed, as a Protestant, Staël did turn to elements of Protestantism and to Protestant thinkers such as Herder and Schleiermacher for inspiration for her moral thinking; however, the central tenets of this moral thinking—conscience, moral freedom, sentiment, reason, beauty, the sublime, independent thinking, and the perfectibility of the human species—were above all rooted in philosophy and literature.[28] Interestingly, an irony of Jainchill's chapter on Staël is that he presents her as one of two thinkers who articulated resolutely modern versions of a liberal republic, but rather than Germaine de Staël, he qualifies the other thinker, Charles-Guillaume Théremin, as the "Kantian" thinker because he grounded his version of a liberal republic in moral universalism. To understand the degree to which Staël's moral philosophy was "Kantian" would necessitate broad understanding of her aesthetic thinking, which is only revealed in her literary writings.

In *Germaine de Staël: A Political Portrait*, Biancamaria Fontana takes a more holistic approach to describing Staël's liberal republican thinking by following how it evolved over her career through her nonfiction works, published and unpublished, and through her correspondence. The very detailed portrait that Fontana paints of Staël as a political thinker also includes a more nuanced look at the moral foundations that Staël sought to lay for a liberal republic. She emphasizes how Staël saw the perfectibility of the human species as proof that France was on a path to freedom, equality, and greater

---

[27] Germaine de Staël, *Des Circonstances actuelles qui peuvent terminer la Révolution et des principes qui doivent fonder la République en France (Of Present Circumstances That Can End the Revolution and Principles That Must Found the Republic)*, ed. Lucia Omacini (Paris: Droz, 1979). Henceforth *Of Present Circumstances*. This text was written by Staël in 1798 but only first published in 1906. It has not been translated into English. All quotations will be my translations of the French text.

[28] For an introduction to how Protestantism and Protestant thinkers influenced her philosophical thinking, see her chapter "On Protestantism," in *Germany*, vol. 2, 267–274.

justice.[29] Fontana calls attention to Staël's focus on self-interested passions—such as ambition and vanity—and how, for Staël, these passions were the reason why no great leaders (dedicated to the causes of freedom, political equality, and justice) arose out of the French Revolution.[30] Further, Fontana highlights that the essential moral problem of the French Revolution, for Staël, which became a political problem, was the people's susceptibility to partisanship and fanaticism. This partisanship and fanaticism relied on leaders who were capable of inspiring people to sacrifice their moral judgment to national interest, which was problematic, as Staël writes: "when once we have said that morals ought to be sacrificed to national interest, we are very liable to contract the sense of the word Nation from day to day, and to make it signify at first our own partisans, then our friends, and then our family; which is but a decent synonym for ourselves."[31] Fontana even signals a bridge to Staël's aesthetic thinking when she writes that, for Staël, literary creation represented the best way to address individual and group passions like self-love and party spirit, a precondition to becoming a functional citizen.[32]

In *A Virtue for Courageous Minds: Moderation in French Political Thought, 1748–1830*, Aurelian Craiutu comes the closest of the analysts of Staël's political thought to offering a bridge from morality in her political thinking to morality in her aesthetic thought. Similar to Fontana, Craiutu takes a meticulous and overarching look at her political writings, which span from the early Revolution through to her death under the restoration of the Bourbon monarchy, to underscore Staël's unflinching commitment to pluralism, moderation, freedom, and constitutional government.[33] Like Jainchill and Fontana, Craiutu highlights that the importance of morality in Staël's thinking arrives on the scene with the Reign of Terror and with her subsequent attempts to think through how a revolution that began in the name of the universal values of freedom and equality could give way to the trampling of legality and morality by the Jacobins and the acceptance of this trampling by the people.[34] For Staël, as Craiutu explains, the power of the Jacobin leaders resided in their self-interested ability to develop a "virtual religion, that fueled the rise of fanaticism, by joining political enthusiasm, inspired by faith in metaphysical abstractions, to the[ir] political ambitions."[35] These metaphysical abstractions included the concept of liberty "invoked by its overzealous friends to justify

---

[29] The perfectibility of the human species, for Staël, was the moral movement since the beginning of time and catalyzed by the advent of Christianity that led to greater liberty, equality, and justice for all. Staël proves the existence of the perfectibility of the human species in *On Literature*, a work of impressive literary erudition.

[30] Staël analyzes these passions and the role they were playing in the Revolution in her work *On the Influence of Passions* (1795).

[31] Staël, *Germany*, vol. 2, 222. Staël, *De l'Allemagne*, vol. 2, 194.

[32] Fontana, *Germaine de Staël*, 132–157.

[33] He examines Staël's political texts: *Of Present Circumstances that can end the Revolution and Principles that must Found the Republic in France; A Reflection on Interior Peace; Reflections on Peace, Addressed to M. Pitt and to the French; Considerations on the French Revolution*. He also touches briefly on *Germany*.

[34] Craiutu, *A Virtue for Courageous Minds*, 167.

[35] Craiutu, *A Virtue for Courageous Minds*, 168.

the elimination of their opponents, denounced as enemies of the republic."[36] As a result, highlights Craiutu, Staël concluded that the problem was that "while most people want to be free . . . many abuse liberty," and, "in fact, during the revolution no word had been abused more than 'liberty.'"[37]

Indeed, the Revolution had exposed the tendency to want to polarize and oversimplify the messy complexity of conceiving of and implementing new political and social practices and institutions designed to promote and protect freedom.[38] Worse, the tendency to polarize and oversimplify was exacerbated by impatience with this complexity. Finally, the polarization and oversimplification of concepts led to the degradation of language, which, in turn, allowed self-interested leaders to deploy concepts like freedom, devoid of moral significance, to convince followers to commit the most heinous acts of violence in the name of public interest, or worse, public salvation. The solution, for Staël, was philosophical: the French people needed to understand the moral origins of freedom. Only then would the French population and their future leaders be able to develop patience for complexity and compromise. Only then would they be able to tolerate opposing views with the goal of embracing "the ideal of a liberty *above* or *beyond* all parties," and "believing that one must support whatever government had the best chance of promoting civil and political liberty."[39] Only then would they privilege the virtues of pity, courage, justice, and generosity over the passions of self-interest, self-love, ambition, and fanaticism.[40]

In his conclusion to this chapter, Craiutu sketches the beginning of a bridge to Staël's aesthetic thinking. He highlights that, for Staël, a predisposition to understanding the moral origins of freedom depended on the capacity to feel enthusiasm because enthusiasm allowed for the experience of "the elevation of soul" and "the comprehension of superior truths." Indeed, Staël affirms: "let me repeat: enthusiasm has nothing to do with fanaticism and cannot lead people astray. Enthusiasm is tolerant—not out of indifference, but because it makes us feel the interest and beauty of everything."[41]

All three of the works that I have presented analyze in great detail Staël's liberal and moderate thought during the post-Terror years, and how, for Staël, moral regeneration was a condition sine qua non for the conception and implementation of a free republic. None of these works gives any time, though, to an easily overlooked text that was published during the same post-Terror period as the political texts that sketch Staël's liberal and moderate thought: *Essay on Fiction* (*Essai sur les fictions*, 1795). In addition, these texts do not reference two key chapters, titled "On Writers" and "On the Power of Reason," in *Of Present Circumstances* even though these two chapters close the work. *Essay on Fiction* and *Of Present Circumstances* jointly represent an inflection

---

[36] Craiutu, *A Virtue for Courageous Minds*, 173.
[37] Craiutu, *A Virtue for Courageous Minds*, 172–173.
[38] Craiutu, *A Virtue for Courageous Minds*, 196.
[39] Craiutu, *A Virtue for Courageous Minds*, 172.
[40] Staël, *Des Circonstances*, 298.
[41] Craiutu, *A Virtue for Courageous Minds*, 196.

point, though, where—as I will highlight—through a focus on the moral regeneration of the nation, Staël's literary thinking becomes inextricably conjoined with her political thinking.

2 The Political and Moral Role of Fiction

In *Of Present Circumstances*, Staël calls on philosophical writers to help bring an end to the Revolution and a beginning to a durable liberal republic. Famously, she writes: "it is philosophers who made the Revolution, it is they who will end it."[42] She argued that works of philosophical analysis dedicated to the study of political theory, what she called *la science politique*, should serve the elaboration and implementation of political institutions.[43] She writes: "for all of legislation ... for the organization of a free constitution ... to end the Revolution by bringing reason and certitude to political questions, it is to philosophical analysis that we must turn."[44] For a moral revolution that could buttress a future liberal republic, Staël reasoned that France would need to turn to philosophical writers of fiction, a genre that could be widely consumed. As she writes, "one class of writers, those who dedicate themselves uniquely to works of imagination can be ... of great service to the national spirit," because "it is philosophical reason joined with the talents of the writer from which the impulse of national spirit in France must spring."[45] Writers of philosophical fiction could reform national spirit by inspiring virtue.[46]

One of the first tasks for philosophical writers of fiction was to address the degradation of language. Staël argues in *Of Present Circumstances* that the Reign of Terror, "a reign of crime," infused language with "all of these uncouth or ferocious expressions that continue to soil the language."[47] As an example of this degraded language, she cites discourse from one of the radical republican clubs, of which I will quote just the beginning: "Citizens, federalism is raising its hideous head; anarchy is ready to devour us; the monster of royalism is going to precipitate us into this; it is time to reveal to you the entire truth: aristocrats, those vampires of the people, are hiding themselves in order to better deal their blows in the shadows."[48] Of this passage, Staël writes that this type of degraded language "depraves both the person who utters these expressions as well as the person who hears them."[49] The person who hears these expressions and takes them

---

[42] Staël, *Des circonstances*, 273.

[43] Staël, *Des circonstances*, 281. It should be noted that during the French Revolution, *la science politique* is a neologism and not a discipline.

[44] Staël, *Des circonstances*, 282.

[45] Staël, *Des circonstances*, 289.

[46] Staël, *Des circonstances*, 286–287.

[47] Staël, *Des circonstances*, 287–288.

[48] Staël, *Des circonstances*, 295. Staël quotes this passage in italics in the original text.

[49] Staël, *Des circonstances*, 295.

seriously can be pushed to "the bloodiest fury" whereas the person who does not take them seriously and who is an "honest soul" becomes, through this corrupted language, indifferent to "the most worthy principles of enthusiasm."[50] To address the problem of the degradation of language, Staël writes: "there is, by the way, a great service that philosophical writers can provide France: to introduce reforms in the use of speech and to preserve us first from its perfidy and even from its inanity."[51] Among the reforms that she invokes is the introduction of the use of natural language because "it is a noble, elegant and harmonious style that produces within us the sort of exalted feeling that a beautiful day, the pure air, a still evening elicit for souls in harmony with the wonders of creation."[52] The task for writers, in terms of language, was monumental because the stake was infusing truth back into the language of feeling, as she writes: "sincere writers, the only ones who can have superior talent, will have a lot of difficulty putting truth back into the language of feeling."[53] The task was urgent, though, because a revolution in language could inaugurate a revolution in feeling, which could usher out the reign of passions buttressed by self-interest and usher in respect for the virtues and the feelings that Staël deemed essential to a functioning moral citizen, namely pity, courage, justice, and generosity.[54]

While in *Of Present Circumstances*, Staël articulates very clearly the political role that fiction needs to play, it is in *Essay on Fiction* where she presents the "philosophical novel" as the genre that can have the greatest influence on moral ideas.[55] For Staël, the philosophical novel—the category in which she placed *The New Héloïse*, *Paul and Virginia*, English novels like *Clarissa* and *Tom Jones*, and in which she would later place as the prime example *The Sorrows of Young Werther*—was the only form of fiction, in her opinion, that could both move an individual to discover truth of feeling in the private sphere and also have far-reaching influence on the moral ideas of the French population as a whole.[56] She writes that the philosophical novel "as we can conceive of it, as we have a few models, is one of the most influential on the morality of individuals, which must then shape public morals."[57] Rather than individual virtue being inculcated patriarchally by the father of the family, then, Staël proposed the philosophical novel because its dramatic effect and art of moving the soul to action through natural language could inspire virtue more effectively than patriarchal discipline: "the gift of affecting is the great strength of fiction; it is possible to make almost all moral truths sensitive by

---

50 Staël, *Des circonstances*, 294.

51 Staël, *Des circonstances*, 293.

52 Staël, *Des circonstances*, 289.

53 Staël, *Des circonstances*, 294.

54 Staël, *Des circonstances*, 298.

55 Staël, "Essai sur les fictions" ("Essay on Fiction") in *Oeuvres de jeunesse*, 145. Translations henceforth are mine.

56 Staël's moral revolution depended indeed on the literate public. In her opinion, if she could educate and inspire moral reform in the literate population, these men and women could then serve as virtuous models of emulation for the general public.

57 Staël, "Essai sur les fictions," 146.

putting them in action."[58] Furthermore, the philosophical novel was naturally superior to metaphysical writings on morality as a means to inspire virtue because "metaphysical precision, applied to the moral affections of man, is completely incompatible with his nature."[59] She adds: "we can extract a purer, more heightened morality from good novels than from any didactic work on virtue."[60] It should not go unnoticed that by making these statements about the superiority of philosophical novels on moving people to virtuous action, she was also positioning the writer of fiction in a role superior to that of the father, the teacher, and models of emulation for revolutionary festivals.

Specifically concerning how a philosophical novel needed to go about inspiring truth of feeling, Staël sketched a preliminary framework of the interplay between form and content in *Essay on Fiction*. In terms of content, the philosophical novel, for Staël, should depict the full panoply of human passions and follow the principles of verisimilitude. Only a literature that painted an individual's habitual feelings (*sentiments habituels*) could both appeal to and move the masses who, for Staël, could not be expected to be moved by the dramatic theater of kings, the supernatural stories of the ancients, or the heroic subjects of historical novels. By painting characters and feelings with force and detail, by focusing on the "quiet, delicate and gentle morals on which the happiness of individuals and their relationships between each other depend," Staël reasoned that "there was no other type of reading capable of producing an impression as deep of hate for vice and love for virtue."[61] The love of virtue, which she described as the love of the feelings of pity, courage, justice, and generosity, and the hate of vice thus became for Staël the effect that all philosophical novels should produce. Finally, in terms of form, the philosophical novel should be guided by philosophy. She explains that though she advises writers to exploit the passions, "philosophy must be the invisible power that directs their effects" because "if it showed itself first, it would destroy the prestige of [the passions]."[62] She thus warned writers not to let themselves be seduced by the fiction they were writing; on the contrary, they needed to remember that fiction was nothing more than the art of seduction for a philosophical and moral end: "fiction is used to seduce; the more we want its result to be moral or philosophical, the more we must adorn it with all that can affect, and lead to the result without indicating it in advance."[63] Taken together then, *Essay on Fiction* and the last two chapters of *Of Present Circumstances* can be read as the first draft of a poetics of the philosophical novel.

In her subsequent major work on literature and philosophy, *On Literature* (1800), and in the preface to her first novel, *Delphine* (1802), Staël fleshes out more fully her conception of the philosophical novel and the role it should play. In her preface to *Delphine*, Staël reminds the reader of one of the major problems facing the moral regeneration

---

[58] Staël, "Essai sur les fictions," 150.
[59] Staël, "Essai sur les fictions," 131.
[60] Staël, "Essai sur les fictions," 152.
[61] Staël, "Essai sur les fictions," 148.
[62] Staël, "Essai sur les fictions," 132.
[63] Staël, "Essai sur les fictions," 132.

of the nation: the perversion and corruption of the French language.[64] Specifically regarding French literature at the turn of the century, as France was coming out of the Revolution and into the authoritarian rule of Napoleon Bonaparte, Staël highlights that a return to the past when respect for the French language was at its peak in terms of good taste would not suffice to reinvigorate degraded contemporary language. A new genre was needed for nineteenth-century France that would turn to the strengths of the literatures and philosophies of other nations that were further along in their pursuit of freedom and truth.[65] For Staël then, the future French philosophical novel should find its genesis in the eighteenth-century English novel, a genre that embodied natural language—the talent of painting nature with truth—and that sought to have a moral influence.[66] In addition to its proximity to nature, Staël argued that the superiority of the eighteenth-century English novel could be found in its embodiment of English melancholy. Staël argued that melancholy was a perfecting force necessary in free republics because "liberty and virtue, the two great results of human reason, require meditation, and meditation leads necessarily to serious objects."[67] Furthermore, she reasoned, the English understood that individual happiness was necessarily at odds with universal values such as freedom, equality, and justice because these ideals and the institutions that sought to protect them demanded self-sacrifice and duty to the love of freedom. The English novel thus integrated the themes of self-sacrifice and suffering as virtuous actions necessary to freedom, and as a consequence, she saw the English novel and novelist as contributing to the public good, thereby strengthening the free English nation. With its natural language, melancholy, and public utility, Staël saw in the English novel the seed of a new genre that could be adapted to France. Future French novelists needed to be aware, though, that the English novel lacked the perfection of style and taste that a French public would demand and that was inherent in French thought.[68] In addition, the English national spirit of public utility demanded this same utility of English philosophy, which certainly compromised the English novel's pursuit of truth above and beyond existing manners of thinking and governing. For Staël, English philosophy had not advanced much beyond materialist metaphysical thought that placed the center of morality in the sphere of sensations. Luckily for the English, she affirmed, "the cultivation of all pure and elevated sentiments is so consolidated in England by political and religious institutions that the skepticisms of the intellect revolve around these imposing columns without ever shaking them."[69]

---

[64] Staël, *Delphine*, ed. Béatrice Didier (Paris: GF Flammarion, 2000), vol. 1, 53.

[65] Staël, *Delphine*, 54; Staël, *De l'Allemagne*, vol. 2, 75.

[66] Staël, *Delphine*, 53; Staël, *Des circonstances*, 287.

[67] Staël, *De la littérature*, 241. For an analysis of melancholy in Staël's literature, see Eric Gidal, "Civic Melancholy: English Gloom and French Enlightenment," *Eighteenth Century Studies* 37 (2003): 23–45. See also Karen de Bruin, "The Melancholy of Happiness: *Corinne* and the *Femme Supérieure*," in *Staël's Philosophy of the Passions: Sensibility, Society and the Sister Arts*, ed. Tili Boon Cuillé and Karyna Szmurlo (Lewisburg: Bucknell University Press, 2013), 75–92.

[68] Staël, *De la littérature*, 249.

[69] Staël, *Germany*, vol. 2, 119. Staël, *De l'Allemagne*, vol. 2, 97.

For the pursuit of natural truths and especially the truth of feeling, the French philosophical novel would need to turn to German philosophy, as Staël confirms: "the English are less independent than the Germans in their general manner of considering all that relates to religious and political ideas. The English find peace and liberty in the order of the things that they have adopted, and they consent to the modification of some philosophical principles. . . . The philosophers from Germany, encompassed by faulty institutions . . . have devoted themselves to a rigorous examination of natural truths."[70] While German philosophy and literature exhibited errors of style and taste, much like English literature and philosophy, for Staël, German literature and thought showed the "character . . . of a free people" in their pursuit of ideals and truth.[71] More important, she found within the new German school of philosophical thought the revolutionary metaphysical doctrine that would ground her notions of personal responsibility and duty to freedom.

3   The New German School

Staël indeed began to turn seriously to German literature in 1799 as she was composing *On Literature*. As German literature and philosophy were not widely known in France, to familiarize herself with German thinking and writing, she requested from her German-speaking friends works like Schiller's *Marie Stuart, Wallenstein*, and *Joan of Arc*, Goethe's *Werther* and *Wilhelm Meister*, Friedrich Klopstock's *Messiade*, and Charles de Viller's *Philosophy of Kant*. At this stage in her career, her *Essay on Fiction*, translated by Johann Wolfgang von Goethe and published by Friedrich Schiller in *Die Horen*, had been well received in Germany. However, she had not yet visited Germany, she could not read German, and she was reading all the works she ordered in translation. Later in 1799, however, and enchanted by what she had been reading, Staël began her study of the German language with her tutor, Gerlach, who exposed her to German philosophical thought. After his death in 1802, she continued her studies with August Wilhelm Schlegel, whose lectures on drama she attended in Vienna and who also served as tutor to her children and who frequented her salon at Coppet. She described her experience of reading in German the works of writers such as Kant, Schiller, Goethe, Schelling, Lessing, Herder, Müller, and the Schlegel brothers: "when I started the study of German, it felt like I was entering into a new sphere where I encountered the most striking insights on all that I had previously felt confusedly."[72] Finally, her forced exile under Napoleon Bonaparte's Consulate afforded her the opportunity to travel to Germany during the winter of 1803–1804 to visit the writers and thinkers—especially Goethe and Schiller—whom she had come to respect profoundly. While there, she gleefully discovered that,

[70] Staël, *De la littérature*, 257.
[71] Staël, *De la littérature*, 256, 264.
[72] Staël, *De l'Allemagne*, vol. 2, 68.

contrary to its censure in France by a press controlled by Napoleon, her novel, *Delphine*, had been widely read in Germany, and furthermore, to much acclaim.[73]

After hinting to friends such as Friedrich Heinrich Jacobi that she would publish a work that would present German culture, thought, and literature to the French nation, she finally did so in 1810 only to have the published work immediately seized by Napoleon's police.[74] Much to his misogynistic discomfort, Napoleon increasingly recognized that Staël's devotion to freedom, truth, and justice was becoming dangerous to his autocratic regime even though, to avoid his censors, Staël made not one mention of him and his political influence on the German states.[75] His repression did not stop Staël from seeing to it that her work was published. Thanks to her governess, Fanny Randally, and to August Wilhelm and Friedrich Schlegel, who ensured the safekeeping of the manuscript, Staël had the text reprinted in London in 1813 and immediately translated into English and German.[76]

It is in this major work, *Germany*, a work dedicated to analyzing the public spirit of Germans, that Staël elaborates in detail the elements of German philosophy and literature that she found essential to her poetics of the philosophical novel. Importantly, it is also in this work that Staël hones her conception of individual virtue, the basis for the moral regeneration of the nation, and for the implementation of a free republic. Finally, it was this work that elevated Staël to the unenviable status of archenemy of Napoleon Bonaparte.

Staël makes clear in *Germany* that of all the German philosophers, the thinker who exerted a disproportionate influence on her moral thinking was Immanuel Kant.[77] In Kant's philosophy, as she understood it, Staël found the tools to disarm eighteenth-century French metaphysical thought, which she had been writing against for years.[78]

---

[73] Germaine de Staël, *France et Allemagne, Le Léman et L'Italie*, vol. 5 of *Correspondance Générale*, ed. Béatrice W. Jasinski (Geneva: Champion-Slatkine, 2009), 142. Staël, *De l'Allemagne*, vol. 1, 30.

[74] Staël, *Correspondance Générale*, vol. 5, 175. Winock, *Madame de Staël*, 377.

[75] Florence Lotterie, "Madame de Staël et l'esprit de Coppet," in *L'Empire des Muses: Napoléon, les Arts et les Lettres* (Paris: Belin, 2004), 137.

[76] Winock, *Madame de Staël*, 393; Theresa M. Kelley, "Women, Gender and Literary Criticism," in Brown, *The Cambridge History of Literary Criticism*, vol. 5, *Romanticism*, 324.

[77] Staël also presents the moral and aesthetic philosophies of precursors to Kant and philosophers inspired by Kant. For example, she presents Lessing, Hemsterhuis, and Jacobi as precursors to Kant because they attacked materialist doctrine but, according to her, none of the three founded a new metaphysical system. Staël argued that the most prominent successors of Kant, Fichte and Schelling, ineffectively attempted to reduce the dualism of Kant's system, rooted in both the soul and nature, to one principle: either the soul or nature. Staël found the philosophies of both of these thinkers inferior to that of Kant because they did not leave room for conscience and duty which, for her, was the divinely governed interaction between the individual and the material world. Staël, *De l'Allemagne*, vol. 2, 141–154.

[78] While Staël played an outsize role in introducing German thought to England and France, she has also been criticized for her oversimplification of Kant's *Critique of Practical Reason* and *Critique of the Power of Judgment*. David Simpson summarizes, for example: "even the cosmopolitan Madame de Staël, in her important book *De l'Allemagne*, translated into English in 1813 and a key text in introducing the second generation of Romantics to German thought, managed only the vaguest summary of Kant's philosophical priorities"; David Simpson, "Transcendental Philosophy," in Brown, *The Cambridge History of Literary Criticism*, vol. 5, *Romanticism*, 74.

Staël described Enlightenment metaphysics in *Germany* as the materialist current of thought, espoused by the likes of Helvetius, Diderot, and Saint-Lambert, that was responsible for having advanced in France the notion that the origin of all ideas came from the sensations and the passions they provoked—the strongest passion being self-interest.[79] Individual virtue then consisted in aligning self-interest with self-love (*amour de soi*) and public virtue consisted in the alignment of self-interest with national interest. The major problem with this line of thought, reasoned Staël, was that it situated morality outside the individual and deprived the individual of both free will and individual responsibility.[80] Furthermore, it excluded sentiment, and more specifically the role of conscience, from any conception of individual and public virtue. In addition, this line of thought left no place for enthusiasm—the simultaneous feeling of love for the beautiful, the elevation of the soul, and the pleasure (*jouissance*) of devotion—thereby giving overwhelming space to the passion of fanaticism. Enlightenment "metaphysics" for Staël was thus to blame for its role in the propagation of Revolutionary violence because it allowed individuals to justify heinous acts of violence, such as mass beheadings in the name of public salvation, as virtuous acts of fanaticism because these acts conformed with the national interest at the time.

Staël saw it as essential to find a different philosophical system that could place personal responsibility, moral judgment, and duty to freedom at its center.[81] In Kant's philosophy she found both the philosophical system she was seeking and an aesthetic system that aligned with the poetics of the philosophical novel that she was elaborating, as she writes laudatorily: "Kant wished to re-establish primitive truths and spontaneous activity in the soul, conscience in morals, and the ideal in the arts."[82] One of Staël's major preoccupations concerned the centrality of feeling to a philosophy of moral behavior. She was thrilled to find in her readings that German thinkers of the "new school," inspired by Kant, "consider sentiment as a fact, the primitive phaenomenon of mind; and they look upon the power of philosophical reasoning as destined solely to investigate the meaning of this fact."[83] Staël quickly understood that for German thinkers, and especially Kant, feeling was different from feelings: "sentiment and conscience are terms employed almost as synonyms in his writings; but sensibility approaches much nearer the sphere of emotions, and, consequently the passions brought about by these emotions."[84] This distinction allowed Staël to argue for the primacy of feeling in any project to provoke moral regeneration of a nation because, as she had seen during the Revolution, reason was a "pliable instrument, which can equally attack and defend" the same interest.[85] Only feeling could tell the just from the unjust, the moral from the immoral. In

---

[79] Staël, *De l'Allemagne*, vol. 2, 181.
[80] Staël, *De l'Allemagne*, vol. 2, 89–92, 109–11.
[81] Staël, *Germany*, vol. 2, 112. Staël, *De l'Allemagne*, vol. 2, 91.
[82] Staël, *Germany*, vol. 2, 150. Staël, *De l'Allemagne*, vol. 2, 129.
[83] Staël, *Germany*, vol. 2, 91. Staël, *De l'Allemagne*, vol. 2, 91.
[84] Staël, *Germany*, vol. 2, 226 (translation modified). Staël, *De l'Allemagne*, vol. 2, 198.
[85] Staël, *Germany*, vol. 2, 156. Staël, *De l'Allemagne*, vol. 2, 133.

a famous statement, Staël wrote of Kant's belief in the primacy of feeling: "in referring to sentiment, which does not admit of doubts, the knowledge of transcendent truths . . . he makes conscience the innate principle of our moral existence; and the feeling of right or wrong is, according to his ideas, the primitive law of the heart."[86] Kant, as she read him, gave a status to conscience that aligned fully with the conception of innate conscience that Staël had been elaborating from an early age, inspired by Rousseau. Moreover, Kant's moral philosophy armed Staël with what she saw as irrefutable proof that feeling was what allowed individuals to know that they were free because innate conscience—a divine voice—was coupled with an innate feeling of duty. The primary moral duty of reason then was to translate the voice of conscience, which existed in a space of freedom unbound by norms and laws, into moral action.[87] It followed then, for Staël, that if individuals were free, they could exercise free will, and thus they were ultimately responsible for their actions. Duty to one's conscience became then the ultimate definition of virtue, for Staël, and it necessarily led to sacrifice and suffering and not the pursuit of individual happiness because the work of conscience was the work of resistance in the name of perfecting of the soul.[88] As a corollary, public virtue, namely the commitment to the universal values of freedom and justice held true by conscience, also required suffering and sacrifice. To uphold public virtue, citizens would need to sacrifice their self-interest and resist injustice in the name of the perfectibility of the human species, that moral movement since the beginning of time, catalyzed by the advent of Christianity, that tended toward universal ideals, and specifically greater freedom, equality, and justice for all.

Inspired by Kantian thought, Staël reasoned that the philosophical novel would need to represent virtue as duty to one's conscience, and thus to self-sacrifice and suffering. It would also need to inspire respect for duty to conscience, self-sacrifice, and suffering. Better yet, the philosophical novel should also somehow awaken the feeling of conscience and duty to one's conscience in its readers. As Staël writes: "the morality of a novel consists then in the sentiments it inspires."[89] In terms of models of emulation for French novelists, they could find inspiration for representation of duty to one's conscience and thus to self-sacrifice and suffering in the eighteenth-century English novel, in English melancholy, and in German novels like *The Sorrows of Young Werther*. Staël would begin to find an answer for French novelists to the question of how to provoke the experience of conscience and duty to one's conscience in her readers, though, in Kant's aesthetics of the beautiful and the sublime.

Kant's aesthetics of the beautiful and the sublime, simplified, gave Staël a mechanism that she could present to French novelists for inspiring the experience of moral freedom (*la liberté morale*). The beautiful in Kantian philosophy, summarized by Staël, was "the realization of that image which is constantly present to the soul" and the "outward

---

[86] Staël, *Germany*, vol. 2, 158. Staël, *De l'Allemagne*, vol. 2, 135.
[87] Staël, *De l'Allemagne*, vol. 2, 135.
[88] Staël, *De l'Allemagne*, vol. 2, 196.
[89] Staël, *De l'Allemagne*, vol. 2, 47.

image of that ideal beauty, the type of which exists in our mind."[90] It both embodied and provoked the "feeling of the infinite."[91] Staël transposed this feeling of the infinite to the moral terrain of enthusiasm, whereby the feeling of the infinite inspired by beauty, now the feeling of enthusiasm, promoted virtuous devotion and divine love in religion.[92] Finally, enthusiasm promoted "all the sacrifices of personal interest" and "the power of duty."[93] Most important, in terms of Staël's poetics of the philosophical novel, enthusiasm flowed from the "universal harmony" of beauty, the harmony between content and form, between fiction and philosophy, between truth and imagination, and between sentiment and reason.[94] It was precisely this harmony that French writers should seek to embody in their novels, and for which she had been advocating since her *Essay on Fiction*.

If beauty allowed for the experience of the infinite, and thus the feeling of enthusiasm, thereby providing a nourishing moral force, it was the Kantian sublime that provided Staël with the aesthetic device that she could adapt to enable novelists to confront readers with their moral freedom and their duty to their conscience, and thus to suffering and sacrifice. Staël presented the Kantian sublime as moral freedom grappling with destiny or nature. She described the sublime as having two effects on an individual: first to overwhelm and then to uplift.[95] It was thanks to "one spark of the sacred fire in our bosoms" that an individual could overcome the overwhelming nature of the sublime because "with that one spark, we are able to resist the impressions which all the powers in the world could make upon us."[96] It was precisely this resistance to overwhelming exterior forces that interested Staël because it was in this resistance that moral action happened. Sublime scenes within a philosophical novel could inevitably force readers into moments of moral struggle with no other recourse than their own conscience and their knowledge that virtue was nothing more than duty to this conscience. Of course, given the inapprehensible nature of the sublime, it could only conceivably appear in glimmers in the novel, and it could only come through in divine moments. The capacity to conjure the sublime in fiction thus would have to depend on the novelist's genius, which, of course, was rooted in the novelist's own duty to her conscience and capacity to resist. And unsurprisingly, as Staël obliquely suggests through her character Corinne in the novel *Corinne, or Italy* (1807), a thinly veiled metaphor for the exceptional female writer, it was this writer, protected only by devotion to her conscience and the knowledge that she was turning herself over to a higher cause— that of freedom and of the moral education of future generations—who, through her

---

[90] Staël, *Germany*, vol. 2, 160. Staël, *De l'Allemagne*, vol. 2, 136–37.
[91] Staël, *Germany*, vol. 2, 262. Staël, *De l'Allemagne*, vol. 2, 218.
[92] Staël, *De l'Allemagne*, vol. 2, 239.
[93] Staël, *Germany*, vol. 2, 263. Staël, *De l'Allemagne*, vol. 2, 239.
[94] Staël, *De l'Allemagne*, vol. 2, 301.
[95] Staël, *De l'Allemagne*, vol. 2, 137.
[96] Staël, *Germany*, vol. 2, 161. Staël, *De l'Allemagne*, vol. 2, 137.

resistance, was most predisposed to the type of genius needed to inspire sublime scenes within the novel.[97]

4 CONCLUSION

Napoleon dreamed of legitimizing his empire through neoclassical literature and the arts, through writers and artists who sang his praise; Germaine de Staël mounted a formidable pole of resistance through her philosophy and fiction as well as her salon at Coppet that brought together preeminent thinkers in Europe.[98] As Florence Lotterie highlights, for Staël as for her friends at Coppet, "writing was an insurrectional act that consecrated individual independence," and this insurrectional writing was justified by duty to one's conscience in the name of the perfectibility of the human species.[99] The Reign of Terror gave urgency to Staël's search for a metaphysical system that would consecrate conscience and duty to one's conscience as central to liberal morality, and it spurred her search for a new national literature capable of morally reforming the French nation. The discordance between the result of the Revolution (the Napoleonic empire) and the political philosophy of freedom in the name of which the Revolution erupted pushed Staël to work even more fervently in favor of a liberal morality rooted in conscience and resistance and a literature that would support the propagation of this morality. Indeed, fifty years later, Victor Hugo would famously qualify romanticism as "liberalism in literature," but for Staël, at the moment she was writing, the stakes of the philosophical novel were higher: the writer was the guardian of the moral seeds of a free republic, which had to be disseminated and sowed at all costs. In opposition then to an emperor who thought that all women should stay home and knit, Staël instead birthed a new genre of fiction as philosophy.

Retrospectively, there could be no more fitting day than July 14 for Germaine de Staël's passing. This is the day when the French nation celebrates what Staël relentlessly worked for over her lifetime: a liberal republic rooted in individual freedom and political equality. While the French nation does not nationally celebrate Staël's death, enshrined in this date is the sublimity of Germaine de Staël's work and existence, which Benjamin Constant describes in an obituary: "those who mourn her feebly will not know how to portray her; those who mourn her as she was worthy of being mourned will not be able to paint her."[100]

---

[97] For a full analysis of how Corinne comes to embody melancholic genius and the artists capable of provoking the experience of the sublime, see de Bruin, "The Melancholy of Happiness," 75–92.

[98] Lotterie, "Madame de Staël," 140 (translation mine).

[99] Lotterie, "Madame de Staël," 142; Staël, *De la littérature*, 323.

[100] Constant, "Nécrologie," 180.

BIBLIOGRAPHY

Balayé, Simone. *Ecrire, lutter, vivre*. Geneva: Librairie Droz, 1994.

Constant, Benjamin. "Nécrologie." *Mercure de France*, July 1817.

Craiutu, Aurelien. *A Virtue for Courageous Minds*. Princeton: Princeton University Press, 2012.

De Bruin, Karen. "The Melancholy of Happiness: *Corinne* and the *Femme Supérieure*." In *Staël's Philosophy of the Passions: Sensibility, Society and the Sister Arts*, edited by Tili Boon Cuillé and Karyna Szmurlo, 75–92. Lewisburg: Bucknell University Press, 2013.

Fontana, Biancamaria. *Germaine de Staël: A Political Portrait*. Princeton: Princeton University Press, 2016.

Gidal, Eric. "Civic Melancholy: English Gloom and French Enlightenment." *Eighteenth Century Studies* 37 (2003): 23–45.

Jainchill, Andrew. *Reimagining Politics after the Terror*. Ithaca: Cornell University Press, 2008.

Kelley, Theresa M. "Women, Gender and Literary Criticism." In *The Cambridge History of Literary Criticism*, vol. 5, *Romanticism*, edited by Marshall Brown, 321–337. Cambridge: Cambridge University Press, 2000.

Lotterie, Florence. "Madame de Staël et l'esprit de Coppet." In *L'Empire des Muses: Napoléon, les Arts et les Lettres*, edited by Jean-Claude Bonnet, 133–150. Paris: Belin, 2004.

Simpson, David. "The French Revolution." In *The Cambridge History of Literary Criticism*, vol. 5, *Romanticism*, edited by Marshall Brown, 49–71. Cambridge: Cambridge University Press, 2000.

Simpson, David. "Transcendental Philosophy." In *The Cambridge History of Literary Criticism*, vol. 5, *Romanticism*, edited by Marshall Brown, 72–91. Cambridge: Cambridge University Press, 2000.

Staël, Germaine de. *Considerations on the Principal Events of the French Revolution*. Edited by Aurelian Craiutu. Indianapolis: Liberty Fund, 2008.

Staël, Germaine de. *De la littérature*. Edited by Gérard Gengembre and Jean Goldzink. Paris: GF Flammarion, 1991.

Staël, Germaine de. *De l'Allemagne*. Edited by Simone Balayé. 2 vols. Paris: GF Flammarion, 1968.

Staël, Germaine de. *De l'influence des passions suivi de Réflexions sur le suicide*. Edited by Chantal Thomas. Paris: Editions Payot et Rivages, 2000.

Staël, Germaine de. *Delphine*. Edited by Béatrice Didier. 2 vols. Paris: GF Flammarion, 2000.

Staël, Germaine de. *Des Circonstances actuelles qui peuvent terminer la Révolution et des principes qui doivent fonder la République en France*. Edited by Lucia Omacini. Paris: Droz, 1979.

Staël, Germaine de. "Essai sur les fictions." In *Oeuvres de jeunesse*, edited by Simone Balayé and John Isbell, 131–156. Paris: Editions Desjonquères, 1997.

Staël, Germaine de. *France et Allemagne, Le Léman et l'Italie*, vol. 5 of *Correspondance générale*. Edited by Béatrice W. Jasinski. Geneva: Champion-Slatkine, 2009.

Staël, Germaine de. *Germany*. Vol. 2. New York: Eastburn Kirk and Company, 1814.

Staël, Germaine de. *The Influence of Literature upon Society*. 2 vols. London: Henry Colburn, 1812.

Staël, Germaine de. *Lettres diverses, 1794*. Vol. 2 of *Correspondance Générale*, edited by Béatrice W. Jasinski. Paris: Pauvert, 1965.

Staël, Germaine de. *Letters on the Works and Character of J. J. Rousseau.* London: G. G. J. and J. Robinson, 1789.

Staël, Germaine de. "Lettres sur les ouvrages et le caractère de J.-J. Rousseau." In *Oeuvres de jeunesse,* edited by Simone Balayé and John Isbell, 33–99. Paris: Editions Desjonquères, 1997.

Winock, Michel. *Madame de Staël.* Paris: Fayard, 2010.

CHAPTER 3

···

SOPHIE MEREAU (1770–1806)

···

ADRIAN DAUB

LITERARY history has long positioned Sophie Mereau as a consummate mediator. As Jacqueline Vansant has noted, Mereau's reception has treated her "as a functional adjunct: as a muse, as erotic impulse, as tragic victim who inspires the male poetic genius to greater flight of fancy."[1] Half early idealist, half late Enlightenment *Popularphilosophin*, Mereau has often been regarded as a literary figure with strong philosophical ambitions who probably proved more influential on the development of philosophical romanticism than on, say, romantic literary forms. She is often located "in between" the Enlightenment and romanticism, a kind of bridge. She belongs, as Anthony J. Harper notes, "to a generation set on the borderline between the Enlightenment and classicism and the first generation of the German Romantics."[2] But at least when it comes to philosophy, this framing risks reducing Mereau's own agency: while she first emerged onto the intellectual scene among a generation that sought to combine the impulses of Kant's critical philosophy with the existing framework of German philosophy,[3] her activity continued well into the heyday of romanticism and idealism. The fact that she maintained dueling commitments, to the new currents on the one hand and to more outmoded philosophical concerns on the other, was likely strategic. Mereau clung to sensualist and sentimentalist impulses of the Enlightenment, to its strategies of communication and its pedagogic commitments, because she sought to evade certain constitutive elisions and weaknesses of German romantic and idealist thought.

We underestimate the level of careful calibration, of active mediation performed by this singular thinker at our own peril. Mereau was no passive alembic in which the

---

[1] Jaqueline Vansant, "Sophie Mereau," in *Bitter Healing: German Women Writers, 1700–1830: An Anthology*, ed. Jeannine Blackwell and Suzanne Zantop (Lincoln: University of Nebraska Press, 1990), 371.

[2] Anthony J. Harper, "Sophie Mereau," in *Encyclopedia of German Literature*, ed. Matthias Konzett (London: Routledge, 2015), 697.

[3] Manfred Frank, *Unendliche Annäherung* (Frankfurt: Suhrkamp, 1997).

various intellectual currents of her age entered into unusual combinations. She was a canny, thoughtful and purposeful triangulator, part of a generation of thinkers who sought to bring competing and differing philosophical programs to bear on a lifeworld that was undergoing profound transformation. The most important biographical fact of her life likely was the French Revolution, and like many of her contemporaries she spent her life trying to understand the ramifications of that event. In this, she resembles other actors in the Kantian aftermath—from the fideists à la Jacobi, to the theologically oriented Kant critics who first roused the Tübingen Idealists to essay at "completing" the critical philosophy.[4] All of these groups of thinkers sought to combine established philosophy and preexisting commitments with a profound revolution in what constituted philosophical thought. What set Mereau apart was simply the nature of those commitments—where the triangulations of, say, Johann Friedrich Flatt or Gottlieb Christian Storr (two theologians who taught Hegel and Hölderlin at the Tübingen *Stift*, (in)famous for slipping all of theology back into the Kantian system as postulates of pure practical reason) were profoundly backward-looking, looking to protect an outmoded theology from the Kantian challenge, Mereau's pointed forward: toward early feminism's engagement with the terminal moraines of German Idealism, specifically the fracturing and dueling strands of Hegelianism.[5]

This overview of her ideas will avoid proceeding biographically—an approach that has been too readily applied to women authors in general, and seems deeply inappropriate for a woman whose philosophical ambitions were never exhausted by her biography, and moreover didn't much change over the course of her life. The largest portion of this article will be given over to Mereau's theory of consciousness, theory of affect, and political theory—and in particular to the way Mereau combined these three, which would prove deeply influential for romantic philosophy in the later 1790s and beyond.

1 Mereau as Philosopher

One difficulty in assessing Mereau as a philosopher is of genre: few of the genres in which the efflorescence of philosophical publishing of the 1790s moved were open to women, and Mereau largely restricted herself to those genres that were traditionally acceptable for women. Even when she blazed new trails she was careful not to emphasize the newness—for instance, upon editing her own journal, *Kalathiskos*, she named it after an ancient Greek term for a gathering basket for spinning yarn.[6] The idea seemed

---

[4] Dieter Henrich, *Ursprung aus dem Ich* (Frankfurt: Suhrkamp, 2004), 65.

[5] Adrian Daub, *The Dynastic Imagination: Family and Modernity in 19th Century Germany* (Chicago: University of Chicago Press, 2020).

[6] Mereau explicates the multiple meanings she intended and their gendered basis in the opening poem to the first volume: Sophie Mereau, *Kalathiskos, Erstes Bändchen* (Berlin: Fröhlich, 1801), iii–iv.

to emphasize traditional gender roles; all the while putting them in the service of deeply radical ends. Hers was the type of philosophical thought that moved in literary, epistolary, and poetic genres, often in those characteristic of late Enlightenment literary and philosophical publics. Even her politics, with their emphasis on common sense and the directness of feeling, at times anticipated less those of the romantics than they reflected those of the neo-Lockean or late Leibnizian *Popularphilosophen* like Christian Garve and Johann Georg Heinrich Feder.[7]

At the same time, her contemporaries, above all the various romantic circles with which she was well-acquainted, had expanded the playing field for philosophical intervention. After all, Schlegel had declared Goethe's *Wilhelm Meister*, a novel, a coequal "great tendency" of the age alongside Fichte's *Wissenschaftslehre* and the French Revolution.[8] Mereau's novels (*The Blossoming Age of Sensibility* [*Blüthenalter der Empfindung*] of 1794 and *Amanda and Eduard* [*Amanda und Eduard*] of 1803) were deeply philosophical, and her lyric poetry too was extremely ambitious in making points about consciousness, commonweal, politics, and history. Her contemporaries recognized as much: when she submitted her poem "Schwarzburg" for inclusion in Friedrich Schiller's *Musen-Almanach*, Schiller decided that it was a better fit for the more philosophically ambitious periodical *Die Horen*.[9]

But Mereau's success in these arenas of course should not overshadow the fact that many others still were closed to her—and that the genres her age offered her gender were not widely thought to comport with public philosophizing. Mereau made clear, for instance, that she regarded her letter-writing as an extension of her publications, not the publications a reflection of her private communications. "A letter," she wrote to her later husband, Clemens Brentano, in November 1799, "is to me always like a novel—and I would rather say too little than too much."[10] While Mereau knew how to scandalize in her personal and public life, it's noticeable that when compared to her friends Friedrich and Dorothea Schlegel, for instance, she accepted the conventions by which the propriety and adequacy of women's communications was judged. Frequently, as I will show, she was able to wring critical potential from superannuated conventions not by breaking with them, but by employing them exactly as intended.

---

[7] For an overview of the positions of the *Popularphilosophen*, see: Frederick C. Beiser, *The Fate of Reason: German Philosophy from Kant to Fichte* (Cambridge, MA: Harvard University Press, 1993), 199.

[8] Friedrich Schlegel, *Kritische Friedrich-Schlegel-Ausgabe*, ed. E. Behler, J. J. Anstett, and H. Eichner (Paderborn: Schöningh, 1958–), vol. 17, 85.

[9] Janet Besserer Holmgren, *The Women in Schiller's "Horen": Patrons, Petticoats, and the Promotion of Weimar Classicism* (Newark: University of Delaware Press, 2007), 37.

[10] "Ein Brief ist mir immer wie ein Roman,—und ich mag lieber zuwenig als zuviel sagen." Mereau to Brentano, November 1799. All translations, unless otherwise indicated, are my own. *Der Briefwechsel zwischen Clemens Brentano und Sophie Mereau, Erster Band* (Leipzig: Insel, 1908). 12.

2 MEREAU'S LIFE

Sophie Mereau was born Sophie Schubart in 1770. She came from an academic family—her father was a finance official for the Duke of Saxony—and, like other women intellectuals of the upper bourgeoisie of her generation, seemed to have a natural sense of entitlement to participation in the intellectual sphere. She and her sister Henriette were educated to the full extent the late eighteenth century permitted young women. Early on Mereau sought connections to the intellectual heavyweights of her age and quickly established herself among them.[11]

Her 1793 marriage to Friedrich Ernst Carl Mereau, a law professor and librarian in Jena, made clear that, her intellectual ambitions notwithstanding, her life path was still extremely rigid and traditional. Judging from her correspondence and her retrospective framings in her fictions, she agreed to marriage for entirely pragmatic reasons. Through her husband, Mereau found a connection to the burgeoning intellectual scene in Jena, first with Friedrich Schiller, later Johann Gottlieb Fichte, Jean Paul, Johann Gottlieb Herder, Friedrich Wilhelm Joseph Schelling, and the Schlegels. She wrote and published continuously and participated in philosophical salons and seminars—often encouraged, albeit in condescending and sexist terms, by the famous male authors around her. Schiller's assessment to Goethe has become somewhat infamous in this regard: "Our friend Mereau has indeed a certain inwardliness and at times I cannot deny that she has a certain dignity of feeling and some depth. But she developed all of them on her own and in contradiction to the world."[12] Even her critics seemed incapable of not showing some admiration, but her admirers seemed incapable of treating her as their equal.

Her first published poem appeared in Schiller's periodical *Thalia* in 1790: "On France's Festival" ("*Bey Frankreichs Feier*") already contained *in nuce* many preoccupations of her mature work. The poem is an open celebration of the emancipatory impulses of the French Revolution, and it characteristically touches both on the personal and on the political. For Mereau, the French Revolution makes clear that both freedom and love must be thought of in terms of autonomy. Before long, Mereau would begin to employ language and ideas inspired by Johann Gottlieb Fichte to explore the radical political implications of Kant's account of autonomy. But "Bey Frankreichs Feier" suggests she sensed these implications well before encountering Fichte and his work. What impinges on individual autonomy is more than just political pressure. Traditional morality is just one more way in which the ancien régime lives on: as she wrote in a fragment, "you human beings who simply carry along your prejudices from your enslavement, what

---

[11] The two most important synoptic overviews of Mereau's life, overall project, and poetic oeuvre are: Dagmar von Gersdorff, *Dich zu lieben kann ich nicht verlernen. Das Leben der Sophie Brentano-Mereau* (Frankfurt: Insel, 1984), and Katharina von Hammerstein, *Sophie Mereau-Brentano: Freiheit-Liebe-Weiblichkeit. Trikolore sozialer und individueller Selbstbestimmung um 1800* (Heidelberg: Winter, 1994).

[12] Cited in Holmgren, *The Women Writers in Schiller's "Horen,"* 28 (translation modified).

good is liberty for you? You are simply rushing into a renewed enslavement."[13] In the poem, love and freedom become important corollaries to one another: only affect can undergird a robust sense of freedom, but affects without autonomy are unproductive. And while the poem, like many of her earlier works, appeared anonymously, the incipit ("by Demoiselle ***" ["von Demoiselle ***"]) left no doubt that the author was a woman. This too was characteristic of her mode of intervention: while she was careful to remain (at least in her writing) within the bounds of *Schicklichkeit* (decorum) set by contemporary society, playing with pseudonyms and gender-flipped narrators and speakers, she was always also careful to make clear that it was a woman who held the pen. And so she left no doubt that in "Bey Frankreichs Feier," a female writer understood the reverberation of political emancipation to extend into the realm of the erotic.

> Mächtig zwar rührt auch der Liebe Zauber
> Menschenseelen, adelt Herz und Muth,
> aber selbst der Flammenhauch der Liebe
> wird verschlungen von der Freiheit Gluth.[14]

> Powerfully too moves the magic of love
> The soul of men, ennobled heart and courage,
> But even the flaming breath of love
> Is engulfed by the embers of freedom.

From the first, erotic autonomy and political autonomy were deeply entwined in Mereau's thinking. Given that Fichte in his *Rechtslehre* (1797) would spend an entire tortured appendix trying to bring together the proposition that woman could be politically autonomous even though her erotic drive "committed" her to a lack of autonomy,[15] Mereau's starting position—never abandoned—was deeply inimical to the mystificatory idealizations of femininity that was to become characteristic to certain aspects of German idealist and romantic thought. The emancipatory ambitions of the French Revolution were meaningless unless they were extended into the realm of the interpersonal, unless they touched on matters of gender. But rethinking gendered morality likewise could never be kept separate from the political sphere—it pointed to a changed mode of governance, yes, of understanding the relationship of individual and polity. This was a point that Mereau was not content to simply make in her poetry. She brought it into the public sphere.

Mereau was unhappy in her marriage, carrying on multiple affairs, among them with Friedrich Schlegel and her later second husband, Clemens Brentano. Her divorce from Mereau in 1801, in which she was represented by none other than Herder, is often thought to be the first recorded divorce in the Duchy of Saxe-Weimar. After the divorce,

---

[13] Sophie Mereau, *Liebe und allenthalben Liebe* (Munich: Deutscher Taschenbuch Verlag), vol. 3, 191.

[14] Sophie Mereau, "Bey Frankreichs Feier," *Thalia* 3, no. 11 (1790): 141.

[15] Adrian Daub, *Uncivil Unions: The Metaphysics of Marriage in German Idealism and Romanticism* (Chicago: University of Chicago Press, 2012).

Mereau settled down with her daughter in Camburg, a smaller town just down the river Saale from Weimar. In 1803 she agreed to marry Clemens Brentano, probably because she became pregnant with his child. The years with Brentano, first in Marburg, later in Heidelberg, were marked by his jealousy, a profound feeling of unfreedom on her part, and repeated, increasingly traumatic pregnancies. She died in childbirth on October 31, 1806, in Heidelberg.

3 Mereau's Philosophical Thought

Mereau's thinking drew on many strands of German philosophy of the late eighteenth century, but two factors make her thinking particularly potent for her age. One is the primacy of the autobiographical and of embodiment in her philosophy—she openly drew on her life for her novel plots and raised questions that mattered to her as an ambitious woman. Her philosophy was aimed both at transcending the structures and strictures of the world as she encountered it, and at comprehending them. The other factor is the primacy of the erotic, which functioned both as an emblem of personal autonomy and a symbol of the individual's relationship to other persons and the cosmos. Gender played into both of these: even when she published anonymously (e.g., her 1794 novel *Blüthenalter der Empfindung*), she made sure readers knew that they were reading a woman writer. And throughout her fictions, Mereau has her women characters push back against men's universalism, articulating the specificities of their societal position.

In fact, Mereau's poetry and prose specialized in these gestures that, with Gayatri Chakravorty Spivak, we could call "interruptions," drawing on Schlegel's notion of "parabasis":[16] Mereau strategically and momentarily shifts rhetorical registers, but equally registers of analysis, destabilizing her own earlier assertions. She leaves the ideal for the real, the universal for the particular, the rational for the passionate—but only for a brief, decentering moment. In a telling moment in *Blüthenalter der Empfindung*, for instance, Mereau has her protagonist, Albert, espouse what is essentially her theory of marriage—it is frequently male characters that speak most directly for Mereau. But then she has two women—Albert's love interest, Nanette, and her aunt—check Albert's grandiose claims about how the world ought to be. "In refuting them," she writes, the women "only made reference [Rücksicht] to reality, and did not confuse the present state of the world with an ideal one."[17] This kind of roleplay juxtaposes Mereau's own beliefs about what was true and possible with a sense of the world in which such possibility would have to be realized.

---

[16] Gayatri Chakravorty Spivak, *A Critique of Postcolonial Reason* (Cambridge, MA: Harvard University Press, 1999), 14.

[17] Sophie Mereau, *Das Blüthenalter der Empfindung; Amanda und Eduard: Romane*, ed. Katharina von Hammerstein (Munich: Deutscher Taschenbuch Verlag, 1997), 100.

Whether or not she is thinking of idealism or romanticism—Mereau is loath to surrender to the tidal pull of the zeitgeist, and instead keen to assert control over broadly shared ideas. Above all, she applied this skepticism to her generation's interest in plenitude, in a rescission of the divisions characteristic of Enlightenment thought and civil society, which one can find in the thought of Fichte as much as Hölderlin, in the early Hegel as much as in the Schlegel brothers. Mereau acknowledged that impulse as personally and politically compelling, but remained cognizant of just how dependent the productiveness of this drive was on one's station within society. Precisely because she connected these broad ideas to what we would today call "positionality," Mereau was able to unearth contradictions within the high-flying philosophemes of her age. Thus, Mereau could on the one hand echo the idea that gender complementarity (and thus the inequality of the sexes) was a sign of how individuals could be (re)united in bigger wholes. "Men and women must not be equal. How else does love arise? Love is a desire to replace that which we ourselves lack—both together make a human being."[18] But at the same time, she could express instinctual horror at unification, at the rescission of individual boundaries implicit in "Romanticism of unification." In a journal note from July 1805, she writes: "perhaps human beings are like flowers of a great tree? Many flowers, few ripen into fruits. Dissolved, their ownness [Eigenheit] annihilated, most sink back into the element, only a few retain themselves and give birth to new lines [Geschlechter]."[19] The passage reads like a nightmare-version of a Romantic dream: annihilation, dissolution, unification with the "element" were all things her male contemporaries tended to celebrate unproblematically; here they emerge for the poet, who was, not incidentally, pregnant at the time, as figures of horror.

The journal note comes from the period during which Mereau lived with, and was married to, Clemens Brentano, an inveterate propagandist of gender complementarity.[20] The "interruptions" of tidy speculations like Brentano's have to be taken quite literally: Mereau lived with, in, and around discourses of unification, and fully understood their political appeal. But this made her interventions a praxis as well as theoretical—they consisted in checking romantic thought in the moment of its articulation. And just like their articulations, her interruptions were suggestive of a broader epistemological program. In a letter to Clemens Brentano, Mereau—at this point fully immersed in the *topoi* of the heyday of Romanticism—sounds a note of caution that always already subverts her desire for oneness, for the Romantic ideal (and Idealistic claim) of unity between subject and object. "An irresistible urge compels me to surrender entirely to my imagination, to surround shapeless existence with the colors of poetry, to stop worrying about the necessary and focus on the beautiful. But oh! The rowboat of my fate does not glide across a bright, placid surface where I could lay down my oars unbothered and play with the light of the moon and the stars, while a kind breeze guides the boat through

---

[18] Cited in Julia Augart, *Eine Romantische Liebe in Briefen: Zur Liebeskonzeption im Briefwechsel von Sophie Mereau und Clemens Brentano* (Würzburg: Königshausen & Neumann, 2006), 80.

[19] Mereau, *Liebe und allenthalben Liebe*, vol. 3, 82–83.

[20] Augart, *Eine Romantische Liebe in Briefen*, 80.

the gently curling waves. [My boat] makes its voyage through shoals and eddies, shaken by storms, and I must grasp the rudder or sink."[21] The voyage Mereau describes here may be quintessentially Romantic, but the image is resolutely Kantian. The small boat Mereau describes is the one that pushes off of the island of the pure understanding in the Analytic of Principles in Kant's *Critique of Pure Reason*. This land, Kant tells us, "is an island, and enclosed in unalterable boundaries by nature itself. It is the land of truth (a charming name), surrounded by a broad and stormy ocean, the true seat of illusion, where many a fog bank and rapidly melting iceberg pretend to be new lands."[22] The Romantic revision of this picture consists essentially in discounting the shoals and fog banks in these waters, to deny that their treachery deprives them of truth content. Mereau reworks the image differently: she is less concerned with the waters she traverses in surrendering to her imagination; she is concerned with the person doing the rowing. Specifically, she seems concerned with the anthropological rather than transcendental status of the person in the boat—they are an embodied, particular individual, rather than simply a mind. And here the genre of the text seems to matter—Mereau is addressing Clemens Brentano, and is comparing the level of, to use a twentieth-century term, privilege involved in this kind of expedition into fantasy. There may be others, such as Clemens, who can surrender to the waves far from the island of truth—Mereau herself cannot.[23]

Note that Mereau is not suggesting that this makes the ocean of illusion inaccessible to her. She too feels "an irresistible urge" to set off in her little boat. Not surrendering for her means actively steering and intervening. Her self-disruptions, her consistent gestures of self-correction, are intended precisely as assertions of this kind of autonomy: they characterize both the form of her philosophizing and constitute its prime motive.

This interruptive structure in many respects accounts for the aforementioned sense of "in-between-ness" in Mereau's thinking. To be sure, in some cases her borderline existence may have been owed to a generative intellect open to a great number of influences. But there is also a great deal of strategy involved. Moreover, it is important to note that while the gesture has its aesthetic cognates in certain conceptual lodestars of the Romantic generation—above all irony and parabasis—in the philosophical realm at the end of the eighteenth century the gesture is much more associated with the common sense philosophy and the antimonist thrust of the final generation of German *Popularphilosophen* and the separate but in many ways related *Glaubensphilosophen*. The *Popularphilosophen*, men like Christian Garve and Friedrich Nicolai, were essentially neo-Empiricist defenders of Enlightenment, whose primary move against Kant's

---

[21] Sophie Mereau, *Wie sehn' ich mich hinaus in die freie Welt: Tagebuch, Betrachtungen und vermischte Prosa* (Munich: Deutscher Taschenbuch Verlag, 1997), 67.

[22] Immanuel Kant, *Critique of Pure Reason*, trans. Paul Guyer and Allen Wood (Cambridge: Cambridge University Press, 1999), A 236/B 296.

[23] Daniel Purdy, "Plucking the Strings of Desire: Abstraction and Sensuality in Sophie Mereau's 'Bildungsgeschichte,'" in *Sophie Mereau: Verbindungslinien in Zeit und Raum*, ed. Katharina von Hammerstein (Tübingen: Winter, 2008), 145–162.

critical philosophy consisted in checking speculation by reference to common sense.[24] Meanwhile fideists in the mode of Friedrich Heinrich Jacobi suggested that at some point speculation had to be abandoned in favor of a *salto mortale* into faith.[25] Both of these were rejected by the nascent idealist and romantic philosophies. Mereau's style is thus probably not to be understood simply as an anticipation of Romantic *topoi*, but a careful update to the style of thinking gradually being displaced by the Critical Philosophy and Romantic thought.

Take for instance the aforementioned poem "Schwarzburg," which appeared in *Die Horen* in 1796. "Schwarzburg" celebrates the natural beauty of the Schwarza Valley in Thuringia and expands its observation into a picture of human autonomy. Throughout, the poem contrasts the imposed and arbitrary conventions of society with the purity of nature. "Nature," as Mereau writes in one of her notes, is what keeps human beings authentic and free. "Nature created me open and free. The liveliness of my affect, the activity of my imagination do not depend on artificial aids to satisfy my joys. Obstacles and force and prohibition would only render those joys bitter."[26] The natural beauty of the Schwarza Valley promises a dissolution of the bonds of individuality, as the "truth of nature" works on the poet and on an imagined lover.

> Hier lege, was ihm Menschen aufgedrungen,
> Des Vorurteils erträumte Forderung,
> Der frohe Wand'rer ehrerbietig ab,
> Und geh' allein, sich selbst zurückgegeben,
> Der Wahrheit und Natur mit reinem Sinn zu leben,
> Ein freier Mensch mit seinem Pilgerstab.[27]

> What weight human beings have placed upon him,
> The dreamed-up postulates of prejudice,
> May the joyful wanderer discard them here in reverence,
> May he go alone, returned to himself,
> To live the truth and nature with a pure sense,
> A free man with his pilgrim's staff.

The picture of a human being endowed by nature with a freedom that convention and "the dreamed-up postulates of prejudice" serve to restrict at every turn runs as a constant through Mereau's novelistic and poetic output. In "To a Trellissed Tree" ("An einen Baum am Spalier," 1800), Mereau contrasts the organic, free development of a tree to the brutalizing form in which human manipulation confines that development. Just in case we miss the metaphor she closes the poem by focusing on "a human shape":

---

[24] Beiser, *The Fate of Reason*, 168.
[25] Elizabeth Millán, *Friedrich Schlegel and the Emergence of Romantic Philosophy* (Albany: State University of New York Press, 2012), 56.
[26] Mereau, *Liebe und allenthalben Liebe*, vol. 3, 193.
[27] Mereau, *Liebe und allenthalben Liebe*, vol. 2, 16.

> Eine menschliche Gestalt schnell vor mich hin,
> Die, auf ewig von dem freien Sinn
> Der Natur entfernt, ein fremder Drang
> Auch wie dich in steife Formen zwang.[28]
>
> Of a human shape before my gaze,
> Who forever severed from the liberal ways
> Of nature, is coerced by alien norms,
> Just as you are, into rigid form.[29]

Throughout her work Mereau treated this critique of imposed "rigid forms"—very much in the spirit of Kant's Enlightenment essay—as both a theory of cognition and a political theory. The "forms" imposed on the "free sense of nature" included both structures of thinking and very specific social obstacles. Above all in the realm of the erotic Mereau never tired of registering the free impulses of human autonomy and the restrictions imposed by political, religious, and social authorities upon them. Prime among her target was the institution of marriage—but it is important to notice that by taking aim at marriage, she intends far more than just social critique. Bound up with her insistence on freely chosen love relations free of conventional interference was a sense of political subjecthood (for both partners), a sense for the resonance an individual could have in a broader social and natural cosmos, and thus ultimately a theory of cognition.

Horst Albert Glaser has suggested that Mereau's critique of marriage was largely based on "an Enlightenment idea."[30] I have argued elsewhere that Mereau treated marriage as a part of a much larger political whole—that her critique of the strictures of tradition has to be understood in terms of the French Revolution and Kant's Copernican Revolution.[31] When a pair of lovers in *Blüthenalter der Empfindung* claim that "we ourselves vouchsafe for ourselves," the autonomy of their relationship from "custom and creed" seems to echo Fichte's concept of the "dignity of man"—which explicitly equates the emancipated self of Kant's "Enlightenment" essay with the *citoyen* of the French Revolution. But it adds a far more clearly gendered dimension than Fichte's text, which while not blind to issues of race seems altogether insensate to inequalities having to do with gender. While the charges leveled at the bounds of marriage in *Blüthenalter* and *Amanda und Eduard* indeed resembled the sentimentalist critiques of the *Sturm-und-Drang* and the late Enlightenment's moralism of feeling, she accorded marriage the kind of centrality it would later hold for figures like Friedrich Schlegel and Novalis.

Especially once she encountered the work of Fichte (whom she met personally when he arrived in Jena amid much fanfare in 1794, and whose lectures and seminars she attended),

---

[28] Sophie Mereau, *Gedichte*, vol. 1 (Berlin: Unger, 1800), 15.

[29] Sophie Mereau, "To a Trellissed Tree," in *Bitter Healing: German Women Writers 1700–1803*, ed. Jeannine Blackwell and Susanne Zantop (Lincoln: University of Nebraska Press, 1990), 379.

[30] Horst Albert Gläser and György Vajda, eds., *Die Wende von der Aufklärung zur Romantik, 1760–1820* (Amsterdam: John Benjamins, 2001), 143.

[31] Daub, *Uncivil Unions*, 220.

Mereau tended to organize her lyric poetry around Fichtean ideas. For instance, she frequently alternates between moments of plenitude on the one hand and its unraveling on the other, mimicking the dialectic between the "thetic" moment of self-positing and the act of self-determination by which the "absolute I" devolves into "I" and "Not-I." Her 1802 longform poem *Serafine* suggests that Mereau understood this as a feature of human cognition as such—even though she imbues that cognition with explicit social and political ramifications. In opening *Serafine*, Mereau describes a beautiful natural scene in Edenic terms that are at the same time clearly indebted to a theory of cognition in the mode of Hölderlin, Novalis, or Schlegel. We are watching a self and an environment constitute one another. The Not-I becomes what it is only through the positing power of the I, but the I (unlike in Fichte) is itself determined by the Not-I. This coconstitution is about more than emotion or mood (a feeling of belonging or dependence), it has to do with the very categories by which the understanding is able to lay claim to its world of objects. What makes the scene paradisiacal is not just its beauty, it is also its comprehensibility: it is a place where "the chain of events holds" ("der Begebenheiten Kette hält"). It is pleasing not just in its hues and colors, it is pleasing also in its causal intelligibility.

> Ein fremdes Land liegt vor mir aufgeschlossen,
> von milderm Himmel lieblich überstralt,
> Wo heil'ge Bluem voll Bedeutung sprossen;[32]
>
> A foreign land lies opened up before me,
> Arched over lovely by a milder heaven,
> Where sacred flowers full of meaning grow;

Whatever allows for the poetic subject to find purchase in this "foreign land" appears to be some combination of meaning, comprehensibility, and beauty. The self and its categories are unproblematically at home in these "pleasant pastures." However, we are told almost immediately that "disquiet too dwells in these pleasant pastures" ("doch wohnt auch Unruh in den schönen Fluren"). In this case, the disquiet is not introduced by society, by its echoes, or premonitions within the natural space. It springs rather from human psychology itself.

> Nicht lange! Von dem stürmischen Gemüthe,
> Das, mit sich selber kämpfend, stets verliert,
> Hat alle Ruhe mit der Neuheit Blüthe,
> Ein kurzer Hauch der Zeit hinweggeführt.[33]
>
> Not long! Through stormy conscience,
> Which, wrestling with itself, will always lose,
> A simple breath of time has driven away
> All quiet with the blooming of the new.

[32] Mereau, *Gedichte*, 4.
[33] Mereau, *Gedichte*, 7.

Inconstancy, mood, and inclination precipitate a counter-motion to the drive toward unity with the world. This sudden reversal of thrust from oneness to division, from contentment to agitation, is in German literature mostly associated with eighteenth-century *Empfindsamkeit*. Even though written at the height of Mereau's involvement with the Romantics, *Serafine*, much like *Amanda und Eduard*, owes a profound debt to the aesthetics of Rococo. Helene Riley has suggested that Mereau was always more at home in a Romantic poetics à la Friedrich Schlegel than in the classicist aesthetics with which she began her career, and seems to regard the author's early literary efforts (including "Schwarzburg") as being mannered and formalistic.[34] But Mereau's predilection for what in another context Ernst Bloch called "asynchronicity" (*Ungleichzeitigkeit*) likely was far more deliberate than Mereau is usually given credit for. *Serafine* combines the morality of the mid-eighteenth century with the philosophical preoccupations of the end of the century. Where *Serafine*'s opening is atypical for Mereau's thinking is that it considers epistemology and psychology largely independent of social and political theory.

Compared to her poetry, which brims with the same obsessions and preoccupations as does that of her contemporary interlocutors, Mereau's novels and novel fragments can feel a little antiquated. Compared to the philosophical novels Friedrich Schlegel, Friedrich Hölderlin, Novalis, and others were writing around the same time, her tales have the cloak-and-dagger trappings of an eighteenth-century novel. As I have argued elsewhere, Mereau's reliance on comparatively old-fashioned novel plots is likely deliberate. There was, in spite of all the formal experimentation, a cleanness and neatness to her male Romantic contemporaries' philosophical plots of alienation and joyous, loving reunification. Consider how organically young men are allowed to develop in Friedrich Hölderlin's *Hyperion* (1797–1799), Friedrich Schlegel's *Lucinde* (1799), or Ludwig Tieck's *Franz Sternbalds Wanderungen* (1798). These novels are vertiginous formally, but the overall gestalt of the story is fairly simple, precisely because what asserts itself in their plots of development is supposed to flow as much as possible from nature, unobstructed by narrative or social convention. The pronounced messiness that exists in Mereau's books—*Blüthenalter der Empfindung* especially is rife with melodramatic plot twists, dramatic misunderstandings, and grand reveals—is not owed to form, but rather to intricate, yet deeply conventional plotting. The conventional plot allowed Mereau's novels to remain alive to the hold that convention still retained on life, at least for some. In her novels as well, Mereau's sentimental streak thus quickly reveals itself as a piece of political philosophy disguised as literary criticism: the creaky melodramatic contraptions of the eighteenth century may stick out amid the heady philosophical speculations, but they are meant to. They are outdated conventions, but no less powerful for being outdated—and they tell of equally noxious conventions, strictures of ritual and faith, of commerce and false propriety. Mereau is careful not to discount what yet holds power, no matter how illegitimate that power.

---

[34] Helene Kastinger Riley, "Saat und Ernte. Sophie Mereaus Forderung geschlechtlicher Gleichberechtigung," in *Die weibliche Muse*, ed. Helene Riley (Columbia, SC: Camden House, 1986), 55–88.

This mediation of experiences of authenticity and plenitude with those factors that denature and constrain those experiences and are, at least at her historic moment, still equally real, enters into characteristic alignment in Mereau's great philosophical poem "Schwarzburg." Even though it ultimately celebrates a unification with nature and the cosmos, the poem remains far more dynamic than similar nature poems composed by her various contemporaries. This is partly because she grants nature more of an active role, the valley and its flora alternately beckoning and rejecting the poet. But mostly it is because the subject that experiences this newfound sense of liberation keeps evolving as the poem goes on. Rather than Fichte's flinty, monadic, self-positing I, the wanderer we meet is, in keeping with German grammar ("*der* Wanderer" is always masculine), a "he" throughout. As Janet Besserer Holmgren has pointed out, Mereau in fact worked to heighten this effect: the original version of the poem makes clear in one single stanza that the wanderer is in fact a woman; the version in *Die Horen* omits that entire stanza.[35]

But the ambiguities in terms of gender and individuation do not end there. Toward the end, the pronouns "we" and "I" appear with increasing frequency, and the poem closes with a rapturous invocation of the "I." Nature thus works on the self in three different ways in this poem: it impinges on the self as a "he," as a "we," and as an "I." Questions of universality and particularity hover above this mode of address: is the (male) wanderer universal, even though he walks through a poem written by a woman author? How universal is the "we" invoked in the poem's close? How does this "we" combine its gendered particulars, the male wanderer and the (probably female) love object he at certain moments imagines?

The Romantics had of course many ways to describe the approach to the "unconditioned" by means of "the conditioned," as Novalis put it: a kind of infinite approach to a plenitude that any articulation in language and thought had to fall short of.[36] It is important that "Schwarzburg" is making a very different point, asking a very different question. Mereau is not being ironic; she is not undoing the approach to the infinite by pointing to the persistence of the particular. Throughout the poem, degrees of particularity (an individual that is different from the universal) are carefully mapped out, while the promise of nature is that all particularity is in the end transcended:

> Ich seh' die leichten Schranken niederfallen,
> Mich aufgelös't im reinen Äther wallen,
> Und Gottheit liegt in diesem Augenblick![37]

> I see the last soft barriers falling,
> I see myself drift dissolved in the ether,
> Divinity in this moment lies!

---

[35] Holmgren, *The Women in Schiller's "Horen,"* 42.
[36] Manfred Frank, *Unendliche Annäherung* (Frankfurt am Main: Suhrkamp, 1997), 687.
[37] Mereau, *Gedichte*, 119.

Earlier in the poem, Mereau has turned the wanderer's walking stick into a "pilgrim's staff." Nature's equality thus provides to its "pilgrim" a religious ideal to which to aspire. It is an ideal of unity, of shared life, and—most important—of equality that reflects back on the society the wanderer has left behind. It is an ideal by which society could, and indeed should, be reordered and reorganized. At the same time, Mereau's wanderer carries that society with him into the Schwarza Valley. As insistently as the wanderer celebrates the falling away of stricture (of convention, of social obligation, of unfreedom in general), just as insistently does he seem to be borne back into hemmed-in, alienated particularity. Again and again, those particularities are social in character: the wanderer divests himself, Mereau writes, "of the dreamed-up demands of prejudice." That which determines human beings from without—that which assigns them a place and limits their options—for Mereau seems to mean religion, civil society, as well as conventions around gender. "The human being," Mereau writes, is "from outside and inside set upon and blocked" ("der Mensch, von außen und von innen / bestürmt, geengt").[38] Again and again, the poet revels in "the ecstasies of freedom" ("der Freiheit Seligkeiten")[39] in nature while noting that most human beings forgo it "for a factitious happiness that always escapes." Mereau is disinterested in tarrying with moments of authenticity and perfect autonomy without casting an eye, forward or backward, away from the undetermined and toward social, epistemological, sexual determination.[40]

This is characteristic of Mereau's approach to the particular. She shares the Romantic preoccupation with undivided unity, derived ultimately from Spinoza and Shaftesbury. But she is not content to cancel out particularity (which for her seems to mean broadly the specificity of social standing, of profession, of gender) entirely: the thing that is supposed to be swallowed whole, to dissolve entirely into the *hen kai pan,* nevertheless attracts her curiosity and philosophical acumen. Nor, however, is she content to rely on concepts like irony to harness and capture this dynamic. Partly this seems to be because the particularity that separates the individual from the *hen kai pan* is more embodied, social, and specific than the particularity that cleaves, say, Fichte's "I" from the "absolute I." For one thing, it is gendered. And gender for Mereau is always also social. The wanderer we meet in "Schwarzburg" has a specific backstory, and it is once again about an "alien fate":

> Des müden Herzens Wunden zu beweinen,
> Die feindlich ihm ein strenges Schicksal schlug,
> Und, eingewiegt in freie Träumereien,
> Sich sehnsuchtsvoll hier der Natur zu weihen,
> Sein Leid in diese schöne Wildnis trug.[41]

---

[38] Mereau, *Gedichte,* 112.

[39] Mereau, *Gedichte,* 112.

[40] Daniel Purdy, "Sophie Mereau's Authorial Masquerades and the Subversion of Romantic *Poesie,*" *Women in German Yearbook* 13 (1997): 29.

[41] Mereau, *Gedichte,* 115.

> To grieve the wounds of a tired heart,
> Which implacably a foreign fate imposed,
> And, rocked by unfettered dreaming,
> Commit himself yearningly to nature,
> Carried his pain into this beautiful wilderness.

This wanderer has a story, and it is a deeply gendered one: moving through space in this way is clearly gendered itself, aloneness in the late eighteenth century isn't gender neutral. More important, the gestures here are autobiographical: observing nature in this way at the turn of the nineteenth century means carrying oneself into nature to some extent. And yet, the self that enters into this space is clearly marked as male—from the overall stance of the individual to the mere fact of the pronouns used throughout.

Mereau's poetry thus instantiates two things at once: a drive toward universality and unity with all things, and a commitment to parsing out who exactly gets to have access to universality and unity. If Mereau is largely remembered as a thinker about intimacy, sexuality, and marriage, then this is probably because it was in that sphere where the encomia to unification clashed most decisively with how such a union was actually lived. But Mereau's poetry makes clear that the sexual relationship only furnished the most obvious disconnect between Romantic ambitions and the prose of the world. The French Revolution loomed large in her thinking and her poetry from the very beginning. Behind her careful autopsy on questions of affect, plenitude and freedom, stands the question of how the passions that sustained the Revolution failed in making it last, a question that the authors of the "Oldest Systematic Program of German Idealism" (some combination of G. W. F. Hegel, F. W.J . Schelling, and Friedrich Hölderlin) posed around the same time that she did.

4   CONCLUSION

Whether in *Serafine*, in "Schwarzburg," or in her novels, Mereau indulged moments both of oneness and of plenitude, but also paid close attention to the friction that attends such moments. And especially in her poetry it is clear that this friction had a larger story to tell: about the way inequality operated within contemporary society, about how power and privileges were distributed, about what kind of a political project could claim to redistribute them. Mereau understood that the idea of the self-positing I held immense power of the, as did the idea of the Not-I as an effect of absolute positing. She shared Fichte's sense of the profound political implications of Kant's notion of autonomy. Like him (and unlike many fellow Romantics) she made explicit the link between this notion of autonomy and the events in France after 1789, above all in her novel *Blüthenalter der Empfindung*. But at the same time, she was far more attuned to the resistances and recalcitrances that obstruct the progress of human autonomy.

Throughout her oeuvre, Mereau relies on an eclectic mix of literary forms, and especially the skillful combination of contemporary and outdated, to chart a path both toward a characteristically Romantic fusion with the cosmos, and to lend importance to the social and political factors that inhibit the individual from any such unification. The tendency to arrange Mereau's career as a path of *Bildung*, moving from a neoclassicist aesthetic to a gradual Romantic awakening, risks occluding the fact that Mereau strategically mixed styles, genres, and philosophical ideas throughout her career. And the fact that she did so with a clear goal in mind: both to take seriously the political ramifications of the revolutions in epistemology among her contemporaries, and to register misgivings about how easily or unproblematically one could move from one to the other. Her work is roughly contemporaneous with the Hölderlin circle's elaboration of the Romantic politics of post-Fichtean epistemology, and most of the texts discussed here emerged around the same time as the Tübingen roommates wrote "The Oldest Systematic Program of German Idealism." Nevertheless, Mereau articulated something of a precritique of their generation's most dizzy raptures.

BIBLIOGRAPHY

Augart, Julia. *Eine Romantische Liebe in Briefen: Zur Liebeskonzeption im Briefwechsel von Sophie Mereau und Clemens Brentano*. Würzburg: Königshausen & Neumann, 2006.

Beiser, Frederick C. *The Fate of Reason: German Philosophy from Kant to Fichte*. Cambridge, MA: Harvard University Press, 1993.

Blackwell, Jeannine, and Susanne Zantop. *Bitter Healing: German Women Writers 1700–1803*. Lincoln: University of Nebraska Press, 1990.

Daub, Adrian. *The Dynastic Imagination: Family and Modernity in Nineteenth-Century Germany*. Chicago: University of Chicago Press, 2020.

Daub, Adrian. *Uncivil Unions: The Metaphysics of Marriage in German Idealism and Romanticism*. Chicago: University of Chicago Press, 2012.

Frank, Manfred. *Unendliche Annäherung*. Frankfurt: Suhrkamp, 1997.

Gersdorff, Dagmar von. *Dich zu lieben kann ich nicht verlernen. Das Leben der Sophie Brentano-Mereau*. Frankfurt: Insel, 1984.

Gläser, Horst Albert, and György Vajda, eds. *Die Wende von der Aufklärung zur Romantik, 1760–1820*. Amsterdam: John Benjamins, 2001.

Hammerstein, Katharina von. *Sophie Mereau-Brentano: Freiheit-Liebe-Weiblichkeit. Trikolore sozialer und individueller Selbstbestimmung um 1800*. Heidelberg: Winter, 1994.

Harper, Anthony J. "Sophie Mereau." In *Encyclopedia of German Literature*, ed. Matthias Konzett, 697–698. London: Routledge, 2015.

Henrich, Dieter. *Ursprung aus dem Ich*. Frankfurt: Suhrkamp, 2004.

Holmgren, Janet Besserer. *The Women in Schiller's "Horen": Patrons, Petticoats, and the Promotion of Weimar Classicism*. Newark: University of Delaware Press, 2007.

Kant, Immanuel. *Critique of Pure Reason*. Translated by Paul Guyer and Allen W. Wood. Cambridge: Cambridge University Press, 1999.

Mereau, Sophie. *Das Blüthenalter der Empfindung; Amanda und Eduard: Romane*. Edited by Katharina von Hammerstein. Munich: Deutscher Taschenbuch Verlag, 1997.

Mereau, Sophie. *Gedichte*. 2 vols. Berlin: Unger, 1800.

Mereau, Sophie. *Kalathiskos, Erstes Bändchen*. Berlin: Fröhlich, 1801.

Mereau, Sophie. *Liebe und allenthalben Liebe*. 3 vols. Munich: Deutscher Taschenbuch Verlag, 1996.

Mereau, Sophie. *"Wie sehn' ich mich hinaus in die freie Welt": Tagebuch, vermischte Prosa und philosophische Betrachtungen*. Edited by Katharina von Hammerstein. Munich: Deutscher Taschenbuch Verlag, 1997.

Millán, Elizabeth. *Friedrich Schlegel and the Emergence of Romantic Philosophy*. Albany: State University of New York Press, 2012.

Purdy, Daniel. "Plucking the Strings of Desire: Abstraction and Sensuality in Sophie Mereau's 'Bildungsgeschichte.'" In *Sophie Mereau: Verbindungslinien in Zeit und Raum*, edited by Katharina von Hammerstein, 145–162. Tübingen: Winter, 2008.

Purdy, Daniel. "Sophie Mereau's Authorial Masquerades and the Subversion of Romantic *Poesie*." *Women in German Yearbook* 13 (1997): 29–48.

Riley, Helene Kastinger. "Saat und Ernte. Sophie Mereaus Forderung geschlechtlicher Gleichberechtigung." In *Die weibliche Muse*, edited by Helene Kastinger Riley, 55–88. Columbia, SC: Camden House, 1986.

Spivak, Gayatri Chakravorty. *A Critique of Postcolonial Reason*. Cambridge, MA: Harvard University Press, 1999.

Vansant, Jaqueline. "Sophie Mereau." In *Bitter Healing: German Women Writers, 1700–1830: An Anthology*, ed. Jeannine Blackwell and Suzanne Zantop, 371–373. Lincoln: University of Nebraska Press, 1990.

CHAPTER 4

RAHEL LEVIN VARNHAGEN (1771–1833)

PAULA KELLER

1 VARNHAGEN AND HER TIME

PHILOSOPHICALLY minded women in the eighteenth and nineteenth century, like Rahel Levin Varnhagen,[1] present us with an interesting hermeneutical problem. Varnhagen didn't leave behind a body of systematic work. Nowhere does she present her ideas in a structured, concise, argumentative way. What we have are scattered, aphoristic, sometimes even contradictory philosophical remarks, thrown into her letters next to personal conversation. I argue that to reconstruct her philosophical work, we must look not only at these, but also at how she presents herself throughout her writing. These autobiographical passages are philosophy as they offer an answer to Varnhagen's main philosophical question: how should we live in an unjust world?

Varnhagen is a well-known public figure in Early German Romanticism.[2] Yet, partly due to the outlined hermeneutical problem, she is not typically remembered today for her philosophical work. Rather, she is—in Hannah Arendt's biography—presented to us as a Jewish woman in an anti-Semitic society; in works of literary scholars, she appears a *salonnière* and letter writer at the center of Romantic life, compared in literary ability to Germaine de Staël or George Sand; in others, she is rendered a protofeminist.[3]

---

[1] A quick note on names: through her writing and its posthumous publication, Varnhagen is known simply as "Rahel." "Varnhagen" is her husband's name, "Levin" her maiden name. I have chosen to refer to her as "Rahel Levin Varnhagen," or "Varnhagen" for short.

[2] Renata Fuchs, "'Soll ein Weib wohl Bücher schreiben; Oder soll sie's lassen bleiben? The Immediate Reception of Rahel Levin Varnhagen as a Public Figure," *Neophilologus* 98, no. 2 (2014): 303–324.

[3] We find the first presentation in Hannah Arendt, *Rahel Varnhagen*, trans. Richard and Clara Winston (New York: Harcourt Brace Jovanovich, 1974); the second in Heidi Tewarson, *Rahel Levin*

Never is she considered a serious philosopher[4]—not even really by herself. She writes: "[an] artist, philosopher or poet is not above me. We are made of the same element. On the same rank and we belong together. And he, who wanted to exclude the other, only excludes himself. But living was assigned to me."[5] Varnhagen asserts that she is *like* a philosopher. In part her own and especially others' (mis)reception is due to her writing style. She often prefers the mysterious, profound-sounding fragment to clear definitions, consistent term employment, or structured argument.[6] The scholarship on her work therefore still today praises her "bonmots," her beautiful words, and in so doing belittles her philosophical contributions.[7]

Yet, what are these contributions? The quoted passage points in a promising direction: "living was assigned" to her. Perhaps Varnhagen lived—rather than wrote—*philosophically*. Writing can explicitly assert a point (as philosophical writing typically does). But it can also show this point, as Varnhagen notes in response to Humboldt's review of Jacobi's novel *Woldemar*: "a work of art must not always *tell* me, what it wants, it must *show* it.... One needs to have something to prove in mind, if one writes a novel, but one must be young enough in oneself to only feel it, and not to carry it on one's tongue eternally analyzed; otherwise it becomes a theory on how to prove, and not a living example for the proof, taken from nature."[8] A novel, says Varnhagen, is aesthetically inferior if it tells rather than shows. This is because a novel ought to be a "living example." I want to treat this passage as a cue for how to read Varnhagen's own writing: perhaps

---

Varnhagen (Lincoln: University of Nebraska Press, 1988); Margaretmary Daley, *Women of Letters* (Rochester, NY: Camden House, 1998); Barbara Becker-Cantarino, "Leben als Text," in *Frauen Literatur Geschichte*, ed. Hiltrud Gnüg and Renate Möhrmann (Stuttgart: Metzler, 1999), 129–146; Fuchs, "'Soll ein Weib'"; and the third presentation in Dena Goodman, "Letter Writing and the Emergence of Gendered Subjectivity in Eighteenth-Century France," *Journal of Women's History* 17, no. 2 (2005): 9-37; Lorely French, "'Meine beiden Ichs': Confrontations with Language and Self in Letters by Early Nineteenth-Century Women," *Women in German Yearbook* 5 (1989): 73-89 ; Julia Kristeva, "The Meaning of an Example: Rahel Varnhagen," in her *Hannah Arendt* (New York: Columbia University Press, 2001), 48-69.

[4] However, parts of her writing are occasionally described as "a kind of philosophical essay"; Daley, *Women of Letters*, 13. Thanks to Anne Pollok's "The Role of Writing and Sociability for the Establishment of a Persona: Henriette Herz, Rahel Levin Varnhagen, and Bettina von Arnim," in *Women and Philosophy in Eighteenth-Century Germany*, ed. Corey W. Dyck (Oxford: Oxford University Press, 2021), 195–210, Varnhagen has now also made it into philosophical handbooks.

[5] Rahel Varnhagen, *Gesammelte Werke, Rahel-Bibliothek* (Munich: Matthes & Seitz, 1983), vol. 1, 266. In subsequent citations from these collective volumes, I use only the volume number. All translations of Varnhagen's writings in this chapter are my own—to my knowledge no modern self-standing translations exist (yet).

[6] See Daley, *Women of Letters*, x–xi; Tewarson, *Varnhagen*, 13–14, 43.

[7] See for example Ursula Isselstein, "'Durch Gedruckte Worte Sprechen': Die Tagebücher und Aufzeichnungen Rahel Levin Varnhagens," in *Tagebücher und Aufzeichnungen*, by Rahel Varnhagen, ed. Ursula Isselstein (Göttingen: Wallstein, 2019), 953. Varnhagen's work was already so received during her own lifetime. Interestingly, she is aware of that and explicitly uses the term "Bonmots" to describe other's impression of her; see VII, 2, 33.

[8] I, 107, my italics.

it too shows us something of philosophical interest, rather than telling us that thing.[9] I argue that we should treat Varnhagen's letters as the records of a life that constitutes a philosophical example. Her central question is: "how should we live in an unjust world?" (section 2 here).[10] Her answer—expressed mostly through her self-presentation in her letters—is that we should live authentically (section 3), cultivate friendships (section 4), and focus on our self-development (section 5). This amounts to a strategy of communal retreat from unjust social reality.

Readers may be familiar with Hannah Arendt's *Rahel Varnhagen: The Life of a Jewish Woman*. Arendt's biography introduces the person Varnhagen, but does not present the *philosopher* Varnhagen. Arendt rather tells "Rahel's *life* as she herself might have told it" in order to make a point about being a Jew in Germany.[11] This, following Arendt's main thesis, is a social position between the two equally bad alternatives of pariah and parvenu. I argue that Varnhagen's own understanding of life in the face of injustice is more optimistic: she shows how one can escape Arendt's dilemma of pariah and parvenu through communal retreat.

Varnhagen's preferred genre—the letter—is itself part of this demonstration. She uses it to show the importance of friendship and self-development in an unjust world, as I argue in sections 4 and 5. Yet, the letter is also the typical genre for a woman at her time. Such letters were mostly semipublic, passed among friends, sometimes published anonymously, and written in a style of "educated naturalism" aiming to demonstrate their writer's true character and inner life.[12] Otherwise mostly excluded from the public sphere, women could enter a literary public sphere through correspondence.[13] Letter writing was a rare chance for women to become "subjects of their own discourse, rather than remaining objects within the patriarchal discourse."[14] This epistolary culture also inspired stylized philosophical letters by men, most famously Schiller's Letters *On the Aesthetic Education of Man*.[15]

[9] Varnhagen's method fits with ideas of Romantic Poetry, which, in a narrow sense, refers to the mixture of literary styles (in Varnhagen's case: autobiographical letters mixed with theory), and, in a broad sense, to the romanticization or aesthetization of life (in Varnhagen's case exemplified by her turning her life into written work); see Frederick Beiser, *The Romantic Imperative: The Concept of Early German Romanticism* (Cambridge, MA: Harvard University Press, 2003), 6–22; and Friedrich Schlegel, *Kritische Friedrich-Schlegel-Ausgabe*, ed. Ernst Behler et al., vol. 1, *Studien des Klassischen Altertums* (Paderborn: Schöningh, 1958), *Athenäum*-Fragment 116.

[10] For a similar interpretation of this as the central question underlying Varnhagen's intellectual production see Daley, *Women of Letters*, 57.

[11] Arendt, *Varnhagen*, xv, my italics.

[12] Tewarson, *Varnhagen* 1988, 39; see Daley, *Women of Letters*, 1998.

[13] Goodman, "Letter Writing"; Weissberg, "Writing on the Wall: Letters of Rahel Varnhagen," *New German Critique* 36 (1985): 165.

[14] French, "'Meine beiden Ichs,'" 75.

[15] Friedrich Schiller, *On the Aesthetic Education of Man*, ed. and trans. Elizabeth Wilkinson and L. A. Willoughby (Oxford: Clarendon Press, 1982).

2 SOCIAL CRITIQUE

I begin with Varnhagen's diagnosis and critique of her social environment. The two key elements of social reality which she identifies and critiques are the social restrictions on women's lives and the subordination of Jews.

As a Jewish woman, the inferiority of her social position is obvious to Varnhagen and, unlike many of her contemporaries, she understands both components—gender and religious inferiority—as contingent, human-made, unjust, and in need of remedy. Arendt's influential account of Varnhagen's life and work focuses on religious subordination, presenting the social position of Jews as that of outcasts—not at the bottom of, but outside society.[16] Yet, reading Varnhagen's work, social restrictions on women's lives also feature prominently. In a particularly graphic passage, Varnhagen outlines what a woman is degraded to in the social world: "a powerless being, that is credited for nothing, to sit at home now, and that would have heaven and earth, humans and animals against it, if it desired to go away (and that has thoughts like any another human), and [yet] must properly stay at home, and that if it makes *movements* that are noticeable must swallow accusations of all kinds made against it with *raison* [reason]; because it truly is not *raison* [appropriate] to shake [its determinants]; because then the glasses, the distaffs, the flowers, the sewing kit falls away, everything hits in."[17] While Jews are outcasts, women have a very particular, severely limited place *within* society and any deviation from it will be sanctioned. For Jewish women these restrictions intersect with their position as outcasts: "happily you [a Jewish woman] would have wanted to be 'a homely wife, loving and kissing your husband' as Goethe says in his *Distichon*; but you couldn't. And where to put the terrible reserves, the abilities of heart and life!"[18] In this case, is the Jewish woman restricted in her agency because she is a *Jew*? Not really—Jews (or indeed anyone) would not aspire to be homely wives, a social position Varnhagen just recognized as inferior. Is the Jewish woman restricted because she is a *woman*? Not really either; other women can be homely wives, even if that might be all they can be. Rather, it seems her restriction arises from being a *Jewish woman*. Varnhagen's analysis makes clear the "compoundedness" or nonseparability of different dimensions of oppression (in this case gender and religion)—a point also at the heart of contemporary intersectional theorizing.[19]

Following Arendt's reading of Varnhagen's life, there are only two options for how to live in such an unjust social reality. These form a "diabolic dilemma to which [Varnhagen's] life had been confined: on the one hand she had been deprived of

---

[16] Arendt, *Varnhagen*.

[17] VII, 1, 12–13.

[18] Rahel Varnhagen, *Briefwechsel mit Pauline Wiesel*, ed. Barbara Hahn (Munich: C. H. Beck), 91.

[19] Kimberle Crenshaw, "Demarginalizing the Intersection of Race and Sex: A Black Feminist Critique of Antidiscrimination Doctrine, Feminist Theory and Antiracist Politics," *University of Chicago Legal Forum* 1 (1989): 166.

everything by general social conditions, and on the other hand she had been able to purchase a social existence only by sacrificing [her] nature."[20] These are the options of pariah—the social outcast—and parvenu—the upwardly mobile assimilationist. Being a parvenu is costly, as Arendt suggests here. It is also fragile or unstable, as she and Varnhagen agree.[21]

Varnhagen sees the dilemma Arendt diagnoses. But she proposes a way out which Arendt overlooks: a strategy of communal retreat. In her writing, Varnhagen endorses and tries out an alternative life, separate from social roles and practices, with authenticity, self-development, friendship, and community as central values—more on these in the next sections. This strategy is first a direct *response* to injustice, as Varnhagen writes: "should they, the governments, prevent change, then it is good to be together, to help one another, to discuss, and to know oneself there, to see."[22] Second, this strategy is itself a form of *resistance* against injustice: Varnhagen and her friends don't give in and adapt, but come together. Third, the strategy of communal retreat is instrumental to achieving *progressive change*.[23] The passage just quoted continues: "living, loving, studying, being industrious, marrying, if that comes along, doing every little thing rightfully and lively, that is always alive, and that nobody prevents. And from this big, ever bigger union of the willing human being nothing, nothing at all, should develop?"[24] Varnhagen's answer to this rhetorical question is of course that social change *will* develop from defying social restrictions and living to the fullest. These developments will likely be slow and gradual, as Varnhagen suggests when thinking about the prospects of social change.[25] Nevertheless, communal retreat is resistance that aims at social change.

Arendt overlooks this way out of the pariah-parvenue dilemma. She expresses disappointment about Varnhagen's politics: "like all parvenus, [Varnhagen] never dreamed of a radical alteration of bad conditions but rather of a shift of personnel that would work out in her favor, so that the situation would improve as if by the stroke of a magic wand."[26] But the philosopher Rahel Levin Varnhagen whom I present in this chapter is neither as self-interested nor as passive as Arendt makes her out to be. She does not wait for improvement, but through communal retreat enacts it herself.

Varnhagen's retreat strategy differs from Arendt's options of pariah or parvenu. The intentional outsider is no pariah: she has chosen her own path, shares it with others, and regards it as an elevation from the rest of society while the pariah is cast out by society.

---

[20] Arendt, *Varnhagen*, 213.

[21] Arendt, *Varnhagen*, 202. See for example Rahel Varnhagen, *Tagebücher und Aufzeichnungen*, ed. Ursula Isselstein (Göttingen: Wallstein, 2019), 69, for a brilliant illustration of fragility using the example of Joséphine Bonaparte, socially elevated through marriage with Napoleon, and cast back into social nullity by divorce.

[22] I, 505; see Jennet Kirkpatrick, *The Virtues of Exit: On Resistance and Quitting Politics* (Cambridge: Cambridge University Press, 2017), esp. chap. 2.

[23] See Tewarson, *Varnhagen*, 90.

[24] I, 505; see also II, 381–383.

[25] II, 383–384.

[26] Arendt, *Varnhagen*, 201–202.

This outsider is also no parvenu: she has her own ends of self-development, and of communal and authentic life while "the only goal [the parvenu] can possibly have is to rise."[27] In section 3, I focus on the authentic life of the outsider, in section 4 on the value of friendship for her, and in section 5 on the project of self-development she engages in.

3 Authenticity

Varnhagen shares with other Romantics a fascination for authenticity or naturalness. On at least one interpretation of authenticity, authentic individuals should become what they truly are: they should cultivate those, and only those, character traits and attributes they are naturally endowed with. Varnhagen invokes this Romantic ideal when she stresses the importance of "being oneself," calling up "one's deepest essence," developing the "raw material within us," cultivating one's "natural dispositions."[28] If everyone lives according to this principle, say the Romantics, society becomes a rich tapestry of iridescent personalities in harmony with one another.[29] I will call such authenticity strong-sense authenticity. Being authentic in the strong sense means having developed one's natural dispositions.

Especially in an unjust society, attempts at the development of one's natural dispositions come with the risk of misshaping or even crushing them—a worry that Varnhagen is aware of and tries to accommodate, as I show in section 5. Yet, perhaps in an attempt to avoid this problem entirely, we also find discussion of a weaker sense of authenticity in Varnhagen's work. Then, authenticity only means being honest and true to one's *present* self. This self is now understood as a socially shaped—perhaps even misshaped—being. Weak-sense authenticity means only that one's external presentation and behavior conform to one's internal sense of self. Whether natural disposition or endowment are developed does not matter for weak-sense authenticity. External presentation and inner sense of self can easily drift apart, as Varnhagen describes metaphorically: one can " entirely get away from what one truly is; away, far away, like a feeble little ship driven far off on a vast ocean by wind and tempest! The one thing that in truth still concerns me personally, that has sunk deep into my heart and lies down at the bottom, dark and heavy as granite—that far down, I cannot see; I let it lie; like a poor worker who loses himself in the operations of life all week long and perhaps on Sunday can come close to its real essence."[30] Lack of such weak-sense authenticity is something one can come to be reflectively aware of: on Sundays when no work needs doing, the worker has time to understand that he has lived inauthentically. His authentic

---

[27] Arendt, *Varnhagen*, 209.

[28] Varnhagen, *Tagebücher*, 984; 13; III, 1.

[29] See Schiller, *On the Aesthetic Education of Man*, 2–5; Schlegel, *Kritische Friedrich-Schlegel-Ausgabe*, vol. 2, Ideen 60.

[30] Varnhagen quoted in Arendt, *Varnhagen*, 211.

self further exists "down at the bottom" of his heart. It has not been left in an embryonic state, nor has it been lost, as would be true for a lack of strong-sense authenticity. I will concentrate on weak-sense authenticity for now and return to strong-sense authenticity only in section 5.

Social forces may bring about a lack of weak-sense authenticity: the worker must work to survive and feed his family even if his work does not correspond to his talents or preferences; women must adapt to social expectations even when this behavior does not represent their true character. Varnhagen describes cases of inauthentic pretense for women: "one [as woman] loves, keeps, and preserves the wishes of one's kin; adapts to those; turns them into one's highest worry and urgent occupation; but they cannot fulfill, recover, give us rest for further activity, and conduct; or strengthen and vitalize us for our entire life."[31] It is interesting to observe that for Varnhagen social forces have limited power: they cannot shape women so thoroughly that the inferior social roles do in fact come to fulfill, recover, and give rest. I take this to mean that, following Varnhagen, socially conforming women must somehow be aware of the deficiency of their lives. Present-day feminism is often less optimistic than Varnhagen seems to have been. Especially discussions about internalization, causal social construction, or psychological oppression today suggest that social forces can create socially restricted, yet weak-sense-authentic human beings. Women, says for example Sandra Bartky, can fully internalize oppressive social norms, such that living accordingly entirely fulfills them.[32] This internalization can go so far as to make the "oppressed . . . doubt that [they] . . . have the capacity to do the sorts of things that only persons can do, to be what persons, in the fullest sense of the term, can be."[33] Applied to Varnhagen's example, for Bartky women can even come to think of themselves as incapable of anything but loving, keeping, and preserving "the wishes of one's kin."

Varnhagen's more optimistic position leads her to be critical of socially conforming women, in particular of women writers who express themselves in a tone of artificial timidity. She has little sympathy for this particular inauthenticity: "it seems exactly of this kind of condemnable flattery when a woman, when she writes, writes for print—so then surely means to record something thought out—, still always posits herself as entirely subordinated compared to the man or to men and so pretends to be something she is not; and [when she] aims to mention [that] in her writing, as if she regarded herself as an amiable usurper, tolerated simply because of non-threatening weakness! . . . why these long shallow excuses, in this intellectual, non-partisan circulation and exchange, and why the old-franconian coquetry?"[34] Even Varnhagen herself is occasionally tempted by such coquetry. She expresses this most clearly in the following passage: "my sadness, frustration, despondency, discontent, fragility, in short everything, everything

---

[31] Rahel Varnhagen, *Rahel und ihre Zeit. Briefe und Zeugnisse*, ed. Bertha Badt (Munich: E. Rentsch, 1912), 170–171.

[32] Sandra Bartky, *Femininity and Domination* (New York: Routledge, 1990), 22–32.

[33] Bartky, *Femininity*, 29.

[34] III, 116. 'Old-franconian' means 'out-dated' in this context.

has reached its highest point. I cannot pretend any longer. And yet, some [people] still come to me. I only write this, because I am writing; if you were to see me, you wouldn't notice it at all: I speak and am as always."[35] Only in her letters does Varnhagen have to courage to be authentic. In this case weak-sense authenticity involves showing one's actual sadness and frustration. In the face-to-face interactions she describes Varnhagen as lacking such weak-sense authenticity: she accords with social norms of innocent, unassuming cheerfulness while not actually being cheerful. Varnhagen is not a flawless "living example" of her own philosophical program: we see her struggling to live up to her values and so are able to thoroughly understand the demands of the program she endorses. This is an advantage of her writing being both statement and performance: a reader might not have reached this level of understanding of her proposed strategy and of its intricate difficulties had she not presented the reader with herself as concrete example.

Artificial timidity is a socially caused but not seemingly *internal* impediment on authenticity: it is only their own lack of courage that keeps women from writing differently. Varnhagen identifies a second socially caused impediment to authenticity that is more external: hermeneutical inadequacy due to the socially available language. Most writers will be familiar with the frustration of struggling for words and Varnhagen has excellent metaphors to describe it: "there is a play of colors—that's what I want to call it—in our chest, which is so tender that, as soon as we want to express it, turns into a lie; I see the words, when they have worked themselves out of my heart, as they hover in the air in front of me, they form a lie; I search for different ones, time passes; and yet they would not have gotten any better! This dread keeps me from speaking."[36] What a writer wishes to express is a play of colors, something delicate within themselves; its first attempt of expression is laborious, the expression hovers in the air, is eventually discovered to be a lie. Elsewhere, Varnhagen compares literary expression to nothingness or to something once warm that has now become cold.[37] This inability to find the right, true, warm words is exacerbated for the socially marginalized and subordinated writer. Such a writer's hermeneutical struggles spring not only from her own inadequacy but from social forces: "the German, my own, language is not at my disposal; our language is our lived life; I have invented mine for myself; I could therefore make less use than many others of ready-made phrases; my phrases are then frequently bumpy and flawed in many ways, but always true."[38] Here, we see Varnhagen presenting herself as neither pariah nor parvenu, but as having defied social norms and retreated from society, "inventing" her own life. We also see her concern for authenticity; her phrases are "always true." But to write truly, she can't make use of ready-made phrases in her language. This is because socially common or dominant ways of life shape the terms and concepts available in language. When leading a different life,

---

[35] IX, 26.
[36] I, 298.
[37] Varnhagen, *Tagebücher*, 33.
[38] VIII, 159; see also I, 76, 334.

as Varnhagen does, much needed terms are absent from one's language. This point is familiar from discussions of hermeneutical injustice in contemporary social epistemology. Hermeneutical injustice, says Miranda Fricker, is "the injustice of having some significant area of one's social experience obscured from collective understanding owing to hermeneutical marginalization" where such marginalization refers to unequal participation in how "some significant area(s) of social experience" are commonly interpreted.[39] Jewish women, like Varnhagen, have little opportunity for hermeneutical participation.

To find Fricker's ideas prefigured in a woman's writing from the Romantic era is interesting in itself. Varnhagen's work further shows a way to deal with such injustice that is different from Fricker's. Fricker suggests that we all ought to cultivate a virtue of hermeneutical justice.[40] Here, she is concerned with how an *audience* ought to engage with potentially hermeneutically marginalized individuals. Varnhagen, on the other hand, is concerned with what hermeneutically marginalized *speakers* like her ought to do. Her hermeneutical inadequacy paradoxically motivates Varnhagen to do better. She becomes fascinated with "beautiful language and good expression" and works to meet those standards in her own work.[41] In so doing, she develops an idiosyncratic writing style, she 'invents' her own language, as she says. It is filled with exclamations, unusual imagery, and occasional words from foreign languages—a writing style of creative authenticity. Faced with hermeneutical injustice, one ought to stubbornly create one's own language for oneself, suggests Varnhagen. Following commentator Liliane Weissberg, this unfamiliar language, which I have identified as having been born out of resistance to hermeneutical restrictions, is partly responsible for Varnhagen's renown as a writer.[42]

For the writer Varnhagen, authenticity is a guiding principle of literary production. This point is emphasized by literary commentators Christa Bürger and Heidi Tewarson.[43] I have embedded this idea about literary style in Varnhagen's larger philosophical program: for her, authenticity, in its weak sense, is a general principle guiding a life in an unjust world. According to weak-sense authenticity, one ought to act according to who one is, avoiding pretence. The literary realm is only one among many in which this principle ought to be realized. There, one ought to write according to who one is. Revisiting Arendt's dilemma of pariah and parvenu, we can start to see how Varnhagen presents a solution. Living authentically may involve defying unjust social norms. The authentic female writer may, for example, defy social norms of overly humble and deferential writing style when she actually feels no inferiority. In defying such a social norm, she is neither pariah nor parvenu but intentional outsider.

[39] Miranda Fricker, *Epistemic Injustice* (Oxford: Oxford University Press, 2007), 158; 153.

[40] Fricker, *Epistemic Injustice*, 169–175.

[41] Varnhagen, *Tagebücher*, 33.

[42] Weissberg, "Writing on the Wall."

[43] Christa Bürger, *Leben Schreiben* (Stuttgart: J. B. Metzler, 1990), 131; Tewarson, *Varnhagen*, 82.

4 FRIENDSHIP AND COMMUNITY

We already encountered a worry about authenticity's practicability: since living authentically sometimes involves defying unjust social norms, it can be very arduous or perhaps even impossible to do so. Varnhagen's own struggles demonstrate this well. Any form of resistance to unjust social norms, she says, is hard: at the very least one must expect constant criticism and sanctioning.[44] Fortunately, resistance often gets easier when one is not alone. This is one reason why Varnhagen emphasizes the importance of community and friendship throughout her work—a theme I turn to now.

Varnhagen writes to her Jewish friend Regine Frohberg in 1806: "let this be consolation in this horror, that a creature lives, who knows your existence as a loving witness, and—I dare say—understands it! And I will not leave you. I will lead this process for you, by the world, and by god and by nature."[45] Varnhagen makes clear that friendship can alleviate suffering simply because someone else listens supportively to one's testimony.[46] Here we see again Varnhagen's characteristic double layer of philosophical statement and performance. She states (albeit implicitly) that friendship alleviates suffering while she simultaneously *is* a loving witness, a good friend, and so hopes to alleviate her friend Regine's suffering.

Yet, friendship does not alleviate suffering only because friends are a supportive audience. Friendships also allow one to recognize that some of one's suffering is shared with others. This new-found commonality provides consolation. Varnhagen notes this in a letter to her sister Rose: "talk to me lots; that and my answers will do you good, and will free you. It is sweet, and full of consolation, in the dreary world, to be allowed to speak to a mind, which knows every pain; and which clearly responds with a tongue,—a kind of notice—, that one does not err alone, and does not have to withstand unheard-of (and entirely new) sorrows. This consolation and no other! humans can grant to one another, when they want to be friends."[47] Here again we find both statement and performance of consolation through friendship—and we find them together: it is exactly through making the general point about supportive friendships that Varnhagen performs her own particular supportive friendship. She outlines that such friendships can alleviate suffering because they reveal it to be shared suffering; in saying this very thing she communicates to Rose that Rose's suffering is shared and thereby helps her.

So friendships alleviate suffering in two ways: being a supportive witness and revealing suffering to be shared. Varnhagen also outlines a third, more minimal way, in which friendships provide support. Friends are an audience; they enable one to speak of one's suffering, even if one cannot count on their support nor on the existence of shared suffering: "write, and express it! This benefits the mind, the body, the soul and the heart.

---

[44] VII, 1, 12; Varnhagen, *Rahel und ihre Zeit*, 170–171.

[45] IX, 28; see I, 360.

[46] See Kay Goodman, "Poesis and Praxis in Rahel Varnhagen's Letter," *New German Critique* 27 (1982): 126–127.

[47] I, 225.

... If one feels like remaining silent, then I approve; if one must speak, then it seems to me, that that is better: and so it is. Speaking and expressing oneself in particular, is better; one develops oneself specifically through that, and leaves behind as many likenesses of oneself, in the sequence of time."[48] Three aspects—(1) supportive (2) audience (3) with similar experiences—make friendship valuable. Such friendship is especially needed in a social reality in which one is likely to suffer from marginalization, subordination, or restriction as a Jewish woman. Statements and performances of such friendship therefore appear mostly in Varnhagen's correspondence with other Jewish women.

When Varnhagen advocates retreating from a social reality that subordinates and restricts, this is not meant to be a total retreat. As just shown, it is communal, rather than solitary; second, it is a recuperative retreat to alleviate suffering caused by social reality and gain strength in preparation for inevitable new suffering. Retreating is a partial strategy, perhaps meant to create an enclave for autonomy in some areas—writing authentically, having friends—so that restriction and subordination in other areas can be endured. As commentator Renata Fuchs points out, Varnhagen successfully aimed for public success and recognition as *salonnière* and writer during her lifetime.[49] So if her (recorded) life is indeed a philosophical example, then her strategy of retreat can only be partial.

I've shown that in the case of authenticity, Varnhagen takes a core Romantic value, prominently advocated at her time, and gives her own spin to it. For her, authenticity is not so much the authentic unfolding of one's natural endowments—what I called strong-sense authenticity—but rather being true to oneself when faced with restrictive social forces. I referred to this as weak-sense authenticity. The same—Varnhagen using a core Romantic value—is also true for friendship or community. In Romantic thought, interaction with others—through friendship or general sociability—is often presented as the place to freely unfold human nature. Schleiermacher, for example, thinks of social interaction as "one of the first and noblest needs" of human beings.[50] Free sociability (*freie Geselligkeit*)—the ideal form of social interaction—is characterized as "the free association of rational and mutually-cultivating persons."[51] Such sociability, says Schleiermacher, is governed by three laws: a formal law of reciprocity, a material law of freedom, and a quantitative law of limited pluralism of individual characters. Schleiermacher was a frequent guest at Varnhagen's salon and his *Toward a Theory of Sociable Conduct,* in which he outlines his idea of free sociability, was likely inspired by these visits. It is then no coincidence that we find similar anthropological ideas about sociability and community in Varnhagen's own work:

> what we actually understand by the word "human," is after all the creature that stands in rational relation with those like it, in a relation of consciousness, which

[48] I, 336.

[49] In her " 'Soll ein Weib.' "

[50] Friedrich Schleiermacher, *"Toward a Theory of Sociable Conduct" and Essays on Its Intellectual-Cultural Context,* trans. Jeffrey Hoover, ed. Ruth D. Richardson (Lewiston, NY: Edwin Mellen, 1995), 20.

[51] Schleiermacher, *Toward a Theory of Sociable Conduct,* 21.

we ourselves are able to form, and are also necessitated to always form. We might be as we want, we might do what we like, we have the longing to be amiable. All of us follow this beautiful, pure, most human, most lovely instinct. Taken in the highest sense—but also as far down [into details] as its splinters—the entire mesh of human life, as human beings, is nothing but that, modified into eternity.[52]

So community and friendship are important in two ways for Varnhagen. I've shown that the socially restricted or subordinated individual finds consolation through friendship; friendship alleviates her suffering. We can add now the second way: through friendship any individual can satisfy her human need for free social interaction among diverse individuals. In their discussions of this second aspect, Varnhagen and Schleiermacher also mention a third: such a friendly community is a location for self-development or formation. Formation (*Bildung*) constitutes another core Romantic idea that Varnhagen adopts and embeds in her strategy of retreat. For her, through formation in exchange with others and in literary production a socially restricted and subordinated individual is able to pursue her own project, separate from otherwise constant restriction and subordination.

5 FORMATION

Bildung—German for culture, formation, education, self-development—fascinates Early German Romantic thought for at least two historical-contextual reasons. First, processes of secularization, well under way at the end of the eighteenth century, popularized the idea that each human being has autonomy over her own life.[53] With such autonomy comes responsibility and the possibility to evaluate others according to how they live. *Bildung*—the effort one invests into unfolding one's potential, one's talents, or one's ideal self-image—was used as a new standard for evaluation. Second, the Early German Romantics, initially eagerly enthusiastic about the French Revolution, were soon disillusioned about the prospects of republican government in light of the Revolution's failures and atrocities.[54] One lesson they drew from these historical events was that a republic needs a suitably educated demos to be stable—the French people didn't yet have the appropriate *Bildung*.

At the turn to the nineteenth century, *Bildung* is at the heart of philosophical projects; poets write about it; social and educational reformers aim to realize it; and broader society starts pouring into salons where *Bildung* is gained, maintained, and (perhaps above all) presented. Varnhagen, her salon, and her letters are in the midst of

---

[52] I, 323–24.

[53] Kristin Gjesdal, "*Bildung*," in *The Oxford Handbook of German Philosophy in the Nineteenth Century*, ed. Michael N. Forster and Kristin Gjesdal (Oxford University Press, 2015), 697–698.

[54] Beiser, *Romantic Imperative*, 88–90.

this infatuation and so it comes as no surprise that she incorporates the idea of *Bildung* into her writings.

As with the Romantic values of authenticity and community, Varnhagen thinks of *Bildung* as a way to retreat from restricting and subordinating society. Again, this is not only what Varnhagen suggests. It is what she herself tries out, as she notes when reflecting on her life:

> what I do like is that I got to know myself. The last proof of my courage to stand shall serve me to make me more courageous; courageous, not to tolerate worthless things in the place of happiness. Who only lives in the heart, and only gives from the heart, should not at all take bad coins. Birth expelled me from the world, luck did not let me in, or down; I side eternally with the power of my heart and with what my mind shows me. This is the circle shown to me by nature: within it I am powerful and others are void.[55]

Getting to know oneself, unfolding one's emotional and intellectual abilities—heart and mind, as Varnhagen says—is a retreat, an intentional distancing of oneself from a world that only subordinates or excludes. The world "expelled" her (Arendt's pariah), she was not "let in" (Arendt's parvenu), instead she "got to know" herself. Such self-development is not just valuable as a retreat from oppressive conditions, it also gives strength and courage to endure these when seclusion isn't possible, says Varnhagen. In these two respects—retreat and recuperation—*Bildung* plays a role similar to that of friendship and community.

But how does the marginalized person get to know herself, how does *Bildung* best proceed? I argue that Varnhagen favors *Bildung* via social, rather than pedagogical, means. Varnhagen's pathway to *Bildung* is conversation, and, in particular, written conversation in the form of letters. This means that her entire epistolary oeuvre can be understood as one large performance of *Bildung*. To see how she develops this point, I start from what Varnhagen regards as bad *Bildung*.

Bildung often proceeds wrongly. This, says Varnhagen, is particularly true of women's education, which has two main flaws. First, it suffocates or distorts natural facilities (*Naturanlagen*), as she observes using the example of an acquaintance's daughter:

> the daughter: properly alive, conversational. But it seems to me, not developed out of her nature. . . . She is to be praised, and pleasant; and not affected, but unnatural in her expression. Only it seems to me that had her very own nature been developed she would be an entirely different girl. . . . Not only the most fortunate circumstances are part of bringing forth the very own endowments of humans, and to form them in harmony: but most human beings are formed entirely artificially, and they don't have strong enough character traits, not even those exercised in harmony, to resist the education of parents or circumstances; rather they remain embryonic, monstrous,

---

[55] I, 321; see also I, 328.

with crippled, rotten, scarcely scattered, feeble natural dispositions. . . . A common appearance to me, and truly tragic, multiply tragic.[56]

I demonstrated in section 3 that Varnhagen endorses the value of weak-sense authenticity, understood as the correspondence between external presentation and inner sense of self. But in disucssing the *Bildung* of the young woman in this example, Varnhagen invokes ideas of strong-sense authenticity, understood as the realization of natural endowment. Her young female protagonist lacks strong-sense authenticity. Varnhagen seems to suggest: while it is already desirable (and often difficult) to be weak-sense authentic, it is even better to work on becoming strong-sense authentic through *Bildung*.

As a second fault of existing *Bildung* Varnhagen notes that normal women's education due to parents and circumstances does not at all prepare one for real life. It is impractical and therefore useless, as Varnhagen writes in her diary: "if real life actually appears before their eyes, comes to their throat, always anew from soil, and clouds, and from the unique poor flesh, then they [those so educated] . . . do not know how to decide anything, they do not understand how to treat anything, so they do everything wrongly even if only out of mere perplexity."[57] From this presentation of bad *Bildung*, we can derive two desiderata for good *Bildung*. A backward-looking desideratum: *Bildung* ought to unfold one's natural endowments. And a forward-looking desideratum: *Bildung* ought to prepare one for the life one will lead and the actions and decisions one may have to take within it.

Where might such *Bildung* be gained? Interestingly, Varnhagen has sympathies for Rousseau's educational program: "via Rousseau's *Emile* one finds out how the entire world must have been equipped to educate [erziehn] a child into a—in all senses— healthy human being; yet, how far we are removed from this condition, and are only able to effect very piecemeal and very little in education."[58] Rousseau proposes an ideal education in isolation from society. This isolation has two parts: isolation from social forces, restrictions, or norms, and isolation from other human beings, except for one's teacher.[59] Varnhagen endorses the first, but rejects the second isolation, as I show now. Aware that Rousseau's ideal is unattainable in the nonideal present, Varnhagen suggests that education ought to proceed in contact with others. Accordingly, she advises her sister Rose:

> go to places where new things, words and human beings touch you, where those renew your blood, life, nerves and thoughts. For us women this is doubly necessary;

---

[56] III, 1–2.

[57] Varnhagen, *Tagebücher*, 74.

[58] III, 133. Strictly speaking, *Bildung* and *Erziehung* denote different ideas. *Erziehung*, following Gjesdal's "*Bildung*", 695, refers mostly to the specific formation of "child-rearing, upbringing, and school education." However, Varnhagen seems to use *Erziehung* in a more general sense, where it becomes synonymous with *Bildung* (as in III, 1–2, quoted earlier), as do other Romantics, most notably Schiller in his *On the Aesthetic Education [Erziehung] of Man*.

[59] Rousseau, Jean-Jacques. *Emile, or Education*. J. M. Dent, 1762. Accessed at https://oll.libertyfund. org/title/rousseau-emile-or-education.

men's occupation on the other hand is also business, which they must deem important, in the exercise of which their ambition feels flattered; they see an advance in it, into which they are moved by the movement of humans: while we only always have bits and pieces in front of us that drag us down, small expenses and facilities. . . . This is why you and I need to be refreshened a bit.[60]

Bildung comes from contact with new people and new things. In this way, men are in the advantage; they have daily opportunities for self-development when engaged in their work in the public sphere. Women, on the other hand, must seek education in places different from their prescribed private, largely socially isolated life. Such social education can fulfill at least the forward-looking desideratum just discussed: interaction with others presents an opportunity to practice exactly those social skills one may need in life—skills one might not learn through Rousseau's education in isolation. Whether the backward-looking desideratum about unfolding natural endowment is also fulfilled depends on what kind of social environment one forms oneself in. Varnhagen agrees with Rousseau that at least the education of women must proceed away from ordinary social life which would only suppress or distort women's natural facilities.

If *Bildung* is to proceed in a social, communal setting, but somewhat removed from social norms and restrictions,[61] the salon might seem the ideal place. The salon aims to create a "free play of thoughts and feelings whereby all members mutually stimulate and enliven each other," writes Schleiermacher.[62] Romantic salons have been celebrated as standing outside rigid social rules, allowing for (some) social mobility and free association of individuals from different classes.[63] Yet, in her own salon, Varnhagen is often viewed—in rather sexist ways—as a mediator or stimulator of others' *Bildung*, not an active self-forming participant.[64] One commentator even reports that Varnhagen has mastered the "female art, the art of stepping back" needed for a lively salon.[65] Varnhagen's position in the salon sounds as if it is no good place for women's *Bildung*. Worse, it sounds as if she has given up on her own *Bildung*. She seems to have made her

---

[60] Varnhagen, *Rahel und ihre Zeit*, 170–171.

[61] In endorsing such interactive *Bildung* removed from society, Varnhagen agrees with early modern women philosophers like Mary Astell, who argues that "good education should occur in a religious retreat, a women's-only educational institution," as Karen Detlefsen shows in her "Cartesianism and Its Feminist Promise and Limits: The Case of Mary Astell," in *Descartes and Cartesianism: Essays in Honour of Desmond Clarke*, ed. Stephen Gaukroger and Catherine Wilson (Oxford: Oxford University Press, 2017), 202; see Mary Astell, *A Serious Proposal to the Ladies, For the Advancement of Their True and Greatest Interest. In Two Parts* (London, 1697), https://www.gutenberg.org/files/54984/54984-h/54984-h.htm. Yet, Varnhagen is opposed to Astell's religious solution; she expresses skepticism about religious education for example in her *Tagebücher*, 71–72.

[62] Schleiermacher, *Toward a Theory of Sociable Conduct*, 25.

[63] Jürgen Habermas, *Struktuwandel der Öffentlichkeit* (Frankfurt: Suhrkamp, 1990), 86–121; see Seyla Benhabib, "The Pariah and Her Shadow," *Political Theory* 23, no. 1 (1995): 5–24.

[64] Fuchs, " 'Soll ein Weib,' " 307–308.

[65] Berta Badt, foreword to Varnhagen, *Rahel und ihre Zeit*, ed. Badt, 20.

peace with the social restrictions placed on women's lives, happily occupying the role of mere female mediator between great male minds.

We mustn't be so quick in condemning her. She lives her program of retreat and *Bildung* elsewhere: not as *salonnière* bogged down by gender norms and restrictions, but as writer in conversation with other writers. Here she can form herself in exchange with others, according to the forward-looking desideratum described earlier. Private, literary exchange is less exposed to social pressures that might distort or suppress natural facilities, thereby also fulfilling the backward-looking desideratum on *Bildung*. Again, *Bildung* through writing is only a partial retreat from social restriction and subordination; one is still part of society—either pariah or parvenu—when one stops writing.

Karen Detlefsen uses the concepts of ideal and nonideal theory to contrast Rousseau's and Mary Astell's philosophy of education.[66] These concepts are also useful to make sense of Varnhagen's work. Ideal-theory, following Elisabeth Anderson, "attempts to construct a model of what an ideally just society would look like, or what principles ideally just procedures would follow."[67] When Varnhagen says of *Emile* that it shows "how the entire world must have been equipped to educate a child into a . . . healthy human being" yet that we are far "removed from this condition,"[68] she agrees that Rousseau is an ideal theorist. We can understand Varnhagen's own program as nonideal theory whose task it is "to articulate the problems we face, then diagnose their causes, and finally to formulate solutions."[69] One problem is the unjust social world. Varnhagen focuses less on the diagnosis of its causes and more on the formulation of a solution: a strategy of communal retreat aimed at authenticity and filled by a project of self-development. A more specific problem is the distorting education of women. This problem's cause is also the unjust social world. The solution Varnhagen formulates is communal education, not in salons where social forces still dictate women's inferior role, but in one-on-one conversations, often through correspondence.

Varnhagen repeatedly reflects on this formative function of her epistolary production. She refers to it as "the soul taking a walk" on "fresh, small, abstract paths, we didn't yet know."[70] She notes that "what I do like: that I came to know myself [through my letters]."[71] And in a longer passage she emphasizes the oral, conversational character of her writing: "my writing should often resemble fresh, aromatic strawberries, on which sand and roots still hang: this you once said; I accept it. . . .—Yet, I need to say one thing about my way of writing: . . . I never want to write a speech, but I want to write conversations, as they live in a human being, and as they are only laid out through

---

[66] Detlefsen, "Cartesianism," 203–206.

[67] Elizabeth Anderson, 'Toward a Non-ideal, Relational Methodology for Political Philosophy: Comments on Schwartzman's "Challenging Liberalism," *Hypatia* 24, no. 4 (2009): 135.

[68] III, 133.

[69] Anderson, "Toward a Non-ideal, Relational Methodology," 135.

[70] II, 414–415.

[71] I, 321; see also French, "'Meine Beiden Ichs,'" 86.

will and art. . . . If someone's writing, be it book, memoir, or letter, is only a complete, delivered speech, then for me it always has an aftertaste of dislike."[72] These passages make clear that Varnhagen's letter writing does not present finished, polished results, rather it documents a process that she herself recognizes as the development and formation of her own self through conversation. Reading these passages in conjunction with her letter to Rose, her negative characterization of existing *Bildung*, and her positive words about Rousseau, we can suspect that written conversation is not only incidentally the means through which one concrete person—Rahel Levin Varnhagen—chose to form herself, as literary commentators note.[73] Rather, it is the means, says Varnhagen, through which restricted, subordinated, or marginalized individuals can and should form themselves. Epistolary production is sufficiently social to prepare for life, yet sufficiently removed from restrictive social reality not to suppress or distort natural characteristics. As such it fulfills both Varnhagen's forward- and backward-looking desiderata of good *Bildung*.

6 Conclusion

Varnhagen uses core Romantic concepts and ideas—I've looked at authenticity, community, and *Bildung*—and makes them speak to her particular question about how to live in a restrictive and subordinating social reality.

Her answer presents a solution to the pariah-parvenu dilemma Arendt sketches. By living authentically, in a community of friends, and in having the project of *Bildung* one can partly retreat from restrictive, subordinating society. Following Varnhagen, such retreat has the potential to affect social progress in the long term. In this chapter, I have refrained from any evaluation of her strategy of retreat, exit, or withdrawal—this is work for another day. Yet, what we can certainly conclude is that Arendt's assessment of Varnhagen as passive, apolitical, and self-interested stands in contrast with Varnhagen's self-presentation which I have reconstructed here.

To sketch a strategy of simultaneous retreat and resistance, Varnhagen uses her own life, as recorded in and lived through her letters. There, she demonstrates her authenticity, she acts as a friend, and she forms herself through literary production and conversation. We can summarize three reasons as to why Varnhagen might present her ideas in this way. First, as a woman without formal philosophical training, she has few other socially acceptable literary options besides the production of personal letters. Second, due to the hermeneutical inadequacies she notes, she might be better able to show than tell what she wishes to convey. Third, showing by example might be more detailed, more alive, and so more convincing than flat-out telling.

---

[72] III, 456.
[73] Daley, *Women of Letters*, 60; Bürger, *Leben Schreiben*, 118.

I have argued that, in Varnhagen's work, we find core Romantic ideas put to original politically and socially relevant uses, presented in an unusual declarative-cum-performative style. This warrants more *specifically philosophical* attention paid to her.

I am most grateful to Julia Borcherding, Anna Ezekiel, Kristin Gjesdal, Anne Pollok, as well as audiences and commentators at the ChiPhi 'Philosophy and Genre' Workshop at York, April 6 and 7, 2021, the Stirling SWIP conference, January 9–22, 2021, the Manchester BPPA 'Radical Philosophy Conference', November 25–28, 2020, and the conference 'From Enlightenment to Romanticism: Women at the Turning Point' at Western University, October 13 and 14, 2022 for comments and feedback on earlier versions of this chapter.

BIBLIOGRAPHY

Anderson, Elisabeth. "Toward a Non-ideal, Relational Methodology for Political Philosophy: Comments on Schwartzman's 'Challenging Liberalism.'" *Hypatia* 24, no. 4 (2009): 130–145.

Arendt, Hannah. *Rahel Varnhagen: The Life of a Jewish Woman.* Translated by Richard and Clara Winston. New York: Harcourt Brace Jovanovich, 1974.

Astell, Mary. *A Serious Proposal to the Ladies, for the Advancement of Their True and Greatest Interest. In Two Parts.* London: 1697. https://www.gutenberg.org/files/54984/54984-h/54984-h.htm.

Badt, Bertha. Introduction to *Rahel und ihre Zeit. Briefe und Zeugnisse*, by Rahel Varnhagen, edited by Bertha Badt, 7–34. Munich: E. Rentsch, 1912.

Bartky, Sandra. *Femininity and Domination.* New York: Routledge, 1990.

Becker-Cantarino, Barbara. "Leben als Text—Briefe als Ausdrucks- und Verständigungsmittel in der Briefkultur und Literatur des 18. Jahrhunderts." In *Frauen Literatur Geschichte*, edited by Hiltrud Gnüg and Renate Möhrmann, 129–146. Stuttgart: Metzler, 1999.

Beiser, Frederick C. *The Romantic Imperative: The Concept of Early German Romanticism.* Cambridge, MA: Harvard University Press, 2003.

Benhabib, Seyla. "The Pariah and Her Shadow." *Political Theory* 23, no. 1 (1995): 5–24.

Bürger, Christa. *Leben Schreiben.* Stuttgart: J. B. Metzler, 1990.

Crenshaw, Kimberle. "Demarginalizing the Intersection of Race and Sex: A Black Feminist Critique of Antidiscrimination Doctrine, Feminist Theory and Antiracist Politics." *University of Chicago Legal Forum* 1 (1989): 139–167.

Daley, Margaretmary. *Women of Letters: A Study in the Personal Writing of Caroline Schlegel-Schelling, Rahel Levin Varnhagen, and Bettina von Arnim.* Rochester, NY: Camden House, 1998.

Detlefsen, Karen. "Cartesianism and Its Feminist Promise and Limits: The Case of Mary Astell." In *Descartes and Cartesianism: Essays in Honour of Desmond Clarke*, edited by Stephen Gaukroger and Catherine Wilson, 191–206. Oxford: Oxford University Press, 2017.

French, Lorely. "'Meine beiden Ichs': Confrontations with Language and Self in Letters by Early Nineteenth-Century Women." *Women in German Yearbook* 5 (1989): 73–89.

Fricker, Miranda. *Epistemic Injustice: Power and the Ethics of Knowing.* Oxford: Oxford University Press, 2007.

Fuchs, Renata. "'Soll ein Weib wohl Bücher schreiben; Oder soll sie's lassen bleiben? The Immediate Reception of Rahel Levin Varnhagen as a Public Figure." *Neophilologus* 98, no. 2 (2014): 303–324.

Gjesdal, Kristin. "*Bildung*." In *The Oxford Handbook of German Philosophy in the Nineteenth Century*, edited by Michael N. Forster and Kristin Gjesdal, 695–719. Oxford: Oxford University Press, 2015.

Goodman, Dena. "Letter Writing and the Emergence of Gendered Subjectivity in Eighteenth-Century France." *Journal of Women's History* 17, no. 2 (2005): 9–37.

Goodman, Kay. "Poesis and Praxis in Rahel Varnhagen's Letter." *New German Critique* 27 (1982): 123–139.

Habermas, Jürgen. *Struktuwandel der Öffentlichkeit*. Frankfurt: Suhrkamp, 1990.

Isselstein, Ursula. "'Durch Gedruckte Worte Sprechen': Die Tagebücher und Aufzeichnungen Rahel Levin Varnhagens." In *Tagebücher und Aufzeichnungen*, by Rahel Varnhagen, 941–1010. Edited by Ursula Isselstein. Göttingen: Wallstein, 2019.

Kirkpatrick, Jennet. *The Virtues of Exit: On Resistance and Quitting Politics*. Cambridge: Cambridge University Press, 2017.

Kristeva, Julia. "The Meaning of an Example: Rahel Varnhagen." In *Hannah Arendt: Life Is a Narrative*, by Kristeva, 48–69. New York: Columbia University Press, 2001.

Pollok, Anne. "The Role of Writing and Sociability for the Establishment of a Persona: Henriette Herz, Rahel Levin Varnhagen, and Bettina von Arnim." In *Women and Philosophy in Eighteenth-Century Germany*, edited by Corey W. Dyck, 195–210. Oxford: Oxford University Press, 2021.

Rousseau, Jean-Jacques. *Emile, or Education*. J. M. Dent, 1762. https://oll.libertyfund.org/title/rousseau-emile-or-education

Schiller, Friedrich. *On the Aesthetic Education of Man in a Series of Letters*. Edited and translated by Elizabeth Wilkinson and L. A. Willoughby. Oxford: Clarendon Press, 1982.

Schlegel, Friedrich. *Studien des Klassischen Altertums*. Vol. 1 of *Kritische Friedrich-Schlegel-Ausgabe*, edited by Ernst Behler, Jean Jacques Anstett, Hans Eichner, and Ursula Behler. Paderborn: Schöningh, 1958–.

Schleiermacher, Friedrich. *"Toward a Theory of Sociable Conduct" and Essays on Its Intellectual-Cultural Context*. Translated by Jeffrey Hoover. Edited by Ruth D. Richardson. Lewiston, NY: Edwin Mellen, 1995.

Tewarson, Heidi Thomann. *Rahel Levin Varnhagen: The Life and Work of a German Jewish Intellectual*. Lincoln: University of Nebraska Press, 1988.

Varnhagen, Rahel. *Briefwechsel mit Pauline Wiesel*. Edited by Barbara Hahn. Munich: C. H. Beck, 1997.

Varnhagen, Rahel. *Gesammelte Werke. Rahel-Bibliothek*. 10 vols. Munich: Matthes & Seitz, 1983.

Varnhagen, Rahel. *Rahel und ihre Zeit. Briefe und Zeugnisse*. Edited by Bertha Badt. Munich: E. Rentsch, 1912.

Varnhagen, Rahel. *Tagebücher und Aufzeichnungen*. Edited by Ursula Isselstein. Göttingen: Wallstein, 2019.

Weissberg, Liliane. "Writing on the Wall: Letters of Rahel Varnhagen." *New German Critique*, no. 36 (1985): 157–173.

CHAPTER 5

KAROLINE VON GÜNDERRODE (1780–1806)

ANNA EZEKIEL

THE German writer Karoline von Günderrode has long had a reputation as a lyric poet and writer of dramas; however, the philosophical aspects of her work, although acknowledged by her earliest readers,[1] have tended to be ignored, at least until the recent revival of interest in philosophy written by historical women. Attention not only to Günderrode's philosophical thought but also to her literary work has been overshadowed by interest in her life and suicide, which has generated biographical interpretations of her writings and a "Günderrode mythos"[2] surrounding events related to her death. Her life and works have inspired poems,[3] plays,[4] novels,[5] music,[6] and paintings;[7] she has been called "the German Sappho" and described as a prophetess and a priestess.[8]

However, quite aside from this near-mythical status and the events of Günderrode's biography, Günderrode was a powerful writer and original thinker with an astute and

---

[1] Karoline von Günderrode, *Sämtliche Werke und ausgewählte Studien*, ed. Walter Morgenthaler (Frankfurt: Stroemfeld/Roter Stern, 1990–91) (hereafter SW, followed by volume number and page number), III, 65.

[2] Adrian Hummel, "Lebenszwänge, Schreibräume, unirdisch. Eine kulturanthropologisch orientierte Deutung des 'Mythos Günderrode,'" *Athenäum* 13 (2003): 61–91.

[3] Johannes Bobrowski, "Die Günderode" (1956), in *Sarmatische Zeit. Schattenland Ströme* (Stuttgart: Deutsche Verlagsanst, 1961), 29.

[4] Waltraud Schade, *Tod am Rhein. Ein Schauspiel* (Norderstedt: Books on Demand, 2006).

[5] Christa Wolf, *Kein Ort. Nirgends* (Berlin: Aufbau, 1979).

[6] Manfred Trojahn, *Spätrot. vier Gesänge auf Gedichte der Karoline von Günderrode: für Mezzosopran und Klavier* (1987).

[7] Meret Oppenheim, *Für Karoline von Günderrode* (1983), in Christoph Leitgeb, "Das Jenseits-Lichte der Liebe," *Der Standard*, August 4, 2006.

[8] Otto Berdrow, "Eine Priesterin der Romantik. Karoline von Günderrode," *Die Frau* 2 (1894/95): 681–688; Marina Rauchenbacher, *Karoline von Günderrode. Eine Rezeptionsstudie* (PhD diss., University of Vienna, 2012), 124f.

critical grasp of German Idealism and Romanticism. Her writings reflect on the same problems that preoccupied other philosophers working in these traditions, including the question of free will, the nature of the self, the nature of consciousness, the vocation of humankind, the relationship between the self and nature and between these and the Absolute or the divine, what happens to us after we die, the role of gender in human life and society, and ideals for political arrangements and the pursuit of virtue and beauty. Günderrode's contributions on these topics are exciting and original, providing a unique and as yet relatively unexplored perspective on topics in early nineteenth-century German thought.

This chapter provides an introduction to these philosophical contributions. After a brief biography and an overview of Günderrode's writings, the chapter summarizes key areas of Günderrode's philosophical thought. Starting with Günderrode's metaphysical claims and the unique accounts of love and death that these entail, the chapter moves on to Günderrode's accounts of consciousness and identity and then to her political theory and nascent ethics and aesthetics. Günderrode's work has interested scholars working on gender, and the chapter also outlines Günderrode's contributions to this area. The last section of the chapter describes Günderrode's personal connections to well-known thinkers of the early nineteenth century and suggests ways in which she might have influenced them.

1 BIOGRAPHY

Karoline Friederike Louise Maximiliane von Günderrode was born in 1780 in Karlsruhe, in the southwest of modern Germany, to a family of minor nobility. The family prized education, with a particular interest in literature and philosophy: both Günderrode's parents were amateur writers.[9] The family employed a tutor to teach Günderrode and her five younger siblings, who grew up creating stories and dramas to read to each other at home. Günderrode's unpublished satirical play *Story of the Beautiful Goddess and Noble Nymph Calypso* (*Geschichte der schönen Göttin und edlen Nympfe Kalipso*) stems from this period.

Günderrode experienced a number of tragedies in her early life. Her father died in 1786, and her sisters Louise, Charlotte, and Amalie died in 1794, 1801, and 1802, respectively. Günderrode nursed Charlotte and Amalie as they succumbed to tuberculosis; her letters express her misery and frustration at having to wait helplessly while her beloved sisters passed away: "I must sit almost the whole day beside the sickbed, and with a patient whose spiritual forces are so worn out that not a single gratifying expression is heard from them. . . . I'm inwardly totally miserable. Advise me, help me, and don't say

---

[9] Dagmar von Gersdorff, *"Die Erde ist mir Heimat nicht geworden." Das Leben der Karoline von Günderrode* (Frankfurt: Insel, 2006), 30, 63.

your cold *it must be so,* or at least let's spin dreams around this dire theme [Ich muß fast den ganzen Tag am Krankenbette sitzen und bei einer Kranken, deren Geisteskräfte so abgespannt sind, daß man keine einzige erfreuliche Äußerung derselben gewahr wird. . . . ich bin ganz elend innerlich. Rate, hilf mir, und sage nicht Dein kaltes Es-Muß-So-Sein, oder laß uns wenigstens dies fatale Thema mit Träumen umspinnen]."[10]

It is possible that Günderrode also suffered from tuberculosis, as she had symptoms such as headaches and painful eyes. As a result, many of her writings, letters, and notes were dictated to friends or written on green paper, which was supposed to be better for her eyes.

After the death of Günderrode's father, the family struggled financially. To supplement her widow's pension, Günderrode's mother took up a post as companion to Princess Auguste von Hessen-Kassel (the sister of the king of Prussia) in Hanau, but her difficulties in managing her finances continued and led to tensions with her daughters.[11] For these reasons, from 1797 Günderrode lived in the Cronstett-Hynspergische Damenstift: a convent that provided respectable living quarters in Frankfurt for the daughters of cash-strapped nobility. The convent had strict rules about dress and behavior, but allowed the women who lived there to travel to visit family and friends, make outings to the theater, receive (female or chaperoned) visitors at home, and study and write.

While at the convent, Günderrode was able to continue her studies in philosophy, ancient languages, and ancient history and religions, and begin a literary career, due in large part to wealthy or academic connections. These connections helped her acquire texts, provided feedback on her work, and negotiated for her with publishers. For example, the husband of her friend Elisabetha von Mettingh, the *Naturphilosoph* Christian Gottfried Daniel Nees von Esenbeck, helped publish her first collection, *Poems and Fantasies* (*Gedichte und Phantasien*), and the famous writer Sophie von La Roche—a friend of Günderrode's mother—published Günderrode's short story "Story of a Brahmin" ("Geschichte eines Braminen") in her journal *Herbsttage* (*Autumn Days*). Günderrode was close friends with La Roche's granddaughters Bettina and Kunigunde ("Gunda") Brentano and their brother Clemens. Both Bettina Brentano von Arnim and Clemens Brentano became well-known writers in their own right.

In 1799, Günderrode met the jurist Friedrich Carl von Savigny (another friend of the Brentanos) and was immediately attracted to him.[12] They became romantically involved, but Savigny eventually married Gunda instead. Günderrode sent her lyric poem "The Kiss in the Dream" ("Der Kuß im Traume") to Savigny on the date of their wedding in April 1804.[13] The reasons for Savigny's decision were probably pragmatic: Günderrode's

---

[10] Günderrode, Letter to Gunda Brentano, August 29, 1801, in Birgit von Weißenborn, ed., *"Ich sende Dir ein zärtliches Pfand." Die Briefe der Karoline von Günderrode* (Frankfurt: Insel, 1992), 78–79; see also Günderrode, Letter to Gunda Brentano, October 21, 1801, 81–82.

[11] Gersdorff, *"Die Erde ist mir Heimat,"* 16–17, 124–126.

[12] Günderrode, Letter to Karoline von Barkhaus, July 4, 1799, in Weißenborn, *"Ich sende Dir,"* 49–50.

[13] Günderrode, Letter to Friedrich Carl von Savigny, April 1804, in Weißenborn, *"Ich sende Dir,"* 124.

health was not robust and she was experiencing financial difficulties, while her intellectual leanings were considered inappropriate for a woman and especially a wife.

In 1804, Günderrode met and began an affair with the philologist and mythologist Georg Friedrich Creuzer: a married man. There was talk of divorce and even of a ménage à trois with Creuzer's wife, Sophie;[14] however, Creuzer prevaricated and eventually abandoned the idea. On July 26, 1806, Günderrode received a letter from Creuzer ending the affair, and committed suicide the same day. She had been staying with a friend in Winkel am Rhein, whom she calmly told she was going for a walk; she walked to the banks of the Rhine, where she weighted her skirt with stones and stabbed herself in the heart with a dagger that she had been carrying around for this purpose for some time.[15] She left a note and a bloodstained handkerchief for Creuzer as a pledge of their reunion after death.[16]

2 GÜNDERRODE'S WRITINGS

Günderrode published in a wide range of genres, including epic and lyric poetry, dramas, dialogues, and short stories, and also left behind various unpublished works, notes, and letters. She published two collections of writings in her lifetime: *Poems and Fantasies* in 1804 and *Poetic Fragments* (*Poetische Fragmente*) in 1805, both under the pseudonym "Tian." These met with mixed reviews. Initial responses to *Poems and Fantasies* were positive; however, when Günderrode's identity was revealed, and it was discovered that she was a woman, the appraisal of her work suffered.[17]

At the time of her death, Günderrode had completed a third collection, *Melete*, which she intended to publish under the new pseudonym "Ion." However, Creuzer, who had been dealing with the publisher on Günderrode's behalf and feared a scandal associated with his role in her suicide, suppressed its publication at the news of her death. *Melete* did not appear in print until 1906.

In addition to these collections, Günderrode published four separate pieces in journals. As mentioned earlier, La Roche included Günderrode's short story "Story of a Brahmin" in her 1805 *Herbsttage*, and Creuzer published the plays *Udohla* and *Magic and Destiny* (*Magie und Schicksal*) in *Studien*, a journal he edited with Carl Daub.

---

[14] Gersdorff, *"Die Erde ist mir Heimat,"* 204–206.

[15] Bettina Brentano von Arnim, "Report on Günderrode's Suicide (1808/1839)," in *Bitter Healing: German Women Writers 1700–1830. An Anthology*, ed. Jeannine Blackwell and Susanne Zantop (Lincoln: University of Nebraska Press, 1990), 464, 471.

[16] Günderrode, Letter to Georg Friedrich Creuzer, July 1806, in Weißenborn, *"Ich sende Dir,"* 344.

[17] Early reviews of Günderrode's work had noticeably sexist overtones (SW III, 61–62, 64–66, 130–133). See Anna Ezekiel, introduction to *Poetic Fragments, by Karoline von Günderrode* (Albany: State University of New York Press, 2016), 1–38; Dagmar von Hoff, Sara Friedrichsmeyer, and Patricia Herminghouse, "Aspects of Censorship in the Work of Karoline von Günderrode," *Women in German Yearbook: Feminist Studies and German Culture* 11 (1995): 99–112.

Finally, Günderrode's play *Nikator* was published in Willmann's *Taschenbuch für das Jahr 1806* (*Pocketbook for the Year 1806*), where it appeared alongside pieces by the writer Sophie Mereau (who was married to Clemens Brentano) and the philosopher and historian Joseph Görres.

Günderrode also wrote several unfinished or unpublished poems, dramas, and prose fragments, as well as letters and notebooks that include, among other topics, notes from her philosophical studies and readings on the history and religions of Europe, Asia, and North Africa. Günderrode's philosophical interests included Kant, Fichte, Herder, Hemsterhuis, Schleiermacher, Fichte, Schelling, and the Early German Romantics Novalis and Friedrich Schlegel. In many cases, especially in relation to Fichte and Schelling, her notes show independent engagement with the texts and the beginnings of the development of her considered position on the topics they discuss.[18]

Surprisingly, given the young age at which Günderrode died and the variety of genres in which she wrote, her writings reveal a remarkably consistent underlying philosophical schema. This schema includes a metaphysics, a unique theory of identity, political and social theories, and the beginnings of an ethics and an aesthetics. Günderrode's work is also interesting for its focus on the social construction of identity and social conditions of agency, as well as on the role of gender in determining the events of one's life.[19]

3 GÜNDERRODE'S PHILOSOPHY

3.1 Metaphysics

Günderrode's metaphysical position underlies her claims about human nature, love, friendship, politics, virtue, art, gender, agency—in short, all the ideas expressed in her literary and philosophical works. Understanding her metaphysics is therefore crucial for interpreting her writing. The clearest descriptions of Günderrode's metaphysics are found in the unpublished piece "Idea of the Earth" ("Idee der Erde") and in "Letters of Two Friends" ("Briefe zweier Freunde"), which was intended for publication in *Melete*.

---

[18] Dalia Nassar, "The Human Vocation and the Question of the Earth: Karoline von Günderrode's Philosophy of Nature," *Archiv für Geschichte der Philosophie* 104, no. 1 (2022): 108–130.

[19] See, e.g., B. Becker-Cantarino, "Karoline von Günderrode: Dichtung—Mythologie—Geschlecht," in *Schriftstellerinnen der Romantik. Epoche, Werke, Wirkung* (Munich: C. H. Beck, 2000), 199–225; Karin Obermeier, "'Ach diese Rolle wird mir allzu schwer': Gender and Cultural Identity in Karoline von Günderrode's Drama 'Udohla,'" in *Thalia's Daughters: German Women Dramatists from the Eighteenth Century to the Present*, ed. Susan Cocalis and Ferrel Rose, with Karin Obermeier (Tübingen: Francke, 1996), 99–114; Michaela Schrage-Früh, "Subversive Weiblichkeit? Die Frau als Muse, Geliebte und Künstlerin im Werk Friedrich Schlegels und Karoline von Günderrodes," in *Subversive Romantik*, ed. Volker Kapp, Helmuth Kiesel, Klaus Lubbers, and Patricia Plummer (Berlin: Duncker und Humblot, 2004): 365–390.

The "Letters" are partly based on "Idea of the Earth" and in some places repeat parts of the latter word for word.

According to these texts, every individual object or living being in the world is comprised of indestructible "elements [Elemente]" that are only temporarily assembled into the animals, plants, and objects we encounter in everyday life. When living beings die and decompose, or when inanimate objects are destroyed and break down, the elements that constitute them fall apart. They then become available to be recombined with other elements to form new beings or objects. "Thus," Günderrode claims, "life is immortal and surges up and down in the elements, for they are life itself. But determinate and individual life is only a life-form given through this determinate connection, attraction and contact, which can last no longer than the connection [So ist das Leben unsterblich und wogt auf und nieder in den Elementen denn sie sind das Leben selbst, das bestimmte und einzelne Leben aber ist nur eine durch diese bestimte Verknüpfung, Anziehung und Berührung gegebne Lebensform, welche nicht länger dauern kann als eben die Verknüpfung]."[20]

Two further aspects of Günderrode's metaphysics play important roles in the areas of her thought discussed below. The first is the account Günderrode gives of the mechanism by which the elements are combined into their various forms. As the last quotation indicates, the elements are drawn together into particular forms by "attraction [Anziehung]" (or the "law of attraction [Gesetze der Anziehung]").[21] Günderrode expands on this claim, explaining that the elements "seek what is similar to them according to laws of affinity [suchen . . . die Ähnlichern auf nach Gesezen der Verwantschaft]"[22] and, elsewhere, that "all harmonious things are connected in a certain way [alle harmonische Dinge in einer gewissen Verbindung stehen]."[23] In other words, certain elements—those that are similar, have an affinity, or "harmonize" with each other—are attracted to each other and, once the bonds are broken that were constraining them within two (or more) different objects or living beings, they are released to move together and join to create new forms. This claim has important implications for Günderrode's accounts of love and death in particular (see the next section).

Another important aspect of Günderrode's metaphysics, which plays a role in Günderrode's ideas about politics, virtue, and beauty (discussed further below), is her conceptualization of the relationship of the individual entities that are constituted from the elements that make up the world, on the one hand, and this world (or the "earth [Erde]") as a whole, on the other. Günderrode claims that during their time as part of individual entities, the elements "become livelier [sind lebendiger geworden]," which she justifies with the claim that "living force is strengthened in every exercise [die lebendige

---

[20] Karoline von Günderrode, "The Idea of the Earth," trans. Anna Ezekiel in *Women Philosophers of the Long Nineteenth Century: The German Tradition*, ed. Dalia Nassar and Kristin Gjesdal (Oxford: Oxford University Press, 2021), 82. SW I, 446–447.

[21] SW I, 358.

[22] Günderrode, "The Idea of the Earth," 82. SW I, 447.

[23] SW I, 33.

Kraft stärkt sich in jeder Übung]" and an analogy to warriors growing stronger by fighting each other.[24] She further claims that, when the entities die or break down, the elements out of which they were made retain this enhanced animation or liveliness. As a result, through the process of individual entities living and dying (or, in the case of inanimate objects, being created and dissolving), the earth as a whole also becomes more animated: "each mortal gives back to the earth a raised, more developed elemental life [jeder Sterbende [giebt] der Erde ein erhöteres, entwikleteres Elementarleben zurück]."[25]

Accordingly, Günderrode describes the earth as an "organism [Organismuß]" that, over time, gradually becomes more complex and animated: "more perfect and universal [vollkommener und allgemeiner]"[26]—and also (following from the "laws of affinity" that drive the recombination of elements) more harmonious. This process, if it were completed, would result in a single, perfect, eternal organism in perfect harmony with itself. However, Günderrode deliberately equivocates on whether the process will in fact reach this endpoint: "I do not assert whether the earth will be altogether successful in organizing itself immortally like this [ob es der Erde überhaupt gelingen wird sich so unsterblich zu organisieren behaupte ich nicht]."[27] This ambivalence toward progress is an important factor in Günderrode's claims about political organization; it forms a contrast with thinkers such as Fichte or Hegel who see history as necessarily progressing toward an ideal end-point.

3.2 Death and Love

One of the implications of the above account is that, for Günderrode, death is not an end to our existence, as beings temporarily constituted out of eternal elements. Instead, death is a site of change and re-creation. The individual entity dies or falls apart, but on the level of its constituent parts it continues to exist. These parts are now scattered among many other entities and join together with elements that previously formed parts of several other individuals. Günderrode views this as a form of reincarnation, claiming that "The Indian notion of the transmigration of souls corresponds to this opinion [Die Idee der Indier von der Seelenwanderung entspricht dieser Meinung]."[28]

This model also informs Günderrode's understanding of friendship and love, which she presents as our experience of the attraction of some of our constituent elements to, or harmony or affinity of these elements with, some of the elements that currently constitute someone else. In other words, on a chemical or physical level, similar elements within ourselves and within a friend or lover are attracted to each other, and this

---

[24] SW I, 447.
[25] Günderrode, "The Idea of the Earth," 83; SW I, 447.
[26] SW I, 447.
[27] Günderrode, "The Idea of the Earth," 83; SW I, 448.
[28] Günderrode, "The Idea of the Earth," 83; SW I, 447–448.

attraction manifests itself in our human experience as an emotion. One of Günderrode's characters explains the feeling of being drawn to someone: "A similar or identical thought in different heads, even if they never know of each other, is, in a spiritual sense, a connection [ein ähnlicher oder gleicher Gedanke in verschiedenen Köpfen, auch wenn sie nie von einander wußten, ist im geistigem Sinne schon eine Verbindung]."[29]

This connection continues after death, at which point it allows us to physically join with our loved ones. In "Letters," one of the correspondents writes of their fear that, after death, "your I and mine should be dissolved in the ancient primordial matter of the world [dein Ich und das Meine sollten aufgelösst werden in die alten Urstoffe der Welt]"; but: "then I consoled myself that our befriended elements, obeying the laws of attraction, would find each other even in infinite space and join with each other [dann tröstete ich mich wieder, daß unsere befreundete Elemente, dem Gesetze der Anziehung gehorchend, sich selbst im unendlichen Raum aufsuchen und zu einander gesellen würden]."[30] Similarly, in the poem "The Malabarian Widows" ("Die Malabarischen Witwen") Günderrode writes: "Death becomes love's sweet celebration, / The separated elements unified [Zur süßen Liebesfeyer wird der Tod, / Vereinet die getrennten Elemente]."[31]

Günderrode is often viewed as a poet of love and death par excellence, and her suicide—especially in light of the pledge of reunion she left for Creuzer—seen as partly motivated by her commitment to these metaphysical views.[32] Whether or not that is so, Günderrode's work reflects more than just a conventional or sentimental hope for union with loved ones after death. Instead, she thoroughly integrates her depictions of human emotional life with her metaphysical account of the constituents of the world and the processes that drive its development.

3.3 Consciousness and Identity

One of the aspects of Günderrode's account of death that biographical interpretations of her work tend to miss is the significance of this account for consciousness and personal identity, and for explanations of what it is, most essentially, to be human. As I have explained, for Günderrode the elements that constitute each individual being, human or otherwise, are scattered after death and reused as parts of new entities. If this were just a question of redistributing physical components (perhaps at the level of cells, molecules, or atoms), then the reincarnation and union with loved ones that Günderrode promises would seem rather meaningless. Why should we care if the physical components that

---

[29] Karoline von Günderrode, *Philosophical Fragments*, ed. and trans. Anna Ezekiel (New York: Oxford University Press, forthcoming); SW I, 33.

[30] Günderrode, *Philosophical Fragments*; SW I, 358.

[31] Günderrode, *Philosophical Fragments*; SW I, 325.

[32] B. Becker-Cantorino, "The 'New Mythology': Myth and Death in Karoline von Günderrode's Literary Work," in *Women and Death 3: Women's Representations of Death in German Culture since 1500*, ed. Clare Bielby and Anna Richards (Rochester, NY: Camden House, 2010), 52; Schrage-Früh, "Subversive Weiblichkeit?," 384.

make up our bodies are used for something else after we die? But Günderrode suggests that, in some sense, we will in fact experience this reincarnation and union with loved ones. Her attempts to imagine and communicate this experience underlie some of the most evocative passages in her work.

In several pieces, Günderrode indicates that some form of consciousness or awareness continues after our individual self is fragmented and redistributed after death. For example, in "An Apocalyptic Fragment" ("Ein apokalyptisches Fragment") the narrator, who has first witnessed and then personally experienced death and resurrection, remembers having had "muffled and tangled dreams [dumpfe und verworrene Träume]" while they were dead.[33] In the prose poem "A Dream" ("Ein Traum"), Günderrode describes "spirits of antiquity [Geister der Vorwelt]" lying "spellbound [gebant]" and "numbed [betäubt]" in "heavy stupefaction [schwerer Betäubung]." Although they are unable to interact with their surroundings, they are aware of them in an attenuated sense: "the confused roaring of [events'] voices pressed only weakly into the ears of the sleepers. They . . . stretched their arms out longingly to life [in das Ohr der Schläfer drang nur schwach das verworrne Brausen ihrer Stimen, sie . . . strekten Sehnsuchtsvoll ihre Arme nach dem Leben aus]"—but "in vain! [vergeblich!]."[34]

As the above descriptions suggest, for Günderrode, consciousness is distributed throughout existence, although it persists in the nonhuman world in altered and often diminished forms. A person's individual consciousness survives after that person's death, dispersed among both organic beings and inanimate objects. Günderrode undermines the differences between these categories of entities, on the grounds that so-called inanimate objects always have the potential to be enlivened and made animate. "Thus," she writes in "Idea of the Earth," "however my elements may be dispersed, when they join to what is already living they will elevate it; when they join to those things whose life resembles death, they will animate them [wie also auch mein Elemente zerstreut werden mögen, wenn sie sich zu schon lebendem gesellen, werden sie es erhöhen, wann zu dem dessen leben noch dem Tod gleicht, so werden sie es beseelen]."[35] According to Günderrode, one's self is subject to fragmentation and re-formation, but persists through all the transformations, separations, and joinings that one's elements undergo in the long process of the organic development of the earth, and is itself transformed in this process.

This is a radical and unusual account of consciousness, personhood, and individuality. Although the similarities of Günderrode's metaphysics to those of Schelling are often noted, including the reduction of the distinction between the conscious and the unconscious, what is uniquely Günderrode's is the way she builds on this metaphysics to imagine altered states for individual human beings.

Interestingly, for Günderrode the radical changeability of the self also characterizes the self while it is alive. Like the models of Clemens Brentano and Heinrich von Kleist,

---

[33] SW I, 53.
[34] Günderrode, *Philosophical Fragments*; SW I, 439.
[35] Günderrode, "The Idea of the Earth," 83; SW I, 447.

who developed their accounts of the self at around the same time,[36] the self, according to Günderrode, is discontinuous and opaque. It is mysterious even to itself and changes from one moment to the next. Günderrode writes to Savigny: "I believe my essence is uncertain, full of fleeting phenomena that come and go changeably [ich glaube, mein Wesen ist ungewiß, voll flüchtiger Erscheinungen, die wechselnd kommen und gehen]."[37] And to Clemens Brentano: "It often seems to me as if you had many souls; when I begin to like one of these souls, then it departs and another steps into its place [es kömmt mir oft vor, als hätten Sie viele Seelen, wenn ich nun angange, einer dieser Seelen gut zu sein, so geht sie fort]."[38] The implications of this fragmentary or momentary model of the self for one's self-image and one's relationships to others are still to be fully explored.[39] However, it is clear that Günderrode sees the self, and the supposedly essentially human characteristic of consciousness, not as discrete or whole, but as capable of fracture and dispersal. To Günderrode, we exist in a state of flux, and new ways of understanding ourselves and our world are needed if we are to take account of the radical changes that the self goes through both while alive and after death.

3.4 Political Theory

Günderrode's political views have been described as "revolutionary,"[40] and they are so in a philosophically interesting way. Günderrode viewed political entities such as states or religious communities in much the same way she viewed individual beings and objects: as temporary constellations of elements (in this case, the individual members of a state or community) subject to entropy and decay and undergoing periodic transformation. Thus, for Günderrode, political revolutions, like death and new birth, are necessary for continued life and the ever-changing development of the whole. Both revolution and death allow old, failing entities to be dissolved, after which new, young, and powerful entities can emerge from their remains. This theory underlies passages such as the following, taken respectively from Günderrode's plays *Udohla* and *Muhammad, the Prophet of Mecca* (*Mahomed, der Prophet von Mekka*):

> Oh, when will the earth reshape itself again?
> When will dawn the morning of better times?

---

[36] Karl Heinz Bohrer, *Der romantische Brief. Die Enstehung ästhetischer Subjektivität* (Frankfurt: Suhrkamp, 1989).

[37] Günderrode, Letter to Savigny, February 1804, in Weißenborn, *"Ich sende Dir,"* 120.

[38] Günderrode, Letter to Clemens Brentano, May 19, 1802, in Weißenborn, *"Ich sende Dir,"* 89.

[39] But see Anna Ezekiel, "Narrative and Fragment: The Social Self in Karoline von Günderrode," *Symphilosophie: International Journal of Philosophical Romanticism* 2 (2020): 65–90..

[40] Lucia Maria Licher, "Der Völker Schicksal ruht in meinen Busen.' Karoline von Günderrode als Dichterin der Revolution," in *"Der Menschheit Hälfte blieb noch ohne Recht." Frauen und die französische Revolution*, ed. Helge Brandes (Wiesbaden: Deutscher Universitätsverlag, 1991), 113–132; Obermeier, "'Ach diese Rolle,'" 100–101.

> Patience my heart! eventually it must come,
> Your old gods are still alive.
> They live, to generate the world anew[.]
>
> (O wann wird neu die Erde sich gestalten?
> Wann bricht der Zeiten bessrer Morgan an?
> Geduld mein Herz! er muß ja endlich kommen,
> Es leben deine alten Götter noch.
> Sie leben, neu die Welt sich zu erzeugen.)[41]
>
> The weakness of age
> Of ailing times,
> Becomes bold youth
> By the breath of enthusiasm
> Awakened to life.
>
> (Die Schwäche des Alters
> Der kränkelnden Zeiten,
> Wird muthige Jugend
> Vom Hauch der Begeistrung
> Zum Leben erweckt.)[42]

Unlike her metaphysics, Günderrode did not leave behind a clear articulation of her political theory, and we must piece it together from fragmentary remarks and her literary works, especially her plays. With regard to her thinking on revolution, in particular, we can also draw on what we know of her contemporaries' ideas on the subject.[43] It was relatively common at the time to consider politics as a continuation, in the human realm, of processes of development that took place in the natural world, both in living beings and in geological events. Thus, for example, the historian August Ludwig von Schlözer (1735–1809) opened his book on "universal history" with the claim: "we will survey as a whole the revolutions of the globe that we inhabit and of the human species to which we belong [wir wollen die Revolutionen des Erdbodens, den wir bewohnen, und des menschlichen Geschlechtes, dem wir angehören, im Ganzen uebersehen]."[44] Friedrich Schlegel indicates something similar in his "Speech on Mythology" ("Rede über die Mythologie"), which Günderrode excerpted in her notebooks,[45] and Herder makes similar claims in another of Günderrode's favorite

---

[41] SW I, 223.

[42] SW I, 131.

[43] See Ezekiel, "Revolution and Revitalization: Karoline von Günderrode's Political Philosophy and Its Metaphysical Foundations," *British Journal of the History of Philosophy* 30, no. 4, Special Issue on Post-Kantian Practical Philosophy, ed. James A. Clarke and Gabriel Gottlieb (2022; preprint 2020): 666–686.

[44] August Ludwig von Schlözer, *Vorstellung seiner Universal-Historie* (Göttingen: Dieterich, 1772), 1; see also 13, 84, 265–266, 348.

[45] Friedrich Schlegel, "Rede über die Mythologie" (1800), in *Kritische Friedrich-Schlegel-Ausgabe, Abteilung 1. Kritische Neuausgabe* (Munich: 1967), vol. 2, 322; SW II, 281.

texts, *Outlines of a Philosophy of the History of Humankind* (*Ideen zur Philosophie der Geschichte der Menschheit*).[46]

The view of human history as part of and continuous with natural history allows Günderrode to present the processes driving the rise and fall of civilizations as motivated by the same underlying principle as that governing the birth and death of individual entities. In other words, political revolution is driven by the same process of maturing strength and cohesiveness followed by weakening, dissolution, and decay as the cycle of life in the natural world.

Günderrode's interest in politics also extended to other aspects of social life, especially friendship,[47] the social conditions for the emergence of agency, and the limitations of the rightful use of power. The latter two aspects of her work have generated analysis by scholars working on gender; these are discussed in the next section.

3.5 Gender, Power, and Agency

The area in which Günderrode's work has generated the most scholarly interest to date is in relation to her ideas about gender. Initial interest centered on Günderrode's difficulties as a woman writer in the early nineteenth century, her supposedly conflicted personality (caught between traits coded feminine and those coded masculine), and her suicide as perhaps a response to these gendered constraints.[48] Another area of interest has been Günderrode's contributions to new, specifically female expressions of identity that many scholars claim emerged around 1800.[49] Scholars have also argued that Günderrode challenges gendered signifiers in her depictions of commemorative practices;[50] that she constructs a "feminine sublime" that can counter exclusionary tendencies in Kant's sublime;[51] and that she works against Early German Romantic gender dualism.[52]

---

[46] Johann Gottfried Herder, *Ideen zur Philosophie der Geschichte der Menschheit* (Riga: Johann Friedrich Hartknoch, 1784), *passim*, esp. vol. 1, 18–24.

[47] Ezekiel, "Narrative and Fragment."

[48] E.g., Helga Dormann, "Die Karoline von Günderrode-Forschung 1945–95. Ein Bericht," *Athenaeum* 6 (1996): 234; Christa Wolf, "Karoline von Günderode—ein Entwurf," in *Der Schatten eines Traumes. Gedichte, Prosa, Briefe, Zeugnisse von Zeitgenossen* (Munich: Deutscher Taschenbuch, 1997 [originally published 1979]), 5–60.

[49] E.g., Lorely French, "'Meine beiden Ichs': Confrontations with Language and Self in Letters by Early Nineteenth-Century Women," *Women in German Yearbook* 5 (1989): 73–89.

[50] Liesl Allingham, "Countermemory in Karoline von Günderrode's 'Darthula nach Ossian': A Female Warrior, Her Unruly Breast, and the Construction of Her Myth," *Goethe Yearbook* 21 (2014): 39–56.

[51] Christine Battersby, "Stages on Kant's Way: Aesthetics, Morality, and the Gendered Sublime," in *Feminism and Tradition in Aesthetics*, ed. Peggy Zeglin Brand and Carolyn Korsmeyer (University Park: Pennsylvania State University Press, 1995), 227–244.

[52] Anna Ezekiel, "Women, Women Writers, and Early German Romanticism," in *The Palgrave Handbook of German Romantic Philosophy*, ed. Elizabeth Millán Brusslan (Palgrave Macmillan, 2020), 475–509.

Günderrode's plays, which often deal with political events surrounding the actions of "great men" such as Muhammad, Attila the Hun, or kings and sultans of Günderrode's own invention, are concerned with the ways gender affects freedom and agency. Günderrode is particularly interested in how powerful individuals exceed reasonable use of power and cause unjustified suffering to others, and how less powerful individuals, especially women, can navigate the constraints imposed on them by the powerful in order to realize their own agency.

For example, Günderrode's play *Magic and Destiny* opens with an argument between a mage, Alchmenes, and his son, Ligares, who wants to learn the secrets of prophecy. Alchmenes claims Ligares's destiny lies elsewhere: "the stars do not choose *you* [sich die Sterne *Dich* nicht ausersehen]"; Ligares retorts, "Should stars decide what I may do? / And judge over my worth and unworth? [entscheiden sollten Sterne, was ich darf? / Und über meinen Werth und Unwerth richten?]."[53] Ligares, of course, ignores his father's advice and tragedy ensues. But what is interesting is not so much the question of whether Ligares acts freely or whether his life course is determined by destiny, which is the overt theme of the play, but the understated commentary on this debate that Günderrode presents through the other characters. Ligares's former fiancée, Ladika, has jilted him, but Ligares will not accept this and ruins her hopes for happiness by killing her new fiancé. Ligares's mother, Cassandra, has dark premonitions that no one listens to (as her name hints). The efforts of two servants, Mandane and Zeno, to calm and help their masters are in vain. Thus, while Günderrode's play seems to follow the conventions of a classical tragedy, it subtly interrogates who gets to ask whether their actions are free or determined by external events, and what the effects of insistence on self-determination by these privileged individuals are on those individuals who, by contrast, are so constrained by their social roles that the question is not even at issue.

A similar commentary runs through *Muhammad, the Prophet of Mecca*. Muhammad believes he enacts God's will, while other characters increasingly wonder whether he is simply pursuing his own interests—and we eventually have to wonder this ourselves, as Muhammad's actions lead to the deaths of two sympathetic characters.[54]

In *Udohla*, Günderrode suggests an alternative to the selfish pursuit of one's own desires by powerful individuals. Here, the Sultan's fiancée, Nerissa, can only wait for him to decide her fate, until he offers her the choice to stay or leave: his abdication of his power over others is what enables Nerissa to assert her own agency.[55] As Barbara Becker-Cantarino argues, Günderrode shows that, in a patriarchal society, men can act freely, but women can only do so if men make space for them.[56]

Günderrode presents this conditioned agency of women most clearly in her play *Hildgund*. Here, Attila offers to spare Hildgund's homeland if she will marry him. The

---

[53] SW I, 235.
[54] See Ezekiel, "Introduction to *Muhammad, the Prophet of Mecca*," in *Poetic Fragments, by Karoline von Günderrode*, ed. and trans. Anna Ezekiel (Albany: State University of New York Press, 2016), 121–151.
[55] SW I, 230–231.
[56] Becker-Cantarino, "Dichtung—Mythologie—Geschlecht," 215.

main focus of the play is Hildgund's deliberations as she decides how she will respond. Eventually, she accepts Attila's offer but decides to kill him on their wedding night. However, in order to implement this decision, she must first be given permission to make the decision by her father, the King, and then resist her fiancé Walther's insistence on acting on her behalf.[57] Something similar happens in Günderrode's reworking of Ossian's poem "Darthula," in which the titular heroine must watch helplessly as her people are killed in battle until her father hands her a sword with which to fight.[58] In both pieces, Günderrode shows how women must negotiate with external constraints imposed by gender roles and the self-assertion of men in order to assert their agency or act in the political sphere.

3.6 Ethics

Günderrode's ethics must be pieced together from unpublished fragments and short sections in her published and unpublished writings. The most revealing passages on this topic are in "Idea of the Earth," "Letters of Two Friends," and "Story of a Brahmin."

The latter piece relates the narrator Almor's development from childhood to his later life, which he spends in spiritual contemplation and near-isolation, in the process providing important clues for interpreting Günderrode's statements on "virtue [Tugend]" in the other pieces just mentioned. After a period occupied with business dealings and the enjoyment of aesthetic experiences, Almor experiences a moral awakening: "the moral world, until then invisible to me, was unveiled to me; I saw a community of spirits, a realm of effect and countereffect, an invisible harmony, a purpose to human striving, and a true good [die mir bisher unsichtbare moralische Welt enthüllte sich mir, ich sah eine Gemeinschaft der Geister, ein Reich von Wirkung und Gegenwirkung, eine unsichtbare Harmonie, einen Zweck des menschlichen Strebens und ein wahres Gut]."[59] The rest of the passage makes it clear that this "moral world" is Kant's kingdom of ends: Almor attempts to become "a citizen of the moral realm [Bürger des moralischen Reiches]" and discover the answer to the questions "who was I? what should I be? what position befitted me? [wer ich sey? was ich seyn solle? welche Stelle mir gebühre?]"[60]—a modified version of Kant's three questions "What can I know? What ought I to do? What may I hope?"[61] Also using Kantian language, Almor says:

> With what joy I stepped out of the narrow circle of my allocated daily work into the free activity of a thinking being that sets its own purpose for its conduct, out

---

[57] See Ezekiel, "Introduction to *Hildgund*," in *Poetic Fragments, by Karoline von Günderrode*, ed. and trans. Anna Ezekiel (Albany: State University of New York Press, 2016), 39–57.

[58] SW I, 13.

[59] SW I, 304.

[60] Günderrode, *Philosophical Fragments*; SW I, 305.

[61] Günderrode's notebooks contain detailed notes on Kiesewetter's *Grundriß einer reinen allgemeinen Logik nach Kantischen Grundsätzen* (SW II, 302–349), a popularization of Kant's work.

of limited personal self-interest into the great fraternity of all human beings for the good of all. The merely mechanical and animal life that I had escaped lay behind me like a musty dungeon; I stepped into the world in every sense and exercised my forces in many a self-conquest, in many a difficult virtue.

(Mit welcher Freude trat ich aus dem engen Kreis zugemessener täglicher Arbeiten in die freye Thätigkeit eines denkenden Wesens, das sich selbst einen Zweck seines Thuns setzt, aus dem beschränkten persönlichen Eigennutz in die große Verbrüderung aller Menschen, zu aller Wohl. Das bloß mechanische und thierische Leben, dem ich entronnen war, lag wie ein dumpfer Kerker hinter mir; ich trat in jedem Sinne in die Welt, und übte meine Kraft in mancher Selbstüberwindung, in mancher schweren Tugend.)[62]

However, Almor subsequently realizes that this Kantian form of morality cannot satisfy him. He asks:

Why, then, is everything on earth good except human beings? Why should they alone become different than they are? Is a person only virtuous if they stand on the ruins of their own spirit and can say: Look, these [ruins] rebelled, but they fell, I have become victor over them all! —Barbarian! Do not rejoice in your victory; you have waged a civil war: those that have been conquered were children of your own nature, you have killed yourself in your victory, you have fallen in your battle.

(Warum ist denn alles gut, was auf Erden ist, nur der Mensch nicht? Warum soll er allein anders werden, als er ist? Ist nur der tugendhaft, der auf den Ruinen seines eignen Geistes steht und sagen kann: Seht, diese hatten sich empört, aber sie sind gefallen, ich bin Sieger worden über sie Alle!—Barbar! freue dich nicht deines Siegs, du has einen Bürgerkrieg geführt, die Ueberwundenen waren Kinder deiner eignen Natur, du hast dich selbst getödtet in deinen Siegen, du bist gefallen in deinen Schlachten.)[63]

"Morality,"[64] Almor claims, applies in a limited realm of specifically human-to-human relations, of concern for "humankind [Menschheit]." He contrasts this, first, with the "animal [thierisch]" level of existence that Kantian morality helped him surmount, described as a "relationship to earth [Verhältniß zur Erde],"[65] or a concern for "health, preservation, propagation [Gesundheit, Erhaltung, Fortpflanzung]." He also contrasts the moral world of human relations with a "spiritual [geistig]" or religious relationship to the infinite. The latter is the subject of the remainder of the story. Clearly, for Günderrode, Kantian morality is an intermediate stage in human development.

---

[62] Günderrode, *Philosophical Fragments*; SW I, 305.
[63] Günderrode, *Philosophical Fragments*; SW I, 305–306.
[64] Günderrode uses the German terms *Sittlichkeit* and *Moralität* interchangeably.
[65] Günderrode, *Philosophical Fragments*; SW I, 310–311.

Günderrode does not describe the ethical or interpersonal aspects of the "relation to the infinite" that she advocates in "Story of a Brahmin"; instead, Almor settles into a life of religious contemplation. However, "Story of a Brahmin" includes a description of the universe that is consistent with the metaphysics outlined in "Idea of the Earth" and "Letters of Two Friends,"[66] justifying recourse to these texts to further develop Günderrode's ideas about what virtue looks like beyond Kantian morality.

Toward the ends of both these pieces, after presenting the metaphysical outline described earlier in this chapter, Günderrode sketches the implications of this model for truth, justice, benevolence, love, beauty, and virtue. Virtuous acts, she states, are those that contribute to the increasing harmony and unification of the whole: "virtue of all kinds is only one thing, i.e., a forgetting of personhood and particularity for the All [die Tugend aller Art ist nur Eine, d.h. ein Vergessen der Persönlichkeit und Einzelheit für die Allheit]."[67] This relationship of the individual to the infinite emerges in ordinary human life in virtuous acts (as well as acts that manifest justice, truth, love, and beauty): "the condition of the dissolution of multiplicity in unity," Günderrode claims, "is already prepared here in a spiritual way by love and virtue [durch Liebe und Tugend also wird schon hier auf eine geistige Weise der Zustand der Auflößung der Vielheit in der Einheit vorbereitet]."[68] We can relate this to the personal development described in "Story of a Brahmin," in which Almor first overcomes his individual desires in consideration of humanity as a whole (the kingdom of ends) before discovering the possibility of a relationship to the broader whole of the universe by contemplating, and acting in relation to, a conception of a spiritual infinite. The pursuit of virtue, truly understood, is the means by which we help realize the perfect, eternal, organic unity that Günderrode previously described as the idea of the earth: "from this perspective . . . it also became clear to me what the great thoughts of truth, justice, virtue, love and beauty claim, which germinate in the soil of personhood and, soon overgrowing it, stretch up to the free heavens [in dieser Betrachtungsweise . . . ist mir nun auch deutlich geworden was die großen Gedanken von Wahrheit, Gerechtigkeit, Tugend, Liebe und Schönheit wollen, die auf dem Boden der Persönlichkeit keimen, und ihn bald überwachsend sich hinaufziehen nach dem freien Himmel]."[69]

3.7 Aesthetics

Some aspects of Günderrode's thinking about the nature of beauty are indicated in the passage just cited: beauty, for Günderrode, is self-identity and harmony; it is "the outer expression of equilibrium achieved with itself [der äussere Ausdruck des erreichten

[66] SW I, 312.
[67] Günderrode, *Philosophical Fragments*; SW I, 361.
[68] Günderrode, *Philosophical Fragments*; SW I, 361.
[69] Günderrode, *Philosophical Fragments*; SW I, 361.

Gleichgewiches mit sich Selbst]."[70] But I want to note one further aspect of Günderrode's thought on aesthetics: the creative and (re-)vitalizing role that she ascribes to music.

In several of her unpublished fragments and poems, Günderrode relates music to the emergence of life. In "The Realm of Tones" ("Das Reich der Töne"), she writes: "a mysterious life inhabits all materials, but it is trapped within them, snared in matter's firm bonds, from which it cannot wrest itself on its own. But when an external impetus touches the material, then the bonds are undone. The tones emerge from their prisons, embrace the air with trembling joy, and spill over into each other in harmonious vibration [allen Materien wohnt ein geheimnißvolles Leben ein, aber es ist in ihnen gefangen, umstrikket mit des Stoffes festen Banden denen es sich nicht allein entwinden kann. Wann aber der äussere Anstos die Materie berühret dann werden die Bande gelöset, die Töne entspringen ihren Kerkern, umarmen mit zitternder Freude die Luft, u in harmonischen Schwingungen fließen sie in einander über]."[71] This passage is echoed in the poem "The Tones" ("Die Töne"), which describes the "soul" of music as "imprisoned in matter [im Stoff gefangen]" before being released to "breathe from the nightingale's breast [hauchen aus der Nachtigallen Brust]" and finally be transformed by dwelling in human beings.[72] In both this piece and the fragment "Music" ("Die Musik"), Günderrode describes the human artist as made pregnant by and giving birth to music.[73]

In other pieces, the "rebirth [Wiedergeburt]" of music through human beings is inverted to depict the resurrection of human beings through music. In "Music for Me" ("Die Music für Mich"), Günderrode describes the "images [Bilder]" evoked by music as a "storm [Sturm]," and claims that this "storm is a true awakener of the dead. For when I hear its roaring, the images of the past emerge from their graves before me, and I wander once more among them [der Sturm ist mir ein wahrer Aufferwekker von den Toden. Denn wenn ich sein Brausen vernehme gehn mir die Bilder der Vergangenheit aus ihren Gräbern hervor, u ich wandle noch einmal unter ihnen]."[74] This regenerative power of music emerges even more powerfully in "The Cathedral in Cologne" ("Der Dom zu Cölln"). After describing the tombs in the cathedral in claustrophobic terms that recall both the entombment of "life" in matter in "The Realm of Tones" and the description of the "sleepers" in "A Dream," Günderrode writes:

> . . . I shiver deeply, for the dead are so silent.
> But then song rises, and organ tones; they float,
> Celebrating, up into the domes, where resplendent saints pray
> But the tones transform, and into the wings of angels
> And sweep, surging melodiously, around the holy images.
> And everything is glorified to heaven—music, and colors, and forms,

---

[70] Günderrode, *Philosophical Fragments*; SW I, 361. See also SW I, 448.
[71] Günderrode, *Philosophical Fragments*; SW I, 441. See also "The Nightingale" ("Die Nachtigall"), SW I, 440.
[72] SW I, 380.
[73] SW I, 441.
[74] Günderrode, *Philosophical Fragments*; SW I, 443.

For entranced eyes the graves, the dead, disappear,
And from the silent crypts a joyful cheer rises. —
Yes, I have seen the resurrection with the eyes of spirit.
And the life of art leads the soul to heaven.

[. . . mich schauert so tief daß also stumm sind die Toden.
Doch da hebt sich Gesang, u Orgeltöne, sie schweben
Feiernd die Dome hinauf, wo glänzende Heilige beten
Und es wandeln die Töne sich um in Fittche der Engel
Und umrauschen melodisch woogend die heiligen Bilder.
Und zum Himmel verkläret sich alles Musik, und Farben, u Formen,
Aus dem entzükten Auge verschwinden die Gräber, u Toden,
Und den stummen Grüften entsteiget ein freudiges Jauchzen. —
Ja ich habe die Auferstehung gesehen im Auge des Geistes.
Und das Leben der Kunst, es führte die Seele zum Himel.][75]

Unfortunately, Günderrode left only these tantalizing fragments on music, with no real indication of whether or how they fit with the rest of her claims about beauty, death, or reincarnation. Judging from the consistency of her thought on other topics, it seems likely that she would have integrated these fragments with the rest of her account. It is intriguing to speculate how she might have worked these concepts into her thought as a whole.

4 GÜNDERRODE'S INFLUENCE

As I hope is shown by the above discussion, Günderrode's work is philosophically interesting for its own sake; however, it is also important due to its possible influence on the development of ideas by better known nineteenth-century thinkers. Günderrode was an important link between Early German Romanticism and Heidelberg Romanticism, which was active around 1804–1809 and counted among its members Creuzer, Brentano von Arnim, Achim von Arnim (Bettina's husband), Clemens Brentano, and Sophie Mereau. (Other members included Joseph Görres, the Brothers Grimm, Joseph and Wilhelm von Eichendorff, and, on some accounts, Hölderlin.)

Günderrode's work and thought are very likely to have exerted a strong influence on Clemens Brentano and Bettina Brentano von Arnim in particular. At around the same time that Günderrode was writing, Clemens Brentano developed an account of a fragmented selfhood and individuality that is considered a defining influence on the emergence of a modern understanding of the inner experiences of the individual. Brentano's model of the self has some similarities to (as well as some differences from) Günderrode's model of the momentary, or "catastrophic" self: for example, Karl Heinz

---

[75] Günderrode, *Philosophical Fragments*; SW I, 379.

Bohrer claims that Günderrode "shares with both [Brentano and Kleist] the discovery of the autonomous 'I' that can only find itself in its subjectivity [mit beiden teilt sie die Entdeckung des autonomen 'Ichs,' das sich nur in seiner Subjektivität finden kann]."[76] Since, as mentioned earlier, Günderrode discussed this topic in her letters to Brentano, it is very possible that she influenced his account or that a mutual influence on their concepts of the self obtained between the two young writers.

Günderrode's influence on Bettina Brentano von Arnim is indisputable, and through Brentano von Arnim she also likely influenced the Young Hegelians and American Transcendentalism. In her later life, Brentano von Arnim was a well-known political activist and writer with close connections to the Young Hegelians, several of whom, including David Strauss, Edgar Bauer, Eduard Meyen, Arnold Ruge, and Karl Friedrich Köppens (in a letter to Marx), acknowledged the influence of her epistolary novel *Günderode* (*Die Günderode*) on their attacks on organized religion.[77] This novel was based on Brentano von Arnim's correspondence with Günderrode and includes edited versions of some of Günderrode's letters; the text describes the two women's intellectual development and includes prominent reflections on history, religion, mythology, music, language, and love. *Günderode* was translated into English by the American Transcendentalist Margaret Fuller,[78] who also developed an account of friendship based on the relationship between Günderrode and Brentano von Arnim portrayed in this book.[79]

It is difficult to know the extent of Günderrode's influence on Creuzer, since Creuzer's friends, fearing a scandal due to his implication in her suicide, destroyed most of her letters to him. However, from their remaining letters and the drafts of *Melete*, in the production of which Creuzer was closely involved, we know that the pair discussed religion, mythology, ancient languages, ancient history, and questions such as the nature of the self and what happens after death. The first volume of Creuzer's magnum opus, *Symbolism and Mythology of the Ancient Peoples* (*Symbolik und Mythologie der alten Völker*), was published in 1810, only four years after the affair with Günderrode. Throughout the nineteenth century, this text was a dominant influence on European ideas about the history and development of mythology and culture, standing in opposition to nationalistic theories that claimed that each culture generated its own national mythology expressing its distinctive nature. Günderrode's syncretism (which is evident in her work from before she met Creuzer in 1804) is echoed in Creuzer's account of the emergence of ancient Greek culture, mythology, and religion from even older cultures in the region. One of Günderrode's biographers notes that Creuzer uses Günderrode's

---

[76] Bohrer, *Der romantische Brief*, 76.

[77] Heinz Härtl, "Bettina Brentano-von Arnim's Relations to the Young Hegelians," trans. Dorothee E. Krahn, in *Bettina Brentano-von Arnim: Gender and Politics*, ed. Elke P. Frederiksen and Katharine R. Goodman (Detroit: Wayne State University Press, 1995), 145–184.

[78] Bettina Brentano von Arnim, *Correspondence of Fräulein Günderode and Bettine von Arnim*, trans. Margaret Fuller and Minna Wesselhoeft (Boston: T.O.H.P. Burnham, 1861).

[79] Margaret Fuller, "Bettine Brentano und Günderode," *The Dial: A Magazine for Literature, Philosophy, and Religion* 2 (1842): 313–357.

wording in his description of Egypt in *Symbolism and Mythology*;[80] another claims that their letters suggest that Günderrode may have read drafts of this text.[81]

We will likely never know the full extent of Günderrode's influence on her immediate circle or her wider readership. At that time, women's contributions to philosophical, scientific, or literary production often went unacknowledged or were appropriated by their male colleagues. Nonetheless, we can detect likely threads of influence on writers, philosophers, and other scholars whose work is already well-known. This is only one of the reasons why we should read the work of this fascinating, original, and overlooked thinker.

BIBLIOGRAPHY

Allingham, Liesl. "Countermemory in Karoline von Günderrode's 'Darthula nach Ossian': A Female Warrior, Her Unruly Breast, and the Construction of Her Myth." *Goethe Yearbook* 21 (2014): 39–56.

Battersby, Christine. "Stages on Kant's Way: Aesthetics, Morality, and the Gendered Sublime." In *Feminism and Tradition in Aesthetics*, edited by Peggy Zeglin Brand and Carolyn Korsmeyer, 227–244. University Park: Pennsylvania State University Press, 1995.

Becker-Cantarino, B. "Karoline von Günderrode: Dichtung—Mythologie—Geschlecht." In *Schriftstellerinnen der Romantik. Epoche, Werke, Wirkung*, 199–225. Munich: C. H. Beck, 2000.

Becker-Cantorino, B. "The 'New Mythology': Myth and Death in Karoline von Günderrode's Literary Work." In *Women and Death 3: Women's Representations of Death in German Culture since 1500*. Edited by Clare Bielby and Anna Richards, 51–70. Rochester, NY: Camden House, 2010.

Berdrow, Otto. "Eine Priesterin der Romantik. Karoline von Günderrode." *Die Frau* 2 (1894/95): 681–688.

Bobrowski, Johannes. "Die Günderode" (1956). In *Sarmatische Zeit. Schattenland Ströme*, 29. Stuttgart: Deutsche Verlagsanst, 1961.

Bohrer, Karl Heinz. *Der romantische Brief. Die Enstehung ästhetischer Subjektivität*. Frankfurt: Suhrkamp, 1989.

Brentano von Arnim, Bettina. *Correspondence of Fräulein Günderrode and Bettine von Arnim*. Translated by Margaret Fuller and Minna Wesselhoeft. Boston: T.O.H.P. Burnham, 1861. First published in German in 1840.

Brentano von Arnim, Bettina. "Report on Günderrode's Suicide (1808/1839)." In *Bitter Healing: German Women Writers 1700–1830. An Anthology*, edited by Jeannine Blackwell and Susanne Zantop, 455–472. Lincoln: University of Nebraska Press, 1990.

Creuzer, Georg Friedrich. *Symbolik und Mythologie der alten Völker, besonders der Griechen. In Vorträgen und Entwürfen*. 3 vols. Leipzig: Darmstadt, 1810–12.

Dormann, Helga. "Die Karoline von Günderrode-Forschung 1945–95. Ein Bericht." *Athenaeum* 6 (1996): 227–248.

---

[80] Gersdorff, "Die Erde ist mir Heimat," 227.
[81] Lucia Maria Licher, *Mein Leben in einer bleibenden Form aussprechen. Umrisse einer Ästhetik im Werk Karoline von Günderrodes (1780–1806)* (Heidelberg: Winter, 1996), 134.

Ezekiel, Anna. "Introduction to *Hildgund*." In *Poetic Fragments, by Karoline von Günderrode*, edited and translated by Anna Ezekiel, 39–57. Albany: State University of New York Press, 2016.

Ezekiel, Anna. "Introduction to *Muhammad, the Prophet of Mecca*." In *Poetic Fragments, by Karoline von Günderrode*, edited and translated by Anna Ezekiel, 121–151. Albany: State University of New York Press, 2016.

Ezekiel, Anna. Introduction to *Poetic Fragments, by Karoline von Günderrode*, 1–38. Albany: State University of New York Press, 2016.

Ezekiel, Anna. "Narrative and Fragment: The Social Self in Karoline von Günderrode." *Symphilosophie: International Journal of Philosophical Romanticism* 2 (2020): 65–90.

Ezekiel, Anna. "Revolution and Revitalization: Karoline von Günderrode's Political Philosophy and Its Metaphysical Foundations." *British Journal of the History of Philosophy* 30, no. 4, Special Issue on Post-Kantian Practical Philosophy, ed. James A. Clarke and Gabriel Gottlieb (2022; preprint 2020): 666–686.

Ezekiel, Anna. "Women, Women Writers, and Early German Romanticism." In *The Palgrave Handbook of German Romantic Philosophy*, edited by Elizabeth Millán Brusslan, 475–509. Palgrave Macmillan, 2020.

French, Lorely. "'Meine beiden Ichs': Confrontations with Language and Self in Letters by Early Nineteenth-Century Women." *Women in German Yearbook* 5 (1989): 73–89.

Fuller, Margaret. "Bettine Brentano und Günderode." *The Dial: A Magazine for Literature, Philosophy, and Religion* 2 (1842): 313–357.

Gersdorff, Dagmar von. *"Die Erde ist mir Heimat nicht geworden." Das Leben der Karoline von Günderrode*. Frankfurt: Insel, 2006.

Günderrode, Karoline von. "Karoline von Günderrode (1780–1806)." In *Women Philosophers of the Long Nineteenth Century: The German Tradition*, edited by Dalia Nassar and Kristin Gjesdal, translated by Anna Ezekiel, 62–84. Oxford: Oxford University Press, 2021.

Günderrode, Karoline von. *Philosophical Fragments*. Edited and translated by Anna Ezekiel. Oxford: Oxford University Press, forthcoming.

Günderrode, Karoline von. *Poetic Fragments, by Karoline von Günderrode*, translated by Anna C. Ezekiel. Albany: State University of New York Press, 2016.

Günderrode, Karoline von. *Sämtliche Werke und ausgewählte Studien*. 3 vols. Edited by Walter Morgenthaler. Frankfurt am Main: Stroemfeld/Roter Stern, 1990–91.

Härtl, Heinz. "Bettina Brentano-von Arnim's Relations to the Young Hegelians." Translated by Dorothee E. Krahn. In *Bettina Brentano-von Arnim: Gender and Politics*, edited by Elke P. Frederiksen and Katharine R. Goodman, 145–184. Detroit: Wayne State University Press, 1995.

Herder, Johann Gottfried. *Ideen zur Philosophie der Geschichte der Menschheit*. 4 vols. Riga: Johann Friedrich Hartknoch, 1784–1791.

Hoff, Dagmar von, Sara Friedrichsmeyer, and Patricia Herminghouse. "Aspects of Censorship in the Work of Karoline von Günderrode." *Women in German Yearbook: Feminist Studies and German Culture* 11 (1995): 99–112.

Hummel, Adrian. "Lebenszwänge, Schreibräume, unirdisch. Eine kulturanthropologisch orientierte Deutung des 'Mythos Günderrode.'" *Athenäum* 13 (2003): 61–91.

Kiesewetter, Johann Gottfried. *Grundriß einer reinen allgemeinen Logik nach Kantischen Grundsätzen zum Gebrauch für Vorlesungen begleitet mit einer weitern Auseinandersetzung für diejenigen die keine Vorlesungen darüber hören können von J. G. C. C. Kiesewetter*. 2nd ed. Berlin: F. T. Lagarde, 1795.

Licher, Lucia Maria. *Mein Leben in einer bleibenden Form aussprechen. Umrisse einer Ästhetik im Werk Karoline von Günderrodes (1780–1806)*. Heidelberg: Winter, 1996.

Licher, Lucia Maria. "'Der Völker Schicksal ruht in meinen Busen.' Karoline von Günderrode als Dichterin der Revolution." In *"Der Menschheit Hälfte blieb noch ohne Recht." Frauen und die französische Revolution*, edited by Helge Brandes, 113–132. Wiesbaden: Deutscher Universitätsverlag, 1991.

Nassar, Dalia. "The Human Vocation and the Question of the Earth: Karoline von Günderrode's Philosophy of Nature." *Archiv für Geschichte der Philosophie* 104, no. 1 (2022): 108–130.

Nassar, Dalia, and Kristin Gjesdal, eds. "Chapter Two: Günderrode." In *Women Philosophers of the Long Nineteenth Century: The German Tradition*, 62–84. New York: Oxford University Press, 2021.

Obermeier, Karin. "'Ach diese Rolle wird mir allzu schwer': Gender and Cultural Identity in Karoline von Günderrode's Drama 'Udohla.'" In *Thalia's Daughters: German Women Dramatists from the Eighteenth Century to the Present*, edited by Susan Cocalis and Ferrel Rose, with Karin Obermeier, 99–114. Tübingen: Francke, 1996.

Oppenheim, Meret. *Für Karoline von Günderrode* [1983; painting]. In Christoph Leitgeb, "Das Jenseits-Lichte der Liebe," *Der Standard*, August 4, 2006. https://www.derstandard.at/story/2528022/das-jenseits-licht-der-liebe.

Rauchenbacher, Marina. "Karoline von Günderrode. Eine Rezeptionsstudie." PhD diss., University of Vienna, 2012.

Schade, Waltraud. *Tod am Rhein. Ein Schauspiel*. Norderstedt: Books on Demand, 2006.

Schlegel, Friedrich. "Rede über die Mythologie" (1800). In *Kritische Friedrich-Schlegel-Ausgabe, Abteilung 1. Kritische Neuausgabe*, vol. 2, 311–329. Munich: 1967.

Schlözer, August Ludwig von. *Vorstellung seiner Universal-Historie*. Göttingen: Dieterich, 1772.

Schrage-Früh, Michaela. "Subversive Weiblichkeit? Die Frau als Muse, Geliebte und Künstlerin im Werk Friedrich Schlegels und Karoline von Günderrodes." In *Subversive Romantik*, edited by Volker Kapp, Helmuth Kiesel, Klaus Lubbers, and Patricia Plummer (Berlin: Duncker und Humblot, 2004): 365–390.

Trojahn, Manfred. *Spätrot: Vier Gesänge auf Gedichte der Karoline von Günderrode: für Mezzosopran und Klavier*. 1987.

Weißenborn, Birgit, ed. *"Ich sende Dir ein zärtliches Pfand." Die Briefe der Karoline von Günderrode*. Frankfurt: Insel, 1992.

Wolf, Christa. "Karoline von Günderode—ein Entwurf." In *Der Schatten eines Traumes. Gedichte, Prosa, Briefe, Zeugnisse von Zeitgenossen*, 5–60. Munich: Deutscher Taschenbuch, 1997. Originally published 1979.

Wolf, Christa. *Kein Ort. Nirgends*. Berlin: Aufbau, 1979.

CHAPTER 6

....

BETTINA BRENTANO VON ARNIM (1785–1859)

....

ANNE POLLOK

BETTINA Brentano von Arnim is one of the most fascinating writers of German Romanticism. After a late, but spectacular start to her career as an author with the biographically inspired *Goethe's Correspondence with a Child: For His Memorial* (*Goethes Briefwechsel mit einem Kinde. Seinem Denkmal*, 1835)[1] that boldly claims the legacy of Germany's most admired poet, Brentano von Arnim continues to explore the realm of autobiographical fiction (*Günderode, Clemens Brentano's Spring Wreath* [*Clemens Brentanos Frühlingskranz*]), but also widens the perspective to the pressing social questions of her time.[2] She is highly versatile: a social conscience paired with playful innocence and ingenuity. Given that most of her works play with mixing in biographical information with philosophical reflection, one key to understanding her writings is indeed her biography. In opposition to its first appearance, Brentano von Arnim's works are not sentimental-autobiographical musings, but manifestations of a play with fiction

---

[1] The original subtitle "Seinem Denkmal" plays with the ambiguity between this book being the "Denkmal," and the intended actual memorial in form of a sculpture (the proceeds of the book were meant to contribute to the realization of it, but it never came to fruition in her lifetime). Brentano von Arnim indeed designed a memorial for Goethe—one that depicts the poet sitting on a Roman throne with a small "Bettine-as-Psyche" at his feet; see Anne Pollok, "On Self-Formation: The Role of Writing and Sociability for the Philosophy of Henriette Herz, Rahel Levin Varnhagen, and Bettina von Arnim," in *Women and Philosophy in Eighteenth-Century Germany*, ed. Corey Dyck (Oxford: Oxford University Press, 2021), 207, and Monika Shafi, "The Myth of Psyche as Developmental Paradigm in Bettine Brentano von Arnim's Epistolary Novels," in *Gender and Politics*, ed. Elke Frederiksen and Katherine Goodman (Detroit: Wayne State University Press, 1995), 95–114.

[2] Reference to Brentano von Arnim's works (with the exception of *Conversations with Demons*) will be made in the text as WB followed by a volume number and a page number. WB refers to *Bettine von Arnim: Werke und Briefe in vier Bänden*, ed. Walter Schmitz and Sibylle Steinsdorff (Frankfurt/M: Deutscher Klassiker Verlag, 1986–2004). Reference to *Conversations with Demons* (*Dämonenbuch*) will be made to Bettina von Arnim, *Gespräche mit Dämonen*, in *Werke und Briefe*, vol. 1, ed. Gustav Konrad, 258–407 (Frechen: Bartmann, 1959).

and fact, with expectation and the lack of its fulfillment. After a short introduction to her life and works, I will concentrate on her concept of identity through symphilosophy. This notion of a self is not only reflected in others, but in nature and in art, as well as her political agenda.

1 Life-Stations: The Very Material of Literature?

Elisabeth Catharina Ludovica Magdalena Brentano was born on April 4, 1785, as the thirteenth child of the businessman Peter Anton Brentano (1735–1779) and the seventh child of his second wife, Maximiliane, née La Roche (1756–1793), the daughter of Sophie von La Roche (1730–1807).[3] When her mother died in 1793, Brentano was sent to a convent together with two of her sisters. The young girl seems to have shown decisive marks of an independent spirit already at an early age: she was an outsider in the circle of siblings, did not follow her older brothers' rule, and always attempted to do things her own way.[4] She spent some of her childhood and adolescence at her grandmother's in Offenbach as well as in the family home in Frankfurt. She traveled throughout Germany to visit her siblings (one of her sisters, Kunigunde [1780–1863], was married to Friedrich Carl von Savigny [1779–1861]), attended her grandmother's salon, and also became friends with the poet Karoline von Günderrode (1780–1806), who published her works under a male-sounding pseudonym—Tian. After a short-lived affair with Brentano's brother, Clemens Brentano (1778–1842), which Günderrode ended after receiving an erotically aggressive letter in which Clemens degrades her ingenuity and style,[5] Günderrode got caught up in an unhappy love affair with the married scholar Friedrich Creuzer (1771–1858), who demanded that she end her friendship with Brentano.[6] The liaison with Creuzer ended in 1806. In the same year, maybe out of disappointment in her former lover, but also perhaps on account of her inability to find a sure footing in the literary scene, Karoline von Günderrode committed suicide. Brentano revisited these events in both her first and second publication.

---

[3] Sophie von la Roche's novel *History of Miss Sternheim* [*Geschichte des Fräulein Sternheim*] (1771), and several journal and travel diaries, made her one of the most famous writers of the late German Enlightenment.

[4] Wolfgang Bunzel, "Von Herz zu Herz? Zum textlogischen Status und sozialhistorischen Kontext der Familienbriefe Bettine von Arnims," in *Dieses Buch gehört den Kindern. Achim und Bettine von Arnim und ihre Nachfahren*, ed. Ulrike Landfester and Hartwig Schultz (Berlin: Albin, 2004), 49.

[5] See Barbara Becker-Cantarino, *Schriftstellerinnen der Romantik: Epoche, Werke, Wirkung* (Munich: Beck, 2000), 203.

[6] See his letters, cited in WB I, 865, in which he urges Günderrode to "free herself from such company."

Brentano had a rather intimate—in the eyes of some family members, too intimate—relationship with her older brother Clemens. He stylized her as the character Annonciata, the "power of life," in his *Godwi, or The Stone Image of a Mother* (1800–1801). While he also encouraged her to write, he did not intend for her to become a self-standing author but wished her to write in a "female style." This included the usage of the letter format for an attempt at a *Briefroman*, but he also intended to use her ideas for his own works (this was quite common among the early Romantics). Clemens was less than enthusiastic when she published *Goethe's Correspondence with a Child*, which unabashedly used personal notes and letters, not even shying away from exposing the erotic aspects of this peculiar relationship.[7] She was strong enough to resist her brother's attempts to shape and direct her talent as early as when their bond first formed in her teens.[8] They eventually grew apart, in particular in the wake of Clemens's turn to Catholicism. However, the most decisive breach in their relationship came with Clemens's engagement to Sophie Mereau (1770–1806), whom Brentano von Arnim seems to have perceived as a threat to her own relationship with her brother.[9] After her brother's death in 1842, she dedicated her third book to recapturing the early years of their relationship, covering roughly the years 1800–1803.

In 1811, Bettina Brentano married Achim von Arnim (1781–1831), a good friend of Clemens. Having met in 1802, they were in close contact during the writing and publication of *The Boy's Magic Horn* (*Des Knaben Wunderhorn*) in 1805–1808; she contributed to the project, and also set music to some of von Arnim's poems, albeit her name was never officially connected to the project.[10] After a long friendship and courtship, the couple finally settled in Berlin and the manor in Wiepersdorf—we should note that their marriage was accompanied by a contract that prevented von Arnim from using his wife's money to pay for the debts he had already amassed – quite some for the necessary renovations of the decrepit manor.[11] The marriage seemed harmonious, but

---

[7] Brentano von Arnim defends herself, arguing that these erotically charged moments were important for her development as a writer. Her portrayal took them "away from the coarse earthly realm of unsagacious, mendacious people"; see her letter from June 17, 1834 [WB IV, 303].

[8] The siblings did not meet before 1797; see Hartwig Schultz, *"Unsere Lieb aber ist außerkohren": Die Geschichte der Geschwister Clemens und Bettine Brentano* (Frankfurt/M: Insel, 2004), and his "Nachwort" to *Bettine von Arnim, Werke und Briefe* (Frankfurt/M: Deutscher Klassiker Verlag, 1985), 344–358; Ursula Isselstein, "Briefwechsel als Bildungsprojekt. Dialogische Konstellationen im *Frühlingskranz* Bettine von Arnims," in *Die Brentanos. Eine europäische Familie*, ed. Konrad Feilchenfeldt and Luciano Zagari (Tübingen: Niemeyer, 1992), 208–218.

[9] See commentary in WB I, 818–819, and Becker-Cantarino, *Schriftstellerinnen*, 231.

[10] Ann Willison, "Bettina Brentano von Arnim: The Unknown Musician," in Frederiksen and Goodman, *Gender and Politics*, 304–345.

[11] See Roswitha Burwick, "Achim von Arnim," in *Bettina von Arnim Handbuch*, ed. Barbara Becker-Cantarino (Berlin: de Gruyter, 2019), henceforth cited as Hb. In this instance the reference is to Hb 117–118. This did not stop Brentano von Arnim, however, later when she decided to "force" him to use her money, when their debts became too crushing. This fits well with her motto: "human beings should not give themselves up for the other, but they should strive to work together" (letter to Max Brokop 1811, in *Der Briefwechsel zwischen Bettine Brentano und Max Prokop von Freyberg*, ed. Sibylle Steinsdorff (Berlin: de Gruyter, 1972), 206).

von Arnim became more immersed in his endeavors as a proper squire, and—despite producing a barrage of novels, novellas, and poems—he seemed to have stopped sharing his intellectual endeavors with his wife, who was starving for challenges and exchange. Even though the couple stayed close, they grew apart intellectually the more their interests continued to diverge. What Brentano von Arnim thought about the anti-Semitic *Christian-German Tischgesellschaft* (access to which was prohibited to "Jews, Frenchmen, and Liberals"), which her husband founded with Adam Heinrich Müller (1779–1829) in 1811, the year of their marriage, is not known, but it is clear from her letters that her political views differed quite radically from her husband's. Accordingly, access to her own salon in Berlin was less restrictive.

During her many travels, for instance to Berlin, Frankfurt, and Munich, Brentano von Arnim was also fully immersed in the poetic and political circles of her time, with intellectuals such as Rahel Varnhagen-von Ense, Friedrich Schleiermacher, Ludwig Tieck, Savigny, the Grimm brothers, and others. When the Grimm brothers lost their positions in Göttingen as a punishment for being part of the infamous "Göttingen Seven,"[12] Brentano von Arnim wrote numerous letters to the Berlin Academy of Sciences, as well as to the king and the then crown prince Friedrich Wilhelm (later King Friedrich Wilhelm IV), and published an open letter in Gutzkow's *Telegraph for Germany* (1839) in order to help secure them a position in Berlin. She finally succeeded in 1840, the very year of Friedrich Wilhelm's ascendance to the throne.[13] Brentano von Arnim's letter network was formidable and influential.[14] She had a close friendship with Goethe's mother, Catharina Elizabeth Goethe, called "Frau Rath" (1731–1808); their conversations in Goethe's home in Frankfurt, some of which centered around the famous son's youth, were so thorough that the son himself ended up using them for his autobiography *Poetry and Truth* (1808–1833). Frau Rath herself plays an important role in almost all of Brentano von Arnim's works. In *Goethe's Correspondence with a Child*, the letters between the two women serve as a prolonged introduction to the actual exchange of letters between the "lovers," and to a fictional "diary", entitled "book of love" as a third part. Furthermore, in her more straight-forwardly political works, *This Book Belongs to the King* (*Dieses Buch gehört dem König,* 1843) and *Conversations with Demons* (*Gespräche mit Dämonen,* 1852), Frau Rath serves as a semifictional mouthpiece of the frank and insightful commoner—the antidote to the mysterious female of the Romantics: an unsophisticated, yet

---

[12] Today the Göttingen Seven's act of civil disobedience in respect to their responsibility for the nation is understood as one of the initial events leading to a broader interest in the value of the freedom of opinion. But in particular the brothers Grimm, especially the more nationalistic and traditionalistic Jacob, represent this new trend in a rather limited way; see Klaus von See, *Die Göttinger Sieben: Kritik einer Legende* (Heidelberg: Winter, 1997), 75.

[13] See, for instance, Solveig Ockenfuß, *Bettine von Arnims Briefromane: Literarische Erinnerungsarbeit zwischen Anspruch und Wirklichkeit* (Opladen: Westdeutscher Verlag, 1992), 17.

[14] See Becker-Cantarino, "Netzwerk in Berlin," in Hb 205, who counts over 200 of her contemporaries who were in more or less close contact with Brentano von Arnim.

strikingly clever predecessor of the openly political protagonists in the literature of the *Vormärz*.[15]

Brentano von Arnim befriended leading figures of the so-called Heidelberg Circle,[16] such as Joseph Görres (1776–1848), and important representatives of the "Young Germany," for example the author Theodor Mundt (1808–1861), who sometimes frequented her salon in the 1830s.[17] In her later years, she was friends with Karl Marx (1818–1883)—there are quite entertaining reports that the young Marx had to leave his fiancée waiting alone in a hotel so that he could accompany Brentano von Arnim on a lengthy walk, much to his chagrin. But he must also have been fascinated by a person who actually shared his interest in fundamentally improving the conditions of the working class.

From 1836 onward, Brentano von Arnim led a liberal salon, in which she used her fame to influence younger bourgeois men. Later, this salon was even called "salon of the demagogues"; but, as Becker-Cantarino points out, this name is a bit overdone: Brentano von Arnim's salon was significant, but not in itself the breeding ground of liberalism.[18] It is noteworthy that she allowed for heated debates, which her daughters seemed to have witnessed rather anxiously—even more so as two of them sided with Savigny's conservatism and started entertaining a gathering for the establishment. Ironically, the conservative salon met on the left, the oppositional salon on the right site of the main hall in their shared residence in Berlin.[19]

Her engagement with the poor did not only result in impressive masses of notes and empirical observations of their living conditions (many of these observations came from her friends and acquaintances, most notably Heinrich Grunholzer), which she planned ultimately to include in the so-called *Book of the Poor* (*Das Armenbuch*), which was never published during her lifetime. Her attitude also brought her into legal trouble—the most famous case being the so-called Magistratsprozess of 1846–1847. After several publishing houses did not agree to publish her late husband's collected works, she endeavored to do this privately. According to the Common Law of the Land (Allgemeines Landrecht), any such activity required her to purchase official citizenship of Berlin. When she was informed of this, she ironically suggested that the state give her an honorary citizenship, while insisting that the publication of her husband's work was

[15] Frau Rath was in fact noble by birth. Nonetheless, her forthright and sometimes naïve attitude made her the perfect candidate for Brentano von Arnim. As Brentano von Arnim put it, Frau Rath "knows how to infuse respect" (BW I, 452).

[16] The concept "Heidelberger Romantik" as used by Alfred Baeumler and others is to be taken with a good deal of caution. One central figure, Heinrich von Eichendorff, was never as close to the others as some later notes make it seem. See *Heidelberger Romantik. Mythos und Symbol*, ed. Karl Otto Frey and Theodore Ziolkowski (Heidelberg: Winter, 2009). We should also keep in mind that some studies of this time pay too much heed to the idea of a "Volk" and anti-Semitic tendencies.

[17] See Petra Wilhelmy-Dollinger, *Die Berliner Salons. Mit kulturhistorischen Spaziergängen* (Berlin: de Gruyter, 2000), 163.

[18] Becker-Cantarino, "Gespräch, Geselligkeit, Salon," in Hb 352.

[19] From Maximiliane Brentano's diary; see Johannes Werner, *Maxe von Arnim: Tochter Bettinas/ Gräfin von Oriola (1818–1894)* (Leipzig: v. Hase & Koehler, 1937), 173.

a family matter and did not fall under the city's jurisdiction (see WB IV, 559–562, 573–588). The case went back and forth; ultimately, Brentano von Arnim, who was absent during the trials, was declared guilty of "willful disregard of the city" and sentenced to two months in prison, as well as full payment of all legal expenses. The case was highly publicized. Brentano von Arnim's defense stressed her status as a celebrated author, and a "darling" of the German public, but to no avail.[20] It was thanks to the intervention of Savigny, her brother–in–law, that she did not have to serve her sentence, but "only" had to pay the legal expenses and the contested business tax.[21]

Brentano von Arnim's genuine interest in the situation of the poor is quite clear. In her own childhood, she never knew poverty. She initially experienced lack of resources during the first years of her marriage in Wiepersdorf, when the family income was not sufficient—and their knowledge of farming and organizing a manor left a lot to be desired. But neither then, nor later was she unwilling to share what she possessed. She also did not show the typical yet distanced benevolence of the noblewoman, as she clearly understood that the existing situation would not be alleviated by mere charity. The transformation of agricultural Prussia into a modern industrialized state needed adequate political guidelines (Engels worked on similar issues at the time).[22] Creating convincing arguments within entertaining stories, but also making information available was part of her agenda to improve the conditions of the poor. She used her voice to influence the ruling nobility, as she clearly understood that in order to improve the situation of the poor, you still have to get the upper classes on board. Her letters to leading figures in Prussian politics show her concern for real people and their problems.[23] This engagement seems largely private in its nature as the letters were not published; however, the addressees knew well enough that the famous author could eventually use them in her future works.[24] Brentano von Arnim also wrote short political pieces, most famously the address *For the Dissolved National Assembly of Poland: Voices from Paris* (1848) that draws attention to the aftermath of the revolution of 1848 not in Germany, but in Poland.[25] During the cholera epidemic of 1831 (Hegel was among the victims), she

[20] See Becker-Cantarino, "Rechtsstreitigkeiten," in Hb 308–309.

[21] On the so-called *Magistratsprozess*, see Becker-Cantarino, "Rechtsstreitigkeiten," in Hb 306–309, and Gertrud Meyer-Hepner, *Der Magistratsprozess der Bettina von Arnim* (Weimar: Arion, 1960).

[22] See Ingeborg Drewitz, *Bettine von Arnim: Romantik, Revolution, Utopie* (Berlin: Bertelsmann, 1984), 212. It is clearly not true that Brentano von Arnim was uninformed—a typical gendered assumption on our side. She studied political writings, pamphlets, and recent brochures to prepare for her *Book of the Poor*. Her artistic genius sometimes belies her stunning knowledge and level of information.

[23] See a list of her interventions in Loreley French, "Strategies of Female Persuasion: The Political Letters of Bettina Brentano von Arnim," in Frederiksen and Goodman, *Gender and Politics*, 74.

[24] See also the *Magistratsprozess*, in which she used publicity as a well-worn weapon. Concerning its proceedings, which were ultimately aimed at shaming her publicly (but were all too transparent in this goal) see Drewitz, *Bettine*, 219–220, and Becker-Cantarino/Helga Brandes, "Kampf gegen die Zensur," in Hb 295–315.

[25] We should note here that of course not all of Brentano von Arnim's appeals were successful. In particular in her attempts to sway Friedrich Wilhelm IV, she went overboard, needling him relentlessly

was involved in organizing medical and financial help, always with an eye to including the poor.

Brentano von Arnim and her husband had seven children, and she insisted on her own pedagogical method of bringing them up. As we know from some of her earliest writings, she was dead set against nearly all forms of authoritarian education, in particular when it concerned religion—a topic that is echoed throughout *This Book Belongs to the King*. Children should be treated independently of their gender or religion, and most of all they should be treated with respect. In loose adoption of Rousseau, she trusted a natural formation to bring forth the best in her children; a trust that even forbade her to discipline her sons when they got older and became more reckless.[26] The children lived free of almost all social constraints in Wiepersdorf, and it was only in later years that her husband played a more prominent role in their upbringing. With the children—some of whom deviated quite notably from her ideals—and their guardian Savigny, Brentano von Arnim had many quarrels, in particular after her husband's death in 1831, and when in 1835 she herself emerged as an author and a public figure. Her children mostly lived a life of the nobility, much more comfortable in their (traditional) roles than their mother had ever been.

Brentano von Arnim herself might have been unconventional; still, she only became a published writer and the intellectual persona she seemed to have always wanted to be *after* her husband's sudden death in 1831. Then, she understood her writing not only as a personal matter, but also as a means to voice the concerns of her time. By publishing her private correspondence, she engages with her audience. The last example of this is her *Ilius Pamphilius and Ambrosia* (*Ilius Pamphilius und die Ambrosia*) (1847–1848),[27] in which she as Ambrosia takes the younger Ilius Pamphilius, the student Philipp Engelhard Nathusius (1815–1872), under her wing. Brentano von Arnim here seeks to impart to the next generation her values of a romantic-progressive encounter with the world. The time gap between the actual letters and the book is not as wide as in the earlier works; she and Nathusius exchanged letters between 1836 and 1839, ten years prior to the publication of *Pamphilius*. The role of the child is here taken up by the student (who wrote "I am completely free with her, but stupid as a child and do not know

---

until he lost his patience (see commentary, WB III, 1210). That she was the actual author of this address could only be verified in 1929 (Commentary, WB III, 1221).

[26] See Becker-Cantarino, "Erziehung, Kinder, Nachfahren," in Hb 147; Landfester and Schultz, *Dieses Buch gehört den Kindern*, and *Bettine von Arnims Briefwechsel mit ihren Söhnen*, ed. Wolfgang Bunzel and Ulrike Landfester, 3 vols. (Göttingen: Wallstein, 1999–2012).

[27] The title went through quite some changes. First, Brentano von Arnim envisaged a volume collecting further correspondences, such as with the students Philipp Hössli and Julius Döring, embarrassingly titled "Meine letzten Liebschaften" (My last liaisons); then, to draw attention to the mistreatment of either the brothers Grimm or the poet Hoffmann von Fallersleben, titled "Briefwechsel mit zwei Demagogen" (Letters with two demagogues). Ultimately, Döring never allowed for the publication of his letters, and even the revised title "Ilius, Pamphilius, and Ambrosia" had to let go of its commas to reference only two, not three partners in dialogue; see Hedwig Pompe, "Ilius Pamphilius," in Hb 445.

how to utter a word"),[28] whereas Brentano von Arnim now assumes the role of nurturer and teacher, providing guidance and inspiration. But more than in the previous works this book shows how such a relationship can falter in light of reality: Pamphilius can take as much as he wants from Ambrosia's nurturing advice—he might still not become the poet he aspires to be for lack of talent; Ambrosia ends up showing *against* his example how romantic self-formation is supposed to work.

Brentano von Arnim's influence, both on the youth, but also on the king, diminished decisively in the 1850s. This became painfully apparent by the severe lack of success of her last work, *Conversations with Demons*. Even two years after its publication, according to Varnhagen, not one copy had been sold; and Moriz Carriére (1817–1895), one of her protégés and later a professor of art history in Gießen and Munich, attested that this work "went by without a trace."[29] Following a stroke in 1855, Brentano von Arnim never fully recovered and spent her last years in relative silence, while still supporting artists, mainly musicians and composers, until her death on January 20, 1859, with the model of the Goethe monument that she designed still close to her bed.

2 Brentano von Arnim as an Author

Brentano von Arnim's work is deeply creative, a wild play with perspectives and styles, but it is also a manifestation of her involvement in matters of public welfare. Whether written as a quasi-biographical memory (*Goethe's Correspondence, Günderode, Spring Wreath, Pamphilius*) or as a phantasmagorical vision of a possible dialogue with the still living (*This Book Belongs to the King, Conversations with Demons*), her work engages the main character, "Bettine," with acquaintances from the author's life in an imaginative, at times quite fantastical setting. It is not merely to entertain, but to address the reader as directly and affectively as possible. Her way of presenting herself as a naïve and playful child is better understood as a calculated move to direct attention away from the scandalous issue of a philosophizing political woman and toward the far more digestible (and gender-less) image of a playful and guileless suggestion to think things through anew.

In contrast to other woman writers of her time, Brentano von Arnim was relatively free of all external motivations to publish. She did not have to earn money, nor did she, at least in her early writings, campaign for a cause;[30] she simply chose to make her voice heard. She went into publication with the self-assured manner of a professional: even before *Goethe's Correspondence* appeared, she had commissioned reviews by some of her acquaintances, such as Wilhelm Grimm or Joseph Görres. Everyone should buy her

---

[28] BW III, 687.
[29] Carriere quoted in Konstanze Bäumer and Hartwig Schultz, *Bettina von Arnim* (Stuttgart: Metzler, 1995), 136.
[30] See note 1 above; the planned Goethe-memorial was, however, not a political cause.

book, she stated, "because it is beautiful."[31] The Young Germans (Jungdeutsche), who enthusiastically followed the July Revolution of 1830 in France and were hoping for more progressive changes in Germany, saw her as a mouthpiece for their new ideas. Journal editors like Karl Gutzkow (1811–1878) sought to win her as a contributor—however, they wanted her to tone down the lyricism and develop more straightforwardly political ideas. She was mostly unwilling to do this, even though some shorter writings such as the aforementioned address to the general assembly in Poland are indeed less playful, and more straightforwardly political in nature. But even then she does not stray far from the rhetoric that she employs in her books. Brentano von Arnim never fully aligned her ideas with the Young Germans, as she did not agree with their critique of German Classicism and Romanticism as apolitical.

Accordingly, her dedication of *Günderode* to the "students," which clearly included the Young Germans as well as the Young Hegelians,[32] did not amount to a full embrace of their ideals. Brentano von Arnim did not want a complete revolution of society, as her later political writings show. Fanny Lewald (1811–1889) celebrated Brentano von Arnim's legacy in her essay "The Cult of Genius: a Letter to Bettina von Arnim" (Der Cultus des Genius. Ein Brief an Bettina von Arnim), which appeared in 1849 in *Blätter für literarische Unterhaltung*. However, she also describes how Brentano von Arnim's character was inexplicable to all of them, and ends up celebrating her supposedly female virtues as the giving nurturer, making her unusual mannerisms more digestible.

Brentano von Arnim's writing mixes fiction and reality, past and present, and crossed the boundaries between self and others.[33] The result is a multifaceted structure, a new form of an open monologue.[34] It presents the author's perspective, split up between a subjective, but somewhat auctorial character ("Bettine"), and her respective counterparts. These counterparts serve as "echoes," as she in turn is their "reverberation" (*Wiederhall*); they engage in a conversation that clearly shows their different outlooks and interests. Each partner in dialogue serves as more than a mere line-giver or shape-enhancer, for without them we would have trouble seeing the depth of "Bettine's" character and the nature of her actions.[35] As was the case with other women of her

---

[31] WB II, 914; see also WB IV, 303.

[32] See the comments by contemporaries in Heinz Härtl, "Dies Völkchen mit der vorkämpfenden Alten: Bettina von Arnim und die Junghegelianer," in *Jahrbuch des Freien Deutschen Hochstifts* (1992), 215.

[33] This "intermingling of time frames, the overlay of personalities, the blurring of reality and fiction" are all typical of Bettina. See Elke Frederiksen and Katherine Goodman, "Locating Bettina Brentano von Arnim, A Nineteenth Century German Woman Writer," in Frederiksen and Goodman, *Gender and Politics*, 22, who also stress the comparison to Christa Wolf, one of the first and most fair Bettina Brentano von Arnim interpreters.

[34] Christa Bürger and Birgitt Diefenbach, editors' introduction to *Bettina von Arnim Lesebuch* (Leipzig: Reclam, 1987), 6.

[35] This is also why her partners and she herself are sometimes addressed as a mere "Echo" in her own writings; see particularly *Die Günderode*.

class, Brentano von Arnim learned, and actively refined, the art of conversation in the salon.[36]

Since her work is still not widely known (and even less accepted as containing philosophical ideas), and particularly not in the anglophone world,[37] this overview should include some general references to her main works and point out the most striking and innovative aspects of her writing.

With her first published work, *Goethe's Correspondence with a Child*, Brentano von Arnim entered the literary market with a bang.[38] Feeding on the intense interest in Johann Wolfgang von Goethe (1749–1832) as a writer and public persona, the work's appearance close to the master's death in 1832, but also its startling openness and constructed intimacy, garnered an extensive and intensive reception. Brentano von Arnim enthusiastically celebrates her relationship with the "national poet"; in the first part she paints the artist's memory in her letter exchange with Catharina Elisabeth Goethe, covering roughly the years 1807–1808 (Frau Rath died that year). The second part is dedicated to the actual exchange of letters between Goethe and Brentano von Arnim between 1808 and 1826—she edited the letters and expanded them, in particular those by Goethe, who appears much less involved in the exchange (he broke off all contact in 1830). The last part, the "book of love," Bettine's stylized diary, encapsulates her emotional reactions to Goethe's death, but also includes more general thoughts on music and artistry, culminating in an intricate philosophy of love.[39]

Instead of reading this book as a book of devotion to an idealized male figure,[40] recent literature focuses on Brentano von Arnim's method of fictionalizing memory, and therewith reshaping personal constellations. She also plays with the expectations an audience has of a female protagonist. Sometimes she portrays "Bettine" as a "vessel" for other people's thoughts, for instance when she merely takes over Herrn Voigt's political musings in *Günderode* (WB I, 348–349; later she reflects on them in her own voice

[36] She started her own salon around 1836 when she was at the peak of her fame for *Goethe's Correspondence*. As such, it was guaranteed to make an impression, as most visitors wanted to get to know the infamous "child" (see Becker-Cantarino, "Gespräch, Geselligkeit, Salon," in Hb 350–351).

[37] Even though some of the best works on Brentano von Arnim stem from anglophone writers such as Katherine Goodman, Elke Frederiksen, Alison Stone, and Anna Ezekiel.

[38] Schmitz and Steinsdorff count thirty-eight reviews in the years 1835–1840. See WB II, commentary, 910–913.

[39] Bakunin translated this part into Russian in 1838; see Bäumer and Schultz, *Bettina*, 174.

[40] This has been the common reception of *Goethe's Correspondence*, and of Brentano von Arnim in general, in particular in western Germany, for the most part of the nineteenth and twentieth centuries. As a poignant highlight see Hans-Wilhelm Kelling, "Bettina von Arnim: A Study in Goethe-Idolatry," *Bulletin of the Rocky Mountain Modern Language Association* 23, no. 2 (1969): 73–82; as a good antidote see Ingrid Fry, "Elective Androgyny: Bettine Brentano von Arnim and Margaret Fuller's Reception of Goethe," *Goethe Yearbook* 10 (2001): 246–262; Konstanze Bäumer, *Bettine, Psyche, Mignon: Bettina von Arnim und Goethe* (Stuttgart: Akademischer Verlag, 1986), in particular 120–130, who portrays the decisive move of Bettine as Mignon from the supporting to the central character, and Miriam Seidler, "Goethes Briefwechsel," in Hb 367–383.

[WB I, 384]).[41] She lets her alter ego be the naïve child who does not even understand "Caroline's" poems, but reads them anyway because their creator is so nice (WB I, 351); she approaches Goethe as a child and revisits this child-like persona often throughout other writings—creating with this alter ego the perfect persona in which she can play out different aspects of herself. She is not a blank canvas for others, nor is she ignorant of her own desires. Quite the opposite: under the guise of a child, she is allowed to go beyond decorum, she can slide behind other people's defenses, and can continue to ask the question "why?" With her character "Bettine" and her partners in dialogue, she also helps the reader to feel directly involved, to actually *be* out there on her nightly walk through the woods, or high on top of a tree, conversing freely and with no academic (or conventional) decorum with others.

Her taking up the persona of a "child" should thus not be seen as an inappropriate claim to childishness and some misapplied "womanly naïveté"; but it is designed to allow for an unconventional perspective, creating a closeness between her and "the mother" Frau Rath, and Goethe, the "older brother." As Voigt in *Günderode* puts it: "wisdom should bloom forth from a child" (WB I, 340). Accordingly, instead of just representing mere reflections of Goethe's genius, both "Frau Rath" and "Bettine," the main characters in the conversation (apart from the cold and distant Goethe himself), establish a firm hold on the direction and quality of the memories here presented. "Bettine" develops a notion of love as a "divine fundamental feeling." This serves to justify the creative freedom she takes to develop herself in light of the divine image of the great poet. Only in her exuberance does she love him appropriately and is thus able to present him the right way.[42] She freely mixes truth and fiction, combining the actual letters with lines taken from letters to others (such as Beethoven, Frau Rath, Schleiermacher, and Hermann Fürst von Pückler-Muskau), but also extracts material from Goethe's works,[43] so as to form a truthful image of love as a form of self-expression. As Brentano von Arnim admits in a letter to the lawyer and literary scholar Karl Hartwig Gregor von Meusebach (1781–1847), she was not that much in love with the actual Goethe, "but I needed somebody, on whom I could project my thoughts etc."[44] This is what Goodman calls "radical autobiography."[45] Two aspects are decisive

---

[41] The model for this character, Niklas Vogt, was professor of history in Mainz from 1784 and from 1806 von Dalberg's closest assistant. Brentano von Arnim appreciated his political views (he favored a European Republic; see WB I, 1136), as well as his willingness to put conventional views aside in order to entertain her ideas: "and when he, inspired by my enthusiasm, sits down and engages in a conversation with a . . . leg of a chair, then I deem him worthy of being my playmate," she writes to her brother Clemens; WB I, 1137.

[42] On this "theology of love," see Ingrid Leitner and Sibylle von Steinsdorff, "Die vollkommenste Grammatik der Liebe, die jemals komponiert wurde. Thesen zum poetischen Verfahren Bettine von Arnims in 'Goethe's Briefwechsel mit einem Kinde,'" *Jahrbuch Bettina von Arnim Gesellschaft* 6/7 (1994/95): 143–157.

[43] In particular those close to the first journey to Italy; see Bäumer and Schultz, *Bettina*, 62.

[44] Cited in Bunzel, "Briefwechsel," in Hb 496.

[45] Katherine Goodman, *Dis/Closures: Women's Autobiography in Germany between 1790 and 1914* (New York: Lang, 1986), 91.

here. On the one hand, the self that emerges from this kind of literature only becomes fully visible when it actively engages with others. "Bettine" as a character "emerges with and in contrast to others; it defines itself and evolves because of their influence and in opposition to them."[46] On the other hand, this relation to the other(s) does not have to be a faithful depiction of "real" relationships, but the biographical material is used in order to further the self. Brentano von Arnim's letter-books thus do not necessarily tell us "how things actually were" (to use a phrase coined by nineteenth-century historicism), but they show us what "Bettine" made of them. For her, the imagined self is indeed part of the "true" self, as she considers the imagination one of our finest features.

"Bettine's" last letters to Frau Rat in *Goethe's Correspondence* (WB II, 62–84) retell the events around Karoline von Günderrode's death, concentrating on the horror and helplessness that it harbored for Brentano von Arnim herself. Following her lover's wishes, Karoline ended her friendship with Brentano von Arnim, renouncing a deep relationship and devaluing the mutual trust between the friends. Günderrode's suicide soon thereafter, which took Brentano von Arnim by complete surprise, was a huge scandal— a scandal that she wanted to move away from, as it overshadowed the appropriate appreciation of Günderrode's legacy.[47] As Brentano von Arnim stresses in *Goethe's Correspondence*, she decided to forgo her sadness, a sadness that she will surely own and turn into something fruitful in due time.

This process of taking ownership of this relationship and of this sadness that retrospectively color everything is reflected in Brentano von Arnim's second book, *Günderode* (1840).[48] It celebrates a relationship between a sage teacher ("Caroline") and her unruly student ("Bettine")—although the roles are constantly reversed over the course of the book. These switches are designed to showcase the intellectually rich friendship and ultimate equality of the two women. So "Bettine" exclaims: "we two philosophers will have . . . huge and deep speculations by which the old world will break from its old rusty hinges; they might even reverse the direction of its rotation.—You know what, you are going to be Plato . . . and I will be your friend and student Dion, we will love each other dearly and will forsake our lives for each other" (WB I, 331–332). Their student-teacher relationship is dynamic and ever-changing, with "Caroline" repeatedly stressing how worthy her friend is to serve as an example for every poet. The book is also a reflection on wisdom and philosophy, offering an alternative to the ruling school of Idealism. We can assume that Brentano von Arnim read Jean Paul (1763–1825), Johann Gottfried Herder (1744–1803), Friedrich Heinrich Jacobi (1743–1819), Friedrich

---

[46] Goodman, *Dis/Closures*, 106.

[47] The book was also instrumental in bringing the then-forgotten published works by the real Günderrode, such as poems or her *Poetische Fragmente*, to the attention of the public; some poems and reflections of hers are even published for the first time here. It is due to this reminder that 1857 Friedrich Goetz published a first, if incomplete, edition of Karoline von Günderrode's works.

[48] Note that the title gives the last name of the poet without the double *r*., a change as subtle as the fictional "Bettine" for the real "Bettina."

Hölderlin (1770–1843), and others,[49] under Günderrode's tutelage. Brentano von Arnim clearly prefers these thinkers over Immanuel Kant (1724–1804), Friedrich Wilhelm Joseph Schelling (1775–1854), and Johann Gottlieb Fichte (1762–1814).[50] Her views also align much more with Friedrich Schleiermacher (1768–1834) and the Young Hegelians, many of whom attended her salon during the time she revisited the correspondence with her friend, which would eventually turn into *Günderode*.[51]

In the book, Brentano von Arnim practices symphilosophy modeled on the early Romantics; but this time, it is an imaginary dialogue between two women.[52] Once again, the letters are carefully edited, extended, and ordered. "Bettine" engages with and reprints Günderrode's works, and thus "creates a space for interaction between independently thinking women."[53] Together, they reflect and refine the ideals of the early Romantics—the elevation of reality through poetry, the mystification of the common, the higher sense that shines through the everyday, and the disregard of the documentary for the ideal, just to name a few[54]—in order to explore their "true selves."

Given that her friend Günderrode had been in a relationship with Brentano von Arnim's brother Clemens, it is no wonder that his name is mentioned quite often between the friends. She gives this relationship more space in her next book: *Clemens Brentano's Spring Wreath, Wrought from the Letters of Our Youth, as He Asked Me to Do in Writing* (1844).[55] It does not merely represent a reminiscence of her early relationship with her brother at the beginning of the 1800s (mainly 1800–1803), but continues

---

[49] Even if accompanied by a "Nervenfieber," we should even assume that Brentano von Arnim read Kant, Fichte, Schelling, and Schleiermacher (see WB I, 278; Bäumer and Schultz, *Bettina*, 26); see also Ockenfuß, *Briefromane*, 42–43, in particular regarding her positive reception of Hölderlin.

[50] "The Idealists merely imprint their systems onto the world, regardless of whether they might actually fit" (see WB I, 307); she mentions a discussion about Schleiermacher's "Monologen" with Günderrode (WB I, 485).

[51] See Härtl, "Völkchen," 215.

[52] We should also mention that Brentano von Arnim also uses letters by others or to others to "fill up" the conversation, for example Günderrode's letters to Clemens, or her own ones to Max Prokop von Freyberg, Clemens, and Claudine Piautaz (see Bäumer and Schultz, *Bettina*, 34). On the matter of symphilosophy as a continuation of the early romantics, see in particular Alison Stone, "Bettina von Arnim's Romantic Philosophy in *Die Günderode*," *Hegel Bulletin* 43.3 (2022): 1–24, https://doi.org/10.1017/hgl.2021.19.

[53] Renata Fuchs, "'I Drink Love to Get Strong': Bettina Brentano von Arnim's Romantic Philosophy and Dialogue in *Die Günderode*," *Women in German Yearbook* 32 (2016): 32; see also Ockenfuß, *Briefromane*, 12 and chap. 4.

[54] Brentano von Arnim's actual engagement with, roughly speaking, literature and philosophy of her time is slim. Bäumer and Schultz, *Bettina*, 24, mention a meeting she had with Hölderlin's friend Sinclair in 1806, just after Günderrode's suicide and during the advent of Sinclair's final separation from his best friend, Hölderlin. It is hard to imagine that suicide was not part of their conversation, as well as the possible causes and preceding events of suicides. Hölderlin, in a similar vein to Günderrode's, is mentioned in *Die Günderode* as one failed attempt to grasp and form oneself—see BW I, 318, 392–395: "Bettine" tells her friend of regular meetings with "St. Clair."

[55] *Clemens Brentanos Frühlingskranz aus Jugendbriefen ihm geflochten, wie er selbst schriftlich verlangte*—the bulky title should stress that her brother himself asked her to write this book; this was mostly directed against the reservations among the rest of the family, who feared that this work was too scandalous, see BW I, 9.

her reorientation toward the ideas of the early Romantics, in particular their interest in folk poetry from the Middle Ages, the compilation and selection of poems and stories for posterity to form a "German folk spirit," their insistence on a creative exploration of these texts rather than a critical examination of their sources, and the poeticizing of life through its imaginative reformulation. Brentano von Arnim sharpens her dismissal of the then-current "Romantics-turned-conservatives" who, as she thought, only paraded empty thoughts.[56] Just as in *Günderode*, so here Brentano von Arnim uses the book to set issues right between herself as an intellectual and writer, and the more conventional expectations of her brother. *Spring Wreath* allows her to take ownership of their relationship: she stresses how much Clemens himself wanted her to immortalize their younger years, and brings this unusual relation between two siblings into the open, against her family's wishes.[57] Her work was also instrumental in the public perception of Clemens Brentano as a lyricist.[58] But it also helped to present Brentano von Arnim as free of her brother's expectations: "if you had grasped me in my own language then you would not like me for a moment, . . . the talk would have been of other things. A swarm of misunderstandings" (WB I, 199).[59]

We can finally witness the breakdown of dialogue in *Ilius Pamphilius and Ambrosia*: both partners end up representing not two sides of a persona but become alter ego and ego—representing the insurmountable difference between strangers who bring with them two completely different sets of skills, talents, and expectations.[60] This complex relationship of expectations and disappointments has not yet been fully explored in the secondary literature.[61]

3 Central Philosophical Ideas of the Letter Books

3.1 Identity through Symphilosophy

For Brentano von Arnim, writing is a mode of self-formation through reflection and expression, but also a testing out of various personae. For her, reasoning cannot be an

---

[56] Bäumer and Schultz, *Bettina*, 15–16.

[57] In particular her older brother Franz, senator in Frankfurt and obviously concerned for their public appearance; see Becker-Cantarino, "Frühlingskranz," in Hb 417.

[58] See Becker-Cantarino, "Frühlingskranz," in Hb 419.

[59] The plan for a second part of this book, presumably building on the exchange between Clemens and Achim, kept Brentano von Arnim busy throughout the 1840s, but never quite came to fruition.

[60] See Hedwig Pompe, "Ilius Pamphilius," in Hb 446.

[61] See Konstanze Bäumer, "*Ilius Pamphilius und die Ambrosia*: Bettina von Arnim als Mentorin," *Jahrbuch Bettina von Arnim Gesellschaft* 3 (1989): 263–282; Hedwig Pompe, *Wille zum Glück: Bettine von Arnims Poetik der Naivität im Briefroman Die Günderode* (Bielefeld: Aisthesis, 1999), and "Ilius Pamphilius," in Hb 439–451.

isolated activity, but has to be a "thinking together" (WB I, 341). This thinking is a continual game of question-and-answer, representing the back-and-forth between two lovers (WB I, 341). "Where should my spirit find its footing if it is not the self-conquered property of love?—Do I understand myself?—I don't even know" (WB I, 344). In the words of Immortalita, the main character of a short play by Günderode that features prominently in the first part of the letter-book, "I do not know! Why don't I know myself," to which Hekate replies: "Because you cannot see yourself" (WB I, 355). The ability to see oneself, to reflect oneself in dialogue and in artful self-presentation is exactly what Brentano von Arnim seeks in her letter-books. In the play, it is love that will offer Immortalita the mirror to finally see herself, as it encompasses everything. Brentano von Arnim portrays this love through the relationships that play out in her works. These are representations of all forms of love: eros in *Goethe's Correspondence*, philia in *Günderode* and *Spring Wreath*, agape in the *This Book Belongs to the King* and, at least in principle, some combination of eros and philia in *Pamphilius*.

Her "philosophy" is thus not one of studies and systems, but one of interaction, shared reflections, and the joint development of imaginative tableaus and situations. On the formal level, this is reflected in a liberal understanding of artistic form. "Bettine" reads a letter from "Caroline" while she herself and the pages of "Caroline's" letter are floating in a pool, mixing the sequence of pages randomly (WB I, 366). She presents snippets from the past, but in reverse order. She lets others be her mouthpiece. But her way of presentation does not invite an "anything goes" approach, as she also asks: "can we consider anything just as we want?—I can consider the clouds above the same way as my duvet, but still the former will not come down to cover me" (WB I, 398). She lets Herr Voigt tell us that philosophy is nothing without feeling (*Empfindung*), that it has to become poesy before it is actually meaningful for us (WB I, 378).[62] In the same vein, she has to incorporate and digest her fellow thinkers' thoughts into her work to make them hers in the sense of understanding them truly. As she puts it, the goal is "to let the inner spirit work by itself, and not let a foreign one take over" (WB I, 616), as it is our vocation "to create our own ideal," and build "a divine human nature" from sound human reason, as well as emotion and imagination" (WB I, 517).

In her art, other people become symbolic of a meaning, an atmosphere, or a type. In *Günderode*, for instance, Bettine's friend "Caroline" as well as the elusive Hölderlin represent two versions of an artist who did not succeed, in that they either could not hold themselves together in light of role-limitations and expectations (Günderrode) or lost the ability to make themselves understood and descended into madness (Hölderlin). In *Goethe's Correspondence*, Goethe and Beethoven represent different aspects of both Brentano von Arnim's personality (the classical poet and the inspired musician, the nobleman and the grumpy simpleton) and her time (the Classicist aiming at immortality, the Romantic—as she understands Beethoven—who seeks to "overwhelm" with his music). What seems narrowly subjective is representative of much larger structures.

---

[62] Niklas Vogt (see n. 42) is taken as a representative of nonacademic early romantic philosophy.

The incorporation of other people's works into her own is thus an expression of the early romantic praxis of productive reception and symphilosophy. But, as she claims, this collage of thoughts and situations is not guided by some grand yet abstract idea; she doesn't have to be important or clever. Rather, without thinking, but with inspiration, she ought to tell a story: "I am so glad that I am unimportant, since then I do not need to pick up clever thoughts whenever I write, I just need to tell a story. Otherwise I would think I should not write without imparting some morality or something wise that makes the content more weighty. Now I no longer care to sculpt or glue together my thoughts artistically . . . I stopped thinking" (WB I, 380).

Her version of symphilosophy does not initiate a complete union of views and personalities, however, but often showcases potential for conflict. She does not seek harmony at all costs. Whenever she fails to "feel" the spirit who is trying to guide her, she ceases to listen to him at all, as she tells her brother (BW I, 197, also 212); marking her unwillingness to just fall in line with all of his judgments, she writes: "I need to keep my freedom" (WB I, 213, 275). The fallout with Goethe is always there in the background of *Goethe's Correspondence*, in Goethe's shorter replies and in the lack of resonance in the diary; with "Caroline" it is at times even more visible, in particular in their diverging views on vitality and immortality. "Bettine" favors complete immersion in the endless rise and fall of nature—but "Caroline" increasingly does not share this view: "mind enhances [steigert] this world; it is through mind alone that actual life is alive; . . . everything else is passing shadows."[63] Whereas "Caroline" wants to trust reason, we sense in "Bettine" the lingering of vitalism à la Herder, or even the advent of a Nietzschean "gay science."

Consequently, when "Bettine" rejects the dry teachings of history, "Caroline" reminds her younger friend of the importance of our past as the framing story of our lives— "How are you going to capture yourself, if you do not stand on safe ground?" Caroline asks (WB I, 404). For "Bettine," however, this ground can very well be pure fantasy—the better even if it moves and changes. In her ventures into nature, in the long nights spent noting down thoughts that even manage to surprise the writer herself (WB I, 457, 480), "Bettine" seeks what cannot be grasped rationally. The ground thus created is suffused in imagination, dreams, and passion (WB I, 480).

3.2 Levitating Religion and Music

This is also the central point of her *Schwebereligion* (inadequately translated as "levitating religion"),[64] that she develops in *Günderode*: constant change, mobility, but at the same time a centeredness in a life that is fundamentally shared (WB I, 455). By actively forming this shared world, we remain the masters of our life (WB I, 456).

---

[63] GW I, 728; I follow Stone's translation here; see Stone, "Romantic Philosophy," 15.
[64] Stone, "Romantic Philosophy," 12, translates it as "hovering religion."

Whenever "Bettine" references this "religion" in her letters, she gets caught up in little stories and similes; she celebrates the *feelings* experienced in nature, during sunset, in the spring, and so on. All these deviations from a strictly logical or deductive justification of her religion are intentional, as the center of this religion is its dynamics. It is a decidedly nonrational and nondirected thinking that serves to figure out the basis of this faith. "Bettine" aims to find that moment where thoughts are quiet (WB I, 465), where she—immersed in the immensity of nature—discovers her creative power to form a full picture out of her impressions (WB I, 467) without conceptual guidance, let nature pass through her, and be idealized through her imagination. The author repeats the divine command "there shall be . . . ! (es werde . . . !)" when she grasps and artfully expresses what lies in front of her. This cannot be reached by education of the intellect, and that is also why "Bettine" refuses to read "Schiller's aesthetics" (WB I, 468; see 250) or other such highlights of her culture, since philosophers, the living proof of such one-sided education, are just haughty (WB I, 307–308). "What is all politics against the silver gaze of nature! Don't you agree, it shall be a fundamental principle of our levitating religion that we won't allow education" (WB I, 468). Somewhat begrudgingly, "Caroline" appreciates "Bettine's" reckless willingness to give herself over to her unconscious (WB I, 436), as ultimately "Bettine" *becomes* the poetry that "Caroline" herself tries so hard to create—"Bettine" can get closer to nature by using her imagination and sensibility, letting them become natural forces rather than intellectual laws of style, whereas "Caroline" is presented as being constrained by the demands of style and tradition, and rather seeks to reach out to a purely spiritual realm. Her stern lecture on the value of history (WB I, 401–402), but even more so her poetry makes this clear. Particularly telling in this regard is a poem that Brentano von Arnim weaves into the book at an earlier point, "Change and Faithfulness" ("Wandel und Treue," WB I, 326–329), that ends with Narzissus's rejection of the eternal and senseless change in nature in favor of (the idea of) eternal beauty.[65] In this sense, *Günderode* is the manifestation of this back-and-forth between the willingness to give up control and the acute awareness of the dangers and insecurities that come with this very process.

The enthusiasm that "Bettine" embodies, in particular in *Günderode* and in the third part of *Goethe's Correspondence*, is thus a testament to Brentano von Arnim's dedicated search for true insight, which she calls the "holy spirit." We find it in nature, where it is pure rhythm (WB I, 482; see also 571, 577, 626), but we also find it in music.[66] "God is passion!" "Bettine" exclaims (WB I, 475; see also *Dämonenbuch*, 271). And it is through the "levitating religion" that we can realize this highest form of being (475–480). The issue of such a "religion" is its hermetic nature: on the one hand, it strives to articulate a state akin to a *unio mystica* with creation, on the other it lacks a definite and enduring shape, as it always develops and changes, and thus cannot be taught. The two central

---

[65] This is a very convincing argument in Stone, "Romantic Philosophy," 10–11: for "Bettine," philosophy serves life, whereas "Caroline" "is drawn away from life."

[66] Not any music, as "Bettine's" critique of Frederick's "soldier music," which might reference Frederick's only symphony in D Major, premiered in 1747, makes clear; WB I, 473, and commentary, 1157.

tenets of this religion are the maxims: have no fear (WB I, 465), and have experiences, as these are "giving our spirit sustenance" (WB I, 527). "Bettine" evokes (and practices in her work) the assistance of poetry and music to such a goal:

> I believe that great thoughts we think for the first time are so surprising that we feel our words which with we try to capture them are nothing; they search for their expression by themselves; we are too timid to use one that has been unheard of—but what does it matter? I have always wanted to talk in a way that is uncommon, if that means I get closer to these thoughts within my soul. I am certain that music must dwell within the soul, as any tune or mood is unthinkable in its motion without a melody. There must be something inborn in the soul in which our stream of thoughts flows. (WB I, 306)

To "Caroline,"[67] but also in *Goethe's Correspondence* she confesses her love for music, naming Beethoven in particular (e.g., WB I, 473–774, WB II, 345–347); music for her is the sensual embodiment of a divine nature, hence she refers to a notion that others might call perfection or harmony as a "music or concert of spirits" (WB I, 520). Music is Brentano von Arnim's safe haven;[68] she lets "Bettine" break out in song during frightening situations. And when "Bettine" plays the piano (or various other instruments), she feels more centered than when she writes or is otherwise intellectually engaged (WB I, 392–393). Out of all art forms, music is the ultimate tool to grasp the immensity of nature and the divine (WB I, 392), and it is also the art form that engages mind and body, and allows for freedom: "but my soul is a passionate dancer, it leaps around to an inner dance music that only I can hear and the others don't. Everyone is yelling for me to be quiet, and you [Clemens] do too, but because of my desire to dance, my soul doesn't listen to you" (WB I, 61). This soul actually does not listen to any of her male friends, be it Clemens, Pamphilius (Nathusius), or even Goethe. She tells the latter even that her passionate states do not lay claim on anything, but that they rather put a seed in whoever cares to listen. This is a seed that germinates and comes to full fruition only if this person lets it (*Goethe's Correspondence*, Diary, WB II, 542).

---

[67] Stone, "Romantic Philosophy," 11–12, stresses the tension between their stances. Whereas "Caroline," mainly in her fragment "The Realm of Tones" (Günderrode, GW, vol. III, 582–583), stresses the confluence of notes, "Bettine" favors the intervals between notes—not what is explicitly there, but what is between things, unsaid and unknown.

[68] Brentano von Arnim was a trained and very talented singer with a wide vocal range (see Renate Moehring, Hb 578–580) and was trained in piano and composition by various teachers such as Philipp Carl Hoffmann (1769–1842) and Rudolf August Friedemann Koch (1752–1811), who also supported her compositions for poems by Achim von Arnim, Goethe, and Hölderlin and her contributions to *Des Knaben Wunderhorn*. Ludwig van Beethoven (1770–1827) discussed music with her and dedicated to her his composition for Goethe's "Neue Liebe, neues Leben," (op. 75, no. 2, 1810). Brentano von Arnim used some of his letters for *Pamphilius* (see Renate Moehring, "Bettina von Arnim und die Musik," in Hb 595, with references to the uncertain origin of these letters). She also befriended Franz Liszt (1811–1886), as well as Robert and Clara Schumann (1810–1856; 1819–1896). Johannes Brahms (1833–1897) dedicated his *Sechs Gesänge* (op. 3, 1853) to her.

4 The Political Dimension: Worth of the Individual

In her publications during the last two decades of her life, Brentano von Arnim most decisively moves further into the political arena, albeit never renouncing the value of artistic dialogue and imagery. The most important aspect of her stance is her insistence on the absolute value of (each) individual. Every human being needs to be accepted and heard—the monarch might be the first of all, but in truth this manifests and strengthens his duty toward his people, who are more than a faceless mass to govern.

When her star rose in the wake of the publication of *Goethe's Correspondence*, the Young Germans were hopeful that they had found a spokesperson who would pave a way for their thoughts into aristocratic circles. Brentano von Arnim was well-known and well-connected; having her voice in the publication organs of the Young Germans (such as Gutzkow's *Telegraph*) would lend the latter credibility. She stayed in contact with many of the Young Germans in the self-proclaimed role of mentor. The same goes for the Young Hegelians, including David Friedrich Strauß (1808–1874), Adolf Stahr (1805–1876), Fanny Lewald, Bruno and Edgar Bauer (1809–1882, 1820–1886). She sent her *Günderode* to Strauß, as it touches on issues of genius that Strauß developed in his concept of a "Cultus des Genius."[69] They saw each other in 1843 in Stuttgart and conversed on related topics, even though Brentano von Arnim stayed away from fundamental religious skepticism and from Hegel's "absurd" philosophy in general (WB III, 733, commentary). Adolf Stahr was also among her protégés; she enabled him to publish his brochure *Bettina and Her Königisbuch* (*Bettina und ihr Königsbuch*) in 1843, and a defense of her *Spring Wreath* in 1844—as this book also had its fair share of trouble to endure from the censors.[70] Stahr's later wife, Fanny Lewald, published a review of *Pamphilius* that also included a nod to *This Book Belongs to the King*. As noted, Lewald read Brentano von Arnim as an author devoted to the service of others, a supporter of the revolutionary ideals of the students—and a true representative of the feminine ideal of selflessness in her care for others, as presumably expressed in the *Pamphilius*. We do not know Brentano von Arnim's reaction to this characterization.[71]

While Brentano von Arnim does not develop a clear-cut political program, even less so in the scandalous work *This Book Belongs to the King*, she considers the role of

---

[69] See Härtl, "Völkchen," 216.

[70] The book was printed by Egbert Bauer's publishing house (which was already on the censors' radar due to the progressive works that it housed); as its title image also appeared to harm the audiences' sense of propriety and the dedication to Prince Waldemar of Prussia was seen as a form of *lèse-majesté*, the books were held back and could only be finally published due to the intervention of Friedrich Wilhelm IV. Brentano von Arnim launched a public discussion of her treatment by the censors, working together with the publication organs of the Young Germans; see Becker-Cantarino and Helga Brandes, "Kampf gegen die Zensur," in Hb 298–301.

[71] Becker-Cantarino, "Die Junghegelianer," in Hb 247.

the king and church, the developments of factory workers in the light of her earlier assessment of Mirabeau as an important theorist behind the French Revolution in *Spring Wreath*, and her thoughts on Napoleon, but also the state of mind of the Young Germans. She firmly believed in her power to influence the king to realize a "monarchy of the people" (Volkskönigtum) in which the king as *primus inter pares* wisely leads a free people. He might have more information, knowledge, and power than his subjects, but this puts an even greater responsibility on his shoulders, as it binds his will to do everything in *their* spirit and interest. Any king, argues the daemon in the subsequent *Conversations with Demons*, who can only point to his lineage, but fails to be accepted by his people, is bound to turn into dust: "the obedience, given to the king by his people, is the spirit of the people [Volksgeist] guiding him, and the people obey in him only their *own* genius . . . and only those who never stop re-enlivening the binding powers between themselves and their people, those *alone* are the bearers of brightly spirited laws [hellgeistiger Gesetze], to which the ruler is bound, and if he ever desists from them, according to the peoples' faith, he will lose divine radiance [Glanz] and be punished by revolt, war, and fall, and death" (*Dämonenbuch*, 336). Brentano von Arnim's insistence on the "conscience of the king" might strike the reader as naïve. But in light of her insistence on the importance of individual worth, her stance is at least somewhat understandable. Moreover, she had facts on her side: *This Book Belongs to the King* concludes with "Experiences of a Young Swiss Man in the 'Voigtland,' "[72] which gives an exact breakdown of financial hardship (impressive lists of income, taxes owed, necessary expenses, debt, items produced within a year, etc.) which explains the abject misery of the poor. With this clear account on the unbearable living and working conditions of the poor, Brentano von Arnim allows her readers to see how important the king's conscience is *in concreto*. Rejecting her advice would be tantamount to a rejection of reality, which would ultimately harm concrete people, and, in the long run, political stability (and thus challenge the king's justification of his own power).[73]

To present her case, Brentano von Arnim once again chooses an engaging format that mixes empirical observations, philosophical arguments, and literary escapades. She lets Frau Rath have a conversation with the representatives of the establishment (the legendary Queen Louise, but also, in the second part, a Lutheran minister and the mayor of Frankfurt, Frau Rath's hometown). Frau Rath then engages in a "Sokratie" (a loose form of a Socratic dialogue that puts her enemies to shame—but also allows us readers to question Frau Rath's beliefs), and the book closes with an even more fantastic "Conversation between Frau Rath and a French Magpie." The magpie ultimately takes

---

[72] She uses Heinrich Grunholzer's notes on the "Vogtländischen Armen" living in the outskirts of Berlin, among others. See Drewitz, *Bettine*, 196, and Pia Schmid, "Erfahrungen eines jungen Schweizers," in Hb 411–416.

[73] A jarring portrait of the inability of the poor to feed themselves we find in the "Story of the Lucky Purse," see WB III, 536–555. It was not published during Brentano von Arnim's lifetime; see Birgit Ebert, "Bettina Brentano-von Arnim's Tale of the Lucky Purse and Clemens Brentano's Story of Good Kasperl and Beautiful Annerl," in Frederiksen and Goodman, *Gender and Politics*, 185–212.

off into "freedom" (WB III, 325–326), while Frau Rath and a "daemon" (WB III, 325) set out in a fantastic and ironic-triumphant journey toward the open sea, accidentally setting Frankfurt on fire—the "fire of freedom" no less (328).

It is quite telling that the reception of the *Königsbuch* is neatly divided among party lines: whereas conservative monarchists read it as half-baked, brazen, and superficial, the opposition could not praise it enough. See, for instance, Gutzkow's comment (in his journal, banned in Prussia) that explicitly links Brentano von Arnim's books with communism (at that point still a vague term): if communism is an expression of the "most burning, most ardent [glühendste] love for humankind,"[74] then Brentano von Arnim's books are in turn an expression of it.

A year after the book's publication, Brentano von Arnim puts her ideas to the test and publishes a note in all newspapers about her plans to publish her observations on the situation of the poor, asking for further input by the public. But since her work concentrated on the weavers who engaged in a revolt that very same year, she pushed her plans back, as they would have been understood as a call for open warfare against the monarchy.[75] She had to be careful to avoid censorship, but she also faced the decline of her influence on the king. Perhaps it was in light of these developments that her last book, the *Dämonenbuch*, seems more careful and more daring at the same time: she reaches out in some directions, while slamming doors shut in others.[76]

In this work she again argues that the true means by which to bring a people together is the perfect king,[77] a king who is held accountable for his actions and lets his subjects make their own decisions. More concretely, she argues against a king who only appeases the nobility at the cost of the citizens (see *Dämonenbuch* 331). Rather, the king should accept the superiority of a "World Religion"[78] that undercuts any attempts to exclude any group of people from state action. She does not formulate a concrete political program, but a general hope for inclusion of the people in the king's reign: "all people must be the organ of the law, all acts must safeguard the law, realize the law, interpret the law" (*Dämonenbuch* 310). Not political power, but the ethics (*Sittlichkeit*) of the people can ultimately guarantee the welfare of the state. We should also read the daemon's dismissal of "dogma and clerical law" as sources of education in this spirit—they can only misguide and twist our education and the ability for self-formation and give birth to "sophism" (*Dämonenbuch* 330; see her rants against common education in *Günderode*, WB I, 468; see 250). It may be that the people are too drawn into the passions of revolution. Both daemon and king seem to agree that the actions of the people in 1848 were motivated by helplessness and passion, and by being too uneducated, impatient, and restless to think

[74] Drewitz, *Bettine*, 200.

[75] See Drewitz, *Bettine*, 203.

[76] With a good sense of irony, the author herself censors the book and blanks out some random lines.

[77] See "An die aufgelöste Preussische National-Versammlung," a brochure that harshly comments on the suppression of the Polish revolution in 1848 (see WB III, esp. 632–636, and Drewitz, *Bettine*, 23–36).

[78] *Dämonenbuch*, 336. This religion seems to have some Spinozistic undertones, which befits her defense of Judaism at the beginning of the book.

about alternatives to revolution. But in the end, once the people are allowed to educate and feed themselves, their actions will be in harmony with the state. "A king who carries the equality of all people in himself shall be invincible" (*Dämonenbuch* 335). Or, in the words of the "proletarian," "we shall put ourselves in a sovereign place within the unity of the people. You will be able, with a strong and calm hand, to . . . guide us wherever you want us to [go], if you enable us to feel ourselves as yours" (*Dämonenbuch* 387).

5 BRENTANO VON ARNIM'S LEGACY

Brentano von Arnim is one of the most interesting, if somewhat late, representatives of early Romanticism. Even though her publications appeared decades after her models, her publications' spirit is expressive of the lively imagination, the fearless mixing of fact and fiction, the daring reach toward a totality of a self with others that is so typical of that earlier age. She is one of the few who did not fall prey to the *salto mortale* (the deadly jump) into religiousness; and she became a beacon of hope for the less privileged with her political work. Ultimately, her work falls somewhere between Romanticism and socialism, and people have grappled with this unique situation, as Fanny Lewald's praise of Brentano von Arnim as a "miracle flower" clearly shows (see section 2 here). As her brother Franz and her brother-in-law Savigny feared, Bettina Brentano von Arnim was an embarrassment for her family to a certain degree: unable to build herself a little pocket-sized heaven,[79] she did not stay within the supposedly "natural" limitations of femininity, but branched out to explore foreign "lands," "in which no feminine happiness is to be found."[80]

At least her first two letter-books were widely recognized, even internationally. Before *Goethe's Correspondence* even appeared, inquiries were made for a translation into English.[81] However, this early project did not come to fruition—mostly due to Brentano von Arnim's unwillingness to allow for a shortened version, and her insistence on phrases that were simply unintelligible to an anglophone ear. As the translator Sarah Austin (1793–1867), herself the author of an influential book on Goethe (*Characteristics of Goethe*, 3 vols., London, 1833), noted, "her conversation is that of a clever woman, with some originality, great conceit, and vast unconscious ignorance. Her sentiments have a bold and noble character. . . . Gleams of truth and sense, clouds of nonsense—all tumbled out with equally undoubting confidence."[82]

Brentano von Arnim tried to translate the book herself, which, given she had no command of the language, turned out to be problematic. Nevertheless, in 1837 and 1838 she had it printed and sent to London for commission. Predictably, sales were

---

[79] See Savigny's letter of January 31, 1807, cited in Härtl, "Briefe Savignys," 117.
[80] Cited in Härtl, "Briefe Savignys," 108.
[81] See a list of translations in Bäumer and Schultz, *Bettina*, bibliography 1.2, 174–177.
[82] Cited in Becker-Cantarino, "Zur Rezeption," in Hb 611.

bad, and reviews even worse.[83] Things were much better in New England, where the Transcendentalists welcomed *Goethe's Correspondence* and in particular *Günderode*, realizing the latter's philosophical potential.[84] It was Margaret Fuller in particular who also brought Brentano von Arnim to the attention of the "leading" American Transcendentalist (at least if we speak of the breadth of reception), Ralph Waldo Emerson.[85] In due time, Brentano von Arnim became the new "cult figure" of the Transcendentalists, who often compared their greatest minds to German figures.[86] Fuller wrote an influential article, "Bettine Brentano and Her Friend Günderode."[87] She did not appreciate, however, *Goethe's Correspondence* as much. To her mind, it should instead have been titled "A Child's Correspondence with Herself."[88] "Bettine's" conversation with "Caroline" in *Die Güderode* Fuller regarded as much more natural, less self-indulgent; a true dialogue between intellectuals about aesthetic appreciation, poetics, and the nature of intellectual inquiry itself. It is unfortunate that even though Fuller contacted Brentano von Arnim in 1840, we do not know of any reply (see Becker-Cantarino, "Zur Rezeption," in Hb, 614). In 1859, Emerson wrote to Brentano von Arnim's daughter Gisela: "I mourned that I could not have earlier established my alliance with your circle, that I might have told how much I and my friends owed her."[89] His review of *This Book Belongs to the King* in the *Dial* (1843) is supportive and correctly identifies "freedom" as Brentano von Arnim's main interest—an interest he also detects in her earlier works, albeit in a less overtly political form. However, he rejects her political ideas as too idealistic. Theodore Parker (1810–1860), the liberal preacher and abolitionist, visited Brentano von Arnim in Berlin in 1843 and summed up her political critique in a similarly skeptical manner: "How the Government will welcome such a book [he references the *Book of the Poor*] is not difficult to see."[90] And he was right.

In Germany, Brentano von Arnim was first mythologized and then marginalized. Gutzkow called her one of the three "German Parcae,"[91] and Mundt referred to her as the "German Sibylle,"[92] but neither engaged with the actual *author* Brentano von Arnim.[93]

---

[83] See Becker-Cantarino, "Zur Rezeption," in Hb 612.

[84] See Becker-Cantarino, *Schriftstellerinnen* and *Handbuch*.

[85] See Charles Capper, *Margaret Fuller: An American Romantic Life*, vol. 2, *The Public Years* (Oxford: Oxford University Press, 2007), 22, and Becker-Cantarino, "Zur Rezeption," in Hb 613.

[86] Capper, *Fuller*, 26: "Sturgis's *Dial* poem *Bettina!* would earn her the sobriquet the 'American Bettina' to match Fuller's tag as the 'American Corinne,' after Mme. de Staël's vivaciously brilliant heroine."

[87] Capper, *Fuller*, 73.

[88] Cited in Capper, *Fuller*, 74.

[89] Cited in Becker-Cantarino, "Zur Rezeption," in Hb614.

[90] Cited in Franklin Benjamin Sanborn, *Recollection of Seventy Years*, vol. 2 (Boston, 1909), 552.

[91] See Gutzkow, *Gesammelte Werke*, vol. 9: *Oeffentliche Charaktere* (Jena, n.d.), 215–232. The others were Rahel Varnhagen and Charlotte Stieglitz (the latter author committed suicide in 1834 to give her husband new inspiration to write).

[92] Mundt, *Geschichte der Literatur der Gegenwart. Vorlesungen* (Berlin, 1842), here 317.

[93] See for instance Marjanne Goozé, "The Reception of Bettina Brentano von Arnim as Author and Historical Figure," in Frederiksen and Goodman, *Gender and Politics*, 349–420, and Ulrike Landfester,

For the following generations, her political interests (as far as they were known) began to look more and more untimely: her idea of a monarchy of the people was outdated, and, as much as she highlighted the situation of the poor, she proved to be blind to other important social factors of her time: the rise of the middle class, and the slowly developing emancipatory movement. One of the few fair treatments of her work is Ricarda Huch's *Die Romantik* (2 vols., 1899, 1902). Only in the 1920s do we find an increased interest in (and the willingness to allow discussion of) her work, not least due to the edition of her works in seven volumes by Waldemar Oehlke.[94] Up into the twentieth century, the German reception of Brentano von Arnim was defined by her family's continued hold on her papers and notes, as well as by the fundamental difference of perspectives in West Germany and East Germany, the former highlighting her romantic genius (even though the positivist Germanistik exhausted itself primarily in the battles concerning the "real" letters underneath her letter-books), the latter her political agenda. Despite the family's attempts to hide the latter, Ruth Krenn was able to confirm Brentano von Arnim's authorship of the papers regarding the revolution in Poland. With the land reforms of the Soviet occupation in eastern Germany, the family manor in Wiepersdorf became "People's Property" (Volkseigentum) and was turned into the Bettina von Arnim Archive. (The first researcher there was Gertrud Meyer-Hepner, pursuing her work on the Magistratsprozess.)[95] No other woman writer was as present in the cultural life in East Germany, in particular during the early years of its formation, as Brentano von Arnim, even though the romantic dimension of her writing was almost entirely ignored. Christa Wolf deeply understood Brentano von Arnim's literary strategies and endorsed them in her own works.[96] During the last years of the German Democratic Republic (1986–1998), Heinz Härtl started a careful and brilliant edition for the *Stiftung Weimarer Klassik* (still unfinished); the now canonical edition in West Germany was produced by Walter Schmitz and Sibylle von Steinsdorff in four volumes between 1986 and 2004 (and still lacks an edition of *Conversations with Demons*).

Befittingly, many encounter Brentano von Arnim not through her own work but through a quasi-fictional character of the same name in another novel: Milan Kundera's *Immortality* (1988), which offers an ambivalent, but reluctantly admiring portrait of the cunning and verbose wannabe-child that only wants "to bathe in the light of [Goethe's] celebrity." Kundera understood Brentano von Arnim's play with perspectives and personae as a power play, as he often stresses that Goethe had every right to be afraid of

"Von Frau zu Frau? Einige Bemerkungen über historische und ahistorische Weiblichkeitsdiskurse in der Rezeption Bettina von Arnims," in *Jahrbuch Bettina von Arnim Gesellschaft* 8/9 (1996/97), 201–222.

[94] Bettina von Arnim, *Sämtliche Werke*, ed. Waldemar Oehlke, 7 vols. (Berlin: Propyläen, 1920), 22.

[95] See Hannelore Scholz-Lübbering, "Rezeption und Forschung in der DDR," in Hb 639.

[96] See in particular her *Kein Ort. Nirgends—No Place on Earth*, which appeared simultaneously in 1979 in West Germany (Darmstadt: Luchterhand) and East Germany (Berlin: Aufbau) (English translation by Jan van Heurck, New York: Farrar Strauss Giroux, 1982), her collecction "Der Schatten eines Traumes. Karoline von Günderrode—Ein Entwurf," München: dtv, 1997 and "Nun ja! Das nächste Leben geht aber heute an. Ein Brief über die Bettine" (1979; trans. in Frederiksen and Goodman, *Gender and Politics*, 35–67).

Bettine since she used her public persona to shape Goethe's legacy—not just to share his status, but also to establish her own.

Research on Brentano von Arnim had grown and become more serious and seemingly less ideologically restricted in the last thirty years. The most impressive testament to this is Barbara Becker-Cantarino's *Bettina von Arnim Handbuch*, published with de Gruyter in 2019, which brings together some of the most important scholars of Brentano von Arnim in Germany and offers many valuable articles on all aspects of her life and work, many of which I have cited here. Reception in anglophone countries will surely increase with Nassar and Gjesdal's *Women Philosophers in the Long Nineteenth Century: The German Tradition* (2021), which will enable students to learn about Brentano von Arnim and her colleagues.

Even though female philosophers are still not quite taken up in the canon, Brentano von Arnim's work is by now relatively well-known and studied, the main blank spaces still being the later works. Goozé might still be right that the first encounter with her work will almost always feel personal—we still tend to pose already well-known and well-answered questions *as if for the first time*; we still tend to discuss "the relationship between form and subjectivity, life and art, politics and idealism, and feminism and the 'feminine'" in order to get closer to the center of her work.[97] Here is to hope that this article may invite its readers to do the same.

BIBLIOGRAPHY

Bäumer, Konstanze. *Bettine, Psyche, Mignon. Bettina von Arnim und Goethe.* Stuttgart: Akademischer Verlag 1986.
Bäumer, Konstanze. "*Ilius Pamphilius und die Ambrosia.* Bettina von Arnim als Mentorin." *Jahrbuch Bettina von Arnim Gesellschaft* 3 (1989): 263–282.
Bäumer, Konstanze. "Interdependenzen zwischen mündlicher und schriftlicher Expressivität." In "*Der Geist muss Freiheit genießen!" Studien zu Werk und Bildungsprogramm Bettine von Arnims,* edited by Walter Schmitz and Sibylle von Steinsdorff, 154–173. Berlin: Albin, 1992.
Bäumer, Konstanze, and Hartwig Schultz. *Bettina von Arnim.* Stuttgart: Metzler, 1995.
Becker-Cantarino, Barbara, ed. *Bettina von Arnim Handbuch.* Berlin: de Gruyter, 2019.
Becker-Cantarino, Barbara. *Schriftstellerinnen der Romantik: Epoche, Werk, Wirkung.* Munich: Beck, 2000.
Bunzel, Wolfgang. "Von Herz zu Herz? Zum textlogischen Status und sozialhistorischen Kontext der Familienbriefe Bettine von Arnims." In *Dieses Buch gehört den Kindern. Achim und Bettine von Arnim und ihre Nachfahren,* edited by Ulrike Landfester and Hartwig Schultz, 37–81. Berlin: Albin, 2004.
Bunzel, Wolfgang, and Ulrike Landfester. *Bettine von Arnims Briefwechsel mit ihren Söhnen.* 3 vols. Göttingen: Wallstein, 1999–2012.
Bürger, Christa, and Birgit Diefenbach, editors' introduction to Bettina von Arnim Lesebuch (Leipzig: Reclam, 1987).

[97] Goozé, "Reception," 349–350.

Capper, Charles. *Margaret Fuller: An American Romantic Life*. Vol. 2, *The Public Years*. Oxford: Oxford University Press, 2007.

Daley, Margaretmary. *Women of Letters: A Study of Self and Genre in the Personal Writings of Caroline Schlegel-Schelling, Rahel Levin Varnhagen, and Bettina von Arnim*. Rochester, NY: Camden House, 1998.

Diefenbach, Birgitt. "Zur Einführung." In *Bettina von Arnim Lesebuch*, edited by Birgit Diefenbach and Christa Bürger, 5–8. Leipzig: Reclam, 1987.

Drewitz, Ingeborg. *Bettine von Arnim: Romantik, Revolution, Utopie*. Berlin: Bertelsmann, 1984.

Frederiksen, Elke, and Katherine Goodman, eds. *Bettina Brentano von Arnim: Gender and Politics*. Detroit: Wayne State University Press, 1995.

Frederiksen, Elke, and Katherine Goodman. "Locating Bettina Brentano von Arnim, a Nineteenth Century German Woman Writer." In *Bettina Brentano von Arnim: Gender and Politics*, edited by Elke Frederiksen and Katherine Goodman, 13–34. Detroit: Wayne State University Press, 1995.

French, Lorely. "Strategies of Female Persuasion: The Political Letters of Bettina Brentano von Arnim." In *Bettina Brentano von Arnim: Gender and Politics*, edited by Elke Frederiksen and Katherine Goodman, 71–94. Detroit: Wayne State University Press, 1995.

Frey, Karl Otto, and Theodore Ziolkowski, eds. *Heidelberger Romantik. Mythos und Symbol*. Heidelberg: Winter, 2009.

Fuchs, Renata. "I Drink Love to Get Strong": Bettina Brentano von Arnim's Romantic Philosophy and Dialogue in *Die Günderode*." *Women in German Yearbook* 32 (2016): 1–24.

Gjesdal, Kristin, and Dalia Nassar, eds. *Women Philosophers in the Long Nineteenth Century: The German Tradition*. Oxford: Oxford University Press, 2021.

Goodman, Katherine. *Dis/Closures: Women's Autobiography in Germany between 1790 and 1914*. New York: Lang, 1986.

Goodman, Katherine. "Through a Different Lens: Bettina Brentano von Arnim's Views on Gender." In *Bettina Brentano von Arnim: Gender and Politics*, edited by Elke Frederiksen and Katherine Goodman, 115–141. Detroit: Wayne State University Press, 1995.

Goozé, Marjanne. "The Reception of Bettina von Arnim as Author and Historical Figure." In *Bettina Brentano von Arnim: Gender and Politics*, edited by Elke Frederiksen and Katherine Goodman, 349–420. Detroit: Wayne State University Press, 1995.

von Günderrode, Karolin *Gesammelte Werke*. Edited by L. Hirschberg. 3 vols. Berlin: Goldschmidt-Gabrielli, 1920–22.

Gutzkow, *Gesammelte Werke*. Jena: Hermann Costenoble, 1876.

Härtl, Heinz. "Briefe Friedrich Carl von Savignys an Bettina Brentano." *Wissenschaftliche Zeitschrift der Universität Halle* 28 (1979): 105–128.

Härtl, Heinz. "Dies Völkchen mit der vorkämpfenden Alten: Bettina von Arnim und die Junghegelianer." *Jahrbuch des Freien Deutschen Hochstifts* (1992): 213–254.

Isselstein, Ursula. "Briefwechsel als Bildungsprojekt. Dialogische Konstellationen im Frühlingskranz Bettine von Arnims." In *Die Brentanos. Eine europäische Familie*, edited by Konrad Feilchenfeldt and Luciano Zagari, 208–218. Tübingen: Niemeyer, 1992.

Landfester, Ulrike. *Selbstsorge als Staatskunst. Bettine von Arnims politisches Werk*. Würzburg: Königshausen&Neumann, 2000.

Landfester, Ulrike. "Von Frau zu Frau? Einige Bemerkungen über historische und ahistorische Weiblichkeitsdiskurse in der Rezeption Bettina von Arnims." *Jahrbuch Bettina von Arnim Gesellschaft* 8/9 (1996/97): 201–222.

Leitner, Ingrid. "Liebe und Erkenntnis: Kommunikationsstrukturen bei Bettine von Arnim: Ein Vergleich fiktiven Sprechens mit Gesprächen im Salon." In *Salons der Romantik: Beiträge eines Wiepersdorfer Kolloquiums zu Theorie und Geschichte des Salons*, edited by Hartwig Schultz, 235–251. Berlin: de Gruyter, 1997.

Leitner, Ingrid, and Sibylle von Steinsdorff. "Die vollkommenste Grammatik der Liebe, die jemals komponiert wurde. Thesen zum poetischen Verfahren Bettine von Arnims in 'Goethe's Briefwechsel mit einem Kinde.'" *Jahrbuch Bettina von Arnim Gesellschaft* 6/7 (1994/95): 143–157.

Lewald, Fanny. "Der Cultus des Genius. Ein Brief an Bettina von Arnim." *Blätter für literarische Unterhaltung* 171–174 (July 18–21, 1849), 681–683, 685–687, 689–690, 694–695.

Liebertz-Grün, Ursula. *Ordnung im Chaos. Studien zur Poetik der Bettine Brentano von Arnim.* Heidelberg: Winter, 1989.

Meyer-Hepner, Gertrud. *Der Magistratsprozess der Bettina von Arnim.* Weimar: Arion, 1960.

Mundt, Theodor. *Geschichte der Literatur der Gegenwart. Vorlesungen.* Berlin: M. Simion, 1842.

Ockenfuß, Solveig. *Bettine von Arnims Briefromane: Literarische Erinnerungsarbeit zwischen Anspruch und Wirklichkeit.* Opladen: Westdeutscher Verlag, 1992.

Pollok, Anne. "On Self-Formation: The Role of Writing and Sociability for the Philosophy of Henriette Herz, Rahel Levin Varnhagen, and Bettina von Arnim." In *Women and Philosophy in Eighteenth-Century Germany*, edited by Corey W. Dyck, 195–209. Oxford: Oxford University Press, 2021.

Pompe, Hedwig. *Der Wille zum Glück: Bettine von Arnims Poetik der Naivität im Briefroman Die Günderode.* Bielefeld: Aisthesis, 1999.

Sanborn, Franklin Benjamin. *Recollection of Seventy Years*, vol. 2. Boston: R.G. Badger, 1909.

Schultz, Hartwig. *"Unsere Lieb aber ist außerkohren": Die Geschichte der Geschwister Clemens und Bettine Brentano.* Frankfurt/M: Insel, 2004.

Shafi, Monika. "The Myth of Psyche as Developmental Paradigm in Bettine Brentano von Arnim's Epistolary Novels." In *Bettina Brentano von Arnim: Gender and Politics*, edited by Elke Frederiksen and Katherine Goodman, 95–114. Detroit: Wayne State University Press, 1995.

Stone, Alison. "Bettina von Arnim's Romantic Philosophy in *Die Günderode*." *Hegel Bulletin* 43.3 (2022): 1–24. https://doi.org/10.1017/hgl.2021.19.

von Arnim, Bettina. *Werke und Briefe in vier Bänden.* Edited by Walter Schmitz and Sibylle Steinsdorff. 4 vols. Frankfurt/M: Deutscher Klassiker Verlag, 1986–2004.

von Arnim, Bettina. *Gespräche mit Dämonen.* In von Arnim, *Werke und Briefe*, vol. 1, edited by Gustav Konrad, 258–407. Frechen: Bartmann, 1959.

Waldstein, Edith. *Bettine von Arnim and the Politics of Romantic Conversation.* Columbia, SC: Camden House, 1988.

Werner, Johannes. *Maxe von Arnim: Tochter Bettinas/Gräfin von Oriola (1818–1894).* Leipzig: v. Hase & Koehler, 1937.

Wilhelmy-Dollinger, Petra. *Die Berliner Salons. Mit kulturhistorischen Spaziergängen.* Berlin: de Gruyter, 2000.

Willison, Ann. "Bettina Brentano von Arnim: The Unknown Musician." In *Bettina von Arnim: Gender and Politics*, edited by Elke Frederiksen and Katherine Goodman, 304–345. Detroit: Wayne State University Press, 1995.

CHAPTER 7

FANNY LEWALD (1811–1889)

ULRIKE WAGNER

THIS essay takes up a line of investigation that has played a crucial role in the critical literature on Fanny Lewald (1811–1889), namely the relationships among her life, her work, and the philosophical tradition of the Enlightenment. As Ulrike Stamm astutely points out, Lewald is an exception among nineteenth-century female authors because reason constitutes the leading category of her self-understanding and activities as a writer.[1] To be sure, critics have always acknowledged her commitment to Enlightenment values and beliefs; but the specific ways in which key philosophical tenets and controversies of the time shape her writing and thinking has hardly been detailed (though Stamm's investigation of Lewald's uses and conceptualizations of reason stands as an important exception). In conversation with recent criticism, I focus on this neglected area of scholarship and ask what it really means to examine Lewald as a thinker of the Enlightenment.

More specifically, the subsequent sections investigate from different angles how Lewald reworks central themes, narratives, and arguments from contemporary debates in religious philosophy, and how she engages Kant's response to what was arguably the most pressing concern of her generation, namely the formulation of answers to the question "What is Enlightenment?" Section 1 is an introduction to Lewald's life, work, reception, and the Enlightenment tradition. Section 2 centers on resonances of Baruch Spinoza, Gotthold Ephraim Lessing, Moses Mendelssohn, and discourses of the Haskalah or Jewish Enlightenment in Lewald's early novel *Jenny*. In dialogue with these thinkers and debates, Jenny envisions a model of trans-confessional tolerance that gestures beyond the conflicts and struggles she and other members of her social circles find themselves in. The dualist categories of successful or unsuccessful emancipation which critics have commonly applied in assessing the novel cannot sufficiently accommodate the theological position and mode of faith introduced here. Hence, I suggest examining *Jenny*'s position within the wide-ranging contemporary critical religious

---

[1] Ulrike Stamm, "Fanny Lewald: Autorschaft im Zeichen der Vernunft," *Zeitschrift für Germanistik* 22, no. 1 (2012): 130.

discourses Lewald was tapping into. Following in the footsteps of leading voices of her generation, she reflects on questions of religious truth as processes tied to ethical practices in daily life.

Taking their cue from Mendelssohn and, crucially, Lessing's *Nathan the Wise*, a prototypical work of Enlightenment thinking, Jenny and her father discuss the individual's responsibility in separating religion in its historical manifestations from the spirit of religion, and Jenny envisions a future where her own liberal views and her fiancé's orthodoxy can peacefully coexist. Section 3 examines how Lewald draws on the same stock of religious arguments, images, and narratives to reshape her contemporaries' views of women's roles. Just as the history of religion does not answer questions of divine legitimacy and authenticity, the history of women does not provide a definition of how women ought to be and live. In rewriting Lessing's "Parable of the Palace," *Jenny* suggests that there is no historical foundation for a narrowly defined understanding of womanhood and promotes plural forms of existence. Lewald's political writings, I demonstrate, are pragmatically oriented and aimed at supporting such plural forms. Throughout texts such as the *Easter Letters for Women* (*Osterbriefe für Frauen*, 1863) and the letters *For and against Women* (*Für und Wider Frauen*, 1870), she is concerned with mapping out cogent plans for the social, political, and institutional conditions under which women have equal rights to education and work. Her focus, in other words, is less on how woman ought to *be* and more on the circumstances under which she can *become*.

Contemporary readers might wonder why Lewald was not more invested in depicting assertive women, guided by the primacy of reason, freed from the normative chains of society, and leading exemplarily emancipated lives. An answer, I propose, lies in how she experienced people's struggles of maturing or becoming *mündig* (to borrow a key word from Kant). In section 4, this essay turns to resonances of Kant's response to the question "What is Enlightenment" in Lewald's life and work. Frequently echoing Kant's text, her political, fictional, and autobiographical writings are all deeply concerned with the vexed issue of the individual's striving for maturity, or *Mündigkeit*, as it occupied women and men of all social and religious backgrounds. Her writings record her own emancipatory battles and those of other women as well as the ones she witnessed in religious debates or the rebellious activities in the revolutionary years, recorded in her *Recollections of the Year 1848* (*Erinnerungen aus dem Jahre 1848*, 1850). She observed how people vacillated between breaking away from habitual behaviors and withdrawing into what seemed to be the normal and familiar. Being a pragmatic, realistic, and deeply historical thinker, she felt obliged to give her fictional characters a historical grounding: "in my opinion the main figure or group of characters who make up the main motif [of a novel] have to be given a broad cultural-historical basis, like the column on which a work of [sculptural] art is raised, because we are historians through and through, and because in every novel there is also a biographical element."[2] *Feelings and Thoughts (Gefühles und*

---

[2] Fanny Lewald, *Gefühltes und Gedachtes 1838–1888*, ed. Ludwig Geiger (Dresden: Minden, 1900), 146–147. Translated in Margaret E. Ward, *Fanny Lewald: Between Rebellion and Renunciation* (New York: Peter Lang, 2006), 285.

Gedachtes, 1838–88), her collection of remarks and aphorisms, demonstrates that she views her works as growing out of, and deeply embedded in, her biography and time. It follows naturally from such an outlook and her experiences with people's struggles for independence that she would prioritize pragmatic concepts for change in some areas of social life over grandiose definitions of abstract terms such as *autonomy* or *emancipation*. Given her enormous literary output, much research is still to be done, but the works assembled here suggest that her main focus lies in creating the social and educational conditions that would promote plural and open-ended forms of *Selbstaufklärung*, a lasting process of self-education in the Enlightenment tradition.

1 LIFE, WORK, RECEPTION, AND THE ENLIGHTENMENT TRADITION

Fanny Lewald was a best-selling, popular, and respected woman writer in nineteenth century Germany.[3] She was born in 1811 into an educated, bourgeois Jewish merchant family in the East Prussian port town of Königsberg, the oldest of the eight children of Zippora and David Marcus. Her father later changed his legal name to the more German-sounding Lewald and was overall unconcerned about Jewish religious traditions (ML I: 366–368).[4] The family was not observant, and Fanny, like some of her siblings, converted in her youth to Christianity.[5] Her immense oeuvre includes twenty-seven novels and over thirty novellas and stories, as well as travelogues, autobiographical texts, shorter memoirs, personal letters, journalistic writings, and journal articles.[6] She was deeply engaged in the most pressing political questions of her time, as works such as her eyewitness account of Europe's revolution, *Recollections of the Year 1848*, testify. Brought up in the spirit of the Enlightenment, she was a fervent advocate for liberal ideas and universal human rights. In her three-volume autobiography, *The Story of My Life* (*Meine Lebensgeschichte*, 1861–62), she characterizes her writing as *Tendenzliteratur*, as engaged literature composed always with an eye toward a defined set of political and moral purposes (ML III: 35–36). The didactic orientation of her works grew out of her experience as both a female and a Jewish writer. This twin identity forced her to deal

---

[3] On the distribution and financial success of Lewald's publications, see Dagmar C. G. Lorenz, *Keepers of the Motherland: German Texts by Jewish Women Writers* (Lincoln : University of Nebraska Press, 1997), 37.

[4] Fanny Lewald, *Gesammelte Werke*, vols. 1–3, *Meine Lebensgeschichte* (Berlin: Verlag von Otto Janke, 1871), hereafter ML (vol. no. in roman numeral, followed by page number). Unless otherwise indicated, translations from Lewald's works are my own.

[5] On the family's relationship to matters of religious observance, see also Ward, *Fanny Lewald*, 31.

[6] For a bibliography of Lewald's works, see Marieluise Steinhauer, *Fanny Lewald, die deutsche George Sand: Ein Kapitel aus der Geschichte des Frauenromans im 19. Jahrhundert* (Berlin: K&R Hoffmann, 1937), 131–137. For an overview of Lewald's published texts and unpublished manuscripts see Ward, *Fanny Lewald*, 17.

with limitations, hostilities, and prejudices throughout her life, and questions of empowerment for women, especially for those with a Jewish or otherwise socially disadvantaged background, became the dominant topic in her writings.

Shortly after her death, Helene Lange and Gertrud Bäumer, pioneer figures and leading activists in the international and German civil rights feminist movement, acknowledged Lewald's groundbreaking impact on the movement.[7] Her later essays, such as the widely discussed *Easter Letters for Women* and *For and Against Women*, are dedicated specifically to the cause of women, and other works such as her autobiography and her early novels *Clementine* (1843), *Jenny* (1843), and *A Life Question* (*Eine Lebensfrage*, 1845) are also often discussed in this context. The three anonymously published fictional works are concerned with topics such as the marriage of convenience, divorce, and how the social and legal situation of Prussia's Jewish population informed intermarriage between Jews and Christians.

Lewald's father had prohibited her claiming authorship for her first publications. Fearing his family's reputation and diminishing marriage prospects for his daughters, he expressed his doubts about his first-born's intentions to publish her work and her involvement in politics and other matters of public interest. Reluctantly, he gave her permission to publish under the condition that she keep her activities to herself and remain anonymous. In recapitulating the life-changing conversation she had with her father as a thirty-year-old aspiring writer, Lewald reverts to direct speech in her autobiography; readers recognize quickly that she uses this form of direct address frequently to highlight moments of significance or turning points in her life.[8] The discussion over her first major publication obviously marks such a life-changing moment, and it also paradigmatically stages the complex power dynamic between her and her father. The structure of their conversation exemplifies how her father's opinions formed her thinking and guided her decision-making throughout her life: " 'You are really thinking of beginning a longer work; do you want to be a writer?' 'Yes, if you have nothing against it, dear Father.' He shrugged his shoulders as he was wont to do, when he was involved with something he did not like. That hurt me" (*An Autobiography* 214).[9]

Lewald's autobiographical recollections of her father's reluctant response to her professional plans evokes understanding and sympathy in her rather than a decidedly oppositional stance as one might expect, given how strongly she feels about her work (ML II: 397–398). At the same time, however, she was adamant about following her own agenda in her writing. She firmly conveys to him that her writings will treat any relevant topic the way it ought to be treated, regardless of hurt feelings or concerns any family

---

[7] Helene Lange and Gertrud Bäumer, eds., *Handbuch der Frauenbewegung* (Berlin: Moeser, 1901); Gertrud Bäumer, "Fanny Lewald," *Die Frau. Monatsschrift für das gesamte Frauenleben unserer Zeit* 18 (1910–11): 487–491. Bäumer highlights Lewald's crucial role in paving the way for an entire generation to "come to their senses." Cited in Gabriele Schneider, *Fanny Lewald* (Reinbek: Rowohlt, 1996), 143.

[8] On Lewald's use of direct speech in her autobiography, see Ward, *Fanny Lewald*, 81.

[9] Fanny Lewald, *The Education of Fanny Lewald: An Autobiography*, ed. and trans. Hanna Ballin Lewis (Albany: State University of New York Press, 1992). This abridged translation of *Meine Lebensgeschichte* will hereafter be cited in the text as *An Autobiography*.

members might have: "'I mean, when I work, I take off my kid gloves and take hold firmly with my bare hand. If I am to write, I will have to be able to state exactly what I think and touch on every subject that seems appropriate to me. I cannot pay attention to what you want to hear from me, or what you want to let the children (that is what we were referred to as a whole) hear'" (*An Autobiography* 215). Taking the *Bildungsroman* tradition as her model, the adult Lewald looks at this biographical crossroad of her younger self with a clear awareness of her calling and the price it comes with. But instead of confronting her father with no alternative to her chosen path, she highlights her willingness to renounce her plans and ambitions if her father feels unable to give his seal of approval: "I saw that my demands and plans were awkward and undesirable for my father, and I explained that if he was not agreeable to them, I was still willing to give up the fulfillment of my wishes" (*An Autobiography* 215).

Finally—albeit with reservations and restrictions—David Lewald acquiesced to his daughter's career choice; her novels were successful from the beginning, and he soon permitted her to publish under her own name. Such tentative support did not, however, fundamentally destabilize the hierarchical power dynamic between father and daughter, which runs like a red thread through her autobiographical writings and resonates in the relationships of her fictional characters.

This tension between her comprehensive emancipatory agenda on the one hand and her subservient behavior and affirmation of patriarchal norms on the other informs much critical writing on her life and work.[10] Many scholarly publications gesture at her ambivalent stance on issues of emancipation already in their titles, which juxtapose terms such as *respectability, resignation, discipline*, and *renunciation* with *rebellion, deviance*, or *daydreaming*.[11] These dichotomies have structured critical accounts of her biography as well as investigations of her political writings, her essays on female education, and her fictional works.[12] Ward points out that Lewald's inconsistent position on matters related to the emancipation of women and their participation in many domains of work

---

[10] For an overview of Lewald's international reception, see Christina Ujma, ed., *Fanny Lewald (1811–1889): Studien zu einer großen europäischen Schriftstellerin und Intellektuellen* (Bielefeld: Aisthesis, 2011), 18–35; Ward, *Fanny Lewald*, 17–26; Brigitta van Rheinberg, *Fanny Lewald. Geschichte einer Emanzipation* (Frankfurt am Main: Campus, 1990), 21–36.

[11] Compare Ruth-Ellen Boetcher Joeres, *Respectability and Deviance: Nineteenth-Century German Women Writers and the Ambiguity of Representation* (Chicago: University of Chicago Press, 1998); Christina Ujima, "Zwischen Rebellion und Resignation: Frauen, Juden und Künstler in den historischen Romanen Fanny Lewalds," in *Travellers in Time and Space. The German Historical Novel*, ed. Osman Durrani and Julian Preece (Amsterdam: Rodopi, 2001), 283–299; Regula Venske, "Discipline and Daydreaming in the Works of a Nineteenth-Century Woman Author: Fanny Lewald," in *German Women in the Eighteenth and Nineteenth Centuries*, ed. Ruth-Ellen B. Joeres and Mary Jo Maynes (Bloomington: Indiana University Press, 1983), 175–192; Ward, *Fanny Lewald*.

[12] According to Gabriele Schneider's biography, *Fanny Lewald* (Hamburg: Rowohlt, 1996), the contradictory nature of her continuous vacillation between "conformity and revolt" determined Lewald's life, writing, and political engagement throughout, making it challenging for modern readers to relate to her (8). Vanessa van Ornam's conclusion to her monograph *Fanny Lewald and Nineteenth-Century Constructions of Femininity* (New York: Peter Lang, 2002), is structured around the same dichotomy (168).

and social life clarifies why leading voices of feminist criticism and activism in the 1980s and 1990s turned away from her: "those who were looking for more radical foremothers were dissatisfied with her willingness to quell her rebellious impulses and to present herself as conforming to traditional norms, both social and linguistic. She was thought to be too male-identified, her positions cautious and pragmatic."[13]

Lewald's criticism of the past decade has become more diverse, and scholars have approached her life and work from a variety of fresh perspectives. Her inconsistency in matters of emancipation is not always the dominant concern, and some have critically scrutinized the secondary literature and its persistent concentration on the shortcomings and contradictory dynamics of Lewald's works. Traci O'Brien, for instance, argues that the insistent scholarly focus on questions of resistance and conformity has obscured our view of other relevant aspects of her writing such as the role that categories of race play in her emancipatory project.[14] Julia Kuehn's recent essay is the first to provide a serious engagement with Lewald's understudied reflections on poesis and the realist aesthetics of her novels.[15] And the collected volume edited by Christina Ujma displays the wide-ranging international networks in which Lewald's writings evolved, and also the mentoring function she had for other contemporary authors.[16] We have thus gained a more comprehensive and nuanced view of her many political and social engagements, and also of writings that had previously been ignored.

2 *JENNY* AND THE PHILOSOPHY OF RELIGION

A bestseller at the time, *Jenny* is among Lewald's most widely read and admired novels. This story of a young Jewish woman, Jenny Meier, who falls in love with her tutor, Gustav Reinhard, also occupies a prominent place in the critical literature. Among Lewald's

---

[13] Ward, *Fanny Lewald*, 24. Sigrid Weigel refers to Lewald and her female fictional characters as prime examples of women who have completely internalized the male gaze and cannot but view the world through the eyes of a man; "Der schielende Blick. Thesen zur Geschichte weiblicher Schreibpraxis," in *Die verborgene Frau: Sechs Beiträge zu einer feministischen Literaturwissenschaft* (Berlin: Argument, 1983), 98. Similarly, Regula Venske and Renate Möhrmann draw into view how her emancipatory ambitions are continuously undermined by her inability to break free from patriarchal norms, rendering a truly emancipatory stance impossible. Compare Regula Venske, *Ach Fanny! Vom jüdischen Mädchen zur preußischen Schriftstellerin: Fanny Lewald* (Berlin: Elefanten Press, 1988); Renate Möhrmann, *Die andere Frau. Emanzipationsansätze deutscher Schriftstellerinnen im Vorfeld der Achtundvierziger Revolution* (Stuttgart: Metzler, 1977).

[14] See Traci S. O'Brien, *Enlightened Reactions: Emancipation, Gender, and Race in German Women's Writing* (Bern: Peter Lang, 2011), 157–234.

[15] Julia Kuehn, "Realism's Connections: George Eliot's and Fanny Lewald's Poetics," *George Eliot—George Henry Lewes Studies* 68, no. 2 (2016): 91–115. On Lewald's aesthetics and its relation to gender, see Peter M. McIsaac, "Rethinking Tableaux Vivants and Triviality in the Writings of Johann Wolfgang von Goethe, Johanna Schopenhauer, and Fanny Lewald," *Monatshefte* 99, no. 2 (2007): 152–176.

[16] Ujma, *Fanny Lewald*.

fictional texts, *Jenny* is the one that brings together the themes of gender inequality and religious prejudice most powerfully. Discrimination against women and Jews, the two subjects that preoccupied Lewald throughout her career, advance the plot development of her second novel at every stage, leading up to dramatic clashes between different characters. While Reinhard trains to become a Protestant minister and is a stern proponent of Christian dogma, Jenny comes from a wealthy, highly educated bourgeois Jewish family. Raised by her father in the tradition of Enlightenment thinking, she must summon all her willpower to repress her doubts of the tenets of Reinhard's belief and to convert to Christianity so that they can get married.

Critics have mostly focused on how—and how well—the novel succeeds in its implicit plea to respect the diverse religious beliefs and practices of individuals, even if they differ from one's own, and how the plot addresses women's emancipation. Scholars have highlighted how Lewald exposes discriminatory practices and demonstrates their absurdity and untenability against the backdrop of the Enlightenment's advocacy of universal human rights and rational principles. Particularly insightful in this context are critical works focusing on the novel's engagement with the ongoing legal restrictions leveled against Prussia's Jewish population and the daily social struggles and discrimination they faced.[17] The Prussian Jewish population's day-to-day life was determined by constantly changing provisions and prohibitions concerning taxes, customs regulations, protection money, limited professional options, and strict governmental control over the number of Jewish families allowed to reside in a given city.[18]

I want to turn from this well-explored sociohistorical context to the philosophical tradition Lewald's *Jenny* responds to. How does the novel engage central themes and arguments from contemporary debates in religious philosophy?[19] We find key ideas of the period's most prominent philosophical voices, such as Lessing, Mendelssohn, and Spinoza, refracted in the text. In this philosophical context, it is important to note that Lewald herself is at pains to stress that terminological minutiae and a systematic philosophical approach are not among her principal concerns:

> Neither in my youth nor any later point have I been able to absorb grandiose, perfected systems or use philosophical textbooks to my advantage. That is because I always had to fully appropriate what was foreign to me before it could become meaningful or useful for me. I also think that the independent development of a single proposition is more useful for people—especially for people without particular talent and unaccustomed to studying foreign theories—than familiarizing themselves with large quantities of thoughts that others have come up with. Systematic textbooks and theories have always frightened and confused me because I often felt

---

[17] For further references, see the critical overview in O'Brien, *Enlightened Reactions*, 177–184.

[18] On the situation of Jews in Prussia see Christopher Clark, *Iron Kingdom: The Rise and Downfall of Prussia, 1600–1947* (Cambridge, MA: Harvard University Press, 2006), 258–259, 583–587.

[19] On Lewald's engagement with Spinozist pantheism and its manifestations in Goethe, Ludwig Feuerbach, and David Strauss, see Stamm, "Fanny Lewald," 138.

that they were too powerful. The single, active word, however, or witnessing a specific action was useful and encouraged me. (ML I: 350–351)

This passage from her autobiography sums up succinctly where her philosophical interests lie. Philosophical terms and fragments of complex argumentative constructs are a source of inspiration for her, but she appropriates them for the purpose of authorizing and strengthening her emancipatory ideas and agenda. Her practical approach to philosophy corroborates Jürgen Habermas's observation regarding the special role Enlightenment thinking played for Germany's Jewish population. Their commitment to philosophy, he states, led not to detached study confined to academic circles, but rather to a practical project that tied in directly with issues of urgent social and political change; they regarded the "realization of philosophy" as essential to their lives and well-being in family and society.[20]

For Jenny it is nothing less than her marriage that depends on both partners' capacity and motivation to embrace principles of the Enlightenment ideal of religious tolerance. To be sure, gender inequality and their family's different religious confessions also help explain why their relationship fails—yet these are not, I would argue, the deciding factors.[21] Rather, that failure stems from Reinhard's unwillingness to let reason guide his thinking and adopt Jenny's uncompromising opposition to any form of religious dogmatism, be it Christian or Jewish.

Jenny has grown up with a perspective on religion that resonates with Lewald's understanding of Spinozist pantheism. Frankly admitting to her lack of philosophic discipline and training, and her rather rudimentary grasp of Spinoza's *Ethics*, Lewald asks her friend "Doctor Waldeck" to formulate in a concise sentence what he takes to be the "basic premise of Spinozism"; and Waldeck's response that "everything that exists, is God!" then becomes the "regulator" for her "thinking, loving, actions" (*An Autobiography* 302–303). In the novel it is Jenny's father who has taught his daughter since childhood what it means to view her surroundings as manifestations of the divine. As a young adult, Jenny has fully embraced her father's teachings and defends them passionately in the regular meetings with her pastor, hired by Reinhard with the purpose of familiarizing her with Protestant dogma.[22]

---

[20] Compare Jürgen Habermas, *Theorie und Praxis. Sozialphilosophische Studien* (Frankfurt a.M.: Suhrkamp, 1993), 89.

[21] In discussing the existing *Jenny* criticism, O'Brien also highlights its dual argumentative structure of conformity and resistance. As pointed out in the first part of this essay, this direction of argument prevails in the majority of research on Lewald. Generally speaking, the critical assessments of *Jenny* center on how the novel exposes stereotypes of Jewishness and femininity while also reproducing them in different ways. Compare Möhrmann, *Die andere Frau*; Gudrun Marci-Boehncke, *Fanny Lewald: Jüdin, Preußin, Schriftstellerin: Studien zu autobiographischem Werk und Kontext* (Stuttgart: Heinz, 1998); Irene Stocksieker Di Maio, "Jewish Emancipation and Integration: Fanny Lewald's Narrative Strategies," in *Autoren damals und heute. Literaturgeschichtliche Beispiele veränderter Wirkungshorizonte* (Amsterdam: Rodopi, 1991), 273–302.

[22] On Lewald's reception of pantheism and its relationship to Judaism, see also Karin Tebben, *Literarische Intimität: Subjektkonstitution und Erzählstruktur in autobiographischen Texten von Frauen* (Tübingen: Francke, 1997), 62–64.

She tries hard to deceive herself into thinking she can accept Reinhard's strict views on incarnation and the Trinity while also finding a way to harmonize his faith with her own pantheistic outlook. However, both her father and her cousin Joseph, as well as Reinhard's mother, recognize early on that her plans equal attempts at squaring the circle. When Joseph learns of his cousin's upcoming conversion, he lets her know in no uncertain terms that he does not see a way for someone who is used to "evaluat[ing] everything according to standards of reason" to become a Christian capable of meeting Reinhard's expectations: "You were raised in a certain school of thought, if I may say so, and you have therefore been deprived of the option to adopt faith without scrutiny. You will hopefully become a human being in accordance with the heart of God, but you will never be a Christian or Jewess."[23] He recalls to her that she was raised with the idea that identity is a continuous process of becoming, and that honing the faculty of reason takes center stage in this process. Such faith in rational scrutiny and *Bildung* of the self as a way of relating to God, he states, contrasts sharply with the rigid rules and orthodox beliefs associated with the revealed religions, whether Christianity or Judaism.

Fully absorbed by her love for Reinhard, however, Jenny is determined to overcome their differences and confronts her pastor with a model of transconfessional tolerance that echoes Lessing's drama *Nathan the Wise* (1779). Her story of what her father taught her about God's omnipresence in all forms of existence and the soul's immortality culminates in her recapitulation of the key moment when she had asked him what distinguishes one religion from another:

> "and what does this division between religions consist in that has been strong enough to cause war and oppression over centuries? It consists in forms, I was told, which people in their blindness place above the spirit. Follow the example of the good that you are given and try to stay clear of the evil. Imagine a small delicate vessel, my father once said, in which an invisible hand planted precious seed. One would anxiously protect the divine seed and prevent any harm . . . if one knew that it would only grow in a vessel that was completely pure! You are such a vessel, and the divine can grow in you only because you are free of evil thoughts."
>
> Jenny could tell from her listener's expression that he did not share this view, but she did not let that perturb her and continued calmly: "This allegory made me happy,—I was a child back then, Mister Pastor!—and I asked if the seed had finally grown into a powerful tree; a tree which had burst the small vessel, freed itself and stretched into the blue sky from which the seed had once descended? Yes! said my father, and becoming free is called striving!" (*Jenny* 130–131)

Though phrased differently, Jenny asks her father essentially the same question that leads up to the parable of rings in Lessing's drama. In Lessing's work, Sultan Saladin famously asks the Jewish merchant Nathan which one of the three monotheistic

---

[23] Fanny Lewald, *Jenny*, ed. Ulrike Helmer (Frankfurt am Main: Helmer, 1988), 84 (hereafter *Jenny* in the text).

religions—Islam, Judaism, or Christianity—he holds to be the true one. Lewald's Jenny, similarly, wonders on what ontological grounds people have placed the authority and legitimacy of their religion above that of others. Like Nathan, Jenny's father draws in his response a clear distinction between, on the one hand, religious forms as manifest in different historical times and places, and, on the other, the spirit of religion. Religions have developed from various oral and written traditions and exhibit vastly different customs and precepts; what they all share however, is their origin in history.[24] This distinction between the spirit and its historical expressions suggests that nobody may lay claim to an exclusive ownership of truth and thereby feel entitled to govern others. In following this line of thinking, both men replace divinely ordained accounts of history, in which religions compete for recognition and authority, with a future-oriented and open-ended model of religious understanding centered on the subject.

Both Nathan and Jenny's father illustrate this transfer of religious truth from historical origin narratives to the self by means of the genre of fairy tales. At the time, the genre was understood in general terms and could denote basically any type of story, tale, or fable.[25] In choosing this most broadly defined narrative form that grew out of a complex web of oral and written traditions, they use a medium that perfectly fits the Enlightenment project of self-empowerment; the reader's and listener's active engagement and participation in writing and rewriting the story is inscribed in the genre.

In Lessing's *Nathan*, the powerful story of the three indistinguishable rings, each representing one religion, culminates in Nathan's account of the judge who calls on the three brothers to look forward and continue writing their ring's story by taking on responsibility and finding true faith through humanist actions.[26] No religion has built-in transtemporal merits, and the only way for the brothers to find an answer to their question regarding the right one is by continuously proving themselves in the praxis of daily life. The verdict on who wins this ongoing, competitive striving is not for the judge to give, and he releases the brothers into an open-ended future.[27] Similarly, Jenny's father employs the image of a vessel holding divine seed that may ripen if his daughter takes care of it by leading an ethical life. Jenny continues this narrative thread by imagining how the seed will one day burst the vessel, and how she will

---

[24] See the dialogue between Nathan and Saladin in the middle of the parable in Gotthold Ephraim Lessing, *Werke 1778–1780*, ed. Klaus Bohnen (Frankfurt am Main: Deutscher Klassiker Verlag, 1993), 554–558.

[25] Willi Goetschel, *Spinoza's Modernity: Mendelssohn, Lessing and Heine* (Madison: University of Wisconsin Press, 2004), 242.

[26] Lessing, *Werke 1778–1780*, 560.

[27] Goetschel and Leventhal demonstrate that the concern with the nature and status of truth is of paramount importance for Lessing and lies at the heart of his *Nathan*. Goetschel suggests that central aspects of Spinoza's critical agenda in the *Tractatus Theologico-Politicus* inform Lessing's reconceptualizing of the nature of truth throughout, *Spinoza's Modernity*, 230–250; see also Robert S. Leventhal, *The Discipline of Interpretation: Lessing, Herder, Schlegel and Hermeneutics in Germany 1750–1800* (Berlin: de Gruyter, 1994), 107–139.

grow above and beyond herself toward the open sky and into an unknown future full of possibility.[28]

There are direct references to *Nathan* or echoes of Lessing's thinking throughout Lewald's novel. Lewald also references the role model for *Nathan*'s main character: Moses Mendelssohn. With *Nathan the Wise*, Lessing, famously created a lasting memorial to the philosopher's commitment to fostering transconfessional dialogue and the overcoming of religious differences. Mendelssohn was at the center of the Haskalah (from the Hebrew *sekhel*, "reason" or "intellect") or Jewish Enlightenment. This movement fostered a broad range of new encounters between Jewish and German culture, with Berlin—the city where *Maskilim*, as enlightened male Jews referred to each other, ushered in a new period in the history of German Judaism. Inspired by the tenets of the Enlightenment, and its propagation of reason and religious tolerance, orthodox positions and the rabbinical elite's monopoly on the exegesis of the Torah came under attack. Publications such as Mendelssohn's translation of the Pentateuch "brought the sacred language of the synagogue out into the open air of an enlightened public sphere," propagating the idea that being observant and committed to the Jewish faith might coexist with being a secular citizen of the state.[29] Mendelssohn and his generation used the contemporary language of reason, humanism, and tolerance to fight discrimination and the exclusion of Berlin's Jewish community from public life, and reinterpreted the foundations of their faith through the lens of enlightened discourse.[30]

The prominence of Mendelssohn's thinking in *Jenny*, and especially of his adaptation of Plato's *Phaedo*, has been demonstrated by Karin Tebben.[31] Lewald, like Lessing, found in Mendelssohn's works historical evidence and arguments, suggesting that orthodox views such as Reinhard's and a commitment to liberal, tolerant, and rational thinking don't have to exclude one another. This broadminded and flexible attitude features in Mendelssohn's most influential and enduring work, *Jerusalem*, which shows a strong commitment to the Jewish faith but without compromising spiritual freedom and rationality.[32]

Thus in echoing this progressive Haskalah discourse, Jenny imagines conditions under which her relationship with Reinhard could thrive. Yet the different dialogic constellations between Reinhard, his mother, Jenny, and the pastor stage scenarios in

---

[28] Like the parable Lessing adapted from Giovanni Boccaccio's *Decameron*, the allegory of the vessel has a long narrative tradition. Tebben highlights its function in religious writings and in Maimonides's doctrine of faith, *Subjektkonstitution und Erzählstruktur*, 64.

[29] Clark, *Iron Kingdom*, 261.

[30] On Mendelssohn, Lessing, and the Haskalah, see Ulrike Wagner, "Schleiermacher's Geselligkeit, Henriette Herz, and the 'Convivial Turn,'" in *Conviviality at the Crossroads: The Poetics and Politics of Everyday Encounters*, ed. Oscar Hemer et al. (Houndmills, Basingstoke: Palgrave Macmillan, 2020), 66–67.

[31] Tebben, *Subjektkonstitution und Erzählstruktur*, 84–87.

[32] On Mendelssohn's dual commitment to traditional Judaism and Enlightenment thinking in *Jerusalem*, see Shmuel Feiner, *Moses Mendelssohn: Sage of Modernity*, trans. Anthony Berris (New Haven: Yale University Press, 2010), 153–186; Shmuel Feiner, *The Jewish Enlightenment*, trans. Chaya Naor (Philadelphia: University of Pennsylvania Press, 2002), 166–171.

which the most enlightened concepts of *Bildung* and religious understanding are not strong enough to alter stern orthodoxy and resolve conflicts. The novel culminates in Jenny's tragic death and leaves the reader with no more than a vision of what her life and relationships could have looked like under different social circumstances.

The prevailing promises as well as the limitations of the Haskalah resonate throughout Lewald's work and life. She recalls in great detail meeting with seventy-six-year-old Henriette Herz (1764–1847), one of Berlin's most prominent Jewish *salonières*, who opened her house to bring people from various social, religious, and cultural backgrounds together; and Lewald explicitly places her own work and social gatherings in the tradition of influential Jewish women such as Herz, Rahel Levin Varnhagen, Dorothea Schlegel (*née* Brendel Mendelssohn), and Sara Levy (*née* Itzig)—many of them the wives, sisters, and daughters of the *Maskilim* (ML III: 108–126). Together with her husband, Adolf Stahr (1805–1876), a classical scholar whom Lewald met in Rome at the age of thirty-four and married over a decade later, she became a public figure in Berlin and hosted the city's most prominent intellectuals and artists at her house on popular "Monday evenings" in the late 1850s and 1860s.[33] With few exceptions, the scholarly literature has not sufficiently acknowledged the contributions these women made to the Haskalah's formation and direction.[34] By reviving and continuing this tradition, Lewald envisions forms of life, social interaction, and belonging beyond confessional confines—and, crucially, also beyond those of the rigid gender roles of the period.

3 On Rewriting the History of Women and Reinventing Femininity

Jenny's recollections of her religious education resonate strongly with the theological positions articulated prominently by figures such as Spinoza, Mendelssohn, and Lessing. Lewald engages these Enlightenment and Haskalah discourses to stake out a theological

---

[33] On the Lewalds' continuation of the Berlin salon tradition, see Ingeborg Drewitz, *Berliner Salons. Gesellschaft und Literatur zwischen Aufklärung und Industriezeitalter* (Berlin: Haude & Spener, 1965), 101. Key letters of the couple's private exchange have been published in *Ein Leben auf dem Papier: Fanny Lewald und Adolf Stahr; der Briefwechsel 1846 bis 1852*, 3 vols., ed. Gabriele Schneider and Renate Sternagel (Bielefeld: Aisthesis, 2014–17). The published collection gives insight into their experience of the revolution in Paris, Berlin, and Bremen. Their epistolary exchange contains nearly 900 letters, stored at the Berlin State Library; only a small fraction has been published.

[34] None of these women are mentioned in Pelli Moshe, *Haskalah and Beyond: The Reception of the Hebrew Enlightenment and the Emergence of Haskalah Judaism* (Lanham, MD: University Press of America, 2010); Feiner introduces the private get-togethers hosted by Jewish women as social hubs of Berlin's Romantic scene but not as nodal points of the Haskalah; see *The Jewish Enlightenment*, 303; Natalie Naimark-Goldberg's *Jewish Women in Enlightenment Berlin* (Oxford: Littman Library of Jewish Civilization, 2013) draws awareness to this omission of the role of women in the Haskalah and develops a more inclusive and nuanced understanding of the movement and its sites of articulation.

position and mode of faith that points beyond her characters' immediate struggles and conflicts. But she also taps into and modifies that same discourse with the objective of retelling the history of women, and of reimagining their present and future roles. The scene in *Jenny* in which Reinhard's mother references Lessing's "Parable of the Palace" cogently illustrates how Lewald rewrites a well-known story to fit her feminist agenda. As Tebben points out, the assessment of the widowed mother, the *Pfarrerin* (wife of a Lutheran pastor), prophetically warns her son against marrying Jenny. Her speech, however, is also a programmatic declaration addressing the novel's female readership:[35]

> "That is what I fear!" said the clergywoman. "Jenny's intellect is relentlessly clear; she is not deceived by her heart, and that worries me. These intellectual girls from Jewish families who were raised like Jenny almost always lack proper female conduct: . . . Each other's company and the care for daily housekeeping duties no longer gives them pleasure; they prefer male company. . . . Their intellect and enlightenment progresses rapidly in these male circles; they quickly tear down old prejudices and discard narrow views. The house with its peaceful old walls where the young girl felt at home and where she appears most loveable is destroyed and replaced by a new shining palace. Bright sunlight shines through the building's large windows and reflects from its smooth marble walls. Everything is light! There is no half-darkness, no gloomy shadow, and no quiet room to build an altar for the creator, no intimate place for shy love." (*Jenny* 90)

Reinhard's mother feels threatened by the girl's figurative destruction of her familiar house, representing her departure from an existence within a closely defined radius of domestic activities. In the mother's narrative, the girl replaces her old space—congenial to the thriving of a feminine character in the traditional sense—with a new palace that is all light, shiny, and reflective. Lessing published the parable about the palace a year before *Nathan*, calling it a barely encoded poetic statement about the history of Christianity;[36] the narrative was part of a series of highly controversial exchanges with Johann Melchior Goeze, chief pastor of Hamburg and major spokesman of Lutheran orthodoxy.[37]

Lessing's parable introduces the palace as an immeasurable architectural construction that is all light and equipped with numerous doors and windows, leading to an impression of disorientation and confusion for those entering and moving in it. Throughout history, humans have been searching for the right *Grundriss*, the right floor plan, with the goal of orienting oneself in this unique palace, which Lessing employs as an image of the spirit of religion in its manifold forms and articulations. These ongoing battles over the right exegesis of the Scriptures or right "floor layouts," as the story puts it metaphorically, pose the greatest threat to the spirit of religion and human

---

[35] Tebben, *Subjektkonstitution und Erzählstruktur*, 16.

[36] Lessing, *Werke 1778–1780*, 828–829.

[37] On the controversy with Goeze, see Lessing, *Werke 1778–1780*, 768–803. On the origin of the parable and its reception history, see 822–831.

well-being. Different religious groups have interpreted the Bible's "words" and "signs" to fit their views and needs, forgetting that answers to their fundamental questions are not to be found in fundamentalist explications of so-called historical evidence and origin. The parable concludes with a scenario in which the palace appears to almost burn down because, rather than protecting the construction as a whole, everyone is only interested in rescuing what they regard as the true floor plan. This parable—with its powerful image of the palace that does not correspond to a single floor layout—is part of a number of groundbreaking and highly controversial works that Lessing published to refute conflations of Biblical exegesis and historical origin narratives with the question of religious truth in the field of apologetics.[38]

In Lewald's rewriting of the parable, Reinhard and his family are only concerned to safeguard their "layout of the house" and the notion of womanhood associated with it. In destroying her home and building a palace in Lessing's sense, Jenny does something much more radical than replace a traditional understanding of how woman ought to be and what she ought to do with a more progressive one: she seeks to rewrite the history of women altogether as an antifoundationalist one. The image of the reflecting palace representing womankind does not map onto a specific floor plan; there is no historical ground, in other words, no foundation for a narrowly defined understanding of womanhood such as the one articulated by Reinhard's mother. The palace with its immeasurable dimensions signifies plural forms of femininity, growing out of different ways of life, education, social interactions, and everyday practices.

To examine Lewald's numerous writings on the topic of women through such a pluralist lens is more productive, I suggest, than judging them against the backdrop of modern notions of emancipation. She approaches the theme of emancipation from various angles, calling for more differentiated research of her practical agenda for education and women in the labor market, as well as of her fictional explorations of female self-understanding. *Jenny*, for example, introduces changing conceptions of womanhood; the novel's heroine slips into different roles over the course of the novel. After ending the relationship with Reinhard, she gives up on the idea of marriage and finds peace and fulfillment in intellectual activities and in painting Lewald juxtaposes Jenny's interests and daily routines with those of her friend Clara Horn, who altogether fulfills social expectations in her exemplary role as loving wife to William and mother to his children. Without judging their respective lives, Lewald puts the two women in dialogue and highlights how difficult it was for Jenny to imagine an existence such as Clara's and vice versa (*Jenny* 230).

When Walter enters her life, Jenny gives up her single existence only reluctantly and after careful deliberation. He is a count, comes from one of Germany's oldest aristocratic

---

[38] In his function as head librarian of the ducal library of Wolfenbüttel, Lessing famously commentated on and published sections from the *Apology or Defence for the Rational Worshippers of God* by the deist Hermann Samuel Reimarus, as "fragments," instigating one of the most important controversies of the age between the Enlightenment movement and orthodox Lutheran theology. On the controversy over the Reimarus fragments, see Goetschel, *Spinoza's Modernity*, 196–206.

families and embodies a new type of man; unperturbed by Jenny's Jewishness and eager to live the enlightened ideals of his age, he wants to replace the traditional marriage model with an egalitarian one. In conversation with Jenny, he points out that the ways humans have organized their bonds or imagined a relationship in correspondence with nature has always been subject to change; poetry, he explains, illustrates these changes with its vastly different interpretations of nature: the Greeks sensed the presence of dryads in their trees, whereas his generation sees clarity and freedom in their upward-pointing branches. Such radical shifts of perspective make him hopeful that "we will finally get rid of a number of old stereotypical images" and their harmful effects (*Jenny* 226–227). Jenny develops Walter's imagery further in a picture that reinvents marriage as an equal partnership: her drawing replaces the gendered image of a powerful oak tenderly enwrapped by ivy with two equally strong trees, growing and embracing one another happily side by side.[39]

This ideal of marriage fails because of society's lack of tolerance, culminating in the death of both lovers at the end of the novel. But despite this tragic conclusion, *Jenny* illustrates Lewald's varied approaches to using popular images and narratives to develop new debates over women's roles in the family and in society at large. Here and across her varied writings she concentrates on the dynamics of particular situations and practical reform projects rather than on a more comprehensive and abstract emancipatory agenda. More specifically, her keen analyses of the dependent and desolate existence of the majority of girls and women constitutes the backdrop for her urgent call for access to formal education and to the labor market. The primary focus of her political writings is to map out the social and educational prerequisites for broadening women's options and the project of self-emancipation.

Throughout her autobiography and writings such as the early essay "Some Thoughts about the Education of Girls" ("Einige Gedanken über Mädchenerziehung," 1843) or the letters *For and against Women*, Lewald draws attention to women's paradoxical situation: One the one hand, they are entrusted with the "most important task of life . . . the education of human beings" (*An Autobiography* 156) and with the vital duty of managing large households; on the other hand, they receive no preparatory guidance for their job and the responsibilities it carries. Unlike professionals in any other job, they are expected to perform perfectly without any systematic educational training. As disastrous as women's lack of a right to education, she states further, is society's celebration of so-called virtuous qualities of delicacy and untainted purity. Girls are "raised for dependence" and not expected to outgrow states of childlike naivety and immaturity.[40]

---

[39] On Jenny's drawing of the oak tree and its symbolic function in the history of German nationalism, see Rebecca Ann Zajdowicz, "Constructing the Ideal German Woman: National Identity and Fanny Lewald's novel *Jenny*," in *Fanny Lewald (1811–1889): Studien zu einer großen europäischen Schriftstellerin und Intellektuellen*, ed. Christina Ujma (Bielefeld: Aisthesis, 2011), 166–168.

[40] Fanny Lewald, *Für und wider die Frauen. Vierzehn Briefe* (Berlin: Verlag von Otto Janke, 1870), 41. See also Lewald, "Einige Gedanken über Mädchenerziehung," May 1843, in *Archiv für vaterländische Interessen oder Preußische Provinzialblätter*, ed. O. W. L. Richter (Königsberg, 1843), 380–395. Excerpts from Lewald's essays on the education of girls are reprinted in *Frauenemanzipation im deutschen Vormärz. Texte und Dokumente*, ed. Renate Möhrmann (Stuttgart: Reclam, 1978), 25–27.

Educated wives and mothers, by contrast, would not only fulfill their roles more successfully but also have career options beyond the domestic sphere. The *Easter Letters*
and the letters *For and against Women* promote women's access to the labor market as
the foundation for emancipation. Lewald emphatically and repeatedly highlights that
there is no equality without women's "emancipation to work" (*An Autobiography* 157).
Professional training and gainful employment free women from being in a position
in which marriage is their only path to financial security. Moreover, women's participation in the workforce lowers the pressure on families with financial constraints. Job
qualifications also enable women to provide for themselves in case they do not get married or their marriages do not work out. Bourgeois women ought to take the lead in the
emancipation process Lewald envisions, for they can model for those who are less privileged that having a professional career is not a stigma but an honor, one that can even
be fulfilling and enjoyable, as examples of working women in other countries such as
America suggest (ML II: 192–196).

Scholars have highlighted the progressive aspects of Lewald's plans for equal rights
to education and work as well as the constraints and limitations of her vision. Her inconsistent statements about women's role in society appear rather puzzling and incompatible with what we would today consider an emancipatory stance. While she pleads
passionately for economic independence and access to the labor market and career
perspectives, she celebrates traditional family values and doubts that any professional
career can possibly replace a woman's natural vocation as wife and mother. "Evolution,"
the biological urge to procreate, seems to frequently win out over feminism and "revolution" in her writing.[41] Psychological readings find explanations for her contradictory
stance in her relationship to her father, and sociohistorical ones draw attention to her
female readers and assessment of how typical middle-class women of her day thought
about their domestic existence; the majority, she states repeatedly, felt comfortable in
their role and would not have it any other way.[42] Looked at from the angle of her engagement with contemporary philosophical and religious discourses, her stance, I suggest, is
consistent with her Enlightenment agenda of self-emancipation, powered by practical
changes in the domains of education and paid labor.

Education and the option to work are the prerequisites for any further emancipatory steps because formal training is the only way for women to develop their cognitive
abilities and acquire a set of skills necessary to emerge from a life of dependency and
turn what feels normal and familiar upside down.[43] Echoing Kant, she critiques those
who refuse to draw on their reason and prefer to withdraw "behind the bars of blessed
habit" (ML I: 241). Reflecting on her own career path and its potential model function

---

[41] See O'Brien for a discussion of criticism on Lewald's contradictory position in her political writings
in *Enlightened Reactions*, 218–219. On Lewald's doubts regarding a professional career as replacement
for a woman's "natural" role, see for example *Für und wider die Frauen*, 11, and "Einige Gedanken über
Mädchenerziehung," 25–27.

[42] Compare, for example, *Für und wider die Frauen*, 11.

[43] Compare Lewald, *Für und wider die Frauen*, 41–42.

for others she wonders if "other women felt the urge for independence and personal freedom" (ML III: 253). Yet in the long run she is optimistic that with greater access to education and professional options, the number of women able and willing to emerge from their state of immaturity will increase: "We may demand the emancipation of women for the purpose of employment. It is to be expected that by pursuing paid work they will emancipate themselves from a number of mistakes which at this point make them completely unfit for a rational understanding of life. Idleness and intellectual emptiness have brought a large number of women down to the level of play toys. A lack of knowledge and destitution have ruined thousands of women."[44] This observation that ennui and a lack of intellectual stimulation have turned women into submissive "play toys," incapable of claiming a voice of their own, is followed by a cogent statement on how to gradually exit the current state: "enlightenment, instruction, work, and a sufficient income" create the "preconditions," she formulates programmatically, for "free self-determination."[45] What such an emancipated state and self-determination implies for an individual is contingent on factors such as her "stage of *Bildung*" and "power of reason," Lewald states in the *Easter Letters*.[46]

I follow Stamm in her observation that emancipation is for Lewald first and foremost an "outward liberation," gradually followed by an "inner" one whose content and direction she does not specify.[47] Her main mission is to put women in a position from which they can choose rather than be told what their choice ought to look like. In this regard, it is illuminating to discuss her reluctance to specify what an enlightened emancipated life would look like in the context of her engagement with the philosopher who had perhaps the most pervasive impact on her life and work, Kant.

4 What Is Enlightenment?

The opening paragraph of Lewald's autobiography leaves no doubt about her primary sense of belonging. Readers learn in the very first sentence that she was born in Königsberg and that both of her parents were also Königsbergers (ML I: 8) and hence inhabitants of the town instantly associated with the name Immanuel Kant; the information that they were also Jewish comes second.[48] She recalls from her childhood how her mother took pride in the fact that her father was always greeted in a friendly manner by Professor Kant on his daily walks because "at that time, it was still a distinct honor

---

[44] Lewald, *Für und wider die Frauen*, 53–54.

[45] Lewald, *Für und wider die Frauen*, 54.

[46] Fanny Lewald, *Osterbriefe für Frauen*, reprinted in *Politische Schriften für und wider Frauen*, ed. Ulrike Helmer (Frankfurt am Main: Helmer, 1989), 22.

[47] Stamm, "Fanny Lewald," 136.

[48] On Lewald's identification with Königsberg and her description of the town in her novel *Transformations* (*Wandlungen*, 1853), see Ward, *Fanny Lewald*, 29–30.

for a Jew to be treated with respect by Christians" (*An Autobiography* 4). Fanny's own father introduced her to Kant's categorical imperative when she was only eight years old, and she read the *Anthropology from a Pragmatic Point of View* (*Anthropologie in pragmatischer Hinsicht*, 1798) when she was sixteen on his recommendation (ML I: 276).[49]

Clearly taking her cue from one of the most recited formulations in "Answering the Question: What Is Enlightenment?" ("Beantwortung der Frage: Was ist Aufklärung?," 1784), she sums up her father's pedagogy in one sentence: "children must see, hear, and learn to obey!" (*An Autobiography* 50). While making obedience and submission his guiding parenting principles, however, David Lewald also sends his eldest to school and grants her the intellectual training to emerge from such a state of *Unmündigkeit*, immaturity. Uncommon for a girl of her social background, Lewald attends Königsberg's coeducational Ulrich School for seven years until the age of fourteen (ML I: 99–100). The passages in her autobiography describing her teacher's method are of particular interest in the context of the Enlightenment's impact on pedagogical ideals because her recollections suggest that she experienced elements of the most progressive approaches to learning in her classroom. The teacher's inductive style was centered on letting his students make their own discoveries and on fostering their self-learning skills in the most innovate ways. His method of teaching, she recalls, was "the most pleasant and stimulating I have ever encountered" (*An Autobiography* 39).

These recollections provide insight into her ambivalent experience of being raised to become an independently thinking individual while also being expected to submit to a set of restrictive rules and conventions at the same time. Kant provided her with terms to articulate and critically reflect on her experiences and to bring them into dialogue with those of others. Upon closer inspection, we find echoes of his vexed notion of immaturity refracted throughout her discussions, structuring her thinking about her upbringing, about the lives of other women, and also about Berlin society at large. Paradoxically, Kant holds the individual responsible for remaining caught up in a state of immaturity (*selbstverschuldete Unmündigkeit*) while also blaming the individual's guardians (*Vormünder*) who do not want to relinquish their position of authority: "statutes and formulae . . . are the shackles of a perpetual state of immaturity." It is not a lack of understanding that makes individuals accept guidance from others, in Kant's eyes, but "idleness," "cowardice," and "a lack of resolve and courage." And even an individual daring enough to throw off the shackles of oppression is most likely doomed to fall prey to minor obstacles and retreat because "he is not used to such freedom of movement."[50]

In her *Recollections of the Year 1848*, Lewald draws on Kant's terminology and assesses the revolutionary events of her time in light of his understanding of immaturity. In the

---

[49] On her father's introduction of Kant's categorical imperative, see Lewald, *Gefühltes und Gedachtes*, 244.

[50] Immanuel Kant, "An Answer to the Question: What Is Enlightenment," in *Toward Perpetual Peace and Other Writings on Politics, Peace, and History*, ed. Pauline Kleingeld, trans. David L. Colclasure (New Haven: Yale University Press, 2006), 17–18.

spring of 1848, she traveled to France with the hope of witnessing "the most significant event of the time at the place where it had broken out."[51] While in Paris she learned about the political riots in Berlin, yet she was doubtful from the beginning that the movement would be powerful enough to dethrone the German princes and turn their fragmented principalities into a unified nation state: "According to everything I have seen so far, the German republicans returning from France to their fatherland will notice soon how wrong they are in assuming that Germany, a country used to the monarchy, is enthusiastic about the republic."[52] Back in Berlin, her skepticism turned out to be more than justified when she was an eyewitness to battles that had seemed full of promise but ended in the victory of reaction and autocracy. Conservative circles, the church, and the aristocracy acted as unified forces while the movement's advocates of liberalism and democracy lacked coordination and cohesive plans.[53] Employing Kant's childhood imagery, Lewald comments on the government's hypocritical paternalism: "the government is treating the people just as indulgent parents treat a weeping child, to whom they say, 'Oh, the dear child is too good. It isn't crying at all any more.' And all the while, the child is still screaming and hitting and kicking around with its hands and feet. It has good reason to scream, too, because it is still suffering."[54] By describing the relationship between Berlin's population and the government in such infantilizing terms, Lewald corroborates Kant's point regarding the limits of the rebelling oppressed who have never learned how to resist and articulate their opposition. In light of such inexperience, rulers can afford to act like authoritarian parents who calmly indulge their child's tantrums, fully aware that there is nothing to fear. As much as the ruling class must to be held to account, those being ruled also have their share of the blame: "in contrast [to the Parisians], the Berliners stand there not knowing what to do. They are as frightened and at loss as children who have been using a walker too long and are finally set on the ground to walk by themselves. They do not trust their own feet, because they are not being supported any more; they would really like to know if the king, if the various branches of the government are satisfied with what has happened."[55] Unlike the French, the German public did not seem ready for free self-determination. People were afraid to act without guidance and had not suffered enough to put all their energies into emancipating themselves from the domination of others; in comparing the populace

---

[51] Fanny Lewald, *Erinnerungen aus dem Jahre 1848, In Auswahl*, ed. Dietrich Schaefer (Frankfurt am Main: Insel, 1969), 28.

[52] Lewald, *Erinnerungen aus dem Jahre 1848*, 11–12.

[53] On Lewald and the development of the revolutionary events, see Heidi Thomann Tewarson, "Die Aufklärung im jüdischen Denken des 19. Jahrhunderts: Rahel Levin Varnhagen, Ludwig Robert, Ludwig Börne, Eduard Gans, Berthold Auerbach, Fanny Lewald," in *Juden und jüdische Kultur im Vormärz*, Forum Vormärz Forschung, Jahrbuch 1998, ed. Horst Denkler et al. (Bielefeld: Aisthesis, 1999), 56.

[54] Fanny Lewald, *A Year of Revolutions: Fanny Lewald's Recollections of 1848*, ed. and trans. Hanna Ballin Lewis (New York: Berghahn, 1997), 71.

[55] Lewald, *Recollections of 1848*, 89. Both passages are also cited in Ruth Whittle and Debbie Pinfold, *Voices of Rebellion: Political Writings by Malwida von Meysenbug, Fanny Lewald, Johanna Kinkel and Louise Aston* (Bern: Peter Lang, 2005), 87. The authors note Lewald's adaptations of Kant, and my analysis of the two text passages is an elaborated version of selected points briefly mentioned in their book.

to toddlers who have been harnessed in their *Gehkorb*, their walker, for too long, she recalls Kant's much cited image for people's immaturity, the "Gängelwagen."[56] In a letter written in 1849, she explicitly warns her friend Johann Jacoby, a tireless advocate of liberty, about the lack of enthusiasm and unreliability of the people to stand up for liberty without reservation when it matters: "to date the populace has always sacrificed the idea of freedom, the law, for material benefits at the decisive moment."[57]

Like Kant, however, she places her hopes in future generations. She notes that members of the bourgeois class like herself play a key role in supporting the education of the inarticulate working class in this process of release from immaturity. Taking the French as a model, she advocates for a "spiritual armament created by means of the language." Like the leaders of the revolution, people ought to find their own voice, free "the language of all abstraction, from all academic dust" and turn it from being a means for class distinction into "public property."[58] As Ruth Whittle and Debbie Pinfold demonstrate, Lewald detects the first signs that such appropriation and transformation of language is under way on a Good Friday walk through Berlin-Friedrichshain in the spring of 1849. Looking at the graves of those who died in the Berlin street fights, she draws attention to their inscriptions; irrespective of the orders by the police controlling the graves and monitoring epitaphs, the words inscribed in the stones tell how people feel about and how they want to commemorate their dead: "because the people had to learn to perceive themselves as a power in regard to authority, they gained the courage to speak their own language."[59] Lewald notes such fleeting moments of rebellion and empowerment throughout her work and in different contexts and constellations.

Regarding the emancipation of women, she notes significant progress in the series of *Easter Letters*: "what used to be . . . the property of a selected few has now become a common good, to a certain degree. The number of those feeling entitled to think about themselves and the world they live in to the extent which their rational powers permit them to . . . has increased immensely."[60] Participation in civil society has grown and more women feel entitled to make their voices heard and exercise critical judgment. Aside from such observations, however, Lewald is not invested in defining Enlightenment and formulating her answer to the famous question "What Is Enlightenment?" initially posed by the theologian and educational reformer Johann Friedrich Zöller in a note to an article he published in the *Berlinische Monatsschrift* in 1782. In statements that are strongly reminiscent of Kant's response, she is concerned with people's *Ausgang* or

---

[56] Immanuel Kant, "Beantwortung der Frage: Was ist Aufklärung?," in *Was ist Aufklärung? Ausgewählte kleine Schriften*, ed. Horst D. Brandt (Hamburg: Meiner, 1999), 20.

[57] The letter to Jacoby is cited in Tewarson, "Die Aufklärung im jüdischen Denken des 19. Jahrhunderts," 58.

[58] Lewald, *Recollections of 1848*, 51.

[59] Lewald, *Recollections of 1848*, 106. See Whittle and Pinfold in *Voices of Rebellion* for a more elaborate discussion of Lewald's recollections from visiting the graves in Friedrichshain, 90.

[60] Fanny Lewald, *Osterbriefe für Frauen*, 22 (emphasis in the original).

departure from ingrained habits rather than specifying what such efforts of breaking away would lead to.

James Schmidt's analysis of Kant's position and comparison to Moses Mendelssohn, I suggest, is a productive lens through which to explore Lewald.[61] In his comparative reading, Schmidt demonstrates that Mendelssohn defines "enlightenment with reference to the goal it fosters," namely, the "destiny of man"; Kant, by contrast, "defines enlightenment not in terms of what it achieves, but rather in terms of what it escapes." Drawing on the brief discussion of enlightenment in the *Critique of Judgment*, Schmidt highlights Kant's reluctance to posit autonomy as the goal of enlightenment and calls attention to the "merely negative" character of Kant's notion: "the demand that one 'think for oneself' was understood by Kant as a 'liberation from prejudice' in general, and a 'liberation from superstition' in particular." Kant, in other words, looks primarily at the causes for immaturity and says less about the actual state of maturity.[62]

5 CONCLUDING REMARKS

This chapter has demonstrated that Lewald's ambivalent stance on matters of emancipation looks different through the prism of the philosophical traditions she engages and inscribes herself in. The root causes of her reluctance to specify consistent emancipatory objectives are by no means limited to her patriarchal upbringing but are also deeply anchored in the most controversial debates of her time. Her dedication to pragmatic changes as grounds for open-ended processes of education and self-emancipation follows naturally from her experience and intellectual reflection on the vexed issue of maturity and becoming independent. Each of this chapter's sections has zeroed in on selected passages of her political and fictional writings that testify to her commitment to creating conditions congenial to plural forms of existence: Jenny's vision of transconfessional tolerance modeled on *Nathan*'s famous fairy tale and Lewald's revival of conviviality in the Haskalah tradition promote respect and acceptance in matters of confessional difference. The retelling of the "Parable of the Palace" in *Jenny*, Lewald's autobiography, and her political writings bring different models of femininity into dialogue and thereby contest narrowly defined notions of womanhood. To date, only a small fraction of her extensive literary output has become the object of critical scrutiny; the texts analyzed here, however, exemplify her deep investment in the most urgent philosophical and intellectual historical questions of her age, calling for further research beyond the field of women's literature.

---

[61] James Schmidt, "What Enlightenment Was: How Moses Mendelssohn and Immanuel Kant Answered the *Berlinische Monatsschrift*," *Journal of the History of Philosophy* 30, no. 1 (January 1992): 77–101.

[62] Schmidt, "What Enlightenment Was," 88–89, 93.

BIBLIOGRAPHY

Bäumer, Gertrud, and Helene Lange, eds. *Handbuch der Frauenbewegung*. Berlin: Moeser, 1901.

Boetcher Joeres, Ruth-Ellen. *Respectability and Deviance: Nineteenth-Century German Women Writers and the Ambiguity of Representation*. Chicago: University of Chicago Press, 1998.

Clark, Christopher. *Iron Kingdom: The Rise and Downfall of Prussia, 1600–1947*. Cambridge, MA: Harvard University Press, 2006.

Drewitz, Ingeborg. *Berliner Salons. Gesellschaft und Literatur zwischen Aufklärung und Industriezeitalter*. Berlin: Haude & Spener, 1965.

"Hascala: Judaic Movement." In *Encyclopaedia Britannica*. https://www.britannica.com/topic/Haskala.

Feiner, Shmuel. *Moses Mendelssohn: Sage of Modernity*. Translated by Anthony Berris. New Haven: Yale University Press, 2010.

Feiner, Shmuel. *The Jewish Enlightenment*. Translated by Chaya Naor. Philadelphia: University of Pennsylvania Press, 2002.

Goetschel, Willi. *Spinoza's Modernity: Mendelssohn, Lessing and Heine*. Madison: University of Wisconsin Press, 2004.

Habermas, Jürgen. *Theorie und Praxis. Sozialphilosophische Studien*. Frankfurt a.M.: Suhrkamp, 1993.

Kant, Immanuel. "An Answer to the Question: What Is Enlightenment." In *Toward Perpetual Peace and Other Writings on Politics, Peace, and History*, edited by Pauline Kleingeld, translated by David L. Colclasure, 17–23. New Haven: Yale University Press, 2006.

Kant, Immanuel. "Beantwortung der Frage: Was ist Aufklärung?" In *Was ist Aufklärung? Ausgewählte kleine Schriften*, edited by Horst D. Brandt, 20–22. Hamburg: Meiner, 1999.

Kuehn, Julia. "Realism's Connections: George Eliot's and Fanny Lewald's Poetics." *George Eliot—George Henry Lewes Studies* 68, no. 2 (2016): 91–115.

Lessing, Gotthold Ephraim. *Werke 1778–1780*. Edited by Klaus Bohnen and Arno Schilson. Vol. 9 of *Werke und Briefe in zwölf Bänden*. Frankfurt am Main: Deutscher Klassiker Verlag, 1993.

Leventhal, Robert S. *The Discipline of Interpretation: Lessing, Herder, Schlegel and Hermeneutics in Germany 1750–1800*. Berlin: de Gruyter, 1994.

Lewald, Fanny. *Jenny*. Edited by Ulrike Helmer. Frankfurt am Main: Helmer, 1988.

Lewald, Fanny. *Meine Lebensgeschichte*. Vols. 1–3 of *Gesammelte Werke*. Berlin: Verlag von Otto Janke, 1871.

Lewald, Fanny. *The Education of Fanny Lewald: An Autobiography*. Edited and translated by Hanna Ballin Lewis. New York: State University of New York Press, 1992.

Lewald, Fanny. *Für und wider die Frauen. Vierzehn Briefe*. Berlin: Verlag von Otto Janke, 1870.

Lewald, Fanny. *Gefühltes und Gedachtes 1838–1888*. Edited by Ludwig Geiger. Dresden: Minden, 1900.

Lewald, Fanny. *Politische Schriften für und wider Frauen*. Edited by Ulrike Helmer. Frankfurt am Main: Helmer, 1989.

Lewald, Fanny. *Erinnerungen aus dem Jahre 1848, In Auswahl*. Edited by Dietrich Schaefer. Frankfurt am Main: Insel, 1969.

Lewald Fanny. *A Year of Revolutions: Fanny Lewald's Recollections of 1848*. Edited and translated by Hanna Ballin Lewis. New York: Berghahn, 1997.

Lewald, Fanny. "Einige Gedanken über Mädchenerziehung." In *Archiv für vaterländische Interessen oder Preußische Provinzialblätter*, 380–395, edited by O. W. L. Richter. Königsberg, 1843.

Lewald, Fanny. "Einige Gedanken über Mädchenerziehung." In *Frauenemanzipation im deutschen Vormärz. Texte und Dokumente,* edited by Renate Möhrmann, 25–27. Stuttgart: Reclam, 1989.

Lorenz, Dagmar C. G. *Keepers of the Motherland: German Texts by Jewish Women Writers.* Lincoln: University of Nebraska Press, 1997.

Marci-Boehncke, Gudrun. *Fanny Lewald: Jüdin, Preußin, Schriftstellerin: Studien zu autobiographischem Werk und Kontext.* Stuttgart: Heinz, 1998.

McIsaac, Peter M. "Rethinking Tableaux Vivants and Triviality in the Writings of Johann Wolfgang von Goethe, Johanna Schopenhauer, and Fanny Lewald." *Monatshefte* 99, no. 2 (Summer 2007): 152–176.

Möhrmann, Renate. *Die andere Frau. Emanzipationsansätze deutscher Schriftstellerinnen im Vorfeld der Achtundvierziger Revolution.* Stuttgart: Metzler, 1977.

Möhrmann, Renate, ed. *Frauenemanzipation im deutschen Vormärz. Texte und Dokumente.* Stuttgart: Reclam, 1978.

Moshe, Pelli. *Haskalah and Beyond: The Reception of the Hebrew Enlightenment and the Emergence of Haskalah Judaism.* Lanham, MD: University Press of America, 2010.

Naimark-Goldberg, Natalie. *Jewish Women in Enlightenment Berlin.* Oxford: Littman Library of Jewish Civilization, 2013.

O'Brien, Traci S. *Enlightened Reactions: Emancipation, Gender, and Race in German Women's Writing.* Bern: Peter Lang, 2011.

Ornam, Vanessa van. *Fanny Lewald and Nineteenth-Century Constructions of Femininity.* New York: Peter Lang, 2002.

Pinfold, Debbie, and Ruth Whittle. *Voices of Rebellion: Political Writings by Malwida von Meysenbug, Fanny Lewald, Johanna Kinkel and Louise Aston.* Bern: Peter Lang, 2005.

Rheinberg, Brigitta van. *Fanny Lewald. Geschichte einer Emanzipation.* Frankfurt am Main: Campus, 1990.

Schmidt, James. "What Enlightenment Was: How Moses Mendelssohn and Immanuel Kant Answered the Berlinische Monatsschrift." *Journal of the History of Philosophy* 30, no. 1 (1992): 77–101.

Schneider, Gabriele. *Fanny Lewald.* Reinbek: Rowohlt, 1996.

Schneider, Gabriele, and Renate Sternagel, eds. *Ein Leben auf dem Papier: Fanny Lewald und Adolf Stahr; der Briefwechsel 1846 bis 1852.* 3 vols. Bielefeld: Aisthesis, 2014–17.

Stamm, Ulrike. "Fanny Lewald: Autorschaft im Zeichen der Vernunft." *Zeitschrift für Germanistik* 22, no. 1 (2012): 129–141.

Steinhauer, Marieluise. *Fanny Lewald, die deutsche George Sand: Ein Kapitel aus der Geschichte des Frauenromans im 19. Jahrhundert.* Berlin: K&R Hoffmann, 1937.

Stocksieker Di Maio, Irene. "Jewish Emancipation and Integration: Fanny Lewald's Narrative Strategies." In *Autoren damals und heute. Literaturgeschichtliche Beispiele veränderter Wirkungshorizonte,* Amsterdamer Beiträge zur Neueren Germanistik, vol. 31–33, edited by Gerhard P. Knapp, 273–302. Amsterdam: Rodopi, 1991.

Tebben, Karin. *Literarische Intimität: Subjektkonstitution und Erzählstruktur in autobiographischen Texten von Frauen.* Tübingen: Francke, 1997.

Thomann Tewarson, Heidi. "Die Aufklärung im jüdischen Denken des 19. Jahrhunderts: Rahel Levin Varnhagen, Ludwig Robert, Ludwig Börne, Eduard Gans, Berthold Auerbach, Fanny Lewald." In *Juden und jüdische Kultur im Vormärz,* Forum Vormärz Forschung, Jahrbuch 1998, edited by Horst Denkler et al., 17–61. Bielefeld: Aisthesis, 1999.

Ujma, Christina, ed. *Fanny Lewald (1811–1889): Studien zu einer großen europäischen Schriftstellerin und Intellektuellen.* Bielefeld: Aisthesis, 2011.

Ujima, Christina. "Zwischen Rebellion und Resignation: Frauen, Juden und Künstler in den historischen Romanen Fanny Lewalds." In *Travellers in Time and Space. The German Historical Novel*, edited by Osman Durrani and Julian Preece, 283–299. Amsterdam: Rodopi, 2001.

Venske, Regula. "Discipline and Daydreaming in the Works of a Nineteenth-Century Woman Author: Fanny Lewald." In *German Women in the Eighteenth and Nineteenth Centuries*, edited by Ruth-Ellen B. Joeres and Mary Jo Maynes, 175–192. Bloomington: Indiana University Press, 1983.

Venske, Regula. *Ach Fanny! Vom jüdischen Mädchen zur preußischen Schriftstellerin: Fanny Lewald*. Berlin: Elefanten Press, 1988.

Wagner, Ulrike. "Schleiermacher's *Geselligkeit*, Henriette Herz, and the 'Convivial Turn.'" In *Conviviality at the Crossroads: The Poetics and Politics of Everyday Encounters*, ed. Oscar Hemer et al., 65–87. Houndmills, Basingstoke: Palgrave Macmillan, 2020.

Ward, Margaret E. *Fanny Lewald: Between Rebellion and Renunciation*. Edited by Horst S. Daemmrich. New York: Peter Lang, 2006.

Weigel, Sigrid. "Der schielende Blick. Thesen zur Geschichte weiblicher Schreibpraxis." In *Die verborgene Frau: Sechs Beiträge zu einer feministischen Literaturwissenschaft*, edited by Inge Stephan and Sigrid Weigel, 83–137. Berlin: Argument, 1983.

Zajdowicz, Rebecca Ann. "Constructing the Ideal German Woman: National Identity and Fanny Lewald's novel *Jenny*." In *Fanny Lewald (1811–1889): Studien zu einer großen europäischen Schriftstellerin und Intellektuellen*, edited by Christina Ujma, 155–168. Bielefeld: Aisthesis, 2011.

CHAPTER 8

···

HEDWIG DOHM (1831–1919)

···

SANDRA SHAPSHAY

> A member of the Reichstag recently said: "One cannot talk corpses into living," but one can make the living believe that they in fact have no right to live—at least not for themselves, but only for others.
>
> Hedwig Dohm, "On the Agitators of Antifeminism"

THE debate on the nature and value of compassion (*Mitleid*) between Arthur Schopenhauer and Friedrich Nietzsche—as well the contemporary reverberations thereof—is interestingly illuminated through the lens of German feminist philosopher and writer Hedwig Dohm (1831–1919). Although Schopenhauer and Nietzsche never engaged each other directly (as the former died before the latter's philosophically productive period), their thoughts on compassion are very much "in dialogue." In her philosophical essays and fiction—especially in her 1894 novella *Become Who You Are* (*Werde, die du bist*), a title that recalls Nietzsche's instruction in *The Gay Science*, "Du sollst der werden, der du bist" (You should become who you are),[1] as well as the subtitle of *Ecce Homo, How One Becomes What One Is* (*Wie man wird, was man ist*)—Dohm joins this conversation, and, as I shall argue, contributes something rather revolutionary to it.[2]

As a preview, I see her contribution as consisting of three main points. First, she highlights the gendered nature of compassion, and in doing so, takes Schopenhauer's discussion out of the transcendental realm and situates it in a dynamic social context. In this manner, Dohm effectively "out genealogizes" Nietzsche—who also tries to situate Schopenhauer's discussion of compassion historically, but who, despite his

---

[1] Friedrich Nietzsche, *The Gay Science*, trans. Walter Kaufmann (New York: Vintage, 1974), sec. 270. Hereafter GS, followed by section number.

[2] The epigraph to this chapter is from Dohm, "On the Agitators of Antifeminism," in *Women Philosophers in the Long Nineteenth Century: The German Tradition*, ed. Dalia Nassar and Kristin Gjesdal, translated by Anna C. Ezekiel (Oxford: Oxford University Press, 2021), 150. Unless specified otherwise, references to Dohm's texts are to those in this anthology.

genealogical method, lapses into talk of "woman in herself."[3] With exquisite wit, Dohm points out Nietzsche's own transcendental blind spot when it comes to women. Second, Dohm (perhaps implicitly) draws out parallels between the norms of the ordinary nineteenth-century bourgeois woman's life and the increasing degrees of self-lessness in Schopenhauer's *Mitleids-Moral*. In doing so, she joins Nietzsche in the criticisms of its harmful effects on the self—a self that ought to affirm and create itself for the sake of health as well as for the splendor of the human type—but focuses her attention on the half of the human population who are intensively socialized to fall under its sway. Third, she offers a new ideal in place of the Overman or Zarathustra, one which virtuously balances compassion with self-assertion and self-creation. This is the ideal of "The New Mother."

This dialectic on compassion begins with Schopenhauer's claim that it is the feeling of compassion—and, notably, *not* a good will governed by the categorical imperative as Kant would have it—that is *the* true foundation of morality. In a lengthy essay he argues that what he holds as the two cardinal virtues, *Gerechtigkeit* (justice) and *Menschenliebe* (translated often as loving kindness or philanthropy), ultimately spring from the feeling of compassion. There are eudaimonistic benefits for the compassionate person, according to Schopenhauer, insofar as the compassionate person lives in a world of "friendly appearances" whereas the egoist or, even worse, the malicious person lives in a world of "hostile appearances." In addition, there are potential soteriological benefits, for the compassionate person is at least on the road to salvation via resignation. Yet, if an action were done for the sake of such benefits, it would have no moral worth: according to Schopenhauerian ethics, only actions done *from the motive of compassion* have true moral worth.

Nietzsche hailed Schopenhauer as his "educator" in an essay by the same title (1873), and in his earliest published work, *The Birth of Tragedy* (1872), he takes over quite a bit of his teacher's transcendental idealism and metaphysics of will. But Nietzsche always drew the line at Schopenhauer's morality of compassion (*Mitleids-Moral*).[4] Even in *The Birth of Tragedy*, Nietzsche departs quite strikingly from the Schopenhauerian embrace of compassion as the foundation of morality and as the virtuous path toward asceticism and resignation from a world (our world) that involves such tremendous suffering. He resists what he regards as a morally motivated denial of life in favor of an aesthetic, creative *affirmation* of existence, an affirmation that embraces simultaneously the world's joy and creation as well as its suffering and destruction as a sublime, artistic spectacle.

In later works Nietzsche builds a case that compassion is a *sham and a trap* (more on this in what follows). For instance, expanding on a thought from Pindar, he enunciates

---

[3] Dohm, "Nietzsche and Women," in Nassar and Gjesdal, *Women Philosophers in the Long Nineteenth Century*, 129. Hereafter NW, followed by page number.

[4] For an extensive argument for this claim, see Christopher Janaway, *Beyond Selflessness: Reading Nietzsche's Genealogy* (Oxford: Oxford University Press, 2007).

this ideal for free spirits: "we, however, want to become those we are—human beings who are new, unique, incomparable, who give themselves laws, who create themselves" (GS 335). And what stands in the way of our creative self-fashioning?[5] In other words, what is the "greatest danger" on the road to becoming who we are? Nietzsche's answer is clear: the greatest danger lies "im Mitleiden" (GS 271). It's safe to say that the most serious bone of contention between Nietzsche and his educator concerns the value of compassion.

Into this dispute, enters Hedwig Dohm. As just sketched here, notwithstanding Nietzsche's genealogical method—which does import a historical dimension into the dispute, as Schopenhauer pursues a transcendental, even if largely empirical, approach—this philosophical quarrel remains largely aloof from actual social realities. Dohm enriches the discussion by *concretizing* it. As just alluded to here, she casts light on the nature of compassion by drawing attention to the fact that compassion—in nineteenth-century European society—is a highly *gendered* moral emotion (whether it be *the* Ur-virtue à la Schopenhauer or a pseudo-virtue à la Nietzsche). Second, she addresses the value of compassion by investigating its effects on the *actual lived experiences* of nineteenth-century European women, tracing the effects of the *Mitleids-Moral diachronically* throughout the flesh-and-blood life cycles of women, from girl-hood to old age. Dohm thus contributes both substantively and methodologically to this debate on the nature and value of compassion by investigating—and to the best of my knowledge, investigating *for the first time in the philosophical landscape*—how the emotion contributes to and detracts from the lives of the people who are socialized first and foremost to be its most diligent practitioners.

1 DOHM'S LIFE AND WRITINGS

Before turning to Dohm's intervention into the dispute over the *Mitleids-Moral*, I would like to set the stage with a brief sketch of her life and writings. She was born Hedwig Schleh in Berlin in 1831 to tobacco factory owner Gustav Adolph Gotthold Schlesinger and his wife, Wilhelmine Henriette Jülich. Her father's family had previously converted to Christianity, but Gustav decided to go a bit further toward assimilation and changed his surname to the less Jewish sounding Schleh. Hedwig was the third child and eldest daughter in a family of eighteen children. An intellectually curious child, she "resented the unequal treatment of sons and daughters . . . [as well as the] physical limitations

---

[5] How to understand this paradoxical-sounding ideal of "becoming who you are" is a topic of significant scholarly debate in Nietzsche scholarship. For a variety of positions, see Alexander Nehamas, *Nietzsche, Life as Literature* (Cambridge, MA: Harvard University Press, 1985); Brian Leiter, "The Paradox of Fatalism and Self-Creation in Nietzsche," in *Willing and Nothingness: Schopenhauer as Nietzsche's Educator*, ed. Christopher Janaway (Oxford: Clarendon Press, 1998); and Paul Franco, "Becoming Who You Are: Nietzsche on Self-Creation," *Journal of Nietzsche Studies* 49, no. 1 (2018): 52–77.

imposed upon girls."[6] Firsthand experience of the Revolution of 1848 further awakened her sociopolitical consciousness and shaped her lifelong antipathy toward state violence, as witnessed in her outspoken opposition to World War I at the end of her life.

Ultimately, she convinced her restrictive parents to allow her to enter a teacher training school, and to travel to Spain to visit her brother. In Spain she took private Spanish lessons from Wilhelm Friedrich Ernst Dohm (1819–1883), a German literary critic, translator, and writer and the editor-in-chief of the important political-satirical journal *Kladderadatsch*. She married Ernst, whose family of origin had also converted from Judaism to Christianity, and in doing so became exposed to literary social circles and an exciting world of political ideas. Their home was a frequent salon visited by luminaries such as Alexander von Humboldt, Karl August Varnhagen, Theodor Fontane, Countess Sophie von Hatzfeldt, Lily Braun, and Franz Liszt, among others. Yet Dohm was unable to participate as fully as she would have liked, since she was quite occupied by their five children, produced in quick succession: a son, who died in 1866, and four daughters, all of whom, Dohm saw to it, received a serious education and professional training.

In 1867 her writing career began when she took over a work commission from Ernst and published a two-volume history of Spanish literature. In 1872, with her children more self-sufficient, she began writing about women's emancipation, starting with her essay "What the Pastors Think about Women" ("Was die Pastoren von den Frauen denken"). This was followed by several treatises about women's social situation in which she argued for women's suffrage, equality in education, and professional opportunities: "Jesuitism in the Household" ("Der Jesuitismus im Hausstande" (1873)); "The Scientific Emancipation of Women" ("Die wissenschaftliche Emancipation der Frau" (1874)); and "Women's Nature and Rights" ("Der Frauen Natur und Recht" (1876)). With these essays, Hedwig Dohm became a household name in literary and feminist circles in Germany.

In the late 1870s Dohm also wrote four social comedies, which were performed in Berlin and met with public success. In the late 1880s, she published overtly philosophical satirical essays that attacked antifeminist currents in the larger society. She targeted especially intellectuals such as Nietzsche (more on this to follow), German neurologist Paul Julius Möbius, and Guy de Maupassant, aiming to expose the prejudices and fallacies in their writings on women. In the 1890s, she wrote five works of fiction, including the novels *Become Who You Are* and *How to Become Women* (*Wie Frauen Werden*), both published in 1894.

Finally, in the early twentieth century, Dohm became even more politically active, joining and cofounding groups dedicated to the legislative reform of women's education and career training. In "From the Death Bed" ("Auf dem Sterbebett," 1919), her last

---

[6] Quote from Elizabeth G. Ametsbichler, afterword to *Become Who You Are*, by Hedwig Dohm, trans. and ed. Elizabeth G. Ametsbichler (Albany: State University of New York Press, 2006), 82. For this biographical sketch, I have relied mostly on this work and on Samantha Michele Riley, "Hedwig Dohm," in *The Literary Encyclopedia*, https://www.litencyc.com/php/speople.php?rec=true&UID=11985.

essay, she writes about the disappointment she experienced regarding the slow progress of women's rights. Notwithstanding, she lived to see the introduction of women's suffrage in Germany in 1918. Shortly thereafter, Dohm died of a lung infection in Berlin on June 1, 1919.

With this sketch in place, I shall now turn to Dohm's philosophical contribution to the quarrel between Schopenhauer and Nietzsche on the nature and value of compassion.

2 SCHOPENHAUER ON COMPASSION

In "On the Basis of Morality" (*Über die Grundlage der Moral*, 1840–1841) Schopenhauer offers his most extensive treatment of the emotion of compassion, which he describes as follows: "[compassion is] the wholly immediate *sympathy* [Theilnahme], independent of any other consideration, in the first place toward another's *suffering*, and hence toward the prevention or removal of this suffering. . . . As soon as this compassion is alert, the well-being and woe of the other is immediately close to my heart, in just the same way, though not always to the same degree, as only my own is otherwise."[7] Versus psychological egoists, Schopenhauer holds that this immediate sympathy with and desire to prevent or remove the suffering of another is "wholly real," and "by no means . . . rare" (OBM, 200). After providing this analysis, he then aims to show that compassion is the sole source of actions with moral worth; this case is based on empirical evidence of common intuitions, ordinary language analysis, and a thought-experiment involving two would-be murderers, Caius and Titus, who refrain from the crime out of a variety of motivations.[8]

But a question remains: is the compassionate person *objectively* speaking the better person than the egoist and the malicious person? Or might the compassionate person be a "sucker" or "loser" (to put it in more contemporary parlance), who helps others with their struggles rather than affirming himself or herself? To answer this question Schopenhauer offers a "metaphysical basis" for why the compassionate person, epistemically speaking, sees things objectively aright, while the egoist and malicious person are fundamentally in error. For Schopenhauer, the essence of compassion consists in a person *"making less of a distinction than everyone else between himself and others"* (OBM, 249, emphasis mine). By contrast, the malicious person makes a great distinction

---

[7] Arthur Schopenhauer, "On the Basis of Morality," in *The Two Fundamental Problems of Ethics*, edited and translated by Christopher Janaway (Cambridge: Cambridge University Press, 2009), §16, 200, my underlining. Hereafter OBM, followed by page number.

[8] For a fuller treatment see my *Reconstructing Schopenhauer's Ethics: Hope, Compassion, and Animal Welfare* (New York: Oxford University Press, 2019), especially chap. 4; and Colin Marshall, "Schopenhauer's Titus Argument," in *Schopenhauer's Moral Philosophy*, ed. Patrick Hassan (London: Routledge, 2021).

between the "I" and the "other" such that "to him someone else's suffering is immediately a pleasure" (OBM, 249), and for the egoist, "the same distinction is still great enough . . . that to gain a small advantage to himself he will use great harm to others as a means" (OBM, 249).[9]

Unlike the egoist and the malicious person, then, the compassionate person intuitively recognizes a *fundamental parity* between himself and others by virtue of a shared essence. Given Schopenhauer's transcendental idealism and identification of the thing-in-itself with "will" (his metaphysical monism of will), the compassionate person's insight constitutes *a step in the right epistemic direction*. That is to say, the compassionate person's conduct embodies an intuitive insight beyond the "principium individuationis" and into the way the world really is in itself, into the world as "will." In terms that Schopenhauer borrows from the Indian tradition, the compassionate person sees through the "veil of māyā" to the truth enunciated in the Vedas that "Tat tvam asi" (You are that!) (WWR I, 401). Thus, because the compassionate person intuitively perceives this distinction between the "I" and the "other" as "by no means so great"—and even in actions of "noble-mindedness [this distinction] appears to be removed, so that *someone else's I is placed on a par with his own*" (WWR I, 401, emphasis mine)—the compassionate person gets things metaphysically right, for the I and the other *really are on a par* in terms of their value.[10]

Compassion comes in degrees, for Schopenhauer, with respect to its cognitive content and the behavior it motivates. In the lowest degree, a person practices the virtue of justice (refraining from harming others and giving them their due). In a higher degree, a person practices also the virtue of loving kindness, which manifests in "pure, i.e., unselfish love of others" that "equates the other individual and his fate with its own" (WWR I, 402). In the highest degree of unselfish love—magnanimity—one will actually "sacrifice his life completely for the good of many others." Schopenhauer describes the person with a very high degree of compassion as follows:

> [but] the character who has achieved the highest goodness and the most perfect magnanimity will sacrifice his life completely for the good of many others: this is how Codrus died, as well as Leonidas, Regulus, Decius Mus, Arnold von Winkelried, and everyone else who freely and consciously goes to a certain death for the sake of

---

[9] See also Arthur Schopenhauer, *The World as Will and Representation*, vol. 1, trans. and ed. Judith Norman, Alistair Welchman, and Christopher Janaway (Cambridge: Cambridge University Press, 2010), 339. Vol. 1 and vol. 2 (2018) hereafter WWR, followed by volume and page number.

[10] There is a lively scholarly debate over the content of the compassionate person's insight. The more traditional reading is that it is a recognition of metaphysical unity or the nondistinctness of individuals on the basis of Schopenhauer's monistic metaphysics of will. Colin Marshall defends a modified version of this view in "Schopenhauer on the Content of Compassion," *Noûs* (published ahead of print, March 26, 2020): 1–18, https://doi.org/10.1111/nous.12330. My own reading is axiological and sees the content of compassion as intuitive insight into the roughly equal *inherent value of the other* (a value had to some degree by all sentient beings). See my *Reconstructing*, 2019; and my "Was Schopenhauer a Kantian Ethicist?," *International Journal of Philosophical Studies* 28, no. 2 (2020): 168–187. For another variation on the axiological interpretation see Janaway, *Beyond Selflessness*.

family or fatherland. Also on this level is everyone who willingly suffers and dies for asserting claims that are in the collective interest of humanity and are part of the human patrimony, i.e. key, universal truths and the eradication of great errors: this is how Socrates died, as well as Giordano Bruno and the many heroes of truth who met with death at the stake at the hands of the priests. (WWR I, 402)

In the case where the person who has "achieved the highest goodness" does not meet with a violent death on the battlefield or at the stake, the insight that leads the person to universal love and the desire to remedy all of the sufferings of the world, may lead to universal loathing and resignation from life: "such a human being, who recognizes himself, his innermost and true self in all beings, must also regard the endless suffering of all living things as his own, and take upon himself the pain of the whole world. . . . [this] becomes the *tranquillizer* of all and every willing. The will begins turning away from life: it shrinks from each of the pleasures in which it sees life being affirmed. A human being achieves the state of voluntary renunciation, resignation, true composure, and complete will-lessness" (WWR I, 406). The extremely compassionate person, who takes on the "sufferings of all living things as his own," thus takes on a very hard lot. Since there is so much suffering, taking on the "pain of the whole world" is such as to divest a person from the pleasures of life. Further, the person may come to realize that her efforts at reducing suffering are ultimately quite futile: a minute decrease in an ocean of suffering. Accordingly, Schopenhauer writes, a person with such a high degree of insight beyond the *principium individuationis* "is no longer satisfied with loving others as himself and doing as much for them as for himself; instead, he has conceived a loathing for the essence that is expressed as his own appearance, the will to life, the kernel and essence of that world he recognizes as a miserable place" (WWR I, 407).

Thus, when the dial of compassion is turned up to the highest degree—along with the pessimistic insight that the pain of the whole world is tremendous and irremediable in the grand scheme—the very logic of compassion involves a transition from virtue to asceticism. And in this way, Schopenhauer identifies a deep parallel between his ethical thought and that of Christianity: "its ethics are entirely in the spirit of our present discussion and lead not only to the highest degree of loving kindness but also to renunciation" (WWR I, 413). As in Christian ethics, for Schopenhauer, we should love others as we love ourselves, but when we truly do so on the prescribed universal scale, we shall realize that this world is a vale of tears, that compassionate action is ultimately quite futile, and that we should rather resign from it entirely.

3 Nietzsche on Compassion

The Christian echoes in Schopenhauer's ethical thought were not lost on Nietzsche, who was exercised by the fact that even such a thoroughgoing atheist could be caught up in the "ascetic ideal."[11] Nietzsche takes aim at Schopenhauer's version of it by first disputing his account of the *nature* of compassion.[12] In a psychological egoist vein, Nietzsche suggests that the "compassionate person" is at bottom just a person who (truly, secretly) enjoys the feeling of *superiority over another*. What is called "suffering with," on this diagnosis, is really just a form of ressentiment of the weak. On top of the petty power grab that is compassion, for Nietzsche, modern society puts a pleasing varnish. In sum, for Nietzsche, the modern concept of compassion (1) masks the general power-lessness of those who practice it, while simultaneously (2) elevating the impulses of herd members who seek to feel superior to others—and thus who act faute de mieux as "physicians, consolers, and 'saviors' of the sick" (GM, 125)—into a cardinal virtue.

With respect to the true nature of compassion, however, Schopenhauer and Nietzsche are just talking past each other. Schopenhauer admits that some actions may just *look* compassionate—but are really undertaken out of ostentation or from various egoistic motives—yet he believes it is "just as certain that there are actions of disinterested loving kindness and freely willed justice" such as when "a rich man [who] had what belonged to him given back by a poor man" (OBM, 186). He dares a skeptic like Nietzsche to interpret as egoistic the actions of someone like "Arnold von Winkelried [who] cried 'Comrades, dear confederates, care for my wife and child' and then embraced as many enemy spears as he could" (OBM, 196). Schopenhauer finds it totally implausible to chalk this up to a self-interested motive like the desire to feel superior, writing incredulously: "anyone may think that if he can: I am unable to do so. . . . If anyone nevertheless insisted on denying to me the occurrence of all such [truly compassionate] actions, then according to him morals would be a science without a real object, like astrology and alchemy, and it would be a waste of time disputing further about its basis. So I would have finished with him, and am speaking to those who accept the reality of the matter" (OBM, 196–197).

On this score, then, Schopenhauer and Nietzsche reach an impasse. But for the sake of argument, let's suppose that Nietzsche would accept that there are some genuinely compassionate actions (in Schopenhauer's terms, "freely-willed justice" and "disinterested loving kindness"). Then the debate continues since Nietzsche mounts a further critique of the *value* of compassion. One of the clearest statements of this critique comes in the preface to GM, section 5, and bears quoting at length:

> what was especially at stake [in Nietzsche's *The Wanderer and His Shadow*, 1880] was the *value* of morality . . . the value of the "unegoistic," the instincts of pity, self-abnegation, self-sacrifice [den Werth des "Unegoistischen," der Mitleids-, Selbstverleugnungs-, Selbstopferungs-Instinkte] which Schopenhauer had gilded, deified, and projected into a beyond for so long that at last they became for him

---

[11] Friedrich Nietzsche, *On the Genealogy of Morals*, translated by Walter Kaufmann and R. J. Hollingdale (New York: Vintage, 1967), 19 and 102. Hereafter GM, followed by page number.

[12] I should note here that *Mitleid* in Nietzsche is often translated, especially by Kaufmann, as "pity," but this strikes me as a mistranslation since "compassion" better captures the etymology of *Mit-leiden*, "suffering with."

'value-in-itself,' *on the basis of which he said No to life and to himself.* . . . I understood the ever spreading morality of pity [Mitleids-Moral] that had seized even on
philosophers and made them ill, as the most sinister symptom of a European culture that had itself become sinister, perhaps as its by-pass to a new Buddhism? To a
Buddhism for Europeans? to—*nihilism*? (GM, 19, emphasis mine)

And in the next section, Nietzsche adds:

one has taken the *value* of these "values" as given, as factual, as beyond all question;
one has hitherto never doubted or hesitated in the slightest degree in supposing "the
good man" to be of greater value than "the evil man." . . . But what if the reverse were
true? What if a symptom of regression were inherent in the "good," likewise a danger,
a seduction, a poison, a narcotic, through which the present was possibly living *at the
expense of the future*? Perhaps more comfortably, less dangerously, but at the same
time in a meaner style, more basely?—So that precisely morality would be to blame
if the *highest power and splendor* actually possible to the type man was never in fact
attained? So that precisely morality was the danger of dangers? (GM, 20)

In these passages, Nietzsche's main criticism of the morality of compassion is that
it leads to tremendous disvalue: first, it *devalues life* (it says no to life) on the basis of
the great amount of suffering involved in affirming it because affirmation ineluctably
involves domination and exploitation of others. Second, it *devalues the self* (it says no to
the self) in its recommendation of *selfless*[13] living for others, so as to reduce the suffering
of "the herd." Third, due to the devaluation of life and self it *encourages mediocrity*—that
is, it encourages us to live "more comfortably, less dangerously, but at the same time in
a meaner style, more basely." In all of these ways, the *Mitleids-Moral* is a symptom of
"declining life" (GM, 154), and declining selves, that will prevent or at least forestall the
development of the highest splendor of the human type.

In response, Nietzsche proposes a counter–moral code which recommends first and
foremost *self-assertion* and *self-fashioning*, and that eschews the temptations of compassion. In *Ecce Homo*, for example, he writes:

the overcoming of pity [des Mitleids] I count among the *noble* virtues: as
"Zarathustra's temptation" I invented a situation in which a great cry of distress
reaches him, as pity [das Mitleiden] tries to attack him like a final sin that would
entice him away from *himself* [ihn von sich abspenstig machen will]. To remain the
master [Herr bleiben] at this point, to keep the eminence of one's task undefiled

---

[13] Bernard Reginster explicates this Nietzschean objection against Schopenhauer, writing: "the
defining attitude of the compassionate agent [on Schopenhauer's account of compassion] is one of
self-lessness, understood as a relative devaluation of his own interests by the compassionate agent. . . .
[Nietzsche's] chief misgiving appears to focus on Schopenhauer's assumption that the altruistic character
of compassion requires the selflessness of the agent. . . . [that] I must devalue my own interests, at
least relatively to those of others." Bernard Reginster, "Sympathy in Schopenhauer and Nietzsche," in
Sympathy: A History, ed. Eric Schliesser (Oxford: Oxford University Press, 2015), 259.

by the many lower and more myopic impulses that are at work in so-called selfless actions, that is the test, perhaps the ultimate test, which a Zarathustra must pass—his real *proof* of strength. (EH, 228)

The key danger of Schopenhauer's *Mitleids-Moral*, to strong, noble, self-creating men like Zarathustra, for Nietzsche, is its *selflessness*. And to some extent this criticism does hit the mark, for compassion in very high degrees according to Schopenhauer may lead to magnanimous sacrifice of oneself (for the sake of others) and even to a recoiling from life altogether and a resignation from the world. In stark contrast to the egoist, the compassionate person in Schopenhauer's ethical thought recognizes that the "I" has no more (though, it should be said, also *no less*) value than anyone else's "I." Further, the maxim of the good person in this ethics is "harm no one; rather help everyone to the extent that you can" (OBM, 140). Given that one can do quite a lot of harm to other human beings as well as to nonhuman animals *just by living* (see Jainism, and its worry about harming insects in the harvesting of plants); and given that there are so many suffering others—suffering from poverty, disease, violence, and so on—who could be helped, Schopenhauer's morality of compassion can become *very demanding*. So demanding, in fact, that avoiding harm to others and helping them "to the extent that you can" can easily overwhelm the value of the self (as in the case of von Winkelried). Nietzsche is correct to point out that the logic of Schopenhauer's *Mitleids-Moral* is on track to "unself man." Practiced to a high degree, the morality of compassion is indeed, for better or for worse, an "Entselbstungs-Moral" (EH, 292).[14]

4 HEDWIG DOHM ON SELFLESSNESS

Into this hitherto rather abstract moral-psychological dispute, Hedwig Dohm intervenes by putting it into a concrete social context, that is, *with respect to the particular situation* of the lives of European women in her day. For Dohm, such women are socialized to be (1) in their youth, charming sexual objects for men; (2) in their reproductive years, self-less wives and mothers, living through and for their husbands and children; and (3) in their old age, *resigned from life*, encouraged to see themselves as "superfluous" and thus voluntarily to shrink from active social life and indeed, from life itself as expeditiously as possible.

In her novella *Werde, die du bist,* the very title calls attention to the highly gendered nature of the "virtues" that spring from compassion, and which present the greatest obstacle to self-creation: In place of Nietzsche's masculine article in "Du sollst der werden, der du bist" (GS 270), Dohm addresses the imperative specifically to women (via the "die," the feminine form of "der"). In this story—which could easily be the story of any

---

[14] For an extensive and illuminating discussion of Nietzsche's critique of Schopenhauer's ethics in the GM see Janaway, *Beyond Selflessness.*

nineteenth-century bourgeois European woman—it is the typical woman, *not* the typical man, who is first and foremost in need of self-affirmation.

The novella opens with a story that frames the central first-personal narrative as told through journal entries: an older woman (she's about sixty), Agnes Schmidt, has been convalescing in the mental hospital of a certain Doctor Behrend near Berlin. Of the protagonist, we are told, "everyone who knew the spouse of the Privy Councillor Schmidt agreed that she had been a good, well-mannered, somewhat limited and philistine housewife, ignorant and totally absorbed with family life." Further, she had "cared for her paralyzed husband [in his final 8 years] in a self-sacrificing way."[15] But recently, in the mental hospital, she had become "a new individual": "usually, she was taciturn. Occasionally, however, she started to talk; then it was as if she were carrying on a conversation with a supernatural being. Her words breathed immeasurable melancholy or dithyrambic ecstasy. She uttered profound and sublime thoughts in a form that was reminiscent of Nietzsche's *Zarathustra*. One would have believed that this old woman had been a great poetess and that an excess of intellectual provocation caused the mental disturbance. The opposite was the case" (*Become*, 1).

We learn the backstory of her current Zarathustrian "madness" through her journal, which she starts writing as a kind of therapy after she is widowed, and which she gives to Dr. Behrend so that he may better understand his patient. The journal entries give us the main story of the novella and the actual voice of the protagonist, Agnes Schmidt, offering a first-personal account of a widow who, now with leisure time to read, reflect, travel (first to Italy, then to Capri), and write in this very journal, embarks on an examination of her past and hesitatingly but ultimately thrillingly embarks on a journey toward the discovery/creation of her own "I."

With vivid, phenomenological detail, Dohm paints a picture of the societal ideal of the compassionate, loving, self-less, "good woman" as a *trap* set for women by men who seek to maintain, egoistically, their traditional privilege and dominance over women. It starts in childhood: as a girl, Agnes writes, she was "[a] well-behaved, good child, a gentle and pretty child. . . . I did whatever was demanded of me. However, they preferred my brother to me, and when later, I never learned music or drawing or languages or anything else, it was because my brother received everything that could be saved up for" (*Become*, 9–10). Her mother, she recounts, "essentially lived only for father" and father "barely took notice of me," because "parents are always disappointed when daughters instead of sons are born to them." She concludes from this that "girls had to be subordinate" (*Become*, 11). Her subordination continues as married woman: Agnes recounts that her husband was "convinced of his superiority over me, [and] was somewhat willful and strict in his demands on me [but this] did not disturb the peace of our marriage . . . I was healthy, my husband was happy and satisfied, my daughters Grete and Magdalene blossomed. Hearty and lively children whom I loved with my whole heart, but who saw

---

[15] Dohm, *Become Who You Are*, in Nassar and Gjesdal, *Women Philosophers in the Long Nineteenth Century*, 2. Hereafter *Become*, followed by page number.

to it that I had to work vigorously" (*Become*, 12). It was only after the death of her husband, whom she cared for in a "self-sacrificing way," and a string of realizations—that her adult daughters were really no longer daughters since they became mothers; that her grandchildren were actually either frightened or contemptuous of her; and that her sons-in-law simply viewed her as an irritating if at times comical burden—that she draws the conclusion that sparks her self-creation:

> They had chained up my nature. Now I've been unleashed. . . . Living for others ought to be the right, the true thing. If that were so, and everyone lived for others, then indeed others would have had to live for me, and then it just would be the same and much simpler if everyone lived for himself from the beginning.
>
> A mother ought to be there only for her children! So I should only live and work for my daughter, and the daughter in turn should only be there for her children. What a senseless, fruitless circular course. (*Become*, 32)

Agnes finally recognizes the deeply gendered nature of the self-sacrificing virtues into which she has been socialized: It is wives, mothers, and daughters who are taught to "live for others" but no one—certainly not boys and men—in turn, lives for them. Women in her society live least of all for themselves. The result for these women is a "senseless, fruitless circular course."

> So what of her own "I"?

> Did I really only have duties toward others, none toward myself? Were all of the others more worthy than I? If they had been, then—then of course—. . . . Love your neighbor as yourself, it says in the gospel.
>
> I am allowed, I ought then to love myself? What have I ever done for myself out of love? Nothing that I knew of.
>
> But yet I was always satisfied? I? But I wasn't even an "I." (*Become*, 32–33)

Ultimately, Agnes realizes that women—and it seems *only women*—are inculcated by bourgeois society into an even more self-sacrificing rendition of the Christian commandment to love thy neighbor as yourself: women aren't even encouraged to love themselves! This version of compassionate love equates to the highest degrees of compassion on Schopenhauer's scale (magnanimity) where the "I" isn't just considered on a value par with others, rather, the value of the "I" is overwhelmed and outweighed by the value of others. In other words, Agnes realizes that women of her day were instructed not just to "love thy neighbor as thyself"—an injunction that assumes the *value parity of everyone's "I" male or female*—rather, they are inculcated into the most extreme version of this Christian ethos, one that encourages women to imitate Christ himself. Ironically, in the mental hospital, where Agnes reports she has never felt saner, she expresses this to Dr. Behrend: "many women die on the cross . . . for others, like our Savior" (*Become*, 8). Through books, reflection, and writing, however, Agnes realizes that it is high time for her to shed this self-sacrificing ethos for women and to heed the titular imperative of the novella: better late than never, she should become who she is!

Dohm's analysis of women's socialization accords with explicit guides to female morals written in the mid-nineteenth century. To wit, in their classic study *The Madwoman in the Attic,* Sandra Gilbert and Susan Gubar quote Mrs. Sarah Ellis's "Victorian England's foremost preceptress of female morals and manners," composed in 1844 (just a few years after the publication of Schopenhauer's OBM). Ellis prescribes the following for women: "because she is the "least engaged of any member of the household," a woman of right feeling should devote herself to the good of others. And she should do this silently, without calling attention to her exertions because "all that would tend to draw away her thoughts from others and fix them on herself, ought to be avoided as an evil to her."[16] Returning to the dialogue with Schopenhauer and Nietzsche, it is also striking how Dohm's analysis of prescribed women's self-lessness throughout the lifecycle of the good nineteenth-century bourgeois woman, parallels the increasing degrees of virtue—and self-lessness—in Schopenhauer's ethical thought. In Dohm's analysis, on the lowest level, the girl's interests are furthered by her mother but it ought to be the girl's main desire to please others (especially her parents and a would-be male suitor); as a grown woman, even more selflessly, she should gladly sacrifice any interests she might have for herself in favor of those of her children and husband; and finally, and most selflessly of all, as an older woman, after her husband has died and after her adult children and grandchildren no longer require her services, she should resign from life altogether.

Yet, despite the fact that the lifecycle of the ordinary, bourgeois woman in his own era closely mirrored the increasing path of virtue (from compassion to asceticism) laid out in his ethical thought, Schopenhauer's prime examples of heroic self-sacrifice are all *men*—Codrus, Leonidas, Regulus, Decius Mus, Arnold von Winkelried—who died in battle or who willingly suffered and died "for asserting claims that are in the collective interest of humanity and are part of the human patrimony" like Socrates and Giordano Bruno. To be fair, Schopenhauer does acknowledge that women (and he thinks, to their credit) excel at the higher degree of compassion (*Menschenliebe*) whereas men tend to excel rather at the lower level (*Gerechtigkeit*). But his reason for thinking this has nothing to do with women's socialization into selflessness. Rather, it has to do with what he sees as women's innate weaknesses and competencies vis-à-vis men, writing: "women, who because of the weakness of their reason are much less capable than men of understanding universal *principles*, of holding them firm and taking them as their guide, are as a rule inferior to men in the virtue of justice. . . . On the other hand they surpass men in the virtue of *loving kindness*: for the occasion for this is mostly *intuitive* and therefore speaks immediately to compassion, to which women are decidedly more readily receptive" (OBM, 206). Thus, Schopenhauer pays women a kind of backhanded compliment: they have a moral advantage because they are less adept at reasoning. Yet

---

[16] Sandra M. Gilbert and Susan Gubar, *The Madwoman in the Attic: The Woman Writer and the Nineteenth-Century Literary Imagination* (New Haven: Yale University Press, 1979), 24.

he also lauds women's greater intuitive receptivity to compassion, and he has high praise for saintly women mystics like Madame de Guyon (WWR I, 411) who have managed to resign from life. But what Schopenhauer fails to see—and what Dohm brings to light—is that the *ordinary life* of the vast majority of nineteenth-century women was one that *trained them up* to be selfless paragons of the *Mitleids-Moral*. Schopenhauer's ahistorical, transcendental approach to this topic obscures the gendered power relations that have made women in Schopenhauer's terms "more readily receptive" to compassion. And the queasiness that we might feel at this socialized double standard with respect to compassion helps us to feel the pull of Nietzsche's criticisms of its value. (Speaking personally as a Schopenhauer scholar, I can say that it has helped me feel their pull.)

In contrast to Nietzsche, however, and like Schopenhauer, Dohm does seem to subscribe to the reality of truly compassionate actions. Given their socialization, women especially seem genuinely motivated to help others to the extent that they can. But like Nietzsche, Dohm launches some withering criticisms of the self-lessness involved in the *Mitleids-Moral*, especially in light of the damage it does to the lives of those who are most inculcated into it, namely those of women.

Through her vivid portrayals of a woman's lived experience of the *Mitleids-Moral*, Dohm offers a Nietzschean-style critique, namely, that it leads to a sick, life-denying *unselfing*, that constitutes so much wasted potential. Thus she writes in her essay "The New Mother":

> but it is still said that a woman should be absorbed in her child and her husband. So strange, so absurd, that I, with my own individuality, should be absorbed in my children! But my children, my husband, they are totally different than I am! My I is not at all in them. Where is it then, if not in me?"[17]
>
> Yes, when I perceive the rights of children, I also perceive the rights and happiness of mothers. They harm themselves when they cling to their adult children who no longer need them, seek refuge in the lives of these children to escape loneliness and the spiritual wasteland of age. Many women of mental and spiritual poverty (as a result of their upbringing) have nothing else in the world that is attached to them or to which they are attached. And because they themselves have not become their own, have no life purpose of their own, they make their children into their self. (NM, 143)

Here Dohm lays bare how a typical nineteenth-century woman is encouraged to lose her "I" at every stage of life: her upbringing impoverishes her mentally and spiritually and leaves her with no projects or "life purpose" of her own; as a grown woman she is encouraged instead to become "absorbed in her child and husband," and then, even when they no longer need her, she clings to them for a sense of purpose and to "escape loneliness and the spiritual wasteland of age." This is chilling picture of a person who has

---

[17] Dohm, "The New Mother," in Nassar and Gjesdal, *Women Philosophers in the Long Nineteenth Century*, 143. Hereafter NM, followed by page number.

been socialized to un-self herself, and one that is reminiscent of the Nietzschean worries about the *Mitleids-Moral*'s self and life negating effects. Yet, in these passages, Dohm's twist on the Nietzschean critique reveals something else. She reveals the lopsided impact—the real double standard—of this moral code insofar as the *Mitleids-Moral* in her contemporary society is prescribed first and foremost for *women*. It is not the male but really the female cycle of self-lessness that is repeated, generation after generation: "the daughter who has become a mother stops being a daughter. And now the young mother again hopes for the future in her children; and her mother, now a grandmother, sees that children promise nothing. This eternal melancholy cycle: that was the lot of the mother" (NM, 143–144). Further, she raises that famous legal question: Who benefits? That is, who benefits from this melancholy female cycle of selflessness? The answer is obvious: men are the beneficiaries of this gendered morality of self-lessness. Women are trained to live *for men*, so that men may to a greater extent cultivate their own "I's," from generation to generation.

Interestingly, Nietzsche implicitly recognizes this female-gendered ethics of compassion, for he refers offhandedly but repeatedly to the *Mitleids-Moral* as "effeminate," for instance:

> this problem of the value of pity [Mitleid] and of the morality of pity [Mitleids-Moral]
> (--I am opposed to the pernicious modern *effeminacy* of feeling [Gefühlsverweichlichung] . . .)" (GM, 20, emphasis mine)

> that the sick [compassionate ones] should *not* make the healthy sick—and this is what such an <u>emasculation</u> [Verweichlichung] would involve. (GM, 124, emphasis mine)

Nietzsche here implicitly acknowledges that compassion is predominately a woman's virtue—for him it is "effeminate" and "emasculating"—and accordingly should be avoided, at least by men. But contrary to Dohm, Nietzsche is not really concerned to warn women about the dangers of the *Mitleids-Moral*, let alone to help emancipate them from it. Quite the opposite is the case, for Nietzsche groups the *Mitleids-Moral* together with "democracy, international courts in place of war, [and] *equal rights for women*": all symptoms of declining self and "declining life" (GM, 154, emphasis mine).

Of course, it stands to reason that equal rights for women would be a boon to the self-creation *of women*. And this seems precisely to be the problem with them for Nietzsche, which prompts the question: with whose declining self is Nietzsche really concerned? Clearly, his ideal of self-creation is one slated only for a small class of *men*, notably, men who can eschew the temptations of effeminate compassion. Of course, these free spirits will need material support; the kind provided by "slaves" and, importantly for this discussion, *women*—thus, down with democracy and equal rights for women!

One facet of Dohm's intervention in this dispute over the *Mitleids-Moral* is to offer a metacritique of Nietzsche. The problem with Nietzsche's criticisms is that they are applied arbitrarily, according to his prejudices. Accordingly, it is eminently appropriate for slaves and women to live for others and to sacrifice their own "I's" so that free-spirited *men* can attain the highest type of *man*. But what justifies Nietzsche's a priori exclusion of women from the group of would-be free spirits?

It seems to Dohm that Nietzsche's a priori exclusion of women from becoming free spirits is due to an ironic lapse into transcendental thinking about "woman in herself." This lapse is made all the more ironic (and painful, for admitted Nietzsche fans like Dohm) by the fact that he had precious little experience with women—only his "five-fingers breadth of experience" (NW, 128). Unfortunately, Nietzsche was no Socrates, "he does not know what he does not know" (Dohm, "Nietzsche and Women," 1898). Thus, he ends up spewing the most absurd and offensive nonsense about the transcendental nature of woman. Dohm could run a similar argument against Nietzsche's talk of male slaves too, but this is not (and need not) be her focus. She quips instead that "[a]nyone who wants slaves is not a man [*Herr*]" (NW, 134). With this, quip, however, Dohm alludes to Nietzsche's Zarathustra (the ideal "Herr") who, if he were a real "Herr" could not possibly want a slave for a partner; thus offering an internal critique of Nietzsche's own ideal man.

By contrast, when it comes to women (at least white, bourgeois, European women) Dohm knows whereof she speaks. She brings the lived experience of the nineteenth-century European woman to bear on this philosophical debate, and in light of this experience as well as her analysis of the undue burden of compassion on girls and women, she radically transforms Nietzsche's critique of the *Mitleids-Moral* as well as his ideal of the self-creating man. Yet it is important to note that her alternative critique is not anticompassion tout court. In fact, she lauds compassion in several places.

5 Dohm on Compassion

In her essay "Are Professional Employment and Maternal Duties Compatible?" (1900), Dohm praises professional women like her female dentist who raised half a dozen nephews and nieces, while simultaneously practicing her vocation and engaging in all manner of philanthropy. Like Schopenhauer, Dohm sees compassionate care for others as a virtue; but unlike Schopenhauer, she urges that the virtue should be kept in check so as not to overwhelm the value of the "I." That is to say, one should be compassionate, but one should also keep in mind that one's own "I" is on a value par with that of the "other" and thus the other's well-being and woe does not count for more than one's own. Where Dohm really parts ways from Schopenhauer (and promotes a kind of feminist-Kantian duty to oneself) is to stress that *girls as well as boys, women as well as men, have a duty to appreciate the value that resides in themselves—they have a duty to develop their own "I" and thus ought not to sacrifice their own "I" for that of another.* Thus, while it might be exceedingly noble to sacrifice one's "I" in certain rare circumstances (e.g., in the case of Arnold von Winkelried or even Jesus Christ), for Dohm, it certainly shouldn't be the expected norm for anyone to sacrifice their "I" for others, as it plainly was for women in the nineteenth century.

Another facet of Dohm's intervention in this dispute over the *Mitleids-Moral* is that she offers an *alternative ideal* to Schopenhauer's resigned Saint as well as to Nietzsche's self-creating Overman or Zarathustra. This is Dohm's ideal of the "New Mother." New mothers are "women of the next generation [who] will have, besides the obligations that motherhood brings with it, other practical or intellectual areas of work . . . [that] produce a social community. . . . The love of children, forced to become passive, is joined by the love of work, which only runs dry with the ebbing of one's life force" (NM, 144). Obviously, the new mother is not to be understood as the woman who has recently had a child. And as the foregoing has hopefully made clear, Dohm is a staunch critic of essentialist conceptions of women (and men): this is connected both to her Nietzscheanism as well as her critique of Nietzsche for self-contradictorily lapsing right back into the kind of essentialism he himself criticizes when he comes to the topic of women. Rather, the new mother is a new type of woman—though she is perhaps a new type of human being tout court—who strikes the right balance between compassionate love for others and self-creation. She's a mother who also creates herself through "practical or intellectual areas of work"—in contemporary terms, "a working mom" or a mother who has a professional life outside the home—and crucially, she has the moral-psychological insight to break the "melancholy cycle" of feminine self-sacrifice by encouraging instead a virtuous cycle of feminine self-creation. Dohm writes: "the times need the 'new mother' like the bread of life—the mother who gives up her authority voluntarily and in a timely way. With the emergence of the 'new mother,' an event apparently contrary to nature emerges. It is the 'new daughters,' those borne aloft by their times, who create the 'new mother,' often so that clever and good 'old mothers' (by that I don't mean in years) become new in their daughters" (NM, 142). Dohm suggests here that contemporary daughters are themselves *demanding* a new mother—and a new kind of woman. And Dohm explains that the mother/daughter relationship will be fraught unless they are both changed: the mother who continues to live her life through her daughter—her "second edition"—will provoke a conflicted relationship with a "new daughter," who does not wish to become that traditional, "second edition." Unless the mother emerges to meet the newly independent daughter; and the daughter emerges to appreciate and respect the independence of the new mother, the relationship will be fractious.

Breaking this vicious cycle is the new maternal paradigm: the mother no longer lives solely for and through her children. And her children in turn do not expect this of her. She encourages especially her daughter's independence, giving up her "authority voluntarily and in a timely way," thus enabling mothers and daughters to be friends, bonded in a "higher, purer love." And this friendship between mother and daughter breaks the "melancholic cycle" by instead encouraging a cycle of rebirth: It's a rebirth for daughters who are "borne aloft by their times" rather than effaced and pulverized into sand by them; and it's a rebirth for mothers, who, taking a cue from these self-creating daughters, re-create themselves as well, like Agnes Schmidt after she starts writing and travelling. But in order for the new mother to emerge there needs to be the societal shedding of the stark choice for daughters between the myrtle (love/marriage) and the thorns (a life of hardship; the starving vagrant): women need to be able to pursue "practical and intellectual areas of work." In the essay "Are Professional Employment and Material Duties Compatible?" (1900) Dohm goes so far as to suggest that mothers need to work in order to be good mothers. Yet she also recognizes that some mothers who do not have professional employment outside of the home may be happy with their domestic and maternal activities. Whether such happiness and goodness coincide is not clear; but she seems to hold that it's not strictly speaking a necessary condition for good motherhood that a woman have a professional life outside of the home, but that it certainly helps! The key for the emergence of the new mother, it seems for Dohm, *is equal professional opportunity and training for women.* Thus, the conversion from old to new mother depends on justice (equal rights for women), education (equal opportunities for the development of talents), and consciousness (a shedding of the psychic burden of the extreme and female-gendered *Mitleids-Moral*).

In sum, the resolution Dohm proposes for this debate over the nature and value of compassion is not to allow the bona fide virtue of loving kindness to overwhelm and supplant the "I." It was especially hard for women in her society to maintain and cultivate their "I's" (because of their upbringing, societal structures, and also perhaps, as she suggests somewhat transcendentally, due to an innate "mother love"). It is indeed still difficult for women today to strike this balance as evidenced by the popularity of Sheryl Sandberg's *Lean In* (2013) and her related "Lean In Circles" among many other self-help books and groups for working women.[18] Dohm's intervention still feels timely: she offers a glimpse at a new feminine Zarathustra in her portrayal of the "new mother" and her new "mother-love." The new mother-love may originate in biological love, but it grows into something cultural and intellectual: a true friendship between independent, self-actualizing "I's." This figure, just emerging in the late nineteenth century and early twentieth century, has her own intellectual and practical work; she becomes a friend to her adult daughter, no longer losing herself in her husband and child, and no longer trying to mold her daughter into a "second edition of herself." With this new mother ideal—an ideal perhaps for women and men alike—Dohm charts a path between a traditional feminine tendency toward Schopenhauerian selflessness and a traditional masculine tendency toward Nietzschean (pitiless) self-assertion. It is a model of virtuous balance between self-creation and compassionate love for others. Dohm thus contributes to the philosophical landscape a novel approach to becoming who you are.

I would like to thank Kristin Gjesdal for introducing me to the work of Hedwig Dohm and for her insightful and encouraging feedback on earlier drafts of this chapter. Thanks also to Dalia Nassar for incisive commentary that helped me strengthen this essay, and who, along with Kristin, is giving voice to the contributions of nineteenth-century women philosophers who have been neglected for far too long. Finally, I'm grateful to my two (new) daughters—Molly and Marlena—who lavish support and love on their working mom.

---

[18] Sheryl Sandberg, *Lean In: Women, Work, and the Will to Lead* (New York: Knopf, 2013).

Bibliography

Ametsbichler, Elizabeth. Afterword to *Become Who You Are*, by Hedwig Dohm, translated and edited by Elizabeth G. Ametsbichler, 81–100. Albany: State University of New York Press, 2006.

Dohm, Hedwig. *Become Who You Are*. Translated and edited by Elizabeth G. Ametsbichler. Albany: State University of New York Press, 2006.

Dohm, Hedwig. "The New Mother." In *Women Philosophers in the Long Nineteenth Century: The German Tradition*, edited by Dalia Nassar and Kristin Gjesdal, translated by Anna Ezekiel, 139–144. Oxford: Oxford University Press, 2021.

Dohm, Hedwig. "Nietzsche and Women." In *Women Philosophers in the Long Nineteenth Century: The German Tradition*, edited by Dalia Nassar and Kristin Gjesdal, translated by Anna Ezekiel, 128–138. Oxford: Oxford University Press, 2021.

Franco, Paul. "Becoming Who You Are: Nietzsche on Self-Creation." *Journal of Nietzsche Studies* 49, no. 1 (2018): 52–77.

Gilbert, Sandra M., and Susan Gubar. *The Madwoman in the Attic: The Woman Writer and the Nineteenth-Century Literary Imagination*. New Haven: Yale University Press, 1979.

Janaway, Christopher. *Beyond Selflessness: Reading Nietzsche's Genealogy*. Oxford: Oxford University Press, 2007.

Leiter, Brian. "The Paradox of Fatalism and Self-Creation in Nietzsche." In *Willing and Nothingness: Schopenhauer as Nietzsche's Educator*, edited by Christopher Janaway, 217–257. Oxford: Clarendon Press, 1998.

Marshall, Colin. "Schopenhauer on the Content of Compassion." *Noûs* 55, no. 4 (2020): 782–799.

Marshall, Colin. "Schopenhauer's Titus Argument." In *Schopenhauer's Moral Philosophy*, edited by Patrick Hassan. London: Routledge, 2021.

Nehamas, Alexander. *Nietzsche, Life as Literature*. Cambridge, MA: Harvard University Press, 1985.

Nietzsche, Friedrich. *The Birth of Tragedy*. Translated by Walter Kaufmann. New York: Vintage, 1967.

Nietzsche, Friedrich. *Ecce Homo*. Translated by Walter Kaufmann. New York: Vintage, 1967.

Nietzsche, Friedrich. *The Gay Science*. Translated by Walter Kaufmann. New York: Vintage, 1974.

Nietzsche, Friedrich. *On the Genealogy of Morals*. Translated by Walter Kaufmann and R. J. Hollingdale. New York: Vintage, 1967.

Reginster, Bernard. "Sympathy in Schopenhauer and Nietzsche." In *Sympathy: A History*, edited by Eric Schliesser, 254–285. Oxford: Oxford University Press, 2015.

Riley, Samantha Michele. "Hedwig Dohm." In *The Literary Encyclopedia*. Article published January 29, 2008. https://www.litencyc.com/php/speople.php?rec=true&UID=11985.

Sandberg, Sheryl. *Lean In: Women, Work, and the Will to Lead*. New York: Knopf, 2013.

Schopenhauer, Arthur. "On the Basis of Morality." In *The Two Fundamental Problems of Ethics*, edited and translated by Christopher Janaway, 113–258. Cambridge: Cambridge University Press, 2009.

Schopenhauer, Arthur. *Sämtliche Werke*. Edited by Arthur Hübscher. 7 vols. Mannheim: F. A. Brockhaus, 1988.

Schopenhauer, Arthur. *The World as Will and Representation*. Vol. 1. Translated and edited by Judith Norman, Alistair Welchman, and Christopher Janaway. Cambridge: Cambridge University Press, 2010.

Schopenhauer, Arthur. *The World as Will and Representation*. Vol. 2. Translated and edited by Judith Norman, Alistair Welchman, and Christopher Janaway. Cambridge: Cambridge University Press, 2018.

Shapshay, Sandra. *Reconstructing Schopenhauer's Ethics: Hope, Compassion, and Animal Welfare*. Oxford: Oxford University Press, 2019.

Shapshay, Sandra. "Was Schopenhauer a Kantian Ethicist?" *International Journal of Philosophical Studies* 28, no. 2 (2020): 168–187.

CHAPTER 9

LOU SALOMÉ (1861–1937)

KATHARINA TERESA KRAUS

Lou Salomé (1871–1937) was one of the most controversial female intellectuals of her day. Born in Russia, she was one of the most prolific women writers in Germany at the turn of the century, producing both literary works and essays on topics of religion, philosophy, gender theory, and psychoanalysis. She maintained numerous friendships with intellectuals of her time, lived an unconventional lifestyle, and had several love affairs, while she was married to Friedrich Carl Andreas (1846–1930), with whom she refused to have a sexual relationship. Among her close friends, for shorter or longer periods of time, were the philosophers Friedrich Nietzsche (1844–1900) and Paul Rée (1849–1901), as well as the poet Rainer Maria Rilke (1875–1926) and, in later years, Sigmund Freud (1856–1939), the founder of psychoanalysis. She eventually became one of Freud's first female students and the first female practitioner of psychoanalysis.[1]

Salomé is best known for her novels and novellas in which she often portrays the lives of female characters, such as *Ruth* (1895), *Fenitschka* (1898), and *A Deviation* (*Eine Ausschweifung*, 1898), or explores themes of religious faith and doubt, such as *The Struggle over God* (*Im Kampf um Gott*, 1883) and *The Hour Without God* (*Die Stunde ohne Gott*, 1921). Her work is therefore primarily the subject of literary studies, whereas her essays on philosophical topics have received little attention. Her style has often been dismissed as overly metaphorical, too complex, and not sufficiently argumentative. Nevertheless, a wealth of creative thinking, original ideas, intellectual breadth, and novelty make it worthwhile to explore her philosophical views in their own right.

---

[1] On Salomé's life, see Lou Andreas-Salomé, *Lebensrückblick. Grundriß einiger Lebenserinnerungen*, ed. Ernst Pfeiffer (Zurich: Niehans und Insel, 1951); as well as Ursula Welsch and Michaela Wiesner, *Lou Andreas-Salomé: Vom "Lebensurgrund" zur Psychoanalyse* (Munich: Verlag Internationale Psychoanalyse, 1988); Martin Biddy, *Woman and Modernity: The (Life)Styles of Lou Andreas-Salomé* (Cornell University Press, 1991); Christiane Wieder, *Die Psychoanalytikerin Lou Andres-Salomé. Ihr Werk im Spannungsfeld zwischen Sigmund Freud und Rainer Maria Rilke* (Göttingen: Vandenhoeck & Ruprecht, 2011).

Influenced by Nietzsche's philosophy as well as by the *Lebensphilosophie* movement in the nineteenth century, the central terms of Salomé's philosophical oeuvre
are "life," "lived experience [Erleben]" (in the sense of "living or going through something"), and "co-living [Mitleben]" (in the sense of "living with others"). Although
she neither saw herself primarily as a philosopher nor held a formal position at a university, she developed her own original philosophical viewpoint over the course of her
life, which is manifested in several smaller writings as well as in her most extensive
systematic work, the unpublished manuscript *The God* (*Der Gott*, 1910). In addition,
her focus on life also plays a central role in her feminist works, in which she spells
out the conditions of human life specifically in terms of a female way of life, as most
clearly in *The Human Being as a Woman* (*Der Mensch als Weib*, 1899) and *The Erotic*
(*Die Erotik*, 1910).[2]

Her own contribution to philosophy is therefore best understood in the context of
the *Lebensphilosophie* movement, which received growing attraction in the second half
of the nineteenth century and which was significantly influenced by Nietzsche's naturalism and antirationalism. *Lebensphilosophie* gained prominence through the work
of Wilhelm Dilthey (1833–1911), who, although still largely inspired by Kant, sought a
phenomenologically richer account of the psychological and psychosomatic reality
of human life and focused attention on life forces (also called drives), such as natural
instincts and sexual drives.[3] In her early essays, Salomé already anticipated insights
of Freud's psychoanalysis, in which a theory of drives is also central, and she later became heavily involved in the study and practice of psychoanalysis.[4] Salomé was personally acquainted with Dilthey's research assistant, Helene Stöcker.[5] She also valued the
writings of Georg Simmel (1858–1918), whom she knew personally and with whom she
corresponded from her time in Berlin in the 1880s. Simmel was one of the first German
sociologists and best known for his analyses of human individuality and social fragmentation. Moreover, Salomé actively engaged with the work of Henri Bergson (1859–1941),
whose philosophy of life focuses on human creativity and the so-called *élan vital*.[6] While
her own position is inspired by these sources, she carves out an original philosophy of
life and later expands her view in light of Freud's psychoanalysis. Thus, two main phases
can be distinguished in her systematic writings: the first period, in which she develops

[2] Salomé's writings on women were (and still are) controversial because of their essentialist and
biological assumptions about gender, and Salomé herself was not an active supporter of the women's
rights movement. See section 2.

[3] E.g., Wilhelm Dilthey, *Selected Works*, ed. R. A. Makkreel and F. Rodi, vol. 1, *Introduction to the
Human Sciences* (Princeton: Princeton University Press, 1985–2010).

[4] A pivotal work in the development of Freud's drive theory, in which he conceives of drives in terms
of life and death drives, is Sigmund Freud, "Beyond the Pleasure Principle," in *The Standard Edition of
the Complete Psychological Works of Sigmund Freud*, ed. James Strachey, vol. 18 (1920), 1–78 (London:
Hogarth Press and the Institute of Psycho-Analysis, 1953–74).

[5] Welsch and Wiesner, *Lou Andreas-Salomé: Vom "Lebensurgrund" zur Psychoanalyse*, 133.

[6] Salomé owned Bergson's two volumes *Matière er mémoire* and *L'évolution créatrice* in the 1912
editions. See Hans-Rüdiger Schwab, "Lebensgläubigkeit. Über Lou Andreas-Salomés nachgelassenes
Manuskript 'Der Gott,'" in *Der Gott* (Taching am See: MedienEdition Welsch, 2016), 203.

her original philosophy of life, extends roughly from the beginnings of her career as a writer in the 1880s to 1910; the second period, which incorporates the insights of psychoanalysis, begins with her turn to psychoanalysis and her personal encounter with Freud in 1911 and lasts until her death in 1937.

This chapter focuses on the first period. Its goal is to elaborate her philosophy of life as a philosophical position in its own right by exploring its main features, clarifying the major influences on her position (especially the Nietzschean and Spinozist elements) and discussing it in the context of contemporary accounts of life in the nineteenth and early twentieth centuries (Dilthey, Simmel, and Bergson).

Section 1 explores, in *The God* and related texts, her critique of religious experience and her positive account of life and the "faith in life," highlighting specifically the Spinozist and Nietzschean influences on her position. Section 2 focuses on her feminist writings, especially *The Human Being as a Woman*, and examines how her philosophy of life plays out in her gender theory, according to which womanhood is understood in terms of a female way of life and development.

1 Salomé's Original Philosophy of Life

1.1 A Critique of Religious Experience as Life Negating

In her unpublished manuscript *The God*, written in 1909 and completed—according to the author's preface—on New Year's Day 1910, Salomé offers her most comprehensive systematic study of God, religion, and life.[7] Her original view of life derives from her analysis of religious experience and traditional belief in a transcendent God—a God who exists separate from and beyond the sensible world. In the spirit of a Nietzschean critique, she maintains that traditional faith has led to serious distortions in human experience and to the suppression of human life. Following the secular trend at the turn of the century to reinvent a representation of the divine in an impersonal and immanent way, she argues that the traditional transcendent conception of God results from a turning away from life itself and from a splitting off of life-affirming forces in human beings. On the basis of this critique, she develops her own philosophy of life, which culminates in a "*faith in life* [*Lebensglauben*]" that can be understood as an ultimate trusting devotion to life itself and the suspension of the traditional religious faith in favor of life itself (*God*, 73).

In her analysis of religious experience, Salomé follows the stages of human development from childhood through adolescence to adulthood. With this developmental

---

[7] The manuscript was first published in its original German version by the publisher MedienEdition Welsch in 2016: Lou Andreas-Salomé, *Der Gott, in Einzelbände*, vol. 5, edited by Hans-Rüdiger Schwab (Taching am See: MedienEdition Welsch, 2016) (hereafter abbreviated *God*). All translations from *Der Gott* are my own.

approach, she anticipates the way psychoanalysis would later offer explanations in terms of the stages of human development. A child naturally creates a fantasy image of God as a person who is assumed to be opposed to the child's immediate reality, but also to act upon the child's life and the lives of those close to the child, such as parents and siblings. This childlike belief originally arises from an initially shocking experience of the outer—the natural and the social—world and from the fact that external, social expectations mostly run counter to the child's own desires. The child experiences a growing tendency of a separation between the inner and the outer life, which feels increasingly disturbing.[8] Salomé characterizes the original experience of this separation of the inner and the outer as the "double character of life" (*God*, 9) or as "double experience of life [Doppelerleben]" (*God*, 13), as opposed to the "full experience of life [Voll-erleben]" (*God*, 11). At this stage, a child still has a strong sense of the original unity of life and the "wholeness of lived experience [Ganzheit des Erlebens]" (*God*, 9) but increasingly feels a "double experience," according to which the inner and the outer behave in opposite and potentially conflicting ways.[9]

Religious faith thus originates from the human desire to restore the original unity of life, and the imaginary conception of God as a parent-like (or more precisely, father-like) figure acting in everyday life is understood as a means of reconciling the seemingly resistant external world with one's own internal world: "the nucleus and germ of every ancient religious practice" is "the reflection of parenthood, of common and therefore divine descent," which is the "original way of incorporating the external life into the human interior" (*God*, 11). This imaginary conception, however, is only a "reality substitute" that eventually blocks the "reality of life [Lebenswirkliche]" itself (*God*, 20). A healthy human development therefore aims at replacing the imaginary substitute with the experience of life itself: only in the negation and rejection of a God who is opposed to life can human beings realize the deeper "meaning of life [Lebensinn]" and recover the truly "divine" in their own individual lives (*God*, 24; see also 33). Hence, Salomé argues for a conception of life that itself in some sense embraces the divine—an idea reminiscent of the Spinozist conception of God as identical with nature. This already indicates that Salomé's own conception of faith will be a *faith in life* itself, which consists in a radical surrender to the living reality itself in all its manifold manifestations in one's own experiences, as well as in collective experiences.[10]

---

[8] Salomé starts her own memoirs with a chapter titled "The Experience of God." See Lou Andreas-Salomé, *Looking Back*, ed. Ernst Pfeiffer, trans. Breon Mitchell (New York: Marlowe, 1995), 1–11.

[9] Similarly, Simmel diagnoses a characteristic "duality of being inwardly directed and of being outwardly directed, of the individual life form and the supra-individual total life to which it belongs." Georg Simmel, "Das individuelle Gesetz. Ein Versuch über das Prinzip der Ethik," *Logos. Internationale Zeitschrift für Philosophie der Kultur* 4 (1913): 142. Simmel, however, considers this duality to be a defining characteristic of organic life par excellence and calls it the "typical tragedy of the organism" (Simmel, "Das individuelle Gesetz," 142), whereas Salomé holds that life is unitary in itself and follows a Spinozistic monism, as I will discuss hereafter and in section 1.3.

[10] In *Die Erotik*, Salomé develops a similar solution to the problem of the divisive experience of life in religious and social contexts by emphasizing the originally unifying and holistic character of life. See Lou Andreas-Salomé, *Die Erotik*, in *Die Gesellschaft: Sammlung sozialpsychologischer Monographien*, ed.

This radical turning to life itself is typically a sign of the stage of the adolescent life: "what takes place in puberty: the human being is transformed back into a vessel of the generality of life, and just then, awakens to the full consciousness of himself—this new kind of interweaving of self-contemplation and universal coherence [Allzusammenhang] characterizes youth in every dimension" (*God*, 26). The adolescent awakens to a new self-consciousness in which he perceives himself not only as someone in the process of "becoming [Werden]" and "growing [Wachsen]," but also as someone who "no longer transfer[s] his meaning [Sinn] to external symbols, [but rather] expect[s] it from himself" (*God*, 26). Given a healthy human development, an adolescent proceeds toward a "full-healthy life"—a life "in which inside and outside do not split apart for the human being in a pathological way," but rather according to which life consists in a "living unity" (*God*, 31).

Salomé here presents us with a first account of her own view of *life*: life is a creative act of self-constitution, which consists above all in a "intellectual organization" (*God*, 29), resulting in "intellectual-creative states [geistesschöpferische Zustände]" (*God*, 32) and in "an intellectual experience of being [geistiges Seinserlebnis]" (God, 38). This creative act always aims at restoring an original unity—a unity that is inherent in life itself.

Salomé arrives at this positive account of life through a closer analysis of religious people who, instead of following this original intellectual organization, proceed according to opposite reasons: "[the reason] of turning away from life, of not coming to terms with it, of some rupture between self and world, where the inner experience did not stand up to the outer urge, and so a new duality split out precisely there, where in childhood it [the duality] strives to unite into the whole of life" (*God*, 29). According to Salomé's psychological analysis of religious experience, religion arises from suffering from a split between internal and external forces and from an existential need for unity. When one practices a traditional, (mono-)theistic religion, the split, however, is not overcome by the restoration of the original unity of life, but by the projection of an external source, namely God, as a power that remedies this split and comforts humans in their suffering. According to Salomé, this projection of God is only an "illusion" that produces an even deeper duality and causes the ultimate failure to come to terms with the human conditions and to find unity again. Salomé describes the religious person as the "suffering" human being who also engages in a creative act—an act that, however, is not life-promoting. By performing religious acts and maintaining an imaginary relationship with God, that is, "the God illusion," human beings turn away from their own lives and lose their original connection to life and its unity (*God*, 30). Religious acts thus merely create fictions that do not strengthen life's internal forces, but actually hinder them. They are "delusional acts of idealization" through which we try to close the split between inside and outside in human consciousness, but whereby we can only fail (*God*, 59).[11]

Martin Buber (Frankfurt am Main: Literarische Anstalt: Rütten & Loennig, 1910) (hereafter abbreviated *Die Erotik*), 5–68.

[11] A similar critique of religion, according to which religion produces illusions of God from the projections of human desires, is also found in Ludwig Feuerbach (1804–1872)—an author whom Salomé

Salomé's critique of religion bears similarities to both Spinoza's critique of theism and Nietzsche's analysis of Christianity as a life-destroying force. Like Spinoza, Salomé notes an intensifying duality between the divine and the world when people follow the belief in a transcendent God who is assumed to act as a complementary partner on the world to bring about unity and harmony in the world.[12] Spinoza famously argues that traditional theism falls prey to a dualism that is inherently inconsistent.[13] Against Judeo-Christian theism, in particular, he objects to the plausibility that an immutable, incorporeal God can create a mutable and extended universe that is distinct from God himself. Spinoza's own metaphysical system in his *Ethics* (1677) overcomes this fundamental dualism by conceiving of God as the only unique eternal infinite substance that exists (see *Ethics* Ip14), and of both mental and bodily entities as mere modes of God (see *Ethics* IIp10–11).[14] The only way to avoid such fundamental dualism is to recognize the fundamental identity of God and nature or, as Spinoza simply states it: "God, or Nature" (*Ethics* IV Preface). Spinoza argues that the "eternal and infinite being we call God, or Nature, acts from the same necessity from which he exists" (*Ethics* IV Preface) and that from God's infinite power "all things have necessarily flowed, or always followed . . . from eternity and to eternity" (*Ethics* Ip17s1). Spinoza rejects any anthropomorphizing notion of God and in particular the conception of God as an acting person. He subscribes to a mechanical account of

cites on several occasions, for instance, in her short text "Erleben," in *Philosophie: Ideal und Askese. Aufsätze und Essays*, vol. 2, ed. Hans-Rüdiger Schwab (Taching am See: MedienEdition Welsch, 2010) (hereafter abbreviated *AuEII*), 19–27, in which she develops a similar critique of traditional religion and transcendent conceptions of God, see esp. *AuEII*, 25.

[12] Salomé's philosophy is much indebted to Spinoza, whose work she began to study with her mentor Hendrik Gillot in her adolescence. See Welsch and Wiesner, *Lou Andreas-Salomé: Vom "Lebensurgrund" zur Psychoanalyse*, 26; Gisela Brinker-Gabler, *Image in Outline: Reading Lou Andreas-Salomé* (London: Bloomsbury Academic, 2012), 43–46; Schwab, "Lebensgläubigkeit," 199–200. She frequently refers to Spinoza with great admiration in her writings on psychoanalysis, for example her *Freud Journal* (New York: Basic Books, 1964), and "My Thanks to Freud" (Vienna: Internationaler Psychoanalytischer Verlag, 1931). On the Spinozistic elements in her writings, see Sandra A. Wawrytko, "Lou Salomé (1861–1937)," in *Contemporary Women Philosophers, 1900–Today*, ed. Mary Ellen Waithe, vol. 4, *A History of Women Philosophers* (Dordrecht: Kluwer, 1996), 73 and notes 33–37, and Katharina Kraus, "Salomé on Life, Religion, Self-Development, and Psychoanalysis: The Spinozistic Background," in *Spinoza in Germany: Political and Religious Thought across the Long Nineteenth Century*, ed. Jason M. Yonover and Kristin Gjesdal (Oxford: Oxford University Press, forthcoming).

[13] In nineteenth-century German philosophy and literature, there was a broad reception of Spinozistic ideas, beginning specifically with Friedrich Jacobi, *Über die Lehre des Spinoza in Briefen an Herrn Moses Mendelssohn* (Breslau: Löwe, 1785). Spinoza's monistic conception of thought and world had a lasting effect on the German idealists who drew explicitly on Spinozistic ideas; see Eckart Förster and Melamed Yitzhak, eds., *Spinoza and German Idealism* (Oxford: Oxford University Press, 2012). The idea of a mystical union of nature without the postulate of a personal God was very attractive to many German writers at the turn of the nineteenth to twentieth century; see Uwe Spörl, *Gottlose Mystik in der deutschen Literatur um die Jahrhundertwende* (Paderborn, Brill: 1997).

[14] For references to Spinoza's *Ethics* (1677), see Benedictus de Spinoza, *Spinoza's Ethics* (Princeton: Princeton University Press, 2020). I use the standard pagination with the following abbreviations: The Roman number indicates the number of the book, p (= proposition), s (= scholium).

nature according to which all changes in nature necessarily result from immutable natural laws.

Following Spinoza's monism, Salomé conceives of the divine as something that cannot be separated from the sensible world and especially from life itself. To truly live a unified life requires the "negation" of theistic beliefs so that "life can free itself to itself and to the divinity that is inherent in it" (*God*, 33). The divine for Salomé is inherent in life itself and cannot be separated from it, nor should it be assumed to transcend life.[15]

By recognizing that the multiplicity of individual mental and bodily processes within ourselves are expressions of one and the same coherent, unified life, Salomé approaches the idea of a divine that is the ultimate source, ground, or origin of all life, not only of the single individual or of the human species, but of life in general—an idea that Salomé explicates in the notion of *Mitleben*. Salomé, however, departs from Spinoza in her emphasis on life, which for her is not reducible to mechanical changes and to the motion of bodies. She favors a vitalist account of nature according to which nature is understood primarily as living, and even inorganic matter can be properly understood only in relation to living organisms. In this respect, her view shares similarities with the organicist positions of some German idealists, most clearly developed by Friedrich Wilhelm Joseph von Schelling, who conceives of nature as the origin of a self-determining subjectivity and thus as inherently organic and productive rather than as a concatenation of mechanical laws.[16]

Salomé follows Nietzsche in his analysis that religious people try to satisfy a certain internal need, which results from an experienced split, and just by doing so miss out on their own aliveness. Religious acts have mainly a comforting function, which takes place on an affective as well as on a rational level. More precisely, Salomé distinguishes three functions of religion: (1) the "symbolic" function of religious action as an expression of the "natural breath of life for the soul's health," (2) the consolatory function as a "healing mixture for the mentally suffering," and (3) the power-exerting function of God as the "determiner of general validity [Allgemeingeltende] and all-controlling One [Allesbeherrschende]" (*God*, 39). Each of these functions is driven by the fundamental illusion that there is a God who exists detached from the sensible world as a force acting from outside on human life and all other creatures. To escape this illusion and avoid being trapped in a religion that inhibits life, Salomé suggests that we need to refocus on the "organizing force" within us and on our own creativity (*God*, 32).

---

[15] A nontranscendent conception of God is also found in other representatives of the philosophy of life, especially in Wilhelm Dilthey, "Das Problem der Religion" (1911), in *Gesammelte Schriften*, vol. 4 (Göttingen: Vandenhoeck & Ruprecht, 1914–2006), 288–305. Dilthey, however, still appreciates the value of religious experience. Dilthey understands mystical experience not as a feeling of union with a transcendent God, but as a general awareness of the inner coherence of nature and of one's own embeddedness in nature; religious experience is then seen as life-affirming. See Rudolf Makkreel, "Wilhelm Dilthey," *Stanford Encyclopedia of Philosophy*, 2020, https://plato.stanford.edu/entries/dilthey/.

[16] See, for instance, Friedrich Wilhelm Joseph von Schelling, *System des transcendentalen Idealismus* (1800) (Hamburg: Meiner, 2000).

Similarly, Nietzsche argues that the beliefs, moral values, and ethical commitments that we have built on faith in a Christian God have alienated us from a healthy way of life and are destined to collapse. Christian values, and especially the ascetic ideal, undermine life's natural pursuit of growth, domination, expansion, strength—in short, the natural will to power. The Christian religion tends to distract us from this essential nature of life and should therefore be replaced by a true affirmation of life and by the adoption of values that promote human flourishing.[17]

1.2 *Erleben* and the Failure to Live

Going beyond a critique of traditional religion, Salomé presents life as the central concept of her own positive philosophy—a concept that for her is more fundamental than the concepts of the material body or the mind: the character of the living is fundamental for explaining both physical-sensational and mental-psychological activities. Her own position has therefore similarities with the contemporary *Lebensphilosophie*.

Salomé spells out the concept of life in two ways: on the individual level, she develops a concept of *Erleben* (lived experience), according to which each individual is capable of experiencing herself as a living unity and as belonging to life as a whole.[18] On the collective level, she defines the activity of *Mitleben* (co-living), according to which each individual understands herself as belonging to the collective of living beings and as being embedded in the wholeness and oneness of being (e.g., *All-Verbundenheit*, *Einssein-aller*). This collective thus includes not only human life, but all life, even non-organic nature as part of what is enclosed by life and perceived by living beings. By emphasizing the receptive-sensory, emotional, and intellectual-creative aspects of life, Salomé understands her position as being opposed to the overly rationalist positions of the Enlightenment, such as that of Kant (on her account) (*God*, 75). In this respect, too, her view bears similarities to the fundamental critique of Enlightenment thought, and especially of rationalist positions, that we find in Nietzsche and Schopenhauer. Instead of seeing the ground of all being in reason, Salomé invokes an irrational ground of life

---

[17] Esp. Friedrich Nietzsche, *The Gay Science*, trans. Josefine Nauckhoff and Adrian Del Caro (Cambridge: Cambridge University Press, 2001), and Friedrich Nietzsche, *On the Genealogy of Morality*, trans. Carol Dieth (Cambridge: Cambridge University Press, 2006). On Nietzsche's account of life as the will to power, see Bernhard Reginster, *The Affirmation of Life. Nietzsche on Overcoming Nihilism* (Cambridge, MA: Harvard university Press, 2008), 103–147; Nadeem J. Z. Hussain, "The Role of Life in the *Genealogy*," in *The Cambridge Guide to Nietzsche's "On the Genealogy of Morality,"* ed. Simon May (Cambridge: Cambridge University Press, 2011), 142–169. In 1882, Salomé had several encounters and an intense intellectual exchange with Nietzsche, who was romantically interested in her (see Welsch and Wiesner, *Lou Andreas-Salomé: Vom "Lebensurgrund" zur Psychoanalyse*; Martin Biddy, *Woman and Modernity*). She was the first to write a comprehensive interpretation of Nietzsche's work, in which she first suggested a periodization of his philosophical development. See Lou Andreas-Salomé, *Friedrich Nietzsche in seinen Werken* (Vienna: Konegen, 1894).

[18] Both German terms *Erfahren* (*Erfahrung*) and *Erleben* (*Erlebnis*) are usually translated as *experience*. To distinguish between them, I leave the German *Erleben* untranslated.

(*Lebensgrund* or *Urgrund*) from which all being, including physiological and intellectual activities, emerges.[19] In what follows, I first examine her concept of *Erleben* in light of her critique of the Enlightenment emphasis on reason.

Following her critique of religious experience, she diagnoses a general failure to experience oneself as unified. Her critique of religion now expands into a broader critique of rationalism and finally a critique of ethics and morality. Salomé recognizes the "rule of the understanding [Verstandesherrschaft]" against the will and feeling. She conceives of the activities of the understanding in mechanistic terms, since they aim at "division, analysis, and the reduction to logical mechanisms" (*God*, 57). The task of the understanding—similar to that of religion—is to reconcile and "include inwardness in outwardness" (*God*, 57). Similarly, the understanding abstracts from the "inner life," thus inhibiting its free development and realization, and thereby reinforcing the dichotomy between inner and outer. The rational person, like the religious person, tries to overcome this dichotomy, but can only do so through a "certain bravery of non-thinking," the "resignation to the triviality of existence," or a "busy efficiency," which ultimately leads to the "banalization" and "de-internalization of life" (*God*, 59). Salomé arrives at a very broad definition of religion that includes what one may call the "faith in reason," that is, the Enlightenment belief in reason as the ultimate source of truth and morality. All these rational attempts "to close the split of human consciousness into inside and outside," however, are only "delusional act[s] of idealization" and hence yield only "surrogate solutions" (*God*, 59). According to Salomé's critique, humans tend to generate "religious surrogates" in terms of social conventions, moral rules, or ethical ideals, in order to fulfill their need for primal unity (*God*, 60). Such surrogates have the same damaging effect as the God illusion: they reinforce a life-denying dualism, rather than promoting life.[20] The delusion of rationality just turns into the scheme of the delusion of religion (see *God*, 74): while the religious person projects the longing for life into God and thus reifies it externally, the believer in reason transfigures earthly human relations into something divine and thereby elevates morality and rational progress to indispensable principles of life—principles that, however, are equally external and alien to life as a transcendent God.

---

[19] Salomé frequently invokes the notion of an ultimate ground of life, which she calls *Urgrund*. This idea, too, may point to her borrowing from Schelling, who introduces the term in his work *Über das Wesen der menschlichen Freiheit* (1809) (Hamburg: Meiner, 1997), 78, to denote the undifferentiated being that precedes all ground and existence, for which he also uses the term *Ungrund*. Schelling developed an influential model of the relationship between the subject and its inherent, but conceptually elusive life forces. With this model, Schelling influenced thinkers from Schopenhauer and Nietzsche to Freud and beyond.

[20] While many Enlightenment philosophers rejected the mystical aspects of religious experience as irrational, Salomé reverses this Enlightenment critique of religion by arguing that the Enlightenment emphasis on rationality has made inaccessible the primordial unity of life that still shines through in mystical experiences and that has been notoriously misinterpreted by theistic religions. In this sense, Salomé's Enlightenment critique bears similarities to Nietzsche's critique of rationality as a dangerous force that undermines life in Friedrich Nietzsche, *The Birth of Tragedy out of the Spirit of Music*, ed. Raymond Geuss and Ronald Speirs (Cambridge: Cambridge University Press, 1999).

The only way to experience oneself as unified and whole is through what she calls "immediate lived experience [unmittelbares Erleben]" (*God*, 59). Only through this can the current processes of life be grasped as "parts of a wholeness" and life really lived in a holistic sense (*God*, 60). In using the term *Erleben*, Salomé adopts a term that was crucial for the contemporary *Lebensphilosophie*. Dilthey was the first to coin *Erleben* as a technical term to fill a gap in earlier representational and epistemological accounts of experience, which can, for example, be found in Kant's transcendental philosophy. In his effort to do more justice to the phenomenological richness of human inner life, including its sensory, affective-emotional, and conative aspects, Dilthey refines what has been called by Kant (and others) *inner experience (innere Erfahrung)*. Inner experience, for Kant, yields a truth-apt representation (i.e., an objective, conceptual representation) of the inner states and psychological features of the individual subject, in analogy with outer experience that yields a truth-apt representation of the external states of the world.[21] For Dilthey, by contrast, inner and outer experience are no longer equivalent. Rather, by reconceiving of inner experience as actually lived experience (*Erleben*), he emphasizes that inner experience is primarily a mental activity and thus a real mental occurrence in time (as opposed to the representational and epistemic nature of outer experience). In contrast to the German term *Erfahren*, the term *Erleben* indicates the active engagement of the subject in making the contents of her representations a part of her own consciousness, that is, of her own inner world. Hence, rather than focusing on the resulting state of mind that is supposed to veridically represent an object, the term *Erleben* shifts emphasis to the inner event taking place within the experiencing subject, namely the *Erlebnis*. Dilthey also describes this process as a becoming-internal.[22]

Salomé construes *Erleben* in active terms as an "act of life [Lebensakt]" (*God*, 60, 64, 69) or a "life process [Lebensvorgang]" (*God*, 96, 99, 132) in which we experience our feeling, willing, and thinking as an unfragmented, "uncut" wholeness of life (*God*, 69). The division of our experience into physiological stimuli and sensation, psychic experience, and abstract thinking results only from a retrospective analysis of the unified life process. In lived experiencing, passive receptivity and simple stimulus-response schemes combine with active "intellectual-creative processes" into an integrative whole (*God*, 69). More specifically, Salomé distinguishes three aspects of *Erleben* that

---

[21] For an account of inner experience and its relation to outer experience, see Katharina Kraus, *Kant on Self-Knowledge and Self-Formation* (Cambridge: Cambridge University Press, 2020).

[22] See, e.g., Wilhelm Dilthey. *Drafts for Volume II of the Introduction to the Human Sciences (ca. 1880–1890)*, ed. R. A. Makkreel and F. Rodi, 243–457. Vol. 1 of *Selected Works* (Princeton: Princeton University Press, 1985–2010), esp. 253. For Dilthey, it is the lived experience (*Erleben*) of which we can give an immediate expression (*Ausdruck*) and gain immediate understanding (*Verstehen*). Such understanding of our lived experience is the subject matter of the *Geisteswissenschaften*, as he argues in his *Introduction to the Human Sciences*. On Dilthey's account of *Erleben*, see Rudolf Makkreel, *Dilthey: Philosopher of the Human Studies*, 2nd ed. (Princeton: Princeton University Press, 1992), and Makkreel, "Wilhelm Dilthey," and Katharina Kinzel, "Inner Experience and Articulation: Wilhelm Dilthey's Foundational Project and the Charge of Psychologism," *Hopos: The Journal of the International Society for the History of Philosophy of Science* 8, no. 2 (2018): 347–375.

manifest themselves only together in an integrated life process: physiological-passive receptivity, active-intellectual creativity, and what she calls "soulfulness [Seelisches]," which mediates between the passive and active aspects.[23] These distinctions show that for Salomé, psychic and physical experience are not separate phenomena or really distinct states of human beings, but complementary modes of one and the same act of life. This, again, suggests the influence of Spinoza, who likewise conceives of mind and body as two parallel modes of one and the same substance or ground. Using the examples of aesthetic experience of natural beauty and music, Salomé discusses the complementarity of mind and body in terms of the "intellectuality of sensibility [Geistigkeit ihrer Sinnlichkeit]" and the "material experience [stoffliches Erleben]" (God, 91). For Salomé, "all intellectual materializes" and "all material [can be also viewed] in its intellectuality" (God, 107).[24]

Erleben is thus at the same time both a mode of consciousness and a mode of being (e.g., "Seinserlebnis," God, 38). As a mode of being, *Erleben* can have various degrees of "fullness." With the frequent use of superlatives such as "fullest of life [Lebensvollstes]" (God, 100) and "fullest of all life [Allerlebensvollste]" (God, 128), Salomé indicates that the primordial unity of being is achieved only in the highest degree or fullness of life. Only in immediate *Erleben* can we get a sense of the fullness of being, regain some of our wholeness in the partiality of single life events, and restore the primordial unity of life. However, not every act of lived experience provides access to this highest level of being. Rather, Salomé distinguishes different "methods of experience," depending on the kinds of mental phenomena involved and depending on the degree of inwardness or outwardness. Death and God are understood as the "most outwardly directed methods of experience" because they most lack "inner humanity" (see God, 105 and 91). Like Dilthey (and in contrast to other contemporary philosophers of life), Salomé assumes that *Erleben* can be reduced neither to the level of representation, nor to purely organic-biological processes.[25] Life is defined primarily in terms of intellectual-creative activities; therefore

---

[23] This threefold distinction may reflect a traditional distinction of the scholastic-Aristotelian tradition between *anima* (passive-receptive soul), *animus* (re-active, specifically human soul), and *mens* (pure active intellect), which is still present in eighteenth-century German philosophy and which, for example, Kant refers to in his lectures on anthropology, e.g., *Anthropology Parow*, in *Kants gesammelte Schriften*, ed. Königlich Preußischen Akademie der Wissenschaften, vol. 25, 247 (Berlin: de Gruyter, 1902–), and *Anthropology Collins*, in *Kants gesammelte Schriften*, vol. 25, 16.

[24] See, e.g., "the subjective [Erleben] . . . belongs mentally just as bodily to the nature-filled [Naturerfüllte] and nature-limited [Natur-begrenzte]" (God, 91). Salomé expands on this point in *Die Erotik* (see esp. 12–15). An alternative translation for "intellectual" in these quotations would be "spiritual," following the German idealist conception of "spirit".

[25] Herbert Spencer, for example, develops an evolutionary philosophy of life, closely following Charles Darwin's theory of evolution. His philosophy has been criticized as "mechanistic" by, among others, Henri Bergson, who—like Dilthey and Salomé—stresses the importance of immediate lived experience and of conscious creative life-processes; see Henri Bergson, *Matière et Mémoire. Essai sur la relation du corps à l'esprit* (Paris: F. Alcan, 1896), and Henri Bergson, *L'Évolution créatrice* (Paris: F. Alcan, 1907).

"that which is most full of life can only be accomplished in the intellect" (*God*, 100).[26] Salomé rejects a mechanistic conception of life and attributes any mechanistic reduction of psychic experience to a misguided analysis by the dissecting "mechanism of the understanding," which can describe life only from the outside but not from the inside (*God*, 112; see also 107, 121, 128). The wholeness of life therefore shows itself especially in our emotionality, since our feelings gather a manifold experience into a unity and thus express "all-unity [Alleinheit]" and "all-peace [Allfrieden]," in contrast to the dissecting understanding (*God*, 85).[27]

Yet it is a common fact that humans fail to have the kind of immediate *Erleben* that would give them access to the wholeness of their lives and that they fail to act in a truly intellectual-creative way. Human life frequently remains "in its mechanistic division, in the misery of its piecemeal nature, [and] without that supplementary confidence" that leads to fulfillment and joy (*God*, 63). This failure not only deepens the split between the inner life and the outer world from which we have suffered since childhood, but it finds its distinctive expression in, and is even the source of, our ethics, morality, and conventions, as I have shown. When we are not involved in genuinely creative acts of life, we look for goals and purposes that exist in the external world, and try to animate things from the external world in order to imitate aliveness with them. Instead of actually being creative, we adhere to the mere symbolization of life and try to create meaning by following habitual moral rules, social codes, and trained regulations. But this imitation of the inner life can only lead to the pathological externalization of life, to a meaning that has only external validity, and finally to a "shadowy unreality of our existence" that is the opposite of life (*God*, 72). Ethical principles, morals, and social conventions, like religious rituals, are hence misleading guides to a lifeless life, as it were, and not to a life in which we are truly alive, whole, and creative.

Salomé's critical diagnosis of the human condition in her time bears strong resemblance to Nietzsche's critique of morality. In *The Birth of Tragedy* (1872) and in his *Genealogy of Morals* (1887), for example, Nietzsche, too, puts forward a concept of life that stands in stark contrast to the prevailing morality. Similarly, he argues that the common moral values based on Christian faith and Greek rationality undermine our affirmation and enjoyment of life and therefore lead to decadence and degeneration.[28]

In sum, for Salomé, all of human existence proceeds in three possible ways. First, the *symbolic life*: the life that does not rely on external and delusional symbolizations, but that is its own symbol, as in the moment of "the most childlike childhood, the most

---

[26] See also: "in its intellectual-creative states, life means . . . an unbreakable unity of all sensations, which otherwise, for our divided experience and contemplation, split into various opposites" (*AuEII*, 22).

[27] The distinction between feeling as a collection to unity and the understanding as dissecting into multiplicity can also be found, among others, in Simmel, e.g., Georg Simmel, *Gesamtausgabe*, ed. Otthein Rammstedt, vol. 12, 86 (Suhrkamp: Frankfurt a. M., 1999–2015); see also Schwab, "Lebensgläubigkeit," 232 n. 48).

[28] See Friedrich Nietzsche, *The Birth of Tragedy out of the Spirit of Music*, ed. Geuss and Speirs, and *On the Genealogy of Morality* (Cambridge University Press, 2006). For discussion, see Hussain, "The Role of Life in the *Genealogy*," 150–157, and Reginster, *The Affirmation of Life*, 148–200.

youthful adolescence, the most powerful maturity, the most eternal age,"; in other words, a life filled by moments in which we symbolically glimpse its primordial unity (*God*, 73). Second, the *pathological life*: the life that is driven by externalization and delusion, leading to "wavering confidence in life, dichotomy, struggle," that is, the life of traditional religion, rationalist ethics, and conventional morality (*God*, 73). Third, the *divine life* or the *true life*, as it were: the life that is crafted and created by the "faith in life [Lebensglauben]" and hence by the "eternal divinity of life [Lebensgöttlichkeit],"; in this way of life, we grow beyond ourselves, become truly creative and "greater" than ourselves (*God*, 73).

In her short text "Erleben," Salomé describes the self-transcendence of the divine life in terms of a life that has "nothing selfish [Selbstisches]" (*AuEII*, 24) any more and writes: "therein lies already unlocked, where 'life' wants to go, where it stretches itself: beyond the individual living being, but through [such being] itself, through its own highest enhancement in that its sensitive contact with that what affects it simultaneously releases its creative power" (*AuEII*, 22). While the idea of transcending human life as we ordinarily live it is reminiscent of Nietzsche's (1883) quest for the *Übermensch*, Salomé herself was critical of Nietzsche's emphasis on an ever greater individualization of the *Übermensch*.[29] Unlike Nietzsche's *Übermensch*, who strives for the domination of lower forms of life, Salomé complements her theory of life with a conception of *Mitleben*, which means the *living with others*: through empathic commitment to others, we first participate in the wholeness of being and develop a supraindividual way of life.

1.3 *Mitleben* and the Faith in Life

Salome moves from her account of the immediate *Erlebnis* to an account of the *Allerlebnis* (all-experience) that transcends the individual in its singularity and aims at the totality of nature (*God*, 78, 84, 94, 96, 106). This *Allerlebnis* can only be approximated through an activity of *Mitleben* (co-living) through which we empathically relate to the lives of others. Like *Erleben*, *Mitleben* also comes in various kinds and degrees of unity.[30] The central goal of *Mitleben* is all-love (*Allliebe*), which is a "devotion to the One" and a desire to "become whole," as Salomé describes it in this passage: "for as love finds the whole [Ganze] in the One [im Einen] (instead of the One [Eine] in the many) and as it again generates in the child the new egoistic, self-ascending world center, so its devotion to the One also has an effect on itself as a wanting to become whole" (*God*, 81). All-love transcends the human community and strives toward participation in the whole of life as the One from which everything partial follows and flows. More concretely, all-love includes both the individual's active striving toward this wholeness and the affective appreciation of that wholeness in all concrete fellow creatures. It is thus manifested in our

---

[29] On this point, see Wawrytko, "Lou Salomé (1861–1937)," 78–79.
[30] A similar conception of social co-living can be found in *Die Erotik*, esp. 37–40.

loving attitude toward all kinds of living beings, not just human beings: it is "our love far beyond our equals" and equally concerns "the so much less demanding fellow creature" such as lower developed animals (*God*, 83). By pursuing all-love, we begin to transcend ourselves and move toward a supraindividual form of life through which we participate in the wholeness of being. But what exactly is the wholeness of being? Would this not include nonliving, inorganic matter? Salome offers us the following definition of nature, which again shows the Spinozistic thrust of her position: "what we call 'nature' . . . becomes so many-sided, so all-sided (therefore also at the same time . . . apostrophized as 'soulless') because life and death are drawn into it by us,—because thereby it has become for the first time a total symbol for both [life and death] for us" (*God*, 88). Salomé argues that life and death coincide in the totality of all being. Death can be understood as belonging to the wholeness of being only in relation to the living and hence must be conceived as the opposite of life. More specifically, to perceive something as material, inorganic, or dead is only a distortion of our limited insight into the nature of being. As finite beings, we are simply unable to comprehend the whole, and because of our dissecting understanding, we tend to be concerned with the fragmented and divisible, that is, the materiality of being. Inorganic matter is then considered as a lesser degree of reality or even as an "unreality": "the inorganic reality is, so to speak, no longer a reality at all, . . . it becomes an unreality, . . . the opposite to the living [reality]. Its divisibility, fragmentariness, the only thing we know to perceive of it, this limit of our insight, we make from now on the symbol and allegory of the inanimate in itself" (*God*, 88). Given her account of inorganic matter as the unreal aspects of the wholeness of being, and her account of death as the opposite of life and at the same time united with life in such wholeness, Salomé conceives of an even higher form of experience: the total experience (*Gesamterlebnis*) that goes even beyond the activity of *Mitleben*, since *Mitleben* can be exercised only toward living beings, but finds "its limit in the dead," the inorganic (*God*, 90).

For Salomé, there is only one way to liberate *Mitleben* from its limitation: turning to the experience of beauty and thus to art. The activity of creating art becomes a symbol of striving for the wholeness of being; indeed, even life is to be understood—in a sense—as a work of art (*God*, 101). The created artwork, in turn, is understood as a symbol of such wholeness—a symbol that we need in order to ultimately conceive of ourselves as facets of the One and as embedded in the whole: "as a result of the experience of beauty, *Mitleben* does not stop at any boundary, it only reaches a higher, more far-reaching excitement; but as a result of the creation of art, it returns from this height and vastness to man, to him as the part of nature that can be grasped as a whole only if he comprehends himself in its thousandfoldness" (*God*, 93). Art is the only way to transcend our human limitations and symbolically ascend to the whole, to overcome the disharmonies we encounter in reality and proceed toward agreement and harmony. Art is thereby understood as the "sensualization of the intellectual [Versinnlichung des Geistigen]" (*God*, 99). Unlike the other methods of transcending the duality of experience, the religious and rational methods, the method of art is ultimately more successful because it closes, rather than widens, the gap between the inner and outer life, thus symbolically pointing to the "fullest of life" (*God*, 100), rather than exteriorizing it.[31] The reason for this is that a work of art, unlike the illusion of God or the illusion of rational ideals, does not itself pretend to *be* the whole, but only to symbolically, though still imperfectly, *express* the whole that is to be created only through life itself. Therefore, art does not negate or suppress the dynamic unfolding of the living creation, but enhances it: "the work of art is able to represent wholeness and perfection outwardly only because it is not something like that in itself, but in itself only a parable—a parable-like arrangement of parts, whose unity lives only from intellect to intellect, between creator and co-creator, but leaves the parts lifeless in their materiality" (*God*, 104). A work of art can be understood as a parable of wholeness in that it unites the artist and the viewer of art. They are jointly active in the co-creation of the meaning of a work of art—a meaning that can be most fully accessed through the lived experience of beauty.

The turn to aesthetic experience as the only solution to the inner contradictions experienced in life is a well-known line of argument among the German idealists. Schelling, for example, conceives of an artwork as the symbolic presentation of an infinite unity in finite form. Unlike Salomé, Schelling does not reject the necessity of rational ideals, but like Salomé, he argues that we can pursue and approach the unity that such ideals define only through the experience of beauty in artworks.[32]

Salomé finally presents a broader theory of the relation of thought and life, as well as that of mind and body. This theory incorporates Spinozistic elements and yet also contains a scathing critique of rationalist conceptions of reality. In a Spinozistic vein, Salomé identifies the reality of life with the way of experiencing life. While life as such is always whole, diversity enters only at the level of experiencing such a life by a diversity of "methods of experiencing" (*God*, 105).[33] The God illusion and the conception of death are the two most externalist forms of experience. The opposition of death and life is now understood in terms of two different ways of conceiving the same reality. Viewing something as dead or recognizing dead aspects in things is seen as an improper way of conceiving due to a "viewing error" of our finite mental faculties (*God*, 125). Conceiving of reality in the proper sense is conceiving of it as living. By explaining the distinction between life and death as a matter of conceiving rather than real being, Salomé finds a plausible explanation for how death and life, inorganic and organic matter, can be understood as one and the same, or as coinciding in the same wholeness of being. That we conceive of things as inorganic or dead is particularly due to the dissecting activities of our understanding. The understanding analyzes matter into parts each of which are external to one another and conceives of it as a complex mechanism of interacting

---

[31] A similar conception of art as the symbolization of the wholeness of life can be found in *Die Erotik* (see esp. 25–28).

[32] In his *System of Transcendental Idealism*, Schelling develops a philosophy of art as the final keystone of his universal organon of philosophy.

[33] In Spinoza, we find an identification of *conceiving* and *being*. Similarly, diversity for Spinoza is primarily explained at the level of conception, whereas at the level of being there is only one unique substance. For an insightful account of conceiving and diversity in Spinoza, see Samuel Newlands, *Reconceiving Spinoza* (Oxford: Oxford University Press, 2018).

parts (see, e.g., "mechanistic partiality," *God*, 122; "mechanistic complexity," 123).[34] By contrast, the distinctive mark of organic beings is their "inner form" (*God*, 121) and their "living interiority" (*God*, 123). Given this model, we can now understand any seeming contrast as a matter of opposing ways of conceiving, rather than opposing ways of being, such as the "duality of exterior and interior, thought and feeling, matter and intellect, and so on" (*God*, 123; see also 107). The understanding cannot grasp the inner forms of life, but must necessarily decompose the "selfhood" of a living being into its "self-emptying" (*God*, 124). Salomé thus comes to the radical conclusion that "life—seen from the side of thinking—is . . . only a diversely analyzable death, a death dissolved in mortality" (*God*, 127). By contrast, the inner form and wholeness of life can only be felt through immediate *Erleben* and expressed in terms of symbols, but never thought in terms of rational concepts. The place to find truth is thus not thought, but life itself, "because all thinking can necessarily have its deepest truth only there, where it leads itself ad absurdum, containing the deepest truth as self-contradiction in itself, legitimizing its own right by solving its own conditionality in wonderful, liberating paradoxes" (*God*, 113). In contrast to the rationalist conception of a reality that can be fully explained by reason, for Salomé the pursuit of truth in thought naturally leads to absurdities and contradictions that can only be overcome by life itself.

As has become clear, Salomé advocates a gradual conception of the living, ranging from the most basic to the most developed level as follows:

> Inorganic (*Anorganisch*) → Organic (*Organisch*) → Living (*Lebendig*) → Soulful (*Seelisch*) → Intellectual (*Geistig*) → Personal (*Persönlich*) (see God, 117)

Accordingly, the highest level of life is *personal being*—an idea that is in fact in accordance with the traditional (Neo-)Platonic and Christian accounts. Yet Salomé characterizes personhood as a liminal concept of life that tends to transcend itself and the individuality it marks:[35]

> the more individually one comes to oneself, the more factually one departs from oneself; the more vividly one is left to one's own devices, the more actively one is generating; the more creatively one enhances, the more creaturely one is subject to one's own creation [desto geschöpfhafter dem Werk untertan]; the more one is separated into uniqueness, the more only wholeness remains; and finally everything

---

[34] Salomé appears to take her "mechanistic" account of the understanding to track the rationalist conception of rationality, and in particular the Kantian notion of understanding (*Verstand*). It should be noted, however, that Kant himself was critical of a mechanization of reasoning and himself held a teleological conception of the two rational faculties, the understanding and reason.

[35] Schelling, too, holds that the person is best understood through a boundary concept that transcends individuality, rather than through a concept that positively describes an individual. For an insightful discussion, see Thomas Buchheim, "Grundlinien von Schellings Personbegriff," in *"Alle Persönlichkeit ruht auf einem dunkeln Grunde": Schellings Philosophie der Personalität*, ed. Thomas Buchheim and Friedrich Hermanni (Berlin: Akademie-Verlag Berlin, 2004), 11–34.

that we call personality, "the highest happiness of the children of the earth,"[36] is already nothing more than this gratifying, creating, devout contradiction to oneself,—is nothing but a gesture beyond the personal. (*God*, 126)

In this passage, the liminal character of personhood is captured in a series of seemingly contradictory movements: persons by nature tend to become ever more individual, vivid, creative, and unique creators of their own lives, but in doing so they turn precisely to the opposite, becoming ever more separate from their individuality, generating new life (beyond their own), becoming a creature subject to their own creative acts, and finally dissolving into wholeness rather than remaining distinct individuals.

To sum up, reconciling and harmonizing the apparent contradictions we encounter in life by referring to an all-encompassing wholeness is the central theme of Salomé's philosophy of life. Although she develops this account of life through a critical analysis of traditional theistic beliefs, her view may have more in common with certain currents of theistic and other religions than she would have been willing to admit in *The God*.[37] With her distinctive faith in life, Salomé remains open to a certain kind of religious experience that strives for unity and wholeness as the ultimate life-enhancing goal of human existence. Such a view can, for example, be found in the religious experience of Jewish and Christian mystics, who emphasize the bodily-soul union with the divine rather than the notion of a transcendent God. Like Salomé, they describe their encounters with the divine in erotic language and see the erotic as the highest expression of religious experience—a theme that is particularly evident in Salomé's feminist writings, to which I now turn.

2 Salomé's Feminism as a Philosophy of Life

2.1 The Female Way of Life

Women's fates play a major role not only in Salomé's numerous literary works. She also wrote several theoretical works on feminist themes, for example on female eroticism in *Thoughts on the Problem of Love* (1900), *Die Erotik* (1910), and *Eros* (1922/23), and psychoanalytic studies of women, for example *The Female Type* (1914). Although she never appeared publicly as a protagonist of the women's emancipatory movement, she championed the cause of women, their free development and emancipation, in her

---

[36] This quotation refers to Goethe's poem cycle *Westöstlicher Divan* (1819), and is taken from the poem "Suleika."

[37] In her memoire and other later works, she writes more positively about the importance of religious faith in general, including "the feeling of a deeply shared destiny with all things" and a "sense of reference" (*Looking Back*, 10–11).

writings and with her own lifestyle. What is remarkable about her approach to feminism is her characterization of the two genders as two different "ways of life" (*AuEII*, 97). In accounting for womanhood in terms of a distinct female way of life, she allows for both an ontological core definition and the possibility of a free development (*Entfaltung*) of women. Her life-theoretical approach therefore uniquely combines an essentialist theory of gender with an existentialist-developmentalist one, and positions itself midway between essentialism and universalism. It is noteworthy that even her own contemporary feminists dismissed Salomé's essay *The Human Being as Woman* (1899) as "essentialist," since she seemingly postulates an ahistorical and asocial female essence that manifests itself in empirically observable character traits and behavioral tendencies. Yet it would be a serious misunderstanding of Salomé's intention and feminist project to reduce her conception of a female way of life to such an asocial and ahistorical essence.[38] Rather, Salomé conceives of an idealized female way of life (denoted by the term "Weib"), which defines, or better outlines, the potentialities for the concrete empirical life of a real woman (denoted by the term "Frau")—potentialities that can change, progress, and develop in light of historical and social circumstances. My goal in this final section is to show that Salomé's philosophy of life not only provides the terminological framework she draws upon in her feminist essays, but also gives her the theoretical foundation to develop an original gender theory that may still be relevant in today's feminist discourse.

In her essay *The Human Being as Woman* (1899), Salomé examines the ontological difference between man and woman in terms of their respective ways of life on three different levels—the physiological, the psychological, and the intellectual. This approach enables her, on the one hand, to determine the "possibilities of being and living" of women and men in a gender-specific way (*AuEII*, 96) and, on the other hand, to recognize the equal value and independence of each gender-specific way of life and hence to offer a theoretical underpinning for the emancipation of women. The three levels of analysis resemble the threefold distinction in her philosophy of life—between body, mind, and what she calls soulfulness (*Seelisches*). The psychic, or soulful, level is, in both cases, the mediating level between physiological-bodily processes and intellectual-creative acts.

At the physiological level, Salomé acknowledges that the division of genders is at the "root of all life" (*AuEII*, 96), as there is a "gendered root of all existence" (*AuEII*, 103). By recourse to contemporary biological accounts of the process of human procreation, Salomé thus argues against the stereotype that women are merely passive recipients,

---

[38] For example, Hedwig Dohm (1831–1919) raises this type of criticism against Salomé's essentialist and biological assumptions, although Dohm was otherwise a respectful reader of Salomé's work; for discussion, see Brinker-Gabler, *Image in Outline*, 37–40. Salomé tended to side with Nietzschean feminists, who emphasized women's nature, rather than women's social and political rights. On the controversial reception of Salomé's feminist work among contemporary and current feminists and for a discussion of the essentialism objection; see also Lorraine Markotic, "Andreas-Salomé and the Contemporary Essentialism Debate," *Seminar* 36 (2000): 59–78. See also chapter 8 here.

whereas men are the active creators of new life. Rather, although physiologically there are certain characteristic differences between oocytes and sperm cells, "both independently represent the essence of the sexes involved in them" (*AuEII*, 98). Salomé thus considers both sexes as actively contributing to an equal degree to the formation of new life in a fertilized ovum.[39]

The physiological level finds a parallel on the psychological level. From the psychological point of view, woman and man differ in their characteristic developmental movements and are considered "as two independent worlds for themselves" (*AuEII*, 102). While the woman is seen as developing organically from within, the man is characterized as moving forward and progressing linearly and therefore as exhibiting qualities of a "mechanistic, almost automatic" nature (*AuEII*, 104). Women are focused on the "inward effect," but such effects are harder to examine than the outward pushing effects that men strive for (*AuEII*, 106). The female way of life is associated with notions such as "homeland [Heimat]" (or "being at home [heimisch sein]," *AuEII*, 96, 97, 115–118, 128), "harmony" (*AuEII*, 97, 115, 125, 128), and "unity" or intrinsic "uniformity [Einheitlichkeit]" (*AuEII*, 102, 104, 108, 119, 129). Salomé here uses terms like "home" to explain that by turning inward, women are more self-sufficient and find everything they need within themselves to be their own nurturing ground, unlike men who must strive for something external to be nourished.[40] A woman is then considered as a "total appearance [Totalerscheinung]," rather than as a set of individual traits and features (*AuEII*, 103, 107). Instead of being guided by external goals like the man, the woman leads her life "in all individual details in the living context of the whole being [Gesamtwesen]" (*AuEII*, 97; also 102) and therefore is characterized as a harmonious whole that follows her inner principles.

It is in this connection that Salomé, perhaps somewhat surprisingly, suggests that the "the maternal [Mütterliche] [is] the symbol of the feminine," since for the woman "doing and being are much more intimately linked" than for the man (*AuEII*, 104).[41] In the course of the argument, however, it becomes clear that this should not be understood to mean that women are limited to being mothers and can only find fulfillment in their motherhood. After all, Salomé herself consciously renounced becoming a mother and having biological children. Rather, this statement is to be understood as a recognition of the necessity of a maternal element in life itself. Such a maternal element, however, does not have to consist in biological motherhood, but can take on manifold psychological forms, and in fact, it is not confined to those who identify as women. Rather, according

---

[39] To reflect the fact that in the German discourse in which Salomé's participated the distinction between *sex* and *gender* was not yet made in the way we distinguish them today––both are referred to as "Geschlecht" in German––I use the term "sex" as a translation in her discussion of the biological level and the term "gender" in all other contexts.

[40] I thank Madeleine Schmitz for bringing this interpretation of these metaphors to my attention.

[41] In *The God*, "motherliness" is understood as something that calls for special respect and is identified with the "organism," as opposed to the mechanism of the understanding (*God*, 119). An extensive discussion of motherliness can be found in *Die Erotik* (40–50).

to her theory of bisexuality, masculine and feminine traits coexist in each person and the "firmest union of masculinity and femininity consists in motherliness."[42]

Salomé follows many contemporaries in assuming that women are inherently less differentiated, calling them the "more undifferentiated piece of nature" (*AuEII*, 119; also 101). She shares this commitment with other philosophers of life, such as Georg Simmel. While Simmel derives a lower value of female life from this assumption, Salomé, by contrast, turns this characteristic into a real advantage for women: being less differentiated means having more potentiality, having more possibilities for development and thus more "creative power [Schöpferkraft]" (*AuEII*, 101).[43]

Similarly, on the intellectual level, the female way of life tends toward the holistic development of being. On the intellectual level, it is particularly important for Salomé that women should not follow masculine norms, because if they do, they will enter a dangerous and character-destroying competition: "therefore, the principled intellectual and practical competition with the man—this proof-production [Beweis-Erbringen] of their equal efficiency in each isolated individual occupation—is a true work of the devil, and the outward ambition that is aroused in the process, is about the deadliest quality that the woman can cultivate. The absence of this ambition is precisely her natural greatness: the certainty that there is no need for such a proof in order to feel in herself the highest self-entitlement [Selbstberechtigung] as a woman" (*AuEII*, 110). The "self-entitlement" of women derives from their gender-specific way of life and corresponding female values, not from a simulation of the male way of life and the adoption of masculine norms.[44] Hence, Salomé is willing to assert that women differ from men in their intellectual characteristics. In particular, women, according to her, can better endure, process, and harmonize contradictions, whereas men tend to focus on rational logic and struggle with the contradictions they encounter in life. For women, truth is primarily what is "life-enhancing [lebenserweckend]" rather than what is rationally provable (*AuEII*, 112). Recall that according to her philosophy of life, the truth of rational thought (i.e., the truth of the understanding) leads only to the analysis of the dead, whereas the "deepest truth" can be found only in "self-contradiction" and the paradoxical nature of life itself (*God*, 113). This radical conception of truth leaves open the question of the status of logical thinking and rationality in her philosophy. It also raises the question whether she recommends that women not engage in rational discourse, thereby exposing themselves to "the reproach of dilettantism, inconsistency, and superficiality" (*AuEII*, 111). By contrast, according to Salomé, women's ability to harmonize contradictions leads to their distinctive "goodness and wisdom beyond all reason" (*AuEII*, 122).

[42] "Man and Woman—Bisexuality," *The Freud Journal of Lou Andreas-Salomé*, trans. Stanley A. Leavy (New York: Basic Books, 1964), 189. See also *Die Erotik*, 52. Her view of bisexuality was consistent with other contemporary theories, for instance, Otto Weininger's study of bisexuality in *Geschlecht und Charakter. Eine prinzipielle Untersuchung* (Vienna: Wilhelm Braumüller, 1903). For discussion, see Wawrytko, "Lou Salomé (1861–1937)," 73–75.

[43] On the notion of "differentiation" in the contemporary studies of evolutionary theory and on the dispute between Simmel and Salomé, see Brinker-Gabler, *Image in Outline*, 28–30.

[44] A similar point against the male norming of women is found in *Die Erotik* (51).

In her account of the intellectual qualities of women, Salomé recognizes a particularly close relationship between bodily and mental functions, as she also noted in her general philosophy of life. She writes that "abstract thoughts very easily become personal" to a woman, "not only by bringing them into relation with certain persons," but also because the thoughts themselves seem to "rise bodily [leibhaftig] from the ground of life" and thereby first "become valuable to her" (*AuEII*, 112). Again, the Spinozistic theme of a parallelism between bodily and mental aspects of thought and experience recurs.[45]

2 Becoming a Women as Unfolding (*Entfaltung*)

The goal of both genders is to respectively develop into independent, whole beings and to participate in the all-life. However, this goal is pursued in different ways. The emancipation of the woman consists exactly not in following the values and goals of men, but to bring her own developmental possibilities to maturity following her own values. Salomé describes the development (*Entfaltung*) of women as a harmonization and broadening, whereas the male development leads to specialization and individualization (see *AuEII*, 119). Therefore, the goal of women should be, first and foremost, "to bring the innermost vitality to maturity" (*AuEII*, 116). Striving toward harmonization should not mislead one into thinking that a woman has no contradictions within herself. Rather, there is a "whimsical mixture of opposites in the woman: the impression at the same time of the wild, impulsive, contradictory, and also the more harmonious, quieter, balanced; the instinctive protest against law, classification, responsibility, duty, and yet also of higher morality" (*AuEII*, 118). As the more undifferentiated piece of nature, her life and beauty is a symbol of the wholeness of life in general. Women are thus "the more primordial as well as the more perfect" (*AuEII*, 119).

Most important, there should be equal developmental opportunities for both genders: "no room for the woman's development is therefore just as bad as no freedom of movement for the man's development, for as he wants to be allowed to reach to whatever his faculties may aim at . . . so she must be allowed to grow in herself and be allowed to increase to an ever greater extent of being" (*AuEII*, 118). As a final motif, Salomé returns to her faith in life and the person-transcending goal of the all-life: the superpersonal way of life thus defines the highest state of being for both genders. The striving for this highest goal should not be misunderstood as a negation of one's gender-specific way of life, but understood as the harmonization of the apparent contradictions between the

---

[45] See also Katharina Kraus, "The Spinozistic Background". Lloyd has recently suggested that the Spinozist parallelism of mind and body offers an alternative to the distinction between "sex" and "gender" and thus provides an interesting feminist philosophy for overcoming dominance and difference between the genders; see Genevieve Lloyd, "Dominanc and Difference. A Spinozistic Alternative to the Distinction between 'Sex' and 'Gender,'" in *Feminist Interpretations of Benedict Spinoza*, ed. Moira Gatens (University Park: Pennsylvania State University Press, 2009), 29–41.

two ways of life in an even higher unity.[46] It is a reconciliation of the two in the sense of a *Mitleben* with the other in harmony: "the life in the personal as well as in general, the self-assertion as well as the integration into the all-life, is unified in the genders, by virtue of their essential tendencies [Wesenstendenzen], which have differentiated themselves from the start in different ways, [and so the life] combines itself in different ways, and gives each of them its special power in life" (*AuEII*, 122). In the recognition of the specifically feminine in the pursuit of the all-life lies the true meaning of female emancipation: "for nothing can emancipate a woman so deeply and truly as the idea that she is denied by some confinement in which she is artificially kept the way to attain full commitment [Hingabe] and devotion [Andacht] to life—to find the point from which life and she herself could find their mysteriously intermingling harmony" (*AuEII*, 122). The kind of devotion to life that Salomé anticipates here is, for her, erotic in nature. The highest form of life for women is therefore found in the lived experience of erotic love—a theme that she explores in further studies, such as *Die Erotik* (1910), and that has decisively shaped her own way of life, as she describes most intimately in her memoirs: love is something "almost mystical" that "becomes the symbol of everything wonderful" (*Looking Back*, 16). "Love in its fullest sense presumes that we give ourselves to each other totally" (*Looking Back*, 16).

3 CONCLUDING REMARKS

The goal of this chapter has been to reevaluate and appreciate Lou Salomé as a philosopher in her own right. I have offered a detailed analysis of her original philosophy of life and its application within her feminist theory. Life, according to Salomé, is understood in a holistic way as a totality and universal connectedness of reality that precedes all concrete experience and must already be presupposed in any theoretical discourse. In contrast to alternative biologistic tendencies in philosophy of life, Salomé construes life in its highest form as an intellectual-creative process. The immediate lived experience (*Erleben*) first enables the participation in the whole of life and is therefore the most authentic way of life for an individual. Through co-living (*Mitleben*), we feel the omnipresent interconnectedness with others and ultimately strive to harmonize the apparent contradictions in life and to embed ourselves in the wholeness and oneness of being (e.g., *All-Verbundenheit, Einssein-aller*). By postulating a specifically feminine way of life and by emphasizing women's specificity, she avoids both the danger of reducing women to a set of essentialist stereotypes and the danger of measuring women against a system of masculine norms in a male-dominated world. Rather, by redefining the core elements of a female way

---

[46] In *Die Erotik*, Salomé is more critical of the "love ideal" of harmony, characterizing it as an "exaggeration" and a "man's ideal concept" (51). Nonetheless, at the end of her discussion, she returns to the ideas of a "superpersonal unity" and an "all-eternal selfhood" that characterize the successful union of women and men (55).

of life and exploring the many possibilities for women's self-sufficient and independent development, she makes room for a positive revaluation of women and for the recognition of their distinctive, equally valuable subjectivity. Even prior to Salomé's encounter with Freud and her work as a psychoanalyst, one can see in her thought a rich source for further reflection on human life in the context of society, religion, and gender equality.

I thank the editors, Kristin Gjesdal and Dalia Nassar, for encouraging me to pursue my interest in Lou Salomé and for inviting me to contribute to this volume. I am grateful to Kristin Gjesdal and Fred Rush for extremely helpful comments on an earlier version of this chapter, as well as to Madeleine Schmitz for an insightful discussion of section 2.

BIBLIOGRAPHY

Bergson, Henri. *L'Évolution créatrice*. Paris: F. Alcan, 1907.

Bergson, Henri. *Matière et Mémoire. Essai sur la relation du corps à l'esprit*. Paris: F. Alcan, 1896.

Biddy, Martin. *Woman and Modernity: The (Life)Styles of Lou Andreas-Salomé*. Ithaca: Cornell University Press, 1991.

Brinker-Gabler, Gisela. *Image in Outline: Reading Lou Andreas-Salomé*. London: Bloomsbury Academic, 2012.

Brinker-Gabler, Gisela. "Renaming the Human. Andreas-Salomé's 'Becoming Woman.'" *Seminar* 36 (2000): 22–41.

Buchheim, Thomas. "Grundlinien von Schellings Personbegriff." In *"Alle Persönlichkeit ruht auf einem dunkeln Grunde." Schellings Philosophie der Personalität*, edited by Thomas Buchheim and Friedrich Hermanni, 11–34. Berlin: Akademie-Verlag Berlin, 2004.

Dilthey, Wilhelm. *Drafts for Volume II for the "Introduction to the Human Sciences."* Edited by R. A. Makkreel and F. Rodi, 2433–2458. Vol. 1 of *Selected Works*. Princeton: Princeton University Press, 1985–2010.

Dilthey, Wilhelm. *Gesammelte Schriften*. Edited by Bernhard Groethuysen. 26 vols. Göttingen: Vandenhoeck & Ruprecht, 1914–2006.

Dilthey, Wilhelm. *Introduction to the Human Sciences*. Edited by R. A. Makkreel and F. Rodi, 47–242. Vol. 1 of *Selected Works*. Princeton: Princeton University Press, 1985–2010.

Dilthey, Wilhelm. "Das Problem der Religion," 288–305. Vol 4 of *Gesammelte Schriften*. Göttingen: Vandenhoeck & Ruprecht, 1914–2006.

Dilthey, Wilhelm. *Selected Works*. Edited by R. A. Makkreel and F. Rodi. 6 vols. Princeton: Princeton University Press, 1985–2010.

Förster, Eckhart, and Yitzhak Melamed. *Spinoza and German Idealism*. Oxford: Oxford University Press, 2012.

Freud, Sigmund. "Beyond the Pleasure Principle." In *The Standard Edition of the Complete Psychological Works of Sigmund Freud*, edited by James Strachey, vol. 18 (1953–1974), 1–78. London: Hogarth Press and the Institute of Psycho-Analysis, 1920.

Hussain, Nadeem J. Z. "The Role of Life in the *Genealogy*." In *The Cambridge Guide to Nietzsche's "On the Genealogy of Morality,"* edited by Simon May, 142–169. Cambridge: Cambridge University Press, 2011.

Gatens, Moira. *Feminist Interpretations of Benedict Spinoza*. University Park: Pennsylvania State University Press, 2009.

Jacobi, Friedrich. *Über die Lehre des Spinoza in Briefen an Herrn Moses Mendelssohn*. Breslau: Löwe, 1785.

Kant, Immanuel. *Kants gesammelte Schriften*. Edited by the Königlich Preußischen Akademie der Wissenschaften. 29 vols. Berlin: de Gruyter, 1902–.

Kinzel, Katherina. "Inner Experience and Articulation: Wilhelm Dilthey's Foundational Project and the Charge of Psychologism." *Hopos: The Journal of the International Society for the History of Philosophy of Science* 8, no. 2 (2018): 347–375.

Kraus, Katharina. *Kant on Self-Knowledge and Self-Formation: The Nature of Inner Experience*. Cambridge: Cambridge University Press, 2020.

Kraus, Katharina. "Salomé on Life, Religion, Self-Development, and Psychoanalysis: The Spinozistic Background." In *Spinoza in Germany: Political and Religious Thought across the Long Nineteenth Century*, edited by Jason M. Yonover and Kristin Gjesdal. Oxford: Oxford University Press, forthcoming.

Lloyd, Genevieve. "Dominance and Difference: A Spinozistic Alternative to the Distinction between 'Sex' and 'Gender.'" In *Feminist Interpretations of Benedict Spinoza*, edited by Moira Gatenschr, 29–41. University Park: Pennsylvania State University Press, 2009.

Markotic, Lorraine. "Andreas-Salomé and the Contemporary Essentialism Debate." *Seminar* 36 (2000): 59–78.

Makkreel, Rudolf. *Dilthey: Philosopher of the Human Studies*. 2nd ed. Princeton: Princeton University Press, 1992.

Makkreel, Rudolf. "Wilhelm Dilthey." In *Stanford Encyclopedia of Philosophy*. Stanford University, 1997–. Article published January 16, 2008; last modified September 29, 2020. https://plato.stanford.edu/entries/dilthey/.

Newlands, Samuel. *Reconceiving Spinoza*. Oxford: Oxford University Press, 2018.

Nietzsche, Friedrich. *The Birth of Tragedy Out of the Spirit of Music*. Edited by Raymond Geuss and Ronald Speirs. Cambridge: Cambridge University Press, 1999.

Nietzsche, Friedrich. *The Gay Science*. Edited by Bernard Williams. Translated by Josefine Nauckhoff and Adrian Del Caro. Cambridge: Cambridge University Press, 2001.

Nietzsche, Friedrich. *On the Genealogy of Morality*. Edited by Keith Ansell-Pearson. Translated by Carol Dieth. Cambridge: Cambridge University Press, 2006.

Nietzsche, Friedrich. *Thus Spoke Zarathustra*. Edited by Robert Pippin. Translated by Adrian Del Caro. Cambridge: Cambridge University Press, 2006.

Reginster, Bernhard. *The Affirmation of Life. Nietzsche on Overcoming Nihilism*. Cambridge, MA: Harvard university Press, 2008.

Salomé, Lou Andreas-. *Die Erotik*. In *Die Gesellschaft: Sammlung sozialpsychologischer Monographien*, vol. 23, edited by Martin Buber, 5–68. Frankfurt am Main: Literarische Anstalt: Rütten & Loennig, 1910.

Salomé, Lou. *In der Schule bei Freud. Tagebuch eines Jahres 1912/13*. In *Werke und Briefe von Lou Andreas Salomé in Einzelbänden* Vol. 14, edited by Manfred Klemann: Taching am See: MedienEdition Welsch, 2017.

Salomé, Lou Andreas-. *The Freud Journal of Lou Andreas-Salomé*. Translated by Stanley A. Leavy. New York: Basic Books, 1964.

Salomé, Lou Andreas-. *Friedrich Nietzsche in seinen Werken*. In *Einzelbände*, vol. 8, edited by Daniel Unger, 9–246. Taching am See: MedienEdition Welsch, 2020.

Salomé, Lou Andreas-. *Der Gott*. In *Einzelbände*, vol. 5, edited by Hans-Rüdiger Schwab, 9–133. Taching am See: MedienEdition Welsch, 2016.

Salomé, Lou Andreas-. *Lebensrückblick. Grundriß einiger Lebenserinnerungen.* Edited by Ernst Pfeiffer. Zurich: Niehans und Insel, 1951.

Salomé, Lou Andreas-. *Looking Back: Memoirs.* Edited by Ernst Pfeiffer. Translated by Breon Mitchell. New York: Marlowe, 1995.

Salomé, Lou Andreas-. "Der Mensch als Weib." In *Aufsätze und Essays*, vol. 2, edited by Hans-Rüdiger Schwab, 95–130. Taching am See: MedienEdition Welsch, 2010.

Salomé, Lou Andreas-. "My Thanks to Freud; Open Letter to Professor Freud on His 75th Birthday." Translated by William Needham. Vienna: Internationaler Psychoanalytischer Verlag, 1931.

Salomé, Lou Andreas-. *Philosophie: Ideal und Askese. Aufsätze und Essays.* Vol. 2. Edited by Hans-Rüdiger Schwab. Taching am See: MedienEdition Welsch, 2010.

Salomé, Lou Andreas-. *Psychoanalyse: Mein Dank an Freud.* In *Aufsätze und Essays*, vol. 4, edited by Hans-Rüdiger Schwab, 1–395. Taching am See: MedienEdition Welsch, 2010.

Salomé, Lou Andreas-. *Religion: Von der Bestie bis zum Gott.* In *Aufsätze und Essays*, vol. 1, edited by Hans-Rüdiger Schwab, 1–320. Taching am See: MedienEdition Welsch, 2010.

Schelling, Friedrich Wilhelm Joseph von. *Über das Wesen der menschlichen Freiheit* (1809). Hamburg: Meiner, 1997.

Schelling, Friedrich Wilhelm Joseph von. *System des transcendentalen Idealismus* (1800). Hamburg: Meiner, 2000.

Schwab, Hans-Rüdiger. "Lebensgläubigkeit. Über Lou Andreas-Salomés nachgelassenes Manuskript 'Der Gott.'" Postscript in Lou Salomé, *Einzelbände*, vol. 5, edited by Hans-Rüdiger Schwab, 199–242. Taching am See: MedienEdition Welsch, 2016.

Simmel, Georg. *Gesamtausgabe.* Edited by Otthein Rammstedt. 24 vols. Suhrkamp: Frankfurt a. M., 1999–2015.

Simmel, Georg. "Das individuelle Gesetz. Ein Versuch über das Prinzip der Ethik." *Logos. Internationale Zeitschrift für Philosophie der Kultur* 4 (1913): 117–160.

Spinoza, Benedictus de. *Spinoza's Ethics* (1677). Translated by George Elliot. Edited by Claire Carlisle. Princeton: Princeton University Press, 2020.

Spörl, Uwe. *Gottlose Mystik in der deutschen Literatur um die Jahrhundertwende.* Paderborn: Brill, 1997.

Wawrytko, Sandra A. "Lou Salomé (1861–1937)." In *Contemporary Women Philosophers, 1900–Today*, vol. 4 of *A History of Women Philosophers*, ed. Mary Ellen Waithe, 69–102. Dordrecht: Kluwer, 1996.

Weininger, Otto. *Geschlecht und Charakter. Eine prinzipielle Untersuchung.* Vienna: Wilhelm Braumüller, 1903.

Welsch, Ursula, and Michaela Wiesner. *Lou Andreas-Salomé: Vom "Lebensurgrund" zur Psychoanalyse.* Munich: Verlag Internationale Psychoanalyse, 1988.

Wieder, Christiane. *Die Psychoanalytikerin Lou Andres-Salomé. Ihr Werk im Spannungsfeld zwischen Sigmund Freud und Rainer Maria Rilke.* Göttingen: Vandenhoeck & Ruprecht, 2011.

CHAPTER 10

....

ROSA LUXEMBURG
(1871–1919)

....

LYDIA PATTON

Rosa Luxemburg was a Polish socialist activist, political theorist, and political economist. Her life, spent in sympathy with workers' struggles, has been romanticized, and her controversial, pioneering work has been revived repeatedly.[1] Themes of her political theory include:

- The capitalist state as an expression of class antagonism, versus natural, cooperative economies characteristic of preindustrial forms of social organization
- The accumulation of capital as an imperative of the capitalist state and as a motivation for imperialism and colonial exploitation
- Rejection of the view that gradual reform of the capitalist state could serve the people's interests, and a spirited defense of a proletarian revolution

Luxemburg's work was revived as part of the feminist movement in the 1960s and 1970s,[2] and has enduring importance to anticolonial and antiimperialist thought. And Luxemburg's work is a significant expression of the Marxist tradition in philosophy.

This essay will first present a vignette of Luxemburg's life and work, referring to classic and recent biographies. Following that, section 3 examines concepts of the state and nation in Hegel, Marx, Engels, and Lenin. The subject of section 4 is Luxemburg's substantial work of political economy, *The Accumulation of Capital*. It is a most significant achievement, analyzing the contradictions of the capitalist state and its role in driving imperialist expansion and colonialism. Section 5 traces how Luxemburg's political economy in *Accumulation* underwrites her interventions in the heated debates over

---

[1] See Peter Hudis and Kevin Anderson, eds., *The Rosa Luxemburg Reader* (New York: Monthly Review Press, 2004), for an edited selection of Luxemburg's work.

[2] See Raya Dunayevskaya, *Rosa Luxemburg, Women's Liberation, and Marx's Philosophy of Revolution* (Chicago: University of Illinois Press, 1991).

Polish independence. And section 6 concludes with remarks on Luxemburg's significance for philosophy and political thought.

1 LIFE

Rosa Luxemburg was instrumental in the founding of the revolutionary Polish Socialist Party, called the Social Democratic Party of the Kingdom of Poland (SDKPL), of the German Communist Party (with Karl Liebknecht), and of the Social Democratic Party in Germany. She led workers' strikes, published extensively in the popular and socialist press, participated in multiple Internationals of the Socialist Party, and took part in the week-long Spartacist uprising in Germany that began on January 5, 1919. Luxemburg published academic works in political economy, philosophy, and socialist theory. She was imprisoned repeatedly and, later, brutally murdered in response to her political activity.

Luxemburg's short life is so exciting that it has been retold many times, and she has experienced several revivals, one of which is currently under way.[3] In the 1960s, interest in Luxemburg was revived as part of the first wave of Western feminism, which prompted reexaminations of her own work and of her collaborations and friendship with Clara Zetkin.[4]

Paul Buhle notes that Luxemburg's affinity for Trotsky, and her challenges to Lenin and Marx, led to her denunciation under Stalin.[5] Some European thinkers who supported reform (but not overthrow) of capitalist institutions mistook her for a historical ally, in consequence. She was a controversial figure in life, debating the leaders of communist and socialist movements of Russia, Germany, and Poland. It is no surprise, then, that after her death others inside and outside the socialist movement took the opportunity to tell misleading stories about her views and life.[6] "Myths and misrepresentations," as

---

[3] In 1959, Tony Cliff published a pamphlet on Luxemburg's life: "Rosa Luxemburg: A Life of Struggle". The pamphlet was reprinted in *Socialist Review* (January 2009). Link: https://socialistworker.co.uk/social ist-review-archive/rosa-luxemburg-life-struggle/ .

[4] More on this history can be found in Dunayevskaya, *Women's Liberation*. J. P. Nettl published a biography of Luxemburg in 1966, and in the 1980s another well-known account of her life was contributed by Elzbieta Ettinger. Linda Edmondson, "Lives of Rosa Luxemburg," *Revolutionary Russia* 2, no. 2 (1989): 35–44, is a review of biographies available until the mid-1980s. Recently, in 2020, Dana Mills published a new biography of Luxemburg, and in 2019 Nettl's biography was reissued by Verso. Kate Evans published a detailed graphic novel of Luxemburg's life in 2015, *Red Rosa* (London: Verso Books, 2015), with an afterword by historian Paul Buhle.

[5] Paul Buhle, afterword to Evans, *Red Rosa*, 215–219.

[6] In Linda Edmondson's view, the publication of J. P. Nettl's well-known biography of Luxemburg in 1966 came at an "opportune moment," when the "Stalinist stranglehold on Marxist thought had been loosened, allowing new (or old and repressed) ideas of a democratic Marxism to surface for the first time since the 1920s" ("Lives," 1989, 35).

one scholar puts it, have "been Rosa Luxemburg's fate almost from the moment of her death."[7]

Rosa Luxemburg was born in Poland on March 5, 1871. Around 1886, she joined the Polish revolutionary party Proletariat and began participating in its political activities.[8] By 1889 "the police had caught up with her," and she emigrated to Switzerland. Despite her exile, Luxemburg quickly became "the theoretical leader of the revolutionary socialist party of Poland", first called Proletariat and then the SDKPL.[9] The paper of the SDKPL, *Sprawa Rabotnicza*, was a major outlet for her work.

In August 1893, at the age of twenty-two, Luxemburg attended the Congress of the Socialist International as the representative of the SDKPL. There were two Polish socialist parties in attendance: the SDKPL and the rival Polish Socialist Party (PPS), "whose main plank was the independence of Poland." The PPS had historically had the support of "all the experienced elders of international socialism," including even Engels, who, with Marx, had earlier made Polish independence a key part of the platform of the German Communist Party.[10] The twenty-two-year-old Luxemburg stood up to the PPS, arguing against the independence of Poland on the strongest terms. She "struck out at the PPS, accusing it of clear nationalistic tendencies and a proneness to diverting the workers from the path of class struggle; and she dared to take a different position to the old masters and oppose the slogan of independence for Poland. Her adversaries heaped abuse on her, some of them, like the veteran disciple and friend of Marx and Engels, Wilhelm Liebknecht, going so far as to accuse her of being an agent of the Tsarist secret police. But she stuck to her point."[11] During the debates, Luxemburg cited Marx's own arguments and analyses in making critical points against his earlier support for the PPS. Throughout her life, Luxemburg argued against nationalism as a distraction from class struggle, and against populism as a basis for nationalism. Luxemburg's arguments regarding nationalism are inseparable from her economic, sociopolitical, and class analysis.

Luxemburg is best described as a socialist activist, political theorist, and political economist, who begins within a largely Marxist framework, but who, by the end of her career, defines her own sphere of influence. Luxemburg took on most of the orthodox Russian Marxist thinkers of the time, arguing that their interpretations of Marx were retrograde or misguided, including Vasily Vorontsov (*Accumulation*, chap. 19) and Nikolai Frantsevich Danielson, who went by the name "Nikolayon" (*Accumulation*, chap. 20).[12]

[7] Edmondson, "Lives," 35.

[8] Proletariat was "founded in 1882, some 21 years before the Russian Social Democratic Party (Bolsheviks and Mensheviks) came into being" (Cliff, "Rosa Luxemburg.")

[9] Cliff, "Rosa Luxemburg."

[10] Cliff, "Rosa Luxemburg."

[11] Cliff, "Rosa Luxemburg."

[12] Rosa Luxemburg, *The Accumulation of Capital*, trans. Agnes Schwarzschild (London: Routledge, 1951; reprint, New York: Monthly Review), 2. Hereafter *Accumulation* in the text.

In 1903–1904 she entered into a debate with Lenin "on the national question, and on the conception of party structure, and the relation between the party and the activity of the masses."[13] In many ways, however, she was sympathetic with Lenin's position and with the Bolshevik split from the more moderate elements in the Communist Party.[14]

After her key role along with Karl Liebknecht in the formation of the German Communist Party (following a split with the German Socialist Party when they failed to oppose World War I), Luxemburg spent several years in prison during the 1910s, and was freed only on November 8, 1918. She joined in the Spartacist revolution with "all her energy and enthusiasm," but "unfortunately the forces of reaction were strong. Right wing Social Democratic leaders and generals of the old Kaiser's army joined forces to suppress the revolutionary working class. Thousands of workers were murdered; on 15 January 1919 Karl Liebknecht was killed; on the same day a soldier's rifle butt smashed into Rosa Luxemburg's skull."[15] The reception of Luxemburg's thought after her death is tied closely to the fate of the Soviet Socialist Republics—in both positive and negative ways. Luxemburg was denounced under Stalin for Trotskyism. Her work was revived in so-called Eastern Bloc countries and in the West in the 1960s. But revivals of her work have been undermined, to an extent, by suppression of socialist research. To understand Luxemburg, one must understand socialist thinking, which has been kept alive only sporadically in the academic context. Marx and Marxist thought were leading strains of philosophical research in East German and Eastern European academia between the 1960s and 1991. But after 1991, many East German philosophy departments were emptied of socialist, including Marxist, philosophers and replaced with analytic philosophers from the West.[16]

Whatever one's political views are, this is unfortunate given the historical importance of socialist thought. The eroding away of competence in socialist thought and history would have undermined our ability to understand some of the most influential thinkers in history. But that erosion did not happen—or, at least, not as completely as it could have. In the German tradition, the Frankfurt School, and later thinkers including Herbert Marcuse and Jürgen Habermas, were an important conduit to socialist

[13] Cliff, "Rosa Luxemburg."

[14] "When the October Revolution broke out, Luxemburg welcomed it enthusiastically, praising it in the highest terms. At the same time, she did not believe that uncritical acceptance of everything the Bolsheviks did would be of service to the labour movement" (Cliff, "Rosa Luxemburg.").

[15] Cliff, "Rosa Luxemburg."

[16] See Ulrich Schneider, "The Situation of Philosophy, the Culture of the Philosophers: Philosophy in the New Germany," *Social Research* 64, no. 2 (Summer 1997), 281–300. In addition to the evidence presented in Schneider's article, I heard the same in conversation, during an unofficial visit of several months to a department in the former Deutsche Demokratische Republik in 2001. On the question of the entwined fates of academic philosophy, McCarthyism, and the Cold War in the USA, see John McCumber, *Time in the Ditch* (Evanston, IL: Northwestern University Press, 2001), and George Reisch, *How the Cold War Transformed Philosophy of Science* (Cambridge: Cambridge University Press, 2005). I am grateful to Dalia Nassar for guidance on this subject.

thought and to Marx in particular, presented in a form that was acceptable to Western philosophers.[17]

However, the radical tradition of socialism to which Luxemburg belongs was kept alive in a different way. Here the history of thought owes a crucial debt to anticolonial, feminist, and radical traditions of research. Anticolonial and radical thinkers including Angela Davis,[18] C. L. R. James,[19] and Cedric Robinson (*Black Marxism*) kept the study of socialist thought alive in the 1960s, 1970s, and 1980s, and their influence and popularity helped to maintain that study into the 1990s and up to the present day.[20]

Luxemburg's relationship to anticolonial thought is complex. She is a potential ally of anticolonialism because of her insight that the capitalist desire for increasing accumulation drives imperialist conquest.[21] But she is also criticized for belonging to the tradition which sees certain nations (especially Germany and Russia) as central to socialist history and progress, giving less attention to the rest of the world.[22] Her positions on the independence of Poland are closely linked to her views on the relative importance of Germany and Russia to the revolutionary overthrow of capitalism.

Rosa Luxemburg's views on "the national question" are relevant, not just to the renewed assessment of her work and its impact, but to her relationship to contemporary currents in political thought, especially antiimperialist thought and international socialism. The sections that follow will, first, present the analysis of states and nations found in Marx, and then Luxemburg's analysis of imperialism as arising from the capitalist drive for accumulation of surplus value. Following that, Luxemburg's analysis will be related to her criticism of the Polish independence movement, which put her at odds with Socialist Party leadership of the time.

---

[17] Habermas sometimes is seen as part of the tradition of "analytical Marxism" that also includes G. A. Cohen and John Roemer.

[18] Angela Y. Davis, "Marcuse's Legacies," in *Herbert Marcuse: A Critical Reader*, ed. John Abromeit and W. Mark Cobb (New York: Routledge, 2004), 43–50, and *The Angela Y. Davis Reader*, ed. Joy James (Hoboken: Wiley, 1998).

[19] C. L. R. James, *The Black Jacobins* (London: Secker & Warburg, 1938); *World Revolution, 1917–1936: The Rise and Fall of the Communist International* (London: Secker & Warburg, 1937).

[20] Movements like Science for the People, which were influential in the formation of Science and Technology Studies as a field, have also helped to maintain engagement with socialist thinking in the scientific context. See Sigrid Schmalzer, Alyssa Botelho, and Daniel Chard, eds., *Science for the People: Documents from America's Movement of Radical Scientists* (Amherst: University of Massachusetts Press, 2018).

[21] See, e.g., Hannah Holleman, *Dust Bowls of Empire* (New Haven: Yale University Press, 2018), 64–65. More contemporary perspectives often reverse Luxemburg's arrow of causation, arguing that colonialism and settler occupation is a necessary condition for capitalist expansion and the more fundamental of the two. See, e.g., Eve Tuck and K. Wayne Yang, "Decolonization Is Not a Metaphor," *Decolonization: Indigeneity, Education & Society* 1, No. 1 (2012): 1–40. Thanks are due to Dalia Nassar for reference to this significant work.

[22] Those sympathetic to Luxemburg also cite this, as it is a clear conclusion to be drawn from her work. Cedric Robinson criticizes this tendency in Luxemburg, as it lays aside the revolutionary potential of nations beyond her analysis. *Black Marxism* (London: Zed Books, 1983; reprint, Chapel Hill, NC: University of North Carolina Press, 2000), 62–65.

2 THE STATE AND THE NATION
IN MARXIST THOUGHT

It is well known that Marx's early thought was developed in conversation with the Young Hegelians, but also that that conversation led to his significant departure from the Hegelian tradition, especially in his conception of the state. Still, Marx's view can be seen as a further development away from Kant's idealist position regarding moral agency, in a way inspired by Hegel's own criticisms of, and amendments to, the Kantian position. Kant's Kingdom of Ends (*Reich der Zwecke*) rests on the idea that moral agents are self-legislating and autonomous, and thus that the only true law is the moral law.

In the Kantian and Hegelian traditions, the state can embody the moral law and promote individual freedom, and thus is not (necessarily) coercive. In the Marxist tradition, the state is an enemy of freedom, a bureaucratic machine that serves the capitalist ends of exploitation and maintains class antagonisms. (The *nation*, however, may embody the will of the people.)

Hegel's political theory is grounded, as are Rousseau's and Kant's, on the community of autonomous subjects.[23] But Hegel's analysis of the relationship between the individual and the state is quite different. As Lydia Moland notes, "Hegel's description of the citizen's disposition aims first of all, then, to identify what must be true both of the state and of the individual's perception of the state in order to allow the citizen to be at home in his actions," that is, not to be alienated from the state even when following its laws.[24] When the state's laws are seen, not as "external and imposed," but as part of the individual's own agency, the citizen develops an "ideal political disposition," which "combines insistence that the state cultivate its citizens' individuality with the requirement that individuals modify their self-interest for the good of the state. When the citizen and the state mutually recognize each other, the citizen can see the laws of the state as his own and so be at home in them."[25] It is fundamental to Hegel's political—and even his ethical—philosophy that the ethical-political subject should recognize the state as a legitimate actor and should even make the state's interests her own. The ethical subject is essentially a citizen of a state, and her freedom rests on the existence of that state: "Hegel's definition of patriotism makes it clear that this disposition is built on the mutual recognition that is the foundation of Hegel's ethical philosophy. In order for the individual to develop the disposition Hegel describes, he must recognize the state and,

---

[23] The classic text is G. W. F. Hegel, *Elements of the Philosophy of Right* (1820), ed. Allen W. Wood, trans. H. B. Nisbet (Cambridge: Cambridge University Press, 1991).

[24] Lydia Moland, *Hegel on Political Identity: Patriotism, Nationality, Cosmopolitanism* (Evanston, IL: Northwestern University Press, 2011), 47.

[25] Moland, *Hegel on Political Identity*, 47.

just as importantly, he must know that he, as an individual with rights and interests, is recognized by the state."[26] The state must recognize its citizens as free agents, and the individual must see the state as taking action to "promote his freedom."[27] This "mutual recognition" between the individual and the state comes about when the state is seen as acting in line with the individual's agency, not as imposing external sanctions from an alien perspective.[28]

For Hegel, as for Kant, true freedom requires, not only recognition of a law valid for oneself, but recognition of the law as binding on—and protecting the freedom of—all rational agents. In the Kantian and Hegelian accounts, the role of the ideal state is not restricted to wielding power. This can be contrasted to Hobbes's "Naturall force" in *Leviathan*, where the state imposes authority as a father does on a family. The Kantian and Hegelian ideal state is more like a Hobbesian "Common-wealth by Institution," where the state is an "Artificial Man" designed to protect the actions and interests of its citizens.[29]

Hobbes arguably recognizes individual agency independently of the state (although life outside the state is, he famously notes, "nasty, poor, brutish, and short"). In contrast, Hegel argues that individual agency and freedom develop only in interaction with other rational subjects and with institutions. But what is the essence of free subjectivity for Hegel, if it requires engagement with agents and structures outside the subject to develop in the first place? Human subjectivity requires interaction with other human subjects: humans are essentially social beings whose agency develops in and through recognition of others' agency. To Hegel and Kant, the ideal state recognizes the agency of each rational being. The structures that enable mutual recognition include the moral law and legislation as part of the moral community.

Marx's political theory begins from his recognition of the essence of human existence as part of a "collectivity," and "the primary form of human collectivity is the species [Gattung], or, more specifically, the species-being [Gattungswesen]."[30] The essence of the human species is our ability to engage with nature, to change it and to interact with it through labor.[31] For Marx, the development of capitalism results in the alienation of the

---

[26] Moland, *Hegel on Political Identity*, 53. Moland cites Hegel here: "as a result, this other immediately ceases to be an other for me, and in my consciousness of this, I am free" (Hegel, *Elements of Philosophy of Right*, §268).

[27] Moland, *Hegel on Political Identity*, 53.

[28] "Ideally . . . the citizen does not look at the state as an external power imposing laws and sanctions. He instead understands the institutions and procedures that govern the state and, in recognizing that they are designed to promote his freedom, does not view them as an imposition" (Moland, *Hegel on Political Identity*, 53).

[29] Thomas Hobbes, *Leviathan, Parts I and II* (1651) , ed. A. P. Martinich and Brian Battiste, rev. ed. (Peterborough, Ontario: Broadview Press, 2010), 18.

[30] "There is a fundamental continuity in Marx's writings deriving from his philosophical position as an Hegelian and Feuerbachian." Joseph Petrus, "Marx and Engels on the National Question," *Journal of Politics* 33, no. 3 (1971): 800. See also David Harvey, *A Companion to Marx's Capital: The Complete Edition* (London: Verso Books, 2018), 114–117.

[31] Harvey, *Companion*, 114, 175.

laborer from nature and from his own labor.[32] The marketplace destroys mutual recognition: "in the marketplace, people relate to one another not as people but as buyers and sellers of things."[33] Capitalists have the aim of accumulating surplus value from the labor of workers.[34] A capitalist nation is oppressive in its essence since it supports the upper classes in their project of extracting and accumulating surplus value from nature and from people.

Marx argues that global communism resolves the conflict between the interests of the state and those of the people: "the teleological development of history leads towards the re-establishment of the species on a higher plane of existence, and the overcoming of alienation and divisions. Universal, cosmopolitan society, on the highest level of global communism, will be without the divisions and conflicts between such secondary forms of human existence as distinct social systems, classes, nationalities, nations, and states."[35] Marx and Friedrich Engels wrote "The German Ideology" in 1845 and 1846, a work critical of the "Young Hegelians," who reduced every conflict to contradictions produced by "consciousness," or to a contradiction found in the religious outlook (pt. 1, A). Marx and Engels characteristically respond that the conflicts facing Germans are, instead, to be found in the material conditions in which they find themselves: in particular, in the conditions of human labor and production (pt. 1, A). Some Hegelians argue that freedom is found by seeing the state as an extension of one's own conscious moral agency. Marx and Engels argue here that human freedom is found in global organization under communism. In "The German Ideology," "one finds . . . explicit references to the ultimate universalism to be attained under global communism. Before the final resolution of the antagonism between men, civil society expresses itself in separatism and organizes itself vis-à-vis other peoples as discrete nationalities. It organizes itself internally in the form of the state."[36] Organization into particular states or nations will always separate workers from each other and set up artificial differences between their material needs and conditions of labor.

Socialist thinkers differed in their analyses of what would happen as workers began to organize and revolt. Lenin contributes a famous analysis in *The State and Revolution* (1917). Engels had argued against the Hegelian notion that the state is "the reality of the ethical idea," "the image and reality of reason." Instead, Engels argues, the state

> is a product of society at a certain stage of development; it is the admission that this society has become entangled in an insoluble contradiction with itself, that it has split into irreconcilable antagonisms which it is powerless to dispel. But in order that these antagonisms, these classes with conflicting economic interests, might not consume themselves and society in fruitless struggle, it became necessary to have a

---

[32] See, e.g., Harvey, *Companion*, chap. 4.
[33] Harvey, *Companion*, 112.
[34] Harvey, *Companion*, chap. 10.
[35] Petrus, "Marx and Engels," 800.
[36] Petrus, "Marx and Engels," 800.

power, seemingly standing above society, that would alleviate the conflict and keep it within the bounds of "order"; and this power, arisen out of society but placing itself above it, and alienating itself more and more from it, is the state.[37]

Lenin cites the foregoing passage approvingly in *The State and Revolution* (1917), noting that "the state is a product and a manifestation of the irreconcilability of class antagonisms. The state arises where, when and insofar as class antagonism objectively cannot be reconciled. And, conversely, the existence of the state proves that the class antagonisms are irreconcilable."[38] The "contradictions" cited by Engels and Lenin are *class* conflicts within society: conflicts arising from the material exploitation of the people who do the labor (the working class) by those who accumulate surplus value from that labor (the capitalist class). The state has been mistakenly seen as a way to mediate those conflicts (*State and Revolution*, chap. 1 §1), but the presence of a state is instead an indication that class conflict is present.

Following the revolution of the working classes and the seizure of the means of production, Engels famously argued that the bourgeois state—the institutions that maintained civil society—would "wither away": "as soon as there is no longer any social class to be held in subjection, as soon as class rule, and the individual struggle for existence based upon the present anarchy in production, with the collisions and excesses arising from this struggle, are removed, nothing more remains to be held in subjection — nothing necessitating a special coercive force, a state. . . . State interference in social relations becomes, in one domain after another, superfluous, and then dies down of itself. . . . The state is not "abolished." It withers away.[39] As Lenin points out, Engels meant to say that *once* the proletarian revolution was accomplished, there would be nothing more for the state to do (*State and Revolution*, chap. 1 §4). The state exists as a consequence of class antagonism, so if that antagonism is removed, the state has no further reason to exist. The state will not wither away by itself in the absence of revolution and overthrow of the capitalist order.

In *The Communist Manifesto*, Marx and Engels argue for the destruction of the bourgeois state as necessary to postrevolutionary workers' society, and Lenin cites this in *The State and Revolution*, arguing for "the destruction of the bureaucratic-military state machine" (chap. 3 §2). Marx and Engels take the Paris Commune as a model for a people's revolution. Following a people's revolution, the social and political organization that replaces the "state machine" should be an expression of the people's will. Lenin argues for the voluntary organization of the people in communes and for their eventual organization into a central body, constituting voluntary "proletarian centralism."[40] Lenin's

---

[37] Friedrich Engels, *The Origin of the Family, Private Property and the State* (1884) (Moscow: Progress, 1976), 177–178.

[38] Vladimir Ilyich Lenin, *The State and Revolution* (August 1917), in *Collected Works*, vol. 25 (Moscow: Progress, 1964), , chap. 1, §1.

[39] Friedrich Engels, *Anti-Dühring. Herr Eugen Dühring's Revolution in Science* (Moscow: Progress, 1947), 301–303.

[40] "Now if the proletariat and the poor peasants take state power into their own hands, organize themselves quite freely in communes, and unite the action of all the communes in striking at capital, in

"national" unity is based on the development of the "higher phase of communist so-ciety," one that arises "when people have become so accustomed to observing the funda-mental rules of social intercourse and when their labor has become so productive that they will voluntarily work according to their ability" (chap. 5, §4).

Lenin condemns the "bureaucratic-military state machine" of the capitalist state and exalts the unified people's nation. The "bureaucratic-military state machine" is antithet-ical to freedom. But the organization of a free people's nation requires, first, the develop-ment of consciousness among the proletariat to the point that they voluntarily observe rules of social interaction and work voluntarily for goods held in common. Lenin concludes that "so long as the state exists there is no freedom. When there is freedom, there will be no state" (chap. 5, §4). In the people's nation, voluntarily gathering in communes with centralized organization, freedom comes from the people rather than from the state. Still, the people must be organized: their freedom comes from voluntary organization that is developed over time.[41]

The organization of the "people's nation" is behind Lenin's defense of "the right of na-tions to self-determination," which Luxemburg will famously challenge (section 5 here). Nationalism can be defended, in Lenin's (and Marx's and Engels's) politics, insofar as it is an expression of the will and interests of working people. As I will show in section 5, Luxemburg provides a scorching critique of even this attenuated "nationalism," and she does so on two grounds: first, *Realpolitik* concerning the role of Germany, Poland, and Russia in workers' struggles, and second, her analysis of the role of the state in imperi-alism and capitalist accumulation. I will turn to Luxemburg's analysis of imperialism and accumulation first, in section 4, and then to the question of *Realpolitik* and Polish independence in section 5.

3 IMPERIALISM AND ACCUMULATION: LUXEMBURG ON POLITICAL ECONOMY

In 1913, only about five years before her death, Luxemburg published *The Accumulation of Capital: A Contribution to the Economic Explanation of Imperialism*.[42] The work

---

crushing the resistance of the capitalists, and in transferring the privately-owned railways, factories, land and so on to the entire nation, to the whole of society, won't that be centralism? Won't that be the most consistent democratic centralism and, moreover, proletarian centralism?" (*State and Revolution*, chap. 3 §4).

[41] Thus, one might ask whether Lenin has, in fact, moved so far away from Hegel. After all, one of the most significant functions of the state for Hegel is *Bildung*, which could be seen as analogous to Lenin's appeal to the people's will and its development, for instance, through the organization of people's councils and the Commune. I am grateful to Dalia Nassar for this insight into the comparison between Hegel and Lenin.

[42] The centenary of the publication of *The Accumulation of Capital* in 2013 was marked by conferences and publications, including Judith Dellheim and Frieder Otto Wolf, eds., *Rosa Luxemburg: A Permanent Challenge for Political Economy* (London: Palgrave MacMillan, 2016), and Riccardo Bellofiore, ed., *Rosa*

makes valuable contributions, many of which I will note here, even though it has known limitations.[43]

The Accumulation of Capital is a substantial contribution to political economy, to social thought, and to anti-imperialist theory. The achievements of the book are grounded in Marx's analysis of capital, labor, and value. But Luxemburg went further, achieving (among other things):

(1) An expanded account of Marx's analysis of production, adding the production of the "means of exchange"[44]

(2) Thoroughgoing criticism of Sismondi's theory of crises[45]

(3) A defense of "natural economies" as a basis of socialism[46]

(4) A decisive refutation of "Russian populism" as a basis for socialism[47]

(5) An argument that imperialism results in degradation of the social control of production and reproduction, and, thus, an argument for a "socially planned economy"[48]

(6) Sharp criticism of militarism as a site of accumulation of capital under imperialism[49]

Luxemburg is a natural ally of anticolonial and antiimperialist thought. She views capitalist economies as extractive and exploitative at their core. Luxemburg's analysis views imperialism as "the product of capital's need to realize surplus value in an accumulating economy."[50]

In section 1, Luxemburg begins with the question of reproduction. Cultures in what Rousseau called the state of nature realized that some sort of reproduction of value through labor (for instance, preserving food or building infrastructure) was necessary to avoid starvation or other misfortunes. But in these "communist agrarian" societies,

---

Luxemburg and the Critique of Political Economy (London: Taylor & Francis, 2009). Luxemburg's work on political economy is becoming more well-known and studied. These collections provide an admirable review of the strengths, contributions, and limitations of Luxemburg's *Accumulation*.

[43] Like many works of political economy, *The Accumulation of Capital* at times rests on a somewhat shaky empirical foundation, drawing on partial examples and single cases to support more general conclusions. See Dellheim and Wolf, *Rosa Luxemburg*, and Bellofiore, *Rosa Luxemburg and the Critique of Political Economy*, for detailed discussion.

[44] This discussion is found in Section 1. A general note: In the translation used, *The Accumulation of Capital* is divided into sections, which then are divided into chapters with sequential numbering. So there are larger 'sections' divided into smaller 'chapters', but the chapter numbering does not restart with each section.

[45] Section 2.

[46] Section 3, especially chapters 27, 28, and 29.

[47] Section 2.

[48] Section 1.

[49] Section 3, especially chapter 32.

[50] Roberto Veneziani, "Rosa Luxemburg on Imperialism," in Bellofiore, *Rosa Luxemburg and the Critique of Political Economy*, 130.

the nature and scope of reproduction is determined by "the community of all workers," in a system of "planned cooperation" (*Accumulation*, 32). Luxemburg argues that this "planned cooperation" is in fact "natural," in the sense that planning for cooperative social interaction is a natural human capacity and desire. At the conclusion of the work, Luxemburg notes that capitalist societies must resist natural, cooperative, social organization of economies, since capitalism cannot survive without the enslavement of one class to another, and enslavement is not a feature of the natural organization of society (*Accumulation*, chap. 27).

Capitalism emerges as an inherently exploitative system in which the ruling class exploits the working class, extracting surplus value from workers and from the natural environment. Luxemburg's argument thus draws on Marx's analysis of labor and value in *Capital*.[51] She goes beyond Marx in her analysis of the role of social organization. First, Luxemburg argues that capitalism depends on the "anarchy" of the market (*Accumulation*, 45). In capitalist societies, as opposed to "natural" economies, the market is lawless: that is, it is not planned or governed by social or cooperative organization. A capitalist society may produce more than enough food for its citizens, but that food may not get to those citizens because the market is organized to make money, not to distribute food efficiently. Despite sufficient production, then, people go hungry.

Much of the argument of *The Accumulation of Capital*—the entirety of section 2—is aimed at political economists like Adam Smith and François Quesnay, who had argued that the capitalist market economy is not lawless, as Luxemburg argued, but rather governed by rational principles, and thus serves the interests of its citizens. Interestingly, given that he is often regarded as a precursor to Marx,[52] Luxemburg also devotes much of *Accumulation* to criticizing Jean Charles Léonard de Sismondi, who had argued that interventions could avert irrational crises caused by unregulated markets. Luxemburg argues that nothing short of the overthrow of capitalism could overcome market crises in the long run.[53]

Luxemburg's criticisms of Adam Smith are reminiscent of Marx's. She acknowledges as correct Smith's view that labor constitutes value.[54] But Smith didn't realize that labor can *impart* value as well. Labor can create new means of production (equipment, like printing presses or tractors; infrastructure; intellectual capital). The means to create new means of production—wages for labor, money for component parts of tools—then

[51] For more detailed analysis of the relationship between Luxemburg and Marx on this question see Paul Zarembka, "Value: Marx's Evolution and Luxemburg's Legacy," in Dellheim and Wolf, *Rosa Luxemburg*, 55–91.

[52] Sismondi anticipated Marx's division between bourgeois and proletariat, and argued against laissez-faire economics in favor of market regulation.

[53] In this sense, Luxemburg's arguments against Sismondi in *Accumulation* are akin to her criticisms of Eduard Bernstein in *Social Reform or Revolution?*

[54] See Rosa Luxemburg, "Wage Labor: Selections from *Introduction to Political Economy*," trans. Anna Ezekiel, in *Women Philosophers of the Long Nineteenth Century: The German Tradition*, ed. Dalia Nassar and Kristin Gjesdal (New York: Oxford University Press, 2021), 214–240.

becomes part of a new tally of total capital (*Accumulation*, 66). Luxemburg notes that few of the classical economists have the capacity to account for capital of this kind. Even Marx does not provide a complete account of the flow of capital in this sense, Luxemburg argues. Marx allows for production and consumption, but his chart mapping capital does not account for "means of production of the means of exchange" (*Accumulation*, 99). This type of production is the material manifestation of the social aspects of the economy. As Govind summarizes Luxemburg's argument: "where reproduction on an expanded scale with the two departments (means of production and consumption) took place, a portion of the surplus value had to be proportionately realised. It is here that a third market (as effective demand)—a means of production of the means of exchange—was required and so there was imperial-colonial expansion."[55]Capitalism even within a nation's borders, Luxemburg notes, provides incentives to expansion: larger enterprises have the advantage (*Accumulation*, 40). But, following the law of capitalism that surplus value must increase continuously over time (*Accumulation*, 76–78), Luxemburg explains that enterprises must reach out beyond the borders of their own states (chap. 25). At some point, surplus value must be realized, that is, more tools and equipment must be produced, and more value extracted from nature and from workers, in order to exchange more value on the market. Luxemburg notes that, in this sense, surplus value that will become wages or equipment is in fact a form of capital, which complicates the calculations of Smith and Marx alike.

Luxemburg's analysis of value and labor leads to her characteristic claim that capitalist economies—and capitalist state organization—inherently lead to imperialism and expansion. She marshals this argument against figures outside socialism like Smith and Quesnay, but also against socialist figures, like Nikolayon, and social democrats, including Eduard Bernstein. Bernstein, a protégé of Friedrich Engels, became a significant figure in the early Social Democratic Party in Germany, helping to write its 1891 Erfurt Program. The debates between Bernstein, Luxemburg, Lenin, August Bebel, and Karl Kautsky between 1898 and 1903 were formative for this party.[56]

Eduard Bernstein published several articles in *Die Neue Zeit* between 1896 and 1898, and a book, *Die Voraussetzungen des Sozialismus und die Aufgabe der Sozialdemokratie*, in 1899. Luxemburg's celebrated *Social Reform or Revolution?* of 1900 was written as a contribution to these debates, and features her revolutionary critiques of Bernstein's reformist program.[57] Bernstein argued that the final aim of revolution was unnecessary, and that gradual, evolutionary reforms could achieve the workers' goals. Luxemburg opposed this view strongly.

The question arose quickly, whether Luxemburg's analysis of the exploitative aspects of the state would apply to what Lenin would call a nation, as well. As I've shown, Lenin

---

[55] Rahul Govind, "Nation State in the Age of Imperialism," *Economic and Political Weekly* 48, no. 14 (2013): 51.

[56] David W. Morgan, "The Father of Revisionism Revisited: Eduard Bernstein," *Journal of Modern History* 51, no. 3 (1979): 526.

[57] Rosa Luxemburg, *Social Reform or Revolution?* (1900) (London: Militant Publications, 1986).

seems to allow for a "nation" to arise within a state, one that expresses the will of the working people, even before the revolution. The occasion of the debate over the independence of Poland revealed the question of the "right" of nations to self-determination as a contested one within socialist circles. Luxemburg's position was drawn from her own distinctive analysis and rooted in her account of political theory.

4 ROSA LUXEMBURG ON NATIONALISM

Luxemburg's writings on nations and states discussed in this section are drawn from the materials reprinted in *The National Question*, a 1976 collection edited by Horace Davis that has recently come back into print.[58]

One can read Luxemburg's writings on nationalism in multiple contexts. There is a particularly instructive contrast between readings of Luxemburg that center internal Russian and German politics (the Bolshevik/Menshevik debates, her fights with Lenin and affinities with Trotsky)[59] and readings that emphasize the relevance of Luxemburg's work to broader questions of imperialism and colonialism.[60]

In many ways, the debate over the independence of Poland that animated Luxemburg's debates with Marx, Engels, and Lenin was inspired more by *Realpolitik* than by theory. In the 1790s, Poland was partitioned, leaving it with areas ("partitions") effectively governed by Prussia, Russia, and Austria. At the 1896 International Socialist Congress in London, the PPS asked for a motion endorsing Polish independence. Marx and Engels supported the independence of Poland, arguing that the workers had the right to dismantle the bureaucratic, capitalist state set up by the occupying powers. But their arguments also rested on the idea that Poland had a "right" to establish itself as an independent "nation."[61]

Luxemburg's criticisms of Marx's and Engels's positions focused on two questions:

1. Whether there was a Marxist argument for an independent Poland
2. Whether there is a "right of nations to self-determination"

[58] Rosa Luxemburg, *The National Question: Selected Writings*, edited by Horace Davis (New York: Monthly Review Press, 1976). Hereafter National Question.

[59] See Heinz Schurer, "Some Reflections on Rosa Luxemburg and the Bolshevik Revolution," *Slavonic and East European Review* 40, no. 95 (June 1962), 356–372.

[60] E.g., Govind, "Nation State in the Age of Imperialism"; Veneziani, "Rosa Luxemburg on Imperialism"; Holleman, *Dust Bowls of Empire*, 64–65; Robinson, *Black Marxism*, 62–65.

[61] Marx and Engels wrote frequently supporting the restoration of a Polish nation, linking it with the fate of Germany and Russia. In "A Polish Proclamation," in an issue of *Der Volksstaat*, the organ of the German Social Democratic Workers Party, from June 11, 1874, Engels wrote: "Poland has demonstrated in 1863 and further proves every day that it cannot be done to death. Its claim to an independent existence in the European family of nations cannot be refused. But its restoration has become a necessity particularly for two peoples: for the Germans, and for the Russians themselves."

Luxemburg argues "no" on both fronts. She realized more clearly than anyone the conflicts between Marx's, Engels's, and Lenin's positions on Poland, and other aspects of their political thought. In setting out her position, Luxemburg articulated her own inter-pretation of the "essence" of Marxism. A Marxist argument for an independent Poland must rest on the conditions of the political economy and on the working conditions and interests of the proletariat. But in Luxemburg's view, the argument Marx and Engels gave rested mainly on the fact that the Russian partition of Poland was under the tsardom. The purportedly "socialist" argument for an independent Poland was that it would un-dermine the tsardom from within, and that this would galvanize proletarian revolution in Russia, and, in turn, in Germany.[62] Luxemburg objects that it was not Poland that was propping up the tsardom, but the old peasant order and the interests of the landed classes and bourgeoisie in Russia: "the tsardom finds itself forced to support a capitalist economy, but in doing so it is sawing off the limb on which it sits."[63]

The difference between Luxemburg's position and Marx's depends less on socialist doc-trine than on their differing views of the role of Russia in global proletarian revolution. As Marx and Engels put it in a letter to a Polish group, "the cry 'Let Poland live!' which then resounded throughout Western Europe was not only an expression of sympathy and support for the patriotic fighters . . . the cry . . . in and of itself meant: 'Death to the Holy Alliance, death to the military despotisms of Russia, Prussia, Austria.'"[64] To Marx and Engels, Polish independence held out the promise of effective resistance to that military despotism. Luxemburg, who was much more familiar with the situation in Poland, argued that Polish independence from Russia would not achieve any substantial goal for socialism.

In Luxemburg's view, socialist conclusions on particular political questions may change with the historical, material conditions. Marx and Engels tended to tie the in-dependence of Poland to the fate of Prussia, Russia, and Austria, and to argue that the workers of Poland would inevitably want to rise up against the "despotic" rule then spreading over western Europe. Luxemburg objected that this perspective was rooted in international politics, not in an analysis of the workers' interests and mate-rial conditions. On *Marxist* grounds—and here Luxemberg appears more Marxist than Marx—it is incumbent on anyone writing on the issue to explain how the independence of Poland would be in the interests of the proletariat, including whether it would aid in bringing about a workers' revolution.

What about the "right of nations to self-determination"? When the PPS asked the London Congress to support an independent Poland, the Congress instead adopted a very grand-sounding statement: "the Congress—the resolution states—declares itself in favor of 'the complete right of all nations to self-determination, and expresses its sym-pathy for the workers of every country now suffering under the yoke of military, national,

---

[62] For a clear statement of this view, see Engels, "A Polish Proclamation."

[63] Luxemburg, "The Polish Question at the International Congress in London," repr. in *The National Question*, 52.

[64] Letter from Marx and Engels to the group "Rovnosc," received November 1880, cited in Luxemburg, foreword to *The Polish Question*, repr. in *The National Question*.

or other despotism; the Congress calls on the workers of all these countries to join the ranks of the class-conscious workers of the whole world in order to fight together with them for the defeat of international capitalism and for the achievement of the aims of international Social Democracy." [65] As Luxemburg points out, the Congress punted the question by appealing to a universal "right" of "all" nations to "self-determination," and by linking this right to the liberation of the working classes. She subjects this strategy to strong criticism, supporting the conclusion that socialist thought does not justify a universal "right of nations to self-determination."

Luxemburg notes that the Congress statement is very vague. It grandly tells the working classes to rise up, but not how or when or why to do so: they are to stand up for their national interests in order to "self-determine" in whatever way seems right to them ("The Polish Question", 109). But within the capitalist state, the ability of workers to organize freely is severely restricted.

There are two senses of "right" at issue here. One is based on the mutual recognition between citizens and state found in Kant and Hegel, and in the Enlightenment tradition generally. That cannot be the Marxist sense of "right": in Marxist terms, the capitalist state denies its citizens mutual recognition. Another sense, more attuned to Marxist thinking, is the workers' prerogative to organize themselves, to seize the means of production, and to take control of the machinery of the state. Global communism requires a workers' revolution. As Luxemburg argues, in Marxist terms the workers' right to found a *nation* depends on their first rising up to overthrow the *state*.

Luxemburg argues that the formation of free "nations" in Lenin's sense is limited under capitalism and imperialism. There is no universal democratic "right" of organization into a nation, independently of the historical, material, economic conditions that can make those rights manifest. If one tries to find a Marxist justification for nationalism, we find that on socialist grounds there are "no 'eternal' truths and there are no 'rights.'" [66]

Thus, in a socialist context, the formula "right of self-determination" either expresses nothing, or an "unconditional duty of all socialists to support all national aspirations," which is unfounded. [67] Luxemburg points out that even Marx and Engels implicitly support this conclusion: in the revolutions of 1848, Marx and Engels did not support Czech independence, but did support Polish independence, even though on Marxist doctrinal grounds the justification for the two cases is the same. [68] The conclusion Luxemburg reaches is, therefore: there is no universal, socialist right of nations to self-determination.

Luxemburg does acknowledge a right of the people to organize themselves and to assert their class interests. After the workers' revolution, [69] it will then be possible for people

[65] Rosa Luxemburg, "The National Question and Autonomy," in *National Question*, 107.
[66] "The Polish Question", repr. in *The National Question*, 111.
[67] "The Polish Question", repr. in *The National Question*, 112.
[68] "The Polish Question", repr. in *The National Question*, 115.
[69] *The Communist Manifesto* is Marx's and Engels's classic analysis of the place of revolution in communist politics. Luxemburg herself wrote a key text in this regard, *Social Reform or Revolution?*

to organize into nations without thereby asserting an idealist "right" of the individual to determine her national interests. Nations will be based on the achievement of the right historical-material conditions, which will allow for self-determination in a global democracy. [70] There is no such thing as a universal, conceptual "right" of nations to self-determination on socialist grounds: such rights are won by the workers through struggle.

To Luxemburg, certainly, workers are free to form a nation: but only *after* the revolution. Luxemburg thus criticizes Marx's, Engels's, and Lenin's implicit conclusion (which would be developed into a political program by Bernstein) that a worker's nation, along the lines of the Paris Commune, can come about within a capitalist state. The will and interests of the people are insufficient, according to Luxemburg's account, to bring a nation about before the overthrow of the capitalist state. Luxemburg's writings on nationalism are thus consistent with her conclusion, in *Social Reform or Revolution?*, that gradual reform of the state from within is insufficient: revolution is necessary.

Beyond her broader points on nationalism and the state, Luxemburg criticizes Marx's personal stance on Poland. On her assessment of the situation, Marx's support for an independent Poland derives from two sources:

1. Ignorance of the conditions on the ground, and consequent disregard for the bloodshed that would result if Polish socialists were to start an independence movement. Marx would regard this from the comfort of the West.
2. Marx's view that the independence of the Russian Polish partition would help the cause of a socialist revolution in Germany. Given (1), Luxemburg effectively accuses Marx of sacrificing the Polish proletariat to the interests of Germany.

Luxemburg's positions on Polish independence reflect her deep knowledge of the Polish situation, her diagnosis of flaws in Marx's and Lenin's analyses (e.g., the impossibility of forming a worker's nation within the capitalist state), and her position on world politics (her view that Polish independence would not further the cause of revolution in Germany).

5   CONCLUSION

Luxemburg's position on the role of the capitalist state never wavered: it was the manifestation of class conflict and antagonism. A proletarian uprising—via her favored tactic of mass strikes and workers' movements—was necessary to overthrow the state. As Horace Davis remarks, this distinctive position was one of Luxemburg's most influential:

it is perhaps little known that despite Lenin's attacks on her, the philosophical position so ably expounded by Rosa Luxemburg in her articles of 1908–1909 was never

---

[70] "The Polish Question", repr. in *The National Question*, 108.

refuted; that it was, on the contrary, adopted by a substantial section of the Bolshevik Party, which fought Lenin on the issue, using Rosa Luxemburg's arguments—and eventually, in 1919, defeated him, so that the slogan of the right of self-determination was removed from the platform of the Communist Party of the Soviet Union (CPSU). Later, when the issue was no longer so acute, the slogan was revived and today represents part of the CPSU's stock in trade. But the basic arguments in its favor are precisely those which were successfully opposed by Rosa Luxemburg and her partisans. The Soviet leadership is working with a blunted tool.[71]

Luxemburg rejected Marx's and Lenin's position (expressed earlier on) that workers could form a nation with a "right of self-determination" within the capitalist state.[72] To Luxemburg, the right of cooperative social organization is, in one sense, inalienable and "natural"; but in another, is only achievable with the overthrow of the state.

Kant and Hegel had argued that rights are guaranteed by the mutual recognition between citizens and state, where the laws of the state are not imposed by arbitrary authority, but rather derive their binding force by recognizing the moral status of free citizens. Marx, Engels, and Lenin responded that the capitalist state cannot engage in mutual recognition because capitalism is oppressive by nature. The capitalist state alienates workers from their labor and uses them as a mere means to an end: the accumulation of surplus value.

However, Engels famously argued that violent overthrow of the state may not be necessary in all cases. If the workers were to organize and claim ownership of the means of production and of their own labor, the state might simply "wither away," as it would have no more to do.[73] Eduard Bernstein, a protégé of Engels, worked this position into a larger politic: that gradual reform of the state, rather than revolution, could address workers' exploitation.

Rosa Luxemburg's classic *The Accumulation of Capital* provides a deep analysis of why the state will not "wither away" without a fight. Capitalist states have an interest in acquiring, not only surplus value, but the means to accumulate more capital. The inherent contradiction between the freedom of the workers and the capitalist state, which Marx, Lenin, and Engels identified, becomes with Luxemburg a deeper problem. She provides a novel dynamic analysis of why modern capitalist states will attempt, not only to survive, but to become stronger over time: to annex more property, more land, and more surplus value from workers' labor.

Luxemburg's analysis in *The Accumulation of Capital* is the motivation behind her positions in the debates over whether reform or revolution was necessary (in, of course,

---

[71] Horace Davis, introduction to *National Question*, 9.

[72] Löwy, "Why Socialism Must Be Internationalist," sees this as a weakness in Luxemburg's view; I argue that it is a distinctive position and one that characterizes her entire career.

[73] As is well known, Marx himself argued that capitalism contains inherent contradictions that will inevitably result in revolution and the establishment of socialism. For discussion of Marx's thesis see G. A. Cohen, R. Veryard, D. H. Mellor, A. G. M. Last, Randolph Quirk, and John Mason, "Historical Inevitability and Human Agency in Marxism [and Discussion]," *Proceedings of the Royal Society of London* 407, no. 1832 (September 8, 1986), 65–87.

Social Reform or Revolution?) and in the debates over Polish independence. Marx and Engels argued that the Polish workers could establish a nation within the Polish state that would fight for the workers' interests. Luxemburg pointed out that the workers had not yet overthrown the Polish state, and that without a revolution, Polish independence would mean the reestablishment of a capitalist state.

If one had Engels's confidence that that state would wither away in time, one might argue that establishing a capitalist state would be beneficial to the workers' interests in the long run. This may, in fact, be the reasoning behind Marx's, Lenin's, and Engels's support of Polish independence. But Luxemburg saw only the call to reestablish an entity that was fundamentally opposed to the workers' interests, an entity that inevitably would move to accumulate surplus value and to exploit labor.

Marx famously thought, along with Luxemburg, that capitalism replaced the existing feudal order in Europe, not a state of nature. One might respond to Luxemburg on Marx's behalf, that the dynamic of history is not a return to an earlier social order, but rather a dialectic: a move toward socialism. Luxemburg's theory threatens, one might think, to appeal to a mythical "natural" order of things to justify her opposition to capitalism. But some might see this as just as irrational and romantic as an appeal to "nationalism" or "culture" to justify the establishment of a state. Certainly, the history of precapitalist societies is not peaceful or perfect, and one might mount a criticism of Luxemburg's account along these lines. Marx could argue, for instance, that the move toward socialism is not a move backward toward a previously existing "natural economy", but rather a move toward an aim the workers have chosen for themselves. In this sense, Marx, Engels, and Lenin defend the ideal of "self-determination" of a people. On this reading, Luxemburg arguably does not have the scope for "self-determination," as she argues that states should be overthrown and replaced by nations following a "natural economy," not principles chosen by the workers.

In *The Accumulation of Capital*, Luxemburg argues that the capitalist state owes its existence, not to "rational" principles as Smith alleged, but to its violent resistance to earlier forms of social organization. Luxemburg argues that human beings have historically not been found in the mythical "state of nature" of Hobbes, Locke, and Rousseau, but rather, in a "natural economy," "institutions maintain their economic power by subjecting the labor power, and the most important means of production, the land, to the rule of law and custom" (*Accumulation*, 369). Capitalism did not replace the state of nature, coming as a beneficial means of protecting citizens from violence. Instead, capitalism itself overthrows the natural economy that existed previously.

Luxemburg argues that colonialism and capitalism must violently resist this natural economy. There are laws and customs that govern natural economies, and they provide a method of social organization that does not exploit the labor of its workers, or the most fundamental means of production (the land). In Luxemburg's view, the "nation" set up by the workers is an institution capable of enforcing the "laws and customs" that develop in, and govern, all natural economies. Thus, there can be governance in Luxemburg's analysis, but not coercion. The original sin, in Luxemburg's view, is the violent replacement of natural economy by a commodity economy, which sets in motion the inevitable cycle of exploitation and accumulation. Chapter 27 of *Accumulation* is a brief but bloody history of the advent of commodity economies across Europe and Asia.

In one sense, Luxemburg's theory resembles that of Kant and Hegel: Luxemburg's nation, like the state in Kant and Hegel, is set up only to recognize laws that already implicitly govern exchanges between citizens (and, in Luxemburg's case only, their relation to the land). But there are significant differences. Luxemburg does not build her nation on the alleged rights of the citizen, but rather on the laws that come about in the course of natural social activity. She does not appeal to any feature that is not found in *any* natural economy. Thus, her view does not endorse any form of nationalism, even though it does allow for nations.

Read in the context of *Accumulation*, Luxemburg's position in the debates on Polish independence comes into clearer focus. As Luxemburg sees it, nations should be founded on the social enforcement of laws that effortlessly come to organize natural economies in the absence of capitalist, colonialist exploitation. The "independence" of Poland, to Luxemburg, would not be the establishment of a natural economy, but rather the restoration of a state and commodity economy. To Marx, Engels, and Lenin, Polish independence would aid in the international struggle for workers' rights since the Polish workers' movement was strong. To Luxemburg, the Polish government her socialist comrades were so eager to restore would inevitably resist the workers, since any capitalist state must do so to survive. Luxemburg's position is clear: only revolution restores the natural order of things.

I am grateful to Kristin Gjesdal and Dalia Nassar for the opportunity to write this chapter. Dalia Nassar's comments on a draft of the chapter were insightful and led to marked improvements. An earlier version of this chapter was read at a workshop, "Women Philosophers in the Long Nineteenth Century," at Temple University in September 2018. The questions at that workshop, from Kristin Gjesdal, Samantha Matherne, Lydia Moland, and others among the authors of this volume, were instrumental in guiding revisions.

References

Bellofiore, Riccardo, ed. *Rosa Luxemburg and the Critique of Political Economy.* London: Taylor & Francis, 2009.

Buhle, Paul. Afterword to *Red Rosa*, by Kate Evans, 215–219. London: Verso Books, 2015.

Cliff, Tony. "Rosa Luxemburg: A Life of Struggle" (1959). Pamphlet reprinted in *Socialist Review* (January 2009). https://socialistworker.co.uk/socialist-review-archive/rosa-luxemb urg-life-struggle/.

Cohen, G. A., R. Veryard, D. H. Mellor, A. G. M. Last, Randolph Quirk, and John Mason, "Historical Inevitability and Human Agency in Marxism [and Discussion]." *Proceedings of the Royal Society of London* 407, no. 1832 (September 8, 1986): 65–87.

Davis, Angela Y. *The Angela Y. Davis Reader*. Edited by Joy James. Hoboken: Wiley, 1998.

Davis, Angela Y. "Marcuse's Legacies." In *Herbert Marcuse: A Critical Reader*, edited by John Abromeit and W. Mark Cobb, 43–50. New York: Routledge, 2004.

Davis, Horace. Editor's introduction to *The National Question*, by Rosa Luxemburg, 9–48. New York: Monthly Review Press, 1976.

Dellheim, Judith, and Frieder Otto Wolf, eds. *Rosa Luxemburg: A Permanent Challenge for Political Economy*. London: Palgrave MacMillan, 2016.

Dunayevskaya, Raya. *Rosa Luxemburg, Women's Liberation, and Marx's Philosophy of Revolution*. Chicago: University of Illinois Press, 1991.

Edmondson, Linda. "Lives of Rosa Luxemburg." *Revolutionary Russia* 2, no. 2 (1989): 35–44.

Engels, Friedrich. *Anti-Dühring. Herr Eugen Dühring's Revolution in Science*. Moscow: Progress, 1947.

Engels, Friedrich. *The Origin of the Family, Private Property and the State* (1884). Moscow: Progress, 1976.

Engels, Friedrich. "A Polish Proclamation." *Der Volksstaat*, July 11, 1874.

Ettinger, Elzbieta. *Rosa Luxemburg: A Life*. Boston: Beacon Press, 1986.

Evans, Kate. *Red Rosa*. London: Verso Books, 2015.

Govind, Rahul. "Nation State in the Age of Imperialism." *Economic and Political Weekly* 48, no. 14 (April 6, 2013): 48–58.

Harvey, David. *A Companion to Marx's Capital: The Complete Edition*. Vol. 1. London: Verso Books, 2018.

Hegel, G. W. F. *Elements of the Philosophy of Right* (1820). Edited by Allen W. Wood. Translated by H. B. Nisbet. Cambridge: Cambridge University Press, 1991.

Hobbes, Thomas. *Leviathan, Parts I and II* (1651). Edited by A. P. Martinich and Brian Battiste. Rev. ed. Peterborough, Ontario: Broadview Press, 2010.

Holleman, Hannah. *Dust Bowls of Empire*. New Haven: Yale University Press, 2018.

Hudis, Peter, and Kevin Anderson, eds. *The Rosa Luxemburg Reader*. New York: Monthly Review Press, 2004.

James, C. L. R. *The Black Jacobins*. London: Secker & Warburg, 1938.

James, C. L. R. *World Revolution, 1917–1936: The Rise and Fall of the Communist International*. London: Secker & Warburg, 1937.

Lenin, Vladimir Ilyich. *The State and Revolution*, trans. Brian Baggins. In *Collected Works*, vol. 25. Moscow: Progress, 1964. Originally published August 1917.

Löwy, Michael. "Why Socialism Must Be Internationalist . . . And What Rosa Luxemburg Can Teach Us about It." *Rosa Luxemburg Stiftung*, January 23, 2020. URL: https://www.rosalux.de/en/publication/id/41529/why-socialism-must-be-internationalist.

Luxemburg, Rosa. *The Accumulation of Capital*. Translated by Agnes Schwarzschild. London: Routledge, 1951; reprint, New York: Monthly Review, 1968.

Luxemburg, Rosa. *The National Question: Selected Writings*. Edited by Horace Davis. New York: Monthly Review Press, 1976.

Luxemburg, Rosa. *Social Reform or Revolution?* Translated by Integer. London: Militant, 1986.

Luxemburg, Rosa. "Wage Labor: Selections from *Introduction to Political Economy*" (1925). Translated by Anna Ezekiel. In *Women Philosophers of the Long Nineteenth Century: The German Tradition*, edited by Kristin Gjesdal and Dalia Nassar, 214–240. New York: Oxford University Press, 2021.

Marx, Karl, and Friedrich Engels. The German Ideology. In 1845–47, vol. 5 of *Marx and Engels Collected Works*, edited by Maurice Cornforth, translated by Clemens Dutt, 19–539. London: Lawrence & Wishart, 1975.

McCumber, John. *Time in the Ditch: American Philosophy and the McCarthy Era*. Evanston, IL: Northwestern University Press, 2001.

Mills, Dana. *Rosa Luxemburg*. London: Reaktion Books, 2020.

Moland, Lydia. *Hegel on Political Identity: Patriotism, Nationality, Cosmopolitanism*. Evanston, IL: Northwestern University Press, 2011.

Morgan, David W. "The Father of Revisionism Revisited: Eduard Bernstein." *Journal of Modern History* 51, no. 3 (1979): 525–532.

Nettl, J. P. *Rosa Luxemburg: The Biography* (1966). London: Verso, 2019.

Nixon, Jon. *Rosa Luxemburg and the Struggle for Democratic Renewal*. London: Pluto Press, 2018.

Petrus, Joseph. "Marx and Engels on the National Question." *Journal of Politics* 33, no. 3 (1971): 797–824.

Reisch, George. *How the Cold War Transformed Philosophy of Science: To the Icy Slopes of Logic*. Cambridge: Cambridge University Press, 2005.

Robinson, Cedric J. *Black Marxism: The Making of the Black Radical Tradition*. London: Zed Press, 1983; reprint, Chapel Hill, NC: University of North Carolina Press, 2000.

Schneider, Ulrich Johannes. "The Situation of Philosophy, the Culture of the Philosophers: Philosophy in the New Germany." *Social Research* 64, no. 2 (Summer 1997): 281–300.

Schurer, Heinz. "Some Reflections on Rosa Luxemburg and the Bolshevik Revolution." *Slavonic and East European Review* 40, no. 95 (June 1962): 356–372.

Tuck, Eve, and K. Wayne Yang. "Decolonization Is Not a Metaphor." *Decolonization: Indigeneity, Education & Society* 1, no. 1 (2012): 1–40.

Veneziani, Roberto. "Rosa Luxemburg on Imperialism." In *Rosa Luxemburg and the Critique of Political Economy*, edited by R. Bellofiore, 130–143. London: Taylor & Francis, 2009.

Zarembka, Paul. "Value: Marx's Evolution and Luxemburg's Legacy." In *Rosa Luxemburg*, edited by J. Dellheim and F. O. Wolf, 55–91. London: Palgrave MacMillan, 2016.

CHAPTER 11

....

EDITH
LANDMANN-KALISCHER
(1877–1951)

....

DANIEL O. DAHLSTROM

EDITH Landmann-Kalischer is one of many women philosophers whose work has been woefully neglected over the past century. The neglect is not surprising, given the male-dominated context of German-speaking academia and philosophy in this era. Other Jewish women philosophers, her contemporaries Edith Stein, Hedwig Conrad-Martius, and Gerda Walther, faced similar obstacles to being accepted and promoted as peer thinkers and scholars. Disregarded in Landmann-Kalischer's case are extraordinary studies in the philosophy of art, aesthetics, and epistemology that are as challenging to orthodoxy today as they were in the previous century. In recent years her reflections on poetry have begun to garner attention, with the recognition of her vital presence within the so-called George-Kreis (the literary circle around Stefan George) and her devastating ostracism from the circle following the rise of National Socialism and its co-option of George. This essay, designed to introduce readers to the person and the thinker, is divided into three parts: after sketching her life and works before 1925, I review her significant philosophical contributions during that time. The final part chronicles her writings and responses to the tragic events in Germany during the last twenty-five years of her life.

1 BIOGRAPHICAL SKETCH: PART 1

....

Born on September 19, 1877, Edith Landmann-Kalischer (hereafter "LK") was the youngest daughter of Berlin banker Moritz Kalischer. From a young age she had a particular fondness for poetry. Late in life she reminisces that a poem by Goethe "likely determined" all her subsequent intellectual choices, convinced as she was that what is "deepest and highest" in humanity is to be found in poetry alone.[1] Dissatisfied with the early schooling offered to young women around Berlin, she successfully applied to attend a gymnasium from 1894 to 1897. Although she enrolled in the University of Zurich in October 1897, she audited classes of such luminaries as Georg Simmel and Carl Stumpf at the University of Berlin from April 1898 to April 1901, before returning to Zurich to complete her doctoral degree. She identifies her area of studies as "philosophy, specifically psychology, and art history," a description demonstrating not only a time without fixed boundaries between philosophy and psychology, but her own interdisciplinary approach to these subjects.

In 1901 she received her doctorate with the dissertation "Analysis of Aesthetic Contemplation (Painting and Sculpture)" under the direction of Ernst Meumann.[2] In a list of the lectures and seminars she visited during her studies, she gives special thanks to Simmel, Meumann, and Stumpf, among others. The dissertation's title reflects a critical appropriation of Kant's notion of the contemplativeness characteristic of the disinterestedness of aesthetic judgment. In the dissertation, LK makes use of the "complementary" methods of self-observation and consideration of art history (since the processes exceed the scope of an individual consciousness) in an effort to determine and analyze the psychological process that is found in all aesthetic observation and only there, thereby providing a positive account of what the purely negative determination (dis-interestedness) attempts to introduce.

Two years after receiving her doctorate, LK married Julius Landmann, an economist at the International Labor Office in Basel who would become a leading figure in the Swiss National Bank and hold a chair in economics at the University of Basel. At Basel during the first decade of the century LK wrote two major essays, "On the Cognitive Value of Aesthetic Judgments" (1905) and "On Artistic Truth" (1906); a short monograph, *Artistic Beauty as the Elementary Aesthetic Object*; and a lengthier monograph, *Philosophy of Values* (both in 1910), while writing scads of reviews and corresponding extensively with Alexius Meinong.[3] In the *Philosophy of Values*, LK prefaces her own axiology with an extensive critical commentary on Hugo von Münsterberg's theory

---

[1] Edith Landmann-Kalischer, "Eine Aufzeichnung aus dem Jahr 1948 über Assimilation und Zionismus," *Emuna. Horizonte zur Diskussion über Israel und das Judentum* 10 (1975): 45. In the same reflections she notes that everything else she took up ("philosophy or natural science, music, logic, and even experimental psychology") was a chore in comparison with the fulfillment that poetry brought.

[2] Meumann, who would gain renown as a founder of experimental pedagogy, developmental psychology, and the *Archiv für die gesamte Psychologie*, also wrote works on aesthetics, including *Einführung in die Ästhetik der Gegenwart* in which he laments the lack of attention paid to LK's work in aesthetics. See Ernst Meumann, *Einführung in die Ästhetik der Gegenwart*, 3rd ed. (Leipzig: Quelle & Meyer, 1919), 72.

[3] Meinong praises LK's discussion of the "cognitional value" of feeling as the most important argument for that general view. See Alexius Meinong, "Für die Psychologie und gegen den Psychologismus," *Logos: Internationale Zeitschrift für Philosophie der Kultur* 3, no. 1 (1912): 10. From 1905 to 1913 LK's reviews of works on ethics, aesthetics (by Lipps, Dessoir, and Segal), axiology, the narrator in epics, and art history (Donatello) as well as reviews of each of Emil Lask's influential books on the logic of philosophy and on the doctrine of judgment appear in Meumann's *Archiv für die gesamte Psychologie*.

of four irreducible, absolute values (logical, aesthetic, ethical, religious). During this flurry of creative work, she gave birth to Georg Peter (1905) and Eva (1906); a second son, Michael, was born in 1913.[4] It bears noting that responsibility of raising the children fell principally on her shoulders. Indeed, when she broached the possibility of pursuing her own work free of domestic duties for a while, her husband responded with a death threat, leaving LK to lament: "so, here, too . . . nowhere roots, nowhere sympathy, nowhere love."[5]

In the years that followed, the celebrated poet Stefan George was a frequent houseguest in the Landmann-Kalischer home. From around 1915, LK appears to have fallen in love with Stefan George and, though the love was unrequited, she became, as it is frequently put, George's "Eckermann" (a reference to Goethe's devoted unpaid literary assistant and author of *Conversations with Goethe*). Whenever George visited the Landmanns, LK would apparently not retire until she recorded their conversations and his pronouncements during the day.[6]

In 1920 she published *Georgika*, a work in three parts that begins with a study of the essence of a poet, followed by overviews of George's work and his impact. Before a second edition appeared four years later, she also published *The Transcendence of Knowing* (1923) and "Carl Spitteler's Poetic Mission [*Sendung*]," a study of the Nobel Prize–winning Swiss poet. I will have more to say about *Georgika* later, but the work on epistemology in the 1923 monograph deserves mention for its strident defense of an unfashionably realistic position. "Transcendence," she maintains, "is the essence of all knowledge."[7] In the work she criticizes phenomenological and Kantian theories of knowledge alike for their assumption that knowing is to be understood in a "presuppositionless" way, apart from any philosophical or scientific discipline. In opposition to this reigning assumption, LK labels her position "transcendent realism" and "a realistic epistemology," committed to the notion that knowing is firmly planted "as a factical event in objective nature."[8] In her view, the existence of the external world is neither to be refuted nor to be proven; instead it is the *Urphänomen*, the very "sense and goal of consciousness," and the notion of something purely subjective not moving beyond itself is a "fiction."[9]

---

[4] Georg Peter (d. 1994) would become a noted philologist and Michael (d. 1984) a prominent proponent of philosophical anthropology, drawing on the work of Simmel.

[5] Susanne Hillman, "Wandering Jews: Existential Quests between Berlin, Zurich, and Zion" (PhD Diss., University of California, San Diego, 2011), 312n862; Korinna Schonharl, "'Wie eine Blume die erfroren ist'—Edith Landmann als Jüngerin Stefan Georges," in *Stefan George. Dichtung—Ethos—Staat. Denkbilder fur ein geheimes Europa*, ed. Bruno Pieger and Bertram Schefold (Berlin: Verlag fur Berlin-Brandenburg, 2010), 213.

[6] Robert E. Norton, *Secret Germany: Stefan George and His Circle* (Ithaca: Cornell University Press, 2002), 516; Schonharl, "'Wie eine Blume die erfroren ist,'" 225.

[7] Edith Landmann-Kalischer, *Die Transcendenz des Erkennens* (Berlin: Bondi, 1923), 75, 236.

[8] Landmann-Kalischer, *Die Transcendenz des Erkennens*, 75. The term 'factical' (*faktisch*) here has its typical meaning at the time, designating not an impersonal, observable matter of fact (*Tatsache*) but a fact that is a lived experience of the world.

[9] Landmann-Kalischer, *Die Transcendenz des Erkennens*, 74. For contemporary reviews of the work, see Margaret Schuster, "Edith Landmann als Philosophin," *Castrvm Peregrini* 25 (1955): 44n1.

2 CONTRIBUTIONS TO PHILOSOPHY

No treatment of LK's many contributions to twentieth-century thought can afford to ignore her philosophical investigations of three topics in particular: the cognitive value of aesthetics, the concept of artistic truth, and the essence of the poet.

2.1 The Cognitive Value of Aesthetics

In her 1905 essay "On the Cognitive Value of Aesthetic Judgments" (hereafter "CV"), LK argues that aesthetic judgments are, indeed, cognitive judgments, capable of being true or false, and she bases her argument on the striking parallels between aesthetic judgments and sensory judgments.[10] Beauty, she contends, should be considered a property of things in the same transsubjective sense in which sensory qualities are. The claim that the sky is beautiful is no less objective than the claim that it is blue.

   In the essay she first addresses the possible ways of grounding values. After arguing that values cannot be grounded in volition and desires or ideals and norms (since all of the latter presuppose values), LK claims that only one alternative remains: grounding the value "in the object's connection to our feeling" where "the pure, disinterested judgment of taste" serves as "the paradigm of the value judgment" (CV 270). She then takes aim at the view that feelings are "purely subjective elements of consciousness." In contrast to times past, the law-governed dependency of sensations on the object and thus the possibility of objective cognition through the senses are widely acknowledged. Given this success, LK sees no reason to rule out the possibility of cognition through feelings. If a positivist like Mach can regard sensory qualities as constant connections of objects to our sense organs, allowing us to speak of them as properties of objects, why can't feelings be analogously properties of objects? "Why should being red count as a property of the thing but not being beautiful?" (CV 274).

   There are several objections to LK's proposal, all hailing from subjectivist accounts of values, and she builds her case by responding to each of them. The *first* objection is that her proposal would bind values to the existence of the object. But the objection lacks legs, in LK's eyes, since it fails to distinguish between real and represented values. "The value can be *represented* in an object that does not exist" just as much as in one that does (CV 275). A *second* objection derives from the seemingly greater variability of feelings in contrast to sensations. But there is also variation, LK points out, in representations and sensations, often caused by the state of the subject. Moreover, given the considerable

---

[10] Edith Landmann-Kalischer, "Über den Erkenntniswert ästhetischer Urteile: Ein Vergleich zwischen Sinnes- und Werturteilen," *Archiv für die gesamte Psychologie* 5 (1905): 263–328. All translations of LK's texts are mine. For an excellent review of this essay, see Samantha Matherne, "Edith Landmann-Kalischer on Aesthetic Demarcation and Normativity," *British Journal of Aesthetics* 60, no. 3 (2020): 315–334.

progress that has been made in discovering "the law-governed dependency of sensations on the object and thus the possibility of objective knowledge through the senses," there is no reason to think that a similar discovery is not forthcoming for feelings. "*Just as we distinguish between subjectively and objectively conditioned sensations, so, too, we may distinguish between subjectively and objectively conditioned feelings*" (CV 276; italics in original).[11]

The cognitive judgment in the value judgment is, LK claims, not scientific cognition but what underlies the latter: perceptual cognition. But this claim introduces a *third* and a *fourth* objection, namely, that aesthetic properties do not have the same fundamental significance as sensory properties for cognition and that they are no more essential to the mechanical worldview than sensory qualities. If it is a mistake to put secondary qualities and primary qualities on the same level, how much more mistake would it be to rank tertiary qualities with the primary qualities? LK responds to the *third* objection by noting how a color may be necessary for recognition of things but not necessary—as a value may be—for concept formation (as in the case of artworks). As for the *fourth* objection, LK notes that if beauty is contingent and dispensable from a mechanistic point of view, the same holds in spades for colors and sounds. "For the sensory properties are no more derivable than value from being that is thoroughly determined in a causal way" (CV 278).[12]

LK notes a *fifth* objection to her proposal of placing beauty on a par with sensory qualities, namely, the fact that the latter mediate the former. But beauty, no less than colors, depends upon chemical properties without being any less real than those properties. To be sure, the more mediated the aesthetic perception, the more possibilities of deception are at hand. But this fact in no way contradicts the perceptibility of aesthetic qualities. Regardless of the mediation, the judgment that something is beautiful, that is, objectively pleasing, is no less true or false than the judgment that something is red.

Having shown that none of the likely objections to the supposition of a strict parallel between sensory judgments and aesthetic judgments holds up, LK devotes the second section of her essay to demonstrating the parallel in terms of subjective and objective reliability. By "subjective" in this case, she means the judgments of inner perception, for example, "I see blue," "this pleases me," in contrast to their corresponding objective forms, for example, "this is blue," "this is beautiful." An aesthetic judgment can be subjectively less reliable when a feeling is colored by others (not least those named, represented, or conceived). But the reliability of a sensory judgment is itself affected in a parallel way when one sensation overpowers another, as in cases of mishearing or

---

[11] To be sure, science's centuries-old efforts to rid cognition of feelings make this prospect appear paradoxical. But in fact it has had to do something analogous for sensations; "in mechanics, the color of things is as irrelevant as thermal qualities are for optics" (CV 276). So, too, "the knowledge of feeling, the knowledge through feeling as an inner sense" that is in question here has nothing to do with the animism and anthropomorphism that science has battled (CV 276).

[12] LK points out that while values have the characteristics of primary qualities in several worldviews (Plato, Nietzsche, Lotze), no one has ever attempted to explain the world on the basis of secondary qualities.

overlooking. Yet the presence of degrees of subjective reliability in neither case rules out the possibility of approximating through practice and instruction what Stumpf calls a "maximal subjective reliability" (CV 284).

As for objective reliability, LK first elaborates its conditions negatively, by noting the analogous sorts of deceptions for sensory and aesthetic judgments, grounded in "psychological, physiological, and material circumstances," respectively (CV 287). Her point is that, if we can agree that there are these sorts of deceptions, then we have to concede that aesthetic judgments, like sensory judgments, can be true or false. *Psychological deceptions* arise when, instead of expressing a feeling's immediate connection to its object (the artwork), it expresses a connection to something else, for example, the work's historical position, its content, its instructiveness, its utility, and the like (much as we may mistake the utility of seeing a color for simply seeing it). *Physiological deceptions* on the sensory level occur when, for example, a sensation that flows into another becomes confused with or taken for it, thanks to a predisposition. In a similar fashion, an aesthetic feeling may be confused with other feelings, frequently thanks to an emotion, a mood, or volition, blinding us to unconventional beauties (or at times making us more receptive to them just because they are novel).[13] Finally, just as there are *physical* deceptions on the sensory level (the rod looking bent in water), so, too, on the level of feelings, there are parallel deceptions, where the feeling does not correspond to the aesthetic stimulus—because, for example, the sensory mediation of the latter is faulty (as when a gallery is too dark or a music hall too cavernous) or the mediation is misconstrued (as when a director misses the significance of the dialogue in a particular scene).[14]

Having established the parallel between aesthetic and sensory judgments in this negative fashion (i.e., in parallel sorts of deception), LK turns to the analogy between the positive criteria for the two types of judgment. In both cases, she submits, the truth of any judgment consists in its agreement with other judgments. The immediacy of sensory and aesthetic judgments, LK acknowledges, might seem to rule out this view. Yet their objective reliability is not determined simply on the basis of immediate impressions without comparison with other judgments. Citing with approval Brunetière's observation that "to enjoy something is one thing, but to judge it is quite another," LK upholds

---

[13] Each custom, fashion, style produces a predisposition that colors each new impression insofar as it meets or does not meet expectations. Not meeting expectations is typically displeasing until a kind of fashion-fatigue sets in (supposing, of course, that, belonging to a particular culture and age, one does not find the content completely alien). To guard against these and other sources of physiological deception, critics rightly mistrust first impressions. Much as it takes more than one sip to determine a wine's character, so it takes time for the feeling adequate to the stimulus to "dawn" on us (CV 296). "Being predisposed to specific feelings will hinder the reproduction of feelings opposed to these. . . . Entire ages are so dominated by a mood that artworks with a different feeling-content are no longer enjoyed at all and the satisfaction of what is felt in that mood blinds them to other artistic deficiencies" (CV 299).

[14] LK also adds a section on deceptions about intensity; in terms of scope, there are upper and lower aesthetic thresholds, just as there are for sensory thresholds. So, too, there are parallel differences in regard to sensitivity to the degrees of intensity, a sensitivity that, like the difference in range, can be heightened through practice.

the difference between the subjective judgment "x pleases me" and the objective judgment "x is beautiful" (CV 306).

She identifies four criteria of the objective reliability of sensory judgments: their agreement/disagreement with (1) other judgments of the same sense, (2) judgments of other senses, (3) other individuals' sensory judgments, and (4) other things and stimuli that we are acquainted with, particularly through science (the most compelling criterion). She then identifies analogous criteria for value judgments: their agreement with (1) judgments by the same person about the same object at different times and in different circumstances ("'Rhapsody in Blue' sounds grand to me every time I hear it"), (2) judgments by the same person about different objects ("No contemporary of Fra Angelico is his equal"), and (3) judgments by other persons, not least critics and experts with knowledge of time-trusted techniques ("Everyone appreciates the beauty of the symmetry of a Greek temple").[15]

LK adds some important qualifications. She acknowledges that paralleling value judgments with sensory judgments seems both to underrate and to overrate them— underrate them because they seem to have greater claim on universality than sensory judgments and overrate them since they seem to lack the universality of the latter judgments. But that greater claim can be explained by the fact that we connect them much more profoundly than a person's sensory judgments with her humanity. As for the seeming lack of parallel unanimity, she rejects universality of agreement as a criterion since "the concepts of objectivity and universality do not coincide" and since "contradiction within our own judgments"—whether sensory or aesthetic—overrules agreement with others (CV 309–310, 320–321). She points out, moreover, that there are in fact "elementary agreements" even where we perceive a development of the aesthetic sense, leading her to conclude that the number of aesthetic judgments not in agreement should probably not exceed those in the domain of the senses (CV 316). Differences obtain, nonetheless, but they can be traced in no small measure, she submits, to the greater complexity of aesthetic judgments and to the fact that aesthetic receptivity to nature as well as art develops not only in an individual life but in the lives of peoples. More important, these differences do not justify "any intrinsic contrast" between aesthetic judgments and sensory judgments (CV 315).

2.2 Artistic Truth

A year after the defense of aesthetic judgments' cognitive value, LK publishes "On Artistic Truth" (hereafter: "AT"), in which she argues that the experience of art yields cognition of a certain sort.[16] Artworks are not judgments and, hence, cannot be true or

---

[15] Under value judgments in this essay, LK places both aesthetic and ethical judgments (CV 314). A criterion analogous to the fourth criterion of sensory judgments, namely, their agreement with scientific judgments regarding their stimuli, is not available at the present time in the aesthetic domain (CV 321).

[16] Edith Landman-Kalischer, "Über künstlerische Wahrheit," *Zeitschrift für Ästhetik und allgemeine Kunstwissenschaft* 1 (1906): 457–505.

false, but their contents, what they express, can be.[17] As in the 1905 essay, LK supposes that truth consists in a judgment's agreement with another. So the question of the possibility of artistic truth amounts to the question: with what do the judgments, contained in what an artwork "says," agree?

LK answers this question by setting up a parallel between two sorts of representations, those belonging to mental reality and those belonging to art. To varying degrees of adequacy, mental reality represents objective reality. Art stands in relation to mental reality in the same manner as the latter stands to objective reality. "Art does not afford objective reality. It mirrors and portrays the mental world instead, and it is true insofar as it portrays that world faithfully, insofar as it succeeds in freeing the mental world from its entanglement with objective reality (which overreaches often enough precisely in naive consciousness) and in establishing it purely on its own terms. . . . Just as we would never see our face were it not for a mirror, so, too, we would never see our own inner life opposite us —were it not for the mirror of art (AT 463)." Art is, in effect, a kind of mirror, a mirror of the soul, our only means of seeing what is otherwise only available to "inner perception" (AT 463).

LK elucidates the various forms of artistic truth by identifying three peculiarities of consciousness that are present in each of three zones of consciousness (sensations/perceptions, memories, and phantasy) and mirrored respectively in art. Those peculiarities, indicative of the "narrowness of consciousness," are the fact (1) that consciousness represents only a segment of objective reality, (2) that it has a center and periphery, and (3) that it is subject to conditions of the entire life of consciousness (including various feelings and interests, personal and cultural). Art's reproductions of sensations and perceptions are true when they present the latter "just as they are in consciousness, when they do not yet or no longer serve as a means of cognition, when the correction that thinking makes in them, for the purpose of the construction of objective reality, is not yet or no longer performed on them" (AT 466). For this reason, she adds, painters and musicians typically consider more colors and sounds respectively than come into consideration for objective reality. Impressionist paintings may be considered paradigmatic examples here but so is a painting that depicts the bent look of the rod in water or music that captures the rhythm of wave after wave coming to shore. There is scarcely any need, LK adds, to demonstrate the presence of the second peculiarity, that is, the presentation of a segment of reality arranged around a center, not as it is in reality but as it appears to the senses of the perceiver.[18]

Turning from sensations/perceptions to memory's representations, LK notes that the latter are selective, filling in gaps in what memory retains, based upon what constantly recurs and what corresponds to representations already on hand (what a culture considers the norm or paradigmatic) or upon feelings and interests. As such, "our

---

[17] "Its [the artwork's] truth can lie only in its content, its outcome, in the result of the process through which we take it up into ourselves, only in what it says, relates, shows, or expresses" (AT 459).

[18] Oddly, perhaps, LK does not specifically discuss the third peculiarity of consciousness as it applies to art's representation of sensations and perceptions.

memory's representations are little suited to afford a faithful picture of reality," but that makes them no less something that art represents and emulates (AT 468). An artwork is typically considered untrue if it is not one-sided and selective, that is to say, if it violates paradigms and norms (representations of what its theme should be) that govern memory's representations.[19] So, too, an artwork stumbles, like memory does, if it runs counter to the prevailing interests or the feelings that give the artwork a certain unity. "Only a strong feeling, relative to a theme [*Gegenstand*], makes an artistically true portrayal of it possible since its representation lives in our memory only under the influence of such a feeling" (AT 473). Shakespeare's tragedies are artistically true because they emulate our selective and agonizing memories of tragic events.

Phantasy's representations, the next zone of mental life considered by LK, differ from memory's representations only by degrees, bringing about consciously what memory does for the most part nondeliberately. What principally drives phantasy is feeling and its role is evident in "art that is predominantly phantasy (the fairytale)," where "everything goes on as we would like it to go on" and our longing "for surprises, for the extraordinary, for everything that breaks up the everyday and breaks through what is merely possible" is realized. "In a fairytale," she continues, "we feel free because it plays freely with the things that we stand powerless against in life, the things that we have been delivered to without any hope of rescue" (AT 478). As a genre, moreover, the fairytale "merely cultivates in the most perfect manner what every art lives from" (AT 479). Wishes are part of the life of the soul and so it is left to art—especially Romantic art—to express these wishes, the truth of what is wished for. "The golden age and a land of milk and honey are phantasy's ways of rewriting the natural course of what happens and doing so in ways that flatter every longing (and to that extent are artistically true)" (AT 481).

Even if fairytales signal what every art lives from, artistic truth remains subject, nonetheless, to a certain constraint, namely, possibility. Moreover, in contrast to reality in the sense of what merely occurs, the artist must represent what could happen, that is, what is probable. "For us the probable can mean nothing other than what appears as true, what is psychologically and thus artistically true. The probable is the truth of art because it is *what appears as true*" (AT 483).[20]

---

[19] "Every eclectic art that combines all viewpoints, all interests, is devoid not only of style but of truth. It corresponds to what is conceptually [*dem begrifflich Seienden*], not to the mental reality. Unity of style is a postulate of artistic truth because it is a property of memory's representation" (AT 473).

[20] Having noted that fables suppose the probable as what appears true, LK addresses the need to represent what seems necessary—"since it resists being believed"—when it comes to the content of tragedy as well as the tragic content of epics, and novels, in contrast to the content of comedy. After locating the fundamental difference between tragedy and comedy in the feelings underlying them, she completes this review of the forms of combination of representations and their corresponding genres by observing that the combination of representations in lyric poetry alone is "not guided by any sort of representation of a purpose and is subject solely to the natural course of associations and to feelings" (AT 487).

Having dealt with sensations/perceptions and with combinations of representations in memory and phantasy, LK turns finally to feelings. Although they lack representations' capacity to be objectively as well as artistically true, feelings do not remain fully captive to the inner world. Passive and active feelings are expressed in physiognomic-physiological expressions and in actions, respectively. Art is capable of portraying these expressions, truthfully or not, and, indeed, of doing so through "the completely novel creation of an adequate expression of feeling" not found in life otherwise (AT 491). Art dispenses, for example, with life's social and ethical constraints. "Custom and ethical life, pride and shame hold us back a thousand times over from the action that would express our feeling adequately . . . the more the spontaneous expression of feeling in actions is inhibited by reinforced feelings of humanity, justice, self-respect and respect of others, and the less the demand for such expression can be satisfied in life, the more a people will be in need of art" (AT 492).

If art represents the entire sweep of the life of the mind (sensations/perceptions, representations, and feelings), how does it differ from psychology? In the essay's final segment LK addresses this question head-on. Her view of art is obviously no less at odds with the view that art is a childlike version of scientific truth than with the view of it as an assortment of lies and exaggerations. To be sure, its truth may coincide with scientific and historical truth (if, for example, Shakespeare's portrayal of what he imagined as Caesar's fate happens to be historically accurate). But while it differs from these truths in the way that the mind's reality differs from objective reality, it differs no less from psychology, the science of mental reality. Whereas psychology translates that reality into concepts with law-like connections among them, "art merely makes what is given to inner perception accessible to another organ, to outer perception; it makes perceptible for eye and ear what was only present to 'inner sense.' . . . It gives feelings an audible or colorful form" (AT 495). So, too, LK concludes, the truth disclosed by art is only conveyed by it—and, indeed, by its beauty.[21]

2.3 The Essence of the Poet

The first part of LK's *Georgika* (hereafter: "G"), outlining the essence of a poet and the distinctiveness of poetry in relation to other arts, serves as an extended preface to the other parts of the work, devoted to Stefan George's work and his impact, respectively.[22]

---

[21] LK concludes the essay with a discussion of the "correlative" character of the concepts of artistic truth and beauty (AT 504). It is noteworthy that this account of artistic truth finds little echo in contemporary aesthetics. There is, for example, no entry on artistic truth in the *Stanford Encyclopedia of Philosophy*, and the sort of conception of artistic truth proposed by LK plays no role in its entries on the definition of art.

[22] Edith Landmann-Kalischer, *Georgika. Das Wesen des Dichters, Stefan George* (Heidelberg: Weiss, 1920).

The first part (to which I now turn) also complements LK's previous work on visual and plastic arts by presenting her philosophy of poetry.

LK begins her account of the essence of poetry by stressing the need to locate that essence not in a peripheral, contingent feature, however universal it may be, but in central features on which those peripheral features are founded. That central feature is not the form alone (e.g., meter, rhyme) but "the indissoluble secret unity of content and form." Only where the poet is the "creator of a people" can that form be conceived by others from within as something that is alive and nourished by the same spirit that created it (G 5). LK thus takes issue with pure formalism and with overstating the analogy of poetry with visual arts thanks to "the allure of the peripherally formal."[23] The analogy is inherently limited because poetry's means of expression and its theme (*Gehalt*) are essentially different from those of other arts. Since language, the poet's material (*Stoff*), is already the product of the human soul, there is not the same degree of tension between spirit and material as in plastic arts. Hence, when it comes to poetry we delight less in the overcoming of the tension and consider a poet of a lesser rank if his chief merit lies in this artistry. "When the poet wrestles with language, it is spirit wrestling with spirit," and such material is predisposed to be formed by the spirit (of the poet), being nothing else but a means of expression; indeed, "it is the primeval creation of the human soul, the first, most encompassing receptacle of the human spirit [*Gefäß des Geistes*]" (G 7).

Yet the difference in the theme is no less important. While painters and sculptors open the visual world to us, the poet discloses something all-embracing that radiates throughout the entire world from within. To be sure, plastic artists also give visual expression to the spirit of an age, but that spirit itself first "issues," LK insists, from its poets. While poetry's theme is thus not circumscribed, like that of painting and sculpture, by the world laid out before our eyes (*Welt des Auges*), how the eyes see that world is conditioned by "that encompassing element that is the home [*Heimat*] of the poet" (G 8). Citing Rodin, Hölderlin, and the Greeks (and also anticipating Heidegger), LK utilizes the contrast between an artifact and an organism to clarify the difference. Whereas painters, sculptors, and architects build the house of the human spirit, the poet creates its body (*Leib*).

Like everything that lives, poetry flows from heterogeneous sources, as both dionysian darkness and "apollonian daylight"—"rhythm and shape, song and image"—flow together into poetry (G 10). Although one source may dominate the other, both can be found wherever poetry exists. "What we deem the 'poetry's theme' is what results from the confluence of both sources, the sensuous object illumined through and through by the primal light" (G 11).

Modern times, LK laments, have lost sight of this theme, replacing it with a concentration on the poetic material alone, as the art of poetry gives way to literature (something fully avoided by George). Without denying certain merits of modern literature

---

[23] G 6; in part 2, LK stresses that George's poetry is unpopular because it avoids everything peripheral, contingent, and banal (G 31).

(e.g., instructiveness, finesse, technical expertise), LK makes the sweeping charge that "it is handed over to the darkness of the human spirit, devoid of any higher knowledge"; concerned not with what is soulful and divine but with what is novel, fashionable, and interesting, this literature is "only a witness to the monstrous *avilissement des coeurs*" (G 12). The modern age accordingly deems poetry merely "the painting that talks, the mirror of the world" and, instead of announcing what would not be in the world without him, the poet is only there to give voice to what is already there. On this view, the poet is merely someone able to provide the dumb with a language and to say what he is suffering. They are the protean masters of mimesis, gifted with the ability to give expression to others, while disappearing themselves behind what they exhibit. "Phantasy and the pleasure of being someone else thus count for the modern world as the primary characteristic of the poet" (G 13)."[24]

Modern literature is thus concerned, not with portraying human perfection—the theme of George's poetry—but with portrayals as such in order to activate naive interest in the surrounding world. Through humor and stirring, it endeavors to convert what is beneath the value of poetic portrayal into something valuable. In what amounts to a "shameful connivance," it thus makes the small important, thereby disfiguring "the supreme truth of ideas" and robbing human beings not only of greatness but even the idea of greatness (G 14).

LK conceives poetry as nothing less than a kind of divine incarnation. In the service of the gods, the poet facilitates the process as "the paradigm of humanity" and the "purest human being." The poet is "more complete than other human beings," with a capacity to bear within himself the tension of things opposed to one another, and, hence, his reality is "the mystical unity of opposites."[25] Encompassing opposites in himself is only possible, however, by bursting the limits of reality. "Hence, the life of the poet is in phantasy and his object is the perfect humanity."[26] The very antithesis of the shapeless Proteus who enters into all gestalts, the poet is gestalt through and through (*voller Gestalt*) and, as such, brings the forms from out of himself. Instead of thinking himself into the hearts of others, the poet is his own heart alone, expressing and portraying it.

Contesting once again the confusion of the universal and the essential, LK advises that this conception of the poet embraces not so much all that is as all that should be, insofar as it can be incorporated in one person. Someone who withdraws from this idea (perfection) in favor of being all humans (universality) is "not a poet but a caricature of

---

[24] Taking a jab at *l'art pour l'art*, LK notes that critics of the mimetic character of naturalism do not depart from the "sphere of the imitative" as long as they strive for "portrayal for the sake of portrayal" (G 13).

[25] G 14; in part 2, touting the "inner equanimity" of George's poetry, its "balance of dionysian forces and apollonian clarity" and perfect medley of "sensation, image, and thought," LK identifies George not only as a classical poet but as "the perfect human being" (G 32–35)! Nor does the adulation of the person wane in part 3; see, for example, G 76–80.

[26] G 15. Picking up on this theme in part 2, LK depicts "the basic feeling without which George's work cannot be grasped: the radical denial of everything present . . . the creation of a new realm of its own" (G 44).

a poet."[27] Viewed from this Socratic-Platonic perspective (that of the primacy of perfection over universality), the meaning of "empirically actual humanity for the portrayal of perfect humanity can only be quite slight"—indeed, the very antithesis of the poet's sole object (G 17).

Throughout different epochs, the essence of the poet is the same, that of a "hymnist"—the composer of text and music—for his times, whether in the form of epic, dramatic, or lyric poetry. Here, too, LK finds herself on the side of the ancients who, in contrast to moderns, located the chief difference of poetry in the object of the portrayal rather than the manner of depiction.

George is obviously the paradigmatic poet in LK's eyes and the account of "the essence of the poet" in the first part of her monograph is composed very much with George in mind. Not surprisingly, given the absence of anything but lyric poetry in George's oeuvre, LK rounds out the first part by stressing the primacy of lyrical poetry. "Just as the Attic tragedy and comedy arose from dithyrambs and songs, so the basic form even of every drama is the poem. There is no great dramatist and no writer of epics who is not in the first place a poet, i.e., someone who knows [kennt] the magic of words. We do not name a poem a drama but of every drama we can say [that] it is a poem" (G 21). The view that lyric poetry is necessarily only subjective is of a piece with the view that poetry exists to satisfy an interest in the peripheral and depict a colorful reality rather than to portray primordially human potential—something that can be sketched (as in George's poetry) in a few lines "just as well or even better" than through dramatic or epic fulsome detail. "Certainly," LK adds, "the lyric always gives only himself but does the dramatist do otherwise, indeed, can or should he?"[28]

Wrapping up this discussion of poetic genres, LK reiterates that "true poetic composition [Dichtung]" is as far from something purely imitative as it is from the pure expression of emotion and arbitrary individuality. "We may start from drama, from an epic, or from lyric poetry, but from wherever we proceed, we are led back to the one basic form of poetic composition: the animated word and the one object of poetic composition: the complete [ideal] humanity."[29] LK adds a significant qualifier. While a poet working in any genre is a poet only to the extent that he participates in this "unified idea of poetic composition," there are various degrees and stages in which it is realized (G 23).

LK concludes this first part by observing that, once it has been established that "a complete ideal humanity" is the one great object of poetry, its place in the spiritual life

---

[27] G 16. LK contrasts Hebbel's Proteus from his 1834 poem by that name with "the tremendously poetic acknowledgement of the totality in the I" in George's 1913 poem "Stern des Bundes."

[28] G 21. In what might appear to some an instance of the genetic fallacy, LK proceeds to argue for viewing Shakespeare's plays and poetry as expressions of the poet's own being, lying in the depths of his heart.

[29] G 23. I add "ideal" here because LK subsequently speaks of "the ideal of complete humanity" and employs a cognate adjective, urbildlich (G 24), thereby capturing the idea, expressed earlier, that the humanity that is the object of poetry is humanity not only as it is but as it should be (G 16). In the second part of Georgika, LK uses the same expression "the animated word" to describe the "primal form of poetry" that George's poetry, having excluded everything literary, presents to us (G 29).

of a people is also set. Citing Goethe (*Wilhelm Meisters Lehrjahre*), LK notes that the poet shows us all sides of human beings but in view of "the holy norm that he bears in his heart" and that all humanity strives for, consciously or not, "like the plant reaches for the sun."[30] Because no one else understands us so deeply and leads us so far beyond ourselves as a poet, and because poetry's object is given to it alone—and neither science nor philosophy nor religion—to proclaim and preserve, a poet-less people is a people that has lost sight of its guiding star.[31] Hence, LK concludes, poets essentially are what they were in antiquity, the sole educators of a people, "the unacknowledged legislators of the world."[32]

3 BIOGRAPHICAL SKETCH: PART 2

Unrequited love is tragic enough, exacerbated, as LK notes in her diary, by the fact that her husband was able to get closer to George on a personal basis in the latter's male-centered circle than any female could, even one as devoted as LK.[33] Yet in the ensuing years tragedy struck again and again. In 1925 her daughter succumbed to a rare form of tuberculosis. As LK blames herself for her daughter's death, her ardor for George wanes. In 1931 her husband, also a victim of depression, commits suicide. But her husband's suicide is hardly the end of the tragedies befalling her. With Hitler's rise to power and the National Socialist appropriation of George's work (not without his endorsement), LK found herself as a Jewish intellectual of the wrong gender, no less, increasingly abandoned, not by George himself, but by the members of his circle. While George was blasé about the prospect of Jews in the Third Reich, LK recognized the existential character of the threat, precisely for Georgian Jews (i.e., Jews in George's circle) like herself.[34] In the summer of 1933, shortly before George's death, she composes and distributes to friends her first—but by no means her last—response to the threat: "Omaruru: To the German Jews who stood with the Secret Germany."

"Omaruru" opens with an acknowledgment of the anti-Semitism that she shared with other members of the circle. "You know that, out of love for the German people, I have

---

[30] G 25; in part 2, LK returns to this notion of a norm, with the observation that George's poetry fulfills the highest demand "in which ethical and aesthetic values are united: measure" (but not to be confused with moderation) (G 37); see, too, her observation of the dispensability of individual ethical categories in favor of *das Sein, das Ethos* (G 50).

[31] These strong claims suppose a distinction between poetry and these other undertakings that LK scarcely takes time to explain or justify. In a similar fashion she remarks rather cavalierly that the pictorial art (*die bildende Kunst*) reaches the same object "only indirectly" and that music, unfolding in isolation from representations and objects, "passes it by" (G 26)!

[32] LK is citing Shelley's "Defense of Poetry" (1821, published 1840); LK iterates how, from the outset of the world, the determination of norms has been reserved for poets (G 95).

[33] Hillman, "Wandering Jews," 313; Schonharl, "'Wie eine Blume die erfroren ist,'" 231.

[34] Edith Landmann-Kalischer, *Gespräche mit Stefan George* (Düsseldorf: Küpper), 209.

been an anti-Semite just like you, when it comes to the type of Jews who have spread across Germany after and already long before the war. Do you seriously believe that it would still be possible for me to have anything in common with this type of Jew, and especially with today's Jewish youth who, having grown up with nothing but Zionism and Communism, have no more inkling of the German spirit than the Germans themselves do?"[35] Although Georgian Jews, she continues, had long shared numerous thoughts with those of the Third Reich, not least the necessity of the policy toward Jews, she nonetheless sees the suicidal dilemma that National Socialism presents. "Yet with all the German spirit we have, we cannot divest ourselves of our Jewish blood. Are we now supposed somehow to rip the German spirit from us and transform ourselves back into old pious or modern national or even international Jews? We would rather kill ourselves."[36] There must be a third path, a path on which a person remains and becomes further what she has become, "German and Jew," leading LK to the conclusion: "the task placed before us arises from the fate that has befallen us: to remain what we have become: Germans of Jewish blood, Jews of German spirit."[37] Since there was no home for "German Jews for whom the spirit of German poetry was sacred," LK proposes moving to a ghetto in Germany or, better yet, to some other place such as "Omaruru," a town in Namibia.

Members of the circle panned "Omaruru," rejecting the proposal as childish, and she did not further disseminate it. Increasingly distressed by events in Germany and heartened by the successful emigration of German Jews to Palestine, LK eventually finds a "path to Zionism," even though, despite this being a path that she thinks George himself would have applauded, she does not take the step of emigrating herself. After the war she would celebrate Israel's independence: "once more we have a fatherland."[38] When arrest appeared likely in 1938 while she was residing in Berlin, she returned to Basel where she remained until her death in 1951. During this time she published numerous book reviews and several essays on George.[39]

There is more than a little truth to the observation that for most of her life, LK was more interested in serving in Stefan George's world than leading in the academic world of philosophy.[40] Nonetheless, in her final work, *The Doctrine of the Beautiful* (hereafter "LvS"), published a year after her death, she presents a masterful philosophical argument for beauty's place in the world, its creation in art, the grasp of it in aesthetic intuition, and its place in the realm of values.[41] Beauty's place in nature arises from the fact that, as the Greeks discovered, "all beauty rests upon harmony" (LvS 13). There are accordingly, LK submits in the opening chapter, levels of harmonies of countervailing

---

[35]   Ulrich Raulff, *Kreis ohne Meister: Stefan Georges Nachleben* (Munich: Beck, 2010), 150n102.

[36]   Quoted in Raulff, *Kreis ohne Meister,* 152.

[37]   Quoted in Raulff, *Kreis ohne Meister,* 152.

[38]   Michael Landmann, *Erinnerungen an Stefan George. Seine Freundschaft mit Julius und Edith Landmann* (Amsterdam: Castrum Peregrini, 1980), 138.

[39]   See the bibliography.

[40]   Schuster, "Edith Landmann als Philosophin," 36.

[41]   Edith-Landmann-Kalischer, *Die Lehre vom Schönen* (Vienna: Amandus, 1952).

forces, ascending through nature to the endpoint and highest level: the beauty of the human spirit.

Artists bring into the world an even more complex harmony (the theme of the second chapter). "Just as the nature surrounding [the human being] found a mirror in his spirit, so he creates a mirror of his own beauty in art" (LvS 48). The key word here is "create" (*erschafft*) and LK singles out two self-imposed constraints in this respect (that in turn are the defining aspects of an artwork). The first—"the *Urphänomen* of art"—is the fact that the artist portrays what she portrays in some other material (*Stoff*) (LvS 50). The second "completely paradoxical" constraint is the respective art's focus on a singular sense modality, in contrast to the usual representation of things via a confluence of such modalities. Thus, when it comes to painting, for example, "we are all eyes," just as when it comes to music, we are all ears (LvS 52).

The effective combination of these two aspects/constraints in artistic beauty involves three elements: the formal character of what is portrayed (symmetry and organization), the relevant artistry (the artist's technique of animating a material for a particular sense modality), and the artistic theme ("a unity of an I and a world"). This artistic theme falls apart, LK adds, when the artistic means (the first two elements) are left out of consideration, mistakenly rendering art "either naturalistic or expressionistic, either mere imitation of nature or mere expression of the soul" (LvS 72).

One might argue, LK concedes, that beauty is not art's concern, particularly given the fact that classic artworks show human existence in all its imperfection rather than in its beauty. She responds to this challenge by arguing that interpretations of art that locate the meaning of art in something other than beauty can be traced to mistaking one of its elements for the whole—a case she proceeds to make by critically examining interpretations of art as imitation and as expression.[42]

In the third chapter of LvS, LK shifts from creator to beholder. She argues that the object of aesthetic intuition is neither actual nor tied to personal interests like the everyday objects of perception; but it is also not fixed on mere sensations. "The musical effect is not connected to mere sounds; a melody is taken up as the song of a soul" (LvS 213). Just as art expresses the soul in sensory form, so aesthetic intuition empathetically grasps its object as a living—expressive and meaningful—whole. Taking aim at the modern, overly subjective definition of the beautiful object as the correlate of aesthetic contemplation, LK points out that the latter relates to the ugly as well as the beautiful but only fully unfolds when its object is something beautiful, whether or not it is an artwork. Channeling Schiller (one of her heroes, along with Goethe), she discusses how the aesthetic state of mind is one of play but nonetheless deadly serious. To the familiar objection that the pursuit of beauty is not merely a distraction but an obstacle to the real business of life, she counters that the otherworldly harmony of beauty alone "separates us from the inhuman" (LvS 241). LK concludes this third chapter by revisiting arguments

---

[42] This second chapter continues with discussion of the tasks of art and the beauty of particular arts: poetry, painting, sculpture, music, architecture.

from her earlier essay that, however fallible, aesthetic judgments, no less than judgments of the senses, can be true or false.

As for beauty's place finally in the realm of values (the theme of her concluding chapter), it is "the tipping-point-on-the-scale" (*Zünglein-an-der-Waage*) for all other higher values: the holy, the true, and the good (LvS 346–349). To be sure, depending upon the epoch, the experience of one value seems to dominate (e.g., religion in some epochs, reason in others). Yet while art owes its origins to the experience of the holy and while it necessarily pays homage to what we know and what we should do, beauty is misconstrued whenever it is subordinated to these other values. A glimpse of LK's own view of the matter can be gathered from the contrast she draws at the conclusion of the book between beauty and the Enlightenment conception of the true and the good. The Enlightenment failed to supplant religion because it remained fixed on this or that part (e.g., pure reason or pure will) rather than life as a whole. By contrast, she concludes, while "the beautiful cannot, to be sure, occupy the role of religion . . . it can express [*wiedergeben*] the full feeling of the holy and, like the holy, as the supreme norm, it can pervade all the domains of life" (LvS 349).

BIBLIOGRAPHY

Hillman, Susanne. "Wandering Jews: Existential Quests between Berlin, Zurich, and Zion." PhD diss., University of California, San Diego, 2011.

Landmann-Kalischer, Edith. "Eine Aufzeichnung aus dem Jahr 1948 über Assimilation und Zionismus." *Emuna. Horizonte zur Diskussion über Israel und das Judentum* 10 (1975): 45–48.

Landmann-Kalischer, "Edith. Essays on Art, Aesthetics, and Value," In Edited with an introduction by Samantha Matherne and translated by Daniel O. Dahlstrom. New York: Oxford University Press, 2023.

Landmann-Kalischer, Edith. *Georgika. Das Wesen des Dichters, Stefan George*. Heidelberg: Weiss, 1920.

Landmann-Kalischer, Edith. *Gespräche mit Stefan George*. Düsseldorf: Küpper, 1963.

Landmann-Kalischer, Edith. *Die Lehre vom Schönen*. Vienna: Amandus, 1952.

Landmann-Kalischer, Edith. *Die Transcendenz des Erkennens*. Berlin: Bondi, 1923.

Landmann-Kalischer, Edith. "Über den Erkenntniswert ästhetischer Urteile: Ein Vergleich zwischen Sinnes- und Werturteilen." *Archiv für die gesamte Psychologie* 5 (1905): 263–328.

Landmann-Kalischer, Edith. "Über künstlerische Wahrheit." *Zeitschrift für Ästhetik und allgemeine Kunstwissenschaft* 1 (1906): 457–505.

Landmann, Michael. *Erinnerungen an Stefan George. Seine Freundschaft mit Julius und Edith Landmann*. Amsterdam: Castrum Peregrini, 1980.

Matherne, Samantha. "Edith Landmann-Kalischer on Aesthetic Demarcation and Normativity." *British Journal of Aesthetics* 60, no. 3 (2020): 315–334.

Meinong, Alexius. "Für die Psychologie und gegen den Psychologismus." *Logos: Internationale Zeitschrift für Philosophie der Kultur* 3, no. 1 (1912): 1–14.

Meumann, Ernst. *Einführung in die Ästhetik der Gegenwart*. 3rd ed. Leipzig: Quelle & Meyer, 1919.

Norton, Robert E. *Secret Germany: Stefan George and His Circle*. Ithaca: Cornell University Press, 2002.

Raulff, Ulrich. *Kreis ohne Meister. Stefan Georges Nachleben*. Munich: Beck, 2010.

Schonharl, Korinna. "'Wie eine Blume die erfroren ist'—Edith Landmann als Jüngerin Stefan Georges." In *Stefan George. Dichtung—Ethos—Staat. Denkbilder fur ein geheimes Europa*, edited by Bruno Pieger and Bertram Schefold, 207–242. Berlin: Verlag fur Berlin-Brandenburg, 2010.

Schuster, Margaret. "Edith Landmann als Philosophin." *Castrvm Peregrini* 25 (1955): 34–49.

CHAPTER 12

ELSE VOIGTLÄNDER
(1882–1946)

ÍNGRID VENDRELL FERRAN

ELSE Voigtländer belongs to the first generation of women to enter the German university. After spending her first years in Leipzig, she moved to Munich to study philosophy and psychology in 1905. In 1909, Voigtländer became the first woman to earn a PhD within the phenomenological movement. Her work *On the Types of Self-Feelings* (*Über die Typen des Selbstgefühls*, 1910)[1] was written under the supervision of Theodor Lipps.[2] She turned to psychoanalysis shortly after this and, between 1912 and 1914, was a member of the Berlin psychoanalytical group led by Karl Abraham.[3] Her divergences from Freud regarding the role of experience in the formation of character led her to leave psychoanalysis. Her discussions of psychoanalytical concepts make her not only one of the first phenomenologists to engage with psychoanalysis, but also one of the first trained professional psychologists to study Freud's teachings in depth. She later pursued a career as a psychologist, specializing in welfare theory and in the neglect of women and young people, often in collaboration with the psychiatrist Adalbert Gregor, who is known for his work on eugenics.[4] In the late 1920s, she became director of the women's prison in Waldheim. From 1937 onward, she was a member of the Nationalsozialistische Deutsche Arbeiterpartei (NSDAP),[5] and therefore collaborated with National

---

[1] Else Voigtländer, *Über die Typen des Selbstgefühls* (Leipzig: R. Voigtländers Verlag, 1910). This book is identical to *Vom Selbstgefühl*, which was published the same year by the Voigtländer family publishing company

[2] Voigtländer defended her PhD in November 1909, two months before Margarete Calinich, another of Lipps's female students, submitted her dissertation on the relationship between colors and moods.

[3] Ludwig M. Hermanns, "Karl Abraham und die Anfänge der Berliner Psychoanalytischen Vereinigung," *Abhandlungen zur Geschichte der Medizin und der Naturwissenschaften* 81 (1997): 174–188.

[4] It is unknown whether Voigtländer, like Stein, aimed at a career in academia.

[5] Though Voigtländer's thought contains ideological elements close to those defended by Nazism, these elements can also be found in other authors of that time, for example the activist and pacifist Helen Stöcker. It is unclear whether her membership was the result of profound National Socialist convictions or rather the product of external motivations. It would have been impossible for her to keep her job as

Socialism.[6] After 1920, she worked mainly as a psychologist and continued to publish on philosophical issues relating to affectivity and gender. With her contributions to research on the emotions in particular, she remains faithful to the principles, methods, and insights of the phenomenological tradition as developed by its early proponents. Voigtländer's commitment to the phenomenological tradition raises questions which will be taken up in this chapter. How should she be placed within the larger context of early phenomenology? How did she contribute to the development of the phenomenology of affectivity?

To answer these questions, I will work with the idea of a "philosophical constellation." This expression was coined by Dieter Henrich in the context of his study of German idealism to refer to the network of thinkers and debates which were in lively exchange and through which philosophical issues were developed. In this chapter, I will treat early phenomenology as a constellation of people, discussions, topics, and theories, to investigate Voigtländer's place within it. More specifically, I will focus on her relationship to other members of this network and examine her participation in the main debates, as well as her involvement in the development of phenomenological methods and concepts.[7] This will lead me to explore in particular her connections to other phenomenologists of the Munich Circle of phenomenology and her contribution to the development of phenomenology in its early stages. This task is particularly important because, exceptions aside, Voigtländer has been largely neglected in histories of the phenomenological movement. It is high time that the history of phenomenology included her as a full-fledged member of this movement and that her work received the attention it deserves.

The chapter is structured as follows. Section 1 examines a series of documents, such as reports, seminar records, and letters, in order to shed light on Voigtländer's relationships with Lipps and prominent members of the Munich Circle, such as Pfänder, Max Scheler, Moritz Geiger, and Johannes Daubert. Sections 2–6 consist of a careful analysis of her participation in the development of a branch of phenomenology. In particular, I focus on her phenomenology of affectivity.[8] Attention is paid to her methodology, her

director of a women's prison without being a member of the party. Interestingly, her date of birth on her membership card is false. Either this was a Freudian lapsus or an act of vanity (in the card, she appears to be three years younger), or it was a clear sign that she did not identify with the membership.

[6] For an accurate study of Voigtländer's biography, which focuses on her involvement with National Socialist Germany during her time in Waldheim, see Georg Heffernan, "Phenomenology, Psychology, and Ideology: A New Look at the Life and Work of Else Voigtländer," *Phenomenological Investigations* 1 (2020). See also Georg Heffernan, "An Ordinary Woman: Else Voigtländer and the National Socialism", in *Else Voigtländer. Self, Emotion, and Sociality*, ed. Íngrid Vendrell Ferran (Cham: Springer, 2023), 223–242 and Sophie Loidolt and Petra Gehring, "Psychologizing Politics, Neglect, and Gender: Applications of Voigtländer's Scientific Characterology", in: *Else Voigtländer. Self, Emotion, and Sociality*, 199–222.

[7] Dieter Henrich, "Konstellationsforschung zur klassischen deutschen Philosophie," in *Konstellationsforschung*, ed. Martin Mulsow and Marcelo Stamm (Frankfurt am Main: Suhrkamp, 2005), 23.

[8] Voigtländer also published extensively on sexual difference and gender as Edith Stein (one of the main representatives of the Göttingen Circle of phenomenology) did some years later. See Ute Gahlings, "Else Voigtländer on Sexual Difference: An Early 20th Century Gender Theory?", in *Else Voigtländer. Self, Emotion, and Sociality*, 181–198.

contributions to an emotivist theory of self-consciousness, her scrutiny of the social dimension of the self, the development of a concept of affectivity as intimately linked to value, and the debate on ressentiment and love. Section 7 discusses the mechanisms that led to her omission from the canon and reflects upon the necessity of rewriting the history of the phenomenological movement. The main findings are briefly summarized in the concluding section.

1 VOIGTLÄNDER'S PLACE WITHIN THE MUNICH CIRCLE OF EARLY PHENOMENOLOGY

To begin, it is necessary to examine Voigtländer's relationship to other members of the early phenomenological circle working and studying at Munich where she wrote her dissertation. Early phenomenology was comprised of a heterogeneous group of thinkers.[9] Chronologically, the "early" period coincides with the beginning of the movement around 1900 and ends in about 1925. However, after 1915 the group experienced a loss of cohesion due to both the vicissitudes of World War I—Adolf Reinach, who was one of its main representatives, died at the front—and internal tensions about how to understand the task and method of phenomenology itself.

It has become customary to divide early phenomenology into different circles, each with its own particularities. The Munich Circle was organized around the figure of Lipps and authors such as Alexander Pfänder, Reinach, Moritz Geiger, Johannes Daubert, Max Scheler, Theodor Conrad, Hedwig Conrad-Martius, and Gerda Walther. The Göttingen Circle was developed under the auspices of Edmund Husserl. To this circle belonged Edith Stein and many Munich phenomenologists, such as Reinach, Conrad, and Conrad-Martius, who went to Göttingen to study with Husserl. The Freiburg Circle was developed later when Husserl moved there from Göttingen in 1916, first attracting Stein, who moved there in the same year, and later Walther. Among the three circles, the Munich and the Göttingen circles in particular have much in common. The "Munich-Göttingen phenomenologists" (an expression coined by Conrad and Conrad-Martius in the 1950s) had a strong realist orientation and were opposed to Husserl's later developments toward idealism and transcendentalism.

Despite the lively exchange and the movement of researchers between groups, there were thinkers in Munich who did not move to Munich.[10] This was the case for

---

[9] Alessandro Salice, "The Phenomenology of the Munich and Göttingen Circles," in *Stanford Encyclopedia of Philosophy* (Stanford University, 1997. Article published August 3, 2015; last modified Nov 5, 2020). https://plato.stanford.edu/archives/win2020/entries/phenomenology-mg/.

[10] See Eberhard Avé-Lallemant and Karl Schuhmann, "Ein Zeitzeuge über die Anfänge der phänomenologischen Bewegung: Theodor Conrads Bericht aus dem Jahre 1954," *Husserl Studies* 9 (1992): 77–90; 75.

Voigtländer. Moreover, there are certain features and institutions which can be found only in the Munich Circle. Munich phenomenologists were influenced by Lipps's psychology: at that time, the term "psychology" meant the study of what appears to consciousness and as a discipline it was not clearly delimited from philosophy as it is today. Also, some of them were interested in empirical research: for instance, Geiger was trained in experimental psychology by Wundt before moving to Munich.

Moreover, alongside Lipps's seminars for advanced students, another institution that played a crucial role in the Munich Circle's development of phenomenology was the "Akademischer Verein für Psychologie," which was founded in 1895 and also led by Lipps. It was under the auspices of this association that in 1904 Daubert invited Husserl to give a talk on his *Logical Investigations* (1900–1901), which led to Lipps being accused of psychologism and many of the Munich phenomenologists moving to Göttingen. In the summer and winter terms of 1906 and 1906–1907, this association was led by Lipps's nephew Conrad. When Conrad moved from Munich to Gottingen, he organized a similar "Verein" there, which in the winter term of 1909–1910 turned into the "Philosophische Gesellschaft Göttingen."[11]

How are we to locate Voigtländer within the Munich Circle? This question cannot easily be answered by looking at books on the history of the phenomenological movement because she scarcely appears in them. Thus, it is necessary to resort to other sources of information. I will focus here in particular on the autobiographical note that appears at the end of her dissertation *On the Types of Self-Feelings*, the "Belegblätter" (the record of her course attendance), Lipps's dissertation report, and her correspondence with Daubert.

In the autobiographical note, Voigtländer states that her dissertation has been written under the direction of Lipps, but she also makes it clear that she sought out Pfänder's supervision during the final stages of her PhD. With this statement, she places herself close to one of the main representatives of the Munich Circle of phenomenology.

A look into the "Belegblätter," the list of courses she attended at Munich, shows that she was a student of Lipps, Pfänder, Scheler, and Geiger.[12] In the winter term of 1905–1906, she attended Lipps's course on psychology and Pfänder's course on logic. In the summer term of 1906, she attended Pfänder's course on pedagogics and Lipps's seminar on psychology. In the winter term of 1906–1907, again she attended Lipps's and Pfänder's courses. The summer term of 1907 is particularly interesting because she attended courses offered by Lipps, Pfänder, Geiger, and Scheler. Bearing in mind Voigtländer's use of literary examples in her dissertation, it is worth noting that in the summer term of 1907, Pfänder discussed Henrik Ibsen's play *The Master Builder* in his "psychologische Übung" (psychological exercise). This course was attended not only by Voigtländer, but also by Dietrich von Hildebrand (who is today also considered to be a representative of

---

[11] Avé-Lallemant and Schuhmann, "Ein Zeitzeuge," 78–79.

[12] The sources consulted are Else Voigtländer, Belegblätter Else Voigtländer, Universitätsarchiv München (UAM), STUD-BB-237 WS 1905/06; STUD-BB-272 SS 1907; STUD-BB-284 WS 1907/08; STUD-BB-298 SS 1908; STUD-BB-310 WS 1908/09; and STUD-BB-341 WS 1909/10.

the Munich Circle).[13] In the winter term of 1907–1908, she attended courses by Lipps, Pfänder, and Scheler, and in the summer term of 1908, she attended those by Lipps and Scheler. During her last three terms as a student (from 1908–1909 to 1910), she attended only Pfänder's courses. Moreover, she was also a student of the well-known economist Lujo Brentano (Franz Brentano's younger brother). In short, Voigtländer was a student of the main representatives of the Munich phenomenological tradition. This implies not only that she was directly acquainted with these thinkers, but also that they were acquainted with her. Moreover, we have good reason to think that in these seminars she established contact with other students and PhD candidates. At a time when the university was a privilege for the few and dominated by men, Voigtländer was certainly known to teachers and male colleagues.

The third source of information is Lipps's dissertation report. Here Lipps claims to know Voigtländer and thinks favorably of her from his seminars and from the "Verein," one of the most important organs of the Munich Circle of phenomenology.[14] This means that she attended not only regular courses at the university but actively attended with teachers and colleagues the activities, conferences, and readings about phenomenological issues that were organized by the "Verein."

Voigtländer's correspondence with Daubert, whom she had befriended, provides important insights into her place within the network of Munich phenomenologists. To my knowledge, this correspondence consists of five letters. The first two letters, from Daubert to Voigtländer, were written in 1913 and 1914, respectively. The last three letters—one from Daubert and two from Voigtländer—were written in 1930 when she was already director of the women's prison in Waldheim.[15] However, there are probably more letters since there was apparently no interruption in their communication in the intervening years.

In the first two letters, they discuss philosophical issues and Daubert updates Voigtländer about the philosophical activities in Munich, but they also exchange thoughts about the political and economic situation and make plans to go skiing in the mountains. In the first letter, Daubert comments to her that Pfänder and some "other men of the old circle" plan to offer philosophical discussions again (mainly presentations and critical reviews of Husserl, Emil Lask, Paul Natorp, and Henri Bergson). Daubert also asks her to come to Munich to practice skiing with him and remarks how happy he feels each time he hears from her (he seems to be very fond of her). In the second letter, Dauber apologizes for his slow response ("you know how difficult writing is for me"). This letter contains discussions about characterology, authentic and inauthentic

---

[13] Karl Schuhmann, "Daubert-Chronik," in *Karl Schuhmann. Selected Papers in Phenomenology*, ed. Cees Liejenhorst and Piet Steenbakkers (Dordrecht: Kluwer Academic, 2005), 319.

[14] See Else Voigtländer, Promotionsakte Else Voigtländer, Universitätsarchiv der Ludwig-Maximilians-Universität München, Bestand O-I-90p (Voigtländer's doctoral proceedings, 1909).

[15] See Else Voigtländer, Correspondence Daubert–Voigtländer, Bayerische Staatsbibliothek München, 30.12.1913, 13.5.1914, 3.8.1930, 20.8.1930, and 17.9.1930, transcribed by Rodney Parker and Thomas Vongehr.

character traits, Russian literature, Daubert's thoughts about his planned book on logic, and plans for potential excursions and ski trips. He mentions that the philosophical discussions with Pfänder, Geiger, Fischer, Brunsig, Specht, and Löwenstein take place regularly and that they have discussed Scheler's ethics and Lask. In the last three letters (August and September 1930), Daubert and Voigtländer discuss the idea of erotic love as sentiment (*Gesinnung*), and the nature of values and their relation to affective states. From these letters, it is clear that Voigtländer took an active part in the activities of the Munich Circle, that she knew their main representatives, and that she forged friendships with other members of the group. The fact that Daubert kept her posted about the developments of the group suggests that she was interested in what was going on in Munich despite living elsewhere.

These documents leave little doubt that Voigtländer was a member of the Munich Circle. As I have shown, she attended courses offered by the main phenomenologists working at Munich, actively participated in the debates organized around Lipps's seminars and the "Verein," and was known by Lipps, Pfänder, and Daubert. It is likely that other phenomenologists also knew her as a student or colleague: although there is no evidence of exchanges with Scheler, Geiger, or any other Munich phenomenologist, her attendance at their courses and participation in the "Verein" make it difficult to imagine that they had not noticed her. Having examined her relations with other members of the Munich network, in the next sections I will examine how she should be situated conceptually within this group.

2 PHENOMENOLOGY AND LITERATURE: DESCRIPTION, METHOD, AND STYLE

In *On the Types of Self-Feelings* (1910), Voigtländer employs the term "phenomenology" on multiple occasions and asserts the phenomenological nature of her analysis of the feeling of self-worth.[16] Though it might seem that she employs this term without giving it a clear definition, I suggest that it is in fact employed in two different ways.[17] On the one hand, like Lipps and other Munich phenomenologists (such as Pfänder in his early texts), Voigtländer uses the term "phenomenology" in a very general sense to refer to the description and analysis of mental phenomena, that is, of the contents of consciousness. This usage—which was widely extended among Munich phenomenologists—is independent from and prior to Husserl's development of the phenomenological method in the *Logical Investigations*.

---

[16] Voigtländer, *Selbstgefühl*, 34, 38, 45–46, 48, 68, 81, 115–116, and 119.
[17] I disagree with Heffernan on this point. He argues that Voigtländer employs the term without giving it a specific sense. See Heffernan, "Phenomenology, Psychology, and Ideology."

On the other hand, she also employs the term in a narrow sense to refer to a specific methodology. As mentioned, Munich phenomenologists found in Husserl a method of research to study mental phenomena without falling prey to Lipps's psychologism. In fact, Munich phenomenologists were more attracted to Husserl's method of the intuition of ideas or eidetic intuition (*Wesenschau*) than to his ideas about phenomenology as a discipline or his claims about reality and mind.[18] Eidetic intuition consists in generating variations of a phenomenon and observing what is essential to it and what is not. Voigtländer's book can be regarded as a specific application of the phenomenological methodology in this narrow sense of practicing an intuition of ideas. This is particularly clear in the second part of the book. The eidetic variation is used here to examine different possibilities of the feeling of self-worth as oscillating between the extreme categories of self-abandonment and self-affirmation.[19]

It is worth noting that phenomenologists understood themselves as having a certain degree of freedom when applying the phenomenological method to a particular field. In this respect, Scheler understood phenomenology in terms of an "attitude,"[20] and Reinach described it as the "art of seeing [Kunst des Schauens],"[21] rather than as a method per se. Voigtländer can be regarded as taking this freedom in the application of the phenomenological method at face value. More precisely, her freedom consists in resorting to literary examples extracted from the works of Henriette Feuerbach, Goethe, Ibsen, Thomas Mann, Gottfried Keller, and Gotthold Ephraim Lessing, among others, to support her theses. She also writes in a style that is close to Nietzsche's, which was unprecedented within her phenomenological circles.

Indeed, at that time, it was uncommon among phenomenologists to use literary examples or even to write in a literary style. In his report, Lipps described her dissertation as "almost feuilletonistic [fast feulletonistisch]," remarking that the first distinction between self-feeling and self-knowledge is elaborated by drawing on an "example taken from G. Keller."[22] This qualification has a clearly negative tone which Lipps immediately tries to attenuate by writing that Voigtländer is a psychologist to be taken seriously. Yet, what Lipps calls "feuilletonistic" should be regarded as her original contribution to the phenomenological methodology. She employs literary examples not only to illustrate her claims but also to attain philosophical knowledge about the human being. Rather

---

[18] For this view, see: Avé-Lallemant and Schuhmann, "Ein Zeitzeuge," 80 and 82, and more recently, Daniele de Santis, "Theodor Conrad. Zum Gedächtnis Edmund Husserls (Ein unveröffentlichter Aufsatz aus der Bayerischen Staatsbibliothek)," *Husserl Studies* 38, no. 1 (2021): 55 – 66..

[19] For a similar reading, see: Lambert Wiesing, *Ich für mich. Phänomenologie des Selbstbewusstseins* (Berlin: Suhrkamp, 2020), 209.

[20] Max Scheler, "Phenomenology and the Theory of Cognition," in *Selected Philosophical Essays*, trans. David R. Lachterman (Evanston, IL: Northwestern University Studies in Phenomenology and Existential Philosophy, 1973), 137

[21] Adolf Reinach, "Über Phänomenologie," in *Sämtliche Werke* I, ed. Karl Schumann and Barry Smith (Munich: Philosophia Verlag, 1989), 532.

[22] See Voigtländer, Promotionsakte Else Voigtländer.

than making claims in a vacuum, she uses vivid and colorful descriptions with the aim of showing the richness of our affective life and getting us imaginatively and emotionally involved. By these means, we come to participate actively in the phenomenological analysis of the intuition of ideas about human affective life. In so doing, Voigtländer developed a unique style among early phenomenologists—it was only much later with authors like Sartre that phenomenology exploited the cognitive powers of literature for philosophical purposes.

After this book, her style became more sober and less literary. However, in her philosophical output she continued to use the phenomenological method.[23] This commitment is already clear in an article published one year later titled "On Freud's Significance for Psychology" ("Über die Bedeutung Freuds für die Psychologie," 1911) where she provides the first phenomenological interpretation of Freud's mechanism of *Verdrängung* (repression),[24] applying phenomenological concepts to the field of psychopathology before Karl Jaspers. This phenomenological orientation remains in later works in which she provides insightful analysis of political emotions, erotic love, the alpine experience, and sentiments.[25]

3 SELF-FEELING AND THE EMOTIVIST TRADITION OF SELF-CONSCIOUSNESS

With her dissertation, Voigtländer also contributed to the development of the phenomenology of affectivity. The term *Selbstgefühl* literally means self-feeling, that is, a feeling which involves a sense of self. Yet, in her book, she is particularly interested in those self-feelings where one's own value is disclosed to the subject, for which she employs the term "feeling of self-worth" (*Selbstwertgefühl*).[26] Though the concepts *Selbstgefühl* and

---

[23] Her publications on education and correction are developed in line with the empirical psychology of the time.

[24] Else Voigtländer, "Über die Bedeutung Freuds für die Psychologie," in *Münchener philosophische Abhandlungen. Theodor Lipps zu seinem sechzigsten Geburtstag gewidmet von früheren Schülern*, ed. Alexander Pfänder (Leipzig: Barth, 1911), 294–316. See Thomas Barth, "Else Voigtländer's Thoughts on Psychoanalysis," in *Else Voigtländer. Self, Emotion, and Sociality*, 47–69.

[25] See Else Voigtländer, "Zur Psychologie der politischen Stellungnahme: Eine massenpsychologische Studie," *Deutsche Psychologie* 3 (1920), 184–206; "Zur Phänomenologie und Psychologie des 'alpinen Erlebnisses,'" *Zeitschrift für angewandte Psychologie* 33 (1923), 258–270; "Über das Wesen der Liebe und ihre Beziehung zur Sexualität," in *Verhandlungen des I. Internationalen Kongresses für Sexualforschung, veranstaltet von der Internationalen Gesellschaft für Sexualforschung Berlin vom 10. bis 16. Oktober 1926, Dritter Band: Psychologie, Pädagogik, Ethik, Ästhetik, Religion*, ed. Max Marcuse (Berlin: A. Marcus, 1928), 189–196; and "Bemerkungen zur Psychologie der Gesinnungen," in *Neue Münchener Philosophische Abhandlungen: Alexander Pfänder zu seinem sechzigsten Geburtstag gewidmet von Freunden und Schülern*, ed. Ernst Heller and Friedrich Löw (Leipzig: Barth, 1933), 143–164.

[26] For this translation, I follow Sebastian Aeschbach, *Ressentiment: An Anatomy* (PhD diss., University of Geneva, 2017). As Heffernan has pointed out, the concept can also be translated as "self-feeling": Heffernan, "Phenomenology, Psychology, and Ideology."

Selbstwertgefühl can already be found in Lipps, in Voigtländer we witness an interesting conceptual shift.[27]

In *Fühlen, Denken und Wollen* (1903), Lipps argued that feelings (*Gefühle*) are constitutive qualities of the self (insofar as all feelings are qualities of the self, all feelings are also feelings of the self).[28] In addition, he elaborates a classification of feelings, distinguishing between the following classes: feelings related to objects, intellectual feelings, psychological feelings, and "feelings of self-worth" (*Selbstwertgefühle*). A characteristic of this last class of the feelings of self-worth is that pleasure and pain are directed toward the self, that is, they have the self as their object. Thus, when we experience a feeling of self-worth, we not only feel in a certain way, but we also feel this way in relation to ourselves. Moreover, these feelings emerge only in retrospection and "looking backward." (Otherwise they would presuppose a duplication of the self, which Lipps considered to be impossible.)[29] If we do not reflect on the previous experience and remain immersed in pursuing a certain goal, then the feeling of self-worth will not emerge. Finally—and in a way which seems to contradict this claim—feelings of self-worth are, for Lipps, always feelings of the value of our actions or activities. In fact, our activities are always the object of a feeling of self-worth. The concept of activity should be understood broadly here as encompassing not only actions but also perceiving, thinking, and so on.

Voigtländer takes Lipps's terminology as her point of departure. However, instead of analyzing the "feelings of self-worth" as one class of feelings of the self, she considers them separately. In her view, feelings of self-worth are "an affective valuating consciousness of one's own self which each of us has and which is subjected to fluctuations."[30] Examples of this kind of feeling are: confidence, self-affirmation, pride, vanity, shame, cowardice, haughtiness, remorse, embarrassment, ambition, self-abandonment, and self-esteem. In these feelings, we experience ourselves as elevated or low-spirited. We apprehend the fluctuations of our own value according to the possession of certain traits and abilities, failures and achievements. In confidence, we experience ourselves as elevated, while in embarrassment we feel diminished in worth.

Voigtländer characterizes "feelings of self-worth" according to three main features. First, they have an "affective moment," according to which they can be classified as pleasant or unpleasant (e.g., feeling uplifted is a pleasurable experience, while feeling depressed is unpleasurable). Today we would refer to this moment as "hedonic valence." Second, they involve a "cognitive moment" in which we grasp our own worth nonconceptually. This clearly indicates that, for her, feelings of self-worth fulfill a "cognitive function." Finally, these feelings are accompanied by an "awareness of the self."

---

[27] See Philipp Schmidt, "Value in Existence: Lotze, Lipps, and Voigtländer on Feelings of Self-Worth", in *Else Voigtländer. Self, Emotion, and Sociality*, 25–46.

[28] Theodor Lipps, *Fühlen, Wollen und Denken. Eine psychologische Skizze* (Leipzig: Johann Ambrosius Barth, 1903), 1.

[29] Lipps, *Fühlen*, 177.

[30] Voigtländer, *Selbstgefühl*, 19.

That is, in these feelings we become conscious of ourselves, that is, they involve a "self-consciousness."

Considering the "feelings of self-worth" on their own allows her to elaborate a detailed analysis of their main types.[31] The first type is constituted by "vital feelings of self-worth" (*vitales Selbstgefühl*), which are instinctive, natural, innate, and unconscious (a term that Voigtländer uses to indicate their prereflexive nature). These feelings manifest a natural affective orientation unrelated to our achievements. Feelings of self-affirmation, courage, confidence, and their opposites belong to this class. In these feelings the affective moment, that is, their being pleasant or unpleasant, is predominant. The second type is configured by the "conscious feelings of self-worth." These feelings emerge from an objective appreciation of our achievements and talents and presuppose a "division" or "split of the self [Teilung des Selbst]."[32] Central to them is not their hedonic valence but our awareness of our own value. The descriptions of both types indicate that Voigtländer is working with a stratified model of affectivity. However, this model is not made explicit in her work. (By contrast, Scheler, Stein, and Geiger will develop more sophisticated and complex accounts about the stratified nature of affectivity and they will also identify more strata than the two recognized by Voigtländer.)[33] In this model, the vital domain is more primitive than the psychological. Moreover, both levels might enter into conflict: one can have a strong vital self-worth but a weak conscious feeling of self-worth (and vice versa; I return to this issue later to explain Voigtländer's analysis of ressentiment).

Before comparing her account with Lipps's account of the "feelings of self-worth," it should be acknowledged that some of Voigtländer's descriptions of the "feelings of self-worth" have an unsettling character for today's reader. As stated earlier, for Voigtländer, the vital domain is more primitive than the psychological. Yet, for her, the vital is based on the biological constitution of the subject, which, in turn, "stems from the blood, race, the life."[34] These and similar descriptions not only attach an exaggerated importance to the biological, but also appear to be linked to ideological claims about race. These descriptions may reflect ideological prejudices which were quite common at that time. However, in the light of Voigtländer's later collaboration with Gregor, who was a proponent of eugenics, other comments on race within in her work, and her membership of the NSDAP during her time in Waldheim, such remarks reveal a continuous ideological thread in her life and thought.

A comparison may be established on the basis of the characterizations made in Lipps's and Voigtländer's accounts. First, while Lipps sees feelings of self-worth as one class of

---

[31] Voigtländer, *Selbstgefühl*, 21–22.

[32] Voigtländer, *Selbstgefühl*, 21.

[33] See Scheler, *Formalism in Ethics and Non-formal Ethics of Values*, trans. Manfred S. Frings and Roger L. Funk (Evanston, IL: Northwestern University Press, 1973), 295; Stein, *On the Problem of Empathy: The Collected Works of Edith Stein* (Washington, DC: ICS, 1989), 100; Moritz Geiger, *The Significance of Art*, ed. Klaus Berger (Lanham, MD: University Press of America, 1986), 46.

[34] Voigtländer, *Selbstgefühl*, 30.

feelings of the self, Voigtländer offers a more nuanced consideration of their distinctive types. Second, while Lipps provides only a general description, Voigtländer examines the affective, cognitive, and self-conscious dimensions in each of the types. Third, Lipps describes feelings of self-worth in a twofold manner: he argues that they emerge only after we reflect on ourselves in retrospection, though he simultaneously acknowledges that they accompany all our activities. By contrast, in distinguishing between two types of feelings, Voigtländer also distinguishes between two kinds of self-consciousness involved in them: vital feelings are prereflexive, while conscious feelings of self-worth involve a reflective stance toward oneself. Finally, by arguing that our own value is apprehended by a feeling, Voigtländer defends the idea of a cognitive function of affectivity. This idea resonates with similar claims defended by other early phenomenologists (see section 6), but nothing similar can be found in Lipps.

Against the backdrop of this comparison, we can better understand the critique that Lipps makes of Voigtländer's account in his PhD report.[35] Here, Lipps praises her work for being an initial attempt to investigate the matter of self-feeling, but regrets that many of the issues raised remain unanswered. Two of his critiques are particularly relevant. First, Lipps claims that, although Voigtländer clearly states the difference between self-feeling and self-knowledge, the relation between the two requires further consideration. Second, he questions Voigtländer's project to analyze "feelings of self-worth" as a phenomenon in their own right. In my view, the first remark indicates Lipps's skepticism about the cognitive function of "feelings of self-worth," that is, their capacity to apprehend, grasp, and disclose fluctuations of one's own value. With the second remark, Lipps overlooks what to my mind should be considered Voigtländer's main contribution. In examining the "feelings of self-worth" separately, she identified an essential aspect of our affective life: that human beings are able to sense fluctuations in their own value through feeling.

To understand the novelty of Voigtländer's claims, we need to take into account the debate on self-consciousness at the time. Early phenomenological accounts of self-consciousness can be divided into two camps.[36] On the one hand, transcendental accounts such as the one put forward by Husserl explained the self as a transcendental condition of our experiences. On the other hand, emotivist accounts such as those put forward by Lotze and Lipps were connected to empirical considerations and regarded feelings as a source of subjective experience. This "emotivist tradition of self-consciousness," as Guillaume Fréchette (adopting an expression from Gustav Kafka)

---

[35] See Voigtländer, Promotionsakte Else Voigtländer. Voigtländer received grade III from Lipps in the major discipline of Philosophy. In Art History (Berthold Riehl) and in Economic History (Lujo Brentano) which were her minor disciplines, she received grade II from each examiner. Her final grade was III.

[36] Guillaume Fréchette, "Searching for the Self: Early Phenomenological Accounts of Self-Consciousness from Lotze to Scheler," *International Journal of Philosophical Studies* 21, no. 5 (2013): 658. See also Guillaume Fréchette, "Phenomenology and Characterology. Austrian and Bavarian," in *Else Voigtländer. Self, Emotion, and Sociality*, 163–180.

called it, was widely developed by authors belonging to the Munich Circle, such as Pfänder and Reinach,[37] as well as by Geiger and Scheler, who defended it in combination with the theory of immanent psychic realism.[38]

Voigtländer may be regarded as contributing to the emotivist tradition. Her approach to self-consciousness is empirical rather than transcendental. Moreover, she explains self-consciousness in terms of feeling. And, like many other Munich phenomenologists, she embraces the idea that the self has a reality distinct from the reality of objects we might be directed toward. Within this tradition, her account stresses the cognitive function of feelings by claiming that these grant us access to an aspect of reality that is not accessible via other forms of consciousness. This reality is one's own self-worth. In short, it is in feelings that we apprehend our own value.[39]

4 EMPATHY, AUTHENTICITY, AND THE SOCIAL DIMENSION OF THE SELF

Voigtländer also contributes to the debate on what can be called the social dimension of the self. More precisely, she offers an account of how the perceptions that others might have of us come to constitute part of our self. For this, her distinction between "genuine [eigentliches Selbstgefühl]" and "non-genuine or mirror feelings of self-worth [uneigentliche oder Spiegelselbstgefühl]" is crucial.[40] This terminology, I suggest, describes the experience of one's own feelings as either having or not having their origin within one's own self. While genuine feelings are experienced as having their origins in the self, nongenuine feelings arise when we experience ourselves from the perspective of a hypothetical other. Nongenuine feelings are those that arise by way of joking, make-believe, pretending, acting as if we are moved by an affect, posing, attitudinizing, boasting, imagining experiences, deceiving ourselves, living a lie, and experiencing ourselves from the perspective of a possible other. As she puts it: a nongenuine feeling is "a feeling of self-worth experienced with regard to what one is in the imagination, in the opinion of others, to what refers to an 'image' of oneself."[41] As a result, these feelings are not anchored in the kernel of the self and we experience them as having a "coreless,"

---

[37] Fréchette, "Self," 657.

[38] According to immanent psychic realism, the inner perception is subject to illusions and deceptions, as is the outer perception. See Moritz Geiger, "Fragment über den Begriff des Unbewussten und die psychische Realität," *Jahrbuch für Philosophie und phänomenologische Forschung* 4 (1921): 1–137; Max Scheler, "The Idols of Self-Knowledge," in *Selected Philosophical Essays*, trans. David R. Lachterman (Evanston, IL: Northwestern University Studies in Phenomenology and Existential Philosophy, 1973).

[39] Voigtländer, *Selbstgefühl*, 10, 19.

[40] Voigtländer, *Selbstgefühl*, 22.

[41] Voigtländer, *Selbstgefühl*, 76 (my translation).

"airy," and "playful nature."[42] In different respects, she provides here a conceptual tool to analyze some phenomena which are similar to what Jean-Paul Sartre, much later, called *mauvaise foi* (bad faith).[43] Yet, it should be underscored that Voigtländer's nongenuine feelings are not reduced to cases in which we deceive others and ourselves.

The term *uneigentlich*—which I have translated here as "nongenuine" to stress the fact that such feelings are experienced as arising outside the self—can also be translated as "inauthentic." However, it should remain clear that for Voigtländer this term is not employed in a normative, epistemic, or moral sense.[44] "Nongenuine" or "inauthentic" neither indicates how a feeling must be nor is an epistemic category. Indeed, in her account, non-genuine feelings are not reduced to cases of self-deception. Moreover, the term "nongenuine" does not refer exclusively to feelings that are the product of an intentional deception or to feelings in which we are not truly ourselves. Rather, the term is used in a descriptive sense to refer to those feelings which stem from a hypothetical external view from ourselves. The term also stresses the intrinsically social nature of the self.

The very existence of such feelings indicates not only that we are able to imagine how we are seen by others, but also that we may incorporate these imaginings about ourselves into the way we feel. To explain how this incorporation takes place, Voigtländer resorts to the mechanism of empathy (*Einfühlung*). In her view, such feelings emerge because we are able to "feel into" the image that we think others might have of us.[45] This concept of empathy is elaborated in line with Lipps, for whom empathy was a form of "projection" of oneself into something. The way in which she and Lipps use the concept differs from other conceptions of empathy in the early phenomenological tradition, such as the one developed by Scheler to indicate a form of "perception" of other minds (which can but does not have to involve imagination-like states).[46] In Voigtländer's account, through empathizing with the image others might have of us, we can attain a twofold perspective about ourselves: the perspective that we have from the first person point of view and the one that we achieve through projection.

Voigtländer's work on genuine and nongenuine feelings is the first of a series of accounts on this topic developed within early phenomenology. By the time that she published her work (1910), Willy Haas was writing a dissertation titled "On the Authenticity and Inauthenticity of Emotions" ("Über Echtheit und Unechtheit von

---

[42] Voigtländer, *Selbstgefühl*, 97. At least since Hume, these qualifications were widely extended to describe the distinctive phenomenology of feelings which arise under the influence of the imagination (which are generally described as being less firm and solid).

[43] Jean-Paul Sartre, *Being and Nothingness*, trans. Hazel E. Barnes (New York: Washington Square Press, 1993).

[44] See for alternative interpretations: Hilge Landweer, "Authenticity and Mask: Critical Self-Reflections on Else Voigtländer," in *Else Voigtländer. Self, Emotion, and Sociality,* 141–162 and Alessandro Salice, "Else Voigtländer on Social Self-Feelings," in *Else Voigtländer. Self, Emotion, and Sociality,* 125–140.

[45] Voigtländer, *Selbstgefühl*, 86.

[46] For an overview of this thesis in the phenomenological tradition, see: James Jardine and Thomas Szanto, "Empathy in the Phenomenological Tradition," in *The Routledge Handbook of Philosophy of Empathy*, ed. Heidi Maibom (London: Routledge, 2017), 86–97.

Gefühlen," 1910) under the supervision of Pfänder. The phenomenon that Haas describes is quite similar to what Voigtländer calls nongenuineness. Unlike Voigtländer, however, Haas developed what can be called a coherence model of inauthenticity. In his view, an emotion is authentic when it coheres with the general affective condition of the subject and inauthentic when it does not. Thus, a joy is authentic when it fits with the positive thoughts, desires, attitudes of the subject, but inauthentic if the subject is in a bad mood.[47] The inauthenticity of sentiments was also a topic in Pfänder's "Psychology of Sentiments" ("Zur Psychologie der Gesinnungen," 1913–16). Like Haas, Pfänder endorses a coherence model, but Pfänder stresses the possibility that an inauthentic sentiment can turn into an authentic one. Thus, an inherited hatred might be inauthentic because it does not fit with other aspects of the subject's psychology, but when the subject changes her thoughts, her feelings into the direction of that hatred, it might turn into an authentic one. Using some adjectives that recall Voigtländer's descriptions, Pfänder argues that inauthentic sentiments are experienced as "schematic, hollow, thin, coreless or light."[48] The view that an emotion might be inauthentic was also one of Scheler's major concerns in a series of essays devoted to self-knowledge and psychic reality.[49]

The social dimension of the self is also the topic of Voigtländer's article "On the Nature of a Person and the Experience of the 'Mask'" ("Über die 'Art' eines Menschen und das Erlebnis der 'Maske'").[50] Rather than focusing exclusively on feelings, this essay gives an account of the relation between those values that we attribute to others according to the impression that we have of them (a phenomenon for which she coins the expression: "impressional value" (*Eindruckswert*)) and the real qualities of the other's character. However, this article was developed against the backdrop of certain ideological beliefs about human character that we have already found in her dissertation.

5 INTENTIONALITY, VALUE, AND AFFECTIVITY

Voigtländer also actively participated in the development of the phenomenological concept of affectivity as intimately linked to values. Many early phenomenologists took at face value Brentano's idea that affective states exhibit a genuine form of intentionality

---

[47] Willy Haas, *Über Echtheit und Unechtheit von Gefühlen* (Nurnberg: Benedikt Hilz, 1910), 12.

[48] Alexander Pfänder, "Zur Psychologie der Gesinnungen: Erster Artikel," *Jahrbuch für Philosophie und phänomenologische Forschung* 1 (1913), 383. For an analysis of Pfänder's account, see: Genki Uemura and Toru Yaegashi, "Alexander Pfänder," in *The Routledge Handbook of Phenomenology of Emotion*, ed. by Thomas Szanto and Hilge Landweer (London: Routledge, 2020), 63–71.

[49] Scheler, "Idols."

[50] Else Voigtländer, "Über die 'Art' eines Menschen und das Erlebnis der 'Maske': Eine psychologische Skizze," *Zeitschrift für Psychologie und Physiologie der Sinnesorgane* 92 (1923): 326–336.

which should be distinguished from the intentionality of cognitive states, such as presentations and judgments. For Brentano, the sui generis intentional structure of affective states consists in presenting their objects as either good or bad, that is, as inviting us to position ourselves positively or negatively toward them. For instance, the object of love is presented as lovable, the object of hate as hateworthy. In brief, affective states involve for Brentano a valuation of their objects. Like Brentano, many early phenomenologists defended objectivist positions about values. However, unlike Brentano, they developed their accounts in the direction of value realism. More precisely, they defended the view that values exist as independent realities and that they are apprehended by feelings. In their view, intentional feelings fulfill the cognitive function of making the realm of values accessible to us. Yet, among early phenomenologists, the relationship between values and affective states was interpreted in different ways: while Scheler argued that the feelings responsible for the apprehension of values are sui generis and prior to the emotional response,[51] Stein considered these feelings as one moment of the emotional experience.[52]

In this context, Voigtländer was one of the first phenomenologists to acknowledge that self-feelings have cognitive value and are able to apprehend fluctuations of one's own value.[53] With these claims, she comes to endorse a position which is closer to Scheler than to Stein (in fact, this position is today widely attributed to Scheler). However, Voigtländer was not a value objectivist throughout. For her, some affective states such as sentiments (*Gesinnungen*) impress their character on the targeted objects.[54] Love, admiration, or tenderness make objects appear to us in a certain light, that is, they confer specific "impressional values" (*Eindruckswerte*) onto their objects. Love is what makes the other appear charming, beautiful, lovely, marvelous, and so on.[55] In this respect, she defends a hybrid position regarding the ontology of values. Some values—such as those grasped by the feelings of self-worth—seem to have an objective reality, while those experienced via sentiments are the result of a projection of our own affective states. In short, feelings of self-worth are explained by means of an objectivist model, while to explain impressional values she resorts to projectionist and subjectivist accounts.[56]

These ontological claims about values have implications for Voigtländer's general picture of affectivity. In fact, on the basis of this distinction between two types of values, she establishes a distinction between two kinds of affective states: while feelings apprehend objective values, sentiments project impressional values onto their objects.

---

[51] Scheler, *Formalism.*

[52] Stein, *Empathy.*

[53] Voigtländer, *Selbstgefühl*, 11.

[54] In her dissertation, she does not use this term but refers to the phenomenon as a kind of feeling. The term "sentiment" is adopted in later works. See Voigtländer, *Selbstgefühl*; Voigtländer, "Liebe"; Voigtländer, "Gesinnungen."

[55] Voigtländer, *Selbstgefühl*, 111; Voigtländer, "Maske."

[56] See for an alternative interpretation: Genki Uemura, "Between Love and Benevolence: Voigtländer, Pfänder, and Walther on the Phenomenology of Sentiments," in *Else Voigtländer. Self, Emotion, and Sociality*, 71–88.

Voigtländer's subjectivism about values in the case of sentiments was discussed in her correspondence with Daubert (September 3 and 17, 1930). Daubert criticizes her claim that love is what makes the other appear charming, attractive, and so on, on the grounds that it falls prey to subjectivism. She responds to this accusation by claiming that, in the case of sentiments, values fall between the objective and the subjective. This intermediate position of the values that we attribute to the objects of our sentiments is what she tries to capture with the concept of "impressional value" explained earlier. We can explain her position in the following terms. The "impressional values" are evaluative qualities (i.e., qualities that lead us to position ourselves positively or negatively toward the object which embodies them) that we attribute to an object by virtue of our affective orientation toward it. "Impressional values" stem from the impression that we have of the other and this impression always arises in the frame of a sentiment that we have for him or her. In this respect, in love we will tend to see in the other positive impressional values (e.g., charming, loving, etc.) while in hate, we will tend to see the opposite. Such "impressional values" differ from objective values such as "dangerous," "disgusting," and so on, which are based on particular nonevaluative features of an object and which, as such, enjoy certain intersubjective consensus.

Although early phenomenology has been clearly associated with an objectivist and realist ontology of value and the movement has been associated with the epistemic claim that values are grasped by feelings, Voigtländer also left space for subjectivist positions of value in her philosophical work. Interestingly, she was not alone in acknowledging the ability of affective states to project their character onto their objects. In this respect, Moritz Geiger argued that affective states are able to project their "feeling tone" onto the targeted objects.[57] When we are in a good mood, we project a rosy glow over everything.

6 Ressentiment and Erotic Love

Voigtländer also provides analyses of specific affective states in the tradition of early phenomenology. Attention will be paid here to two opposed phenomena: ressentiment and love.

The study of ressentiment was of great interest to early phenomenologists because it serves as a stage to examine the intimate relation between affectivity and value. With this term, the early phenomenologists refer to a specific hostile attitude which leads to a devaluation of its targets. The phenomenon is illustrated by the fable of the fox who, unable to reach the grapes, claims that they are sour. In this respect, ressentiment presupposes a devaluation and an inversion of values. Scheler and Reinach devoted attention to it, but it was Voigtländer who first provided an account of its nature in her dissertation.

---

[57] Moritz Geiger, "Zum Problem der Stimmungseinfühlung" (1911), in *Die Bedeutung der Kunst. Zugänge zu einer materialen Wertästhetik*, ed. Klaus Berger and Wolfhart Henckmann (Munich: Fink, 1976), 41.

Drawing on Nietzsche, Voigtländer's dissertation links ressentiment with self-deception. In ressentiment, the devaluation of those objects previously experienced as worthy is an attempt to reduce unpleasant feelings of inferiority and impotence. Voigtländer's account is based on the idea, already mentioned in section 3, that there are two kinds of "feelings of self-worth" and that they take place at different levels of the subject's psychology. In her view, ressentiment results from a tension between a negative vital feeling for which the subject tries to compensate with a positive conscious feeling of self-worth.

Only a couple of years after Voigtländer published her account, but without taking her views into consideration, Scheler published his analysis of ressentiment. In his account, Scheler stresses the relevance of the feelings of impotence and explains ressentiment in terms of a progression of feeling: when feelings of revenge, hatred, malice, envy, rancor, and spite cannot be expressed and are sustained, ressentiment emerges as a self-poisoning attitude.[58] This leads to an inversion of values, which involves a change in the perception of values and a replacement of these values with illusory negative ones.[59] Reinach too devoted some thought to this phenomenon. Unlike Scheler, he argues that, for ressentiment, it is not the repression of negative feelings that is essential but what he calls "the dislocation of the I," that is, the promotion of one's own value, which results from having been diminished in worth after acknowledging the other's value.[60] Though Reinach's thoughts on ressentiment have gone unnoticed, Scheler's analysis has been widely discussed and often taken as an example of how eidetic variation and intuition of ideas work. It was not until very recently that Voigtländer's account caught the attention of philosophers and psychologists working on ressentiment.[61]

Voigtländer devotes one of her last analyses of specific affective states to erotic love.[62] In "On the Nature of Love and Its Relation to Sexuality" ("Über das Wesen der Liebe und ihre Beziehung zur Sexualität," 1928), she identifies in erotic love the three main features that Pfänder attributed to sentiments: erotic love flows from the subject to the object; it has the intention of uniting with the object; it accepts and supports its object. In fact, erotic love is presented as a subgroup of the sentiment of love and as such exhibits its own specificities: it is a warming movement of the heart that presents the other as embodying certain features (*Verkörperungserlebnis*); it involves the tendency to melt with the other (*Verschmelzung*); its goal is to create a perfect unity

---

[58] Max Scheler, *Ressentiment*, trans. Lewis B. Coser and William W. Holdheim (Milwaukee: Marquette University Press, 2010), 45–46.

[59] Scheler, *Ressentiment*, 25, 45–46.

[60] Adolf Reinach, *Three Texts on Ethics*, trans. James Smith and Mette Lebech (Munich: Philosophia Verlag, 2017), 203.

[61] See Aeschbach, *Ressentiment*, and Natalie Rodax et al., "Ressentiment as Morally Disclose Posture? Conceptual Issues from a Psychological Point of View," *Review of Philosophy and Psychology* (2021). See Íngrid Vendrell Ferran, "Ressentiment and Self-Deception in Early Phenomenology: Voigtländer, Scheler, and Reinach," in *Else Voigtländer. Self, Emotion, and Sociality*, 103–124.

[62] See Toru Yaegashi, "Erotic Love and the Value of the Beloved," in *Else Voigtländer. Self, Emotion, and Sociality*, 89–102.

with the other (*vollkommenen Einigung*). To illustrate the specific nature of erotic love, Voigtländer compares it to friendship (another subspecies of love). She writes, metaphorically, that while friendship is a bridge that unifies two poles, erotic love is described as the convergence of two flows.[63] In her view, attractiveness is the main value of the erotic domain. The beloved person appears charming, interesting, lovable, and so on, and due to these qualities, we feel attracted to her. The fact that we can feel attracted to someone who is ugly speaks to a fundamental distinction between the erotic and aesthetic domains.

In considering erotic love as a sentiment, Voigtländer rejects those views that explain it as owing its origins to sexual instinct. Rather, what happens is that, although erotic love originates from a distinct source, as does sexual instinct, both come together when the sentiment is expressed at the bodily level. All affective phenomena are linked to expressive movements. In the specific case of erotic love, these expressive movements come to converge with the already existing sexual impulse. Given that Voigtländer understands erotic love as sentiment with an intrinsic tendency to melt together and create a unity with the other, it seems natural that, among the existing expressive movements, it becomes associated with sexual instinct, which fulfills these tendencies bodily. Voigtländer's account is particularly original when compared to those of Pfänder and Scheler. Her focus on erotic love differs from the accounts provided by these authors, whose main aim was to offer a general description of the phenomenon of love. Only in Scheler can we find an analysis of bodily shame and its connection to sexual love and sexual drive, but unlike Voigtländer, he does not interpret erotic love in terms of sentiment.[64]

7 Rewriting the History of the Phenomenological Movement

Drawing on the idea of a philosophical constellation, the previous sections placed Voigtländer within the early phenomenological movement. In particular, I focused on her relation to other authors of this movement, her participation in different debates, and her contribution to the development of a phenomenology of affectivity. As a result, it is beyond doubt that she was a full-fledged member of the Munich Circle. She made decisive contributions to key topics in early phenomenology, such as self-consciousness, inauthenticity, values, ressentiment, and love. And, in so doing, she contributed to the development of the specific picture of affectivity that emerged within early phenomenology.

---

[63] Voigtländer, "Liebe," 193.

[64] Max Scheler, "Shame and the Feelings of Modesty," in *Person and Self-Value*, trans. Manfred S. Frings (Dordrecht: Nijhoff, 1987).

Yet, Voigtländer's name rarely appears in the works of her male colleagues, peers, and supervisors. They do not mention her in their articles or books, even when it is clear that they knew her personally, as a student, mentee, or classmate, or were familiar with her writings in their roles as supervisors and teachers, or worked on similar topics. Not mentioning her work while working on related issues was clearly a way of excluding her from the philosophical community. And whether intentional or not, it is clear that she was subjected to "collegial exclusion," that is, an exclusion carried by those very members of the group to which she belonged. This means that she belonged to the phenomenological community but occupied a marginal position within it. Within this male-dominated milieu, she was accepted as a student and as an active member of the seminars and groups. She also had the opportunity to publish her works in specialized collections and journals. However, her work did not gain the academic recognition it deserved.

There are a number of factors which might have influenced this exclusion. The fact that she was a female philosopher certainly contributed to rendering her philosophical output invisible. When she entered the German university, it was a domain fully dominated by men, imbued with patriarchal structures, and marked by a still prevalent and habitual tendency to downplay female achievements. Moreover, the fact that she belonged to the very first generation of women participating in the development of the phenomenological movement at a time when phenomenology was not well established as a discipline might have led to her invisibility. Female phenomenologists such as Conrad-Martius, Stein, and Walther, who worked only a few years after her and were involved in the Göttingen and Freiburg circles, gained more attention.

Besides the factors determined by her gender, there are other elements related to Voigtländer's biography which might have contributed to her exclusion. First, her specialization as a professional psychologist and her career in correction favored her invisibility among philosophers. Moreover, she navigated between different psychological currents, moving from Lipps to psychoanalysis and later to empirical research and applied psychology. This meant that she may have fallen between the cracks: only the Berlin Group of psychoanalysis registered her name. Furthermore, her publications did not appear in the *Jahrbuch für Philosophie und phänomenologische Forschung*, which was the main publishing organ of the phenomenological movement.

Did the fact that she defended eugenics, sympathized with National Socialism, and imbued her work with ideological elements play a role in the scant attention she received? We can only speculate about this issue. Voigtländer was not the only phenomenologist who exhibited sympathies with National Socialist ideas. Heidegger, for instance, did too, and this did not prevent him from being taken seriously as a philosopher; nor does this fact prevent philosophers today from engaging with his work.

That said, Voigtländer's exclusion had disastrous consequences. First, when phenomenology became an established philosophical movement and the interest in documenting its origins and development increased, Voigtländer was omitted. For instance, she was not included in Spiegelberg's comprehensive volume on the phenomenological movement, which did so much to give a unitary view of the development of phenomenology.[65] Her works are not conserved in any archive. (She does not appear in the record of the "Nachlässe" of the Munich phenomenologists.)[66] As a result, she has been left out of the canon of phenomenology. One of the fortunate exceptions to this omission is Smid's chapter on the Munich phenomenologists in a volume edited by Avé-Lallemant and Spiegelberg.[67] Smid not only mentions Voigtländer as a phenomenologist of the first order, but also acknowledges her as a pioneer of the phenomenological movement, indicates the relevance of her publications, and praises her originality. Second, her work remained invisible and inaccessible to later authors working on similar topics. Searching for a source of inspiration in early phenomenological accounts, Sartre, Maurice Merleau-Ponty, and other philosophers working on topics such as self-consciousness, emotion, value, ressentiment, and love did not know of her existence because she was not mentioned by any of the other members of the early phenomenological movement. Finally, many of Voigtländer's merits as a pioneer of the phenomenology of affectivity have tended to be attributed to her male colleagues. In this respect, her work has not only received scant attention, but it has also not been subject to impartial assessment.[68]

Exceptions aside, the fact that Voigtländer does not appear in the major volumes dedicated to the history of the phenomenological movement might lead to a kind of self-fulfilling prophecy: even if one were to come across her name, one might be led to think that she was not relevant because she is not mentioned in reference works, compendia, or handbooks. Against this background, there is an urgent need to rewrite the history of the phenomenological movement and to include her as a full member. This is not only a question of historical accuracy. As indicated by Ruth Hagengruber, there is also a "moral demand" to uncover the exclusion to which female philosophers have been subjected.[69] This moral demand, I suggest, must be realized in three different directions. First, it should become a rule of thumb to mention her as member of the Munich Circle in every handbook, book, compendium, and article dealing with the history of the phenomenological movement. This issue has started to be addressed in some recent publications.[70]

---

[65] Herbert Spiegelberg, *The Phenomenological Movement* (The Hague: Nijhoff, 1982).

[66] Eberhard Avé-Lallemant, *Die Nachlässe der Münchener Phänomenologen in der Bayerischen Staatsbibliothek* (Wiesbaden: Otto Harrassowitz, 1975).

[67] Reinhold N. Smid, "'Münchener Phänomenologie'—Zur Frühgeschichte des Begriffs," in *Pfänder-Studien*, ed. Herbert Spiegelberg and Eberhard Avé-Lallemant (The Hague: Nijhoff, 1982), 109–53.

[68] This bias is known in the philosophy of science as the "Matilda effect." See Margaret Rossiter, "The Matilda Effect in Science," *Social Studies of Science* 23 (1993): 325–341.

[69] Ruth E. Hagengruber, "The Stolen History—Retrieving the History of Women Philosophers and Its Methodological Implications," in *Methodological Reflections on Women's Contribution and Influence in the History of Philosophy*, ed. Sigridur Thorgeirsdottir and Ruth Edith Hagengruber (Cham: Springer, 2020), 43.

[70] Heffernan, "Phenomenology, Psychology, and Ideology"; Rodney Parker and Dermot Moran, "Editors' Introduction," *Studia Phaenomenologica* XV (2015); Salice, "Phenomenology"; Íngrid Vendrell Ferran, *Die Emotionen. Gefühle in der realistischen Phänomenologie* (Berlin: Akademie, 2008) See also the recently published edited collection on her work: Íngrid Vendrell Ferran, *Else Voigtländer. Self, Emotion, and Sociality.*

Second, her work on self-worth, self-consciousness, inauthenticity, ressentiment, love, and so on should be put into dialogue with contemporary philosophy.[71] Finally, she should be included alongside Conrad-Martius, Stein, Walther, and others as one of the first female phenomenologists. (There is still no complete list of women who worked in the context of early phenomenology!)[72] In this way, Voigtländer will not only be an object of our recognition; we will also have a more complete and accurate picture of the first stages of the phenomenological movement and, in particular, of the Munich Circle.

8 Concluding Remarks

This chapter has examined Voigtländer's place within the constellation of early phenomenology. By considering her relation to other members of the Munich Circle, her active participation in the main debates, and her contributions to the development of a phenomenology of affectivity, I have presented Voigtländer as a full-fledged member of the early phenomenological movement. I have also discussed some of the mechanisms that may have led to her exclusion and emphasized the need to rewrite the history of the phenomenological movement following the principles of historical accuracy and moral recognition.

I am indebted to Guillaume Fréchette for lively exchanges about Pfänder and Daubert, to Wolfhart Henckmann for providing information about Scheler and the Munich phenomenologists, and to Rodney Parker and Thomas Vongehr for making me aware of the correspondence between Daubert and Voigtländer. I am also grateful to Kristin Gjesdal and Dalia Nassar for their valuable comments on an early draft of this chapter and to Simon Mussell for copyediting it.

References

Aeschbach, Sebastian. "Ressentiment: An Anatomy." PhD diss., University of Geneva, 2017.

Avé-Lallemant, Eberhard. *Die Nachlässe der Münchener Phänomenologen in der Bayerischen Staatsbibliothek*. Wiesbaden: Otto Harrassowitz, 1975.

Avé-Lallemant, Eberhard, and Karl Schuhmann. "Ein Zeitzeuge über die Anfänge der phänomenologischen Bewegung: Theodor Conrads Bericht aus dem Jahre 1954." *Husserl Studies* 9 (1992): 77–90.

---

[71] See, for instance: Aeschbach, *Ressentiment*, and Wiesing, *Ich*, 186–192 and 209–214.

[72] Kristin Gjesdal, "History, Dialogue, and Feeling: Perspectives on Hermeneutic Relativism," in *The Routledge Handbook of Philosophy of Relativism*, ed. Martin Kusch (London: Routledge, 2019), 107–113; Íngrid Vendrell Ferran, "Möglichkeiten von Frauen in der ersten Phase wissenschaftlicher Schulenbildung. Emotionen und Sozialität in der frühen Phänomenologie," *Feministische Studien* 26, no. 1 (2008): 48–64.

Barth, Thomas. "Else Voigtländer's Thoughts on Psychoanalysis." In *Else Voigtländer. Self, Emotion, and Sociality*, edited by Ingrid Vendrell Ferran, 47–69. Cham: Springer, 2023.

Fréchette, Guillaume. "Searching for the Self: Early Phenomenological Accounts of Self-Consciousness from Lotze to Scheler." *International Journal of Philosophical Studies* 21, no. 5 (2013): 654–679.

Fréchette, Guillaume. "Phenomenology and Characterology. Austrian and Bavarian." In *Else Voigtländer. Self, Emotion, and Sociality*, edited by Ingrid Vendrell Ferran, 163–180. Cham: Springer, 2023.

Gahlings, Ute. "Else Voigtländer on Sexual Difference: An Early 20th Century Gender Theory?" In *Else Voigtländer. Self, Emotion, and Sociality*, edited by Ingrid Vendrell Ferran, 181–198. Cham: Springer, 2023.

Geiger, Moritz. "Fragment über den Begriff des Unbewussten und die psychische Realität." *Jahrbuch für Philosophie und phänomenologische Forschung* 4 (1921): 1–137.

Geiger, Moritz. *The Significance of Art*. Edited by Klaus Berger. Lanham, MD: University Press of America, 1986.

Geiger, Moritz. "Zum Problem der Stimmungseinfühlung." In *Die Bedeutung der Kunst: Zugänge zu einer materialen Wertästhetik*, edited by Klaus Berger and Wolfhart Henckmann, 18–59. Munich: Fink, 1976.

Gjesdal, Kristin. "History, Dialogue, and Feeling: Perspectives on Hermeneutic Relativism." In *The Routledge Handbook of Philosophy of Relativism*, edited by Martin Kusch, 107–113. London: Routledge, 2019.

Haas, Willy. *Über Echtheit und Unechtheit von Gefühlen*. Nurnberg: Benedikt Hilz, 1910.

Hagengruber, Ruth E. "The Stolen History—Retrieving the History of Women Philosophers and Its Methodological Implications." In *Methodological Reflections on Women's Contribution and Influence in the History of Philosophy*, edited by Sigridur Thorgeirsdottir and Ruth Edith Hagengruber, 43–63. Cham: Springer, 2020.

Heffernan, Georg. "Phenomenology, Psychology, and Ideology: A New Look at the Life and Work of Else Voigtländer." *Phenomenological Investigations* 1 (2020).

Heffernan, Georg. "An Ordinary Woman: Else Voigtländer and the National Socialism", In *Else Voigtländer. Self, Emotion, and Sociality*, edited by Ingrid Vendrell Ferran, 223–242. Cham: Springer, 2023.

Henrich, Dieter. "Konstellationsforschung zur klassischen deutschen Philosophie." In *Konstellationsforschung*, edited by Martin Mulsow and Marcelo Stamm, 15–30. Frankfurt am Main: Suhrkamp, 2005.

Hermanns, Ludwig M. "Karl Abraham und die Anfänge der Berliner Psychoanalytischen Vereinigung." *Abhandlungen zur Geschichte der Medizin und der Naturwissenschaften* 81 (1997): 174–188.

Jardine, James, and Thomas Szanto. "Empathy in the Phenomenological Tradition." In *The Routledge Handbook of Philosophy of Empathy*, edited by Heidi Maibom, 86–97. London: Routledge, 2017.

Landweer, Hilge. "Authenticity and Mask: Critical Self-Reflections on Else Voigtländer," in *Else Voigtländer. Self, Emotion, and Sociality*, ed. by Ingrid Vendrell Ferran, 141–162. Cham: Springer, 2023.

Lipps, Theodor. *Fühlen, Wollen und Denken. Eine psychologische Skizze*. Leipzig: Johann Ambrosius Barth, 1903.

Loidolt, Sophie, and Petra Gehring. "Psychologizing Politics, Neglect, and Gender: Applications of Voigtländer's Scientific Characterology." In *Else Voigtländer. Self, Emotion, and Sociality*, edited by Ingrid Vendrell Ferran, 199–222. Cham: Springer, 2023.

Parker, Rodney, and Dermot Moran. "Editors' Introduction." *Studia Phaenomenologica* XV (2015): 11–24.

Pfänder, Alexander. "Zur Psychologie der Gesinnungen: Erster Artikel." *Jahrbuch für Philosophie und phänomenologische Forschung* 1 (1913): 325–404.

Reinach, Adolf. *Three Texts on Ethics*. Translated by James Smith and Mette Lebech. Munich: Philosophia Verlag, 2017.

Reinach, Adolf. "Über Phänomenologie." In *Sämtliche Werke* I, edited by Karl Schuhmann and Barry Smith, 530–551. Munich: Philosophia Verlag, 1989.

Rodax, Natalie, Markus Wrbouschek, Katharina Hametner, Sara Paloni, Nora Ruck, and Leonard Brixel. "Ressentiment as Morally Disclosive Posture? Conceptual Issues from a Psychological Point of View." *Review of Philosophy and Psychology* (2021).

Rossiter, Margaret. "The Matilda Effect in Science." *Social Studies of Science* 23 (1993): 325–341.

Salice, Alessandro. "The Phenomenology of the Munich and Göttingen Circles." In *Stanford Encyclopedia of Philosophy*. Stanford University, 1997–. Article published August 3, 2015; last modified Nov 5, 2020. https://plato.stanford.edu/archives/win2020/entries/phenomenology-mg.

Salice, Alessandro. "Else Voigtländer on Social Self-Feelings," in *Else Voigtländer. Self, Emotion, and Sociality*, ed. by Íngrid Vendrell Ferran, 125–140. Cham: Springer, 2023.

Santis, Daniele de. "Theodor Conrad. Zum Gedächtnis Edmund Husserls (Ein unveröffentlichter Aufsatz aus der Bayerischen Staatsbibliothek)." *Husserl Studies* 38, no. 1 (2021): 55–66.

Sartre, Jean-Paul. *Being and Nothingness*. Translated by Hazel E. Barnes. New York: Washington Square Press, 1993.

Scheler, Max. *Formalism in Ethics and Non-formal Ethics of Values*. Translated by Manfred S. Frings and Roger L. Funk. Evanston, IL: Northwestern University Press, 1973.

Scheler, Max. "The Idols of Self-Knowledge." In *Selected Philosophical Essays*, translated by David R. Lachterman, 3–97. Evanston, IL: Northwestern University Studies in Phenomenology and Existential Philosophy, 1973.

Scheler, Max. "Phenomenology and the Theory of Cognition." In *Selected Philosophical Essays*, translated by David R. Lachterman, 136–201. Evanston, IL: Northwestern University Studies in Phenomenology and Existential Philosophy, 1973.

Scheler, Max. *Ressentiment*. Translated by Lewis B. Coser and William W. Holdheim. Milwaukee: Marquette University Press, 2010.

Scheler, Max. "Shame and the Feelings of Modesty." In *Person and Self-Value*, translated by Manfred S. Frings, 1–86. Dordrecht: Nijhoff, 1987.

Schmidt, Philipp. "Value in Existence: Lotze, Lipps, and Voigtländer on Feelings of Self-Worth", in *Else Voigtländer. Self, Emotion, and Sociality*, edited by Íngrid Vendrell Ferran, 25–46. Cham: Springer, 2023.

Schuhmann, Karl. "Daubert-Chronik." In *Karl Schuhmann. Selected Papers in Phenomenology*, edited by Cees Liejenhorst and Piet Steenbakkers, 279–354. Dordrecht: Kluwer, 2005.

Smid, Reinhold Nikolaus. "'Münchener Phänomenologie'—Zur Frühgeschichte des Begriffs." In *Pfänder-Studien*, edited by Herbert Spiegelberg and Eberhard Avé-Lallemant, 109–153. The Hague: Nijhoff, 1982.

Spiegelberg, Herbert. *The Phenomenological Movement*. Boston: Nijhoff, 1982.

Stein, Edith. *On the Problem of Empathy*. Translated by Waltraut Stein. Washington, DC: ICS, 1989.

Uemura, Genki, "Between Love and Benevolence: Voigtländer, Pfänder, and Walther on the Phenomenology of Sentiments," in *Else Voigtländer. Self, Emotion, and Sociality*, edited by Íngrid Vendrell Ferran, 71–88. Cham: Springer, 2023.

Uemura, Genki, and Toru Yaegashi. "Alexander Pfänder." In *The Routledge Handbook of Phenomenology of Emotion*, edited by Thomas Szanto and Hilge Landweer, 63–71. London: Routledge, 2020.

Vendrell Ferran, Íngrid. *Die Emotionen. Gefühle in der realistischen Phänomenologie*. Berlin: Akademie, 2008.

Vendrell Ferran, Íngrid. "Möglichkeiten von Frauen in der ersten Phase wissenschaftlicher Schulenbildung. Emotionen und Sozialität in der frühen Phänomenologie." *Feministische Studien* 26, no. 1 (2008): 48–64.

Vendrell Ferran, Íngrid. "Ressentiment and Self-Deception in Early Phenomenology: Voigtländer, Scheler, and Reinach," in *Else Voigtländer. Self, Emotion, and Sociality*, edited by Íngrid Vendrell Ferran, 103–124. Cham: Springer, 2023.

Vendrell Ferran, Íngrid. *Else Voigtländer. Self, Emotion, and Sociality*. Cham: Springer 2023.

Voigtländer, Else. "Bemerkungen zur Psychologie der Gesinnungen." In *Neue Münchener Philosophische Abhandlungen: Alexander Pfänder zu seinem sechzigsten Geburtstag gewidmet von Freunden und Schülern*, edited by Ernst Heller and Friedrich Löw, 143–164. Leipzig: Barth, 1933.

Voigtländer, Else. "Über das Wesen der Liebe und ihre Beziehung zur Sexualität." In *Verhandlungen des I. Internationalen Kongresses für Sexualforschung, veranstaltet von der Internationalen Gesellschaft für Sexualforschung Berlin vom 10. bis 16. Oktober 1926, Dritter Band: Psychologie, Pädagogik, Ethik, Ästhetik, Religion*, edited by Max Marcuse, 189–196. Berlin: A. Marcus, 1928.

Voigtländer, Else. "Über die 'Art' eines Menschen und das Erlebnis der 'Maske': Eine psychologische Skizze." *Zeitschrift für Psychologie und Physiologie der Sinnesorgane* 92 (1923): 326–336.

Voigtländer, Else. "Über die Bedeutung Freuds für die Psychologie." In *Münchener philosophische Abhandlungen: Theodor Lipps zu seinem sechzigsten Geburtstag gewidmet von früheren Schülern*, edited by Alexander Pfänder, 294–316. Leipzig: Barth, 1911.

Voigtländer, Else. *Über die Typen des Selbstgefühls*. Leipzig: R. Voigtländer, 1910.

Voigtländer, Else. "Zur Phänomenologie und Psychologie des 'alpinen Erlebnisses.'" *Zeitschrift für angewandte Psychologie* 33 (1923): 258–270.

Voigtländer, Else. "Zur Psychologie der politischen Stellungnahme: Eine massenpsychologische Studie." *Deutsche Psychologie* 3 (1920): 184–206.

Wiesing, Lambert. *Ich für mich. Phänomenologie des Selbstbewusstseins*. Berlin: Suhrkamp, 2020.

Yaegashi, Toru. "Erotic Love and the Value of the Beloved," In *Else Voigtländer. Self, Emotion, and Sociality*, edited by Íngrid Vendrell Ferran, 89–102. Cham: Springer, 2023.

CHAPTER 13

··

HEDWIG CONRAD-MARTIUS (1888–1966)

··

RONNY MIRON

THE *San Francisco Examiner* reported on September 22, 1912, under the headline "German Fraulein Is a Clever Thinker," the following:

> People who dislike clever woman [*sic*] are in a tragic mood. The Cleverest philosopher in Germany is a woman, and a brand-new woman, too.
>
> Hedwig Martius has had her book on philosophy crowned and prized by Goettingen University [*sic*]. A 21-year-old girl, with the round, pleasant features of an everyday German hausfrau, has beaten the cleverest brains of Germany.[1]

These words report the event marking the first appearance in the phenomenological discourse of one of the first women to have studied at a grammar school (*Gymnasium*) in Germany: Hedwig Conrad-Martius (1888–1966).[2] In 1912, she won an essay competition of the Philosophy Department of the University of Göttingen with her treatise titled *The Epistemological Foundations of Positivism* (*Die Erkenntnistheoretischen Grundlagen*

---

[1] This citation is taken from a photograph of a newspaper cutting that is stored in the Bavarian State Archive in Munich and catalogued under the title *Zeitungsveröffentlischungen zur Preisschrift* 1912. The fact that the "prize essay" had been composed by a young woman also bred resentment among senior faculty at Göttingen University. In this regard, the journalist cited the following: "if women begin with philosophy, they will go further. They will degenerate to the condition of their English suffragist sisters, and take to breaking windows." Hedwig Conrad-Martius, [Aus der Studienzeit, Zeitungsbericht], 1912, Conrad-Martiusiana, D.I 2 [Nachlass], Bavarian State Archive, Munich.

[2] In 1903, Conrad-Martius enrolled in the Gymnasialkurse für Frauen at the Helene Lange School in Berlin, and in fall 1907/1908 she received her Abitur at the Sophien-Realgymnasium in Berlin. See: Ursula Avé-Lallemant, "Hedwig Conrad Martius," *Jahrbuch der Evangelischen Akademie Tutzing* 15 (1965/1966): 206; Alexandra Elisabeth Pfeiffer, *Hedwig Conrad-Martius: Eine Phänomenologische Sicht auf Natur und Welt* (Würzburg: Orbis Phenomenologicus, Königshausen and Neumann, 2005), 23. See here my extensive introduction to her thinking: Ronny Miron, *Hedwig Conrad-Martius: The Phenomenological Gateway to Reality*, second edition (Springer International, 2023), 3–89.

des Positivismus).[3] The essay, later referred to as the "Prize Essay" (*Preisschrift*),[4] was found worthy of the prize due to its being "profound, original, and striking."[5] Her formative studies of philosophy were at the Ludwig Maximilian University of Munich, where it dawned on her that philosophy was her calling. With the encouragement of Moritz Geiger (1880–1937), whose courses on psychology and art history at Munich University she attended, Conrad-Martius moved to Göttingen in the fall of 1910/1911 to attend the courses of Edmund Husserl (1859–1938) and Adolf Reinach (1883–1917).[6] Conrad-Martius went to Göttingen in the winter semester of 1910–1911 together with a group of young philosophers from the University of Munich. This event was nicknamed by the local phenomenologists "The Munich Invasion of Göttingen."[7] The group, in fact the first generation of phenomenologists contemporary with Husserl, is known as the Munich-Göttingen Circle or the Munich Circle.[8] Soon after her arrival in Göttingen, Conrad-Martius became the living spirit and the driving force of the group. Thus, in 1911 she chaired the seminar of the Göttingen young phenomenologists

---

[3] Hedwig Conrad-Martius, *Die Erkenntnisstheoretischen Grundlagen des Positivismus* (Bergzabern: Heinrich Müller), 1920, private print. References to Conrad-Martius's sources include the year of publication with the year of composition in brackets. All translations from the German original into English are mine. Emphases follow the original.

[4] Avé-Lallemant was the first to coin the phrase. See: Eberhard Avé-Lallemant, *Phänomenologie und Realität, Vergleichende Untersuchungen zur 'München-Göttinger' und 'Freiburger' Phänomenology* (Habilitationsschrift). Ludwig Maximilian University of Munich, 1971, 52, 213. See also Eberhard Avé-Lallemant, "Die Nachlässe der Münchener Phänomenologen in der Bayrischen Staatsbibliothek, Catalogus Codicum manu scriptorium Bibliothecae Monacensis," VOL. 10, pt. 1 (*Wiesbaden: Otto Harrassowitz, 1975), 193.

[5] Conrad-Martius, H. (1912). [Aus der Studienzeit, Zeitungsbericht], Conrad-Martiusiana, D.I 2 [Nachlass]. Bavarian State Archive (BSM) in Munich.

[6] Hedwig Conrad-Martius, "Acceptance Speech at the Ceremony for the Award of the Order of Merit of the Federal Republic of Germany, March 1st 1958," *Studia Phenomenologica* 15 (2015): 52–63, here 61. For more information regarding Conrad-Martius's studies at Munich, see Susi Ferrarello, "Introduction Hedwig Conrad-Martius: 'Having and Being Existence,'" *Studia Phenomenologica* 15 (2015): 51–55, here 52 n. 1. For the courses Husserl delivered in Göttingen during that time period, see Karl Schuhmann, *Husserl-Chronik- Denk- und Lebensweg Edmund Husserls* (Dordrecht: Springer Science + Business Media, 1977), 67–198.

[7] Wilhelm Schapp, "Erinnerungen an Edmund Husserl," in *Edmund Husserl 1859–1959—Recueil Commémoratif Publié A L'occasion De Centenaire De La Naissance Du Philosophe*, ed. Herman Leo van Vreda and Jacques Taminiaux (The Hague: Nijhoff, 1959), 20.

[8] Among the leading members of the Circle were Alexander Pfänder, Johannes Daubert, Moritz Geiger, Theodor Conrad, Adolf Reinach, Maximilian Beck, Max Scheler, and Jean Hering. The younger members of the group were Hans Lipps, Dietrich von Hildebrand, Alexandre Koyré, Roman Ingarden, Edith Stein, and Hedwig Conrad-Martius. The group received various names; see Miron, *Hedwig Conrad-Martius*, 7–11; Juris Rosenwald, "The Phenomenological Ontology of the Göttingen Circle," *Analecta Husserliana* 27 (1989): 11–35; Eberhard Avé-Lallemant, "Die Antithese Freiburg-München in der Geschichte der Phänomenologie," in *Die Münchener Phänomenologie, Vorträge des Internationalen Kongresses in München 13.-18. April 1971*, ed. Helmut Kuhn, Eberhard Avé-Lallemant, and Reinhold Gladiator (The Hague: Nijhoff, 1975), 23; Herbert Spiegelberg, *The Phenomenological Movement*, 1st ed., vol. 1 (The Hague: Nijhoff, 1960), 168; Franz Georg Schmücker, "Die Phänomenologie als Methode der Wesenerkenntnis, unter besonderer Berücksichtigung der Auffassung der München-Göttinger Phänomenologenschule" (diss., 1956), 7.

and was eventually appointed chair of the Philosophical Society in Göttingen (Die philosophische Gesellschaft Göttingen).[9] In all these early settings, where the participation of a woman was unusual, Conrad-Martius stood out as an original and daring intellectual. She was known as the "first lady" of German philosophy.[10]

This chapter discusses three constitutive layers in Conrad-Martius's phenomenological study of reality or Being: the phenomenal, the ontological, and the metaphysical. Each of the layers is distinguished by an inaugurating question: "where do we encounter [essences] in concrete realization?," "what is reality?," and "where does the world remain?," respectively. The discussion unveils the inadequacies pertaining to each of the three layers and the dynamic between them that ends with their joining together in the metaphysical plane. Finally, since Conrad-Martius remained faithful to her early philosophical insights, the layered observation based on her early writings is suggested as a key for understanding her thinking as a whole.

1 HUSSERL'S PHENOMENOLOGY AND THE MUNICH-GÖTTINGEN CIRCLE

Edmund Husserl, the founding father of phenomenology, rose to prominence in Göttingen with the publication of *Logical Investigations* (1900–1901). In this work, he first established the call of "go back to the 'things themselves' [auf die 'Sachen selbst' zurückgehen]."[11] This call encapsulated his early struggle against psychologism, relativism, and various forms of reductionism,[12] and particularly his demand that

---

[9] Previously, the related *Society* was chaired by Theodor Conrad (1881–1969) up to the summer semester of 1912, with breaks, during which his place was filled by Conrad-Martius (summer semester 1911, winter semester 1911–12) and Dietrich von Hildebrand (1889–1977). Feldes describes the group as constantly admitting new members, who later composed the group that became known as the Munich-Göttingen Group. In this context, see Joachim Feldes, *Das Phänomenologenheim, Der Bergzaberner Kreis im Kontext der frühen Phänomenologische Bewegung* (Nordhausen: Traugott Bautz, 2015), 30–32; Eberhard Avé-Lallemant and Karl Schuhmann, "Ein Zeitzeuge über die Anfänge der phänomenologische Bewegung: Theodor Conrad Bericht aus dem Jahre 1954," *Husserl Studies* 9 (1992): 77–90.

[10] James G. Hart, "Phenomenology and the Unearthing of Heaven," in *Hedwig Conrad-Martius' Ontological Phenomenology*, ed. Rodney Parker, 217–233 (Cham: Springer, 2020); James G. Hart, "Hedwig Conrad-Martius," *Minerva's Owl* D-I (1973): 14–19, here 14.

[11] The phrase appeared in Husserl's writings in several contexts; see Edmund Husserl, *Logische Untersuchungen, Untersuchungen zur Phänomenologie und Theorie der Erkenntnis* (The Hague: Nijhoff, 1984), §4, 17–18, §22–23. This saying has also been discussed extensively in connection to the realistic orientation in phenomenology; see Josef Seifert, "Was ist Philosophie? Die Antwort der realistischen Phänomenologie," *Zeitschrift für philosophische Forschung* 49, no. 3 (1995): 92–103; Helmut Kuhn, "Phänomenologie und Realität," *Zeitschrift für philosophische Forschung* 23, no. 3 (1969): 397–402; Schmücker, *Die Phämenologie*.

[12] Edmund Husserl, *Logische Untersuchungen, Prolegomena zur reinen Logik* (The Hague: Nijhoff, 1975), §23, §31.

consciousness be studied independently of the thinking subject.[13] Already at the time of *Logical Investigations*, this call was referred to as the slogan of phenomenology, implying an unmistakable revolt against the neo-Kantian "back to Kant." The latter was addressed to the then-dominant idealistic and materialistic theories of knowledge in the name of the possibility of a universal scientific truth, whose supreme ideal was the Kantian "thing-in-itself."[14] By contrast, Husserl's endeavors paid attention to what is already known or even clearly seen. To this end, whatever presents itself to consciousness must be approached and understood on its own terms while avoiding addressing any category external to it. The subsequent elaboration of Husserl's early call in *Ideas* from 1913 was consolidated as "the principle of all principles," that is "accepting *every* primordial dator [sic] intuition . . . *as it gives itself out to be*, though *only within the limits in which it then presents itself.*"[15] For Husserl, this attitude to the given not only marks "an *absolute beginning*" for phenomenological study but also promises that knowledge that is based on an awareness of phenomena can be presented to us "as it were in its bodily reality."[16] Against this background, the phenomenologists from Munich, who perceived themselves as "confirmed realists [entschiedende Realisten],"[17] would establish the so-called "turn to the object [Die Wende zum Objekt]."[18] This trend of the Munich School would echo in Conrad-Martius's later designation of the phenomenological approach to reality as a "veil" falling "away from the eyes."[19]

Among the various topics Husserl addressed in *Logical Investigations*, "essence intuition" (*Wesensfassung*) had a formative influence on the phenomenologists of the Munich-Göttingen Circle, who regarded it not just as Husserl's most essential achievement but also as the genuine core of phenomenology. Following him, they were convinced that the objects perceived and the ways in which they are known are founded upon the lawfulness of essence (*Wesensgesetze*),[20] stemming from the things themselves

---

[13] Husserl, *Logische Untersuchungen*, §66

[14] For further reading, see Thomas E. Willey, *Back to Kant: The Revival of Kantianism in German Social and Historical Thought, 1860–1914* (Detroit: Wayne State University Press, 1978).

[15] Edmund Husserl, *Ideen zu einer reinen Phänomenologie und Phänomenologischen Philosophie: Allgemeine Einführung in die reine Phänomenologie*, bk. 1, ed. Karl Schuhmann (The Hague: Nijhoff, 1952), §24, 51.

[16] Husserl, *Ideen* (1), §24, 51.

[17] Edith Stein, *Aus dem Leben einer jüdischen Familie: und weitere autobiographische Beiträge*, ESGA (Edith Stein Gesamtausgabe) I, ed. Neyer Maria Amata OCD (Freiburg: Herder, 2002), 200.

[18] Moritz Geiger, "Alexander Pfänder methodische Stellung." In *Neue Münchener Philosophiche Abhandelungen*, ed. E. Heller and F. Löw, 1–16. (Leipzig: Johann Ambrosius Barth, 1933), 13. The trend is widely discussed in the literature in: Seifert, "Was ist Philosophie?"; Kuhn, "Phänomenologie und Realität"; Íngrid Vendrell-Ferran, *Die Emotionen, Gefühle in der realistischen Phänomenologie* (Berlin: Akademie, 2008), 71–78.

[19] Conrad-Martius, "Acceptance Speech," 61. The image of a "veil" falling appears in Conrad-Martius's critique of Idealism (see Hedwig Conrad-Martius, "Seinsphilosophie," In *Schriften zur Philosophie*, vol. 1, 44; Hedwig Conrad-Martius, "Dasein, Substantialität, Seele," in *Schriften zur Philosophie*, vol. 1, 195) and Positivism (see Conrad-Martius, *Die Erkenntnisstheoretichen Grundlagen*, 1), within which they were accused of philosophical "blindness."

[20] Husserl, *Logische Untersuchungen* 1, 10.

and capable of being directly grasped by the art of phenomenological intuition. The objective of this method was designated by Reinach as revealing the essential "what" (*was/Washeit*) that makes something into this specific object, "while break[ing] through with theories and constructions."[21] Reinach further explained this method as follows: "there is no accidentally-being-so in essences, but rather a necessarily-having-to-be-so, and an essentially-cannot-be-otherwise." Moreover, he maintained that direct access to things is aimed at leading us not only to the essences we have "already" intended but also to new essences that must be discovered and brought into the gaze.[22]

The literature expresses no unanimity regarding the meaning attributed by the members of the Circle to the call to "go back to the 'things themselves'" and to Husserl's *Logical Investigations* in general.[23] However, whatever the Circle's understanding of Husserl's early thinking, in no way could it align with his transcendental turn in *Ideas*.[24] In this book, Husserl's focus was given to whatever presents itself to consciousness while avoiding addressing any category external to it.[25] Moreover, the ideal of "absolute beginning" that guided Husserl's search for "*'unities of meanings'*"[26] was meant to overcome the "abyss of sense" gaping between Being as consciousness and Being as reality.[27] Accordingly, his transcendental phenomenology was consolidated as "the sphere of absolute clarity, of immanence in the true sense"[28] and as "the sphere of the absolutely given."[29] These determinations entailed Husserl's identification of givenness with absoluteness or his regarding givenness as a measure of the absolute. However, since appearance takes place before one's consciousness, consciousness itself is conceived in Husserl's transcendental phenomenology as a realm of givenness and therefore also of absoluteness. To this extent, Husserl regarded consciousness as the only plane in which

[21] Adolf Reinach, "Concerning Phenomenology," trans. Willard Dallas, *Personalist* 50, no. 2 (1969): 194–221, here 220.

[22] Reinach, "Concerning Phenomenology," 210.

[23] Avé-Lallemant and Schuhmann rightly noted that the esteem in which the members of the Munich Circle held Husserl's *Logical Investigations* should not be seen as mere acceptance (Avé-Lallemant and Schuhmann, "Ein Zeitzunge," 78). A more critical approach was expressed by Landgrebe, who accused them of "method-less intuition" (Ludwig Landgrebe, *Der Weg der Phänomenologie, Das Problem Einer Ursprünglichen Erfahrung* [Güterslohe: Gred Mohn, 1963], 21), and Rosenwald, who maintained that their view of phenomenology "was easily transformed into religious faith. This opened to phenomenology a path towards irrationalism" (Rosenwald, "The Phenomenological Ontology," 19).

[24] Husserl's transcendental turn was revealed publicly in the lectures given at Göttingen University in 1906/07 (posthumously published in Edmund Husserl, *Die Idee der Phänomenologie, Fünf Vorlesungen*, ed. Walter Biemel [The Hague: Nijhoff, 1950]) and announced in print with the publication of his *Ideas* in 1913 (Husserl, *Ideen zu einter reinen*). However, the change in his thinking had occurred already in 1905; see Walter Biemel, "Einleitung des Herausgegebers to *Die Idee der Phänomenologie*," by Edmund Husserl, ed. Walter Biemel, vii–xi (The Hague: Nijhoff, 1950), vii; Nakhnikian, George. Introduction to *The Idea of Phenomenology*, by Edmund Husserl, ix–xxii. ed. George Nakhnikian, transl. William P. Alston and George Nakhnikian (The Hague: Nijhof, 1964).

[25] See here also: Stein, *Aus dem Leben*, 201.

[26] Husserl, *Die Idee der Phänomenologie*, §55, 120.

[27] Husserl, *Die Idee der Phänomenologie*, §49, 105. See also: Husserl, *Die Idee der Phänomenologie*, §85.

[28] Husserl, *Die Idee der Phänomenologie*, 10.

[29] Husserl, *Die Idee der Phänomenologie*, 14.

phenomenology should take place. Moreover, precisely within the boundaries of consciousness, the desired absoluteness might be achieved. Hence, beyond the study of consciousness, there is nothing of importance for phenomenology. Finally, for Husserl, metaphysics is merely the science of beings that are absolutely given to consciousness and thus consolidated as pure consciousness.

In the face of these developments in the thinking of the "masters," as nicknamed by the members of the Munich-Göttingen Circle,[30] the phenomenologists from Munich discovered that the very thing for which they had gathered around Husserl in Göttingen had largely dissipated. The reaction to the new position revealed in Husserl's turn to transcendentalism is voiced by Conrad-Martius as follows:

> there is not only the pure consciousness, there is not only the existing human person. There is not only what is relative to pure consciousness directed intentionally, not only everything that is relative to the existential [existenziell] that is caring for the world, that is projected, and experiencing existence personally. There is also the world itself in its very own independency-of-Being [Seinsunabhängigkeit] in regard to consciousness and also from the existing "I" [Ich]. . . . Such independence of Being belongs to the essence of the real world! If the world in which we live possessed no independence of Being . . . then there would be no real world, only a fake real [vorgetäuscht Wirklische].[31]

An explicit and consistent precedence provided by the members of the Munich Circle to ontology over epistemology underlies these unmistakable words. Conrad-Martius describes this deliberate philosophical stance as the atmosphere among the phenomenologist friends. In her words: "we got completely out of the habit of making any kind of epistemological, scientific, arbitrary speculative assumptions or drawing respective conclusions."[32] Elsewhere, she adds that Husserl himself "was indifferent toward epistemology just as we ontological phenomenologists were always indifferent. This too we learned from our great teacher [Meister]."[33] However, her personal voice in this regard was loud and clear when she argued that in principle epistemological questions can be grasped only from the objective stance of the real to which the metaphysical dimension

---

[30] Conrad-Martius, "Acceptance Speech," 61; Hedwig Conrad-Martius, "Die transzendentale und die ontologische Phänomenologie," in *Schriften zur Philosophie*, vol. 3, 402; Herbert Spiegelberg, "Epilogue: For the Third Generation of Phenomenologists Contributing to This Volume," in *Phenomenology in Practice and Theory*, ed. W. S. Hamrick, 251–254 (London: Springer, 1985), 253. See here also Stein, E. (2001). *Selbstbildnis in Briefen III: Briefe an Roman Ingarden*, ESGA 4, Bearbeitung und Anmerkungen von Maria Amata Neyer OCD [Ordo Carmelitarum Discalceatarum], Fußnoten mitbearbeitet von Eberhard Avé-Lallemant. Freiburg, Basel, and Vienna: Herder, 38–42; Stein, *Aus dem Leben*, 201.

[31] Hedwig Conrad-Martius, "Phänomenologie und Spekulation," in *Schriften zur Philosophie*, vol. 3, 374–375.

[32] Conrad-Martius, "Acceptance Speech," 62. In the literature, the shift from epistemology to ontology is referred to as "the process of 'ontologization' in twentieth-century western philosophy" (Rosenwald, "The Phenomenological Ontology," 11).

[33] Conrad-Martius, "Die transzendentale," 402.

relates directly.[34] She further explains that "the *epistemological* sphere in no way relates to the question of being able to prove these 'essences' as concrete elements of the real world. We believe that philosophy, in a genuine and rigorous sense, stands outside any (epistemological) question of reality."[35] Later, Conrad-Martius would go so far as to present epistemology as a burden whose removal would enable entry into the realm of metaphysics, the destination of phenomenology.[36] Finally, the connection of these unequivocal and sweeping arguments regarding Husserl's epistemology is also not left unarticulated by Conrad-Martius. Thus, against the background of her criticism of his transcendentalism, she maintains: "finally, Husserl appears as one who found the entrance to a genuine epistemological philosophy."[37]

For his part, Husserl was incapable of tolerating the new facets his students from Göttingen University revealed in phenomenology and described them as "remaining stuck in ontologism and realism,"[38] "half-measures [Halbheiten] fearing the radicalism of the necessary essence of phenomenology."[39] Regarding Conrad-Martius in particular, he asserted: "[she] was never really my student and she consciously rejected the ethos of philosophy 'as a rigorous science.'"[40] In addition, he delivered in person these unpalatable words: "I cannot join your metaphysical ways. Your philosophizing is fundamentally different from what I call phenomenology. I no longer expect you will have the time and inner freedom to enter my large, arduous works that are based on extensive research, in which you will understand what I call phenomenology—this is, of course, the assumption of any acceptance or rejection."[41] Thus, for Husserl, not only did the writings of the Munich phenomenologists not constitute real phenomenology or even philosophy, but they could only be valid as individual scientific achievements. Over the years, the break with the students from Munich who followed Husserl to Göttingen proved irreparable.[42]

---

[34] Hedwig Conrad-Martius, Nachwort to *Die erkenntnisstheoretischen Grundlagen des Positivismus* (Bergzabern: Heinrich Müller, 1920), 130.

[35] Conrad-Martius, "Zur Ontologie und Erscheinungslehre der realen Außenwelt. Verbunden mit einer Kritik positivistischer Theorien," *Jahrbuch für Phänomenologie und philosophische Forschung* 3 (1916): 355.

[36] Hedwig Conrad-Martius, "Was ist Metaphysik?," in *Schriften zur Philosophie*, vol. 1, 48.

[37] Conrad-Martius, "Die transzendentale," 395.

[38] Husserl is cited from: Herbert Spiegelberg, "Perspektivenwandel. Konstitution eines Hesserlbildes," in *Edmund Husserl 1859–1959—Recueil Commémoratif Publié A L'occasion De Centenaire De La Naissance Du Philosophe*, ed. Herman Leo van Vreda and Jacques Taminiaux (The Hague: Nijhoff, 1959), 60.

[39] Edmund Husserl, Husserl to Dorion Cairns, March 21, 1930, in Vreda and Taminiaux, *Edmund Husserl 1859–1959—Recueil Commémoratif Publié*, 285.

[40] Edmund Husserl, *Briefe an Roman Ingarden, Miterläuterungen und Erinnerungen an Husserl*, ed. Roman Ingarden (The Hague: Nijhoff, 1968), 23. Notwithstanding, in the literature, Conrad-Martius is frequently mentioned as Husserl's student. See Avé-Lallemant and Schuhmann, "Ein Zeitzeuge," 79.

[41] Edmund Husserl, "Briefwechsel," in *Edmund Husserl Dokumente*, ed. Karl Schuhmann (The Hague: Kluwer, volume 3, 2: Die Münchener Phänomenologen. Dordrecht: Kluwer, 1994), 19–20.

[42] See Spiegelberg's testimony about his last meeting with Husserl in 1926: Spiegelberg, "Perspektivenwandel," 60–61.

2 THE PHENOMENAL LAYER: "WHERE DO WE ENCOUNTER [ESSENCES] IN CONCRETE REALIZATION?"

The phenomenal layer in the study of reality is established in "On the Ontology and Doctrine of Appearance of the Real External World,"[43] (hereafter: *Doctrine of Appearance*). Based on Husserl's method of "essence intuition" (*Wesenserfassung*), which Conrad-Martius described as "the genuine philosophical task [Aufgabe],"[44] Conrad-Martius articulates two questions whose objective is similar: In what real way are essences given to us? and "where do we encounter them in concrete realiza-tion?"[45] Both questions are addressed to the realm that is referred to as "sensory givenness [sinnlicher Gegebenheit]." In particular, the realm in which the "sensorially given [sinnlicher Gegeben]" is scrutinized as "a sort of "sensory appearance givenness [sinnlicher Erscheinungsgegebenheit]" rather than as manifesting a sensation experi-enced by the subject.[46]

Alternatively, in the phenomenal layer, primacy is given to the object of "sensory givenness," as distinguished from focusing on the senses as an expression of a subjective experience involving objects. Conrad-Martius argues that "the totally peculiar and very own nature of the sensory given"[47] enables it to establish " 'real contact' [Realkontakt]" with the external world.[48] In the first place, among all the existences of the external world, the "sensory given" has the ability to approach me as a content of givenness, since it can make its real existence, in its "here and now," clear and comprehensible in-itself and from itself outward.[49] Second, the sensory given as such, as it were, "raises

---

[43] This treatise is based on Conrad-Martius's dissertation, "The Epistemological Foundation of Positivism. On the Ontology and the Doctrine of the Appearances of the Real External World": Hedwig Conrad-Martius, "Die erkenntnisstheoretischen Grundlagen des Positivismus. Zur Ontologie und Erscheinungslehre der realen Außenwelt," 1913, Conrad-Martiusiana, A.I 2 [Nachlass], Bavarian State Archive, Munich (hereafter "Zur Ontologie"). The dissertation was an elaboration of the first chapter of the "Prize Essay," titled "The Epistemological Elements of Positivism" (Conrad-Martius, *Die Erkenntnishtheoretischen Gundlangen*, 10–24) and was directed by Alexander Pfänder. In July 1912, the dissertation was submitted to the University of Munich and eventually published with minor revisions in Husserl's *Jahrbuch* (Conrad-Marius, "Zur Ontologie").

[44] Conrad-Martius, "Zur Ontologie," 348.

[45] Conrad-Martius, "Zur Ontologie," 356.

[46] Conrad-Martius, "Zur Ontologie," 399.

[47] Conrad-Martius, "Zur Ontologie," 398.

[48] Conrad-Martius, "Zur Ontologie," 423, 425. Like Conrad-Martius, Spiegelberg justified relying on sensory data within a realistic perception. In this regard, he argues that a careful phenomenological scrutiny of immediate phenomena of reality might dismiss objections regarding the reliability of perception mediated by the senses. See Herbert Spiegelberg, *Doing Phenomenology: Essays on and in Phenomenology* (The Hague: Nijhoff, 1975), 153.

[49] Conrad-Martius, "Zur Ontologie," 412.

from itself" the claim of its real and factual existence. She maintains that it belongs to the "'façade' [Gesicht] of the sensory *appearance*" in a way that cannot be factually separated from the worldly-external existence of real existence, to inform me about itself and thus "personally brings its existence into presentation."[50] These qualities of the "sensory given" enable it to mediate between me and the factual and organized being of the real external world. Moreover, since the essence of the sensory given is manifested in what Conrad-Martius refers to as "the character of self-performance [Selbstdarbietungs eigenschaft]," which enables the self-presentation of the external world,[51] it appears to be the ultimate means that can guarantee for me the external world in its spatial and temporal factuality. Likewise, it is maintained that sensory givenness possesses a mediative role in regard to reality due to its fundamental "real contact [Realkontakt]" with the real world.[52] Thus, provided that essentiality belongs to a particular phenomenal state of affairs,[53] as postulated by Conrad-Martius, givenness and existence are bound together. However, she clarifies that sensory appearances lack the aim of "discovering" the "thing in-itself" existing within these appearances. Rather, they aim to bring the "world itself to 'exposure' [Aufdeckung]"[54] as "a self-standing entity [selbstständige Entität]."[55] Hence, arguing for the reality of appearances does not entail identifying with each other real things and their appearances, but they remain standing for what they are, that is, appearances of reality.

In this regard, Conrad-Martius introduces her view of the "surface [Oberfläch]" of things that is first encountered in appearances.[56] She asserts that one can never reach the internal side of things through any real possible cutting open of the given thing.[57] However, the "surface" is not merely a "random cut of a complete thing" but "the visible

---

[50] Conrad-Martius, "Zur Ontologie," 422. Spiegelberg explains that actual things in the world do not modify when they enter into relation with us and are presented to us. Spiegelberg calls the phenomena in which we are involved "subjectival," not in the sense that they do not have real existence or that they are deceptive, but that they are objective parts of the subject and of his world, see Spiegelberg, *Doing Phenomenology*, 134–135. Moreover, in his view the reality of the subjectival phenomena of reality is completely certain (Spiegelberg, *Doing Phenomenology*, 149). Yet the subjectival reality constitutes only a very small part of our total reality and of reality as a whole (Spiegelberg, *Doing Phenomenology*, 135).

[51] Conrad-Martius, "Zur Ontologie," 411, 494.

[52] Conrad-Martius, "Zur Ontologie," 423, 425. Like Conrad-Martius, Spiegelberg also emphasizes what can be referred to as the "claim" of reality entailed in real existence. In this context, he defines a "phenomenon of reality" as one where the phenomenal object presents itself along with the argument about its being real. Therefore, a reality-phenomenon is one that is both positioned as real and distinguished from "mere phenomena" that do not claim reality. See Spiegelberg, *Doing Phenomenology*, 133.

[53] Conrad-Martius, "Zur Ontologie," 349.

[54] Conrad-Martius, "Zur Ontologie," 463.

[55] Conrad-Martius, "Zur Ontologie," 466.

[56] The concept of "surface" is central to Conrad-Martius's illumination of the material being and of materiality in general; see in this regard: Hedwig Conrad-Martius, *Realontologie*, bk. 1, *Jahrbuch für Philosophie und phänomenologische Forschung* 6 (1923): §55–§56, 205–206. This concept is also discussed in: Conrad-Martius, *Realontologie*, §37, 194; §57–§61, 206–209; §72, 214; §107, 235–236.

[57] Conrad-Martius, "Zur Ontologie," 465 n. 1.

external side of matter in general, which encounters the in principle invisible 'interior' [Innere] of the matter."[58] This contact of the "surface" with the internal depth of real things might explain also the related self-performance of the sensory given, regarded as simultaneously describing the material internality that constitutes the appearances of the external world. This implies that the sensory "surface" does not only denote the presented aspect of the thing, but it also embodies its reality, namely it "exists in-itself."[59] Conrad-Martius clarifies that the "self-presentation" of a thing is closely related to the phenomenon of reality. To this extent, she distinguishes sensory givenness from everything that "has no being for itself." This concerns first and foremost perceived objects that rely on objective consciousness, and hence might lack outwardly presenting existence from and by itself.[60] Therefore, what appears as dependent on its existence, including dependence on the objectivization of consciousness, cannot appear as self-presenting.[61] Finally, despite the sensory appearance not being the totality of the external world, Conrad-Martius considers pure observation of what they present by themselves and in themselves, as distinguished from what is above and beyond them, as "a frame for the whole of the study" and as "guidance to the order of this embroiled and complicated state of affairs" of sensory givenness.[62]

Along with consolidating the view regarding the real external world being manifested throughout the sensory givenness, Conrad-Martius introduces another line of argumentation within which the very aspect of externality, understood as mediating the being of the world via the sensory givenness, is problematized. The inceptive argument in this regard concerns the understanding that sensory givenness manifests merely what she refers to as a "semblance of reality [Aussehen einer Realität]"[63] or "a semblance [Anschein] of real presence-being [Gegenwärtigsein] that does not correspond to a factual presence-being [tatsächliches Gegenwärtigsein]."[64] Thus, she distinguishes between "phenomenal starting material [phänomenales Anfangsmaterial]" and a "genuine phenomenon [echte Phänomene]" or "primordial phenomena [Urphänomene]." The phenomenal given serves as a departure point in the philosophical investigation of the objective forms of possible consciousness[65] and of their essence, whose present condition is of "concealment [Verhültheit] and distance."[66] That is, the thing is connected to the object itself, yet its essence is not totally revealed, except to the conscious or sensory

---

[58] Conrad-Martius, "Zur Ontologie," 463.

[59] Conrad-Martius, "Zur Ontologie," 464.

[60] Conrad-Martius, "Zur Ontologie," 413.

[61] Conrad-Martius, "Zur Ontologie," 413 n. 2. Spiegelberg construes that lack of dependence on the side of the subject is "a very fundamental and essential *consequence* of reality" (except in the case of real action of the subject that obviously depends upon him). See Spiegelberg, *Doing Phenomenology*, 132 n. 2.

[62] Conrad-Martius, "Zur Ontologie," 399.

[63] Conrad-Martius, "Zur Ontologie," 441, n. 1.

[64] Conrad-Martius, "Zur Ontologie," 356, 380. Regarding the "semblance of reality" typical of objects of representation, see Conrad-Martius, "Zur Ontologie," 356, 441 n. 1.

[65] Conrad-Martius, "Zur Ontologie," 351.

[66] Conrad-Martius, "Zur Ontologie," 352.

relation toward it. In her opinion, "the specific phenomenological-philosophical work starts for us in the progress from the still covered, although as such it is already visible primordial-phenomenon [Urphänomen], to the 'pure primordial phenomenon.'" This operation first requires the specific phenomenological stance (*Haltung*), in which the entirely direct and undeterred gaze is aimed at the phenomenon in its "pure 'what [Was].'"[67] Conrad-Martius determines that "unveiling" the reality of a thing entails discerning all that is coincidental in it, all that appears only to me or merely "'from a certain side'" of the phenomenon, "whereas the remaining essential totality lies in darkness." However, after removing these contingencies, and only then, when the phenomenon "steps out in full objectivity and absoluteness," does the philosophical work reach its completion[68] and the related "genuine phenomenon" or "primordial phenomenon" is revealed.

Against this background, Conrad-Martius distinguishes between two types of objects: overt, characterized as "unveiled-self-emerging [unverhüllte Selbsthervortreten]," and covert, described as "covered presentiveness [verdeckter Anschaulichkeit]."[69] The status of the two types of objects is not equivalent in the study of the external world. Conrad-Martius states that only "uncovered-self-emerging [unverhüllte Selbsthervortreten]," which she later terms "self-announcing [Selbstkundgabe]," grants an unmediated guarantee through the object's factual thusness and self-existence.[70] Thus, the study of the external world must first rely on the study of the "uncovered-self-emerging" of the sensory given, meaning on overt objects. Hence, not only is the sought essence revealed and clarified through the study of the appearance itself. More generally, the study of reality can never obtain independence from the phenomenal appearance itself, but a careful observation of the phenomenal appearance is indispensable in the phenomenological investigation of the external world.

At the same time, what is being uncovered throughout the study of appearances is also their incapacity to deliver the reality of the given in its entirety. This results primarily from the fact that not everything that is given belongs to the phenomenal primordial material or is rooted in it.[71] Nor can a "'factual' [sachliche]" that is often referred

---

[67] Conrad-Martius, "Zur Ontologie," 352.

[68] Conrad-Martius, "Zur Ontologie," 353.

[69] Conrad-Martius, "Zur Ontologie," 371, 380–881.

[70] Conrad-Martius, "Zur Ontologie," 371. Conrad-Martius continued to deal with the relation between the object's thusness and its selfness in her other writings. See, for example, Hedwig Conrad-Martius, *Das Sein* (Munich: Kösel, 1957), 57. For further reading, see Ebel's critique of phenomenological realism, Gerhard Ebel, "Untersuchungen zu einer Realistischen Grundlegung der Phänomenologischen Wesensschau" (diss., Ludwig Maximilian University of Munich, 1965), 2, 42, Seifert's enthusiastic view of the same (Seifert, "Was ist Philosophie?," 97–98), and Heinemann's stance that favored providing precedence to the study of appearances; Fritz Heinemann, "Erscheinen und Sein: Prologmena zu einer Konkreten Phänomenologie," in *Sinn und Sein, Ein philosophisches Symposion*, ed. Richard Wisser, 183–192 (Tübingen: Max Niemeyer, 1960).

[71] Conrad-Martius, Hedwig. "Zur Ontologie und Erscheinungslehre der realen Außenwelt. Verbunden mit einer Kritik positivistischer Theorien." *Jahrbuch für Phänomenologie und philosophische Forschung* 3 (1916): 345–542, here 351.

to as "'objective' groundedness [Habitus]" be considered as "real rootedness [reale Gegründetheit]"[72] in the sense that a "real moment in concrete reality corresponds with it."[73] These discoveries amount to the understanding that the ontology of the external world cannot be exhausted in the study of phenomenal appearances but raises from itself the need for completion.

The philosophical achievement of Conrad-Martius in *Doctrine of Appearance* exists not only in the rich complexity unveiled in the realm of appearance and the articulation of the foundational principles pertinent to its study. No less than that, the novelty bursting forth from this extremely loaded piece concerns the manifestations of the boundaries inherent in the very attempt to study the external dimensions of reality as such. In particular, as a metaphysical disposition, on the one hand, realistic observation cannot be exhausted in the level of externality, while on the other, the realism of the "covered" objects should be affirmed. Moreover, arriving at a metaphysical view of the external world is bound up with the complex insight that the "overt" object is not simply tantamount to the manifest and the "covert" to the "primordial." Rather, as much as overt objects possess an internal core, so also the covert ones possess presentiveness (*anschaulichkeit*), that is, external aspects. Unavoidably, the reflective path that accompanies the endeavor to account for boundaries that were manifested throughout the phenomenal study of appearances eventually leads Conrad-Martius's thinking beyond the confines that constituted *Doctrine of Appearance*. This takes place in *Realontologie* from 1923, composed subsequently to *Doctrine of Appearance*.

3 THE ONTOLOGICAL LAYER: "WHAT IS REALITY?"

The inaugurating postulate in the ontology of Conrad-Martius is that the one and only philosophically meaningful primordial difference concerns existence and nonexistence.[74] In her view, what distinguishes that which "is" from that which "is not" encompasses "the entire fullness of further specific real-ontological determinations and contradictions."[75] In this regard, Conrad-Martius portrays real beings as "elevating" themselves from nonexistence or from mere ideal and formal existence.[76] Thus, placing

---

[72] For further reading, see Miron, "The Metaphysical Absolutizing." Or the updated version, Miron, *Hedwig Conrad-Martius*, 399–424.

[73] Conrad-Martius, "Zur Ontologie," 351.

[74] The view of finite being as created by God out of nothingness (*ex nihilo negative*) underlies this determination. Likewise, she maintains, "there is truth in speaking about boundless beyond measure *fullness* of Being [Seinsfülle]. The Being of God is . . . *however* every height and depth, the external and the internal inexhaustible penetrating 'element.'" Hedwig Conrad-Martius, "Sein und Nichts," in *Schriften zur Philosophie*, vol. 1, 97.

[75] Conrad-Martius, *Realontologie*, 160.

[76] Conrad-Martius, *Realontologie*, 173.

the related difference at the outset of her discussion is meant to pave her way to tackling the question "what is reality?"[77] In connection with this all-inclusive question, she intends to discern the "constitutive moments that are essentially included in real existence" in order to clarify "the point with which real existence stands and falls."[78] These moments enable the real being to meet what Conrad-Martius postulates as the "task of Being [Seinsaufgabe]" of the real being, namely: to describe personally and precisely the essence that generates it; to be outside the absolute and "boundless void";[79] to be carried within substantial fullness; to be unified with itself and to be contained in-itself.[80]

Each of these "requirements," so to speak, involves both abstract and concrete dimensions that take part in the consolidation of the real being. In addition, they mirror Conrad-Martius's view of the structure of the real being as composed of two inseparable constituents: the essence or the "whatness" of the thing, and the "bearer [Träger]" upon which the essence is "loaded" and that signifies the content of the real being. She establishes that when the essence constitutes itself, it personally carries a bearer that fills the real being with content.[81] A reciprocal relation takes place between these two elements: the bearer is specified by the essence that is loaded onto it and by which it exists, while the essence is carried to the extent that it specifies its bearer. Together, the two consolidate an absolute shape (*Gebilde*) in-itself,[82] a unity in which the specifier and the specified are at the same time the borne and the loaded.[83] In this respect, the constituting elements of real being are portrayed as "formally completely chained together and instructing one another" and as "emerging [into existence] [*entstehen*]" at the same time."[84] Finally, just as the essence and the bearer are bound together in the real being, so also it is impossible to distinguish its abstract aspects from the concrete ones. Nonetheless, in some of the elements elaborated throughout the discussion in *Realontologie* the abstract aspect is more recognizable, while in others the concrete aspect is first manifested. The discussion hereafter will exemplify the abstract aspect through illumination of the element of "Selfness [Selbsthaftigkeit]" while the concrete one will be elucidated in connection with the element of "Corporeality [Leibhaftigkeit]."

3.1 Selfness

This element is first introduced in *Doctrine of Appearance* in connection with the autonomy of the external world vis-à-vis the consciousness and the "I" in general. In this

---

[77] Conrad-Martius, *Realontologie*, 159.

[78] Conrad-Martius, *Realontologie*, 161.

[79] Conrad-Martius, *Realontologie*, 225 n. 2.

[80] Conrad-Martius, *Realontologie*, 225.

[81] Conrad-Martius, *Realontologie*, 167.

[82] Conrad-Martius, *Realontologie*, 167–168.

[83] Conrad-Martius, *Realontologie*, 171.

[84] Conrad-Martius, *Realontologie*, 172.

context, Conrad-Martius regarded the external world as a real being,[85] self-standing in being (*Seinselbstständigkeit*)[86], closed in-itself and transcendent to consciousness and spirit.[87] However, in *Realontologie,* the reality of the element of the self is explicitly articulated as constitutive of the real being that accordingly is referred to as "self-full [selbsthäftig]" or subordinated to itself. Conrad-Martius explains that by the very fact of loading an essence on its bearer (*Träger*), the latter establishes itself as "standing [stehend]." The inseparability of "standing" and "subordination [Unterstehen]" means in this regard that the bearer carries the essence by the very fact of being subordinated to it, while the essence finds in the bearer its "seat [Sitz]" or "a position of your own [Eigenposition]."[88] In addition, only reality has a stance of its own, and vice versa: everything that has a stance of its own is real by that fact alone.[89] Moreover, the real being has an aspect of selfness, since an essence is being carried in it and through this fact achieves a stance in it. However, as here "stance" is not necessarily regarded as denoting a concrete place but primarily an essential rootedness of a thing, no requirement of an outward realization is ascribed to the real being in *Realontologie.* Rather, possessing or, better, being "'a position of your own' [Eigenposition]" indicates "'self-bearingness' [Selbst-Trägerschaft]."[90] Thus, while the essence achieves "personal dwelling [Wohnstätte]" in the real being,[91] the formal and ideal representations are exhausted in mere shape (*Eingeformtsein*), lack a real bearer, and their existence is only functional or formal and not personal.[92] Finally, the reality of the element of "selfness" is crystalized in the following determination: "a real entity became a carrier [Hypokeimenon] of its own self like Atlas that takes earth upon its 'back.'"[93]

3.2 Corporeality

This aspect concerns the capability attributed to the essence of real beings to "achieve a pattern." Whereas in the real being this might be a material pattern, in the ideal being it should be a formal pattern.[94] However, far from denoting a "mere mirror image" or a "virtual image," Conrad-Martius clarifies that corporeality is "'a real' picture" projected into the space and carried inside itself,[95] resulting in "this" corporeal being. Just like the element of "selfness," "corporeality" underlies the dual structure of the real being that

---

[85] Conrad-Martius, "Zur Ontologie," 396.
[86] Conrad-Martius, "Zur Ontologie," 391.
[87] Conrad-Martius, "Zur Ontologie," 424.
[88] Conrad-Martius, *Realontologie,* 179.
[89] Conrad-Martius, *Realontologie,* 177.
[90] Conrad-Martius, *Realontologie,* 177.
[91] Conrad-Martius, *Realontologie,* 178.
[92] Conrad-Martius, *Realontologie,* 178.
[93] Conrad-Martius, *Realontologie,* 176.
[94] Conrad-Martius, *Realontologie,* 162 n. 1.
[95] Conrad-Martius, *Realontologie,* 193 n. 1.

is composed of essence and bearer. Therefore, "when an essence reaches realization or becomes corporeal, by that fact itself a 'bearer' is established, that is upon the essence—as the content of the real existence—the bearer is 'loaded.' "[96]

In addition, the concrete facet of corporeality is manifested through the aspect of the "body [Leib]," and accordingly the real being is referred to as "a possessor of a body [Leib habende]"[97]—a possession that is manifested in its acquired "specific form."[98] In this regard, the body is construed as totally "founded on power [Kraftfundierter],[99] by means of which it bears its own activity and is enabled to a positive stepping out"[100] and as "genuinely carried outside itself."[101] In short: due to its possession of a body, the real being is established as an "absolute immanent transcendence"[102] that is capable of being realized outwardly. Having said that, it should be clarified that this outward realization in no way amounts to a condition for something to be a real being. This is implied in the affinity existing between corporeality and "corporeal givenness" articulated by Conrad-Martius as follows: since the real is corporeal, in certain conditions it can achieve corporeal givenness. However, something is not real because it is corporeally given, rather since something is real it carries inside itself the element of corporeality that can either be actually realized or not.[103] In any event, when corporeal givenness takes place, not only is this being realized as an appearing entity (*Erscheinende*) but also the thing (*Ding*) itself becomes real (*Seiende*).[104]

The affinity between the two discussed elements of "selfness" and "corporeality" is explicitly established by Conrad-Martius herself when she asserts that the real being exists "as in its very own self" and "because this self factually and genuinely is operated in it . . .—the body possessor—the corporeal!"[105] Accordingly, "corporeality" is typified as "what stamps itself . . . [as] the almost personal character of reality."[106] In this regard, she further maintains that "one can first speak about a selfness in the genuine sense where what is concerned is corporeal or a respective bearer of an unfolded essence." The opposite is true as well: only that which by its essence became corporeal and brought this essence "personally and factually" into expression has selfness that might operate as a constitutive selfness.[107] Finally, Conrad-Martius visualized her idea of the real being as "corporeality," that is, a manifestation of the "selfness," as follows:

[96] Conrad-Martius, *Realontologie*, 167.
[97] Conrad-Martius, *Realontologie*, 188.
[98] Conrad-Martius, *Realontologie*, 220.
[99] Conrad-Martius, *Realontologie*, 220.
[100] Conrad-Martius, *Realontologie*, 182.
[101] Conrad-Martius, *Realontologie*, 224.
[102] Conrad-Martius, *Realontologie*, 225–226.
[103] Conrad-Martius, *Realontologie*, 166.
[104] Conrad-Martius, *Realontologie*, 194.
[105] Conrad-Martius, *Realontologie*, 188–189.
[106] Conrad-Martius, *Realontologie*, 187.
[107] Conrad-Martius, *Realontologie*, 186.

"forasmuch as the real entity is a factual carrier [Hypokeimenon] of its own essence, it enters inside it like into its personal "gown" [Kleid]. Namely: clothing of Being [Seinskleid]. The reason is that this certain real being is nothing but (but no more) than the personal that is dressed so. The essence [of the real being] became a clothing that has grown on it or onto the—'body.' "[108] In light of these words, the real being appears as bodily and personally fulfilling its essence—a fulfillment that is nothing but its corporeality.

The years to come would show that Conrad-Martius's early assessment of the search for the pure ontological side of real things as "an absolute evolution"[109] was rather accurate, as the ontological perspective would never be left behind in her writings. Thus, later in her writings, she established the importance of the " 'science of essences of the real being' [Wesenswissenschaft vom realen Sein]" provided by ontology by its designation as an "unabbreviated complete concept of finite reality."[110] Notwithstanding, her writings from the 1930s and onward enable a case for arguing that the ontological orientation of phenomenology could not satisfy her either, hence she sought to open paths from it to metaphysics.

4 The Metaphysical Layer: "Where Does the World Remain?"

An explicit and decisive critique of post-Kantian philosophy, in particular idealism and Husserl's transcendental phenomenology, underlies the prompting question of the metaphysical layer in the thinking of Conrad-Martius, that is, "where does the world remain?"[111] She argues that "modern philosophy totally divests itself of the inconvenient 'in-itself.' Instead, this aspect has been 'transcendentally idealized' and thereby turned into an 'eternally escaping target.' "[112] At the same time, the metaphysical thesis regarding

---

[108] Conrad-Martius, *Realontologie*, 188.

[109] Conrad-Martius, *Realontologie*, 130.

[110] Hedwig Conrad-Martius, "Bemerkungen über Metaphysik und ihre methodische Stelle," in *Schriften zur Philosophie*, vol. 1, 82.

[111] Conrad-Martius, "Phänomenologie und Spekulation," 371. Conrad-Martius's direct criticism is mainly presented in Hedwig Conrad-Martius, "Die aktuelle Krisis des idealistischen Denkens," in *Schriften zur Philosophie*, vol. 1, 32–37; Hedwig Conrad-Martius, "Skizze über den Sensualismus, Phänomenalismus, Idealismus, Subjektivismus, Rationalismus, Pantheismus einerseits und einer teleologischen, Kategorialen, realistischen, kosmischen Weltauffassung un dem Theismus enderseits," 1931, Conrad-Martiusiana, A.III 4, 3 p. [Nachlass], Bavarian State Archive, Munich. In the background of this criticism is her early critical view of positivism in the "Prize Essay" (Conrad-Martius, *Die Erkenntnistheoretischen Grundlagen*) and its subsequent elaboration in *Doctrine of Appearance*. See Conrad-Martius, "Zur Ontologie," 345–347; 352; 357–358; 361–365; 378; 382–386; 390–391; 398–400; 423; 425. For further reading see Miron, "The Metaphysical Absolutizing." Or the updated version, Miron, *Hedwig Conrad-Martius*, 399–424.

[112] Conrad-Martius, "Bemerkungen über Metaphysik," 61.

the existence of the world has been rejected "in favor of a converted transcendental antithesis"[113] within which reason "remains the measure" of Being.[114] Consequently, in what she refers to as the "Platonic-Idealistic metaphysics,"[115] the study of Being has been confined to the boundaries of pure consciousness.[116] Against this background, Conrad-Martius presents her own approach as executing a "necessary methodical turn" that stands in opposition to "idealist philosophy";[117] as overcoming the "idealist world-aspect [Weltaspekt] in general that became blind to the true (substantial) Being"[118] and whose "blinding darkness" generated the false distinction between the ideal and the real that blocked the philosophical access to reality.[119] Her objective is to altogether reject "the metaphysical absolutizing of the ideal" in idealism[120] in favor of rehabilitating the facticity (*Faktizität*) within what transpires as the core concept of her metaphysics, that is, real reality (*wirkliche Wirklichkeit*).[121]

In the first place, Conrad-Martius introduces a distinction between two concepts of reality. The first concerns "reality [Wirklichkeit] as a noematic existence," while the second inquires into "the noematic moments of reality that are transcendent to consciousness." The latter is referred to as "real reality [wirkliche Wirklichkeit]"[122] and is meant to communicate the nonmental reality whose appearance and concretization outward is possible.[123] In this regard Conrad-Martius postulates the following: "the real reality . . . can never belong to the noematic-phenomenal totality [Gesamtbestand] of the world, because it concerns the factual 'standing-on-its-own' [Auf-sich-selber-Stehen] or ontological 'being grounded in-itself' [seinsmäßige 'in-sich-selber Gegründetsein'] of

---

113   Conrad-Martius, "Bemerkungen über Metaphysik," 78.
114   Conrad-Martius, "Seinsphilosophie," 19.
115   Conrad-Martius, "Seinsphilosophie," 22.
116   Conrad-Martius, "Bemerkungen über Metaphysik," 75.
117   Conrad-Martius, "Seinsphilosophie, 23.
118   Conrad-Martius, "Dasein," 195.
119   Conrad-Martius, *Realontologie*, 160.
120   Conrad-Martius, "Skizze," 2.
121   The expression *wirkliche Wirklichkeit* occurred previously in a lecture by Theodor Lipps from 1899 (Karl Schuhmann and Barry Smith, "Against Idealism: Johannes Daubert vs. Husserl's *Ideas I*," *Review of Metaphysics, A Philosophical Quarterly* 38, no. 4 [1985]: 792) and subsequently is in a manuscript of Johannes Daubert from 1904 (cited from: Schuhmann and Smith, "Against Idealism," 792 n. 39). It is mentioned also by Husserl (Edmund Husserl, *Ideen zu einer reinen Phänomenologie und phänomenologischen Philosophie: phänomenologische Untersuchungen zur Konstitution. Zweites Buch*, ed. Marly Biemel [The Hague: Nijhoff, 1952], §18 55), in the sense of the objective material thing that transcends the initial subjectivity and indicates the actual and intersubjective sphere.
122   Conrad-Martius, "Die transzendentale," 397.
123   Avé-Lallemant explains that "real reality" refers to the independent and in-itself existence of real being that preconditions any possible fulfillment of spatial-temporal existence, whereas Husserl's phenomenology accounts only for reality that can exist as an intentional unity of sensory appearances (Avé-Lallemant, "Die Antithese," 33 n. 41). Likewise, Kuhn stressed that "real reality" concerns the real as standing on its own reality rather than a phenomenon represented by the ego (Helmut Kuhn, "Phänomenologie und 'wirklich Wirklichkeit,'" in *Die Münchener Phänomenologie: Vorträge des Internationalen Kongresses in München, 13–18 April 1971*, ed. Helmut Kuhn, Eberhard Avé-Lallemant, and Reinhold Gladiator [The Hague: Nijhoff, 1971], 2).

the world and all its parts [Bestände]."[124] Acquiring a metaphysical stance is, therefore, bound with accounting for the aspect of factuality in it. In addition, the aforementioned primacy of ontology over epistemology is strictly recognizable in this foundational distinction between two ideas of reality that in turn further substantiate it.

Indeed, the aspect of factuality first occurred within the discussion of the phenomenal layer, where it was referred to as "sensory self-presenting [ein sich selbst Präsentierendes]" that is in principle capable of bringing "the 'world in-itself' into exposure."[125] In this regard, Conrad-Martius established that any claim for matter-of-factness and objectivity must find some expression in the concrete reality[126] in which finally the phenomenon "steps out in complete objectivity and totality."[127] In addition, what justified the consideration of the phenomenal aspects of appearances in *Doctrine of Appearance* concerns the essence (*Wesensbeständen*) underlying them[128]—an essence that, so she argues, "bursts forth" from the external side of the thing, referred to as the manifest "surface-appearance [Erscheinungsoberfläche]."[129] That is to say that these are the essences, which are both the object of the study of the external world and the constitutive core of its method of essence intuition, that require accounting for factuality.

Nonetheless, there exists no conflict between this articulated subordination of factuality to essences and the view of the real existence of the external world[130] as an autonomous, absolute, and independent being (*Seinselbstständigkeit*).[131] In the first place, Conrad-Martius asserts the original belonging of essences to a given phenomenal state of affairs,[132] hence the related subordination does not bring about a rupture within reality nor is it meant to be overcome. On the contrary, the primordial established importance of factuality that underlies the discussion of the phenomenal layer is reinstated and further emphasized in the later writings connected with what is here discussed as the metaphysical layer.

Conrad-Martius draws a clear line between factuality and metaphysics when arguing that "we find the genuine field of metaphysics only under the assumption of the factual reality of the world in which we are and to which we ourselves belong."[133] In this regard, metaphysics refers to the real world within its factual existence itself and for-itself. Moreover, "only in the view of that factual Being in its facticity can genuine metaphysical wonderment emanate."[134] This means that not only can no metaphysics be established without accounting for facticity, but also in the face of facticity we cannot

---

[124] Conrad-Martius, "Die transzendentale," 397.
[125] Conrad-Martius, "Zur Ontologie," 463.
[126] Conrad-Martius, "Zur Ontologie," 351.
[127] Conrad-Martius, "Zur Ontologie," 353.
[128] Conrad-Martius, "Zur Ontologie," 354.
[129] Conrad-Martius, "Zur Ontologie," 354.
[130] Conrad-Martius, "Zur Ontologie," 386.
[131] Conrad-Martius, "Zur Ontologie," 391–992.
[132] Conrad-Martius, "Zur Ontologie," 349.
[133] Conrad-Martius, "Was ist Metaphysik?," 38.
[134] Conrad-Martius, "Was ist Metaphysik?," 39.

help but establish metaphysics. In this respect, facticity appears as an indispensable consideration. In addition, given its close connection with phenomenality, facticity should be counted as the first datum of metaphysics. In her words: "facticity is an extensive partaking [mitbestimmender] factor in the qualitative basic set-up [Grundaufbau] of the existing types of Being! Hence any new type of real Being precisely conditions a new kind of metaphysical reasoning."[135]

However, in no way does the service, so to speak, provided to metaphysics by facticity concern unambiguousness. On the contrary, Conrad-Martius accentuates the mysterious element bursting forth from facticity itself, referred to also as the "something [Etwas]."[136] This aspect, so she contends, is inherent in the primordial situation (*Ursituation*) turning facticity into "the questionable in the strict sense [katexochen]!" and inducing primordial questioning (*Urfraglichkeit*) such as: How does it arrive at Being? Why does it have Being? What does it substantiate in Being? What does it obtain in Being? Why is it the way it is, as it exists?[137] In this regard, Conrad-Martius observes that "here we come across a pure, stubborn, unresolvable [unaufschließbares], readily acceptable 'that [Daβ]'! And it is precisely in this pure, insoluble stubbornness of the 'that' that the 'offensiveness' [Anstößigkeit] of facticity lies."[138] Moreover, true addressing of the problematic concerning the existence of the given world,[139] that is avoiding any escape to reasonable explanations of the sort suggested by transcendental philosophies, can meet the related autonomy and independence of the real world. Thereby not only is the postulate that "the entire metaphysical problematic applies only in a world that exists in-itself and for-itself"[140] confirmed, but facticity also transpires as making "our not-questioning [nichtfragen] almost impossible."[141]

Nonetheless, despite the articulated indispensability of metaphysics, facticity cannot serve as a reliable anchor for it, certainly not in the way it does for the positive sciences.[142] Conrad-Martius argues that metaphysics is not concerned with the very existence of the external world or bothered with proving reality as such, which is impossible anyway. Instead, facticity's bearing on metaphysics concerns its ultimate existence vis-à-vis an essential transcendent element, that is, a realm of reality external to consciousness. Accordingly, she postulates that "the metaphysical problem . . . includes in itself the permanent positioning of the transcendence [beleibende Transzendenzstellung] of the absolute."[143] Therefore, a true meeting between the problematic of facticity and that of metaphysics or even the manifestation of the one by the other requires avoiding

---

[135] Conrad-Martius, "Was ist Metaphysik?," 44.

[136] For additional references to the "something," see Conrad-Martius, "Sein und Nichts," 89; Hedwig Conrad-Martius, "Die Zeit," in *Schriften zur Philosophie*, vol. 1, 158.

[137] Conrad-Martius, "Was ist Metaphysik?," 39–40.

[138] Conrad-Martius, "Was ist Metaphysik?," 42.

[139] Conrad-Martius, "Was ist Metaphysik?," 40.

[140] Conrad-Martius, "Was ist Metaphysik?," 39.

[141] Conrad-Martius, "Was ist Metaphysik?," 42.

[142] Conrad-Martius, "Was ist Metaphysik?," 43.

[143] Conrad-Martius, "Bemerkungen über Metaphysik," 53.

consolidating their relation as that of conditioning. Alternatively, it is exactly the inadequacy of both facticity and metaphysics that binds them together. In any event, facticity cannot on its own substantiate metaphysics such that the latter becomes dependent on the former. This is unequivocally confirmed by Conrad-Martius's assertion that the real reality of the world lies in the factual "standing-on-its-own" of the world "whether it is factually given or not."[144]

EPILOGUE

The interpretation of Conrad-Martius's thinking suggested here distills three layers in her main phenomenological writings: phenomenal, ontological, and metaphysical.[145] This division primarily describes the chronological evolution of her thinking from her breakthrough with the "Prize Essay" up to the late 1930s. Specifically, the essay traces her development from the phenomenal study in *Doctrine of Appearance* from 1916, to her ontological inquiry in *Realontologie* from 1923, and concludes with her articulated metaphysical discussions in the writing composed along the 1930s. At first, the phenomenological analysis of each of the layers attempts to offer a close reading of Conrad-Martius's writings, which serve as milestones in the evolution of her thinking. Indeed, this method was revealed as a useful guide for addressing the original contents explored in each of the layers. However, the relations of the "Prize Essay" to her subsequent writings, especially the inadequacies manifested within the confines of each of the layers, remain unclear. This might require pondering the dynamic taking place from the first to the last layer, a dynamic that is not fully manifest in the overt arguments. Both the inadequacies and the dynamic generated by them were revealed as mirroring the essential constitution of the real being itself, whose unfolding eventually requires a metaphysical study.

Thus, in regard to the phenomenal plane, the inadequacy concerning the concretely given as such, which "does not always hold what it, as appearing [Erscheinende] thus and so, seems to promise,"[146] served as an impetus to push Conrad-Martius's thinking beyond the realm of the phenomenal discussion. At this point, it is worth drawing attention to the fact that the main source on which the phenomenal layer relies, that is, *Doctrine of Appearance*, is presented as an "ontology of the external world," thus hinting at the subsequent stage of the ontological layer that will be manifested in *Realontologie*. In any event, only in the writing from the period related to the metaphysical layer (i.e., the 1930s) was Conrad-Martius able to establish explicitly that the sensory can be fully accounted for "only through 'participation' in . . . eternal forms, values, and norms"[147] and

---

[144] Conrad-Martius, "Die transzendentale," 397.

[145] For a comprehensive list of Conran-Martius's writings, see Eberhard Avé-Lallemant, "Hedwig Conrad-Martius (1888–1966): Bibliographie," *Zeitschrift für philosophische Forschung* (1977): 301–309. A complete list of her literary estate: Avé-Lallemant, "Die Nachlässe," 191–256.

[146] Conrad-Martius, "Zur Ontologie," 358.

[147] Conrad-Martius, "Die aktuelle Krisis," 35.

in a priori essential relations[148] that as such are imperceptible, in that they have no phenomenal expression. Likewise, the insight that addresses the philosophical gaze beyond the current context of philosophizing recurs within the ontological layer. In this regard, Conrad-Martius asserts that coming to terms with the essential ontological constitution of the various types of facticity clears "the entry point [Eingangsstellen] and breakthrough point [Durchbruchsstellen] into the realm of metaphysics."[149] Moreover, she adds that in the case that no moment of rupture (*Bruch*) and ontological incommensurability is inherent in the philosophical investigation, no metaphysics is possible at all.[150] It turns out then that the inadequacy experienced in the first two layers, the phenomenal and the ontological, casts the thinking of Conrad-Martius onto the metaphysical plane. This implies the original presence of the metaphysical layer in the layers preceding it—a presence that is manifested as an inadequacy of that philosophical framework. If this insight is correct, then unavoidably the three layers are as primordial as they are in need of each other. Moreover, this primordiality, which concerns both originality and an incomplete stage, might be recognizable via the inadequacy swarming in each layer. At the same time, the reciprocal need of the layers activates the dynamic that ends up with their joining together in the metaphysical plane. However, for these insights to transpire there is a need for time—both the physical time that concerns the years spanning from her breakthrough with the "Prize Essay" to her writing throughout 1930s and the philosophical time that is required for philosophical understanding to ripen.

Finally, the analysis presented in this chapter suggests that the division of the thinking of Conrad-Martius into three layers exceeds methodical considerations. Therefore, in addition, shifting from one layer to the other does not leave behind the previous layer. Moreover, it is argued that the joining together of the three layers into one complex philosophical argument is recognizable via the displayed inadequacies in each of the layers. These, in turn, generated the evolution from one layer to the other and at the same time entailed continuing to ponder matters that were addressed in the previous layer. In a way, one might find an early hint of the force that first enabled the eventual joining together of the three discussed layers in Conrad-Martius's observation from 1920 regarding her philosophical path as a "progressive insight of intensified consciousness."[151]

BIBLIOGRAPHY

Avé-Lallemant, Eberhard. "Die Antithese Freiburg-München in der Geschichte der Phänomenologie." In *Die Münchener Phänomenologie: Vorträge des Internationalen Kongresses in München 13.–18. April 1971*, edited by Helmut Kuhn, Eberhard Avé-Lallemant, and Reinhold Gladiator, 19–38. The Hague: Nijhoff, 1975.

---

[148] Conrad-Martius, "Die aktuelle Krisis," 33.
[149] Conrad-Martius, "Was ist Metaphysik?," 44.
[150] Conrad-Martius, "Was ist Metaphysik?," 43.
[151] Conrad-Martius, "Nachwort," 130.

Avé-Lallemant, Eberhard. "Hedwig Conrad-Martius (1888–1966): Bibliographie." *Zeitschrift für philosophische Forschung* 31(2) (1977): 301–309.

Avé-Lallemant, Eberhard. *Die Nachlässe der Münchener Phänomenologen in der Bayrischen Staatsbibliothek, Catalogus Codicum manu scriptorium Bibliothecae Monacensis*. Vol. 10, pt. 1. Wiesbaden: Otto Harrassowitz, 1975.

Avé-Lallemant, Eberhard. "Phänomenologie und Realität, Vergleichende Untersuchungen zur 'München-Göttinger' und 'Freiburger' Phänomenology." Habilitationsschrift, Ludwig Maximilian University of Munich, 1971.

Avé-Lallemant, Eberhard, and Karl Schuhmann. "Ein Zeitzeuge über die Anfänge der phänomenologische Bewegung: Theodor Conrad Bericht aus dem Jahre 1954." *Husserl Studies* 9 (1992): 77–90.

Avé-Lallemant, Ursula. "Hedwig Conrad Martius." *Jahrbuch der Evangelischen Akademie Tutzing* 15 (1965/66): 203–212.

Biemel, Walter. "Introduction." In *Die Idee der Phänomenologie, by Edmund Husserl*, edited by Walter Biemel, vii–xi. The Hague: Nijhoff, 1950.

Conrad-Martius, Hedwig. "Acceptance Speech at the Ceremony for the Award of the Order of Merit of the Federal Republic of Germany, March 1st, 1958." *Studia Phenomenologica* 15 (2015): 51–63.

Conrad-Martius, Hedwig. [Aus der Studienzeit, Zeitungsbericht], Conrad-Martiusiana, D.I 2 [Nachlass]. Bavarian State Archive (BSM) in Munich, 1912N.

Conrad-Martius, Hedwig. "Die aktuelle Krisis des idealistischen Denkens." In *Schriften zur Philosophie*, vol. 1, 32–37.

Conrad-Martius, Hedwig. "Bemerkungen über Metaphysik und ihre methodische Stelle." In *Schriften zur Philosophie*, vol. 1, 49–88.

Conrad-Martius, Hedwig. "Dasein, Substantialität, Seele." In *Schriften zur Philosophie*, vol. 1, 194–227.

Conrad-Martius, Hedwig. *Die Erkenntnistheoretischen* Grundlagen des Positivismus. Bergzabern: Heinrich Müller, 1920 (private print).

Conrad-Martius, Hedwig. "Forward." In *Die Erkenntnistheoretischen Grundlagen des Positivismus*, 130–131. Bergzabern: Heinrich Müller, 1920 (private print).

Conrad-Martius, Hedwig. "Phänomenologie und Spekulation." In *Schriften zur Philosophie*, vol. 3, 370–384. Munich: Kösel, 1965.

Conrad-Martius, Hedwig. *Realontologie*, bk. 1. In *Jarbuch für Philosophie und phänomenologische Forschung* 4 (1923): 159–333.

Conrad-Martius, Hedwig. *Schriften zur Philosophie*. Vol 1. Edited by Eberhard Avé-Lallemant. Munich: Kösel, 1963.

Conrad-Martius, Hedwig. *Schriften zur Philosophie*. Vol. 3. Munich: Kösel, 1965.

Conrad-Martius, Hedwig. *Das Sein*. Munich: Kösel, 1957.

Conrad-Martius, Hedwig. "Seinsphilosophie." In *Schriften zur Philosophie*, vol. 3, 15–31.

Conrad-Martius, Hedwig. "Sein und Nichts." In *Schriften zur Philosophie*, vol. 1, 89–100.

Conrad-Martius, Hedwig. "Die transzendentale und die ontologische Phänomenologie." In *Schriften zur Philosophie*, vol. 3, 393–402.

Conrad-Martius, Hedwig. "Was ist Metaphysik?" In *Schriften zur Philosophie*, vol. 1, 38–48.

Conrad-Martius, Hedwig. "Die Zeit." In *Schriften zur Philosophie*, vol. 1, 101–184.

Conrad-Martius, Hedwig. "Zur Ontologie und Erscheinungslehre der realen Außenwelt. Verbunden mit einer Kritik positivistischer Theorien." *Jahrbuch für Phänomenologie und philosophische Forschung* 3 (1916): 345–542.

Ebel, Gerhard. "Untersuchungen zu einer Realistischen Grundlegung der Phänomenologischen WesensschauDiss., Ludwig Maxilian Univeristy of Munich, 1965.

Feldes, Joachim. *Das Phänomenologenheim, Der Bergzaberner Kreis im Kontext der frühen Phänomenologische Bewegung*. Nordhausen: Traugott Bautz, 2015.

Ferrarello, Susi. "Introduction to Hedwig Conrad-Martius: 'Having and Being Existence.'" *Studia Phenomenologica* 15 (2015): 51–55.

Geiger, Moritz. "Alexander Pfänder methodische Stellung." In *Neue Münchener Philosophiche Abhandelungen*, edited by E. Heller and F. Löw, 1–16. Leipzig: Johann Ambrosius Barth, 1933.

Hart, James G. "Hedwig Conrad-Martius." *Minerva's Owl* D-I (1973): 14–19.

Hart, James G. "Phenomenology and the Unearthing of Heaven." In *Hedwig Conrad-Martius' Ontological Phenomenology*, edited by Rodney Parker, 217–233. Cham: Springer, 2020.

Heinemann, Fritz. "Erscheinen und Sein: Prologmena zu einer Konkreten Phänomenologie." In *Sinn und Sein, Ein philosophisches Symposion*, edited by Richard Wisser, 183–192. Tübingen: Niemeyer, 1960.

Husserl, Edmund. *Briefe an Roman Ingarden, Mit Erläuterungen und Erinnerungen an Husserl*. Edited by Roman Ingarden. The Hague: Nijhoff, 1968.

Husserl, Edmund. "Briefwechsel." In *Edmund Husserl Dokumente*, edited by Karl Schuhmann. The Hague: Kluwer Academic, volume 3, part 2: Die Münchener Phänomenologen. Dordrecht: Kluwer Academic, 1994.

Husserl, Edmund. Edmund Husserl to Dorion Cairns, March 21, 1930. In *Edmund Husserl 1859–1959—Recueil Commémoratif Publié A L'occasion De Centenaire De La Naissance Du Philosophe*, edited by Herman Leo van Vreda and Jacques Taminiaux, 283–285. The Hague: Nijhoff, 1959.

Husserl, Edmund. *Die Idee der Phänomenologie, Fünf Vorlesungen*. Edited by Walter Biemel. The Hague: Nijhoff, 1950.

Husserl, Edmund. *Ideen zu einer reinen Phänomenologie und Phänomenologischen Philosophie: Allgemeine Einführung in die reine* Phänomenologie. Vol 1. Edited by Karl Schuhmann. The Hague: Nijhoff, 1952.

Husserl, Edmund. *Ideen zu einer reinen Phänomenologie und phänomenologischen Philosophie: Phänomenologische Untersuchungen zur Konstitution*. Vol 2. Edited by Marly Biemel. The Hague: Nijhoff, 1952.

Husserl, Edmund. *Logische Untersuchungen, Prolegomena zur reinen Logik*. The Hague: Nijhoff, 1975.

Husserl, Edmund. *Logische Untersuchungen, Untersuchungen zur Phänomenologie und Theorie der Erkenntnis*. The Hague: Nijhoff, 1984.

Kuhn, Helmut. "Phänomenologie und Realität." *Zeitschrift für philosophische Forschung* 23, no. 3 (1969): 397–402.

Kuhn, Helmut. "Phänomenologie und 'wirklich Wirklichkeit.'" In *Die Münchener Phänomenologie: Vorträge des Internationalen Kongresses in München, 13–18 April 1971*, edited by Helmut Kuhn, Eberhard Avé-Lallemant, and Reinhold Gladiator, 1–7. The Hague: Nijhoff, 1971.

Landgrebe, Ludwig. *Der Weg der Phänomenologie, Das Problem einer Ursprünglichen Erfahrung*. Güterslohe: Gred Mohn, 1963.

Miron, Ronny. "Essence, Abyss and Self: Hedwig Conrad-Martius on the Non-spatial Dimensions of Being." In *Women Phenomenologists on Social Ontology*, edited by Sebastian Luft and Ruth Hagengruber, 147–167. Cham: Springer International, 2018. (An updated version appears in Miron, *Hedwig Conrad-Martius*, 373–397).

Miron, Ronny. "'The Gate of Reality': Hedwig Conrad-Martius' Idea of Reality in Realontologie." *Phänomenologische Forschungen* (2014): 59–82. (An updated version appears in Miron, *Hedwig Conrad-Martius*, 67–192).

Miron, Ronny. *Hedwig Conrad-Martius: The Phenomenological Gateway to Reality.* Cham: Springer International, Second edition, 2023.

Miron. Ronny. "The Metaphysical Absolutizing of the Ideal. Hedwig Conrad-Martius' Criticism of Husserl's Idealism." In *The Idealism-Realism Debate in the Early Phenomenological Movement*, edited by Rodney Parker, 261–284. Berlin: Springer International, 2021. (An updated version appears in Miron, *Hedwig Conrad-Martius*, 399–424).

Miron, Ronny. "The Vocabulary of Reality." *Human Studies* 38, no. 3 (2015): 331–347. (An updated version appears in Miron, *Hedwig Conrad-Martius*, 193–213).

Nakhnikian, George. "Introduction." In *The Idea of Phenomenology, by Edmund Husserl*, edited by George Nakhnikian, ix–xxii. Translated by William P. Alston and George Nakhnikian. The Hague: Nijhoff, 1964.

Pfeiffer, Alexandra Elisabeth. *Hedwig Conrad-Martius. Eine Phänomenologische Sicht auf Natur und Welt.* Würzburg: Orbis Phenomenologicus Studien, Königshausen and Neumann, 2005.

Reinach, Adolf. "Concerning Phenomenology." Translated by Willard Dallas. *Personalist* 50, no. 2 (1969): 194–221.

Rosenwald, Juris. "The Phenomenological Ontology of the Göttingen Circle." *Analecta Husserliana* 27 (1989): 11–35.

Schapp, Wilhelm. "Erinnerungen an Edmund Husserl." In *Edmund Husserl 1859-1959—Recueil Commémoratif Publié A L'occasion De Centenaire De La Naissance Du Philosophe*, edited by Herman Leo van Vreda and Jacques Taminiaux, 12–25. The Hague: Nijhoff, 1959.

Schmücker, Franz Georg. "Die Phänomenologie als Methode der Wesenerkenntnis, unter besondere Berücksichtigung der Auffassung der München-Göttinger Phänomenologenschule." Diss., Ludwig Maximilian University of Munich, 1956.

Schuhmann, Karl, and Barry Smith. "Against Idealism: Johannes Daubert vs. Husserl's *Ideas I*." *Review of Metaphysics, A Philosophical Quarterly* 38, no. 4 (1985): 763–793.

Schuhmann, Karl. *Husserl-Chronik: Denk- und Lebensweg Edmund Husserls.* Dordrecht: Springer Science + Business Media, 1977.

Seifert, Josef. "Was ist Philosophie? Die Antwort der realistischen Phänomenologie." *Zeitschrift für philosophische Forschung* 49, no. 3 (1995): 92–103.

Spiegelberg, Herbert. *Doing Phenomenology: Essays on and in Phenomenology.* The Hague: Nijhoff, 1975.

Spiegelberg, Herbert. "Epilogue: For the Third Generation of Phenomenologists Contributing to This Volume." In *Phenomenology in Practice and Theory*, edited by W. S. Hamrick, 251–254. London: Springer, 1985.

Spiegelberg, Herbert. "Perspektivenwandel. Konstitution eines Hesserlbildes." In *Edmund Husserl 1859-1959—Recueil Commémoratif Publié A L'occasion De Centenaire De La Naissance Du Philosophe*, edited by Herman Leo van Vreda and Jacques Taminiaux, 56–63. The Hague: Nijhoff, 1959.

Spiegelberg, Herbert. *The Phenomenological Movement.* The Hague: Nijhoff, 1960.

Stein, Edith. *Aus dem Leben einer jüdischen Familie: und weitere autobiographische Beiträge*, ESGA (Edith Stein Gesamtausgabe) I. Edited by Neyer Maria Amata OCD. Freiburg: Herder, 2002.

Stein, E. (2001). *Selbstbildnis in Briefen III: Briefe an Roman Ingarden*, ESGA 4, Bearbeitung und Anmerkungen von Maria Amata Neyer OCD [Ordo Carmelitarum Discalceatarum], Fußnoten mitbearbeitet von Eberhard Avé-Lallemant. Freiburg, Basel, and Vienna: Herder.

Vendrell-Ferran, Íngrid. *Die Emotionen, Gefühle in der realistischen Phänomenologie*. Berlin: Akademie, 2008.

Willey, Thomas E. *Back to Kant: The Revival of Kantianism in German Social and Historical Thought, 1860–1914*. Detroit: Wayne State University Press, 1978.

CHAPTER 14

··

GERDA WALTHER
(1897–1977)

··

RODNEY K. B. PARKER

GERDA Walther was a realist phenomenologist associated with the Munich and Freiburg phenomenological circles. A student of Alexander Pfänder and Edmund Husserl, she applied the phenomenological method to issues in social, abnormal, and parapsychology, with a particular interest in mystical and religious experiences. Walther's contributions to philosophy remained largely unrecognized until the 1990s.[1] Since then, scholars have begun the process of revisiting and critically engaging with her two major works, *Toward an Ontology of Social Communities*[2] and *Phenomenology of Mysticism*.[3]

---

[1] Linda Lopez McAlister, "Dr. Gerda Walther: German Feminist Philosopher," in *Against Patriarchal Thinking: Proceedings of the VIth Symposium of the International Association of Women Philosophers*, ed. Maja Pellikaan-Engel (Amsterdam: VU University Press, 1992): 65–69; Linda Lopez McAlister, "Gerda Walther (1897–1977)," in *A History of Women Philosophers*, ed. Mary E. Waithe, 4 vols., vol. 4 (Dordrecht: Kluwer, 1995): 189–206.

[2] Gerda Walther, *Ein Beitrag zur Ontologie der sozialen Gemeinschaften (mit einem Anhang zur Phänomenologie der sozialen Gemeinschaften)* (Halle: Niemeyer, 1922); Gerda Walther, "Zur Ontologie der sozialen Gemeinschaften (mit einem Anhang zur Phänomenologie der sozialen Gemeinschaften)," *Jahrbuch für Philosophie und phänomenologische Forschung* 6 (1923): 1–158.

[3] Gerda Walther, *Zur Phänomenologie der Mystik* (Halle: Niemeyer, 1923); Gerda Walther, *Phänomenologie der Mystik*, Second, revised edition (Olten and Freiburg im Breisgau: Walter, 1955); Gerda Walther, *Phänomenologie der Mystik*, Third, supplemented edition (Olten and Freiburg im Breisgau: Walter, 1976). An English translation of the introduction and first chapter has been published as Gerda Walther, "Phenomenology of Mysticism, Introduction and Chapter One," in *Gerda Walther's Phenomenology of Sociality, Psychology, and Religion*, ed. Antonio Calcagno (Cham: Springer, 2018): 115–133. The growing secondary literature on Walther includes: Niamh Burns, "A Modernist Mystic: Philosophical Essence and Poetic Method in Gerda Walther (1897–1977)," *German Life and Letters* 73, no. 2 (2020): 246–269; Antonio Calcagno, *Gerda Walther's Phenomenology of Sociality, Psychology, and Religion*; Emanuele Caminada, "Joining the Background: Habitual Sentiments Behind We-Intentionality," in *Institutions, Emotions, and Group Agents*, ed. Anita Konzelmann Ziv and Hans B. Schmid (Dordrecht: Springer, 2014): 195–212; Felipe León and Dan Zahavi, "Phenomenology of Experiential Sharing: The Contribution of Schutz and Walther," in *The Phenomenological Approach to Social Reality: History, Concepts, Problems*, ed. Alessandro Salice and Hans B. Schmid (Cham: Springer,

The former, her doctoral dissertation, is a pioneering work in social ontology that investigates we-experiences and the feeling of inner unification or connectedness characteristic of belonging to a community. The latter is an attempt at an objective and scientific analysis of mystical lived-experiences along with supposed instances of thought or emotional transference typically classified as parapsychological.

What follows is a brief introduction to *Toward an Ontology of Social Communities* and *Phenomenology of Mysticism*, and the lines of thought that connect them, specifically her concept of persons as psycho-spiritual beings. These texts neatly display Walther's mix of phenomenology, psychology, and sociology, highlighting her interest in anomalous or nonuniversal lived-experiences (mystical experiences, thought transference, experiences arising from mental illness, etc.) and crowd psychology. Her early works on social ontology and mysticism are also crucial to understanding her overall philosophical project, all the contours of which I will not have space to cover here, and reveal how deeply her mystical views are embedded in all her work. Herein I will not discuss Walther's later work on parapsychology in any detail. This intentional omission should not be interpreted as dismissiveness.

Many of Walther's peers, however, dismissed her work because of her belief in psychic and paranormal phenomena. Shortly after *Phenomenology of Mysticism* was published, Heidegger—whose early lectures in Freiburg Walther had attended[4]—attacked the work for mixing phenomenological research, which was supposed to be rigorous and scientific, with esotericism. He considered this a "public scandal of philosophy."[5] Similar contempt was expressed by Walther's colleagues in Munich. Circa 1930, when asked to contribute an essay to a Festschrift in honor of Pfänder's sixtieth birthday, Walther responded to the editors that she would write on the "Psychology of Telepathy." She was informed that an essay on such a subject could not be accepted.[6] It is worth mentioning the broader academic context in which this rejection of Walther's ideas occurred.

2016): 219–234; Sebastian Luft and Ruth Hagengruber, eds., *Women Phenomenologists on Social Ontology: We-Experiences, Communal Life, and Joint Action* (Cham: Springer, 2018); Linas Tranas and Emanuele Caminada, "Gerda Walther and Hermann Schmalenbach," in *The Routledge Handbook of Phenomenology of Emotion*, ed. Thomas Szanto and Hilge Landweer (London: Routledge, 2020): 133–143; Dan Zahavi and Alessandro Salice, "Phenomenology of the We: Stein, Walther, Gurwitsch," in *The Routledge Handbook of Philosophy of the Social Mind*, ed. Julian Kiverstein (London: Routledge, 2016): 515–527; Dan Zahavi, "Intersubjectivity, Sociality, Community: The Contribution of the Early Phenomenologists," in *The Oxford Handbook of the History of Phenomenology*, ed. Dan Zahavi (Oxford: Oxford University Press, 2018): 734–752.

[4] Walther attended the first three courses that Heidegger delivered in Freiburg in 1919 after being discharged from military service: "The Idea of Philosophy and the Problem of Worldview," "Phenomenology and Transcendental Philosophy of Value," and "On the Nature of the University and Academic Study"; Rodney Parker, "Gerda Walther (1897–1977): A Sketch of a Life," in Calcagno, *Gerda Walther's Phenomenology of Sociality, Psychology, and Religion*, 5n11.

[5] Martin Heidegger, *Ontology—the Hermeneutics of Facticity*, trans. John van Buren (Bloomington: Indiana University Press, 1999), 58.

[6] Gerda Walther, "On the Psychology of Telepathy," *Journal of the American Society for Psychical Research* 25, no. 10 (1931): 438n1. Walther indicates in her autobiography that she suspects Pfänder may have been involved in the decision to reject her proposal, since he had expressed that he thought

In the late nineteenth and early twentieth centuries, as psychology was distinguishing itself as a scientific discipline separate from philosophy, parapsychology was a popular subject. Respected philosophers and psychologists such as Henry Sidgwick, William James, Henri Bergson, F. C. S. Schiller, Hans Driesch, and C. D. Broad, were involved in the study of psychic and paranormal phenomena. However, the place of parapsychology within scientific psychology was not without controversy. During the early years of the International Congress for Psychology debate erupted over psychic, occult, and religious phenomena. While the study of psychic and occult phenomena was designated as pseudoscience by the majority, religion was saved by shifting the focus of research to religious *experience* and away from mystical *phenomena* as such.[7] The phenomenologists were certainly aware of this debate. In 1896, the Third International Congress for Psychology was held in Munich and presided over by none other than Carl Stumpf and Theodor Lipps.[8] Stumpf reportedly attempted to curb the influx of the spiritualists and hypnotists, but the academic society relied on their membership.[9] Whereas religious experience and belief was widely accepted by the phenomenological community, it seems publicly expressing belief in the reality of psychic and paranormal phenomena was taboo.

Thus, despite her attempts to approach the subject of mysticism objectively and scientifically, given Walther's involvement in parapsychological research beginning in the mid-1920s and her belief that she herself had encountered psychic and paranormal phenomena,[10] it is not altogether surprising that her work fell into relative obscurity. This is unfortunate given that her dissertation is one of the most extensive phenomenological accounts of social connectedness, and her *Phenomenology of Mysticism* engages with the question of whether religious experiences can be distinguished from pathological experiences.[11] As with James, Bergson, Broad, and so on, Walther's interest in psychic,

telepathy was "nonsense" on previous occasions; Gerda Walther, *Zum anderen Ufer: Vom Marxismus und Atheismus zum Christentum* (Remagen: Otto Reichl, 1960), 467.

[7] Ann Taves, "A Tale of Two Congresses: The Psychological Study of Psychical, Occult, and Religious Phenomena, 1900–1909," *Journal of the History of the Behavioral Sciences* 50, no. 4 (2014): 376–399.

[8] *Dritter Internationaler Congress für Psychologie in München vom 4. bis 7. August 1896* (Munich: Lehmann, 1897), XXI. Stumpf and Lipps supervised the Habilitations of Husserl and Pfänder respectively.

[9] Ludy Benjamin and David B. Baker, "The Internationalization of Psychology: A History," in *The Oxford Handbook of the History of Psychology: Global Perspectives*, ed. David B. Baker (Oxford: Oxford University Press, 2012), 4.

[10] One can find ample evidence for this throughout Walther's autobiography. For example, she claims to have encountered a dark "presence" at her uncle's estate in Dreiskau (Walther, *Zum anderen Ufer*, 261–262), she reports having a premonition about the future wife of a man who was courting her (268–269), and she describes one of her first experiences of thought transference (telepathy) during one of Weber's lectures (274).

[11] Walther worried that her own mystical experience, her "break from reality" as I have called it (Rodney Parker, "Gerda Walther and the Phenomenological Community," *Acta Mexicana de Fenomenología*, no. 2 (2017): 52), may have resulted from a psychotic episode (Walther, *Zum anderen Ufer*, 328–239, in reference to the experience of "falling into another world" described at 223–225). This question spurred on her research into schizophrenia (see especially Gerda Walther, "Zur innenpsychischen Struktur der Schizophrenie," *Zeitschrift für die gesamte Neurologie und Psychiatrie* 108

occult, and paranormal phenomena should not be reason to dismiss the valuable contributions she made to philosophy. This value lies in her phenomenological analyses of the essence of we-experiences, religious and mystical lived-experiences, and persons.

1 Toward an Ontology of Social Communities

Walther's foray into the topics of shared experiences and personhood began with her doctoral thesis. In the preface to her dissertation, Walther points out that Marxist philosophy has aroused her interest in the relationship between the individual and the community as well as her belief that understanding the life of the individual as a part of a community was important for a number of ethical and metaphysical problems. More specifically, she has been concerned with the problem of individual free will and social determinism. She gives special mention here to the writings of Max Adler.[12] Elsewhere she explains that she has long believed, under the influence of Marx and Adler, that people are fundamentally social-political beings, having an a priori inner spiritual connection with others. This had led to her interest in investigating the notion of a "social self."[13] Walther's Marxist background is worth noting from the outset insofar as her dissertation is an extension of her original interest in social and political theory. Walther had been raised in a deeply Marxist and atheistic household. Her father, Otto Walther, was a well-connected member of the social democratic movement in Germany, and this afforded her the opportunity to learn Marxist theory from Karl Kautsky and Gustav Eckstein prior to attending university.[14] Before connecting with Alexander Pfänder and becoming interested in philosophy and psychology, Walther's intention was to study sociology, economics, and politics.

(1927): 83–85), from which she ultimately concluded that mystical experiences are to be differentiated from the delusions of fanatics and imaginings spawned by pathological mental states (Walther, *Phänomenologie der Mystik*, 16–18). This topic is still debated in psychiatric literature; see, for example, Joseph Pierre, "Faith or Delusion? At the Crossroads of Religion and Psychosis," *Journal of Psychiatric Practice* 7, no. 3 (2001): 163–172; Ryan McKay, "Hallucinating God? The Cognitive Neuropsychiatry of Religious Belief and Experience," *Evolution and Cognition* 10, no. 1 (2004): 1–12; Ryan McKay and Robert Ross, "Religion and Delusion," *Current Opinion in Psychology* 40 (2020): 160–166.

[12] Walther, *Ein Beitrag zur Ontologie der sozialen Gemeinschaften (mit einem Anhang zur Phänomenologie der sozialen Gemeinschaften)*, III. Walther would later discuss these issues with Adler in person (Walther, *Zum anderen Ufer*, 313–314).

[13] Walther, *Zum anderen Ufer*, 270–272.

[14] Walther, *Zum anderen Ufer*, 133. Otto Walther's inner circle of friends also included the high-profile Social Democrats Wilhelm Liebknecht, August Bebel, Adolf Geck, Clara Zetkin, and Rosa Luxemburg (Walther, *Zum anderen Ufer*, 20–21). It seems that Walther spent considerable time with these figures in the years prior to her father's death.

It was with her exposure to Husserl's phenomenology and Pfänder's phenomenological psychology that Walther's approaches to social communities began to take root. Her dissertation attempts to clarify the essence of social communities and their constitution, along with the lived-experience of being part of a "we." Hence it is ontological on the one hand and phenomenological on the other. Not surprisingly, she draws heavily on the work of Husserl and Pfänder, but also from the writings of sociologist Max Weber (whose final lecture courses she attended in 1919 and 1920),[15] Edith Stein (with whom she studied in Freiburg and with whom she was acquainted as part of Husserl's inner circle of students),[16] and Max Scheler (with whom she had no direct acquaintance). Unlike Husserl, whose point of departure is the ego considered as a *solus ipse*, Walther begins from the position that there is an a priori inner connectedness among egos in the deepest layer of the self, and believes that the shared social and cultural world is the external expression of this.[17] Though this is not elaborated in detail in the text, Walther's notion of an a priori inner connectedness among egos, understood as spiritual beings, appears to have roots in her reading of Hegel, particularly his idea that individual selves are part of a single, absolute spirit.[18] This allows for not only the inner connectedness of social communities, but thought and emotional transference (in contagion or telepathy), and our ability to commune with the Divine—themes that she takes up in *Phenomenology of Mysticism*.

The word "community," Walther points out, indicates that there is something communal, something held in common that unites its members. An investigation into the essence of social communities must pay special attention to this something. She argues that this commonality must be some aspect of the mental or spiritual life of the members, some partially identical intentional content of consciousness (such as a common goal), rather than an external trait.[19] However, this identical intentional content is not a sufficient condition for the establishment of a social community. There could be situations where individuals share intentional content but have no knowledge of each other and we would not count this as a social community. In addition to knowing the other members of the community, Walther also stresses that there must be intentional reciprocal interaction among the members. By this she means the ability for the mental-life of each individual in the group to have an influence on the mental-lives of the others such that

---

[15] Parker, "Gerda Walther and the Phenomenological Community," 65.

[16] When she arrived in Freiburg, Husserl instructed Walther to take part in Stein's "philosophical kindergarten," in which Stein introduced new students to Husserl's phenomenology (Walther, *Zum anderen Ufer*, 204).

[17] Walther, *Zum anderen Ufer*, 272.

[18] Walther, "Zur Ontologie der sozialen Gemeinschaften (mit einem Anhang zur Phänomenologie der sozialen Gemeinschaften)," 112. See Walther, *Phänomenologie der Mystik*, 98, and Walther, *Zum anderen Ufer*, 237–238.

[19] Walther, "Zur Ontologie der sozialen Gemeinschaften (mit einem Anhang zur Phänomenologie der sozialen Gemeinschaften)," 19–20.

they come into an inner agreement or inner connectedness. This gives rise to a feeling of togetherness and belonging.[20]

For Walther, inner connectedness and a "feeling of belonging together" are essential to social communities. If this inner connectedness is not present, then the social group is not yet a community. Walther describes this "feeling of belonging together" as a mental wave that flows through the subject, enveloping their entire mental-life and its respective complex of lived-experiences in a warm light. The feeling of belonging and connectedness we experience when we identify as part of a community, part of something greater than ourselves and fulfilling a greater purpose, generally has a positive valence, as Walther indicates. It colors our experience of the world and ourselves in the world in a way that stands in contrast to feelings of alienation and isolation.[21] According to Walther, this feeling of belonging together is experienced as emerging not from without, but from within, from the background of the ego, penetrating into the foreground of wakeful consciousness and uniting the subject with its object.[22] She goes on to stress that it is *habitual* lived-experiences of unification with others that underpin communities and communal life.[23]

A characteristic component of communal life are we-experiences, that is, lived-experiences that I do not simply experience as *mine* but as *ours*. Insofar as we-experiences require inner connectedness and a feeling of belonging together, Walther also calls them communal lived-experiences.[24] We-experiences are to be distinguished from a mere coexperiencing, where two or more individuals experience the same object or share a similar experience, sympathy, and so on. When the members of, say, a sports team win an important game, the excitement and sense of achievement that some member of the team might experience would constitute a we-experience if they feels the others participating in that experience with them as a part of their first-person (plural) inner experience. It is not the team considered as some higher order "person" independent of the members that feels the excitement and sense of achievement. The we-experience arises and is realized in and through the members of the team.[25] This is made possible by the inner connectedness of the members. Walther writes:

[20] Walther, "Zur Ontologie der sozialen Gemeinschaften (mit einem Anhang zur Phänomenologie der sozialen Gemeinschaften)," 32–33.

[21] Of course, there may be feelings of, say, collective guilt or shame as well, embarrassment over one's membership or participation in a community.

[22] Walther, "Zur Ontologie der sozialen Gemeinschaften (mit einem Anhang zur Phänomenologie der sozialen Gemeinschaften)," 34–35. This description of the "feeling of belonging together" mirrors the one Walther gives of her first mystical experience, a communion with the Divine, which I discuss hereafter. See Walther, *Zum anderen Ufer*, 223–225.

[23] Walther, "Zur Ontologie der sozialen Gemeinschaften (mit einem Anhang zur Phänomenologie der sozialen Gemeinschaften)," 48 and 69.

[24] Walther, "Zur Ontologie der sozialen Gemeinschaften (mit einem Anhang zur Phänomenologie der sozialen Gemeinschaften)," 70.

[25] Walther, "Zur Ontologie der sozialen Gemeinschaften (mit einem Anhang zur Phänomenologie der sozialen Gemeinschaften)," 70.

"My" lived-experiences, to the extent and *only* to the extent they are precisely communal lived-experiences, do not merely arise from myself, from my isolated self, my I-myself-alone behind the Ego-point; instead they arise simultaneously from the other *in me*, from the we . . . with whom I am one. I live and experience from myself *and* from *them in me* at the same time, from "us." Already *before* these lived-experiences enter into the Ego-point, are actualized within it, they are thus communal lived-experiences, for they arise already as stimuli from myself *and* the others *in me*. . . . Thus, it is not the case that I have lived-experiences arising first from me as *isolated* single Ego and individual self, that I then compare with those of others grasped in empathy . . . and unite myself only then with these others in their lived-experiences, and grasp these lived-experiences only now retroactively as communal lived-experiences and call them such. . . . Communal lived-experiences in our sense are rather *only* those lived-experiences that come about *on the basis of my unification with the others*, from them *in me* and of me *in them*, from us . . .[26]

Walther is careful to distinguish we-experiences from instances of sympathy and empathy, feeling with and into others, respectively. In those experiences, I grasp the mental-life of the other precisely as *theirs* and *not mine*. While I might come to have an inner experience that is similar to their lived-experience, this is not a we-experience in that it is not originarily unified with the other as *ours*. They would be two fundamentally separate experiences belonging to different subjects, each having exclusive ownership over their own lived-experience. With we-experiences the others and I are a unit, common owners of our communal lived-experience.[27] Examples might be found in political movements, fandoms, religious communities, and so on.

From this brief sketch of just some of the topics discussed in Walther's dissertation, it is easy to see how her work bridges phenomenology, sociology, and social psychology. The same is true of her work on religious and mystical experiences. The lived-experience of communion with the Divine is closely related to we-experiences, as are various group experiences reported by members of religious or mystical communities. A phenomenological analysis of various types of shared experiences and the differences between them could cover topics ranging from empathy and sympathy, to emotional contagion and telepathy, to we-experiences and mass hysteria. A feeling of others *in me* could be used to describe schizophrenia, certain paranormal and psychic phenomena, and so on. Thus, the trajectory of Walther's interests is foreseeable from her initial work. I turn now to Walther's second major philosophical work.

---

[26] Walther, "Zur Ontologie der sozialen Gemeinschaften (mit einem Anhang zur Phänomenologie der sozialen Gemeinschaften)," 71–72.

[27] Walther, "Zur Ontologie der sozialen Gemeinschaften (mit einem Anhang zur Phänomenologie der sozialen Gemeinschaften)," 73–75.

2 PHENOMENOLOGY OF MYSTICISM

Walther began writing the manuscript that would eventually turn into the *Phenomenology of Mysticism* in early 1920. Thus, the text was written roughly contemporaneously with her dissertation on social ontology. The work was originally conceived as a response to an unnamed friend in Freiburg who was having doubts about "God and the world." Walther felt compelled to help this friend who, she was convinced, was struggling with an existential crisis. She decided the best approach would be to present in an impersonal and scientific manner a study of religious and mystical experiences.[28] This was a subject that Walther herself had become intimately connected with a little over a year earlier. In November 1918, while on the train back to Freiburg from Baden-Baden after visiting her dying father, Walther could feel herself sinking into a depression and worried about her mental health. She then claims she was touched by a presence that permeated and enveloped her inner being with a sense of warmth, light, and goodness.[29] Walther immediately reported this experience to Pfänder, who assured her that it was an experience of the Divine.[30] Reflecting on her own personal mystical experience, Walther quickly jotted down her initial thoughts. A copy to this manuscript was presented to Pfänder for his fiftieth birthday and another was given to Walther's friend from Freiburg.[31] Walther later searched for historical accounts of the experiences of mystics to support her work.[32]

It is worthy of note that in addition to writings of other early phenomenologists one would expect to find Walther referencing in her *Phenomenology of Mysticism*, one other name stands out prominently—Stefan George. Sometime after her experience on the train, Walther stumbled upon copies of Rudolf Steiner's *Theosophy*[33] and George's *The Seventh Ring*.[34] While Steiner's writings provided Walther with a vocabulary for describing her personal mystical experiences—even causing her to understand that she had seen the aura of Karl Kautsky's nephew in 1915[35]—George and his circle had a much more profound influence on her thought and methodology, as we see reflected in *Phenomenology of Mysticism*.[36] Interestingly, in his criticism of *Phenomenology of*

---

[28] Walther, *Zum anderen Ufer*, 262–263.

[29] Walther, *Zum anderen Ufer*, 223–325.

[30] Walther, *Zum anderen Ufer*, 263. The word Walther uses here is *Wesensgrund*—a term she identifies as Pfänder's name for the Divine (Walther, *Zum anderen Ufer*, 260).

[31] Walther, *Zum anderen Ufer*, 264. The manuscript, titled "Ein Beitrag zur (bewusstseinsmäßigen) inneren Konstitution des eigenen Grundwesens als Kernpunkt der Persönlichkeit (und Gottes)," can be found in Walther's *Nachlass* in the Bavarian State Library in Munich as Ana 317 A III 2.1.

[32] Walther, *Zum anderen Ufer*, 264. Teresa of Ávila's work *The Interior Castle* and Martin Buber's *Ecstatic Confessions* became important sources for Walther.

[33] Walther, *Zum anderen Ufer*, 254–255.

[34] Walther, *Zum anderen Ufer*, 291.

[35] Walther, *Zum anderen Ufer*, 255 (see 151).

[36] Walther attended lectures given by Friedrich Gundolf (born Gundelfinger), a member of the George-Kreis, while undertaking her ill-fated Habilitation at the University of Heidelberg. While in

Mysticism mentioned earlier, Heidegger refers derisively to the influence of the George-Kreis and Steiner.[37]

There are three editions of Walther's *Phenomenology of Mysticism*, and there are significant changes between the first and second. These revisions and additions reflect Walther's intellectual development in the years between 1923 and 1955. During those three decades Walther worked in a state mental hospital and became involved in parapsychological research. However, despite the changes the core theses of the book remain intact. In no particular order, Walther argues (1) that the capacities for free will, self-consciousness, and empathy distinguish spiritual beings from merely sentient beings; (2) that mystical experiences are distinct from both sense perceptions and the representations of dreams, imagination, memory, and hallucination; (3) that thought and emotional transference is possible without any external communication via the senses; and (4) that the purported phenomenological similarity between mystical experience and the experiences of the mentally ill is not as great as some would claim. I will only touch on some of these positions below.[38]

In the introduction to the *Phenomenology of Mysticism*, Walther explains that she is neither attempting to give a naturalistic or causal explanation concerning the origins of mystical experiences, nor attempting to prove or refute the veridicality of such experiences in terms of their correspondence with reality. We can leave aside the supernatural, metaphysical questions about whether these experiences refer to some ultimate, transcendent reality. Instead, Walther is undertaking a phenomenological analysis of religious and mystical lived-experiences, experiences that make up part of our shared world, in order to highlight the essential characteristics that distinguish them from other types of experience. She stipulates that by *mystical* experiences, she means only those experiences that claim to be direct, bodily lived-experiences of the Divine.[39]

Walther argues that to conduct an unbiased investigation of mystical experiences one must be aware of two common prejudices. The first is that it is impossible to have

---

Heidelberg, Walther also studied with Karl Jaspers and Heinrich Rickert; Parker, "Gerda Walther (1897–1977): A Sketch of a Life," 6–7. Walther later published an essay dealing with the work of another member of the George-Kreis, Ludwig Klages; Gerda Walther, "Ludwig Klages Und Sein Kampf Gegen Den 'Geist,'" *Philosophischer Anzeiger* 3, no. 1 (1928): 48–90. However, Walther's primary connection to the George-Kreis was Percy Gothein, with whom she became friends (Walther, *Zum anderen Ufer*, 297). In an earlier article, I have incorrectly stated that Walther was "romantically involved" with Gothein. Their relationship was not romantic in nature.

[37] Husserl makes similar pejorative remarks about the spread of mysticism and "spiritual" renewal movements, specifically "Steinerianism," in letters to Winthrop Bell and Thomas Masaryk; Edmund Husserl, *Briefwechsel Bd. 3: Die Göttinger Schule*, Husserliana Dokumente III (Dordrecht: Kluwer, 1994), 24–25; Edmund Husserl, *Briefwechsel Bd. 1: Die Brentanoschule*, Husserliana Dokumente III (Dordrecht: Kluwer, 1994), 114). As a historical aside, Steiner attended lectures given by Franz Brentano at the University of Vienna. See Rudolf Steiner, *Autobiography: Chapters in the Course of My Life: 1861–1907*, trans. R. Stebbing (Great Barrington, MA: SteinerBooks, 2006), 25–28.

[38] For the sake of simplicity, references throughout will be to the third edition of Walther's *Phenomenology*.

[39] Walther, *Phänomenologie der Mystik*, 21–22.

a bodily experience of the Divine, and that what mystics experience is merely a manifestation of their own psyches. There are numerous ways we might flesh out Walther's worries here. On the one hand, one might deny that bodily experiences of the Divine are possible simply because there is no Divinity. This would be the prejudice of the non-believer or anyone who presupposes the sort of metaphysical naturalism characteristic of what phenomenologists refer to as the natural attitude. Such a presupposition must be tentatively bracketed or put out of play for the purposes of phenomenological investigation. On the other hand, she might mean specifically that there can be no bodily experience of the Divine due to some underlying metaphysical issue of interaction, and what mystics "feel" taking place inside them must be caused by their own minds. In either case, the prejudice described here seems to amount to the belief that all mystical experiences are mere imaginings, hallucinations, manifestations of the subconscious, and so on. The second is the belief that all experience must be founded on sense data. Walther suggests that we must make room at least for the possibility of something like extrasensory or spiritual perception,[40] where the "data" are in some sense ineffable. She points out that mystics often speak of smells, tastes, sounds, feelings of warmth, and the "seeing" of light, but that these are all vague approximations and imperfect analogies.[41]

Since mystical experiences are anomalous, unlike universal experiences of sense perception, imagination, or memory, there are difficulties in describing them adequately. We rely on the testimony of mystics, trusting that the descriptions they can articulate of their lived-experiences more or less accurately capture and can intimate what is given in those experiences. In describing their experiences, mystics must rely on a language we all share in common, such as the language of sense data. Walther asks us to imagine a world where four-fifths of the population are born blind and only one-fifth are able to see. If those born with sight were to attempt to convey their experience of color to the blind, they would have to do so by recourse to experiences familiar to the other four-fifths, that is, they would need to translate colors into the language of sound, or touch, and so on. However, the blind would never fully know what it is like to see colors. Walther writes:

> but those who only ever hear sounds and tones could have but a very faint and unclear picture of the colours being presented to them. Only if they were suddenly able to "see" could they fully comprehend what was meant, and they would then realize that the use of certain sounds and tones as a symbol for certain colours was entirely appropriate based on an inner lawfulness and truth regarding the relations between sounds and colours. If they were only capable of seeing one colour, or a group of colours, at first, even if they were still partially colour-blind, then they would have already been given the key to the whole world of colours and its representation in the world of sounds.[42]

---

[40] Walther, *Phänomenologie der Mystik*, 28.

[41] Walther, *Phänomenologie der Mystik*, 24.

[42] Walther, *Phänomenologie der Mystik*, 26. I would be remiss here not to note the similarity between Walther's argument and Frank Jackson's famous thought experiment about Mary; Frank Jackson, "Epiphenomenal Qualia," *Philosophical Quarterly* 32, no. 127 (1982): 127–36.

Walther goes on to argue that the mere fact that the majority of people have not had mystical experiences is no proof against the correctness of their descriptions or their having had such experiences. She compares the situation with the fact that the majority cannot comprehend in the slightest the most advanced levels of mathematics. However, we do not consider mathematicians working in these areas to be engaging in mere phantasy, lies, or self-deception. The fact that such things are beyond our comprehension, that we have not experienced them, does not justify us in being skeptical of the mathematician's claims. Mystics, according to Walther, should be afforded the same treatment.[43]

Just one example of mystical or religious experience that Walther takes up is "hearing" the "voice" of God. If we look at reports of experiences of this type, we notice that what is being described is generally not an auditory hallucination like we might find in someone experiencing a psychotic episode. The language of "hearing" here is symbolic. Instead, a "voice" or a presence that is not properly described in any way other than like an auditory sensation, is *felt* in the inner being of the person undergoing the religious experience. While it is felt as arising in their heart or their head, it is not experienced as originating from their ego, but from the spiritual background of consciousness.[44] This particular type of inner experience, what some call "inner witnessing," is a nonverbal communion with the Divine. God communicates from God's spirit to the spirit of the person, and their spirit communicates this to the foreground of consciousness. As the nineteenth-century theologian William Burt Pope writes: "whether called the witness of the Spirit, the assurance of faith, or the inward light [the inward witness is] a real testimony of the Spirit to the individual soul."[45] Walther admits that hearing the voice of God could be a manifestation of the subconscious in some cases.[46] While not a hallucination, a person might be identifying their inner monologue as coming from God rather than originating in themselves. But the question of the origin of the experience is separate from the description of the experience as it is lived.

3 WALTHER'S CONCEPT OF PERSONHOOD

I have just now referenced the spirit and the inner spiritual background of the person. In Walther's dissertation on social ontology, it is in this spiritual background that I find the others *in me* when we form a community.[47] We-experiences are thus possible because we are psycho-*spiritual* beings.[48] In her *Phenomenology of Mysticism*, Walther develops

---

[43] Walther, *Phänomenologie der Mystik*, 28.

[44] Walther, *Phänomenologie der Mystik*, 165–168.

[45] William Burt Pope, *The Inward Witness: And Other Discourses* (London: Wollmer, 1885), 15.

[46] Walther, *Phänomenologie der Mystik*, 173.

[47] Walther, "Zur Ontologie der sozialen Gemeinschaften (mit einem Anhang zur Phänomenologie der sozialen Gemeinschaften)," 71.

[48] Walther, "Zur Ontologie der sozialen Gemeinschaften (mit einem Anhang zur Phänomenologie der sozialen Gemeinschaften)," 22.

her concept of the person and describes this spiritual aspect in detail. For Walther, the person is not only a social being and a being with the capacity for rational deliberation, but a spiritual being whose basic essence (*Grundwesen*)[49] unfolds within a particular cultural and historical context. This basic essence, which she also calls *entelechy*,[50] is essentially grounded in the Divine.[51]

Walther writes that "the innermost, essential core of human personhood, its *basic essence*, so to speak, is equally spiritual. Therefore, we must sharply distinguish the intellect (or reason) from the spirit in this sense."[52] In *Toward an Ontology of Social Communities* she divides the person into the trinity of ego-center, self, and basic essence.[53] I will not elaborate on this threefold division here. Instead, I will focus on Walther's concept of person as she presents it in *Phenomenology of Mysticism*. Therein she argues that the defining features of personhood are (1) free will, (2) self-consciousness, and (3) spirit.

The ability of the I to spontaneously shift and direct its attention toward objects of its own choosing, Walther writes, is the greatest achievement of the I.[54] Here she does not simply mean our ability to turn our gaze this way or that, but our ability to focus our attention on, or withdraw it from, the contents of our lived-experiences. In this way, we have some control over the formation of the self. This capacity for self-determination, the freedom of the I, marks a boundary between animal consciousness and human consciousness. Indeed, Walther argues that this is one starting point of the *spirit*. Merely sentient creatures seem to lack this capacity. They also lack the ability to identify their experiences as their own and reflect on them. This leads to the second defining feature of personhood, namely, self-consciousness. All our lived-experiences have the form "I experience something." I recognize that I am experiencing, and that my experiences belong to me. It is because we have this capacity for self-consciousness along with the freedom of the I that we can reflect on consciousness itself.[55] Finally, persons have a *spiritual core* or *spiritual basic essence*. Alluding to the affinity argument in Plato's *Phaedo*, Walther reasons that it is through our corporeal bodies that we are able to experience and come to know physical objects, and it is through the spirit that we are able to experience and know spiritual objects (other spiritual beings, cultural objects, etc.).[56] Our spiritual basic essence, along with our ability to reflect on our own mental-lives, is what allows us to have lived-experiences of other psycho-spiritual beings, that is, to empathize with them and have we-experiences, as well as mystical and religious experiences.

---

[49] Walther, "Zur Ontologie der sozialen Gemeinschaften (mit einem Anhang zur Phänomenologie der sozialen Gemeinschaften)," 15–16.

[50] Walther, "Phenomenology of Mysticism, Introduction and Chapter One," 117.

[51] Walther, *Phänomenologie der Mystik*, 34.

[52] Walther, *Phänomenologie der Mystik*, 34.

[53] Walther, "Zur Ontologie der sozialen Gemeinschaften (mit einem Anhang zur Phänomenologie der sozialen Gemeinschaften)," 55–56.

[54] Walther, *Phänomenologie der Mystik*, 38.

[55] Walther, *Phänomenologie der Mystik*, 43.

[56] Walther, *Phänomenologie der Mystik*, 44.

4 Conclusion

Herein I have only scratched the surface of Walther's thought and her large body of writings. My aim has been to highlight some of the core concepts developed in *Toward an Ontology of Social Communities* and *Phenomenology of Mysticism*, while also showing how the two works are connected. It is clear that Walther's concept of persons as psycho-spiritual beings, as beings with a spiritual basic essence, plays a pivotal role in her philosophy. While Walther's interest in psychic and paranormal experiences likely led to the scholarly neglect of her work, her interest in these experiences from a phenomenological perspective needs to be understood within the context of her broader interests, such as social psychology, abnormal psychology, and mysticism. Moreover, her early works, written before her shift to parapsychology, contain important contributions to social ontology and the study of religious experience. They are worthy of renewed consideration and should be studied alongside other pioneering texts in these fields, such as Ferdinand Tönnies's *Community and Society* and William James's *Varieties of Religious Experience*.

Bibliography

Benjamin, Ludy, and David B. Baker. "The Internationalization of Psychology: A History." In *The Oxford Handbook of the History of Psychology: Global Perspectives*, edited by David B. Baker, 1–17. Oxford: Oxford University Press, 2012.

Burns, Niamh. "A Modernist Mystic: Philosophical Essence and Poetic Method in Gerda Walther (1897–1977)." *German Life and Letters* 73, no. 2 (2020): 246–269.

Calcagno, Antonio, ed. *Gerda Walther's Phenomenology of Sociality, Psychology, and Religion*. Cham: Springer, 2018.

Caminada, Emanuele. "Joining the Background: Habitual Sentiments behind We-Intentionality." In *Institutions, Emotions, and Group Agents*, edited by Anita Konzelmann Ziv and Hans B. Schmid, 195–212. Dordrecht: Springer, 2014.

Dritter Internationaler Congress für Psychologie in München vom 4. bis 7. August 1896, Munich: Lehmann, 1897.

Heidegger, Martin. *Ontology—the Hermeneutics of Facticity*. Translated by John van Buren. Bloomington: Indiana University Press, 1999.

Husserl, Edmund. *Briefwechsel Bd. 1: Die Brentanoschule*. Husserliana Dokumente III. Dordrecht: Kluwer, 1994.

Husserl, Edmund. *Briefwechsel Bd. 3: Die Göttinger Schule*. Husserliana Dokumente III. Dordrecht: Kluwer, 1994.

Jackson, Frank. "Epiphenomenal Qualia." *Philosophical Quarterly* 32, no. 127 (1982): 127–136.

León, Felipe, and Dan Zahavi. "Phenomenology of Experiential Sharing: The Contribution of Schutz and Walther." In *The Phenomenological Approach to Social Reality: History, Concepts, Problems*, edited by Alessandro Salice and Hans B. Schmid, 219–234. Cham: Springer, 2016.

Lopez McAlister, Linda. "Dr. Gerda Walther: German Feminist Philosopher." In *Against Patriarchal Thinking: Proceedings of the VIth Symposium of the International Association of*

Women Philosophers, edited by Maja Pellikaan-Engel, 65–69. Amsterdam: VU University Press, 1992.

Lopez McAlister, Linda. "Gerda Walther (1897–1977)." In *A History of Women Philosophers*, edited by Mary E. Waithe, 4 vols., vol. 4, 189–206. Dordrecht: Kluwer, 1995.

Luft, Sebastian, and Ruth Hagengruber, eds. *Women Phenomenologists on Social Ontology: We-Experiences, Communal Life, and Joint Action*. Cham: Springer, 2018.

McKay, Ryan. "Hallucinating God? The Cognitive Neuropsychiatry of Religious Belief and Experience." *Evolution and Cognition* 10, no. 1 (2004): 1–12.

McKay, Ryan, and Robert Ross. "Religion and Delusion." *Current Opinion in Psychology* 40 (2020): 160–166.

Parker, Rodney. "Gerda Walther (1897–1977): A Sketch of a Life." In Calcagno, *Gerda Walther's Phenomenology of Sociality, Psychology, and Religion*, 3–9.

Parker, Rodney. "Gerda Walther and the Phenomenological Community." *Acta Mexicana de Fenomenología*, no. 2 (2017): 45–66.

Pierre, Joseph. "Faith or Delusion? At the Crossroads of Religion and Psychosis." *Journal of Psychiatric Practice* 7, no. 3 (2001): 163–172.

Pope, William B. *The Inward Witness: And Other Discourses*. London: Wollmer, 1885.

Steiner, Rudolf. *Autobiography: Chapters in the Course of My Life: 1861–1907*. Translated by R. Stebbing. Great Barrington, MA: SteinerBooks, 2006.

Taves, Ann. "A Tale of Two Congresses: The Psychological Study of Psychical, Occult, and Religious Phenomena, 1900–1909." *Journal of the History of the Behavioral Sciences* 50, no. 4 (2014): 376–399.

Tranas, Linas, and Emanuele Caminada. "Gerda Walther and Hermann Schmalenbach." In *The Routledge Handbook of Phenomenology of Emotion*, edited by Thomas Szanto and Hilge Landweer, 133–143. London: Routledge, 2020.

Walther, Gerda. *Ein Beitrag zur Ontologie der sozialen Gemeinschaften (mit einem Anhang zur Phänomenologie der sozialen Gemeinschaften)*. Halle: Niemeyer, 1922.

Walther, Gerda. "Ludwig Klages und sein Kampf gegen den 'Geist.'" *Philosophischer Anzeiger* 3, no. 1 (1928): 48–90.

Walther, Gerda. "On the Psychology of Telepathy." *Journal of the American Society for Psychical Research* 25, no. 10 (1931): 438–446.

Walther, Gerda. *Phänomenologie der Mystik*. Second, revised edition. Olten and Freiburg im Breisgau: Walter, 1955.

Walther, Gerda. *Phänomenologie der Mystik*. Third, supplemented edition. Olten and Freiburg im Breisgau: Walter, 1976.

Walther, Gerda. "Phenomenology of Mysticism, Introduction and Chapter One." In Calcagno, *Gerda Walther's Phenomenology of Sociality, Psychology, and Religion*, 115–133.

Walther, Gerda. *Zum anderen Ufer: Vom Marxismus und Atheismus zum Christentum*. Remagen: Otto Reichl, 1960.

Walther, Gerda. "Zur innenpsychischen Struktur der Schizophrenie." *Zeitschrift für die gesamte Neurologie und Psychiatrie* 108 (1927): 56–85.

Walther, Gerda. "Zur Ontologie der sozialen Gemeinschaften (mit einem Anhang zur Phänomenologie der sozialen Gemeinschaften)." *Jahrbuch für Philosophie und phänomenologische Forschung* 6 (1923): 1–158.

Walther, Gerda. *Zur Phänomenologie der Mystik*. Halle: Niemeyer, 1923.

Zahavi, Dan. "Intersubjectivity, Sociality, Community: The Contribution of the Early Phenomenologists." In *The Oxford Handbook of the History of Phenomenology*, edited by Dan Zahavi, 734–752. Oxford: Oxford University Press, 2018.

Zahavi, Dan, and Alessandro Salice. "Phenomenology of the We: Stein, Walther, Gurwitsch." In *The Routledge Handbook of Philosophy of the Social Mind*, edited by Julian Kiverstein, 515–527. London: Routledge, 2016.

CHAPTER 15

....

EDITH STEIN (1891–1942)

....

DERMOT MORAN

EDITH Stein (1891–1942), who, upon entering the Carmelite order in 1934, took the name "Saint Teresa Benedicta of the Cross," was a brilliant, original philosopher and phenomenologist. Born into a Jewish family, she was persecuted by the National Socialist regime and died, aged fifty-one, in Auschwitz concentration camp in 1942.[1] During her short life Stein was extraordinarily productive; her complete works run to twenty-eight volumes,[2] including translations.[3] Her philosophical writings range over phenomenology (1916–1925), political philosophy,[4] women's education and feminism (1920–1933),[5] Christian metaphysics and anthropology (1927–1942), and Christian mystical writings (1933–1942).[6] Stein made original philosophical contributions in many areas, but especially in

[1] Freda Mary Oben, *Edith Stein: Scholar, Feminist, Saint* (New York: Alba House, 1988). In recognition of her martyrdom, Teresa Benedicta of the Cross was beatified by Pope John Paul II in 1987 and canonized in 1998. This was controversial among those who considered that she died because she was of Jewish descent rather than as a martyr to her Christian faith.

[2] Edith Stein, *Gesamtausgabe* (Freiburg: Verlag Herder, 1950–2018). Hereafter GA, followed by volume and page number. Twelve volumes of the English translation, *The Collected Works of Edith Stein* (Washington, DC: Institute of Carmelite Studies, 1986–2014) (hereafter CWES) have been published to date.

[3] Stein translated, from Latin, Thomas Aquinas's *De veritate* (GA 23, 24) and *De ente et essentia* (GA 26); from English, John Henry Newman's *The Idea of the University* (GA 21) and other letters and tracts by Newman (GA 22); and, from French, Alexandre Koyré's *Descartes and the Scholastics.*

[4] See Edith Stein, "Eine Untersuchung über den Staat," *Jahrbuch für Philosophie und phänomenologische Forschung* 7 (1925): 1–123; reprinted GA 7; trans. Marianne Sawicki, *An Investigation Concerning the State*, CWES vol. 10 (Washington, DC: ICS, 2006). See Francesca De Vecchi, "Edith Stein's Social Ontology of the State, the Law and Social Acts: An Eidetic Approach," *Studia Phaenomenologica* 15 (2015): 303–330.

[5] Stein's essays on woman, women's education, and spirituality, are collected in Edith Stein, *Die Frau: Fragestellungen und Reflexionen*, ed. Lucy Gelber and Romaneus Leuven, GA 13 (Freiburg: Herder, 2010), trans. Freda Mary Oben, *Essays on Woman*, 2nd ed. (Washington DC: ICS, 2017).

[6] Her mystical writings include studies of St. John of the Cross, *The Science of the Cross*, trans. Sister Josephine Koeppel, CWES vol. 6 (Washington, DC: ICS, 2002), and Teresa of Ávila, as well as a 1941 essay, "Ways to Know God: On the Symbolic Theology of Dionysius the Areopagite," trans. Rudolf Allers,

phenomenology and philosophical anthropology. In this chapter I focus primarily on Stein's contribution to phenomenology.

In 1916, Stein completed her doctoral dissertation, *On the Problem of Empathy* (published 1917),[7] and then became Husserl's first paid personal assistant (1916–1918),[8] transcribing and editing his manuscripts, notably *Ideas II* (not published until 1952),[9] and the *Lectures on the Internal Consciousness of Time* (published 1928, edited by Martin Heidegger, with slight acknowledgment of Stein's contribution).[10] Between 1917 and 1919, Stein wrote a proposed Habilitation thesis, *Philosophy of Psychology and the Humanities*, published in Husserl's *Yearbook* in 1922.[11] This work consists of two long essays: "Psychic Causality" and "Individual and Community."

The next most significant event in Stein's intellectual development was her conversion to Catholicism in 1922, following a chance reading of the *Life of Saint Teresa of Ávila by Herself.*[12] Encouraged by her spiritual mentor, Erich Przywara SJ,[13] in the 1920s, Stein embarked on a sustained study of Aristotle, Augustine, Dionysius, St. Thomas, Duns Scotus, Newman, and modern Neo-Scholastic authors, leading to original ontological studies on the nature of substance, potency and act, essence, existence, including the principle of individuation. Stein did not abandon phenomenology, however; rather she developed an original synthesis of Husserlian phenomenology and Thomistic ontology, focusing on the nature of the human person, "essence" (*Wesen*), "being" (*Sein*), finitude, and infinitude. Stein's Christian period produced two major works of metaphysics:

Thomist 9, no. 3 (July 1946): 379–420; Edith Stein, *Faith and Knowledge*, trans. Walter Redmond, CWES vol. 8 (Washington, DC: ICS, 2000), 83–118.

[7] The title of Stein's dissertation was *Das Einfühlungsproblem in seiner historischen Entwicklung und in phänomenologischer Betrachtung* (*The Empathy Problem as It Developed Historically and Considered Phenomenologically*), published as *Zum Problem der Einfühlung* (Halle, 1917), reprinted GA 5; *On the Problem of Empathy*, trans. Waltraut Stein, CWES vol. 3 (Washington, DC: ICS, 1989), with the first historical chapter (now lost) omitted.

[8] Roman Ingarden, "Edith Stein on Her Activity as an Assistant of Edmund Husserl," *Philosophy and Phenomenological Research*, 23 no. 2 (1962/63): 155–175.

[9] Edmund Husserl, *Ideen zu einer reinen Phänomenologie und phänomenologischen Philosophie*, vol. 2, *Phänomenologische Untersuchungen zur Konstitution* (The Hague: Nijhoff, 1991), trans. R. Rojcewicz and A. Schuwer, *Ideas Pertaining to a Pure Phenomenology and to a Phenomenological Philosophy, Second Book* (Dordrecht: Kluwer, 1989). Hereafter *Ideas II*.

[10] Originally published in 1928 as E. Husserl, *Vorlesungen zur Phänomenologie des inneren Zeitbewußtseins*, ed. M. Heidegger, *Jahrbuch für Philosophie und phänomenologische Forschung* 9 (1928): 367–498; *Phenomenology of Internal Time Consciousness*, trans. James Churchill (Bloomington: Indiana University Press, 1964).

[11] Edith Stein, *Beiträge zur philosophischen Begründung der Psychologie und der Geisteswissenschaften*. GA vol. 6 (Freiburg: Herder, 2010); *Philosophy of Psychology and the Humanities*, trans. M. C. Baseheart & M. Sawicki, CWES vol. 7 (Washington, DC: ICS). Hereafter PPH.

[12] Teresa of Ávila, *The Life of Saint Teresa of Ávila by Herself*, trans. J. M. Cohen (New York: Penguin Classics, 1998). See Florent Gaboriau, *The Conversion of Edith Stein* (South Bend, IN: St. Augustine's Press, 2002).

[13] Stein was influenced by Erich Przywara's *Analogia Entis* (1932); *Analogia Entis. Metaphysics: Original Structure and Universal Rhythm*, trans. John R. Betz and David Bentley Hart (Grand Rapids, MI: Eerdmans, 2014).

Potency and Act (1931)[14] and what she regarded as her masterpiece, *Finite and Eternal Being* (1935),[15] published posthumously.

Although Stein had "found a home in Aquinas's thought world" (PA 3; GA 10 4), she remained loyal to Husserl's phenomenological method and continued to employ it in her later works. Stein's first attempted comparison between Thomism and phenomenology was her essay "Husserl's Phenomenology and the Philosophy of St. Thomas Aquinas," contributed to Husserl's seventieth-birthday *Festschrift*, published in Husserl's *Yearbook for Philosophy and Phenomenological Research* (1929).[16] In her Münster lectures, *Constitution of the Human Person* (1932),[17] for instance, she explicitly uses the phenomenological method (guided by St. Thomas) to explore anthropology: "we will grasp the things themselves [die Sachen selbst] in our gaze" (*Aufbau* 28). This involves bracketing theories and putting oneself in the position to experience human existence and practice essential viewing (*Wesensschau*; *Aufbau* 29). Indeed, much of her comparison between Thomas and Husserl is focused on the meaning of essence and the nature and scope of the form/matter distinction.

Stein was an enthusiastic and perceptive reader of Heidegger's *Being and Time* (1927). Stein wrote a highly perceptive critique of it in the thirties,[18] offering a Christian alternative, defending human fullness and the possibility of infinite Being against Heidegger's account of Being as finitude and human existence as empty. She opposes Heidegger's emphasis on *Angst* and "nothingness" with human beings' more basic sense of "security" and "fullness" in Being, encountered in experiences of joy and love. I shall return to Stein's review later.

Despite her meditative life in the cloister, Stein remained philosophically active through her life. Stein also gained a reputation as a prominent public intellectual, with lectures and radio talks on women's education. She gave an address in Paris to the Thomist Society on the relation between St. Thomas and phenomenology, and

---

[14] Edith Stein, *Potenz und Akt. Studien zu einer Philosophie des Seins*, GA 10 (Freiburg: Herder, 2010); *Potency and Act: Studies Towards a Philosophy of Being*, trans. L. Gelber and R. Leuven, CWES vol. 11 (Washington, DC: ICS, 2009). Hereafter PA, followed by English pagination and GA volume and page number.

[15] Edith Stein, *Endliches und ewiges Sein. Versuch eines Aufstiegs zum Sinn des Seins*, ed. Andrea Uwe Müller, GA 11/12 (Freiburg: Herder, 1986); *Finite and Eternal Being: An Attempt at an Ascent to the Meaning of Being*, trans. Kurt F. Reinhardt, CWES vol. 9 (Washington, DC: ICS, 2002). Hereafter FEB.

[16] Edith Stein, "Husserls Phänomenologie und die Philosophie des hl. Thomas von Aquino," *Jahrbuch für Philosophie und phänomenologische Forschung* (1929): 315–338; Edith Stein, "Husserl and Aquinas: A Comparison," trans. Walter Redmond, in *Knowledge and Faith* (Washington, DC: ICS, 2000), 1–63. Stein originally wrote it as a dialogue between Husserl and St. Thomas, but the editor of the Festschrift, Martin Heidegger, advised her to recast it as an essay.

[17] Edith Stein, *Aufbau der menschlichen Person. Vorlesungen zur philosophische Anthropologie. Münster 1932/1933*, GA vol. 14 (Freiburg: Herder, 2000). Hereafter *Aufbau*.

[18] Edith Stein, "Martin Heideggers Existentialphilosophie," in Edith Stein, *Endliches und Ewiges Sein. Versuch eines Aufstiegs zum Sinn des Seins*, GA 11/12 (Freiburg: Herder, 2006), 445–500; "Martin Heidegger's Existential Philosophy," trans. Mette Lebech, *Maynooth Philosophical Papers* 4 (2007): 55–98. Stein's unpublished book review was not included in the original 1950 German publication of *Finite and Eternal Being* or in the English translation by Kurt F. Reinhardt (2002).

corresponded with important philosophers of the day, including Martin Heidegger, Roman Ingarden,[19] Alexandre Koyré, Jacques Maritain, and others. Her work was taken seriously by Husserl and Scheler and her fellow phenomenologists, for example, Ingarden and Conrad-Martius. In the second edition (1923) of Scheler's *The Nature of Sympathy*,[20] for instance, Scheler acknowledges Stein's critique of his work. Similarly, Merleau-Ponty cites Stein's *Philosophy of Psychology and the Humanities* (1922) in his *Phenomenology of Perception* (1945)[21] on the difference between cause and motivation (a topic also discussed by Husserl in *Ideas II* §56)

1 EDITH STEIN'S LIFE AND HER AUTOBIOGRAPHY, *LIFE IN A JEWISH FAMILY*

Stein's autobiographical *Life in a Jewish Family* (1933, published posthumously in 1950),[22] a protest against Nazi anti-Semitism, recounts her philosophical development. Born into a large family, she entered the University of Breslau (1911–1913) as a student of psychology and classical literature (*Life* 172; GA 1 102). William Stern's psychology course[23] introduced her to the personalism that would become an enduring feature of her philosophy.[24] Another Breslau psychologist, Dr. Georg Moskiewicz (1878–1918), who had spent a semester in Göttingen with Husserl, introduced Stein to Husserl's *Logical*

---

[19] She corresponded with Ingarden, a close friend from her Göttingen days, from 1917 to 1838; see Edith Stein, *Selbstbildnis in Briefen III. Briefe an Roman Ingarden*, GA 4 (Freiburg: Herder, 2001); *Self-Portrait in Letters: Letters to Roman Ingarden*, trans. H. C. Hunt, CWES vol. 12 (Washington, DC: ICS, 2014).

[20] Stein discusses Scheler's 1913 *Zur Phänomenologie und Theorie der Sympathiegefühle und von Liebe und Hass. Mit einem Anhang über den Grund zur Annahme der Existenz des fremden Ich* (Halle: Niemeyer, 1913). Scheler later produced an expanded edition in 1923 in which he acknowledges Stein's criticisms. See M. Scheler, *Wesen und Formen der Sympathie—Die deutsche Philosophie der Gegenwart*, 6th ed., ed. Manfred Frings, Max Scheler Gesammelte Werke, vol. 7 (Bern: Franke, 1973); *The Nature of Sympathy*, trans. Peter Heath (London: Routledge, 1954).

[21] Maurice Merleau-Ponty, *Phénoménologie de la perception* (Paris: Gallimard, 1945), 39; *Phenomenology of Perception*, trans. C. Smith (London: Routledge & Kegan Paul, 1962), 31.

[22] Edith Stein, *Aus dem Leben einer jüdischen Familie und weitere autobiographische Beiträge*, GA 1 (Freiburg: Herder, 2002); *Life in a Jewish Family 1891–1916. An Autobiography*, trans. Josephine Koeppel, CWES vol. 1 (Washington, DC: ICS, 1986). Hereafter *Life*.

[23] Wilhelm (later "William" in the USA) Stern (1871–1938) was a student in Berlin of the psychologist Hermann Ebbinghaus and did groundbreaking research on memory. He was also a pioneer in the psychology of personality and in child psychology (carrying out detailed observations on his own children). As a Jew, he was forced to emigrate in 1933, first to the Netherlands, and then to the United States, where he taught at Duke University. See James T. Lamiell, *William Stern (1871–1938): A Brief Introduction to His Life and Works* (Lengerich: Pabst Science, 2010).

[24] Wilhelm Stern, *Person und Sache: System der Philosophischen Weltanschauung* (Leipzig: Ambrosius Barth, 1906) (*Life* 199).

Investigations (1900/1901)[25] and remarked to her that, in Göttingen, the students "philosophize, day and night, at meals, in the street, everywhere," and talk only of the "phenomena" (*Life* 218; GA 1 132). Having read *Logical Investigations* independently, Stein decided to study with Husserl in Göttingen.

Stein transferred to the University of Göttingen in April 1913 and met with Husserl. He assigned her to his then assistant Adolf Reinach (1883–1917), who prepared students for Husserl's more advanced seminars.[26] Stein also attended external lectures by Max Scheler (1874–1928).[27] Scheler fascinated Stein, with his air of genius, lively talks, and brilliant remarks, quite the opposite of the ponderous and remote Husserl (*Life* 259). Scheler's *Formalism,* part 1 (1913), which also advocated personalism, had just been published in Husserl's *Yearbook* (part 2, 1916).[28] Scheler would feature prominently in Edith Stein's doctoral thesis on empathy (PE 27–34; GA 5 42–51). Scheler claimed to have independently discovered phenomenology, and "availed of every opportunity to insist he was not one of Husserl's disciples" (*Life* 259; GA 1 159). He opposed Husserl's idealism in a condescending manner that upset Stein, although she too opposed her mentor's idealism (*Life* 259; GA 1 158). Indeed, Stein's embrace of realist phenomenology eventually led her to see its congruence with Thomism.

Having failed to find a professor to sponsor her Habilitation, Stein accepted a teaching position at a Dominican school in Speyer, where she spent the next eleven years (1921–1932), somewhat stifled academically. In 1932, she moved to a third-level lectureship at the German Institute for Scientific Pedagogy in Münster. There, Stein gave several important series of lectures on philosophical anthropology, including *The Constitution of the Human Person (Aufbau)* and *What Is the Human?* However, following the National Socialist coming to power in Germany in 1933, Stein was forced to resign her teaching

---

[25] Edmund Husserl, *Logische Untersuchungen,* vol. 2 (Halle: Max Niemeyer, 1900–1901). The Husserliana (Hua) edition is *Logische Untersuchungen, Erster Band, Prolegomena zur reinen Logik,* Text der 1. und der 2. Auflage, hrsg. Elmar Holenstein, Hua XVIII (The Hague: Nijhoff, 1975), and *Logische Untersuchungen, Zweiter Band: Untersuchungen zur Phänomenologie und Theorie der Erkenntnis,* in 2 Bänden, hrsg. Ursula Panzer, Hua XIX (Dordrecht: Kluwer, 1984); as Edmund Husserl, *Logical Investigations,* 2 vols., trans. J. N. Findlay, with a new introduction by Dermot Moran (London: Routledge, 2001).

[26] Adolf Reinach wrote his doctorate under Theodor Lipps at Munich before moving to Göttingen in 1909 to complete his Habilitation with Husserl. He lost his life in Flanders in World War I in 1917. According to Stein, he was a brilliant teacher. Originally Jewish, he converted to Christianity shortly before his death on November 16, 1917. Stein assisted in editing Reinach's collected works. The Christian resignation of Reinach's widow was a major influence on Stein's decision to convert.

[27] These extracurricular lectures were given in cafes and guest houses in Göttingen over the years from 1911 to 1914, arranged by Scheler's friend, Dietrich von Hildebrand, after Scheler had ignominiously lost his job in Munich.

[28] Max Scheler, *Der Formalismus in der Ethik und die materiale Wertethik. Neuer Versuch der Grundlegung eines ethischen Personalismus, Jahrbuch für Philosophie und phänomenologische Forschung,* vol. 1 (1913); vol. 2 (1916), now in *Gesammelte Werke,* ed. Maria Scheler, vol. 2 (Bern: Francke Verlag, 1954); *Formalism in Ethics and Non-Formal Ethics of Values: A New Attempt toward a Foundation of an Ethical Personalism* trans. Manfred S. Frings and Roger L. Funk (Evanston, IL: Northwestern University Press, 1973).

position because of her "Jewish descent."[29] In 1934, she entered the Carmelite convent at Cologne, taking the religious name Teresa Benedicta of the Cross. Shortly after Kristallnacht (November 1938), Stein left Germany for the safety of the Carmelite convent in Echt, Netherlands. However, the condemnation of Nazi anti-Semitism by the Dutch bishops of occupied Netherlands, on July 26, 1942, provoked Hitler to order the arrest of all non-Aryan Roman Catholics there. On August 5, 1942, Stein was interned at Westerbork. Two days later, she was deported to Auschwitz concentration camp in Poland, where she perished, probably on August 9, 1942.

2 EDITH STEIN'S PHENOMENOLOGICAL WRITINGS

During her phenomenological period (1917–1925), Stein published philosophical treatises in Husserl's *Yearbook* covering a remarkable range: embodiment, empathy, the constitution of the human person, the methodology of psychology and the human sciences, the nature of community, and the nature of the state. Her treatment of "empathy" (broadly understood as the conscious awareness of others' subjective experiences, feelings, and thoughts) is particularly original, providing a broadly Husserlian phenomenological analysis, but going further than Husserl in terms of her understanding of the human person as constituted primarily at the emotional level and having psychic depths below the conscious ego.[30]

Stein adopts the basic framework of Husserl's phenomenological method, but she gives it her own realist focus. She applies the *epoché* and the reduction and treats phenomena in their givenness without regard to existence. She then proceeds to eidetic insight into the phenomena. She begins from intentionality, understood as "experiencing a sense" (*Erleben eines Sinnes*). Everything is a correlate of consciousness: "to every object and to every class of objects there correspond certain adapted coherences of consciousness" (*Bewußtseinszusammenhänge*, PPH 7; GA 6 9). Intentionality is governed by an a priori "lawfulness of sense" (*Sinngesetzlichkeit*, PPH 110; GA 6 94). Transcendental phenomenology, for her, explores the ideal a priori lawfulness between subject and object, but, contra Husserl, she does not interpret the correlation as an idealism.

---

[29] See Stein's letter to Elli Dursy, in *Self-Portrait in Letters, 1916–1942*, 141.

[30] As Husserl's work on empathy was not available, Stein's 1917 doctoral dissertation was for many years the only published Husserlian account (alongside Scheler's *The Nature of Sympathy*, 1923). Husserl's *Cartesian Meditations* was published in French in 1931, *Méditations Cartésiennes* (Paris: Vrin, 1931); *Cartesian Meditations*, trans. Dorion Cairns (Dordrecht: Nijhoff, 1967); *Ideas II* was published posthumously in Hua in 1952; *On the Phenomenology of Intersubjectivity* was published as *Zur Phänomenologie der Intersubjektivität. Texte aus dem Nachlass*, ed. I. Kern, Husserliana XIII, XIV, and XV (The Hague: Nijhoff, 1973).

Phenomenology continued to play a significant role in her later work, notably in her *Introduction to Philosophy* (1930) lectures[31] and her 1932/1933 Münster lectures on philosophical and theological anthropology (*What Is the Human Being?* and *Aufbau*).[32] Besides her review of Heidegger's *Being and Time* (1927), written around 1937, she wrote a short review of the parts of Husserl's *Crisis of European Sciences* that appeared in *Philosophia* in 1937.[33] There she comments about Husserl's neglect of the Christian Middle Ages and it is clear she has a higher regard than Husserl for the Scholastic contribution to philosophy: "the Christian thinker must immediately notice that this exploration of the conscience [Gewissenserforschung] of modern philosophy speaks of the connection of modern philosophizing to ancient thought motifs, but is completely silent on everything in between. All the striving for truth of the Christian centuries is as if it had not been or as if it had left no trace in the spiritual endeavors of the last centuries" (GA 9 124, my translation).

3 STEIN'S PHENOMENOLOGICAL ANALYSIS OF EMPATHY (*EINFÜHLUNG*)

Stein's *On the Problem of Empathy* (1917) is a rich, condensed phenomenological analysis of the essence of empathy, the constitution of the psychophysical individual (embodied self), and the understanding of "spiritual" being (i.e., interpersonal culture). The final chapter on the nature of "motivation" (mental causation) anticipates her later discussion in "Psychic Causality" (trans. as "Sentient Causality," PPH 2–128). She also discusses the apprehension of values (*Wertnehmen*), the strata of the soul, and the nature of the person, all themes she returns to in later works. Stein's overall aim is to give a phenomenological account of *empathy* (*Einfühlung*), that is, the apprehension of other subjects as subjects with inner conscious lives of their own, and their psychic states. For her: "empathy is a kind of act of perceiving *sui generis*. . . . Empathy . . . is the experience of foreign consciousness in general, irrespective of the kind of the experiencing subject or of the subject whose consciousness is experienced" (PE 11; GA 5 20). Stein's thesis reviews critically previous discussions of empathy (Lipps, Scheler, Dilthey, Münsterberg). She especially admires Scheler's account: a "bold theory . . . [that] has something extremely

---

[31] Edith Stein, *Einführung in die Philosophie*, ed. H. B. Gerl-Falkovitz and C. M. Wulf, GA 8 (Freiburg: Herder, 2004).

[32] Edith Stein, *Was ist der Mensch? Theologische Anthropologie*, in *Edith Stein*, ed. B. Beckmann-Zöller, GA 15 (Freiburg: Herder, 2005). See Donald Wallenfang, *Human and Divine Being: A Study on the Theological Anthropology of Edith Stein* (Eugene, OR: Cascade Books, 2017).

[33] Edith Stein, "Besprechung von: Edmund Husserl, 'Die Krisis der europäischen Wissenschaften und die transzendentale Phänomenologie. Eine Einleitung in die phänomenologische Philosophie' (1937)," in Edith Stein, *Freiheit und Gnade und weitere Texte zu Phänomenologie und Ontologie*, GA 9 (Freiburg: Herder, 2014), 122–125.

seductive about it" (PE 28; GA 5 43). However, Scheler locates empathy in inner perception, whereas Stein sees it as closer to external perception. She rejects Scheler's pos-
tulation of a neutral stream of experience prior to the emergence of the ego.[34] For her,
following Husserl, experiencing is necessarily *egoic* or first-personal.[35]

Stein applies Husserl's fundamental distinction between straightforward perception
(*Wahrnehmung*), understood as a "presentation" (*Gegenwärtigung*), in which the object
is given directly as "there in the flesh" (*leibhaftig da*), and other forms of "representation," "presentiation," or "presentification" (*Vergegenwärtigung*), such as memory, expectation, fantasy, and empathy (*Erinnerung, Erwartung, Phantasie, Einfühlung*, PE 8;
GA 5 16), where the object is not presented with fleshly givenness (e.g. a fantasy object,
for instance, floats outside the usual spatiotemporal framework within which perceptual objects are experienced). Empathy, for Stein, is a form of presentification or "quasi-
perception" since the other person's consciousness does not come to full givenness
for me: "perception has its object before it in embodied givenness [in leibhafter
Gegebenheit]; empathy does not" (PE 19; GA 5 31).

Following Husserl, Stein then distinguishes between experiences grasped
"originarily" or "primordially" (*originär*), that is, in the first person, and those that are
grasped "nonoriginarily" or "nonprimordially" (*nichtoriginär*): "all genuinely present
experiences are originary as such – What can be more primordial than the experiencing
[Erleben] itself?" (PE 7; GA 5 15). Some experiences point to another subject (or an
earlier state of oneself). Furthermore, originary and nonoriginary experiences often
intertwine. For instance, I can have a *nonprimordial* experience of my *primordial* experience, for example, when I *remember being happy*, the *remembering* is primordially
experienced but the *happiness* is only nonprimordially experienced (PE 8; GA 5 7). The
remembered happiness, of course, points back *to me earlier* as its subject, whereas, in the
case of the empathic apprehension of *another's* joy, I nonprimordially apprehend the joy
as being experienced primordially by *the other subject*.

For Stein, empathy is a nonprimordial experience "which announces [bekundet]
a primordial one" (PE 14; GA 5 24–25). The empathized experience *is located in* another subject and not in myself. This distinguishes empathy from memory or fantasy
(whereas Lipps had compared them). She writes: "so now to empathy itself. Here, too,
we are dealing with an act which is primordial [originär] as present experience though
nonprimordial [nicht-originär] in content. And this content is an experience which,
again, can be had in different ways such as in memory, expectation, or in fantasy" (PE
10; GA 5 18–19). Empathy, then, draws me to attend to the other subject as subject of the
experienced content. Stein goes on to distinguish empathy (*Einfühlung*) from a number
of other related states (mentioned in Lipps, Scheler, and others), including "fellow

---

[34] Scheler claimed we can experience a thought as our own or as someone else's or as nobody's. Stein
rejects this (PE 27; GA 5 43).

[35] In *Ideas II*, Husserl distinguishes between the pure ego (which is the necessary first-person
perspective—it is a point of view) and the personal ego, which has dispositions, capacities, abilities,
habits.

feeling" or "feeling-with" (*Mitfühlen*), which she identifies with Scheler's "sympathy" (*Sympathie*, PE 14; GA 5 25).[36] You pass an examination and are happy. I am happy too; I am happy for your happiness. In this case, our two individual experiences of happiness have related but different contents (PE 14–15; GA 5 25). The "content" of *your* intentional state of happiness is "passing the examination," whereas the content of *my* happiness is your "happiness." This is fellow feeling, not empathy understood in her sense as grasping the other's experience and its intentional object.[37]

Theodor Lipps also saw empathy as involving "feeling of oneness with" or "identification" (*Einsfühlen*, PE 16; GA 5 27), for example, when the audience mimics the movements of the acrobat. But, for Stein, *identification* elides the distinction between the two subjects. I am not actually *one with* the acrobat but only "there" with him. Even if I mimic the acrobat's movements (albeit "internally") my movement is *led* by the other's real movements, whereas the acrobat does not have the sense of her movements being led. The acrobat's experiences are primordial; the observer's experiences are nonprimordial. Stein accurately diagnoses that Lipps has misdescribed the phenomenological situation (PE 16–17; GA 5 27–28).

In *On the Problem of Empathy*, Stein moves from the phenomenological description of one's own lived body to the description of the sensuous experience of another embodied subject as a "bearer of fields of sensation" (*Träger von Empfgindungsfeldern*, PE 66; GA 5 83) and a center of voluntary movement. Just as seeing a spatial object includes a copresentation of the unseen side, so I experience the other's sensations in a "cooriginarity" (*Konorginarität*, PE 58; GA 5 75) with the other's presented body. I see someone's hand *pressing* on the table and I have the sense of their sensations in a kind of "sensing-in" (*Einempfindung*, PE 58; GA 5 76). I can empathize with hands different from my own (e.g., a child's hand) within limits, set by the "type": "hand." My experience is not necessarily limited to a human hand; I can see a dog's paw (PE 59; GA 5 76) or a claw as "hand-like" in its sensations (the bird is gripping the branch). I can sense pain in an injured animal. For Stein, similarities are grasped through associative analogy based on a general "type."[38] Stein maintains that this empathic sensing-in has been missing from previous discussions of empathy. Some philosophers have sought to exclude sensation from empathy (and reserve it

---

[36] Scheler tended to employ the German terms *Sympathie* or *Mitfühlen* ("sympathy") for what Husserl and Stein call "empathy" (*Einfühlung*). Scheler reserved the term *Einfühlung* for what he thought of as imaginative projection (following Lipps), where one person imaginatively simulates what the other person is experiencing. See Max Scheler, *Wesen und Formen der Sympathie/The Nature of Sympathy*, trans. P. Heath.

[37] For a further discussion of Stein's account of empathy, see Dermot Moran, "The Problem of Empathy: Lipps, Scheler, Husserl and Stein," in *Amor Amicitiae: On the Love That Is Friendship. Essays in Medieval Thought and Beyond in Honor of the Rev. Professor James McEvoy*, ed. Thomas A. Kelly and Phillip W. Rosemann (Leuven: Peeters, 2004), 269–312; and Íngrid Vendrell Ferran, "Empathy, Emotional Sharing and Feelings in Stein's Early Work," *Human Studies* 38, no. 4 (2015): 481–502.

[38] Husserl discusses "types" as inexact essences, see Alfred Schutz, "Type and Eidos in Husserl's Late Philosophy," *Philosophy and Phenomenological Research* 20, no. 2 (December 1959): 147–165.

exclusively for feelings). But I can see someone is *cold* (shivering, blue) without going through their feeling of discomfort (PE 61; GA 5 78). I also grasp the other as another zero-point of orientation with its own "world picture" (*Weltbild*, PE 62; GA 5 80). This world of the other is not a fantasy but is actually perceived. When I see the other's position, I do not lose my own. I come to see myself as one among many and the world as intersubjectively constituted. I further grasp the other as a center of voluntary, living movement.

Stein's careful distinctions between empathy and various other psychological states shows herself to be a refined phenomenological psychologist. Her account is very close to Husserl's *Ideas II* (as edited by Stein), which was not then available in print (it was published posthumously in 1952), so Stein's account remained the only accessible Husserlian account for many years. In that regard, it is not strikingly original, but is much more detailed and richer in examples than Husserl's musings.

4 THE CONSTITUTION OF THE EMBODIED PERSON

A central theme that unifies Stein's earlier and later work, already evident in *On the Problem of Empathy* (PE 98; GA 5 116), is the "constitution" (*Konstitution*) of the person, a theme she found in Husserl's *Ideas II* and in Scheler's *Formalism* but that she treats with greater subtlety and depth. The individual person is a multidimensional, layered unity, an *interweaving* (*Verflechtung*) of body, soul, and spirit. As she puts it in her 1932/33 lectures, the human being is at once "living being" (*Lebewesen*), "ensouled being" (*Seelenwesen*), and "spiritual person" (*Aufbau* 30–31). We are determined from above and from below, led by spiritual values and bodily instincts. Stein begins from the "ego" as subject of experience. Following Husserl, this pure ego is the "otherwise indescribable, qualityless subject of experience" (PE 38; GA 5 54). For Stein, as for Husserl, the ego is always living, always actual living present (*immer lebendig-gegenwärtig-wirklich*, FEB 52; GA 11/12 55). Experiences break in on it from the outside, "transcendent" (*Jenseits*, FEB 54; GA 11/12 56). As Stein explains in *Finite and Eternal Being*: "The I is capable of viewing the multitude of external impressions in the light of its understanding and of responding to them in personal freedom. And because the human I is capable of doing this, people are spiritual persons, i.e., carriers of their own lives in a preeminent sense of a personal 'having-oneself-in-hand [In-der-Hand-habens]'" (FEB 370; GA 11/12 316). Our lives have depth and fullness. The human can say "I," which no animal can (*Aufbau* 78). It can take stances toward its drives and impulses. The center of consciousness is the ego, but the human being is also embodied and has a soul which reaches deeper than consciousness. My being is not equivalent to my conscious life (FEB 364; GA 11/12 311). The I is the "carrier" (*Träger*) of experiential fullness. The ego experiences a permanent boundness (*Gebundenheit*, PE 42; GA 5 58) to the body. This "bodily-boundness"

(*Leibgebundenheit*, GA 5 118) is communicated primarily in pains, aches, feelings of weariness.

In *On the Problem of Empathy*, Stein presents a detailed account of the living body (*Leib*) that is very close to Husserl's (then unpublished) *Ideas II*, distinguishing *Leib* and *Körper*. Later, in *Aufbau*, she emphasizes that the living body is an abstraction from the concrete person (*Aufbau* 33). The person is a complex unity of passively received sensations, impulses and drives, vital feelings, emotions and dispositions, rational states, judging, willing, and "position-takings" or "stances" (*Stellungnahmen*)—cognitive, evaluative, and volitional.

My body is experienced as a spatial, material, physical object, with "gaps" (I cannot see my back). It is an imperfectly constituted thing, as Husserl also says. "The impossibility of being rid of the body indicates its special givenness" (PE 46; GA 5 63). While it is possible to conceive of an ego that is not embodied, one cannot conceive of a living body without an I (PE 47; GA 5 64). Anticipating *Ideas II*, she writes that the I is the "zero point of orientation" (*Nullpunkt der Orientierung*, PE 43; GA 5 58).[39] I always experience my body as *here* and everything else as *there*. The lived body is a center of sensations and feelings. Bodily spatiality (*Leibraum*) differs from objective space (*Aussenraum*, PE 43; GA 5 59).

Touch and vision are intertwined; everything seeable is touchable and vice versa. They call each other as "witnesses" (*als Zeugen*, PE 41; GA 5 57). We *see* the hardness of the table. Anticipating Merleau-Ponty on intertwining of the senses, Stein writes: "the robes in Van Dyck's paintings are not only as shiny as silk but also as smooth and as soft as silk" (PE 44; GA 5 61). Sensuous perceptions are not stimuli but present the properties of objects: "we see colors as colors of things" (*Aufbau* 74). My body not only senses external things, it also senses itself (*Aufbau* 46). The body has a "double givenness" (*doppelte Gegebenheit*) as an objective entity and as an experienced center (PE 43; GA 5 59). My consciousness can attend to either sensation. (This is the basis of the "double sensation" phenomenon, discussed by Husserl and developed by Merleau-Ponty.)[40] Stein remarks, anticipating Merleau-Ponty, that this could open up a phenomenology of perception.

Sensations, for Stein, do not issue from the ego, as "egoic" acts of judging or willing do. Sensations are localized (e.g., a pain in my foot) but are experienced "at a distance from the ego" (PE 42; GA 5 58). Indeed, different parts of my body seem further away, for example, my chest is "nearer" to "me" than my feet). Sensations belong to the outer part of my lived body. Sensations come from without. I *have* a toothache rather than I *am* a toothache. Furthermore, I touch the table and there is a difference between the *sensation of touching* and the *sensation of the hard surface*.

Partially adapting Scheler's classification, Stein distinguishes carefully between "sensations" (*Empfindungen*), "sensory feelings" (*sinnliche Gefühle*, PE 100, GA 5

---

[39] Compare Husserl, *Ideas II* 166; Hua IV 158. The body is always "here." I cannot distance myself from it.

[40] See Dermot Moran, "Phenomenologies of Vision and Touch: Between Husserl and Merleau-Ponty," in *Carnal Hermeneutics*, ed. Richard Kearney and Brian Treanor (New York: Fordham University Press, 2015), 214–234.

118; *Aufbau* 75), "general or common feelings" (*Gemeingefühle*, PE 68; GA 5 86), and "sentiments" (*Gesinnungen*, PPH 265; GA 6 221). Sensory feelings are localized. *General feelings* (vigor, weariness, moods) pervade the whole body (PE 48; GA 5 65) and do not intend objects. General feelings face in two directions—toward myself and toward the world; I radiate inward and outward. *Moods* (*Stimmungen*), on the other hand, for Stein, are intentional as they reveal the world in a certain light. Stein's account of moods anticipates Heidegger's in many ways and may have been an influence on him. Moods are unpredictable and are not accessible to the will. A child can be playing happily but suddenly fall into a bad mood. One does not have to be motivated to fall into a mood (PPH 106; GA 6 92).

Stein discusses "spiritual feelings" (*geistige Gefühle*, PE 50; GA 5 66), in terms of their "depth" (*Tiefe*), "reach" (*Reichweite*), "duration" (*Dauer*), and "intensity." *Sentiments* (*Gesinnungen*, GA 5 120; GA 6 221) are higher feelings directed to other persons in their spiritual lives, for example, love, hate, gratitude, resentment, contempt, indignation. (Here Stein is developing Scheler.)

Stein's account of emotions and moods is more detailed and richer than Heidegger's and she also sees emotions in a more positive light than Heidegger. She elaborates on Husserl's and Scheler's accounts (also Dietrich von Hildebrand), according to which feelings and emotions apprehend values (*Wertnehmen*). Humans are sensitive to values and live in a "world of values" (*Wertewelt*, PE 108; GA 5 136). Values are objective entities (*Aufbau* 25). Feelings are evaluative and can be appropriate or inappropriate. There is a fittingness of the emotion to the situation. We also feel ourselves motivated *from above* by spiritual values as well as by other persons we admire. We grasp their positive value. Each person is an absolute value.

Depth of soul and the apprehension of values at different levels are topics Stein analyzes at length already in *On the Problem of Empathy* (PE 102; GA 5 120), but which she returns to in depth in her later Christian writings. Persons live at different degrees of depth. Each person unfolds from his or her depth. The soul has "depth-reception" (*Tiefen-Aufnahme*, PA 391; GA 10 255) and can receive something at the depth appropriate to it. The more a person lives at depth, the more their personal "core" unfolds.

5 STEIN'S PHENOMENOLOGICAL PSYCHOLOGY

Stein's *Philosophy of Psychology and the Humanities* (1922), contains her most detailed published phenomenological analyses of the human person in its cultural (spiritual) world.[41] She distinguishes between "consciousness" as such and the larger

---

[41] In her *Introduction* (*Einführung in die Philosophie*), Stein acknowledges the deep influence of Husserl's *Ideas II*, the manuscripts of which she had been editing from 1916 to 1918 (PPH 2; GA VI 3–4).

psychic domain (soul and spirit) that includes unconscious drives, feelings, and value-apprehensions. In her detailed analysis of the relations between perceptions and feelings, Stein distinguishes between the *content* (*Gehalt*) of experience (e.g., color red), the act of *experiencing* (*Erleben*), for example, *seeing* red, and the *consciousness* (*Bewusstsein*) of that experience (PPH 16; GA 6 18). One can, for instance, have an *anxious* consciousness of an experience, for example, *she nervously looked around the room.* The more intense the experience, the more *luminous* the consciousness of it (PPH 18; GA 6 19). In perceiving, the perceptual object is transcendent and stable although the "sense-content" (*Sinnesbestand*) is changing. Similarly with affections. The experiential contents of the affection may constantly change, but the affection remains the same. The affection can also survive and change in me; the *experiencing* itself changes and not just the intentional content (PPH 106; GA 6 91). Our mental possessions can sit in us like an external object, for example, a remembered mood. A feeling or mood can expire but its sense-content can linger. Stein is also aware that moods can go dormant but can revive. Trauma can resurface.

In her 1922 treatise "Psychic Causality," Stein focuses on the unity of the flow of conscious life and especially on the manner in which human beings are affected by causation and by motivation (a topic Husserl discussed in *Ideas II* §49; and treated earlier by Alexander Pfänder).[42] Hume had denied that we perceive causation (rather than just a sequence of events) because he could not find the *phenomenon* of causation. Kant, in response, made it an a priori structure. For Stein, both physical causation and psychological motivation are *experienced*. Consciousness unrolls in a stream of "pure becoming" (*reines Werden*, PPH 9; GA 6 11) that is ever changing but there is no sense that one temporary state is the *cause* of the next, rather the stream flows in "one undivided and indivisible continuum" (PPH 9; GA 6 11). Experiences are temporal segments of this continuous flow and come clustered together. Experiences do not just replace each other in staccato fashion, there is a certain "dying away." Stein's focus is on "experiential causality" (*Erlebniskausalität*) as opposed to mechanical, physical causation. Experiential causality has its own regularities, for example, weariness dulls experience. Motivation expresses the manner in which one experiential act emerges from another, fulfilling the other in the nature of "for the sake of" relations (PPH 41; GA 6 36). Each individual consciousness is a distinct center of causation, whereas, for physical causation, there is only one entire causal network. Motivation extends through the whole of our psychic lives. "The entire life of acts [Aktleben] comes under rational laws" (PPH 43; GA 6 38). However, there is not a tight connection between cause and effect; a motivating state may motivate a range of possible responses. It is rational to act within this range of responses. Thus, Stein states, grasping a value can motivate a disposition (e.g., joy); a feeling can set in motion a voluntary decision (PPH 46; GA 6 41). Motivation,[43] for

---

[42] Alexander Pfänder, "Motives and Motivation," *Phenomenology of Willing and Motivation and Other Phenomenologica*, trans. H. Spiegelberg (Evanston, IL: Northwestern University Press, 1967), 12–40.

[43] Baseheart and Sawicki, in their translation of PPH, point out that "motivation" is not the usual German word. Alternative terms are *innerer Antrieb, Beweggrund, Leistungsbereitschaft.*

Stein, includes not just actual willing but the largely unobserved, passive connections between our psychic acts. (Stale air in the room motivates me to open the window, in Husserl's example.) These acts, for Stein, have their basis in the ego and radiate outward toward the world. The ego is the "pivot" for motivation (PPH 41; GA 6 36). Motivation can be implicit or explicit. Perceptual givenness, for instance, is a passively experienced motive for assuming a thing's existence. Motivation, unlike causation, is not entirely predictive of the effect, rather it unfolds a series of possibilities, any of which is "rational" to follow.

6 LIFE-POWER (*LEBENSKRAFT*)

One of Stein's most interesting and original contributions is her discussion of "life-power" (*Lebenskraft*, PPH 92–98; GA 6 80–85), that seems to be a combination of Theodor Lipps's concept of "psychic power" and Henri Bergson's concept of "vital impulse" (*élan vital*).[44] At the basis of conscious life are "feelings of life" (*Lebensgefühle*, PPH 19; GA 6 19) and, underlying them, the enduring life-power (PPH 22; GA 6 22). Life-feelings are transitory experiential states, such as "vigor, weariness, freshness, nervousness" (PPH 34; GA 6 31), that flow through the body as a whole and cannot be located in a specific limb. These feeling states cause effects in the stream of conscious but not in a mechanical way. I am tired so I cannot read a book. Each individual has a finite quantity of life-power (which is both physical and psychical). But Stein prefers to say that life-power cannot be quantified, although it has a qualitative character. This life-power manifests itself in life-feelings from sluggishness to alertness, weakness to vigor. Life-power fluctuates; rest can renew it (PPH 68; GA 6 59). It can be elevated through caffeine or high tension or excitement. This effort can be mitigated by "habit" (*Gewohnheit*, PPH 31; GA 6 28). Life-power regulates everything that happens in the psychic stream. All sensory experiences draw down this life-power. A feeling of weariness affects one's whole daily functions for example. Although it is governed by lawfulness, our knowledge of our current life-power does not allow us to make predictions about its future states (PPH 37; GA 6 33). To my knowledge, Husserl has no equivalent to Stein's concept of life-power. It is a psychosomatic quotient of energy that is unique to each individual. Some people radiate energy; others struggle.

In *Philosophy of Psychology and the Humanities* Stein has a rich account of "impulses" or "drives" (*Triebe*), close to Husserl's and Scheler's accounts and offering an alternative to the Freudian conception. Impulses are determined by life-power: "each impulse is a

---

[44] Stein appropriated the notion of life (*Leben*) from Lipps, Husserl, Scheler, Dilthey, and Bergson (she cites Bergson frequently in PPH). Stein's friend, Roman Ingarden, had written a doctoral thesis on Bergson with Husserl in 1918. See Christof Betschart, "Was ist Lebenskraft? Edith Steins erkenntnistheoretische Prämissen in *Psychische Kausalität*" (1), *Edith Stein Jahrbuch* 15 (2009), 154–183.

direct utilization of life-power" (PPH 67; GA 6 59). An impulse can consume one's life-power. Mental vigor seems to be closely dependent on physical vigor (PPH 81; GA 6 70). Mental life consumes a great deal of psychic life-power. Willing demands the heaviest consumption of life-power (PPH 87; GA 6 76). Decision-making requires considerable life-power and hence is most challenging to the person.

7 POSITION-TAKING AND THE "HEART"

For Stein, following Husserl, the ego (*das Ich*) becomes most itself in its position-takings, attitudes, or stances (*Stellungnahmen*). An attitude is a stance toward a state of affairs, for example, a decision, belief, conviction, even a doubt. An attitude has an objective basis for its existence (PPH 64; GA 6 56). The ego develops by taking stances. Stein's account of attitudes (building on Husserl, Reinach, and von Hildebrand) stresses the manner in which they take hold of us rather than being voluntarily adopted: "I cannot decide for or against them as I please" (PPH 48; GA 6 42), although I can neutralize it in a Husserlian *epoché*. I can also take a stance *toward* an attitude: accepting it or rejecting it. (Husserl's example is his desire to smoke; I can disapprove of my desire to smoke.) Stein's example is poignant. A mother learns of the death of her son from his comrades. But she wants not to believe it, so she does not go into grieving mode (PPH 49; GA 6 43). If I adopt or reject an attitude, I have to do it willfully. I can comfort someone I know is dying and express the belief that they will get better, even if I do not believe it (PPH 54; GA 6 47). In order to affirm something, I must be convinced of it (even if on inadequate grounds). Stein develops the complexity of stance-taking and its intertwining with both causal conditions and our psychic states far beyond its treatment by Husserl.

In *Philosophy of Psychology* Stein speaks of the sphere of emotion or affect (*Gemütssphäre*, PPH 79; GA 6 68). Pains and emotional experiences are in part defined by their closeness or remoteness from the spiritual center, namely, "heart" (*Herz*, *Gemüt*).[45] Persons process experiences at different degrees of emotional depth. In *Finite and Eternal Being*, for instance, she gives the example of two people hearing of the assassination of the Archduke Franz Ferdinand that gave birth to World War I. One person hears it, registers it, and goes on planning his vacation, whereas "the other is shaken in his innermost being" (FEB 437; GA 11/12 369) and foresees the outbreak of war. The news has struck deep in his inner being; the "entire human being is engaged, and this engagement expresses itself even in external appearance. . . . He thinks with his 'heart'" (*Herz*, FEB 437; GA 11/12 369).

---

[45] On the phenomenology of the "heart," see Steinbock, *Moral Emotions.* The concept of "heart" is found in Stein, Scheler, and von Hildebrand.

8 THE NATURE OF THE PERSON:
UNFOLDING FROM THE "PERSONAL CORE"
(PERSÖNLICHKEITSKERN)

In her philosophical writings, from *Empathy* (1917) and *Philosophy of Psychology* (1922) to *Finite and Eternal Being* (1935), Stein's primary focus is on the "analysis of the person,"[46] in part inspired by Husserl, Scheler, and Stern. She also treated the topic extensively in her Münster lectures (1932/33). Already in *Empathy*, she argues for the "constitution" (*Konstitution*) of the person in emotional experiences. Feelings "announce personal attributes" (PE 99; GA 5 117) in a way that bodily sensations do not. Stein departs from Husserl's *Ideas I* (Husserl's *Ideas II* has much to say on the person) in finding at the center of the person not the empty pure ego or "ego-pole" (*Ichpol*), but rather what Jean Héring and Hedwig Conrad Martius call the "core of the person" (*Kern der Person*, PE 183; GA 5 122; *Persönlichkeitskern*, PPH 92; GA 6 80), akin to what Christian mystics called the "ground of the soul" (*Grund der Seele*).[47] Stein maintained throughout her work that each human being has an individual personal "core" (*Kern*) that remains unchanged but which contains all the person's potentiality that can be actualized. The person "unfolds" or "ripens" (*sich entfaltet*) from this personal core, which is never completely "disclosed or disclosable" (PPH 200; GA 6 166). This core is directly knowable only by God (*Aufbau* 14); at best human beings draw from it through their lives.

Stein defends the unrepeatable singularity of each person. In *Finite and Eternal Being*, she writes: "Every I is unique [Jedes Ich ist ein Einmaliges]" (FEB 343; GA 11/12 294), with its "peculiarity" (*Eigentümlichkeit*) that is incommunicable, even though it also has a nature of "what" (*quid*) that it shares with other egos. Stein always distinguishes the conscious ego from the whole person (the unity of body-soul-spirit). For Stein, every person is an ego, but not every ego is a person. The person has a unique experience of herself different from her experience of others (*Aufbau* 32). A person has self-awareness; and there may be egos (e.g., animal egos) that do not have this self-awareness and transparency.

An original feature of Stein's metaphysics is her concept of "individual essence" (*Einzelwesen, individuelles Wesen*), an essence that makes something be an individual,

---

[46] Stein, *Self-Portrait in Letters, 1916–1942*, 23.
[47] Stein speaks of the "core point of the I" (*Kernpunkt*) or the "I-core" (*Ichkern*) or "core of the person," (*Kern der Person*), or "personal core" (*personaler Kern, Aufbau* 103). Jean Héring is the first to have employed the expression "core" (*Kern*) to designate the set of fundamental properties of an individual essence, in his doctoral dissertation, *Lotzes Lehre vom Apriori. Eine philosophische Studie* (1914), typescript, 168–169, recently located in the Protestant media library in Strasbourg. Héring also mentions "essential core" (*Wesenskern*) in his "Bemerkungen über das Wesen, die Wesenheit und die Idee" (which Stein read in text in 1917), published in Husserl's *Jahrbuch für Philosophie und phänomenologische Forschung*, vol. 4 (1921), 495–543; see especially 502 on *Wesenskern*. Stein cites Héring's *Bemerkungen* on "whatness" (*Washaftigkeit*, FEB 56; GA 11/12 84). Stein later saw parallels between the "personal core" and St. Teresa of Ávila's "castle of the soul," "die Seelenburg" (FEB 373; GA 11/12 318).

particular "this." Individual entities have "thisness" or *haecceitas* (PA 39; GA 10 29), a *species in individuo*, invoking Dun Scotus. Stein, following Scheler and Husserl, distinguishes between the generic or universal essence of a human being (the "species"—what all humans have in common) and the "individual essences" of individual human beings (e.g., Socrates, FEB 157; GA 11/12 140). Her defense of the essence of the individual involves the differentiation of individuals through a "spiritual matter," a deliberate departure from Aquinas, who thinks individuals are differentiated through their *material* principles only. Furthermore, for Stein, persons have a "possibility of essence" (*Wesensmöglichkeit*, FEB 83; GA 11/12 80), the capacity to actualize their nature. She proposes the "unfolding" or "blooming" (*Entfaltung*; PA 209; GA 10 139) of the soul from its "core" or "seed" (*Kern*). The essence *unfolds* itself in its faculties and capacities (later called its "potentiality"). Stein distinguishes between "unfolding" (*Entfaltung*) and "development" (*Entwicklung*). A person *unfolds* from an essence that is already there.

9 STEIN'S CRITICAL RECEPTION OF HEIDEGGER (C. 1937)

Stein's critical evaluation of Heidegger's major publications, *Being and Time* (1927) and *Kant and the Problem of Metaphysics* (1929), shows her remarkable intellectual prowess and critical capacities.[48] Speaking of *Being and Time*, she writes that "perhaps no other book has influenced contemporary philosophical thought in the last ten years so strongly as this one." In the first part of her review she offers a careful, clear, and accurate summary of Heidegger's main arguments; the second part is her critical assessment or "position-taking" (*Stellungnahme*). She highlights the ambiguity in Heidegger's characterization of Dasein as standing for *humans* (*Menschen*), the *being of the human* (*menschliches Sein*), or a *way of being* (*Seinsweise*). By identifying Dasein's essence with its existence, human being has replaced God as the only being that can reveal the meaning of being. Stein thinks Heidegger's "thrownness" (*Geworfenheit*) needed to be understood as "createdness" (*Geschöpflichkeit*). On the other hand, she describes as "masterly" the treatment of the fundamental constitution of Dasein and its two different modes of everyday and authentic being. She applauds Heidegger's account of everyday Dasein. By excluding talk of the "self" Heidegger does not have a way of negotiating between *das Man* and authentic Dasein. Stein gives a penetrating analysis of the use of *das Man* or "the one." "One" normally means an indeterminate group to which one

---

[48] Edith Stein, "Martin Heideggers Existentialphilosophie," in Edith Stein, *Endliches und Ewiges Sein. Versuch eines Aufstiegs zum Sinn des Seins*, GA 11/12 (Freiburg: Herder, 2006), 445–500; trans. Mette Lebech, "Martin Heidegger's Existential Philosophy," *Maynooth Philosophical Papers* 4 (2007), 55–98. Hereafter MHE. Stein's review also includes discussion of Heidegger's 1928 essay "On the Essence of Ground" ("Vom Wesen des Grundes") and his 1929 Freiburg inaugural lecture "What Is Metaphysics?"

belongs (*es bezeichnet einen unbestimmten Umkreis von Menschen*, GA 11/12 467). Daily life is normative. Stein notes that the person who says "one" is feeling being bound by a norm or a "general law" (*allgemeines Gesetz*): one ought to read a certain book. Stein points out that this norm has to be contextualized: "those who 'must' have read this or that book are those belonging to a certain social stratum within a certain culture: 'barbarians' need not; our builders, insofar as they still live according to their state and do not claim to build cities, need not either; but the 'cultivated European' [der "gebildete Europäer"] must" (MHE, 72; GA 11/12 467). The "one" here is not an individual in authority but the "community" (*Gemeinschaft*): "the 'one' is not existing outside of and next to the individual human beings, nor is it an authentic self; it designates a 'community' [Gemeinschaft]" (MHE 72; GA 11/12 468). Heidegger's inauthentic individual is really the normal, communal self. Moreover, for Stein, this communal being is not *inauthentic*. As she puts it, "being-with [Mitsein] is not as such counterfeit [unecht]" (MHE 72; GA 11/12 468), not a deterioration of the self; rather *Mitsein* is essential for authentic individual being. Stein emphasizes contra Heidegger: "the individual needs the community's support—right from becoming awake to his or her own identity 'as such' and 'in a specific sense' (i.e., as a member)" (MHE 73; GA 11/12 469). The responsibility in a community rests with the informed experts and leaders, and the real deterioration occurs when that expertise is displaced and credence given to the "judgment of nonprofessionals," leading individuals to deliberately forego their own responsibility. Stein understands this flight or "deterioration" (*Verfall*), contra Heidegger, as a "fall from a previous purer and higher position" (*Fall aus einem reineren und höheren Urstand*, MHE 74; GA 11/12 470). For Stein, Heidegger's notion of "falling" without a Fall "corresponds to his 'thrownness' without an actual 'throw'" (*Es entspricht genau dem "Geworfensein" ohne einen "Wurf"*; GA 11/12 470).

Stein critiques Heidegger's account of authentic Dasein resolutely facing its own death. She finds Heidegger's analysis of death lacking in depth. Heidegger equates the *anticipation* of dying with the *experience* of dying, because he overvalues the future and ignores the phenomenon of fulfillment. Stein notes that in severe illness, one already withdraws from being-in-the-world, all concern for the world and for others is withdrawn. One is exclusively concerned for one's own body. Heidegger never mentions the sense of *fullness* (*Fülle, Erfüllung*) of our being that is lost in death. If Dasein were simply emptiness, it would experience no loss in dying. We are not anxious about emptiness. What is feared is loss of fullness. Heidegger's investigation "leaves no room for what gives human life fullness: joy, happiness, love. Dasein is for him emptied to the point of being a sequence from nothing to nothing" (*Das Dasein ist bei ihm entleert zu einem Laufen aus dem Nichts ins Nichts*, MHE 80; GA 11/12 479). Rather, the experience of limited joy inculcates the desire for joy without end. Furthermore, we usually learn of death from the death of others. People's dying can have a powerful effect on others. The dead person, Stein says, can communicate a sense of "majestic calmness and deep peace" (MHE 78; GA 11/12 476). For Stein, it is natural to think of death as a transition to another mode of existence. Stein sees the importance of a link between Dasein and a being-beyond-oneself: "all this means *a bond* [Bindung] *between Dasein and a being which is not its own*, but which is the foundation and goal [Grund und Ziel] for its own being" (MHE 79; GA 11/12 477). Our experience leads us to a being that is not us, leading us to grasp our dependency, that is, createdness.

Heidegger insists that everything is temporal and that eternity makes no sense, but, for Stein, temporality cannot be understood without its counterpart, eternity. She writes: "our being is not simply temporal, that it does not exhaust itself in temporality" (MHE 79; GA 11/12 478). The inability to unfold one's essence points to the fact that one has a possibility beyond temporality. Stein even quotes Nietzsche to the effect that all desire wills eternity. Similarly, in her discussion of Heidegger's *Kantbook*, she criticizes Heidegger's identification of Dasein's transcendence with finitude. For Stein, on the other hand, "transcendence means the breakthrough [Durchbrecken] from finitude, which is *spiritual*, and, *as such*, knowing *personal* being is given in and through its understanding of being" (MHE 86; GA 11/12 489). For Stein, by limiting the access to being to human being, Heidegger has actually cut himself off from understanding the question of the meaning of being. Stein criticizes Heidegger for reducing all "sense" (*Sinn*) to "understanding" (*Verstehen*). For Stein, there is objective sense independent of understanding, otherwise understanding simply accesses meanings it itself has generated (MHE 87; GA 11/12 490). Such constituted meaning cannot provide the foundation that Heidegger is looking for. Heidegger is affirming that there is no being (*Sein*) independent of Dasein. This, for Stein, is unacceptable, given that there are beings other than Dasein. By claiming only Dasein has access to the Being of things, moreover, Heidegger precisely closes off access. He excludes understanding things in their being. She writes: "in fact the human being is caricatured already in what it shares with the being of things: in the deletion [Streichung] of its essentiality and substantiality" (MHE 82; GA 11/ 12 482).

Stein generally criticizes Heidegger's rejection of traditional (especially medieval) discussions of being. Rather than being neglected, the question of being is treated in the medieval *analogia entis* (drawing on Przywara). Furthermore, the medieval tradition did not treat all being as merely present-at-hand (*Vorhandensein*), that is, as thingly persistence (*dinglichem Verharren*, GA 11/12 483). In fact, Stein thinks St. Thomas, in *De Veritate*, has a concept of truth as revelation, "truth revealing and explaining itself" (*sich offenbarende und erklärende Sein*), very similar to Heidegger's own conception of truth as "revealedness" or "uncoveredness" (*Entdeckheit*). In summary, Stein thinks that *Being and Time* is an attempt to make human being the measure of all being: "to show the human being as the ultimate foundation [letztbegründende] to which all other ways of being lead back" (MHE 83; GA 11/12 484). Stein writes: "Heidegger's existential philosophy withdraws and stops in front of what gives being meaning and towards which all understanding of being is directed: in front of the 'infinite,' without which nothing 'finite' and the finite as such can be comprehended" (MHE 88; GA 11/12 492). For Stein, knowing oneself as "finite" means knowing oneself as "something, and not everything." This means one already has some intuition of the "everything" (*Alles*, MHE 89; GA 11/ 12 493). Similarly, to recognize that one is finite is already to grasp the possibility of the nonfinite: "human understanding of being is only possible as a breakthrough from finite to eternal being" (MHE 89; GA 11/12 493). Stein notes the anti-Christian rhetorical tone of *Being and Time*, and her own *Finite and Eternal Being* is meant as an alternative Christian ontology.

CONCLUSION

Edith Stein stands out as a brilliant philosopher, phenomenologist, and ontologist, with a remarkable capacity for fine distinctions, refined psychological observation, always attentive to "the personal touch" (*die "personliche" Note*, PPH 235; GA 6 197). She was the rising star of the Göttingen school of eidetic phenomenology important and for mediating between Husserl and Scheler. In the 1920s, following her conversion to Catholicism, she immersed herself in Aristotelian-Thomistic metaphysics, approached from the phenomenological viewpoint, producing an original account of human personal existence, fulfilled in being through love, and seeking infinite transcendence, that was a deliberate riposte to Heidegger's finite, anxious Dasein. Stein's account of human persons as absolutely unique beings who develop from a given core, are emotionally oriented to values, and are sensitively attuned to others, is a lasting contribution.

BIBLIOGRAPHY

Betschart, Christof. "Was ist Lebenskraft? Edith Steins erkenntnistheoretische Prämissen in *Psychische Kausalität*" (1). *Edith Stein Jahrbuch* 15 (2009): 154–183.

De Vecchi, Francesca. "Edith Stein's Social Ontology of the State, the Law and Social Acts. An Eidetic Approach." *Studia Phaenomenologica* 15 (2015): 303–330.

Gaboriau, Florent. *The Conversion of Edith Stein*. South Bend, IN: St. Augustine's Press, 2002.

Héring, Jean. "Bemerkungen über das Wesen, die Wesenheit und die Idee." *Jahrbuch für Philosophie und phänomenologische Forschung* 4 (1921): 495–543.

Husserl, Edmund. *Cartesian Meditations*. Translated by Dorion Cairns. Dordrecht: Nijhoff, 1967.

Husserl, Edmund. *Ideas Pertaining to a Pure Phenomenology and to a Phenomenological Philosophy, Second Book*. Translated by R. Rojcewicz and A. Schuwer. Dordrecht: Kluwer, 1989.

Husserl, Edmund. *Ideen zu einer reinen Phänomenologie und phänomenologischen Philosophie. Zweites Buch: Phänomenologische Untersuchungen zur Konstitution*. Husserliana IV. The Hague: Nijhoff, 1991.

Husserl, Edmund. *Logical Investigations*. 2 vols. Translated by J. N. New York: Routledge, 2001.

Husserl, Edmund. *Logische Untersuchungen*. 2 vols. Halle: Max Niemeyer, 1900–1901.

Husserl, Edmund. *Logische Untersuchungen*. Vol. 1. *Prolegomena zur reinen Logik*. Text der 1. und der 2. Auflage. Edited by Elmar Holenstein. Husserliana XVIII. The Hague: Nijhoff, 1975.

Husserl, Edmund. *Logische Untersuchungen*. Vol. 2. *Untersuchungen zur Phänomenologie und Theorie der Erkenntnis*. 3 vols. Edited by Ursula Panzer. Husserliana XIX. Dordrecht: Kluwer, 1984.

Husserl, Edmund. *Méditations Cartésiennes*. Translated by Gabrielle Peiffer and Emmanuel Levinas. Paris: Vrin, 1931.

Husserl, Edmund. *Zur Phänomenologie der Intersubjektivität. Texte aus dem Nachlass*. Vol. 1. *1905–1920*. Edited by I. Kern. Husserliana XIII. The Hague: Nijhoff, 1973.

Husserl, Edmund. *Zur Phänomenologie der Intersubjektivität. Texte aus dem Nachlass*. Vol. 2. *1921–1928*. Edited by I. Kern. Husserliana XIV. The Hague: Nijhoff, 1973.

Husserl, Edmund. *Zur Phänomenologie der Intersubjektivität. Texte aus dem Nachlass*. Vol. 3. *1929–1935*. Edited by I. Kern. Husserliana XV. The Hague: Nijhoff, 1973.

Husserl, Edmund. *Phenomenology of Internal Time Consciousness*. Translated by James Churchill. Bloomington: Indiana University Press, 1964.

Husserl, Edmund. *Vorlesungen zur Phänomenologie des inneren Zeitbewußtseins*. Edited by M. Heidegger. *Jahrbuch für Philosophie und phänomenologische Forschung* 9 (1928): 367–498.

Ingarden, Roman. "Edith Stein on Her Activity as an Assistant of Edmund Husserl." *Philosophy and Phenomenological Research* 23, no. 2 (1962/63): 155–175.

Lamiell, James T. *William Stern (1871–1938): A Brief Introduction to His Life and Works*. Berlin: Pabst Science, 2010.

Merleau-Ponty, Maurice. *Phénoménologie de la perception*. Paris: Gallimard, 1945.

Merleau-Ponty, Maurice. *Phenomenology of Perception*. Translated by Colin Smith. London: Routledge & Kegan Paul, 1962.

Moran, Dermot. "Phenomenologies of Vision and Touch: Between Husserl and Merleau-Ponty." In *Carnal Hermeneutics*, edited by Richard Kearney and Brian Treanor, 214–234. New York: Fordham University Press, 2015.

Moran, Dermot. "The Problem of Empathy: Lipps, Scheler, Husserl and Stein." In *Amor Amicitiae: On the Love That Is Friendship: Essays in Medieval Thought and Beyond in Honor of the Rev. Professor James McEvoy*, edited by Thomas A. Kelly and Phillip W. Rosemann, 269–312. Leuven: Peeters, 2004.

Oben, Freda Mary. *Edith Stein. Scholar, Feminist, Saint*. New York: Alba House, 1988.

Pfänder, Alexander. "Motives and Motivation." In *Phenomenology of Willing and Motivation and Other Phenomenologica*, translated by Herbert Spiegelberg, 12–40. Evanston, IL: Northwestern University Press, 1967.

Przywara, Erich. *Analogia Entis. Metaphysics: Original Structure and Universal Rhythm*. Translated by John R. Betz and David Bentley Hart. Grand Rapids, MI: Eerdmans, 2014.

Scheler, Max. *Formalism in Ethics and Non-formal Ethics of Values: A New Attempt toward a Foundation of an Ethical Personalism*. Translated by Manfred S. Frings and Roger L. Funk. Evanston, IL: Northwestern University Press, 1973.

Scheler, Max. *Der Formalismus in der Ethik und die materiale Wertethik. Neuer Versuch der Grundlegung eines ethischen Personalismus*. Vol. 2 of *Gesammelte Werke*, edited by Maria Scheler. Bern: Francke, 1954.

Scheler, Max. *Der Formalismus in der Ethik und die materiale Wertethik. Neuer Versuch der Grundlegung eines ethischen Personalismus. Jahrbuch für Philosophie und phänomenologische Forschung*. Vol. 1 (1913). Vol. 2 (1916).

Scheler, Max. *The Nature of Sympathy*. Translated by Peter Heath. London: Routledge, 1954.

Scheler, Max. *Zur Phänomenologie und Theorie der Sympathiegefühle und von Liebe und Hass. Mit einem Anhang über den Grund zur Annahme der Existenz des fremden Ich*. Halle: Niemeyer, 1913.

Scheler, Max. *Wesen und Formen der Sympathie—Die deutsche Philosophie der Gegenwart*. 6th ed. Vol. 7 of *Gesammelte Werke*, edited by Manfred Frings. Bern: Francke, 1973.

Schutz, Alfred. "Type and Eidos in Husserl's Late Philosophy." *Philosophy and Phenomenological Research* 20, no. 2 (December 1959): 147–165.

Stein, Edith. *Beiträge zur philosophischen Begründung der Psychologie und der Geisteswissenschaften. Jahrbuch für Philosophie und phänomenologische Forschung* 5 (1922): 1–283.

Stein, Edith. *The Collected Works of Edith Stein.* Washington, DC: Institute of Carmelite Studies, 1986–.

Stein, Edith. "Eine Untersuchung über den Staat." *Jahrbuch für Philosophie und phänomenologische Forschung* 7 (1925): 1–123.

Stein, Edith. *Gesamtausgabe.* Freiburg: Verlag Herder, 1950–2018.

Stein, Edith. "Husserls Phänomenologie und die Philosophie des hl. Thomas von Aquino." *Jahrbuch für Philosophie und phänomenologische Forschung* 10 (1929): 315–338.

Stein, Edith. "Martin Heidegger's Existential Philosophy." Translated by Mette Lebech. *Maynooth Philosophical Papers* 4 (2007): 55–98.

Stein, Edith. *Zum Problem der Einfühlung.* Halle: Buchdruckerei des Waisenhauses, 1917.

Stein, Edith. "Ways to Know God: On the Symbolic Theology of Dionysius the Areopagite." Translated by Rudolf Allers. *Thomist* 9, no. 3 (July 1946): 379–420.

Steinbock, Anthony. *Moral Emotions: Reclaiming the Evidence of the Heart.* Evanston, IL: Northwestern University Press, 2014.

Stern, Wilhelm. *Person und Sache: System der Philosophischen Weltanschauung.* Leipzig: Ambrosius Barth, 1906.

Teresa of Ávila. *The Life of Saint Teresa of Ávila by Herself.* Translated by J. M. Cohen. New York: Penguin Classics, 1998.

Vendrell Ferran, Íngrid. "Empathy, Emotional Sharing and Feelings in Stein's Early Work." *Human Studies* 38, no. 4 (2015): 481–502.

Wallenfang, Donald. *Human and Divine Being: A Study on the Theological Anthropology of Edith Stein.* Eugene, OR: Cascade Books, 2017.

PART II

MOVEMENTS

CHAPTER 16

TOWARDS A MORE INCLUSIVE ENLIGHTENMENT

German Women on Culture, Education, and Prejudice in the Late Eighteenth Century

COREY W. DYCK

WHEN attempting to capture the concept of enlightenment that underlies and motivates philosophical (and political and scientific) developments in the eighteenth century, historians of philosophy have frequently relied upon a needlessly but apparently intentionally exclusive account. This, namely, is the conception of enlightenment first proposed by Kant in his famous essay of 1784. There, Kant takes enlightenment to consist in the "emergence from the self-imposed state of minority," but this state, Kant claims, is out of reach for "by far the greatest part of humankind (including the entire fair sex)" (AA 8:35).[1] That Kant should proceed to argue that it is, consequently, only possible for a "public" to attain enlightenment as a result of the public use of reason, a privilege enjoyed by citizens and exemplified in the activity of the scholar (*Gelehrter*), offers little consolation as women (among other groups) did not hold the status of citizens,[2] and were seldom granted recognition for scholarly achievements.[3] For Kant, women evidently have no part in enlightenment, neither as its principal propagators nor as its intended recipients.

---

[1] Kant's works are cited according to volume and page number in *Kant's Gesammelte Schriften*, Deutsche (formerly Königlich-Preussische) Akademie der Wissenschaften ed. (Berlin: Reimer, 1900–1919; de Gruyter, 1920–) (abbreviated as AA).

[2] For a discussion of the importance of (active) citizenship for Kantian enlightenment, see Charlotte Sabourin, "Kant's Enlightenment and Women's Peculiar Immaturity," *Kantian Review* Vol. 26, no. 2 (2021): 235–260.

[3] Compare in this context Kant's earlier remark that women who engage in learned controversies like Mme. Dacier and Du Châtelet "might just as well also wear a beard" (AA 2:229–230).

Regrettably, this deficiency is reflected in our philosophical histories of the period. For instance, the Kantian conception of enlightenment evidently lies behind Ernst Cassirer's influential studies, as it is taken to characterize "most clearly the decisive intellectual tendency as well as the historical character and mission of the philosophy of the enlightenment."[4] Considering the philosophical developments of the eighteenth century through this particular lens has the effect of foregrounding a set of philosophical themes—the critique of religion, the epistemological turn, and the autonomy of reason—that no doubt figure prominently in texts written by men in the period.[5] However, at least in the German context, these were not topics that women chose to, or were even able to, engage with, not only because discussion of them was biased toward a highly specialized and public form of scholarly expression but also because the controversial character of the topics, especially the critique of religion, was inconsistent with the still-developing norms of female authorship. More narrowly, the result of thus exclusively relying on the Kantian conception of enlightenment is that the topics on which German women did tend to publish in the late eighteenth century, including pedagogy and civil equality, are categorized as of merely popular, rather than properly philosophical, interest (in spite of often being thoroughly informed by the philosophical views of the time) and the diverse forms of nonpublic female intellectuality developed in the period are assigned little, if any, significance.

All this leads one to wonder what a history of the philosophy of this period *could* look like when considered from the perspective of a different, and indeed more inclusive, conception of enlightenment, and in this chapter I propose to conduct an experiment of sorts along just these lines. As opposed to Kant's conception and its exclusionary legacy, I will instead take the conception proposed by his contemporary Moses Mendelssohn as my starting point. As a Jew, Mendelssohn did not enjoy the privileges of true citizenship in the Prussian state, nor did he have access to the usual institutions of education. Understandably, then, Mendelssohn's conception of enlightenment is distinguished both by its wider scope and progressive character, but as I will show, it has the considerable advantage of bringing the manifold intellectual contributions of a diverse set of women into focus. It does more than this, however, as it also reveals these women as actively and critically engaging with key aspects of Mendelssohn's (and others') philosophical views and, crucially, working to transform and expand his conception of enlightenment in a more inclusive direction. To the end of showing all this, I will begin with a consideration of Mendelssohn's comparatively unfamiliar essay on enlightenment.

[4] See Ernst Cassirer, "Enlightenment," in *Encyclopaedia of the Social Sciences*, ed. E. Seligman (New York: Macmillan, 1935), vol. 5, 547. See also L. W. Beck, "From Leibniz to Kant," in *Routledge History of Philosophy*, ed. R. Solomon and K. Higgins (London: Routledge, 1993), 6.

[5] On Cassirer's philosophical reasons for privileging this conception of enlightenment, see Ursula Renz, "Cassirer's Enlightenment: On Philosophy and the 'Denkform' of Reason," *British Journal for the History of Philosophy* 28, no. 3 (2020): 636–652.

1 A Primer on Mendelssohnian Enlightenment

Mendelssohn's essay "On the Question: What Does It Mean to Enlighten?" ("Ueber die Frage: Was heißt aufklären?"),[6] appeared in the *Berlinische Monatschrift* in September 1784, in a response to the question which was posed in a contribution to the same journal in December 1783.[7] Mendelssohn's discussion begins by situating the notion within a constellation of related terms, namely, *"enlightenment, culture, education [Aufklärung, Kultur, Bildung],"*[8] which he identifies as "new arrivals" in the German language. While the coinages may be novel, he denies that these terms designate completely new concepts (just as, he claims, a people might not have a term for "virtue" or "superstition" but are not for that reason thought to lack them). In addition to their novelty, these three concepts have in common the fact that they designate "modifications of social [geselligen] life" or "effects of the industry and efforts of human beings [Menschen][9] to improve their social condition" (JubA 6.1, 115).

Mendelssohn next turns to a consideration of how these concepts are related, and he contends that they are closely interconnected; specifically, he claims that *Bildung* is the combination of culture and enlightenment. These latter are, in turn, distinguished inasmuch as the former concerns the *practical* and enlightenment the *theoretical*, though in both cases Mendelssohn considers objective and subjective expressions of the attainment of each, that is, respectively, what is produced or acquired through each and what sort of skills or habits might be developed in a subject enjoying this condition. So, culture can be understood either (objectively) as relating to goodness, refinement, and beauty in arts, craftsmanship, and "social mores [Geselligkeitssitten]" or (subjectively) concerning industriousness and skillfulness in arts and craftsmanship, and in the inclinations, drives, and habits relating to social mores. By contrast, enlightenment, at

---

[6] All references to Mendelssohn's works are to the *Gesammelte Schriften, Jubiläumsausgabe*, ed. A. Altmann et al. (Stuttgart: Friedrich Frommann Verlag), 1971– (cited within the text as JubA followed by volume and page number). I have also made use of the following translations (and abbreviations): [EVM] (with Thomas Abbt), "Exchange on the Vocation of Man," trans. A. Pollok, *Graduate Faculty Philosophy Journal* 39, no. 1 (2018): 237–261; [MH] *Morning Hours: Lectures on God's Existence*, trans. D. Dahlstrom and C. W. Dyck (Dordrecht: Springer, 2011); [JRP] Moses Mendelssohn, *Jerusalem, or on Religious Power and Judaism*, trans. A. Arkush (Waltham, MA: Brandeis University Press, 1983). All other translations are my own.

[7] For background on this discussion, see James Schmidt, "The Question of Enlightenment: Kant, Mendelssohn, and the *Mittwochsgesellschaft,*" *Journal of the History of Ideas* 50, no. 2 (1989): 269–291.

[8] There are well-known difficulties in translating the German term *Bildung* ("formation," "self-formation"). For simplicity's sake, I have rendered it as "education" here, though, I will opt to reproduce the German in what follows in order to distinguish it from terms like *Erziehung* and *Ausbildung*, which conform better to the English "education."

[9] I have opted throughout to render *Mensch* as "human being" rather than "man," though most authors in the period used it to designate males only.

least on an initial pass, has to do (objectively) with the acquisition of theoretical cognition and (subjectively) with the skill to reflect rationally on all that which pertains to the concerns of human life.

Significantly, for Mendelssohn enlightenment, culture, and *Bildung* are not all-or-nothing conditions but admit of degrees, where these depend on the extent to which enlightenment, culture, or state of *Bildung* agrees with the "vocation of the human being [Bestimmung des Menschen]." As I will show, what Mendelssohn generally understands through this is the further development of the human being's distinctive capacities. In any case, Mendelssohn does make clear that this vocation constitutes a standard against which human progress can be judged: "at all times, I set the vocation of the human being as the measure and goal of all our strivings and efforts, as a point towards which we must direct our eyes if we would not lose ourselves" (JubA 6.1, 115–116). A people, then, attains to a higher state of *Bildung* "the more its social condition is brought into harmony with the vocation of the human being through art and industry"; similarly with respect to culture, the more inclinations, drives, and habits in social mores "in a people correspond to the vocation of the human being, the more culture is attributed to it" (JubA 6.1, 115). Enlightenment likewise comes in degrees, depending on the extent to which we become skillful in reflecting "on matters pertaining to human life, according to the standard of their importance and influence upon the vocation of the human being" (JubA 6.1, 115), though rather than pertaining to a *people* (*Volk*), as was the case with *Bildung* and culture, Mendelssohn claims that enlightenment primarily pertains to the individual (and only derivatively to a people or *Nation*; see JubA 6.1, 117).

By way of making this last claim more precise, Mendelssohn distinguishes between the human being's vocation considered either as a human being or as a citizen (*Bürger*), which is to say considered in relation to life in a society. As he notes, the distinction is only relevant to enlightenment since "the *human being* as *human being* [i.e., considered as an individual] does not stand in need of *culture*, but does need *enlightenment*" (JubA 6.1, 116). This introduces a distinction between two sorts of enlightenment—that of the human being as human being and that of the human being as citizen—where the precise demands of the latter depend upon the "estate and occupation [Stand und Beruf]" of the individual in society, but those of the former pertain to the human being in abstraction from such differences: "the *enlightenment* that interests the human being as human being is *universal*, without distinction in terms of estate; the enlightenment of the human being considered as citizen is modified according to *estate* and *occupation*" (JubA 6.1, 117). Accordingly, while enlightenment for Mendelssohn is understood, broadly, in terms of the accumulation of theoretical cognition and improvement of our capacity to appraise the importance of matters in relation to our vocation, it is clearly the enlightenment of the human being *as human being* that is of foremost interest, where this pertains to improving ourselves in virtue of those dispositions and capacities we all have in common rather than with respect to that which sets us apart.

Yet Mendelssohn also recognizes that "certain truths that are useful to the human being as human being can at the same time be harmful to him as citizen" (JubA 6.1, 117), which raises the specter of conflicts or collisions (*Kollisionsfälle*) between one's vocations. In order to arrive at a comprehensive account of the possible conflicts and their potential remedies, Mendelssohn further distinguishes the "essential [wesentlichen]" and "accidental [zufälligen]" or "extra-essential [außerwesentlichen]" vocations or determinations (*Bestimmungen*) of each.[10] Concerning the possible (and actual) conflicts between our extraessential vocation as human beings and either our essential or extraessential vocation as citizens, he calls generally for rules to be established to decide these cases (JubA 6.1, 117). More problematic are the conflicts that involve our *essential* vocation as human beings, and Mendelssohn considers what is to be done when these clash with our essential vocation as citizens and our extraessential vocation as human beings. Concerning the former, which takes place when the regime fails to recognize that enlightenment is "indispensable [unentbehrlich]" for humanity "through all estates of the realms [über alle Stände des Reichs]," Mendelssohn rather cryptically asserts that in such cases philosophy should "lay its hand on its mouth [Hier lege die Philosophie die Hand auf den Mund!]," presumably lest, in publicly disclosing the conflict, it forces the regime's hand in imposing stricter measures to stifle enlightenment (JubA 6.1, 117).[11] Concerning the latter conflict—that between the essential and extraessential aspects of the human being's vocation as human being—Mendelssohn cites as an example the case where truths that are salutary for humanity nonetheless tear down the "principles of religion and ethics." Here Mendelssohn recommends that the virtuous would-be enlightener should "proceed with caution and forebearance, and prefer to tolerate prejudice" rather than run the risk of being driven out along with the truth, even as he recognizes himself that this maxim is ripe for abuse (JubA 6.1, 118).

In order to better appreciate the distinctive character of Mendelssohn's conception of enlightenment it will be helpful to briefly contrast it with that of Kant, as elaborated in "Answering the Question: What Is Enlightenment?" Kant's conception of enlightenment involves casting off the fetters through which one willingly subjects the use of one's own understanding to the authority of others, that is, enlightenment "is the human being's emergence from his self-incurred minority" (AA 8:35). While Kant enjoins us each to "have courage to make use of [our] *own* understanding" (AA 8:35), he proceeds to observe that it is rare for an individual to attain enlightenment, given the appeal of, and habituation to, letting others make decisions on one's behalf. It is, he claims, less unlikely that a public (*Publicum*) should attain enlightenment, and it can do so through the freedom of its members to make public (*öffentlich*) use of their reason. This is, namely, a use of their reason apart from, and which does not interfere with, their occupation of a given office or profession, and which is exemplified, according to Kant, in the use of one's reason "as a scholar before the entire public of the world of readers" (AA 8:37). So, while

---

[10] Notably, in a subsequent letter, Mendelssohn presents the distinction between essential and extraessential in terms of the former relating to human *existence* (*Daseyn*) and the latter to human *well-being* (*Besserseyn*) (see JubA 13, 236).

[11] A number of other alternative interpretations of this enigmatic claim have been canvassed; for discussion see A. Pollok, *Fazetten des Menschen. Zur Anthropologie Moses Mendelssohns* (Hamburg: Meiner, 2010), 457–461.

we remain beholden to the guidance and censorship of others in the private exercise of reason in the context of the office we might occupy, no such constraints (ought to) obtain concerning reason's public use, and provided that a people enjoys such freedom in the public use of reason, it is possible for it to achieve enlightenment, albeit only slowly given the difficulty in overcoming implanted prejudices (AA 8:36).

Kant's essay would appear three months after Mendelssohn's, in December 1784, though he was apparently unaware of Mendelssohn's response when he composed his own. This led him to wonder publicly in a note added to his own contribution, whether "chance may bring about agreement in [their] thoughts" (see AA 8:42). There are, no doubt, some initial similarities, such as in their respective distinction between the context of professional life and the extraprofessional context,[12] yet the differences are arguably more striking, three of which we might point out here.[13] First, I have shown that Mendelssohn approaches enlightenment through a wider perspective, as a "modification of social life," and even if he will proceed to emphasize that enlightenment pertains to the human being considered not only as (individual) human being but also as a member of society, it remains the case that for Mendelssohn enlightenment is enacted *within* society, and indeed would remain incomplete were this not the case inasmuch as culture relates to enlightenment as theory does to practice. Kantian enlightenment, by contrast, is enacted publicly, but the fact that it consists in debate engaged by scholars does not suggest any corresponding social forum. Second, for Mendelssohn enlightenment itself, as consisting in the individual's attainment of cognition and the development of one's cognitive powers, can only be attained by degrees as a result of a gradual process of training and education. For Kant, however, enlightenment is apparently the result of a spontaneous act of will or practical reason, and presumably either attained all at once or not at all, and which in spite of rarely being executed is nonetheless the function of a capacity that belongs to every human being as such.[14] Third, and finally, Mendelssohn's focus in his essay, as opposed to Kant's, is squarely on the *enlightener*, that is on the individual who would, after attaining enlightenment, seek to guide others to the same. This much is signaled in the title of his essay—"What does it mean *to enlighten*?"—as it is in his discussion of how the enlightener should proceed when the enlightenment of others would conflict with the duties of the citizen.[15] For Kant's part, he

---

[12] This commonality may not be coincidental as some have traced the distinction to a common source; on this see A. Pollok, *Fazetten*, 455–456.

[13] For a rather more detailed comparison of the two pieces, see W. Goetschel, *The Discipline of Philosophy and the Invention of Modern Jewish Thought* (New York: Fordham University Press, 2016), 210–229.

[14] For this, see P. Guyer, *Reason and Experience in Mendelssohn and Kant* (Oxford: Oxford University Press, 2020), 264–265. In a note in his essay "What Does It Mean to Orient Oneself in Thinking?," in an apparent response to Mendelssohn's discussion, Kant allows that (a specific form of) education can play a role in the enlightenment at the level of the *individual* but denies that it is effective in bringing about the enlightenment of an *age* (see AA 8:146–147).

[15] For a detailed discussion of this, see A. Pollok, "How the Better Reason Wins: Mendelssohn on Enlightenment," *Deutsche Zeitschrift für Philosophie* 68, no. 4 (2020): 540–563.

allows that the example of the enlightened individual might inspire others and "dissem-inate the spirit of a rational valuing of one's own worth and of the calling of each indi-vidual to think for himself" (AA 8:36), though such individuals are ultimately so rare, and prejudice so widespread, that the gradual enlightenment of a public instead is the best that can be realistically hoped for. As I will show, these three distinctive features of Mendelssohn's conception of enlightenment do not merely mark a difference of opinion between him and Kant but, actually prove rather consequential as they happen to con-stitute three themes—the importance of culture for enlightenment, the necessity of ed-ucation, and how the enlightener should proceed in the face of prejudice—with which a number of women were vigorously engaged near the turn of the nineteenth century.

2 THE CULTURE OF ENLIGHTENMENT: HENRIETTE HERZ AND RAHEL LEVIN VARNHAGEN

As it happens, Mendelssohn's distinction between *Aufklärung* and *Kultur* was chal-lenged in a letter responding to his essay by the enthusiastic enlightener August Hennings (about whom more will be said in the fourth section). Hennings challenges the strict distinction between enlightenment and culture given that he understands cul-ture to be just the cultivation in us effected *through* enlightenment (JubA 13, 228). In re-sponse, Mendelssohn upheld the difference between the two, claiming that culture has "something intentional [etwas vorsätzliches]" about it, in contrast with enlightenment, a fact he takes to be confirmed in our ordinary linguistic usage; moreover, he claims that it is sometimes the case that enlightenment is the *effect* of culture rather than vice versa (JubA 13, 235).

This last claim points to an important feature of Mendelssohn's discussion: as im-portant as the *distinction* between culture and enlightenment is, he also takes pains to emphasize their crucial *inter*dependence (which is not limited to their mutual poten-tial to produce one another). Not only does he compare the relationship between the two to that between "theory and practice," but he also contends that they "stand in the most precise connection, even if subjectively they can very often be separated" (JubA 6.1, 116). Indeed, Mendelssohn assigns an indispensable role to culture in spreading and securing the gains of enlightenment, a service it yields by promoting the *sociability* of human beings through the refinement of manners and the expansion of opportunities for engagement and concourse.[16] Culture likewise serves as an important check on en-lightenment for Mendelssohn, making it important that both are cultivated at once. For

---

[16] See for instance JubA 13.1, 235, where he attributes a hesitancy among a people to associate with others to a deficiency in culture.

instance, doctrines that pass as enlightened might nonetheless have the consequence of degrading public morals or fomenting the development of manners hostile to concourse among individuals (even as they adopt the mask of "gentleness of spirit").[17] As he writes in the essay, "where enlightenment and culture advance in equal strides, then they serve one another as the best means for preventing prejudice" (JubA 6.1, 118)—a claim he reiterates in his response to Hennings, with particular emphasis on the potential for the misuse of enlightenment: "if enlightenment outstrips culture by too wide a measure, the former can of course become dangerous" (JubA 13, 237).

For Mendelssohn, then, the pursuit of culture is integral to the efforts to attain enlightenment, and it is for this reason that Mendelssohn also lays considerable emphasis on the importance of various forms of association. In the enlightenment essay, Mendelssohn has already indicated the importance of developing the culture of human beings with respect to their specific "estates and professions," where the aim was to further association with one's fellows *within* a given estate and profession, and where Mendelssohn seems to deny the need for the pursuit of culture insofar as it might involve the association across different estates (JubA 6.1, 116–117). However, in a subsequent essay, Mendelssohn thinks better of this as he recognizes the potential harms caused by the strict separation of the estates; so, after (re)introducing the distinction between "offices [Ämter]" and "estates [Stände]," he continues: "what is useful for offices can be damaging for the estates, and vice versa. In large nations, where businesses are abundant, distinguishing them ever more carefully is convenient; but the estates must be brought into connection all the more as the distinction between offices inclines us to separate them" (JubA 6.1, 151).[18] When it comes to the types of associations that best promote this intermingling, Mendelssohn makes specific mention of "brotherhoods [Brüderschaften], orders, and guilds" which, whatever their precise purposes, have the common function of enabling sociability between estates in the pursuit of a shared end (JubA 6.1, 151).[19] In any case, Mendelssohn likely does *not* have in mind the "reading societies" and other sorts of more formal (and sometimes secret) learned gatherings, such as his own *Mittwochsgesellschaft*. In addition to appealing to a rather more limited clientele, these groups contribute little to the refinement of manners given their focus on the delivery of lectures or the (dramatic) reading of poetry and plays. Indeed, this dependence on the written word strikes Mendelssohn as inconsistent with the sort of conversational intercourse that promotes culture; as he writes (in a rather different context in *Jerusalem*), "Everywhere there is the dead letter; never the spirit of lively conversation [lebendige Unterhaltung]" (JubA 8, 169–170; JRP 103).

[17] See JubA 8, 131; JRP, 63: "wie Atheisterei und Epikurismus den Grund untergraben, auf welchem die Glückseeligkeit des gesellschaftlichen Lebens beruhet" (see also as well as JubA 8, 201–202; JRP 136–137).

[18] Notably, Mendelssohn also identifies a class of profession or office that requires "vieljähriger Umgang mit Menschen aus allen Ständen" (see JubA 6.1, 152).

[19] Mendelssohn's essay is itself a response to an essay published in the *Berlinische Monatschrift* that had ridiculed "Schützengilden" for serving little purpose in modern Germany.

An overlooked example of the sort of (informal) association that conforms to Mendelssohn's model would be the salon, an institution that flourished in Berlin (with some interruptions) beginning in 1780. What is particularly relevant about the salon in this context is that it frequently hosted individuals holding diverse social standing.[20] One distinguishing feature of Berlin salons was that rather than being hosted by female members of the aristocracy, as was the case in France, they were often hosted by Jewish women. The two most famous such gatherings of turn-of-the-century Berlin were those hosted by Henriette Herz (1764–1847) and Rahel Levin Varnhagen (later Fredericke Varnhagen von Ense) (1771–1833). Notably, Herz and Varnhagen were childhood friends, were both Jewish, and were also closely acquainted with Mendelssohn and his daughters. It was Mendelssohn's open house that served as a particular model and inspiration for their own.[21] The intermingling of the estates within these salons run by Jewish women from families of means is perhaps unsurprising—their comparative wealth and (informal) education (particularly compared to women brought up in Christian families) meant that they had cultivation of manners combined with access to the highest social strata, even as their religion marked them as outsiders.[22]

As one of the few quasi-public spaces in which women could directly engage with the contemporary culture and also employ their own agency, especially in creating and exploring different models of self-formation,[23] the salon was an important feature of intellectual life in Berlin from the late eighteenth century onward (even if it was frequently mythologized in subsequent accounts).[24] Moreover, and in spite of the considerable differences in their respective gatherings (reflecting their own interests and particular talents), both Herz and Varnhagen can be understood as quite self-consciously seeking to promote culture in the distinctively Mendelssohnian sense. In the case of Herz, her salon developed out of the regular gathering hosted by her husband, the philosophical physician and favorite student of Kant, Marcus Herz (1747–1803), in which a prominent and diverse clientele heard lectures and witnessed scientific experiments (which she also attended).[25] Herz's salon, which ran from roughly 1780 until her husband's death, started as an alternative for those members of the younger generation in attendance with interests in discussing the latest literature, including the young Humboldt brothers

[20] Petra Wilhelmy-Dollinger elevates this to a characteristic mark of Berlin salons "im Idealfall"; see *Die Berliner Salons: Mit historisch-literarischen Spaziergängen* (Berlin: de Gruyter, 2000), 38.

[21] See for instance Julius Fürst, ed., *Henriette Herz. Ihr Leben und ihre Erinnerungen* (Berlin: Hertz, 1850), 123; and Wilhelmy-Dollinger *Die Berliner Salons*, 19 and 56.

[22] On these points, see Fürst, *Henriette Herz*, 121–124, Wilhelmy-Dollinger, *Die Berliner Salons*, 49, and Heidi Thomann Tewarson, *Rahel Levin Varnhagen. The Life and Work of a German Jewish Intellectual* (Lincoln: University of Nebraska Press, 1998), 26–33.

[23] On this, see Anne Pollok, "The Role of Writing and Sociability for the Establishment of a Persona: Henriette Herz, Rahel Levin Varnhagen, and Bettina von Arnim," in *Women and Philosophy in Eighteenth-Century Germany*, ed. C. W. Dyck, 195–210 (Oxford: Oxford University Press, 2021).

[24] See the literature cited in I. von der Lühe, "Biographie als Versuch über weibliche Intellektualität," in *Jahrbuch für Frauenforschung*, edited by I. von der Lühe and A. Runge (Stuttgart: J.B. Metzler, 2001), 113, n. 23, for critical perspectives on the "myth of the salon."

[25] For an account of the founding of Herz's salon, see Wilhelmy-Dollinger, *Die Berliner Salons*, 61–62.

(to whom she taught the Hebraic alphabet), Schleiermacher, and the Schlegels (and it is here that Friedrich met his future wife, Brendel Veit-Mendelssohn). Herz herself does not refrain from boasting that "at that time in Berlin there was no man or women who would later distinguish themselves . . . who had not belonged to this circle."[26] Significantly, she also emphasizes the fact that her "society" was a place where *spiritedness (Geist)* served to level all distinctions, and the resulting equalization yielded a sort of satire of courtly life, directed "against the whole class of the high nobility with its cold formality [Formalwesen]."[27] The result, at least the intended one, was a group of like-minded individuals committed to the spirited and free exchange of ideas in a context untainted by the sorts of prejudice (especially anti-Semitic) that held sway in broader society: "What is then to be wondered that amidst such social relations (or more accurately, mis-relations [Mißverhältnisse], a spiritual society presented itself, an opportunity which, in spite of the predominant prejudice against the Jews at the time, was eagerly snapped up by those who generally sought spiritual cultivation [geistige Förderung] down the path of a conversational exchange of ideas?"[28]

Varnhagen was even more explicit about the purpose of her salon, particularly the first salon she hosted, which ran from the early 1790s until 1806. Convening in her parents' house over a simple service of tea, Varnhagen's salon expressly had sociability as its goal. In a frequently quoted passage in a later letter, she extols sociability (*Geselligkeit*) and its centrality for all human endeavors: sociability, Varnhagen writes, is "actually the most human thing among human beings! The sum-total and the origin of everything moral! Without fellows, without companions for earthly existence, we would ourselves not be persons and ethical action, law, or thinking would be impossible without the assumption that another—the image of a person—is like us, that he is *what we are*."[29] The central value placed on sociability meant that during her first salon, the emphasis was on wide-ranging conversation and not dramatic readings or the presentation of lectures, which Varnhagen found distasteful.[30] Varnhagen characterizes hers as a "free society,"[31] and in order to ensure that it promoted the end of sociability, Varnhagen discouraged personal satires and mockery,[32] but sought to ensure that "a productive good will" predominated.[33] Varnhagen's salon was especially notable for the wide intermingling between estates that it fostered. Among its guests (a number of whom overlapped with Herz's salon) were artists and thinkers (including her brother, Ludwig Robert, and Jean

---

[26] Fürst, *Henriette Herz*, 127.

[27] Fürst, *Henriette Herz*, 126.

[28] Fürst, *Henriette Herz*, 126.

[29] Rahel Varnhagen, *Rahel. Ein Buch des Andenkens für ihre Freunde*, ed. K. Varnhagen (Berlin: Duncker & Humblot, 1834), vol. 2, 616. See also Tewarson, *Rahel Levin Varnhagen*, 43.

[30] See Karl Varnhagen, *Vermischte Schriften*, 3rd ed. (Leipzig: Brockhaus, 1876), 167–68, and Tewarson, *Rahel Levin Varnhagen*, 36.

[31] See K. Varnhagen, *Vermischte Schriften*, 166–167, and R. Varnhagen, *Rahel. Ein Buch des Andenkens*, vol. 2, 462, respectively.

[32] K. Varnhagen, *Vermischte Schriften*, 168; see also Tewarson, *Rahel Levin Varnhagen*, 36.

[33] R. Varnhagen, *Rahel. Ein Buch des Andenkens*, vol. 1, 62–63.

Paul), members of her family and Jewish friends, but also diplomats, officers, and nobility, with whom Varnhagen enjoyed an exceedingly casual *rapport*. An unwelcome and unpleasant baron who threatened to spoil the mood one evening was productively engaged by Varnhagen "simply and well, without apprehension or insincerity,"[34] while Clemens Brentano reports that concerning the aristocratic guests, such as Prince Louis Ferdinand (1772–1806), Varnhagen "does not care any more than if they were lieutenants or students . . . they would be equally welcome to her."[35]

In addition to realizing the kind of sociability essential to the promotion of Mendelssohnian culture, both Herz's and Varnhagen's salons represent a notable extension of Mendelssohn's call for intermingling between the estates to include the concourse between the sexes.[36] It is notable in this respect that both Herz and Varnhagen enjoyed an atypically casual relationship with members of the opposite sex. For Herz, this was partly the result of her husband's benign unconcern for her, a circumstance that led to Herz having to delicately extricate herself from numerous entanglements with admirers.[37] In Varnhagen's case, she points to her unmarried status as removing an obstacle for her to engage with male guests more freely; this is suggested, for instance, when she equates the limitations of the state of marriage with those of membership in a specific estate: "an office or estate [Amt oder Stand] seems to me to be as restricting as a marriage."[38]

This interest in exploring the possibilities of refined, nonromantic concourse between the sexes is likewise behind the rather more experimental *Tugendbund* ("compact of virtue"), initiated by Herz and Wilhelm von Humboldt, and which included his brother Alexander, as well as Carl von La Roche and Brendel Veit-Mendelssohn, among others (some of whom were outside Berlin and were personally unacquainted with Herz). The *Tugendbund* had as its purpose "reciprocal moral and spiritual [sittliche und geistige] development, and the exercise of love in effective works."[39] As the participants themselves attested, the *Tugendbund* itself had all the trappings of a formal society (Wilhelm von Humboldt refers to it as a *Loge* or lodge), complete with encrypted letters and a set of statutes.[40] In contrast with some of these other societies, there were no hierarchies observed among those involved, as the participants employed the familiar (*Du*) form, no matter the relative difference in standing, a circumstance that applied to new members as well as older ones. While the group struck some as a mere forum for half-disguised

[34] K. Varnhagen, *Vermischte Schriften*, 163.

[35] Quoted in Tewarson, *Rahel Levin Varnhagen*, 37.

[36] It is not obvious, however, that Mendelssohn would not have welcomed this; thus, he favorably mentions, in his reply to Hennings, the French who have distinguished themselves in the pursuit of culture by promoting "conversation between human beings of all estates and *sexes* [Geschlechter]" (emphasis mine; JubA 13, 236).

[37] See Hans Landsberg, ed., *Henriette Herz. Ihr Leben und ihre Zeit* (Weimar: Kiepenheuer, 1913), 140–145.

[38] R. Varnhagen, *Rahel. Ein Buch des Andenkens*, vol. 1, 120.

[39] Fürst, *Henriette Herz*, 149.

[40] See Landsberg, *Henriette Herz*, 196–197.

flirtatious oversharing and as a juvenile pursuit which Herz herself never outgrew (as was suggested by Varnhagen herself, who opted not to join),[41] Herz did credit it for the inspiration of at least one "exercise of love in effective works," namely, when she took in a child of Jewish beggars who were stranded beyond the gates of Berlin, though she regrets that her efforts to "raise [the child] to virtue" were ultimately unsuccessful.[42] What is, in any case, important is that alongside the crucial role that Herz's and Varnhagen's salons had in the reception and development of early romanticism, these experiments in sociability (including the *Tugendbund*) still have a foot in the eighteenth century, as they serve as prime examples of institutions which fostered and indeed extended the kind of culture which Mendelssohn identified as vital for enlightenment.[43]

3 EDUCATION AS VOCATION: AMALIA HOLST

Returning to Mendelssohn's characterization of enlightenment itself, it will be recalled that the conception of the human being's distinctive *vocation* (*Bestimmung*) plays a central role. With this phrase, Mendelssohn is obviously invoking a set of issues, first formulated by Johann Joachim Spalding (1714–1804) in his *Die Bestimmung des Menschen* (1st ed. 1748), that are central to German philosophy and philosophical anthropology throughout the second half of the eighteenth century. Mendelssohn was quite familiar with this famous work, as is evidenced by an exchange between himself and his friend Thomas Abbt on the topic published in 1764, in the course of which Mendelssohn identifies the human being's vocation as follows: "the *proper* vocation of the human being on this earth, which the foolish and the wise alike fulfill—albeit to a different degree—is hence the *cultivation [Ausbildung] of all faculties of the soul according to divine intentions*, since this is the aim of all their earthly work [Verrichtung]" (JubA 6.1, 20; EVM 250). This account of the human being's vocation *as human being* serves as a crucial frame for Mendelssohn's corresponding conception of enlightenment. As I have shown, in the essay on enlightenment Mendelssohn claims that our vocation as human beings is "set as the measure and aim of all our strivings and efforts, like a point to which we must direct our eyes if we would not become lost" (JubA 6.1, 115–116). It is not, therefore, the mere "acquisition of *information*," in Kant's subsequent dismissive formulation (see AA 8:146n), that is constitutive of enlightenment for Mendelssohn, but rather the opportunity for the cultivation of the soul's faculties that such acquisition affords. Clearly, Mendelssohn's particular conception of the human being's vocation has as its distinct implication that education of some sort, through the development of our distinctively human, higher capacities, is necessary for all in order to fulfill this

---

[41] See Wilhelmy-Dollinger, *Die Berliner Salons*, 65.

[42] For an account, see Fürst, *Henriette Herz*, 152.

[43] Compare Tewarson, who also stresses both Herz's and Levin's "deep commitment to Enlightened Humanism" (*Rahel Levin Varnhagen*, 27).

vocation; given this, however, it is rather odd that Mendelssohn himself never devoted a treatise to education.[44]

Significantly, this connection between the conception of the human vocation in terms of the development of our higher capacities and the issue of education was clearly recognized by Amalia Holst (1758–1829). In her self-identification as a "practical educator [praktische Erzieherin]," Holst engaged in a thorough criticism of the philosophical foundations and applicability of modern educational theories. In her (anonymously published) *Observations on the Mistakes of our Modern Education* (*Bemerkungen über die Fehler unserer modernen Erziehung*) of 1791, she takes aim specifically at Johann Bernhard Basedow and Joachim Heinrich Campe, whose ambitious pedagogy sought to replace the emphasis on rote memorization of useless material with a wide-ranging education in the sciences, religion, and morality with the aim of producing useful citizens. This was accomplished through the publication of textbooks, including model conversations between pupil and instructor as well as a wealth of visual aids, and through the use of (sometimes competitive) games particularly for the mastery of languages.[45] While Holst shares Basedow's and Campe's reservations regarding the old methods, she charges them with an overcorrection; so, while memorization had the effect of making students content with a superficial sort of learning that did not penetrate to its source, "modern education has fallen into the opposite error, [namely] it leads the pupil to the font [Quelle] too early, from which they can take as much as they want, but unused to this heady brew they become drunk at first and think themselves able to hold their own with anyone; but habituation soon dulls the effect and, as they still have no feeling for the truly beautiful and useful, they grow to neglect and despise them and rush to the next stream without ever bothering to return."[46] According to Holst, then, modern educational practices promote the development of harmful drives and passions among students, including obstinacy (as in the aforementioned case), vanity and self-conceit (through competitive learning), and an imagination overheated by the images of the divine presented in the textbooks. On this last point in particular, Holst approvingly cites "the blessed Mendelssohn" who had also denounced the inclination to render supersensible things sensible in the preface to his *Morgenstunden*.[47]

---

[44] Of course, Mendelssohn was actively involved in a number of pedagogical projects, including the founding of the first public school for Jewish boys in Berlin, and counted a number of educational innovators among his friends and correspondents, including Johann Bernhard Basedow and Joachim Heinrich Campe. Mendelssohn does touch on the issue in a variety of contexts; see for instance, JubA 8, 118–119; JRP 50. For more on this topic, see Britta Behm, *Moses Mendelssohn und die Transformation der jüdischen Erziehung in Berlin. Eine bildungsgeschichtliche Analyse zur jüdischen Aufklärung im 18. Jahrhundert* (Münster: Waxmann, 2002), especially 189–210.

[45] See Robert Louden, *Johann Bernhard Basedow and the Transformation of Modern Education: Educational Reform in the German Enlightenment* (London: Bloomsbury, 2020), 12–18.

[46] A. Holst, *Bemerkungen über die Fehler unserer modernen Erziehung von einer praktischen Erzieherin* (Leipzig: Müller, 1791), 90.

[47] Holst, *Bemerkungen*, 90. For the reference to Mendelssohn, see MH xx; and Robert Louden, "A Mere Skeleton of the Sciences? Amalia Holst's Critique of Basedow and Campe," in *Women and*

Behind Holst's criticisms of modern education lies a conception of the human being's vocation similar to Mendelssohn's, though Holst thinks that this conception has distinct implications for pedagogical presuppositions and practices. Accordingly, she recognizes the importance of education for cultivating the child's intellect and will, but contends that the wide range and abstract character of the topics treated by modern educators, as well as the reliance upon argumentation, are poorly suited to the stage of development of the child's powers and dispositions. As she notes, these modern educators wrongly presume that their pupils have access to distinct conceptions of the subject matter and seek to lead them to various conclusions through the use of long chains of inference they are unable to follow.[48] This has the effect of rushing children's maturation, forcing their intellectual development beyond its natural pace and leading to the generation of passions which they are poorly equipped to handle, a circumstance that leads Holst to compare children educated in the modern fashion to plants in a hothouse as they are forced to grow quickly and ripen too early.[49] Holst attributes this failing on the part of modern educators to their bent toward theory rather than practice,[50] and to neglecting to observe carefully the children they will be shaping.[51] Had they done so, rather than "being unable to move quickly enough in teaching students in the elements of all sciences as soon as possible" they would instead have recognized the wisdom of their own advice that "with a child, the enlightenment of the understanding must be pursued only very slowly" and through "lessons that are accommodated to the capacities of the child."[52]

With Holst's *On the Vocation of Women for a Higher Education of the Mind* (*Über die Bestimmung des Weibes zur höhern Geistesbildung*) of 1802, the implicit reliance in the *Bemerkungen* upon the conception of the vocation of the human being as consisting in the individual development of higher capacities becomes explicit. Early in the treatise, for instance, she claims that nature's purpose with respect to humanity was "to endow us with enough dispositions and powers so that we can develop [ausbilden] them and thereby transition to a condition of culture."[53] Moreover, the right of every human being to education is directly a function of the duty to fulfill this purpose: "all higher education of the human being, and consequently also of women, must flow from the all-encompassing and true source, as a duty of humanity to develop all of his powers and to contribute to the well-being of the whole as an active member. Therefore the ennobling of ourselves, and co-operation in the great plan of the author of nature, is our

---

Philosophy in Eighteenth-Century Germany, ed. C. W. Dyck (Oxford: Oxford University Press, 2021), 86–87 on this point.

[48] See Holst, *Bemerkungen*, 27–30. Notably, Holst's criticism here might even be extended to Mendelssohn's own conversations with his young audience on abstract topics that constitute the basis for his last work, *Morgenstunden*, though she refrains from pointing this out herself.

[49] Holst, *Bemerkungen*, 74.

[50] Holst, *Bemerkungen*, 39.

[51] Holst, *Bemerkungen*, 53.

[52] Holst, *Bemerkungen*, 37–38.

[53] A. Holst, *Über die Bestimmung des Weibes zur höhern Geistesbildung* (Berlin: Frölich, 1802), 14.

purpose."[54] Holst now makes the case for women's right to education in particular, and indeed she does so in terms familiar from Mendelssohn's essay on enlightenment. In doing so, she pointedly does not challenge the traditional conception of women's vocation in terms of the threefold occupations of "spouse, mother, and house-wife" but she does banish these to what Mendelssohn would call the "extraessential determinations" of woman's vocation, emphasizing instead that women, as human beings, should also be recognized as entitled to enlightenment to the same extent that men are. She writes that "only in the first obligation of human beings, which demands that we develop [auszubilden] all of our powers in the most beautiful harmony toward the highest perfection, will we all be free. Here we share in the same rights, and this duty binds us as well as men. Before we are man or woman, male or female citizen of a nation, husband or wife, we are human beings."[55] In this way, Holst appropriates the core distinctions in Mendelssohn's account—between our vocations as human beings and as citizens, and between essential and extraessential determinations—and the presumed priority of the former in each case in order to unlock the emancipatory potential of this conception of enlightenment for women. For his own part, Mendelssohn did not explicitly (or implicitly) exclude women from among the subjects of enlightenment; nonetheless, Holst now makes it clear that gender is to be considered among the human being's "extraessential" determinations when it comes to the issue of our essential vocation as human beings: "[we] must, as thinking beings, completely abstract from what pertains to us as women [ganz vom Weibe abstrahiren], and merely consider ourselves as humans, that is, as perfectible beings."[56]

4 ELISE REIMARUS AND THE ADVANCE OF ENLIGHTENMENT

The previous discussion raises the issue of how to act in cases of conflict between our interest in enlightenment and our duties as citizens of a state. Mendelssohn's contention that deference should be shown to the regime in conflicts between what the regime deems to be central to its subjects and what reason determines to be essential to us as human beings proved to be controversial. Mendelssohn's own view, of course, should be situated within the context of his *Jerusalem* and the strict exclusion of the state (and religion) from authority over matters of conscience, but even so Mendelssohn's position was taken by some to validate the toleration of harmful prejudices that stood in the way of the progress of enlightenment. In a letter in response to Mendelssohn's essay, August

---

[54] Holst, *Bestimmung,* 65.

[55] Holst, *Bestimmung,* 59.

[56] Holst, *Bestimmung,* 2. Even so, Holst arguably violates this distinction in limiting her call for improved access to education "an die höheren Stände, und den Mittelstand" (*Bestimmung,* 68).

Hennings (1746–1826), an envoy of the Danish court in Berlin and (later) Saxony, and an enthusiastic *Aufklärer*, denied the possibility of such a conflict, if our enlightenment as citizens is to have any meaning:

> the opposite of enlightenment is delusion [Verblendung], active or passive, barbarousness, or stupidity. In such a conflict, therefore, the human being would have to be misled by barbarousness or preserved in a state of unknowing. Here, God would be put in contradiction with Himself. He would have put a power into some just so that it could be rendered impotent or inactive in commerce with others. If it is not to come to that, then the constitution of the state must be unjust, and we could no longer call it the enlightenment but rather the delusion of the citizen. Thus, no conflict is possible. (JubA 13, 228–229)

In response to this uncompromising approach to the progress of enlightenment—one that seeks the immediate eradication of all prejudice and denies the possibility in principle of any abuse of enlightenment[57]—Mendelssohn advises the need for forbearance and even toleration of prejudice, lest the would-be enlightener harm their own cause. Thus, he claims, the enlightener must "observe the time and circumstances carefully, and only raise the curtain in those respects in which the light would be salutary to the sick," and even confesses that, if he had the power to uncover all prejudice "with a single stroke of the pen," he would be loath to do so (JubA 13, 237).

As it happens, the contrasting positions here set out by Mendelssohn and Hennings relating to how, and how fast, enlightenment should advance are only the late developments of an ongoing discussion on the topic between the two, a discussion that was notably also engaged by Elise Reimarus (1735–1805), an admirer and correspondent of Mendelssohn, and Hennings's close friend and sister-in-law. Reimarus was a central figure in Hamburg intellectual life from the 1770s onward, in no small measure due to the "tea table [Teetisch]" that she cohosted (with Hennings's sister, Sophie). The table counted Klopstock, Campe, and F. H. Jacobi among its guests, and provided a forum for discussing recent literary and philosophical works, including plays by Lessing (who was, as it were, a corresponding member of the group).[58] Reimarus's own literary activity included works for the stage and pedagogical texts (including the sorts of model conversations criticized by Holst).[59] However, she would be best known for her involvement in the two major intellectual controversies of her time: the Fragmentenstreit (Fragment Controversy), involving Lessing's publication of a radical deistic text written by her father, and the Pantheismusstreit (Pantheism Controversy), between Jacobi and Mendelssohn relating to the former's report that Lessing had confessed himself a Spinozist. As is particularly evident in her correspondence relating to the former

---

[57] As Hennings writes to Mendelssohn, "Misbrauch der Aufklärung verstehe ich so wenig als Dunkelheit des Lichts" (JubA 13, 229).

[58] On this, see Almut Spalding, *Elise Reimarus (1735–1805) The Muse of Hamburg: A Woman of the German Enlightenment* (Würzburg: Königshausen and Neumann, 2005), 177–198.

[59] For an example, see Spalding, *Elise Reimarus*, 231–232.

controversy, Reimarus developed and honed a distinctive and consistent position relating to the advance of enlightenment.[60]

The Fragment Controversy relates to a manuscript written by Reimarus's father, the orientalist and philosopher Hermann Samuel Reimarus (1694–1768), titled *Apology for the Those Who Honour God Rationally* (*Apologie oder Schutzschrift für die vernünftigen Verehrer Gottes*), in which he, among other things, disputes the authority of Scripture as a source of revelation and outlines a conspiracy among Jesus's disciples at the origin of Christianity. The manuscript came into Lessing's hands in 1770 or 1771—and it is now thought that Elise Reimarus was the driving force in delivering it to him[61]—and in 1774 he began publishing a series of "fragments by an unknown" from the manuscript, a circumstance made possible through his position as director of the ducal library in Wolfenbüttel (which exempted him from the censor). The first fragment ("On the Toleration of Deists," 1774) elicited little in the way of response, a fact that disappointed Lessing. A series of publications in 1777 of the most inflammatory sections, along with his critical commentary (and an excerpt from his own *Erziehung des Menschengeschlechts*, without identifying himself as the author), did provoke the opposition of orthodox Lutheran theologians with whom Lessing traded publications through to 1780. This ultimately led to the confiscation of the manuscript and the revocation of the exemption, and Lessing was further forbidden to publish on theological topics (and at one point threatened with further sanction from the imperial Corpus Evangelicorum).

Whatever Lessing's intentions in stoking the controversy,[62] Elise Reimarus's interest was to strike a blow in the "fight against the repression of reason and human freedom"[63] through the publication of her father's radical views, which she shared (possibly even going further than him in some doctrines).[64] Even so, Reimarus recognized from the outset that caution had to be exercised, not only because of her family's potential exposure, but also, and especially, because proceeding too hastily might have the opposite effect. She reports in a letter to Hennings that in an early discussion concerning how best to publish the *Apologie*, she initially resisted publication altogether, given that in her opinion, "the making-known of certain things, and the dispelling of prejudices, always happens too early or too late."[65] It does not seem that Reimarus had any say in the matter in the end, as Lessing first attempted to publish the manuscript in its entirety before turning to

---

[60] In what follows, I am particularly indebted to Reed Winegar's discussion of Reimarus, as presented in his "Elise Reimarus: Reason, Religion, and Enlightenment," in *Women and Philosophy in Eighteenth-Century Germany*, ed. C. W. Dyck (Oxford: Oxford University Press, 2021), 110–133.

[61] On Elise Reimarus's role in this, see Gerhard Alexander, "Wie kam Lessing zur Handschrift der Wolfenbütteler Fragmente?," *Philobiblon. Eine Vierteljahrsschrift für Buch- und Graphiksammler* 16, no. 3 (1972): 160–173, and Almut Spalding, "Der Fragmenten-Streit und seine Nachlese im Hamburger Reimarus-Kreis," *Aufklärung* 24 (2012): 16, on the likely date of the exchange.

[62] On Lessing's intended targets (the neologists) see H. B. Nisbet, introduction to *Philosophical and Theological Writings*, by G. E. Lessing, trans. and ed. H. B. Nisbet (Cambridge: Cambridge University Press, 2005), 6–7.

[63] Wilhelm Wattenbach, "Zu Lessings Andenken," *Neues Lausitzisches Magazin* 38 (1861): 200.

[64] See Bertha Badt-Strauß, "Elise Reimarus und Moses Mendelssohn (Nach ungedruckten Quellen)," *Zeitschrift für die Geschichte der Juden in Deutschland* 4 (1932): 174–176.

[65] Wattenbach, "Zu Lessings Andenken," 197.

the publication of fragments,[66] but in any case Reimarus would defend Lessing's eventual strategy to Hennings, who, unsurprisingly, advocated for a more straightforward way of proceeding. Foremost among Reimarus's reasons for approval of the piecemeal strategy is that the publication of the manuscript in its entirety would make it likely that the author would suffer the same fate as other radical thinkers, like Matthew Tindal, who, in stepping forward fully with their works, were simply "printed, denounced, and forgotten."[67] Lessing has thus provided, through the faceless Fragmentist, the opportunity for the public's durable engagement with the truth, rather than inviting immediate proscription from those authorities hostile to enlightenment.[68] Against Hennings, who advocates for "the open, frank, heroic love of truth," Reimarus thus prefers in these times of division, the "gradual undermining of the edifice" which, like the full-frontal assault proposed by Hennings, promises its eventual and total destruction, but bears a better chance of lasting success such that "no hope can remain for rebuilding it."[69]

What in any case becomes clear through Reimarus's involvement in the Fragment controversy is that, like Mendelssohn, she thinks that the advance of enlightenment must be pursued cautiously and with a close eye on the general and local circumstances. Notably, Reimarus would come to share some of Hennings's concerns in light of the uproar that resulted from the publication of the second fragment in 1777, conceding that they should have adopted the "direct route [den geraden Weg]" from the outset.[70] Even in this distance-taking, however, her frustration should be understood as directed at Lessing's own unhelpful interventions into the affair through his dissenting commentary, his insertion of his own disguised and highly "confusing" speculations, and the distracting sideshow of bitter polemics. In her later verdict, Reimarus realizes that "a mask like Lessing's is least suited to the truth,"[71] and indeed, this disappointment is entirely a function of her worry that the best chance for the *Apologie* to have the desired effect on the public has been, as a result of the transformation of the controversy into a personal dispute, irretrievably lost.[72]

And yet, despite also rejecting Hennings's more extreme approach, which Mendelssohn pointedly characterizes as amounting to a "prejudice against prejudice,"[73] Reimarus's views on the advance of enlightenment are to be distinguished from Mendelssohn's more concessive approach. This departure is evident in her role in

---

[66] Heinrich Sieveking, "Elise Reimarus (1735–1805) in den geistigen Kämpfen ihrer Zeit." *Zeitschrift des Vereins für Hamburgische Geschichte* 39 (1940): 101.

[67] Wattenbach, "Zu Lessings Andenken," 206.

[68] Along these lines, Reimarus praises the fact that Lessing's original publication (quite contrary to his intentions) seems to have "aroused little distrust among the orthodox" (Wattenbach, "Zu Lessings Andenken," 197).

[69] Wattenbach, "Zu Lessings Andenken," 204 and 206.

[70] Wattenbach, "Zu Lessings Andenken," 208.

[71] Wattenbach, "Zu Lessings Andenken," 209.

[72] Wattenbach, "Zu Lessings Andenken," 212 and 216.

[73] Quoted in Alexander Altmann, *Moses Mendelssohn: A Biographical Study* (Portland, OR: Littman Library of Jewish Civilization, 1998), 391.

connection with her activity relating to Mendelssohn's new translation of the Pentateuch, for the advertisement of which a pamphlet was circulated in 1778.[74] A rumored ban of the translation on the part of the Jewish community in Altona precipitated a discussion of prejudice and the limits of toleration among Mendelssohn, Hennings, and Reimarus. Mendelssohn, after floating an uncharacteristically intolerant query about whether state police might limit the proselytizing of a tolerated minority (which provoked a strong dissent from Reimarus),[75] adopted the rather more characteristic position that prejudices should be tolerated, can often be corrected by other prejudices (in the way an initial reckoning error might be offset by a subsequent one), and indeed, may sometimes even be indispensable.[76] At this juncture, Reimarus, who had been mediating the correspondence, intervened with a letter to Mendelssohn in which she expresses her agreement that prejudice is to some extent ineradicable, and concedes that Hennings's position of a general crusade against prejudice is "chimerical," but nonetheless stresses that the responsibility of combatting them remains: "But how? Not through fire and sword, but rather insofar as one exposes them, as much as possible, to the light of truth which they cannot bear. . . . If, then, I say: I wish to utterly uproot prejudices, I understand by this that one should strive as far as possible for distinct concepts, seek as far as possible the highest degree of truth and spread its light."[77] Thus, against Mendelssohn who, as Altmann has noted, had long cherished the idea that "in certain instances prejudice might be preferable to enlightenment,"[78] Reimarus contends that in spite of the unavoidability of prejudice, and in spite of some prejudices being harmless or even capturing some of the truth, it remains the task of enlighteners to proactively, but prudently, set themselves in opposition to them.

This policy of cautious but persistent advancement is evident in Reimarus's activity in the Fragment Controversy, though not only there. I have shown that her initial hesitation to publish the full *Apologie* had to do with her concern that the text would be decried and forgotten without effect, a concern that Lessing's strategy successfully (initially, at least) mitigated.[79] For Reimarus, then, the inclination was consistently in favor of putting the radical text in the hands of the public in a form in which it could most effectively do the work of dispelling the prejudices fomented by the defenders of organized (and revealed) religion. Yet, this attitude of cautiously but consistently advancing enlightenment can also be discerned in her activity in the context of the Pantheism Controversy. Reimarus does not shy away from Lessing's alleged Spinozism; rather, she greets Jacobi's report with some relief since she has heard reports that he had inclined

---

[74] For detailed presentation, see Altmann, *Moses Mendelssohn*, 368–420.

[75] See his letter to Hennings of July 29, 1779, and Reimarus's comments to Hennings in her letter of August 31, 1779 (both quoted in Altmann, *Moses Mendelssohn*, 388–390).

[76] See Altmann, *Moses Mendelssohn*, 391.

[77] Quoted in Badt-Strauß, "Elise Reimarus und Moses Mendelssohn," 178.

[78] Altmann, *Moses Mendelssohn*, 391. On this, one might see JubA 6.1, 111 and 139 (where Mendelssohn distinguishes the true from the false in prejudices).

[79] For Reimarus's subsequent and wholly positive appraisal of Lessing's manner of proceeding, see her letter to August Hennings, March 12, 1785 (in Wattenbach, "Zu Lessings Andenken," 223).

toward rather more "superstitious" practices in his last days, though she adopts the prudent course of action in submitting it to Mendelssohn, who is better placed to judge "whether the public should be allowed to know it or not" (in his planned work on Lessing's character) (JubA 13, 120–121). Reimarus also seems to relish her role as the arbiter of the (at that point private) debate between the two relating to the truth and nature of Lessing's Spinozism, though she indicates later that Jacobi's Lessing "seemed truer and therefore appealed more" to her.[80] Even her shock at Jacobi's publication of the correspondence between them and Mendelssohn can be explained through her disappointment, similar to that felt in the course of the Fragment Controversy, that the inclusion of material relating to Lessing's private interactions with his friends would distract from the larger issue of his Spinozism; thus, she felt a deep concern that "a contest over the truth [Wettstreit um die Wahrheit] . . . could now become a private quarrel [Privatstreit] in which only Lessing's enemies and the enemies of truth might win."[81]

This view on the appropriate way to advance enlightenment arguably also informs Reimarus's political thought, outlined in an unpublished manuscript thought to have been written between 1789 and 1792.[82] There, she identifies the jurisdiction of state authority as extending (only) to "external right," or that aspect of those actions that might impinge on others' action and omission, but rather than strictly separating this from the inner domain of conscience (as Mendelssohn does), such that political life might be insulated from (private) enlightenment, Reimarus instead emphasizes the necessity for the enlightened individual to guide and inform the policies of the state: "the *morally* and *psychologically* necessary conditions of a higher degree of political perfection are public consensus [Überzeugung], led by *Selbstdenker* who are morally disposed [moralisch gesinnte], and a set of customs that are supported by rationality in policy and the rearing of children [Kinderzucht]."[83] Given the indispensability of such active *Selbstdenker*, Reimarus claims that any enlightenment that is limited merely to the sphere of external action (that is, in Kantian terms, the sphere of right rather than virtue) is "absurd and pernicious," as "external freedom is only the means *of the internal* and a mere condition of moral culture."[84] On account of her conception of the relation between the spheres of morality and right, Reimarus is sometimes compared to Kant (either in terms of offering an alternative Kantian view or an alternative to the Kantian view).[85] Without denying the appropriateness or the fruitfulness of such a comparison, it should now be clear that

---

[80] Quoted in Sieveking, "Elise Reimarus (1735–1805)," 126.

[81] Reprinted in Badt-Strauß, "Elise Reimarus und Moses Mendelssohn," 185. For a thorough discussion of this issue, see Winegar, "Elise Reimarus: Reason, Religion, and Enlightenment," 120–124 and 130–133.

[82] See Spalding, *Elise Reimarus*, 285.

[83] Reimarus, *Versuch einer Läuterung und Vereinfachung der Begriffe vom natürlichen Staatsrecht*, §28 (in Spalding, *Elise Reimarus*, 513).

[84] Reimarus, *Versuch*, §29; Spalding, *Elise Reimarus*, 513.

[85] For the former see Lisa Curtis-Wendlandt, "Legality and Morality in the Political Thought of Elise Reimarus and Immanuel Kant," in *Political Ideas of Enlightenment Women: Virtue and Citizenship*, ed. L. Curtis-Wendlandt, P. Gibbard, and K. Green (Farnham: Ashgate, 2016), 91–107, and for the latter see Winegar, "Elise Reimarus on Freedom and Rebellion," in *Practical Philosophy from Kant to Hegel:*

there is also a relevant context (and important foil) for the development of her views in her engagement with Mendelssohn.

5 CONCLUSION

As I hope to have shown, shifting focus to Mendelssohn's conception of enlightenment has the effect of acknowledging the importance of diverse forms of (historically female) intellectuality and sociality, foregrounding philosophical topics of special interest to women, and revealing women to be involved participants in discussions of central importance to the Enlightenment. I have also shown that the women considered here did not content themselves with implementing Mendelssohn's conception of enlightenment but instead actively and critically engaged with it, frequently in ways that served to extend and enhance its inclusivity (of women in particular). This was the case for Herz's and Varnhagen's efforts to expand women's role in promoting the flourishing of culture (while also testing and revising the boundaries between the sexes), for Holst's attempts to realize the emancipatory potential in the notion of the vocation of a human being as a human being and to furnish it with an appropriately ambitious theory of education, and finally for Reimarus's forthright account of the responsibility of the would-be enlightener to gradually but decisively persist in undermining the edifice of prejudice that stands in the way of enlightenment. So, even as all this helps to underline the fruitfulness of the Mendelssohnian alternative to Kant, both in inspiring critical discussion in its own time and as a lens through which we gain a more diverse picture of German philosophy in the late eighteenth century, the transformations of this conception by the women profiled here also point to the possibility of an even more inclusive conception of enlightenment.

I am grateful to Anne Pollok, Charlotte Sabourin, and to the editors of this volume for their helpful comments on previous drafts of this chapter.

BIBLIOGRAPHY

Abbt, Thomas, and Moses Mendelssohn. "Exchange on the Vocation of Man." Translated by Anne Pollok. *Graduate Faculty Philosophy Journal* 39, no. 1 (2018): 237–261.

Alexander, Gerhard. "Wie kam Lessing zur Handschrift der Wolfenbütteler Fragmente?" *Philobiblon. Eine Vierteljahrsschrift für Buch- und Graphiksammler* 15, no. 3 (1972): 160–173.

Altmann, Alexander. *Moses Mendelssohn: A Biographical Study*. Portland, OR: Littman Library of Jewish Civilization, 1998.

Freedom, Right, and Revolution, ed. G. Gottlieb and J. Clarke (Cambridge: Cambridge University Press, 2021), 99–117.

Badt-Strauß, Bertha. "Elise Reimarus und Moses Mendelssohn (Nach ungedruckten Quellen)." *Zeitschrift für die Geschichte der Juden in Deutschland* 4 (1932): 173–189.

Beck, Lewis White. "From Leibniz to Kant." In *Routledge History of Philosophy*, edited by Robert C. Solomon and Kathleen M. Higgins, 5–39. London: Routledge, 1993.

Behm, Britta L. *Moses Mendelssohn und die Transformation der jüdischen Erziehung in Berlin. Eine bildungsgeschichtliche Analyse zur jüdischen Aufklärung im 18. Jahrhundert.* Münster: Waxmann, 2002.

Cassirer, Ernst. "Enlightenment." In *Encyclopaedia of the Social Sciences*, edited by Edwin Seligman, vol. 5, 547–552. New York: Macmillan, 1935.

Curtis-Wendlandt, Lisa. "Legality and Morality in the Political Thought of Elise Reimarus and Immanuel Kant." In *Political Ideas of Enlightenment Women: Virtue and Citizenship*, edited by L. Curtis-Wendlandt, P. Gibbard, and K. Green, 91–107. Farnham: Ashgate, 2016.

Fürst, Julius, ed. *Henriette Herz. Ihr Leben und ihre Erinnerungen.* Berlin: Hertz, 1850.

Goetschel, Willi. *The Discipline of Philosophy and the Invention of Modern Jewish Thought.* New York: Fordham University Press, 2016.

Guyer, Paul. *Reason and Experience in Mendelssohn and Kant.* Oxford: Oxford University Press, 2020.

Hahn, Barbara. "Der Mythos vom Salon: 'Rahels Dachstube' als historische Fiktion." In *Salons in der Romantik*, edited by Hartwig Schultz, 213–234. Tübingen: Niemeyer, 1997.

Holst, Amalia. *Bemerkungen über die Fehler unserer modernen Erziehung von einer praktischen Erzieherin.* Leipzig: Müller, 1791.

Holst, Amalia. *Über die Bestimmung des Weibes zur höhern Geistesbildung.* Berlin: Frölich, 1802.

Kant, Immanuel. *Kant's Gesammelte Schriften.* Edited by (formerly Königlich-Preussische) Akademie der Wissenschaften. Berlin: Reimer, 1900–1919; de Gruyter, 1920–.

Kant, Immanuel. *Practical Philosophy.* Edited and translated by Mary J. Gregor. Cambridge: Cambridge University Press, 1999.

Landsberg, Hans, ed. *Henriette Herz. Ihr Leben und ihre Zeit.* Weimar: Kiepenheuer, 1913.

Lessing, Gotthold Ephraim. *Philosophical and Theological Writings.* Edited and translated by Hugh Barr Nisbet. Cambridge: Cambridge University Press, 2005.

Louden, Robert. *Johann Bernhard Basedow and the Transformation of Modern Education: Educational Reform in the German Enlightenment.* London: Bloomsbury, 2020.

Louden, Robert. "A Mere Skeleton of the Sciences? Amalia Holst's Critique of Basedow and Campe." In *Women and Philosophy in Eighteenth-Century Germany*, edited by Corey W. Dyck, 72–92. Oxford: Oxford University Press, 2021.

Mendelssohn, Moses. *Gesammelte Schriften. Jubiläumsausgabe.* Edited by Alexander Altmann et al. Stuttgart-Bad Cannstatt: Frommann-Holzboog, 1971–.

Mendelssohn, Moses. *Jerusalem, or on Religious Power and Judaism.* Translated by Allan Arkush. Waltham: Brandeis University Press, 1983.

Mendelssohn, Moses. *Morning Hours: Lectures on God's Existence.* Translated by Daniel O. Dahlstrom and Corey W. Dyck. Dordrecht: Springer, 2011.

Pollok, Anne. *Fazetten des Menschen. Zur Anthropologie Moses Mendelssohns.* Hamburg: Meiner, 2010.

Pollok, Anne. "How the Better Reason Wins: Mendelssohn on Enlightenment." *Deutsche Zeitschrift für Philosophie* 68, no. 4 (2020): 540–563.

Pollok, Anne. "The Role of Writing and Sociability for the Establishment of a Persona: Henriette Herz, Rahel Levin Varnhagen, and Bettina von Arnim." In *Women and Philosophy in Eighteenth-Century Germany*, edited by Corey W. Dyck, 195–210. Oxford: Oxford University Press, 2021.

Reimarus, Hermann Samuel. *Apologie oder Schutzschrift für die vernünftigen Verehrer Gottes.* Edited by Gerhard Alexander. Hamburg: Insel, 1972.

Renz, Ursula. "Cassirer's Enlightenment: On Philosophy and the '*Denkform*' of Reason." *British Journal for the History of Philosophy* 28, no. 3 (2020): 636–652.

Sabourin, Charlotte. "Kant's Enlightenment and Women's Peculiar Immaturity." *Kantian Review* 26, no. 2 (2021): 235–260.

Schmidt, James. "The Question of Enlightenment: Kant, Mendelssohn, and the *Mittwochsgesellschaft*." *Journal of the History of Ideas* 50, no. 2 (1989): 269–291.

Sieveking, Heinrich. "Elise Reimarus (1735–1805) in den geistigen Kämpfen ihrer Zeit." *Zeitschrift des Vereins für Hamburgische Geschichte* 39 (1940): 86–138.

Spalding, Almut M. G. *Elise Reimarus (1735–1805) The Muse of Hamburg: A Woman of the German Enlightenment*. Würzburg: Königshausen and Neumann, 2005.

Spalding, Almut M. G. "Der Fragmenten-Streit und seine Nachlese im Hamburger Reimarus-Kreis." *Aufklärung* 24 (2012): 11–28.

Spalding, Johann Joachim. *Die Bestimmung des Menschen*. 7th ed. Leipzig: Weidmanns Erben und Reich, 1763.

Thomann Tewarson, Heidi. *Rahel Levin Varnhagen. The Life and Work of a German Jewish Intellectual*. Lincoln: University of Nebraska Press, 1998.

Varnhagen, Karl A. *Vermischte Schriften*. 3rd ed. Leipzig: Brockhaus, 1876.

Varnhagen, Rahel. *Rahel. Ein Buch des Andenkens für ihre Freunde*. 3 vols. Edited by Karl Ernst Varnhagen von Ense. Berlin: Duncker & Humblot, 1834.

von der Lühe, Irmela. "Biographie als Versuch über weibliche Intellektualität." In *Jahrbuch für Frauenforschung*, edited by I. von der Lühe and A. Runge, 103–114. J. B. Metzler: Stuttgart, 2001.

Wattenbach, Wilhelm. "Zu Lessings Andenken." *Neues Lausitzisches Magazin* 38 (1861): 193–231.

Wilhelmy-Dollinger, Petra. *Die Berliner Salons: Mit historisch-literarischen Spaziergängen*. Berlin: de Gruyter, 2000.

Winegar, Reed. "Elise Reimarus on Freedom and Rebellion." In *Practical Philosophy from Kant to Hegel: Freedom, Right, and Revolution*, edited by Gabriel Gottlieb and James Clarke, 99–117. Cambridge: Cambridge University Press, 2021.

Winegar, Reed. "Elise Reimarus: Reason, Religion, and Enlightenment." In *Women and Philosophy in Eighteenth-Century Germany*, edited by Corey W. Dyck, 110–133. Oxford: Oxford University Press, 2021.

CHAPTER 17

IDEALISM AND ROMANTICISM

ALISON STONE AND GIULIA VALPIONE

MOST accounts of German idealism and early German romanticism deal exclusively with male figures: Fichte, Schelling, Hegel; Hölderlin, Novalis, Friedrich Schlegel. Yet women belonged to and helped to shape these movements, taking part in this period of creative post-Kantian ferment.[1] Caroline Schlegel-Schelling and Dorothea Veit-Schlegel were core members of the Jena romantic circle.[2] Other women who were part of the romantic and idealist conversation were Sophie Mereau, Sophie Tieck (Ludwig Tieck's sister),[3] Dorothea Tieck (his daughter), Karoline von Günderrode, and Bettina Brentano von Arnim. (These last two were not members of the Jena circle but linked to it through intellectual exchanges and friendships and were connected to Heidelberg romanticism.)

Considerable scholarship exists on these women,[4] but to date it has rarely been integrated into *philosophical* accounts of idealism and romanticism.[5] This is partly

---

[1] Throughout, "romanticism" is used as shorthand for "early German romanticism."

[2] Many of these women had multiple surnames due to marriage or shared first, or family, names. We reduce surnames for reading ease (e.g., to Dorothea *Veit*) or use first names to avoid ambiguity.

[3] Through her brother, Tieck was close to the Jena circle, publishing "View of Life" in *Athenaeum*, vol. 3 (1800), 205-215. She also wrote stories, plays, poems, and fairy tales.

[4] On Schlegel-Schelling, see Douglas Stott, "Caroline. Briefe aus der Frühromantik," (2009-2023), https://www.carolineschelling.com; on Sophie Tieck, Monika Halberstok, *Sophie Tieck—Leben und Werk. Schreiben zwischen Rebellion und Resignation* (Munich: Iudicium, 2001); on Günderrode, Anna C. Ezekiel, introduction to *Poetic Fragments*, by Karoline von Günderrode, ed. and trans. Anna C. Ezekiel (Albany, NY: State University of New York Press, 2016), 1–38; on Veit, Martha Helfer, "Dorothea Veit-Schlegel's Florentin: Constructing a Feminist Romantic Aesthetic," *German Quarterly* 69, no. 2 (1996): 144–160, and Laurie Johnson, "Dorothea Veit's *Florentin* and the Early Romantic Model of Alterity," *Monatshefte* 97, no. 1 (Spring 2005): 33–62; on Dorothea Tieck, Christian Smith, "Translation and Influence: The Influence on German Theory of Dorothea Tieck's Translations of Shakespeare," *Borrowers and Lenders* 11, no. 2 (2018): 1–29; and on Bettina von Arnim, Barbara Becker-Cantarino, ed., *Bettina von Arnim Handbuch* (Berlin: de Gruyter, 2020).

[5] However, see Juliana de Albuquerque and Gert Hofmann, eds., *Anti/Idealism: Re-interpreting a German Discourse* (Boston: de Gruyter, 2019).

because much of this scholarship comes from literary theory, history, German studies, and women's studies. Philosophers, however, have integrated literary, historical, or Germanist orientated scholarship when it comes to the male Jena romantics. Such integration makes sense given that Jena romanticism was a literary *and* philosophical movement, and thinkers like Schlegel and Novalis composed fragments, poems, stories, novels, and letters in addition to what had become the conventional philosophical form: essays and treatises. Furthermore, literary devices such as irony and fragmentation embodied the romantic philosophical view of the limitations of the discursive intellect and the primacy of aesthetic intuition. With the male romantics, it is widely recognized that their literary work had a philosophical dimension and rationale;[6] now we need to extend that recognition to their female coworkers.

The literary side of romanticism created openings for women to philosophize in media other than the long-form systematic treatise in a period when higher education was closed to them. Women (of a certain class) were expected to engage in reading and discussion of literature—this was part of both the Enlightenment ideals of cultivation, civilization, and sociability and of the romantic ideals of sensitivity and spontaneity. *Authoring* literature, however, was less acceptable, so that romantic women often wrote anonymously or under pseudonyms (e.g., "Tian" for Günderrode) or male camouflage, with Caroline Schlegel-Schelling publishing many literary reviews and cotranslating Shakespeare under her husband August Wilhelm Schlegel's name, to avoid the hostility aroused by named authorship.[7] Still, compared to philosophy, literature was relatively open to women—letter-writing most of all, for writing letters was a "conventional attainment" for middle-class women.[8] Accordingly, romantic and idealist women's philosophical contributions can often be found in novels, short stories, poems, letters, and translations, not only essays. This is not to say that women only contributed to romanticism and not idealism, although idealism, as in the works of Kant, Fichte, Schelling, and Hegel, more often assumed the form of the treatise. Romanticism and idealism were closely interrelated, emerging in a common field of debate, notwithstanding their differences, which will emerge later in this chapter. Thus by participating in romantic circles women were simultaneously engaging with central ideas of German idealism.

Still, one might ask why we should see literary works like Dorothea Veit's novel *Florentin* as making philosophical contributions at all. Here we follow Mary Ellen

---

[6] As Friedrich Schlegel wrote, romanticism aims "to bring poetry and philosophy together"; *Fragmente*, in *Kritische Friedrich-Schlegel-Ausgabe* (hereafter cited as KFSA, followed by volume and page number), ed. Hans Eichner (Paderborn: Schöningh, 1958–), vol. 2, 182, no. 116. As an example of the way in which literary work by male romantics has been recognized as philosophically relevant, see Ernst Behler, *Frühromantik* (Berlin: de Gruyter, 1992).

[7] For details, see https://www.carolineschelling.com/carolines-literary-reviews-vol-1/. Caroline wrote of her wish to remain in "the feminine sphere of anonymity" (letter 128 to Gotter, Kronenberg, 15–16 June 1793, https://www.carolineschelling.com/letters/volume-1-index/letter-128/).

[8] Margaretmary Daley, *Women of Letters: A Study in the Personal Writing of Caroline Schlegel-Schelling, Rahel Varnhagen, and Bettina von Arnim* (Columbia, SC: Camden House, 1998), 1.

Waithe in "considering a woman as a philosopher if the content of her writings or teaching corresponds to that of any recognized philosophical subject matter of [her own] or any other historical period"[9]—in this case, to core romantic and idealist ideas. At the same time, we will show the originality of the women's philosophies in relation to the male German romantics and idealists. Mereau interprets Fichte's idea of autonomy from a directly political perspective; Veit and Sophie Tieck criticize Fichte's idea of the self-producing self; Schlegel-Schelling and Dorothea Tieck contribute to romantic translation theory; Günderrode develops a philosophy of nature, a core part of German idealism and romanticism; and Bettina Brentano von Arnim, together with her friend Günderrode, deepen the idealist philosophy of freedom, taking in gender difference and socioeconomic conditions.

We will look at women's interventions regarding (1) the self, (2) translation, (3) nature and existence, and (4) freedom, before (5) drawing overall conclusions about women in idealism and romanticism.

1 ROMANTICISM, IDEALISM, AND THE SELF

As to how women around idealism and romanticism conceived the self, a common theme is the rejection of Fichte's idea of the self-positing self. For the early Fichte in his *Wissenschaftslehre*, the experiencing subject must ascribe all its representations to itself and in doing so it posits itself, constituting itself as the same unified subject that it takes itself to be. Thus the subject is originally free, spontaneous, and self-constituting. This idea forms the common starting point for both German idealism and romanticism. The women of these movements see it as inflating the self to a false position of sovereignty.

The first woman to take a critical direction vis-à-vis Fichte is Sophie Mereau, who knew Fichte's early philosophy well,[10] as is evident in her novel *The Blooming Age of Sensation* (1794). The emotional relationships between its protagonists are portrayed in terms that echo Fichte's philosophy, with the difference that the protagonists (in particular the female character, Nanette) have to alternate the self-reflection of the I with a relationship with the political-social world that conditions the autonomy of the subject

---

[9] Mary Ellen Waithe, ed., *A History of Women Philosophers*, vol. 4, *Contemporary Women Philosophers, 1900–Today* (Dordrecht: Kluwer, 1995), xx. On this, see also Mary Ellen Waithe, "Sex, Lies, and Bigotry: The Canon of Philosophy," in *Methodological Reflections on Women's Contribution and Influence in the History of Philosophy*, ed. Sigridur Thorgeirsdottir and Ruth Edith Hagengruber (Dordrecht: Springer, 2020), 8.

[10] In a letter to his wife, Fichte wrote that only one woman, Sophie Mereau, attended his seminar (the *Privatissimum*); Johann Gottlieb Fichte to Marie Johanne Fichte, 17 June 1794, in *Gesamtausgabe der bayerischen Akademie der Wissenschaften* (hereafter cited as GA, followed by volume and part number), vol. 3.2, ed. Reinhard Lauth and Hans Jacob (Stuttgart: Friedrich Frommann/Günther Holzboog, 1970), 135.

and endangers the affective relationship itself.[11] Mereau's tale contrasts with such other romantic novels as Friedrich Schlegel's *Lucinde*, which shows the development of the male protagonist at the expense of the passive female characters. *The Blooming Age of Sensation* on the contrary tells of Nanette, who "demanded equal rights with the man she wanted to love."[12]

Another female-authored romantic novel that advances a philosophical critique of Fichtean idealism is Dorothea Veit's *Florentin*, published anonymously in 1801 (with Dorothea's husband-to-be Friedrich Schlegel named as editor). Rather than foregrounding a female protagonist, *Florentin* mimes, parodies, and critiques the male-centered *Bildungsroman*. The protagonist Florentin visits the Schwartzenbergs and tells them his complicated life-story. Raised by a housekeeper with occasional visits from a woman he thought was his mother, he was eventually taken to live with that woman, and with a sister whom he now met. His extremely pious mother imposed a punitive monastic regime on Florentin and his sister; at last escaping, he made a failed attempt to rescue his sister, where-upon his mother angrily revealed that she was not his mother at all. Fleeing to Venice, Florentin went through various troubled escapades culminating in a violent separation from his wife, who has aborted their child. Afterward Florentin flees the Schwartzenbergs to stay with their aunt Clementina—a sublimely beautiful, holy, philanthropic woman, now old and ill. He is drawn to her; there are hints that she may be his mother, but she remains remote and the story ends with Florentin simply disappearing again.

Far from finding himself, Florentin endlessly loses himself, and indeed he is "the product of a bizarre family structure of substitutes and absences."[13] Florentin needs to learn about his origins to know himself. If he could construct a narrative about his provenance, or find the people at its center, he could achieve self-knowledge and so ful-fillment. Without it he is ever restless and unsettled, left in an endless cycle of failed relationships. In effect, *Florentin* criticizes Friedrich Schlegel's version of romanticism in *Lucinde* (in response to which Veit wrote *Florentin*). *Lucinde*'s protagonist Julius moves through successive romantic relationships, using the women to realize different aspects of himself and so reach fulfillment, whereas Florentin moves through different women undergoing one disappointment after another.

Florentin also differs from the romantic fairy tale, in which the protagonist is typ-ically involved in a futile intellectual quest but manages to break out of this into the more fulfilling realm of feeling and/or love. The romantics used the fairy tale to em-body a critique of the limitations of the discursive intellect and affirm the primacy of affect. One female-authored romantic fairy tale compares interestingly with *Florentin*: Sophie Tieck's tale *The Old Man in the Cave* (1800).[14] The protagonist Leonhard visits

---

[11] Adrian Daub, *Uncivil Unions: The Metaphysics of Marriage in German Idealism and Romanticism* (Chicago: Chicago University Press, 2012), 216.

[12] Sophie Mereau, *Das Blüthenalter der Empfindung* (Gotha: Justus Perthes, 1794), 93.

[13] Helfer, "Dorothea Veit-Schlegel's *Florentin*," 154.

[14] English translation in Jeannine Blackwell and Shawn C. Jarvis, eds., *The Queen's Mirror: Fairy Tales by German Women, 1780–1900* (Lincoln: University of Nebraska Press, 2001), 75–88.

an old magician to request "knowing everything in its innermost and outermost essence, and particularly everything within one's own self," and "the gift of seeing my own thoughts standing before me after I have crafted them." The gift backfires as Leonhard finds himself constantly surrounded by a group of unpleasant and confusing figures, the embodiment of his half-formed thoughts, which he cannot escape. Fortunately he meets and falls in love with a mysterious girl, the magician's estranged daughter. Father and daughter are now reconciled, and the sorcerer frees Leonhard from the curse of his thoughts. The sorcerer counsels him: "a person does not really achieve anything through too great introspection, except great confusion,"[15] and Leonhard realizes that love is much more important.

The story is another critique of Fichte's self-positing self as well as of the systematizing ambitions of German idealism—these two being connected, since Fichte sought to ground and complete the unity of knowledge by deriving it systematically from the self-positing self. Tieck objects that the pursuit of complete, systematic knowledge is quixotic. One will only become lost in theory, unable to make contact with the real, sensible world. Feeling and affect precede and motivate thought, and Leonhard needs to escape from excessive thought back into feeling.

Here Tieck endorses core romantic ideas. Indeed her story has common features with another paradigm romantic fairy tale, Novalis's "Hyacinth and Rose-blossom."[16] Hyacinth abandons his childhood sweetheart Rose-blossom to travel the world in pursuit of insight into the mysteries of the universe, at last lifting the veil of Isis only to discover—Rose-blossom. In other words: the complete knowledge to which German idealism aspires is impossible, and we need to "invert" ourselves back into the realm of feeling and affect which precedes the intellect. Love shows the way, for in love we feel our dependency on another being and our affective nature.

Yet the happy endings of both romantic fairy tales are heart-warming, magical, but hollow. The beloved women in them are mere aesthetic images who bring happiness to the male protagonists. Thus, although romanticism stressed the primacy of feeling over intellect, the concern was generally with men's emotional fulfillment, women merely serving as means. Veit criticizes this by depicting as empty and unfulfilling Florentin's attempted aesthetic "use" of the women around him. Here Veit challenges romanticism from within, suggesting that rather than romantic love-relationships constituting a point when the self feels its dependence on someone outside it, the masculine self actually remains self-enclosed within these relationships, absorbed in its own imaginings.

If the idealist self-positing self and the romantic aesthetic imagining self are rejected, how is the self conceived instead? Part of an answer comes from Caroline Schlegel-Schelling's letters, one of her chief forms of writing (although only collected and published posthumously). Caroline's letters do not theorize the self but rather embody a conception

---

[15] Sophie Tieck, "The Old Man in the Cave," in Blackwell and Jarvis, *The Queen's Mirror*, 78, 87.

[16] Novalis, *Die Lehrlinge zu Saïs*, in *Schriften* (hereafter cited as HKA, followed by volume and page number), ed. Richard Samuel, Hans-Joachin Mähl, and Gerhard Schulz (Darmstadt: Wissenschaftliche Buchgesellschaft, 1975), vol. 1, 91–109.

of it as relational, affective, and linguistic. In the letters she tells others about life-events, her reading, her relationships, and tells her different interlocutors about one another. The self, here, is located in an ever-shifting web of relationships and it exercises agency by negotiating and renegotiating these relationships. This is not the autonomy of a sovereign, self-making self but that of a self inherently related with others; this is not a transcendental subject that builds reality following its own transcendental categories, but a subject whose identity *follows* (and does not *precede*) the relationships,[17] and whose agency cannot be rationally preestablished—a view we will find further developed by Günderrode[18] and Brentano von Arnim. Language is the central medium for negotiating these relationships, through the circulation of letters, as well as verbal and written communications. As well as being linguistic,[19] the relational self embodied here is also sensitive and affective, caught up in successive emotional responses to others and affecting them in turn.

It might be replied that the male romantics and idealists also regard the self as relational, for instance, when Hegel theorizes the constitutive role of relationships of recognition for the self, or when Schlegel states that the human being can be known only within its relations with others.[20] Although this is obviously a complicated issue, our suggestion is that the female romantics and idealists take the relationality of the self further, and more emphatically give relationships priority over individual selfhood. For example, Veit shows the hollowness of a self whose relationships with others take place primarily in the medium of their own aesthetic imagination. For Caroline Schlegel-Schelling, the self arises from within its epistolary exchanges and relationships *before* any subsequent theorization of their structures. Relationships with actual concrete others, who exist outside the self, come first.

Schlegel-Schelling's epistolary practice[21] further relates to the central romantic idea of *Symphilosophie* and of fragmentation, where the intrinsic incompleteness

---

[17] A consistency with contemporary feminist philosophy can be traced here: "the central notion on which . . . [feminism] rests is that of experience; the lived experience of real-life women that Adrienne Rich expresses . . . in the notion of 'the politics of location.' The politics of location means that the thinking, the theoretical process, is not abstract, universalized, objective, and detached, but rather that it is situated in the contingency of one's experience. . . . In other words, one's intellectual vision is not disembodied mental activity; rather, it is closely connected to one's place of enunciation, i.e., where one is actually speaking from"; Rosi Braidotti, "The Subject in Feminism," *Hypatia* 6, no. 2 (Summer 1991): 160.

[18] See Anna C. Ezekiel, "Narrative and Fragment: The Social Self in Karoline von Günderrode," *Symphilosophie. International Journal of Philosophical Romanticism* 2 (2020): 65–90.

[19] We find here traces of the importance given to language by Hamann and Herder, also echoed in August Wilhelm Schlegel's thought: to him, only through language can the subject separate from the object and thus constitute itself. See his *Vorlesungen über Philosophische Kunstlehre*, in *Kritische Ausgabe der Vorlesungen*, ed. Ernst Behler, vol. 1 (Munich: Schöningh, 1989), 5, and *Briefe über Poesie, Silbenmaß und Sprache*, in *Sämmtliche Werke*, ed. Eduard Böcking, vol. 7 (Hildesheim: Olms, 1971), 104.

[20] "The human being should be considered as human society." Friedrich Schlegel, *Transzendentalphilosophie*, KFSA XII, 44.

[21] Letters were women's privileged means of written expression. See Elke Frederiksen, "Deutsche Autorinnen im 19. Jahrhundert: Neue kritische Ansätze," *Colloquia Germanica* 14, no. 2 (1981): 97–113; see also, Barbara Becker-Cantarino, *Schriftstellerinnen der Romantik, Epoche—Werk—Wirkung* (Munich: C. H. Beck Verlag, 2000), 164–165.

of knowledge parallels the dynamism of the absolute. In this view, on the one hand, fragmentariness is not a sign of weakness of thought, nor is the fragment a piece of a static system which is completed by simply increasing the number of pieces in our possession. Each fragment is not simply a part of truth, but implies a continuous interpretation, infinite potential connections, and a dynamic system that does not serve as perfect and total knowledge. Contrary to German idealist aspirations to total systematicity, the "system" should be in endless transformation because of its incompleteness. On the other hand, the "system" of fragments reproduces the dynamism of the absolute and of life in nature, so that neither the single fragment nor the whole in which it is placed can be reduced to an object or to a static concept; on the contrary, they are in continuous transformation. This parallels the dynamism of the epistolary exchanges in which Caroline took part, so that her practice of letter writing performs the romantic idea of fragmentation. It thus exemplifies not only the self's relationality and sociability but also the romantic metaphysical view that the absolute is a dynamic whole-in-movement.

2 Women, Translation, and Romanticism

Caroline Schlegel-Schelling and Dorothea Tieck were pivotal in the so-called Schlegel-Tieck translation of Shakespeare's plays, which has decisively influenced both the German and European reception of Shakespeare and the principles of translation. Producing the translation was far from easy. Caroline encouraged August Wilhelm to embark on it in 1797, but he tired of the project and it had lapsed by 1802, then Ludwig Tieck eventually took over in 1825. In 1828 Tieck had still managed no new translations, so he enlisted help from his daughter Dorothea and from Wolf Heinrich Graf von Baudissin (a diplomat who had previously translated *Henry VIII* and whose involvement came at August Wilhelm's recommendation). The three—Ludwig, Dorothea, and Baudissin—then translated the remaining nineteen plays. To further complicate the authorship, Schlegel's original translations involved much work from Caroline, who edited and finalized many of his drafts and did some initial translating. Her importance is indicated by August Wilhelm's accomplishing virtually nothing further on the project after their 1803 divorce.

Thus the celebrated "Schlegel-Tieck" Shakespeare edition owes as much to Caroline and Dorothea as to August Wilhelm and Ludwig, not to mention Baudissin.[22] Yet the translations appeared under only August's and Ludwig's names. Caroline's contributions

---

[22] Baudissin's initial omission, however, gets corrected much more regularly and comprehensively than those of Caroline and Dorothea; see, e.g., Simon Williams, *Shakespeare on the German Stage* (Cambridge: Cambridge University Press, 2004), 150.

were silently incorporated into August Wilhelm's,[23] while Ludwig was comfortable "accepting nearly full credit for the translation."[24] He only belatedly clarified the key role of "an other translator who does not want to be named" (i.e., Dorothea, misleadingly described using masculine pronouns).[25] But to be fair, Caroline and Dorothea would have faced fierce criticism if named as authors. In the reception history of "Schlegel-Tieck," as long as Caroline's and Dorothea's work goes unacknowledged, the translations are celebrated; but once their work is acknowledged, the translations get criticized. Take Hermann Conrad's essay on Caroline; acknowledging her role, he speaks of "an edition brought to production allegedly by Schlegel but in reality largely by Caroline"; but he regards her interventions as "distortions," erroneous, childishly naïve, and repeatedly steering the translation project off course.[26] Others have branded Dorothea's translations "very inadequate"[27] or called her "an accomplished translator, but hardly in Schlegel's league."[28]

Little wonder that Dorothea Tieck preferred to stay hidden. She was similarly reticent about how she saw the task of the translator. She did, though, say that (1) the translator should reproduce the original as faithfully as possible, with minimum loss; so (2) women are better suited than men for translating, for it is women's nature to *recreate*, not create.[29] With (1), Dorothea states the core of romantic translation theory: a translation should reproduce the original as faithfully as possible. This was radically innovative. Translators then standardly improved, corrected, and freely amended their source texts. In contrast, for August Schlegel, "the translator should aspire . . . to [complete] equivalence . . . ; it was the translator's task to exercise a kind of 'negative capability'

[23] Some editions of the *Romeo and Juliet* translation credit Caroline as lead author (see Stott, "Caroline", in particular https://www.carolineschelling.com/caroline-and-shakespeare/). Likewise some editions of "Tieck's" Shakespeare translations are now attributed to Dorothea or Baudissin, respectively, depending who was lead translator in each case.

[24] Kenneth Larson, "The Origins of the 'Schlegel-Tieck' Shakespeare in the 1820s," *German Quarterly* 60, no. 1 (Winter 1987): 30. One of Tieck's credentials for taking on the Shakespeare project, his 1796 translation of *The Tempest*, was actually an unacknowledged collaboration with his sister Sophie; see Alan Corkhill, "Keeping It in the Family? The Creative Collaboration of Sophie and Dorothea Tieck," in *Collective Creativity: Collaborative Work in the Sciences, Literature, and the Arts*, ed. Gerhard Fischer and Florian Vassen (Amsterdam: Rodopi, 2011), 123.

[25] In the third volume of the new series, he admitted that the basic translating was done by "young friends," later identified in notes to volume 7 as Baudissin and an unnamed other. Ludwig Tieck, "Vorrede" to *Shakespeares dramatische Werke*, vol. 3 (Berlin: Reimer, 1825–33), iii–iv; "Nachwort," vol. 7, 378. In fairness, Dorothea really did not want to be named; see her letter to Friedrich von Uechtritz, Dresden, 8 March 1833, ed. Sophia Zell, in *Letters and Texts: Intellectual Berlin around 1800*, ed. Anne Baillot, online edition of letters, https://www.berliner-intellektuelle.eu/manuscript?Brief07DorotheaT ieckanUechtritz + en#1.

[26] Hermann Conrad, "Caroline and the Translation of Shakespeare," trans. Douglas Stott, https://www.carolineschelling.com/caroline-and-shakespeare/conrad-caroline-shakespeare/.

[27] *Encyclopedia Americana* (1919), vol. 24, s.v. "Schlegel, August Wilhelm," 376.

[28] Louise Adey, "Reading between the Lines: Tieck's Prolegomena to the Schlegel-Tieck Edition of Shakespeare," *Bulletin of the John Rylands University Library of Manchester* 71, no. 3 (1989): 90.

[29] For (1) see Dorothea's letter to Uechtritz cited earlier; for (2) her letter to him of July 15, 1831 (on the website cited earlier).

which would allow him to disappear behind his material. The translation, when complete, should stand as a work of art in its own right, without anything to suggest that it was...a copy."[30]

This translation theory is bound up with romantic metaphysics and epistemology. The idea is that an artwork, such as *Romeo and Juliet*, is an organic whole where every element of the work flows from its overarching unity.[31] This unity can only be apprehended intuitively, since it is a synthetic unity that does not correspond to a mere aggregate of parts that can be analyzed through concepts. The translator must intuit this animating spirit and then recreate it. This view of translation belongs within romantic metaphysics, according to which the world is an organic and unitary whole whose unity we can only apprehend intuitively.

The translator, then, reproduces the original faithfully by recreating its spirit, not mechanically copying its every letter. This brings us back to the debate at the end of the eighteenth century resulting from the Kantian separation between the spirit and the letter of a philosophical work,[32] from which the romantics developed their ideas of criticism and translation.[33] These imply the enhancement (*Potenzierung*) of a text: in Friedrich Schlegel's words, we must understand the literary work better than the author himself,[34] because the work "knows more than it says and wants more than it knows."[35]

On this view fidelity to the original is consistent with, indeed requires, that translation be creative. In fact, Novalis argues that translation is an artistic production, a way of making poetry.[36] Here he distinguishes two types of translation. The first, called "grammatical" (*grammatisch*), requires a discursive faculty and a lot of erudition to make a semantic and syntactical translation without any pretension to its becoming a literary work of its own.[37] The second type Novalis calls "transformative" (*verändernd*). It requires a poetic ability to recreate the whole of the work: "the true translator of this

---

[30] Adey, "Reading between the Lines," 90–91. See also August Wilhelm Schlegel, "Etwas über William Shakespeare bei Gelegenheit Wilhelm Meisters," *Die Horen* 6, no. 4 (1796): 57–112.

[31] Schlegel, "Etwas," and "Über Shakespeares Romeo und Julia," *Die Horen* 10, no. 6 (1797): 560.

[32] Fichte highlighted the difference between spirit and letter, too. Indeed, he claimed his philosophy was Kantian in spirit and that the *Wissenschaftslehre* could be told (*mitteilt*) only through the spirit, and not through the letter (*Grundlage der gesammten Wissenschaftslehre*, GA I.2, 414). See also: Johann Gottlieb Fichte, *Von den Pflichten der Gelehrten. Vorlesungen und Entwürfe*, GA II.3, 295–342, and *Über Geist und Buchstab in der Philosophie. In einer Reihe von Briefen*, GA I.6, 333–361.

[33] "The *critique* should not judge the works of art according to a universal ideal, but seek the individual ideal of each work." Friedrich Schlegel, *Fragmente zur Poesie und Literatur*, KFSA XVI, 270, no. 197. The relationship between criticism and translation is very close, as each translation implies a critical relationship with its object; see Friedrich Schlegel, *Philosophische Lehrjahre*, KFSA XVIII, 386, no. 784.

[34] Schlegel, *Philosophische Lehrjahre*, KFSA XVIII, 63, no. 434.

[35] Friedrich Schlegel, *Über Goethes Meister*, KFSA II, 140.

[36] "Translating is as much about writing poetry as creating one's own works—and it is more difficult, less frequent. After all, all poetry is translation"; Novalis to A. W. Schlegel, 30 November 1797, HKA IV, 237.

[37] André Stanguennec, *La philosophie romantique allemande* (Paris: Vrin, 2011), 89.

kind must be an artist himself, and be able to give the idea of the whole in any way he chooses. He must be the poet of the poet."[38]

Hence, we have August's principles that a translation should appear to be a complete, self-contained work and that translation is a creative activity in which a new artwork is made.[39] He stated those views in two essays connected with the Shakespeare translation project. The first sketches the project's guiding translation principles (1796); the second elaborates their bearing on *Romeo and Juliet* (1797). But *Romeo and Juliet* was, as mentioned already, primarily translated by Caroline.[40] In turn, significant portions of August's second essay are lifted from two letters Caroline wrote to him in 1797,[41] and August later admitted that Caroline coauthored the essay.[42]

In these two letters (numbers 186 and 187) Caroline indeed states the key romantic ideas about translation: the work is an organic unity; all its parts belong in it necessarily, flowing out of its unity; the unity must be apprehended intuitively; and, further, *Romeo and Juliet*'s unifying principle is the unity of opposites—the sensual and the spiritual, love and death, bliss, and suffering. What has gone down in intellectual history as August's bold and original view of translation, then, owes much to Caroline. We have shown that Dorothea subscribed to this translation theory too, using it to claim women's greater capacity as translators on the grounds that they can better receive the spirit of the original text.[43] But Caroline, in particular, helps to formulate romantic translation theory in the first place, and she thereby contributes to articulating romantic metaphysics more broadly. For in romanticism translation is not a marginal issue but models the entire role of intuition as our basic relation to the world, as well as our creativity as knowing subjects and the dynamic vitality of the absolute. Romantic metaphysics is never credited to Caroline, but in fact she helped to formulate it by contributing to the translation theory that is part of it.[44]

---

[38] Novalis, *Blüthenstaub*, HKA II, 437, no. 68.

[39] The high quality of translations by romantic philosophers was noticed by Germaine de Staël: "the art of translation is developed further in German than in any other European dialect," *De l'Allemagne*, vol. 1 (Paris: Libraire Stéréotype, 1814), 254.

[40] See Conrad, "Caroline and the Translation of Shakespeare" (although for Conrad the extent of her involvement is something negative). He partly draws on Rudolf Genée, *A. W. Schlegel und Shakespeare: ein Beitrag zur Würdigung der Schlegelschen Übersetzungen* (Berlin: Reimer, 1903).

[41] Caroline, letters 186 and 187 to Schlegel, Jena, 1797 (day and month uncertain), https://www.caroli neschelling.com/letters/volume-1-index/letter-186/, and https://www.carolineschelling.com/letters/vol ume-1-index/letter-187/.

[42] August Wilhelm Schlegel, *Kritische Schriften* (Reimer: Berlin, 1828), I, xvii–xviii.

[43] On the feminization of translation, see Lorely French, "The Magic of Translation: Dorothea Schlegel's *Geschichte des Zauberers Merlin*," *Pacific Coast Philology* 40, no. 1 (2005): 36–56. Here French is discussing Veit's "translation," *Story of the Magician Merlin*, which in fact has no single original and includes an "alternative" ending that Veit derived from obscure sources. This then is another creative translation.

[44] Caroline's letters on *Romeo and Juliet* predate F. Schlegel's essay on Goethe's *Meister* (1798) and Novalis's *Blüthenstaub* (1798) and are roughly contemporaneous with Novalis's 1797 letter to A. W. Schlegel concerning translation. Caroline's views were not merely derivative of the men's; she was a coworker in producing these ideas.

Another dimension of romanticism manifested in the Shakespeare project was collaboration and collective creativity—philosophizing together, *Symphilosophie*. Philosophical discussion was considered in terms of a dialectic between the understanding and the incomprehension of the other, thus allowing perennial openness to the problem under discussion and continuous renewal of philosophical research. ("If in the communication between thoughts there is an alternation between absolute understanding and absolute non-comprehension, then this can be called philosophical friendship.")[45] The romantics sought to think and write together, using their journal, the *Athenaeum*, to embody *Symphilosophie*. This collaborative spirit, which extended to the Shakespeare translation, created openings for women, as with Caroline and Dorothea Tieck as translators. Yet these remained asymmetrical and unequal exchanges: the women depended on the men much more than the men depended on them, and the women did not receive equal acknowledgment as authors or creators. As Jane Kneller reminds us,[46] Dorothea Veit described the Early German romantic symphilosophical circle as a "republic of nothing but despots."[47]

3 NATURE, BIRTH, AND DEATH

In an 1800 letter to Schelling, Schlegel-Schelling says she will answer his previous letter "cross-wise X as in Friedrich [Schlegel]'s philosophemes." She continues:

> I must also test to see whether from
>
> death   bliss
>   x
> pain   love
>
> I can extract life and peace. You will doubtless not want to press me too hard to reveal whence I derive my primal axioms in this regard. How irksome when one knows something for certain and then is also supposed to render an account of the source from whence one has it.[48]

---

[45] This fragment is by Fr. Schlegel but published in *Blüthenstaub* by Novalis: KFSA II, 164, no. 20.

[46] Jane Kneller, "Feminism," in *The Oxford Handbook of German Philosophy in the Nineteenth Century*, ed. Michael N. Forster and Kristin Gjesdal (Oxford: Oxford University Press, 2015), 546.

[47] Dorothea Veit to Schleiermacher, 16 January 1800, in Friedrich Daniel Ernst Schleiermacher, *Kritische Gesamtausgabe*, vol. V.3, ed. Andreas Arndt and Wolfgang Virmond (Berlin: de Gruyter, 1992), 347. Women were important for the formulation of Schleiermacher's philosophy, too. For example, his concept of "sociability" (*Geselligkeit*) was strongly influenced by Henriette Herz; see Ulrike Wagner, "Schleiermacher's *Geselligkeit*, Henriette Herz, and the 'Convivial Turn,'" in *Conviviality at the Crossroads: The Poetics and Politics of Everyday Encounters*, ed. Oscar Hemer, Maja Povrzanović Frykman, and Per-Markku Ristilammi (Cham: Palgrave, 2020), 65–87.

[48] Caroline, letter 274d to Schelling, Braunschweig, 18 November 1800, https://www.carolineschelling.com/letters/volume-2-index/letter-274d/.

And, after four sentences concerning a collaborative nature-poem between Goethe and Schelling, "amid your most recent intentions, did you also think of your good father and your good mother, those who perhaps more simply but certainly just as forcefully and lovingly gave you your *first* life?"

The context is the recent death of Caroline's beloved daughter Auguste, although her "primal axiom" also draws on her reading of *Romeo and Juliet*, extending its organizing principle—the unity of death and love, bliss and pain—to the cosmos generally. The axiom is a cross, first, as in Christianity—an emblem of both suffering and reconciliation. Second, it is chiasmatic: on the one hand, death and pain cut across the bliss of love; on the other hand, death and bliss go together, as death brings us bliss (oblivion) by relieving us from the pains of love. This is *her* primal axiom, Caroline says, effectively setting it against other idealist first principles: Fichte's "I am I," and, for Schelling, the first principles governing the construction of nature, namely infinite productivity and infinite inhibition by which it becomes dammed up into finite products. Compared to these other first principles, Caroline's is more concrete and existential: the primal splitting is between love and death, not subject and object. We love others, yet they die—and by then she had lost all four of her children. By implication, again, the self is relational; what is primal is the self's involvement in and vulnerability to love-relationships, rather than an abstract principle of self-constitution. The tangible matters of birth, vulnerability, and death to which Caroline refers do not usually figure in the abstract systems of German idealism, despite their pervasiveness in people's lives.

The death-love relation does, however, receive systematic elaboration from Karoline von Günderrode. She sets out a philosophy in which death is reunification into the whole (*Alles*) from which we were separated at birth. This reunification leads to further cycles of rebirth, part of a vast cosmic progression whereby nature progressively spiritualizes itself.

Günderrode was syncretistic, drawing on Novalis (especially his *Hymns to the Night*), Schleiermacher (*On Religion*), the *Athenaeum*, Fichte (*Vocation of Humankind*), and Schelling (including his *Ideas for a Philosophy of Nature*).[49] Thus she combined idealist and romantic ideas. She also read extensively in religion and mythology, combining Eastern ideas of rebirth with a philosophy of nature influenced by Schelling. Among the women considered here, Günderrode came closest to idealist system-building, although she also wrote poems, dramas, and letters. Here we reconstruct her cosmology as sketched in *Story of a Brahmin* (published as "Tian"), and the fictitious exchange of

---

[49] Günderrode composed a *Studienbuch* indicating her reading; see Steven D. Martinson, "'. . . aus dem Schiffbruch des irdischen Lebens': The Literature of Karoline von Günderrode and Early German Romantic and Idealist Philosophy," *German Studies Review* 28, no. 2 (2005): 303–326, and Helga Dormann, *Die Kunst des inneren Sinns. Mythisierung der inneren und äusseren Natur im Werk Karoline von Günderrodes* (Würzburg: Königshausen und Neumann, 2004), 8–9. She read all of Schelling's philosophy of nature texts plus his *System of Transcendental Idealism* and *Bruno* (Dormann, *Die Kunst*, 8). See also Karoline von Günderrode, *Ausgewählte Studien*, in *Sämtliche Werke und ausgewählte Studien* (hereafter cited as SW, followed by volume and page numbers), ed. Walter Morgenthaler, vol. 2 (Basel: Stroemfeld/Roter Stern, 1991), 359–406 for her notes on philosophy of nature.

letters with Eusebio (i.e., Creuzer, her then lover), included in her final poetry collection, *Melete*; these letters draw on her essay "Idea of the Earth" (from her *Nachlass*).[50]

For Günderrode, there is a unitary whole with which we are all originally one, but from which we become separated in being born as finite individuals. In the poem "The Wayfarer's Descent," she writes:

> Too late! You are born to the day,
> Separated from the element of life,
> We command becoming, not being,
> And you are already separated from the mother's womb
> Parted from dreams by your consciousness.[51]

Günderrode describes the whole in maternal terms as a womb, a primal sea, and ground. She also identifies it with the earth; as universal, infinite, eternal life; and as "the all," *das Alles*, or *die Allheit*, like other romantics. The whole is revealed to us in intuition[52] but lost to us as conscious, thinking subjects.[53] We cling to our thoughts, but we also long for the lost unity, pulled between finitude and the infinite.[54]

We are drawn beyond our finitude because we all remain part of universal life, even though we are finite individuals.[55] Günderrode articulates this through the notion of "elements." For her, all human beings retain and contain elements of universal life, a universal force which contains and encompasses everything that has existed, still exists, and will exist in the future, and which at the same time is the cause of everything: it is creator and created.[56] The elements of life are embodied in electrical currents and magnetic and chemical forces flowing through and animating us. At lower levels of nature too, inanimate, mechanical bodies that are mere matter in motion are attracted together because they share elements of infinite life; magnetism realizes this attraction further, electricity still further,[57] and most of all that "most inner mixture of different elements with the highest grade of connection and attraction which we call life."[58] Thus "attraction" is pervasive and obtains because the elements of infinite life that are shared out among individual beings draw them together, trying to reunite into their original oneness.

For Günderrode, "individual life is given over to the law of mortality."[59] Ultimately individual beings must dissolve back into the whole, on which, after all, they depend. But once

---

[50] Having arranged to publish *Melete*, after Günderrode's suicide in 1806 Creuzer withdrew it; it only came out in 1906. See also Anna Ezekiel's chapter on Günderrode in this *Handbook*.

[51] Karoline von Günderrode, *Gedichte und Phantasien*, SW I, 73.

[52] Karoline von Günderrode, *Geschichte eines Braminen*, SW I, 309.

[53] Karoline von Günderrode, *An Eusebio*, SW1, 359.

[54] Günderrode, *Gedichte und Phantasien*, SW 1, 52–53.

[55] Günderrode, *An Eusebio*, SW 1, 359.

[56] Günderrode, *Geschichte eines Braminen*, SW I, 309.

[57] Karoline von Günderrode, *Ausgewählte Studien*, SW II, 366.

[58] Karoline von Günderrode, *Idee der Erde*, SW I, 446.

[59] Günderrode, *An Eusebio*, SW I, 359.

returned to infinite life, these beings strengthen and replenish it. Having had to struggle against their previous individuation to reunite, the currents of universal life within the now-dead individuals have been strengthened and so, now returned to universal life, they enhance *its* vitality and power. As a result, the earth now rebirths new individuals but more highly animated and energized ones.[60] Hence, for Günderrode, nature begins by producing mechanical beings; their elements when reabsorbed into the earth enable it to produce magnetic (i.e., more animated) beings, then electrical, chemical, organic, and finally human beings. This process must continue until the earth has become as vital as it can be: "The earth rebirths [gebiert . . . wieder] the life-material that has been given back to it in new appearances, until, through ever-new transformations, all that is capable of life within it has become living. This would be achieved if all masses became organic."[61] This happens through the rebirth of individual human beings, as she continues:

> so every mortal gives back to the earth a heightened, more developed elementary life, which the earth develops further into rising forms; and through this, by taking ever more developed elements into itself, the organism must become more complete and universal. . . . The Indian idea of the transmigration of soul corresponds to this view . . . [but ultimately] the earth can only finally reach its authentic, actual existence when it has dissolved all its appearances in a communal organism, when spirit and body so completely penetrate one another that all bodies, all forms are at once also thought and soul and all thoughts are at once also form and body and a truly clarified body, without defects and illness and immortal, therefore quite different from what we call body or matter, to which we attach transience, illness, weight and deficiency.

When human individuals die, then, the vital currents that had been in them replenish the earth, so that it now re-produces beings in which the elements and the life force are stronger.[62] The particular mixture of which every human being is made up and the human being's particular form of life dissolve, but the *Lebenstoff* (life-material) is born again in ever new phenomena and individuals. In every cycle, life is strengthened, until everything that can receive life has become a living being, and until the entirety of existing matter has become organic. Everyone is involved in this process of rebirth toward the realization of the idea of the earth, in which both organic and inorganic phenomena dissolve into a single organism,[63] and spirit and body pervade each other. At this point, the spirit will be body, the body will also be thinking, thinking will be an enlightened body, and the form will correspond to the essence: the realization of the earth will bring

---

[60] We find something similar in Friedrich Schlegel's Cologne lectures of 1804. He had dealt for a long time with Indian philosophy, an interest Günderrode shared. See Friedrich Schlegel, *Entwicklung der Philosophie in zwölf Büchern*, KFSA XIII, 17.

[61] Günderrode, *An Eusebio*, SW I, 359–360. See also Günderrode, *Geschichte eines Braminen*, SW I, 310.

[62] Günderrode, *Idee der Erde*, SW I, 447.

[63] "The Earth can only attain its appropriate existence [*Dasein*] when its organic and inorganic phenomena [*Erscheinungen*] dissolve into a common organism." Günderrode, *Idee der Erde*, SW I, 448.

truth, justice, and beauty.[64] For this reason, the realization of the idea of the earth is not only a path of rebirth of vital forces but also a moral path.[65]

Günderrode thus combines a Christian conception of posthumous resurrection of the spiritual body with an Eastern idea of rebirth. She shares themes with Hölderlin: our separation from the original unity (of being, for Hölderlin; of the earth, for Günderrode) and longing to reunite into "the all" and dissolve our individuality: "life is immortal and rises and falls in the elements, for they are life itself, but the particular and individual life is only a form of life [*Lebensform*] given by this particular combination, attraction and contact, which cannot last longer than the combination itself."[66] However, compared to Hölderlin, Günderrode connects these themes more closely with birth, death, and rebirth. Günderrode also draws on Schelling's idea of constitutive forces of attraction and repulsion within nature, but whereas he stresses their polarity, Günderrode emphasizes attraction, and she foregrounds "elements," understood broadly as attractive currents that reflect the presence in us of universal life.[67] Günderrode puts her own interpretation upon Schelling's idea that nature is visible spirit and spirit is invisible nature. She agrees with him that infinite life advances beyond embodied finite life into higher, more spiritual forms—thought, sensation and, consciousness. But she joins this to the view that after death we are each reborn, assuming increasingly spiritualized forms with each rebirth.[68]

Overall, Günderrode sets out an original philosophy of nature, distinctive in its focus on not only death and immortality but also birth and rebirth, and in uniting the metaphysics of nature with moral questions.[69]

4 Idealism, Romanticism, and Freedom: The Floor to Women

Freedom is a central theme of idealism and romanticism. The difficulty of how freedom and nature can coexist is already at stake in Kantian philosophy. In the *Critique of the*

---

[64] "Truth is the expression of always being equal to oneself; justice is the striving of the totality in the particular to be equal to itself; beauty is being equal and harmonious to oneself." Günderrode, *Idee der Erde*, SW I, 448.

[65] Günderrode, *Idee der Erde*, SW I, 448.

[66] Günderrode, *Idee der Erde*, SW I, 446.

[67] Günderrode is close to Franz von Baader's philosophy of nature. For him the main forces of nature are three (attraction, repulsion, and impulse to unity) and are also called "elements." See Franz von Baader, *Beiträge zur Elementar-physiologie*, in *Sämtliche Werke*, ed. Franz Hoggmann and Julius Hamberger, vol. 3 (Aalen: Scientia Verlag, 1987), 205. Also notably, Fichte grew much closer to Günderrode's standpoint after 1800, now seeing "life" as preceding the two poles I/not-I and, instead of their opposition, seeing a flow of multiplicities and differences: Fichte, *Die Bestimmung des Menschen*, GA 1.6, 306.

[68] Günderrode has often been seen as obsessed with death, but for her, death is just part of the process by which life strengthens itself and progressively rises up to immortality.

[69] This wasn't the case for Schelling, but we can find a similar attempt in Friedrich Schlegel. See Giulia Valpione, "Bildung et vie dans la philosophie politique de Friedrich Schlegel," in *L'Homme et la nature*

Power of Judgment (1790), Kant attempts to bridge the gap between the practical perspective that contemplates freedom and the cognitive perspective that assumes determinism in nature. Yet the contrast between the moral subject and the natural world remains. For Kant, being free implies overcoming one's own nature, giving up one's impulses, attitudes, and habits ("second nature") to submit to the rational and sovereign will. Freedom is likewise at the heart of Fichte's philosophy.[70] The freedom of the "I" in his 1794 *Grundlage* is described as a tendency to autonomy, the ability to impose one's own laws on oneself;[71] while in the *Sittenlehre*, it is a tendency to absolute spontaneous activity,[72] in a relationship of mutual determination between the "I" and the "not-I." The topic of freedom recurs in Schelling's works: to him, freedom is the beginning and the end of all philosophy.[73] Unlike Fichte, but like the romantics,[74] he places the germ of freedom already in nature, and the human being participates in it as part of nature. Moreover, to Schelling, the development of nature and its freedom is characterized by the division into poles, negative and positive. The division into genders is the result of this polarization.[75] Although this radical difference is structural to the development of nature's freedom so that both poles are necessary, the female pole is identified as the negative of the male pole.[76]

This theme registers in romanticism beyond the philosophy of nature, as the disparity of male and female gets borne out in the inequality between male and female contributors to romanticism. If male-female polarity is necessary for the development of nature's freedom, this hides the preponderance of the male pole, which in the end dictates and imposes its own perspective on freedom upon the whole of which it is part. As we have shown, the voice that deals with freedom is still considered exclusively masculine, a voice that considers the diversity between the sexes yet claims to speak on behalf of both. Although the position of women is included in the symphilosophical dialogue, the women of romanticism are almost always excluded from the possibility of saying what freedom is for them. And considering the centrality of this concept for idealism and romanticism, this is no small thing. For example, Schlegel wrote in *On Philosophy: To Dorothea* that women are the privileged recipients of philosophy, yet

dans le romantisme allemand. Politique, critique et esthétique, ed. Giulia Valpione (Zürich: Lit Verlag, 2021), 147–162.

[70] "My [philosophical] system is the system of freedom." Fichte to Baggesen, April-May 1795, GA III.2, 298.

[71] See the last (practical) part of the *Grundlage der Wissenschaftslehre*, GA I.2, 385–451.

[72] Fichte, *Sittenlehre*, GA I.5, 54.

[73] Friedrich Wilhelm Joseph Schelling, *Vom Ich als Prinzip der Philosophie*, in *Historisch-kritische Ausgabe* (hereafter cited as AA, followed by volume with part no., and page number), ed. Hartmut Buchner et al., vol. 1.2 (Stuttgart: Fromman-Holzboog, 1980), 101.

[74] Schlegel, *Transzendentalphilosophie*, KFSA XII, 56. Novalis, *Notes for a "Romantic Encyclopedia,"* trans. and ed. David W. Wood (Albany: State University of New York Press, 2007), 27, no. 172.

[75] On this, see Alison Stone, *Nature, Ethics and Gender in German Romanticism and Idealism* (London: Rowman & Littlefield, 2018), 173–174, and Peter Hanns Reill, *Vitalizing Nature in the Enlightenment* (Berkeley: University of California Press, 2005).

[76] Stone, *Nature, Ethics*, 174.

he represents them as passive subjects, ready to accept the teaching of the speaker—inevitably a man—who describes what they have to study (or not): "I will certainly not expect you to devote yourself to the external history of the humankind";[77] "you would hardly adapt to a division of your being. Without someone to act as your intermediary it would perhaps be completely impossible."[78]

On the one hand, Friedrich Schlegel admits women's intellectual equality with men, even arguing that sexual difference is only an external aspect of human existence,[79] and that women's vocation is not directed to domestic life. On the other hand, "woman is a domestic being,"[80] so that women rarely look up from prejudices and banality, whereas men, as members of the estates (*Stände*)—from which women were excluded—are endowed with a sense of honor and duty that brings them closer to religion.[81] Confirming the romantic men's attitude toward women is *Athenaeum Fragment* no. 364, by Schleiermacher, specifying a "Rational Catechism for Noble Women"[82] that includes ten commandments and a creed in which, over and over again, the formula "you must not" is imposed on the female reader. This is despite Schleiermacher—like Friedrich Schlegel—articulating a nongendered account of the self that precedes the split between male and female.[83]

Similarly, Novalis relegates the feminine to the private sphere. The queen's role within the monarchy is to deal with the domestic sphere of action and not the political one.[84] The queen can speak in the institutional sphere, but only about what modern political philosophy defines as "private" (the education of women and children and domestic customs) or as the sphere of care—as the queen must ensure that the poor and the ill are sufficiently nourished.[85] Again, while Schlegel in his Cologne lectures criticizes the exclusion of women from laws of inheritance and property ownership, a point in favor of women's freedom, he does not recognize the possibility of women assuming a different role in society from the strictly domestic one. Above all, little space was given to what women *themselves* had to say in this regard, even within the early German romantic circle and despite the importance of *Symphilosophie*.

Yet even if they were not listened to, romantic women gave freedom a key role in their philosophy: a concept of freedom that (in contrast with the male romantics and idealists) implied political reflection and engagement by women, and in which

[77] Friedrich Schlegel, *Über die Philosophie. An Dorothea*, KFSA VIII, 48.

[78] Schlegel, *Über die Philosophie*, KFSA VIII, 57; see Daub, *Uncivil Unions*, 235.

[79] Schlegel, *Über die Philosophie*, KFSA VIII, 45.

[80] Schlegel, *Über die Philosophie*, KFSA VIII, 299.

[81] Schlegel, *Über die Philosophie*, KFSA VIII, 300.

[82] In Schlegel, *Fragmente*, KFSA II, 231, no. 364.

[83] Thandeka, "Schleiermacher, Feminism and Liberation Theologies: A Key," in *The Cambridge Companion to Friedrich Schleiermacher*, ed. Jacqueline Mariña (Cambridge: Cambridge University Press, 2005), 287–306.

[84] "The queen does not have a political, but a domestic sphere of influence"; Novalis, *Glaube und Liebe*, HKA II, 491, no. 27.

[85] Novalis, *Glaube und Liebe*, HKA II, 491, no. 27.

freedom is exercised from within circumstances and relationships rather than preceding or preconstituting them. The most interesting reflections on this subject come from Günderrode and her close friend and interlocutor Bettina Brentano von Arnim.

Freedom and its relationship with nature and destiny is central to Günderrode's thinking, a *fil rouge* in all her plays. In them, the necessity of destiny is equated with natural necessity,[86] and the heroes have to face their inability to be the masters of their own fates. The prophet Muhammad perceives himself to be without any will (*willenlos*), feeling himself not a subject *of* action but as subject *to* it: "it came over me."[87] The Sultan of the Mongols bends laws and customs to marry Nerissa, whom he believes to be his sister; nevertheless, they will be unable to get married because he has killed her brother (without knowing the blood bond with Nerissa).[88] Furthermore, the magician of *Magic and Destiny* expends all his vital force (*Lebenskraft*) to change the destiny of his son Ligares, who at first opposes his father's maxim: "the stars do not circle because humans act: Humans change according to the course of the stars . . . Thoughts rise and fall with the course of the heavenly bodies."[89] Even Ligares, however, must eventually admit that his actions were not actually the fruit of freedom: "so I think, I was merely forced to do it."[90] Finally, Nikator (the protagonist of the homonymous play) declares that he feels like a servant of destiny: "from battle to battle I am being dragged. . . . We would like to stand against the Lord of Chance, but *he* wins. . . . The steersman does not master the wave, it pulls him away with its wild force."[91]

However, Günderrode is not a determinist; in her works, we find two ways in which freedom manifests itself. The first concerns Nikator, who is free when he decides to follow the voice of his heart even at the price of disobeying the king's orders—whereas following the sovereign's will would have made Nikator a slave.[92] The second way in which one of Günderrode's characters expresses freedom is in the play *Hildgund*. Hildgund is portrayed as a heroine for two reasons. (1) Dragged by the power of fate back into the arms of Attila, from whom she has fled, she manages to exploit this condition in her own favor, deciding to kill Attila. (2) As a woman, she is subject to external powers and forces, whereas man can claim to manage his own existence autonomously: man dictates (or at least claims to dictate) the law of his own actions, like the Kantian sovereign subject. In contrast, a woman's life is not in her hands, says the protagonist Hildgund: "how lordly is man, he shapes his destiny, / by just his own powers is his law at its goal. / Woman's destiny, ah! Does not rest in her own hand! / Now she follows need,

---

[86] Karoline von Günderrode, *Muhammad, the Prophet of Mecca*, in *Poetic Fragments*, 177. A similar thought is expressed in her play *Magic and Fate*: "The gods' will has given you to me, / For God's will speaks also through fate." Karoline von Günderrode, *Magie und Schicksal*, SW I, 268.

[87] Günderrode, *Muhammad*, 177; see also 194.

[88] The novel is *Udohla* and can be found in SW I, 203–231.

[89] Günderrode, *Magie und Schicksal*, SW I, 235.

[90] Günderrode, *Magie und Schicksal*, SW I, 275.

[91] Karoline von Günderrode, *Nikator*, SW I, 279–280; italics added.

[92] Günderrode, *Nikator*, SW I, 290.

now strict custom's will, / Can one revoke what superior power commands?"[93] Here Günderrode shows awareness that women are not only subject to destiny but also to the will of men who decide on their futures. Unlike Nikator, therefore, Hildgund not only manages to assert a form of freedom even within the constraint of destiny, but she also does this from a position of greater vulnerability. As Anna Ezekiel points out, Hildgund uses precisely her disadvantageous position as a woman to fulfil her desire to free herself, her family, and her homeland from Attila's threat.[94]

What does Günderrode's difference from the male philosophers of romanticism consist in? The difference is not that Günderrode rejected the idea of the sovereign and autonomous Kantian subject (as Ezekiel claims), since the male romantic philosophers also underline the natural and vital forces to which the human being is perpetually subjected. In 1801, Friedrich Schlegel criticized the idea of freedom of will as the "absolute faculty of causality" enabling human beings to determine themselves.[95] For Schlegel, this presupposes a vision of nature as a machine subject to strict determinism, from which, therefore, it is possible to escape only through a radical break. In declared contrast with Kant, for Schlegel nature is an organism and is free, and the human being is free, too, only because it is the highest expression of nature.[96] Thus human freedom is conditioned by the organic whole of nature. This means that the human individual cannot be fully free until the world of which it is part is free too. But since the world is not yet perfect, the human being has a role in perfecting it.[97] For Novalis, too, nature has to progress toward morality,[98] and the human being's crucial role is to form, or cultivate (*bilden*), the earth.[99]

Schlegel and Günderrode therefore agree that freedom is not the imposition of a sovereign will that can subvert destiny and subjugate nature. What distinguishes Günderrode, though, is that the most striking act of freedom in her plays is performed by someone who not only follows and exploits the course of destiny (Hildgund accepts the need to return to Attila) but also exploits her position of social inferiority (a woman who cannot claim to govern her future) to change the course of events. Ligares, who believed he could subdue the course of the stars to his action, cannot do it; nor can the Sultan of the Mongols, who was willing to subvert the laws and customs in order to marry Nerissa. Hildgund, by contrast, succeeds. She does not claim to master the order of things, but proceeds secretly—she does not announce to her father that she intends to kill Attila, and neither is the tyrant's murder narrated in the play. She exploits her condition of inferiority and uses the idea that she, as a woman, is completely harmless. It is a question not of absolute autonomy imposing its own laws on the world, but a more

---

[93] Günderrode, *Hildgund*, in *Poetic Fragments*, 76.
[94] Anna Ezekiel, "Metamorphosis, Personhood, and Power in Karoline von Günderrode," *European Romantic Review* 25, no. 6 (2014): 773–791.
[95] Schlegel, *Transzendentalphilosophie*, KFSA XII, 50.
[96] Schlegel, *Transzendentalphilosophie*, KFSA XII, 72.
[97] Schlegel, *Transzendentalphilosophie*, KFSA XII, 42.
[98] Novalis, *Fragmente und Studien 1799–1800*, HKA III, 601, no. 291.
[99] Novalis, *Blüthenstaub*, HKA II, 427, no. 32.

complex awareness of the particular condition and set of relationships with which one has to deal. This is evident not only in Günderrode's plays, but also in her conception of virtue in the "Idea of the Earth," as we have shown.

This is Günderrode's originality with respect to the male philosophers of romanticism. The men conceive of the division of the sexes as steps in the development of freedom, but this is, after all, only an echo of their own voices because women do not enjoy their own freedom and self-determination. Günderrode shows us an untraveled alternative path, in which women can also enjoy freedom, although in a different way, where precisely because they are women, their mode of self-determination is less spectacular but ultimately more effective.

The close link between nature and freedom returns in Brentano von Arnim, who combines this theme with a strong interest in social questions, bringing her thought closer to the so-called Jungdeutsche (Heinrich Heine and others) and the Left Hegelians.[100]

In her correspondence with her brother Clemens, Brentano von Arnim is angry that her brother could never see her for what she was, only for what she should have been: "you never read me in my language; you got another nature out of me."[101] That misunderstanding manifests her brother's lack of love for her; for the fusion of two beings in the feeling of love[102] is at the basis of that reciprocity between subject and object that is proper to the cognitive process: "I want to be loved, or I want to be understood, it is the same."[103]

The idea of what and who "Bettina" really was is connected to the difficulty of understanding the "I" in its opacity.[104] Brentano von Arnim links freedom to self-knowledge, a path along which the subject tries to overcome its opacity to itself. This is essential to the human being; it describes her role in nature and must take priority over customs.[105] The need for freedom must always be affirmed, even when it involves a contrast with *Sittlichkeit* and good manners.[106] Human beings must know themselves:[107] unconsciousness and ignorance are prisons, and getting out of them means achieving freedom;[108] learning to understand oneself is humankind's highest task, through which nature can reflect on and spiritualize itself.[109] Becoming aware of one's own nature— one's freedom but also one's own sensitive component—allows the human being to form

---

[100] Becker-Cantarino, *Bettina von Arnim Handbuch*, 241–251.

[101] Bettina von Arnim, *Clemens Brentanos Frühlingskranz*, in *Werke und Briefe in vier Bänden* (hereafter cited as AWB, followed by volume and page number), vol. 1, ed. Walter Schmitz (Frankfurt a. M.: Deutscher Klassiker Verlag, 1986), 199.

[102] As von Arnim writes to Goethe: *Goethes Briefwechsel mit einem Kinde*, AWB II, 430.

[103] Von Arnim, *Goethes Briefwechsel*, AWB II, 432.

[104] "After all, every human being is a big secret"; von Arnim, *Die Günderode*, AWB I, 441.

[105] Letter from von Arnim to Goethe: *Goethes Briefwechsel*, AWB II, 317.

[106] Von Arnim, *Frühlingskranz*, AWB I, 212.

[107] Von Arnim, *Dies Buch gehört dem König*, AWB III, 222.

[108] Von Arnim, *Frühlingskranz*, AWB I, 161.

[109] Von Arnim, *Goethes Briefwechsel*, AWB II, 472, 508.

her own nature in the direction of inner harmony.[110] Whoever does not take the path of self-knowledge, or lets sensual forces overwhelm her moral nature, loses her freedom and may even commit crimes.[111] Without self-knowledge there is no freedom.

However, Brentano von Arnim so links self-knowledge and freedom as to avoid a moralizing attitude. She sees guilt as the result of a Kantian-descended philosophy that erects the fortress of rational practical law from whose high towers one judges experience and prosecutes the outlaw, humanity. Here the human being's reason and her nature (which includes many other elements besides reason) are set at odds, leaving the subject continuously dissatisfied even when rational moral precepts are faithfully respected. This is because all the human being's other sensitive and volitional components are mutilated: "you have killed yourself in your victory."[112] Morality, for Günderrode and Brentano von Arnim, must pass through a self-knowledge that is not simply reason's reflection on itself but takes into consideration all aspects of the human being.

Brentano von Arnim goes further to the point of justifying the actions of the criminal. The criminal cannot be blamed for her actions, because she did not enjoy the material and economic conditions that would have allowed her to know herself and thus be free: that is why she is nothing more than a slave, an ignorant person, lacking self-awareness and not even knowing how the crime happened, what its causes are. Whoever lacks self-awareness is devoid of will as she cannot understand her own freedom;[113] being unfree, she should not be blamed for her act, responsibility for which instead falls on the State. In fact, although self-knowledge is a recurrent theme in romanticism and idealism, Brentano von Arnim stands out for investigating the material conditions that allow or disallow the possibility of self-knowledge and freedom.

Here Brentano von Arnim's philosophy is again heir to romanticism, for which the subject should no longer be considered in isolation, as the subject is unthinkable if abstracted from the relationships and the historical context in which it is placed. But Brentano von Arnim shifts her attention to the social conditions in which individuals live, and this determines her political position. The conviction of necessary self-awareness, for Brentano von Arnim, requires a liberal attitude (*Gesinnung*) that should be particularly attentive to the subject's socioeconomic conditions. If a human being cannot satisfy her most basic needs, her soul will be enslaved, as it will be too concerned with material needs to deal with knowledge, so that she cannot possibly be convinced of her own freedom.[114]

A section of *This Book belongs to the King*, titled "Experiences of a Young Swiss Man in the Vogtland," illustrates well what Brentano von Arnim means. These pages consist of reportage (one of the first texts in the tradition of empirical and qualitative social

---

[110] Von Arnim, *Dies Buch gehört dem König*, AWB III, 131. "Thinking is . . . shaping itself in harmony," von Arnim, *Günderode*, AWB I, 577.

[111] Von Arnim, *Dies Buch*, AWB III, 249.

[112] Günderrode, *Geschichte eines Braminen*, SW I, 305.

[113] Von Arnim, *Dies Buch*, AWB III, 286, 198.

[114] Von Arnim, *Dies Buch*, AWB III, 188.

research)[115] on the living conditions of an *Armen-Kolonie* that has settled on the out-skirts of Berlin, in the so-called Vogtland, creating a society increasingly isolated from the rest of the population. The author's opinion is peremptory: the presence of so many poor people (many of them former textile factory workers) in a country is not simply a sign of regional economic difficulty but an indication that that country is not free. That the poor are not helped out of their condition—except through gestures of charity and almsgiving that do not really help them to overcome their status—only chains them to their condition,[116] by legitimizing their negative perception of the State: "what is the State to the people? A domineering slave trader who bartered with him, and there-fore tortured his servant's mind; who pronounced speeches of power at him until his starving, contested, thousandfold angered heart sank into the swamp of pious morality, then slammed the lid of his coffin over his rising spirit or even closed his throat with the collar of a dog."[117]

The responsibility for criminal acts, especially in view of these conditions of neces-sity, falls fully to the State. Instead of pursuing beggars, treating begging as a crime using brutal police regulations;[118] instead of imposing litanies on the poor; instead of forcing women to marry (as their only means of economic subsistence) and thus isolating them, the State should initiate and make possible the teaching of science to the poorer classes,[119] thus tearing them away from the mechanical occupations that numb them to the point of making them forget their condition.[120] However, in the place of doing this, the State shows ferocity against criminals through the use of laws that do not really pursue justice, but simply attest to and legitimize the usurpation by which some citizens have reached a condition of privilege. For laws against theft, for Brentano von Arnim, do not simply protect the right to property, but also legitimize a previous misappropri-ation which consists in the accumulation of goods. And as a solution to theft and other crimes, prison is put forward, though it in no way helps to develop love in the criminal, or her power to become herself, to follow her innate and free nature.[121]

Formal laws, linked to a legal despotism that makes men and women slaves, are use-less, Brentano von Arnim argues. These mechanical laws distance themselves from the people, guiding the people according to formal principles that have no contact with their spirit (*Volksgeist*), reducing them to nothing but obedient and predictable machines.[122] Instead of submission to laws derived from mechanistic theory, Brentano von Arnim supports implementation and guidance of the rules that the living being gives to itself. Here she takes up a classic romantic theme, but she uses this approach—favoring the

---

[115] Becker-Cantarino, *Bettina von Arnim Handbuch*, 413.
[116] Von Arnim, *Dies Buch*, AWB III, 212, 335, 367.
[117] Von Arnim, *Dies Buch*, AWB III, 200.
[118] Von Arnim, *Dies Buch*, AWB III, 196, 357.
[119] Von Arnim, *Dies Buch*, AWB III, 366, 364, 336, 212, 239–240.
[120] Von Arnim, *Dies Buch*, AWB III, 237.
[121] Von Arnim, *Dies Buch*, AWB III, 202, 227.
[122] Von Arnim, *Dies Buch*, AWB III, 170, 229, 221, 237.

development of life against the dead machine—to criticize social conditions, property laws, and the prison system. To avoid crime, we need scientific awareness,[123] paying attention to ensure that the science is not the mechanistic one so criticized by romanticism.[124]

In a series of letters to Günderrode, in which the two women plan the possibility of a new religion, Bettina proposes a new meaning for the term *Bildung*: this must be an exercise of the forces within us, of curiosity about ourselves, and must focus on the full development of the spirit with no imposition of a catechism or formal laws.[125] The latter are the focus of a certain kind of philosopher, one who reduces everything, including nature, to a machine, and who does not feel the power of the spirit: "all he wants is to present the hocus-pocus of his superlative machine."[126] She writes: "back away now, you great boasters of philosophy, you philistines of dogmatics, you pedants of legal presumption, before the wisdom that speaks to us from everything in the most beautiful and modest garments, which leads us out of your madness back to ourselves. What are your laws and systems against a bird that knows how to build its nest and fill the warm summer nights with song?"[127] Instead of building prisons and organizing a police system against the desires of human beings, she suggests ensuring the necessary conditions so that every single man and woman can dedicate themselves to self-knowledge, to spirit's development toward freedom.[128]

As should be evident, Brentano von Arnim does not limit the moral side of human beings to their rationality or spirituality. As she clearly pointed out, the corporeality and physical desires of men and women shouldn't be despised in favor of their intellects or immaterial souls—"according to your holy church ancestors . . . we had to renounce the beautiful temple of the body and declared it to be a bag of grubworms, a sinful excrement of nature."[129] This position emerges in her attention to birth, as a physical event. The male romantics tended also to invoke birth, but by construing creativity as spiritual birthing, contrasted to the literal, physical birthing done by females.[130] However, Brentano von Arnim (like other women romantics and idealists) conceptualizes birth very differently. In her epistolary exchange with Goethe, "Bettine" refers to the words of Frau Rat (Goethe's mother) to recount Goethe's birth and first days of life, producing

---

[123] "The only thing to try would be if you could get him [the criminal] to reach science [*den großen Karpfenteig der Wissenschaft*]." Von Arnim, *Dies Buch*, AWB III, 239.

[124] On this, see: Schelling, *Ideen zu einer Philosophie der Natur*, AA I.5, 93–106; *Von der Weltseele. Eine Hypothese der höhern Physik zur Erklärung des allgemeinen Organismus*, AA I.6, 67–71. But see also Baader on philosophy of nature: Franz von Baader, *Ideen über Festigkeit und Flüssigkeit zur Prüfung der physikalischen Grundsätze des Herrn Lavoisier*, in *Sämtliche Werke*, vol. 3, 187–188; *Tagebücher*, in *Sämtliche Werke*, vol. 11, 392–393; *Vorreden. Zu den Beiträgen zur dynamischen Philosophie*, in *Sämtliche Werke*, vol. 1, 385.

[125] von Arnim, *Die Günderode*, AWB I, 468.

[126] von Arnim, *Die Günderode*, AWB I, 384.

[127] Von Arnim, *Dies Buch*, AWB III, 51.

[128] On this, see also: Giulia Valpione, "Expanding the Canon: The Political Philosophy of Bettina von Arnim," *Symphilosophie* 2 (2020): 131–156.

[129] Von Arnim, *Dies Buch*, AWB III, 291.

[130] See Christine Battersby, *Gender and Genius* (London: Women's Press, 1989).

an overlap between Katharina Elisabeth Goethe and Brentano von Arnim herself. The overlay between the two women comes out in Brentano von Arnim's expressions suggesting her (impossible) direct testimony to the birth of the much older Goethe: "your mother's puerperium, in which she gave birth to you, had blue squared curtains. She was eighteen years old and married for a year, and she remarked that you would probably remain young forever, and your heart would never grow old, since you were buying your mother's youth. For three days you pondered before you came into the world and you gave your mother difficult hours. . . . You appeared totally black and without any sign of life. They laid you in a small trough and sewed the pit of your heart with wine, despairing for your life. Your grandmother stood behind the bed, and when you first opened your eyes, she called out 'he lives!' "[131]

She continues: "your grandfather planted a pear tree in the well-kept garden in front . . . to commemorate your birth."[132] Only through the story of his own birth can Goethe complete his confessions (*Bekenntnisse*): Goethe becomes fully aware of his self not through the conflict with a not-I, but through the story of Bettine/Frau Rat who have held the secret of his birth.[133]

Veit also addresses the theme of birth. Veit's Florentin, we mentioned, tries but fails to solve the mystery of his origins and above all his birth mother. To know himself, he would need to tell a story beginning from his birth origins, and he cannot. Veit hints that the alternative to Fichte's self-birthing "I am I" is a natal self, constituted by its birth from a genuinely external other person, a mother.

Birth figures for Caroline Schlegel-Schelling too. After writing to Schelling of her primal axiom, which alludes to the deaths of the children she has borne, she admonishes Schelling for not acknowledging his debts to, or dependence on, his parents. He may think he has penetrated to the first principles of the cosmos, but he has forgotten the original relationships that first constituted him as a thinking self. And, we have shown, birth along with death and rebirth are key to Günderrode's philosophy of nature, on which we are all moving through successive cycles of rebirth within a vast cosmic progression. In giving salience to birth within romanticism and idealism, the women reorientated these philosophical standpoints in ways that brought their female experience to bear and gave it theoretical expression.

5 CONCLUSION

Women were part of Early German romantic circles and discussions of German idealism. No woman was as central as Hegel, Schelling, or Fichte, but then the latter three were professional philosophers, an option not available to women. Still, the case of

---

[131] Von Arnim, *Goethes Briefwechsel*, AWB II, 375.
[132] Von Arnim, *Goethes Briefwechsel*, AWB II, 699.
[133] Von Arnim, *Goethes Briefwechsel*, AWB II, 372.

German romantic and idealist women bears out Eileen O'Neill's general argument regarding women in the history of philosophy: that women were there all along but have been overlooked and forgotten by historians.[134] In this case, women have mainly been excluded through romantic and idealist positions being attributed only to men and not also to the women who helped to articulate the positions. We have shown this with Schlegel-Schelling's translation theory; Günderrode's philosophy of nature; Mereau's, Tieck's, and Veit's critiques of the self-positing self; and Günderrode's and Brentano von Arnim's idea of freedom. Standardly, though, romantic translation theory is referred only to August Wilhelm Schlegel; philosophy of nature only to Schelling; criticism of the self-positing self only to Novalis and Friedrich Schlegel; and philosophy of freedom only to Fichte, Schelling, Hegel, and Friedrich Schlegel.

To include women in romanticism and idealism, then, we need, first, to go beyond a narrow few "major" figures who were professional philosophers and acknowledge a whole swath of interlocutors.[135] Second, we must attend to diverse forms of philosophical expression, not only long-form systematic treatises but also letters, fiction, poetry, fragments, and essays. Third, we should acknowledge the complexity of authorship, for although the romantics extolled *Symphilosophie* and this opened spaces for women, at worst *Symphilosophie* degenerated into unacknowledged exploitation of women's intellectual labor.

Women contributed to romanticism and idealism in the shapes under which we already know these movements, but women's contributions also have certain distinctive features. Rejecting the absolute self, they reconceive the self as relational; they explore the complexities of love-relationships and insist that true relationships must be with real external other people, not mere imaginary projections; they envisage freedom as exercised through negotiation of one's place in natural and social relationships; and they introduce an orientation toward birth.[136] Women romantics developed a consistent and partly sociopolitical philosophy, even if male romantics and idealists sought to limit them to an affective and private sphere.

We thank Anna Ezekiel for her comments on an earlier draft.

REFERENCES

Adey, Louise. "Reading between the Lines: Tieck's Prolegomena to the Schlegel-Tieck Edition of Shakespeare." *Bulletin of the John Rylands University Library of Manchester* 71, no. 3 (1989): 89–104.

---

[134] Eileen O'Neill, "Disappearing Ink: Early Modern Women Philosophers and Their Fate in History," in *Philosophy in a Feminist Voice*, ed. Janet Kourany, 17–62 (Princeton: Princeton University Press, 1998).

[135] This idea was notably followed by Dieter Henrich, who nevertheless included no women philosophers in his reconstruction, despite their evident importance; see Dieter Henrich, *Konstellationen, Probleme und Debatten am Ursprung der idealistischen Philosophie 1789–1796* (Stuttgart: Klett-Cotta, 1991).

[136] This again prefigures some recent feminist philosophy, such as Adriana Cavarero, *In Spite of Plato: A Feminist Rewriting of Ancient Philosophy* (Cambridge: Polity Press, 1995).

Albuquerque, Juliana de, and Gert Hofmann, eds. *Anti/Idealism. Re-interpreting a German Discourse*. Berlin: de Gruyter, 2019.

Arnim, Bettina von. *Werke und Briefe in vier Bänden*. Edited by Walter Schmitz. Frankfurt a. M.: Deutscher Klassiker Verlag, 1986–2004.

Baader, Franz Xavier von. *Sämtliche Werke*. Edited by Franz Hoggmann and Julius Hamberger. Aalen: Scientia Verlag, 1987.

Baillot, Anne, ed. *Letters and Texts: Intellectual Berlin around 1800*. https://www.berliner-intellektuelle.eu.

Battersby, Christine. *Gender and Genius*. London: Women's Press, 1989.

Becker-Cantarino, Barbara, ed. *Bettina von Arnim Handbuch*. Berlin: de Gruyter, 2019.

Becker-Cantarino, Barbara. *Schriftstellerinnen der Romantik: Epoche, Werke, Wirkung*. Munich: C. H. Beck, 2000.

Behler, Ernst. *Frühromantik*. Berlin: de Gruyter, 1992.

Blackwell, Jeannine, and Shawn C. Jarvis, eds. *The Queen's Mirror: Fairy Tales by German Women, 1780–1900*. Lincoln: University of Nebraska Press, 2001.

Braidotti, Rosi. "The Subject in Feminism." *Hypatia* 6, no. 2 (Summer 1991): 155–172.

Cavarero, Adriana. *In Spite of Plato: A Feminist Rewriting of Ancient Philosophy*. Translated by Serena Anderlini-D'Onofrio and Áine O'Healey. Cambridge: Polity Press, 1995.

Conrad, Hermann. "Caroline and the Translation of Shakespeare." Translated by Douglas Stott. 2009-2023. https://www.carolineschelling.com/caroline-and-shakespeare/conrad-caroline-shakespeare/.

Corkhill, Alan. "Keeping It in the Family? The Creative Collaboration of Sophie and Dorothea Tieck." In *Collective Creativity: Collaborative Work in the Sciences, Literature and the Arts*, edited by Gerhard Fischer and Florian Vassen, 115–128. Amsterdam: Rodopi, 2011.

Daley, Margaretmary. *Women of Letters: A Study in the Personal Writing of Caroline Schlegel-Schelling, Rahel Varnhagen, and Bettina von Arnim*. Columbia, SC: Camden House, 1998.

Daub, Adrian. *Uncivil Unions: The Metaphysics of Marriage in German Idealism and Romanticism*. Chicago: Chicago University Press, 2012.

Dormann, Helga. *Die Kunst des inneren Sinns. Mythisierung der inneren und äusseren Natur im Werk Karoline von Günderrodes*. Würzburg: Königshausen und Neumann, 2004.

Ezekiel, Anna C. "Metamorphosis, Personhood, and Power in Karoline von Günderrode." *European Romantic Review* 25, no. 6 (2014): 773–791.

Ezekiel, Anna C. "Narrative and Fragment: The Social Self in Karoline von Günderrode." *Symphilosophie: International Journal of Philosophical Romanticism* 2 (2020): 65–90.

Fichte, Johann Gottlieb. *Gesamtausgabe der bayerischen Akademie der Wissenschaft*. Edited by Erich Fuchs et al. Stuttgart: Friedrich Frommann/Günther Holzboog, 1962–2012.

Frederiksen, Elke. "Deutsche Autorinnen im 19. Jahrhundert: Neue kritische Ansätze." *Colloquia Germanica* 14, no. 2 (1981): 97–113.

French, Lorely. "The Magic of Translation: Dorothea Schlegel's *Geschichte des Zauberers Merlin*." *Pacific Coast Philology* 40, no. 1 (2005): 36–56.

Günderrode, Karoline von. *Poetic Fragments*. Translated and edited by Anna C. Ezekiel. Albany: State University of New York Press, 2016.

Günderrode, Karoline von. *Sämtliche Werke and ausgewählte Studien*. Edited by Walther Morgenthaler. 3 vols. Frankfurt: Roter Stern, 1990–91.

Halberstok, Monika. *Sophie Tieck—Leben und Werk. Schreiben zwischen Rebellion und Resignation*. Munich: Iudicium, 2001.

Helfer, Martha. "Dorothea Veit-Schlegel's *Florentin*: Constructing a Feminist Romantic Aesthetic." *German Quarterly* 69, no. 2 (1996), 144–160.

Henrich, Dieter. *Konstellationen. Probleme und Debatten am Ursprung der idealistischen Philosophie 1789–1796.* Stuttgart: Klett-Cotta, 1991.

Johnson, Laurie. "Dorothea Veit's *Florentin* and the Early Romantic Model of Alterity." *Monatshefte* 97, no. 1 (Spring 2005): 33–62.

Kneller, Jane. "Feminism." In *The Oxford Handbook of German Philosophy in the Nineteenth Century,* edited by Michael N. Forster and Kristin Gjesdal, 534–551. Oxford: Oxford University Press, 2015.

Larson, Kenneth. "The Origins of the 'Schlegel–Tieck' Shakespeare in the 1820s." *German Quarterly* 60, no. 1 (Winter 1987): 19–37.

Martinson, Steven D. "'. . . aus dem Schiffbruch des irdischen Lebens': The Literature of Karoline von Günderrode and Early German Romantic and Idealist Philosophy." *German Studies Review* 28, no. 2 (2005): 303–326.

Mendelssohn-Veit-Schlegel, Dorothea. *Florentin: A Novel.* Translated by Edwina Lawler and Ruth Richardson. Lewiston, ME: Edwin Mellen, 1988.

Mereau, Sophie. *Das Blüthenalter der Empfindung.* Gotha: Justus Perthes, 1794.

Novalis. *Notes for a "Romantic Encyclopedia."* Translated and edited by David W. Wood. Albany: State University of New York Press, 2007.

Novalis. *Schriften.* Edited by Richard Samuel, Hans-Joachin Mähl, and Gerhard Schulz. Darmstadt: Wissenschaftliche Buchgesellschaft, 1960–2006.

O'Neill, Eileen. "Disappearing Ink: Early Modern Women Philosophers and Their Fate in History." In *Philosophy in a Feminist Voice,* edited by Janet Kourany, 17–62. Princeton: Princeton University Press, 1998.

Reill, Peter Hanns. *Vitalizing Nature in the Enlightenment.* Berkeley: University of California Press, 2005.

Schelling, Friedrich Wilhelm Joseph. *Historisch-kritische Ausgabe.* Edited by Hartmut Baumgartner, Wilhelm G. Jacobs, Jörg Janzen, Hermann Krings. Stuttgart: Frommann-Holzboog, 1976–.

Schlegel, August Wilhelm. "Etwas über William Shakespeare bei Gelegenheit *Wilhelm Meisters.*" *Die Horen* 6, no. 4 (1796): 57–112.

Schlegel, August Wilhelm. *Kritische Ausgabe der Vorlesungen.* Edited by Ernst Behler. Munich: Schöningh, 1989.

Schlegel, August Wilhelm. *Kritische Schriften.* 2 vols. Reimer: Berlin, 1828.

Schlegel, August Wilhelm. *Sämmtliche Werke.* Edited by Eduard Böcking. Hildesheim: Olms, 1971.

Schlegel, August Wilhelm (and Caroline Schlegel-Schelling). "On Shakespeare's *Romeo and Juliet.*" Translated by Julius Charles Hare. *Ollier's Literary Miscellany I*: 1–39. London: 1820.

Schlegel, August Wilhelm (and Caroline Schlegel-Schelling). "Über Shakespeare's Romeo und Julia." *Die Horen* 10, no. 6 (1797): 530–560.

Schlegel, Friedrich. *Kritische Friedrich-Schlegel-Ausgabe.* Edited by Ernst Behler et al. Munich: Schöningh: 1958–.

Schleiermacher, Friedrich Daniel Ernst. *Kritische Gesamtausgabe.* Edited by Andreas Arndt et al. Berlin: de Gruyter, 1980–.

Smith, Christian. "Translation and Influence: The Influence on German Theory of Dorothea Tieck's Translations of Shakespeare." *Borrowers and Lenders* 11, no. 2 (2018): 1–29.

Staël, Germaine de. *De l'Allemagne.* Paris: Librairie Stéréotype, 1814.

Stanguennec, André. *La philosophie romantique allemande.* Paris: Vrin, 2011.

Stone, Alison. *Nature, Ethics and Gender in German Romanticism and Idealism*. London: Rowman & Littlefield, 2018.

Stott, Douglas. "Caroline. Briefe aus der Frühromantik." 2009-2023. https://www.carolinesc helling.com.

Thandeka. "Schleiermacher, Feminism and Liberation Theologies: A Key." In *The Cambridge Companion to Friedrich Schleiermacher*, edited by Jacqueline Mariña, 287–306. Cambridge: Cambridge University Press, 2005.

Thorgeirsdottir, Sigridur, and Ruth Edith Hagengruber, eds. *Methodological Reflections on Women's Contribution and Influence in the History of Philosophy*. Dordrecht: Springer, 2020.

Tieck, Ludwig, ed. *Shakespeare's dramatische Werke*, 9 vols. Berlin: Reimer, 1825–33.

Tieck, Sophie. "Lebensansicht." In *Athenaeum. Eine Zeitschrift von August Wilhelm Schlegel und Friedrich Schlegel*, vol. 3: 205–215. Digital edition by Jochen A. Bär. http://www.zbk-onl ine.de/texte/A1654.htm.

Tieck, Sophie. "The Old Man in the Cave." In *The Queen's Mirror: Fairy Tales by German Women, 1780–1900*, edited by Jeannine Blackwell and Shawn C. Jarvis, 75–88. Lincoln: University of Nebraska Press, 2001.

Valpione, Giulia. "Bildung et vie dans la philosophie politique de Friedrich Schlegel." In *L'Homme et la nature dans le romantisme allemand. Politique, critique et esthétique*, edited by Giulia Valpione, 147–162. Zurich: Lit Verlag, 2021.

Valpione, Giulia. "Expanding the Canon: The Political Philosophy of Bettina von Arnim." In *Symphilosophie* 2 (2020): 131–156.

Wagner, Ulrike. "Schleiermacher's *Geselligkeit*, Henriette Herz, and the 'Convivial Turn.'" In *Conviviality at the Crossroads: The Poetics and Politics of Everyday Encounters*, edited by Oscar Hemer, Maja Povrzanović Frykman, and Per-Markku Ristilammi, 65–87. Cham: Palgrave, 2020.

Waithe, Mary Ellen, ed. *A History of Women Philosophers*. 4 vols. Dordrecht: Springer, 1995.

Williams, Simon. *Shakespeare on the German Stage*. Cambridge: Cambridge University Press, 2004.

CHAPTER 18

....

MARXISM AND THE WOMAN
QUESTION IN IMPERIAL AND
WEIMAR GERMANY

....

CAT MOIR WOLFE

ON 19 July 1889, Clara Zetkin, one of the leading activists and theorists of the German proletarian women's movement, gave a speech to the International Workers' Congress on the liberation of women. As Zetkin's speech demonstrates, the question of women's emancipation in the international socialist movement was a thorny one. Since August Bebel published *Die Frau und der Sozialismus* (*Woman and Socialism*) in 1879,[1] the socialist line on the issue had been that the "woman question" concerning the capacity of women and their rights in society was subordinate to the "social question" concerning he division of labor and distribution of wealth.[2] Whereas the early feminist movement in Germany and elsewhere fought for women's rights within the existing social framework, concentrating on issues such as education, suffrage, and prostitution, Bebel had argued that women's position in society could only be improved by challenging the foundations of capitalism, which made many women financially dependent on men and exploited their paid and unpaid labor.

Zetkin did not fundamentally challenge this assertion. "Women workers," she argues, clearly echoing Bebel, "are totally convinced that the question of the emancipation of

---

[1] Bebel was the chair of the Social Democratic Party of Germany, and from 1892 to 1913 served as its most important parliamentary spokesman and strategist.

[2] August Bebel, *Woman and Socialism*, Jubilee 50th ed., trans Meta L. Stern (New York: Socialist Literature, 1910), 3. *Woman and Socialism* soon became one of the most widely bought, borrowed, read, and translated books in the German socialist movement. It was published in numerous editions in many languages and updated continuously during Bebel's lifetime, and many of these editions contained only a part of the original. This English edition is complete, and was produced to mark the 50th Jubilee of the formation of German Workers Clubs in America. Studies on the reading habits of workers demonstrate that Bebel's was one of the works most frequently borrowed in this milieu. See Hans-Josef Steinberg and Nicholas Jacobs, "Workers' Libraries in Germany before 1914," *History Workshop* 1 (1976): 166–180.

women is not an isolated one but rather constitutes a part of the great social question."[3] However, Zetkin shrewdly used Bebel's widely accepted argument to vehemently challenge those men within her own party who militated for the limitation, and in some cases prohibition, of women's work. For instance, at the 1869 Allgemeine Deutscher Sozialdemokratischer Arbeiterkongress (General German Social-Democrat Workers' Congress) in Eisenach, followers of Ferdinand Lassalle, the founder of the German social democratic movement, had called for women's industrial labor to be outlawed, a demand that the Marxist faction successfully opposed on the grounds that women in need would be forced into prostitution if they had no other economic option.[4]

In 1889, Zetkin did not resort to such paternalistic (even if accurate)[5] reasoning.[6] Rather, she relied on economic arguments to convince her comrades. Neither capitalists nor male citizens could do without women's work, Zetkin argued: the capitalist needs female wage labor to maintain competitiveness, while the male citizen depends on women's unpaid, reproductive labor in the home. Against the assumption among many male workers that women's industrial labor depressed men's wages because women were prepared to work for less, Zetkin countered that prohibiting women's work would not raise the wages of men. "The capitalists would very soon replace the lack of cheap female labor by the employment of more efficient machinery," she claimed, "and very shortly everything would be just as it was before."[7]

Zetkin's intervention bears witness to the intellectually vibrant proletarian women's movement that existed in Imperial and Weimar Germany, nourished by the Marxist idea that radical social transformation was necessary if women were to achieve full equality with men. However, like Zetkin, these women both advanced and engaged critically with the Marxist tradition, developing positions in social and political philosophy intended to serve them in their practical aims: women's liberation, in the context of the broader pursuit of economic and social justice.

In this chapter, I examine the thought of the socialist and working-class women's movement in Imperial and Weimar Germany through the lens of Marxism's relation to the woman question. Methodologically, this is a challenging task, due to both the gender and class status of the thinkers in question. Women like Zetkin, Lily Braun, Helene Grünberg, Gertrud Hanna, Marie Juchacz, Toni Sender, and Luise Zietz were not trained philosophers, though they were steeped in the Marxist and socialist theory of their time.

---

[3] Clara Zetkin, "For the Liberation of Women," in *Selected Writings* (Chicago: Haymarket Books, 2015), 46.

[4] Rosemarie Nave-Herz, *Die Gechichte der Frauenbewegung in Deutschland* (Hanover: Niedersächsischen Landeszentrale für politische Bildung, 1997), 18; Sabine Schmitt, *Die Arbeiterinnenschutz im deutschen Kaiserreich* (Stuttgart: Metzler, 1995), 43–61.

[5] Most prostitutes in Imperial Germany were working-class, and many reported beginning sex work after losing other gainful employment. See Julia Roos, *Weimar through the Lens of Gender: Prostitution Reform, Woman's Emancipation, and German Democracy, 1919-33*. University of Michigan Press, 2010.

[6] Richard J. Evans, "Prostitution, State and Society in Imperial Germany," *Past & Present* 70 (1976): 106–129.

[7] Zetkin, "For the Liberation of Women," 49.

These women were rather what Italian Marxist Antonio Gramsci referred to as organic intellectuals: with exceptions like Zetkin and Braun, they were largely autodidacts from rural and urban proletarian backgrounds who made theoretical contributions to the social struggles of which they were both product and part. Reconstructing the ideas of the German proletarian women's movement is thus an exercise in *intellectual history from below*, where labor history meets the history of ideas, and social history meets the history of philosophy.

The fact that women were not admitted to universities until the late nineteenth century—and then only women of means—requires us to look beyond academic philosophy for evidence of women thinkers' contributions. When it comes to working-class women, the problem is doubly compounded. However, their frequent lack of formal academic education did not prevent working-class, socialist, and Marxist women from being formidable theorists capable of formulating sophisticated and trenchant positions on central questions of social and political philosophy. In addition to their pamphlets, articles, and books, we can also find detailed treatments of philosophical matters in these women's correspondence, diaries, and autobiographies, where they exist.

Examining the thought of the proletarian wing of the German women's movement reminds us that ideas have a life outside the texts in which they are usually first formulated. In the spirit of Marx's eleventh thesis on Feuerbach, according to which the task of philosophy is not only to interpret, but also to change the world, for these women, there was no strict separation between theory and practice. This means that the contribution of women thinkers to Marxist theory is inseparable from the history of the proletarian women's movement. The chapter thus begins by offering a brief account of the history of the proletarian women's movement in German-speaking Europe before moving on to examine the ideas advanced by its participants. As I will show, while the concerns of proletarian women thinkers often centered upon topics of characteristic feminist interest such as suffrage, motherhood, and prostitution, they were far from limited to women's issues. Socialist and Marxist women published and spoke on matters as varied as the theory of the state, revolution, nationalism, colonialism, war, and welfare.

1   A Brief History of the German Proletarian Women's Movement

During the nineteenth century, as ideas of freedom and equality inspired by the French Revolution swept through Europe, and industrialization brought about radical shifts in social relations, the question of where women fit into this new world picture began to be raised. The woman question, or *Frauenfrage* as it was known in the German-speaking lands, concerned women's rights to vote, to own property in their own names, to get education and work outside the home without their husbands' permission, to have a say over their children's upbringing, and over their own bodies with access to abortion—all rights that were denied to German-speaking women in the period. All over Europe, women began to organize themselves to fight for these rights, all of which they eventually won.

However, women's experiences were by no means uniform, and neither were their demands. As Richard J. Evans has observed, the mainstream of nineteenth-century feminism had two major characteristics: it was liberal, and it was middle-class. Pioneering German feminists included Louise Otto-Peters, the founder of the *Frauen-Zeitung* (*Women's Magazine*), the first publication in German to advocate for women's rights, and Auguste Schmidt, who with Otto-Peters founded the Allgemeiner Deutscher Frauenverein (General German Women's Association; ADF), the first association to militate for women's rights in German-speaking Europe. These early feminists came from bourgeois backgrounds, and their chief concerns were women's education, suffrage, and social issues such as prostitution (though some, like Otto-Peters, were concerned with women's rights to and at work).

Proletarian women undoubtedly wanted access to education and the vote—their associations included suffrage as a demand long before the mainstream women's movement did so. Yet working-class women also had quite different immediate needs from those represented by the ADF. Between 1882 and 1925, the proportion of working women in Germany rose from 36.3 percent to 48.2 percent, driven by growth in low-paid urban and rural jobs. In particular, the number of women factory workers grew steadily. As early as 1875, about one million women—roughly 20 percent of all those employed— worked in industry. Another 1.4 million women were employed as maids, and at least half a million women earned money through cottage industry. Women in industry and home-based work, as well as in the service sector, were mostly low-skilled. General wage inequality meant that women received on average only 35–50 percent of the wages of male workers.[8] The daily reality of exploitative wage labor outside the home and what Marxist theorists call "reproductive" labor (unpaid but essential for reproducing the economic and social order) within it meant that for working-class women in Imperial and Weimar Germany, the "woman question" was inextricably tied to the broader "social question" of economic inequality.

From the 1860s onward, then, a proletarian women's movement in Germany emerged to give voice to what working-class women saw as their specific needs. As Zetkin, one of this movement's pioneers, details in her *Zur Geschichte der proletarischen Frauenbewegung in Deutschland* (*On the History of the Proletarian Women's Movement in Germany*), as early as 1869, the Internationale Gewerksgenossenschaft der Manufaktur-, Fabrik- und Handarbeiter (International Trade Union Cooperative of Manufacturing, Factory, and Manual Workers), based in Saxon Crimmitschau, directed its propaganda to proletarians "of both sexes" and included two women—Wilhelmine Weber and Christiane Peuschel—in its organizing committee. From the 1870s, women's demands

---

[8] See Ulla Knapp, "Frauenarbeit in Deutschland zwischen 1850 und 1933: T. I." in *Historical Social Research*, 8(4), 42-82 (1983), and "Frauenarbeit in Deutschland zwischen 1850 und 1933: T. II." in *Historical Social Research*, 9(1), 3-42 (1984).

such as equal wages for equal work, suffrage rights, and maternity protection also began to be included among the general demands of the labor movement.

In 1873, two working-class Berlin women, Paula Staegemann and Berta Hahn, founded the Berliner Arbeiterfrauen- und Mädchenverein (Berlin Working Women and Girls' Association), the first proletarian women's organization in Germany, which demanded equal wages for women. Though its founders were promptly jailed under the antisocialist laws introduced by Chancellor Otto von Bismarck in 1878, in 1885 Staegemann, together with Emma Ihrer, Marie Hofmann, and Gertrude Guillaume-Schack, set up the Verein zur Wahrung der Interessen der Arbeiterinnen (Association for the Protection of the Interests of Women Workers), which also campaigned for equal wages, mutual legal advocacy in wage disputes, and education. This organization, too, was dissolved by police after only a year.

Even after the antisocialist laws expired in 1890, it remained difficult for women to organize politically, since they were banned from membership in political organizations until 1908. Socialist women were thus forced to organize outside of the official Social Democratic Party (SPD) party structure. At the 1892 Party Congress, however, the decision was made to extend the system of *Vertrauensmänner*—confidants who maintained the important link between the local associations and the party executive—to women. A *Frauenagitationskommission* (women's agitation committee) was established, and was replaced two years later by the election of individual *Vertrauensfrauen* (female confidants) in order to escape the possible charge of association by the authorities. From 1900, SPD women also held biennial conferences in spite of the ongoing threat of repression.

In 1892, Zetkin took over the editorship of *Die Arbeiterin*, the newspaper of the proletarian women's movement, from her comrade Emma Ihrer, renaming it *Die Gleichheit*. Within a few years, *Die Gleichheit* became the quasi-official newspaper not only of the German, but also of the international working women's movement, with a circulation of 80,000 in 1910. A lively proletarian women's movement and press also developed outside Imperial Germany in Austria and Switzerland.

From the 1890s, socialist and working-class women sometimes cooperated and sometimes conflicted with the mainstream women's movement, housed from 1894 under the umbrella organization of the Bund deutscher Frauenvereine (Federation of German Women's Associations; BDF). For instance, while the demand for political equality remained controversial within the BDF, for the proletarian women's movement, women's suffrage had always been a central demand. Meanwhile, socialist and nonsocialist women frequently cooperated in other civil society organizations, such as the Verband für Frauenwahlrecht (Association for Women's Suffrage), Helene Stöcker's Bund für Mutterschutz und Sexualreform (League for Motherhood and Sexual Reform), which campaigned for sexual education and fought against the ban on abortion, and pacifist organizations such as the Bund neues Vaterland (New Fatherland League), established in 1914 to oppose World War I and promote internationalism. The socialist and mainstream women's movements also faced common enemies: not only the generalized patriarchy (the world of socialist politics, too, remained heavily male-dominated), but also the organized antifeminist movement.

Ultimately, however, the political differences between the proletarian and mainstream women's movements proved intractable, and proletarian women's groups remained excluded from the BDF. Despite its rhetorical commitment to nonpartisanship, at the local level the mainstream women's movement often "pursued bourgeois interests by openly working against the SPD, seeking to limit its influence among young working women."[9] Socialist and proletarian women also often sought to distance themselves from their liberal counterparts. In her speech at the 1896 Party Congress, Zetkin argued that bourgeois women were campaigning against men of their own class, while working-class women and men fought alongside one another to advance their shared social position. Not all proletarian women opposed cooperation with the liberal movement, however: Lily Braun fiercely opposed Zetkin's isolationist stance on this issue, which ultimately led to her being excluded from the working women's movement.

It is worth pausing over the Braun-Zetkin conflict, because although it also had significant personal and political dimensions, it demonstrates succinctly how philosophical differences shaped the direction of the movement. The key question was whether class or sex was the more fundamental social division. Zetkin was firmly convinced that women's liberation could not be achieved in capitalist society; that only by achieving full economic equality and democratic control of the labor process would gender inequality—which was above all grounded for Zetkin in a gendered division of labor—be finally abolished. As a result of this conviction, Zetkin insisted that all work undertaken by socialist women be conducted in the service of the broader class struggle. Activities such as education on the situation of women and advice in legal matters were therefore, in Zetkin's view, best left to existing institutions such as educational clubs, trade unions, and bourgeois social reform groups. Social Democratic women should rather militate for the party and its program, which included measures specifically designed to liberate working women, such as suffrage and equal pay.

By her own admission, Braun, who was involved with the left wing of the bourgeois feminist movement prior to 1895, when Ottilie Baader convinced her to join the Social Democrats, never understood the Marxist idea of the primacy of class struggle: in Braun's view, the goal of women's liberation cut across class divides. From the outset, she sought to bring working-class women into the broader feminist movement via organizations like the Berlin-based *Frauenwohl* (Women's Well-being), while after 1895 Braun advocated among Social Democratic women for cooperation with middle-class feminists. Certainly, Braun's vision for the women's section of the party was less directly political than Zetkin's: her 1897 reform proposals, which met with fierce resistance from Zetkin and Baader in 1897, primarily envisaged it as a vehicle for education and consciousness raising, rather than direct militancy for party and unions.

Sometimes Braun did appear to support Zetkin's principles. For instance, in Hamburg, where women were free to join political organizations, Braun rejected a

[9] Nancy R. Reagin, *A German Women's Movement: Class and Gender in Hanover, 1880–1933.* Chapel Hill: University of North Carolina Press, 1995, p. 8.

separate structure for women, arguing that "we are all Social Democrats." She was, however, motivated here by a rejection of feminist separatism rather than by Marxist conviction. In a similar vein, Braun questioned why, if the women's movement was an integral part of the organized working class, male SPD comrades were disenfranchised from decision-making at the women's congress. Braun's insistence on the class-transcendent character of the woman question thus ultimately revealed a contradiction at the heart of the proletarian women's movement. While insisting that the woman question was subordinate to the social question, Social Democratic women always maintained the integrity of their own structures within the movement, which tacitly admitted the specificity of women's struggles.

Despite these challenges, the German proletarian women's movement continued to expand in the early years of the twentieth century. In 1907, the first International Socialist Women's Conference took place in Stuttgart, which established a Women's International Secretariat with the German Zetkin at the helm and *Die Gleichheit* as the international organization's official publication. At the second conference in Copenhagen in 1910, a resolution was adopted to establish an annual International Women's Day to campaign for the political emancipation of women—the same International Women's Day that continues today. In 1912, the Socialist Women's International held an extraordinary conference in Basel, Switzerland, to monitor peace and pledge to campaign for an end to the Balkan war.

War—above all World War I—proved to be a critically divisive issue, both among socialists themselves and between bourgeois and socialist women. The nationalistic support for the war among Social Democrats led to an internal party conflict, which ended in the foundation of the Unabhängige Sozialdemokratische Partei Deutschlands (Independent Social Democratic Party; USPD), in April 1917, which was first joined by the Spartacus group around Rosa Luxemburg, Karl Liebknecht, and Zetkin. The women's movement was similarly split, with some women supporting peace and others patriotism. However, although bourgeois and socialist women faced the same challenge, existing differences between these camps were sharpened in the conflict, with socialist women broadly supporting peace and many middle-class women prioritizing the Vaterland.

When the German revolution broke out at the war's end in November 1918, socialist women played a critical role in radical agitation. Lida Gustava Heymann recounted that in Hamburg, in the first days of the revolution, a large public assembly was convened at which only women were supposed to speak. In addition to well-known names such as Zetkin, Heymann (1868–1943), and radical feminist and pacifist Anita Augspurg (1857–1943), autobiographies and other accounts show that lesser-known women such as the Kiel Social Democrat Gertrud Völcker (1896–1979), the Munich rebel Hilde Kramer (1900–1974), the Frankfurt trade unionist Toni Sender (1888–1964), the young Ruhr socialist Emilie Böckle (1901–1971), and the Berliners Martha Globig (1901–1991) and Franziska Rubens (1894–1971), both of whom later became communists, played an active role.

With the foundation of the Weimar Republic in 1919, women won the right to vote and to stand for election. In the elections to the constituent National Assembly, 78 percent of the women entitled to vote took part, and 9.6 percent of the members of Parliament were female. However, women continued to be underrepresented in all parties in the 1920s and were hardly represented in high party offices. After the war, urban women working in large plants who might have supported the USPD or the Kommunistische Partei Deutschlands (German Communist Party; KPD) were fired to make room for returning war veterans, which dampened grassroots female radicalism until 1923. After a brief surge in female support for the left in the aftermath of devastating hyperinflation in 1923, the KPD was banned and women workers threw their weight behind the SPD, whose support among women increased as it tracked to the right.

The trend toward fragmentation continued throughout the women's movement in the 1920s. The BDF became more conservative and dedicated itself to preserving traditional women's roles, while the proletarian women's movement fragmented further with the founding of the KPD. Dismissed as editor of *Die Gleichheit* in 1917 for her role in forming the Spartacus League, which merged with the KPD in 1919, Zetkin founded a new publication in 1921, *Die Kommunistische Fraueninternationale* (*The Communist Women's International*), which aimed to convince women of the virtues of joining Soviet Russia in worldwide revolution rather than succumbing to the empty promises of feminist movements in capitalist nations.

Meanwhile, women in the SPD, including Zetkin's successor at *Die Gleichheit*, Marie Juchacz, founded the mutual aid organization Arbeiterwohlfahrt (Workers' Welfare) in 1919. The political organization of radical women also continued: in the Weimar years, anarcho-syndicalist women began to organize en masse for the first time. In publications such as *Der Syndikalist* (*The Syndicalist*) *and Der Frauenbund* (*The Women's League*), anarchists tended to address women in their roles as wives and mothers in order to try and win them to the cause. Nevertheless, for women of all political persuasions, social work became the most important political field of work in the Weimar Republic.

Adolf Hitler's appointment as Reich chancellor in 1933 brought an end to the independent women's movement in Germany. The BDF dissolved itself to avoid *Gleichschaltung* (strategic alignment with the regime), while socialists, communists, and anarchists of all genders became automatic enemies of the state. Many of the rights that women had won, such as the right to stand for election or the principle of equal pay, were abolished and would only be regained after the war.

2 Philosophy of the German Proletarian Women's Movement

Though German socialist and working-class women developed their own body of theory in the context of their movement, their ideas all to a greater or lesser extent engaged favorably and/or critically with Marxist theory. As I have shown, Bebel's *Woman and Socialism* had laid some of the groundwork for a specifically Marxist engagement with the woman question. There, Bebel argued that proletarian women were doubly subjugated: as workers and as women. In the home, women performed unpaid labor in the service of their husbands, while in the workplace they were exploited as wage laborers. In this vein, Bebel argued that the bourgeois institution of marriage bound women into servitude, and praised the increasing divorce rate as evidence of women beginning to "cast off a yoke that has become unbearable." He argued that the natural free sexuality of both women and men was stifled by monogamous marriage, and led to prostitution as the only way to satisfy one's desire outside of the union. On the question of women's labor, Bebel was especially strident. He accused the ruling classes of promoting the inclusion of women in the labor process only to depress the income of male and female labor alike. Meanwhile, in a chapter on the legal status of women, Bebel gives a detailed account of the situation of suffrage and political rights of women around the world, highlighting the numbers of proletarian women still effectively excluded from public life by the fact that suffrage, where it was afforded, was still largely tied to property.

Another Marxist work that influenced socialist thinking on the woman question was Friedrich Engels's book *The Origin of the Family, Private Property and the State* (*Ursprung der Familie, des Privateigenthums und des Staats*) (1884). The key idea of the *Origin* was that the family values of the nineteenth-century European middle classes— the industrious breadwinning husband, demure domesticized wife—were merely an ideological cover for the truth of a situation in which men were in legal, political, and economic control of women and children. Like Bebel, Engels criticized the institution of monogamous marriage, arguing that it constituted the very origin of class conflict. "The first class antithesis which appears in history coincides with the development of the antagonism between man and woman in monogamian marriage, and the first class oppression with that of the female sex by the male."[10] Because Engels paired patriarchy inseparably with class division, he insisted that the subjugation of women could not be overcome using the mechanisms of the bourgeois legal system.

The modern individual family, Engels argued, is "founded on the overt or covert domestic slavery of the woman," who was typically economically dependent on her husband. The husband's position as breadwinner put him de facto in a position of supremacy such that, within the family "he is the bourgeois; the wife represents the proletariat." [11] The liberation of women, Engels therefore claimed, depended on women possessing economic equality with men, which he argued could only be achieved by abolishing a capitalist social system in which both sexes were merely free to be exploited equally. With the transition to a communist society, Engels predicted not only the socialization of property and abolition of wage labor, but also the socialization of domestic work and childcare.

---

[10] Friedrich Engels, *The Origin of the Family, Private Property and the State*. In *Engels: 1882–1889*, vol. 26 of *Marx & Engels Collected Works*. London: Lawrence & Wishart, 1990, p. 176.

[11] Engels, p. 181.

Bebel's and Engels's work indelibly influenced the ideas of the proletarian women's movement. Luise Zietz, later a member of the Reichstag and one of the leading organizers of the women's section of the SPD, remarked in her essay "What Bebel Gave to Proletarian Women": "when I got hold of [the book] at the end of the eighties . . . I felt as so many, many proletarian women had done: the scales fell from our eyes and we gained an understanding of the interrelationships of economic and political conditions."[12] For many working-class women, Bebel's book was an invitation into the movement, and a powerful means by which to understand their social conditions.

Zetkin, too, built on these existing Marxist theories. In her speech to the SPD Congress at Gotha on October 1896, Zetkin claimed that Bebel's *Woman and Socialism* was "more than a book, it was an event—a great deed" that had convinced her that socialism could only win with the support of women workers.[13] Meanwhile, in a tribute to Engels after his death in 1895, Zetkin wrote that proletarian women owed him a special debt of thanks for the *Origin*, which she claimed had been of "fundamental importance for the struggle to emancipate the entire female sex."[14]

Undoubtedly the movement's most visible and prolific female theoretician, Zetkin was born Clara Eißner in 1857 in rural Saxony. In 1872, her family moved to Leipzig, where as a girl she was introduced to the women's movement via her mother's contact with Auguste Schmidt, who enrolled the young protégé Zetkin in the renowned teacher's seminar from 1874 to 1878. At the time, Leipzig was one of the most important centers of the workers' movement, and there Clara Eißner was introduced to socialist ideas, listening to lectures by August Bebel and Wilhelm Liebknecht, among others, at the Workers' Education Association. In 1878 she joined the organization that would become the SPD. Her party entry, along with her relationship with the Ukrainian social revolutionary Ossip Zetkin, led Clara to break with her mentor Schmidt. When Ossip Zetkin died after a long illness in 1889, Clara Zetkin compensated for her grief by redoubling her commitment to socialism and women's issues. She went on to play a leading role in the SPD, including as a member of the party executive from 1909 to 1917. A staunch opponent of militarism, Zetkin was instrumental in mobilizing women against World War I, later concentrating her political commitment on the communist world movement. A friend of Lenin, Zetkin became not only a top communist functionary and professional politician in the Weimar Republic, but also the leading communist women's rights activist. As a founding member of the KPD, Zetkin was one of the first women to become a member of the German parliament: from January 1919 she was a member of the Constituent Assembly of Württemberg, and from 1920 to 1933 she was a member of the German Reichstag. Though Zetkin had been a radical in the SPD,

---

[12] Louise Zietz, "Das alles erfuhren wir ers taus Bebels 'Frau'". Genkow, Heinrich and Miller, Angelika (eds.), August Bebel – "ein prächtiger alter Adler". Nachrufe – Gedichte – Erinnerungen. East Berlin. 1990. p. 303.

[13] Clara Zetkin. *Selected Writings*, edited by Philip S. Foner. Chicago: Haymarket Books, 2015, 79.

[14] Zetkin, "Selected Writings", 105.

in the KPD she represented a more moderate wing, and toward the end of her life, her opposition to Stalinism saw her become politically isolated in the Soviet Union.

A formidable thinker, orator, and strategist, Zetkin pushed beyond Bebel and Engels in theorizing the place of working women in the struggle for equal rights and class emancipation. Her speech to the meeting of the Second International in Paris in 1889 became the basis of the party's approach to women's liberation, contributing significantly to the party's commitment to including women and girls in the socialist movement. Like Bebel and Engels, Zetkin viewed the historical development of women's position in society as a function of the underlying economic structure. However, she presented a nuanced argument about the dialectical nature of women's work in response to voices within the Social Democratic movement who sought to abolish it—ostensibly for their protection (*Arbeiterinnenschutz*), the same terms in which the abolition of children's labor was cast, though in reality out of anxieties about the competition posed by cheaper female labor.

With the transition to industrial capitalism, Zetkin argued, mechanization had driven down wages to the point that a male worker's single wage was no longer sufficient to support his family, meaning that women also had to work in order to make ends meet. However, far from being a disadvantage for women, Zetkin acknowledges that women's increasing participation in the workplace had in fact freed her sex from the enforced and exclusive vocation of domestic life. To be sure, this argument alone would not have been enough to convince those in the party who were ill disposed toward women's increasing demands. But Zetkin shrewdly turns the argument into a potential strategic advantage for the labor movement. By participating in the workforce, women are freed from the "social slavery" of economic dependence or independence, but they are also subjected to the vagaries of the capitalist labor market, which politicizes them. The woman question, for Zetkin, was "born by the machine age," and its resolution required complete social revolution. Thus, Zetkin deployed and expanded on classic Marxist theory in order to shape the discussion about the abolition of women's work within the party.[15]

Labor rights were a key issue for the proletarian women's movement from the beginning. Equal salaries made the bargaining power of workers of both sexes collectively stronger, and the demand for "gleicher Lohn für gleiche Leistung" (equal pay for equal performance)—a principle also defended by bourgeois women such as Alice Salomon—was raised at party level as early as 1865. A particular point of contention in the dispute over equal pay was the contradiction between the fact that this demand presupposed equal output and the idea that women needed protective labor market measures to account for their reduced physical performance capacity. Trade unionist Gertrud Hanna attempted to resolve this contradiction through the concept of equal work (*gleichwertigen Arbeitsleistung*), a concept intended to enable a comparison between different categories of men's and women's work.

A book printer's assistant, Hanna came into contact with the trade union movement in the mid-1890s, joining the board of the book printers' union and from 1907 working

---

[15] Zetkin, "Selected Writings," 46.

as a full-time trade union employee. From 1909 until the end of the Weimar Republic, she was the only female member of the Allgemeiner Deutscher Gewerkschaftsbund (General Commission of Trade Unions, ADGB) or the organization's Federal Executive Committee. In the pages of the *Gewerkschaftliche Frauenzeitung* (*Union Women's Magazine*), of which Hanna was chief editor from 1915 until 1933, she put women's labor issues center stage. Hanna also militated for women's political participation in the SPD after joining the party in 1908. Between 1919 and 1921, Hanna was a member of the constituent Prussian state assembly and then of the Prussian state parliament until 1933, where she campaigned in particular for maternity protection and for the protection of women at work. She was also a member of the main committee of Arbeiterwohlfahrt and a committed antifascist: before the Reichstag elections on 31 July 1932, Hanna published an anti-Nazi appeal calling on women to join the Iron Front, a paramilitary organization in the Weimar Republic that aimed to defend liberal democracy against totalitarian ideologies on the far right and far left.

An article in *Die Gleichheit* published on 8 November 1918—literally on the eve of the German revolution—looked to England for inspiration on the question of equal pay. In August 1918, women workers on London buses and trams started the first equal pay strike in the country's history, over the offer of an unequal war bonus. The strike was successful in that it forced the government to conduct a special inquiry into whether the principle of equal pay between women and men should be established in all industries. The inquiry concluded, along the lines suggested by Hanna, that there should be a principle of equal pay for equal work, but since it deemed women's work to be less productive than that of men, rejected the idea of equal pay in the absolute. *Die Gleichheit* thus exaggerated when it reported that English workers had effectively won the fight for equal pay: the full results of the government report were not published until 1919. It is a sad irony that the English women's fight for equal pay was ultimately defeated by a report based on the principle of equal work—rather than equal performance or output—advocated by Hanna. In Germany, too, Hanna's solution only resulted in women's jobs being classified into upper and lower wage categories.

Die Gleichheit insisted that the fight for equal wages in England had been made easier by the fact that English women now had the vote, which indeed some of them (those over the age of thirty who were property owners or the wives of property owners, or graduates voting in a university constituency) had acquired in February that year with the Representation of the People Act. It was a right for which German women would have to wait only a matter of weeks after the publication of *Die Gleichheit*'s article: on 30 November, all German women over the age of twenty, without qualification of property ownership, obtained suffrage rights.

It was an issue for which Hanna, Zetkin, and many others in the proletarian women's movement had long campaigned. Already in March 1911, Hanna had explicitly linked the right to vote with the struggle for equal pay. The labor movement, Hanna claimed, had improved the lives of women workers by militating for strengthened rights in every sector. However, she wrote, "even today, the working class does not have the influence in the parliaments that it deserves according to its strength and its importance for the whole economic life of society."[16] The parliamentary labor movement would be able to advance the cause of workers—and thus of women workers—only when women themselves won the right to vote and to stand as candidates in elections.

Helene Grünberg argued along similar lines. Born the daughter of a Berlin restaurateur in 1874, Grünberg trained as a seamstress before joining the SPD in the 1890s. In 1896 she joined the trade union movement where she organized maids and cleaners. One of the SPD's first female public speakers, Grünberg took over the post of workers' secretary in the Nuremberg trade union, and became the first salaried female workers' secretary in Germany—a role in which she succeeded in increasing the number of women organized in trade unions by 60 percent within one year. In 1906, at Grünberg's instigation, the first free trade union for domestic servants was founded in Nuremberg. In November 1919, Grünberg also became a member of the Weimar National Assembly.

Writing alongside Hanna in a publication issued from the first meeting of SPD women in 1911, Grünberg argued that the slow development of women workers' rights was evidence of the importance of women's suffrage. Women's working hours at the time were poorly regulated if at all: according to Grünberg, there were no legally regulated working hours for agricultural workers and domestic servants, and the ten- and sixteen-hour days won by the SPD for women factory workers and waitresses, respectively, could often become longer with overtime. "If the right to vote gave women influence over the composition of the Reichstag," Grünberg speculates, "if there were more Social Democratic representatives of the working class, women as well as men, then the ten-hour day for women workers would have been law for many years and the introduction of the legal eight-hour day for all women wage workers would be within reach."[17] For these women, then, women's suffrage was not an end in itself but was essential to advancing the cause of the labor movement.

Luise Zietz, a weaver's daughter who joined the labor movement in 1892, framed the issue slightly differently. Zietz made her first public appearance as a speaker during the Hamburg dockworkers' strike of 1896, during which she organized the women's resistance. From 1898 to 1904 she was treasurer of the Verband der Fabrik- Land- und gewerblichen Hilfsarbeiter (Federation of Factory, Agricultural and Industrial Laborers) in Hamburg-St. Georg, representing this local union at the trade union congresses in 1902 and 1910. When the Reichsvereinsgesetz (Imperial Associations Act) came into force in 1908, she officially became a member of the SPD. Zietz was a popular and successful agitator for the party, especially among women. At the Nuremberg Party Congress she was the first woman in Germany to be elected to a party executive committee. In 1919/1920, Zietz became a member of the Weimar National Assembly

---

[16] Gertrud Hanna. "Die Bedeutung des Frauenwahlrechts für die Arbeiterinnen." In: *Frauenwahlrecht! Herausgegeben zum Ersten Sozialdemokratischen Frauentag von Clara Zetkin*, 1911, 6.

[17] Helene, Grünberg. "Frauenwahlrecht und Sozialpolitik." Frauenwahlrecht! Herausgegeben zum Ersten Sozialdemokratischen Frauentag von Clara Zetkin, 1911, 8.

and remained a member of the Reichstag for the rest of her life. Zietz was a radical in addition to her parliamentary success. However, in 1917 she was one of the founding members of the USPD, of whose Central Committee she also remained a member until her death.

Rather than focusing on the necessity of suffrage for improving working women's situation, as Hanna and Grünberg did, Zietz emphasized that their position as workers meant that working women should be entitled to vote. Given that a growing number of women workers produced the goods necessary for the maintenance and development of society, Zietz claimed, they too should have a say in politics. Not only women's productive—that is, waged—labor but also their reproductive function represented for Zietz a major factor in favor of their right to suffrage. "Women bear, care for, and raise the future generation," she argued, a task that was of the utmost importance for society, and which was both dangerous (Zietz points to the numbers of women who died during or became seriously ill after childbirth) and unpaid.[18] In this, Zietz anticipated later Marxist feminist critiques of reproductive labor, which emphasize the gendered nature of the largely unpaid domestic care and emotional labor required to reproduce the workforce in capitalist society.

Women's bodies, in the context of both motherhood and sexuality, were another topic of concern for proletarian women. Proletarian women did not speak and write as openly about sexuality as some other feminists. Occasional articles in *Die Gleichheit* dealt with women's sexual life, but these tended to concentrate on the need for education and a less restrictive morality in rather vague terms. Helene Stöcker wrote extensively about women's sexuality in a way not encountered among proletarian women. Stöcker was not a socialist, though both of the civil society organizations she helped to found included socialists, and Stöcker herself was critical of capitalism, which she saw as inherently militaristic. Philosophically, Stöcker was a "left-wing Nietzschean" who applied Nietzsche's theory of self-creation to sex and gender.[19]

In various publications and in the pages of the Bund für Mutterschutz's newspaper *Die neue Generation (The New Generation)*, Stöcker argued that the sexuality of men and women should be considered equal, and that sexuality outside marriage should be permitted. Many socialist women—and men—saw questions of private sexuality as secondary to the struggle, as Zetkin's comments to the Nuremberg Party Congress in 1908 indicate. Speaking about the socialist youth movement, Zetkin said that "young proletarians have to be trained to bridle the intellectually and morally coarse, blind, instinctive sexual life, and to suffuse it with the values of our culture."[20] Certainly, "our"

---

[18] Zietz, *"Zur Frage des Mutter- und Säuglingsschutzes,"* 6.

[19] Seth Taylor. *Left-Wing Nietzscheans: The Politics of German Expressionism, 1910–1920.* de Gruyter, 1990.

[20] Clara Zetkin. *Protokoll über die Verhandlungen des Parteitages der Sozialdemokratischen Partei Deutschlands abgehalten zu Nürnberg,* 11 bis 12 September 1908 (Berlin, 1908), 529. Cf. R. P. Neuman, "The Sexual Question and Social Democracy in Imperial Germany." *Journal of Social History* 7, no. 3 (1974), 276.

culture referred to socialist culture; whether "young proletarians" was meant to include both sexes is unclear.

Women's sexuality came up more frequently in the proletarian milieu in relation to prostitution. In Imperial and Weimar Germany, prostitutes were defined as female: male prostitution was dealt with under Paragraph 175 of the criminal code dealing with homosexuality.[21] Prostitution grew rapidly in Germany in the second half of the nineteenth century, largely as a consequence of urbanization: working-class autobiographies frequently tell of young women who moved to the city to find work in domestic service or other industries, and moving into prostitution if they lost their jobs or were exploited.[22] By the turn of the century, estimates of the total number of prostitutes active in Germany varied between 100,000 and 200,000; on the eve of World War I, there were said to be more than 330,000 prostitutes in business throughout the country, the vast majority of whom were from working-class backgrounds.[23]

Socialist women tended to criticize the criminalization of prostitution, seeing the latter in Bebel's terms as an unavoidable product of a capitalist society in which women who could not find other work were forced to sell their labor in the sex industry. When more restrictive measures were introduced by the Lex Heinze in 1900, the proletarian women's press reacted strongly.[24] In March 1900, Adele Gerhard, a Jewish women's rights campaigner close to the SPD, criticized the disproportionate impact of prostitution restrictions on working-class women in *Die Gleichheit*. In particular, Gerhard objected to the watering down of punishment for pimps in the process of drafting the bill, since it was well known, she argued, that many working women and servant girls were lured or forced into prostitution by their employers.[25]

Another front on which sexuality was tackled by proletarian women was abortion. Paragraph 218 of the 1871 German Criminal Code made abortion at any stage of pregnancy illegal, aiming in particular to target "illicit" sex outside marriage or pregnancies conceived as a result of prostitution.[26] This paragraph was preserved in the Weimar constitution. By this time, however, more and more married women wishing to limit the size of their families used abortion as a post facto contraception method. Throughout the 1920s, the USPD, majority SPD, and KPD brought motions to the Reichstag to repeal Paragraph 218, all of which were ultimately unsuccessful. In 1931, in an atmosphere of

---

[21] Martin Lücke, "Hierarchien der Unzucht: Regime männlicher und weiblicher Prostitution in Kaiserreich und Weimarer Republik," in *L'homme: Zeitschrift für feministische Geschichtswissenschaft* 21, no. 1 (2010): 49–64.

[22] Evans, "Prostitution, State and Society in Imperial Germany," 108; Alfred Kelly, ed., *The German Worker: Working-Class Autobiographies from the Age of Industrialization* (Berkeley: University of California Press, 1987), 23.

[23] Evans, "Prostitution, State and Society in Imperial Germany," 108; 115–116.

[24] The law was named after a pimp and his wife (who was a prostitute), who in 1887 broke into a church to steal silver and murdered a night watchman who interrupted them.

[25] Adele Gerhard, "Um Freiheit und Kultur," *Die Gleichheit*, 28 March 1900: 50.

[26] Cornelia Usborne, "Abortion in Weimar Germany—The Debate amongst the Medical Profession," *Continuity and Change* 5, no. 2 (1990): 199–224.

economic crisis and political turmoil, thousands of women joined together in a concerted campaign to call for the abolition of 218.[27] That year, an issue of *Der sozialistische Arzt* (*The Socialist Doctor*) carried a number of voices against Paragraph 218, including doctors, politicians, and members of the proletarian women's movement, including Toni Sender and Marie Juchacz.

Sender, also from a Jewish background, had joined the labor movement already as a schoolgirl. During the German revolution, she took part in the workers' councils, and in 1920 was elected to the Reichstag on a USPD ticket, appealing in her campaign material to women in their role as mothers. In her contribution to the issue, Sender claimed that the prohibition of abortion was completely ineffectual, calling it a *Klassengesetz* (classed law) that disproportionately impacted working-class women.[28]

Juchacz, a carpenter's daughter who worked variously as a domestic servant, factory worker, nurse, and tailor, was milder in her tone.[29] Having joined the SPD in 1908, Juchacz remained with the majority after the party split in 1917, succeeding Zetkin as editor of *Die Gleichheit* in 1917. She admitted that the only way to combat abortion was to improve the social conditions of women and educate them about sexuality and contraception. However, the more moderate Juchacz was also quick to reassure her readers that Social Democratic women were not advocates of abortion as such.

Mothers' rights—to participate in the upbringing of their children, to maternity protection, and to welfare if they were single—were an issue that sometimes united and sometimes divided socialist and bourgeois women. In 1911, Zietz published a pamphlet setting out socialist demands of state support for working women, which—along with limits to the working hours and ages—included the extension of health insurance to all female workers whose household income was under a certain threshold, as well as eight weeks' compulsory maternity leave paid at full salary.[30] For other women in the period, motherhood was a "spiritual" matter, as Ann Taylor Allen has put it.[31]

This was certainly the case for Lily Braun. Born into an aristocratic family, Braun had in part joined the socialist cause out of a perceived affinity between her own powerlessness as an aristocratic woman destined only to reproduce her social class through childbearing and the position of proletarian women who also reported experiencing themselves as objects.[32] Nevertheless, Braun's upbringing did shape her views, and her embrace of the doctrine of spiritual motherhood distinguished her from many of her working-class comrades, for whom raising children was a practical matter of putting

---

[27] Atina Grossman, "Abortion and Economic Crisis: The 1931 Campaign against §218 in Germany," *New German Critique* 14 (1978): 119–137.

[28] Toni Sender, "Stimmen gegen den § 218," *Der sozialistische Arzt* 7, no. 4 (1931): 103–104.

[29] Marie Juchacz, "Stimmen gegen den § 218," *Der sozialistische Arzt* 7, no. 4 (1931): 102–103.

[30] Luise Zietz, *Zur Frage des Mutter- und Säuglingsschutzes* (Leipzig: Verlag der Leipziger Buchdruckerei AG, 1911), 28–29.

[31] Ann Taylor Allen, "Mothers of the New Generation: Adele Schreiber, Helene Stöcker, and the Evolution of a German Idea of Motherhood, 1900–1914," *Signs* 10, no. 3 (1985): 418–438.

[32] Jean H. Quataert, *Reluctant Feminists in German Social Democracy 1885–1917* (Princeton: Princeton University Press, 1979), 89-90.

food on the table as much as it was an affair of the heart. As Jean Quataert has argued in her classic study on the German socialist women's movement, "Braun's whole philosophy on love, marriage, and the family was centered around the need for motherhood to help women realize their true nature."[33] Braun's position on this issue reveals once again how the apparent contradiction between sex and class shaped the views of individual women. If, as I have shown, Braun rejected feminist separatism, seeing sex and gender concerns as class-transcendent, she applied a double standard to women from different class backgrounds when it came to motherhood. Braun's deep commitment to motherhood meant that she was generally critical of women who chose a childless existence, though she approved the limitation of births in the case of working-class women.[34] This arguably rather reactionary view contrasted with some of Braun's other ideas, including experimenting with communal living, which were too radical for many in both the liberal and proletarian wings of the women's movement.

Not only mothers' rights, but also those of children were at the forefront of proletarian women's concerns. Zietz, who had to work as a child in her father's wool shop to supplement the family income, was particularly concerned with the Kinderschutzgesetz (Child Protection Act) that came into force in 1904.[35] It was the first Reich law to regulate child labor in various trades beyond factory work. In her interventions on the topic in *Die Neue Zeit* (*The New Times*, the theoretical journal of the SPD) in 1904–1905, Zietz clarifies that her party fraction voted in favor of the law because it represented a measure of social protection from capitalist exploitation.[36] However, Zietz also stridently criticized the law's shortcomings. As she notes, no uniform age limits were applied so that in commerce, children over the age of twelve could be employed, whereas in the haulage industry an age limit of fourteen years was mandatory. Meanwhile, agriculture and forestry were not covered by the law at all, although, as Zietz laments, "children working in agriculture have it not one iota better than their comrades-in-suffering in industry."[37] She claimed that the law was virtually unenforceable on account of a lack of statistics on children's work, the fact that teachers were being held responsible for reporting children in school who appeared tired or unfocused—an unreliable and unjust method, in Zietz's view—and the exploitation of loopholes by employers who redefined their type of work in order to escape the restrictions.[38] For Zietz, the complete abolition of child labor, which she called the "most egregious form of capitalist exploitation," that damaged children's physical and intellectual development, must be the explicit goal of the labor movement.[39]

---

[33] Quataert, *Reluctant Feminists*, 96.

[34] See Ann Taylor Allen, "German Radical Feminism and Eugenics, 1900–1908," *German Studies Review* 11, no. 1 (1988): 31–56.

[35] Luise Zietz, "Das Kinderschutzgesetz und dessen Handhabung," *Die neue Zeit* 22 (1904): 705–708; "Die Wirksamkeit des Kinderschutzgesetzes," *Die neue Zeit* 18 (1906), 587–594.

[36] Zietz, "Das Kinderschutzgesetz und dessen Handhabung," 705.

[37] Zietz, "Das Kinderschutzgesetz und dessen Handhabung," 706.

[38] Zietz, "Die Wirksamkeit des Kinderschutzgesetzes," 588; 594.

[39] Zietz, "Die Wirksamkeit des Kinderschutzgesetzes," 594.

The ambivalent socialist response to questions of motherhood and sexuality is no-where better illustrated than in the "birth strike" debate of 1913.[40] The term "birth strike" was first used in 1892 when French neo-Malthusians and feminists Marie Huot and Paul Robin called for a "grève des ventres," believing they had found a means to overturn the social structure in the class struggle.[41] Limiting births, they argued, would strengthen the situation of workers, since less labor would be available, and wages would therefore inevitably rise.

In 1912, two social democratic doctors from Berlin, Alfred Bernstein and Julius Moses, whose practices brought them into contact with many working-class women, advocated women's right to use birth control along similar lines. Though contraception was tech-nically illegal in Germany at the time, in reality working-class families already used various forms, from the natural withdrawal and temperature methods, and postcoital douching, to condoms and cotton or sponge tampons. In the 1920s, practical education around contraception became one of the key tasks of workers' organizations, advocated by Juchacz among others.[42] Doctors increasingly advocated legalizing the practice, not only to give women greater control over their bodies, but also for eugenic reasons, emphasizing the importance of population "quality," particularly where demands for welfare were being made. In addition to these reasons, Bernstein and Moses argued—in terms reminiscent of the earlier French debate—that smaller families would improve the conditions of workers by depriving the capitalist class of soldiers for their wars.

In July of the following year, the local Berlin SPD organization arranged two meetings dedicated to the birth strike. Zetkin, Zietz, and Rosa Luxemburg, whose contribution was all the more powerful given that she rarely spoke on sexuality or the family, were vehemently opposed to the demographic reasoning behind the idea. Zietz argued that it was not the high birth rate, but economic inequality that was responsible for working-class exploitation. Limiting the number of children could aid individual women and families, she claimed, but it could not improve the situation of the class as a whole.[43] Luxemburg agreed, declaring that the social question could never be solved by "self-help," but only via structural economic change.[44] As the report on the debate in *Die Gleichheit* shows, other women, particularly Minna Güldner and Clara Bohm-Schuch, insisted on the importance of working women being able to control their fertility in order to improve their lives and free themselves to participate in politics, though they too rejected the birth strike as a weapon in the class struggle.[45] But it was Clara Zetkin

[40] Anna Bergmann, "Am Vorabend einer neuen Sexualmoral? Die Debatte um den 'Gebärstreik' im Jahr 1913," *INDES* 2, no. 2 (2013): 90–97; R. P. Neuman, "Working Class Birth Control in Wilhelmine Germany," *Comparative Studies in Society and History* 20, no. 3 (1978): 408–428.

[41] Francis Ronsin. La Grève des ventres. Propagande néo-malthusienne et baisse de la natalité en France (XIXᵉ-XXᵉ siècles). Aubier, 1980

[42] Marie Juchacz, "Geburtenfrage—Sexualberatung eine Aufgabe der Arbeiterwohlfahrt," *Arbeiterwohlfahrt* 23, no. 4 (1929): 730–734

[43] See "Sozialistische Frauenkonferenz für Groß-Berlin," *Die Gleichheit*, 26 November 1913, 72–73.

[44] Neuman, "Working Class Birth Control in Wilhelmine Germany," 414.

[45] "Sozialistische Frauenkonferenz für Groß-Berlin," 73.

who rejected this perspective most vociferously, arguing that those who advocated a birth strike as a means of depriving capitalists of foot soldiers for their wars forgot that fewer soldiers also meant fewer revolutionaries.[46]

When war did break out in July 1914, Zetkin called on proletarian women to resist what she saw from the beginning as an unjust war.[47] In the pages of *Die Gleichheit*, she declared that Germany was illegitimately making Austria's war, waged in an attempt to block tsarist Russia's expansionist pretensions, its own. Zetkin saw Russian tsarism and Austro-Hungarian monarchism as equally oppressive regimes, and accused Imperial Germany of capitalizing on the conflict in order to advance its own nationalist expansion. The German working class must, she claimed, resist a war that would only see their fathers, husbands, and sons slaughtered and the wealthy and powerful further strengthened.

A year later, at the International Socialist Women's Conference, Zetkin intensified these arguments, asking her fellow delegates "Where are your husbands? Where are your sons?"[48] Though a year earlier, she had defended the national emancipation movements in Austria-Hungary, Zetkin questioned the nationalist concept of the *Vaterland* in the name of which Germany was waging its war.[49] "Of what does the fatherland consist?" she asked, if not the "well-being of its millions . . . who are being changed to corpses, cripples, unemployed beggars and orphans by this war?"[50] Contrary to the rhetoric of the political class, Zetkin claimed the war was waged not in order to defend the fatherland, but to expand the wealth of a tiny minority of big industrialists, including arms manufacturers such as Alfred Krupp, and to conquer new colonies for the exploitation of resources. Zetkin's stance on the war thus clearly illustrates the split that had occurred in the broader socialist movement: though the majority SPD supported the war on patriotic grounds, Zetkin's antinationalism and anticolonialism typified a Marxist stance that Lenin would soon articulate when he identified imperialism with the highest stage of capitalist development.[51]

Rosa Luxemburg, too—undoubtedly German socialism's most prominent female theorist—vehemently opposed colonialism and imperialism, viewing the imperialist World War I as a direct consequence of capitalism's need for constant expansion. Luxemburg expounded her economic theory in her 1913 book *The Accumulation of Capital (Die Akkumulation des Kapitals)*, in which she argued that capitalism depended not only on "primitive accumulation" (the acquisition of wealth by the conquest of land), but also on the incorporation of previously unproductive workers—such as women—into the production process.[52] For Luxemburg, war was just another means

---

[46] Neuman, "Working Class Birth Control in Wilhelmine Germany," 413.

[47] Zetkin, "For the Liberation of Women," 110–113.

[48] Zetkin, "For the Liberation of Women," 130–132.

[49] Zetkin, "For the Liberation of Women," 110.

[50] Zetkin, "For the Liberation of Women," 131.

[51] Vladimir Lenin, *Der Imperialismus als höchstes Stadium des Kapitalismus. Gemeinverständlicher Abriß* (Berlin: Dietz Verlag, 1962).

[52] Rosa Luxemburg, *The Accumulation of Capital* (New York: Routledge, 2003).

for capitalism to expand in this way. In her most important antiwar pamphlet, *The Crisis of Social Democracy* (*Die Krise der Sozialdemokratie*) (1915), Luxemburg vilifies the support for war by the majority of her party, singling out the Social Democratic women's movement for collaborating in national service activities such as soup kitchens instead of militating for peace.[53]

In this, as in her general approach to the woman question, Luxemburg took much the same line as Zetkin, viewing class allegiance as more important than sex. Though she supported the struggle for women's suffrage, arguing in her 1912 pamphlet *Women's Suffrage and Class Struggle* that the matter was "one of the vital issues on the platform of Social Democracy," Luxemburg nevertheless saw the struggle for suffrage alone, without a concomitant fight for workers' rights, as a political cul-de-sac. Pointing in 1904 to examples of countries where women already had the vote, Luxemburg reminds her reader that the "domination of capital" was in no way challenged by their enfranchisement.[54]

Neither the end of the war nor the Russian Revolution would resolve the tension at the heart of socialist thinking on the woman question. Certainly, Zetkin welcomed the Russian Revolution as a major victory for the international labor movement. Writing to Lenin in 1922, she acknowledged the "mistakes" and "stupidities" that had been committed in the process, but still saw October 1917 as "the first great world-historical attempt to raise Marxism from theory to practice."[55] From the early 1920s, Zetkin visited the Soviet Union regularly, before moving there definitively after the Nazis took power in January 1933, and she died in Moscow in July that year. Though Zetkin's commitment to the international labor movement never wavered, during the last years of the Weimar Republic, she became a sharp critic of her party, opposing the erosion under Soviet control of democratic decision-making, the termination of cooperation with trade unions, and the Stalinist rejection of a popular front against fascism. Even if she sometimes toed the party line, denouncing "traitors" when it was expected, overall Zetkin's oppositional stance in the second half of the 1920s brought her into conflict with a changing international communist and labor movement.[56]

During these years, however, Zetkin never tired of campaigning for working women, and she continued to see the class struggle and the international labor movement as women's best route to achieving their goal of equality. In the pages of her periodical *Die Kommunistische Fraueninternationale* (*The Communist Women's International*) (1921–1925), Zetkin continued to convince women of the virtues of joining Soviet Russia in worldwide revolution rather than succumbing to what she continued to see as the

---

[53] Rosa Luxemburg, *The Crisis of German Social Democracy* (1915), https://www.marxists.org/archive/luxemburg/1915/junius/index.htm.

[54] Rosa Luxemburg, "The Proletarian Woman," in *The Rosa Luxemburg Reader*, ed. Peter Hudis and Kevin B. Anderson (New York: Monthly Review Press, 2004), 244.

[55] Clara Zetkin, "Für die Sowjetmacht," in *Artikel, Reden und Briefe* (Berlin: Dietz, 1977), 242–245.

[56] Marcel Bois, "Clara Zetkin und die Stalinisierung von KPD und Komintern," in *Clara Zetkin in ihrer Zeit: Neue Fakten, Erkenntnisse, Wertungen*, ed. Ulla Plener (Berlin: Dietz, 2008), 149–156.

empty promises of feminist movements in capitalist nations. Among other things, Zetkin highlighted the successes of the Bolshevik sexual revolution as a great triumph of working-class struggle.[57] In her interview with Lenin on the woman question in 1920, she disagreed with her comrade when he cautioned that the "private" questions of sexuality and marriage could serve as a diversion from revolutionary action. Zetkin, who had made versions of the same argument herself over the years, now reminded Lenin that sex and marriage were problematic for women of all classes under capitalism, and that the war had accentuated women's difficulties in these areas.[58]

Yet if Zetkin at first appears here rather uncharacteristically to give ground to the view that the woman question was class transcendent, it is clear from her writings that she continued to see the improved fortunes of women as inextricably connected to the class struggle. In her antifascist writings of the period, too, she decried Mussolini's commitment to partial, local suffrage for women, which had already been surpassed in Germany in 1918.[59] In this respect, Zetkin remains an exemplar for the way in which representatives of the German socialist women's movement theorized the woman question through the lens of the political and social struggles of their day.

BIBLIOGRAPHY

Allen, Ann Taylor. "German Radical Feminism and Eugenics, 1900–1908." *German Studies Review* 11, no. 1 (1988): 31–56.

Allen, Ann Taylor. "Mothers of the New Generation: Adele Schreiber, Helene Stöcker, and the Evolution of a German Idea of Motherhood, 1900–1914." *Signs* 10, no. 3 (1985): 418–438.

Baader, Ottilie. *Ein steiniger Weg. Lebenserinnerungen einer Sozialistin.* Bonn: Dietz, 1979.

Bebel, August. *Woman and Socialism.* Translated by Meta L. Stern. New York: Socialist Literature, 1910.

Bergmann, Anna. "Am Vorabend einer neuen Sexualmoral? Die Debatte um den 'Gebärstreik' im Jahr 1913." *INDES Zeitschrift für Politik und Gesellschaft* 2, (2013): 90–97.

Bhattacharya, Tithi, ed. *Social Reproduction Theory.* London. Pluto Press, 2017.

Bois, Marcel. "Clara Zetkin und die Stalinisierung von KPD und Komintern." In *Clara Zetkin in ihrer Zeit: Neue Fakten, Erkenntnisse, Wertungen,* edited by Ulla Plener, 149–156. Berlin: Dietz, 2008.

Braker, Regina. "Helene Stöcker's Pacifism in the Weimar Republic: Between Ideal and Reality." *Journal of Women's History* 13, no. 3 (2001): 70–97.

Canning, Kathleen. "Gender and the Imaginary of Revolution in Germany." In *Germany 1916-23: A Revolution in Context,* edited by Klaus Weinhauer, Anthony McElligott, and Kirsten Heinsohn, 103–126. Berlin: Transcript Verlag, 2015.

---

[57] Legislation on sex and gender introduced in early revolutionary Russia was the most progressive in the world at that time. Civil marriage was introduced, and divorce and abortion were legalized, while prostitution and homosexuality were also decriminalized. See Gregory Carleton, *The Sexual Revolution in Bolshevik Russia* (Pittsburgh: University of Pittsburgh Press, 2005).

[58] Clara Zetkin, *Lenin on the Woman Question* (New York: International, 1934), https://www.marxists.org/archive/zetkin/1920/lenin/zetkin1.htm.

[59] Zetkin, "For the Liberation of Women," 170–175.

Chickering, Roger. "'Casting Their Gaze More Broadly': Women's Patriotic Activism in Imperial Germany." *Past & Present* 118 (1988): 156–185.

"Die Frau im Beruf." *Die Gleichheit*, August 11, 1918.

Dollard, Catherine L. *The Surplus Woman: Unmarried in Imperial Germany, 1871–1918*. New York: Berghahn, 2009.

Engels, Friedrich. *The Origin of the Family, Private Property and the State*. In *Engels: 1882–1889*, vol. 26 of *Marx & Engels Collected Works*, 129–276. London: Lawrence & Wishart, 1990.

Evans, Richard J. "Bourgeois Feminists and Women Socialists in Germany 1894–1914: Lost Opportunity or Inevitable Conflict?" *Women's Studies International Quarterly* 3 (1980): 355–376.

Evans, Richard J. *The Feminist Movement in Germany, 1894–1933*. London: Sage, 1976.

Evans, Richard J. "German Social Democracy and Women's Suffrage 1891–1918." *Journal of Contemporary History* 15, no. 3 (1980): 533–577.

Evans, Richard J. "Prostitution, State and Society in Imperial Germany." *Past & Present* 70 (1976): 106–129.

Evans, Richard J. *Sozialdemokratie und Frauenemanzipation im Deutschen Kaiserreich*. Bonn: Dietz, 1979.

Feministischen Institut der Heinrich-Böll-Stiftung, ed. *Wie weit flog die Tomate? Eine 68erinnen-Gala der Reflexion*. Berlin: Heinrich-Böll-Stiftung, 1999.

Frei, Annette. *Rote Patriarchen. Arbeiterbewegung und Frauenemanzipation in der Schweiz um 1900*. Zurich: Chronos, 1987.

Gemkow, Heinrich, and Angelika Müller, eds. *August Bebel, "ein prächtiger Adler". Nachrufe—Gedichte—Erinnerungen*. Berlin: Dietz Verlag, 1990.

Gerhard, Adele. "Um Freiheit und Kultur." *Die Gleichheit*, March 28, 1900.

Globig, Marta. "Zietz, Luise, geb. Körner." In *Geschichte der deutschen Arbeiterbewegung. Biographisches Lexikon*, edited by Roland Grau, Günter Hortzschansky, W. Rieß, and Gerhard Roßmann, 501–502. Berlin: Dietz Verlag, 1970.

Grossman, Atina. "Abortion and Economic Crisis: The 1931 Campaign against §218 in Germany." *New German Critique* 14 (1978): 119–137.

Grünberg, Helene. "Frauenwahlrecht und Sozialpolitik". In: *Frauenwahlrecht! Herausgegeben zum Ersten Sozialdemokratischen Frauentag von Clara Zetkin*, 7–8. 1911.

Guido, Diane J. *The German League for the Prevention of Women's Emancipation: Antifeminism in Germany 1912–1920*. Bern: Peter Lang, 2010.

Hanna, Gertrud. "Die Bedeutung des Frauenwahlrechts für die Arbeiterinnen." In: *Frauenwahlrecht! Herausgegeben zum Ersten Sozialdemokratischen Frauentag von Clara Zetkin*, 5–6. 1911.

Heide, Schlüpmann. "Nietzsche-Rezeption in der alten Frauenbewegung. Die sexualpolitische Konzeption Helene Stöckers." *Nietzscheforschung* 19, no. 1 (2012): 75–90.

Helfert, Veronika. "Between Pacifism and Militancy: Socialist Women in the First Austrian Republic, 1918–1934." *Diplomacy & Statecraft* 31, no. 4 (2020): 648–672.

Juchacz, Marie. "Geburtenfrage—Sexualberatung eine Aufgabe der Arbeiterwohlfahrt." *Arbeiterwohlfahrt* 23, no. 4 (1929): 730–734.

Juchacz, Marie. "Stimmen gegen den § 218." *Der sozialistische Arzt* 7, no. 4 (1931): 102–103.

Juchacz, Marie, and Johanna Heymann. *Die Arbeiterwohlfahrt. Voraussetzungen und Entwicklung*. Berlin: Dietz Verlag, 1924.

Kaplan, Temma. "On the Socialist Origins of International Women's Day." *Feminist Studies* 11, no. 1 (1985): 163–171.

Kelly, Alfred, ed. *The German Worker: Working-Class Autobiographies from the Age of Industrialization.* Berkeley: University of California Press, 1987.

Kleinhempel, Friedrich. "Als Arbeiterinnen um Gleichen Lohn kämpften." *Neues Deutschland,* August 1, 2007. https://www.nd-aktuell.de/artikel/103113.als-arbeiterinnen-um-gleichen-lohn-kaempften.html.

Knapp, Ulla. "Frauenarbeit in Deutschland zwischen 1850 und 1933: T. I." *Historical Social Research* 8, no. 4 (1983): 61–64.

—"Frauenarbeit in Deutschland zwischen 1850 und 1933: T. II." *Historical Social Research,* 9, no. 1 (1984): 3–42

Lafleur, Ingrun. "Adelheid Popp and Working-Class Feminism in Austria." *Frontiers: A Journal of Women Studies* 1, no. 1 (1975): 86–105.

Lenin, Vladimir. *Der Imperialismus als höchstes Stadium des Kapitalismus. Gemeinverständlicher Abriß.* Berlin: Dietz Verlag, 1962.

Lenz, Ilse, ed. *Die Neue Frauenbewegung in Deutschland.* Wiesbaden: VS Verlag, 2010.

Limbach, Jutta. *"Wahre Hyänen": Pauline Staegemann und ihr Kampf um die politische Macht der Frauen.* Berlin: Dietz, 2016.

Losseff, Gisela. "Gleichberechtigung oder Frauenemanzipation in der historischen Entwicklung." *Gewerkschaftliche Monatshefte* 11 (1972): 725–732.

Lücke, Martin. "Hierarchien der Unzucht: Regime männlicher und weiblicher Prostitution in Kaiserreich und Weimarer Republik." *L' homme: Zeitschrift für feministische Geschichtswissenschaft* 21, no. 1 (2010): 49–64.

Luxemburg, Rosa. *The Accumulation of Capital.* Translated by Agnes Schwarzschild. New York: Routledge, 2003.

Luxemburg, Rosa. *The Junius Pamphlet: The Crisis of German Social Democracy.* Translated by Dave Hollis. Marxists Internet Archive, 2003. https://www.marxists.org/archive/luxemburg/1915/junius.

Luxemburg, Rosa. "The Proletarian Woman." In *The Rosa Luxemburg Reader,* edited by Peter Hudis and Kevin B. Anderson, 242–247. New York: Monthly Review Press, 2004.

Nave-Herz, Rosemarie. *Die Gechichte der Frauenbewegung in Deutschland.* Hanover: Niedersächsischen Landeszentrale für politische Bildung, 1997.

Neuman, R. P. "The Sexual Question and Social Democracy in Imperial Germany." *Journal of Social History* 7, no. 3 (1974): 271–286.

Oulios, Miltiadis. "Die anarchistische Frauenbewegung in Deutschland vor 1933." PhD diss., University of Cologne, 1999.

Peterson, Brian. "The Politics of Working-Class Women in the Weimar Republic." *Central European History* 10, no. 2 (1977): 87–111.

Planert, Ute. *Antifeminismus im Kaiserreich. Diskurs, soziale Formation und politische Mentalität.* Göttingen: Vandenhoeck & Ruprecht, 1998.

Quataert, Jean H. *Reluctant Feminists in German Social Democracy 1885–1917.* Princeton: Princeton University Press, 1979.

Reagin, Nancy R. *A German Women's Movement: Class and Gender in Hanover, 1880–1933.* Chapel Hill: University of North Carolina Press, 1995.

Regin, Cornelia. "Hausfrau und Revolution. Die Frauenpolitik der Anarchosyndikalisten in der Weimarer Republik." *Internationale Wissenschaftliche Korrespondenz zur Geschichte der Deutschen Arbeiterbewegung* 25 (1989): 379–397.

Roos, Julia. *Weimar through the Lens of Gender: Prostitution Reform, Woman's Emancipation, and German Democracy, 1919-33.* University of Michigan Press, 2010.

Salomon, Alice. "Gleicher Lohn für gleiche Leistung." In *Frauenarbeit und Beruf*, edited by Gisela Brinker-Gabler, 194–199. Frankfurt am Main: Fischer Taschenbuch Verlag, 1979.

Schmitt, Sabine. *Die Arbeiterinnenschutz im deutschen Kaiserreich*. Stuttgart: Metzler, 1995.

Schulz, Kristina. "Sozialistische Frauenorganisationen, bürgerliche Frauenbewegung und der Erste Weltkrieg. Nationale und internationale Perspektiven." *Historische Zeitschrift* 298, no. 3 (2014): 653–685.

Sender, Toni. "Stimmen gegen den § 218." *Der sozialistische Arzt* 7, no. 4 (1931): 103–104.

Sharp, Ingrid, and Matthew Stibbe. "'In diesen Tagen kamen wir nicht von der Straße': Frauen in der deutschen Revolution von 1918/1919." *Ariadne: Forum für Frauen- und Geschlechtergeschichte* 73/74 (2018): 32–39.

Sproat, Liberty P. "The Soviet Solution for Women in Clara Zetkin's Journal *Die Kommunistische Fraueninternationale*, 1921–1925." *Aspasia* 6 (2012): 60–78.

Steinberg, Hans-Josef, and Nicholas Jacobs. "Workers' Libraries in Germany before 1914." *History Workshop* 1 (1976): 166–180.

Stoehr, Irene. "Fraueneinfluß oder Geschlechterversöhnung? Zur 'Sexualitätsdebatte' in der deutschen Frauenbewegung um 1900." In *Frauenkörper Medizin Sexualität*, edited by Johanna Geyer-Kordesch and Annette Kuhn, 159–191. Düsseldorf: Schwann (1986).

Taylor, Seth. *Left-Wing Nietzscheans: The Politics of German Expressionism, 1910–1920*. Berlin: de Gruyter, 1990.

Usborne, Cornelia. "Abortion in Weimar Germany—The Debate amongst the Medical Profession." *Continuity and Change* 5, no. 2 (1990): 199–224.

Weikart, Richard. "Marx, Engels, and the Abolition of the Family." *History of European Ideas* 18, no. 5 (1994): 651–672.

Zetkin, Clara. *Die Arbeiterinnen- und Frauenfrage der Gegenwart*. Berlin: Verl. d. *Berliner Volks-Tribüne*, 1889.

Zetkin, Clara. *Selected Writings*, edited by Philip S. Foner. Chicago: Haymarket Books, 2015.

Zetkin, Clara. "Friedrich Engels: Nachruf zu seinem Tode." In *Auswahl aus den Jahren 1889 bis 1917*, vol. 1 of *Ausgewählte Reden und Schriften*, 82–83. Berlin: Aufbau Verlag, 1957.

Zetkin, Clara. "Für die Sowjetmacht." In *Artikel, Reden und Briefe: 1917–1933*, 242–245. Berlin: Dietz, 1977.

Zetkin, Clara. *Lenin on the Woman Question*. New York: International, 1934.

Zetkin, Clara. *Zur Geschichte der proletarischen Frauenbewegung in Deutschland*. Berlin: Dietz, 1958.

Zietz, Luise. "Das Frauenwahlrecht, ein Rechtstitel und eine Notwendigkeit." In *Vollmar: Vorwärts! In: Frauenwahlrecht!*, edited by Clara Zetkin, 4–5. Stuttgart: Dietz, 1911.

Zietz, Luise. "Das Kinderschutzgesetz und dessen Handhabung." *Die neue Zeit* 22 (1904): 705–708.

Zietz, Luise. "Die Wirksamkeit des Kinderschutzgesetzes." *Die neue Zeit* 18 (1906): 587–594.

Zietz, Luise. *Zur Frage des Mutter- und Säuglingsschutzes*. Leipzig: Verlag der Leipziger Buchdruckerei AG, 1911.

Zietz, Luise. "Das alles erfuhren wir ers taus Bebels 'Frau'". In *August Bebel - "ein prächtiger alter Adler"*, edited by Heinrich Genkow and Angelika Miller. Nachrufe - Gedichte - Erinnerungen. East Berlin, 1990.

CHAPTER 19

FEMINIST PHILOSOPHIZING IN NINETEENTH-CENTURY GERMAN WOMEN'S MOVEMENTS

LYDIA MOLAND

In her 1915 book titled *Feminism in Germany and Scandinavia*, the American biographer Katharine Anthony paid tribute to the philosophical nature of the women's movement in Germany. "The German women," she wrote, "as we should expect, are the metaphysicians of the woman movement. Their contribution to the philosophy of feminism is a significant chapter in the history of their efforts. Their belief in the power of ideas, their respect for clear thinking, and their appreciation of scientific leadership reflect their national background. The feminists' methods, like all other cultural methods and reform movements of the country, are dyed in the intellectualism of the most scientific civilization of the world."[1] Anthony, a native of Arkansas who had written biographies of Margaret Fuller, Louisa May Alcott, and Catherine the Great, knew some of this movement firsthand. She had lived in Germany and studied at the universities of both Heidelberg and Freiburg before returning to the United States to complete a Ph.B. at the University of Chicago. Based on her experience in Germany, she was clearly impressed with German feminism and its philosophical roots.

Although the word *feminism* was not typically used in German discourse until the twentieth century, arguments by women against the systematic and ubiquitous disadvantages they faced had their roots in at least the eighteenth century.[2] There was much to protest. Women in the shifting political landscape of German states existed in

---

[1] Katharine Anthony, *Feminism in Germany and Scandinavia* (New York: Holt, 1915), 14.

[2] On the use of the word, see Susanne Schötz, "'Human Beings Is What Women Want to Become, and to Partake of the Garland of Work and Victory': Visions of Emancipation, Community Spirit, and Social Reform in the First German Women's Movement," *Frontiers in Sociology* 4, no. 64 (2019): 2.

a web of restrictions that kept them ignorant and dependent. Education for girls was minimal and usually did not extend past their early teenage years; at the beginning of the nineteenth century, German girls were among the least educated in Europe.[3] Marriages were often determined by the family with little or no input from daughters. Social norms dictated that middle-class men not marry until they were financially secure, meaning that younger women were often coerced into marriages with much older men. Husbands retained almost total legal control over decisions in the family and over their wives' finances.[4] Employment out of the home was considered unseemly for middle- and upper-class women, leaving them few economic options if they were single or widowed. A "surplus" of women, caused by wars and emigration, meant that the number of women in this situation had become a widespread problem.[5] Protections for working-class women as the region industrialized were scarce. Women had essentially no political rights and, for most of the century, were barred from even participating in political organizations.

In the nineteenth century, women took up philosophical questions in the service of confronting this widespread, multipronged injustice. They grappled with definitions of freedom, self-determination, and individuality and worked to articulate how progress, both within a culture and in humanity, was to be defined. They also articulated questions specifically about women. How did women differ from men? Did women have an "essence," and if so, what was it? What was women's relation to work or to politics? They also confronted practical questions. What did women need to realize their potential? What unjust social practices, moral codes, and repressive laws needed to be reformed? In asking these questions, women drew on eighteenth-century German philosophical thought, including Kant, Schiller, and Goethe; they then worked with the ideas of nineteenth-century philosophers including the German Romantics, Hegel, and Nietzsche. Beginning with political organizing around the Revolution of 1848, women also began to put this philosophizing into action. They formed organizations that fought for goals from education reform to suffrage to labor emancipation; through these organizations, they sought to address other issues that directly impacted women's lives, such as birth control, maternal insurance, and abortion. The result is a century of robust philosophical thought and burgeoning political organization.

In what follows, I focus on what I will call feminist philosophizing: explicitly theoretical thinking about the status, nature, and particular concerns of women. I begin with a brief overview of such theorizing among women of the Romantic period, isolating general themes that became influential in the mid-nineteenth century when women began to organize into reform societies. I then shift to considering the philosophical

---

[3] Jutta Schroers Sanford, "The Origins of German Feminism: German Women 1789–1870" (PhD diss., Ohio State University, 1976), 180.

[4] Schötz, "'Human Beings Is What Women Want to Become,'" 8.

[5] Anthony, *Feminism in Germany and Scandinavia*, 85. For an extensive treatment of this topic, see Catherine Dollard, *The Surplus Woman: Unmarried in Imperial Germany, 1871–1918* (New York: Berghan Books, 2009).

commitments of leaders of three of these societies. These include Louise Otto-Peters's Enlightenment-based agitation for women's education and employment; Clara Zetkin's fight for women's place in a socialist revolution; and Helene Stöcker's Nietzsche-inspired individualism. All three women were known as the theoreticians of their respective organizations; each edited an influential journal through which she gave her branch of the movement a philosophical foundation. Each, in her way, thus carried forward what Katharine Anthony identifies as the "belief in the power of ideas" characteristic of German philosophical thought.[6]

1 FEMINIST PHILOSOPHIZING IN THE EARLY NINETEENTH CENTURY

The early nineteenth century saw the birth of German Romanticism, a philosophical movement formed in reaction to Kant's Enlightenment morality and the aesthetic classicism of Schiller and Goethe. Its originators, including Friedrich Schlegel, Friedrich von Hardenberg (Novalis), and Ludwig Tieck, encouraged, to a limited degree, the extension of women's engagement into philosophy and poetry. This atmosphere nurtured the scholarly brilliance of several self-taught female intellectuals.[7] Some of these women, in addition to their work in metaphysics, aesthetics, political philosophy, and translation, theorized about their status as women. Among these was Dorothea Schlegel, Friedrich Schlegel's wife, whose 1801 novel *Florentin* thematized love, marriage, and the relationship between men and women, as well as criticizing loveless marriage as unethical. *Florentin* also theorized about the contingency of gender as opposed to the inevitability of physical differences based on sex.[8] Caroline von Wolzogen, Friedrich Schiller's sister-in-law, suggested in her novel *Agnes von Lilien* (1796) that women should be freed of traditional limitations and that marriage should be a

---

[6] For a 2014 update of biographical research on participants in German women's movements, see Irina Hundt, "Zum Stand der biografischen Forschungen in der Frauenbewegung: Berichte vom 21. Louise-Otto-Peters-Tag 2013," *Louiseum* 34 (2014): 46–73.

[7] For the roots of feminist philosophizing in the seventeenth and eighteenth centuries, including the influence of Locke and Rousseau, see Sanford, "Origins of German Feminism," 8–9, 27. Early progressive theorizers about women's capacities included Anna Maria Schürmann, Johann Christoph Gottsched, Theodor Gottlieb von Hippel, and Ester Berhard. On Schürmann, see Sanford, "Origins of German Feminism," 9; on Gottsched and Hippel, see Doris Starr Guilloton, "Toward a New Freedom: Rahel Varnhagen and the German Women Writers before 1848," in *Woman as Mediatrix: Essays on Nineteenth-Century Women Writers*, ed. Avriel H. Goldberger (Westport, CT: Greenwood, 1987), 134.

[8] Dorothea Schlegel, *Florentin* (Leipzig: Friedrich Bohn, 1801), 8; see Sanford, "Origins of German Feminism," 95, and Bryan Norton, "Geschlecht, Sinnfeld, Kontingenz: Zur Ontologie in Dorothea Schlegels *Florentin*," *Symphilosophie: Internationale Zeitschrift für philosophische Romantik* 2 (2020): 120. For feminist implications of the novel, see Margaret Helfer, "Dorothea Veit-Schlegel's Florentin: Constructing a Feminist Romantic Aesthetic," *German Quarterly* 69, no. 2 (1996). See also chapter 17 here.

partnership between equals.[9] Karoline von Günderrode, whose theoretical writings built on philosophizing by Fichte and Schelling, claimed to have "a deplorable but incorrigible discrepancy in my soul; and it will and must remain so, for I am a woman, and have desires like a man, without manly strength. That's why I'm so changeable, and so at odds with myself."[10]

Theorizing about women's equality and possible partnership with men is also evident in the correspondence of women and their prominent husbands, for instance between Wilhelm and Caroline von Humboldt and between Caroline Schlegel-Schelling and her second husband, August Wilhelm von Schlegel.[11] Both Caroline Schlegel-Schelling and Dorothea Schlegel published feminist opinions in the Schlegel brothers' journal *Athenaeum*.[12] Among these women's legacies was their determination to be individuals, including the right to choose marriage based on love. Both ended unhappy marriages through divorce and married again for love, asserting the right to pursue individual happiness over social convention.[13]

Another prominent figure of this generation was Rahel Levin Varnhagen (1771–1833), whose famous Berlin salon was frequented by prominent philosophers and whose intellectual circle included Fichte, Schleiermacher, Schlegel, Schelling, and Heine. Levin Varnhagen's vast correspondence, some of which was published during her lifetime and some posthumously, shows her to be vigorously engaged in both Enlightenment and Romantic philosophical debates.[14] Levin Varnhagen, who was Jewish, was painfully aware of the ways in which being both Jewish and a woman placed limitations on her brilliant intellect. Commentary on women's position in society and ideas for improving that position through more freedom of thought and action recur throughout her writing.[15] In addition to these concrete issues, she kept apprised of philosophical thinking about women among philosophers in her circle: she saw in Hegel and Fichte

---

[9] See Anna von Sydow, ed., *Wilhelm und Caroline von Humboldt in ihren Briefen*, 7 vols. (Berlin: E. S. Mittler und Sohn, 1907–18), quoted in Sanford, "Origins of German Feminism," 79.

[10] Anna C. Ezekiel, "The Social Self in Karoline von Günderrode," *Symphilosophie* 2 (2020): 74–75.

[11] See Albert Leitzmann, ed., *Die Brautbriefe Wilhelms und Karolinens von Humboldt* (Leipzig: Insel Verlag, 1920), quoted in Sanford, "Origins of German Feminism," 83–84.

[12] See *Athenaeum*, ed. A. W. and F. Schlegel, vol. 1, no. 2 (Berlin, 1798–1800), 25, 111, 113; vol. 2, nos. 1, 4, 20. See Guilloton, "Toward a New Freedom," 142. That these women had extensive influence on the men in their circles is evident in Friedrich Schlegel's 1799 novel *Lucinde* (Berlin: Heinrich Fröhlich, 1799) as well as in Schleiermacher's *Catechism of Reason for Noble Women* ("Idee zu einem Katechismus der Vernunft für edle Frauen," in Arthur Schopenhauer, *Kritische Gesamtausgabe*, ed. Hans-Joachim Birkner et al. Berlin/New York: de Gruyter, 1980–I.2, xxxviii, 153–154).

[13] For another account of these women's influence on the German women's movement, see Carol Diethe, *The Life and Work of Germany's Founding Feminist Louise Otto-Peters (1819–1895)* (Lampeter, UK: Edwin Mellen Press, 2002), 3.

[14] See Catalina Elena Dobre, "Rahel Levin Varnhagen's Philosophical Reflections on Moral Character, *Bildung*, and Sociability," *Symphilosophie* 2 (2020): 92. On the publication of Varnhagen's letters, see Heidi Thomann Tewarson, *Rahel Levin Varnhagen: The Life and Work of a German Jewish Intellectual* (Lincoln: University of Nebraska Press, 1998), 48, 129, 201.

[15] Tewarson, *Varnhagen: Life and Work*, 215–218.

relatively progressive views about women and praised Schleiermacher's *Catechism of Reason for Noble Women* (1798).[16]

Levin Varnhagen, whose early intellectual guide was Goethe and who especially admired the complexity and vigor of his female characters, struggled throughout her life to navigate the "progressive" attitude among Goethe and younger Romantics that acknowledged women's intellectual potential but nevertheless confined them to an idealized type.[17] She repeatedly rejected the claim that women's minds were different and that their lives could be fulfilled only in marriage and motherhood. "This claim derives from the assumption that a woman's soul knows nothing higher than the demands and claims of her husband . . . or the talents and wishes of her children," she wrote; "this would render any marriage, as such, the highest achievable human state. But this is not so."[18] She blamed women's reputed frivolity on the fact that they had "no space for their own feet, they must put them only where the man has just stood and wants to stand . . . every attempt, every wish, to undo this unnatural state is called frivolity or even considered culpable behavior." She frequently articulated grave misgivings about marriage, at one point declaring that loveless marriages were "indecent" and all too often the source of repression and abuse.[19] The publication of a collection of her letters in 1834, revealing a brilliant and unconventional woman deeply critical of sexual norms, had a wide influence on the next generation of female writers. Among these were women who subsequently authored novels that explored women's roles, for instance Ida Hahn-Hahn and Malwida von Meysenbug.[20]

In the next generation, the celebrated and notorious author Bettina Brentano von Arnim (1785–1859) also theorized about being a woman. In 1844, already well known for her work *Goethe's Correspondence with a Child* (*Goethes Briefwechsel mit einem Kinde*), she published *Spring Wreath* (*Clemens Brentanos Frühlingskranz*), a reconstruction of a correspondence with her brother, the Romantic poet Clemens Brentano. Here Brentano von Arnim rejects the Romantics' idealization of women, including her brother's desire that she dedicate herself to art and poetry. She also rejects the suggestion that women and men's different essences could be fully perfected in each other, asserting personal freedom above even this ostensibly progressive goal. "I know what I need!—I need to keep my freedom," writes Brentano von Arnim. "You want to force on me the great difference between a 'superior woman' and a 'good man.' May these two find each other on

---

[16] Guilloton, "Toward a New Freedom," 134–135; see also Tewarson, *Varnhagen: Life and Work*, 216–217.

[17] Tewarson, *Varnhagen: Life and Work*, 129.

[18] Rahel Varnhagen, *Gesammelte Werke*, ed. Konrad Feilchenfeldt, Uwe Schweikert, and Rachel E. Steiner (1983), vol. 2, 564–565, quoted in Tewarson, *Varnhagen: Life and Work*, 165.

[19] Tewarson, *Varnhagen: Life and Work*, 215.

[20] Kay Goodman, "The Impact of Rahel Varnhagen on Women in the Nineteenth Century," *Amsterdamer Beiträge zur neueren Germanistik* 10 (1980): 128–129. Goodman also writes about Levin Varnhagen's influence on German women generally (133) and on Lewald in particular (140). For references to her among later women's movement leaders such as Hedwig Dohm and Ellen Key, see Goodman's discussion at 152.

some happy star! I only request one thing of you, that you don't tell me about it. Once and for all, I want to be totally excluded from this sacred state!"[21] Echoes of these sentiments, inspired by both Brentano von Arnim and Levin Varnhagen, are also found in later writing by female novelists such as Luise Müller, Luise Aston, and Fanny Lewald.[22]

2 WOMEN'S RIGHTS IN THE SERVICE OF HUMANITY: LOUISE OTTO-PETERS

Among the women influenced by feminist philosophizing in this earlier generation was Louise Otto-Peters (1819–1895). Raised by a progressive father who encouraged his daughters to memorize Schiller's poetic calls to freedom and to inform themselves politically, Otto-Peters showed an eager interest in philosophy. An early anecdote recounts a visitor finding her in the garden, knitting and reading Hegel.[23] Her political consciousness appears to have been awakened by witnessing the deplorable conditions of female lace-makers near Freiberg.[24] She resolved to become an author; her first two novels, *Ludwig the Waiter* (*Ludwig der Kellner*, 1843) and *Castle and Factory* (*Schloss und Fabrik*, 1846) were socially conscious works that highlighted the plight of such women. The latter may have been influenced by her reading of Engels's *The Condition of the Working Classes.*[25]

As movements for political reform and national unity began building across German-speaking states in the early 1840s, Otto-Peters and other women chafed against restrictions on their political involvement. In 1843, Otto-Peters read an article by the political radical Robert Blum in which he asked whether women had the right to participate in the rights of the state. In her published response, Otto-Peters answered: "yes, women have not only the right but also the duty to participate in affairs of state," arguing there and in a series of subsequent publications that this duty was founded in women's love for their homeland and in their desire for a united Germany that was free from

[21] Bettina von Arnim, "Clemens Brentanos Frühlingskranz," in *Werke*, vol. 2, ed. Heinz Härtl (Berlin: Aufbau, 1989), 696, quoted in Katherine R. Goodman, "Through a Different Lens: Bettina Brentano-von Arnim's Views on Gender," in *Bettina Brentano-von Arnim: Gender and Politics*, ed. Katherine R. Goodman and Elke P. Fredericksen (Detroit: Wayne State University Press, 1995), 125.

[22] Guilloton, "Toward a New Freedom," 139–41.

[23] Ruth-Ellen Boetcher Joeres, ed., *Die Anfänge der deutschen Frauenbewegung: Louise Otto-Peters* (Frankfurt a.M.: Fischer Taschenbuch, 1983), 63. Born Louise Otto, she married the political activist August Peters in 1858 after he was freed from several years' incarceration following his revolutionary activities.

[24] Diethe, *Life and Work*, 31. For an account of her self-education as a young woman, including her encounters with the work of philosophers such as Hegel and Romantic figures such as Brentano von Arnim and Levin Varnhagen, see Irina Hundt, "Die autodidaktischen Studien 'eines deutschen Mädchens' um 1840," *Louise-Otto-Peters-Jahrbuch* 1 (2004): 29–38.

[25] Diethe, *Life and Work*, 54.

foreign rule.[26] Otto-Peters also lamented that women's political engagement was much more advanced in the United States and England where reformed governments gave them more opportunities to fulfill their duties. This series of articles by Otto-Peters is sometimes considered the beginning of the official German women's movement, but other women, such as Meysenbug and Kathinka Zitz-Halein, also began to organize around this time.[27]

Otto-Peters supported the revolutionary activities of 1848 by publishing a poetry collection titled *Songs of a German Girl* (*Lieder eines deutschen Mädchens*) which, among other things, criticized the revolutionary call for freedom for referring only to men.[28] In May 1848, she published "A Girl's Appeal to the Highly Respected Minister Oberlander and Labor Commission Set Up by Him and to All Workers" ("Adresse eines Mädchens an den hochverehrten Minister Oberländer, an die von ihm berufene Arbeiterkommission und an alle Arbeiter"). This appeal began: "Sirs, if you are examining the organization of labor you must remember that it is not sufficient for you to organize the labor of men, you must do the same for women."[29] She urged politicians not to "declare one half of humanity immature children and make them completely dependent on the other half. . . . In the name of morality, in the name of the fatherland, in the name of humanity, I call upon you: as you organize workers, do not forget the women!"[30] "Women's participation in the state is a duty," she repeated in May 1848, "but today I will add this: the state also has the duty to give attention to the position of women. It must thoroughly take the position of women into the scope of its considerations, it must not only bear in mind the rights of men, but also the rights of women."[31]

Calls for women's inclusion in this moment of political change, however, went mostly unheeded. The National Assembly, convened in the wake of revolutionary victories to write a constitution for a united Germany, did not allow women to participate, nor did it specifically discuss women's rights.[32] The subsequent failure of this assembly and of the revolution generally set the cause of women's political rights back substantially.

---

[26] Louise Otto-Peters, "Die Theilnahme der weiblichen Welt am Staatsleben," *Sächsische Vaterlandsblätter* 3 (1843): 633, quoted in Ute Gerhard, *Unerhört: Die Geschichte der deutschen Frauenbewegung* (Hamburg: Rohwohlt Taschenbuch Verlag GmbH, 1995), 38.

[27] Gerhard, *Unerhört*, 16. On Zitz-Halein, see Stanley Zucker, "German Women and the Revolution of 1848: Kathinka Zitz-Halein and the Humania Association," *Central European History* 13, no. 3 (1980): 237–254.

[28] Goodman, "Bettina Brentano-von Arnim's Views," 118.

[29] Louise Otto-Peters, "Adresse eines Mädchens an den hochverehrten Minister Oberländer, an die von ihm berufene Arbeiterkommission und an alle Arbeiter," *Leibziger Arbeiterzeitung* 4 (1848), quoted in Diethe, *Life and Work*, 61. See also Johanna Ludwig, "Auch die Rechte der Frauen bedenken'. Louise Otto (1812–1878) in der Revolution von 1848/49," in *Akteure eines Umbruchs: Männer und Frauen der Revolution von 1848/49*, ed. Helmut Bleiber, Walter Schmidt, and Susanne Schutz (2003), 495–496.

[30] Otto-Peters, "Adresse eines Mädchens," translation mine. See also Ludwig, "'Auch die Rechte der Frauen bedenken,'" 499.

[31] Louise Otto-Peters, "Weibliches Proletariat," *Der Volksfreund* (1848): 52, translation mine. See also Ludwig, "'Auch die Rechte der Frauen bedenken,'" 500.

[32] See Sanford, "Origins of German Feminism," 132. See also Schötz, "'Human Beings Is What Women Want to Become,'" 7.

Blum himself was executed in 1848, after which Otto-Peters and others feared that the revolution's goals would never be realized.

Despite these failures, Otto-Peters founded the *Women's Newspaper* (*Frauen-Zeitung*), a journal with the subtitle "I Am Recruiting Women Citizens for the Empire of Freedom!" ("Dem Reich der Freiheit werb' ich Bürgerinnen!") in 1849. The goals of the *Frauen-Zeitung* were clear. "We demand our share," Otto-Peters wrote in its first issue: "the simple human right to develop all our powers freely, to have legal rights and independence within the state." Crucial to this demand, she continued, was the right to "earn our share; we want to energetically promote the redemption of humanity, primarily by trying to spread wherever possible the great idea for the future: freedom and humanity."[33]

In justifying her demand for women's participation in these Enlightenment goals, Otto-Peters adopted and expanded a prevailing conception of gender difference inherited from Goethe. In the conclusion to *Faust Part I*, Goethe had praised "the eternal feminine" (*das Ewig-Weibliche*), depicting women as the more morally pure sex, responsible for inspiring men to higher virtue. This conception of women had, by Otto-Peters's adulthood, become a kind of orthodoxy in German society.[34] Without challenging its central premise, Otto-Peters interpreted Goethe's dictum in a reformist direction. First, she used it to argue for the equality of the sexes: "The woman is completely the man's equal [ebenbürtig] in respect to all of life's higher concerns," she wrote in an 1851 essay titled "The Eternal Feminine" (Das Ewig-Weibliche).[35] But women's strengths were different: they were found in "the capacity for enthusiasm, the receptivity for what is great and beautiful, an excitable imagination and a soaring, ideal direction."[36]

Otto-Peters did not, like more conservative interpreters of Goethe, believe that these characteristics should confine women to motherhood or philanthropy. On the contrary, she argued that if women were denied opportunities for education and political participation, they would be unable to develop the very skills and wisdom necessary to playing their prescribed role. "It is a sin not only against the woman but against humanity, and in principle against all of creation, to thrust the woman into servitude and hold her there, to want to confine her to domesticity and so to exclude her from all other human goals which do not relate to the family," she wrote.[37] It was not just women's potential

[33] Louise Otto-Peters, "Programme," *Frauen-Zeitung* 1 (1849), quoted in Diethe, *Life and Work*, 67.

[34] Diethe, *Life and Work*, 4–5.

[35] Louise Otto-Peters, "Das Ewig-Weibliche," *Frauen-Zeitung* 3, no. 45 (1851): 321. For discussion, see Schötz, "'Human Beings Is What Women Want to Become,'" 11; Teruko Yamada, "Louise Otto-Peters und die deutschkatholische Bewegung: Die bürgerliche Frauenbewegung des Vormärz und der Revolutionszeit," *Louise-Otto-Peters-Jahrbuch* 1 (2004): 107; and Margrit Twellman, *Die deutsche Frauenbewegung. Ihre Anfänge und erste Entwicklung 1843–1899* (Meisenheim am Glan: Quellen, 1972), 36.

[36] Louise Otto-Peters, "Das Recht der Frauen auf Erwerb. Blicke auf das Frauenleben der Gegenwart" (1866), https://scholarsarchive.byu.edu/sophnf_essay/10, quoted in Schötz, "'Human Beings Is What Women Want to Become,'" 11.

[37] Otto-Peters, "Das Ewig-Weibliche," quoted in Twellman, *Die deutsche Frauenbewegung*, 36. See also Yamada, "Louise Otto-Peters und die deutschkatholische Bewegung," 207.

for self-perfection that was lost through enforced servitude: at stake was nothing less than the perfection of humanity. In a later publication, she claimed that women were "the priestly guardian[s] of the sacred and sanctifying flames of enthusiasm . . . without which the whole of humankind is lost!"[38]

In understanding the "eternal feminine" in the service of humanity's perfection, Otto-Peters aligned her vision for women's reformed role squarely with progressive depictions of history common among eighteenth- and nineteenth-century philosophers from Kant to Hegel. Her aspiration, as one biographer puts it, was "for nothing less than the re-demption of humanity" through women's activity, fueled by the "Hegelian belief 'that the absolute spirit fulfils itself within the development of human history.'"[39] A woman's right to self-development, in other words, was in the service of her right to use her specific nature to benefit humanity. Women had a right to develop their talents outside the home and in the greater cause of the perfection of humanity just as men had the right to apply their capacities for logic and thought to the same.

What, then, was needed for women to achieve this self-perfection that would allow women to contribute to the perfection of humanity?[40] Among the most pressing needs, Otto-Peters thought, was education that would prepare them for employment opportunities. She and other authors in the *Frauen-Zeitung* also advocated for reform of laws that made women dependent on male family members as well as reform of marriage and family laws. All of these goals were highly controversial, and some were opposed by other women such as Helene Lange, who became the leader of more conservative women's organizations.

Because of its progressive views, censors forced the paper to shut down in 1852, but not, as one author puts it, before Otto-Peters had "established a widespread network of female supporters whose letters and contributions often showed a surprising political sophistication."[41] Building on this foundation, Otto-Peters continued agitating for women's participation in society throughout the next decade. Her efforts culminated in 1865 when, together with Auguste Schmidt, Ottilie von Steyber, and others, she founded the German Association of Female Citizens (Allgemeiner deutscher Frauenverein; ADF). Schmidt's address at the initial conference made the movement's foundation in Enlightenment philosophy and natural law explicit, referencing women's "*natural entitlement* . . . to raise themselves up from their current subordination to the equality

---

[38] Otto-Peters, "Das Recht der Frauen auf Erwerb. Blicke auf das Frauenleben der Gegenwart," 71, quoted in Schötz, "'Human Beings Is What Women Want to Become,'" 6.

[39] Diethe, *Life and Work*, 69. For more on Hegel's possible influence, see Schötz, "'Human Beings Is What Women Want to Become,'" 15.

[40] As is frequently the case, the very words used to describe this movement were contested: some use the general Women's Movement (*Frauenbewegung*), others Women's Emancipation (*Frauenemanzipazion*) or Women's Rights (*Frauenrechte*) or the Woman Question (*Frauenfrage*). For discussion, see for instance Schötz, "'Human Beings Is What Women Want to Become,'" 2, 5. See also Renate Möhrmann, ed., *Frauenemanzipation im deutschen Vormärz* (Stuttgart: Reclam, 1978), 3–12.

[41] Ruth-Ellen Boetcher Joeres, "Louise Otto-Peters," in *Nineteenth-Century German Writers, 1841–1900*, ed. Siegfried Mews and James N. Hardin, Dictionary of Literary Biography (Detroit: Gale, 1993).

due to them alongside men."[42] As they were endowed with reason and so dignity, their lack of access to the political sphere and consequent dependence on men violated those rights. In an 1868 article titled "An Existence Worthy of Humanity for All!" ("Menschenwürdiges Dasein für Alle!") Otto-Peters wrote: "in our striving, we women . . . take the view of pure humanity, or if you will of natural law," demanding only a "dignified existence for everyone, including for women."[43] She continued to make use of philosophical thought to justify her reform work, including the work of K. F. C. Krause, whose nonhierarchical description of male and female "peculiarities" confirmed her own philosophical views of gender equality.[44]

The ADF settled on a two-pronged approach to the woman question, namely work and education. Writing in the organization's journal *New Paths* (*Neue Bahnen*), which she edited for almost four decades, Otto-Peters declared that "work, which is the very corner stone of the new society, is a duty and honor of the female sex, and we therefore demand the right to work and hold it as vital that all barriers which stand in the way of female work should be removed."[45] This position took aim at the assumption that it was shameful for middle-class women to work outside the home, regardless of the family's financial need: a norm that both crippled women's potential for self-determination and impoverished families in which men were absent or unable to work. Otto-Peters instead wedded Enlightenment values to a philosophy of self-help: "*Only what is achieved through one's own endeavors has any value.*"[46]

In choosing to focus on the right to work, Otto-Peters conceded that the ADF would concentrate on middle-class women since, as she acknowledged, in "the so-called lower orders, the proletariat, it is completely taken for granted that a woman will work as hard as a man."[47] The organization resolved to agitate for work opportunities for women

---

[42] Louise Otto-Peters, *Das erste Vierteljahrhundert des Allgemeinen deutschen Frauenvereins gegründet am 18. October 1865 in Leipzig* (Leipzig: Schäfer, 1890), quoted in Schötz, "'Human Beings Is What Women Want to Become,'" 12. Another woman who philosophized about concepts such as freedom and self-determination as regards women was Louise Dittmar, whose writings include a strident attack on marriage as a "system of economic and social control that serves to suppress and mistreat women and children." See Ruth-Ellen Boetcher Joeres, "Spirit in Struggle: The Vision of Louise Dittmar (1807–1884)," *Amsterdamer Beiträge zur neueren Germanistik* 28 (1989): 298. Dittmar published several theoretical works in the mid–1840s and briefly edited a journal titled first *Soziale Reform* and later *Das Wesen der Ehe*. See also Hundt, "Autodidaktischen Studien," 66–67, and Ute Rosenbusch, *Der Weg zum Frauenwahlrecht in Deutschland* (Baden-Baden: Nomos Verlagsgesellschaft, 1998), 32–33.

[43] Louise Otto-Peters, "Menschwürdiges Dasein für Alle!," *Neue Bahnen* 3, no. 122 (1868) , quoted in Schötz, "'Human Beings Is What Women Want to Become,'" 12.

[44] Schötz, "'Human Beings Is What Women Want to Become,'" 10. See also Siegfried Wollgast, "Louise Otto-Peters und Karl Christian Friedrich Krause als ihre philosophische Quelle," *Louise-Otto-Peters-Jahrbuch* 1 (2004).

[45] Louise Otto-Peters, *Neue Bahnen* 1, no. 1 (1866): 2, quoted in Diethe, *Life and Work*, 121. For a history of *Neue Bahnen*, see Diethe, *Life and Work*, 139.

[46] Otto-Peters, "Das Recht der Frauen auf Erwerb. Blicke auf das Frauenleben der Gegenwart," quoted in Schötz, "'Human Beings Is What Women Want to Become,'" 7; italics in the original.

[47] Otto-Peters, "Das Recht der Frauen auf Erwerb. Blicke auf das Frauenleben der Gegenwart," 29, quoted in Diethe, *Life and Work*, 123.

"through societies for women's education and the press, the founding of co-operatives to support consumer goods recommended by women, the establishment of a system to advertise vacancies for female work, the founding of industrial training schools for girls, the establishment of girls' hostels and finally, the cultivation of higher scientific education."[48] Otto-Peters also made arguments for these aspirations available to a wider public in a 1866 publication titled *Women's Right to Employment: Perspectives on Contemporary Women's Lives* (*Das Recht der Frauen auf Erwerb: Blicke auf das Frauenleben der Gegenwart*).

As the ADF grew and became more mainstream toward the end of the century, it lost much of its reformist zeal and was criticized by more progressive women reformers such as Lida Gustava Heymann and Anita Augspurg for being too timid and overly focused on the concerns of middle-class women.[49] While Hedwig Dohm, for instance, used both the natural law tradition and John Stuart Mill's utilitarianism in the 1870s to argue for women's suffrage—declaring that "human rights have no gender"—the ADF initially declined to organize for women's suffrage.[50] Otto-Peters herself became more conservative, urging her readers to support the unification of Germany under Bismarck in 1871 and using *New Paths* to urge women to sacrifice for the nation.[51] As her social progressiveness stalled, however, Otto-Peters continued to write philosophically, encouraging women to educate themselves about the natural sciences, physiognomy, economics, and medicine. She wrote an influential autobiography, *Women's Lives in the German Empire: Memoirs From the Past with References to the Present and Future* (*Frauenleben im deutschen Reich: Erinnerungen aus der Vergangenheit mit Hinweis auf Gegenwart und Zukunft*), which concluded with a chapter titled "Future" in which she laid out her hopes for coming generations in recognizably philosophical terms: "the goal is the harmony of humankind and this will not be established as long as human beings are still prevented by law or society from achieving harmony with themselves and their environment; and they are prevented from this as long as it is not possible for them . . . to develop themselves and their abilities, and to use them in their own interest in free self-determination, as well as in the general interest in voluntary subordination and devotion."[52]

[48] Diethe, *Life and Work*, 121.

[49] Patricia A. Herminghouse and Magda Mueller, introduction to *German Feminist Writings*, ed. Patricia A. Herminghouse and Magda Mueller (New York: Continuum, 2001), xxvi.

[50] Hedwig Dohm, "The Right of Human Suffrage," in Patricia A. Herminghouse and Magda Mueller, eds., *German Feminist Writings*, trans. Constance Campbell (New York: Continuum, 2001), 123, translation altered. For more on suffrage, see Rosenbusch, *Der Weg zum Frauenwahlrecht in Deutschland*, 287, 302. For more on Dohm, see Gjesdal and Nassar, "Introduction," in *Women Philosophers in the Long Nineteenth Century: The German Tradition*, ed. Kristin Gjesdal and Dalia Nassar (Oxford: Oxford University Press, 2021), 122–128, and Rosenbusch, *Der Weg zum Frauenwahlrecht in Deutschland*, 292–293. Dohm later became critical of essentialist and natural law–based conceptions of women.

[51] Diethe, *Life and Work*, 128.

[52] Louise Otto-Peters, *Frauenleben im deutschen Reich. Erinnerungen aus der Vergangenheit mit Hinweis auf Gegenwart und Zukunft* (Leipzig: Schäfer, 1876), 256, quoted in Schötz, "'Human Beings Is What Women Want to Become,'" 5. See also Ingrid Deich, "Annäherung an Louise Otto-Peters' Buch *Genius der Natur*," *Louise-Otto-Peters-Jahrbuch* 1 (2004): 62.

In 1894, the ADF was subsumed under the larger Federation of German Women's Associations (Bund Deutscher Frauenvereine; BDF); Otto-Peters died one year later. The BDF endorsed efforts to obtain voting rights for women in 1902 and could, also by the turn of the century, take credit for increased access among women to education and some professions.[53]

3 WOMEN IN THE SOCIALIST REVOLUTION: CLARA ZETKIN

As the ADF used Enlightenment philosophy and natural law theory to improve women's educational and employment opportunities, women in the socialist movement philosophized about their part in the greater proletarian struggle against capitalism. The woman who came to embody this theoretical position was Clara Zetkin (1857–1933). Influenced initially by Friedrich Engels's *The Origin of the Family, Private Property, and the State* (1884) and August Bebel's *Women and Socialism*, Zetkin came to prominence in the Social Democratic Party of Germany (Sozialdemokratische Partei Deutschlands; SPD) after delivering an address to the 1889 Socialist International called "The Current Question concerning Women and Female Workers" ("Die Arbeiterinnen- und Frauenfrage der Gegenwart").[54]

Zetkin, following Engels, was initially convinced that full socialist reform, as well as women's emancipation, required the abolition of the monogamous family.[55] Childcare in a socialist state, she for instance argued, should be communal and owned publicly.[56] Because she believed that women's emancipation would only be possible with the emancipation of labor from capital, Zetkin also initially argued that campaigning for social reforms such as women's suffrage was futile, writing that women "expect our full emancipation neither from the admittance of women to what are called the free professions, nor from an education equal to that of the male sex—although to demand these two rights is only natural and right—nor from the granting of political rights."[57] In articulating these positions, Zetkin isolated systematic economic injustice as the root of all particular injustices, denying that problems experienced by individual groups, such as women, could be solved within the social system as it existed.

---

[53] See Rosenbusch, *Der Weg zum Frauenwahlrecht in Deutschland*, 302, and Sanford, "Origins of German Feminism," 180.

[54] The party became known by this name officially in 1890.

[55] Daniel Gaido and Cintia Fancia, "'A Clean Break': Clara Zetkin, the Socialist Women's Movement, and Feminism," *International Critical Thought* 8, no. 2 (2018): 279.

[56] Richard Evans, "Theory and Practice in German Social Democracy 1880–1914: Clara Zetkin and the Socialist Theory of Women's Emancipation," *History of Political Thought* 3, no. 2 (1982): 293.

[57] Clara Zetkin, *Ausgewählte Reden und Schriften*, vol. 1, *Auswahl aus den Jahren 1889 bis 1917* (Berlin: Dietz Verlag, 1957), vol. 1, 108, quoted in Evans, "Theory and Practice in German Social Democracy," 293. On suffrage, see also Rosenbusch, *Der Weg zum Frauenwahlrecht in Deutschland*, 306.

As of 1896, perhaps as a result of reporting about women's work in newly industrialized sectors that she published as editor of the journal *Equality* (*Die Gleichheit*), Zetkin declared that her views on the family had been "one-sidedly negative" and articulated a more positive judgment of the family as an institution.[58] The goal of socialism, she now asserted, was to allow women to fulfill their roles as women "better than before, in the interests of the emancipation of the proletariat. The better the circumstances in the family ... the more capable it will be of taking part in the struggle."[59] Zetkin's position, as Catherine Dollard puts it, thus came to represent "an orthodox Marxist understanding of capitalist exploitation instilled with a maternalist sensibility central to the women's activism of Zetkin's time."[60]

Enabling women to achieve socialist goals meant promoting equality within marriage. In an 1899 pamphlet titled "The Student and the Woman" ("Der Student und das Weib"), she wrote that "when two strong, free personalities find themselves in love[,] marriage will ... elevate the individual personalities in mutual giving and receiving beyond themselves. . . . The social revolution creates the social preconditions for full female humanity ... and places by the side of the citizen a collaborative, coequal partner." In such a society, she argued, the woman's "individuality will flourish while at the same time, she will fulfill her task as wife and mother to the highest degree possible," enabling her children to achieve their "powerfully unfurled humanity."[61] Zetkin thus envisioned an individuality that at the same time was in the service of the collective.

To this end, Zetkin articulated demands for women's education, freely chosen marriage, legal protection for female workers, and equal rights to association, assembly, and political participation. Zetkin also led the movement within the SPD for women's suffrage, although she remained clear that voting was not an end in itself. In a 1906 speech on suffrage, she differentiated her priorities from that of other mainstream feminists by pointing out that instead of basing their arguments on natural law, Marxists based their demand on a materialist conception of history, with the result that "the alpha and omega of our demand for women's suffrage remains: we demand equal political rights with men, so that we can take part without legal restrictions in the struggle for the destruction of this society."[62]

---

[58] Clara Zetkin, *Die Gleichheit* 4, no. 25 (1896), 197–200, quoted in Evans, "Theory and Practice in German Social Democracy," 293.

[59] Clara Zetkin, *Ausgewählte Reden und Schriften* (Berlin: Dietz, 1953), vol. 1, 108, quoted in Evans, "Theory and Practice in German Social Democracy," 293.

[60] Catherine Dollard, "German Maternalist Socialism: Clara Zetkin and the 1896 Social Democratic Party Congress," in *Feminist Moments: Reading Feminist Texts*, ed. Katherine Smits and Susan Bruce (London: Bloomsbury Academic, 2016), 93.

[61] Clara Zetkin, "Der Student und das Weib," *Marxistische Blätter* (1899), quoted in Dollard, "German Maternalist Socialism: Clara Zetkin and the 1896 Social Democratic Party Congress," 97–98.

[62] Clara Zetkin, *Zur Frage des Frauenwahlrechts, bearbeitet nach dem Referat auf der Konferenz sozialistischer Frauen zu Mannheim, Dazu drei Anhänge: I. Resolution der Konferenz sozialistischer Frauen zu Mannheim, das Frauenwahlrecht betreffend; II. Entwicklung des Frauenwahlrechts; III. Eine*

This philosophical commitment meant that, despite some overlap with the goals of other women reformers, Zetkin was adamant that there could be no cooperation between socialists and groups such as the ADF, whose members she denigrated as "Frauenrechtlerinnen." There was, Zetkin proclaimed, no single "woman question": the crucial question was not about women but about workers. Bourgeois women, she argued, were waging a struggle against men, whereas proletarian women were working with men toward a revolutionary goal. Advocating, in a subtitle of one of her essays, for "Social Revolution instead of Women's Rights Nonsense" ("Statt Frauenrechtelei: Soziale Revolution"), Zetkin denied that there was any such thing as a "feminine nature" that united exploiting and exploited women.[63] "Just like the emancipation of the proletariat is only possible by eliminating the capitalist relations of production," she argued, "the emancipation of women is also only possible through the abolition of private property."[64] Or, as she put it at the Paris Congress of the Second International in 1889: "the working women, who aspire to social equality, expect nothing for their emancipation from the bourgeois women's movement, which allegedly fights for the rights of women. That edifice is built on sand and has no real basis. Working women are absolutely convinced that the question of the emancipation of women is not an isolated question which exists in itself, but part of the great social question. They realize perfectly clearly that this question can never be solved in contemporary society, but only after a complete social transformation."[65]

This commitment to Marxist principles put Zetkin at odds also with less radical socialists such as Lily Braun who disavowed historical materialism and advocated for reform instead of revolution. Braun favored giving attention to women's issues over working-class issues more generally, collaborating with other feminists such as Minna Cauer in the Women's Welfare Association (Frauenwohl) and publishing in journals such as *The Women's Movement* (*Die Frauenbewegung*).[66] Together, Braun and Cauer used a combination of socialist and liberal thought to fight for contraception, childcare, communal living arrangements, and suffrage.[67] The tensions between Zetkin and Braun

---

sozialistische Enquete über die sofortige Einführung des Frauenwahlrechts (Berlin: Buchhandlung Vorwärts, 1907), 12, quoted in Gaido and Fancia, "A Clean Break," 286. On socialists' involvement in the suffrage movement generally, see Rosenbusch, *Der Weg zum Frauenwahlrecht in Deutschland*, 302–312.

[63] See Gaido and Fancia, "A Clean Break," 283.

[64] Clara Zetkin, *Zur Geschichte der proletarischen Frauenbewegung Deutschlands* (Berlin: Dietz Verlag, 1928), chap. 4, quoted in Gaido and Fancia, "A Clean Break," 283.

[65] Clara Zetkin, "Die Arbeiterinnen- und Frauenfrage der Gegenwart," (Berlin: Verlag der Berliner Volks-Tribune, 1889), 81, quoted in Gaido and Fancia, "A Clean Break," 280.

[66] Braun also had very developed philosophical views. One biographer describes her as "not a Kantian in her philosophy, but a Nietzschean," and recounts her use of Hegel's lord-bondsman dialectic to understand class struggle. See Alfred Meyer, *The Feminism and Socialism of Lily Braun* (Bloomington: Indiana University Press, 1985), 95–97. Meyer disputes the characterization of Braun as a reformer rather than a revolutionary. Cauer (1841–1922) advocated especially for rights for female nurses, suffrage, and women's political inclusion, publishing *Die Frauenbewegung* from 1895 to 1919. See Gerhard, *Unerhört*, 218–219.

[67] For a description of reform initiatives by Braun and others, see Ann Taylor Allen, "German Radical Feminism and Eugenics, 1900–1908," *German Studies Review* 11, no. 1 (1988): 40.

at the turn of the century caused one of the most damaging rifts in the women's movement to that date and presaged friction that still exists between "bourgeois" feminism and other progressive movements today.

4 NIETZSCHE FOR WOMEN AND A NEW ETHICS: HELENE STÖCKER

As socialists agitated for proletarian revolution and the BDF continued to work for educational, employment, and political rights, another feminist movement began to develop in response to the philosophy of Friedrich Nietzsche. This movement was led by Helene Stöcker (1869–1943) who, after a conservative upbringing in which she clandestinely read Goethe and Brentano von Arnim, went to Switzerland where it was possible for a woman to pursue a higher degree in philosophy. Her research, which included work on women intellectuals such as Brentano von Arnim, Günderrode, and Varnhagen, focused on the individualism, self-determination, and artistic vision found in German Romanticism. She was the first woman to be a scholarly assistant to Wilhelm Dilthey and returned to Germany as the first woman with a doctorate in a philosophical subject. Her dissertation focused on art, tolerance, and humanitarian thought in post-Enlightenment German aesthetics.[68]

Stöcker encountered Nietzsche's writings in 1891 and was transfixed by his call to reevaluate ethical values. She was especially inspired by his exhortation to reject Christianity's life-denying ethics for an affirmative worldview. Through Nietzsche, she envisioned a philosophy that was life-affirming and joyful, not tied to duty, imagining nothing less than a "new humanity—men and women—Nietzsche's higher humans, who are allowed to say yes to life and themselves."[69] "Life!" she wrote in an 1897 essay titled "Our Reevaluation of Values" ("Unsere Umwertung der Werte") "What that word means—how much jubilation, delight, trembling, revulsion, annihilation . . . !"[70] Her lectures on Nietzsche in Berlin in 1902 were pivotal in bringing his thought to the public's attention.[71]

Stöcker developed this vision into what she called New Ethics (Neue Ethik) in which Christianity's doctrine of original sin would be replaced by love as the highest value.

---

[68] See Annegret Stopczyk-Pfundstein, *Philosophin der Liebe: Helene Stöcker: Die 'Neue Ethik' um 1900 in Deutschland und ihr philosophisches Umfeld bis heute* (Germany: Books on Demand GmbH, 2003), 20, 85, 91–97, 163.

[69] Helene Stöcker, "Unsere Umwertung der Werte," in *Die Liebe und die Frauen* (Minden in Westf.: J. C. C. Bruns' Verlag, 1906), 7, quoted in Heide Schlüpmann, "Radikalisierung der Philosophie: Die Nietzsche-Rezeption und die sexualpolitische Publizistik Helene Stöckers," *Feministische Studien* 3, no. 1 (1984): 24.

[70] Stopczyk-Pfundstein, *Philosophin der Liebe*, 188.

[71] Stopczyk-Pfundstein, *Philosophin der Liebe*, 104.

She combined this Nietzschean conviction with an ongoing commitment to Kant's moral philosophy which elevated each human to a position of dignity and placed responsibility for morality within every human.[72] Annegret Stopczyk-Pfundstein divides Stöcker's resulting philosophy into four central claims: Each personality (*Persönlichkeit*) (1) determines itself; (2) knows its own purpose in life; (3) builds its own worldview (*Weltanschauung*); (4) strives to realize its ethical ideas in society.[73] Integral to this reevaluation of values was a multifaceted understanding of love, including romantic and maternal love but also sexual love, as crucial to a fulfilled life. This capacious understanding of the power of love also broadened into a pacifism that Stöcker continued to advocate for until her death.

Although Nietzsche's reputation as a misogynist thinker became quickly established as his reputation grew, Stöcker saw in his philosophy the potential to address the situation of German women.[74] In a 1897 speech titled "Friedrich Nietzsche and Women" ("Friedrich Nietzsche und die Frauen"), she sought to lay the foundation for a Nietzschean feminism.[75] The freedom from traditional ethical roles and the impetus to develop into the intellectually and emotionally rich individuals that Nietzsche envisioned could, Stöcker thought, liberate women from the customs that held them back. Nietzsche, she wrote, "brought women freedom in his 'Become, who you are.'. . . That is our redemption: that we can rejoice to be born as women, because that gives us the possibility to be human perhaps in an even richer quantity . . . now we realize that we can break these chains."[76] Stöcker was in fact not alone in isolating Nietzsche's potential for women: other prominent theorists of the women's movement, including Hedwig Dohm, Malvida von Meysenbug, Ellen Key, and Lily Braun, understood him as a "Liberator of Women" as well.[77]

True to her conviction that a life-affirming philosophy should seek to realize itself in society, Stöcker began to work for the social reforms necessary for women to be able to pursue this self-fulfillment. In 1904, together with other reformers such as Braun, Key, and Dohm, she founded the League for the Protection of Motherhood (Bund für Mutterschutz; BfM) to this end.[78] As the organization's leader, she agreed with the middle-class women's movement that women should be allowed to marry for love, arguing that relationships between men and women would succeed only if both were

---

[72] Stopczyk-Pfundstein, *Philosophin der Liebe*, 71, 141, 82–83.

[73] Stopczyk-Pfundstein, *Philosophin der Liebe*, 142.

[74] Stopczyk-Pfundstein, *Philosophin der Liebe*, 114. See for instance Hedwig Dohm's chapter "Nietzsche and Women" (Nietzsche und die Frauen), in *Die Antifeministen: Ein Buch der Verteidigung* (Berlin: F. Dümmlers Verlagsbuchhandlung, 1902).

[75] Schlüpmann, "Radikalisierung der Philosophie," 13.

[76] Stöcker, "Unsere Umwertung der Werte," 14, translation mine, quoted in Stopczyk-Pfundstein, *Philosophin der Liebe*, 117.

[77] Stopczyk-Pfundstein, *Philosophin der Liebe*, 119.

[78] For leading participants in the BfM, see Edward Ross Dickinson, "Reflections on Feminism and Monism in the Kaiserreich, 1900–1913," *Central European History* 34, no. 2 (2001): 192–193. Braun later left the organization after disagreements with Stöcker about its direction: see 193.

allowed to develop their personalities and support each other in that development.[79] But she went much further than other movement leaders in identifying reforms that would make women's sexual expression and reproductive freedom possible. In a social atmosphere that described childbearing as a patriotic duty, she used Kant to argue for birth control, arguing that women should not be made means to the ends of the state.[80] She also advocated for the loosening of restrictions on abortion, for sexual education, and for legal rights of single mothers and illegitimate children.[81] She fought against the double standards that punished women who were forced into prostitution but turned a blind eye to men's promiscuity.[82] Central to her vision was also the demand that women be allowed to choose whether, when, and with whom to have children as well as be provided with the material conditions necessary to raising these children. "Followers of New Ethics demand that every German mother should be able to nourish her own child, and to that end there must be basic legal conditions" that made this possible, she wrote, such as maternal insurance and legal protection for female workers.[83]

Stöcker was the editor of two journals for the BfM: *The Protection of Mothers* (*Mutterschuutz*) (1905–1908) and *The New Generation* (*Die neue Generation*) (1909–1933). In these and other publications, she made frequent references to Goethe, Schiller, Kant, Novalis, Schopenhauer, Schlegel, and Schleiermacher.[84] She specifically thought of her Nietzschean foundation as in contrast to utilitarianism; later in life, she also quoted American philosophers such as William James.[85] Despite her sympathies with socialism, her deep individualism put her at odds with Zetkin's aims; her embrace of sexual reform and her suspicion of any reductive definition of women's essence or roles made her too radical for inclusion in the BDF.[86] She thus never considered herself part of the "women's movement" narrowly, but instead committed to a more general reform of morality for both women and men.

Stöcker's theorizing about sexuality, for instance in *Toward the Reform of Sexual Ethics* (*Zur Reform der sexuellen Ethik*), also included a progressive view of history, now founded in new fields such as sociology and sexology. Through such publications, Stöcker aimed to convince readers that women's sexual independence was the next stage of evolutionary progress and that Germany, as a modern progressive society, should embrace it fully.[87] In the service of this argument, she utilized ethnological research tied

---

[79] See, for instance, Stopczyk-Pfundstein, *Philosophin der Liebe*, 142–143.

[80] Schlüpmann, "Radikalisierung der Philosophie," 29; Stopczyk-Pfundstein, *Philosophin der Liebe*, 183; on sexual education see Allen, "German Radical Feminism and Eugenics, 1900–1908," 44.

[81] "German Radical Feminism and Eugenics, 1900–1908," 44–46; Stopczyk-Pfundstein, *Philosophin der Liebe*, 101.

[82] Stopczyk-Pfundstein, *Philosophin der Liebe*, 196.

[83] Stopczyk-Pfundstein, *Philosophin der Liebe*, 224.

[84] Stopczyk-Pfundstein, *Philosophin der Liebe*, 22.

[85] On Stöcker and American philosophers, see Stopczyk-Pfundstein, *Philosophin der Liebe*, 172.

[86] On Stöcker and socialism, see Schlüpmann, "Radikalisierung der Philosophie," 23. On relations with the BDF, see Allen, "German Radical Feminism and Eugenics, 1900–1908," 36.

[87] See Kirsten Leng, "Culture, Difference, and Sexual Progress in Turn-of-the-Century Europe: Cultural Othering and the German League for the Protection of Mothers and Sexual Reform, 1905–1914,"

to Germany's imperial and colonial aspirations.[88] Her conclusions from this material were mixed: on the one hand, she claimed that Europeans had progressed in their sexual ethics beyond other cultures; on the other, she held up sexual practices in other cultures as being more natural in a way that both exoticized and patronized these cultures.[89] "We in Europe have remained stuck halfway through the journey," she wrote, adding: "we have shed some external barriers but have not yet abandoned our crude, uncivilized attitudes toward women and love."[90]

Stöcker was also part of what has been called the "social-radical wing" of the eugenics movement: a group largely consisting of feminists, both in Europe and the United States, who wanted to ensure for women the opportunity to choose both their sexual partners and their family size in the interest of producing healthier children.[91] Only with such opportunities, Stöcker thought, could women and children have the opportunity to develop their individuality. Eugenics so understood also included the right to contraception and abortion as ways of preventing the continuation of hereditary diseases.[92] Stöcker has since been criticized by disability theorists for her support of birth control practices that would prevent births of severely disabled children or children who would inherit their parents' sexually transmitted diseases.[93] Stöcker did not advocate for forced sterilization or euthanization. But she did, at least initially, give space in *Die neue Generation* to others who later advocated those positions, and some of her own pronouncements evidence her willingness to argue that "society should prevent conception" among those with hereditary illnesses.[94] Her use of Nietzschean terms such as *Übermensch* and *Weltanschauung*, as well as her friendship with Nietzsche's sister, Elisabeth Förster-Nietzsche, despite her knowledge of Förster-Nietzsche's association with National Socialism, have also tainted her reputation.[95]

Journal of the History of Sexuality 25, no. 1 (2016): 65. For the influence of evolutionary theory on Stöcker's thought, see Dickinson, "Reflections on Feminism and Monism in the Kaiserreich, 1900–1913," 192.

[88] Leng, "Culture, Difference, and Sexual Progress," 74.

[89] Leng, "Culture, Difference, and Sexual Progress," 73.

[90] Helene Stöcker, "Liebe und Ehe in der Türkei," *Die Neue Generation* 5, no. 5 (1909): 178, quoted in Leng, "Culture, Difference, and Sexual Progress," 79.

[91] Allen also lists Lily Braun, Ellen Key, Adele Schreiber, and Grete Meisel-Hess as part of this movement. For American parallels, see Allen, "German Radical Feminism and Eugenics, 1900–1908," 46–67, 50–51.

[92] Allen, "German Radical Feminism and Eugenics, 1900–1908," 46. For a history of the evolution of the eugenics movements toward racist eugenics, see Dickinson, "Reflections on Feminism and Monism in the Kaiserreich, 1900–1913," 200.

[93] Stopczyk-Pfundstein, *Philosophin der Liebe*, 241.

[94] Quoted in Dickinson, "Reflections on Feminism and Monism in the Kaiserreich, 1900–1913," 205. For discussion of eugenics in *Neue Generation*, see Stopczyk-Pfundstein, *Philosophin der Liebe*, 257. On her use of the word "race" at least initially to indicate the human race and her abandonment of the term in the 1920s, see Dickinson, "Reflections on Feminism and Monism in the Kaiserreich, 1900–1913," 76.

[95] On Stöcker and eugenics, see Allen, "German Radical Feminism and Eugenics, 1900–1908," Stopczyk-Pfundstein, *Philosophin der Liebe*, 76, 228, 39–65, and Dickinson, "Reflections on Feminism and Monism in the Kaiserreich, 1900–1913," 200. On Stöcker's relationship to Förster-Nietzsche, see Stopczyk-Pfundstein, *Philosophin der Liebe*, 108.

That Stöcker herself was no Nazi was evidenced not only in her committed pacifism, deep individualism, and radical feminism but also by the fact that in 1933, directly following the Reichstag fire, she fled Berlin after learning that some of her friends had already been shot. She never returned.[96] After concerted advocacy by American pacifists, she was ultimately allowed to emigrate to New York, where she died in 1943.

5 CONCLUSION

By the time Katharine Anthony published *Feminism in Germany and Scandinavia* in 1915, German feminism had blossomed into a multifaceted and often contentious array of positions on what women were and should be. I have only given the outlines of some of the movement's most prominent theoreticians and their primary publications here: much remains to be done to trace the philosophical development and depth of their thought. Many others besides those mentioned here also used philosophical claims recognizable from these women's thinking to address additional women's issues. The pacifist Lida Gustava Heymann argued, for instance, against the carnage of World War I by advocating for the "female, constructive principle" against the "male, destructive principle."[97] Gabriele Reuter promoted suffrage as necessary for women to reach their potential.[98] Anna Rüling extended arguments against loveless marriages to draw attention to the "degree to which absurd attitudes toward homosexual women are responsible for tragic marriages," advocating for the dignity and rights of all humans as the basis for extending these rights to lesbians.[99]

Through this feminist philosophizing, these and many other women articulated theoretical frameworks that illuminated the situation of German women in the long nineteenth century. They absorbed rich strains of philosophical thought and extended them to encompass the half of humanity male philosophers were often happy to ignore. By the beginning of World War I, they had substantially improved education and employment opportunities for women; they had laid the foundation for women's suffrage, which was ratified in 1919; and they had shifted the discourse around marriage, sexual ethics, and maternal rights.[100] They left the legacy of intellectual rigor and practical application that so impressed Katharine Anthony; it is a legacy that challenges us to understand our own philosophizing broadly and inclusively, and as a stimulus for social change.

My thanks to Daniel Ellison for research and editorial assistance with this chapter.

---

[96] Stopczyk-Pfundstein, *Philosophin der Liebe*, 238.

[97] Lida Gustava Heymann, "Female Pacifism," in *German Feminist Writings*, ed. Patricia A. Herminghouse and Magda Mueller (New York: Continuum, 2001), 149.

[98] Herminghouse and Mueller, introduction, 152.

[99] Anna Rüling, "What Interest Does the Women's Movement Have in the Homosexual Question? (1904)," quoted in Herminghouse and Mueller, introduction, 207.

[100] Schötz, " 'Human Beings Is What Women Want to Become,' " 8.

BIBLIOGRAPHY

Allen, Ann Taylor. "German Radical Feminism and Eugenics, 1900–1908." *German Studies Review* 11, no. 1 (1988): 31–56.

Anthony, Katharine. *Feminism in Germany and Scandinavia*. New York: Holt, 1915.

Arnim, Bettina Brentano von. "Clemens Brentanos Frühlingskranz." In *Werke*, vol. 2, edited by Heinz Härtl, 783–1012. Berlin: Aufbau, 1989.

Deich, Ingrid. "Annäherung an Louise Otto-Peters' Buch *Genius Der Natur*." *Louise-Otto-Peters-Jahrbuch* 1 (2004): 58–75.

Dickinson, Edward Ross. "Reflections on Feminism and Monism in the Kaiserreich, 1900–1913." *Central European History* 34, no. 2 (2001): 191–230.

Diethe, Carol. *The Life and Work of Germany's Founding Feminist Louise Otto-Peters (1819–1895)*. Lampeter, UK: The Edwin Mellen Press, 2002.

Dobre, Catalina Elena. "Rahel Levin Varnhagen's Philosophical Reflections on Moral Character, *Bildung*, and Sociability." *Symphilosophie* 2 (2020): 91–113.

Dohm, Hedwig. *Die Antifeministen: Ein Buch der Verteidigung*. Berlin: F. Dümmlers Verlagsbuchhandlung, 1902.

Dohm, Hedwig. "The Right of Human Suffrage." In *German Feminist Writings*, edited by Patricia A. Herminghouse and Magda Mueller. Translated by Constance Campbell. New York: Continuum, 2001, 121–123.

Dollard, Catherine. "German Maternalist Socialism: Clara Zetkin and the 1896 Social Democratic Party Congress." In *Feminist Moments: Reading Feminist Texts*, edited by Katherine Smits and Susan Bruce, 91–98. London: Bloomsbury Academic, 2016.

Dollard, Catherine. *The Surplus Woman: Unmarried in Imperial Germany, 1871–1918*. New York: Berghan Books, 2009.

Evans, Richard. "Theory and Practice in German Social Democracy 1880–1914: Clara Zetkin and the Socialist Theory of Women's Emancipation." *History of Political Thought* 3, no. 2 (1982): 285–304.

Ezekiel, Anna C. "The Social Self in Karoline Von Günderrode." *Symphilosophie* 2 (2020): 65–90.

Gaido, Daniel, and Cintia Fancia. "'A Clean Break': Clara Zetkin, the Socialist Women's Movement, and Feminism." *International Critical Thought* 8, no. . (2018): 277–303.

Gerhard, Ute. *Unerhört: Die Geschichte der deutschen Frauenbewegung*. Hamburg: Rohwohlt Taschenbuch Verlag GmbH, 1995.

Gjesdal, Kristin and Dalia Nassar. "Introduction." In *Women Philosophers in the Long Nineteenth Century: The German Tradition*, edited by Kristin Gjesdal and Dalia Nassar, 122–127. Oxford: Oxford University Press, 2021.

Goodman, Katherine R. "Through a Different Lens: Bettina Brentano-Von Arnim's Views on Gender." In *Bettina Brentano-Von Arnim: Gender and Politics*, edited by Katherine R. Goodman and Elke P. Fredericksen, 115–41. Detroit: Wayne State University Press, 1995.

Goodman, Kay. "The Impact of Rahel Varnhagen on Women in the Nineteenth Century." *Amsterdamer Beiträge zur neueren Germanistik* 10 (1980): 125–153.

Guilloton, Doris Starr. "Toward a New Freedom: Rahel Varnhagen and the German Women Writers before 1848." In *Woman as Mediatrix: Essays on Nineteenth-Century Women Writers*, edited by Avriel H. Goldberger, 133–143. Westport, CT: Greenwood, 1987.

Helfer, Margaret. "Dorothea Veit-Schlegel's Florentin: Constructing a Feminist Romantic Aesthetic." *German Quarterly* 69, no. 2 (1996): 144–160.

Herminghouse, Patricia A., and Magda Mueller, eds. *German Feminist Writings*. New York: Continuum, 2001.

Herminghouse, Patricia A., and Magda Mueller. Introduction to *German Feminist Writings*, edited by Herminghouse and Mueller, xvii–xxxviii. New York: Continuum, 2001.

Heymann, Lida Gustava. "Female Pacifism." In *German Feminist Writings*, edited by Patricia A. Herminghouse and Magda Mueller, 149–152. New York: Continuum, 2001.

Hundt, Irina. "Die Autodidaktischen Studien 'eines deutschen Mädchens' um 1840." *Louise-Otto-Peters-Jahrbuch* 1 (2004): 29–38.

Hundt, Irina. "Zum Stand der biografischen Forschungen in der Frauenbewegung: Berichte vom 21. Louise-Otto-Peters-Tag 2013." *Louiseum* 34 (2014): 46–73.

Joeres, Ruth-Ellen Boetcher, ed. *Die Anfänge der deutschen Frauenbewegung: Louise Otto-Peters*. Frankfurt a.M.: Fischer Taschenbuch, 1983.

Joeres, Ruth-Ellen Boetcher. "Louise Otto-Peters." In *Nineteenth-Century German Writers, 1841–1900*, edited by Siegfried Mews and James N. Hardin, 295–301. Dictionary of Literary Biography. Detroit: Gale, 1993.

Joeres, Ruth-Ellen Boetcher. "Spirit in Struggle: The Vision of Louise Dittmar (1807–1884)." *Amsterdamer Beiträge zur neueren Germanistik* 28 (1989): 279–301.

Leitzmann, Albert, ed. *Die Brautbriefe Wilhelms und Karolinens von Humboldt*. Leipzig: Insel Verlag, 1920.

Leng, Kirsten. "Culture, Difference, and Sexual Progress in Turn-of-the-Century Europe: Cultural Othering and the German League for the Protection of Mothers and Sexual Reform, 1905–1914." *Journal of the History of Sexuality* 25, no. 1 (2016): 62–82.

Ludwig, Johanna. "'Auch die Rechte der Frauen Bedenken'. Louise Otto (1812–1878) in der Revolution von 1848/49." In *Akteure eines Umbruchs: Männer und Frauen der Revolution von 1848/49*, edited by Helmut Bleiber, Walter Schmidt, and Susanne Schutz, 493–514. Berlin: Fides, 2010.

Meyer, Alfred. *The Feminism and Socialism of Lily Braun*. Bloomington: Indiana University Press, 1985.

Möhrmann, Renate, ed. *Frauenemanzipation im deutschen Vormärz*. Stuttgart: Reclam, 1978.

Norton, Bryan. "Geschlecht, Sinnfeld, Kontingenz: Zur Ontologie in Dorothea Schlegels *Florentin*." *Symphilosophie: Internationale Zeitschrift für philosophische Romantik* 2 (2020): 115–129.

Otto-Peters, Louise. "Adresse eines Mädchens an den Hochverehrten Minister Oberländer, an die von ihm Berufene Arbeiterkommission und an alle Arbeiter." *Leibziger Arbeiterzeitung* 4 (May 20, 1848).

Otto-Peters, Louise. *Das Erste Vierteljahrhundert des Allgemeinen Deutschen Frauenvereins Gegründet Am 18. October 1865 in Leipzig*. Leipzig: Schäfer, 1890.

Otto-Peters, Louise. "Das Ewig-Weibliche." *Frauen-Zeitung* 3, no. 45 (November 23, 1851): 321.

Otto-Peters, Louise. *Frauenleben im Deutschen Reich. Erinnerungen aus der Vergangenheit mit Hinweis auf Gegenwart und Zukunft*. Leipzig: Schäfer, 1876.

Otto-Peters, Louise. "Menschwürdiges Dasein für Alle!". *Neue Bahnen* 3, no. 122 (1868).

Otto-Peters, Louise. *Neue Bahnen* 1, no. 1 (1866).

Otto-Peters, Louise. "Programme." *Frauen-Zeitung* 1 (April 21, 1849): 1.

Otto-Peters, Louise. "Das Recht der Frauen auf Erwerb. Blicke auf das Frauenleben der Gegenwart." Hamburg: Hoffmann und Campe, 1866. https://scholarsarchive.byu.edu/sophnf_essay/10.

Otto-Peters, Louise. "Die Theilnahme der Weiblichen Welt am Staatsleben." *Sächische Vaterlandsblätter* 3 (1843).

Otto-Peters, Louise. "Weibliches Proletariat." *Der Volksfreund*, May 17, 1848, 52.

Rosenbusch, Ute. *Der Weg zum Frauenwahlrecht in Deutschland*. Baden-Baden: Nomos Verlagsgesellschaft, 1998.

Rueling, Anna. "What Interest Does the Women's Movement Have in the Homosexual Question? (1904)." In *German Feminist Writings*, edited by Magda Mueller and Patricia A. Herminghouse, 206–210. New York: Continuum, 2001.

Sanford, Jutta Schroers. "The Origins of German Feminism: German Women 1789–1870." PhD diss., Ohio State University, 1976.

Schlegel, Dorothea. *Florentin*. Leipzig: Friedrich Bohn, 1801.

Schlegel, Friedrich. *Lucinde: Ein Roman*. Berlin: Heinrich Fröhlich, 1799.

Schopenhauer, Arthur. "Idee zu einem Katechismus der Vernunft für edle Frauen." In Arthur Schopenhauer, *Kritische Gesamtausgabe* I.2, edited by Hans-Joachim Birkner et al. Berlin/New York: de Gruyter, 1980–,153–4.

Schlüpmann, Heide. "Radikalisierung der Philosophie: Die Nietzsche-Rezeption und die Sexualpolitische Publizistik Helene Stöckers." *Feministische Studien* 3, no. 1 (1984): 10–38.

Schötz, Susanne. "'Human Beings Is What Women Want to Become, and to Partake of the Garland of Work and Victory': Visions of Emancipation, Community Spirit, and Social Reform in the First German Women's Movement." *Frontiers in Sociology* 4, no. 64 (2019): 1–21.

Stöcker, Helene. "Liebe und Ehe in der Türkei." *Die Neue Generation* 5, no. 5 (1909): 171–178.

Stöcker, Helene. "Unsere Umwertung der Werte." In Helene Stöcker, *Die Liebe und die Frauen*, 6–18. Minden in Westf.: J. C. C. Bruns' Verlag, 1906.

Stopczyk-Pfundstein, Annegret. *Philosophin der Liebe: Helene Stöcker: Die "Neue Ethik" um 1900 in Deutschland und ihr philosophisches Umfeld bis heute*. Germany: Books on Demand GmbH, 2003.

Sydow, Anna von, ed. *Wilhelm und Caroline von Humboldt in ihren Briefen*. 7 vols. Berlin: E. S. Mittler und Sohn, 1907–18.

Tewarson, Heidi Thomann. *Rahel Levin Varnhagen: The Life and Work of a German Jewish Intellectual*. Lincoln: University of Nebraska Press, 1998.

Twellman, Margrit. *Die deutsche Frauenbewegung. Ihre Anfänge und erste Entwicklung 1843–1899*. Meisenheim am Glan: Quellen, 1972.

Varnhagen, Rahel. *Gesammelte Werke*. Edited by Konrad Feilchenfeldt, Uwe Schweikert, and Rachel E. Steiner. Munich: Matthes and Seitz,1983.

Wollgast, Siegfried. "Louise Otto-Peters Und Karl Christian Friedrich Krause als ihre philosophische Quelle." *Louise-Otto-Peters-Jahrbuch* 1. Markkleeberg: Sax Verlag, 2004: 39–57.

Yamada, Teruko. "Louise Otto-Peters und die deutschkatholische Bewegung: Die Bürgerliche Frauenbewegung des Vormärz und der Revolutionszeit." *Louise-Otto-Peters-Jahrbuch* 1. Markkleeberg: Sax Verlag, 2004: 90–114.

Zetkin, Clara. "Die Arbeiterinnen- und Frauenfrage der Gegenwart." Berlin: Verlag der Berliner Volks-Tribune, 1889.

Zetkin, Clara. *Ausgewählte Reden und Schriften*. Berlin: Dietz, 1953.

Zetkin, Clara. *Ausgewählte Reden und Schriften*. Vol. 1. *Auswahl aus den Jahren 1889 Bis 1917*. Berlin: Dietz Verlag, 1957.

Zetkin, Clara. *Zur Geschichte der proletarischen Frauenbewegung Deutschlands.* Berlin: Dietz Verlag, 1928.

Zetkin, Clara. *Die Gleichheit* 6, no. 25, December 9, 1896.

Zetkin, Clara. *Zur Frage des Frauenwahlrechts, Bearbeitet nach dem Referat auf der Konferenz Sozialistischer Frauen zu Mannheim.* Berlin: Buchhandlung Vorwärts, 1907.

Zetkin, Clara. "Der Student und das Weib." *Marxistische Blätter* (1899): 17–29.

Zucker, Stanley. "German Women and the Revolution of 1848: Kathinka Zitz-Halein and the Humania Association." *Central European History* 13, no. 3 (1980): 237–254.

CHAPTER 20

....

WOMEN PHILOSOPHERS AND THE NEO-KANTIAN MOVEMENT

....

KATHERINA KINZEL

THIS chapter introduces four women philosophers whose work stands in a more or less close relationship to the German neo-Kantian movement: Hedwig Bender and Grete Hermann in Germany, Camille Bos in France, and Hilda Oakeley in the UK. In his introduction to *The Neo-Kantian Reader*, which aims to provide a representative selection of texts from philosophers of different neo-Kantian proclivities, Sebastian Luft claims that—unlike in the phenomenological tradition—there was no female presence in neo-Kantianism.[1] In two recent volumes on neo-Kantianism and its history, female representatives of the movement are absent as well.[2] This deserves some critical examination.

The difficulties start right with the question as to what neo-Kantianism is exactly, and what criteria we might draw upon when subsuming individual philosophers under the term. By the late nineteenth century, the landscape of academic philosophy in the German-speaking world was shaped by two schools of thought that sought to adapt Kant's project to the problems of their time: the "Baden school," featuring Wilhelm Windelband, Heinrich Rickert, and Emil Lask as its core members, and the "Marburg school," founded by Herman Cohen and continued by Paul Natorp and Ernst Cassirer. The former transformed Kantianism into a philosophy of values and history, the latter into a transcendental philosophy of science and culture. Central to both schools was an antipsychologistic reading of Kant's first *Critique* and the thought

---

[1] Sebastian Luft, editor's introduction to *The Neo-Kantian Reader* (London: Routledge, 2015), xxvii.

[2] Nicolas de Warren and Andrea Staiti, eds., *New Approaches to Neo-Kantianism* (Cambridge: Cambridge University Press, 2015); Rudolf Makkreel and Sebastian Luft, eds., *Neo-Kantianism in Contemporary Philosophy* (Bloomington: Indiana University Press, 2010).

that philosophy is concerned with the questions of validity that arise in empirical science and other cultural domains. When I speak of "orthodox" neo-Kantianism, it is these two schools that I am referring to. No women were part of the neo-Kantian orthodoxy.

However, the early history of Kant-reception as well as its ramifications in the late nineteenth and early twentieth century is more difficult to categorize and licenses a broader use of the term. Early debates on what exactly the letter of Kant's philosophy stated led to a proliferation of Kantianisms. Notably, Johann Gottlieb Fichte thought of himself as a successor completing Kant's project. He was opposed by thinkers like Jakob Friedrich Fries and Johann Friedrich Herbart. Their defenses of "critical philosophy" against the idealisms of Fichte, Schelling, and Hegel gave Kantian themes an empiricist spin. Otto Liebmann demanded a "return to Kant" against such appropriations, claiming to recover the pure doctrine of transcendental philosophy against both speculative idealist and empiricist (mis)readings. A generation later, Friedrich Albert Lange turned to Kantianism in an attempt to resolve the materialism debates, while Hermann von Helmholtz aligned it with a theory of perception based on the results of empirical sense-physiology. The historical approach of Benno Erdmann gave new impulses to Kant scholarship, just when interpretive conflicts over Kant's oeuvre gained broader attention in the controversy about the reality of space and time between Friedrich Adolf Trendelenburg and Kuno Fischer. The neo-Kantian orthodoxy became consolidated in the Baden and Marburg schools between the 1880s and the turn of the century. But many late nineteenth-century figures who are commonly considered part of the movement cannot be grouped with either. Bruno Bauch, Jonas Cohn, and Hans Vahinger took up ideas from both schools, while Alois Riehl and Leonard Nelson sought to establish their own. At the same time, Kantian philosophies gained prominence in France with Émile Boutroux and Charles Renouvier, and in the UK in the works of British Idealists like Thomas Hill Green and Edward Caird.

Characterizing such a diverse range of philosophies as "neo-Kantian" carries the risk of conceptual inflation. On a broad construal of the term, which includes all of these different strands, women philosophers were part of the neo-Kantian movement. Each of the women I will discuss in this chapter took up and transformed Kantian ideas while pursuing independent philosophical aspirations. But were they "neo-Kantians" in a sense that is specific or demanding enough not to include the majority of philosophical theorizing from the nineteenth to the early twentieth century? Note that this problem arises not only when discussing women philosophers. We might ask, for example, whether there is a meaningful sense of the term on which Helmholtz comes out as a neo-Kantian, but Wilhelm Dilthey does not, on which Vahinger is classified as a neo-Kantian, but not Arthur Schopenhauer. What might be the criteria that warrant inclusion into or exclusion from the movement?

Strict adherence to Kant's doctrine cannot serve as a criterion. First, it remains contested what exactly this doctrine amounts to. And second, even the orthodox neo-Kantians did not rest content with the "letter" of Kant's philosophy. Rather, they revised and adapted it in response to the challenges of their own age. Windelband aptly summarizes the spirit of the movement: "understanding Kant means going be-yond him."[3]

Sociological considerations concerning institutional affiliations and training, as well as patterns of influence and reception, can help to establish the actual historical lineages through which Kantian thought was disseminated. But taken by themselves, they do not provide the sought-after criterion either. Training and influence do not guarantee con-tinuity in philosophical content. And since intellectual traditions also involve transfor-mation, we are right back to the question at which point "going beyond" Kant amounts to leaving him behind.

Perhaps the question "was X a neo-Kantian?" is not a particularly fruitful one. In what follows, I pursue a different strategy. I identify key issues that were of concern to the orthodox neo-Kantians and take these as a starting point for an exploration of how different women philosophers in the late nineteenth and early twentieth centuries addressed them. My discussion will trace the dispersion of Kantian philosophies throughout different intellectual, institutional, and national contexts; highlight their versatile character; and suggest a reconsideration of our understanding of "neo-Kantianism" that takes account of its centrifugal tendencies.

One overarching concern that shaped discussions in German philosophy from the mid-nineteenth century was the relation between philosophy and the empirical sci-ences. Novel developments in mathematics and physics, advances in experimental psy-chology and neurophysiology, and the professionalization of disciplines like history and—later—sociology forced philosophers to reconsider their role in relation to these fields. This reconsideration was also one of the central drivers of the "return to Kant."

First, the orthodox neo-Kantians championed an antipsychologistic interpretation of Kant's first *Critique* that secured the independence of transcendental philosophy from psychology and related empirical disciplines. On the antipsychologistic reading, the a priori conditions of knowledge do not consist in innate structures of the human psycho-physical apparatus. Rather, they are of a strictly formal or logical character. This view was forcefully defended by the founding figures of the two orthodox schools. The second edition of Cohen's *Kants Theorie der Erfahrung* from 1885 identifies the formal conditions of experience with the synthetic principles that are implicit in the content of mathematical natural science, while Windelband's "Kritische und genetische Methode" (1883) locates them in values that are irreducible to the empirical realm.

Second, central to the Marburg school was a concern with the historicity of natural science and its implications for transcendental philosophy. This problem became par-ticularly pressing because Kant had spelled out the conditions of experience in such a way that certain posits of Newtonian physics—Euclidean geometry and the three laws of motion—seemed to receive synthetic a priori status. Subsequent scientific developments challenged the elevation of Newtonianism to a pure natural science. In

---

[3] Wilhelm Windelband, *Präludien. Aufsätze und Reden zur Philosophie und ihrer Geschichte* (Tübingen: Mohr Siebeck, 1924), vol. 1, iv. All translations in this chapter are my own.

the works of Cohen, Natorp, and Cassirer, we thus witness attempts to reconcile apriorism with the historicity of science.

Third, the professionalization of the historical disciplines raised the question as to what distinguishes the "historical sciences" from the natural sciences. There was widespread agreement that Kant's foundation of the natural sciences did not extend to the disciplines that study the human, historical, and cultural world. And yet, in the preoccupation with conditions of validity, the Baden neo-Kantians found a fruitful strategy for determining the peculiarities of historical method. Central to their philosophy was the thought that history does not study law-like regularities but "individualities," and that historical life is inherently related to the domain of values.

Starting from these concerns—the philosophy-science relation, antipsychologism, scientific change, and historical method—we can begin to explore the relationships of late nineteenth-century women philosophers to the neo-Kantian movement. In what follows, I present the philosophical ideas of Bender, Hermann, Bos, and Oakeley in their broad contours. In the conclusion, I return to the key concerns of the orthodoxy that I have just outlined and analyze how, in taking up and developing Kantian ideas, the four women presented in this chapter contributed to them. As I will show, the differences in the philosophical orientations of Bender, Hermann, Bos, and Oakeley, and between their respective transformations of Kantianism, are profound. This plurality is indicative of the versatile character of Kantian philosophies at the turn to the twentieth century and points to the centrifugal tendencies that had been at work in the reception of Kant since the turn to the nineteenth.

1 BENDER IN DEFENSE OF METAPHYSICS

Hedwig Bender (1854–1928) was born in Luxemburg. In 1872, she took the exam to become a teacher at the Higher Girls' School (Höhere Mädchenschule) in Hannover and subsequently worked in Minden, Dresden, and Eisenach. Bender's philosophical writings focus on Kant, Spinoza, and Giordano Bruno, and seek to render Spinozist metaphysics compatible with an appreciation for the successes of the natural sciences. Bender was part of the conservative wing of the women's movement. She petitioned for women's rights to a university education but did not endorse universal suffrage.[4]

Bender's main philosophical work, *Toward the Resolution of the Metaphysical Problem* (*Zur Lösung des metaphysischen Problems*; 1886), contains two articles that Bender had published in *Zeitschrift für Philosophie und philosophische Kritik* in 1884 and 1885, as well as two additional chapters. Bender's project as sketched in these writings is a revision of Kant's account of the limits of knowledge and of the thing-in-itself. Ultimately, Bender

---

[4] "Bender, Frl. Hedwig," in *Lexikon deutscher Frauen der Feder*, vol. 1, ed. Sophie Pataky (Berlin: Pataky, 1889); Ursula Meyer, *Die andere Philosophiegeschichte* (Aachen: ein-FACH-verlag, 2007), 188–191.

seeks to defend philosophy as metaphysics—the quest for first principles—and seeks to secure metaphysics a farther reach than Kant had allowed. To this end, she deems it necessary to simultaneously reject materialism and Kant's own "extreme idealism."

Her discussion of these issues in *Toward the Resolution* starts from a dilemma in Kant's conception of the thing-in-itself that was familiar since Jacobi: by introducing the thing-in-itself Kant makes use of the categories, in particular causation and substance. Thus, either the use of the categories is, pace Kant himself, not restricted to experience, or the notion of a thing-in-itself is untenable.[5] Bender intends to resolve this dilemma in favor of the first option: the thing-in-itself exists, and we can know of its existence because the use of the categories beyond experience is rationally warranted and amounts to knowledge. To bolster this view, Bender proposes a revised account of the categories, as well as of the transcendental aesthetics.

According to Bender, Kant's transcendental deduction does not demand "that the unity, which is thought in the syntheses of representations, is *only* [a unity] **created** by our understanding . . . *to which does not correspond any objective unity*."[6] The thought that the categories are subjective expressions of objectively real relations has not been ruled out by Kant. And in fact, only this view can preserve the idea of a mind-independent object. For Bender, Kant's transcendental idealism destroys this idea by separating the transcendental object—the unity afforded by the categories—from the thing-in-itself.[7]

Bender goes on to develop a novel account of the relation between understanding and sensibility. She argues that there are only three originary categories that the entire activity of the understanding is based upon: substance, causality, and interaction. The categories of causality and interaction are represented in the forms of intuition of space and time. More precisely, the relations that are merely "thought" in the concepts of the understanding are represented as "real" in the sensible forms of space and time. The relation that is thought in the category of interaction is represented as the coexistence of a manifold in space, and the relation that is thought in the category of causation is represented as the succession of a manifold in time.[8] Relations are objectively real; they are captured subjectively through the categories and represented intuitively in space and time. Since causality and interaction, space and time, are given in a unity, there needs to be an "ultimate ground" of the inner unity of all relations. This is provided by the category of substance which is the most fundamental of the categories.[9]

The category of substance also features centrally in what Bender considers her refutation of "extreme idealism." She argues that the relations between perceptions are dependent on their "content," and that this content must be caused by something external

[5] Hedwig Bender, *Zur Lösung des metaphysischen Problems. Kritische Untersuchungen über die Berechtigung des Transcendental-Idealismus und der atomistischen Theorie* (Berlin: Mitterer und Sohn, 1866), 1–2.

[6] Bender, *Lösung*, 12, original emphasis.

[7] Bender, *Lösung*, 7–9.

[8] Bender, *Lösung*, 150–151.

[9] Bender, *Lösung*, 144–145.

affecting our sensibility. Thus the category of causation leads us from our subjective sensibility to the "objective reality" affecting it. This objective reality, in turn, is thought in the category of substance.[10] Ultimately, Bender embraces a Spinozist picture of metaphysics: the appearances are conditioned by the unconditioned thing-in-itself.[11] The relation between thing-in-itself and appearance is a causal relation between substance and accident: the thing-in-itself is the unconditioned cause of the appearances.[12]

Bender defends her mitigated idealism not only against more extreme forms of idealism, but also against "materialism." In the third chapter of *Toward the Resolution* she turns to a discussion of atomism and materialism. She seeks to show that the rejection of materialism leaves a philosophically plausible version of atomism intact, the ultimate goal being the dissolution of apparent conflicts between her conception of metaphysics and atomistic natural science. In a first step, she claims that the materialist concept of the atom incurs a tension between force and matter. According to Bender, only idealism allows for reconciling the two concepts, tracing them back to different faculties. The concept of matter extended in space is how we represent objective being in sensibility; the concept of force is the nonsensible representation of objective being as provided by the understanding.[13] A philosophically robust account conceptualizes the atom as an immaterial, nonextended self-moving force, while acknowledging that it can only be represented in intuition as matter extended in space.[14]

Bender then shows that this conception of the atom does not warrant materialism. Drawing on Emil du Bois-Reymond, she identifies three problems of the materialist worldview: the essence of the atom cannot be known, consciousness cannot be made intelligible on the basis of mechanical principles, and materialism leads to contradictory ideas about the initial state of the universe.[15] In order to go beyond these limits, atomism must be supplemented with metaphysics. We need to think of the totality of the world not as a conglomerate of isolated atoms, but as thoroughly determined and ordered. This presupposes that the totality of the world of appearances is the expression of an organically structured unity, which determines all individual objects in part-whole relations: the thing-in-itself as unconditioned or absolute substance provides the principle of unity of the world-totality.[16]

Philosophy, Metaphysics, and Individual Research (*Philosophie, Metaphysik und Einzelforschung*) from 1897 continues Bender's engagement with the possibility of metaphysics, focusing on the question of philosophical method and on the relation between philosophy and the special sciences. Bender now conceptualizes philosophy as a general science that, although founded in experience, differs from the natural sciences in its

[10] Bender, *Lösung*, 13.
[11] Bender, *Lösung*, 32–35.
[12] Bender, *Lösung*, 157.
[13] Bender, *Lösung*, 108.
[14] Bender, *Lösung*, 120.
[15] Bender, *Lösung*, 123.
[16] Bender, *Lösung*, 141–142.

starting-point and method. On account of these differences, philosophy is in a position to provide the presuppositions made by the natural sciences with a rational justification. Bender thinks that the presuppositions in question are not merely of an epistemological character but also consist in general ontological principles.

As Bender observes, the idea that the limits of experience are the limits of knowledge motivates both the neo-Kantian and the positivist attacks on metaphysics. Against this idea, she seeks to demonstrate that first, philosophy and natural science are on a par in deriving nonempirical knowledge from experience, and second, that this procedure is rationally warranted both in science and in philosophy.

On Bender's reading, the neo-Kantians—she refers in particular to Lange, Fischer, and Windelband—reduce philosophy to epistemology, rejecting any form of metaphysics that would go beyond the critical self-clarification of reason. Against these views she maintains that philosophical metaphysics in a stronger sense, as an inquiry into first principles, is possible. Surprisingly though, her defense of this position jettisons apriorism.

In *Toward the Resolution*, Bender had already noted her disagreement with the Kantian conception of pure a priori cognition. She takes issue with Kant's famous idea that, while all knowledge begins with experience, it does not all arise from experience. According to her, the categories and forms of intuition cannot be said to be a source of knowledge that would be independent of experience. This is because the relations that are grasped through them cannot be cognized a priori. They can only be cognized by consulting experience.[17]

Philosophy, Metaphysics, and Individual Research elaborates this thought further. But Bender's main concern is not with Kant or the neo-Kantians, but with positivism. Since the positivist values science while devaluing philosophy, her strategy is to emphasize the commonalities between the two forms of inquiry. Most important, natural science also necessarily goes beyond experience. Not only does it introduce nonempirical hypotheses for the purpose of explanation and prediction, but central concepts of science, in particular those of causality, natural law, and force go beyond experience as well.[18]

Bender agrees with both Hume and Kant that causality is synthetic, but not given in experience. That is, the causal influence by which the cause necessitates the effect is never encountered in observation. All that is ever observed is a constant conjunction, not the necessity associated with the concept of a causal connection.[19] Bender then argues with Kant that Hume was led from this insight to assuming the groundlessness of causal inference only because he conceived of the human mind as passive, rather than actively contributing to the order of experience. But against Kant, she now maintains

---

[17] Bender, *Lösung*, 66–69.
[18] Hedwig Bender, *Philosophie, Metaphysik und Einzelforschung. Untersuchung über das Wesen der Philosophie im Allgemeinen und über die Möglichkeit der Metaphysik als Wissenschaft und ihr Verhältnis zur naturwissenschaftlichen im Besonderen* (Leipzig: Haake, 1897), 20–23.
[19] Bender, *Philosophie*, 23–24, 33.

that the categories that order experience, most centrally those of causality and substance, are not given a priori. Rather, they are indirectly derived from experience by a procedure that is analogous to the process of building hypotheses in natural science. Causality is not found in experience, but indirectly derived from it, and such a procedure is—despite Hume's problem of induction—rationally warranted.[20]

Bender's deduction of causality from experience takes the following form: all our experience is experience of happenings. The concept of a happening, however, is only intelligible if contrasted to the idea of a persistent being. By comparing the two ideas, we realize that happenings are not independent and unconditioned, but conditioned. The concept of a cause makes these features of our experience intelligible. It naturally springs from considering happenings as the general form of our experience. Bender further argues that the idea of causality is rationally justified: without it we are led to the contradictory thought of a real being that is not independent, yet without a cause.[21]

The difference between science and philosophy then, is not their starting point, which is empirical, but their level of analysis. Since science seeks to explain particular cases, while philosophy aims to grasp the "world of appearance as a whole,"[22] the hypotheses formed by philosophy are more general in kind. But according to Bender, they also carry a different epistemic warrant. She maintains that philosophical truths are "formal truths" and known with apodictic certainty. And being both general and apodictically certain, philosophical principles can serve as foundations of natural science.[23]

2 HERMANN ON CAUSALITY

With Grete Hermann (1901–1984) we turn to a very different way of engaging with the philosophy-science relation and the category of causality. Hermann studied mathematics, physics, and philosophy at the University of Göttingen. She received her doctoral degree in mathematics under the supervision of Emmy Noether in 1925. Her philosophical teacher was the neo-Kantian moral philosopher and socialist Leonard Nelson, who had been spearheading the rediscovery of Fries's philosophy in Germany. Hermann was involved in the political activities of the antifascist International Socialist Militant League (Internationaler Sozialistischer Kampfbund). She emigrated to London in 1938 the same year that the Nazi regime dissolved the League. Returning to Germany after the war, she became full professor at the *Pädagogische Hochschule* Bremen.[24] Hermann

[20] Bender, *Philosophie*, 40–41.
[21] Bender, *Philosophie*, 43–45.
[22] Bender, *Philosophie*, 72.
[23] Bender, *Philosophie*, 50–52.
[24] Inge Hansen-Schaberg, "A Biographical Sketch of Prof. Dr Grete Henry-Hermann," in *Grete Hermann—Between Physics and Philosophy*, ed. Elise Crull and Guido Bacciagaluppi (Dordrecht: Springer 2016).

published in political and moral philosophy and edited Nelson's *Collected Works* (*Gesammelten Schriften*). Her critical commentary on his ethics is entitled "Overcoming the Contingent" (Die Überwindung des Zufalls; 1953). In the present context, her work in philosophy of science deserves a closer look.

Before her emigration, Hermann had visited Leipzig, where her discussions with the physicists Werner Heisenberg and Carl Friedrich von Weizsäcker led to the publication of *The Natural-Philosophical Foundations of Quantum Mechanics* (*Die naturphilosophischen Grundlagen der Quantenmechanik*) in 1935. In this essay and in her 1937 work *The Significance of Modern Physics for the Theory of Knowledge* (*Die Bedeutung der modernen Physik für die Theorie der Erkenntnis*), Hermann starts from the observation that recent advances in physics seem to call into question central tenets of Kant's philosophy. Quantum mechanics challenges the aprioricity of the category of causation while general relativity calls into question the Euclidean character of space as an a priori form of intuition. In both cases, Hermann seeks to show that the physical theories in question require a reconsideration of the questions of natural philosophy, but do not refute the Kantian a priori.

Here is the problem arising from quantum mechanics, as recapitulated by Hermann: the concept of causality is closely linked to that of prediction. The idea of causality as a necessary connection between cause and effect seems to entail that knowledge of the initial conditions of a physical system and of the causal laws holding in it allows one to derive the final state of this system. But quantum mechanics allows only for probabilistic prediction. Together with the possibility of deterministic prediction, the idea that natural processes are subject to throughgoing causal connection is called into question.[25]

The question, then, is whether the probabilistic nature of quantum mechanical prediction expresses merely a contingent limitation of human knowledge. This would mean that additional variables could be found which, if known, would enable deterministic prediction. Hermann's nuanced discussion of the question of hidden variables contains her solution to the problem of causality.

Hermann starts with a recapitulation of Heisenberg's uncertainty principle. With the discovery of the wave-particle dualism, the same physical entities can be described as waves or as particles. However, the two descriptions can only be made compatible if each limits the application of the other: Heisenberg's uncertainty relations calculate these limits, with the effect that an object's position and an object's momentum cannot be both determined with exactness at the same time.[26] For Hermann, Heisenberg's uncertainty relations are not restrictions of our subjective capacities for knowledge. Rather, they characterize the physical system itself, meaning that a particle does not have a determinate position and momentum at the same time. This in turn suggests that the

---

[25] Grete Hermann, "Die naturphilosophischen Grundlagen der Quantenmechanik," in *Grete Henry-Hermann: Philosophie—Mathematik—Quantenmechanik. Texte zur Naturphilosophie und Erkenntnistheorie, mathematisch-physikalische Beiträge sowie ausgewählte Korrespondenz aus den Jahren 1925 bis 1982*, ed. Kay Hermann (Wiesbaden: Springer, 2019), 209.

[26] Hermann, "Grundlagen," 212–213.

subsequent trajectory of the particle is not determined by its position and momentum. It might be caused by factors other than these, that is, hidden variables.[27] Hermann discusses a variety of different arguments against the possibility of hidden variables, including the famous proof of von Neumann, and rejects them. "There can ... be only one sufficient reason to stop the further search for the causes of an observed process as fruitless in principle: *that one already knows these causes.*"[28] And Hermann's point is exactly that quantum mechanics is complete. It does contain the relevant causal knowledge and hence no further hidden variables need to be discovered.

To explain why this is the case, she draws on Bohr's correspondence principle. The correspondence principle ensures that in the limiting case of large quantum numbers, that is, for macroscopic objects, quantum mechanics agrees with classical mechanics. Hermann points to the relevance of the correspondence principle for interpreting the measurement results of quantum mechanical experiments. When interpreting the result of a measurement in light of the quantum mechanical mathematical formalism, one presupposes a theory of measurement—a theory of the interaction between the physical system and the measurement instrument. And this theory is classical and deterministic. Hence, the concepts of classical physics that describe the macroscopic objects of the measurement system are transferred as causes to the quantum system.[29]

While the measurement result cannot be predicted quantum theoretically, as soon as a result has been obtained, the theory of the measurement process provides a causal deterministic account of how it has come about. This retroactive ascription of a causal process means that quantum mechanics is complete, permitting no hidden variables. It also means that causality is preserved. While quantum mechanics denies deterministic prediction, it maintains "the in principle unlimited application of causal ideas, under which any natural process can be subsumed in principle, and with respect to all physical properties that characterize it."[30]

At times, Hermann presents this conclusion as a mere conceptual clarification that disentangles causality and prediction. In other parts of the essay, however, she maintains that her interpretation has stronger implications for natural philosophy. She suggests that the real philosophical issue is not with causality at all. Rather, it concerns the relativity of knowledge to the measurement context.[31] After all, the reason why the causes that are known after the measurement result has been obtained could not serve for its prediction is that "they determine the system only relative to the observation that has been made in the measurement."[32]

In a classical description, the characterization of the physical system under investigation is independent of the context of measurement. But in quantum mechanics, the

[27] Hermann, "Grundlagen," 215–216.
[28] Hermann, "Grundlagen," 226.
[29] Hermann, "Grundlagen," 227.
[30] Hermann, "Grundlagen," 235.
[31] Hermann, "Grundlagen," 267.
[32] Hermann, Grundlagen," 264.

characterization of the physical system in terms of specific causal relations depends on which measurements one chooses to perform in order to acquire knowledge of this system. Moreover, the respective observational contexts exclude one another. An experiment designed to measure the momentum of a particle will allow for an explanation of the measurement result as a causal effect of the particle's momentum. But the uncertainty relations preclude the system from being causally described with respect to the particle's position. Hence, the characterization of the physical system is causally complete, but it is so only relative to the measurement context.

Hermann's *The Significance of Modern Physics for the Theory of Knowledge* extends this thought to the case of Einstein's relativity theory. Here, it is not causality but Euclidean space that is at issue. Kant seemed to take Euclidean geometry to provide the a priori framework for physical space, that is, for the space in which we encounter physical objects that are subject to natural laws. But the general theory of relativity relies on non-Euclidean (Riemannian) geometry to describe physical processes. When general relativity was confirmed experimentally for the first time in 1919, this was taken to prove that physical space is not Euclidean. What does this imply for space as an a priori form of intuition?

Hermann argues that the mathematical formalism of general relativity theory only has physical significance if its variables are coordinated with observables. In this process of coordination, the idea of inertial frames, and with it the classical concepts of space and time, remain presupposed.[33] Hermann concludes that it is not the Euclidean character of space that is at issue. What must be dropped is the presupposition that the determination of natural processes has an absolute character: "classical physics tacitly presupposed that physical theory would succeed in determining natural processes univocally and adequately in their spatial and temporal relations and that because of the mutual interaction of the extended in space could explain them as a strictly causally determined happening."[34] It is thus not apriorism, but the assumption of absoluteness that is overthrown by relativity theory and quantum mechanics.

3 Bos's Doxastic Voluntarism

With Camille Bos (1868–1907), we turn from physics to psychology, from objective cognition to belief, and from the German to the French context. Bos acquired her doctoral degree in philosophy at the University of Bern in 1901 and worked as a translator, translating works of Thomas Carlyle and Ernst Häckel into French. Her doctoral thesis, titled *Psychology of Belief* (*Psychologie de la Croyance*) was published in a second, enlarged edition in 1905. Her second book, *Pessimism, Feminism, Moralism* (*Pessimisme,*

[33] Grete Hermann, *Die Bedeutung der modernen Physik für die Theorie der Erkenntnis* (Leipzig: Hirzel, 1937), 39–40.
[34] Hermann, *Bedeutung*, 41.

Féminisme, Moralisme), from 1907, positioned her as a commentator on the ideologically contested issues of her time. Bos died in the year of its publication at the age of thirty-nine.[35]

Bos draws on Kantian ideas only indirectly. In her view, the development of mathematics has reduced what Kant believed to be synthetic a priori principles to conventions, while the emergence of non-Euclidean geometries has transformed space into a mere construction.[36] Kant has been superseded by the development of natural science. Bos's own method is psychological, rather than transcendental, and the voluntaristic gist of her account of belief-formation is opposed to the intellectualism of Kant's theoretical philosophy.

Nevertheless, Bos emphasizes that the conceptual space in which her own investigation situates itself was opened up first by Kant. Kant had laid the foundations not just for modern science, but also for the moral law. He demonstrated that theoretical reason is constitutive of experience, but that it can neither provide insight into the supersensible, nor lay down authoritative principles for action. Thus, he arrived at a conception of faith as independent from knowledge, rather than a deficient form thereof. This then also allows for a reconceptualization of belief on the grounds of practical rather than theoretical reason. According to Bos, the categorial imperative establishes the primacy of practical reason, understood as the "primacy of belief over cognition,"[37] or the "primacy of volition over the understanding."[38]

Bos's *Psychology of Belief* gives this primacy a psychological interpretation. She opposes any form of intellectualism, according to which our doxastic states are regulated by rational considerations alone, or even primarily. For Bos, the formation and acceptance of beliefs implies the totality of the self, including a person's emotional life and, most important, their volitions. Bos argues in favor of doxastic voluntarism, the idea that we enjoy voluntary control over at least our higher-level beliefs. To spell out this claim, Bos proceeds from simple beliefs based in sensation to the complex and abstract ideas of science, metaphysics, and religion. The ascent from simple to complex, sensuous to abstract then also corresponds to a transition from determined to free: beliefs are first generated by unconscious psychological mechanisms, yet on higher levels of reflection, free volition, and the expression of one's personality play a central role.

The starting point of *Psychology of Belief* is sensation as a necessary foundation of belief. For Bos, even the most abstract ideas are believed only to the extent that they refer back to sensation. "It is impossible for us to believe in that of which we cannot immediately or mediately have a sensible perception."[39] In the formation of our abstract belief systems of science, metaphysics and religion, the import of sensation on belief is an indirect one. Every sensation leaves behind an image, and a sufficiently intense mental

---

[35] "Nécrologie Mlle Camille Bos," *Revue Philosophique de la France et de l' Étranger* 64 (1907): 660.
[36] Camille Bos, *Psychologie de la Croyance* (Paris: Alcan, 1905), 129.
[37] Bos, *Psychologie*, 12.
[38] Bos, *Psychologie*, 37.
[39] Bos, *Psychologie*, 23–24.

image can play the role of a sensation. We then believe in abstract ideas because our capacity for symbolization allows us to associate images with them.[40]

While all belief is thus rooted in sensation, sensation is not sufficient for belief. This already shows on the most fundamental level: sensation is not perception, and the former
is transformed into the latter through a psychic process that involves the totality of the
self. Emotion and volition determine how sensory stimuli are processed into the perceptual contents of what we see, hear, and feel.[41]

Bos continues to highlight the role of emotion and volition on every level of the process of belief-formation, but she assigns them different roles. Emotion, affect, and desire,
for Bos, are part of the unreflective, habitual mechanisms of belief-formation. There is
no disinterested theoretical belief or disinterested judgment. Emotion fortifies beliefs
already held, guides the acceptance or rejection of novel ideas, and helps to decide between competing hypotheses.[42]

The process by which belief systems are constructed in line with our affective
tendencies amounts to an unreflective automatism. Yet Bos is keen to emphasize that we
have authorship over the belief-systems that we adopt.

Bos argues for this view on the basis of a holistic account of belief revision. Our beliefs
form an interconnected network or system. To keep this network consistent, the incorporation of novel ideas sometimes requires that previously held beliefs are abandoned.
What decides which ideas are given up and which are preserved? Bos points to the
will, which arrests the habitual mechanism of belief formation and allows for reflective
decisions between ideas.[43] In his review of the first edition of *Psychology of Belief,* Henri
Bergson reads his own philosophy of life into Bos's account of volition and identifies the
will with the vitality of the soul.[44] Note, however, that Bos ascribes a rather restricted
role to volition: it merely directs our attention to a specific object. When our attention
rests longer on a particular object, this object is imbued with the intensity and clarity of
the sensuous image. This then elicits belief in the object.[45] Volition thus intervenes into
the psychological mechanism of belief-formation, arresting one mechanism and setting
into motion another one. This suffices for establishing that we are the authors of the
belief-systems we end up adopting. The abstract belief systems of metaphysics and religion are underdetermined by sensation, and deciding between competing metaphysical
or religious views requires the free expression of personality.[46]

Bos's doxastic voluntarism culminates in the thesis of the essential identity of belief
and action: belief is an internal action, while action is externalized belief.[47] On the most

---

[40] Bos, *Psychologie,* 65.
[41] Bos, *Psychologie,* 34.
[42] Bos, *Psychologie,* 55, 62.
[43] Bos, *Psychologie,* 71–73.
[44] Henri Bergson, "Camille Bos. Psychologie de la croyance," *Revue Philosophique de la France et de l'
Étranger* 27 (1902), 531–532.
[45] Bos, *Psychologie,* 78–79, 82.
[46] Bos, *Psychologie,* 140–141.
[47] Bos, *Psychologie,* 94.

fundamental level, action externalizes our common-sense belief in the reality of the self and the body, in the existence of an external world and the personhood of others, and in the reality of past and future.[48] While there is no certainty, there is the strength of our convictions as tied to the sphere of volitional action. On Bos's view, skepticism is not doubt but weakness of the will.

4 Oakeley on Historical Experience

The concept of personality is also central to the work of the British philosopher Hilda Diana Oakeley (1867–1950). But Oakeley does not draw on psychology to explore personality, rather, she approaches the issue in connection with problems of value and history. In 1894 Oakeley went to Oxford, where she studied with British Idealists such as Caird and Bernard Bosanquet. Although finishing her studies in 1898, she would be awarded her degree only twenty-two years later when Oxford opened its degrees to women. In 1899 she took up a position as head of the Royal Victoria College at McGill University, Canada's first residential women's college, and she became the first woman member of McGill's Faculty of Arts.

Oakeley returned to England in 1905 and took up a position as philosophy lecturer first at Manchester and later at King's College, Oxford. From 1925 to 1931, she was acting head of King's Philosophy Department. In 1940–1941 she was President of the Aristotelian Society, and from 1909 until her death she served as vice president of the British Federation of University Women.[49]

Before becoming a full-time academic in 1921, Oakeley had been active in educational reform and social work. In line with her interests in pedagogy, her philosophical writings show a continuing concern with "creative personality" and its ethical significance. But her philosophy is hard to classify. Oakeley takes her account of experience to "follow Kant in his general idea,"[50] but she also engages with the idealisms of Plato and Leibniz, as well as with various contemporaneous authors. She covers a broad range of topics. Her books *A Study in the Philosophy of Personality* (1928) and *History and the Self* (1934) concern questions of ethics, selfhood, history, and values. In political philosophy, she published two monographs, *The False State* (1937) and *Should Nations Survive?* (1942). In what follows, I focus on Oakeley's philosophy of temporal experience and history.

---

[48] Bos, *Psychologie*, 109–111, 117–121.

[49] Janet Howarth, "Oakeley, Hilda Diana (1867–1950)," *Oxford Dictionary of National Biography* (2009), https://www.oxforddnb.com/view/10.1093/ref:odnb/9780198614128.001.0001/odnb-9780198614 128-e-48502.

[50] Hilda Oakeley, "The World as Memory and as History," *Proceedings of the Aristotelian Society* 27 (1926–27): 292.

In "The World as Memory and as History" from 1927, Oakeley argues that experience is "creative memory,"[51] that it has an essentially historical form. She starts from the claim that what we experience as the present contains the past. The past must be assumed to be no less real and knowable than the present. This is because experience is never of an isolated instance. Rather, consciousness is temporally extended such that the mind at least partially "lives" in the past.

In Oakeley's account, the past is real, but the present has an uneasy status. On the one hand, it is only experienced as real by way of its reception into the past, that is by becoming memory. But on the other hand, unlike the past, which cannot be altered, present existence is accessible to action. Oakeley solves this tension by thinking of "memory" not as a dead stock of experience, but as an active force. "We live and we have the greater part of our being in the world of memory—this world, whether we call it past or present, being active for us in our now."[52] The activity by which the self alters existence in the present and the incorporation of the present into the past are one and the same process: the process of creative memory.

Oakeley gives a temporal interpretation of the metaphysical dualism between mind and nonmind. The finite mind lives in the past, but the present is where it encounters nonmind, or otherness as a "bare event."[53] On the basis of and conditioned by memory, the foreign world and "otherness" of nonmind is partially transfigured into mind. And because memory is active and creative in the now, finite minds can construct an ordered world of experience out of an alien material.

Creative memory does not merely bestow order upon its raw materials, it also endows the event with value and meaning. For Oakeley, the mind is necessarily located in a plurality of finite centers, it is personal and individual. Value and meaning are created by "the personal principle,"[54] that is, by individual selves that seek to overcome both the otherness of nonmind and their own finitude.[55] Thus creative memory produces history. "The action and reaction between bare event and memory, memory and fresh event produces history, and history is again absorbed by memory."[56]

In her *History and the Self* from 1934, Oakeley extends her conception of creative memory to questions concerning human freedom, the driving forces of the historical process, and the prospects of historical knowledge. About the prospects of historical knowledge, she is rather pessimistic. She distinguishes between history as the process experienced by individual selves, and history in its "categorial" form as a record. Historical knowledge in the former sense would require access to the "inner side" of history as experienced by individuals.[57] Oakeley discusses and rejects a range of possible

---

[51] Oakeley, "World," 292.
[52] Oakeley, "World," 296.
[53] Oakeley, "World," 298.
[54] Oakeley, "World," 305.
[55] Oakeley, "World," 307–309.
[56] Oakeley, "World," 304.
[57] Hilda Oakeley, *History and the Self* (London: Williams & Norgate, 1934), 60.

ways in which individual experience might be known. She disagrees with Dilthey over the relevance of psychology for history, arguing that the individual self escapes the universal concepts of psychology.[58] More fundamentally, she claims that we neither have direct experience of other minds, nor can we know them by analogy with our own experience. This is because the self cannot form the unproblematic basis of analogical inference. For there to be a self, there must already be given other selves in the commonality of language and culture. Other selves cannot be inferred, they are presupposed. Moreover, self-knowledge tends to eradicate the very experience it seeks to represent: by turning myself into an object of knowledge I end up knowing only an abstraction.[59] Attempting to transform first-person experience into knowledge destroys the very character of this experience as an activity and process. This also means that historical knowledge cannot capture the personal experience that is implied in the process of history. Oakeley concludes that "history in the original and primary sense, as a true record of the conscious experience of mankind, is not possible."[60]

In this context, she also engages with Rickert, who had argued that historical "individualities" can be known conceptually by relating them to cultural values. Oakeley observes that when Rickert speaks of values, he seems to have abstract historical categories in mind—state, religion, science, art, or morality. Rickert's individualities are not the personal selves that form the centers of historical experience. Rather, they are the historical formations recorded in categorial history.[61]

Oakeley is more optimistic with respect to this second form of historical knowledge. But here too she points to limitations, identifying five Baconian "Idols" that threaten historical objectivity.[62] Among them are the incompleteness and contingency of the historical record, the subjectivity and relativity of the ordering principles of historical reconstruction, and "animism"—our tendency to imbue historical forces and events with personality, giving room to "irrational invasions of the cultural life."[63]

Ultimately, Oakeley holds both knowledge and value to be relative to the personal principle. And this curtails the possibility of finding order or universal meaning in history. However, she thinks that the personal principle, although being the source of historical relativity, is itself beyond relativity.[64] Examining how this nonrelative principle gives rise to relativity, Oakeley turns to the problem of moral freedom. In opposition to Kant and to Nicolai Hartmann's Platonist essentialism of values, she argues that, first, freedom cannot be reduced to freedom of the will, but needs to be conceived more broadly as the capacity to bestow value and meaning upon events.[65] Second, she questions the distinction between noumena and phenomena, claiming that the

---

[58] Oakeley, *History*, 50.
[59] Oakeley, *History*, 50–53.
[60] Oakeley, *History*, 79.
[61] Oakeley, *History*, 67–68.
[62] Oakeley, *History*, 79.
[63] Oakeley, *History*, 85.
[64] Oakeley, *History*, 249.
[65] Oakeley, *History*, 171.

noumenal self is a causal beginning in the empirical world. And third, she maintains that freedom must mean freedom to do both good and evil.[66]

The latter point is of particular importance when it comes to explaining the nonpersonal forces of history. Oakeley's argument is as follows. History occurs when mind creates meaningful and value-laden historical events out of a material which is otherwise indifferent to value. But the historical world is such that, although created by human minds, it exceeds their control.[67] Oakeley does not merely think of unintended consequences here, but of the world of social institutions and historical developments more broadly. Its structure and developmental dynamic exceed the intentions, purposes, and values of the historical actors. How does this nonpersonal world come about?

As stated earlier, the personal principle endows events with value. And because there is a material alien to value, values do not come into the world as fully realized. Since they carry normative force, there must be a process toward their realization. Oakeley argues that value could, in principle, control the material alien to it. It does not do so, however, because personality "is the source from which disvalue as well as value proceeds."[68] The reason for the existence of nonpersonal factors in history is thus to be found in the personal principle—in the freedom to create both good and bad, both value and disvalue. History follows no predetermined course, and it does not express universal values, but the fundamental principle of a holistically conceived, personal freedom.[69]

5 NEO-KANTIANISM RECONSIDERED

Having introduced the philosophies of Bender, Hermann, Bos, and Oakeley in their main contours, we can now return to the central concerns of the neo-Kantian orthodoxy. As stated earlier, key issues were the philosophy-science relation, the problem of scientific change, antipsychologism, and the question of historical method. In the remainder of this chapter, I will survey how the women philosophers presented here contributed to these topics, and how their contributions related to and differed from those of the orthodox neo-Kantians of the Baden and Marburg schools.

The philosophy-science relation, and the clarification of the status of metaphysics in relation to empirical science is Bender's central question. As I have shown, her project employs the Kantian conceptual apparatus of categories, forms of intuition, synthesis, and the thing-in-itself. But it revises this apparatus so as to extend the reach of metaphysics and to establish philosophy as a form of inquiry that, although grounded in experience, arrives at apodictically certain knowledge of first principles. In both goals

---

[66] Oakeley, *History*, 167–168.
[67] Oakeley, *History*, 38–39, 91.
[68] Oakeley, *History*, 116.
[69] Oakeley, *History*, 273–174.

and method, Bender's philosophy is diametrically opposed to the Marburg neo-Kantian approach.

Following Cohen, the Marburg philosophers located the defining feature of Kantianism not in any part of Kant's doctrine, but in the transcendental method. As they understood it, this method identifies "experience" with the theoretical content of mathematical natural science and inquires into the a priori presuppositions that make this content possible. As I have shown, Bender is critical of any approach that ties philosophy too closely to epistemology.[70] Although she thinks that philosophy ought to start from and explain experience, she does not identify experience with the content of science but takes it to refer to our everyday perceptual experience.[71]

The opposition can further be illuminated by going back to the controversy about the transcendental aesthetics between Trendelenburg and Fischer in the late 1860s. In this debate, Trendelenburg had argued that space and time are a priori and ideal, but that this does not rule out their reality as noumena. Bender's own account of the categories and forms of intuition parallels Trendelenburg's "neglected alternative," for as I have shown, she regards them as subjective representations of objectively real relations.

Cohen intervened in the Fischer-Trendelenburg debate, maintaining against both that intuition is a source of knowledge, rather than a mere form of representation.[72] In later works, he develops a conceptualist interpretation of transcendental idealism, according to which sensibility is not independent of the understanding, and the laws of pure thinking fully determine the object of knowledge.[73] This antipsychologistic conceptualism stands opposed to any account that, like Bender's, takes intuition to provide representations of a mind-independent reality.

Cassirer later conceptualizes the laws of thinking as functions, and argues that progress in science and philosophy occurs when substance-concepts are replaced with function-concepts, and when sensible experience is overcome in favor of abstract conceptual determination.[74] In light of Cassirer's historical narrative about the progress of science, Bender's adherence to the concept of substance appears like a remnant of long-dead epistemology and metaphysics that fails to account for, or in any meaningful way relate to, the dynamic character of modern science.

In exploring the implications that recent developments in physics bear for transcendental philosophy, Hermann stands closer to the Marburg school and their conception of the science-philosophy relation. She is part of a broader neo-Kantian project that seeks to salvage and, if necessary, to reform Kant's account of the a priori conditions of experience in light of scientific change. Natorp discusses relativity theory with this aim

---

[70] Bender, *Philosophie*, 4–5.

[71] Bender, *Philosophie*, 71–72.

[72] Hermann Cohen, "Zur Kontroverse zwischen Trendelenburg und Kuno Fischer," *Zeitschrift für Völkerpsychologie und Sprachwissenschaft* 7 (1870).

[73] Hermann Cohen, *Kants Theorie der Erfahrung*, 2nd ed. (Berlin: Dümmler, 1885).

[74] Ernst Cassirer, *Substanzbegriff und Funktionsbegriff. Untersuchungen über die Grundfragen der Erkenntniskritik* (Berlin: Bruno Cassirer, 1910).

in his book *The Logical Foundations of the Exact Sciences* (*Die Logischen Grundlagen der Exakten Wissenschaften*) from 1910.[75] Some years later, Cassirer, in his celebrated book *Einstein's Theory of Relativity* (*Zur Einsteinschen Relativitätstheorie*; 1921) attempts to show that general relativity theory is a direct confirmation of transcendental idealism. In the same year, Ilse Schneider published *The Space-Time Problem in Kant and Einstein* (*Das Raum-Zeit Problem bei Kant und Einstein*; 1921), which takes a more conservative approach, attempting to insulate Kant's views on space and time from disconfirmation by general relativity. Hermann joins the debate on general relativity rather late, yet she pioneers the neo-Kantian interpretation of quantum mechanics: Cassirer's *Determinism and Indeterminism in Modern Physics* (*Determinismus und Indeterminismus in der modernen Physik*) appeared in 1937, two years after the publication of *The Natural-Philosophical Foundations of Quantum Mechanics*. Cassirer cites Hermann's article once in his work, reiterating the point that causality must be distinguished from the criterion of its application, while also criticizing Hermann's assumption that prediction and causality had been unified in classical physics.

Compared to the Marburg school, which pushed for a thoroughgoing reform of Kant's account of intuition and tended to take the principles as primary to the categories, Hermann's solution appears more limited. Quantum mechanics does not demand a revision of causality, nor does it challenge its applicability to experience. Likewise, relativity theory does not force us to reconsider space as a form of intuition or the faculty theory presupposed by Kant. The philosophically challenging problem is located elsewhere: in the assumption that physical knowledge is absolute.[76]

However, we must note that here Hermann departs quite substantially from Kant. As several commentators have noted, Kantian causality allows for prediction only because the principles of pure understanding achieve the univocal determination of natural processes in space and time.[77] For Kant, the universal application of the categories to intuition engenders a spatiotemporally unified world of experience in which physical objects can be determined univocally or absolutely. If together with prediction, the possibility of univocal determination goes out the window, Hermann's notion of causality is not the Kantian one. What is more, in the second analogy of experience, Kant had argued that only the universal applicability of causality allows for a distinction between the subjective apprehension of temporal sequences and an objective temporal succession in the appearances themselves. If causality is observer-relative, this move from the subjective to the objective becomes problematic.

---

[75] Paul Natorp, *Die logischen Grundlagen der Exakten Wissenschaften* (Leipzig: Teubner, 1910), 399–404.

[76] Hermann, "Grundlagen," 256; *Bedeutung*, 42–44.

[77] Michael Cuffaro, "Grete Hermann, Quantum Mechanics and the Evolution of Kantian Philosophy," in *Women in the History of Analytic Philosophy*, ed. Jeanne Peijnenburg and Sander Verhaegh (Dordrecht: Springer, 2022), ; Léna Soler, "The Convergence of Transcendental Philosophy and Quantum Physics: Grete Henry-Hermann's 1935 Pioneering Proposal," in *Grete Hermann—Between Physics and Philosophy*, ed. Elise Crull and Guido Bacciagaluppi (Dordrecht: Springer 2016).

Nevertheless, Hermann thinks of her account as a radicalization of transcendental philosophy that is true to its sprit. First, quantum mechanics is in agreement with transcendental idealism to the extent that it reveals cognition to be restricted to the identification of systems of relations rather than things in themselves.[78] And second, by revealing the relative character of these relations, it points to the possibility of independent, yet compatible ways of knowing the natural world. This follows quite naturally from the brand of Friesian neo-Kantianism that Hermann shares with Nelson. For Nelson and Hermann, the key insight of the Kantian antinomies is that the application of the categories must be restricted.[79] But for Hermann, the resolution of the antinomies demands not merely that objective cognition be restricted to experience, thus delimiting theoretical from practical reason. It demands that the a priori conditions of knowledge are taken to be relative. The "splitting of truth . . . extends into the physical knowledge of nature itself; instead of merely delimiting it against other possibilities for grasping reality."[80] Hermann's interpretation of quantum mechanics and her neo-Friesian reading of the antinomies thus point in the same direction: to a reinterpretation of the limits of knowledge. There is a broad parallel between this project and Cassirer's philosophy of symbolic forms. Both push for a pluralization and dynamization of the a priori conditions of knowledge, allowing for more than one way of constructing and knowing the natural world.

With Bos, we remain concerned with the science-philosophy relation. But since Bos formulates a psychological theory of belief formation, the question of psychologism, and the relation of the psychological to the transcendental becomes central here as well. Bos's work can plausibly be placed in the context of the French neo-Kantian school of Renouvier. She cites Renouvier in the context of her critique of certainty and frequently refers to William James—whose ties to Renouvier are well documented[81]—when fleshing out her doxastic voluntarism. Renouvier's neo-criticism is characterized by two essential tenets. First, the "principle of relativity," according to which knowledge is essentially relational and relative to the knowing subject. Second, the claim that reason does not issue absolute certainties. Instead of absolute certainty, there is only certitude, understood as the conviction of the individual who is responsible for the beliefs that they hold. For Renouvier, certitude presupposes individual freedom and is to be made sense of in terms of the obligations of practical reason. Bos does not frame her account of belief in terms of duty and obligation. However, she adopts Renouvier's views on certitude and follows his suggestion that "there is no certainty; there are only people who are certain."[82] Bos also shares the idea that the formation and adoption of beliefs

---

[78] Hermann, "Grundlagen," 255.

[79] Hermann, "Grundlagen," 249.

[80] Hermann, "Grundlagen," 256.

[81] Jeremy Dunham, "Idealism, Pragmatism, and the Will to Believe: Charles Renouvier and William James," *British Journal for the History of Philosophy* 23, no. 4 (2015).

[82] Charles Renouvier, *Essais de critique générale* (Paris: Colin, 1912), vol. 1, 366; Bos, *Psychologie*, 131.

presupposes individual freedom. And like Renouvier, she takes this view to be contin-uous with the Kantian project.[83]

Bos's reduction of certainty to the conviction of empirical subjects, and her account of belief as regulated by psychological laws conflict with the antipsychologistic commitments of the neo-Kantian orthodoxy. For the Marburg and the Baden school, the method of philosophy ought not to collapse into that of empirical science, as philosophy deals with transcendental conditions rather than psychological processes. Note also another point of disagreement. Although the charge, voiced by Bender, and later but more famously by Martin Heidegger, that the neo-Kantians reduced critical philosophy to epistemology is overblown, neither the Marburg nor the Baden philosophers developed a clear stance on the relation between theoretical and practical philosophy. Bos takes a decided position on this matter. Her doxastic voluntarism takes its cues from the primacy of practical reason over theoretical. Bos interprets this primacy psychologistically: as a form of mental causa-tion by which volition intervenes into the psychological mechanisms of belief-formation.

Finally, with Oakeley, we turn to questions concerning historical method and the role of values in history that were of central concern to the Baden neo-Kantians. As noted, Oakeley develops her philosophy of history by drawing on a broad variety of philo-sophical sources. She discusses the works of Bergson, Dilthey, Rickert, Hartmann, and Ernst Troeltsch alongside those of Bosanquet, C. D. Broad, Francis H. Bradley, John M. E. McTaggart, and Alfred North Whitehead. But her particular brand of idealism aligns itself neither with that of the British Idealists, nor with the German neo-Kantians and historicists.[84] Oakeley notes that her account of experience follows Kant's "general idea"[85] yet goes beyond Kant in holding that experience and knowledge are "conditioned by a positive quality in the activity of the subject, resulting from the limitation of finite mind and its strain to overcome this limitation, determining the experience of value, or the categories of the principle of personality."[86] Her insistence on the creative sponta-neity of mind in its striving to overcome its limitation is reminiscent of Cassirer's under-standing of "productive synthesis." And the idea that historical experience is essentially an experience of value puts her in close proximity to the Baden school.

However, by conceptualizing mind as essentially personal, and by identifying this personal principle as the source of value, she positions herself in opposition to both. Discussing Hartmann's Platonism, Oakeley rejects the "objective idealism of value"[87] that conceives of values as essences that exist independently of the mind. On her view, values only have existence in actual moral life.[88] She identifies the "strain to the

---

[83] Bos, *Psychologie*, 127.

[84] On Oakeley's relation to British Idealism, see Emily Thomas, "Hilda Oakeley on Idealism, History and the Real Past," *British Journal for the History of Philosophy* 23, no. 5 (2015):; Emily Thomas, "British Idealist Monadologies and the Reality of Time: Hilda Oakeley Against McTaggart, Leibniz, and Others," *British Journal for the History of Philosophy* 23, no. 6 (2015).

[85] Oakeley, "World," 292.

[86] Oakeley, "World," 292.

[87] Oakeley, *History*, 199.

[88] Oakeley, *History*, 205.

transcendent" that is part of moral life with the idea of the future: the possibility of imagining a different kind of existence awakens the self to the potentials inherent in humanity.[89] Oakeley explicitly embraces the moral relativism that results from her philosophy of personality and thinks of historical knowledge as severely limited by subjectivity. To the Baden neo-Kantians, relativism about values and skepticism about historical knowledge were anathema.

In the works of Bender, Hermann, Bos, and Oakeley, we not only encounter approaches that deviate from the neo-Kantian orthodoxy. We also find that there are profound philosophical differences between these four philosophers and between the ways in which they take up and transform Kantian ideas. The differences between them are reflective of the centrifugal tendencies that shaped the reception of Kant since its beginnings. Already in the heyday of German idealism Kant was appropriated and transformed in a plurality of different ways: attempts to drive Kant beyond the limits of knowledge that he himself had set were confronted by interpretations insisting on the distinction between science and metaphysics, those who thought that transcendental philosophy implied a strong emphasis on the subject faced criticisms based on empiricist readings, Kantianism was developed along both psychological and logical lines. Studying the works of women philosophers, we witness some of these early themes reappearing in the late nineteenth and early twentieth century. Bender and Oakeley present metaphysical appropriations of Kant's concepts, while Bos and Hermann situate themselves in the tradition of scientific philosophy. Bos and Oakeley make the subject central to their philosophies, and Bos does so based on a psychological reading of the primacy of practical reason. The centrifugal forces that had been at work already in the early reception of Kant were now further amplified by the dispersion of Kantian thought in different intellectual, institutional, and national contexts. Taking into account the contributions of women philosophers, "neo-Kantianism" appears less as a unified movement than a set of heterogeneous strands of development in which Kantian ideas were taken up, transformed, and actualized in different contexts.

I want to thank Paul Ziche, Kristin Gjesdal, and Dalia Nassar for their insightful comments on an earlier draft of this chapter.

BIBLIOGRAPHY

"Bender, Frl. Hedwig." In *Lexikon deutscher Frauen der Feder*, vol. 1, edited by Sophie Pataky, 50–51. Berlin: Pataky, 1889.

Bender, Hedwig. *Philosophie, Metaphysik und Einzelforschung. Untersuchung über das Wesen der Philosophie im Allgemeinen und über die Möglichkeit der Metaphysik als Wissenschaft und ihr Verhältnis zur naturwissenschaftlichen im Besonderen.* Leipzig: Haake, 1897.

---

[89] Oakeley, *History*, 213.

Bender, Hedwig. *Zur Lösung des metaphysischen Problems. Kritische Untersuchungen über die Berechtigung des Transcendental-Idealismus und der atomistischen Theorie.* Berlin: Mitterer und Sohn, 1886.

Bergson, Henri. "Camille Bos. Psychologie de la croyance." *Revue Philosophique de la France et de l' Étranger* 27 (1902): 529–533.

Bos, Camille. *Pessimisme, Féminisme, Moralisme.* Paris: Alcan, 1907.

Bos, Camille. *Psychologie de la Croyance.* Paris: Alcan, 1905.

Cassirer, Ernst. *Determinismus und Indeterminismus in der modernen Physik. Historische und systematische Studien zum Kausalproblem.* Göteborg: Elanders Boktryckeri Aktiebolag, 1937.

Cassirer, Ernst. *Substanzbegriff und Funktionsbegriff. Untersuchungen über die Grundfragen der Erkenntniskritik.* Berlin: Bruno Cassirer, 1910.

Cassirer, Ernst. *Zur Einsteinschen Relativitätstheorie. Erkenntnistheoretische Betrachtungen.* Berlin: Bruno Cassirer, 1921.

Cohen, Hermann. *Kants Theorie der Erfahrung.* 2nd ed. Berlin: Dümmler, 1885.

Cohen, Hermann. "Zur Kontroverse zwischen Trendelenburg und Kuno Fischer." *Zeitschrift für Völkerpsychologie und Sprachwissenschaft* 7 (1870): 249–296.

Cuffaro, Michael. "Grete Hermann, Quantum Mechanics and the Evolution of Kantian Philosophy." In *Women in the History of Analytic Philosophy*, edited by Jeanne Peijnenburg and Sander Verhaegh. Dordrecht: Springer, 2022: 113–145.

De Warren, Nicolas, and Andrea Staiti, eds. *New Approaches to Neo-Kantianism.* Cambridge: Cambridge University Press, 2015.

Dunham, Jeremy. "Idealism, Pragmatism, and the Will to Believe: Charles Renouvier and William James." *British Journal for the History of Philosophy* 23, no. 4 (2015): 756–778.

Hansen-Schaberg, Inge. "A Biographical Sketch of Prof. Dr Grete Henry-Hermann." In *Grete Hermann—Between Physics and Philosophy*, edited by Elise Crull and Guido Bacciagaluppi, 3–16. Dordrecht: Springer, 2016.

Hermann, Grete. *Die Bedeutung der modernen Physik für die Theorie der Erkenntnis.* Leipzig: Hirzel, 1937.

Hermann, Grete. "Die naturphilosophischen Grundlagen der Quantenmechanik." In *Grete Henry-Hermann: Philosophie—Mathematik—Quantenmechanik. Texte zur Naturphilosophie und Erkenntnistheorie, mathematisch-physikalische Beiträge sowie ausgewählte Korrespondenz aus den Jahren 1925 bis 1982*, edited by Kay Hermann, 207–258. Wiesbaden: Springer, 2019.

Hermann, Grete. "Die Überwindung des Zufalls. Kritische Betrachtung zu Leonard Nelsons Begründung der Ethik als Wissenschaft." In *Leonard Nelson zum Gedächtnis*, edited by Minna Specht and Willi Eichler, 25–111. Frankfurt am Main: Verlag Öffentliches Leben, 1953.

Howarth, Janet. "Oakeley, Hilda Diana (1867c–1950)." *Oxford Dictionary of National Biography* (2009). https://www.oxforddnb.com/view/10.1093/ref:odnb/9780198614128.001.0001/odnb-9780198614128-e-48502.

Luft, Sebastian, ed. *The Neo-Kantian Reader.* London: Routledge, 2015.

Makkreel, Rudolf, and Sebastian Luft, eds. *Neo-Kantianism in Contemporary Philosophy.* Bloomington: Indiana University Press, 2010.

Meyer, Ursula. *Die andere Philosophiegeschichte.* Aachen: ein-FACH-verlag, 2007.

Natorp, Paul. *Die logischen Grundlagen der Exakten Wissenschaften.* Leipzig: Teubner, 1910.

"Nécrologie Mlle Camille Bos." *Revue Philosophique de la France et de l' Étranger* 64 (1907): 660.

Oakeley, Hilda. *The False State.* London: Williams and Norgate, 1937.

Oakeley, Hilda. *History and the Self.* London: Williams & Norgate, 1934.

Oakeley, Hilda. *Should Nations Survive?* London: George Allen & Unwin, 1942.

Oakeley, Hilda. *A Study in the Philosophy of Personality.* London: Williams & Norgate, 1928.

Oakeley, Hilda. "The World as Memory and as History." *Proceedings of the Aristotelian Society* 27 (1926–27): 291–316.

Renouvier, Charles. *Essais de critique générale*, vol. 1. Paris: Colin, 1912.

Schneider, Ilse. *Das Raum-Zeit Problem bei Kant und Einstein.* Berlin: Springer, 1921.

Soler, Léna, "The Convergence of Transcendental Philosophy and Quantum Physics: Grete Henry-Hermann's 1935 Pioneering Proposal." In *Grete Hermann—Between Physics and Philosophy*, edited by Elise Crull and Guido Bacciagaluppi, 55–69. Dordrecht: Springer 2016.

Thomas, Emily. "British Idealist Monadologies and the Reality of Time: Hilda Oakeley against McTaggart, Leibniz, and Others." *British Journal for the History of Philosophy* 23, no. 6 (2015): 1150–1168.

Thomas, Emily. "Hilda Oakeley on Idealism, History and the Real Past." *British Journal for the History of Philosophy* 23, no. 5 (2015): 933–953.

Windelband, Wilhelm. "Kritische oder genetische Methode?" In *Präludien. Aufsätze und Reden zur Philosophie und ihrer Geschichte*, vol. 1, 99–135. Tübingen: Mohr Siebeck, 1924.

Windelband, Wilhelm. *Präludien. Aufsätze und Reden zur Philosophie und ihrer Geschichte*, vol. 1. Tübingen: Mohr Siebeck, 1924.

CHAPTER 21

··

TWO FEMALE PESSIMISTS

··

FREDERICK C. BEISER

1 THE PESSIMISM CONTROVERSY

ONE of the longest, most intense, and widespread philosophical controversies in Germany in the second half of the nineteenth century was the so-called *Pessimismusstreit*.[1] Almost everyone who was anyone in the intellectual world, in one form or another, participated in the controversy. It began in the 1860s, strengthened in the 1870s and 1880s, and weakened only in the 1890s, though it lasted even into the early twentieth century. According to some contemporary accounts, pessimism overshadowed materialism and historicism as the most pressing and important issue of the age.[2] Pessimism became the talk of the town, the subject of academic lectures, and even the object of satire.[3]

The pessimism controversy had two main phases. The first phase arose in the 1860s with Arthur Schopenhauer's rise to fame, when many articles, pamphlets, and books were published attacking his pessimism. While Schopenhauer had many detractors, he also had many defenders.[4] The second phase began in 1870 in reaction against Eduard von Hartmann's *Philosophy of the Unconscious* (*Philosophie des Unbewussten*, 1870),[5]

---

[1] On the controversy as a whole, see O. Plümacher, *Der Pessimismus in Vergangenheit und Gegenwart, Geschichtliches und Kritisches* (Heidelberg: Georg Weiß Verlag, 1883). A second edition appeared in 1888.

[2] Theodor Tautz, *Der Pessimismus* (Karlsruhe: G. Braun'schen Hofbuchhandlung, 1876), 6–7; and Edmund Pfleiderer, *Der moderne Pessimismus* (Berlin: Carl Habel, 1875), 7–8.

[3] The satire is by M. Reymond, *Das Buch vom gesunden und kranken Herrn Meyer* (Bern: Frobeen & Cie., 1877). Herr Meyer, Reymond's hapless antihero, holds a literary salon where Hartmann's pessimism is discussed. The book is in verse and comes with many amusing illustrations.

[4] The chief defenders were Julius Frauenstädt, *Briefe über die Schopenhaurer'sche Philosophie* (Leipzig: Brockhaus, 1854); Julius Bahnsen, *Der Widerspruch im Wissen und Wesen der Welt* (Berlin: Theobold Grieben, 1880); Phillip Mainländer, *Philosophie der Erlösung* (Berlin: Thebold Grieben, 1880); and Paul Deussen, *Die Elemente der Metaphysik* (Bonn: Marcus, 1876).

[5] Eduard von Hartmann, *Die Philosophie des Unbewussten. Versuch einer Weltanschauung* (Berlin: Carl Duncker, 1870).

which reaffirmed but qualified Schopenhauer's pessimism. During the 1870s alone hundreds of reviews, scores of articles, and dozens of books were published on Hartmann's pessimism.[6] The torrent persisted throughout the 1880s.

There should be no mystery why pessimism became such an important issue: nothing less was at stake than the value of life itself. "To be or not to be?" That famous question from Hamlet summarizes perfectly the essence of the dispute. Is life worth living? The central contention of the pessimists was that life is not worth living because it is filled with suffering which far outweighs its pleasures. Their opponents—neo-Kantians, materialists, positivists, Lotzeans, Lutheran clergy—responded that life, despite all its troubles, tribulations, and tragedies, is nevertheless worth living.

Despite its great philosophical and cultural importance, the pessimism controversy has been largely forgotten. It had one great historian in the late nineteenth century: Olga Plümacher. Her *Der Pessimismus in Vergangenheit und Gegenwart*, which was first published in 1883, remains the single attempt to explain and describe the various viewpoints and episodes of the controversy.[7] Today, if the controversy is remembered at all, it is solely through its most famous participant: Friedrich Nietzsche. In his day, however, Nietzsche was known as only one among many contributors to the controversy.[8]

It is a consequence of the neglect of the pessimism controversy that two of its most interesting participants have been largely forgotten. They were, as they signed their names, A. Taubert and (the already mentioned) O. Plümacher. It turns out that they were female pioneers, women philosophers in an age when women were still not widely recognized in the intellectual realm. The *A* in Taubert's pen name stood for Agnes; and the *O* in Plümacher's stood for Olga. Because they signed themselves only with their initials, they were not known as women; contributors to the controversy simply assumed that they were men.[9]

Agnes Taubert (1844–1877) was the wife of Eduard von Hartmann. Although she often defended her husband's philosophy during the controversy, she did not always do so; she was an independent voice who stated her own views on many issues. She wrote two contributions to the pessimism controversy: *Philosophy against Natural-Scientific Hubris* (*Philosophie gegen naturwissenschaftlichen Ueberhebung*) (1872) and *Pessimism and Its Opponents* (*Der Pessimismus und seine Gegner*) (1873). Both books were widely read and reviewed. The first book was a defense of Hartmann's metaphysics against

---

[6] O. Plümacher, "Chronologische Verzeichnis der Hartmann-Literatur von 1868–1880," in *Der Kampf um's Unbewusste* (Berlin: Duncker, 1881), 115–150.

[7] See Plümacher, *Der Pessimismus in Vergangenheit und Gegenwart*, as cited earlier. See also her "Die Philosophie des Unbewussten und ihre Gegner," *Unsere Zeit* 15 (1879): 321–345. Plümacher was also the author of a book on two thinkers in the Schopenhauer school, *Zwei Individualisten der Schopenhauer'schen Schule* (Berlin: Duncker, 1882). The two thinkers were Mainländer and Hellenbach.

[8] See Plümacher, "Die Philosophie des Unbewussten und ihre Gegner," 329–330; and Otto Siebert, *Geschichte der neueren deutsche Philosophie seit Hegel* (Göttingen: Vandenhoeck & Ruprecht, 1898), 243–245.

[9] Polemical literature discussing their writings would refer to the authors with the masculine pronoun "er."

critics who appealed to the authority of natural science. Taubert was a critic of what we nowadays call "scientism," the overextension of the claims of science and the presumption that it alone offers the path to truth. The second book, which was widely discussed in the 1870s, was a counterattack on Hartmann's critics. According to Carl Heymons, Hartmann's publisher, Taubert played a major role in the organization and strategy of the dispute against Hartmann's critics.[10] Sadly, such a promising talent had a very short life. Taubert died May 1877, only thirty-three years old, a victim of "an attack of a rheumatism of the joints."[11]

Olga Plümacher (née Hühnerwadel) (1839–1895) was also a prominent voice in the pessimism controversy.[12] She wrote three major contributions to it: *The Struggle Concerning the Unconscious (Der Kampf um's Unbewusste)* (1881); *Pessimism Past and Present (Der Pessimismus in Vergangenheit und Gegenwart)* (1883); and *Two Individualists from the Schopenhauer School (Zwei Individualisten der Schopenhauer'schen Schule)* (1882). The bibliography appended to the first book is still the only complete one; the second book is still the only history of the pessimism dispute. Plümacher also wrote an article on Hartmann's pessimism for *Mind,* which served as the introduction to his ideas for the Anglophone world.[13] All these works show a complete mastery of the polemical literature and great acumen in discussing the issues. It has been said that if Hartmann's critics read her, they would not have bothered to make their criticisms in the first place.[14]

Plümacher's achievement is all the more remarkable considering the obstacles she had to struggle against. She had no formal university education; she was a single mother; and she spent much of her life in a Swiss colony in the backwoods of Tennessee.[15] It is sad that her library, most of her correspondence, and her personal documents have disappeared. She died, alone and forgotten, in Tennessee in 1895.

Why were Taubert and Plümacher so attracted to pessimism? Their writings offer few clues. But one thing is certain: that the source of the attraction was not least political. Neither Taubert nor Plümacher fit the stereotype of the female intellectual, someone

[10] Carl Heymonds, *Eduard von Hartmann, Erinnerungen aus den Jahren 1868–1881* (Berlin: Duncker, 1882), 49.

[11] Heymonds, *Eduard von Hartmann,* 47.

[12] On Plümacher's life, see Rolf Kieser, *Olga Plümacher-Hünerwadel: Eine gelehrte Frau des neunzehnten Jahrhunderts* (Lenzburger: Lenzburger Ortsburgerkommission, 1990). Kieser's biography is excellent in uncovering the basic facts of Plümacher's life, but he does not discuss her intellectual achievements.

[13] O. Plümacher, "Pessimism," *Mind* 4 (1879): 68–89. The article is a critique of James Sully's *Pessimism: A History and a Criticism* (London: Henry King, 1877).

[14] This was the opinion of Arthur Drews, *Eduard von Hartmann's philosophisches System im Grundriss* (Heidelberg: Carl Winter, 1906), 59.

[15] Plümacher's husband, Eugen Plümacher, founded a Swiss colony in Grundy County, Tennessee. Plümacher lived there from 1869 to 1881, when she returned to Switzerland. Her husband abandoned her in Tennessee and moved to South America, where he later served as US consul in Maracaibo, Venezuela. On the Swiss colony in Tennessee, see Frances Helen Jackson, *The Swiss Colony at Gruetli* (Gruetli-Laager: Grundy County Swiss Historical Society, 2010). Plümacher returned to Tennessee in 1886 in the hope of curing her son's tuberculosis; but he died there in December of that year.

devoted to radical or progressive causes. Both were politically and socially conservative. They shared Hartmann's hostility to social democracy, and they saw themselves as protectors of culture against the masses. The great value of pessimism was that it discouraged the unrealistic aspirations of the working class, who believed that life could be improved through socialism. For some historians, such political views are reason enough to let someone disappear into the obscurity of the past. But it must be said in their defense: their achievements rise above politics; they deserve recognition for their own sake.

2 THE POSSIBILITY OF PESSIMISM

Of all the questions raised by the pessimism controversy, the most fundamental concerned the meaning and possibility of pessimism itself. Some critics held that the central thesis of pessimism—that nothingness is better than being—is meaningless or, at the very least, unverifiable. They argued that such a thesis amounts to metaphysics because it is a theory about the world as a whole or existence in general, for which there can be neither verification nor falsification. Clearly, though, the optimist could derive no polemical advantage from this argument. If it were correct, it would hold against the optimist as much as the pessimist. The argument implied that the whole attempt to determine the value of life—whether in positive or negative terms—cannot succeed because it transcends the limits of knowledge.

One of the first to make this criticism was Rudolf Haym, a prominent neo-Kantian, in an extensive early review of Hartmann's philosophy for the *Preußische Jahrbücher*.[16] Hartmann's central thesis that existence is worse than nonexistence, Haym charged, goes beyond the limits of all possible knowledge. "Who does not become dizzy," he asked, "with the demand to compare the existence of the world with its non-existence"?[17] We can compare one thing with another *within* the world, because both belong to a common genus and we have experience of both. "But the whole world itself!" How do we compare it with anything because we cannot have any possible experience of it. To determine which is better, being or nothingness, Haym argued, we need to have a standpoint beyond both, a privileged perspective where we could somehow *per impossibile* compare them against one another, as if they were species of some common genus or superbeing (*Ueberseiende*).[18] But what is this superbeing? We cannot give it any specific content, and so the comparison is meaningless for us.

---

[16] Rudolf Haym, "Die Hartmann'sche Philosophie des Unbewussten," *Preußische Jahrbücher* 31 (1873): 41–80, 109–139, 257–311. These articles were reprinted in book form as *The Hartmanian Philosophy of the Unconscious* (*Die Hartmann'schen Philosophie des Unbewussten*) (Berlin: Reimer, 1873). All references here are to the original article.

[17] Haym, "Die Hartmann'sche Philosophie des Unbewussten," 258.

[18] Haym, "Die Hartmann'sche Philosophie des Unbewussten," 258.

In her *Pessimism and Its Opponents*, Taubert carefully responded to Haym's objection.[19] She insisted that there is no need to postulate a standpoint beyond the world to compare life with death, existence with nonexistence. This objection derives from the failure to distinguish between life and the *concept* of life, Taubert insists. The philosopher is not comparing life with death but only the *concepts* of life and death, which are easily comparable because they are only abstractions (PG 23). The comparison of the concept of life with its negation is not problematic, since to have any concept at all is to have also the concept of its negation. To have the concept of existence or life itself we simply have to abstract from their particular features. Just as a person with hearing and sight can imagine the world of someone deaf and blind, so philosophers can imagine that the world they know with all their senses does not exist (PG 23).

Whatever the merits of Haym's argument against metaphysics, Hartmann and Taubert responded that they are ultimately irrelevant to the central claims of pessimism (PG 11–12).[20] Pessimism, they stressed, is not a metaphysics, and it does not even presuppose one; it is rather a strictly empirical theory about the unattainability of happiness and the prevalence of suffering in life. Hartmann and Taubert insisted that their pessimism is essentially a eudemonistic theory, according to which there is more pain and suffering than pleasure and happiness in life. Whether this is so, they argued, does not demand going beyond the realm of human experience, because it is a thesis true or false of human experience itself. To determine whether it is true or false, we only have to see whether there is, for most people most of the time, more pain than pleasure, more suffering than happiness. If that is so, then we have reason to conclude from experience itself whether life is worth living or not. With this response, Hartmann and Taubert believed, they had ducked the charges of metaphysics.

It is necessary to add, however, that this attempt to escape metaphysics was really a tactical maneuver to avoid critical blows. For Hartmann's and Taubert's more considered position was that ethics and metaphysics are inseparable, that human beings cannot know the meaning and value of life without knowing their place in the universe as a whole. Sure enough, Taubert reminded Hartmann's critics that his pessimism was the necessary result of his metaphysical principles (PG 26); and Hartmann, despite all his disclaimers, never tired of stressing that ethics without metaphysics "floats in the air."[21]

---

[19] All references to Taubert refer to *Der Pessimismus und seine Gegner* (Berlin: Duncker, 1873), and will appear in parentheses in the body of the text as PG followed by page numbers.

[20] Hartmann, "Ist der Pessimismus wissenschaftlich zu begründen?," *Philosophische Monatshefte* 15 (1879): 589–612. See also Hartmann, "Die Stellung des Pessimismus in meinem philosophischen System," in *Zur Geschichte und Begründung des Pessimismus*, Zweite Auflage (Leipzig: Hermann Haacke, 1891): 18–28. (This article appears only in the second edition of this work.)

[21] See Hartmann's comment in *Phänomenologie des sittlichen Bewusstseins* (Berlin: Wegweiser Verlag, 1924), 610.

3 THE EUDEMONIC CALCULUS

Granted that pessimism is not committed to a metaphysics to determine the value of life, Hartmann's critics were still not satisfied. They also questioned his attempt to measure the value of life in empirical terms according to pleasure and pain alone. All kinds of objections were raised against his eudemonic standards and measurements. His critics were opposed to his conception of pleasure, to how he measured pleasure and pain, and to the consequences he drew from his measurements. Against this barrage of objections, Taubert and Plümacher rushed to Hartmann's defense.

A common objection against Hartmann's eudemonic calculus was that it is pseudo-scientific, presupposing the comparability of incommensurable values. If we consider all the different kinds of value in life, this objection went, it becomes impossible to compare and summarize them, so that we can never say that misery preponderates over happiness.[22]

Hartmann's response to this objection was to stress that only the *quantitative* aspects of pleasure and pain are relevant to assessing the value of life as a whole.[23] He readily admits that sensations have a qualitative dimension which makes them incommensurable with one another; but he still insists that in determining their pleasure or pain alone, we can abstract from their content or qualitative dimension and consider strictly their quantitative one, that is, their intensity and duration. Just as we can determine whether on a given tabletop the weight of the pears is greater than that of the apples—however different pears are from apples—so we can determine whether different sensations bring more pleasure over pain. If the sum of pleasure in the world is negative, then we have to accept pessimism, which is then an inductive truth based on experience alone.

This reply did not silence Hartmann's critics. In his *World Misery and Pain* (*Weltelend und Weltschmerz*, 1872),[24] Jürgen Bona Meyer, a neo-Kantian critic, insisted that in calculating the value of life one still could not leave out the qualitative dimension of pleasure and pain. Not all pleasures and pains are on the same footing, and some pleasures are higher and better than others, just as some pains are lower and worse than

---

[22] For this objection, see Johannes Volkelt, *Das Unbewusste und der Pessimismus* (Berlin: F. Henschel, 1873), 286–287; Julius Duboc, "Eduard von Hartmann's Berechnung des Weltelends," *Deutsche Warte* 6 (1874): 350–361; Adolf Horwicz, "Die psychologische Begründung des Pessimismus," *Philosophische Monatshefte* 16 (1880): 264–88; Friedrich Paulsen, "Gründen und Ursachen des Pessimismus," *Deutsche Rundschau* 48 (1886): 360–381; and Albert Weckesser, *Der empirische Pessimismus in seinem Zusammenhang im System von Eduard von Hartmann* (Bonn: Universitäts-Buchdruckerei von Carl Georgi, 1885).

[23] See his "Ist der Pessimismus wissenschaftlich zu begründen?," in *Zur Geschichte und Begründung des Pessimismus* (1880): 65–85.

[24] Jürgen Bona Meyer, *Weltelend und Weltschmerz. Eine Rede gegen Schopenhauer's und Hartmann's Pessimismus* (Bonn: Marcus, 1872). See also his argument in *Arthur Schopenhauer als Mensch und Denker* (Berlin: Carl Haber, 1872), 44–55.

others. It is not as if we can measure pleasure and pain in precise independent units, and as if one unit of pleasure balances one unit of pain. It is just a fact, Meyer pointed out, that people endure great pains for the sake of higher pleasures. Haym too thought it a mistake to ignore the qualitative dimension of pleasure and pain.[25] The price of ignoring that dimension, he argued, is a completely abstract and artificial comparison which has nothing to do with the real values of life, which lie in the realm of quality and particularity.[26] Haym also accused Hartmann of having a much too sensual and physical conception of pleasure, because only such a conception allowed for precise calculation and measurement.

Taubert did her best to defend Hartmann's eudemonic calculus against these objections (PG 20). Part of her defense was purely methodological. It was Hartmann's aim to reach some general conclusions about the balance between pleasure and pain in the world; and to do that he had to abstract entirely from the qualitative dimension of pleasure and pain. What all pleasures have in common simply as feelings is their *quantitative* dimension, their intensity and duration; they differ from one another in terms of their qualities or contents alone. We have to take quality into account, then, only when we consider specific kinds of pleasures and attempt to make comparisons between instances of them. Though perfectly correct to make this point, Taubert failed to address the wider issue it raised: how accurate is our account of the value of life if we consider solely the quantitative dimension of pleasure?

Taubert was indignant about Haym's claim that Hartmann had a physical or sensual concept of pleasure (PG 21). This was an old "priest's trick" (*Pfaffenkniff*), which tries to discredit eudemonism by claiming that it reduces all pleasure to sensuality. She pointed out that Hartmann recognized the positive pleasures of science, art, and religion, which he was far from reducing down to carnal pleasures. Haym's point, however, was that Hartmann had to treat pleasure as sensual or physical if it was to be measured purely quantitatively and taken into account by his calculus. To the extent that the pleasures of art, science and religion are not so measurable, they simply fall out of the calculus, and to that extent give an incomplete estimate of the pleasures of life.

Another issue in weighing the pleasures and pains in life arose concerning Hartmann's assessment of "the four great values": health, freedom, youth, and security. Hartmann had claimed that these values have a strictly negative or relative worth, because we appreciate them only when we are deprived of them; otherwise, we take them for granted, so that they give us only a "0" when measured by the utilitarian calculus. Although Meyer, Haym and Julius Duboc admitted that these values are indeed negative or relative, they also insisted that people are not as inclined to take them for granted as Hartmann supposed.[27] Everyone in life has experienced illness, oppression, and insecurity, and so they have great pleasure if they are removed. Meyer claimed that, even if

---

[25] Haym, "Die Hartmann'sche Philosophie des Unbewussten," 41–80, 109–139, 257–311, esp. 261–265.
[26] Haym, "Die Hartmann'sche Philosophie des Unbewussten," 263.
[27] Meyer, *Weltelend und Weltschmerz*, 18–19; Haym, "Die Hartmann'sche Philosophie des Unbewusstseins," 266–267; and Duboc, "Hartmann's Berechnung," 356–358.

we were not self-conscious of health, freedom, youth, and security, they should still be weighed heavily in any account of the value of life. "Happiness remains happiness, even when I do not repeat it hourly that it is happiness; it still remains happiness as a lasting source of pleasure."[28] In making this point, Meyer raised a general question that would loom larger in the course of the controversy: namely, to what extent must I be conscious of having a pleasure for it to be one?

Undaunted by these arguments, Taubert defended Hartmann's analysis of the four great values (PG 31). She admitted that we do not live, as Haym put it, in "an Epicurean middle world" where no one experiences illness, oppression, and insecurity. It is indeed often the case that we learn to treasure health, freedom, youth, and security. Nevertheless, it is still true that these are only relative or negative goods, that we value them only because we fear the opposite. Taubert also questioned Meyer's assumption that we can derive great pleasure from these values even if we are not conscious of them. It is "a bold assumption," she said, to think that there can be pleasures of which we are not conscious. If that were so, it would not help the optimist's case, because the pessimist might just as well refer to unconscious pain (PG 32).

4 PLÜMACHER'S COUNTERATTACK

After Taubert's *Pessimism and Its Opponents* appeared in 1873, there was no lull in hostilities between the pessimists and their enemies. Taubert's book was more a provocation than a pacification of Hartmann's critics, whose attacks only grew in number, depth, and intensity. Taubert's early death in May 1877 left Hartmann surrounded by his foes and bereft of his most loyal ally. He was in desperate need of aid to carry on the struggle for the pessimist cause.

That aid finally came in the early 1880s with Olga Plümacher's book *Pessimism Past and Present,* which was first published in late 1883.[29] This book is not only a history but also a defense of pessimism. Its second part is a systematic and thorough examination of all the latest criticisms of pessimism, especially those which had appeared since Taubert's book. Because it is so solid and lucid, Plümacher's counterattack is worthy of careful examination. One of its avid readers was Nietzsche, whose copy was filled with annotations.[30]

Plümacher first raised the question whether individual differences regarding pleasure are so great that they invalidate any generalization about pleasure and pain among

[28] Meyer, *Weltelend und Weltschmerz,* 19.

[29] References to Plumacher's book will be made to the second edition, *Der Pessimismus in Vergangenheit und Gegenwart* (Heidelberg: Georg Weiß Verlag, 1888), and will be appear in parentheses in the body of the text as PVG followed by page numbers.

[30] See Thomas Brobjer, *Nietzsche's Philosophical Context* (Urbana: University of Illinois Press, 2008), 99.

human beings (PVG 181–184). She admitted that, within certain limits, people were indeed very different. What gave one person pleasure gave another displeasure. Such differences in feeling depend on a host of factors, namely, on age, physical constitution, state of health, custom, education, and social class. Nevertheless, Plümacher insisted that the differences were not limitless, that they were not so great that they were absolute (PVG 182). There is a certain point at which all people, regardless of differences in physical constitution, feel pain. No one, for example, can bear putting their hands in boiling water. This is sufficient, Plümacher maintained, to justify the kind of generalizations that the pessimist needs to make about life. All that matters in the first instance is simple pleasure or pain; and only in the second instance does one have to examine variations in the stages of psychic and physical organization (PVG 183). To take these variations into account, one has to specify the circumstances and conditions under which the feelings of pleasure or pain take place; and the more specific these are, the more reliable the generalizations will be, holding for all people regardless of nationality, race, and social class (PVG 183–184).

Plümacher then examined the objection that reliable generalizations are impossible because the values of different pleasures are incommensurable (PVG 184–190). Even if all people feel the same upon the same stimulus and occasion, there is still the problem that feelings arising from different stimuli and occasions will be too heterogeneous to make comparisons and reliable generalizations about them. In response to this objection, Plümacher dug in her heels and fell back to the old line of Maupertuis.[31] It was already clear to him in the eighteenth century, she pointed out, that all pleasures and pains are alike as simple feelings, regardless of their cause and content; they differ from one another in their duration and intensity alone (PVG 184). The pessimist does not deny that there are great qualitative differences between feelings, and that as such they are incommensurable with one another (PVG 184–185). But his chief aim is to determine simply whether there is more pleasure than pain in the world, and to that end he does not have to consider the qualitative dimension of pleasure and pain at all (PVG 185). The great axiological question of the value of life depends on *how much* pleasure or pain is present, regardless of its origins and content (PVG 186). This point is decisive, Plümacher insists, against all Hartmann's critics. Their objections against pessimism, she opined, have not progressed beyond the days of Maupertuis (PVG 185). They think that Hartmann has to make qualitative comparisons between different pleasures; but it is precisely this qualitative dimension from which the pessimist abstracts in order to make comparisons between amounts of pleasure (PVG 187).

---

[31] Though she did not explicitly cite it, Plümacher probably meant Pierre Louis Moreau de Maupertuis, *Essai de philosophie morale* (Berlin: Akademie der Wissenschaften, 1749), which argued that pleasures and pains could be compared purely quantitatively in terms of intensity and duration, and that, because pains outnumbered pleasures, nonbeing was preferable to being. Maupertuis was thus a pessimist avant la lettre. Hartmann was well aware of Maupertuis's work and discusses it in *Zur Geschichte und Begründung des Pessimismus* (Berlin: Duncker, 1880), 21.

While Plümacher helped to clarify the kinds of generalizations the pessimist wants to make, she had also inadvertently revealed a weakness in his argument. Granted that there is much more pain than pleasure in life, this still does not warrant general conclusions about its value. For that reckoning, the critics insisted, still leaves out the qualitative dimension, which cannot be so easily ignored. What if the few pleasures of life, though greatly outnumbered by pain, are of a much greater *quality* or *value* than the pains? Such pleasures might make life worth living after all. Take the case of a man who is ill with cancer and who constantly suffers great pain; nevertheless, he chooses to go on living because of his love for his children, which is a joy of such value to him that all his suffering pales in comparison.

In the course of her argument against Hartmann's critics, Plümacher made some major concessions about the measurement of pleasure and pain. She conceded that there is no "feeling meter" or "sensation scale" even for the intensity of pleasure and pain. Many feelings, even those like one another, remain incommensurable. One could not say, for example, that the feelings of a mother for the loss of her child are more intense than those for the death of her husband, or that the feelings for the loss of a fiancé are less intense than those for the death of a sibling. All that one can say in these cases is that these experiences are intensely painful, even if one cannot make precise comparisons. She also accepted the point that pleasure and pain cannot be added or subtracted like quantities in mathematics.[32] If I have a pleasure that I assign the value of +10, and then I have a pain that I assign the value of - 5, it does not follow that I am left with a pleasure of + 5 and that the pain somehow disappears (PVG 187). Pleasures and pains do not relate to one another in such precise increments, Plümacher realized, and so she states that they are "overleaping" (*überspringende*), that is, their values increase not by continuous increments but by whole quantities, so that a pleasure can completely vanquish a pain or conversely. Hence the pessimist cannot make exact mathematical calculations after all (PVG 188).

Plümacher did not fail to respond to the objection that pessimism rests upon a false theory of feeling (PVG 195–199). Two critics, Hugo Sommer and Johannes Rehmke, had contended that Hartmann went astray in basing all pleasure upon the will, and that he neglects other sources of pleasure which have no connection with the will.[33] Among these pleasures are aesthetic ones, so that it seems as if Hartmann had failed to consider the entire aesthetic dimension of life, one of the most important sources of pleasure, and one that sometimes makes life worth living. Plümacher's first line of defense against this objection is that feeling remains the same—it has the same qualitative and quantitative properties—whether or not it derives from the will (PVG 195). The psychological theory about the origin of pleasure makes no difference to the pessimist, then, who in his calculations counts all pleasure and pains, whatever their source (PVG 196). Rehmke's

---

[32] This was the point of Horwicz, "Begründung," 267–270.

[33] See Hugo Sommer, *Der Pessimismus und die Sittenlehre* (Haarlem: De Erven F. Bohn, 1882), 31, 41, 83; and Johannes Rehmke, *Die Philosophie des Weltschmerzes* (St. Gallen: Zollikofer, 1876), 44–45. A similar point is made by Haym, "Die Hartmann'sche Philosophie des Unbewussten," 68, 262.

theory that there are some pleasures that are independent of the will derives all its plausibility, Plümacher argued, from limiting the will down to its conscious dimension alone, though the causes of pleasure are largely subconscious (PVG 197). She admitted, however, that it is difficult to demonstrate Hartmann's theory that all pleasure ultimately originates in the will, because, in some cases, it is difficult to determine whether the will is always really present as a source of pleasure (PVG 198).

The most interesting phase of Plümacher's counterattack is her reply to those critics who maintain that pessimism is a pathological response to the tragedies of life (PVG 199–210). According to these critics,[34] pessimism is the product of a morbid sensitivity or choleric temperament which exaggerates the negative side of life. A more normal sensitivity and temperament would also grasp the positive side of life, which it would not allow to be overshadowed by its negative side. Plümacher is willing to concede such an abnormal sensitivity and choleric temperament in the cases of Schopenhauer and Julius Bahnsen; but nothing of the kind is to be found in Hartmann, she assures us, whose temper, judging from his writings and autobiography, is sanguine and equable. Plümacher then turns this objection against the optimists: are they not the blind and obtuse ones who fool themselves (and others) because they cannot appreciate the tragedy of life? Is it not the case, she asked, that it takes a good dosage of obtuseness and superficiality (*Stumpfsinn und Leichtsinn*) to keep melancholy and worry within bounds? Whoever has suffered real tragedy in this life knows that all that quietens and softens their justified grief and sorrow is "a mild forgetting," "a sweet melancholy," which derives from the instinct for self-preservation (201). If we do not forget, if we do not grow numb, the sorrows of life destroy us.

Among those who charged pessimism with morbid pathology was Eugen Dühring, whom Plümacher duly subjects to scrutiny (PVG 201–202). Dühring saw pessimism as an ideology of the idle, decadent, and vain who no longer care about life. Theirs is a "Katzenjammerphilosophie," which arises from overindulgence in liquor and narcotics. The only defensible form of pessimism for Dühring is a "pessimism of indignation" (*Entrüstungspessimismus*) because it recognizes the social and political causes of human misery and motivates people to do something against them.

Unfortunately, Plümacher, like Hartmann, does not engage in a detailed discussion about the merits of Dühring's optimism, and she limits herself only to a few general comments (PVG 202). She maintains that Dühring stays only on the surface of the problems of suffering and evil; his pessimism of indignation goes only so far in recognizing the tragedy of life, which does not have only social and political causes. In its naïve belief in the human causes of evil and the power of human beings to remedy them, Plümacher riposted, Dühring's philosophy reveals itself to be an obsolete standpoint, a relic of the French Enlightenment.

---

[34] Plümacher considers the views of Eugen Dühring, *Der Werth des Lebens*, zweite Ausgabe (Leipzig: Fues Verlag, 1877), 1–37; and Julius Duboc, *Der Optimismus als Weltanschauung* (Bonn: Emil Strauß, 1881), 92–108.

5 THE PROBLEM OF WORK

Whatever the problems with his general concept of pleasure, Hartmann held that the case for pessimism has to be based on induction, on the consideration of the particular aspects of life. The pessimist could draw his dreary conclusions about the value of existence only after the examination of each particular aspect. Withholding all general principles, he had to consider each aspect for its own sake. Hence the pessimist controversy covered a wide array of special topics, such as work, art, and love.

One topic that became an intense battleground between the pessimists and their critics was work (*Arbeit*). Obviously, work is a crucial theme in the pessimist's portrait of life. Our days are filled with work, nine to five most days of the week for many of us, so if work proves to be a negative value in the general accounting of life, the scales will be tipped heavily in the pessimist's favor. Mainly for this reason, Hartmann's analysis of work in the *Philosophy of the Unconscious* is very bleak, even cynical.[35] There can be no doubt, Hartmann declares, that work is an evil for whoever must engage in it. Nobody works if they do not have to, and we do it only to avoid a greater evil, whether that be poverty or boredom. So work is not an end in itself, but only a means to other ends. Usually, work is the price someone must pay to have a secure existence; but that is not a positive but a negative good, that is, one to avoid greater evils; and, furthermore, it is a good (unlike health and youth) that we must purchase through much pain. We also must not underestimate, Hartmann adds, the misery work often imposes upon us. He then cites Schopenhauer's lines about the factory work of five-year-olds, who sit twelve to fourteen hours a day doing repetitive tasks, and who thus "buy very dearly the mere pleasure of drawing breath."[36] The best we can do with work, Hartmann thinks, is to get used to it, to make it habitual, so that we become just like the cart horse who leans to bear his load.

For Hartmann's critics, this was an unduly grim, wildly inaccurate conception of work. Haym thought that Hartmann's conception was suitable only for the galley slave, and that he completely neglected the satisfaction work gives us in exercising our powers and in realizing our will.[37] Work, Meyer argued in a similar vein, is not simply a means to other ends but it is a pleasure in itself, because it activates our powers, directs our energies, and satisfies our human need for "the good, beautiful and true."[38] Of course, there is toil and trouble connected with work; but these negative factors do not outweigh the positive ones, and eventually they become part of the pleasure. By exaggerating the negative aspects of work, Hartmann falsifies one of the chief sources of human happiness: pleasure in acting (*Freude am Thun*).

---

[35] Hartmann, *Philosophie des Unbewussten* (1870), CXII, 584–585.

[36] See Schopenhauer, "Von der Nichtigkeit und dem Leiden des Lebens," *Die Welt als Wille und Vorstellung, Sämtliche Werke*, ed. Wolfgang Freiherr von Löhneysen (Stuttgart: Insel, 1968), II, 740.

[37] Haym, "Die Hartmann'sche Philosophie des Unbewussten," 267.

[38] Meyer, *Weltelend und Weltschmerz*, 17.

None of these objections impressed Taubert.[39] She was skeptical whether the alleged pleasure in work came strictly from work itself. There are so many other sources of pleasure, she argued, that it is not likely that it comes from working alone. One must also consider the greater evils that work avoids, namely, the absence of boredom and idleness; the means it provides for obtaining other things, namely, the happiness of one's family; and the anticipation of the rewards for work (PG 33–34). When we keep in mind such factors, the pleasure in work itself seems to evaporate; hence we have to acknowledge, Taubert insisted, that "the activity of work in and for itself is onerous and unpleasant" (PG 35). In responding to Haym and Meyer, Taubert went on to mention another important factor that diminished the value of work in modern life: the division of labor. In the past a craftsman could derive great pleasure from creating something for which he contributed all the parts and labor; in producing it, his talents and skills would be exercised. But such work has been superseded by modern forms of production, which make each worker engage in a single monotonous task. It is impossible for a modern worker to take pleasure in his work when he does one small task over and over again, and when he has little role in a product's design and mode of production. If Haym only considered the consequences of labor in modern forms of production, Taubert tartly retorted, he would have refrained from his tasteless comment about galley labor.

An important voice in these exchanges about the meaning of work was Johannes Volkelt, a young neo-Kantian and social democrat, whose book *The Unconscious and Pessimism* (*Das Unbewusste und der Pessimismus*, 1873) appeared shortly after Taubert's *Pessimism and Its Opponents*.[40] Volkelt, like Haym and Meyer, felt that Hartmann had given a much too negative portrait of work and its value in life. Work is the means by which we exercise, and become self-conscious of, our powers; and in exercising and becoming self-conscious of them, we gain a sense of our self-worth, which is a great source of inner pleasure. Of course, work involves challenges and difficulties; but it is precisely in overcoming them that we develop our powers and grow in self-confidence and self-consciousness. Volkelt did not underestimate, however, the problems posed for work by modern methods of production. All the problems raised by Taubert he fully recognized. Work had become dull, routine, mindless, and even degrading in the modern division of labor. But, Volkelt explains, these problems are not intrinsic to work itself but only its present form. Many of them will disappear in the socialist state of the future. Although there will still be forms of mass production and a division of labor, working hours will be much shorter and working conditions much better; more important, everyone will receive a liberal education where they will learn to develop all their faculties and not only those needed on the factory floor. There will be not only bread for everyone, but, as Heine put it, "roses and myrtle, beauty and pleasure."

For Taubert, however, the socialist state is no solution to the problems of modern work and production.[41] She shared Hartmann's conviction that a socialist state, which

---

[39] See Taubert, *Der Pessimismus und seine Gegner*, III, "Die private Güter und die Arbeit," 33–36.

[40] Johannes Volkelt, *Das Unbewusste und der Pessimismus* (Berlin: F. Henschel, 1873), 287–292.

[41] See Taubert, *Der Pessimismus und seine Gegner*, "X: Die Glückseligkeit als historische Zukunftsperspektive," 101–122, esp. 114–116.

promised happiness for everyone, is an illusion. There will always be social and economic inequality because resources are always scarce, and because people are born with very unequal capacities to attain them. A socialist state, which would control all aspects of the economy, and which would impose social and economic equality, would be a threat to property, liberty, and talent. Remarkably, Taubert and Volkelt had a very similar diagnosis of the social problem: the modern economy has increased the standard of living for everyone, especially the working classes; but it has also increased their needs and expectations beyond the means of the government and economy to satisfy them.[42] This has created a crisis, because the people now demand more than they can possibly have. Nevertheless, despite their common diagnosis, Volkelt und Taubert had very different solutions to the crisis. For Volkelt, the solution is socialism; but for Taubert, it is pessimism, because it alone exposes the illusions of socialism, the pointless striving for happiness in life.

An interesting take on Taubert's solution to the social problem was given by Georg Peter Weygoldt in his *Critique of Philosophical Pessimism* (*Kritik des philosophischen Pessimismus*, 1875).[43] Weygoldt shared Taubert's conservative views, and he too was a critic of socialism. He believed that the demand for higher wages and better working conditions, the result of socialist agitators among the workers, had become excessive. Because of the increased expectations and demands of the working class, and because of the limited means of satisfying them, discontent was growing and revolution was on the horizon. But, for Weygoldt, pessimism was not the solution to that looming danger but part of its cause, chiefly because the pessimists had painted such a bleak portrait of labor. Work has an intrinsic value, and people should work because it is a pleasure; but because the pessimists have portrayed work as an evil to be avoided, they have encouraged the workers to demand a higher reward for their sacrifices. Nowhere are the dangers of pessimism more evident, Weygoldt contended, than in its conception of work. By describing work in such negative terms, the pessimists have encouraged the very evil they so deeply fear: revolution.

In 1884, a decade after Taubert's death, and well after the initial dust of the controversy had settled, Plümacher provided a new analysis of the concept of work from a pessimist perspective (PVG 210–216). She took a broad and mature view of the topic, one which attempted to take into account all that the critics had written, but also one which could reveal the strengths of the pessimist's case. Plümacher began with a general definition of work. In its initial natural form, work is a species of movement, one where the goal expresses a physiological need; and insofar as work provides for a person's needs, it can be an important source of pleasure. To that extent, Plümacher conceded, Hartmann is "perhaps" wrong to underestimate the degree of pleasure that can be involved in work

---

[42] See Johannes Volkelt, "Die Entwicklung des modernen Pessimismus," *Im neuen Reich* II (1872): 952–968. Taubert cites p. 967 of this article, which outlines Volkelt's very similar take on the social problem, but she takes exception to the conclusions that Volkelt draws from it.

[43] Georg Peter Weygoldt, *Kritik des philosophischen Pessimismus der neuesten Zeit* (Leiden: Brill, 1875), 101–104.

(PVG 211). However, it is wrong to assume, as the optimists do, that the sheer activity of work is intrinsically pleasant. Work is often unpleasant for many reasons; it involves more movement than necessary for a person's needs; it requires too much of one kind of movement; or it inhibits other forms of movement (PVG 211). All too often work develops only one side of one's nature, leaving the other sides frustrated or atrophied. Although Plümacher conceded that Hartmann might have exaggerated the negative aspects of work, she stressed that he never meant to demean its value. He had always emphasized its importance as a means for realizing higher social ends; and in that respect he had given work a much greater value than his critics, who measured its worth solely in terms of the pleasure it gave to the individual (PVG 212). Critics like Weygoldt were completely unfair, then, when they charged Hartmann and Taubert with demeaning the value of work.

Recognizing the value of work does not mean, Plümacher was eager to explain, regarding it as an intrinsically pleasant activity (PVG 212, 214). The moral, social, and cultural value of work is one thing, its eudemonic value for the individual is quite another. To be sure, people often take pleasure in knowing their work to be of moral, social, and cultural value; but that is often small compensation for their trouble and toil. In many cases all the effort and struggle in trying to do good comes to nothing because circumstances make it impossible to realize one's plans (PVG 212). For the philosopher, who takes a broad historical perspective, work plays an important role in advancing social ends and world progress. But for the individual, who sees only particular ends in concrete circumstances, work is often just a grueling and unpleasant task (PVG 214).

Plümacher admitted that work sometimes could be very rewarding and pleasant. But to be so, three conditions had to be fulfilled: (1) the activity of one's vocation balances with one's desire for action; (2) the activity also promotes one's personal ends; and (3) the activity has a higher meaning as something socially useful (PVG 212). But the problem is that these conditions are rarely fulfilled; in most cases, where a worker has to earn the means of subsistence, the demands of work exceed the natural need for movement and require a great expenditure of physical and psychic energy. The sad truth of the matter is that, for the great majority of people, the old dictum is sadly true: "if you do not put your life into it [i.e. the work], you will never receive it" (PVG 213).[44] It was for this reason that the goal of the great majority is not work but leisure; in other words, they work only so that they do not have to work anymore (PVG 215).

Plümacher regarded this situation as "a tragic contradiction of cultural life," and not as the temporary result of a historical form of political or economic organization. She had sympathy with the condition of the workers, whose wages could barely cover their needs, and whose work was often exhausting and meaningless to them (PVG 213). But she could see no social or political solution to it and seemed to disapprove of social democracy as a remedy (PVG 213). In one remarkable passage, she seems to admit that the

---

[44] Plümacher implies this is an old saying, which goes in the original German: "Und setzt ihr das Leben nicht selber ein, nicht wird euch das Leben gewonnen sein."

social problem is the result of defective social, economic, and political organization. She writes that "in our cultural situation" the poor work too much for their reward. It then turns out, however, that she thinks that their labors are more the result of climate and geography than politics. With her experience in Tennessee in mind, she noted that in many parts of the southern United States people can earn a living from the soil without much trouble or labor.

Work, Plümacher explained, is not something accidental or arbitrary in the human predicament, but something natural and necessary. It lies in the plan of the world as much as breathing in the plan of the organism. This plan is not something imposed upon us but lies deep within our inner nature (PVG 214). In this respect the optimists are right to speak about "the blessings of work"; hence Hartmann, Plümacher implies, was one-sided in seeing work only in negative terms as something we want to avoid (PVG 214). Nevertheless, though work in one respect fulfills our inner selves and our natural needs, in another respect it demands self-denial and even self-destruction (PVG 214). The fact that work is a blessing does not speak against but for pessimism, Plümacher insisted, because that blessing demands nothing less than "the forgetting of one's self and one's existence," "self-alienation through the mechanical expenditure of energy" (PVG 215).

6 Aesthetic Redemption

In the course of their polemics against Hartmann's pessimism, Jürgen Bona Meyer and Rudolf Haym had both made a point of mentioning the many pleasures in life that Hartmann had left out of his equations. Almost en passant both of them cited the pleasure we derive from nature (*Naturgenuss*), and they stressed its importance for human well-being.[45] It seemed a serious omission that Hartmann never considered this pleasure, especially given the importance that had been bestowed upon it since the romantic era. For Schiller, Goethe, Herder, and the romantics, contact with nature regenerates and inspires human beings. One escapes the drudgery and despair of life, which is the product of culture, by turning to nature. While culture divides us, nature makes us whole again. But if this is so—if nature really restores us, makes us whole and happy—then the pessimist's case against life needs significant qualification.

Even though made en passant, this objection did not go unnoticed. It was fully appreciated by Taubert, who devoted a full chapter to it in *Pessimism and its Opponents*.[46]

It is true, Taubert admitted, that Hartmann, in calculating the pleasures of life, had failed to consider those we derive from nature. But then, she added, he also did

---

[45] Meyer, "Weltelend und Weltschmerz," 20; and Haym, "Die Hartmann'sche Philosophie des Unbewussten," 275. The same point was made in much greater detail by Volkelt in his *Das Unbewusste und der Pessimismus*, 294–298. Though published in the same year as Taubert's work, Taubert does not mention it.

[46] Taubert, *Der Pessimismus und seine Gegner*, VI: "Der Naturgenuss," 55–62.

not mention the suffering often caused by nature, namely, volcanoes, earthquakes, hurricanes, and floods. And that suffering is very great indeed. In Japan millions have lost their lives from earthquakes; in Bengal 10,000 die every year from tiger attacks; and in sailing across the Atlantic, thousands of ships have been lost. So, as these facts attest, nature does not only heal us; she also destroys us. If any objection is to be made against Hartmann, then, it is that he failed to consider such a weighty argument *in favor of* his pessimism (PG 56).

If we find nature beautiful, Taubert went on, that is only because we read our feelings and purposes into it (PG 58, 61). The peace, tranquility and harmony of nature is really only an illusion that we create to calm and charm ourselves. The "laughing meadows" conceal as much suffering as "the torment of the cities"; and "the peace of the night" is the occasion for predators to stalk their prey. A view of a forest from a distance might be beautiful and uplifting; but it is an illusion to think that its denizens are happier than people in the cities. One creature is the prey of another, and thousands of innocent creatures lose their lives from hunger and cold. There is terror, need, struggle in the forest just as in the city.

Taubert regarded pleasure in nature as a fiction because it is, in her view, more a cultural construction than a natural feeling (PG 56–57). Pleasure in nature is a very modern phenomenon, she pointed out, the product of the romantic age and Rousseau's rebellion against modern culture. We derive pleasure from nature only when we want to return to it; and we want to return to it only after we have become alienated from it in the first place. That alienation has been the product of modern urban life, which has enclosed man in a shell of art, technology, customs, and laws. The ancient Greeks felt no longing for nature because they were really part of it; and the medievals did not want to become one with nature because they saw their resting place in heaven. It was only after the infliction of the wounds of modern urban life that people began to long for nature. This only goes to show, Taubert believed, that pleasure in nature is really negative in value: we appreciate nature only if we do not have access to it (PG 57). Nature cannot be regarded, therefore, as a constant source of pleasure, especially for those who live close to it.

But even if we admit that nature is the source of pleasure in the modern age, Taubert continued, it still should not be given much weight in calculating the general value of life. Why? The problem is that this pleasure is becoming more and more rare and inaccessible for most people in contemporary life. Nature has been so polluted by modern industry and technology, it has been so trammeled and spoiled by human habitation, that there are few places left on earth that offer people true tranquility and beauty (PG 59). If we want to find unspoiled nature, we have to travel far to see it; and the further we have to travel, the more stress we have to endure before we get to it. We have to ask ourselves whether travelling to exotic locations to enjoy nature is worth all the trouble; in most cases, it would be more relaxing simply to stay at home (PG 60). What is the pleasure of the Alps if, to enjoy its occasional vistas, one has to endure poor food, rough roads, and dirty hotels? As the reader can see, all the arguments for stay-at-home vacations were already well in place in the nineteenth century.

So far the thrust of Taubert's case against Haym and Meyer is to show that pleasure in nature should not be given much weight on the scales of the value of life. That we take pleasure in nature is a fact that we should not dispute. But that pleasure is not natural and universal; it is not positive and constant; and it is not accessible or common. But, beside these points, Taubert had another kind of argument up her sleeve to show that pleasure in nature should not count as evidence against pessimism. The pessimist is in a better position than the optimist, she contended, to explain why we take pleasure in nature in the first place. That pleasure has its source in our longing to become one with the universe, in our striving to lose our individuality and to rest in peace "in the harbor of nothingness" (PG 57). If life were truly beautiful and desirable, as the optimist assures us, we would never feel this longing; we would not strive to lose our individuality; we would not feel separated from nature; and we would not want to return to her (58). The longing and striving to return to nature stand as evidence for the sorrow and suffering of our normal existence, where we are caught in the toils and troubles of our own individuality. So the pleasure we take in nature, properly examined and explained, turns out to be one of the strongest proofs for pessimism.

The dispute about pleasure in nature was only a foreshadowing, however, of a much bigger issue dividing Taubert and her critics. Haym's complaint about Hartmann's neglect of pleasure in nature had its source in a much broader and deeper criticism: that Hartmann had ignored the aesthetic dimension of life. Hartmann, he insisted, had "stubbornly closed his eyes to the aesthetic element,"[47] and he had done his utmost "to reduce the aesthetic to a minimum."[48] For Haym, this was a major weakness of Hartmann's pessimism, because the aesthetic dimension of life is proof that it is not a scene of sorrow and suffering. Beauty is a source and sign of pleasure, and the omnipresence of beauty is therefore proof of the happiness of life. "The existence of beauty in the world, and the sense for it, is the guarantee of all pleasure that exists, and it is an original phenomenon of pleasure. . . . The enjoyment of art is in truth striking testimony of happiness, which flows in streams through the veins of the earth."[49] A strikingly romantic sentiment from one of the greatest critics of romanticism![50]

Never one to shirk a challenge, Taubert engaged Haym's criticism in the very next chapter of *Pessimism and Its Opponents*.[51] Haym, she charged, had simply confused aesthetic pleasure with happiness. It is one thing to enjoy beauty; it is quite another to equate such enjoyment with happiness, with contentment in life. Even if one sees beauty everywhere, it does not follow that the world is a happy place. After all, beauty lies more in the mind of the perceiver than in things themselves. The conflation of beauty with

---

[47] Haym, "Die Hartmann'sche Philosophie des Unbewussten," 273.

[48] Haym, "Die Hartmann'sche Philosophie des Unbewussten," 275.

[49] Haym, "Die Hartmann'sche Philosophie des Unbewussten," 274.

[50] It is worth noting that Haym was the author of *Die romantische Schule* (Berlin: Gaertner, 1870), the first comprehensive scholarly account of the early romantic movement. Though Haym's treatment is sympathetic, it is often highly critical.

[51] See Tabuert, *Pessimismus und seine Gegner,* VII: "Die Glückseligkeit als ästhetische Weltanschauung," 63–84.

happiness becomes especially apparent, Taubert claimed, from the highest form of art, from tragedy, which depicts not the happiness but the suffering of humanity (PG 64). The purpose of art is to take us beyond the realm of ordinary life, where there is so much sorrow and suffering, and into a higher realm, where we can enjoy forms for their own sake (PG 65). It is art that gives human beings some consolation about the misery of life and that reconciles them to life through the magic of aesthetic illusion (PG 66–67).

Such views about the power of art sound strikingly Nietzschean, though it was probably only a coincidence that Nietzsche's *Geburt der Tragödie* had appeared just a year earlier.[52] Unlike Nietzsche, though, Taubert did not think that art could provide a path of redemption, a remedy for the sorrows and suffering of life. She doubted the possibility of "an aesthetic redemption of the world, that is, an overcoming of suffering through beauty" (PG 77). The problem with such a program, in her view, is that the aesthetic dimension of life is too rarified, accessible only to an elite few, the artist and the highly educated. The great mass of people are too poor and ignorant to appreciate beauty, and so this antidote for their toils and troubles lies out of reach. Haym, for his part, was not so skeptical about the powers of art. Though he admitted that beauty is fully appreciated by only a few, he still insisted that beauty is omnipresent in life and that everyone can take pleasure in it, at least to some degree.[53] But Taubert believed that Haym was too naïve and idealistic, that he had little conception of the poverty and weaknesses of the masses. He had underestimated how poor most people are, and how little time, energy, and money they have for the pleasures of art (PG 77). He was like Queen Antoinette recommending that the people should eat cake when they could not afford bread (PG 76).

The exchange between Taubert and Haym raised the question: why not aesthetic education? In that case the pessimist's reckoning about the value of life would have to be reformulated, throwing much more pleasure into his equations. Aesthetic education was indeed the idea behind Haym's thesis: "happiness is in truth an ethical-artistic task."[54] Haym's point is that beauty is not something given in human life, but that it is something we create by making our lives works of art. Through such an aesthetic education we give our lives a much greater value than they would otherwise have. Hartmann had treated beauty and happiness as a given, as if they were just handed down to us by fate; he had failed to appreciate the simple point behind the old adage that everyone is the forger of his own happiness.[55]

Aesthetic education, though, was not an ideal for which Taubert had much patience. She willfully misread Haym's remarks about it, interpreting them as a proposal for a eudemonistic ethic.[56] Haym had no such intention, and all her criticisms of his attempt

---

[52] Friedrich Nietzsche, *Die Geburt der Tragödie aus dem Geiste der Musik* (Leipzig: Ernst Wilhelm Fritzsch, 1872). Taubert never mentions Nietzsche in her book.

[53] Haym, "Die Hartmann'sche Philosophie des Unbewussten," 274.

[54] Haym, "Die Hartmann'sche Philosophie des Unbewussten," 276.

[55] Haym, 276, refers to the old German adage "Jeder ist seines Glückes Schmied."

[56] See Taubert, *Pessimismus und seine Gegner*, VIII, "Die Glückseligkeit als Tugend," 79–84.

to attach rewards to virtue were beside the point. We should not be misled by Taubert's apparent sympathy with the masses, as if she deplored their poverty and lack of education. The truth of the matter is that Taubert did not sympathize with the people but feared them. She stated that they were not really interested in art and the realm of the ideal, and that they were content with eating, drinking and material well-being (PG 77). Worst of all, their ambitions were to steal the property of the elite and privileged. Goaded by socialist agitators, their goal was complete social and political equality, a world where there be no place for art at all (PG 77).

Nearly a decade after Taubert's exchanges with Haym, Plümacher revisited the aesthetic question in her *Pessimism Past and Present*.[57] The charges against Hartmann for ignoring the aesthetic dimension of life had not abated, and the optimists continued to maintain that taking it into account would tip the eudemonic scales in their favor. Art and pleasure in nature—so the argument went—made life more pleasant than painful, and therefore worth living after all. Plümacher, however, remained skeptical of this argument. She insisted that pessimism does not exclude aesthetic contemplation, and that it can take account of the pleasure derived from it (PVG 227). But the question remained whether aesthetic pleasure really counts that much in weighing the general amount of pleasure versus pain in the world. The aesthetic realm, Plümacher conceded, is indeed very wide, extending to all kinds of objects and experiences. But the problem is that the pleasure of beauty is, for most people, very weak, fragile, and uncommon (PVG 231). To appreciate the fragility and weakness of beauty, one only had to go to a concert with a toothache, visit an art gallery with an upset stomach, or watch a sunset while seasick (PVG 231–232). So, even if the aesthetic realm is wide, the conditions for enjoying it are narrow (PVG 231). Such pleasure requires disinterested contemplation, which is a rare state of mind, one hard to attain and sustain in life (PVG 232). The aesthetic attitude demands tranquility and peace of mind, which are easily overturned by those passions that are inevitably involved in the usual business of life, namely, longing, fear, dread, and anxiety. Whoever insists upon having an entirely aesthetic existence would have to abandon the normal feelings of life and renounce "two-thirds of the richness of the life of the soul" (PVG 232). So, unlike Nietzsche, but like Taubert, Plümacher did not think that life could be made worth living as an aesthetic phenomenon.[58] Art was at best a faint and fleeting escape from the suffering of life, providing no hope for enduring redemption.

Such were some of the highlights of Taubert's and Plümacher's contributions to the pessimism controversy. What I have written here is only an illustration of a much wider and richer discussion, only parts of which I could reproduce here. It should be

---

[57] Plümacher, *Der Pessimismus in Vergangenheit und Gegenwart* (1888), VI, Cap. 8, 233–237.

[58] Plümacher does not respond to Nietzsche in *Der Pessimismus in Vergangenheit und Gegenwart*, though she does briefly refer to him. See PVG 176. She had certainly read him. In an early article, a survey of Hartmann's foes, she took into account Nietzsche's critique of Hartmann in *Unzeitgemässe Betrachtungen*. See Plümacher, "Die Philosophie des Unbewussten und ihre Gegner," *Unsere Zeit* 15 (1879): 321–345, esp. 329.

obvious, though, that these two female pessimists were worthy participants in the controversy, and that the great neglect of them has been nothing less than a sin against history.[59]

BIBLIOGRAPHY

Bacmeister, Albert. *Der Pessimismus und die Sittenlehre.* Haarlem: De Erven F. Bohn, 1882.

Bahnsen, Julius. *Der Widerspruch im Wissen und Wesen der Welt.* 2 vols. Berlin: Theobold Grieben, 1880–82.

Beiser, Frederick C. *Weltschmerz: Pessimism in German Philosophy, 1860–1900.* Oxford: Oxford University Press, 2016.

Brobjer, Thomas. *Nietzsche's Philosophical Context.* Urbana: University of Illinois Press, 2008.

Christ, Paul. *Der Pessimismus und die Sittenlehre.* Haarlem: De Erven F. Bohn, 1882.

Deussen, Paul. *Die Elemnte der Metaphysik.* Bonn: Marcus, 1876.

Drews, Arthur. *Eduard von Hartmanns philosophisches System im Grundriss.* Heidelberg: Carl Winter's Universitätsbuchhandlung, 1902.

Duboc, Julius. "Eduard von Hartmann's Berechnung des Weltelends." *Deutsche Warte* 6 (1874): 350–361.

Duboc, Julius. *Der Optimismus als Weltanschauung und seine religöse ethische Bedeutung.* Bonn: Emil Strauß, 1881.

Dühring, Eugen. *Der Werth des Lebens.* Zweite, völlig umgearbeitete und bedeutend vermehrte Auflage. Leipzig: Fues's Verlag, 1877.

Frauenstädt, Julius. *Briefe über die Schopenhauer'sche Philosophie.* Leipzig: Brockhaus, 1854.

Hartmann, Eduard von. "Ist der Pessimismus schädlich?" *Gegenwart* 16 (1879): 211–214, 233–335.

Hartmann, Eduard von. "Ist der Pessimismus wissenschaftliche zu begründen?" *Philosophische Monatshefte* 15 (1879): 589–612.

Hartmann, Eduard von. "Ist der pessimistische Monismus trostlos?" *Philosophische Monatshefte* 5 (1870): 21–41.

Hartmann, Eduard von. *Phänomenologie des sittlichen Bewusstseins.* Berlin: Duncker, 1879.

Hartmann, Eduard von. *Philosophie des Unbewussten. Versuch einer Weltanschauung.* Berlin: Duncker, 1859.

Hartmann, Eduard von. *Zur Geschichte und Begründung des Pessimismus.* Berlin: Duncker, 1880.

Haym, Rudolf. *Arthur Schopenhauer.* Berlin: Reimer, 1864.

Haym, Rudolf. "Die Hartmann'sche Philosophie des Unbewussten." *Preussische Jahrbücher* 31 (1873): 41–80, 109–139, 257–311.

Haym, Rudolf. *Die romantische Schule.* Berlin: Gaertner, 1870.

Heymonds, Carl. *Eduard von Hartmann. Erinnerungen aus den Jahren 1868–1881.* Berlin: Duncker, 1882.

Horwicz, Adolf. "Die psychologische Begründung des Pessimismus." *Philosophische Monatshefte* 16 (1880): 274–288.

---

[59] The account given here is a condensed version from chapter 8 of my book *Weltschmerz: Pessimism in German Philosophy, 1860–1900* (Oxford: Oxford University Press, 2016).

Jackson, Frances Helen. *The Swiss Colony at Gruetli*. Gruetli-Laager: Grundy County Swiss Historical Society, 2010.

Kieser, Rolf. *Olga Plümacher-Hühnerwadel: Eine gelehrte Frau des neunzehnten Jahrhunderts*. Lenzburg: Lenzburger-Ortsbürgerkommission, 1990.

Mainländer, Phillip. *Die Philosophie der Erlösung*. Berlin: Theobold Grieben, 1880.

Maupertuis, Pierre Louis. *Essai de philosophie morale*. Berlin: Akademie der Wissenschaften 1749.

Meyer, Jürgen Bona. *Weltelend und Weltschmerz: Eine Rede gegen Schopenhauer's und Hartmann's Pessimismus*. Bonn: Marcus, 1872.

Meyer, Jürgen Bona. "Weltlust und Weltleid." In *Probleme der Weltweisheit*, 2 vols., 253–295. Berlin: Allgemeiner Verein fur deutsche Literatur, 1887.

Nietzsche, Friedrich. *Die Geburt der Tragödie aus dem Geiste der Musik*. Leipzig: E. W. Fritzsch, 1872.

Pfleiderer, Edmund. *Der moderne Pessimismus*. Berlin: Carl Habel, 1875.

Plümacher, Olga. *Der Kampf um's Unbewusste*. Berlin: Duncker, 1881.

Plümacher, Olga. "Pessimism." *Mind* 4 (1879): 68–89.

Plümacher, Olga. *Der Pessimismus in Vergangenheit und Gegenwart*. Heidelberg: Georg Weiß Verlag, 1883. 2nd ed. 1888.

Plümacher, Olga. "Die Philosophie des Unbewussten und Ihre Gegner." *Unsere Zeit* 15 (1879): 321–345.

Plümacher, Olga. *Zwei Individualisten der Schopenhauer'sche Schule*. Berlin: Duncker,1882.

Rehmke, Johannes. *Der Pessimismus und die Sittenlehre*. Leipzig: Verlag von Julius Klinkhardt, 1882.

Reymond, M. *Das Buch vom gesuden und kranken Herrn Meyer*. Bern: Georg Frobeen & Cie., 1877.

Schopenhauer, Arthur. *Sämtliche Werke*. Edited by Wolfgang Freiherr von Löhneysen. 5 vols. Stuttgart: Insel, 1968.

Siebert, Otto. *Geschichte der neueren deutschen Philosophie seit Hegel*. Göttingen: Vandenhoeck & Ruprecht, 1898.

Sommer, Hugo. *Der Pessimismus und die Sittenlehre*. Haarlem: De Erven F. Bohn, 1882.

Sully, James. *Pessimism: A History and a Criticism*. London: Henry King, 1877.

Taubert, Agnes. *Der Pessimismus und seine Gegner*. Berlin: Duncker, 1873.

Taubert, Agnes. *Philosophie gegen naturwissenschaftliche Überhebung*. Berlin: Duncker, 1872.

Tautz, Theodor. *Der Pessimismus*. Karlsruhe: G. Braun'she Hofbuchhandlung, 1876.

Volkelt, Johannes. "Die Entwicklung des Modernen Pessimismus." *Im neuen Reich* 2 (1872): 287–292.

Volkelt, Johannes. *Unbewusste und der Pessimismus*. Berlin: F. Henschel, 1873.

Weckesser, Albert. *Der empirische Pessimismus in seinem metaphysisichen Zusammenhang im System von Eduard von Hartmann*. Bonn: Universitäts Buchdruckerei von Carl Georgi, 1885.

Weygoldt, G. P. *Kritik der philosophischen Pessimismus der neuesten Zeit*. Leiden: Brill, 1875.

Windelband, Wilhelm. "Pessimismus und Wissenschaft." *Der Salon für Literatur, Kunst und Gesellschaft* 2 (1877): 814–821, 951–957.

Windelband, Wilhelm. *Präludien*. Neunte Auflage. Tübingen: Mohr, 1924.

CHAPTER 22

··

THE EMERGENCE OF A PHENOMENOLOGY OF SPIRIT: 1910–1922

··

CLINTON TOLLEY

The early nineteenth century in modern German philosophy witnesses a movement away from the philosophy of "consciousness" (*Bewußtsein*) in Immanuel Kant (through Karl Reinhold and Johann Gottlieb Fichte) and toward the philosophy of "spirit" (*Geist*) in Georg Wilhelm Friedrich Hegel (and others).[1] Almost a century after Hegel's plea for this transformation in his 1807 *Phenomenology of Spirit*, a new "phenomenology" began to emerge in Germany from the experimental and "descriptive" psychology of the midcentury. Initially, however, in the 1880s–1900s the new phenomenology in its most well-known form—as articulated by Edmund Husserl, following Franz Brentano— would have likely seemed to Hegel a self-conscious regression back to a philosophy of consciousness, not least due to its increasing willingness to acknowledge its broad kinship to both Kant and Fichte, as well as to the then-contemporary neo-Kantians (such as Paul Natorp). As articulated in Husserl's 1913 *Ideas Pertaining to a Pure Phenomenology and Phenomenological Philosophy*, phenomenology establishes the "absolute" evidential (cognitive-theoretical) priority within philosophy of what is immediately given in consciousness, and then devotes itself primarily to the pure "description" of the fundamental structures of consciousness. Given its restriction of the domain of "first" philosophy, phenomenology considers consciousness almost entirely in abstraction from any real connection it might bear to either the natural world or to whatever substances ("spirits") or powers ("faculties") bring about (or "have") consciousness itself. More specifically, by design Husserl's work leaves mostly to one side, and in most cases explicitly "brackets," questions concerning: (1) the forms of consciousness which incorporate not

---

[1] For a brief historical overview of this development, see Clinton Tolley, "Representation, Consciousness, and Mind in German Idealism," in *Philosophy of Mind in the Nineteenth Century*, ed. S. Lapointe (London: Routledge, 2017), 23–41.

only a relation to truth and falsity (cognition, etc.) but to the good and the pleasant, and so on (that is, the volitional and the affective); (2). the real existent substantiality which has this structure and the causality which brings it about ("spirit"); (3) the intersubjective and social existence out of which ("factically," "historically") consciousness arises; and (4) the possibility of a spiritual existence which is even more "absolute" (and yet perhaps still, somehow, personal) than anything that is immediately ("absolutely") given in consciousness.

As recent scholarship has helped to bring out, however, an exclusive focus on Husserl's 1913 *Ideas* as exemplary of the new phenomenology—however tempting it may be, given its impressively systematic ambition and its pervasive influence throughout the midcentury to follow—ultimately gives a misleading impression as to the true range of concerns of the new phenomenological movement and its philosophical trajectory in the first decades of the twentieth century. First, it is increasingly well-documented that, in his lectures and unpublished manuscripts from the early 1910s forward, Husserl himself works to begin to incorporate many of the topics central to the philosophy of spirit—including in manuscripts for a projected second volume of *Ideas* (which ultimately did not appear until after his death), and also, from 1913 onward, lectures which explicitly include "Spirit" in their titles.[2] What is even less well-known, especially outside of students and scholars of the phenomenological movement,[3] is that, around the same time (in some cases, even earlier), others working in the phenomenological tradition— especially in and around the University of Munich—were already exploring the very themes put to one side in Husserl's early published writings. Anchored in large part by the pioneering work of the experimental and theoretical psychologist Theodor Lipps, the contributions from Munich in the early 1900s also included work by Alexander Pfänder on the phenomenology of "willing" (1900) and "moral sentiment" (Gesinnung) (1913/16), work by Moritz Geiger (in 1911 and 1913) on the phenomenology of "feeling" along with "aesthetic" phenomena, and also what were perhaps the most widely read outside of Munich, the contributions by Max Scheler (1913–16) to the phenomenology of "sympathy" and of "personality." In fact, several of these contributions (by Pfänder, Geiger, Scheler) were published in the very same 1913 (inaugural) volume of Husserl's *Jahrbuch* that contained his own *Ideas*.

---

[2] Compare Michael Weiler, editor's introduction to *Husserliana Band XXXII: Natur und Geist, Vorlesungen Sommersemester 1927* (Dordrecht: Springer, 2001), xi–li. Husserl's *Cartesian Meditations*, for example, with its famous attempt, in its "Fifth Meditation," to incorporate intersubjectivity into what otherwise had seemed to be a "methodologically solipsistic" philosophy, only emerges in lectures in the late 1920s/1930. For a reading of Husserl's development after 1913 as itself moving toward a kinship with Hegelian absolute idealism, see Clinton Tolley, "Husserl's Philosophy of the Categories and His Development toward Absolute Idealism," *Grazer Philosophische Studien* 94 (2017): 460–493.

[3] For some important exceptions, see Herbert Spiegelberg, *The Phenomenological Movement*, 2nd ed. (Dordrecht: Springer, 1965); Brian Harding and Michael Kelly, eds., *Early Phenomenology* (London: Bloomsbury, 2016); Alessandro Salice, "The Phenomenology of the Munich and Göttingen Circles," in *Stanford Encyclopedia of Philosophy* (Stanford University, Winter 2020 ed.), https://plato.stanford.edu/entries/phenomenology-mg/.

What continues to be perhaps least well-known of all, however, is the key contributions made by women during this same period to the broadening of early phenomenology into a philosophy of spirit. Margarete Calinich (born 1868)[4] and Else Voigtländer (1882–1946) were two of the first women to write and defend dissertations in the Munich school—two of the first women, in fact, to defend dissertations in philosophy of any sort in German universities—and their theses, both published in 1910, focused precisely upon questions concerning the affective dimensions of subjectivity and the ontology of values. A decade later, in more direct dialogue with Husserl, as his students and as active participants in the phenomenological "Circles" at Göttingen and Freiburg (though also in continuing conversation with the Munich phenomenologists), Edith Stein (1891–1942) and Gerda Walther (1897–1977) wrote and published dissertations which took up questions of spirit even more explicitly, focusing especially on what phenomenology should say about the basis for what Hegel called the "objective-spiritual" forms of intersubjectivity and community, and giving at least initial hints as to what a phenomenology of "absolute spirit" might look like. Each of these theses contributed to the expansion of phenomenology already in its early decades beyond its focus in Husserl on theoretical-cognitive forms of consciousness, and (especially in Stein and Walther) seemingly beyond the boundaries of the consciousness of the individual human altogether.

My primary goal in what follows is to chart out some of the main contributions by these four women in their dissertations to this movement of "early phenomenology" (for our purposes, work in phenomenology up until the early 1920s) away from a philosophy of consciousness and toward a philosophy of spirit. I will also place these contributions within the historical context of the intellectual community working around Husserl in Göttingen and Freiburg, and also in the Munich school which grew up around Lipps, Pfänder, and Scheler. In the first two sections, I focus on the 1910 contributions of Calinich (section 1) and Voigtländer (section 2) to the broadening of phenomenology to incorporate the aesthetic and affective dimension through their phenomenological investigations of various forms of feeling. In the second half of the essay, I trace out the path from the phenomenology of feeling to the emergence, in Stein (section 3) and Walther (section 4), of a phenomenology of intersubjectivity and sociality, via reflection on the nature and function of a special mode of feeling called (after Lipps) *Einfühlung*— roughly: an act of "feeling into" something, often translated as "empathy"—as a feeling not just of special aesthetic, and perhaps even cognitive, import, but as crucial to the foundations of "objective spirit" and its distinctive phenomenology. I conclude in section 5 with some brief remarks about the further expansion by Stein and Walther of phenomenology in the early 1920s to include explicit reflection on the relation between consciousness and the absolute-spiritual.

---

[4] I have been unable to discover when Calinich died; she seems to have lived at least until the late 1920s.

1 MARGARETE CALINICH, 1910: THE "AFFECTIVE" VALUE OF COLOR-EXPERIENCE

Margarete Calinich was one of the first women working in the early phenomenological tradition to earn her PhD in Germany. Born in Chemnitz, living her early years in Hamburg, educated at Bonn, Leipzig, and eventually Munich, Calinich wrote her thesis on the psychology of affective states under Theodor Lipps at Munich, which she defended and published in 1910 as *Attempt at an Analysis of the Affective Value [Stimmungswert] of Color Experiences* (hereafter *Stimmungswert*).[5] After this she moved to Berlin (at least as of 1913)[6] and published several essays in aesthetics, including "On the Anecdotal in Painting" (1916), a 1920 book on personality, freedom of the will, and education, as well as reviews of books in aesthetics and in social philosophy, including a 1928 review in *Kant-Studien* of Edith Stein's 1925 essay on the state.

While Husserl, following Brentano, had taken phenomenology to focus primarily on what is immediately given in consciousness itself—and even more specifically, focused upon the description of the "intentionality" of consciousness, or the orientation within consciousness from the ego to an object—the phenomenology "circle" in Munich turned its attention to a wider range of distinct topics, albeit ones that they also found immediately present "in" consciousness itself. In his 1903 *Guidelines for Psychology* (hereafter *Psychology*),[7] for example, Lipps echoes Husserl's call for "phenomenological" psychology to consist in the "purely descriptive" task of "registering, analyzing, comparing, and systematically ordering of the contents that are found in consciousness" (*Psychology* 5). This contrasts with an "explanatory" psychology, which would seek to "establish the order of these contents" in a specifically "causal interconnection" (*Psychology* 5). For Lipps, however, intentionality does not function as the universal mark of what is in consciousness; rather, it characterizes only one side of the "most universal" distinction among "contents of consciousness": on the one hand, there are contents (such as those of "sensation") which are "object-related" (*gegenständlich*) in the basic sense of being "experienced as something directly distinguished from me and standing over and against me," but then there are also contents which are "feelings" (*Gefühle*), and which are not experienced as relating to something "over and against" me, but are instead the "experienced qualities and determinations of the ego" itself (*Psychology* 16–17). To mark

---

[5] Calinich, Margarete, "Versuch einer Analyse des Stimmungswertes der Farbenerlebnisse," in *Archiv für die gesamte Psychologie*, band 18, heft 1–2 (Leipzig: Engelmann, 1910), 1–70; all translations from these four theses, and from the other German works without English editions listed in the Bibliography, are my own.

[6] Though her thesis provides a "curriculum vitae" for her years up to 1910, biographical details for Calinich's later life are hard to find; the 1913 listing of new subscribers to *Kant-Studien* places Calinich on Lutherstrasse in Berlin; see Hans Vaihinger and Bruno Bauch, eds., *Kant-Studien* 18 (Berlin: Reuther and Reichard, 1913): 197.

[7] Lipps, Theodor. *Leitfaden der Psychologie* (Leipzig: Engelmann, 1903).

this difference, Lipps calls feelings "absolutely subjective," since the ego itself is "lodged [steckt] in every feeling," rather than the feeling being experienced as something distinct from me (*Psychology* 17). In fact, "feelings" are what "constitute" what "the immediately experienced ego" itself actually is—that is, "how the ego is in each moment of my life being immediately experienced," as Lipps puts it in an earlier 1902 book.[8] Finally, Lipps claims that, because every "experiencing," including those involving object-relations, is not "just something that happens," but is itself "something of which I have an immediate consciousness," every experiencing includes me "feeling myself experiencing."[9] For Lipps, then, already in the phenomenology of feeling (and of self-feeling), we find something distinct from, and yet as "universal" as, the intentionality or object-relatedness "in" consciousness.

Especially in his 1903 *Aesthetics*,[10] Lipps attempts to go further and characterize not just the distinction between object-related consciousness and feeling, but the different dimensions of interplay between them, including possible correlations that seem to obtain between the occurrence of certain basic sensory qualities (e.g., colors, tones) as objects of consciousness, and feelings which are found in "the ego" as qualitative determinations of the subject in consciousness (see *Aesthetics* 425). It is this correlation that Calinich further explores in her 1910 thesis on the affective value of color experiences.

Though Calinich only mentions the term "phenomenological" once (and only in passing), both the choice of topic and the "descriptive psychological" perspective from which she treats her topic bear many close resemblances to the methodology emerging among her other colleagues in Munich and elsewhere ("descriptive psychology" being a term favored not only by Lipps, but also by Brentano and Husserl in his 1900–1901 *Logical Investigations*, though Calinich does not cite them here). The question of the affective value of color experiences is one that Calinich (like Lipps) sees as lying at the intersection of aesthetics, experimental psychology, "descriptive" psychology, and physiology (*Stimmungswert* 4). After reviewing contributions to this question from across these fields (from Eberhard, Goethe, Kant, Helmholtz, Wundt, Hering, Mühler-Ehrenfels, Lipps, and Volkelt, among others), Calinich sets out the more descriptive "point of view" from which her own analysis will proceed: one which takes the physical and the physiological investigations of color experience as supplying "only the preliminaries [Unterbau] for psychological research into this problem" (*Stimmungswert* 19).

In part 1, Calinich gives an overview of some of the findings of these physical and physiological "conditions" for color experience, before turning to a characterization of the "arising of feeling [Gefühlsbetonung] that occurs as the genuinely 'psychical reaction' in relation to "simple color sensations" (*Stimmungswert* 28). Initially Calinich focuses especially on the arising of "pleasure" (*Lust*) or "displeasure" (*Unlust*), though eventually she also considers the feeling of "indifference" (*Ruhe*, "rest") as well (*Stimmungswert* 45).

---

[8] Lipps, *Vom Fühlen, Wollen, und Denken* (Leipzig: Barth, 1902): 2.
[9] Lipps, *Vom Fühlen, Wollen, und Denken*, 6.
[10] Theodor Lipps, *Ästhetik* (Hamburg: Voss, 1903).

After surveying some experimental findings concerning variations at the psychological level among the coordination of feelings with simple color sensations (due to age and other factors concerning cultural influences), Calinich then advances to the more specific question of the "feeling of affect or mood" (*Stimmungsgefühl*) that can arise in a consciousness of the color per se, as immediate object of consciousness, in abstraction or detachment from whatever further physical object if any this color might relate to; in Calinich's words, a "feeling in which the relation to a determinate object goes missing" (*Stimmungswert* 34). This kind of experience is in contrast with those affects or moods which might arise specifically due to the consciousness of more "objective" relations of color sensations to things in nature or to works of art (*Stimmungswert* 34). Calinich's interest here is to isolate "cases in which the color is effective purely through its worth as color" (*Stimmungswert* 36).

This "direct" effectiveness of color experience becomes the focus of part 2, with Calinich concluding (following Lipps and Volkelt) that these pure "colorings of feeling" both correspond to "elementary visual experiences" and are themselves "originary" in that they are unable to be "reduced" to anything further (*Stimmungswert* 43). Even so, Calinich draws upon Lipps to characterize the differential "psychical quantity" of the effectiveness of feelings in relation to their ability (and "strength") to direct (or redirect) our "attention" ("apperception"), due to their "saturation" and "brightness" (*Stimmungswert* 40). Corresponding to this differentiation, Calinich accepts that, for each color there is a particular "grade" of saturation and brightness to which, when the color in this grade is taken "absolutely" as "a pure phenomenon itself" (that is, bracketing whatever further object it might be related to), we "apply the designation 'beautiful'" (*Stimmungswert* 44; see 68).

Calinich concludes part 2 by turning from affective relations in consciousness of pure color phenomena to what occurs when consciousness of the further objects is also present. Here she explores evidence for the correspondence between the aforementioned determination of the affective feeling by "direct factors" in pure color-experience, on the one hand, and the "objective significance" that is accorded to the "bearers of color," on the other—first considering this correlation with respect to things in nature, before moving on to works of art. In part 3, Calinich turns to the special case in which the "object" bearing the color is something which possesses (or is taken to possess) a distinctively "spiritual worth," and in particular is itself something serving as a "symbol" for something else, something which arises by the "combination" (*Verbindung*) or "connection" (*Verknüpfung*) of the sensory impressions with something more than sensory (that is, "elements pertaining to thought" [*gedanklicher Elemente*]; *Stimmungswert* 57).

These additions then lead Calinich to consider whether something similar can occur even in pure color experience—that is, whether it might initiate a new kind of feeling, one which comes about as what Calinich calls (following Lipps) a "feeling into" (*Einfühlung*) the simple color, where what is "felt into" it is still *other* "feelings and sensations" besides its color and besides its immediately felt affective worth—including sensations from the other senses, but also and perhaps more surprisingly other "purely psychical affects or moods" like "cheerfulness, seriousness, dreariness, and so on"

(*Stimmungswert* 58–59). Hence, though later authors (especially after Stein) will also make use of Lipps' analysis of "*Einfühlung*" to articulate the more specific phenomenology of the experience of the psychical life of "others," that is, other persons, by way of the outer experience of their *bodies*, here Calinich explores what seems to be an even more elementary instance of the phenomenon: the experience of a pure *sensation* itself as possessing a significance or meaning that is expressive or otherwise contains psychical determinations.[11] Strikingly, Calinich suggests that this "feeling of psychical life into color" (*Einfühlung psychisches Lebens in die Farben*) can (and at times does) happen directly or immediately in the consciousness of pure sensation itself, without any "collaboration of association" or "reproduction," due to the very "essentiality [Wesenheit] of colors as visual experiences" (*Stimmungswert* 61).

While further analysis of this phenomenon might seem promising for foundational questions in aesthetics more broadly (as is also suggested by Lipps's *Psychology*), Calinich acknowledges that the "affects" or "moods" that are "felt" into the color through such "direct acts of feeling into" (*schlichte Akte der Einfühlung*) are quite indeterminate, and specifically are not yet those of "determinately characterized moods like seriousness and cheerfulness" (*Stimmungswert* 67–69). When more determinate affects are "felt into" a color, this presupposes the work of "association," and it is no longer something that pertains to the "elementary level of color experience" (*Stimmungswert* 66).

While her thesis itself does not present a comprehensively developed differential registration and systematization of the indeterminate feelings that correlate with the range of simple colors, Calinich does continue to take up systematic questions in aesthetics and the philosophy of art in her later essays. Even so, by the time of her 1920 book, Calinich gives evidence of a transition in her orientation: in *Personality and Freedom of the Will as the Foundation and Goal of Education*,[12] written for the "Philosophical-Pedagogical Library" series, we see Calinich shifting her focus not only toward the phenomenology of volition but also to personality and the human individual as a whole. In fact, Calinich here explicitly insists upon the need to "go beyond the purely psychological" to achieve "the phenomenology of the individual human,"[13] challenging the restrictive scope of "descriptive psychology" as it has been practiced so far, even once

[11] Lipps himself uses the term in both contexts: in relation to the "cognition" of other individual persons in his 1903 *Psychology* (see 187), and, in his 1903 *Aesthetics*, in relation to "lower" sensory elements themselves, as able to give "expression pertaining to life," as "a 'symbol' of a psychical content" by means of "what is sensible" becoming "enlivened or ensouled [belebt oder beseelt]," which Lipps then identifies with specifically "aesthetic content" (96). According to Moritz Geiger, in his "Über das Wesen und die Bedeutung der Einfühlung," in *Bericht über den IV Kongress für experimentelle Psychologie*, ed. F. Schumann (Leipzig: Barth, 1910), "Einfühlung" was in fact first used in the aesthetic context (from Herder and the Romantics), with Lipps himself being the one who extended the analysis of "Einfühlung" beyond "the narrow sphere of the aesthetic problematic" and who "drew out in a systematic way its significance for the broad domain of the consciousness of other egos, the knowledge of other personalities" (30), and thus set the stage for both Calinich's thesis and for Stein's later contributions.

[12] Calinich, *Persönlichkeit und Willensfreiheit als Grundlage und Ziel der Erziehung* (Berlin: Mundusverlag, 1920).

[13] Calinich, *Persönlichkeit*, 8; see 84.

it incorporates (as does Lipps) the affective dimension of consciousness. Along these lines, Calinich's development through the 1910s thus parallels that of other Munich phenomenologists, especially Pfänder and Scheler, as well as those influenced by them, such as Stein and Walther, as I will show below.

2 ELSE VOIGTLÄNDER, 1910: THE PHENOMENOLOGY OF "SELF-FEELING [SELBSTGEFÜHL]"

Like Calinich, Else Voigtländer was among the first group of women to take up a research project in the early phenomenological circle at Munich, actually passing her examination a few months before Calinich in 1909 (though Calinich was sixteen years her senior), and then also publishing her thesis in 1910.[14] Voigtländer was born in Kreuznach, and grew up in Leipzig, receiving her early education there and in Dresden, before arriving in Munich in 1905, and pursuing research in psychology and philosophy "under the direction above all of Professor Lipps and later also under that of Professor Pfänder."[15] After defending her thesis, Voigtländer eventually returned to Leipzig, and published numerous articles on psychology and pedagogy, including a critical assessment of the "significance" of Freud "for general psychology and for the phenomenological understanding of psychologists" (1911), the "phenomenology and psychology of 'alpine' experiences" and a "psychological sketch" of the experience of being "masked" from others (both 1923), along with several essays concerning the effects of war on political consciousness.[16] Around the same time, Voigtländer also contributed two entries on psychological topics for a 1923 dictionary of the science of sexuality which also included contributions from Freud himself.[17]

In her dissertation, entitled "On the Types of Self-Feeling," Voigtländer explores what Lipps himself had earlier sketched as the underlying psychical basis for the possibility of just those kinds of "feeling into" elementary sensations which were at the center of Calinich's analysis. In his 1903 *Aesthetics*, Lipps begins his explanation of such "feeling into" by asking how "psychical activities of life" in general can be "meant" in and through

---

[14] See also Íngrid Ferran, "Else Voigtländer," in *The Routledge Handbook of Phenomenology of Emotion*, ed. H. Landweer and T. Szanto (London: Routledge 2020); George Heffernan, "Phenomenology, Psychology, and Ideology: A New Look at the Life and Work of Else Voigtländer," *Phenomenological Investigations* 1 (2021): 1–49.

[15] Else Voigtländer, *Über die Typen des Selbstgefühls* (Leipzig: R. Voigtländers Verlag, 1910), 120; hereafter *Selbstgefühl*.

[16] In her later life, Voigtländer herself actively participated in the National Socialist Party from 1937 through the end of World War II; compare Heffernan, "Phenomenology, Psychology, and Ideology."

[17] In the late 1910s and early 1920s, Voigtländer also became involved in various research efforts into eugenics; compare again Heffernan, "Phenomenology, Psychology, and Ideology."

the perception of various kinds of sensory qualities (colors, spatial figures, tones), and draws attention to an important aspect of what happens in consciousness of our own "doing" (*Tun*). When we "experience a 'self-activity'" as being "full of pleasure," this is due to our "apperception" that in this activity, the "nature of the soul is attaining its rightful state, its validity, its assertion": "in my doing, so far as it is *my* doing, *my* willing and executing, and therefore not wrung out of me, but rather stemming out from me, *in every case* my nature or essence is expressed [sich ausspricht]. . . . In this way, my doing is in every case a ground for a feeling of pleasure. This feeling, however, as a feeling of *my* doing, a *self*-feeling [Selbstgefühl] full of pleasure, in short, a *feeling of self-worth*" (*Aesthetics* 97). In the feeling of pleasure pertaining to the perception (sensation) of the success of our own activity, we thus have an instance of psychical significance ("worth") being "felt into" what is otherwise simply the inner sensory experience of what is happening in my own activity. Mere self-sensation becomes self-feeling because this sensation itself is "apperceived" to indicate ("express") the successful realization of what my essence or nature is striving to do.

Now, in the case of truly "aesthetic" content, Lipps takes the object in question to be "in every case the worth of an object *distinct from me*," and so it is not itself identical with "the feeling from myself of the worth of myself" (*Aesthetics* 101; my italics). This is in part because aesthetic consciousness, though it involves feeling, is itself also object-related rather than merely the experiencing of my own subjective qualities (to recall a distinction from Lipps mentioned earlier). (Note that this obtains even in the elementary aesthetic cases that were of interest to Calinich as mentioned earlier, insofar as the color itself is experienced "over and against" myself, even if not yet as the color "of" some further object.) Nevertheless, for Lipps, the aesthetic case represents an extension of the original self-feeling out onto cases of sensations of other objects as themselves somehow "expressive" of a successful accomplishment of the psychical doings of someone or other. This happens through what Lipps calls "the *objectivated* [objektiviertes] feeling of self-worth"; this "objectivation" is then what makes possible "the expression of the vitality and the possibility of life lying in an object" that is involved in the "enjoyment [Genuss] of the beautiful" (*Aesthetics* 101–102; my italics).

Even so, it is the "feeling of self," and in particular the "feeling of the worth of oneself" in relation to the sensation of the accomplishment of the "expression" of the nature or essence of one's own soul, that provides the model for the explanation of any aesthetic feeling. It is this more basic "self-feeling" and "worth of oneself" that forms the focus of Voigtländer's research in her thesis. Like Calinich, Voigtländer does not officially describe her approach as itself "phenomenological," though she does characterize several points she makes as "phenomenologically" demonstrable, and she also concludes her work by emphasizing that a fully satisfying solution to the problems she addresses would only be possible "in connection with a universal phenomenological psychology and theory of cognition and characterology" (*Selbstgefühl* 119). What is more, Voigtländer's account of her methodology is marked by several features also highlighted not just by Lipps but also specifically by Brentano and Husserl, such as: an emphasis on "inner perception" as the only genuinely scientific mode of givenness of psychical phenomena (see Brentano); and an emphasis on the need for science to forego "presuppositions" (see Husserl); and a priority on the task of "description" (over causal "explanation") of what is immediately given, as it is given ("appears," "looks"): "the scientific, and in general the disinterested, presuppositionless psychological consideration . . . must consider humans from 'within,' i.e., it asks after the connection and formation of their psychical life as it plays itself out and as it 'looks,' taken purely for itself. . . . [It] must merely lay out the structure of the psyche, in its inner connections which obtain for itself" (*Selbstgefühl* 3). Concerning the topic of self-feeling: Voigtländer follows Lipps in claiming that, like all feelings, the feeling of self can be seen (inwardly) to oscillate between the "positive and negative poles" of pleasure and displeasure, and can also be seen to manifest various "grades of intensity" (*Selbstgefühl* 11–12). One cause of this variation is that (as Lipps had intimated) self-feeling also "includes the consciousness of a value" of the self's state; more specifically, self-feeling includes "an apprehension of the worth [Wertauffasung] of one's own person" (*Selbstgefühl* 11); self-feeling thus "includes in itself a kind of "judgment" about the value of one's own self" (*Selbstgefühl* 13). The feeling of self is contrasted with other feelings, therefore, not by its standing as an affective quality as such, nor by its relation to a (judgment of) value (these are both features of all feelings), but instead in terms of the fact that the value felt and judged is the value of one's own self, which affects oneself in a very specific way. Whereas in other feelings that I have, "I live through my reactions to objects and humans," in the case of self-feeling it is "the "self'" which is "set upon" (*angegriffen*) in the feeling itself, and is felt "in a special concentration," in a way that singles out one's "consciousness of personality," a self-consciousness which itself "is contained in [vorliegt] all self-feeling" (*Selbstgefühl* 10–11). Applying this to the case of elementary color experience, the sensing of the color is itself "judged" to express that the self is in a state with a particular value, and it is this self-judgment which gives rise to the feeling of pleasure.

Though Voigtländer emphasizes the inclusion of a kind of consciousness or judgment about the worth of oneself in self-feeling, she immediately rejects the idea that this judgment must be present in any "intellectual" or articulate form. And even when the judgment it contains is brought to consciousness and expressed in words, the "self-cognition" that this judgment expresses is not identical with the "self-feeling" that it contributes to, for example, by "'depressing' me" (*Selbstgefühl* 18). Here Voigtländer draws on Georg Simmel's contrast between "faith or belief" (*Glaube*) in an "intellectual" sense, which requires explicit consciousness of a specific proposition and of grounds for holding it to be true, and the different sense of faith as "a determinate inner relation to something, a devotion of feeling to it, an orienting of life toward it" (*Selbstgefühl* 15). It is the latter sense of faith or belief as a "comportment [Verhalten], a mood [Stimmung]" which manifests itself, for example, in the life of a religious person, or between children and their parents, between friends and lovers, between an individual and their "people" (*Volk*; *Selbstgefühl* 16). What Voigtländer means by "feeling of self" is "something fully analogous with" what might be called "the belief of a human in themselves," in this latter sense of "belief" (*Selbstgefühl* 16).

After outlining these general characteristics of self-feeling in part 1, Voigtländer then turns to the division of "types" of self-feeling in part 2, organized into two main kinds: one which "relates to the person itself as they are in and for themselves and experience themselves," and another which relates the person to themselves by means of how they are "represented" by other people (*Selbstgefühl* 76). The former "direct" relations in self-feeling are themselves divided into four main types. The first basic direct type is the "instinctive or "vital" self-feeling," in which self-feeling is "simply lived through while obtaining in itself," "without knowing why" (*Selbstgefühl* 21). This is the level of self-feeling involved in elementary color experiences. A second contrasting but still direct type is "'conscious' self-feeling," which occurs when "a dividing of self, a standing-over-and-against [oneself] occurs," when one explicitly "takes a part of one's being as an object," and "experiences" this self-cognition as the cause of the feeling of oneself (*Selbstgefühl* 21–22). A further, third type of self-feeling is a modification of the second, which includes not only explicit consciousness and judgment of oneself, but an "advance" or "forming" of consciousness, and the explicit "representation of self," specifically in the direction of the "assertion of oneself" (*Selbstbehauptung*) or "giving up oneself" (*Selbsthingabe*), effecting self-feelings of "pride" and "humility" (*Selbstgefühl* 54). A final, fourth type of self-feeling pertains specifically to "ethical" considerations of oneself. Here she considers two subforms: one which "contains" and is brought about by "moral judgments" about one's accord with traditional rules or laws, and is exemplified by cases of self-approval, shame, regret, respect, and also "self-hatred" (*Selbstgefühl* 70); and then a second which pertains more specifically to "the ethical demand: be yourself! or: be true to yourself!" (*Selbstgefühl* 69), and the self-feelings that pertain to "maturing" and being "immature" (*Selbstgefühl* 74), exposited by references to Lipps but also to Nietzsche and Ibsen.

In the later sections of the work, Voigtländer expands the analysis of the second main "type" of self-feeling—namely, self-feeling that is indirect in the sense that it is specifically mediated by the "representation" (*Vorstellung*), "image" (*Bild*), or "opinion" (*Meinung*) of oneself which is held by *someone else* (*Selbstgefühl* 76). Examples include the kinds of self-feelings which are essentially connected to values that include a relation to others, such as "the need for recognition, ambition, desire for glory, vanity" (*Selbstgefühl* 76). In order to articulate the relevant kind of mediation by another, Voigtländer first takes up the more general question of what it is to have "an "image" in which other individuals are given to us," that is, "how another human is presented to us" (*Selbstgefühl* 77). Voigtländer maintains that another person is "first given only in their corporeal existence"; this "bodily appearance" is that "through which our knowing of their psychical personality proceeds" (*Selbstgefühl* 77). Concerning the various kinds of "values," however, by which we characterize the identity and nature of other persons ("noble," etc.), Voigtländer argues that these values are not "real properties" of "bodies" at all—though because they belong to the other person, she also denies that they are identical with any "psychical process in us" either (*Selbstgefühl* 78–79). In particular, such values are not identical with the "feelings" which their apprehension occasions in us (*Selbstgefühl* 79), nor are they identical with the "moral and other judgments" by means of which we apprehend them (*Selbstgefühl* 82). Rather, the values themselves have "a peculiar phenomenological manner of being," "a particular standing," distinct from both inner and outer (physical) "realities" (*Selbstgefühl* 81).[18]

At this point Voigtländer circles back to topics in aesthetics, insisting, first, that the same is true of those "sensory values" which are involved in the elementary aesthetic "Einfühlung" discussed by Lipps and Calinich. Even here the values in question have a separate standing from both the simple color (or shape) present in sensation and the sensation itself, even though the values are somehow connected to the sensation as what they are "felt into." How exactly perceptual content and value are connected in general is a question that Voigtländer admits goes "further into a cognition-theoretical direction" than can be pursued in her essay (*Selbstgefühl* 81). Nevertheless, Voigtländer does extend this model to a further case, suggesting (echoing Lipps) that the same sort of "understanding" (*Verstehen*) which takes place in these elementary cases—in the movement in feeling, from the merely sensory content in consciousness, to the (aesthetic) value— is what also takes place in the case of our "apprehension of other people" ("Auffassung fremder Menschen"; *Selbstgefühl* 81–82), in relation to their (spiritual) values, including their possession of values of "social position," even though these latter values might seem to be even more loosely connected to what is sensory (*Selbstgefühl* 84).

From here, Voigtländer then extends the same model to the further case of self-feeling which is itself mediated through outer perception, claiming that here too this same transition in feeling (from what is immediately sensorily given to a personality constituted in relation to values) occurs, though now in relation to one's own person. This happens paradigmatically when we "feel into" the sensations and other representations we have which are specifically of our own bodies and their movements in space (*Selbstgefühl* 86). When we do so, we "consider ourselves from the third person, external perspective" (*Selbstgefühl* 97). To distinguish this self-relation by way of "Einfühlung" from the previous forms of internal and direct "self-feeling" mentioned earlier, Voigtländer calls this "an 'inauthentic' experience according to an image" ("ein 'uneigentliches' bildmäßiges Erleben"; *Selbstgefühl* 86–87).[19]

To make the idea more concrete, Voigtländer appeals to an 1879 novel by Friedrich Theodor Vischer (*Auch Einer*) in which the "genesis" of the relevant "image" is brought about by a first encounter with a "mirror" (*Spiegel*) (*Selbstgefühl* 88)—though she credits lectures given by Pfänder in Munich in Winter 1907/8 for the psychological articulation of the general idea of a "mirror self-feeling," along with the idea of the distinctive kind of experience of oneself when one sees oneself in a mirror (*Selbstgefühl* 92). Voigtländer

---

[18] Here Voigtländer foregrounds some of the same central distinctions that will animate Scheler's critiques of empiricism and Kantianism in ethics and value-theory; compare Max Scheler, *Formalismus in der Ethik und die materiale Wertethik*, 2 vols. (Halle: Niemeyer, 1913–16).

[19] Here Voigtländer partially anticipates (conceptually and terminologically) aspects of Heidegger's later phenomenology (in *Being and Time*) of "inauthenticity" as a relation to "my" own existence by way of its determination through "the one '[das man],' rather than through my "ownmost" possibilities; compare Ferran, "Else Voigtländer."

herself describes this as "living in images," and (in anticipation of her later 1923 essay) associates this "unauthentic" self-feeling with what arises through seeing oneself "in the role, the mask, the impression one makes on others," as "present in all posing," and "in every form of play-acting," and ultimately as itself an "unreal experience" (*Selbstgefühl* 92).[20] This is so, even if these (inauthentic) feelings of oneself that arise in the "feeling" of oneself "into" the relevant "image" include, for example, positive feelings of "security," "breadth," "calmness," "serenity" and so on, in relation to one's sense of belonging or "membership" in a social connection such as a family or tradition or class (*Selbstgefühl* 104–105).

While this might seem to threaten to divorce "authentic" self-apprehension from any relation to one's own body, by the end of her essay, Voigtländer would seem to accord at least some kind of "reality" to the experience of oneself in "mirror self-feeling" as well. Voigtländer concludes her thesis by considering whether, having sharply distinguished the two main forms of self-feeling (direct, mirror)—and the two main forms of experiencing of oneself that they involve—they might nevertheless come into "unison" (*Einklang*) in someone's life. At this point Voigtländer goes so far as to claim that "a full self-affirmation [Jasagen zu sich selbst] must also comprehend the image and the effects," at least in the "ideal case," on the grounds that "the inauthentic life, the life in images, does not just hang in the empty air, but is carried and determined by the actual personality on which it rests"—even if it is also determined by the perceptions and opinions of others, along with other social forces (*Selbstgefühl* 116). To the extent that our "vital self-feeling" can find itself in this image, there is a sense in which we are "experiencing our selves in their image" after all (*Selbstgefühl* 116).[21]

3 EDITH STEIN, 1917: THE "PROBLEM" OF "EINFÜHLUNG"

As both dissertations indicate, by 1910 the phenomenon of "feeling into" (*Einfühlung*) was attaining a more and more central place (thanks to Lipps and others) within the psychological and (broadly) phenomenological analysis of many dimensions of psychical life. In addition to these two theses (and further writings by Lipps on the topic), the early 1910s saw two works by other phenomenologists also working in Munich dedicated to the clarification of *Einfühlung* and related feelings. The first was a 1910 survey

---

[20] Here Voigtländer references Simmel's 1908 "Toward a Philosophy of Play-Acting" and Nietzsche's discussions of "masks" (which she returns to in her 1923 essay on masks), and also anticipates elements from more recent work on the phenomenology of "make-believe" by Kendall Walton.

[21] Importantly, the case of unison is distinguished from the case of "blending [Verschmelzung] of the two kinds of experiencing," in which one "poses" as occupying a certain role which then enables one to then come to have that very role in reality; as an example Voigtländer considers Napoleon's explicit "posing" as (and then becoming) a leader (*Selbstgefühl* 118).

of the various approaches to, and explanatory roles for, the topic by Moritz Geiger in an essay titled "On the Essence and Significance of *Einfühlung*." The second, and even more influential, was a short monograph published in 1913 by Max Scheler, entitled *Phenomenology and Theory of the Feeling of Sympathy [Sympathiegefühl] and of Love and Hate*, in which Scheler devotes significant effort to distinguishing his own preferred account of "fellow-feeling" (*Mitgefühl*) from the phenomenon designated by *Einfühlung* by Lipps and others. In both Geiger and Scheler, as in Lipps and Voigtländer, *Einfühlung* was identified as something that is meant not just to help account for the possibility of "aesthetic" experience via sensation, but also to articulate the nature of key forms of self-relations and relations to others, relations which themselves were thought to underwrite not only fundamental types of "cognition" of persons (whether self or other) but also ethical—and more specifically, social—relations in general.

A further important development occurred in the early 1910s with respect to phenomenology's own self-consciousness, due to a much more thorough and explicit articulation of Husserl's conception of its distinctive methodology in his 1913 *Ideas Pertaining to a Pure Phenomenology and Phenomenological Philosophy* (hereafter *Ideas*). Here we find Husserl's influential account of the "phenomenological reduction" of the "natural position" (*Einstellung*) in ordinary consciousness to the field of "pure" consciousness: first through a reduction of attention to the realm of what is immediately given to consciousness ("phenomena") rather than whatever "things" might exist beyond these immediate givens (by "bracketing" (in an "epochē") the natural "thesis" (positing) of the existence of such things; see *Ideas* §31); and then through a further reduction from what is "factically" given in such phenomena to the essences or forms ("eidē") which are universally and necessarily present in phenomena and in consciousness more generally (see *Ideas* 4), by means of an ideational abstraction through the imaginative variation of parts of phenomena and of consciousness itself (*Ideas* §§3–4).[22] Through this methodology, Husserl takes phenomenology to put to one side everything whose existence and givenness to consciousness can be doubted, and to disclose as a "residuum" (*Ideas* §33) the field of pure consciousness itself as what has "absolute being" for consciousness (*Ideas* §44) in the sense of possessing "doubtlessness" (*Ideas* §46).

In her own 1916 dissertation, *On the Problem of Empathy (Einfühlung)* (hereafter *Einfühlung*), published in 1917,[23] Edith Stein brings both of these two developments into conversation, arguing that *Einfühlung* still remains a "problem" (as her title has it), despite the earlier attempts at a more systematic clarification of the phenomenon by the Munich philosophers. After being born and raised and having received her early education in Breslau (now Wrocław, Poland), Stein moved to Göttingen in 1913 to study philosophy, psychology, history, and "Germanistik," before eventually moving again,

---

[22] For a general discussion of these two stages of Husserl's phenomenological reduction, compare Rudolf Bernet, Iso Kern, and Eduard Marbach, *An Introduction to Husserlian Phenomenology* (Evanston, IL: Northwestern University Press, 1993) chap. 2.

[23] Stein, Edith. *Zur Problem der Einfühlung*. Halle: Waisenhaus, 1917.

to Freiburg, in 1916 to join Husserl as his assistant, and to defend her dissertation (*Einfühlung* 133).

As Stein sees it, *Einfühlung* still remains a "problem" even after the various Munich contributions not only because it continues to be used to try to explain phenomena across such a wide variety of domains ("aesthetic *Einfühlung*, *Einfühlung* as a source of cognition of other psychic life, ethical *Einfühlung*"), but also because of the not always conscious intermingling of different disciplinary approaches ("cognitive-theoretical, purely descriptive, genetic-psychological") to the topic itself (*Einfühlung* v). Clarity will be gained, Stein thinks, only by drawing upon the sharpened methodological reflections in Husserl's *Ideas*, as well as its updated systematic account of the elementary structures of consciousness—in short, by adopting the "perspective" (*Einstellung*) of Husserlian phenomenology (*Einfühlung* 1), and approaching *Einfühlung* from within limits of the "phenomenological reduction" (*Einfühlung* 2).

Stein claims that her more specific contribution will be to "draw out the basic problem" around which all the foregoing investigations into *Einfühlung* can be centered—namely, "the question of *Einfühlung* as the experience [Erfahrung] of other subjects and their psychical life [Erleben]"; *Einfühlung* v). As was already intimated by the line of thought from Lipps, Calinich, and Voigtländer, the analysis of the phenomenon of "feeling-into" was taken to lead quickly into questions about the relation between feeling, value, and personality. As was also emerging, however, *Einfühlung* has been suggested to occur at quite elementary layers or levels within our psychical life, levels in which it is not obvious that value and specifically personality come into play. Stein's thesis works its way through distinct conceptions of "subject," which might be thought to correspond to distinct layers of psychical life, and in this way to articulate which kind of subject is "feeling" which kind of subject "into" the sensory objects of consciousness.

In the first main part of the published thesis,[24] Stein begins her attempt to grasp and describe the essence of "my" own elementary experience of the "experiencing" undergone by a "foreign" subject. Stein focuses in particular on the distinctive mode of its "givenness" to me, with a key task being to contrast elementary cases of this with other kinds of psychical acts (outer perception, memory, imagination) which might also have the experiencing undergone by another subject as its object, but which are not elementary or immediate in the relevant sense, as their relation to the other is instead founded upon other acts. Stein also uses the opportunity to engage critically with previous accounts of the topic itself, focusing especially on contributions by Lipps and Scheler, along with engagement with Geiger, Witasek, and Munsterberg, among others.[25]

---

[24] The first part is marked as "Part II," as part 1 of the document that Stein defended in 1916 (which she describes as providing a survey of "the problem of *Einfühlung* in its historical development") was omitted from the published version; see *Einfühlung* v.

[25] Stein does not criticize Voigtländer herself by name, but does take up a position akin to hers under the heading of accounts of *Einfühlung* via "the perspective of representation" as put forward by Witasek (*Einfühlung* 19). Later in the work Stein also takes up briefly the question of the way in which we are "given" to ourselves in both "mirror-like" ways via memory and fantasy, and in mirrors themselves (see *Einfühlung* 71).

One key point of criticism that Stein brings against the other leading views is that they fail to account for the fact that, in an elementary case of *Einfühlung*, the "foreign experiencing" is "itself present here and now" (rather than remembered or inferred); Stein takes the phenomenology of this act to demonstrate that *Einfühlung* includes the "originary givenness" of its object (the foreign experiencing) in a way that is lacking from acts of memory and fantasy and which itself makes *Einfühlung* more like a case of "outer perception" (*Einfühlung* 5). This is so, even if the inner life of the foreign subject is not itself given as a mere object of outer perception; rather, "I am aware of it 'in' some "spatial-temporal thinglike being" which is itself given in outer perception (*Einfühlung* 5).

In line with the earlier authors, Stein looks for illumination in a parallel between what differentiates two kinds of self-apprehension: in our own case, there is a contrast between our immediately "reflecting view" of ourselves, which has "the ego which is living in it be there itself and bodily so [leibhaft]," on the one hand, and the "nonoriginary ways of givenness of our own experiencings" to ourselves that pertain to "remembering, expecting, fantasy," on the other; so too, Stein holds, there is a contrast between the cases in which the experiencing of a foreign subject is "itself there" for me,[26] and the cases in which it is only "there" for me in a "nonoriginary givenness," as in memory and imagination of their experiencing (*Einfühlung* 6). To be sure, the experiencing undergone by the foreign subject is not "there" for me *as* one of my own experiencings; nevertheless, Stein holds that it is *as originarily "there"* for me as is my own experiencing is. Though Stein's own account of the positive nature of the kind of givenness involved in *Einfühlung* is complex, what is crucial here is that it draws essentially on the idea that in my own experiencing I encounter (in *Erfahrung*) the foreign experiencing undergone by another subject as something immediately "announced" (*bekundet*) within my own experiencing (*Einfühlung* 14; see 19).[27]

While other views are criticized by Stein for failing to account for the immediacy of the givenness of the foreign experiencing, Stein takes a different approach in relation to Scheler in particular—in large part because, as it is articulated in his 1913 essay on *Sympathiegefühl*, Scheler's position itself begins from an importantly different starting point. Rather than assuming that the original case of inner perception is restricted to the perception of "my" psychical experiencings, Scheler claims that "the foreign ego with its experiencing is perceived as inwardly as is one's own" (*Einfühlung* 30). This perhaps surprising claim is something that Scheler takes to be made possible by an equally striking fact—namely, that the "stream of experiencing," in its initial "originary" givenness, is "indifferent" to whether the experiencing is "one's own" or "another's," such that these

---

[26] Though interestingly, Stein seems to withhold the idea that the foreign experiencing is there "in *bodily* givenness [in leibhafter Gegebenheit]" for me (see *Einfühlung* 20).

[27] For more on Stein's positive account of the givenness involved in *Einfühlung*, in the context of the views of Lipps and Scheler, see Dan Zahavi, "Empathy, Embodiment and Interpersonal Understanding: From Lipps to Schutz," *Inquiry* 53, no. 3 (2010): 285–306; see also Dermot Moran, "Edith Stein's Encounter with Edmund Husserl and Her Phenomenology of the Person," in *Empathy, Sociality, and Personhood*, ed. Elisa Magrì and Dermot Moran (Dordrecht: Springer, 2017), 31–47; and chapter 15 here.

differentiations only "crystallize" later "out" of what is first a subject-neutral stream (*Einfühlung* 30). The result is that Scheler himself seems to agree with Stein in her claim that the foreign experiencing is *as originarily given* as is my own experiencing.

Even so, the reason for this, on Scheler's account, is that both experiencings are originarily given without being marked as "mine" rather than "not mine." Against the possibility of such an originarily subject-neutral stream of givennesses of experiencings, Stein claims that "every experiencing is in each case essentially the experiencing of an ego and indeed phenomenally [phänomenal] cannot be separated from that ego," and that the alleged examples given by Scheler of experiencings which are not yet "mine" or anyone's (seemingly free-floating experiencings, e.g., of the feeling of hunger) do not in fact point to any absolutely "ego-less experiencings"—even if they do raise the question of what "ego" (*Ich*) might mean in the relevant cases (*Einfühlung* 31–32). Stein does concede, however, that, at some levels of psychical constitution, "the ego" in question will not be "the ensouled individual" that we commonly suppose as the referent of "Ich," but instead will only be "the pure ego" of "absolute consciousness," such that the level of experiencing is "the pure experiencings of the pure ego" (*Einfühlung* 32). While what (or who) this pure ego is, is left unspecified, Stein's main point is that there is always some ego or other as subject in the most elementary givenness of experiencing. Once this fact about essential constitution of experiencing is recognized, Stein claims that "the question of whether an experiencing is "mine" or that of another becomes senseless [sinnlos]" (*Einfühlung* 32), since there is necessarily "mineness" in every experiencing.

Now, as Scheler himself notes in his revised and much expanded 1923 second edition of his work on *Sympathie*, Stein's criticisms are only as effective as her own counter-claim that the essence of the most elementary forms of experiencing indicates that a relation to at least a "pure" ego is always and necessarily included in their very structure.[28] At the outset of part 3 of her thesis, Stein begins by presenting some of the phenomenological basis for these claims about the essential inseparability of experiencing and first-personality—at least in the form of the "pure ego"—drawing (explicitly) on Lipps but also (implicitly) on Husserl's *Ideas*. As Stein understands it, the "pure ego" in question is the "quality-less subject of experiencing," something whose "self-ness" (*Selbstheit*) is itself "experienced" at the most primitive level and "is the foundation of everything which is 'mine'" (*Einfühlung* 41). Though others have claimed that this "self-ness" only comes into being "when an other is given," Stein disagrees, arguing that this self-ness pertains to the "pure ego" per se and is present positively and independently of the pure ego's relation to "other" egos—even if this self-ness only first "comes into relief [Abhebung] over and against another" (*Einfühlung* 41).

Stein concedes that this "pure ego," however, is not yet what is usually meant by "the individual ego," or "the individual" themselves—though what it is to be an "individual" is something that has also not yet been clarified. While the momentary "pure ego" in

---

[28] For some discussion of Scheler's responses to Stein's criticisms, see Antonio Calcagno, "The Role of Identification in Experiencing Community: Edith Stein, Empathy, and Max Scheler," in *Empathy, Sociality, and Personhood*, ed. Elisa Magrì and Dermot Moran (Dordrecht: Springer, 2017), 143–149.

a single case of experiencing is not yet the individual often referred to as "ego, I" (*Ich*), neither is this "individual" formed by the whole "stream" of experiencings which "constitute" a unity due to "the bonding of all of the experiencings of the stream to the presently living pure ego" (*Einfühlung* 42). Hence, though there is a primitive, irreducible "selfness" (relation to ego) involved in each experiencing, though there is a "unity" to the stream of such experiencings, due to their relation ("bond") to the same "pure ego," it is something over and above both of these that is usually meant by "I."

As Stein sees it, we are closer to this further 'something' when we intend "the identical bearer" of all of the experiencings brought together in the same stream; this is what Stein calls "the substantial soul" (*Einfühlung* 43). A soul itself forms a "substantial unity," a unity even beyond (or under) the whole of psychical experiencings; rather, a substantial unity that is "entirely analogous with that of a physical thing" (*Einfühlung* 43). In fact, in the human case at least, the soul is itself in substantial unity with a physical thing, as Stein claims that "the soul is necessarily always the soul in a living body [Leib]" (*Einfühlung* 44; see 54). Thus Stein's technical term for the relevant unit of analysis that is typically meant by using "I" to refer to an individual is neither abstract subject, nor pure ego, nor stream of experiencings, nor even the soul per se, but instead the "psycho-physical individual" (*Einfühlung* 54).

In her exposition of the relation in general of the soul to its living body within a psycho-physical individual, Stein accepts that the two are connected via a kind of causality, though (echoing Lipps's analysis earlier) it is not paradigmatically that of bringing about a mere effect, since the relevant effect in or with the living body, in the exemplary case, is specifically an "expression" (*Ausdruck*) of the relevant psychical phenomenon (*Einfühlung* 50). Having uncovered this "expressive" aspect of the experience of my own psycho-physical individuality given to me via my outer perception of my own body, Stein then uses this idea as a bridge for the phenomenon mentioned earlier under the heading of the similar "announcing" of the "foreign" experiencing in or through an outer givenness of a physical phenomenon: just as my own body "expresses" my psyche (e.g., changes in its experiencings) to me in my outer perception of myself, so too can another body "express" ("announce"; in Lipps's terms, be a "symbol" of) the psyche of an "other" psycho-physical individual (see *Einfühlung* 61).

Here we can see Stein's analysis moving closer to Scheler's, though with key modifications. For Stein, too, ultimately accepts a kind of parallelism or even parity between my perception of my own psycho-physical individuality via its expression in and through (my perception of) my own body, and my perception of another psycho-physical individuality via its announcing in and through (my perception of) their body. That is, though Stein maintains the priority of immediate givenness of the pure ego in the most elementary experiencings, ultimately Stein in fact seems to attribute the "first" case of my own psycho-physical individuality being "given" to me "in the fullest sense" also to a form of *Einfühlung* in relation to what would otherwise be my own merely "physical body" (*Körper*); *Einfühlung* 71).

Even so, with the introduction of the psycho-physical individual and especially with the idea of the "givenness" of a psycho-physical individual (a soul interacting with a body) in an experiencing, Stein insists that we have in fact shifted the field of analysis away from anything that could count as the analysis of mere consciousness. Rather, we have now taken up the analysis of something much more substantial, and something that specifically has "nature over and against itself"; more specifically, we have shifted the analysis to specifically "consciousness as correlate of the object-world" which nevertheless itself has "reality"—that is, to what, at the beginning of the concluding part 4, Stein herself calls "spirit" (*Geist*; *Einfühlung* 101–102).

Even this shift of focus, however, is not yet enough to bring into view what Stein thinks is commonly meant by "person" (*Einfühlung* 109). Echoing the aforementioned analysis from Voigtländer, Stein takes the term "person" to carry with it not only the integration of consciousness with *nature* in a psycho-physical individual or spirit, but also a specific relation of spirit to the world of "*value*," a relation which is itself expressed most originarily in the "feelings" (e.g., of love, hate) had by the given spirit in relation to its values (*Einfühlung* 112). Until value and feeling come on the scene, the analytical differentiation of two individuals as distinct persons is not yet comprehensible.

Having charted out this series of distinctions, we can now better appreciate what Stein takes to remain a "problem" about *Einfühlung* itself: the question of its nature, as it has been usually formulated, is not yet precise enough, since it does not specify either which layer of subject is doing the feeling-into, or what dimension of subjectivity is being "felt-into" the given phenomenon—that is, whether the "ego" (or "egos") involved pertains only to a one-off case of experiencing, or to a whole "stream" of experiencings, or to a soul which bears a stream, or a psycho-physical individual (spirit) in connection with a living body, or (finally) to a whole person (whether mine or another's). It is only at a fairly complex layer of the constitution of experience that persons come into view, either as the subject doing the feeling-into or as that which is felt-into what is given. Hence, if what we are really asking in relation to *Einfühlung* concerns how a person foreign to my own person is "given" to me, this will require that a "full range of a level of values," if not a whole "value-world," be given to me—or at least indicated as the object(s) of the "feeling" of another, a feeling that is (or can be) itself "announced" in my own experiencing (*Einfühlung* 121). What is more, the very same complexly layered objectivity must be "given" if we are to claim "self-cognition" of our own personality—that is, to cognize the person that I am, I myself must be given my own "values," including ones with which, at any moment, I might otherwise seem to be "unacquainted" (*Einfühlung* 130).

In several ways, then, Stein's 1916 dissertation can be seen as part of a common project in the mid-1910s which unites key elements from both Husserlian (Freiburg) phenomenology and the Munich circle, and one which strives to recontextualize inquiries into the elementary forms of consciousness, intentionality, and feeling within a broader phenomenological field of research into the soul, "spirit," their integration with the world of nature and the world of value, and the more social-philosophical questions concerning the constitution in experience of a plurality of differentiated persons. In sharply differentiating the pure ego from soul, psycho-physical individual, spirit, and person, Stein is able to broach a rapprochement between the Freiburg and Munich phenomenologists, insofar as she can then highlight the extent to which a view like Scheler's is more compelling once it is pitched as a thesis about the parity in the "givenness" of one's own personality and the personality of another, rather than as a thesis about any alleged neutrality with respect to the "mineness" or "otherness" of the basic subject-relation (Ich-heit) that would seem to be constitutive of the most elementary experiencings themselves.[29]

4 GERDA WALTHER 1922: TOWARD THE ONTOLOGY (AND PHENOMENOLOGY) OF COMMUNITY

Especially from the vantage point of the end of the 1910s, Stein's work can be seen as providing key impetus to a broader effort to bring Husserl's work into productive dialogue with the already more "spiritually" minded phenomenologists (like Scheler) working in Munich. Stein's own wrestling with positions like Scheler's continued into the early 1920s, as she attempted to make good on her claim in the final part of her thesis that *Einfühlung* must ultimately form "the exemplary basis [Unterlage]" for any "ontology of spirit" (*Einfühlung* 106). Stein grappled, in particular, with what to make of the Hegelian thesis (taken over with modifications by Scheler) that spirit itself (and, with it, personality) could take collective or group forms, such as in families, corporations, and peoples or nations. In Stein's analysis of the inter-personal level of *Einfühlung*—as an experiencing which had one person as subject and another as object—Stein had arrived on the doorstep of what Hegel had called "objective spirit," understood as spirit which has itself "over and against" itself. Yet Stein had not yet taken up the phenomenology of these more complex forms of communal spiritual life, and in particular had not yet raised the question of what might be transformed about consciousness once the personalities involved in the subject or object positions are themselves first person plural—that is, when the "I" changes to the "we."

Stein's next major work culminates in the exploration of precisely this further "communal" dimension of spiritual experience, consisting in two essays published in the fifth volume of Husserl's *Jahrbuch* in 1922, under the title *Contributions to the Philosophical*

---

[29] In this regard, it is worth noting that, during the same several years that she was composing her thesis, Stein's collaborations with Husserl were particularly close, and in particular she extensively revised Husserl's own mid-1910s lecture notes on the constitution of "spirit" into a coherent manuscript that was to serve as the basis for the second volume of *Ideas*. For his part, Husserl was hesitant about accepting Stein's revisions (and also reluctant even to read them or reread his own manuscripts), which led Stein to step away from her role as his official assistant, though they continued to be in touch for years after. Ultimately, the planned second volume of *Ideas* wasn't published during Stein's (or Husserl's) lifetime. For more on Stein's role in the formation of the edition of the text which has since been published, see Marly Biemel, editor's introduction to *Husserliana Band IV* (Dordrecht: Springer, 1991), xvi–xix.

Grounding of Psychology and the Sciences of Spirit [Geisteswissenschaften]; hereafter *Contributions*).[30] Stein's second essay in particular attempts to delineate even more sharply and sustainedly various relations between the individual and the "community" (*Gemeinschaft*), as well as "the ontical structure" or "reality" of a community itself (*Contributions* 175). It also explores the extent to which phenomenology can accept, first, the idea of collective or common "experiencings" (or an ongoing "stream" of such experiencings), where this involves not just one spirit or person experiencing another but two persons sharing the same experience as its common subject, as something "we" are experiencing – with Stein then asking as well whether this would in turn imply the existence of a communal "life-force" which underlies such communal experiencings, or perhaps even a communal "soul" or "spirit" (*Contributions* 246), and at least an "analogue of individual personality" (*Contributions* 175). Stein is also concerned to determine the extent to which it is right to hold (as she had in her thesis) that any such communal phenomenology ("experiencing," "stream," etc.) would of necessity asymmetrically depend for its constitution on the more originary lived experiencings of individuals—or whether (as was advocated by certain strands in neo-Hegelian social theory at the time) there is some sense in which a communal experiencing or stream itself not only helps gives rise to, or "reciprocally" determines the individual streams (see *Contributions* 238), but perhaps even asymmetrically grounds any "individual" experiencing, and perhaps even grounds the experiencing of that first-person-singular "pure ego" which had been previously taken for granted as elementary or even "absolute," in the language of Husserl's 1913 *Ideas*.[31]

Stein's work during this period spurred others to take up the problematic of the phenomenology of the layers of relationships that obtain between the individual and the community. Chief among these was one of Stein's own "students" of sorts, Gerda Walther, who researched just this topic in Freiburg from 1917–1919, during the years between the publication of Stein's own thesis and her 1922 *Contributions*. Walther had already studied social theory and philosophical psychology with Pfänder at Munich from 1915 to 1917, and ultimately moved back to Munich after her time in Freiburg, defending a thesis (with Pfänder) in early 1921 with the title *A Contribution to the Ontology of Social Communities* (hereafter *Communities*; see *Communities* 159).[32] Walther's thesis was also published in Husserl's *Jahrbuch*, albeit not until the volume after the one with Stein's essay, in 1923. Even so, her thesis itself was composed and officially defended before Stein's essay went to print, and was in fact itself also published separately in 1922.[33]

---

[30] Stein, Edith, *Beiträge zur philosophischen Begründung der Psychologie und der Geisteswissenschaften. Jahrbuch für Philosophie und phänomenologische Forschung* 5 (1922), 1–283.

[31] For more on Stein's account of the ontology and phenomenology of community, see Antonio Calcagno, *Lived Experience from the Inside Out: Social and Political Philosophy in Edith Stein* (Pittsburgh: Duquesne University Press, 2014).

[32] Walther, Gerda. *Ein Beitrag zur Ontologie der sozialen Gemeinschaften.* Halle: Niemeyer, 1922.

[33] The pagination of the two printings is the same, though the 1923 *Jahrbuch* version does not include the "Foreword" or the "Curriculum Vitae" from Walther's thesis. In a note in her introduction, Walther mentions Stein's "train of thought" on this subject as being particularly influential on her own

In the foreword to her thesis, Walther describes her interests in "social problems" as predating even her first years in university; in her words: "the life of the individual in social communities, through them, for them, and against them, seemed to me to be one of the most important problems of human life in general. A clarification of the relation between individual and community seemed to me always more important for the solution of all ethical and metaphysical problems of human life" (*Communities* iii). Here Walther also describes her route into the phenomenological approach to these questions, noting that she was drawn first of all to the analysis provided by the historical materialism of Marx and Engels, along with their successors, such as Kautsky, Bebel, and Max Adler, before eventually finding "a light in this chaos of problems" in lectures given by Pfänder (*Communities* iii). From there Walther recounts being drawn to philosophical-sociological writings of Simmel but also Hegel, along with the contributions to philosophical sociology by Scheler and Weber, before eventually joining Husserl and his "students and supporters" in Freiburg for several semesters, and "being drawn ever deeper into the sense and the method of phenomenological research" (*Communities* iv). It is from this perspective, Walther tells us, that she means to attempt "to clarify, ontologically and phenomenologically, the essence of social communities "in general" and their "constitution'" (*Communities* iv). Besides Husserl and Pfänder, Walther singles out only two other philosophers by name—"Dr. M. Heidegger in Freiburg," and then "Dr. Edith Stein"—as of special significance for helping her come to a better understanding of what her own procedure must be for her investigation (*Communities* iv).

Walther's time in Freiburg, then, was of particular importance for setting the course of her own analysis. Her main contact with Stein came through Walther's attendance in the "philosophical kindergarten" that Husserl had Stein run in order to introduce incoming students to the basics of (the Husserlian version of) the phenomenological approach.[34] During her first year in Freiburg, Walther excelled in these introductory exercises, so much so that she was selected to present her work at the inaugural meeting of the Freiburg Phenomenological Society. Walther's talk challenged the Husserlian prioritization of the "pure ego" over and against both all of its contents and also all of the conditions which might make such a pure ego itself possible—with Husserl, Stein, and Heidegger all responding directly to her challenges, and apparently taking up the bulk of the discussion period in an argument among themselves.[35]

Walther continues to explore potential conditions on the pure ego in her 1922 thesis. In the first introductory part (§A), Walther begins by delineating what she means by "ontology" and "phenomenology" respectively, doing so in a way that shows her sensitivity to

---

position, and she even mentions Stein's second essay ("Individual and Community") by name (and gives its publication year as 1921), but says she "could unfortunately not take it into consideration" (*Communities* 17n1).

[34] See Linda McAlister, "Gerda Walther (1897–1977)," in *A History of Women Philosophers*, vol. 4, ed. Mary Ellen Waithe (Dordrecht: Springer, 1995), 189–206; 190; Rodney Parker, "Gerda Walther and the Phenomenological Community," *Acta Mexicana de Fenomenología* 2 (2017): 45–66; 49.

[35] Compare Parker, "Gerda Walther and the Phenomenological Community," 49–50.

the various differentiations of perspective as well as dynamic transformations occurring within the Freiburg/Munich circles.[36] Ontology "investigates the essence of every ob-jectivity [Gegenständlichkeit] in the broadest sense," while phenomenology "pursues research into the ways of being given, appearing, and cognizing of every objectivity in pure consciousness" (*Communities* 1). By beginning with pure consciousness and its "pure ego," phenomenology begins with what is "the most originary" and "absolute," at least with respect to the "phenomenological, cognitive-theoretical" task of setting out the "point of departure for all knowledge," since it begins with "absolute evidence" (*Communities* 1). Immediately, however, Walther qualifies the sense of "absolute" fur-ther by noting that phenomenology need not itself hold that pure consciousness and the pure ego are "absolute" in the "metaphysical" sense of the term (*Communities* 1).

Walther also qualifies the sense of "phenomenology" itself by noting that she is here describing the "Freiburg" version, indicating in a note that "not all phenomenologists would agree," citing Scheler in particular. Finally, Walther also signals that the "con-sciousness" she takes phenomenology to be concerned with is not in any way limited to "consciousness 'of' theoretical objects," but is also fundamentally concerned with "aesthetic, ethical, practical, religious, and other objectivities" (*Communities* 4). For Walther, this indicates that the scope of the regions of ontological investigation into the "essence" of distinct types of phenomena can and should also extend to "the ontology of social communities" (*Communities* 5).

Before moving onto the presentation and analysis of the essence of communities, however, Walther raises two questions already met with earlier, in relation to Stein's engagement with Scheler: first, the question of the "background" conditions for con-sciousness itself to occur, or that "out of which the experiencings emerge as elicitations [als Regungen auftauchen], before they arrive into the ego [ehe sie in das Ich eintreten]" (*Communities* 11); and second, whether, having recognized these conditions, more distinctions need to be introduced concerning what might be meant by "I or ego" (*Ich*) in the first place. Walther calls the background within which "the pure ego" it-self is "embedded," and out of which experiences emerge, the "subconsciousness" (*Unterbewustsein*; *Communities* 11). In relation to the real ego, Walther uses the term "the self" to pick out the whole that comprises both the subconsciousness and the pure ego in consciousness (*Communities* 14), and holds that this self is something that is itself constituted "empirico-'historically'" (*Communities* 15). Underneath even "the self" as an existent whole of (conscious and subconscious) psychical activity, however, is the still further level of something more substantial, what Walther calls "the metaphysically real essence, the 'fundamental essence' [Grundwesen] of a subject," which Walther sees as analogous to what Scheler calls the "spiritual person," or what the Kantians call "the ego in itself" or its "intelligible character" (*Communities* 15).

---

[36] Perhaps surprisingly for a Munich dissertation, Walther's "Introduction" includes a much more detailed and nuanced overview than even Stein's thesis of both the methodology from Husserl's *Ideas* as well as Husserl's technical terminology pertaining to the basic structures of consciousness (e.g., constitution, noesis, noema).

With all of these further distinctions in hand, Walther finally turns to intro-duce the main subject of her thesis: the ontology of social communities. As Walther uses the term "social," one key feature that distinguishes social communities from communities more generally is that their "members" are all humans; hence, there are no "social communities" among nonhumans, nor between humans and nonhumans (*Communities* 18). Given this restriction on the constituents of a social community to humans, Walther thinks that any social ontology "must presuppose a fully worked out ontology and phenomenology of the human person, a phenomenological analysis of *Einfühlung* as the cognition of foreign subjects, and an ontology and phenomenology of society [Gesellschaft], as what in a certain sense forms the foundations of communities" (*Communities* 17). For the account of personality, Walther points us to Scheler as well as to unpublished work by Pfänder, and also to Stein's forthcoming work on "Individual and Community," though she says she has not been able to consult it (*Communities* 17n1); on *Einfühlung*, Walther mentions Stein's 1917 thesis in conjunction with Scheler's work on *Sympathiegefühl*; and on society, Walther mentions Scheler again, along with Simmel, Reinach, and Weber, but then also refers to "Husserl's (unpublished) lecture 'Nature and Spirit'" (*Communities* 17n3).[37]

Having outlined the main presuppositions of her analysis, Walther begins the second main part (§B) of her thesis by setting out "the sense of the concept 'social commu-nity.'" For Walther, a social community involves "a number of humans," all of whom "relate to one identical intentional object in the broadest sense," at least "at some level of their life," and all of whom "know of one another and of their relation to the same inten-tional object," on the basis of which an "interaction with one another" occurs, and out of which "a common life [ein gemeinsames Leben] emerges" (*Communities* 29)—more specifically, "a common psychical-spiritual life" (*Communities* 30). Beyond this, in order to distinguish social community from what (among sociologists like Tönnies) would count merely as a "society" (*Gesellschaft*), Walther also requires an "inner connected-ness" (*Verbundenheit*), or inner "union" (*Einigung*) to be present among the members, which itself gives rise to "a feeling of belongingness" (*Communities* 33). The inner union itself is what allows for a genuinely "common life," with "common experiencings, actions, goals, strivings, willings, wishings, and so on," in contrast to the merely "sim-ilar" or "equivalent" experiencings (etc.) which obtain among members of a mere so-ciety (*Communities* 33).

In her discussion of what makes this "inner union" possible, Walther takes up the possibility, akin to the one floated by Scheler and discussed by Stein (noted earlier), that the most originary form of inner connectedness is that of a kind of "growing together" (*Zusammenwachsen*) which occurs in an "unconscious, subconscious" manner, and in

---

[37] Toward the end of her thesis, Walther also refers to Husserl's manuscript for *Ideas*, vol. 2, though she describes it as something that is not only "unpublished" but "to us unknown [unbekannt]" (*Communities* 127n1). Later in the same passage, Walther also (tantalizingly) connects questions concerning various types of sociological formations to "the unpublished part of E. Stein's dissertation" (*Communities* 128n3).

which "the ego plays no role, whether active or passive" (*Communities* 38). Here Walther allows that, from the "genetic" point of view (what must be temporally or historically in place prior to existence), this sort of union might well be "the necessary presupposition" of all other forms of union. Even so, Walther insists that the "union" that distinguishes specifically social communities from others must ultimately be one that is "freely active," as the kind of union that "alone is worthy of persons" (*Communities* 38). Nevertheless, when Walther later takes up the question of the "depth" in which the "point of arising" is to be found for a single subject's feeling of inner union, she notes that there are reasons for thinking that this "point" lies not only below the "ego-center" level, and even below the broader "self" level (which incorporates the subconscious), but perhaps even below the level of the "fundamental essence" of the individual subject as well. In such a feeling, Walther sees the subject pointed to "their own inner-psychical limit, the limit of their grounding essence, their spiritual person," and opening up onto something "still higher" or "deeper," something "beyond," something "numinous," citing Rudolph Otto's work on "the holy" (*Communities* 60). Walther then suggests that it is in the same "absolute depth of the subject" where a "union of fundamental essence of different subjects with one another" can occur (*Communities* 61)—and not just from the point of one subject, but reciprocally and "responsively," in a "universal 'reciprocal union'" (*Communities* 63).

By placing the "source-point" (*Quellpunkt*) or "ground" for the "common life" of the community in a union that occurs in the depths below or beyond—or at least right at the edge of—the boundaries of any one individual subject (*Communities* 66), one might wonder whether Walther's position has now drawn closer to that of Scheler mentioned earlier. Whether Walther also means to ground the individual's psychic life in general in such a deeper communal life, what Walther herself means by the "collective experiencing" (*Gesamterleben*) that occurs in community is not something that lies "behind" or "above" the individual, or somehow otherwise "separated" from them. Rather, the collective experiencing occurs in the form of a "we" that each of the individuals themselves experiences as their own, albeit in the form: "I and the others." Furthermore, this "we" does not need to form its own real, distinct "ego-center" that is "self-standing" over and against the "individual ego" of the members of the community (*Communities* 70). Later she adds that communities do not take on their "own lived body" (*Leib*) or "center of will" (*Communities* 114).

Even so, Walther acknowledges that, in certain cases of "mystical experiencing," there might very well be "a mysterious, specifically communal source-point of experiencing that streams along behind the individual's self and fundamental essence" (*Communities* 70). In fact, in all cases of communal experiencing, Walther holds that "I am not alone only as 'I myself' [Ich selbst]," and that "I feel myself one with [fühle mich eins mit] the others" in the community, so much so that "'my' experiencings, insofar and only insofar as they are communal experiencings, are sourced not merely from out of myself, from my isolated self, my only-I-myself [Nur-Ich-Selbst] which lies behind the ego-point, but rather spring forth in me equally from another, from the we ... in which I rest, with which I am one" (*Communities* 71). What is more—in a move that parallels and in some ways extends Stein's criticisms of other conceptions of *Einfühlung* for being too "indirect" (with Walther in fact here referring us to Stein's thesis)—Walther claims that such communal experiencings themselves can occur immediately, without being built up out of more originary experiencings of a single ego:

> I do not therefore first somehow have experiencings occurring out from me as an isolated individual-ego and individual-self, which I then somehow compare with the experiencings of others grasped through *Einfühlung*, and so—if I ascertain that the others are experiencing the same as I am "also" experiencing—I also do not unite myself first with these others and their experiencings, and do not apprehend these experiencings only now retrospectively as communal experiencings and designate them as such. . . . Communal experiencings in our sense are rather just those experiencings which entirely proceed from the ground of my union with the others, from them in me and me in them, from us—in me, as in them—even before they arrive in my (or their) ego-center, before they are actualized there. (*Communities* 72)

From here Walther then sets out to mark the resulting distance between what she is calling "communal experiencing" and what Stein (and others) calls "Einfühlung," on precisely the ground that *Einfühlung* is the cognition or apprehension of specifically a "foreign" experiencing, one that is in no way "my own," whereas (as we have just seen) what Walther is calling essentially "communal" experiencing is "my own," even as it involves "others" experiencing together with me in a "we" (see *Communities* 75).

Perhaps surprisingly, at this point Walther even extends the possibility of communal experiencing in the form of "the excitation of experiencing appearing which no one of the "people who are also" [in the community] ever actually having had, or perhaps in this way ever will have" (*Communities* 73). Though she does not ascribe a new "ego" to the community itself, Walther does think we should posit a "communal self"—what she also calls a "common spirit"—which comprises this "layer" of unconscious or subconscious communal experiencings, prior to their becoming "actual" in any individual member, or for "us" (*Communities* 73).[38] Here Walther signals agreement with Scheler at least to the extent that he has something like this "spirit" in mind with his own account (in his *Formalismus*) of the "collective person" (*Gesamtperson*) of a community (*Communities* 73). Later she spells this thought out further, in reference to the fact that some communities not only have their own "self" but also possess their own "fundamental essence" as well, something she takes to be akin to an Aristotelian "dunamis" for the group, which unfolds according to an "entelecheia" (see *Communities* 112). In such cases, the "fundamental essence" of the community is not "simply a sum of the individual fundamental essences taken together"; rather, "it is a 'spiritual collective person' in Scheler's and Hegel's sense" (*Communities* 112). For all of these reasons, though Walther consistently denies that communities have "the center of consciousness and

---

[38] Later Walther clarifies that the community "has its own self *in* the 'self' of the member" (*Communities* 112).

of will" which is distinctive of "a self-standing person," she follows Hegel and Scheler in affirming that "the community is a super-personal, psychical (and spiritual) unity" (*Communities* 114).[39]

5 CONCLUSION: TENTATIVE STEPS TOWARD ABSOLUTE SPIRIT

With these last remarks, Walther's analysis pushes quite far into the metaphysical territory that practicioners of Husserlian phenomenology, at least in its early stages, had hoped to keep in 'brackets'. Strikingly, in the same passage, Walther wades further still into the Hegelian metaphysics of spirit, claiming that "like all metaphysically real fundamental essences," such communal fundamental essences (collective persons or spirits) are "rooted in the divine fundamental essence (in Hegel's 'absolute spirit')" (*Communities* 112). With this we see Walther finally, if only momentarily, returning to the topic of the "metaphysically absolute," a topic she herself bracketed at the outset, as contrasted with the distinctive cognitive-theoretical sense of "absolute" claimed by (Husserlian) phenomenology in relation to the "evident" truth of its chosen starting point.

In her next major work—her 1923 *Toward the Phenomenology of Mysticism*—Walther pursues the relation between phenomenology and the "metaphysically absolute" in a more sustained fashion,[40] though she does touch briefly upon just this question in the appendix to her 1922 thesis (§D). It is not just Walther, however, who was moved increasingly to direct her phenomenological research beyond even the "objective-spiritual" and toward topics pertaining to the "absolute-spiritual" (in the Hegelian sense of these terms). Stein, too, had concluded her own thesis with some hints at an emerging account of the possibility of *Einfühlung* with "purely spiritual persons" (e.g., angels, divinity; see

---

[39] For more discussion on these topics, and for a comparison with Stein's 1922 work, see Anna Maria Pezzella, "On Community: Edith Stein and Gerda Walther," in *Gerda Walther's Phenomenology of Sociality, Psychology, and Religion*, ed. Antonio Calcagno (Dordrecht: Springer, 2018), 47–56.

[40] Walther, Gerda. *Zur Phänomenologie der Mystik*. Halle: Niemeyer, 1923; hereafter *Mysticism*. Here Walther also elaborates and extends her threefold treatment of the human subject as well, in terms of (1) "ego-center" (*Mysticism* 25–26), (2) the set of mental activity that forms the "background to consciousness" within which the acts including an ego are "embedded," which she now associates with "the psychical" region (*Mysticism* 28; also "mind [*Gemüt*]," see 97), and then (3) the "ground essence" as something akin to what others call "spirit" (in humans), which she now also associates more directly with a source of specifically free or spontaneous activity and self-consciousness (*Mysticism* 30–36; in animals and plants lacking these two features, "soul" is the preferred term for their "ground essence"; *Mysticism* 84–85). For a parallel discussion of the nature and importance of the distinction between "psyche" and "spirit," see also *Contributions*; for a comparative discussion of Stein and Walther (and Hedwig Conrad-Martius) on some of these key terms, see Christina Gschwandtner, "Körper, Leib, Gemüt, Seele, Geist: Conceptions of Self in Early Phenomenology," in Calcagno, *Gerda Walther's Phenomenology of Sociality, Psychology, and Religion*, 85–100.

Einfühlung, 131), and then, after also developing her own philosophy of "objective spirit" in her 1922 work, increasingly turned her focus to the "absolute-spiritual," especially after her conversion to Catholicism in 1922.[41]

In summary, then: in the first substantial research contributions of these four women to early phenomenology, we find a broadening of the purview of phenomenology beyond the narrow bounds of the elementary description of the structure of cognitive-theoretical consciousness, to include an analysis of the feeling and value connected with even the most elementary sensory consciousness (Calinich), as well as its role in the awareness of oneself and of others (Voigtländer; Stein)—as well as a further broadening to include both "objective-spiritual" (social-communal) forms (Walther), and also some first attempts at the reinterpretation of the traditional doctrines concerning "absolute spirit" from within the phenomenological point of view.

Highlighting this work helps to reveal the extent to which the early centers of phenomenology in Munich, Göttingen, and Freiburg, along with their official journal (*Jahrbuch*), were also among the early centers of support for research by women in academic philosophy in Germany at the turn of the century. Beyond contributing to the growing recognition of the existence of women working in early twentieth century German philosophy, along with the significance of their works, my hope is that centering attention on these four theses will also help to correct a still-common impression about the scope of early work in phenomenology itself—namely, that it neglected almost entirely topics beyond the pure ego and the structures of theoretical-cognitive consciousness, and that this neglect is corrected only in later contributions (that is, Heidegger's 1927 *Being and Time*, Alfred Schutz's 1932 *The Meaningful Construction [sinnhafte Aufbau] of the Social World*, and Merleau-Ponty's 1945 *The Phenomenology of Perception*, among others). Already in the 1910s and early 1920s, women were well on their way to broadening and deepening the spirit of the phenomenological movement.

---

[41] Compare Mary Catherine Baseheart, Linda Lopez McAlister, and Waltraut Stein, "Edith Stein (1891–1942)," in Waithe, *History of Women Philosophers*, vol. 4, 157–187. It is also worth noting that Walther herself had something of a conversion to the religious in general through a deeply moving experience on a train in 1918, after growing up as non-religious (in her words: "confessionless"; *Communities* 159). A key influence in this broadening toward absolute-spiritual in both Walther and Stein comes from their collaboration and friendship with a fifth woman who was quite active and productive within early phenomenology: Hedwig Conrad-Martius. (In particular, Conrad-Martius's 1921 *Metaphysical Conversations* are taken up by both Stein's *Contributions* and Walther's *Communities*.) I have omitted Conrad-Martius from the present survey due to the fact that her own dissertation (defended in Munich in 1912, published in 1913) focuses on a topic that remains much more squarely within the "classical" purview of Husserlian phenomenology—namely, "the cognitive-theoretical foundations of positivism" and "the ontology and the doctrine of appearances of the external world"— even though (like Stein and Walther) Conrad-Martius's own developments push her later focus well beyond these initial boundaries. For more on Conrad-Martius, see Ronny Miron, *Hedwig Conrad-Martius: The Phenomenological Gateway to Reality* (Dordrecht: Springer, 2021) and chapter 13 here.

BIBLIOGRAPHY

Baseheart, M. C., L. L. McAlister, and W. Stein. "Edith Stein (1891–1942)." In Waithe, *History of Women Philosophers*, 157–187.

Bernet, R., I. Kern, and E. Marbach. *An Introduction to Husserlian Phenomenology*. Evanston, IL: Northwestern University Press, 1993.

Biemel, Marly. "Einleitung der Herausgebers", *Husserliana Band IV*, xiii–xx. Dordrecht: Springer, 1991.

Calcagno, Antonio, ed. *Gerda Walther's Phenomenology of Sociality, Psychology, and Religion*. Dordrecht: Springer, 2018.

Calcagno, Antonio. *Lived Experience from the Inside Out: Social and Political Philosophy in Edith Stein*. Pittsburgh: Duquesne University Press, 2014.

Calcagno, Antonio. "The Role of Identification in Experiencing Community: Edith Stein, Empathy, and Max Scheler." In Magrì and Moran, *Empathy, Sociality, and Personhood*, 143–149.

Calinich, Margarete. "Edith Stein, *Untersuchung über der Staat*." *Kant-Studien* 33 (1928): 297–299.

Calinich, Margarete. "Kühn, Lenore, Die Autonomie der Werte." *Kant-Studien* 32 (1927): 528.

Calinich, Margarete. *Persönlichkeit und Willensfreiheit als Grundlage und Ziel der Erziehung*. Berlin: Mundusverlag, 1920.

Calinich, Margarete. "Über das Anekdotische in der Malerei." *Zeitschrift für Ästhetik und allgemeine Kunstwissenschaft* 11 (1916): 180–188.

Calinich, Margarete. "Versuch einer Analyse des Stimmungswertes der Farbenerlebnisse." In *Archiv für die gesamte Psychologie*, band 18, heft 1–2: 1–70. Leipzig: Engelmann, 1910.

Conrad-Martius, Hedwig. *Die erkenntnistheoretischen Grundlagen des Positivismus*. Halle: Wassenhaus, 1913.

Conrad-Martius, Hedwig. "Die erkenntnistheoretischen Grundlagen des Positivismus." Reprint, with a "Nachwort." Bergzabern: Müller, 1920.

Conrad-Martius, Hedwig. *Metaphysische Gespräche*. Halle: Niemeyer, 1921.

Conrad-Martius, Hedwig. "Zur Ontologie und Erscheinungslehre der realen Aussenwelt." *Jahrbuch für Philosophie und Phänomenologische Forschung* 3 (1916): 345–542.

Geiger, Moritz. "Beiträge zur Phänomenologie des ästhetischen Genusses." *Jahrbuch für Philosophie und Phänomenologische Forschung* 1 (1913): 567–684.

Geiger, Moritz. "Das Bewusstsein von Gefühlen." In *Muenchener philosophische Abhandlungen*, edited by A. Pfänder, 125–162. Leipzig: Barth, 1911.

Geiger, Moritz. "Über das Wesen und die Bedeutung der Einfühlung." In *Bericht über den IV Kongress für experimentelle Psychologie*, edited by F. Schumann, 29–73. Leipzig: Barth, 1910.

Gschwandtner, Christina. "Körper, Leib, Gemüt, Seele, Geist: Conceptions of Self in Early Phenomenology." In Calcagno, *Gerda Walther's Phenomenology*, 85–100.

Harding, Brian, and Michael Kelly, eds. *Early Phenomenology: Metaphysics, Ethics, and the Philosophy of Religion*. London: Bloomsbury, 2016.

Heffernan, George. "Phenomenology, Psychology, and Ideology: A New Look at the Life and Work of Else Voigtländer." *Phenomenological Investigations* 1 (2021): 1–49.

Husserl, Edmund. "Ideen zu einer reinen Phänomenologie und phänomenologischen Philosophie." *Jahrbuch für Philosophie und Phänomenologische Forschung* 1 (1913): 1–323.

Lipps, Theodor. *Ästhetik*. Hamburg: Voss, 1903.

Lipps, Theodor. *Leitfaden der Psychologie*. Leipzig: Engelmann, 1903.

Lipps, Theodor. *Vom Fühlen, Wollen, und Denken*. Leipzig: Barth, 1902.

Magrì, Elisa, and Dermot Moran, eds. *Empathy, Sociality, and Personhood: Essays on Edith Stein's Phenomenological Investigations*. Dordrecht: Springer, 2017.

Marcuse, Max. *Handwörterbuch der Sexualwissenschaft*. Bonn: Marcus und Weber, 1923.

McAlister, Linda. "Gerda Walther (1897–1977)." In Waithe, *History of Women Philosophers*, 189–206.

Miron, Ronny. *Hedwig Conrad-Martius: The Phenomenological Gateway to Reality*. Dordrecht: Springer, 2021.

Moran, Dermot. "Edith Stein's Encounter with Edmund Husserl and Her Phenomenology of the Person." In Magrì and Moran, *Empathy, Sociality, and Personhood*, 31–47.

Parker, Rodney. "Gerda Walther and the Phenomenological Community." *Acta Mexicana de Fenomenología* 2 (2017): 45–66.

Pezzella, Anna Maria. "On Community: Edith Stein and Gerda Walther." In Calcagno, *Gerda Walther's Phenomenology*, 46–56.

Pfänder, Alexander. *Phänomenologie des Wollens*. Leipzig: Barth, 1900.

Pfänder, Alexander. "Zur Psychologie der Gesinnungen." *Jahrbuch für Philosophie und Phänomenologische Forschung* 1 (1913): 325–404; 3 (1916): 1–125.

Salice, Alessandro. 2020. "The Phenomenology of the Munich and Göttingen Circles." In *Stanford Encyclopedia of Philosophy*, Stanford University, 1997–. Article published August 3, 2015; last modified November 5, 2020. https://plato.stanford.edu/archives/win2020/entries/phenomenology-mg/.

Scheler, Max. *Formalismus in der Ethik und die materiale Wertethik*. 2 vols. Halle: Niemeyer, 1913–16.

Scheler, Max. *Zur Phaenomenologie und Theorie der Sympathiegefühle*. Halle: Niemeyer, 1913.

Spiegelberg, Herbert. *The Phenomenological Movement*. 2nd ed. Dordrecht: Springer, 1965.

Stein, Edith. *Beiträge zur philosophischen Begründung der Psychologie und der Geisteswissenschaften*. *Jahrbuch für Philosophie und phänomenologische Forschung* 5 (1922): 1–283.

Stein, Edith. *Zur Problem der Einfühlung*. Halle: Waisenhaus, 1917.

Tolley, Clinton. "Husserl's Philosophy of the Categories and His Development toward Absolute Idealism." *Grazer Philosophische Studien* 94 (2017): 460–493.

Tolley, Clinton. "Representation, Consciousness, and Mind in German Idealism." In *Philosophy of Mind in the Nineteenth Century*, edited by S. Lapointe, 23–41. London: Routledge, 2017.

Vaihinger, H., and B. Bauch, eds. *Kant-Studien*. Vol. 18. Berlin: Reuther and Reichard, 1913.

Vendrell-Ferran, Íngrid. "Else Voigtländer." In *The Routledge Handbook of Phenomenology of Emotion*, edited by H. Landweer and T. Szanto, 96–103. London: Routledge, 2020.

Voigtländer, Else. "Geschlechtsunterschiede (psychische)." In Marcuse, *Handwörterbuch der Sexualwissenschaft*, 176–182.

Voigtländer, Else. "Über die 'Art' eines Menschen und das Erlebnis der 'Maske.'" *Zeitschrift für Psychologie* 92 (1923): 326–336.

Voigtländer, Else. "Über die Bedeutung Freuds für die Psychologie." In *Muenchener philosophische Abhandlungen*, edited by A. Pfänder, 294–316. Leipzig: Barth, 1911.

Voigtländer, Else. *Über die Typen des Selbstgefühls*. Leipzig: R. Voigtländers Verlag, 1910.

Voigtländer, Else. "Verwahrlosung (sexuelle)." In Marcuse, *Handwörterbuch der Sexualwissenschaft*, 475–478.

Voigtländer, Else. "Zur Phaenomenologie und Psychologie des 'alpinen Erlebnissen.'" *Zeitschrift für angewandte Psychologie* 22 (1923): 258–270.

Waithe, Mary Ellen, ed. *A History of Women Philosophers: Modern Women Philosophers, 1600–1900*. Vol. 4. Dordrecht: Springer, 1995.

Walther, Gerda. *Ein Beitrag zur Ontologie der sozialen Gemeinschaften*. Halle: Niemeyer, 1922.

Walther, Gerda. *Zur Phänomenologie der Mystik*. Halle: Niemeyer, 1923.

Weiler, Michael. Editor's introduction to *Husserliana Band XXXII: Natur und Geist, Vorlesungen Sommersemester 1927*, xi–li. Dordrecht: Springer, 2001.

Zahavi, Dan. "Empathy, Embodiment and Interpersonal Understanding: From Lipps to Schutz." *Inquiry* 53, no. 3 (2010): 285–306.

PART III

TOPICS

CHAPTER 23

···

THE IDEA OF THE EARTH IN GÜNDERRODE, SCHELLING, AND HEGEL

···

KAREN NG

AN exciting array of philosophical and historical scholarship has now established be-yond doubt that the concept of nature lies at the center of German idealism and ro-manticism, bringing into view how the systematic (and antisystematic) ambitions of this period all revolve around thinking about the place of humanity within a distinctly modern understanding of nature. In noting that this approach to nature is *modern*, I mean to suggest a number of interconnected features that define this philosophical con-text. First, there is the new, emerging science of biology at the turn of the nineteenth century, a context in which German *Naturphilosophie* played a central role.[1] Second, there is the increasing awareness of a global, universal humanity continuous with na-ture (what Herder called *Humanität*), alongside a creeping sense of alienation from nature resulting from the disintegration of traditional forms of life (well-documented, for example in the writings of Schiller and Hegel).[2] Third, there is, following Andrea Wulf, the very *invention* of the idea of nature itself, an invention led, on her account, by Alexander von Humboldt. Humboldt, she argues, "saw the earth as one great living or-ganism where everything was connected," changing the way we understood our relation

---

[1] See John Zammito, *The Gestation of German Biology: Philosophy and Physiology from Stahl to Schelling* (Chicago: University of Chicago Press, 2018); Robert Richards, *The Romantic Conception of Life: Science and Philosophy in the Age of Goethe* (Chicago: University of Chicago Press, 2002); and Peter Hanns Reill, *Vitalization Nature in the Enlightenment* (Berkeley: University of California Press, 2005).

[2] See Alison Stone, "Alienation from Nature in early German Romanticism," *Ethical Theory and Moral Practice* 17, no. 1 (2014): 41–54. Stone contrasts the approach to alienation from and reconciliation with nature taken by Hegel, Fichte, and Marx with that of Schlegel and Novalis, arguing that the latter, romantic approach in which reconciliation with nature involves an ineradicable dimension of alienation, is better suited to understanding and addressing our present environmental crisis.

to nature while at the same time inventing the very idea of nature as we understand it today.[3] Against the background of these complex but interconnected developments, the question of the relation between human beings and nature gradually came to be understood as a question about our relation to the *earth*.[4] More specifically, the human question came to be understood as part of a larger question about *life on earth*, a question that stretched beyond biology into epistemology, metaphysics, ethics, and social and political philosophy.

Within this wide-ranging context, Karoline von Günderrode's 1805 unpublished fragment "The Idea of the Earth" is noteworthy for a number of reasons. Although her contributions have long been neglected by philosophers, Anna Ezekiel's extensive research and translation work has shown that Günderrode's writings, which include philosophical fragments, dialogues, poetry, dramas, ballads, and fictional and semifictional fragments, were not only in dialogue with the central figures and ideas of German idealism and romanticism, but moreover, make distinctive philosophical contributions to the major questions of the period from a unique and underappreciated perspective.[5] With respect to the philosophy of nature in particular, both Ezekiel and Dalia Nassar have recently argued that her position cannot be easily assimilated with the views of figures such as Herder, Fichte, Schelling, or Hegel, despite engaging seriously with the work of the first three.[6] Building on this attempt to recover her distinctive philosophical contribution to this period, I argue that in focusing on the *earth*, Günderrode's fragment, and her philosophy of nature more broadly, provides a different model for a unified idealist philosophy, shedding new light on both theoretical and practical questions.

On the theoretical side, Günderrode's claim that the *earth* is a "realized Idea" (*eine realisirte Idee*) suggests an alternative approach to the complicated concept of "the Idea" (*die Idee*) that plays an important role in both Schelling and Hegel's philosophies.[7]

---

[3] Andrea Wulf, *The Invention of Nature: Alexander von Humboldt's New World* (New York: Penguin Random House, 2015), 2.

[4] On the importance of the study of the earth and its history in the shift from a descriptive, classificatory approach to nature to the "history of nature" approach that explicitly recognized nature as undergoing change and development, see Zammito, *Gestation of German Biology*, 173.

[5] See Anna C. Ezekiel, introduction to *Poetic Fragments*, by Karoline von Günderrode, trans. Anna C. Ezekiel (Albany: State University of New York Press, 2016), 1–37. On Günderrode's contributions to the philosophy of nature, see Wolfgang Westphal, *Karoline von Günderrode und "Naturdenken um 1800"* (Essen: Verlag Die Blaue Eule, 1993).

[6] See Anna C. Ezekiel, "Revolution and Revitalization: Karoline von Günderrode's Political Philosophy and Its Metaphysical Foundations," *British Journal for the History of Philosophy*, September 17, 2020, https://doi.org/10.1080/09608788.2020.1806033; and Dalia Nassar, "The Human Vocation and the Question of the Earth: Karoline von Günderrode's Philosophy of Nature," *Archiv für Geschichte der Philosophie* 104, no. 1 (2022): 108–130. Günderrode's notes on Fichte's *Bestimmung des Menschen* and her notes on Schelling's *Naturphilosophie* are translated by Ezekiel in Dalia Nassar and Kristin Gjesdal, eds., *Women Philosophers in the Long Nineteenth Century: The German Tradition* (New York: Oxford, 2021).

[7] I will capitalize "Idea" when referring to its technical use in the texts discussed in order to distinguish it from ordinary uses of the term.

In Schelling and Hegel, the Idea represents the foundation of their philosophies, providing an absolute criterion of truth. Although their views differ in a number of ways, the Idea as an absolute criterion of truth is generally presented by both in connection with organic form, with Hegel arguing in the conclusion of the *Science of Logic* that *life* is the immediate manifestation of the Idea. In presenting the *earth* as the realized Idea, I suggest that Günderrode offers an alternative way of understanding both the Idea as a criterion of truth and the role of earthly life as a manifestation of the Idea. "The Idea of the Earth" resists both the more Platonic aspects of Schelling's approach to the Idea, and the tendency in Hegel's approach to strongly identify actuality with rationality. The focus on the earth as the context of truth also provides a different approach to idealism beyond the near exclusive focus on a subject/object schema. Instead, idealism is organized around an earthly context of knowledge that Günderrode calls "the All" (*die Allheit*).

On the practical side, Günderrode's fragment suggests that the activities and processes of earthly life strive toward the realization of a "collective organism" (*gemeinschaftlicher Organismus*). Although this idea is admittedly somewhat obscure, I suggest that the idea of a collective organism provides a different model for thinking about the ethical aims of living beings in relation to the earth, one in which virtue and justice are measured in relation to the achievement of a "collective organism." Here, I will focus on Günderrode's suggestion that the Idea of the earth is yet to be realized, arguing that she puts forward an ecological ethic of sustainability. In presenting her fragment as putting forward *both* theoretical and practical claims via the Idea of the earth, I argue that Günderrode presents a viable and unified idealist philosophy, one that departs from, and also corrects, her contemporaries in novel ways.

This chapter will proceed as follows. In section 1 I briefly take up the Idea in Kant, Schelling, and Hegel. I focus on three features of Schelling's account of the Idea from his *Bruno* in particular, and also point out some of the differences between Schelling and Hegel insofar as these are helpful for understanding Günderrode's employment of the term. Section 2 begins by framing Günderrode's fragment in connection with two claims: first, her claim that the earth is a *realized Idea*; and second, her claim that the Idea of the earth *is in the process of being realized*. Arguing against Nassar's interpretation of the fragment that divides theoretical and practical concerns and emphasizes Günderrode's engagement with Fichte's account of human vocation, I suggest that the former claim addresses a number of theoretical questions in the idealist context, whereas the latter claim addresses practical ones, taken up in sections 2 and 3, respectively. Section 3 further defends the compatibility of the two claims by presenting the unity of Günderrode's thought as taking a *dual aspect* approach and provides an interpretation of the goal of a collective organism. Section 4 concludes by considering the unity of the theoretical and the practical in the Idea of the earth. I argue that Günderrode provides an alternative to the idealist schema of subject/object identity and opposition in her understanding of theoretical and practical aims, and suggest that her fragment gestures toward an ecological holism.

1 The Idea (*Die Idee*):
Kant, Schelling, Hegel

Within the context of German idealist and romantic *Naturphilosophie*, one of the most innovative features of Günderrode's fragment is her deployment of the term "Idea" as directly associated with the earth. Her fragment begins by stating that "the earth is a realized Idea," a claim that immediately calls to mind the broad aims of *Naturphilosophie* to grasp the emergent ideal features of nature's processes and forms. For the German idealists and romantics, the philosophy of nature was essential for combatting the dualistic metaphysics of Kant and earlier thinkers: if features of the ideal (unity, organization, form, mindedness, intelligibility, self-relatedness, self-determination) were manifest in the real (nature broadly understood), then long-standing philosophical dualisms could be discarded and overcome, leading to a unified philosophy in which human activity and behavior were continuous with the natural world. Given these aims, it is no surprise that the philosophy of nature played a central role in nineteenth-century thought in thinkers as varied as Carl Friedrich Kielmeyer, Alexander von Humboldt, Bettina von Arnim, and Lou Salomé.

Günderrode stands out in this context by drawing our attention not just to the ideal features of nature generally, but to the ideality of the earth and its processes in particular. In the period immediately preceding the composition of this fragment, Günderrode engaged in an intensive study of Schelling's philosophy of nature, and many Schellingian themes are evident throughout the text. Most notably, it is Schelling who first makes reference to "the idea of earth" in *Bruno*, published in 1802, which Günderrode read in 1804.[8] Thus, in order to understand Günderrode's fragment in its proper philosophical context, I will begin by charting the most prevalent ways in which the term "Idea" was employed in Kant, Schelling, and Hegel, emphasizing Schelling's discussion in *Bruno* in particular.

In the *Critique of Pure Reason*, Kant introduces his discussion of the transcendental ideas by affirming the Platonic origins of his use of the term:

> Plato made use of the expression *idea* in such a way that we can readily see that he understood by it something that not only could never be borrowed from the senses, but

---

[8] See Ezekiel, "Earth, Spirit, Humanity: Community and the Nonhuman in Karoline von Günderrode's 'Idea of the Earth,'" forthcoming in *Romanticism and Political Ecology*, ed. Kir Kuiken (Romantic Praxis Circle); and Ezekiel, "Revolution and Revitalization," 4. Nassar notes that Günderrode first learned of Schelling's philosophy in the summer of 1804 ("The Human Vocation," 4). In *Bruno*, Schelling writes: "the created earth, for instance, is not the true earth, but only an image of the earth which is uncreated, unoriginated, and never to pass away. But the idea of the earth also contains the ideas of all things that are included in it or that come into existence in it." See F. W. J. Schelling, *Bruno, Or On the Natural and the Divine Principle of Things* (1802), ed. and trans. Michael G. Vater (Albany: State University of New York Press, 1984), 125; F. W. J. Schelling, *Historisch-kritische Ausgabe*, ed. Hartmut Baumgartner, Wilhelm G. Jacobs, Jörg Janzen, and Hermann Krings (Stuttgart: Frommann-Holzboog, 1976–), I:11, 1:347.

that even goes far beyond the concepts of the understanding (with which Aristotle occupied himself), since nothing encountered in experience could ever be congruent to it. Ideas for him are archetypes of things themselves, and not, like the categories, merely the keys to possible experience. In his opinion they flowed from the highest reason, through which human reason partakes in them.[9]

In affirming Plato's general approach to the idea as untouched by anything borrowed from sensation, Kant draws a distinction here between his own account of the categories, which, although a priori, are nonetheless congruent with objects of possible experience, and ideas, which are *archetypes of things themselves* and whose objects cannot be given in experience whatsoever. As archetypes, the ideas originate from reason's activity of making syllogistic inferences, which is driven by the demand to search for the unconditioned—a totality of conditions that provides unity and a complete explanation of all the concepts of the understanding.[10] Although Kant discusses three transcendental ideas in the Transcendental Dialectic of the first *Critique*—the soul, the idea of the world as a whole, and the idea of God—that correspond to the categorical, hypothetical, and disjunctive syllogisms, respectively, there is, ultimately, one, overarching idea of reason, namely, the idea of the *unconditioned*.[11] In associating reason's demand for the unconditioned as a demand for something that can never be an object of cognition, the idea for Kant represents an absolute limit to reason's systematic ambitions, barring it from playing a foundational role in a system of knowledge.[12]

Schelling and Hegel affirm and reject different aspects of Kant's way of employing this term, but for both, the Idea becomes central for how they approach the construction of their philosophical systems. Although they affirm Kant's association of the Idea with the unconditioned, both reject the limitations that Kant places on the possibility of knowing the Idea, and instead present the Idea as a foundational, absolute criterion of truth. The analysis of the Idea as foundational for a system of philosophy is particularly evident in *Bruno*. The discussion of the Idea in this text, written as a dialogue in which Schelling (represented by the titular Bruno, loosely referencing Giordano Bruno) presents his philosophy of absolute identity against Fichte, and showing clear sympathies with Plato's *Timaeus*, is particularly instructive for understanding Günderrode's fragment.

There are three features of the Idea from *Bruno* that I want to highlight in particular. The first is Schelling's appropriation of the Idea as the unconditioned first principle of his absolute idealism. Marking the height of his identity philosophy, Schelling's choice to associate his principle of identity with the Idea is, at least in part, an attempt to

---

[9] Immanuel Kant, *Critique of Pure Reason*, ed. and trans. Paul Guyer and Allen W. Wood (Cambridge: Cambridge University Press, 1998) / *Werkausgabe in 12 Bänden*, ed. Wilhelm Weischedel (Frankfurt am Main: Suhrkamp, 1974), III/IV: A313/B370.

[10] Kant, *Critique of Pure Reason/Werkausgabe*, III/IV: A321–322/B378–379.

[11] Kant, *Critique of Pure Reason/Werkausgabe*, III/IV: A409/B436.

[12] The ideas have a regulative rather than a constitutive use for theoretical reason and also serve as the ground of the postulates of pure practical reason.

respond to Kant's suggestion that the Idea cannot be an object of cognition.[13] In this period of Schelling's philosophical development, he is in the midst of a dispute with Fichte
in which he accuses Fichte of putting forward a merely subjective philosophy of consciousness, while at work constructing a philosophy of identity that comprises both a
transcendental philosophy and a philosophy of nature.[14] The principle of this philosophy is the absolute identity of opposites, an identity that lies at the source of all reality
and knowledge. Discussing the first principle of philosophy as the Idea, Bruno states the
following shortly after entering the dialogue:

> now to lay the foundation for our dialogue! . . . We can all agree on this funda-
> mental notion: the Idea, wherein all opposites are not just united, but are simply
> identical, wherein all opposites are not just cancelled, but are entirely undivided
> from one another. So I begin by praising this principle as first and prior to all else .
> . . 'identity' itself along with 'opposition' will form the highest pair of opposites . . .
> the identity of identity and opposition, or the identity of the self-identical and the
> nonidentical.[15]

As the identity of opposites—Hegel will call this "speculative identity"[16]—the Idea
here opposes Kant's approach to dialectic, in which reason is faced with irresolvable
antinomies in its search for the unconditioned, but also opposes Plato's approach to
the Idea, despite the many Platonic resonances that are scattered throughout the dialogue. (Obviously the dialogue form itself hearkens back to Plato.) One of the central
oppositions united in the Idea is that between the finite and the infinite, and throughout,
Schelling also insists that the Idea is eternal. Many scholars have noted that Schelling's
understanding of eternity here is Spinozist, disassociated with time, duration, and most
important, transcendence, instead referring to the necessary or intrinsic connection
of things.[17] In rejecting the transcendence of the Idea and appropriating the dialectic
of opposites as the key to his philosophical system, Schelling's principle of identity
becomes the basis for linking his transcendental philosophy with his philosophy of nature, providing an alternative to Fichte's merely subjective approach to identity and opposition. Looking ahead, Günderrode will reinterpret the identity of opposites in terms

---

[13] Schelling's choice also reflects his attempt to revive Neoplatonic philosophy in a post-Kantian
context. On Schelling's engagement with Neoplatonic ideas, see Werner Beierwaltes, "The Legacy of
Neoplatonism in F. W. J. Schelling's Thought," *International Journal of Philosophical Studies* 10, no. 4
(2002): 393–428.

[14] This is most clearly stated in the opening of Schelling's *System of Transcendental Idealism*, a text
with which Günderrode was familiar.

[15] Schelling, *Bruno*, 136/*Historisch-kritische Ausgabe*, I:11, 1:358–359.

[16] On the development of Hegel's speculative identity thesis during this same period, see chap. 3 of
Karen Ng, *Hegel's Concept of Life: Self-Consciousness, Freedom, Logic* (New York: Oxford, 2020).

[17] Julie R. Klein, "'By Eternity I Understand': Eternity According to Spinoza," *Iyyun: The Jerusalem
Philosophical Quarterly* 51 (July 2002): 297. On eternity in Schelling's *Bruno*, see also Jason M. Wirth,
"Who Is Schelling's Bruno?" *Rivista di estetica* 74 (2020): 181–190.

of processes of synthesis and dissolution, with the interconnections between mortality and immortality giving shape to the earth as Idea.

In addition to being the absolute principle of the identity of opposition, the Idea for Schelling, as mentioned, is also a criterion of truth. Schelling continues, speaking as Bruno:

> the Idea . . . inasmuch as it unites multiplicity and unity or finitude and infinity, is identically related to both factors. Since we learned earlier that philosophy is concerned solely with the eternal concepts of things, we now realize that philosophy has but one sole object of study, the Idea of all Ideas. And this one Idea is exactly what we conveyed in our formulas for the supreme principle, "the indivisible unity of the identical and the differentiated" and "the inseparability of thought and intuition." The nature of this Idea's identity is that of truth itself, and beauty. For the beautiful is what absolutely identifies the universal and the particular, or unites the species and the individual, as in the [ideal human] forms of the gods. But this same identity is truth too, and the sole truth. And since we regard this Idea as the best criterion of truth available, we will accept only what conforms to this Idea as absolutely true, but what does not measure up to the Idea's truth, we will account merely relative and unreliable truths.[18]

Putting aside the question of beauty, why is the Idea the best criterion of truth available?[19] In defining the Idea in terms of the unity of opposites, Schelling (and Hegel, too) have in mind particular sets of oppositions whose unity and relation are generally taken to be a condition for truth. In this passage, "thought and intuition" as well as "universal and particular" are clear instances of this, but the most general unity and relationship that is at stake for all the German idealists is the one between the *subjective* and the *objective*, with Schelling claiming that "all knowledge is founded upon the coincidence of an objective with a subjective.—For we *know* only what is true; but truth is generally taken to consist in the coincidence of presentations with their objects."[20] Hegel defines the Idea as the unity of concept and objectivity or the unity of concept and reality, going as far as to say that the Idea is the "objectively *true*, or the *true as such*. If anything has truth, it has it by virtue of its Idea, or *something has truth only insofar as it is Idea*."[21] Truth, then, for Hegel and Schelling, is measured in connection with the degree or extent to which the relationship expressed in the Idea is realized. Although I will discuss in a moment a disagreement between Schelling and Hegel in their understanding of the

---

[18] Schelling, *Bruno*, 143/*Historisch-kritische Ausgabe*, I:11, 1:365–366.

[19] *Bruno* opens with a discussion of the relation between beauty and truth, which is often read as a continuation of the account of the relation between art and philosophy in the conclusion of the *1800* System. In Hegel's aesthetics, beauty is understood as the sensuous appearance of the Idea.

[20] F. W. J. Schelling, *System of Transcendental Idealism* (1800), trans. Peter Heath (Charlottesville: University Press of Virginia, 1978), 5/*Historisch-kritische Ausgabe*, I:9, 1:29.

[21] G. W. F. Hegel, *Science of Logic*, trans. George DiGiovanni (Cambridge: Cambridge University Press, 2010), 670/*Werke in 20 Bänden*, ed. Eva Moldenhauer and Karl Markus Michel (Frankfurt am Main: Suhrkamp, 1969), 6:462.

Idea, they agree that it supplies a criterion or model for truth insofar as both also define the Idea in connection with the principle of identity. Schelling concludes *Bruno* by claiming that to know the indifference contained in the principle of identity is to "uncover the original metal of truth."[22]

Third and finally, Schelling, but *not* Hegel, understands the Idea in terms of a relationship between archetypes (*Urbilder*) and their visible appearances, variously described as embodiments, copies, images, and models of the Idea (*Körperwerdung, Abbilder, Vorbilder*).[23] Thus, despite Schelling's anti-Platonism in rejecting the consignment of Ideas to a transcendent heaven, he nonetheless employs a Platonic model in understanding how the Idea appears in the visible, temporal world.[24] In *Bruno*, and consistent with other writings from this period, Schelling grants pride of place to the appearing form of an organism, suggesting that it, more than other finite entities, provides an image of the archetype of the absolute Idea, uniting actuality and possibility, the ideal and the real, soul and body, and concept and reality.[25] Although all finite things in the universe are an embodiment or image of the Idea to some degree, organic nature, Schelling writes, is the "most visible proof" of transcendental idealism, offering an image not only of the archetype of the Idea, but also an image of consciousness, the deduction of which occupies a large part of *Bruno*.[26] The organism provides an image or model for the organization of the universe itself, which "is such a well-organized animal that it can never die."[27] In short, the appearing form of the organism is the key to Schelling's understanding of how archetypes of the Idea become embodied in the visible world, instead of being consigned to a transcendent beyond.

Before turning directly to Günderrode's fragment, I want to note some differences between Schelling and Hegel in their approach to the Idea, ones that are important for situating her presentation of the earth as Idea. First, Hegel eschews Schelling's Platonic model of archetypes and images, largely on account of the fact that the apprehension of such archetypes depends upon what Hegel takes to be a problematic theory of intellectual and aesthetic intuition. Instead, Hegel adopts an expressive or manifestation model of how the absolute appears, arguing that there is an essential relation between the inner and the outer in the manifestation of the absolute.[28] This allows him to avoid a tendency in Schelling to present a reified version of the absolute in terms of a principle of identity or an eternal archetype, with Hegel focusing instead on presenting the absolute as a

---

[22] Schelling, *Bruno*, 221/*Historisch-kritische Ausgabe*, I:11, 1:446.

[23] See Schelling, Bruno, 151, 160, 162, 202, 210–211/*Historisch-kritische Ausgabe*, I:11, 1:373, 383, 384, 425, 435–436.

[24] Another possible model here for understanding Schelling's account of the archetype/image relation is Kant's account of symbolic intuition and aesthetic ideas. See chap. 2 of Eliza Starbuck Little, "The Self-Exhibition of Reason: Hegel on Intuition and Logical Content" (PhD Diss., University of Chicago, 2020).

[25] Schelling, *Bruno*, 150–151/*Historisch-kritische Ausgabe*, I:11, 1:372–373.

[26] Schelling *System*, 122/*Historisch-kritische Ausgabe*, I:9, 1:187.

[27] Schelling, *Bruno*, 176/*Historisch-kritische Ausgabe*, I:11, 1:399.

[28] Hegel discusses the essential relation between inner and outer as manifestation in the transition to the section on "Actuality" in the *Science of Logic*. See Hegel, *Science of Logic*, 460–464/*Werke*, 6:179–185.

method that results from a developmental process, rather than serving as an unconditioned first principle. In line with this shift, Hegel argues at the end of his *Science of Logic* that the immediate manifestation of the Idea is *life*, where the emphasis is placed on understanding living activity as a form of knowing, rather than on grasping the archetypal form of the organism. For Hegel then, the activity of life is a realization or actualization of the Idea, rather than simply an image of the Idea.

Second, in adopting a manifestation model for understanding the appearing of the absolute, Hegel, notoriously, establishes a very tight connection between the actual and the rational. He writes:

> We now reserve the expression 'Idea' for the objective or real concept . . . [and] definitely reject that estimate of it according to which the Idea is something with no actuality . . . we must not regard it as just a *goal* which is to be approximated but itself remains always a kind of *beyond*; we must rather regard everything *as being* actual only to the extent that it has the Idea in it and expresses it.[29]

This passage expresses Hegel's characteristic critique of merely approximating or striving for goals that are in principle unattainable or that lie in a transcendent *beyond* (Kant and Fichte are frequent targets here). In avoiding the Schellingian language of archetypes and images,[30] Hegel focuses on presenting the Idea as actuality and living activity, one manifest in various modes and that expresses varying stages of development, but always contains a kernel of reason. As the manifest reality of rationality as such, the Idea is not something we can strive for directly or intentionally, and finite individuals are ultimately subject to the cunning of reason.

In the following sections, I consider how Günderrode transforms the idealist context that is familiar to us in the works of Schelling and Hegel. Taking a *dual aspect* approach to the Idea of the earth, her theoretical and practical contributions correct some of the problems we find in both Schelling and Hegel, while also developing and transforming idealism in the process.

2 The Earth as a Realized Idea

Günderrode composed "The Idea of the Earth" during a period in which she was engaged in intensive study of both Fichte and Schelling, and resonances of Schelling's philosophy of nature can be heard throughout the fragment.[31] In spite of this, Nassar

---

[29] Hegel, *Science of Logic*, 671/ *Werke*, 6:463–464.

[30] Hegel does not *entirely* eschew this language; in the addition of the opening of the *Philosophy of Mind*, it states that the philosophical approach to *Geist* comprehends it as "ein Abbild der ewigen Idee" (Hegel, *Werke*, 10:§377Z).

[31] The "Idea of the Earth" was meant to be published in Günderrode's third collection of writings, *Melete*, in 1806. However, its publication was stopped by Georg Friedrich Creuzer after her death in

has argued that we should instead understand Günderrode's fragment as a critical engagement with Fichte's idea of human vocation, which she transforms in light of thinking about the moral goals associated with the vocation of the earth itself.[32] Although I agree with Nassar that the fragment can be helpfully read with the question of human vocation in view, Nassar's argument is premised on a division between the theoretical and practical insights of *Naturphilosophie*, a division in which one strand privileges metaphysical and epistemological questions over moral ones (for example, Schelling), and another strand privileges moral questions over theoretical ones (for example, Novalis).[33] Within this presupposed division, Günderrode presents a third path, arguing that human beings ought to transform themselves for the sake of the earth's vocation.[34] However, I think that framing Günderrode's contribution against the background of a division between the theoretical and the practical misconstrues what I take to the be the holistic and monistic framework of German idealism and romanticism, which, despite their differing approaches, defend the ultimate *unity* of theoretical and practical aims. I argue that focusing on Günderrode's approach to the earth as *Idea*, rather than as vocation, can better account for this unity, a unity that is clearly presented in the fragment itself.[35]

One of the most striking features of Günderrode's fragment is her suggestion both that

1) the earth is a realized Idea, and
2) that the Idea of the earth is something that is in the process of being realized.

Trying to understand both of these claims as well as their relation and compatibility for Günderrode's idealism will take up the remainder of the chapter, but for now we can note the following:

1) As a realized Idea, the claim appears to be that the unity and processes of the earth are a manifest reality or actuality of the Idea;
2) but as something that is in the process of being realized, the Idea of the earth appears to be a projected goal, whose complete realization is as yet uncertain.

---

that same year for fear of exposing their affair, and the collection remained unpublished until 1906. See Ezekiel, introduction to *Poetic Fragments*, 7. There are two versions of the fragment, and in what follows I cite from the following text: Karolina von Günderrode, "Idee der Erde," in *Sämtliche Werke und ausgewählte Studien*, ed. Walter Morgenthaler (Frankfurt am Main: Roter Stern, 1990–91), vol. 1, 446–449 (henceforth SW, followed by volume and page number). The English translations used are Anna Ezekiel's, found in Nassar and Gjesdal, *Women Philosophers in the Long Nineteenth Century*.

[32] Nassar contrasts her Fichtean reading with those of Morgenthaler, Westphal, and Helga Dormann, who all interpret Günderrode on Schellingian terms. See Nassar, "The Human Vocation," 5, n.13.

[33] Nassar, "The Human Vocation," 2–3.

[34] Nassar, "The Human Vocation," 6.

[35] Alison Stone and Giulia Valpione also remark that within their consideration of the women philosophers writing during this period, Günderrode's work comes closest to "Idealist system-building." See chapter 17 here.

This section takes up the first claim from the perspective of theoretical questions surrounding the Idea, and the next section will take up the second claim from the perspective of the practical. Günderrode opens the fragment with the first claim, writing:

> the earth is a realized Idea [realisirte Idee], one that is simultaneously effective (force) and effected (appearance). It is thus a unity of soul and body [Leib], of which we call the pole of its activity that it turns outward extension, form, body; the one it turns inwards *intension*, essence, force, soul. Now, as the whole of the earth only exists through this unification of soul and body, so, too, the individual and smallest things only exist through it and cannot be conceived as split in two, for an outer without an inner, an essence without form, a force without some sort of effect, is not comprehensible.[36]

As a realized Idea, the unity that is realized in the earth is that between body and soul, but this unity has two poles of activity: an activity that turns *outward,* appearing as extension, body, and form; and an activity that turns *inward,* manifest as essence, force, and soul. The earth exists in virtue of this unity of inner and outer. Günderrode claims that this unity is the condition of individual things in two senses: first the earth, as an existing, realized unity of inner and outer, sustains the *existence* of earthly individual things; and second, the unity between inner and outer realized in the earth is a condition for the *comprehensibility* of individual things. In combining the conditions of existence and comprehensibility in this way, Günderrode provides an alternative approach to the idealist problem of the relationship between being and thinking, or the real and the ideal, suggesting that the existence and comprehensibility of earthly things are ultimately sustained and conditioned by the earth as a realized Idea. I take it that whereas the former is not so controversial (namely, the claim that the *existence* of earthly things is sustained by and stands in a necessary relation to the unity of the earth), the latter is certainly novel, and at least potentially controversial (namely, the claim that we can only *comprehend* earthly, individual things on the basis of a unity of the inner and outer that is realized in the unity of the earth). Her presentation of the unity of the earth in terms of activity that turns outward and inward also anticipates Hegel's approach to the manifestation of the absolute against Schelling, well before Hegel himself had settled on his own view.[37]

---

[36] SW I, 446.

[37] Hegel's 1804–1805 Jena system of logic and metaphysics contains some of the categories of his mature logic, but the relation between inner and outer as a key component for understanding infinity, life, and the manifestation of the absolute had not yet been fully developed at this time. In the Jena system, Hegel discusses some of the relevant categories (most notably, *Wechselwirkung*) under the heading "Das Verhältnis." See Hegel, *Jenaer Systementwürfe II: Logik, Metaphysik, Naturphilosophie,* ed. Rolf-Peter Horstmann (Hamburg: Felix Meiner Verlag, 1982). In the *Science of Logic,* Hegel discusses the concept (*der Begriff*) as turning inward and outward. See Hegel, *Science of Logic,* 529–549/*Werke,* 6:273–301; and the discussion in chap. 5 of Ng, *Hegel's Concept of Life.*

That the Idea for Günderrode serves as a ground for thinking about the relation be-tween the real and the ideal is also clear from her notes on *Naturphilosophie*.[38] Here she discusses nature as the realized Idea: "now, this eternal nature is neither only real nor only ideal, neither only essence nor only form, but, again, an absolute unity of both: a realized Idea, an essence that molds itself in forms, forms that dissolve themselves in essence, and a unity of both."[39] Her emphasis on the realized Idea is philosophically im-portant for a number of reasons. First, like Schelling and Hegel, she eschews placing the Idea in a transcendent beyond, but she also directly claims that nature, and more specif-ically *the earth as a whole*, is a realized Idea. Although Schelling and Hegel do affirm that nature is a realization of the Idea *to an extent*, both set clear limitations on nature as Idea in a way that Günderrode does not. For Schelling and Hegel, nature is "petrified intel-ligence,"[40] it is an unconscious, weak, and incomplete form of mind, whose *telos* is the spiritual life of human beings. In arguing that the earth is a realized Idea, Günderrode deliberately resists this teleological, anthropocentric view, claiming instead that the unity of the earth is self-sufficient for unfolding the unity of the ideal and the real. In her understanding of the Idea, then, she not only eschews the difficult Schellingian problem of how archetypes relate to their images, but she also displaces the organism as the key to grasping the unity of the ideal the real. Instead, she proposes an *earthly* model of ide-alism in which the unity of essence and form can take myriad shapes in connection with the earth as a whole.

Second, the realized Idea for Günderrode is not defined primarily by opposition, which is the case for both Schelling and Hegel. Instead, the earth expresses its unity through the synthesis and dissolution (*Auflösung*) of different elements, with life being but one result of these processes. She writes: "the most intimate mingling of different elements with the highest degree of contact and attraction we call life."[41] These processes of synthesis and dissolution generate degrees of liveliness, harmony, death, and sepa-ration, but each individual, mortal element is sustained and comprehensible only on account of participating in the unity of the earth. Although she suggests that the ac-tivity of elements on earth must itself be understood within the context of the whole solar system, and even beyond that, the entire universe, it is the unity of the earth that sufficiently manifests the realized Idea.[42] One reason for this can be found in her use of the term "collective organism" (*gemeinschaftlicher Organismus*), which suggests that the earth itself can be treated as an organism only insofar as it forms a unified ecosystem. In the context of what I have called her earthly model of idealism, the "indifference point" or identity between the ideal and the real is realized in the unity of the earth it-self, rather than the unity of the organism. Instead of modeling idealism on the unity

---

[38] These are notes taken from her study of Schelling, published in SW II.

[39] SW II, 379.

[40] Schelling, *System*, 6/*Historisch-kritische Ausgabe*, I:9, 1:31; Hegel, *Philosophy of Nature/Werke*, 9:§247Z.

[41] SW I, 446.

[42] SW I, 448.

and activity of an organism standing in opposition to inanimate, recalcitrant nature, the unity of the earth unfolds through processes of synthesis and dissolution in which the relation between life and death is fluid and deeply interconnected. As in an ecosystem, life and death are intimately comingled and death sustains new life. Günderrode writes: "now, when a person is dead, their mixture returns to the substance of the earth, but that within them which we called force, activity, or rather that of its materials in which the more active pole predominated, reverts to that which is related to it in the earth . . . these elements increase the earth's life in returning to the earth."[43]

Third and finally, the earth as realized Idea is also a condition for truth. Earlier I noted Günderrode's claim that the *comprehensibility* of individual, earthly things depends upon grasping their unity of inner and outer, or essence and form, a unity that is realized most fully in the unity of the earth itself. Near the end of her fragment, Günderrode also speaks directly to the question of truth, stating:

> truth is the expression [Ausdruck] of what *is always the same* as itself; justice is the striving of the All [Allheit] in the particular [Einzelheit] to be the same as itself; beauty is being the same as oneself and harmonious; love, benevolence, compassion is the longing of the particular to enjoy itself in the All, i.e., to become aware of the All in the particular, and, renouncing personhood [Personlichkeit], to surrender itself to the All. . . . Through any kind of truth, justice, beauty, and virtue it becomes more like itself, more harmonious, and freer of the bonds of personhood; through every act of injustice, untruth, and selfishness this state is made more distant.[44]

Truth is situated within a holistic but differentiated context that Günderrode calls the All (*Allheit*), which exists in varying degrees of harmony and dissolution. Truth is measured in relation to the degree of harmony and reality of the All. Whereas expressions of truth, justice, beauty, and virtue bring us closer to the All and to its realization, expressions of untruth, injustice, and selfishness create distance between us and the All and diminish its degree of reality. As the context for the possibility of truth, Günderrode directly associates the All with the realized Idea of the earth, but here, she argues that the immortal All is always in the midst of a process of being realized, something that can manifest degrees of reality. One way to interpret Günderrode's argument that the earth is a context of truth is through the idea of environments, or *Umwelten*, which open up a perceptual field of significance in which forms of theoretical and practical knowledge become possibilities.[45] Taking the earth as the interconnected system of all such environments, the increase of knowledge allows us to better bring that unity and harmony into view, whereas untruth and falsehoods diminish our capacity to see and

---

[43] SW I, 447.

[44] SW I, 448–449.

[45] See Jakob von Uexküll, *A Foray into the Worlds of Animals and Humans*, trans. Joseph D. O'Neil (Minneapolis: University of Minnesota Press, 2010). On *Umwelten* and their connection to species-specific capacities and senses, see Ed Yong, *An Immense World: How Animal Senses Reveal the Hidden Realms Around Us* (New York: Penguin, 2022).

comprehend that same unity. Moving beyond the prevalent idealist schema of thinking about knowledge and truth according to the relation between subject and object, Günderrode's earthly model of idealism does away with the need for the very division between transcendental philosophy and a philosophy of nature, and instead conceives of truth and knowledge in connection with the unity of the earth as a whole.

3 The Idea of the Earth in the Process of Being Realized

Although Günderrode begins her fragment with the claim that earth is the realized Idea, as the fragment progresses, she also suggests that the Idea of the earth is in the process of being realized, where this realization remains an uncertainty. Although Günderrode expresses uncertainty concerning whether or not the Idea of the earth will be fully realized, she does discuss in detail the processes through which the Idea *may* be realized, as well as the ultimate goal of these processes, which she calls the earth as a "collective organism" (*gemeinschaftlicher Organismus*).[46] Importantly, the uncertainty concerning the realization of the earth as a collective organism is not barred in principle, condemned to an infinite striving whose ultimate failure is assured in advance. Nothing in Günderrode's metaphysics suggests that the achievement of this goal is an ontological impossibility, which means that the uncertainty and even unlikelihood of its achievement is due to the contingency of history and individual agents acting within the limitations of prescribed social and political contexts.[47]

Before turning directly to Günderrode's discussion of the processes through which the Idea of the earth may or may not be realized, I want to address a potential objection here, namely, that she cannot claim *both* that the earth is a realized Idea, *and* that the earth is in the process of being realized without falling into a contradiction. To answer this, I propose that she takes a *dual aspect* approach to the Idea of the earth, one that is suggested in her claim that "all things have a double being." She writes:

> all things are, so to speak, finite presentations of the infinite, and so to a greater or lesser extent, all things have a double being [ein doppeltes Dasein]: an individual

---

[46] For a recent attempt to reconsider the idea of the earth as an organism (known as the Gaia hypothesis) from a Darwinian perspective, see W. Ford Doolittle, "Is the Earth an Organism?," *Aeon*, December 3, 2020, https://aeon.co/essays/the-gaia-hypothesis-reimagined-by-one-of-its-key-sceptics.

[47] Günderrode addresses questions concerning agency within the constraints of social and political contexts in a number of her dramas, including *Hildegrund* and *Muhammad, the Prophet of Mecca*, which are published in *Poetic Fragments*. Ezekiel argues that Günderrode's model of agency should be understood in contrast to the Kantian notion of freedom as autonomy, emphasizing instead that agency depends fundamentally upon the finitude and vulnerability of human subjects in relation to environments that escape their full control. See Anna C. Ezekiel, "Metamorphosis, Personhood, and Power in Karolina von Günderrode," *European Romantic Review* 25, no. 6: 773–791.

limited being, insofar as they constitute an independent entity [Wesen] for themselves; and a universal being, insofar as they are dependent on and connected with
the universe, and therefore are, at the same time, participants in the infinite. This
double being is the principle of all entities [Wesen]. Thus all the bodies [Körper] and
materials of the earth are each an individual being for themselves and also, at the
same time, a universal being insofar as they are an element that belongs to the great
whole of the earth. The earth itself has this double life.[48]

Günderrode goes on to discuss the double life of the earth in terms of the earth's movement around its own axis and the earth's movement around the sun, but this general,
philosophical distinction between the aspect of things taken as individual, independent, and limited, in contrast to the aspect of things taken as universal, connected
with the universe, and participants in the infinite, can helpfully situate what I am calling
Günderrode's dual aspect approach to the Idea of the earth. My suggestion is that
whereas her treatment of the earth as a realized Idea considers the earth from the aspect
of its universal, infinite being, her treatment of the earth as something that is in the process of being realized considers it from the aspect of its individual, limited being. That is,
as a universal being that is connected with the broader universe, the earth is a realized
Idea because it participates in the universe and manifests the unity of essence and form
that supports and sustains the individual elements of the earth. As an individual being
that is both limited and independent, the earth is continually in the process of being
realized in virtue of the ongoing synthesis and dissolution of elements that can enliven
or devitalize the earth. Whereas the first perspective presents the general, theoretical
tenets of an idealism in which the unity of the earth as the All supplies a condition and
context for truth, the second perspective takes up the practical dimension of agential activity within the context of earthly life. I now want to turn to this second perspective to
consider Günderrode's understanding of the earth's processes which strive to realize the
earth as a collective organism.
    Although there are undoubtedly ethical undertones in Günderrode's account of what
is at stake in the realization of the Idea of the earth, I will begin by turning to the way she
describes the processes at work in this development. She writes:

> each form that [the elements] produce is only a development of their life-principle.
> But the earth bears the life-material given back to it again in ever new appearances,
> until through ever new transformations everything capable of life in it has come to
> life. This would be when all mass would become organic; only then would the idea of
> the earth be realized.[49]

Thus the All [Allheit] comes to life through the downfall of the particular
[Einzelheit], and the particular lives on immortally in the All whose life it developed

---

[48] SW II, 368.
[49] SW I, 447.

while alive, and even after death elevates and increases, and so by living and dying helps to realize the Idea of the earth.[50]

The earth's ongoing realization takes place by means of the combination of earthly elements into determinate forms and appearances, some combinations of which constitute life, and their dissolution back into the earth by breaking up or dying as the case may be. As I showed earlier within the context of the earth as an ecosystem, life and death are intimately comingled, so much so that Günderrode claims that the particular lives on after death in the All. In addition, Günderrode suggests that the realization of the earth strives toward the increase and elevation of life, with the goal of all mass becoming organic. On the surface, the goal of all mass becoming organic seems not only impossible, but somewhat absurd. Moreover, why would this be a desirable goal at all? I suggest that her further formulation of the collective organism clarifies this somewhat, as well as warns against reading the goal of all mass becoming organic too literally. Instead, it is more fruitful to read Günderrode as suggesting that processes that enliven and harmonize the earth bring us closer to the goal of realizing the earth as a sustainable, well-functioning, and flourishing ecosystem, and that there are clearly processes both human and nonhuman that can undermine that goal—emphasizing of course that human activity overwhelmingly undermines that goal to the point of catastrophe in our present historical stage.

She describes the idea of a collective organism and her doubts concerning its realization as follows:

> the earth can therefore only attain its proper being [*Dasein*] when its organic and inorganic appearances dissolve in a collective organism [*gemeinschaftlichen Organismus*], when both factors—being (body) and thinking (spirit)—penetrate each other to the point of indistinguishability, where all body would also at the same time be thought, all thinking at the same time body, and a fully transfigured body, without lack or illness and immortal. . . I do not assert whether the earth will be altogether successful in organizing itself immortally like this.[51]

The idea of a collective organism suggests thinking about the earth as a collective community of both living and nonliving elements. The elements are mutually sustaining, and so their "dissolving" into a collective organism suggests that they coexist in symbiotic relations giving shape to a living ecosystem. The immortality of the earth can be understood in terms of sustainability: processes and relations that enable the long-term sustainability of the earth as a living ecosystem help to realize the Idea of the earth, whereas processes and relations that destroy the possibility of a sustainable earth devitalize the earth and move us further away from the goal of a collective organism. To be clear, although I think that Günderrode's approach to immortality extends beyond the thought

---

[50]   SW I, 447.
[51]   SW I, 448.

of sustainability, venturing into considerations of reincarnation and the afterlife,[52] the emphasis in this fragment on the goal of a collective organism makes sustainability a central feature of her ethical outlook. In fact, individual acts are measured according to whether or not they bring us closer or further from the goal of a collective organism. She writes: "all single virtues and excellences are therefore mere attempts by the earth-spirit to bring itself nearer to [realizing the earth as Idea]," whereas acts of injustice, untruth, and selfishness make the realization of the earth as Idea more remote.[53] Günderrode presents a novel and clear path for her practical philosophy, which extends the context of ethical life to the context of the earth as a whole. In presenting an ecological, earthly approach to thinking about the ultimate ends of both human and nonhuman activity, the idea of a collective organism is a powerful alternative to the near-exclusive attention in the idealist tradition on the goal of human freedom. Without denying the absolute importance of that latter goal, human freedom can nonetheless only be realized within the context of a habitable, enlivened, and sustainable earth.

4 Conclusion: The Unity of the Theoretical and the Practical in the Idea of the Earth

In focusing on Günderrode's presentation of the earth as Idea, I have argued that she defends both a theoretical and practical dimension of the Idea, addressing on the one hand, questions of knowledge and truth, as well as the long-standing idealist problem of the relation between the ideal and the real; on the other hand, her fragment also addresses questions of ethical agency and the ultimate goals toward which living activity strives. In combining these considerations through a focus on the earth, I want to conclude by suggesting that her approach puts forward two innovations, perhaps even two challenges, to prevailing idealist assumptions of this period.

First, in contrast to the focus on a subject/object schema that defines how Schelling and Hegel (and also Fichte) understand the absolute, Günderrode proposes that questions about the existence and comprehensibility of things can instead be addressed by considering the earth as a context of knowledge and truth. Generalizing somewhat across different figures and texts, the problem of knowledge for the idealists is always framed via the distinction, relation, identity, and opposition between subject and object, which results in different problems to be solved depending on whether one has theoretical or practical questions in view. Taking Hegel as the representative here, the Idea of the true consists in reconciling subject/object opposition into identity through theoretical means—that

---

[52] In "The Idea of the Earth," Günderrode associates her account of the relation between life and death with the "idea of the Indians of the transmigration of souls" (SW I, 447–448). See also "An Apocalyptic Fragment"; and "Piedro," "The Pilgrims," and "The Kiss in the Dream," in *Poetic Fragments*.

[53] SW I, 449.

is, subjects make the world intelligible by rendering it conformable with their theoretical capacities, which, depending on the subject in question, involves capacities such as sensation, as well as more sophisticated means such as definitions and theories, all of which are mediated by concepts, judgments, and syllogistic inferences. The Idea of the good consists in reconciling subject/object opposition into identity by transforming the world through action to make it conformable and hospitable to the living agent's needs and desires, and ultimately, its freedom.[54] For Hegel, this general schema for both theoretical and practical activity both privileges and is modeled on the activity of life. He states: "the perpetual action of life is thus Absolute Idealism; it becomes an other which, however, is always sublated. If life were a realist, it would have respect for the outer world; but it always inhibits the reality of the other and transforms it into its own self."[55] Although he indeed describes the earth itself as an organism that is the basis of life, the relation of living things and the earth consists in overcoming the opposition set by the subject/object divide, such that theoretical and practical aims, for humans and nonhuman animals alike, are fulfilled by transforming the world into an image of the self.[56]

In proposing the earth as a model for and realization of the Idea, Günderrode challenges the insistence on subject/object opposition and identity as the only path for understanding both theoretical and practical aims. On her account, individual things become comprehensible (*begreiflich*) not by sublating them into the form of self, but by grasping their connection to the unity of the earth. In claiming that "truth is the expression of what *is always the same* as itself," she does not mean that truth is static, ever-present, or self-evident; rather, she means to suggest that truth is measured in connection with its ability to reveal the earth's underlying unity and harmony. This is not to privilege unity and harmony over opposition and strife, for the latter are essential to the processes of synthesis and dissolution of elements that make up the life of the earth, contributing to its overall enlivenment or devitalization. Instead, truth, along with justice and virtue, bring us closer to comprehending and realizing the earth as a unified, interconnected, and sustainable totality, whereas untruth and injustice bring us further

[54] See the discussion of the Idea of the true and the Idea of the good in *Science of Logic*, 689–734/ *Werke*, 6:487–548, which take their point of departure from subjective drive. Hegel also discusses the activity of the animal organism in terms of theoretical and practical processes. See *Philosophy of Nature/ Werke* 9:§§357–366.

[55] Hegel, *Philosophy of Nature/Werke*, 9:§337Z.

[56] For attempts to employ Hegel's thought as instructive for environmental philosophy, see Alison Stone, *Petrified Intelligence: Nature in Hegel's Philosophy* (Albany: State University of New York Press, 2004); Nicholas Mowad, "The Natural World of Spirit: Hegel on the Value of Nature," *Environmental Philosophy* 9, no. 2 (Fall 2012): 47–66; and Wendell Kisner, *Ecological Ethics and Living Subjectivity in Hegel's Logic: The Middle Voice of Autopoietic Life* (New York: Palgrave MacMillan, 2014). For attempts to employ Schelling's thought for the same, see Elaine P. Miller, "'The World Must be Romanticised . . .': The (Environmental) Ethical Implications of Schelling's Organic Worldview," *Environmental Values* 14, no. 3 (August 2005): 295–316; Vincent Le, "Schelling and the Sixth Extinction: The Environmental Ethics Behind Schelling's Anthropomorphization of Nature," *Cosmos and History* 13, no. 3 (2017): 107–129; and Dalia Nassar, "An 'Ethics for the Transition': Schelling's Critique of Negative Philosophy and Its Significance for Environmental Thought," in *Schelling's Philosophy: Freedom, Nature, and Systematicity*, ed. G. Anthony Bruno (New York: Oxford University Press, 2020), 231–248.

from that goal. Theoretical and practical aims are comprehensible, determined, and realized not through the form of the self, but in relation to the earth as a living whole.

With the earth as a model for the realization of the Idea, Günderrode's second innovation and intervention pertains to the question of holism. It is relatively uncontroversial that the idealists—especially Schelling and Hegel—are committed to holism in a number of respects. Indeed, the extensive interest and emphasis on the form of the organism is due in part to their contention that it provides the best model for understanding genuine, self-sufficient wholes. Organic unity, as opposed to mere mechanical connection, becomes a standard for both truth and goodness: in connection with the former, Hegel goes as far as opposing his "living" logic to the "lifeless bones" of his opponents; in connection with the latter, he claims that ethical life is the "living good," developing an organic concept of the state as part of his theory of ethical life.[57] In associating the Idea of the earth with what she calls the All, Günderrode subtly shifts her holism in an ecological direction, making the earth the relevant whole of which we, and all other earthly elements, are a part. The elements of this whole include both living and nonliving individuals, self-conscious and unconscious beings, but it is through the processes of living and dying that the Idea of the earth as genuine whole might be realized. Günderrode's ecological holism attempts to uncover what it might mean for the earth to be the context for knowledge and truth, as well as a context for ethical action. The shift from the organic to the ecological, where the ecological does not exclude the organic, but sets its unity and activity in a wider context, opens up a new way of understanding the ultimate aims of living and human activity, which extend beyond individuals and even individual species, but takes into consideration how that activity contributes to, is dependent on, and is sustained by the earth as a whole.

Two features of Günderrode's ecological holism are worth mentioning in particular. First, an ecological approach does not eschew the importance of organic activity and form. Instead, it proposes that the best model for understanding a genuine, self-sufficient whole is not an organism per se, but the essential relations between organisms and their environments, where the earth constitutes the totality of such interconnected environments. As I have shown, the key terms of Günderrode's idealism are not identity and opposition, but synthesis and dissolution: an ecological holism makes categories such as reciprocity and symbiosis central for understanding the essential relations that constitute a genuine whole. A second consequence of this ecological approach is a deprioritizing—though *not erasure*—of the importance of self-sufficient individuals and individuality. This is signaled through Günderrode's talk of "elements," but it is also evident in her suggestion that "renouncing personhood" is a necessary aspect of understanding the truth of the particular in connection with the All.[58] For Günderrode,

---

[57] Hegel, *Science of Logic*, 12/*Werke*, 5:18; and *Elements of the Philosophy of Right*, ed. Allen W. Wood, trans. H. B. Nisbet (Cambridge: Cambridge University Press, 1991)/*Werke* 7:§142. Dean Moyar's *Hegel's Value* (Oxford: Oxford University Press, 2021), develops an interpretation of Hegel's theory of value modeled on the concept of life.

[58] SW I, 449.

the boundaries of an individual are often indeterminate, in constant flux, and always permeable, features that are necessary if we are to grasp the relations that constitute a genuine whole. Although Günderrode's fragment no doubt only presents a gesture toward this ecological holism, rather than its full, systematic articulation, this gesture is nonetheless an important intervention to existing idealist debates, posing a challenge to long-standing frameworks and assumptions.

In this chapter, I have argued that Günderrode's fragment, "The Idea of the Earth," represents a novel contribution to idealist philosophy that addresses both theoretical and practical concerns. Focusing on a dual aspect approach framed by her claim both that the earth is a realized Idea, and that the Idea of the earth is yet to be realized, I suggested that she presents an earthly model of idealism, arguing for the importance of the earth as a context of both truth and ethical life. In situating her work in contrast to Schelling and Hegel, I hope to have shown that Günderrode's work is an original contribution to the philosophical period of German idealism and romanticism. As philosophical research on her work continues to grow, our narratives of this period will no doubt change in interesting and unexpected ways.

BIBLIOGRAPHY

Beierwaltes, Werner. "The Legacy of Neoplatonism in F. W. J. Schelling's Thought." *International Journal of Philosophical Studies* 10, no. 4 (2002): 393–428.

Doolittle, W. Ford. "Is the Earth an Organism?" *Aeon*, December 3, 2020. https://aeon.co/essays/the-gaia-hypothesis-reimagined-by-one-of-its-key-sceptics.

Ezekiel, Anna C. "Earth, Spirit, Humanity: Community and the Nonhuman in Karoline von Günderrode's 'Idea of the Earth.'" In *Romanticism and Political Ecology*, edited by Kir Kuiken. Romantic Praxis Circle, forthcoming.

Ezekiel, Anna C. Introduction to *Poetic Fragments*, by Karoline von Günderrode, translated by Anna C. Ezekiel, 1–37. Albany: State University of New York Press, 2016.

Ezekiel, Anna C. "Metamorphosis, Personhood, and Power in Karolina von Günderrode." *European Romantic Review* 25, no. 6 (2014): 773–91.

Ezekiel, Anna C. "Revolution and Revitalization: Karoline von Günderrode's Political Philosophy and Its Metaphysical Foundations." *British Journal for the History of Philosophy*, September 17, 2020. https://doi.org/10.1080/09608788.2020.1806033.

Günderrode, Karoline von. *Poetic Fragments*. Translated by Anna C. Ezekiel. Albany: State University of New York Press, 2016.

Günderrode, Karoline von. *Sämtliche Werke und ausgewählte Studien*. Edited by Walther Morgenthaler. 3 vols. Frankfurt am Main: Roter Stern, 1990991.

Hegel, G. W. F. *Elements of the Philosophy of Right*. Edited by Allen W. Wood. Translated by H. B. Nisbet. Cambridge: Cambridge University Press, 1991.

Hegel, G. W. F. *Jenaer Systementwürfe II: Logik, Metaphysik, Naturphilosophie*. Edited by Rolf-Peter Horstmann. Hamburg: Felix Meiner Verlag, 1982.

Hegel, G. W. F. *Philosophy of Mind*. Translated by W. Wallace and A. V. Miller. Oxford: Oxford University Press, 2007.

Hegel, G. W. F. *Philosophy of Nature: Part Two of the Encyclopaedia of the Philosophical Sciences* (1830). Translated by A. V. Miller. Oxford: Oxford University Press, 1970.

Hegel, G. W. F. *Science of Logic.* Translated by George di Giovanni. Cambridge: Cambridge University Press, 2010.

Hegel, G. W. F. *Werke in 20 Bänden.* Edited by Eva Moldenhauer and Karl Markus Michel. Frankfurt am Main: Suhrkamp, 1969–71.

Kant, Immanuel. *Critique of Pure Reason.* Edited and translated by Paul Guyer and Allen W. Wood. Cambridge: Cambridge University Pres, 1998.

Kant, Immanuel. *Werkausgabe in 12 Bänden.* Edited by Wilhelm Weisschedel. Frankfurt am Main: Suhrkamp, 1974.

Kisner, Wendell. *Ecological Ethics and Living Subjectivity in Hegel's Logic: The Middle Voice of Autopoietic Life.* New York: Palgrave MacMillan, 2014.

Klein, Julie R. "'By Eternity I Understand': Eternity According to Spinoza." *Iyyun: The Jerusalem Philosophical Quarterly* 51 (July 2002): 295–324.

Le, Vincent. "Schelling and the Sixth Extinction: The Environmental Ethics Behind Schelling's Anthropomorphization of Nature." *Cosmos and History* 13, no. 3 (2017): 107–129.

Little, Eliza Starbuck. "The Self-Exhibition of Reason: Hegel on Intuition and Logical Content." PhD diss., University of Chicago, 2020.

Miller, Elaine P. "'The World Must be Romanticised . . .': The (Environmental) Ethical Implications of Schelling's Organic Worldview." *Environmental Values* 14, no. 3 (August 2005): 295–316.

Mowad, Nicholas. "The Natural World of Spirit: Hegel on the Value of Nature." *Environmental Philosophy* 9, no. 2 (Fall 2012): 47–66.

Moyar, Dean. *Hegel's Value.* Oxford: Oxford University Press, 2021.

Nassar, Dalia. "An 'Ethics for the Transition': Schelling's Critique of Negative Philosophy and Its Significance for Environmental Thought." In *Schelling's Philosophy: Freedom, Nature, and Systematicity,* edited by G. Anthony Bruno, 231–248. New York: Oxford University Press, 2020.

Nassar, Dalia. "The Human Vocation and the Question of the Earth: Karoline von Günderrode's Philosophy of Nature." *Archiv für Geschichte der Philosophie* 104, no. 1 (2022): 108–130.

Nassar, Dalia, and Kristin Gjesdal, eds. *Women Philosophers in the Long Nineteenth Century: The German Tradition.* New York: Oxford University Press, 2021.

Ng, Karen. *Hegel's Concept of Life: Self-Consciousness, Freedom, Logic.* New York: Oxford University Press, 2020.

Reill, Peter Hanns. *Vitalizing Nature in the Enlightenment.* Berkeley: University of California Press, 2005.

Richards, Robert. *The Romantic Conception of Life: Science and Philosophy in the Age of Goethe.* Chicago: University of Chicago Press, 2002.

Schelling, F. W. J. *Bruno, Or On the Natural and the Divine Principle of Things* (1802). Edited and translated by Michael G. Vater. Albany: State University of New York Press, 1984.

Schelling, F. W. J. *Historisch-kritische Ausgabe.* Edited by Hartmut Baumgartner, Wilhelm G. Jacobs, Jörg Janzen, and Hermann Krings. Stuttgart: Frommann-Holzboog, 1976–.

Schelling, F. W. J. *System of Transcendental Idealism* (1800). Translated by Peter Heath. Charlottesville: University Press of Virginia, 1978.

Stone, Alison. "Alienation from Nature and Early German Romanticism." *Ethical Theory and Moral Practice* 17, no. 1 (2014): 41–54.

Stone, Alison. *Petrified Intelligence: Nature in Hegel's Philosophy.* Albany: State University of New York Press, 2004.

Uexküll, Jakob von. *A Foray into the Worlds of Animals and Humans*. Translated by Joseph D. O'Neil. Minneapolis: University of Minnesota Press, 2010.

Westphal, Wolfgang. *Karoline von Günderrode und "Naturdenken um 1800."* Essen: Verlag Die Blaue Eule, 1993.

Wirth, Jason M. "Who Is Schelling's Bruno?" *Rivista di estetica* 74 (2020): 181–190.

Wulf, Andrea. *The Invention of Nature: Alexander von Humboldt's New World*. New York: Penguin Random House, 2015.

Yong, Ed. *An Immense World: How Animal Senses Reveal the Hidden Realms Around Us*. New York: Penguin, 2022.

Zammito, John H. *The Gestation of German Biology: Philosophy and Physiology from Stahl to Schelling*. Chicago: University of Chicago Press, 2018.

CHAPTER 24

··

WOMEN AND NINETEENTH-CENTURY PHILOSOPHY OF SCIENCE IN THE GERMAN TRADITION

··

DANIELA KATHARINA HELBIG

FLIP through the pages of Hedwig Conrad-Martius's guest book in the 1920s and 1930s, at her fruit orchard home in Bergzabern at the southern edge of the Palatinate wine region, and you will find a frequent visitor signed *Anonym*, "The Anonymous." Wryly, Edith Stein had elevated her nickname among her friends to her signature; after all, much of her writing appeared not under her name but under that of men like her teacher Edmund Husserl, her friend Hans Lipps, or Martin Heidegger, who replaced Stein's name as the editor of Husserl's early studies on time consciousness with his own.[1] The setting for Stein's dry acknowledgment of this professional reality is no coincidence. The orchard was not merely an idyllic location for philosophical conversation among a circle of friends. Rather, growing fruit for sale provided an income for Conrad-Martius and her husband while she held out hope for an academic career in Germany.[2] Still impossible when she obtained her doctorate in 1912, professional university careers gradually became more accessible to women after World War I.[3] Stein's anonymous writing too

---

[1] On Stein's anonymous text production, see Marianne Sawicki, *Body, Text, and Science: The Literacy of Investigative Practices and the Phenomenology of Edith Stein* (Dordrecht: Kluwer, 1997), 151–170; esp. 152 on the Bergzabern anecdote. On Heidegger's appropriation of Stein's work, see Emanuele Caminada, "Edith Stein's Account of Communal Mind and Its Limits: A Phenomenological Reading," *Human Studies* 38 (2015): 549–566, at 551–552.

[2] Sawicki, *Body, Text, and Science*, 152. See also Angela Ales Bello, "The Human Being in the Context of Nature: Philosophical Anthropology and the Natural Sciences in Hedwig Conrad-Martius," *Axiomathes* 18 (2008): 425–443, 426.

[3] In Germany, women were generally not admissible to occupy the academic career ladder position of *Assistent* until 1913/1914, of *Privatdozent* until 1919/1920, and of professor until the 1950s. See Annette Vogt, "Von der Ausnahme zur Normalität: Wissenschaftlerinnen in Akademien und in der

was a deliberate strategy toward the goal of an academic position, although it remained unsuccessful. Her work for Husserl did not result in his support for her *Habilitation* as the prerequisite for a professorship; the ruse of collaborating with Hans Lipps to produce his in exchange for him having Stein teach university courses at his institute in Göttingen did succeed in securing him a position, but he did not return the favor as planned.[4] And yet, Stein and Conrad-Martius's ambition to practice philosophy professionally rather than only privately was no longer entirely unrealistic. It marks the end of women's absence not from philosophy, but from institutionalized philosophical disciplines during the nineteenth century.

This absence has particularly important implications for the history of the philosophy of science. As a distinctive new area of inquiry, philosophy of science took shape alongside the proliferation of modern sciences during the nineteenth century. Its defining feature across diverse, and historically changing methodological approaches might best be taken to be its subject matter: the knowledge produced by "science"—a term claimed, in the nineteenth century, by the professionalized, institutionalized, and rapidly multiplying academic scientific disciplines. This formative period of modern science, and of its philosophy, coincided with women being legally barred from most higher education, and limited to informal networks in their participation in philosophical as well as scientific debates. Among the European and North American countries, Germany was the last to admit women as university students across all states by 1909—some years after Austria and decades after parts of Switzerland.[5] There were important nonacademic domains for philosophical debate throughout the nineteenth century, from salons to the growing public market for books, magazines, and newspapers. But the newly emerging field of the philosophy of science relied upon access to academically produced and disseminated knowledge, and it negotiated its own academic, social, and political status with reference to the newly institutionalized sciences. Therefore, women's limited access to academic institutions and research is itself a formative feature of philosophy of science.

Thanks to much recent research by historians of philosophy and gender, we now have an increasingly nuanced picture of work by women during the first few decades of the twentieth century that has been overlooked or written out of the history of the philosophy of science. Important examples include Edith Stein and Hedwig Conrad-Martius's phenomenology, Neo-Kantian approaches like Grete Hermann's or Ilse Schneider's, and

---

Kaiser-Wilhelm-Gesellschaft (1912–1945)," in *Zwischen Vorderbühne und Hinterbühne: Beiträge zum Wandel der Geschlechterbeziehungen in der Wissenschaft vom 17. Jahrhundert bis zur Gegenwart*, ed. Theresa Wobbe (Bielefeld: transcript, 2003), 159–188, at 160–161.

[4] Sawicki, *Body, Text, and Science*, 167. On Edith Stein's eventual success in removing procedural obstacles for women seeking to obtain a *Habilitation*, see Theresa Wobbe, "Von Marianne Weber zu Edith Stein: Historische Koordinaten des Zugangs zur Wissenschaft," in *Denkachsen: zur theoretischen und traditionellen Rede vom Geschlecht*, ed. Theresa Wobbe and Gesa Lindemann (Frankfurt: Suhrkamp, 1994), 15–68, esp. 27–34.

[5] Patricia M. Mazón, *Gender and the Modern Research University: The Admission of Women to German Higher Education, 1856–1914* (Stanford: Stanford University Press, 2003), 14–15.

work by members of the Vienna Circle like Olga Hahn or Rose Rand, to mention only a few. Before I return to these examples in a brief concluding section, the main part of this essay examines the period from the mid-nineteenth century through the early 1900s—the period prior to women's admission to university education and research, and also the formative period of the philosophy of science in the German-speaking context prior to the establishment of the two approaches that were most immediately influential for the Anglophone field of philosophy of science, the Reichenbach School and the Vienna Circle's logical empiricism. I draw on historiographical considerations from the history of science to bring into view women's contributions to philosophical reflections on science, and women's role in the constitution of the philosophy of science as a set of distinctive yet diverse methodological approaches and areas of inquiry during the second half of the nineteenth century.

1 "REALISTIC OPTIONS": WOMEN'S ROLES IN THE CONSTITUTION OF THE PHILOSOPHY OF SCIENCE

Beyond the retrieval of forgotten names and recognition of individual achievements, the category of gender helps foreground the social and political dimensions of the history of the philosophy of science. The departure from romantic-idealist philosophy of nature, *Naturphilosophie*, in the early nineteenth century brought increased philosophical attention to the empirical results of the modern sciences. In the aftermath of Germany's failed 1848 democratic revolution, and alongside the rise of the sciences' industrial importance, this was also a departure from the remnants of Kant's idea of a systematic unity of "science, moral practice, and the reflection about both."[6] An emphasis on epistemological and methodological questions has characterized much academic philosophy of science since; the now standard German term for the field, *Wissenschaftstheorie*, attests as much. The sciences' social and political significance, on the other hand, dominated widely publicized debates that went hand in hand with science's institutionalization and professionalization. The end of the systematic ambition to articulate the relation between problems of theoretical and practical philosophy is thus also marked by a practical separation of discursive spaces.

The formation of a distinctive philosophy of science was a gradual and complex process embedded in the overarching problem for much nineteenth-century philosophy: the reconceptualization of the relationship between philosophy and the sciences, *Wissenschaften* across the spectrum from the natural sciences to the humanities. The

---

[6] Peter McLaughlin, "Nachgedanken zum Bedürfnis der Physiologie nach einer philosophischen Naturbetrachtung," in *Johannes Müller und die Philosophie*, ed. Michael Hagner and Bettina Wahrig-Schmidt (Berlin: Akademie Verlag, 1992), 301–311, at 302.

growing distance between traditional academic philosophical disciplines and institutionalized scientific knowledge production raised the broad questions that have structured the history of nineteenth-century philosophy—albeit to date usually without
any explicit connections being made with the question of women's role in these
developments. The disciplinary identity of philosophy itself was one such pressing
matter of debate. Was philosophy a science? On a par with, or set apart from all other
sciences, perhaps through a foundational or explicatory function?

In the German tradition, *Wissenschaftstheorie* emerged in this context as part of a set
of general epistemological problems. As Elisabeth Ströker has put it, the budding field
of epistemology faced a "transcendental problem under changed circumstances": the
scientific disciplines, particularly those concerned with "human nature," were no longer
taken to merely provide material for philosophical interpretation but now to contribute
actively to the investigation of the possibility of human knowledge.[7] The nature and extent of this contribution, however, were up for debate as much as the question of the
status and methodological foundation of scientific knowledge. These problems provided the impulse for what came to be known as Neo-Kantianism, but scientists too
had stakes in the debate. Their intellectual and professional agendas intersected with
those of philosophers; the Neo-Kantian construction of a disciplinary genealogy beginning with Hermann Helmholtz exemplifies the shared rhetorical insistence on the relevance of the empirical sciences for philosophical inquiry.[8] Terminological ambiguities
speak to the heterogeneity of approaches to bringing scientific results in conversation with established philosophical traditions over the course of the century. The term
Naturphilosophie was still claimed for programs as different as Wilhelm Ostwald's
around 1900 and Hans Reichenbach's in 1931.[9]

The history of nineteenth-century philosophy of science has met with renewed interest in historical continuities such as the Neo-Kantian roots of logical empiricism, or
in problems that resonate with contemporary debates like the role of metaphysics, or

[7] Elisabeth Ströker, "Natur und ihre Wissenschaft in der Philosophie des 19. Jahrhunderts," in
Naturauffassungen in Philosophie, Wissenschaft, Technik. Vol. 3: Aufklärung und späte Neuzeit, ed.
Lothar Schäfer and Elisabeth Ströker (Freiburg: Alber, 1996), 255–292, at 266.

[8] Klaus Christian Köhnke, *The Rise of Neo-Kantianism: German Academic Philosophy between
Idealism and Positivism* (Cambridge: Cambridge University Press, 1991), 96. See Alfred Nordmann,
"Critical Realism, Critical Idealism, and Critical Common-Sensism: The School and World Philosophies
of Riehl, Cohen, and Peirce," in *The Kantian Legacy in Nineteenth-Century Science*, ed. Michael Friedman
and Alfred Nordmann (Cambridge, MA: MIT Press, 2006), 249–274, for a critical assessment of the
actual significance of specific contemporary developments in science within different strands of Neo-
Kantianism. Hermann Helmholtz was ennobled in 1883; I use his birth name without the nobiliary
particle *von* throughout this essay.

[9] Ludwig Wittgenstein's *Tractatus Logico-Philosophicus* was first published in Ostwald's series
Annalen der Naturphilosophie in 1921. On the problems of a standard account of nineteenth-century
philosophy of nature that sees the 1840s and 1850s' "vulgar materialism" as a reaction to idealist
speculation, see Paul Ziche, "The 'New Philosophy of Nature' around 1900—Metaphysical Tradition
and Scientistic Innovation," in *Wilhelm Ostwald at the Crossroads between Chemistry, Philosophy and
Media Culture*, ed. Britta Görs, Nikolaos Psarros, and Paul Ziche (Leipzig: Leipziger Universitätsverlag,
2005), 29–45.

the relation between cognitive science and philosophy of science.[10] These issues from the field's formative years remain at the core of its disciplinary identity. But as as a result of women's limited access to academic philosophy of science until the early twentieth century, it is unsurprising that many earlier contributions made by women do not speak directly to these readily recognizable themes. Women's contributions do, though, provide new perspectives on how and why the philosophy of science took shape as an academic field largely distinct from problems of practical philosophy, and clustered around the developing concerns of *Wissenschaftstheorie*. The avenues open to women's contributions often relate to the unfolding institutionalization of the sciences, and to the construction of spaces for their public discussion. From this perspective, the gendered social order that underpinned the professionalization of the sciences becomes visible as a factor in the constitution of the philosophy of science.[11]

As the growing body of historical scholarship on women engaged in scientific knowledge production shows, the picture of women's exclusion from the public life of science unfolding in academic laboratories and institutions over the course of the nineteenth century, and their relegation to domestic settings that are assumed to be epistemically irrelevant is too simple. Instead, studies of scientific couples and families have analyzed the domestic sphere as a "condition for and consequence of research," and the connections between the epistemological authority of science and the "legitimacy of scientific forms of life" in their various institutionalized and private settings.[12] Turning the focus away from academically recognized work alone has brought into view a variety of significant contributions to science that were made by women as well as the strategies for their "exclusion from the institution of science"—and has underscored the importance of "sites of knowledge production and use beyond the academy."[13]

Similarly, women's contributions to the philosophy of science during the nineteenth century place a question mark over the historiographical privileging of academic contexts, and draw attention to the negotiations over the relation between

---

[10] Michael Heidelberger, "Aspects of Current History of Nineteenth-Century Philosophy of Science," in *The Present Situation in the Philosophy of Science*, ed. Friedrich Stadler (Berlin and Heidelberg: Springer, 2010), 67–74.

[11] On the reliance of the professional role of the scientist on gendered divisions of labor, see Theresa Wobbe, "Instabile Beziehungen. Die kulturelle Dynamik von Wissenschaft und Geschlecht," in Wobbe, *Zwischen Vorderbühne und Hinterbühne*, ed. Wobbe, 13–38.

[12] Donald L. Opitz, Staffan Bergwik, and Brigitte Van Tiggelen, eds., *Domesticity in the Making of Modern Science* (New York: Palgrave Macmillan, 2016), 2. See Deborah R. Coen, *Vienna in the Age of Uncertainty: Science, Liberalism, and Private Life* (Chicago: The University of Chicago Press, 2007), arguing that scientific research could be a site for bridging public and private lives in the Habsburg Empire, and Annette Lykknes, Donald L. Opitz, and Brigitte Van Tiggelen, eds., *For Better or for Worse? Collaborative Couples in the Sciences* (Heidelberg: Birkhäuser, 2012), building on Pnina Abir-Am, Helena Pycior, and Nancy Slack, eds., *Creative Couples in the Sciences* (New Brunswick: Rutgers University Press, 1996).

[13] Christine von Oertzen, Maria Rentetzi, and Elizabeth S. Watkins, "Finding Science in Surprising Places: Gender and the Geography of Scientic Knowledge. Introduction to 'Beyond the Academy: Histories of Gender and Knowledge,'" *Centaurus* 55 (2013): 73–80, at 74.

public discussions and academically sanctioned philosophy of science. To get at these contributions, we need to look at texts that haven't counted (nor aimed to) count as such in their day, and inquire into their relationship to those that did.[14] The point of this historiographical detour is to bring into view the discipline's mutual constitution with a social order that left women with different "entanglements" of social position and cognitive interests from men.[15] This historiographical perspective responds to Catherine Goldstein's demand for the history of science, a demand that is equally relevant for the philosophy of science as a field that developed in close conjunction with the sciences: to recognize that the consequences of the professionalization of the sciences were complex, and require the examination of women's lives not just with regard to barriers, but also with regard to "possibilities, ideas, hopes, and realistic options."[16]

There were compelling avenues for women to realize their intellectual ambitions when it came to the philosophical discussion of the sciences, but they were not necessarily aimed at academic careers—nor were they primarily the result of exclusion from those careers. Rather, women's contributions to, and active cultivation of public debates of the sciences were above all sensible strategic choices and options, and reflected a commitment to intellectual identities that weren't defined by academic conventions, and were at times openly opposed to them. These intellectual identities often served public activist purposes rather than academic goals, including, importantly, the critique of the allegedly scientific basis for the pervasive concept of gender difference that served as an organizational principle across virtually all spheres of society—a topic of philosophical significance, but distinct from the epistemological concerns of the theory of knowledge, and a practical challenge to science's institutionalized organization in its reliance on gendered divisions of labor.

As Klaus C. Köhnke has long argued, the aftermath of the failed democratic revolution of 1848 in Germany entailed the banishing of "questions of practical politics—and with them the entire political philosophy of the opposition—from the life of the university."[17] Academic "self-restraint" in the face of the political repressions left a void filled by philosophical discussions directed at wider, nonacademic publics. The societal relevance of the natural sciences was one particularly important example, as the reception of the "scientific materialists" Karl Vogt, Jakob Moleschott, and Ludwig Büchner attests.[18]

---

[14] This is true to the extent that the history of philosophy largely relies on texts as the non-ephemeral trace of philosophical reflection. Recent histories of women in science have featured a variety of different knowledge production and dissemination practices.

[15] To borrow a metaphor from feminist science studies; see Sabine Höhler and Bettina Wahrig, "Geschlechterforschung ist Wissenschaftsforschung—Wissenschaftsforschung ist Geschlechterforschung," *NTM* 14 (2006): 201–211, at 203.

[16] Catherine Goldstein, "Weder öffentlich noch privat: Mathematik im Frankreich des frühen 17. Jahrhundert," in Wobbe, *Zwischen Vorderbühne und Hinterbühne*, ed. Wobbe, 41–72, at 65; on domestic settings of science, Deborah R. Coen, "The Common World: Histories of Science and Domestic Intimacy," *Modern Intellectual History* 11, no. 2 (2014): 417–438.

[17] Köhnke, *The Rise of Neo-Kantianism*, 71.

[18] Köhnke, *The Rise of Neo-Kantianism*, 79. Wolfgang Lefèvre, "Wissenschaft und Philosophie bei Feuerbach," in *Sinnlichkeit und Rationalität: Der Umbruch in der Philosophie des 19. Jahrhunderts: Ludwig Feuerbach*, ed. Walter Jaeschke (Berlin: Akademie Verlag, 1982), 81–100, situates the scientific

The beginnings of an academically acceptable, distinctive philosophy of science in this context, on the other hand, are associated above all with Hermann Helmholtz and his proposed strategic alliance between philosophy and the empirical sciences—a collaboration between the now-distinct disciplinary successors of eighteenth-century natural philosophy that posed no challenge to the prevailing academic self-restraint. Not yet the towering figure of nineteenth-century German science, but a physiologist and physicist in the early stages of building an academic career, Helmholtz took a mediating stance in the disputes of the 1850s over materialism that confirmed his methodological commitment to a mechanistic world picture while steering clear of politically fraught materialist positions such as the denial of the freedom of the will.[19] At the same time, Helmholtz distanced himself from his teacher, the physiologist Johannes Müller. Helmholtz's critique of Müller's idealist ambitions embodied the anti-*naturphilosophisch* rhetoric that uncouples the theory of knowledge from questions of practical philosophy.

Over the following decades, Helmholtz's programmatic academic alliance of science and philosophy focused primarily on epistemological problems, whereas questions of the sciences' social significance and potential political implications dominated their broad and diverse public debate. The reception of Darwin's evolutionary theory, particularly through Ernst Haeckel, is perhaps the most important example. At the same time, public interventions were part and parcel of scientists' social positioning that went hand in hand with the professionalization of the sciences; in Germany, a rhetorical emphasis on the sciences' practical benefits frequently accompanied their institutional alignment with the material interests of the industrializing state.[20] And, as Tracie Matysik has documented, new ethical concerns developed in conjunction with the biological and human sciences, and became a matter of "vital concerns of public inquiry in Central Europe at the turn of the nineteenth to the twentieth century."[21] In this context, the investigation of the relation between women's contribution to these diverse debates, and the emerging academic field of philosophy of science points to the limits of that field's potential openness to moral and social questions.

To anticipate my juxtaposition of examples that follows, critiques such as Hedwig Dohm's of the prevailing gendered social order in terms of the sciences' moral function

materialists' arguments, frequently criticized as naive or dated, in their philosophical and scientific context.

[19] In the 1855 memorial address that famously posed Kant's transcendental question of the conditions of possibility of knowledge in the material terms of sensory physiology, Helmholtz's concluding example of evidence for the freedom of the will is scientific research itself (Hermann von Helmholtz, "Über das Sehen des Menschen," in *Vorträge und Reden*, 5th ed. (Braunschweig: Vieweg, 1903), 87–117), at 116. On the relation to Müller in the context of this address, see Timothy Lenoir, "Helmholtz, Müller, und die Erziehung der Sinne," in *Johannes Müller und die Philosophie*, ed. Hagner and Wahrig, 207–222.

[20] Andreas Daum, *Wissenschaftspopularisierung im 19. Jahrhundert: Bürgerliche Kultur, naturwissenschaftliche Bildung und die deutsche Öffentlichkeit 1848–1914* (Munich: Oldenbourg, 2002), 436–449; Timothy Lenoir, *Instituting Science: The Cultural Production of Scientific Disciplines* (Stanford: Stanford University Press, 1997).

[21] Tracie Matysik, *Reforming the Moral Subject: Ethics and Sexuality in Central Europe, 1890–1930* (Ithaca: Cornell University Press, 2008), 9.

were at odds with the division of labor in professorial households. In contrast, the practical acceptance of a gendered division of labor was the prerequisite for contributions by women like Anna Helmholtz whose husbands were part of, or seeking to become part of the academic establishment. Their contributions were not likely to associate the discussion of science with challenges to the conservative monarchy's social order, but rather to bolster the social as well as epistemic status of science that was also reflected in the growing philosophical interest in science. Seen through this lens, the focus primarily on epistemological and methodological problems in the philosophy of science that carried forward from the nineteenth into the twentieth century reflects a legacy not only of the end of Kant's systematic ambitions, but also of the gendered social organization of the sciences and their philosophy.

2 "Immoral Sauerkraut": Socially and Politically Critical Philosophical Engagement with Science

Hedwig Dohm is widely known as a writer and women's rights advocate but not commonly associated with the philosophy of science. Her challenges to the allegedly scientific underpinnings of the concept of gender difference deal with topics that have since been widely discussed by philosophers of science, for example, the relation between biological sex and gender, or of innate versus acquired characteristics—but her critique builds on her engagement with John Stuart Mill's political philosophy rather than attempting to engage directly with contemporaneous philosophical discussion of the sciences. Dohm's essays "Women's Scientific Emancipation" (1874) and "Women's Nature and Rights" (1876) intervene in the debates over Mill's *Subjection of Women* that appeared in Jenny Hirsch's German translation in 1869. If the women's movement had been readily ignored among many members of the intellectual classes up to that point, Mill's overt case for women's rights provoked responses ranging across academic disciplines from theologians to medical scientists.[22] After all, not just Mill's political theory, but also his methodological writings on science, and his arguments for understanding the mind in psychological terms had found prominent recipients.[23] Dohm seizes upon the logical inconsistencies in Mill's German reception. Mill could readily

---

[22] On this debate, see Mazón, *Gender and the Modern Research University*, 55.

[23] E. g., on Hermann Helmholtz's psychological approach in comparison with Mill's 1865 *Psychological Theory of the Belief in an External World*, see Liesbet De Kock, "Hermann von Helmholtz's Empirico-Transcendentalism Reconsidered: Construction and Constitution in Helmholtz's Psychology of the Object," *Science in Context* 27, no. 4 (2014): 709–744; on Justus Liebig's critique of Mill's emphasis on inductive methods, see Ströker, "Natur und ihre Wissenschaft," 287; on the Viennese reception of Mill's empirical approach to the foundations of rationality, see Coen, *Vienna in the Age of Uncertainty*, 125.

be declared by many "Europe's greatest thinker," and among those who did most "for the progress of science." Yet at the same time, Mill "advocated for women's political rights without reservation."[24] So why should the cause of women's rights be ridiculed in Germany?

In *The Subjection of Women*, Mill had criticized the portrayal of socially and historically produced differences between women and men as naturally given, and Dohm generally adopts this line of argument. For example, women's alleged "lack of dynamism" is better explained as the result of "absolute, and lifelong dependency" than asserted as a natural characteristic.[25] Like Mill, Dohm is not problematizing the notion of the natural itself. Building on a presumed distinction between the natural and the social, she takes for granted that there are obvious "naturally determined" constraints on organisms, citing as an example Heinrich Heine's revolutionarily minded frog that fails to escape its natal swamp and live the free life of a bird.[26] And also like Mill, Dohm offers little by way of argument for some of her examples for natural constraints or conditions, for example, for what she claims is women's "natural aptitude for medicine."[27] With Mill's general critique of the conflation of the socially produced with the natural as her point of departure, Dohm dismantles a set of arguments made by German scientists that underpin the notion of the "natural" with the social and cognitive authority of the empirical scientific disciplines, anatomy and physiology above all, that take "human nature" to be their subject matter.

Among those arguing against Mill's case for admitting women to professions such as the practice of medicine was the physician Theodor von Bischoff in his 1872 pamphlet *The Study and Practice of Medicine by Women*. To support his claim that such study was "contrary to nature," Bischoff produces an account of anatomical and physiological differences between women and men. From those anatomical and physiological differences, Bischoff infers moral and intellectual differences that allegedly demonstrate women's inaptitude for medicine—making him the main target of Dohm's critique in "Women's Scientific Emancipation," where she argues for women's admission to universities as a step toward equal rights. Having mocked Bischoff's stereotypical list of male versus female traits ("men are courageous, women timid," "men's actions

---

[24] Hedwig Dohm, *Die wissenschaftliche Emanzipation der Frau (1874)*, ed. Berta Rahm (Zurich: Ala, 1982), 3. On Dohm's publication process and strategies to navigate the difficulties in finding publishers for her politically radical work, see Isabel Rohner, *Spuren ins Jetzt: Hedwig Dohm—eine Biografie* (Sulzbach im Taunus: Helmer, 2010), 69.

[25] Hedwig Dohm, *Der Frauen Natur und Recht. Zur Frauenfrage. Zwei Abhandlungen über Eigenschaften und Stimmrecht der Frauen, Berlin 1876*, ed. Berta Rahm (Neunkirch: Ala, 1986), 44.

[26] Dohm, *Die wissenschaftliche Emanzipation*, 181.

[27] Dohm, *Die wissenschaftliche Emanzipation*, 114, concluding Dohm's long list of historical examples of women practicing medicine. Mill's willingness, while probing notions of women's presumed "nature" throughout his essay, to accept without much argument that "the most suitable division of labor" was for a man to earn an income, and for his wife to run the household has long been pointed out (Stefan Collini, editor's introduction to John Stuart Mill, *On Liberty with The Subjection of Women and Chapters on Socialism*, by John Stuart Mill , ed. Stefan Collini (Cambridge: Cambridge University Press, 1989), vii-xxvi, xx).

are guided by conviction, women's by emotion"), Dohm emphasizes the logical flaws of the text. A list of "unproven assumptions" without further argument cannot sustain Bischoff's conclusion that "the true spirit of the exact sciences will always remain inaccessible to women."[28]

In her 1876 "Women's Nature and Rights," Dohm reiterates the central point of her analysis: many assertions regarding women's "nature" are no more than "chatter" even when framed in scientific terms. Why such chatter? In Dohm's view, Mill puts it succinctly: "the vast majority of men cannot tolerate the idea of dealing with women as equals."[29] She holds to account Rudolf Virchow—one of the founders of experimental pathology in Germany and himself politically progressive—first for asserting that women's character traits (which include, according to Virchow, "profundity of sentiment, truth of immediate intuition, gentleness, devotion, fidelity") can be readily deduced from "women's bodily organization," namely the presence of ovaries, and second for "announcing these mere views in the form of a scientific result."[30] Dohm's argument remains open in principle to a thoroughgoing naturalistic account of, for example, mental and cognitive properties formulated in scientific terms, and to a physiological basis for cognitive difference. But as she points out, alleging that such an account has been given when in actual fact it hasn't amounts to an abuse of scientists' professional authority.

Dohm's critique explicitly connects Mill's discussion of women's rights in terms of political theory with problems of the sciences' explanatory scope and social use. And, as Dohm further observes, science—as a widely accepted mode of investigation of "nature"—acquires a kind of moral authority since the natural is readily equated with the morally good. The transgression of socially accepted boundaries is frequently judged in even stronger moral terms once those social boundaries have been naturalized. One of her examples concerns women's hopes for scientific careers. "Even thoughtful men," as she puts it sarcastically, "give in to the eccentric idea that motherly love . . . withers away in the sulphurous odours of physical experiments. On the lunch table of a wife capable of calculating cubic roots, they smell immoral sauerkraut."[31]

Dohm was not alone in drawing attention to scientific naturalizations of gender difference to intervene in public debates over women's rights. Further to her political left, for example, another outspoken critic of the "most ridiculous objections . . . defended in the guise of scientific arguments" to women's attempts at entering the learned

---

[28] Dohm, *Die wissenschaftliche Emanzipation*, 79. As Mazón has highlighted, Dohm was alone among female reformers to take a public stance against Bischoff (Mazón, *Gender and the Modern Research University*, 90).

[29] Dohm, *Der Frauen Natur und Recht*, 140.

[30] Dohm, *Der Frauen Natur und Recht*, 54. Dohm refers to Virchow's "Woman and Cell," first presented in an 1848 talk; see Hans H. Simmer, "Zum Frauenbild Rudolf Virchows in den späten 1840er Jahren," *Medizinhistorisches Journal* 27, nos. 3/4 (1992): 292–319.

[31] Dohm, *Die wissenschaftliche Emanzipation der Frau*, 168–169. On the historical uses of nature to think about standards of the good, see Lorraine Daston and Fernando Vidal, eds., *The Moral Authority of Nature* (Chicago: Chicago University Press, 2004).

professions was the socialist thinker August Bebel.[32] Dohm's astute arguments stand out for their detailed engagement with specific scientific claims as the basis for her critique of the allegedly scientific justification of natural limits to women's aptitude for scientific or philosophical thought.[33] But while she pointedly marked the limits of her opponents' arguments in terms of logic and coherence, she stopped short of integrating specific results of the empirical sciences into her arguments. Such an integration was at the core of both Johannes Müller's attempt to develop physiology on a *naturphilosophisch* basis, and Hermann Helmholtz's critique of his teacher's philosophical views. As Dohm repeatedly stresses, she did not have the training to engage in debates over the content of scientific claims beyond logical analysis. For her to receive that training, and, hypothetically, to seek academic recognition of her arguments probing the moral and political significance of the sciences, would have required the very political intervention she argued for. "Immoral" contributions to the philosophical discussion of the sciences in Dohm's satirical sense, that is, contributions that challenged the prevailing, gendered social order, thus formed part of the public debate of the sciences but remained without academic credentials, and ultimately without recognition within the history of philosophy of science.

A generation onward from Dohm, the naturalization of gender difference in terms of science continued to be a focus for women's contributions to debates of ethics, sexuality, and moral standards—important matters of public concern by the turn of the century, which were informed by widely publicized scientific-philosophical debates such as those around scientific materialism and, from the early 1860s, Darwinism.[34] Like Dohm's, these arguments have remained outside the disciplinary histories that retrospectively define the philosophy of science's subject matter. It is worth noting, however, that the keen public interest in the sciences' societal implications did not necessarily render them a more acceptable topic for academic philosophy of science even when put forward by members of the scientific academic establishment. Ernst Haeckel, professor of zoology at the University of Jena and famous for his influential contributions to the German discussion of evolutionary theory, directed his scientific-philosophical writings at a broad public; his work was attacked by representatives of academic *Fachphilosophie* not least because his undeniable public success posed an obstacle to his dismissal as a philosophically naive dilettante.[35]

---

[32] August Bebel, *Woman and Socialism (1879)*, transl. Meta L. Stern (Hebe) (New York: Socialist Literature Co., 1910), 233.

[33] As historians of philosophy and gender have long noted, this view was pervasive enough also to be projected into the past by Dohm's contemporaries, resulting in the erasure of earlier generations of women in nineteenth-century histories of philosophy. Sabrina Ebbersmeyer, "From a 'Memorable Place' to 'Drops in the Ocean': On the Marginalization of Women Philosophers in German Historiography of Philosophy," *British Journal for the History of Philosophy* 28, no. 3 (2020): 442–462, emphasizes the appeals to women's "nature" or "essence" as a distinctive element to explain the absence of women from nineteenth-century histories of philosophy in the German context.

[34] See Matysik, *Reforming the Moral Subject*.

[35] Paul Ziche, "Die 'Scham' der Philosophen und der 'Hochmut der Fachgelehrsamkeit': Zur fachphilosophischen Diskussion von Haeckels Monismus," in *Monismus um 1900: Wissenschaftskultur*

While Dohm criticized the misuse of allegedly scientific arguments and evidence to justify women's exclusion from professional life, the next generation of left-wing German feminist writers drew on evolutionary theory and physiological, psychiatric, and psychological research to advance their politically activist cases. For example, discussions of the female sex drive in the context of rapid urbanization had immediate political implications, since the view that women's sexual needs were lesser than men's served to rationalize prostitution. But they also spoke to broader concerns, given the widespread and diverse assumptions "that sexuality was somehow central to any consideration of ethics and to the makeup of the moral subject."[36] Still barred from obtaining university degrees in Germany, many women who contributed to these debates had nonetheless gained access to university-level education. Johanna Elberskirchen, for instance, studied natural and medical sciences as well as philosophy at the University of Bern in Switzerland before turning to law in Zurich; Henriette Fürth studied political economics at the Freies Deutsches Hochstift in Frankfurt am Main, and Grete Meisel-Hess studied philosophy, sociology, and biology in Vienna. Despite many individual differences, their arguments in favor of understanding the female sex drive as "active, desiring, and naturally in need of satisfaction" used the sciences in order to assert women's rights to sexual emancipation and self-determination, and contributed to the production of scientific understandings of female sexuality, as Kirsten Leng has argued.[37]

However, physiology and evolutionary theory served a variety of different argumentative purposes in the debates about women's emancipation. The Viennese writer, women's education advocate, and art school director Emilie Exner, née von Winiwarter, drew on both fields to argue that there were inherent differences between women's and men's capacities, and that women's professional choices should be made accordingly.[38] A member of the Exner-Frisch scientific dynasty, she was—as Deborah R. Coen has argued—part of the family's active cultivation of science in the domestic sphere not as a "retreat from politics but a precondition of liberal identity," positing probabilistic science as a model for liberal reasoning in the Habsburg empire.[39] Her

---

und Weltanschauung, ed. Paul Ziche (Berlin: VWB, 2000), 61–79; on Haeckel's publication strategies, see Robert J. Richards, *The Tragic Sense of Life: Ernst Haeckel and the Struggle over Evolutionary Thought* (Chicago: University of Chicago Press, 2008), 217–276.

[36] Matysik, *Reforming the Moral Subject*, 9.

[37] Kirsten Leng, "An 'Elusive' Phenomenon: Feminism, Sexology and the Female Sex Drive in Germany at the Turn of the Twentieth Century," *Centaurus* 55 (2013): 131–152, at 131.

[38] Pharmacy was Exner's main example of a profession that would not remove women from their domestic "essential sphere of action"; Emilie Exner, *Weibliche Pharmaceuten* (Vienna: Verlag des Wiener Frauen-Erwerbs-Vereines, 1902), 4.

[39] Coen, *Vienna in the Age of Uncertainty*, 90. Coen points out that Austrian liberals were less focused than their Prussian counterparts on science's role in industrialization, and on its practical values as a means of prediction and control. Instead, in the politically splintered Habsburg Empire, Austrian liberals strategically stressed the probabilistic character of scientific knowledge as a model of rationality that could "discredit at once the absolute claims of religion while justifying their claim to knowledge that transcended a narrowly class- or nation-based perspective" (Coen, *Vienna in the Age of Uncertainty*, 14).

husband was the physiologist Sigmund Exner; another close family member was Sigmund's brother Franz Serafin Exner, the director of Vienna's Institute for Radium Research and a major proponent of what Michael Stöltzner has termed "Vienna Indeterminism," building on both Ernst Mach and Ludwig Boltzmann's work to argue for a criterion of reality based in probabilistic theory rather than a priori categories, and severing the ties between causality and realism that dominated the German Neo-Kantian tradition.[40]

In her 1906 *The Women's Question: A Reckoning*, Emilie Exner argued that both the radical and moderate wings of the women's movement failed to accept scientific facts that explained the differences in men and women's intellectual capacities—a naturalizing argument of the kind Dohm had attacked some thirty years earlier, but now framed in statistical and evolutionary terms. The "radical claim," according to Exner, was that "men's and women's intellect is equal by nature." She formulated the "moderate claim" statistically: there are differences between "the psyche of the sexes," male and female, but they are no bigger than the differences between individual members of each.[41] In Exner's view, the reasoning underpinning both claims was flawed, and consisted in explaining these differences in terms of the social restrictions that had historically been imposed on women (as Dohm had followed Mill in arguing). Instead, Exner put forward a form of biological materialism that accounts for the alleged differences in women's and men's cognitive abilities in physiological and evolutionary terms.

The "unfathomable difference between the male and female psyche" was one of the firmly established facts of physiology, Exner stated, and it reflected the "modern view that mental activity depends on the physical organization of the body in a tight causal nexus."[42] Evolutionary history had shaped women's mental capacities as much as it had shaped the female body for its functions. Evolutionary biology had done away with philosophical ideas of a "soul hovering, as a pre-given whole, above the physical body," which might have misled women to believe that their "psyche" might have been modified by social circumstances alone.[43] Since the "undeniable" purpose of the organization of women's bodies was motherhood, it was only plausible that women's desire for motherhood, conscious or not, would always prevent them from dedicating themselves fully to an "impersonal goal," as the lack of women among the long list of humanity's greatest names attested.[44] Exner granted that women could be diligent and ambitious, looking back over the first generation of female medical students in Austria as well as elementary education for girls. But nevertheless there remained an incongruity between the

---

[40] Michael Stöltzner, "Vienna Indeterminism: Mach, Boltzmann, Exner," *Synthese* 119 (1999): 85–111. On the context for the relatively large number of women researchers at the Institute for Radium Research between the two world wars, see Maria Rentetzi, "Gender, Politics, and Radioactivity Research in Interwar Vienna: The Case of the Institute for Radium Research," *Isis* 95, no. 3 (2004): 359–393.

[41] Emilie Exner, *Eine Abrechnung in der Frauenfrage* (Leipzig: Leopold Voß, 1906), 5.

[42] Exner, *Eine Abrechnung in der Frauenfrage*, 20.

[43] Exner, *Eine Abrechnung in der Frauenfrage*, 21.

[44] Exner, *Eine Abrechnung in der Frauenfrage*, 22, 24.

acquisition of knowledge, and the ability to put it to use—the lack of the latter, according to Exner, "is apparently a typically female peculiarity."[45]

3 "Scrub Out Your Head": Cultural Positionings of Science

Like Emilie Exner in the Habsburg Empire, Anna Helmholtz was at the very center of imperial Germany's scientific establishment. Her life and work have long been described as exemplifying the gendered division of labor that underpins the professionalization of the sciences in the nineteenth century.[46] Née Anna von Mohl, she was the brilliant and humorous daughter of a distinguished legal scholar, and received an unusually good education that included extended stays with family in Paris and London. She married Hermann Helmholtz in 1861, after the passing of his first wife, Olga.[47] Anna Helmholtz ran the professorial household initially in Heidelberg and later Berlin, where Hermann Helmholtz established the Physikalisch-Technische Reichsanstalt as the empire's most important institution to bridge scientific and industrial interests.[48] His career stands like no other for the rise of the sciences in Germany, and their institutional alignment with the material-technical problems of the rapidly industrializing state. Anna Helmholtz's salon was frequented by the cultural, intellectual, and social elite and illustrates the professorial wife's "duty to provide a certain degree of social entertainment."[49] Frequent

[45] Exner, *Eine Abrechnung in der Frauenfrage*, 45. In his *Physiologie der männlichen Geschlechtsfunktionen*, her husband Sigmund also offered a biological explanation, arguing that "women's thoughts were naturally more closely tied to habit and thus to instinct" (as summarized in Coen, *Vienna in the Age of Uncertainty*, 172).

[46] Maria Osietzki, "Anna von Helmholtz—ein Leben für die Wissenschaft ihres Mannes," in *Naturwissenschaften und Technik: 'doch Frauensache?' Vorträge und Berichte von der Tagung im Kerschensteiner Kolleg*, ed. Margot Fuchs (Wiesbaden: Frauenliteraturvertrieb, 1986), 56–60. More recently, David Cahan, *Helmholtz: A Life in Science* (Chicago: University of Chicago Press, 2018) extensively documents Anna Helmholtz's contributions. Cahan construes her role primarily as supportive (see esp. 312–313) and highlights her influential role in establishing her husband's legacy after his death (735–747).

[47] As laboratory notes from 1850 show, Olga Helmholtz (née von Velten) was actively involved in her husband's physiological experiments; see Henning Schmidgen, "Passagenwerk 1850. Bild und Zahl in den physiologischen Zeitexperimenten von Hermann von Helmholtz," *Berichte der Wissenschaftsgeschichte* 34 (2011): 139–155, 141. The mother of two children, she died of pulmonary disease at the age of thirty-three.

[48] David Cahan, *An Institute for an Empire: The Physikalisch-Technische Reichsanstalt, 1871–1918* (Cambridge: Cambridge University Press, 1989).

[49] Lorraine Daston, "Die wissenschaftliche Persona. Arbeit und Berufung," in Wobbe, *Zwischen Vorderbühne und Hinterbühne*, ed. Wobbe, 109–136, at 125. As Daston observes, the disputes over the lively salon—did its social demands replenish Hermann's spirits, or strain his health?—point to the shared underlying social expectation of professors' wives: to maintain the fine balance between providing necessary distraction from their husbands' work, and taking too much time away from it.

guest Wilhelm Dilthey deemed Anna Helmholtz "one of the most important women of her era," while also pointing out that "she was always conscious of the natural limits of men and women's achievements."[50] It is a matter of speculation whether she accepted those limits as naturally given or as social conventions; her sharp eye for the socially staged performances of gender difference might suggest the latter. For instance, having invited a number of scientific luminaries and their wives to celebrate the discovery of an "ancient animal" to be viewed under a microscope set up in her room, she finds herself rushing between "the ladies admiring the moon in the balcony room, and the gentlemen admiring the *eozoon* in mine."[51]

Within the constraints of the social role that she was practically invested in, Anna Helmholtz found her way of intellectual engagement with the sciences in translating writings by the physicist John Tyndall directed at a generally educated public: *Heat Considered as a Mode of Motion, Fragments of Science for Unscientific People*, and *Sound*.[52] Her portrayal of the beginnings of this translation work in the 1860s—as a joint "sock-knitting" project bringing together family members on long winter days, and providing additional income invested in a "nice carpet from Brussels" for the household she was then still in the process of setting up—should not distract from the significance it acquired.[53] Anna Helmholtz devoted a considerable amount of her time through the 1890s to the demanding task of these translations. The topics ranged widely from technical descriptions of experiments to more overtly philosophical deliberations, for example, on natural laws, or the use of the imagination in the sciences, to practical problems like parasitical illnesses in silkworms.

With this work, Anna Helmholtz took part in the publicization of science that, as historians of science have emphasized, was an important factor in the complex process of establishing the modern sciences' claim to providing authoritative knowledge.[54] From his exceptionally influential position, Hermann Helmholtz intervened frequently

---

[50] Dilthey as quoted in *Anna von Helmholtz. Ein Lebensbild in Briefen.* Vol. 1. Edited by Ellen von Siemens-Helmholtz. Berlin: Verlag für Kulturpolitik, 1929, 211 and 274; see an assessment in similar words by another friend, Rosalie Braun-Artaria, *Von berühmten Zeitgenossen: Lebenserinnerungen einer Siebzigerin* (Munich: Beck, 1918), 138.

[51] Anna Helmholtz, letter on August 2, 1865, in Siemens-Helmholtz (ed.), *Lebensbild*, 126.

[52] Their title pages credited "A. H." for the translation initially, and "Anna von Helmholtz" in later editions (and after her husband's ennoblement in 1883). For more context, see Cahan, *Helmholtz*, 310–313 and 499–508.

[53] Anna Helmholtz, letter on Januar 1, 1867 and October 29 1867, in Siemens-Helmholtz (ed.), *Lebensbild*, 139 and 145.

[54] Rigid distinctions "between the making and communicating of knowledge," and between authorized and "popular" science are a problematic legacy of the process of the professionalization of science during the nineteenth century; (James A. Secord, "Knowledge in Transit," *Isis* 95, no. 4 (2004): 654–672, at 661); see also Andreas W. Daum, "Varieties of Popular Science and the Transformation of Public Knowledge: Some Historical Reflections," *Isis* 100, no. 2 (2009): 319–332, and on the German context, Rosemarie Nöthlich, Olaf Breidbach, and Uwe Hoßfeld, "'Was ist die Natur?' Einige Aspekte zur Wissenschaftspopularisierung in Deutschland," in *"Klassische Universität" und "akademische Provinz": Studien zur Universität Jena von der Mitte des 19. bis in die dreißiger Jahre des 20. Jahrhunderts* (Jena: Dr. Bussert & Stadeler, 2005), 239–250.

in the public discussion of the sciences, and in multiple registers ranging from normative remarks on the university's role in society to epistemological problems. Anna Helmholtz did not see, or seek to portray, herself as a philosopher, especially good ones apparently being a "rare commodity," as she dryly observed.[55] Rather, the division of intellectual labor between her and her husband draws attention to the beginnings of philosophy of science as continuous with the broader effort to make science and scientists part of the cultural establishment within the social order of the industrializing empire. Hermann Helmholtz made connections between sensory physiology and aesthetic principles in his work on sound and optics;[56] more generally, the complex relations between aesthetics, neohumanistic ideals, science, and industry have been investigated as a factor in Germany's ascent to a leading industrial and scientific nation at the end of the nineteenth century.[57]

Anna Helmholtz's 1874 translation of Tyndall's *Fragments* illustrates the appeal to what David Cahan has dubbed the "civilising power of science": the view that humanity derives intellectual understanding as well as "socioeconomic and political power and control" from the pursuit of science.[58] This broad theme runs across Hermann Helmholtz's diverse lectures and writings directed at a wider public. In his introduction to Anna's translation of the *Fragments*, he spells out the social benefits to be expected from this cultivation of a wider public for science. Familiarity with specific scientific results, or so Helmholtz claims, is not what discerning readers are primarily after when they seek out scientists' writings. Rather, they wish to gain insight into the scientist's work process and into his broader attitude and vision—distinguished by careful discipline coupled with experimental imagination. Through texts by scientists who are also gifted writers, like Tyndall, familiarity with the "art of experiment and observation" as it has been methodically developed by the sciences is to become part of general education, *Bildung*—and will have "indestructible significance" for individuals as well as nation-states.[59] Anna Helmholtz, in private, puts her view of the function of engagement with

---

[55] Anna Helmholtz, letter on March 21, 1872, in Siemens-Helmholtz (ed.), *Lebensbild*, 178.

[56] In the context of his broader argument for how physiology gained its institutional and disciplinary status in nineteenth-century Germany by explicating its links to wider society, Timothy Lenoir has drawn attention to the "politics of vision" connecting physiological optics, painting, and aesthetic theory (Lenoir, *Instituting Science*, 131–178). On sensory physiology, music, musical theory, and instrument building, see, e.g., Myles Jackson, *Harmonious Triads: Physicists, Musicians, and Instrument Makers in Nineteenth-Century Germany* (Cambridge, MA: MIT Press, 2006). The connections between modern science and the aesthetic and cultural ideals of the *Bildungsbürgertum* are a theme running through Cahan, *Helmholtz*.

[57] M. Norton Wise, *Aesthetics, Industry, and Science: Hermann von Helmholtz and the Berlin Physical Society* (Chicago: Chicago University Press, 2018); see also Ursula Klein, "Science, Industry, and the German Bildungsbürgertum," *Annals of Science* 77, no. 3 (2020): 366–376.

[58] David Cahan, "Helmholtz and the Civilizing Power of Science," in *Hermann von Helmholtz and the Foundations of Nineteenth-Century Science*, ed. David Cahan (Berkeley: University of California Press, 1994), 559–601, at 560.

[59] *Fragmente aus den Naturwissenschaften: Vorlesungen und Aufsätze. Übersetzt von A. H., mit Vorwort und Zusätzen von Prof. H. Helmholtz* (Braunschweig: Vieweg, 1874), ix–x. On the context of Helmholtz's defense of Tyndall against Karl Friedrich Zöllner, see Cahan, *Helmholtz*, 494--511.

the sciences more colloquially as a means to "scrub out one's head."[60] Her translations of Tyndall integrated the discussion of science into the social and cultural ambitions of the educated middle classes.

This cultural positioning of science complements the emphasis on the significance of specific scientific results that distinguishes Hermann Helmholtz's explicitly philosophical writings. If he privately characterized philosophers as "impotent bookworms who never create any new knowledge," his philosophical contributions exemplified how scientific insights could come to their rescue—an argumentative strategy that, in its insistence on the epistemological relevance of the empirical sciences, became as influential for Neo-Kantianism as it did for logical empiricism.[61] In our context, however, this legacy also marks the limits of a philosophy of science construed as part of a broader effort to position the sciences within the German Empire's social order. To the extent that it required academic training, women's participation in the emerging field generally remained predicated on the radical social and political changes that were demanded by women's rights activists like Dohm, and that ran counter to the politically moderate views held by many members of the scientific establishment such as the Helmholtzes. Anna Helmholtz, in contrast, was in a position to obtain access to the scientific training required for engaging with more technical arguments, but chose instead—and similarly to Emilie Exner in the political context of the Habsburg empire—an avenue for engaging in discussion of the sciences that contributed more directly to furthering their cultural and social establishment.

While certainly also a matter of personal inclination, this choice did not threaten the division of labor that her and her husband's work relied upon practically, and that corresponded to the monarchy's widely accepted, if by no means uncontested gendered social order.[62] Liberal but no democrats, both Anna and Hermann Helmholtz supported the Prussian monarchy after his return to Berlin (and moved in Berlin's upper social circles including members of the imperial family); he saw university and state as closely aligned.[63] At his most explicitly political, Hermann Helmholtz assigned epistemology—for him, the academically based investigation of human cognition in

[60] Anna Helmholtz, letter on March 21, 1872, in Siemens-Helmholtz (ed.), *Lebensbild*, 178.

[61] Helmholtz in a letter to Lipschitz as quoted in Michael Heidelberger, "Helmholtz als Philosoph," *Deutsche Zeitschrift für Philosophie* 43, no. 5 (1995): 835–844, at 835. On Helmholtz's at best reserved stance towards philosophy and philosophers, see Cahan, *Helmholtz*, 531–548.

[62] Maria Osietzki has argued that the social practice of a gendered division of labor was self-evident to the young Helmholtz, and constitutive for his physical theories in his early work "On the Conservation of Force" (1847). This pathbreaking work secured the academic recognition that made possible his first marriage to Olga von Velten—a union that he saw in terms of an economy of forces, with him in charge of the material "production" that would enable him to marry, have a family and "reproduce" (Maria Osietzki, "Körpermaschinen und Dampfmaschinen: Vom Wandel der Physiologie und des Körpers unter dem Einfluß von Industrialisierung und Thermodynamik," in *Physiologie und industrielle Gesellschaft: Studien zur Verwissenschaftlichung des Körpers im 19. und 20. Jahrhundert*, ed. Philipp Sarasin and Jakob Tanner (Frankfurt am Main: Suhrkamp, 1998), 313–346, at 322-–332).

[63] See See David Cahan, "The 'Imperial Chancellor of the Sciences': Helmholtz between Science and Politics," *Social Research* 73, no. 4 (2006): 1093–1128.

scientific terms—the role of bringing into view "humanity's eternal ideals," and as such, firmly associated it with the Prussian monarchy's support of "spiritual riches [Güter geistiger Art]."[64] Anna Helmholtz's translation work with its emphasis on science as cultural education distanced its public discussion from debates that enlisted scientific theories for more radical political goals. While the couple followed these debates keenly, and Hermann Helmholtz defended others' right to discuss potentially radical implications of scientific theories in the name of academic free speech, they did not endorse them.[65] For example, Anna Helmholtz witnessed a speech by the "talented, dangerous, and mean-spirited" August Bebel in the Reichstag, and remained unimpressed with the way he "quoted Haeckel, Virchow and all philosophers ancient and contemporary in order to prove the identity of Darwinism and socialism."[66]

A critique of Hermann Helmholtz's philosophical views placed in the context of the sciences' significant role in the industrializing empire was put forward by Hedwig Bender in her 1897 *Metaphysics and the Scientific Disciplines*.[67] A school teacher in Eisenach, and by that time the published author of several philosophical works, Bender frames her engagement with psychologist-philosopher Wilhelm Wundt's call for a new relationship of philosophy and the sciences with remarks on the place of both in society. The empirical sciences are driven by "material interests and the striving for material comfort" as they are increasingly offering "mastery over nature"; philosophy is "intimately related to the higher human needs" as reflected in cosmology, ethics, and aesthetics.[68] Bender follows Wundt in portraying the task of philosophy as the articulation of the relations between results of specialized disciplines, but qualifies her endorsement by insisting that philosophy "must gain its most important results autonomously and

[64] "The Facts in Perception," delivered as the rectoral address at Berlin's Friedrich-Wilhelms-Universität; (Hermann von Helmholtz, "Die Thatsachen in der Wahrnehmung," in Helmholtz, *Vorträge und Reden*, 215–218). Despite Helmholtz's own rhetorical emphasis, the view of his philosophy as an anti-metaphysical epistemology is reductive; see, e. g., Heidelberger, "Helmholtz als Philosoph," and Nasser Zakariya, "Scenes before Grey Antiquity," *Res: Anthropology and Aesthetics* 69–70 (2018): 5–19.

[65] Richards, *The Tragic Sense of Life*, 329.

[66] Anna Helmholtz, letter on September 12, 1878, in Siemens-Helmholtz (ed.), *Lebensbild*, 227.

[67] On Bender, see Katherina Kinzel, "Women Philosophers and the Neo-Kantian Movement," chapter 20 in this volume. In her emphasis on the prevalence of experience and the development of a scientific world view, Bender was part of a broader movement; a similar motivation to uncover common ground between philosophy and metaphysics informed Wilhelm Ostwald's claim to a new philosophy of nature. (See Ziche, "The 'New Philosophy of Nature.'"). There are, however, important differences; above all, in contrast to Ostwald, Bender does not consider philosophy an empirical science.

[68] Hedwig Bender, *Philosophie, Metaphysik und Einzelforschung. Untersuchungen über das Wesen der Philosophie im allgemeinen und über die Möglichkeit der Metaphysik als Wissenschaft und ihr Verhältnis zur naturwissenschaftlichen Forschung im besonderen* (Leipzig: Hermann Haacke, 1897), 16–17. On Wundt, see Paul Ziche, *Wissenschaftslandschaften um 1900: Philosophie, die Wissenschaften und der nichtreduktive Szientismus* (Zurich: Chronos, 2008), 62–106, describing Wundt as an example of the experiments with a new philosophical role model "distinguished by a union between qualifications in philosophy and specific scientific disciplines" around the turn of the century (Ziche, *Wissenschaftslandschaften um 1900*, 41); other examples are the psychologists Gustav Theodor Fechner, Wilhelm Wundt, Carl Stumpf, and Hermann Lotze, or the physicists Ernst Mach and Ludwig Boltzmann.

independently of them."[69] Accordingly, she argues against empiricist approaches and the notion that philosophy depends on specific results of the empirical sciences, and can only proceed by building upon them.

On Bender's reading, Hermann Helmholtz's ostentatious turn away from Kant and toward "the old empiricist position of simply rejecting all metaphysical claims that cannot be proven experimentally" over the course of his career is characteristic of the—obviously mistaken, in her view—attempt to ground a worldview in scientific knowledge only. It amounts, or so she claims, to giving up on the philosophical task of examining relations between that knowledge and cosmological, aesthetic, and ethical realms.[70] Bender's main counterargument consists in emphasizing that the empirical sciences routinely operate with notions that are beyond sense perception, above all the notions of causality and of laws of nature. She points to inconsistencies in Helmholtz's writings to argue that he and others dodge the question of how to grasp the causal connection between natural phenomena that itself escapes sense perception, "refusing to admit that one cannot make do without transcendental presuppositions."[71] For her, the way out of the predicament lies in accepting the Kantian point that "the notion of causality is a product of the thinking mind."[72] And she warns against the view that scientific experiments—though "the most precious research instrument"—can guard against the excesses of speculation that the *Naturphilosophie* of Schelling and Hegel's days had been accused of: "experiments can never prove or disprove theoretical presuppositions but only show their compatibility with what is already regarded as proven."[73]

On those grounds, Bender goes on to document what she sees as the close relationship between metaphysics and science, yet what was commonly presented as evidence of their utter incompatibility. Her main example is the debate over arguments for the conservation of force (or, in present-day terminology, energy)—an argument that, she claims, can be made in metaphysical terms. And in her view, it was successfully made in metaphysical terms by Julius Robert Mayer when he deduced the equivalence of heat and mechanical force from the premise of the "indestructibleness of given forces" in 1842. Independently, both James Prescott Joule and Hermann Helmholtz reached the same conclusion based on their experiments on the nature of heat—but in their case, Bender points out, the result is a generalization from empirical data that, as such, cannot claim apodicticity.[74] While Helmholtz explains his contempt for the "philosophical-speculative" mode of reasoning adopted by Mayer as a reaction against the "excesses" of speculative philosophy (a common use of the image of natural philosophy that

---

[69] Bender, *Philosophie, Metaphysik und Einzelforschung*, 10–11.

[70] Bender, *Philosophie, Metaphysik und Einzelforschung*, 28.

[71] Bender, *Philosophie, Metaphysik und Einzelforschung*, 39.

[72] Bender, *Philosophie, Metaphysik und Einzelforschung*, 41.

[73] Bender, *Philosophie, Metaphysik und Einzelforschung*, 68–69.

[74] Bender, *Philosophie, Metaphysik und Einzelforschung*, 79. For a case for the importance of Kantian metaphysics for Helmholtz's argument, see Wise, *Aesthetics, Industry, and Science*, 244–298. On Neo-Kantian Alois Riehl's defense of Mayer's argument in 1900, see Ziche, *Wissenschaftslandschaften um 1900*, 55–56.

Bender finds plausible enough), she still does not think it is logically justified.[75] Instead of the retreat to an empirically based epistemology that she finds questionable, Bender expects philosophy to counteract the discursive separation of the scientific investigation of the empirically given from the ethical and aesthetic concerns she takes to be higher human needs.

4 TURN OF THE CENTURY: OPENING DOORS?

University doors opened to women as regular students from 1909 across all German-speaking countries during a time of "crisis of reflection on scientific knowledge."[76] The limits of mechanical modes of explanations became apparent in the physical sciences; World War I threw into question any image of science unproblematically aligned with social and political progress. The corresponding landscape of philosophical approaches to the sciences remained diverse, and this diversity is also characteristic of women's contributions to academic philosophy of science prior to the advent of National Socialism. In response to the proliferation of scientific disciplines over the course of the nineteenth century, questions of the unity of science and philosophy's potential role in articulating this unity acquired a new urgency.[77] They motivated diverging philosophical directions, such as the Vienna Circle and the Reichenbach School's concern with the structure of scientific theories, but also much of Edmund Husserl's phenomenology. His ambition was to articulate a philosophy that was itself scientific in the sense of Husserl's programmatic demand for a *strenge Wissenschaft*, that is, one that was not identical with empirical science, and could ground scientific thinking in general.[78]

Women in the phenomenological movement tackled related questions. Turning toward phenomenology from psychology and psychiatry, Edith Stein's early work on the ontological foundations of psychology and the human sciences examines the "regularities preceding any kind of empirical observation"—a theoretical perspective that remained decisive for her research.[79] Building on her dissertation work on the problem of "empathy," that is, how other minds are given to us, Stein's account of

---

[75] Bender, *Philosophie, Metaphysik und Einzelforschung*, 82.

[76] Hans-Jörg Rheinberger, *On Historicizing Epistemology* (Stanford: Stanford University Press, 2010), 1.

[77] For a historicization of the notion of a general philosophy of science emerging in this context, see Hans-Jörg Rheinberger, "A Plea for a Historical Epistemology of Research," *Journal for General Philosophy of Science* 43 (2012): 105–111.

[78] On Moritz Schlick's critique of Husserl's notion of intuition, see Ziche, *Wissenschaftslandschaften um 1900*, 291–296.

[79] As emphasized by Ruth Hagengruber, "Das Unsichtbare sichtbar machen: die soziale Wirklichkeit und ihre Grundlagen in der Philosophie von Edith Stein," *Edith-Stein-Jahrbuch* 10 (2004): 157–173, at 173; see Edith Stein, *Zum Problem der Einfühlung* (Halle: Buchdruckerei des Waisenhauses, 1917), and Edith Stein, "Beiträge zur philosophischen Begründung der Psychologie und der Geisteswissenschaften," *Jahrbuch für Philosophie und Phänomenologische Forschung* 5 (1922): 1–284. Sawicki reads Stein's

the condition of the possibility of a foundational account of science lies in her notion of community grounded in individual minds' ability to share a common world.[80] As Emanuele Caminada has flagged, the point of departure for Stein's reflections on community is political. Her examples stem from her experience of World War I; her "theoretical struggle" is that of an "engaged patriot for understanding the ontological reality of the subjects of her political passions."[81] Against this background, Stein develops an account of science that does not exempt scientific practice from interpersonal constitution of meaning.[82]

Stein's close friend Hedwig Conrad-Martius, who quickly abandoned her studies of medicine for philosophy, made her name by winning a prestigious prize with a paper on the epistemological foundations of positivism in 1912 in Göttingen.[83] Her central project throughout her lifetime was a phenomenologically grounded *Naturphilosophie* that engaged in depth with scientific research, and that "analyzed the interaction between different modes of givenness" ranging from the empirical to the transcendental, eidetic, and speculative.[84] Not unlike its forerunners such as Ernst Haeckel's philosophy of nature, this work did not have an obvious academic audience. This challenge was compounded by the lack of career options for women, and was met by Conrad-Martius in innovative ways, for example, her 1934 radio lectures on plant souls—work that was, as opposed to academic writing, paid.[85] Like Stein's emphasis on the social constitution

phenomenology of the psyche as offering a starting point for a "unified foundation for the natural and cultural sciences" (Sawicki, *Body, Text, and Science*, 239).

[80] See Ruth Hagengruber, "Sozialphilosophie als 'strenge Wissenschaft': Überlegungen zu Edith Stein und Edmund Husserl," in *Die unbekannte Edith Stein: Phänomenologie und Sozialphilosophie*, ed. Beate Beckmann-Zöller and Hannah B. Gerl-Falkovitz (Frankfurt am Main: Peter Lang, 2006), 59–72, esp. 66–68.

[81] Caminada, "Edith Stein's Account of Communal Mind and Its Limits," 552. Caminada stresses the limits of this potentially idealizing notion of community developed from the wartime experience. On the political dimension of Stein's work, see also Alasdair MacIntyre, *Edith Stein: A Philosophical Prologue* (London: Bloomsbury, 2007), 93–98.

[82] While Stein's explicit engagement is primarily with psychology, Gerda Walther's 1923 *On the Ontology of Social Communities* shows the extent to which the empirical sciences, and specifically social Darwinist positions were discussed in phenomenological circles (Hagengruber, "Das Unsichtbare sichtbar machen," 171).

[83] Prize submissions were anonymous. In order to obtain her doctorate, however, Conrad-Martius had to submit the award-winning paper to the philosophical faculty in Munich. Göttingen would not grant her a doctorate because her high school exams did not include ancient Greek (Alexandra Elisabeth Pfeiffer, "Ontological Phenomenology: The Philosophical Project of Hedwig Conrad-Martius," *Axiomathes* 18 (2008): 445–460, at 447). On Conrad-Martius's turn away from medicine, see Francesco Alfieri, "Hedwig Conrad-Martius: A Philosophical Heredity, Illustrated by E. Avé-Lallemant," *Axiomathes* 18, nos. 515–531 (2008), 521.

[84] Eberhard Avé-Lallemant, "Hedwig Conrad-Martius (1888--1966): Bibliographie," *Zeitschrift für philosophische Forschung* 31, no. 2 (1977): 301–309, at 301. For a concise overview, see Ales Bello, "The Human Being in the Context of Nature."

[85] On the radio lectures, see Alfieri, "Hedwig Conrad-Martius," 523. For the period prior to World War II, the main text is Hedwig Conrad-Martius, "Realontologie," *Jahrbuch für Philosophie und phänomenologische Forschung* 6 (1923). For a discussion of Conrad-Martius's understanding of the plant soul, see also Dalia Nassar, "Plants, Animals, and the Earth," chapter 29 in this volume.

of scientific practice, Conrad-Martius's insistence on clarifying the relationship between human beings and nature marks an edge of the academically acceptable philosophy of science of their days that resonates with some of the field's concerns a century on.

The admission of the first generation of women students to German universities also roughly coincided with the developments in physics that marked the end of the success of mechanical explanation that had characterized much of nineteenth-century science. Relativity theory and quantum physics sparked new debates over notions such as space, time, and causality. Among the women working in the Neo-Kantian tradition, Ilse Schneider and Grete Herrmann stand out for their arguments for the compatibility between Kantian epistemological frameworks and the "new" physics.[86] Schneider was a student of Alois Riehl as well as Albert Einstein and Max Planck in Berlin. In a 1914 article on Henri Poincaré's conventionalism in relation to Einstein, Schneider places Poincaré in the Kantian tradition.[87] Her 1921 doctoral dissertation argues against the view that Kant's transcendental philosophy had to be reviewed in light of Einstein's theory of relativity. Schneider's argument rests on her critique of the conflation of Newton's conceptions of space and time with Kant's, and of misunderstanding Kant's pure forms of intuition as physical realities—a position that aligned her, for example, with Ernst Cassirer, but put her at odds notably with her fellow former Einstein student Hans Reichenbach, whose logical empiricism took the need to revise the Kantian a priori principles as its starting point.[88]

In Göttingen, Grete Hermann took her doctoral supervisor, the eminent mathematician Emmy Noether, by surprise by changing her focus from mathematics and physics to philosophy following her doctorate.[89] Although her primary concern was ethics and political philosophy, she turned her attention to quantum mechanics as part of her broader case for a transcendental *Naturphilosophie* that would encompass both theoretical and practical philosophy, and would build on her teacher Leonard Nelson's

[86]   See chapter 20, on Neo-Kantianism, in this volume for a discussion of the claim that there were no women in the Neo-Kantian movement.

[87]   Ilse Schneider, "Raum, Zeit und ihre Relativität bei Poincaré," in *Herrn Geheimrat Professor Dr. phil. et H. LL. D. Alois Riehl zum siebzigsten Geburtstag,* ed. Kurt Lewin and Alois Riehl (Berlin: H. Lonys, 1914), 91–130. See Andrea Reichenberger, "Zwei Fundstücke zu Henri Poincaré," in *Siegener Beiträge zur Geschichte und Philosophie der Mathematik,* vol. 13, ed. R. Krömer and G. Nickel (Siegen: Siegen University Press, 2020), 127–154, on Schneider's article and for a biographical sketch of Schneider, who emigrated from Nazi Germany to Australia in 1938. Reichenberger also discusses Thekla Schmitz's 1921 doctoral dissertation on Poincaré. On Alois Riehl, see Michael Heidelberger, "Kantianism and Realism: Alois Riehl (and Moritz Schlick)," in Friedman and Nordmann, *The Kantian Legacy in Nineteenth-Century Science,* ed. Friedman and Nordmann, 227–247.

[88]   See Michael Friedman, *Reconsidering Logical Positivism* (Cambridge: Cambridge University Press, 1999). On Reichenbach's and Schlick's attacks on Schneider provoked by her dismissal of Reichenbach's reading of Kant, see Reichenberger, "Zwei Fundstücke zu Henri Poincaré," 149–151.

[89]   Inge Hansen-Schaberg, "A Biographical Sketch of Prof. Dr. Grete Henry-Hermann (1901–1984)," in *Grete Hermann: Between Physics and Philosophy,* ed. Elise Crull and Guido Bacciagaluppi (Dordrecht: Springer, 2016), 3–16, at 7. For a general overview of Hermann's work, see *Grete Henry-Hermann: Philosophie—Mathematik—Quantenmechanik,* ed. Kay Herrmann, ed. Kay Herrmann (Wiesbaden: Springer, 2019).

reading of Kant through Jakob Friedrich Fries.[90] In her 1935 "Natural-Philosophical Foundations of Quantum Mechanics," written following extensive discussions with Werner Heisenberg, Hermann makes a case for the compatibility of Kant's category of causality with quantum mechanics.[91] While she accepts that quantum-physical predictions are statistical rather than strictly deterministic, she argues that the notion of causality in the Kantian sense of the conditions of the possibility of any future physics remains in place because causal chains can be reconstructed retrospectively, though not predicted by quantum physics.[92]

The wider "natural-philosophical novelty of quantum physics," Hermann concludes, lies in the fact that quantum physics "separates various equally legitimate representations within the physical description [namely wave-versus-particle descriptions] that cannot be unified into a single picture of nature."[93] Critical philosophy in the footsteps of Fries had long insisted on the separation between different realms of knowledge: alongside different scientific disciplines like physics or psychology "come evaluative, ethical and aesthetic perspectives whose claims to objectivity find no place in the natural sciences without the latter thereby excluding them from the realm of knowledge." In quantum physics, such "splitting of the truth" is necessary *within* physical description itself. This conceptual requirement reflects the limits of natural knowledge of reality as always only picking out, "in an incomplete way, relational networks whose foundations remain indeterminate within the scope of this knowledge."[94]

With regard to the professionalization of philosophy of science as an academic discipline, the set of approaches grouped together under the label "Vienna Circle" is particularly significant. To the Circle's social and political engagement corresponded its conceptually revolutionary self-stylization that aimed at establishing neopositivist theories of science within academia, against the often considerable resistance of conservative philosophical faculties. However, the concern with the logic of science at the core of the Circle's programmatic efforts is distinct from nineteenth-century traditions of socially and politically invested engagement with science, including women activists' emphasis on the connections between scientific claims about human nature and the corresponding order of society. The Circle's proximity to progressive politics therefore did not align these critiques with the academically based philosophy of science. Neither

---

[90] Giulia Paparo, "Understanding Grete Hermann's Philosophy of Nature," in *Grete Hermann: Between Physics and Philosophy*, ed. Crull and Bacciagaluppi, *Grete Hermann*, 35–51.

[91] Grete Hermann, "Die naturphilosophischen Grundlagen der Quantenmechanik," *Abhandlungen der Fries'schen Schule* 6, no. 2 (1935): 75–152, translated as Grete Hermann, "Natural-Philosophical Foundations of Quantum Mechanics," in Crull and Bacciagaluppi, *Grete Hermann: Between Physics and Philosophy*, ed., Crull and Bacciagaluppi, 239–278.

[92] Paparo, "Understanding Grete Hermann's Philosophy of Nature," emphasizes that Hermann anticipated by some thirty years John Bell's famous 1964 refutation of John von Neumann's 1932 argument against hidden variables. Hermann nevertheless does not proceed to invoke the existence of hidden variables to salvage a deterministic notion of causality.

[93] Hermann, "Natural-Philosophical Foundations of Quantum Mechanics," 277.

[94] Hermann, "Natural-Philosophical Foundations of Quantum Mechanics," 276.

did it support women's participation or career ambitions to the extent that comparable liberal scientific circles in Vienna did, above all the Institute for Psychology.[95] Recent research has foregrounded women's diverse contributions to the Circle's discussions that had previously been historiographically marginalized.[96] Thus, Rose Rand has been described as a logician in her own right, not merely as part of the student group of the Circle and the person who took the official minutes of the meetings gathered around Moritz Schlick in Vienna's Boltzmanngasse.[97] Olga Hahn's contributions to symbolic logic appear as an important part of the interest in universal languages associated with the name of her husband, Otto Neurath, as do Susan Stebbing's.[98] Psychologist Else Frenkel's work with the Circle in the 1930s is reflected in her arguments for the integration of psychoanalysis into the conception of the unity of science, one of the Circle's central concerns.[99]

Looking back on the long process of the constitution of the philosophy of science, the image of doors opening to women in the early twentieth century is not unproblematic. This is not only because, a century on, women remain significantly underrepresented in the discipline and gendered patterns of assessment persist.[100] It is also because this image privileges the disciplinary contours of a philosophy of science that took shape prior to the opening of institutional doors, and during the years of these doors barely just opening—and as such, in contradistinction to different strands of reflection on the sciences, particularly those interrogating their social constitution and political roles. As Gianna Pomata has argued for the case of historical scholarship, we should be careful not to construe all forms of marginalization as externally imposed. While many women were indeed frustrated in their attempts at academic careers in history during the early twentieth century, there were others who deliberately chose to work outside of academic institutions, and whose "intellectual identity centered around a fundamental value—independence as an epistemic ideal—that forms a strong continuity between

---

[95] See Maria Rentetzi, "'I Want to Look Like a Lady, Not Like a Factory Worker.' Rose Rand, a Woman Philosopher of the Vienna Circle," in *EPSA Epistemology and Methodology of Science: Launch of the European Philosophy of Science Association*, ed. M. Suárez et al. (Dordrecht: Springer, 2010), 233–244, at 242; see also Rentetzi, "Gender, Politics, and Radioactivity Research in Interwar Vienna."

[96] Friedrich Stadler, *The Vienna Circle: Studies in the Origins, Development, and Influence of Logical Empiricism* (Dordrecht: Springer, 2015), 54. In addition to the examples mentioned here, Stadler lists Käthe Steinhardt, Maria Kasper, Marie Reidemeister, Olga Taussky-Todd, Hilda Geiringer-Mises, Marja Kokoszynska-Lutman, Janina Hosiasson-Lindenbaum, Izydora Dambska, and Dina Sztejnberg.

[97] Adelheid Hamacher-Hermes, "Rose Rand: A Woman in Logic," in *The Vienna Circle and Logical Empiricism: Re-evaluation and Future Perspectives*, ed. Friedrich Stadler (Dordrecht: Springer, 2003), 365–378.

[98] Jordi Cat, "Neurath and the Legacy of Algebraic Logic," in *Neurath Reconsidered: New Sources and Perspectives*, ed. Jordi Cat and Adam Tamas Tuboly (Dordrecht: Springer, 2019), 241–337.

[99] Dagmar Borchers, "No Woman, No Try?: Else Frenkel-Brunswik and the Project of Integrating Psychoanalysis into the Unity of Science," in Stadler, *The Vienna Circle and Logical Empiricism*, ed. Stadler, 323–338.

[100] Hanne Andersen, "Women in the History of Philosophy of Science: What We Do and Do Not Know," *History Of Philosophy Of Science* 3, no. 1 (2013): 136–139.

nineteenth-century amateurism and present-day independent scholarship."[101] Similarly, much of women's nineteenth-century socially and politically engaged philosophy of science was not directed at academic audiences. Within the confines of twentieth-century philosophy of science as an academic profession predicated upon scientific training, the narrowing focus on a theory of scientific knowledge did not appeal to scholars like, for example, Grete Hermann who remained committed to the question of the relation of problems of theoretical and practical philosophy. If women's contributions foreground how the intellectual contours of the philosophy of science took shape during its formative years, they also invite their future reshaping.

References

Abir-Am, Pnina, Helena Pycior, and Nancy Slack, eds. *Creative Couples in the Sciences*. New Brunswick: Rutgers University Press, 1996.

Ales Bello, Angela. "The Human Being in the Context of Nature: Philosophical Anthropology and the Natural Sciences in Hedwig Conrad-Martius." *Axiomathes* 18, no. 4 (2008): 425–443.

Alfieri, Francesco. "Hedwig Conrad-Martius: A Philosophical Heredity, Illustrated by E. Avé-Lallemant." *Axiomathes* 18, no. 4 (2008): 515–531.

Andersen, Hanne. "Women in the History of Philosophy of Science: What We Do and Do Not Know." *History Of Philosophy Of Science* 3, no. 1 (2013): 136–139.

Avé-Lallemant, Eberhard. "Hedwig Conrad-Martius (1888–1966): Bibliographie." *Zeitschrift für philosophische Forschung* 31, no. 2 (1977): 301–309.

Bebel, August. *Woman and Socialism (1879), transl. Meta L. Stern (Hebe)*. New York: Socialist Literature Co., 1910.

Bender, Hedwig. *Philosophie, Metaphysik und Einzelforschung: Untersuchungen über das Wesen der Philosophie im allgemeinen und über die Möglichkeit der Metaphysik als Wissenschaft und ihr Verhältnis zur naturwissenschaftlichen Forschung im besonderen*. Leipzig: Hermann Haacke, 1897.

Borchers, Dagmar. "No Woman, No Try? Else Frenkel-Brunswik and the Project of Integrating Psychoanalysis into the Unity of Science." In *The Vienna Circle and Logical Empiricism: Re-evaluation and Future Perspectives*, edited by Friedrich Stadler, 323–338. Dordrecht: Springer, 2003.

Braun-Artaria, Rosalie. *Von berühmten Zeitgenossen: Lebenserinnerungen einer Siebzigerin*. Munich: Beck, 1918.

Cahan, David. *Helmholtz: A Life in Science*. Chicago: Chicago University Press, 2018.

Cahan, David. "Helmholtz and the Civilizing Power of Science." In *Hermann von Helmholtz and the Foundations of Nineteenth-Century Science*, edited by David Cahan, 559–601. Berkeley: University of California Press, 1994.

Cahan, David. "The 'Imperial Chancellor of the Sciences': Helmholtz between Science and Politics." *Social Research* 73, no. 4 (2006): 1093–1128.

Cahan, David. *An Institute for an Empire: The Physikalisch-Technische Reichsanstalt, 1871–1918*. Cambridge: Cambridge University Press, 1989.

---

[101] Gianna Pomata, "Amateurs by Choice: Women and the Pursuit of Independent Scholarship in 20th Twentieth-Century Historical Writing," *Centaurus* 55 (2013): 196–219, at 198.

Caminada, Emanuele. "Edith Stein's Account of Communal Mind and Its Limits: A Phenomenological Reading." *Human Studies* 38 (2015): 549–566.

Cat, Jordi. "Neurath and the Legacy of Algebraic Logic." In *Neurath Reconsidered: New Sources and Perspectives*, edited by Jordi Cat and Adam Tamas Tuboly, 241–337. Dordrecht: Springer, 2019.

Coen, Deborah R. "The Common World: Histories of Science and Domestic Intimacy." *Modern Intellectual History* 11, no. 2 (2014): 417–438.

Coen, Deborah R. *Vienna in the Age of Uncertainty: Science, Liberalism, and Private Life.* Chicago: University of Chicago Press, 2007.

Collini, Stefan. Editor's introduction to *On Liberty with The Subjection of Women and Chapters on Socialism,* by John Stuart Mill, vii–xxvi. Cambridge: Cambridge University Press, 1989.

Conrad-Martius, Hedwig. "Realontologie." *Jahrbuch für Philosophie und Phänomenologische Forschung* 6 (1923): 159–333.

Daston, Lorraine. "Die wissenschaftliche Persona. Arbeit und Berufung." In *Zwischen Vorderbühne und Hinterbühne. Beiträge zum Wandel der Geschlechterbeziehungen in der Wissenschaft vom 17. Jahrhundert bis zur Gegenwart,* edited by Theresa Wobbe, 109–136. Bielefeld: transcript, 2003.

Daston, Lorraine, and Fernando Vidal, eds. *The Moral Authority of Nature.* Chicago: University of Chicago Press, 2004.

Daum, Andreas. *Wissenschaftspopularisierung im 19. Jahrhundert. Bürgerliche Kultur, naturwissenschaftliche Bildung und die deutsche Öffentlichkeit 1848–1914.* Munich: Oldenbourg, 2002.

Daum, Andreas W. "Varieties of Popular Science and the Transformation of Public Knowledge: Some Historical Reflections." *Isis* 100, no. 2 (2009): 319–332.

De Kock, Liesbet. "Hermann von Helmholtz's Empirico-Transcendentalism Reconsidered: Construction and Constitution in Helmholtz's Psychology of the Object." *Science in Context* 27, no. 4 (2014): 709–744.

Dohm, Hedwig. *Der Frauen Natur und Recht. Zur Frauenfrage. Zwei Abhandlungen über Eigenschaften und Stimmrecht der Frauen, Berlin 1867.* Edited by Berta Rahm. Neunkirch, Switzerland: Ala, 1986.

Dohm, Hedwig. *Die wissenschaftliche Emanzipation der Frau.* Edited by Berta Rahm. Zurich: Ala, 1982.

Ebbersmeyer, Sabrina. "From a 'Memorable Place' to 'Drops in the Ocean': on the Marginalization of Women Philosophers in German Historiography of Philosophy." *British Journal for the History of Philosophy* 28, no. 3 (2020): 442–462.

Exner, Emilie [Felicie Ewart, pseud.]. *Eine Abrechnung in der Frauenfrage.* Leipzig: Leopold Voß, 1906.

Exner, Emilie. *Weibliche Pharmaceuten.* Vienna: Verlag des Wiener Frauen-Erwerbs-Vereines, 1902.

Friedman, Michael. *Reconsidering Logical Positivism.* Cambridge: Cambridge University Press, 1999.

Goldstein, Catherine. "Weder öffentlich noch privat: Mathematik im Frankreich des frühen 17. Jahrhundert." In *Zwischen Vorderbühne und Hinterbühne. Beiträge zum Wandel der Geschlechterbeziehungen in der Wissenschaft vom 17. Jahrhundert bis zur Gegenwart,* edited by Theresa Wobbe, 41–72. Bielefeld: transcript, 2003.

Hagengruber, Ruth. "Sozialphilosophie als 'strenge Wissenschaft': Überlegungen zu Edith Stein und Edmund Husserl." In *Die unbekannte Edith Stein: Phänomenologie und*

Sozialphilosophie, edited by Beate Beckmann-Zöller and Hannah B. Gerl-Falkovitz, 59–72. Frankfurt am Main: Peter Lang, 2006.

Hagengruber, Ruth. "Das Unsichtbare sichtbar machen: Die soziale Wirklichkeit und ihre Grundlagen in der Philosophie von Edith Stein." *Edith-Stein-Jahrbuch* 10 (2004): 157–173.

Hamacher-Hermes, Adelheid. "Rose Rand: A Woman in Logic." In *The Vienna Circle and Logical Empiricism: Re-evaluation and Future Perspectives*, edited by Friedrich Stadler, 365–378. Dordrecht: Springer, 2003.

Hansen-Schaberg, Inge. "A Biographical Sketch of Prof. Dr. Grete Henry-Hermann (1901–1984)." In *Grete Hermann: Between Physics and Philosophy*, edited by Elise Crull and Guido Bacciagaluppi, 3–16. Dordrecht: Springer, 2016.

Heidelberger, Michael. "Aspects of Current History of Nineteenth-Century Philosophy of Science." In *The Present Situation in the Philosophy of Science*, edited by Friedrich Stadler, 67–74. Berlin: Springer, 2010.

Heidelberger, Michael. "Helmholtz als Philosoph." *Deutsche Zeitschrift für Philosophie* 43, no. 5 (1995): 835–844.

Heidelberger, Michael. "Kantianism and Realism: Alois Riehl (and Moritz Schlick)." In *The Kantian Legacy in Nineteenth-Century Science*, edited by Michael Friedman and Alfred Nordmann, 227–247. Cambridge, MA: MIT Press, 2006.

Helmholtz, Hermann von. "Die Thatsachen in der Wahrnehmung." In Helmholtz, *Vorträge und Reden*, 5th ed., 215–247. Braunschweig: Vieweg, 1903.

Helmholtz, Hermann von. "Über das Sehen des Menschen." In Helmholtz, *Vorträge und Reden*, 5th ed., 87–117. Braunschweig: Vieweg, 1903.

Hermann, Grete. "Die naturphilosophischen Grundlagen der Quantenmechanik." *Abhandlungen der Fries'schen Schule* 6, no. 2 (1935): 75–152.

Hermann, Grete. "Natural-Philosophical Foundations of Quantum Mechanics." In *Grete Hermann: Between Physics and Philosophy*, edited by Elise Crull and Guido Bacciagaluppi, 239–278. Dordrecht: Springer, 2016.

Herrmann, Kay, ed. *Grete Henry-Hermann: Philosophie—Mathematik—Quantenmechanik*. Wiesbaden: Springer, 2019.

Höhler, Sabine, and Bettina Wahrig. "Geschlechterforschung ist Wissenschaftsforschung—Wissenschaftsforschung ist Geschlechterforschung." *NTM Zeitschrift für Geschichte der Wissenschaften, Technik und Medizin* 14 (2006): 201–211.

Jackson, Myles. *Harmonious Triads: Physicists, Musicians, and Instrument Makers in Nineteenth-Century Germany*. Cambridge, MA: MIT Press, 2006.

Klein, Ursula. "Science, Industry, and the German *Bildungsbürgertum*." *Annals of Science* 77, no. 3 (2020): 366–376.

Köhnke, Klaus Christian. *The Rise of Neo-Kantianism. German Academic Philosophy between Idealism and Positivism*. Cambridge: Cambridge University Press, 1991.

Lefèvre, Wolfgang. "Wissenschaft und Philosophie bei Feuerbach." In *Sinnlichkeit und Rationalität. Der Umbruch in der Philosophie des 19. Jahrhunderts: Ludwig Feuerbach*, edited by Walter Jaeschke, 81–100. Berlin: Akademie Verlag, 1982.

Leng, Kirsten. "An 'Elusive' Phenomenon: Feminism, Sexology and the Female Sex Drive in Germany at the Turn of the Twentieth Century." *Centaurus* 55 (2013): 131–152.

Lenoir, Timothy. "Helmholtz, Müller, und die Erziehung der Sinne." In *Johannes Müller und die Philosophie*, edited by Michael Hagner and Bettina Wahrig-Schmidt, 207–222. Berlin: Akademie Verlag, 1992.

Lenoir, Timothy. *Instituting Science: The Cultural Production of Scientific Disciplines*. Stanford: Stanford University Press, 1997.

Lykknes, Annette, Donald L. Opitz, and Brigitte Van Tiggelen, eds. *For Better or for Worse? Collaborative Couples in the Sciences*. Heidelberg: Birkhäuser, 2012.

MacIntyre, Alasdair. *Edith Stein: A Philosophical Prologue*. London: Bloomsbury, 2007.

Matysik, Tracie. *Reforming the Moral Subject: Ethics and Sexuality in Central Europe, 1890–1930*. Ithaca: Cornell University Press, 2008.

Mazón, Patricia M. *Gender and the Modern Research University: The Admission of Women to German Higher Education, 1856–1914*. Stanford: Stanford University Press, 2003.

McLaughlin, Peter. "Nachgedanken zum Bedürfnis der Physiologie nach einer philosophischen Naturbetrachtung." In *Johannes Müller und die Philosophie*, edited by Michael Hagner and Bettina Wahrig-Schmidt, 301–311. Berlin: Akademie Verlag, 1992.

Mill, John Stuart. *On Liberty with The Subjection of Women and Chapters on Socialism*. Edited by Stefan Collini. Cambridge: Cambridge University Press, 1989.

Nordmann, Alfred. "Critical Realism, Critical Idealism, and Critical Common-Sensism: The School and World Philosophies of Riehl, Cohen, and Peirce." In *The Kantian Legacy in Nineteenth-Century Science*, edited by Michael Friedman and Alfred Nordmann, 249–274. Cambridge, MA: MIT Press, 2006.

Nöthlich, Rosemarie, Olaf Breidbach, and Uwe Hoßfeld. "'Was ist die Natur?' Einige Aspekte zur Wissenschaftspopularisierung in Deutschland." In *"Klassische Universität" und "akademische Provinz." Studien zur Universität Jena von der Mitte des 19. bis in die dreißiger Jahre des 20. Jahrhunderts*, edited by Matthias Steinbach and Stefan Gerber, 239–250. Jena: Dr. Bussert & Stadeler, 2005.

Oertzen, Christine von, Maria Rentetzi, and Elizabeth S. Watkins. "Finding Science in Surprising Places: Gender and the Geography of Scientific Knowledge. Introduction to 'Beyond the Academy: Histories of Gender and Knowledge.'" *Centaurus* 55 (2013): 73–80.

Opitz, Donald L., Staffan Bergwik, and Brigitte Van Tiggelen, eds. *Domesticity in the Making of Modern Science*. New York: Palgrave Macmillan, 2016.

Osietzki, Maria. "Anna von Helmholtz: ein Leben für die Wissenschaft ihres Mannes." In *Naturwissenschaften und Technik 'doch Frauensache?' Vorträge und Berichte von der Tagung im Kerschensteiner Kolleg*, edited by Margot Fuchs, 56–60. Wiesbaden: Frauenliteraturvertrieb, 1986.

Osietzki, Maria. "Körpermaschinen und Dampfmaschinen. Vom Wandel der Physiologie und des Körpers unter dem Einfluß von Industrialisierung und Thermodynamik." In *Physiologie und industrielle Gesellschaft: Studien zur Verwissenschaftlichung des Körpers im 19. und 20. Jahrhundert*, edited by Philipp Sarasin and Jakob Tanner, 313–346. Frankfurt: Suhrkamp, 1998.

Paparo, Giulia. "Understanding Grete Hermann's Philosophy of Nature." In *Grete Hermann: Between Physics and Philosophy*, edited by Elise Crull and Guido Bacciagaluppi, 35–51. Dordrecht: Springer, 2016.

Pfeiffer, Alexandra Elisabeth. "Ontological Phenomenology: The Philosophical Project of Hedwig Conrad-Martius." *Axiomathes* 18 (2018): 445–460.

Pomata, Gianna. "Amateurs by Choice: Women and the Pursuit of Independent Scholarship in Twentieth-Century Historical Writing." *Centaurus* 55 (2013): 196–219.

Reichenberger, Andrea. "Zwei Fundstücke zu Henri Poincaré." In *Siegener Beiträge zur Geschichte und Philosophie der Mathematik*, vol 13, edited by R. Krömer and G. Nickel, 27–54. Siegen: Siegen University Press, 2020.

Rentetzi, Maria. "Gender, Politics, and Radioactivity Research in Interwar Vienna: The Case of the Institute for Radium Research." *Isis* 95, no. 3 (2004): 359–393.

Rentetzi, Maria. "'I Want to Look Like a Lady, Not Like a Factory Worker.' Rose Rand, a Woman Philosopher of the Vienna Circle." In *EPSA Epistemology and Methodology of Science: Launch of the European Philosophy of Science Association*, edited by M. Suárez et al., 233–244. Dordrecht: Springer, 2010.

Rheinberger, Hans-Jörg. *On Historicizing Epistemology*. Stanford: Stanford University Press, 2010.

Rheinberger, Hans-Jörg. "A Plea for a Historical Epistemology of Research." *Journal for General Philosophy of Science* 43 (2012): 105–111.

Richards, Robert J. *The Tragic Sense of Life: Ernst Haeckel and the Struggle over Evolutionary Thought*. Chicago: University of Chicago Press, 2008.

Rohner, Isabel. *Spuren ins Jetzt: Hedwig Dohm—eine Biografie*. Sulzbach im Taunus, Germany: Helmer, 2010.

Sawicki, Marianne. *Body, Text, and Science: The Literacy of Investigative Practices and the Phenomenology of Edith Stein*. Dordrecht: Kluwer, 1997.

Schmidgen, Henning. "Passagenwerk 1850: Bild und Zahl in den physiologischen Zeitexperimenten von Hermann von Helmholtz." *Berichte der Wissenschaftsgeschichte* 34 (2011): 139–155.

Schneider, Ilse. "Raum, Zeit und ihre Relativität bei Poincaré." In *Herrn Geheimrat Professor Dr. phil. et H. LL. D. Alois Riehl zum siebzigsten Geburtstag*, edited by Kurt Lewin and Alois Riehl, 91–130. Berlin: H. Lonys, 1914.

Secord, James A. "Knowledge in Transit." *Isis* 95, no. 4 (2004): 654–672.

Siemens-Helmholtz, Ellen von (ed.) *Anna von Helmholtz. Ein Lebensbild in Briefen*. Vol. 1. Berlin: Verlag für Kulturpolitik, 1929.

Simmer, Hans H. "Zum Frauenbild Rudolf Virchows in den späten 1840er Jahren." *Medizinhistorisches Journal* 27, nos. 3–4 (1992): 292–319.

Stadler, Friedrich. *The Vienna Circle: Studies in the Origins, Development, and Influence of Logical Empiricism*. Dordrecht: Springer, 2015.

Stein, Edith. "Beiträge zur philosophischen Begründung der Psychologie und der Geisteswissenschaften." *Jahrbuch für Philosophie und Phänomenologische Forschung* 5 (1922): 1–284.

Stein, Edith. *Zum Problem der Einfühlung*. Halle: Buchdruckerei des Waisenhauses, 1917.

Stöltzner, Michael. "Vienna Indeterminism: Mach, Boltzmann, Exner." *Synthese* 119 (1999): 85–111.

Ströker, Elisabeth. "Natur und ihre Wissenschaft in der Philosophie des 19. Jahrhunderts." In *Naturauffassungen in Philosophie, Wissenschaft, Technik*, vol. 3, *Aufklärung und späte Neuzeit*, edited by Lothar Schäfer and Elisabeth Ströker, 255–292. Freiburg: Alber, 1996.

Tyndall, John. *Fragmente aus den Naturwissenschaften: Vorlesungen und Aufsätze*. Übersetzt von A. H., mit Vorwort und Zusätzen von Prof. H. Helmholtz. Braunschweig: Vieweg, 1874.

Vogt, Annette. "Von der Ausnahme zur Normalität. Wissenschaftlerinnen in Akademien und in der Kaiser-Wilhelm-Gesellschaft (1912–1945)." In *Zwischen Vorderbühne und Hinterbühne. Beiträge zum Wandel der Geschlechterbeziehungen in der Wissenschaft vom 17. Jahrhundert bis zur Gegenwart*, edited by Theresa Wobbe, 159–188. Bielefeld: transcript, 2003.

Wise, M. Norton. *Aesthetics, Industry, and Science: Hermann von Helmholtz and the Berlin Physical Society*. Chicago: Chicago University Press, 2018.

Wobbe, Theresa. "Von Marianne Weber zu Edith Stein: Historische Koordinaten des Zugangs zur Wissenschaft." In *Denkachsen: zur theoretischen und traditionellen Rede vom Geschlecht*, edited by Theresa Wobbe and Gesa Lindemann, 15–68. Frankfurt: Suhrkamp, 1994.

Wobbe, Theresa. "Instabile Beziehungen. Die kulturelle Dynamik von Wissenschaft und Geschlecht." In *Zwischen Vorderbühne und Hinterbühne. Beiträge zum Wandel der Geschlechterbeziehungen in der Wissenschaft vom 17. Jahrhundert bis zur Gegenwart*, edited by Theresa Wobbe, 13–38. Bielefeld: transcript, 2003.

Zakariya, Nasser. "Scenes before Grey Antiquity." *Res: Anthropology and Aesthetics* 69–70 (2018): 5–19.

Ziche, Paul. "Die 'Scham' der Philosophen und der 'Hochmut der Fachgelehrsamkeit.' Zur fachphilosophischen Diskussion von Haeckels Monismus." In *Monismus um 1900. Wissenschaftskultur und Weltanschauung*, edited by Paul Ziche, 61–79. Berlin: VWB, 2000.

Ziche, Paul. "The 'New Philosophy of Nature' around 1900—Metaphysical Tradition and Scientistic Innovation." In *Wilhelm Ostwald at the Crossroads between Chemistry, Philosophy and Media Culture*, edited by Britta Görs, Nikolaos Psarros, and Paul Ziche, 29–45. Leipzig: Leipziger University Press, 2005.

Ziche, Paul. *Wissenschaftslandschaften um 1900: Philosophie, die Wissenschaften und der nichtreduktive Szientismus*. Zurich: Chronos, 2008.

CHAPTER 25

....

TRENDS IN AESTHETICS

....

SAMANTHA MATHERNE

FROM the romanticism and German idealism that marked its beginning to the psychology and phenomenology that marked its end, the long nineteenth century in German philosophy was a century of innovations in aesthetics. And women played a central role at each juncture, spurring these developments as much through their published and unpublished writings, as through their active participation in salons and intellectual circles. In this chapter, I highlight the contributions of four women to these developments in aesthetics: the early romantic Dorothea Veit-Schlegel; the feminist Hedwig Dohm; the early phenomenologist Edith Landmann-Kalischer; and the psychological theorist (among other things) Vernon Lee. Though by no means an exhaustive survey, I use this discussion to underscore two trends in aesthetics during this period.[1] The first trend, which emerges in the discussion of Veit-Schlegel and Dohm, is an emphasis on the social and political value the aesthetic has with respect to *Bildung* ("education," "formation," "development") and achieving ideals, such as freedom and gender equality.[2] The second, which emerges in the discussion of Landmann-Kalischer

---

[1] Another significant trend in this period concerns the various aesthetic means women deploy to the end of "self-formation" and "self-presentation." For a discussion of the role salons, like those hosted by Henriette Herz, Bettina Brentano von Arnim, and Rahel Varnhagen, played to this end, see Anne Pollok, "Femininity and the Salon," in *The Palgrave Handbook of German Romantic Philosophy*, ed. Elizabeth Millán Brusslan (Cham: Palgrave Macmillan, 2020), 119–140. For a discussion of the use of multiple means (salons, letters, and novels) used by Herz, Varnhagen, and Brentano von Arnim to this end, see Anne Pollok, "On Self-Formation: The Role of Writing and Sociability for the Establishment of a Persona (Henriette Herz, Rahel Levin Varnhagen, and Bettina von Arnim)," in *Women and Philosophy in Eighteenth-Century Germany*, ed. Corey Dyck (Oxford: Oxford University Press, 2021), 195–212. For a discussion of the role letter writing played to this end, see Lorely French, *German Women as Letter Writers, 1750–1850* (Madison: Fairleigh Dickinson University Press, 1996); Margaretmary Daley, *Women of Letters: A Study of Self and Genre in the Personal Writing of Caroline Schlegel-Schelling, Rahel Levin Varnhagen, and Bettina von Arnim* (Columbia, SC: Camden House, 1998). For a discussion of the role translation played to this end, see Andrew Piper, "The Making of Transnational Textual Communities: German Women Translators, 1800–1850," *Women in German Yearbook* 22 (2006): 119–144.

[2] Germaine de Staël is another figure in this period committed to thinking through the social and political significance of art and its role in *Bildung*. She stresses this in her writings like *Essay on Fiction*

and Lee, is the desire to offer a psychologically informed account of the nature of aesthetic experience.[3] This said, Veit-Schlegel and Dohm were also interested in how individuals experience the aesthetic, just as Landmann-Kalischer and Lee regarded the aesthetic as something of social and political import. Nevertheless, in their own aesthetic theories Veit-Schlegel and Dohm ultimately orient their views outward toward the social and political significance of the aesthetic, while Landmann-Kalischer and Lee shift focus inward toward the details of individual aesthetic experience. By working through the views of Veit-Schlegel, Dohm, Landmann-Kalischer, and Lee, my aim is to highlight these two trends in aesthetics in the long nineteenth century in German philosophy, as well as the distinctive contribution that these women make to them.

I begin in section 1 with a discussion of Veit-Schlegel's contribution to the aesthetics of the early romantics. I focus, in particular, on the issue of aesthetic education and her account of how novels should be written in order to promote the *Bildung* required for human beings to achieve freedom at both the individual and collective level. In section 2 I turn my attention to Dohm's aesthetics and the role they play in her feminist program. More specifically, I explore Dohm's analysis of the power that aesthetic representations of women can have in either promoting oppression or emancipation, depending on whether these representations are underwritten by an essentialist theory of gender (which she rejects) or a constructive theory of gender (which she endorses).

After exploring the ways in which Veit-Schlegel and Dohm take aesthetic education and aesthetic representation, respectively, to have social and political significance, I turn to Landmann-Kalischer's and Lee's attempts to offer an account of the nature of aesthetic experience that is at once philosophical and psychologically informed. In section 3 I take up Landmann-Kalischer's early phenomenological work in this vein. There, I discuss how she pairs a cognitivist account of aesthetic experience of beauty and art with a realist account of the nature of beauty. I also address her overarching vision of what a "science of aesthetics" should look like. Finally, in section 4 I address Lee's work in psychological aesthetics. Although Lee is not German, I take her aesthetics to belong to the German tradition insofar as she identifies herself as a "disciple" of the German philosopher and psychologist Theodor Lipps. I examine her empirically grounded effort to advance an account of aesthetic experience, which turns on the notion of *Einfühlung* or "empathy."

(*Essai sur les fictions*, 1795) (which was translated by Goethe into German) and her monumental work *The Influence of Literature on Society* (*De la littérature dans ses rapports avec les institutions sociales*, 1800). Her novels, *Delphine* (1802) and *Corrine* (1807), are also underpinned by this vision of the aesthetic. See also chapter 2 here.

[3] Lou Salomé is another figure in this period who approached aesthetics through a psychological lens. See *The Erotic* (*Die Erotik*, 1910) for her psychoanalytic approach to the role bodily and sexual processes, energies, and instincts play in artistic creation. Other aspects of her aesthetic outlook can be found in her work on Ibsen (*Ibsen's Heroines* (*Henrik Ibsens Frauen-Gestalten*, 1892)) and Rilke (*Rainer Maria Rilke*, 1928), as well as in her fiction (e.g., *Fenitschka* and *A Debauchery*) (*Eine Ausschweifung*, 1898). See also chapter 9 here.

1 Dorothea Veit-Schlegel, Romanticism, and Paths to Aesthetic Education

Dorothea Veit-Schlegel (1764–1839) was an active participant in the movement known variously as "early romanticism," "Jena romanticism," or *Frühromantik*, which thrived from around 1796 to 1802.[4] Born Brendel Mendelssohn, she was the daughter of Moses Mendelssohn, a leading German-Jewish thinker of the Enlightenment. Through the arrangement of her father, she married the banker and merchant Simon Veit in 1783. But after meeting Friedrich Schlegel at one of Henrietta Herz's salons in 1797, she started a relationship with him and divorced Veit. Alongside Schlegel, she was at the center of the circle of early romantics, which included other thinkers like August Wilhelm Schlegel, Friedrich von Hardenberg (Novalis), Friedrich Schleiermacher, Ludwig Tieck, Sophie Tieck, and Caroline Schlegel-Schelling. Veit-Schlegel contributed to the movement through various published pieces of literary criticism, translations,[5] and a novel, *Florentin* (1801).[6] She also did a great deal of editorial work for Schlegel and the newly founded romantic journal *Athenaeum*, and she was voluminous in her correspondence. After this period, she and Friedrich moved in increasingly more conservative directions, marrying in 1804 and converting to Catholicism in 1808. But for the purposes of this chapter, I focus on her contributions to the aesthetics of the early romantic movement and their vision of the social-political value of the aesthetic.[7] More

[4] While I focus on Veit-Schlegel's contribution, other German women made important contributions to the aesthetics of the romantic movement, including Caroline Schlegel-Schelling, Sophie Tieck, Rahel Varnhagen, Karoline von Günderrode, Bettina Brentano von Arnim, Sophie Mereau-Brentano, Henriette Herz, among others. For an overview of the aesthetic output of these women, including plays, poetry, novels, letters, and translations, see Gesa Dane, "Women Writers and Romanticism," in *The Cambridge Companion to German Romanticism*, ed. Nicholas Saul (Cambridge: Cambridge University Press, 2009), 133–146; Astrid Weigert, "Gender and Genre in the Works of German Romantic Women Writers," in *The Oxford Handbook to European Romanticism*, ed. Paul Hamilton (Oxford: Oxford University Press, 2016), 240–254. See also chapter 17 here.

[5] Veit-Schlegel translated Germaine de Staël's novel *Corinne, or Italy* (1807) essentially as de Staël was still finishing it. She also translated *Geschichte der Jungfrau von Orleans: Aus altfranzösischen Quellen* (1803), *Geschichte der Margarete von Valois: Gemahlin Heinrichs des Vierten. Von ihr selbst beschrieben* (1803), *Geschichte des Zauberers Merlin* (1804), and *Lother und Maller: Eine Rittergeschichte* (1805).

[6] For a discussion of the issues surrounding Veit-Schlegel's authorship, see Brigitte Sassen, "Dorothea Schlegel and the Challenges of Female Authority and Identity," in *Women and Philosophy in Eighteenth-Century German*, ed. Corey Dyck (Oxford: Oxford University Press, 2021), 179–194.

[7] For surveys of the aesthetic commitments of this movement, see Manfred Frank, *Einführung in die frühromantische Ästhetik* (Frankfurt am Main: Suhrkamp, 1989), Keren Gorodeisky, "19th Century Romantic Aesthetics," in *Stanford Encyclopedia of Philosophy Archive*, Fall 2016 ed., published June 14, 2016, https://plato.stanford.edu/archives/fall2016/entries/aesthetics-19th-romantic/; Elizabeth Millán, "The Aesthetic Philosophy of Early German Romanticism and Its Early German Idealist Roots," in *The Palgrave Handbook of German Idealism*, ed. Matthew Altman (New York: Palgrave Macmillan, 2014),

specifically, I concentrate on the early romantics' account of aesthetic education as the key to the *Bildung* required in order to achieve freedom. And I highlight Veit-Schlegel's analysis of what romantic novels should be like if they are to play a role in aesthetic education.

Let's begin, then, with a brief look at the early romantic view of aesthetic education more generally.[8] According to the early romantics, the ultimate aim of *Bildung* is the achievement of freedom, both in our individual lives and in our social-political systems and institutions. Though this is a common view of *Bildung* at the time, what is distinctive in the early romantics' approach is their aesthetic conception of *Bildung*. Inspired by Friedrich Schiller's *Letters on the Aesthetic Education of Man* (1794), the early romantics regarded aesthetic education as *the* path to *Bildung* and, hence, freedom.[9]

For the early romantics, an aesthetic education is "aesthetic" in, at least, two senses. In the first place, the early romantics regard this education as "aesthetic" in the sense that it uses aesthetic tools, for example, works of art or creative practices. However, the early romantics were not content with the aesthetic tools on offer. In an expansive spirit, they sought to extend the bounds of the aesthetic to include other practices, such as literary criticism and translation. And in a revisionary spirit, they promoted a new aesthetic ideal: the ideal of "romantic poetry" (*Poesie*). As Schlegel famously describes this ideal in *Athenaeum Fragment* #116, romantic poetry is a progressive, universal poetry. . . . It tries to and should mix and fuse poetry and prose, inspiration and criticism, the poetry of art and the poetry of nature. . . . Other kinds of poetry are finished. . . . The romantic kind of poetry is the only one that is more than a kind, that is, as it were, poetry itself: for in a certain sense all poetry is or should be romantic" ("Athenaeum Fragments," 249–250).[10] Though the early romantics explored various literary forms, many of them alighted on the novel (*Roman*) as the form that promised to best embody this ideal and, hence, as having a crucial role to play vis-à-vis aesthetic education.

Moreover, the early romantics conceive of this education as "aesthetic" in the sense that it is an education of sensibility. So understood, an aesthetic education is intended to cultivate our various sensible capacities, such as the senses (outer and inner), imagination, and the faculty of desire. And though the early romantics by no means deny the need to educate our intellectual or rational sides as well, they insist that full freedom requires the cultivation of sensibility.

389–408. For a survey of Veit-Schlegel's contribution, see Karin Stuebben Thornton, "Enlightenment and Romanticism in the Work of Dorothea Schlegel," *German Quarterly* 39, no. 2 (1966): 162–172.

   [8] See Frederick C. Beiser, "The Concept of *Bildung* in Early German Romanticism," in *The Romantic Imperative: The Concept of Early German Romanticism* (Cambridge, MA: Harvard University Press, 2003), 88–105.

   [9] Underscoring the importance of *Bildung*, Veit-Schlegel describes it as "the aspiration of life"; "Dorothea Veit-Schlegel: Selected Diaries and Letters," in *Theory as Practice: A Critical Anthology of Early German Romantic Writings*, ed. Jochen Schulte-Sasse, Haynes Horne, Elizabeth Mittman, and Lisa C. Roetzel (Minneapolis: University of Minnesota Press, 1997), 440.

   [10] "Athenaeum Fragments," in *Classic and Romantic German Aesthetics*, ed. J. M. Bernstein (Cambridge: Cambridge University Press, 2003), 246–260.

As an early romantic, Veit-Schlegel was thus committed to a view of the social-political value of aesthetic education as the path to the *Bildung* required to achieve freedom, both individually and collectively. And, as her body of work evinces, she was also committed to creating aesthetic tools in the form of literary criticism, translations, and novels meant to serve this purpose. However, what is of interest to me in what follows is the philosophical picture she defends of what a "romantic" novel should be like if it is to play a role in aesthetic education, and her criticism of various romantic novels, such as Germaine de Staël's *Delphine* (1802) and Friedrich Schlegel's *Lucinde* (1799), for falling short of this standard. In order to tease out her position, I look at two texts: one of her pieces of literary criticism, titled "A Conversation about the Latest Novels by French Women Writers" ("Gespräch über die neuesten Romane der Französinnen," 1803), and her novel *Florentin* (1801).

Let's begin with the "Conversation."[11] In this text, three women, Felizia, Constanze, and Adelheid (with some rather thin interjections from a man named Albert) discuss contemporary French novels by women, including de Staël's *Delphine*, Sophie Cottin's *Amélie de Mansfield* (1803), and the novels of Madame de Genlis about education. The conversation eventually turns to the topic of the genre of the novel. And at the outset of this discussion, Felizia voices the early romantic line on novels, claiming that they "must be romantic" ("Conversation" 97–98). Felizia is clear that in order for a novel to "be romantic" it is not enough for it to depict "romantic situations" ("Conversation" 97). Rather, she claims that in order for a novel to "be romantic" its "depictions [Schilderungen] of nature, characters, and events" must be "animated" by the "spirit of poetry [Geist der Poesie]" ("Conversation" 97). And over the course of the discussion that ensues the characters make various remarks that paint a picture of what Veit-Schlegel thinks the content, aim, and form of a romantic novel should be like if it is to play a role in aesthetic education.

Beginning with the issue of content, Felizia argues that romantic novels should depict what is "sublime" and "passionate" in life, such as madness or grief ("Conversation" 103). She thus condemns novels that focus on what is banal or trivial, for example, "one's own wishes, prejudices, principles, and renunciations, and . . . petty, confused circumstances of refined society" ("Conversation" 99–100). According to Felizia, the reason that "passionate" and "sublime" content is needed, rather than trivial content, is that romantic novels should lead readers "out of themselves" ("Conversation" 99; see also 105).

At the same time, Felizia claims that a romantic novel should not be written with the aim of simply conveying what is "passionate" or "sublime"; a romantic novel should aim at educating us in the "highest morality," the morality of freedom ("Conversation" 98). She thus warns against novels like *Delphine* that focus so much on the trials and

---

[11] Originally published in *Europa: Eine Zeitschrift* 1, no. 2, ed. Friedrich Schlegel (1803): 88–106. My citations are to this publication; translations are my own. An excerpt has also been translated as "A Conversation about the Latest Novels by French Women Writers," in *Women Critics 1660–1820: An Anthology*, ed. the Folger Collective on Early Modern Critics, tr. Simon Richter (Bloomington: Indiana University Press, 1995), 340–342.

tribulations of the protagonists that we "pity" them to the point of "exhaustion," with no energy for moral elevation to spare ("Conversation" 105).[12]

This said, the characters join in critiquing novels that attempt to realize this educative aim in a didactic way. As Constanze puts it, de Genlis writes her novels as a kind of "guide" or "chart" for young women to follow in navigating social situations ("Conversation" 103). Though Felizia suggests that these charts are "well-done" and even contain a degree of "truth," she claims that something other than a "chart" is needed for an education that leads to the cultivation of sensibility ("Conversation" 103). And in painting her alternative, Felizia suggests that a romantic novel that depicts what is "passionate" and "sublime" through "wonderful images" or "sensible images [Sinnbildern]" is better able to speak to the reader's sensibility on multiple levels. Through these images, she claims that a novel can spark readers' "fantasy" or "imagination" (*Phantasie*), it can leave them "astonished and musing [staunend und nachsinnend]," and it can ultimately lead them into an affective state that is more "cultivated" and "inspired by a higher feeling for the good and beautiful" ("Dialgoue" 99, 105).

Over the course of the "Conversation," Veit-Schlegel thus puts forth a view of the sort of content ("sublime" and "passionate"), aim (educative), and form (sensibility-animating, rather than didactic) that a novel must have in order to "be romantic." And as her criticism of her French contemporaries reveals, she thinks that novels that veer either too far in the "passionate" or the "moralistic" direction fail to reach this ideal. But what about the *Bildungsromane* of her fellow early romantics: does Veit-Schlegel think that these novels are any more successful at "being romantic" and furthering aesthetic education?

Veit-Schlegel's novel *Florentin* would suggest a negative answer to this question.[13] Indeed, *Florentin* is very much an anti-*Bildungsroman*, which appears to serve, in part, as a critique of Schlegel's *Bildungsroman Lucinde*.[14] Though there are a variety of levels on which this critique operates,[15] what is of interest to me here is the implicit aesthetic

---

[12] *Delphine* is a tragic epistolary novel set in Paris during the French Revolution, in which Delphine, a young widow, falls in love with Léonce, who is engaged to Matilde, and which ends with Delphine's suicide. Though the "Conversation" includes numerous critiques of *Delphine*, the characters also praise its "aspirations" as "rare and beautiful" ("Conversation" 97).

[13] Citations are to the 1987 edition. Translations are my own. For the English translation, see *Florentin: A Novel*, ed. and tr. Edwina G. Lawler and Ruth Richardson (Lewiston, NY: Edwin Mellen Press, 1988).

[14] On the ways in which Veit-Schlegel develops *Florentin* as a critique of *Lucinde,* see also chapter 17 here.

[15] For discussion of the way in which *Florentin* serves as a criticism of the gender dynamics in *Lucinde* and early romanticism, see Martha Helfer, "Dorothea Veit-Schlegel's *Florentin*: Constructing a Feminist Romantic Aesthetic," *German Quarterly* 69, no. 2 (1996): 144–160, and "Gender Studies and Romanticism," in *The Literature of German Romanticism*, ed. Dennis Mahoney (Woodbridge: Boydell and Brewer, 2003), 229–250; Liesl Allingham, "Revolutionizing Domesticity: Potentialities of Female Self-Definition in Dorothea Schlegel's *Florentin* (1801)," *Women in German Yearbook* 27 (2011): 1–30; Anna Ezekiel, "Women, Women Writers, and Early German Romanticism," in *The Palgrave Handbook of German Romantic Philosophy*, ed. Elizabeth Millán Brusslan (Cham: Palgrave Macmillan, 2020),475–509. For discussion of the way in which *Florentin* realizes Schlegel's ideal of "reciprocity" (*Wechsel*) better than *Lucinde* does, see Laurie Johnson, "Dorothea Veit's *Florentin* and the Early Romantic Model of Alterity," *Monatshefte* 97, no. 1 (2005): 33–62.

objection Veit-Schlegel levels against *Lucinde* and other *Bildungsromane* of its romantic ilk, such as Novalis's *Heinrich von Ofterdingen* (1802), for falling short of the ideal of "being romantic."[16]

First, though, it may be helpful to offer a very brief summary of the plot of both novels. *Lucinde* is a *Bildungsroman*, written in the form of a fragment, that follows the male protagonist, Julius, across various friendships with men and love affairs with women. Julius's development culminates in his relationship with Lucinde, which allows him to realize himself as an artist.[17] On the surface, *Florentin* shares various similarities with *Lucinde*.[18] *Florentin*, too, is written as a fragment, and follows the male protagonist, Florentin, across various friendships with men and love affairs with women, as he aspires to become an artist and discover his origins. However, unlike Julius, Florentin never develops. He never becomes an artist, he never discovers his roots, and he never has a fulfilling relationship with a woman. Hence the closing line: "Florentin was nowhere to be found" (*Florentin* 153).

In thinking through how Veit-Schlegel uses *Florentin* to critique *Lucinde* on aesthetic grounds the following metaphor she uses in an unpublished preface to *Florentin* is instructive: "this book [is] . . . not a hall of mirrors [Spiegelsaale] where one finds oneself alone in the midst of often repeated forms [Gestalten]" but rather a "picture gallery [Bildergallerie] where the various portraits and figures [Figuren] surround us" (*Florentin* 162). Though she does not say this outright, it seems plausible that she regards *Lucinde*, and other *Bildungsromane* like it, as a "hall of mirrors." At the very least, internal to *Lucinde*, Julius treats women as a "mirror" for himself.[19] Moreover, it seems that these novels invite readers (or at least male readers) to see themselves mirrored in the protagonist.[20] And Veit-Schlegel's choice to not write *Florentin* as a "hall of mirrors" appears to be motivated, in part, by a suspicion about this model for a novel as something that encourages a kind of narcissism or egoism, rather than proper *Bildung*. For one thing, the way that *Florentin* proceeds suggests that, from Veit-Schlegel's perspective, far from being a route to *Bildung*, a male protagonist who constantly looks to women as "mirrors" of himself will fail not only to find himself, but also to recognize these women in their own right. Moreover, in *Florentin* she puts pressure on this mirroring-model of reading, using Florentin's own patterns of reading as a kind of cautionary tale. For at one point, Juliane (one of the three main women characters) tells a ghost story that seems to be an actual account of Florentin's origins, but Florentin is so focused on projecting himself

---

[16] For another reading of the aesthetic significance of *Florentin*, see Helfer's argument that Veit-Schlegel uses this novel to provide a feminist romantic aesthetic, which serves as an alternative to the masculine romantic aesthetic of *Lucinde*.

[17] For a discussion of the fragment style and *Lucinde*, see Dalia Nassar, "From the System of Fragments to the Romantic Novel," in *The Romantic Absolute* (Chicago: Chicago University Press, 2013), 126–154.

[18] For a plot summary of *Florentin*, see Helfer, "Dorothea Veit-Schlegel's *Florentin*," 150.

[19] For discussion of Julius's projection onto Lucinde, see Johnson, "Dorothea Veit's *Florentin*," 41.

[20] A further potential mirroring element pertains to the way in which *Lucinde* was read as a roman à clef for the relationship between Schlegel and Veit-Schlegel, which Veit-Schlegel always denied.

onto what she is saying that he fails to recognize the long-sought truth she is offering him. In these ways, Veit-Schlegel appears to use *Florentin* to criticize *Bildungsromane* that are written on the "hall of mirrors" model for promoting self-centeredness, rather than paving the way toward *Bildung*.[21]

So, why does Veit-Schlegel think that a "picture gallery" model for a novel is more promising with regard to this educative end? Recall that for the early romantics, an aesthetic education is not just aesthetic in virtue of deploying aesthetic tools like novels; it is also aesthetic because it educates sensibility. And it seems that one of Veit-Schlegel's reasons for preferring the "picture gallery" model is that it promises a better education of one's sensory, imaginative, and affective capacities. We saw hints of this in the "Conversation," where Veit-Schlegel emphasizes the need for novels to include images that appeal to one's imagination and cultivate one's feelings. However, in addition to providing the reader with an array of images, Veit-Schlegel emphasizes the open-ended nature of the "picture gallery" that *Florentin* provides. We see this in her remarks in an unpublished dedication to the editor of *Florentin*, where she reflects on her choice not to give *Florentin* a "satisfactory end" (at the end of the novel, Florentin simply leaves, unrealized) (*Florentin* 157). Veit-Schlegel notes that novels typically end with someone being either "married or buried," but she objects that these sorts of "satisfactory ends" leave the reader with too little room to exercise their sensibility in relation to the story (*Florentin* 158). Using a metaphor of dolls to illustrate this idea, she claims that "I am never completely at ease if the poet does not allow me to think or dream about anything. . . . I feel like the little girls who prefer to play with a naked doll, which they dress differently every hour and [to whom they] can give a completely different shape, than with the most magnificent and perfectly dressed doll, which has its clothes and, thereby, its perfect destiny sewn on" (*Florentin* 158). Veit-Schlegel thus intends for the "picture gallery" that is *Florentin* to be not just full of images, but also open-ended enough to provide readers with an opportunity to actively exercise their sensible capacities in the rich and varied ways required for the aesthetic education of those capacities.

In presenting *Florentin* as a "picture gallery" rather than a "hall of mirrors," Veit-Schlegel thus puts pressure on the way in which the *Bildungsromane* of her male counterparts encourage a kind of egoism, rather than a proper *Bildung*. She puts forward an alternative model for a romantic novel, which offers an open-ended array of images that provides readers with the properly aesthetic education required for *Bildung* and the achievement of freedom. And in this effort, as in her critical stance in the "Conversation," we find Veit-Schlegel offering a vision of how a romantic novel should, and should not, be that contributes to the early romantic conception of the social-political value of the aesthetic vis-à-vis aesthetic education.

---

[21] Cautioning against egoism in her diaries, she says, "one comes to the point where one is more interested in ideas than in human beings—and finally, in one's own idea above all, if there is even a moderate degree of egoism" ("Selected Diaries and Letters" 441).

2 HEDWIG DOHM, FEMINISM, AND THE POWER OF AESTHETIC REPRESENTATION

Hedwig Dohm (1831–1919) was a radical feminist, who not only promoted women's rights to education and suffrage, but also defended a view of gender as socially constructed. She was born to an assimilated Jewish family in Berlin, a family of eighteen children in which the sons were given an opportunity for education, while the daughter were denied it. After attending a teacher's college, she married Ernst Dohm, an editor of a satirical magazine, *Kladderadatsch*, in 1853, and the two moved in intellectual circles in Berlin, hosting their own salon. In the 1870s after her children were grown, she began publishing feminist pieces, including *What the Clergy Thinks about Women* (*Was Die Pastoren von den Frauen Denken*, 1872), *Jesuitism in the Household* (*Der Jesuisismus im Hausstande*, 1873), *The Scientific Emancipation of Women* (*Die wissenschaftliche Emancipation der Frau*, 1874), and *The Nature and Rights of Women* (*Der Frauen Natur und Recht*, 1876). In these texts, she defended women's rights and challenged essentialist conceptions of gender in favor of a constructivist view. At the outset of World War I, she wrote articles denouncing German patriotic fervor and defending pacifism. In addition to her political treatises, Dohm wrote various pieces of fiction with female protagonists, which explored issues surrounding marriage, motherhood, and aging, including the novella *Become Who You Are!* (*Werde, die Du bist!*, 1894) and the trilogy of novels *The Fate of a Soul* (*Schicksale einer Seele*, 1899), *Sibilla Dalmar* (1897), and *Christa Ruland* (1902).[22]

Though there are many dimensions to Dohm's feminism, in what follows I shall consider one of its aesthetic dimensions, namely, her views concerning the power of aesthetic representations of women vis-à-vis the construction of gender. For Dohm, aesthetic representations in novels, poetry, and philosophy, give rise to an image of what it is to be a woman, which can have an oppressive or emancipatory effect, depending on whether the background conception of gender is essentialist or constructivist in nature. To explore this aesthetic aspect of Dohm's feminism, I begin with a discussion of a chapter from *The Antifeminists* (*Die Antifeministen*, 1902) titled "Nietzsche and Women" ("Nietzsche und die Frauen"), in which she criticizes Nietzsche, and other authors, for aesthetic representations of women that are underwritten by what she regards as a misguided and pernicious essentialism. I then turn to her own efforts to provide aesthetic

---

[22] For an overview of her feminist writings and her trilogy of novels, see Birgit Mikus, "Hedwig Dohm: 'Bin ich ein Mensch—nichts als ein Mensch,'" in *The Political Woman in Print* (Oxford: Peter Lang, 2014), 209–243. For a discussion of Dohm's novels, see Gaby Pailer, *Schreibe, die du bist* (Pfaffenweiler: Centaurus, 1994); Birgit Mikus, "'Sprechmaschine Du': Sprachkritik in ausgewählten Romanen Hedwig Dohms," *German Life and Letters* 62 (2009): 115–139; and Charlotte Woodford, "Morality and Maternalism: Vera's *Eine für viele* and Hedwig Dohm's *Christa Ruland*," in *Women, Emancipation, and the German Novel* (London: Legenda, 2014), 91–105.

representations in her fiction that promote the constructivist view of what it is to be a woman that she endorses.

In "Nietzsche and Women," Dohm offers a pointed critique of Nietzsche's treatment of women across his writings, blending together astute textual analysis with satirical wit.[23] For my purposes, what is of interest is her critique of Nietzsche's aesthetic representations of women in his writings. Dohm refers to his representation of women as an "image of woman" ("Nietzsche and Women" 21, 26, 29).[24] And she underscores the aesthetic dimensions of this image, by describing Nietzsche as an "ingenious, shocking poet" and a "painter of words," and by situating him in a lineage of "modern poets" who misrepresent women, including Guy de Maupassant and August Strindberg ("Nietzsche and Women" 23, 31, 20). For Dohm, then, Nietzsche uses aesthetic means like poetic or "painterly" language to present, and presumably give force to, an "image of woman" in his writings. And she objects that these aesthetic representations of women are underwritten by a fundamentally mistaken and harmful conception of what women are.

Dohm takes Nietzsche's aesthetic representations of women to be misguided because they rest on an essentialist conception of women as having a fixed nature, which she rejects. Over the course of the piece, she points to various aesthetic images of women that Nietzsche offers, for example, as a "harem woman" who is a "bow whose arrows aim at the *Übermenschen*" and as having "tiger claws under her gloves" ("Nietzsche and Women" 24–25). And she highlights the essentialist ideas about women that underpin these images, including the idea that the natural "vocation" (*Beruf*) of women is to bear children; that they are "determined" to be the "property" of man; and that they are by "nature" "predatory," "cunning," "egoistic," "uneducable" [*Unerziehbarkeit*], "wild," full of "desire," full of "lies," and fixated on "appearance" and "beauty" ("Nietzsche and Women" 23–24, 25–29). However, Dohm rejects all of these essentialist claims as the result of an admixture of certain uncritical patriarchal beliefs that Nietzsche harbors given certain centuries-old prejudices and his own limited experiences with women (see "Nietzsche and Women" 19–23, 31).

Though Dohm critiques these aesthetic representations as misguided, she stresses the power that they nevertheless have in promoting a patriarchal construction of gender. To this end, she highlights Nietzsche's line from *The Gay Science*: "man makes for himself the image of woman, and woman forms [bildet] herself after this image" ("Nietzsche and Woman" 19, 22, 24). For Dohm, this line not only captures the sense in which the "image" that Nietzsche paints of women has a patriarchal lineage, but also the oppressive influence such images can exert on women who construct themselves along these

---

[23] Dohm also critiques Nietzsche in *Sibilla Dalmar*, as Sibilla's lover, Kunz, is a follower of Nietzsche. For a discussion of the feminist critique of Nietzsche by Dohm, Helene Lange, Lili Braun, and Helene Stöcker, see Carol Diethe, "Nietzsche and the Feminists," in *Nietzsche's Women* (New York: de Gruyter, 1996), 137–165.

[24] "Nietzsche and Women," in *Die Antifeministen* (Berlin: Ferdinand Dümmler, 1902), 18–26. Translations are my own. For an English translation of this piece, see *Women Philosophers in the Long Nineteenth Century: The German Tradition*, ed. Kristin Gjesdal and Dalia Nassar (Oxford: Oxford University Press, 2021), 128–138.

lines, for example, taking their natural destiny to be having children, being the property of men, and possessing certain characteristics.

This said, Dohm also sees in this line an emancipatory insight: women do not have a fixed "nature" or "essence," but are rather "formed" or constructed in accordance with images. And although Dohm thinks this construction can proceed in an oppressive way if the images represent women along essentialist lines, it can proceed in an emancipatory way if the images represent women along constructivist lines. Indeed, in her own fiction Dohm attempts to provide images of the latter sort in her women protagonists.

The refrain that recurs across Dohm's fiction is "Become Who You Are!" (*Werde, die Du bist!*). She draws this phrase from Pindar and Nietzsche, but feminizes it, and she uses it to capture the constructivist insight that women are not, by nature, determined to a certain identity, but can determine for themselves who they are. And Dohm attempts to use her novels to aesthetically represent women who illustrate this constructivist position. This said, Dohm's female protagonists are not idealized heroines who are able to transcend societal constraints altogether and fully become who they are. Dohm, instead, offers realistic portraits of women who mostly fail to become who they are on account of the inequitable familial, social, and political forces in their lives, but whose struggles nevertheless portend of progress to come. As she makes this point about the trilogy in the foreword to *The Fate of a Soul*, "in three novels I wanted to depict three generations of women of the nineteenth century, whose representatives, though superior to the average, were supposed to be types [Typen] of their time. I wanted to depict them, rising from the first twilight of the dawn of knowledge, to the bright, promising morning light, which anticipates the brilliance of the midday sun, which will only rise over the women of the twentieth century" (*Fate* 1, my translation).[25] In the trilogy, we meet three generations of female protagonists: Marlene is in her sixties, Sibilla is in her forties, and Christa is in her twenties. Each protagonist becomes aware of the constraints of her expected roles as a wife and mother, and resists those roles with varying, but increasing degrees of success.[26] For example, in *The Fate of a Soul*, in spite of her early participation in the 1848 revolution, once she is married, Marlene is cut off from any political activities. And in spite of her "instinctive struggle" against her traditional role as a mother and wife, she is not able to fully realize herself, and the novel ends with her on a spiritual journey to

---

[25] Dohm, *Schicksale einer Seele* (Berlin: S. Fischer, 1899). Part of her motivation for exploring three generations is her view that the "belief in natural necessity has crumbled" and that this paves the way for the "new" generations of mothers and daughters to construct themselves in a fashion that the older generations could not. Dohm, *Die Neue Mutter* (Nuenkirch: Ala Verlag, 1987), 13. For a discussion of the political implications of Dohm's choice of exploring three "generations," see Birgit Mikus, "Children of the Revolution? A Case Study of the Missing Next Generation in Women's Political Writings in the Nineteenth Century and Hedwig Dohm's Novels," *German Life and Letters* 67, no. 4 (2014): 342–354 and Birgit Mikus and Emily Spiers, "Split Infinities: German Feminisms and the Generational Project," *Oxford German Studies* 45, no. 1 (2016): 5–30.

[26] In *Become Who You Are!*, Dohm highlights the challenges of being an older woman, with the story of the widow, Agnes, who has been locked in an asylum. For further reflections on the prejudices against older women, see Dohm's essay "The Old Woman" (1903), included in *Become Who You Are*. See also chapter 8 here.

India that yields "knowledge" that is merely "theoretical" and "fruitless" on the practical political level (*Fate* 1). By contrast, in *Christa Ruland*, Christa is surrounded by politically engaged "new" women, including a chemist, a medical doctor, an athlete, and an artist. And though Christa by no means becomes a political activist, she is able to reject the traditional roles of wife and mother that have been forced upon her, for example, choosing not to have children because it would be "unnatural" for her and ending her marriage after confronting her husband (*Christa* 195). It is through these sorts of realistic depictions of women, which are underwritten by a constructivist view of gender, that Dohm uses her novels to provide an aesthetic alternative to the sort of misleading aesthetic representations of women she sees in writers like Nietzsche.[27]

Like Veit-Schlegel, Dohm thus regards the aesthetic as something that is not just of individual significance, but as something that has social and political import. For Dohm, however, it is not the general ideal of freedom, but the more specific ideal of gender equality and "becoming who you are" as a woman that aesthetic representations can advance. Moreover, like Veit-Schlegel, she alights on novels as an important means through which she herself attempts to provide aesthetic resources to a wider public, which resist the essentialist view of gender she rejects and promote the constructivist view she endorses. In the theoretical and fictional work of Veit-Schlegel and Dohm we thus find two nineteenth-century visions of why the aesthetic matters if we are to achieve social and political ideals.

3 LANDMANN-KALISCHER, PHENOMENOLOGY, AND THE SCIENCE OF AESTHETICS

As I now turn to the work of Landmann-Kalischer and Lee, I am turning away from aesthetic programs that are oriented around the social-political value of the aesthetic and turning toward programs that offer a philosophical analysis of the nature of aesthetic experience that is informed by psychology.

Edith Landmann-Kalischer (1877–1951) worked primarily on issues in aesthetics, value theory, and epistemology at a moment in German philosophy when philosophical psychology and phenomenology were on the rise.[28] Born to a Jewish family in Berlin, she studied at the Realkursen für Mädchen (Real Courses for Girls), which was founded by the feminist Helene Lange in 1889. Since at that time German universities did not recognize diplomas from the Realkursen, but Swiss universities did, she enrolled at the University of Zurich for her undergraduate work in 1897. This, in turn, enabled her to

---

[27] For a discussion of other political dimensions of these novels, see Mikus, "Hedwig Dohm: 'Bin ich ein Mensch—nichts als ein Mensch," 225–242.

[28] See also chapter 11 here.

take courses at the University of Berlin with Georg Simmel and Max Dessoir as a visitor. Landmann-Kalischer remained at Zurich for her doctorate work, where she wrote her dissertation, "Analysis of Aesthetic Contemplation" ("Analyse der äesthetischen Contemplation," 1902), under the guidance of Ernst Meumann, who had worked as an assistant to Wilhelm Wundt, one of the founders of experimental psychology. In 1903 she married the economist, Julius Landmann, whom she accompanied to his various posts in Berlin, Bern, Basel, and Kiel.

In her early published work, Landmann-Kalischer pursued a psychologically informed program in value theory, publishing pieces on aesthetic value ("On the Cognitive Value of Aesthetic Judgments" ("Über den Erkenntniswert ästhetischer Urteile," 1905) and "On Artistic Truth" ("Über künstlerische Wahrheit," 1906) and on value theory more generally "Philosophy of Values" ("Philosophie der Werte," 1910).[29] In the 1910s, she became involved in the George-Kreis, a circle of artists and academics gathered around the poet Stefan George. And during this period, she turned her philosophical efforts toward developing a theory of cognition, which culminated in *The Transcendence of Cognizing* (*Die Transcendenz des Erkennens*, 1923). At the end of her career, she returned to the aesthetic issues that initially inspired her, and her last work, *The Doctrine of the Beautiful* (*Die Lehre vom Schönen*, 1952), was published posthumously.

Landmann-Kalischer's philosophical efforts are wide-ranging, but in what follows I focus on the broadly phenomenological approach to aesthetics that she develops in the first decade of the 1900s. Though the phenomenological movement was still in a nascent stage when she began writing, her early work can be productively situated in the "Brentano School" of phenomenology, which includes a disparate group of thinkers who take their cue from Franz Brentano, such as Alexius Meinong, Carl Stumpf, Christian von Ehrenfels, Anton Marty, and Kasimir Twardowski.[30] In spite of the many differences between the thinkers in the Brentano School, what Landmann-Kalischer shares with them is Brentano's basic conception of phenomenology as "descriptive psychology," which investigates mental phenomena and lived experience "from an empirical standpoint."[31] Like many of the philosophers in this school, she thinks that this descriptive psychology should be a "science" that analyzes both the "subjective" side of lived experience, which encompasses various mental acts and representations, and

---

[29] Daniel Dahlstrom has translated, and I have edited, a translation of these three essays (which is the first translation of her work into English): *Edith Landmann-Kalischer: Essays on Art, Aesthetics, and Value*, ed. Samantha Matherne, transl. Daniel O. Dahlstrom (Oxford: Oxford University Press, forthcoming). See my introduction in this translation for an overview of her philosophy and these three essays.

[30] For a discussion of the relationship between Landmann-Kalischer's value theory and that of Brentano and Meinong, see Íngrid Vendrell Ferran, "Tatsache, Wert und menschliche Sensibilität: Die Brentanoschule und die Gestaltpsychologie," in *Feeling and Value, Willing and Action*, ed. Marta Wehrle and Maren Ubiali (Cham: Springer, 2014), 141–162. For a discussion of the relationship between her aesthetic theory and that of Brentano, Meinong, and von Ehrenfels, see Maria Reicher-Marek, "Dispositionalist Accounts of Aesthetic Properties in Austro-German Aesthetics," *Paradigmi. Rivista di critica filosofica* 3 (2017): 71–86.

[31] See, e.g., Brentano's *Psychology from an Empirical Standpoint*.

the "objective" side of lived experience, which encompasses the "objects" that those acts and representations are intentionally directed toward.[32] In keeping with this Brentanian approach, in her phenomenological work on aesthetics she investigates both the "subjective" side of aesthetic lived experience, hence, the mental acts and representations it involves, and the "objective" side of lived experience, hence, the aesthetic and artistic "objects" that this experience is directed toward. As I will show, she couples a cognitivist account of aesthetic experience as a source of "cognition" and "truth," together with a realist theory of beauty, as something that is part of the world. And she ultimately paints a picture of what the "science" of philosophical aesthetics should be, which takes its cue from these cognitivist and realist commitments.

In "On the Cognitive Value of Aesthetic Judgments," Landmann-Kalischer focuses on the aesthetic experience of beauty.[33] In the cognitivist vein, she takes aim at noncognitivist views of this aesthetic experience as something that involves a merely subjective feeling of pleasure. Though she agrees that the aesthetic experience of beauty involves a feeling of pleasure, she argues that this pleasure ultimately serves as the basis of a cognitive judgment in which we attribute beauty to objects. It is this feeling-based cognitive judgment that she takes to be at the heart of aesthetic experience of beauty. And she devotes sustained attention to trying to spell out the conditions that we must meet in order to make a cognitive judgment about the beautiful that is "objectively valid" and "true" of the object. To this end, she draws on psychological research to elucidate the "deceptions" that arise, which prevent us from making such judgments in a "reliable" way (see "Cognitive Value" chap. 3).[34] She also offers a logical account of the standards of judgmental "agreement" that an aesthetic judgment must meet in order to be objectively valid (see "Cognitive Value" chap. 4).

In the realist vein, Landmann-Kalischer targets "subjectivist" accounts of beauty, as something that subjects merely project onto objects. Though she thinks that aesthetic value is, in a sense, subjectively conditioned, she claims that it is nevertheless still real, qua a property of objects. And in order to defend this position, she deploys a "secondary quality analogy," according to which beauty is like secondary qualities like color. More specifically, she argues that both beauty and secondary qualities are dispositional properties of objects: properties that are disposed to bring about a response in appropriately situated subjects and which stand in law-governed relations to those responses. In the case of beauty, she identifies the relevant response as a feeling of pleasure, and in

---

[32] See, e.g., "in every lived experience we distinguish a subjective and an objective side. Sensing, representing, feeling, willing are a psychic, subjective lived experience; the sensed, represented, felt, and willed are objective. . . . Act and content [Akt und Inhalt] can be distinguished in every psychic lived experience"; Landmann-Kalischer, "Philosophy of Values," *Archiv für die gesamte Psychologie* 18 (1910): 1–93, 35. Translations of Landmann-Kalischer are my own.

[33] For a lengthier discussion of the theory of aesthetic value and aesthetic judgment that she defends in this piece, see Samantha Matherne, "Edith Landmann-Kalischer on Aesthetic Demarcation and Normativity," *British Journal of Aesthetics* 60, no. 3 (2020): 315–334.

[34] "Über den Erkenntniswert ästhetischer Urteile: Ein Vergleich zwischen Sinnes- und Werturteilen." *Archiv für die Gesamte Psychologie* (1905): 263–328.

the case of secondary qualities, as sensation. And she deploys this secondary analogy in order to argue that, like secondary qualities, beauty is at once real and subjectively conditioned because it is a property of an object that is constituted, in part, by its dispositional relation to responses in subjects.[35]

Whereas in "On the Cognitive Value of Aesthetic Judgment" her focus is on the cognitive nature of the aesthetic experience of the beautiful, in "On Artistic Truth" she defends a different sort of cognitive insight about our aesthetic experience of art and the truths we learn through it. According to Landmann-Kalischer, art gives us a distinctive kind of truth about the "psychic world," that is, truth about our lived experiences as subjects ("Artistic Truth" 463).[36] On her view, art that is "true" gives us a "faithful exhibition [getreue Darstellung] of the psychic world," for example, of what it is like to have a lived experience, such as a feeling, perception, or desire ("Artistic Truth" 463).

More than this, however, Landmann-Kalischer argues that it is through art alone that we cognize certain truths about the psychic world: "just as we would never see our own face [Antlitz] were it not for a mirror, so too we would never see our inner life opposite [gegenüber] us were it not for the mirror of art. Only art exhibits it to us. *Only* through art can we cognize it" ("Artistic Truth" 463, emphasis added). Landmann-Kalischer takes this to be the case because she thinks that art alone presents us with the psychic world "as it is," that is, as we "live" it: art makes what is given to inner perception accessible to another organ . . . it makes perceptible to the eye and the ear what was only present to "inner sense.". . . It makes the content of an abstract representation sensibly present, it gives feelings an audible or colorful gestalt. . . . Art creates agreement by creating a counter-image [Gegenbild] of the psychically given that leaves it as it is ("Artistic Truth" 496).

Though Landmann-Kalischer by no means denies the valuable insight that we might gain into the psychic world through something like phenomenology or psychology, she thinks both of these disciplines are oriented toward the "translation" of what is "given" in lived experience "into concepts" that are more general and abstract ("Artistic Truth" 495).[37] And in this translation, she thinks that certain "individual truths" about our lived experiences in their "given" or "intuitive" form are lost ("Artistic Truth" 497, 495). For Landmann-Kalischer, these truths pertain to what it is immediately like to undergo a particular lived experience. And in a work of art, she claims that instead of translating those lived experiences "into concepts" that are more general and abstract, an artist

---

[35] In the "Philosophy of Values," Landmann-Kalischer describes this view of properties as both subjectively conditioned and objective as a "Kantian" or "critical" view because she takes this view to be in keeping with Kant's "Copernican" idea that the objects of cognition are "constituted" through the subject ("Philosophy of Values," 2–3).

[36] "Über künstlerische Wahrheit," *Zeitschrift für Ästhetik und Allgemeine Kunstwissenschaft* 1 (1906): 457–505.

[37] For a lengthier discussion of the relationship between artists and phenomenologists on Landmann-Kalischer's view, see Samantha Matherne, "Are Artists Phenomenologists? Perspectives from Edith Landmann-Kalischer and Maurice Merleau-Ponty," in *Horizons of Phenomenology*, ed. Patrick Londen, Philip Walsh, and Jeffrey Yoshimi (2023).

uses her medium to produce a "counter-image [Gegenbild]" of these specific lived experiences that make them "sensibly present" to her audience ("Artistic Truth" 496). For example, with a landscape painting, a painter can give us a "counter-image" of what it's intuitively like to see the lush green of a particular meadow, or with a few lines of verse, a poet can give us a "counter-image" of what it's intuitively like to feel hope at the prospect of seeing a dear friend. On Landmann-Kalischer's view, it is through "counter-images" like these that art, and art alone, makes lived experiences intuitively present to us and thereby puts us in a position to acquire knowledge of "individual truths" about them.

Finally, in "Philosophy of Values" Landmann-Kalischer defends an ambitious program for what philosophical aesthetics should be like, as something that contributes to the "science of values" more generally ("Philosophy of Values" 62). Landmann-Kalischer defines a "science of value" as a science that takes as its starting point "the fact [Tatsache] of value as something given" ("Philosophy of Values" 68). The "fact" that she has in mind is the fact that in lived experience we make value judgments about what is beautiful, good, and true. And she claims that the task of a science of value is the "objective determination" of these values, that is, the determination of what the beautiful, good, and true are as objective or real parts of the world ("Philosophy of Values" 68). In this picture of the science of value, we again see echoes of her Brentanian commitment to pursuing a "science" that does justice to the subjective-side of lived experience (here, our lived experience of making value-judgments) and the objective-side of lived experience (here, the beautiful, the good, and the true, as the objects those value-judgments are directed at).

Applying this vision to aesthetics, she argues that a philosophical science of aesthetics needs to investigate both the nature of aesthetic judgments, qua the "subjective" side of aesthetic experience, and the nature of the beautiful itself, qua the "objective" side. With regard to the former project, she claims that the science of aesthetics needs to provide an account of what judgments of the beautiful involve and what is required in order for someone to be "warranted" or "reliable" in making an objectively valid aesthetic judgment ("Philosophy of Values" 55, 59). And, as in "On the Cognitive Value," she claims this, in part, involves looking to psychology to give us insight into the aesthetic "deceptions" we undergo, and to logic for an analysis of the sort of intrajudgmental agreement that pertains to objectively valid aesthetic judgments (see "Philosophy of Values" 59–60).

However, Landmann-Kalischer argues that the ultimate "warrant" for an objectively valid judgment of the beautiful is beauty itself, qua a real or objective part of the world. She thus takes it to be the case that a science of the beautiful must also endeavor to understand what the beautiful is qua a dispositional property of objects that stands in a "lawful-relation" to the pleasure of subjects. For Landmann-Kalischer, this requires getting a clearer picture about the relationship between beauty and the lower-order perceptual properties, such as color, sound, or shape, that beauty supervenes on (see "Cognitive Value" 278–279). She notes that this sort of "objective determination" of beauty is a task that has proved particularly challenging in the aesthetic domain because of the complex set of lower-level properties involved (see "Philosophy of Values" 59). However, she responds by noting that there has been some "success" to this end, citing as examples Aristotle's account of forms of tragedy as beautiful; Polyclitus's, Leonardo da Vinci's, and Albrecht Dürer's artistic renderings of certain "canonical" human forms as beautiful; and a general effort to identify certain mathematical forms like a circle or serpentine line as beautiful ("Philosophy of Values" 81). She argues, moreover, that we should liken the current state of aesthetics to the early state of other sciences like acoustics or optics, which, in spite of countless missteps, eventually arrived at an objective determination of the "stimuli" in objects that give rise to sonic and visual sensations (see "Philosophy of Values" 81, "Cognitive Value" 286–287). And it is this task of the objective determination of the beautiful that she takes to complement the analysis of the nature of aesthetic judgments, which a complete science of aesthetics requires.

In her early phenomenological work on aesthetics, Landmann-Kalischer thus offers a psychologically informed account of the cognitive nature of our aesthetic experience of the beautiful and of the truths we learn through art. She, in turn, pairs this cognitivist view of aesthetic experience with a realist account of the nature of beauty and a vision of what the science of aesthetics should look like, which does justice to the "subjective" and "objective" dimensions of aesthetic experience.

4 VERNON LEE, PSYCHOLOGY, AND EMPATHY IN AESTHETIC EXPERIENCE

Vernon Lee is the pseudonym of Violet Paget (1856–1935), who contributed, among other things, to the field of psychological aesthetics that flourished around the turn of the twentieth century.[38] Although not German herself, as I noted earlier, I am including her in this chapter because she considers herself to be a "disciple" of one of the leading German philosophers and psychologists of the time, Theodor Lipps, who is known for an aesthetics based on *Einfühlung* (empathy) (*Beauty* 74).[39]

Lee was born in France to British parents and spent her childhood in various European countries, including Germany, Switzerland, and Italy, eventually settling in Florence. She was a prolific writer, publishing pieces on the history of art and music, travel essays, supernatural stories, novels, political pamphlets, and philosophical essays

---

[38] For a discussion of how Lee's engagement with the psychological work of Karl Groos, Max Dessoir, Théodule Ribot, and Oscar Külpe (whose psychology lab she visited in 1911) informed her approach to psychological aesthetics, see Susan Lanzoni, "Practicing Psychology in the Art Gallery: Vernon Lee's Aesthetics of Empathy," *Journal of the History of the Behavioral Sciences* 45, no. 4 (2009): 330–354.

[39] Vernon Lee, *Beauty and Ugliness and Other Studies in Psychological Aesthetics* (London: John Lane, The Bodley Head, 1912). Lipps's work on psychology and empathy was also highly influential for the Munich School of phenomenology.

on aesthetics.[40] Her early publications, like *Belcaro: Being Essays on Sundry Aesthetical Questions* (1881), were written while she associated with the circle of the aesthete Walter Pater. But her work in psychological aesthetics commenced in 1887 when she met her collaborator and romantic partner, the Scottish artist Clementina (Kit) Anstruther-Thomson. For the next decade, Lee and Anstruther-Thomson did small-scale empirical research on aesthetic experience by going to galleries, museums, and churches and carefully recording Anstruther-Thomson's introspective reports of her bodily and affective responses to works of art. These efforts culminated in the essay, "Beauty and Ugliness" (1897).[41] Although the two remained close, Lee began developing her psychological aesthetics in a different direction in the first decade of the twentieth century, drawing on Lipps's concept of *Einfühlung* or "empathy."[42] This culminated in a series of pieces, including the book *Beauty and Ugliness* (1912) (which includes a reprint of the eponymous essay), as well as other writings, such as "Gallery Diaries" (1901–1904), "Psychology of an Art Writer" (1903), *The Psychology of Laurus Nobilis: Chapters on Art and Life* (1909), and *The Beautiful: An Introduction to Psychological Aesthetics* (1913).[43]

In keeping with psychological aesthetics in general, Lee seeks to develop an empirically informed account of aesthetic experience.[44] More specifically, she focuses on the experience of the beauty or ugliness of "visible shape (or 'form')" (*Beauty* 80).[45] In both her early and later work, Lee identifies the notion of the "projection" of our inner experience onto the object as the key for understanding this aesthetic experience. Think,

[40] For a bibliography and overview of many of her writings, see "Vernon Lee: A Brief Chronology," in *Vernon Lee: Decadence, Ethics, Aesthetics*, ed. Catherine Maxwell and Patricia Pulham (New York: Palgrave Macmillan, 2006), xvi–xx.

[41] This essay was originally published in *Contemporary Review* 72 (1897): 544–569, 669–688, and it was later reprinted in 1912 in the book *Beauty and Ugliness* with brackets to indicate where Lee and Anstruther-Thomson disagree. *Beauty and Ugliness* also includes essays in which Lee discusses how her 1912 view differs from her 1897 view (see, e.g., "Anthropomorphic Aesthetics," "Aesthetic Empathy and Its Organic Accompaniments," and "The Central Problem of Aesthetics").

[42] See *Beauty*, 18, 46–47, for Lee's discussion of the meaning of *Einfühlung*.

[43] Lee publishes part of the "Gallery Diaries" in the chapter in *Beauty and Ugliness* titled "Aesthetic Responsiveness," and they have been recently republished, along with the "Psychology of an Art Writer" essay, as *The Psychology of an Art Writer*.

[44] This said, Lee also describes her own empirical efforts as limited to the "gallery and the studio," hence not of "the laboratory," and thus not able to achieve the "scientific certainty" that she thinks experimental psychology is able to achieve (*Beauty* viii; see also 358–363). For overviews of Lee's aesthetics, see Carolyn Burdett, "The Subjective inside Us Can Turn into the Objective Outside: Vernon Lee's Psychological Aesthetics," *Interdisciplinary Studies in the Long Nineteenth Century* 12 (2011), https://doi.org/10.16995/ntn.610; Paul Guyer, "Psychological Aesthetics in Britain: Lee," in *History of Modern Aesthetics*, vol. 2 (Cambridge: Cambridge University Press, 2014), 426–437; Dylan Kenny, "The Real Self," in Vernon Lee, *Psychology of an Art Writer* (New York: David Zwirner Gallery/Ekphrasis, 2018), 10–21; Becca Rothfeld, "Mind's Eye," *Art in America*, May 2018, 55–56.

[45] Though she focuses on the aesthetic experience of visible form, she by no means denies the importance of, and need to investigate, the nature of the aesthetic experience of the content of art. See, e.g., her claim that "*Einfühlung* does not explain everything in the artistic phenomenon: the relation of form to what it represents or suggests... constitute a whole group of psychological problems where judgment and recognition play the chief part" (*Beauty*, 69–70).

for example, of projecting qualities of "movement," such as "spreading out," "flowing," "bending," "twisting," and so on onto the "motionless lines and surfaces" of the work of art (*Beauty* 19). However, she understands the nature of this projection in different ways in her early and later work.

In her early work with Anstruther-Thomson, Lee conceives of the projection involved in aesthetic experience as something that is bodily in nature. Thus, in their 1897 essay "Beauty and Ugliness," they document in detail the sort of bodily sensations and resulting feelings of pleasure or displeasure that Anstruther-Thomson has in response to various visible forms. And they argue that these sensations are part of a projective process that is "physiological" or "organic" (*Beauty* 154; see also 65).[46]

However, Lee's understanding of the nature of projection undergoes an important shift after 1897, as she comes to regard it as a "mental phenomenon," rather than a bodily phenomenon (*Beauty* 154). Lee claims that Lipps's account of the mental act of "empathy" served as a crucial "clue" for her in clarifying the mental nature of the projection involved in aesthetic experience (*Beauty* 65, see also 89).[47] According to Lipps, empathy is a mental act in which we project our own inner experiences onto something outside of us, whether it be another person or object. Applying this to aesthetic scenarios, Lipps claims that in aesthetic experience we project our inner experiences that are accompanied by pleasure or displeasure onto objects, like works of art, and experience them as beautiful or ugly, accordingly. And in this account of empathy Lee sees the key to understanding the mental projection involved in the aesthetic experience of visible form.

In a bit more detail, on Lee's mature view, our aesthetic experience involves a mental act of empathy in which we project certain experiences we have had onto a work of art. She claims that if these experiences were initially accompanied by a hedonic feeling of pleasure or displeasure, then this hedonic feeling will be "revived" in the aesthetic experience (*Beauty* 21). In cases where pleasure is revived, Lee claims that we experience the work of art as beautiful, and in cases where displeasure is revived, we experience it as ugly.

Though in her mature work Lee thus draws on Lipps's notion of empathy to clarify the projective nature of aesthetic experience, she is also critical of Lipps for neglecting the bodily dimensions of aesthetic experience altogether, which she takes her early empirical investigation of aesthetic experience to have given evidence of (see *Beauty* 60–73).[48] Although in her mature view she thinks that empathy "explains" the pleasure or displeasure at issue in the experience of beauty or ugliness, she also acknowledges the role that bodily sensations and processes play in "starting and keeping up" empathy

---

[46] Lee aligns this sort of physiological approach to projection with Karl Groos's theory of "inner imitation [innere Nachahmung]" (*Beauty*, 154).

[47] Lee cites, in particular, Lipps's *Spatial Aesthetics and Optical Illusions* (*Raumaesthetik und geometrisch-optische Täuschungen*, 1897) as influential for her view.

[48] She also criticizes Lipps's view that empathy involves the projection of the self onto the object. On her view, it only involves the projection of certain experiences onto the object (see *Beauty*, 54–59).

(*Beauty* 355–356). Indeed, on this issue, she thinks that the philosophical psychologist Karl Groos's theory of "inner imitation," according to which "empathy" is accompanied by certain "motor phenomena of an imitative character," is an important supplement to Lipps's view (*Beauty* 23; see also 63, 77–79). For Lee, then, psychological aesthetics is something that must seek to balance an analysis of the mental phenomena of empathy with an account of the attendant bodily phenomena, which she takes there to be empirical evidence of.

Stepping back, in her work in psychological aesthetics, Lee offers an empirically based analysis of our aesthetic experience of the beauty or ugliness of a visible form. And although she initially analyzes this experience in terms of bodily projection, in her mature work she alights on Lipps's notion of the mental act of empathy as the key to making sense of the projection involved in aesthetic experience. However, contrary to Lipps, she argues that if we are to fully understand the nature of aesthetic experience, we need some account of the role the body also plays. Though Lee thus approaches aesthetic experience through a different lens than Landmann-Kalischer does, we see in the work of both an effort to offer a psychologically informed account of the nature of aesthetic experience.[49]

5 CONCLUSION

In this chapter, I have surveyed the contribution that Veit-Schlegel, Dohm, Landmann-Kalischer, and Lee made to aesthetics in the long nineteenth century in German philosophy. I began with a discussion of the way in which Veit-Schlegel and Dohm contribute to a trend that turns on the recognition of the social and political significance of the aesthetic. In Veit-Schlegel's romantic work, this trend manifested in her analysis of how romantic novels should be in order to contribute to the aesthetic *Bildung* required for human beings to achieve freedom at an individual and collective level. Meanwhile, in Dohm's feminist work, this trend took shape in her account of the power that aesthetic representations of women have in shaping constructions of gender, whether in a patriarchal and oppressive direction à la Nietzsche or in the feminist and emancipatory direction of her own novels. I then turned my attention to the trend in aesthetics oriented toward psychologically informed accounts of the nature of aesthetic experience. In this vein, I discussed Landmann-Kalischer's phenomenological approach to aesthetics and her defense of a cognitivist account of the aesthetic experience of beauty and art, her realist account of the nature of beauty, and her vision of what a science of aesthetics should be. Finally, I considered Lee's interventions in psychological aesthetics and her empirically grounded attempt to use the notion of empathy to make sense of the aesthetic

---

[49] For Landmann-Kalischer's review of Lipps's aesthetics, see her "Theodor Lipps's *Grundlegung der Ästhetik. Ästhetik. Psychologie des Schönen und der Kunst*," *Archiv für die gesamte Psychologie* 5 (1905), 213–227.

experience of the beauty and ugliness of visible form in art. Though by no means exhaustive, I hope this survey helps shed light on the philosophical effort Veit-Schlegel, Dohm, Landmann-Kalischer, and Lee devoted toward elucidating the social-political value of the aesthetic and the nature of aesthetic experience in the long nineteenth century in German philosophy.

I would like to thank Kristin Gjesdal and Dalia Nassar for their insightful feedback on this chapter.

BIBLIOGRAPHY

Allingham, Liesl. "Revolutionizing Domesticity: Potentialities of Female Self-Definition in Dorothea Schlegel's *Florentin* (1801)." *Women in German Yearbook* 27 (2011): 1–30.

Andreas-Salomé, Lou. *The Erotic*. Translated by John Crisp. London: Routledge, 2012.

Andreas-Salomé, Lou. *Fenitschka. Eine Ausschweifung*. Stuttgart: Cotta, 1898.

Andreas-Salomé, Lou. *Ibsen's Heroines*. Translated by Siegfried Mandel. Redding Ridge, CT: Black Swan Books, 1985.

Andreas-Salomé, Lou. *Rainer Maria Rilke*. Leipzig: Im Insel-Verlag, 1928.

Beiser, Frederick C. *The Romantic Imperative: The Concept of Early German Romanticism*. Cambridge, MA: Harvard University Press, 2003.

Brentano, Franz. *Psychology from an Empirical Standpoint*. Translated by Antos C. Rancurello, D. B. Terrell, and Linda L. McAlister. London: Routledge, 2015.

Burdett, Carolyn. "The Subjective Inside Us Can Turn into the Objective Outside: Vernon Lee's Psychological Aesthetics." *Interdisciplinary Studies in the Long Nineteenth Century* 12 (2011).

Daley, Margaretmary. *Women of Letters: A Study of Self and Genre in the Personal Writing of Caroline Schlegel-Schelling, Rahel Levin Varnhagen, and Bettina von Arnim*. Columbia, SC: Camden House, 1998.

Dane, Gesa. "Women Writers and Romanticism." In *The Cambridge Companion to German Romanticism*, edited by Nicholas Saul, 133–146. Cambridge: Cambridge University Press, 2009.

Diethe, Carol. *Nietzsche's Women*. New York: de Gruyter, 1996.

Dohm, Hedwig. *Die Antifeministen*. Berlin: Ferdinand Dümmler, 1902.

Dohm, Hedwig. *Become Who You Are*. Translated by Elizabeth G. Ametsbichler. Albany: State University of New York Press, 2006.

Dohm, Hedwig. *Christa Ruland*. Berlin: S. Fischer, 1902.

Dohm, Hedwig. *Der Frauen Natur und Recht*. Berlin: Wedekind and Schweiger, 1876.

Dohm, Hedwig. *Jesuitism in the Household*. Berlin: Wedekind & Schwieger, 1873.

Dohm, Hedwig. *Die Neue Mutter*. Nuenkirch: Ala Verlag, 1987.

Dohm, Hedwig. *Schicksale einer Seele*. Berlin: S. Fischer, 1899.

Dohm, Hedwig. *Sibilla Dalmar*. Berlin: S. Fischer, 1896.

Dohm, Hedwig. *Was die Pastoren von den Frauen denken*. Berlin: Verlag Reinhold Schlingmann, 1872.

Dohm, Hedwig. *Werde, die Du bist!* Breslau: S. Schottlaender, Schlesische Verlags-Anstalt, 1894.

Dohm, Hedwig. *Die wissenschaftliche Emancipation der Frau*. Berlin: Wedekind and Schweiger, 1874.

Ezekiel, Anna. "Women, Women Writers, and Early German Romanticism." In *The Palgrave Handbook of German Romantic Philosophy*, edited by Elizabeth Millán Brusslan, 475–509. Cham: Palgrave Macmillan, 2020.

Farran, Íngrid Vendrell. "Tatsache, Wert und menschliche Sensibilität: Die Brentanoschule und die Gestaltpsychologie." In *Feeling and Value, Willing and Action*, edited by Marta Wehrle and Maren Ubiali, 141–162. Cham: Springer, 2014.

Frank, Manfred. *Einführung in die frühromantische Ästhetik*. Frankfurt: Suhrkamp, 1997.

French, Lorely. *German Women as Letter Writers, 1750–1850*. Madison, NJ: Fairleigh Dickinson University Press, 1996.

Gorodeisky, Keren. "19th Century Romantic Aesthetics." In *Stanford Encyclopedia of Philosophy Archive*. Fall 2016 ed. Stanford University, 1997–. Article published June 14, 2016. https://plato.stanford.edu/archives/fall2016/entries/aesthetics-19th-romantic.

Guyer, Paul. *History of Modern Aesthetics*. Vol. 2. Cambridge: Cambridge University Press, 2014.

Helfer, Martha. "Dorothea Veit-Schlegel's *Florentin*: Constructing a Feminist Romantic Aesthetic." *German Quarterly* 69, no. 2 (1996): 144–160.

Helfer, Martha. "Gender Studies and Romanticism." In *The Literature of German Romanticism*, edited by Dennis Mahoney, 229–250. Woodbridge, U.K.: Boydell and Brewer, 2003.

Johnson, Laurie. "Dorothea Veit's *Florentin* and the Early Romantic Model of Alterity." *Monatshefte* 97, no. 1 (2005): 33–62.

Kalischer, Edith. *Analyse der ästhetischen Contemplation (Malerei und Plastik)*. Leipzig: Barth, 1902.

Landmann, Edith. *Die Lehre vom Schönen*. Vienna: Amandus, 1952.

Landmann, Edith. *Die Transcendenz des Erkennens*. Berlin: Bondi, 1923.

Landmann-Kalischer, Edith. *Edith Landmann-Kalischer: Essays on Art, Aesthetics, and Value.*, edited by Samantha Matherne and translated by Daniel O. Dahlstrom. Oxford: Oxford University Press, forthcoming.

Landmann-Kalischer, Edith. "Philosophie der Wert." *Archiv für die gesamte Psychologie* 18 (1910): 1–93.

Landmann-Kalischer, Edith. Review of *Grundlegung der Ästhetik. Psychologie des Schönen und der Kunst*, by Theodor Lipps. *Archiv für die gesamte Psychologie* 5 (1905): 213–227.

Landmann-Kalischer, Edith. "Über den Erkenntniswert ästhetischer Urteile: Ein Vergleich zwischen Sinnes- und Werturteilen." *Archiv für die Gesamte Psychologie* 5 (1905): 263–328.

Landmann-Kalischer, Edith. "Über künstlerische Wahrheit." *Zeitschrift für Ästhetik und Allgemeine Kunstwissenschaft* 1 (1906): 457–505.

Lanzoni, Susan. "Practicing Psychology in the Art Gallery: Vernon Lee's Aesthetics of Empathy." *Journal of the History of the Behavioral Sciences* 45, no. 4 (2009): 330–354.

Lee, Vernon. *The Beautiful: An Introduction to Psychological Aesthetics*. Cambridge: Cambridge University Press, 1913.

Lee, Vernon. *Beauty and Ugliness and Other Studies in Psychological Aesthetics*. London: John Lane, The Bodley Head, 1912.

Lee, Vernon. *Belcaro: Being Essays on Sundry Aesthetical Questions*. London: W. Satchell & Co., 1881.

Lee, Vernon. *Laurus Nobilis: Chapters on Art and Life*. London: John Lane, The Bodley Head, 1909.

Lee, Vernon. *Psychology of an Art Writer*. New York: David Zwirner Gallery/Ekphrasis, 2018.

Lee, Vernon, and Clementina Anstruther-Thomson. "Beauty and Ugliness." *Contemporary Review* 72 (1897): 544–569, 669–688.

Lipps, Theodor. *Raumaesthetik und geometrisch-optische Täuschungen*. Leipzig: Johann Ambrosius Barth, 1897.

Matherne, Samantha. "Are Artists Phenomenologists? Perspectives from Edith Landmann-Kalischer and Maurice Merleau-Ponty." In *Horizons of Phenomenology*, edited by Patrick Londen, Philip Walsh, and Jeffrey Yoshimi. Cham: Springer, 2023.

Matherne, Samantha. "Edith Landmann-Kalischer on Aesthetic Demarcation and Normativity." *British Journal of Aesthetics* 60, no. 3 (2020): 315–334.

Maxwell, Catherine, and Pulham Patricia, eds. *Vernon Lee: Decadence, Ethics, Aesthetics*. New York: Palgrave Macmillan, 2006.

Mikus, Birgit. "Children of the Revolution? A Case Study of the Missing Next Generation in Women's Political Writings in the Nineteenth Century and Hedwig Dohm's Novels." *German Life and Letters* 67, no. 4 (2014): 342–354.

Mikus, Birgit. *The Political Women in Print: German Women's Writing 1845–1919*. Oxford: Peter Lang, 2014.

Mikus, Birgit. "'Sprechmaschine Du': Sprachkritik in ausgewählten Romanen Hedwig Dohms." *German Life and Letters* 62 (2009): 115–139.

Mikus, Birgit, and Emily Spiers. "Split Infinities: German Feminisms and the Generational Project." *Oxford German Studies* 45, no. 1 (2016): 5–30.

Millán, Elizabeth. "The Aesthetic Philosophy of Early German Romanticism and Its Early German Idealist Roots." In *The Palgrave Handbook of German Idealism*, edited by Matthew Altman, 389–408. New York: Palgrave Macmillan, 2014.

Nassar, Dalia. *The Romantic Absolute: Being and Knowing in Early German Romantic Philosophy, 1795–1804*. Chicago: University of Chicago Press, 2013.

Nassar, Dalia and Gjesdal, Kristin, ed. *Women Philosophers in the Long Nineteenth Century: The German Tradition*. Oxford: Oxford University Press, 2021.

Pailer, Gaby. *Schreibe, die du bist*. Pfaffenweiler: Centaurus, 1994.

Piper, Andrew. "The Making of Transnational Textual Communities: German Women Translators, 1800–1850." *Women in German Yearbook* 22 (2006): 119–144.

Pollok, Anne. "Femininity and the Salon." In *The Palgrave Handbook of German Romantic Philosophy*, edited by Elizabeth Millán Brusslan, 119–140. Cham: Palgrave Macmillan, 2020.

Pollok, Anne. "On Self-Formation: The Role of Writing and Sociability for the Establishment of a Persona (Henriette Herz, Rahel Levin Varnhagen, and Bettina von Arnim)." In *Women and Philosophy in Eighteenth-Century Germany*, edited by Corey W. Dyck, 195–212. Oxford: Oxford University Press, 2021.

Reicher-Marek, Maria. "Dispositionalist Accounts of Aesthetic Properties in Austro-German Aesthetics." *Paradigmi. Rivista di critica filosofica* 3 (2017): 71–86.

Rothfeld, Becca. "Mind's Eye." *Art in America*, May 2018, 55–56.

Sassen, Brigitte. "Dorothea Schlegel and the Challenges of Female Authority and Identity." In *Women and Philosophy in Eighteenth-Century German*, edited by Corey Dyck, 179–194. Oxford: Oxford University Press, 2021.

Schlegel, Dorothea. "A Conversation about the Latest Novels by French Women Writers." In *Women Critics 1660–1820: An Anthology*, edited by the Folger Collective on Early Modern Critics, translated by Simon Richter, 340–342. Bloomington: Indiana University Press, 1995.

Schlegel, Dorothea. "Dorothea Veit-Schlegel: Selected Diaries and Letters." In *Theory as Practice: A Critical Anthology of Early German Romantic Writings*, edited by Jochen Schulte-Sasse, Haynes Horne, Elzabeth Mittman, and Lisa C. Roetzel, 440–443. Minneapolis: University of Minnesota Press, 1997.

Schlegel, Dorothea. *Florentin*. Translated by Edwina Lawler and Ruth Richardson. Lewiston, NY: Edwin Mellen Press, 1988.

Schlegel, Dorothea. *Florentin: Roman, Fragmente, Varianten*. Edited by Liliane Weissberg. Berlin: Ullstein, 1987.

Schlegel, Dorothea. "Gespräch über die neuesten Romane der Französinnen." *Europa: Eine Zeitschrift* 1, no. 2, edited by Friedrich Schlegel (1803): 88–106.

Schlegel, Friedrich. "Athenaeum Fragments." In *Classic and Romantic German Aesthetics*, edited by J. M. Bernstein, 246–260. Cambridge: Cambridge University Press, 2003.

Schlegel, Friedrich. *Friedrich Schlegel's "Lucinde" and the Fragments*. Translated by Peter Firchow. Minneapolis: University of Minnesota Press, 1971.

Staël, Germaine de. *Corinne, or Italy*. Translated by Sylvia Raphael. Oxford: Oxford University Press, 2008.

Staël, Germaine de. *De la littérature dans ses rapports avec les institutions sociales*. Paris: Maradan, 1800.

Staël, Germaine de. *Delphine*. Translated by Avriel Goldberger. DeKalb: Northern Illinois University Press, 1995.

Staël, Germaine de. *Essai sur les fictions*. In *Œuvres complètes, série I, Œuvres critiques, II, "De la Littérature" et autres essais littéraires*, edited by Stéphanie Genand. Paris: Honoré Champion, 2013.

Stuebben Thornton, Karin. "Enlightenment and Romanticism in the Work of Dorothea Schlegel." *German Quarterly* 39, no. 2 (1966): 162–172.

Weigert, Astrid. "Gender and Genre in the Works of German Romantic Women Writers." In *The Oxford Handbook to European Romanticism*, edited by Paul Hamilton, 240–254. Oxford: Oxford University Press, 2016.

Woodford, Charlotte. *Women, Emancipation, and the German Novel 1871–1910*. London: Legenda, 2014.

CHAPTER 26

SPINOZISM AROUND 1800 AND BEYOND

JASON MAURICE YONOVER

UNLIKE His Canonical Bedfellows René Descartes or Gottfried Wilhelm Leibniz,[1] Benedict Spinoza had no major women correspondents; and in related contrast to Thomas Hobbes, we are not likely to find any explicitly protofeminist tendencies in Spinoza's thought itself.[2] To the contrary: in the last lines of his unfinished *Political Treatise*, Spinoza goes so far as to argue that "women do not, by nature, have equal right with men, but . . . they necessarily submit to men, and so that it cannot happen that each sex rules equally" (TP XI 4).[3] Some readers may wish Spinoza would have quit

---

[1] Elisabeth of Bohemia, for instance, carried out an important exchange with Descartes. On several dimensions of her ethical thought, see Ariane C. Schneck, "Elisabeth of Bohemia's Neo-Peripatetic Account of the Emotions," *British Journal of the History of Philosophy* 27, no. 4 (2019): 753–770. Sophie of Hanover, for example, corresponded with Leibniz. Regarding her metaphysical and epistemological tendencies, see Christian Leduc, "Sophie of Hanover on the Soul-Body Relationship," in *Women and Philosophy in Eighteenth-Century Germany*, ed. Corey W. Dyck (Oxford: Oxford University Press, 2021), 11–28.

[2] For a possible exception in Spinoza's account of the Genesis narrative of the fall, see Hasana Sharp, "Eve's Perfection: Spinoza on Sexual (In)equality," *Journal for the History of Philosophy* 50, no. 4 (Oct. 2012): 559–580. On Hobbes's limited defense of natural maternal right and more, see Susanne Sreedhar, "Hobbes on 'The Woman Question,'" *Philosophy Compass* 7, no. 11 (2012): 772–781.

[3] I cite Spinoza according to common abbreviations. TP = *Political Treatise*, TTP = *Theological-Political Treatise*, and TIE = *Treatise on the Emendation of the Intellect*. Each is referenced by chapter and/or section number. I then utilize the following standard system of reference in citing the E = *Ethics*: app(-endix), c(-orollary), pref(-ace), p(-roposition), and s(-cholium). In addition, "d" stands either for "definition" (when it appears immediately to the right of the part number), or "demonstration" (in all other cases). Hence, E1d3 is the third definition of part 1 and E1p16d is the demonstration of the sixteenth proposition of part 1. I primarily utilize translations of Spinoza's *Ethics* by George Eliot (1819–1880), who was deeply engaged with both Spinoza and the modern German tradition. Translations of any other works of Spinoza are by Edwin Curley. I have amended translations in order to utilize gender-neutral pronouns when Spinoza's relevant claims bear on everyone or everything. Finally, I occasionally cite terms in the original Latin on the basis of Carl Gebhardt's edition of Spinoza's writings.

composing this final work a day earlier—but even if he had done so, Spinoza's earlier reference to "the inconstancy and frivolity of women and all the other much-decried vices of that sex" (E5p10s) would still stand out, along with his pejorative use of "womanish" and more.[4] On the basis of these data, at least, it might at first seem implausible that historical women philosophers, in the German-speaking context or otherwise, would have found inspiration in Spinoza's thought.

And yet here we are. Indeed despite his prejudices, Spinoza's thought and its legacy have proven to be a crucial intellectual resource for a wide range of women philosophers in the modern German tradition.[5] These figures have meanwhile built upon and challenged doctrines central to Spinozism in ways that anyone interested in its history—and indeed the history of modern European thought more generally—ought to contemplate. My focus in this chapter is on the German late eighteenth and early nineteenth centuries. I aim to show here that philosophical dialogues between Spinoza and women philosophers engaging with his thought around 1800, even if indirectly,[6] are especially exciting and understudied. Despite referencing a number of figures throughout the chapter in order to give a sense of just how much work there is to be done in this connection, I dedicate the most attention to Caroline Michaelis-Böhmer-Schlegel-Schelling (1763–1809) and Karoline von Günderrode (1780–1806). In furthering our grasp of these two thinkers so far as the legacy of Spinozism is concerned, I primarily try to sort out their development of ideals of *freedom*. I suggest that these ideals may productively be understood in relation to Spinoza's, but also in relation to one another, such that a kind of conversation around the subject of freedom takes place. In reconstructing a possible discussion and following a thematic thread, I aim to discover something about the liberatory thought not only of the women philosophers in question but also of Spinoza.

Throughout my engagement with these figures, I show that each belongs in discussions of the history of Spinozism in modern German thought—discussions which have developed immensely in recent years,[7] though not far enough. My focus

---

[4] For this use of "womanish" (*muliebris*)—or, per Curley's translation, "unmanly"—in Spinoza's *Ethics*, see E2p49s [IV.C.] or E4p37s1. See also TTP Pref 4 and compare Spinoza's use of "emasculate" (translation altered; *effoeminare*) at TTP III 55.

[5] I draw no distinction here between "philosophers," "thinkers," and so on. In brief, all of the figures I consider in this chapter are clearly philosophically minded—not just because of their links to Spinoza or Spinozism, but also beyond—and so warrant sustained attention on the part of historians of philosophy for this straightforward reason. Note also that I utilize the category "woman" somewhat naively in this context. Although all of the "women figures" I discuss in this chapter were largely regarded as such in their time and so undoubtedly demand engagement in this handbook, these thinkers were also sometimes considered masculine in various respects, and may have identified on their own terms in any number of more complicated ways (though I will not have space to discuss such matters here).

[6] Because this chapter is concerned with Spinozism generally, connections to Spinoza's writings themselves may be looser, or tighter, in various cases. For instance, even figures like Michaelis-Böhmer-Schlegel-Schelling, and Günderrode, who may have only indirect exposure to Spinoza via direct exposure to figures who engage with his writings in detail, require consideration as regards the legacy of Spinozism.

[7] Regarding themes in metaphysics and epistemology, see Eckart Förster and Yitzhak Y. Melamed, eds., *Spinoza and German Idealism* (Cambridge: Cambridge University Press, 2012). On Spinoza and

on the early nineteenth century should not be taken to indicate, however, that there is nothing to say about Spinoza and women philosophers in the German context prior to or following this period. Indeed I will begin by discussing two particularly fascinating thinkers who must be mentioned in precisely this context: Elise Reimarus (1735–1805) and Charlotte von Stein (1742–1827). In addition, in gradually concluding, I will point to some of the most notable engagements with Spinoza's thought toward the latter end of the nineteenth century and into the twentieth, via discussions of Lou Salomé (1861–1937), Resa von Schirnhofer (1855–1948), Anna Tumarkin (1875–1951), and Elisabeth Schmitt (1877–?). While the jump some decades ahead from the previous sections to this final one will leave out significant midcentury thinkers—for example, Fanny Lewald (1811–1889), who would otherwise be important to cover given my thematic focus here on freedom[8]—it will at the same time enable the chapter to consider a wide range of philosophers and their relation to Spinoza's legacy at the long nineteenth century's opening and then its close. This should offer a sense of the bigger picture.

1 PREDECESSORS: REIMARUS AND VON STEIN

Elise Reimarus (1735–1805) is involved in two of the eighteenth century's most consequential affairs that also bear on Spinoza or Spinozism, namely the so-called Fragments and Pantheism Controversies. In the former case, Reimarus and her brother permitted Gotthold Ephraim Lessing to publish, starting in 1774, their late father's rationalist critique of the Bible that was in harmony with Spinoza's thought in several respects; and in the latter case, Reimarus informed Moses Mendelssohn in 1783 of the fateful news that Lessing had, not long before his death, apparently let on a strong affinity for Spinoza's thought in discussions with Friedrich Jacobi. Jacobi now had the fuel he needed to start an antirationalist and counter-Enlightenment fire, for while Lessing was a respected Enlightenment thinker, Spinoza was an atheist pariah. Following correspondence between Reimarus, Jacobi, and Mendelssohn, Jacobi sparked a public controversy such that Lessing's comments were heard far and wide throughout the 1780s and beyond: "the orthodox concepts of the divinity are no longer for me; I cannot stomach them. *Hen kai*

---

more practical matters, see Jason M. Yonover and Kristin Gjesdal, eds., *Spinoza in Germany: Political and Religious Thought Across the Long Nineteenth Century* (Oxford: Oxford University Press, forthcoming).

[8] Lewald was a feminist thinker whose writings, literary and otherwise, engaged with a wide range of political issues. She was also highly sympathetic to Spinoza over an extended period of time, and for instance writes that early exposure to the pantheistic principle according to which "everything that exists is God!" had provided her "all at once [with] the supporting premise for the rest of my future life; the regulator for my thought, my love, my actions," etc. See *Meine Lebensgeschichte*, vol. 3, part 2 (Berlin: Verlag von Otto Janke, 1862), 243–250. For the translation I cite, as well as a brief discussion, see Margaret Ward, *Fanny Lewald: Between Rebellion and Renunciation* (New York: Peter Lang, 2006), 127.

pan [one-and-all]! . . . There is no other philosophy than the philosophy of Spinoza."[9] Finally, in addition to playing a role in these major disputes, Reimarus is likewise a critic of orthodox religion, an apologist for free thought, and yet also a prudent strategist, possibly sympathetic to Spinoza's motto "caution" (*caute*).[10]

Charlotte von Stein (1742–1827), once called a "student [Schülerin] of Spinoza,"[11] is likewise linked to the Pantheism Controversy, if from a greater distance. She reads Spinoza intensively with Johann Wolfgang von Goethe, whose work was prominently referenced in Jacobi's conversations with Lessing wherein Lessing declared his attraction to Spinoza's thought. Goethe develops some of his most important Spinozistic ideas in exchange with von Stein and they collaborate, perhaps partially with Karl Phillip Moritz,[12] on an untitled text referred to in the literature as the "Spinoza Study."[13] While authorship has often been attributed to Goethe, the manuscript is in von Stein's hand, and it is undoubtedly a product of their mutual exchange in the mid-1780s. Goethe seemingly wanted to downplay the importance of von Stein in this context, however; despite letters attesting to their sustained discussions of "our saint" Spinoza,[14] Goethe

---

[9] I try to cite widely available English-language editions of German-language texts throughout this chapter, but in any other case, translations from the German are my own. See the account of Lessing's statements in Friedrich Heinrich Jacobi, *The Main Philosophical Writings and the Novel Allwill*, ed. and trans. George di Giovanni (Montreal: McGill-Queen's University Press, 1994), 187. For a classic treatment, see Frederick C. Beiser, *The Fate of Reason: German Philosophy from Kant to Fichte* (Cambridge, MA: Harvard University Press, 1987), chap. 2.

[10] On Reimarus's writings, and on her role in the two affairs I reference, see chapter 16 in this handbook, as well as important new work by Reed Winegar, "Elise Reimarus: Reason, Religion, and Enlightenment," in *Women and Philosophy in Eighteenth-Century Germany*, ed. Corey W. Dyck (Oxford: Oxford University Press, 2021), 110–133, and "Elise Reimarus on Freedom and Rebellion," in *Practical Philosophy from Kant to Hegel: Freedom, Right, and Revolution*, ed. James Clarke and Gabriel Gottlieb (Cambridge: Cambridge University Press, 2021), 99–117.

[11] This characterization of von Stein appears in a short poetic text by Johann Gottfried von Herder. It was included with a gift of Spinoza's *Opera posthuma* to von Stein and also Goethe in 1784, on the occasion of both von Stein's birthday and Christmas. For a careful reading of Herder's four couplets and an insightful account of the broader context, see Jutta Eckle, "'Und Spinoza sei Euch immer ein heiliger Christ': Charlotte von Steins Beschäftigung mit Philosophie und Naturforschung im Austausch mit Johann Gottfried Herder und Johann Wolfgang von Goethe," in *Charlotte von Stein: Schriftstellerin, Freundin und Mentorin*, ed. Elke Richter and Alexander Rosenbaum (Berlin: de Gruyter, 2018), 339–355. On Herder, Spinoza, and German thought around 1800, see also Michael Forster, "The German Romantic Tradition and Spinoza's *Theological-Political Treatise*," in *Spinoza in Germany*, forthcoming.

[12] See Alessandro Costazza, "Ein Aufsatz aus der Zeit von Moritz' Weimarer Aufenthalt. Eine Revision der Datierung und der Zuschreibung von Goethes *Aus der Zeit der Spinoza-Studien*," *Goethe-Jahrbuch* 112 (1995): 259–274.

[13] The title "Studie nach Spinoza" was chosen by Rudolf Steiner, although the text was first published within Bernard Suphan, "Aus der Zeit der Spinoza-Studien Goethes. 1784–85," *Goethe-Jahrbuch* 12 (1891): 3–12.

[14] See Eckle, "Und Spinoza sei Euch immer ein heiliger Christ," 345, for discussion. For reference to the intensity of their readings focused on the *Ethics*, see also Goethe's 1784 letter to von Stein clarifying, in advance of a visit, that on this occasion he will bring with him "a Latin Spinoza," as "there everything is much clearer and more elegant." In *Goethe's Letters to Frau von Stein*, ed. and trans. Robert M. Browning (Columbia, SC: Camden House), 232. Von Stein and Goethe had initially studied Spinoza in German translation.

will later fail to mention von Stein in his autobiography as he reconstructs his engagement with Spinoza. Finally, and most urgently, von Stein's literary writings, including dramatic works like *Dido* (1794) or the *New System of Freedom* (1798), may have been influenced by her engagement with Spinoza, though they have been rather neglected by scholars in this respect and otherwise.

More work is needed on Reimarus, von Stein, and the relation of their thought to Spinoza and Spinozism. Indeed, Spinoza had become a central reference in German-language thought by 1800,[15] and as a result one may consider a number of thinkers of this era from such an angle. But over the next two sections, I focus on two figures whose thought may be understood in especially productive and complex relation to Spinoza, namely first Michaelis-Böhmer-Schlegel-Schelling and then Günderrode.

2 MICHAELIS-BÖHMER-SCHLEGEL-SCHELLING AND THE INTELLECTUAL-ETHICAL

Caroline Michaelis-Böhmer-Schlegel-Schelling (1763–1809) lived an eventful life; she experienced the French Revolution, imprisonment, an especially tragic loss of a child, and more. Among many other things, this life is documented in her correspondence, which is her primary textual legacy and the focus of my treatment here. I emphasize that her letter writing exhibits her deep interest in grasping especially these events, her intellectual milieu, and her relation to both. The form of the letter was often selected by (or also *for*) women writers in the period, given extensive gender censorship. But correspondence is well-suited to the project Michaelis-Böhmer-Schlegel-Schelling pursues, namely understanding her age and herself, to the end of living more freely—a project that, I argue, can productively be understood in Spinozistic terms. I additionally suggest in this section that the letter itself deserves further attention in accounts of Spinoza, if not also beyond.

While Michaelis-Böhmer-Schlegel-Schelling surely does not develop detailed metaphysical positions—and while she repeatedly presents herself in modest or even self-deprecating terms so far as intellectual matters are concerned (Eps. 219, 240, 317, etc.),[16]

---

[15] On Spinoza and German romanticism generally, for example, see Martin Bollacher, "Der Philosoph und die Dichter. Spiegelungen Spinozas in der deutschen Romantik," in *Spinoza in der europäischen Geistesgeschichte*, ed. Hanna Delf, Julius H. Schoeps, and Manfred Walther (Berlin: Edition Hentrich, 1994), 275–288.

[16] I cite Michaelis-Böhmer-Schlegel-Schelling's correspondence by letter number and according to the extraordinary online edition *Caroline: Letters from Early Romanticism*, ed. and trans. Douglas W. Stott, www.carolineschelling.com (2021). I have also consulted the German original: *Caroline. Briefe an ihre Geschwister, ihre Tochter Auguste, die Familie Gotter, F. L. W. Meyer, A. W. und Fr. Schlegel, F. Schelling u.a., nebst Briefen von A. W. und Fr. Schlegel u.a.*, 2 vols., ed. Georg Waitz (Leipzig: Verlag von S. Hirzel, 1871).

as is common among women thinkers in the period—she has a wide range of philosophical or literary tendencies, and indeed seems to have been attracted to the legacy of Spinoza's thought from early on. Consider the following two expressions of interest in Spinoza or Spinozism. First, already in 1786, she asks her sister to send a copy of Jacobi's controversial account of Spinoza published the prior year (Ep. 69). We have no direct evidence that Michaelis-Böhmer-Schlegel-Schelling, who felt geographically isolated throughout this period, in fact received this text she requested. However, she will some years later discuss Jacobi's *salto mortale*, or leap of faith, from a critical perspective (Ep. 240). Second, and relatedly, she writes to her sister the next year: "I would worship you if you could come up with Herder's *God* for me" (Ep. 74). Of course, she is in this passage promising gratitude; but she may also be playing with the result of pantheism, that is, the metaphysical view according to which everything is God. Versions of pantheism had been defended by Spinoza and then by Herder in his new, partially Spinozistic text *God: Some Conversations* (1787). Again, we cannot be sure Michaelis-Böhmer-Schlegel-Schelling studied this latter work. But she would grow very fond of Herder (Ep. 175), and on one reading of the pantheistic stance, if God is to be worshipped, and if God is all there is, then everything is potentially deserving of worship. Michaelis-Böhmer-Schlegel-Schelling could then mean in her letter that if pantheism is true, she may worship her sister, insofar as her sister is in a sense divine.

Such early reading requests prefigure exchanges Michaelis-Böhmer-Schlegel-Schelling will have about Spinoza's thought and its legacy with German romantics, for example Friedrich von Hardenberg, better known as Novalis, who writes to her about Spinoza's "divine spark of the understanding of nature" (Ep. 216). Although it remains unknown whether she ever engages with Spinoza's writings themselves, she is most explicit in an 1801 letter referencing in-depth discussions with Friedrich Wilhelm Joseph Schelling on recent work of his.[17] She begins by observing that "there is something truly blissful about learning to understand, when an obscure concept is illuminated and one finally beholds the serenity of the concept itself." Here she already seems to hint at Spinoza's ethical project, which I must consider in greater detail momentarily. But meanwhile, I shall gather further momentum to this end in noting that she continues unequivocally: "and how calm does it render one's disposition. Indeed, I do believe in the heaven in Spinoza's soul, whose one-and-all is doubtless that old primordial feeling [das alte Urgefühl] that is now also pushing toward the light in Schelling as well" (translation altered; Ep. 317).[18] She now invokes Spinoza by name alongside the shorthand for pantheism, that is, the "one-and-all" that Lessing referenced when he supposedly expressed

---

[17] Given this context that bears on the passage I explore momentarily, a fuller account of Michaelis-Böhmer-Schlegel-Schelling's relation to Spinoza and Spinozism would profit from a close look at Schelling's *Presentation of My System of Philosophy* (1801), which they read together "line by line." On Schelling's text and Spinoza, see Yitzhak Y. Melamed, "'*Deus sive Vernunft*': Schelling's Transformation of Spinoza's God," in *Schelling's Philosophy: Freedom, Nature, and Systematicity*, ed. G. Anthony Bruno (Oxford: Oxford University Press), 93–115.

[18] Compare two passages in Schelling that reference, respectively, the "primordial" and "peacefulness and calm," highlighted by Melamed, "*Deus sive Vernunft*," 96–97.

his sympathy for Spinoza to Jacobi. Her assertion of "belief" within this passage there-fore draws her directly into the legacy of Spinozism. And in addition to pointing at a Spinozistic pantheism here, she highlights the link between the intellectual and ethical dimensions of Spinoza's liberatory thought—"calm," "heaven," "soul"—if also in partly Christianized terms, not uncommon in the German romantic context.

It is now clear enough that a careful look at Michaelis-Böhmer-Schlegel-Schelling's letters shows she was attracted to Spinoza's ethical undertaking in some form—whether because of a direct encounter with his writings or, more likely, following engagement with contemporary debates around him. But, first: what does this Spinozistic project, with which she was at least indirectly familiar, really encompass? And second: how ex-actly might her stated interest in it manifest itself within her correspondence? I answer these two questions in turn.

First, according to Spinoza, our highest ethical achievement is freedom; but freedom is not anything like producing decisions in an originary manner. In tension with, for in-stance, traditional Cartesian accounts in the European philosophical tradition (at least on Spinoza's reading), Spinoza entirely rejects free will. Freedom for Spinoza is rather existing according to the necessity of one's nature or essence (E1d7).[19] Put more col-loquially, we may say that for Spinoza freedom is being oneself—and we may conjec-ture that Michaelis-Böhmer-Schlegel-Schelling would have known this, at least given her apparent sense of Jacobi's *Concerning the Doctrine of Spinoza in Letters to Herr Moses Mendelssohn* (orig. 1785) at the center of the Pantheism Controversy. In relevant passages of this work—passages another woman thinker of German romanticism, Rahel von Levin Varnhagen (1771–1833), once emphasized with enthusiasm[20]—Jacobi initially clarifies the *negative* dimension of Spinoza's stance on freedom, that is, Spinoza's rejec-tion of free will or the capacity to produce originary decisions. Jacobi rightly reports that Spinoza is "far from denying all freedom . . . but this freedom does not consist in a chi-merical faculty of being able to will." Jacobi then helpfully glosses the *positive* dimension of Spinoza's stance on freedom as well: "the human being's freedom is . . . the degree of their actual power or the force with which a human being is who they are."[21] This latter ideal of freedom that Spinoza thinks we can actually achieve—though it may initially seem obscure—is simply contrasted with choosing this or that, thrown out in the prior passage. True freedom instead consists in expressing oneself. According to Spinoza, the

---

[19] For more detail on Spinoza's notion of freedom, see Michael Della Rocca, *Spinoza* (New York: Routledge, 2008), 187–192.

[20] For Levin Varnhagen's citation of these passages in Jacobi on Spinoza, which she was "extraordinarily glad" to have found, see *Rahel. Ein Buch des Andenkens für ihre Freunde*, vol. 3 (Berlin: Duncker und Humblot, 1833), 150. Work remains to be done on Levin Varnhagen and Spinoza, given this and other references; but on Levin Varnhagen and her status as a Jew in the period, see Hannah Arendt, *Rahel Varnhagen: The Life of a Jewess*, ed. Liliane Weissberg, trans. Richard and Clare Winston (Baltimore: Johns Hopkins University Press, 1997), and Liliane Weissberg, "Stepping Out: The Writing of Difference in Rahel Varnhagen's Letters," in *New German Critique* 53 (Spring 1991): 149–162.

[21] For Jacobi's text in the translation I utilize—and alter slightly—see Jacobi, *Main Philosophical Writings*, 212.

reason we generally do *not* exist according to the necessity of our nature is that we rather exist according to the necessity of external influence, which estranges us from ourselves.

Spinoza's most relevant rationalist move on this basis is to argue something like the following. If we better understand the mechanisms that leave us in what he calls "bondage" (*servitus*) to harmful affects, then we can dampen their power as well as this alienation, and so live in a more suitable manner. This more suitable manner of living, characterized as free, is directly aligned with affirmative affects and power, as the more power we have, the less we are subject to the power of other things that prevent us from expressing ourselves. Spinoza therefore considers knowledge the highest good (*summum bonum*) because, at least according to the *Ethics*, it is most empowering; it allows us to position ourselves appropriately as we recognize how we are externally determined. This way, we can become internally determined in a manner suitable to ourselves. Doing so puts us in the position to reach the ethical summit, namely what Spinoza calls "liberty or blessedness of the soul" (E5pref)—perhaps the "freedom in Spinoza's soul" that Michaelis-Böhmer-Schlegel-Schelling references.

To this end, and with his alignment of knowledge, the affects, and power, Spinoza takes up a tranquil stance that resonates with the one evident in the correspondence of Michaelis-Böhmer-Schlegel-Schelling. In a striking passage, Spinoza proposes to "consider human actions and appetites as if the subject were lines, surfaces, or solids" (E3pref). The comparably composed perspective Michaelis-Böhmer-Schlegel-Schelling develops in her correspondence becomes explicit as early as 1778, in a letter to a friend. She states in clear terms that "I am not some dreamer or rapturous enthusiast, my thoughts are always the result of reflections that I undertake with—if at all possible—a completely cool disposition" (Ep. 4). In this context, she appears to be hinting at an alleged and in any case scandalous sexual encounter while dismissing chatter around herself concerning it. Her move seems to be to take some distance from a histrionic context in order to stand above it. Such an image of an incisive, resolute analyst then stays with us from this early letter over the next decades. In 1783, she criticizes the diaristic writing of a contemporary in the following terms: "she has managed to lift herself into a wonderfully lilting, poetic disposition, and nothing is more pardonable given that she is still so young;[22] but it does need to be moderated; her heart needs to be made more secure and her understanding sharper." The point is that affective reform and a deeper kind of peace is needed in order to grasp one's life and context. A serenity is required which would enable understanding or, she clarifies, "the ability to judge people and things according to their true (unpoetic) nature" (Ep. 35). Margaretmary Daley largely captures this inclination when she writes of Michaelis-Böhmer-Schlegel-Schelling's correspondence that, unlike the course of her life, "the letters are not filled with high drama and passion." Indeed, "on the contrary, [her] dominant emotion is restraint. Her letters portray an ongoing effort to bring order and tranquility to a life that often lacked those

---

[22]   Friederike Sophie Münter-Brun (1765–1835) is less than two years younger than Michaelis-Böhmer-Schlegel-Schelling, who is nineteen at the time of writing!

qualities."[23] Although in this evaluation Daley arguably understates the importance of affirmative affective expressions in the correspondence, for instance of expressions of joy, she is right that we only rarely encounter the various forms of sadness we might expect to encounter more frequently. Michaelis-Böhmer-Schlegel-Schelling thinks only a specific affective perspective will open up the world to successful understanding—and her pursuing this end as she does may be understood in Spinozistic terms, given the historical circumstances I have outlined.

Of course, Michaelis-Böhmer-Schlegel-Schelling was not the only thinker in the modern German-language tradition engaged with the legacy of Spinoza from this practical perspective.[24] For instance, as far as the late eighteenth century is concerned, the radical Jewish philosopher Salomon Maimon arguably pursued an aim related to hers in his likewise highly original *Autobiography* of 1792–1793, and before moving forward, I will quickly review one dimension of his ambitions in order to illuminate the discussion I have begun to develop. In short: Maimon is explicit about his provocative philosophical tendencies, including commitments to aspects of Spinozism, throughout his lifetime. For this reason and others, he too led a turbulent life. He was for instance rejected by leaders in the Jewish community in Berlin after his first arrival to the city—and this despite his thorough training in, as he put it, "understanding *God* and his works." Maimon, a rationalist who developed a significantly intellectualist ethics, documents such struggles throughout his *Autobiography*. But most significantly, in overcoming some of the obstacles to his philosophical training, he finds that he ends up with a deeper "understanding of *humanity*," playing on the previous formulation.[25] Notably, while a philosophical-anthropological impulse inspired Maimon to autobiographical writing, which enabled him to develop and share his social knowledge with an eager reading public, it may be said to have led Michaelis-Böhmer-Schlegel-Schelling to epistolary pursuits, which put her in the position to cultivate her comprehension of the present—albeit with a far greater degree of collaboration (i.e., with the help of her correspondents). Although Maimon may be compared with her in that he too pursues a social understanding of his milieu to intellectual-ethical ends,[26] her focus on correspondence with the aim of developing a grasp of their era then breaks genre barriers that Maimon likewise explored.

---

[23] Margaretmary Daley, *Women of Letters: A Study of Self and Genre in the Personal Correspondence of Caroline Schlegel-Schelling, Rahel Levin Varnhagen, and Bettina von Arnim* (Columbia, SC: Camden House, 1998), 21.

[24] Nor was she the first to question the geometric order that characterizes Spinoza's *Ethics* as well as Schelling's *Presentation*, which takes the former as a model; but see Eps. 294 and 317 for interesting remarks on these matters.

[25] Emphasis mine. Salomon Maimon, *The Autobiography of Salomon Maimon*, ed. Yitzhak Y. Melamed and Abraham P. Socher, trans. Paul Reitter (Princeton: Princeton University Press, 2019), 108.

[26] For some further discussion of this Spinozistic dimension of Maimon's autobiographical writing, see my "Salomon Maimon's 'History in Dialogues,'" *Nexus: Essays in German-Jewish Studies* (2023): 191–216. On Maimon and Spinoza's epistemology, see also my "Goethe, Maimon, and Spinoza's Third Kind of Cognition," in *Goethe Yearbook* 25 (2018): 267–287.

Recognizing this also helps us to recognize the fascinating project developed throughout Michaelis-Böhmer-Schlegel-Schelling's letters. In them, she certainly keeps up-to-date with friends and family or resolves practical matters. But she additionally interrogates her time with uncommon force, attempting to understand it and live more freely throughout it via this understanding. The distinguished historian of philosophy Kuno Fischer may have grasped this most distinctly at the turn of the nineteenth century in explaining that "she is not merely a master, but genuinely a genius in letter writing; *her letters are completely herself . . . and, should the moment or subject matter so dictate, also just as substantial and profound.*"[27] Fischer formulates this perceptive claim in an extended treatment of Schelling and not primarily Michaelis-Böhmer-Schlegel-Schelling, then quickly leaves it behind. Yet his insight that an outstanding form of self-expression—and so in Spinozistic terms: freedom—obtains by way of her correspondence seems exactly right.[28]

Finally, the fact that one may pursue Spinoza's intellectual-ethical project in epistolary form may also help us learn more about Spinoza. While he *explicitly* undertakes self-reflection only on rare occasion,[29] one might wonder to what degree he *implicitly* develops a grasp on his thinking and his context throughout his own letter writing. Spinoza's correspondence is a major part of his (relatively thin) textual legacy, and he maintains an emphasis on the value of society in his main works. While he has sometimes been caricatured as a lone thinker grinding away at lenses, in fact he profited immensely from his exchanges with members of an intimate circle as well as additional interlocutors. Spinoza is indeed unambiguous in arguing that "there is nothing more useful to a human being than another human being" (translation altered; E4p18s)—stressing the significance of *others* to what may nonetheless still be considered *self-expression*, or as some commentators would have it: even superseding orthodox notions of individuality in favor of a deeply relational perspective. Although Spinoza's systematic ambitions are well-known and stand in obvious contrast to the approach of Michaelis-Böhmer-Schlegel-Schelling, we do have straightforward evidence that Spinoza works out technical philosophical matters in letters. Such exchanges then help him to settle his stances on fundamental issues, for example, how to define substance and attribute.[30]

---

[27] Emphasis mine. Kuno Fischer, *Geschichte der neuern Philosophie*, vol. 6 (Heidelberg: Bassermann, 1872), 89. Cited according to the translation by Stott (2021). Although I cannot investigate Fischer's own philosophical sympathies here, it is worth noting—given Michaelis-Böhmer-Schlegel-Schelling's interest in pantheism, discussed earlier—that he was accused of pantheism in 1853 and lost his permission to teach for some time. See Martin Bollacher, "Pantheismus," *Online Lexikon Naturphilosophie* (2020), 7.

[28] See Sara Friedrichsmeyer, "Caroline Schlegel-Schelling: 'A Good Woman, and No Heroine,'" in *In the Shadow of Olympus: German Women Writers around 1800*, ed. Katherine R. Goodman and Edith Waldstein (Albany: State University of New York Press, 1992), 115–136, for further and especially insightful discussion of the status of correspondence in Michaelis-Böhmer-Schlegel-Schelling.

[29] For example, in an important autobiographical reflection, describing his intellectual path, Spinoza says: "after experience taught me that all the things which regularly occur in ordinary life are empty and futile . . ." (TIE 1).

[30] There exist relatively few recent studies on Spinoza's early geometric formulations of his thought, e.g., Ep. 2, where Spinoza's definitions of substance and attribute are the reverse of what will eventually appear in E1d3–4. See also Ep. 4 and Yitzhak Y. Melamed, "A Glimpse into Spinoza's Metaphysical

Additional discussion of these phenomena is in order, as is more extensive analysis of Michaelis-Böhmer-Schlegel-Schelling's letter writing and her broader, at least partially Spinozistic aims—perhaps with reference to her work in literary criticism and beyond, too.

3 Günderrode and the Practical-Liberatory

As with Michaelis-Böhmer-Schlegel-Schelling, in moving on to Karoline von Günderrode (1780–1806) in this section I start off by securing a link to Spinozism. I then begin to discuss the possible significance of this—also for Spinoza. Ultimately, I draw on several of Günderrode's philosophical and literary texts to the end of arguing that she may again be understood as engaged with the liberatory dimension of Spinozism, even if in an interestingly different way that poses a challenge to aspects of Spinoza's account of death in particular.

Although as before we cannot speak of direct exposure to Spinoza's works with any certainty,[31] nonetheless several important parallels are worth noting to begin. They have received little scholarly attention,[32] but these links between Spinoza's thought and Günderrode's may already have been evident during her brief life. An intimate partner, Frederich Creuzer, once writes to her, for instance, remarking upon the "gravity of your interest in philosophy" and encouraging her to "proceed in letting yourself be seized by the great spirit that blows through . . . Spinoza."[33] This could indicate that Günderrode had undertaken studies of Spinoza's writings (alongside works we know she read closely by other figures, for example Johann Gottlieb Fichte and Frans Hemsterhuis). Regardless, Günderrode seems to have been indirectly familiar with and partial to key features of Spinozism, as is evident from texts such as her "Apocalyptical Fragment." Here Günderrode generally develops brief metaphysical reflections concerning a range of themes. But more specifically, the conclusion of this text features what appear to

---

Laboratory: The Development of the Concepts of Substance and Attribute," in *The Young Spinoza: A Metaphysician in the Making*, ed. Melamed (Oxford: Oxford University Press, 2015), 274–276.

[31] Günderrode did in any case copy down a passage from Spinoza's Ep. 43 ("The reward of virtue is virtue itself, whereas the punishment of folly and weakness is folly itself"), which she encountered in a volume presenting quotations from the works of major thinkers. See Max Preitz and Doris Hopp, eds., "Karoline von Günderrode in ihrer Umwelt. III. Karoline von Günderrodes Studienbuch," *Jahrbuch des freien deutschen Hochstifts* (1975), 266.

[32] On a broader range of issues concerning Günderrode and Spinoza than I can consider here, see Joanna Raisbeck, *Karoline von Günderrode: Philosophical Romantic* (Cambridge: Legenda, 2022), arguing that Günderrode is "the most consistent thinker of Spinozist pantheism."

[33] In the elided text, Friedrich Creuzer references also first "the works of Schelling" and then "some of the ancient philosophers." Karoline von Günderrode, *Sämtliche Werke und ausgewählte Studien*, vol. 3, ed. Walter Morgenthaler et al. (Basel: Stroemfeld/Roter Stern, 1991), 344.

be especially strong echoes of Spinoza's metaphysics: "therefore, who has ears to hear, let them hear! It is not two, nor three, nor a thousand, but one-and-all; it is not body and spirit separately, one belonging to time, the other to eternity, but one, belonging to itself."[34] First, we have in this text reference again to the "one-and-all," which I have emphasized was frequently employed as shorthand for Spinoza's pantheism around 1800, following Lessing's well-known use of the locution. Hence, although Günderrode was attracted to several forms of pantheism—and more work is needed on her engagement with Indian philosophy in particular—this reference very likely speaks for an at least indirect familiarity with Spinoza. Second, we have here not just vague mention of a monism according to which all that is is God, namely pantheism, but something more precise. According to Spinoza's monism, there is one substance (compare Günderrode's "not two, nor three"). That substance is eternal despite its expression also in the transitory (consider Günderrode's "one ... at once, time and eternity"). And it has two known attributes, namely thought and extension (note, finally, Günderrode's analogous "spirit" and "body"). In other words, we have in the case of this passage possible evidence of several shared commitments. The historical fact of the letter from Creuzer, along with this gloss of Günderrode's metaphysical tendencies expressed in the "Apocalyptical Fragment," should already suffice to raise the following question: what consequence might an attraction to substance monism and more have for Günderrode as she develops accounts of, among other things, being oneself, and so freedom (the guiding thread of this chapter)?

In order to answer this question, I turn to Günderrode's *Hildgund* (1805), a dramatic fragment featuring an eponymous female protagonist at odds with and initially held captive by Attila the Hun. Following Hildgund's escape and return her homeland, Burgundy, he threatens war. Hildgund's betrothed, Walter, vows to fight as Hildgund exclaims and poses the following 'decisive' question:

> Woman's destiny, ah! does not rest in her own hand!
> Now she follows need, now strict custom's will,
> Can one revoke what superior power commands?[35]

In briefly developing an account of the dramatic fragment hereafter, I propose that the text answers *negatively* the question Hildgund poses. Günderrode accordingly denies or at least deemphasizes here the prospects of the kind of libertarian free will that I have associated (following Spinoza) with Descartes and contrasted with Spinoza's freedom of self-expression. Furthermore, I suggest that through *Hildgund* Günderrode *positively* presents her reader with the idea that one can be subject to "what superior power

---

[34] Translation altered. "Apocalyptical Fragment," in Bettina von Arnim, *Correspondence of Fräulein Günderode and Bettine von Arnim*, trans. Margaret Fuller and Minna Wesselhoeft (Boston: Burnham, 1861), 13.

[35] Karoline von Günderrode, *Poetic Fragments*, ed. and trans. Anna C. Ezekiel (Albany: State University of New York Press, 2016), 76. Hereafter I provide in-text citations of *Hildgund*.

commands" according to the necessity of one's nature—or in Günderrode's more literary terms: one's "fate"—and find liberation in that. This secures a link to Spinoza not just regarding what Günderrode may see as unviable (namely free will, or the capacity to produce originary decisions), but also regarding what she then seems more attracted to (namely freedom understood as being oneself).

Upon hearing the threat of invasion, Hildgund quickly grants that she must obey Attila's "command" and rejects Walter's proposition of war. Hildgund's father has already left the stage, apparently having expected no other result. But we soon find out that Hildgund plans to murder Attila the night she returns to his camp, amid celebrations of her "choice" to "accept" his marriage proposal. Hildgund affirms that "the people's *destiny* rests in [her] breast," and that she "will free them, free me," precisely by accepting her lot—by returning to Attila, though to assassinate him (translation altered; 68). In contrast to, say, Antigone, Hildgund harmonizes in this tragedy the various ethical demands at hand; but very much like Antigone, Hildgund pursues her ethical mission to its end that is arguably a kind of suicide, even though the fragment is in the end unclear on this matter, as the final results of her planned actions are not detailed.[36] Hildgund in any case thereby stresses her self-determination throughout, even given prominent external influence, but in an unexpected manner.

Recall that, for Spinoza, freedom is existing in the one substance there is, and specifically according to the necessity of one's nature—that is, existing in a manner that expresses one's self, despite, or perhaps rather with, the causal forces that be. Günderrode's highest norms likewise bear on self-realization, and not just of the individual, but also of some greater unity. In her "Idea of the Earth" she defines beauty, for instance, as "being the same as oneself and harmonious"; truth, justice, and love then each bear on "the All" as it tries to achieve self-identity, with "the particular" playing various roles to this end, not least because the particular then also "survives immortally" within the all.[37] Hildgund's achievement in this connection may be seen as her fitting into the world such that it also fits her, where this world or her kingdom is able to flourish—which is to say: improve as regards metrics like beauty and justice. Keeping in mind Günderrode's sympathy with several metaphysical commitments essential to Spinozism, we can understand her to be exploring this notion of self-expression within the All through the figure of Hildgund, who recognizes what must happen and finds her power and liberation in this. Although Hildgund cannot quite choose freely, and both she and her father promptly seem to sense she must concede to Attila, she can still act as is necessary in her 'own' way. Arguably, Günderrode's heroine thereby secures a Spinozistic freedom and contributes to the development of the self-identity that Günderrode sees us tasked to accomplish, not just for some individual's sake—Hildgund's individuality is after all highly relational, not least as

---

[36] On Antigone and the drama of politics, see my "Hegel on Tragedy and the World-Historical Individual's Right of Revolutionary Action," in *Hegel on Tragedy and Comedy: New Essays*, ed. Mark Alznauer (Albany: State University of New York Press, 2021), 241–264.

[37] Günderrode, "Idea of the Earth," 83.

she is a *member* of the community that is Burgundy—but for the sake of the whole or "All."

In pointing to the potential importance of this Spinozistic intellectual context, we help satisfy an important demand that has arisen in the literature on Günderrode. Of course, we certainly go beyond any simplistic biographical reading of *Hildgund* as an imagined revenge Günderrode would wish to take on some of her historical contemporaries; as Joanna Raisbeck emphasizes following Susanne Kord, biographism has long been an issue with respect to Günderrode.[38] But more importantly, we assist in filling a lacuna identified by recent scholarly work on Günderrode, too. Christine Battersby has stressed Günderrode's "longing to re-join the earth and simultaneously dissolve her identity into fluidity" such that she can be understood as seeking "an individuality that is in harmony with, and permeated by, the opposing forces that together constitute Nature."[39] Anna C. Ezekiel has followed up on this latter dimension of Günderrode's thought in particular, again without reference to Spinoza, albeit perceptively noting that for Günderrode "freedom, if it exists, must in some way include the influence of external forces on one's actions."[40] However: it is not immediately clear how one might meet these sundry philosophical demands, especially given Günderrode's apparent deemphasis on free will, or the capacity to produce originary decisions, in *Hildgund* and other works. This leaves at least some distance between Günderrode and several of her philosophical interlocutors.[41] But while we should by no means then simply assimilate Günderrode's ideals of self-expression to Spinoza's, I have suggested that freedom and necessity are compatible for both, and in related ways. Freedom arguably even demands necessity, insofar as the former means accepting the latter and yet also remaining or becoming oneself in it. Meanwhile, freedom of will remains impossible, at least for Spinoza (if not also Günderrode), or certainly out of the question given social conditions, at least for Günderrode (as well as her woman protagonist).[42]

[38] See Susanne Kord, *Sich einen Namen machen. Anonymität und weibliche Autorschaft. 1700–1900* (Stuttgart: J. B. Metzler, 1996), 147, cited in Joanna Raisbeck, "Von Mythem umrankt," *Litlog. Göttinger eMagazin für Literatur—Kultur—Wissenschaft*, <www.litlog.de/von-mythen-umrankt>, accessed May 2021. Published July 6, 2019.

[39] Christine Battersby, *The Sublime, Terror and Human Difference* (London: Routledge, 2007), 120f.

[40] Anna C. Ezekiel, "Metamorphosis, Personhood, and Power in Karoline von Günderrode," *European Romantic Review* 25, no. 6 (2014): 782.

[41] For Günderrode's critique of one important contemporary in this connection, see her "On Fichte's *The Vocation of Humankind*," in Dalia Nassar and Kristin Gjesdal, eds., *Women Philosophers in the Long Nineteenth Century: The German Tradition* (New York: Oxford University Press, 2021), 73, note 21: "My best will does not work in the world if I do not have the opportunity to show it in acts [and] if I do not have this opportunity, what is it worth . . . ?" Dalia Nassar, "The Human Vocation and the Question of the Earth: Karoline von Günderrode's Philosophy of Nature," *Archiv für Geschichte der Philosophie* vol. 104, no. 1, 2022, 108–130, discusses this passage and Günderrode's notion of "opportunity" in a similar spirit, albeit in context and in greater detail.

[42] One of Günderrode's most crucial interlocutors will go so far as to write, addressing Günderrode: "No earth-destiny [Erdenschicksal] interests me, because I have yet no freedom to guide it." Von Arnim, *Correspondence of Fräulein Günderode and Bettine von Arnim*, 37.

In highlighting the importance of such circumstances and taking a marked interest in political developments, it seems that Günderrode would then be more interested in the practical potential of a Spinozistic liberatory quest than Michaelis-Böhmer-Schlegel-Schelling. There can be no doubt that Günderrode thoroughly enjoyed her intellectual work and found meaning or even freedom in it, possibly in what could be considered a Spinozistic spirit. But Günderrode's captivating concern in *Hildgund* and related texts is not chiefly intellectual development. It is rather the acquisition of agency by more worldly means,[43] which Michaelis-Böhmer-Schlegel-Schelling eventually sets aside in at least some sense.[44] This practical impulse in *Hildgund* is likewise evident in Günderrode's *Muhammad, the Prophet of Mecca* (1805), which investigates the force of religion, among other things exploring the idea that "where no deed is, there is no power."[45] Such a realist political interest may or may not be a result of necessitarian leanings that could exclude mere potentiality for Günderrode, who repeatedly has her protagonist deny any capacity to produce originary decisions.[46] But her political perspective is in any case in harmony with one compelling dimension of Spinoza's thought that also stresses the importance not of potentiality but of activity, without which power cannot obtain.

Having pointed to these parallels, we must additionally note that Günderrode can definitively be seen as standing in direct tension with Spinoza in at least one major respect, indeed still regarding her notion of power—insofar as she positively reevaluates the metaphysical status of death. I have noted that, strictly speaking, it remains unclear in *Hildgund* whether Günderrode's heroine survives the assassination she has contentedly planned. Does she then try to escape, and if so, does she succeed? Günderrode leaves the narrative open at a crucial juncture, encouraging her reader to define its conclusion as they must, on the basis of their own circumstances—arguably itself the perfect nudge toward freedom as self-expression. Still, although there can be no certainty here, it at least remains very probable that Hildgund's assassination tactic is to be understood as a *fatal* and nevertheless *empowering* one. Among other things, Hildgund has initially stressed Attila's military might in conversation with her father (60). And more generally, Günderrode carries out a robust reconsideration of death in her "Apocalyptical Fragment" as well as numerous other writings. Note that Günderrode affirms in the

---

[43] On a number of issues pertaining to the practical dimension of Günderrode's thought, see Anna C. Ezekiel, "Revolution and Revitalization: Karoline von Günderrode's Political Philosophy and its Metaphysical Foundations," *British Journal for the History of Philosophy* 30, no. 4 (2022).

[44] Michaelis-Böhmer-Schlegel-Schelling had explicit political interests earlier on, which would for instance encourage her exchange with Therese Heyne-Forster-Huber (1764–1829) and Georg Forster, a prominent supporter of revolutionary France in Mainz. This affiliation then led to her imprisonment, and she will later write to a friend in 1793 that she is now "deaf and uninterested with regard to anything political" (Ep. 129). Nonetheless, this is not to say that she abandoned her earlier political tendencies and swung in the other direction, like various Jena romantics on whom she once had a progressive influence.

[45] Günderrode, *Poetic Fragments*, 160. Compare "The Idea of the Earth," in *Women Philosophers in the Long Nineteenth Century*, 82: "a force without some sort of effect, is not comprehensible."

[46] See, for instance, Muhammad's stress on "the providence of God." *Poetic Fragments*, 216.

former text a "release from being" whereby she would be "feeling myself in all, enjoying all in myself."[47] As Amy Jones puts it, "living fully, in her understanding, can include dying."[48]

This possibility of a transition from life into death via joy and ultimately freedom, if properly identified, creates a major tension in Spinoza's thought. Spinoza would not only have an extraordinarily hard time conceiving of suicide as empowering; he cannot even make sense of it at all, strictly speaking. For Spinoza, who must be considered an eliminativist in this respect, suicide per se is impossible—let alone allegedly self-affirming, liberatory suicide. According to Spinoza's *conatus* principle, "[e]very thing . . . strives to persevere in its existence" (E3p6), and perhaps still more urgent, "[n]othing can be destroyed but by an external cause" (E3p4). Spinoza draws from such commitments the conclusion that "no one therefore, unless they be vanquished by external causes, contrary to their nature, neglects to seek what is useful to themselves or to preserve their being" (E4p20s). In other words, for Spinoza, cases of so-called suicide are really just cases of someone yielding. And yet Günderrode, who herself committed suicide at the age of twenty-six and was outspoken about it for years prior, suggests both in *Hildgund* and elsewhere that suicide may not only be possible, but also perfectly in line with one's essence and self-determined. In her "Story of a Brahmin" too, for instance, the protagonist enters into dialogue with an interlocutor who criticizes in ethical terms taking leave of society, considering it a kind of suicide, and the protagonist responds: "as much as the outer development of human beings differs, their inner natures differ just as much."[49] In other words, according to the view suggested by this text, suicide could be the true fulfillment of someone's nature.

Günderrode's reconceptualization of death, and on the basis of a comparable but in the end clearly also divergent monist metaphysics, puts significant pressure on Spinoza. Most urgent is that for Günderrode (and some of her Spinozistic interlocutors like Herder),[50] death is not strictly speaking an end; one's "elements" and influence can form other beings, resulting in a kind of posthumous life.[51] Spinoza made no room for any notion of reincarnation, even along the lines of a more naturalistic "ecosystem theory" on which life and death are intimately intertwined.[52] But Günderrode's views are arguably warranted in a strictly monistic and indeed pantheistic context wherein also degrees of existence play a major role.

---

[47] Von Arnim, *Correspondence of Fräulein Günderode and Bettine von Arnim*, 13.

[48] Amy Jones, "Vampirism Inverted: Pathology, Gender, and Authorship in Karoline von Günderrode's 'Die Bande der Liebe,'" in *Writing the Self, Creating Community: German Women Authors and the Literary Sphere 1750–1850*, ed. Elisabeth Krimmer and Lauren Nossett (Columbia, SC: Camden House, 2020), 143.

[49] Günderrode, *Sämtliche Werke*, vol. 1, 307.

[50] See Gabriel Trop, "Karoline von Günderrode's Aesthetics of *Naturphilosophie*" (unpublished manuscript) for further discussion.

[51] Günderrode, "The Idea of the Earth," 82–83.

[52] I borrow this helpful terminology from Karen Ng. See chapter 23 in this handbook.

Spinoza may in fact have been aware of such tensions in his thought, even regarding the possibility of self-expressing self-sacrifice. As I have shown, what might be called Spinoza's 'bias to existence' is on full display in his *Ethics*, where he goes so far as to claim that a "free person thinks of nothing less than of death" (E4p67). Yet, elsewhere he notes that "people who know themselves [se norunt] to be honorable . . . think it honorable, not a punishment, to die for a good cause, and glorious to die for freedom" (TTP XX 36). While in the former passage Spinoza seems to indicate that death can have no positive value with respect to his ideals, the latter passage hints that one could self-consciously, perhaps even self-*knowingly*, "die . . . for freedom." Following Günderrode, further work ought to pursue the significance of this prospect in Spinoza in more detail, perhaps with additional consideration of his own early self-identified rejection of the sensual.[53] Nevertheless, it is clear that Spinoza will not go so far as Günderrode, whose "The Pilgrims" (1805) has a lyrical I probe with great intensity: "what is the magnificence of the world / And all, that pleases the senses?" before continuing: "I will *gladly* renounce it."[54]

4 Successors and Conclusion

These treatments of Michaelis-Böhmer-Schlegel-Schelling and Günderrode should encourage further work on the relevance of Spinoza or Spinozism to each. But they should also motivate more general discussion of the direct or indirect engagement with Spinoza's thought that is so widespread among modern women philosophers in the German tradition. Before concluding with some remarks regarding that general tendency, I open this section by pointing ahead into the later nineteenth and early twentieth centuries.

Lou Salomé (1861–1937) may not have been familiar with Günderrode, but the following affirmative claims made from her deathbed, having just been read passages from her own work, might lead us to wonder: "yes, I would still say it that way today," and "everything was good, every part of it"—but "the best is indeed death."[55] These comments were made in Göttingen, where she lived out the last years of her life, and so one might likewise grow curious whether she could have been aware of Michaelis-Böhmer-Schlegel-Schelling, a relatedly controversial since 'free-spirited' woman figure

---

[53] See again TIE 1.

[54] Emphasis mine; Günderrode, *Poetic Fragments*, 116–117.

[55] Cited by Brigid Haines, "'Ja, so würde ich es auch heute noch sagen': Reading Lou Andreas-Salomé in the 1990s," *Publications of the Goethe Society* 62 (1991): 77–95. Salomé had developed interests in the negative side to desire already some decades prior, and carried out important work within the psychoanalytic context on narcissism in connection with novel theories of the death drive. On this and more, see the wide-ranging clarificatory discussion in Tracie Matysik, *Reforming the Moral Subject: Ethics and Sexuality in Central Europe, 1890–1930* (Ithaca: Cornell University Press, 2008), chap. 7.

who was born and raised in that city. But in any case, there can be no doubt that Salomé was heavily impacted by an early encounter with Spinoza, and that this led to a long-term interest in his thought. I will first clarify Salomé's own testimony as well as several historical circumstances. Salomé writes that Spinoza was "the one thinker" she approached in her childhood, claiming: "think far enough, correctly enough on any point at all and you hit upon him; you meet him waiting for you, standing ready at the side of the road."[56] It seems Salomé first encountered Spinoza via her early tutor Henrik Gillot, alongside whom she developed a remarkable interest in philosophy. Spinoza then continues to attract Salomé's interest throughout various periods of her thinking. It is possible—indeed extremely likely—that she would have discussed Spinoza with Friedrich Nietzsche and Paul Rée, who were also both engaged with his thought, if perhaps less directly;[57] the three formed a tight trio for some time, and Salomé later lived with Rée. When she eventually moves to Vienna to pursue her work alongside Sigmund Freud, she again reads Spinoza and proposes that he is the "philosopher of psychoanalysis."[58] Since Salomé's interest in Spinoza extends over such a long period, it should come as no surprise that the nature of her engagement with his thought varies widely. But a link to Spinoza's notion of freedom is certainly possible once again, with reference to Salomé's account of liberation that responds to the feminisms of her time. Although Salomé is no antifeminist, she does develop a significant critique of contemporary "so-called women's emancipation movements." She proposes, in tension with some contemporaries, that women "look for themselves in their uniqueness with respect to men, and initially entirely in this," for as long as they do not, "they also will not realize just how extensively and how powerfully they can unfold in the development of their nature." In short: "women are still insufficiently themselves, insufficiently women."[59] This line is complicated by Salomé's thinking in other texts, which demand further attention;[60] but it should certainly also remind us of Spinoza's theory of freedom as self-expression.

[56] Lou Andreas-Salomé, *The Freud Journal of Lou Andreas-Salomé*, trans. Stanley A. Leavy (New York: Basic Books, 1964), 77.

[57] On Nietzsche and Spinoza, see my "Nietzsche, Spinoza, and Etiology (On the Example of Free Will)," *European Journal of Philosophy* 29, no. 2 (2021): 459–474, as well as my "Nietzsche and Spinoza," in *A Companion to Spinoza*, ed. Yitzhak Y. Melamed (Oxford: Wiley-Blackwell, 2021), 527–537. Rée's deterministic views presented in *The Illusion of Free Will* (1885) coincide with Spinoza's on many fronts, and Rée knew this; for instance, he references Spinoza several times in his earlier work *The Origin of Moral Sensations* (1877), available in Rée, *Basic Writings*, ed. and trans. Robin Small (Urbana: University of Illinois Press, 2003).

[58] Salomé, *Freud Journal*, 77.

[59] Lou Andreas-Salomé, *Aufsätze und Essays*, vol. 2, ed. Hans-Rüdiger Schwab (Taching: MedienEdition Welsch, 2014), 35.

[60] See Raleigh Whitinger, introduction to *The Human Family* by Lou Andreas-Salomé, ed. and trans. Whitinger (Lincoln: University of Nebraska Press, 2005), ix, for some discussion.

Like Salomé, Resa von Schirnhofer (1855–1948) studied at Zürich, the first university in the German-speaking context to officially accept women students, and would end up leaving academia. She seems to have ultimately sustained herself by teaching languages and piano.[61] But prior to this, and unlike Salomé, von Schirnhofer was able to complete the doctoral degree. Her dissertation was published under the title *A Comparison of the Thought of Schelling and Spinoza* (1889). The study carefully works out the relation between the two thinkers, with a general emphasis on issues in metaphysics and epistemology, and particular stress on Schelling's "identity philosophy."

Von Schirnhofer anticipates especially two academic philosophers who must be mentioned. Anna Tumarkin (1875–1951) wrote her doctorate at Bern, and was then the first woman professor of philosophy in Europe to secure an academic appointment that involved taking part in defenses and more. Although she is occasionally acknowledged for these achievements,[62] her wide-ranging work on Spinoza and many themes in the history of philosophy, aesthetics, and beyond is rarely if ever appreciated. Tumarkin's *Spinoza: Eight Lectures Held at the University of Bern* (1908) stands out, given its attempt to reconstruct Spinoza on his own terms, against marked neo-Kantian tendencies in this period.

Finally, Elisabeth Schmitt (1877–?), although she was not in the position to pursue an extensive academic career like Tumarkin, wrote a remarkable dissertation at Heidelberg on one of the thorniest issues in Spinoza's thought, again despite then-prominent philosophical pressures that would have cast suspicion on such metaphysical investigations. Her study *Spinoza's Infinite Modes* (1910) has been neglected but remains relevant to discussions in the literature, given both its extensive exploration of the development of the so-called infinite modes across Spinoza's works, as well as its treatment of their systematic importance as regards a range of issues in Spinoza's metaphysics, epistemology, and beyond. Schmitt's dissertation was well-received by her primary evaluator; Wilhelm Windelband writes, concluding a detailed assessment available in Heidelberg at the university library archives, that her dissertation establishes "a highly notable contribution to the interpretation of Spinoza's system," and recommends "most warmly" that she be awarded the doctorate.[63] Windelband likewise notes that her studies were unfortunately interrupted by "sickliness" and "domestic circumstances," each of which may go some

---

[61] Hans Lohberger, "Friedrich Nietzsche und Resa von Schirnhofer," *Zeitschrift für philosophische Forschung* 22, no. 2 (1968): 28.

[62] Tumarkin's status here is also sometimes neglected. Although she had advanced to a nearly full appointment as professor of philosophy at the University of Bern already in 1909, sitting on the University Senate and more, Jeanne Hersch (1910–2000) is referred to as the first woman professor of philosophy in Switzerland in, for instance, resources published by the Karl Jaspers Foundation. I am grateful to Ursula Pia Jauch for noting this. See, e.g., "Jeanne Hersch," https://jaspers-stiftung.ch/de/die-karl-jaspers-stiftung-1/biographie-jeanne-hersch .

[63] I am deeply grateful to Luce deLire and Florian Ehrensperger for their help in gaining access to and transcribing these documents in H-IV-757/4. Schmitt's work was also praised by an important early academic woman philosopher in the United States; see the discussion by Ellen Bliss Talbot (1867–1968) in *The Philosophical Review* 20, no. 6 (1911): 666–668.

distance to explaining her exit from university life.[64] Of course, Schmitt's presence as an academic woman philosopher would also have been tremendously unusual given structural barriers (whose effects are felt up until this day). Certain institutions proved more progressive than others, but it was only starting in 1909—the year Schmitt completed her PhD—that women could initiate studies at all German universities. It should then come as no surprise that surviving documents concerning her enrollment regularly utilize the masculine honorific in print (e.g., "Mr. ___" to list surname); in such cases, this is then generally corrected by hand as the form is filled out (e.g., "M̶r̶. Ms. *Schmitt*"). Not much is known of Schmitt's path following the degree at Heidelberg, but she remained connected to the city for at least some years. She gave weekly lectures at the Institute for Women's Education and Study (Verein Frauenbildung-Frauenstudium) in Heidelberg for some time, introducing the history of modern philosophy to listeners— alongside courses on how to care for an infant, for example, offered by a male medical doctor.[65]

It should now be evident that the engagement with Spinozism among modern women thinkers in the German tradition considered here is as strong as the pronounced interest in Spinoza among more canonical figures—though the literature has yet to explore such a phenomenon. Furthermore, although this has not been my focus in this chapter, the interest in Spinoza among commonly discussed male German thinkers is in many cases mediated through, and possibly anticipated by, women philosophers. Michaelis-Böhmer-Schlegel-Schelling, for instance, arguably prefigures Goethe where he writes of the "peaceful effect [Spinoza] had produced in me" in his autobiography begun after 1810;[66] and in any case, Goethe's reading of Spinoza was of course itself developed in conjunction with von Stein.

In this chapter, I have only just begun exploring plausible engagements with Spinoza or Spinozism among several of the most notable women philosophers in the modern German tradition, in some cases for the first time. I have stressed the apparent significance of the ethical, liberatory dimension of Spinoza's thought: the centrality of his notion of freedom as the expression of one's nature via self-understanding and other forms of power—all of which can be achieved under variable circumstances and allow for a particular kind of self-determination. In pointing

---

[64] In a short biography attached to her dissertation, Schmitt also notes the interruptions of her studies in philosophy, systematic theology, and German literature, which took place between Heidelberg, Freiburg, and Berlin between around 1901 and 1909. See Elisabeth Schmitt, *Die unendlichen Modi bei Spinoza* (Leipzig: Barth, 1910), 136, and a manuscript version of this text in the university library archives at Heidelberg, which diverges from the print version in minor but potentially interesting ways. Schmitt singles out both the theologian Ernst Troeltsch and Windelband for their support in the unpublished materials, but only references Windelband by name in the printed text, for instance.

[65] J. Metzger, *Chronik der Stadt Heidelberg für das Jahr 1910* (Heidelberg: Verlag von J. Hörning, 1913), 222, and Ferdinand Rösiger, *Chronik der Stadt Heidelberg für das Jahr 1911* (Heidelberg: Verlag von J. Hörning, 1914), 174. Schmitt also published again on Spinoza's infinite modes. See Elisabeth Schmitt, "Zur Problematik der Unendlichen Modi," *Chronicon Spinozanum* 2 (1922): 155–173.

[66] J. W. Goethe, *From My Life: Poetry and Truth*, trans. Robert R. Heitner, in *The Collected Works*, vol. 5, ed. Thomas P. Saine and Jeffrey L. Sammons (New York: Suhrkamp Verlag, 1987), 523.

to the viable appeal of Spinoza's account of a relatively flexible freedom under limitation, whereby freedom is distinguished from doing as one pleases (which one very
much could not as a woman thinker around the nineteenth century), I have entirely
avoided questioning this line of thinking. I have not, for instance, attempted to evaluate how productive it may have been, or may still be. Some philosophers today
might well suspect that notions of freedom like the ones I have discussed, lacking
a prominent libertarian dimension, could be counterproductive; at the very least,
there is good precedent in the German tradition for a critical perspective on uniting
freedom with strict necessity along these lines.[67] I have also held off on pursuing a
more intellectual-historical hypothesis, for instance that Spinoza or Spinozism
are attractive to woman philosophers in the modern German tradition because of
Spinoza's outsider status as a Jew. There is certainly evidence to the effect that women
thinkers sometimes *did* see parallels with others who were excluded—the novelized
account by Bettina Brentano von Arnim (1785–1859) of her relation to Günderrode
brings together the woman and the Jew as outsiders, for example[68]—and there could
be much to learn from taking such a perspective in a sufficiently subtle manner. But
I have instead tried to show what might be attractive about the more explicitly philosophical content of Spinoza's thought and its legacy. I hope to thereby encourage further work along both these and other lines.

Bibliography

Andreas-Salomé, Lou. *The Freud Journal of Lou Andreas-Salomé.* Translated by Stanley A.
    Leavy. New York: Basic Books, 1964.
Andreas-Salomé, Lou. *Ideal und Askes.* Vol. 2 of *Aufsätze und Essays*, edited by Hans-Rüdiger
    Schwab. Taching: MedienEdition Welsch, 2014.
Arendt, Hannah. *Rahel Varnhagen: The Life of a Jewess.* Edited by Liliane Weissberg. Translated
    by Richard and Clare Winston. Baltimore: Johns Hopkins University Press, 1997.
Battersby, Christine. *The Sublime, Terror and Human Difference.* London: Routledge, 2007.
Beiser, Frederick C. *The Fate of Reason: German Philosophy from Kant to Fichte.* Cambridge,
    MA: Harvard University Press, 1987.
Bollacher, Martin. "Der Philosoph und die Dichter. Spiegelungen Spinozas in der deutschen
    Romantik." In *Spinoza in der europäischen Geistesgeschichte*, edited by Hanna Delf, Julius H.
    Schoeps, and Manfred Walther, 275–288. Berlin: Edition Hentrich, 1994.

---

[67] To be certain, it is unclear how many of the figures considered in this chapter would go for a fully
deterministic metaphysical view and beyond. In any case—although it is not a feminist critique—see my
discussion of Fichte on rejecting any libertarian dimension to freedom as aristocratic in "Fichte's First
First Principles, in the *Aphorisms on Religion and Deism* (1790) and Prior," in "The Enigma of Fichte's
First Principles," ed. David W. Wood, special issue, *Fichte-Studien* 49 (2021): 21.

[68] See, for some discussion, Kari E. Lokke, *Tracing Women's Romanticism: Gender, History, and
Transcendence* (Routledge: London, 2004), 94–101. On Brentano von Arnim more generally, see chapter
6 of this handbook.

Bollacher, Martin. "Pantheismus." In *Online Lexikon Naturphilosophie*. 2020. www.journals. ub.uni-heidelberg.de/index.php/oepn/article/view/75960.

Costazza, Alessandro. "Ein Aufsatz aus der Zeit von Moritz' Weimarer Aufenthalt. Eine Revision der Datierung und der Zuschreibung von Goethes *Aus der Zeit der Spinoza-Studien*." *Goethe-Jahrbuch* 112 (1995): 259–274.

Daley, Margaretmary. *Women of Letters: A Study of Self and Genre in the Personal Correspondence of Caroline Schlegel-Schelling, Rahel Levin Varnhagen, and Bettina von Arnim*. Columbia, SC: Camden House, 1998.

Della Rocca, Michael. *Spinoza*. New York: Routledge, 2008.

Eckle, Jutta. "'Und Spinoza sei Euch immer ein heiliger Christ': Charlotte von Steins Beschäftigung mit Philosophie und Naturforschung im Austausch mit Johann Gottfried Herder und Johann Wolfgang von Goethe." In *Charlotte von Stein: Schriftstellerin, Freundin und Mentorin*, edited by Elke Richter and Alexander Rosenbaum, 339–355. Berlin: de Gruyter, 2018.

Ezekiel, Anna C. "Metamorphosis, Personhood, and Power in Karoline von Günderrode." *European Romantic Review* 25, no. 6 (2014): 773–791.

Ezekiel, Anna C. "Revolution and Revitalization: Karoline von Günderrode's Political Philosophy and Its Metaphysical Foundations." *British Journal for the History of Philosophy* 30, no. 4 (2022): 666–686.

Fischer, Kuno. *Geschichte der neuern Philosophie: Friedrich Wilhelm Joseph Schelling*. Vol. 6. Heidelberg: Verlagsbuchhandlung von Friedrich Bassermann, 1872.

Förster, Eckart, and Yitzhak Y. Melamed, eds. *Spinoza and German Idealism*. Cambridge: Cambridge University Press, 2012.

Forster, Michael. "The German Romantic Tradition and Spinoza's *Theological-Political Treatise*." In *Spinoza in Germany: Political and Religious Thought Across the Long Nineteenth Century*, edited by Jason M. Yonover and Kristin Gjesdal. Oxford: Oxford University Press, forthcoming.

Friedrichsmeyer, Sara. "Caroline Schlegel-Schelling: 'A Good Woman, and No Heroine.'" In *In the Shadow of Olympus: German Women Writers around 1800*, edited by Katherine R. Goodman and Edith Waldstein, 115–136. Albany: State University of New York Press, 1992.

Goethe, Johann Wolfgang von. *From My Life: Poetry and Truth (Part Four)*. Translated by Robert R. Heitner. In *Goethe: The Collected Works*, Vol. 5, edited by Thomas P. Saine and Jeffrey L. Sammons, 519–606. New York: Suhrkamp Verlag, 1987.

Goethe, Johann Wolfgang von. *Selections from Goethe's Letters to Frau von Stein, 1776–1789*. Edited and translated by Robert M. Browning. Columbia, SC: Camden House, 1990.

Günderrode, Karoline von. *Kommentar*. Vol. 3 of *Sämtliche Werke und ausgewählte Studien*, edited by Walter Morgenthaler et al. Basel: Stroemfeld/Roter Stern, 1991.

Günderrode, Karoline von. *Poetic Fragments*. Edited and translated by Anna C. Ezekiel. Albany: State University of New York Press, 2016.

Haines, Brigid. "'Ja, so würde ich es auch heute noch sagen': Reading Lou Andreas-Salomé in the 1990s." *Publications of the Goethe Society* 62 (1991): 77–95.

Jacobi, Friedrich Heinrich. *The Main Philosophical Writings and the Novel Allwill*. Edited and translated George di Giovanni. Montreal: McGill-Queen's University Press, 1994.

Jaspers Stiftung. "Jeanne Hersch." https://jaspers-stiftung.ch/de/die-karl-jaspers-stiftung-1/ biographie-jeanne-hersch.

Jones, Amy. "Vampirism Inverted: Pathology, Gender, and Authorship in Karoline von Günderrode's 'Die Bande der Liebe.'" In *Writing the Self, Creating Community: German*

Women Authors and the Literary Sphere 1750–1850, edited by Elisabeth Krimmer and Lauren Nossett, 141–162. Columbia, SC: Camden House, 2020.

Kord, Susanne. *Sich einen Namen machen: Anonymität und weibliche Autorschaft. 1700–1900*. Stuttgart: J. B. Metzler, 1996.

Leduc, Christian. "Sophie of Hanover on the Soul-Body Relationship." In *Women and Philosophy in Eighteenth-Century Germany*, edited by Corey W. Dyck, 11–28. Oxford: Oxford University Press, 2021.

Lewald, Fanny. *Meine Lebensgeschichte*. Vol. 3, Part 2. Berlin: Verlag von Otto Janke, 1862.

Lohberger, Hans. "Friedrich Nietzsche und Resa von Schirnhofer." *Zeitschrift für philosophische Forschung* 22, no. 2 (1968): 28–34.

Lokke, Kari E. *Tracing Women's Romanticism: Gender, History, and Transcendence*. Routledge: London, 2004.

Maimon, Salomon. *The Autobiography of Salomon Maimon*. Edited by Yitzhak Y. Melamed and Abraham P. Socher. Translated by Paul Reitter. Princeton: Princeton University Press, 2019.

Matysik, Tracie. *Reforming the Moral Subject: Ethics and Sexuality in Central Europe, 1890–1930*. Ithaca: Cornell University Press, 2008.

Melamed, Yitzhak Y. "'*Deus sive Vernunft*': Schelling's Transformation of Spinoza's God." In *Schelling's Philosophy: Freedom, Nature, and Systematicity*, edited by G. Anthony Bruno, 93–115. Oxford: Oxford University Press, 2020.

Melamed, Yitzhak Y. "A Glimpse into Spinoza's Metaphysical Laboratory: The Development of the Concepts of Substance and Attribute." In *The Young Spinoza: A Metaphysician in the Making*, edited by Yitzhak Y. Melamed, 272–286. Oxford: Oxford University Press, 2015.

Metzger, J. *Chronik der Stadt Heidelberg für das Jahr 1910*. Heidelberg: Verlag von J. Hörning, 1913.

Michaelis-Böhmer-Schlegel-Schelling, Caroline, et al. *Caroline. Briefe an ihre Geschwister, ihre Tochter Auguste, die Familie Gotter, F. L. W. Meyer, A. W. und Fr. Schlegel, F. Schelling u.a., nebst Briefen von A. W. und Fr. Schlegel u.a.* Edited by Georg Waitz. Leipzig: Verlag von S. Hirzel, 1871.

Michaelis-Böhmer-Schlegel-Schelling, Caroline, et al. *Caroline: Letters from Early Romanticism*. Edited and translated by Douglas W. Stott. 2021. www.carolineschelling.com.

Nassar, Dalia. "The Human Vocation and the Question of the Earth: Karoline von Günderrode's Philosophy of Nature." *Archiv für Geschichte der Philosophie* 104, no. 1 (2022): 108–130.

Nassar, Dalia, and Kristin Gjesdal, eds. *Women Philosophers in the Long Nineteenth Century: The German Tradition*. New York: Oxford University Press, 2021.

Preitz, Max, and Doris Hopp, eds. "Karoline von Günderrode in ihrer Umwelt. III. Karoline von Günderrodes Studienbuch." *Jahrbuch des freien deutschen Hochstifts* (1975): 223–323.

Raisbeck, Joanna. *Karoline von Günderrode: Philosophical Romantic*. Cambridge: Legenda, 2022.

Raisbeck, Joanna. "Von Mythem umrankt." *Litlog. Göttinger eMagazin für Literatur—Kultur—Wissenschaft*. www.litlog.de/von-mythen-umrankt. Published online July 6, 2019.

Rée, Paul. *Basic Writings*. Edited and translated by Robin Small. Urbana: University of Illinois Press, 2003.

Rée, Paul. *Die Illusion der Willensfreiheit. Ihre Ursachen und ihre Folgen*. Berlin: Carl Duncker's Verlag, 1885.

Rösiger, Ferdinand. *Chronik der Stadt Heidelberg für das Jahr 1911*. Heidelberg: Verlag von J. Hörning, 1914.

Schmitt, Elisabeth. *Die unendlichen Modi bei Spinoza*. Leipzig: Barth, 1910.

Schmitt, Elisabeth. "Zur Problematik der Unendlichen Modi." *Chronicon Spinozanum* 2 (1922): 155–173.

Schneck, Ariane C. "Elisabeth of Bohemia's Neo-Peripatetic Account of the Emotions." *British Journal of the History of Philosophy* 27, no. 4 (2019): 753–770.

Sharp, Hasana. "Eve's Perfection: Spinoza on Sexual (In)equality." *Journal for the History of Philosophy* 50, no. 4 (Oct. 2012): 559–580.

Spinoza, Benedict. *The Collected Works of Spinoza*. 2 vols. Translated by Edwin Curley. Princeton: Princeton University Press, 1985–2016.

Spinoza, Benedict. *Ethics*. Edited by Clare Carlisle. Translated by George Eliot. Princeton: Princeton University Press, 2020.

Spinoza, Benedict. *Opera*. Edited by Carl Gebhardt. Heidelberg: Carl Winter Verlag, 1924.

Sreedhar, Susanne. "Hobbes on 'The Woman Question.'" *Philosophy Compass* 7, no. 11 (2012): 772–781.

Suphan, Bernard. "Aus der Zeit der Spinoza-Studien Goethes. 1784–85." *Goethe-Jahrbuch* 12 (1891): 3–12.

Talbot, Ellen Bliss. "Review: *Die unendlichen Modi bei Spinoza*." *Philosophical Review* 20, no. 6 (1911): 666–668.

Trop, Gabriel. "Karoline von Günderrode's Aesthetics of *Naturphilosophie*." Unpublished manuscript.

Tumarkin, Anna. *Spinoza. Acht Vorlesungen gehalten an der Universität Bern*. Leipzig: Verlag von Quelle & Meyer, 1908.

Varnhagen von Ense, Karl August, ed. *Rahel. Ein Buch des Andenkens für ihre Freunde. Erster Theil*. Berlin: Duncker und Humblot, 1833.

von Arnim, Bettina. *Correspondence of Fräulein Günderode and Bettine von Arnim*. Translated by Margaret Fuller and Minna Wesselhoeft. Boston: Burnham, 1861.

Ward, Margaret. *Fanny Lewald: Between Rebellion and Renunciation*. New York: Peter Lang, 2006.

Weissberg, Liliane. "Stepping Out: The Writing of Difference in Rahel Varnhagen's Letters." *New German Critique* 53 (Spring 1991): 149–162.

Whitinger, Raleigh. Introduction to *The Human Family* by Lou Andreas-Salomé, edited and translated by Whitinger, vii–xvii. Lincoln: University of Nebraska Press, 2005.

Winegar, Reed. "Elise Reimarus on Freedom and Rebellion." In *Practical Philosophy from Kant to Hegel: Freedom, Right, and Revolution*, edited by James Clarke and Gabriel Gottlieb, 99–117. Cambridge: Cambridge University Press, 2021.

Winegar, Reed. "Elise Reimarus: Reason, Religion, an Enlightenment." In *Women and Philosophy in Eighteenth-Century Germany*, edited by Corey W. Dyck, 110–133. Oxford: Oxford University Press, 2021.

Yonover, Jason M. "Fichte's First First Principles, in the *Aphorisms on Religion and Deism* (1790) and Prior." In "The Enigma of Fichte's First Principles," ed. David W. Wood. Special issue, *Fichte-Studien* 49 (2021): 3–31.

Yonover, Jason M. "Goethe, Maimon, and Spinoza's Third Kind of Cognition." *Goethe Yearbook* 25 (2018): 267–287.

Yonover, Jason M. "Hegel on Tragedy and the World-Historical Individual's Right of Revolutionary Action." In *Hegel on Tragedy and Comedy: New Essays*, edited by Mark Alznauer, 241–264. Albany: State University of New York Press, 2021.

Yonover, Jason M. "Nietzsche and Spinoza." In *A Companion to Spinoza*, edited by Yitzhak Y. Melamed, 527–537. Oxford: Wiley-Blackwell, 2021.

Yonover, Jason M. "Nietzsche, Spinoza, and Etiology (On the Example of Free Will)." *European Journal of Philosophy* 29, no. 2 (2021): 459–474.

Yonover, Jason M. "Salomon Maimon's 'History in Dialogues.'" *Nexus: Essays in German-Jewish Studies* (2023): 191–216.

Yonover, Jason M., and Kristin Gjesdal, eds. *Spinoza in Germany: Political and Religious Thought Across the Long Nineteenth Century*. Oxford: Oxford University Press, forthcoming.

CHAPTER 27

....

ETHICS

....

JOE SAUNDERS

A basic theme in ethics concerns how one relates to others. This chapter explores this through the concepts of empathy and community, as found in the works of Edith Stein and Gerda Walther.[1]

Some ethical theories take as their starting point the idea that human beings are selfish individuals and view ethics as a corrective to that. Iris Murdoch, for instance, writes that: "the problem is to accommodate inside moral philosophy, and suggest methods of dealing with the fact that so much human conduct is moved by mechanical energy of an egocentric kind. In the moral life the enemy is the fat relentless ego. Moral philosophy is properly, and in the past has sometimes been, the discussion of this ego and of the techniques (if any) for its defeat."[2] Murdoch is echoing Martin Luther here. And these echoes also reverberate throughout German philosophy.[3]

Stein and Walther, with their emphasis on empathy and community, offer a different picture of human beings and their relations to each other, one where we feel and live together. This chapter unpacks the ethical significance of their conceptions of empathy and community. In doing so, it compares and contrasts their views with each other's, and also one of the prominent ethical theorists in German philosophy, Immanuel Kant.

---

[1] In focusing on these thinkers, and their conceptions of empathy and community, I leave aside the writings of other women in nineteenth-century German philosophy, whose work has *political* significance, namely Elise Reimarus, Agnes Tauburt, and Olga Plümacher. For a recent discussion of Reimarus's work and its connection to Kant's political philosophy, see Reed Winegar, "Elise Reimarus on Freedom and Rebellion," in *Practical Philosophy from Kant to Hegel: Freedom, Right, and Revolution*, ed. James Clarke and Gabriel Gottlieb (Cambridge: Cambridge University Press, 2021). For a discussion of Taubert and Plümacher, see Frederick C. Beiser, chapter 21 here, and his *After Hegel: German Philosophy 1840–1900* (Princeton: Princeton University Press, 2014), 217–219.

[2] Iris Murdoch, *The Sovereignty of the Good* (London: Routledge, 1970), 51.

[3] For a helpful account of Luther's influence in German philosophy, see Robert Stern, "Luther's Influence on Philosophy," in *The Stanford Encyclopedia of Philosophy Archive*, Fall 2020 ed. (article publ. July 22, 2020), https://plato.stanford.edu/archives/fall2020/entries/luther-influence/.

The chapter begins with a discussion of Stein's *On the Problem of Empathy*. In this work, Stein provides a distinctive account of what empathy is. I lay this out, consider what the ethical implications of her account of empathy might be, and then further explore this through a contrast with Kant's discussion of similar feelings.

I then turn to the work of Walther, who looks to distinguish between empathy and communal lived experiences. Walther sees community as founded by a habitual oneness, where we have a "dark awareness" of a "copresence" of other people.[4] So conceived, we incorporate other people into our background, rather than remaining separate individuals who are able to grasp others through empathy. Both Stein's conception of empathy and Walther's idea of community, in their own ways, help us to overcome the supposed divide between one's self and others. The chapter ends by considering whether Walther goes too far in this, and whether her emphasis on communal experience can be to the detriment of the importance of individuals.

1 STEIN'S CONCEPTION OF EMPATHY

What is empathy? It is a commonly used term, but there are many difference conceptions of it. In a review of the literature on the topic, Cuff, Brown, Taylor, and Howat found forty-three discrete definitions of "empathy"![5] Stein has a distinctive conception of it. She views empathy (*Einfühlung*) as a unique kind of perceiving, a sui generis way we have of comprehending the psychic life of other human beings.[6] This is a key feature of Stein's conception of empathy, that we have experience of other *subjects*.[7]

Stein provides examples of this kind of perception: "a friend tells me that he has lost his brother and I become aware of his pain."[8] She provides more detail in a second example: "my friend comes to me beaming with joy and tells me he has passed his examination. I comprehend his joy empathically; transferring myself into it, I comprehend the joyfulness of the event and am now primordially[9] joyful over it

---

[4] Gerda Walther, "Selections from *A Contribution to the Ontology of Social Communities*," trans. Anna Ezekiel, in *Women Philosophers in the Long Nineteenth Century: The German Tradition*, ed. Dalia Nassar and Kristin Gjesdal (New York: Oxford University Press, 2021), 298.

[5] Benjamin M. P. Cuff, Sarah J. Brown, Laura Taylor, and Douglas J. Howat, "Empathy: A Review of the Concept," *Emotion Review* 8, no. 2 (2016): 144–145.

[6] Edith Stein, *On the Problem of Empathy* (Washington, DC: ICS, 1989), 11. For discussion of Stein's account of the psyche, see Angela Ales Bello, "The Role of Psychology According to Edith Stein," in *The Oxford Handbook of Phenomenological Psychopathology*, ed. Giovanni Stanghellini et al. (Oxford: Oxford University Press, 2019), 20–24.

[7] See Timothy Burns, "From I to You to We: Empathy and Community in Edith Stein's Phenomenology," in *Empathy, Sociality, and Personhood: Essays on Edith Stein's Phenomenology*, ed. Elisa Magrì and Dermot Moran (Springer, 2017), 129.

[8] Stein, *Empathy*, 6.

[9] Stein draws a distinction between *primordial* and *nonprimordial* experiences. The distinction is interesting, but not necessary for the purposes of this chapter. For discussion of the distinction, see

myself."[10] Stein is interested in this kind of awareness that we have of others. To bring out what makes her conception of empathy distinctive, it will help to contrast it with Lipps's, and to draw a few distinctions.

In *On the Problem of Empathy*, Stein is directly engaging with Husserl's and Lipps's work. The word 'empathy' entered the English language through Edward Titchener's translation of Lipps's '*Einfühlung*'.[11] Lipps did not coin the term *Einfühlung* (it had already been used by thinkers in the eighteenth century, such as Herder), but was the first to provide a systemic account of it. This new concept of empathy was a lacuna in Husserl's philosophy,[12] and he was happy to have his student Stein fill it with her dissertation.[13]

Lipps viewed empathy as "the contagion or transference of feeling,"[14] and Stein provides several clear examples of this: "a child seeing another crying cries, too. When I see a member of my family going around with a long face, I too become upset. When I want to stop worrying, I seek out happy company."[15] Stein wants to distinguish this emotional contagion from empathy.[16] Why? For Stein it is important that empathy is experience of *another subject's* emotions rather than just feeling the exact same thing as someone else. In thinking this, she is not alone. Contemporary research also wants to distinguish between empathy and emotional contagion: "a self/other distinction . . . is what separates empathy from emotional contagion . . . . With empathy, the observer is aware that this feeling is a result of perceiving emotion in the other. With emotional contagion, the emotion is captured but the observer lacks this awareness and the observer believes this feeling to be his/her own."[17] Stein conceives of empathy as a three-step process, and characterizes these three steps as

(1) the emergence of the experience,
(2) the fulfilling explication, and
(3) the comprehensive objectification of the explained experience.[18]

Stein, *Empathy*, 7–11, and Fredrik Svenaeus, "Edith Stein's Phenomenology of Sensual and Emotional Empathy," *Phenomenology and the Cognitive Sciences* 17, no. 4 (2018): 744.

[10] Stein, *Empathy*, 13.

[11] Edward Titchener, *Lectures on the Experimental Psychology of Thought-Processes* (New York: Macmillan, 1909). See Remy Debes, "From Einfühlung to Empathy: Sympathy in Early Phenomenology and Psychology," in *Sympathy: A History*, ed. Eric Schliesser (Oxford University Press, 2015).

[12] Edith Stein, *Life in a Jewish Family*, trans. Josephine Koeppel (Washington, DC: ICS, 1986), 218–219.

[13] See Alasdair MacIntyre, *Edith Stein: A Philosophical Prologue, 1913–1922* (Plymouth, UK: Rowman and Littlefield, 2006), 75–77, for a discussion of how Stein's treatment of empathy poses important questions to Husserl's account.

[14] Stein, *Empathy*, 23.

[15] Stein, *Empathy*, 23.

[16] For more on the contrast between Stein and Lipps on this point, see Svenaeus, "Stein's Phenomenology," 753.

[17] Cuff et al., "Empathy: A Review," 149.

[18] Stein, *Empathy*, 10. In referring to these as "steps," I follow Svenaeus, "Stein's Phenomenology," 743.

What exactly are these three steps? In unpacking this, I draw upon Frederik Svenaeus'
helpful analysis.[19] Tweaking Svenaeus's account slightly, we can think of Stein's three-
step process as follows:

(1) The experience of another person emerges to the empathizer (as an experience
     that another person is having).
(2) The empathizer then follows this experience through.
(3) In doing so, they gain more comprehensive understanding of the meaning of the
     experience that the other person is having.

We can see how this works in Stein's earlier example, where her friend has passed his examination.[20] The experience of her friend's joy (1) emerges to Stein as an experience that
her friend is having. Stein then (2) follows this experience through, transferring herself
into it, and as a result, now (3) comprehends the joyfulness of the experience her friend
is having.

It helps to draw a distinction here between *cognitive* and *affective* empathy.[21] The basic
idea is that cognitive empathy concerns one's ability to understand what other people
are *thinking*, whereas affective empathy concerns how other people are *feeling*. Svenaeus
contends that Stein's three-step process of empathy involves feeling in each step.[22] This
raises a question about just how feeling-based Stein's conception of empathy is. Does
empathy involve understanding or knowing what other people are feeling, or also
feeling with them? If it is just understanding or knowing, then one might worry that her
conception of empathy is too cognitive or detached from the feelings of others. (I go on
to consider this in the next section, where I look at the ethical implications of empathy.)
And if it is the latter, where we feel what other people are feeling, then it might collapse
into emotional contagion, which Stein wants to avoid.

Svenaeus makes the case that Stein initially characterizes empathy as just understanding the emotions of others, but goes on to make it clear that it does involve, as he
puts it, "feeling in the footsteps of other people."[23] What distinguishes this from emotional contagion is the three-step process. Our experience of another's feelings affects
how we feel, as does our transferring ourselves into their experience, and our understanding of what they are going through.

Stein's account of empathy involves a full picture of the human being, their consciousness, living body, and feelings.[24] There is something about being embodied in the way

---

[19] See Svenaeus, "Stein's Phenomenology," 742.

[20] For Stein's own characterization of this, see Stein, *Empathy*, 10.

[21] Another important distinction is between empathy and sympathy. For Stein, sympathy involves an
initial act of empathy, but continues into feeling *for someone* or *with them*, but no longer through an act
of empathy; see Stein *Empathy*, 14–15, and Svenaeus, "Stein's Phenomenology," 756.

[22] Svenaeus, "Stein's Phenomenology," 744.

[23] Svenaeus, "Stein's Phenomenology," 745.

[24] For a general account of emotions in Stein, see Antonio Calcagno, "Edith Stein," in *The
Routledge Handbook of Phenomenology of Emotion*, ed. Thomas Szanto and Landweer Hilge (London:
Routledge, 2020).

we are that facilitates empathy with other human bodies.[25] As Svenaeus remarks:[26] "the examples of empathy Stein discusses are all based on the perceptual emergence of the other person in front of me. According to Stein, this is because all forms of empathy are put in motion by lived bodily expressions addressing themselves to the empathizer . . . all cases of empathy are basically sensual in character, meaning they are bodily felt experiences of other living bodies."[27]

2 THE ETHICAL IMPLICATIONS OF STEIN'S CONCEPTION OF EMPATHY

I now turn to consider the ethical implications of Stein's conception of empathy. In 1915, Stein served as a nurse at a Red Cross Hospital in Austria. Alasdair MacIntyre notes that, here,[28] "the questions of how to be aware of the feelings and judgements of others and of what it was in one's own speech and bearing to which those others were responding in acting as they did had become questions of daily practical import." Unfortunately, though, Stein does not provide a full account of the practical or ethical significance of empathy in *On the Problem of Empathy*.[29] Svenaeus notes that:

> Stein's book on empathy is a shortened version of her doctoral dissertation, which additionally contained . . . a fifth, sixth and seventh part about empathy as a social, ethical and aesthetic phenomenon respectively. . . . Nobody knows exactly what thoughts Stein put into these parts, because all existing copies of the dissertation are gone. . . . In these published parts Stein makes clear that her overall aim is not only to study the structure of empathic experience but also the issues of what it means to be a person in a social context and how we ought to live together in the world.[30]

---

[25] Stein, *Empathy*, 58–59. There is some controversy over whether Stein somehow stole this from Scheler (a rumor started by Scheler himself); see Svenaeus, "Stein's Ethics," 167n11. Svenaeus, Fredrik. "Edith Stein's Phenomenology of Empathy and Medical Ethics." In *Empathy, Sociality, and Personhood: Essays on Edith Stein's Phenomenological Investigations*, edited by Elisa Magrì and Dermot Moran, 161–175. Switzerland: Springer, 2017.

[26] Although, it is worth noting that Stein claims that this is not a strict limitation on our ability to empathize; see Stein, *Empathy*, 59.

[27] Svenaeus, "Stein's Phenomenology," 746.

[28] MacIntyre, *Edith Stein*, 71–72.

[29] Svenaeus, "Stein's Ethics," 162, generously remarks that "it is debatable whether Stein actually succeeds in developing an ethics in *On the Problem of Empathy*." But he is a bit too generous here. It is a stretch to say it is debatable whether she succeeds in developing an ethics in the published version of *Empathy*. Unfortunately, she does not.

[30] Svenaeus, "Stein's Phenomenology," 744–745.

In the absence of this, it is left to us to fill in in what a developed ethics based upon Stein's account of empathy would look like.[31]

How then could Stein's conception of empathy extend into ethics? Recall her earlier examples: I see my friend beaming with joy over some good news; I transfer myself into this, comprehend the joyfulness of the event and am now joyful myself over it. Here, I join my friend in their feelings. It seems like a good feature of human beings (and other animals) that we have the capacity to be emotionally attuned to each other in these ways.

Why? The basic thought is that our ability to join others in their feelings can affect our thoughts and actions. Svenaeus unpacks this as follows: "according to Stein, morally relevant feelings are at work already in sensual empathy. As we have seen, the bodily expressions of the other person draw me into her presence and by way of this process I not only attend to but also spontaneously follow her experiences through. This means that if the other is suffering in front of me, I will acknowledge this in the manner of feeling along with her and will possibly also sympathize with her and attempt to help her as a result of this."[32] Imagine you meet up with a friend, and they look distraught. You ask if they are okay, and listen as they tell you what they're going through. Listening to them, and experiencing how they feel affects you, how you think, how you feel. You are now concerned for them, and will perhaps try to help in whatever way you can.

Contemporary research also suggests that affective empathy is linked to moral agency. Elisa Aaltola reports that "affective empathy [rather than projective or cognitive empathy] offers a much more fruitful basis for moral agency. The cases of psychopathy and narcissism act yet again as guides, for whereas psychopaths and narcissists have normal or high cognitive empathy, their affective empathy levels are low or verging on the nonexistent . . . . This fact suggests a link between affective empathy and moral agency."[33] Aalotola draws this connection as follows: "whereas cognitive empathy can remain detached and self-directed, affective empathy is intrinsically involved and other-directed; moreover, it is redolent of openness toward others, consists of it. This is quite simply because, in a very tangible fashion, affective empathy opens us to the influence of others by causing us to resonate with their emotive states. Thereby it impels one to become exposed or receptive to the other, i.e. to allow the other to bear an impact on oneself (hence resisting detachment), and to note and pay heed to others' experiences (hence making other-directedness possible)."[34] Aalotola sketches how empathizing, being emotionally attuned to others, being open to other people and moved by them,

---

[31] Svenaeus himself explores how Stein's theory of empathy could serve as a ground for medical ethics He looks to "explore how the Steinian theory of empathy could serve both as an experientially based anchoring point of medical epistemology and as a founding ground for medical ethics by acknowledging the expressions and needs of suffering persons as the anchoring point for moral theory." Svenaeus, "Stein's Ethics," 162.

[32] Svenaeus, "Stein's Phenomenology," 757.

[33] Elisa Aaltola, "Varieties of Empathy and Moral Agency," *Topio* 33 (2014): 247.

[34] Aaltola, "Empathy and Agency," 247.

and caring for them, are linked. She also goes on, like Stein, to discuss the importance of embodiment for affective empathy.[35]

But empathy does not always facilitate morally laudable behavior. Cuff et al. warn that: "empathy is not necessarily accompanied by a prosocial or helpful behavioural response. While empathy is normally associated with prosocial behaviours . . . this is not always the case. For example, a good understanding of another's emotions can be used by psychopaths to manipulate their victims . . . or used by businesspeople to undermine competitors."[36] This takes us to our next section, where we will consider perhaps the most well-known critic of the idea of grounding morality in sensuous feelings: Kant. We will look at his views on fellow feeling and morality, and consider how Stein might respond.

3 Stein and Kant on Empathy, Fellow Feeling, and Ethics

In her dissertation, Stein's first chapter was a historical overview of the concept of empathy, a "first part surveying the concept of empathy in eighteenth- and nineteenth-century philosophy."[37] Unfortunately, this was also removed when the dissertation was published and now seems lost to history.[38] With this chapter missing, we do not know which thinkers Stein engaged with, and are again left to fill in some of the blanks ourselves.

In filling in some of these blanks, it is fruitful to compare Stein's account with a prominent ethical theory in the German tradition.[39] In Kant, we find an emphasis on the connections between rationality, freedom, and morality. In the *Groundwork*, he seeks a foundation for morality that is not contingent upon human nature. He wants morality to apply to *all* rational beings, including purely spiritual beings (the holy will).[40] Kant also wants morality to apply to us, regardless of how we feel.[41]

---

[35] Aaltola, "Empathy and Agency," 247.

[36] Cuff et al., "Empathy: A Review," 149.

[37] Svenaeus, "Stein's Ethics," 170.

[38] In the preface to the first and second editions, Waltraut Stein notes that "the first historical chapter was omitted in publication and seems no longer to be extant." Stein, *Empathy*, xiii.

[39] Stein does mention Kant once in her letters. In a letter to Roman Ingarden in 1917, she writes: "the 'good work period' began only after Pentecost and was used for an intensive preoccupation with Kant." We also find extensive discussion of sympathy and fellow feeling, and their ethical significance in Hume, but it is not clear that he has a clear distinction between these concepts. In the *Treatise*, he does not discuss "empathy" but offers an account of sympathy that does cover some important parts of what Stein means by "empathy"; see bk. 2, sec. 11; for discussion of Hume (and Adam Smith) on the development on affective empathy, see Aaltola, "Empathy and Agency," 244–247.

[40] IV: 414.1–2. See IV: 389.9–20 for Kant's claim that morality should apply to all rational beings, and IV: 414.1-2 for discussion of the holy will..

[41] IV: 398.20–399.2.

Why is Kant eager to establish morality in this way? He worries that if morality depended upon human nature or sensuous feelings, this would make it contingent, "as though other rational beings did not have to heed it"[42]

Stein does not provide an account of how empathy could serve as the foundation for morality,[43] but she does note that it is a distinctive feature of human life, an embodied and emotional experience that gives us access to others' mental and emotional lives. And as we saw in the last section, it seems like there are important links between ethics and empathy.

One aspect of this is that empathy might help guard against wrongdoing. I might desire my friend's shiny new e-book reader and take it from them. But in doing so, my friend would likely feel betrayed, disappointed, and upset. I would see this, and hopefully comprehend and feel with them, prompting me to return the e-book reader. Likewise, seeing others happy can also make me happy, and as such, empathy could help facilitate prosocial behavior.

Of course, there are limits here. If you see someone step on a nail, you will not literally feel a nail in your own foot. You will likely wince (and maybe your foot will wince in its own way), but you will not literally feel their pain.[44] They will be in pain though, and distressed, and these are feelings that you can enter, understand, and be moved by. And hopefully they will also move you to action.

What would Kant's concern be here? Kant might worry that this way of relating to others makes morality a matter of self-interest. You help others because it makes *you* feel good, and you do not harm others because that makes *you* feel bad. And I think Kant is right to worry about this, after all, we ought to help others because *they* need help, not because it makes us feel better. But it is not necessarily self-interested. For friends help each other not just to make themselves feel better, but because they care about each other. When your friend is doing well, this can make you happy, but your own happiness does not have to be what is motivating you.[45]

This issue of moral motivation is typically the main area of discussions of Kant's ethics and feelings, focusing on Kant's claim in the *Groundwork*, that "to do the action without any inclination but from duty—not until then does the action have genuine moral worth."[46] I want to leave this issue aside here. It has been dealt with excellently and

---

[42] IV: 389.14–15.

[43] Svenaeus might disagree here. He writes that, even in the "published parts. . . . Her goal appears to be no less than to found an ethics built on hierarchies of values that we encounter through feeling towards and with other persons in the world, an overall aim that one suspects was even more present and developed in the dissertation in total" Svenaeus, "Stein's Ethics," 170.

[44] For further discussion of this, see Dan Zahavi, "Empathy and Direct Social Perception: A Phenomenological Proposal," *Review of Philosophy and* Psychology 2, no. 3 (2011): 541–558.

[45] For recent discussion of self-interest, morality, and motivation in Kant, see Martin Sticker and Joe Saunders, "Why We Go Wrong: Beyond Kant's Dichotomy Between Duty and Self-Love," *Inquiry* (2022).

[46] IV: 398.25–27.

extensively elsewhere.[47] But there are additional worries that Kant would have with empathy in ethics that have been less dealt with.

Kant would worry that empathy is too contingent to serve as the foundation for morality. Why? It might happen that human beings are capable of being emotionally attuned to each other, but we cannot expect that all rational beings would be. And if we are looking for moral laws, which hold with absolute necessity, we cannot find these in contingent features of human beings. Let us consider a concrete example: you bump into your neighbor, and they let you know that they have just lost their job. They are worried. You see they are worried, stop and listen, and come to understand how they are feeling. In turn, this affects how you feel. There might be no concrete way in which you could help. You cannot offer them a job or help with money. But they are probably not looking for this sort of help, they just want someone to listen. That is not quite right. They do want someone to listen, but they also would appreciate their listener to be emotionally attuned. And this emotional attunement is a good thing, and thankfully, something that most humans are capable of.

Perhaps there are rational beings who lack the ability to be attuned in this way. (This might be true in extreme cases of psychopathy,[48] and we can also imagine rational non-human beings—aliens, AIs—that lack this capacity). If some beings were incapable of this attunement, it would seem unfair to expect them to empathize. But nevertheless, it still seems good that the majority of humans can be so attuned, and it seems good for us to empathize with each other, and for this to in turn affect our actions.

A related worry is that perhaps this makes morality heteronomous, or hypothetical. Kant claims that if morality is based on anything other than self-legislated (pure practical) reason, then it would be heteronomous, and a system of *hypothetical* imperatives. But the above case seems to put some pressure on this. You see your neighbor is worried, you stop and listen to them, and also come to feel worried. Here, in certain key respects, you are not *self*-determining, your feelings, thoughts, and actions are determined, at least in part, by *another*. You see them struggling, and this changes how you feel, think, and act. But being *other*-determined in this way seems like a good thing.[49]

Kant might worry that this makes the imperative to reach out hypothetical rather than categorical. After all, part of what it means for something to be categorical means that it applies to you regardless of what you desire.[50] But we can apply this to the case at

---

[47] For an excellent extended discussion of the issue of moral motivation in Kant, see Henry Allison, *Kant's Groundwork for the Metaphysics of Morals: A Commentary* (Oxford: Oxford University Press, 201), 88–120; and Robert Stern, *Understanding Moral Obligation* (Cambridge: Cambridge University Press, 2012), 103–147.

[48] For discussion of ethics and psychopathy, see Jim Baxter, *Moral Responsibility and the Psychopath: The Value of Others* (Cambridge: Cambridge University Press, 2021).

[49] Another way of unpacking the distinction between autonomy and heteronomy is to understand heteronomy as being determined by desires/feelings, and autonomy as being determined by (pure practical) reason. I go on shortly to discuss how Kant draws a similar distinction in his discussion of sympathy in the *Metaphysics of Morals*.

[50] See IV: 420. 3-11. Another aspect of categoricity is that, in addition to applying to you regardless of what you desire, categorical moral claims also *override* what you desire.

hand. The claim is not that it is good to attend to people when they are worried, *if you happen to want to do that*. The claim, rather, is that this is a good thing to do, *regardless of what you happen to want*. So conceived, there is something categorical about the claim that we ought to help others.[51] And Stein might agree here. Svenaeus thinks that "Stein is an emotional value realist, and this means that what we ought to be and do shows itself to us through the feelings we develop in encountering the experiences and actions of other persons."[52] So far, I have focused on comparing Stein's understanding of empathy with Kant's rather dismissive treatment of feelings in the *Groundwork*. But of course, this is not his only work on ethics. And in his later *Metaphysics of Morals*, Kant himself discusses sympathetic feeling (*theilnehmende Empfindung*),[53] shared feeling (*Mitgefühl*),[54] and compassion (*Mitleidenschaft*).[55]

Kant sees these feelings as implanted in us by nature, and thinks that we have a (conditional) duty to use these feelings to promote active and rational benevolence, that is, to promote the welfare of others.[56] He calls this the "duty of humanity," because, like Stein, he recognizes that "a human being is regarded here not merely as a rational being but also as an animal endowed with reason."[57] And Kant says some powerful things in favor of this benevolence: "would it not be better for the well-being of the world generally if human morality were limited to duties of right, fulfilled with the utmost conscientiousness, and benevolence were considered morally indifferent? It is not so easy to see what effect this would have on human happiness. But at least a great moral adornment, benevolence, would then be missing from the world. This is, accordingly, required by itself, in order to present the world as a beautiful moral whole in its full perfection, even if no account is taken of advantages (of happiness)."[58] Here, we see Kant strike a slightly different tone than he did in the *Groundwork*. He seems less dismissive of these feelings, perhaps reflecting (as Kantian commentators like to point out) that in the *Groundwork* Kant is seeking a foundation for morality, and while these feelings have no place there,[59] that does not mean that they are completely excluded from his moral system.

But even in *The Metaphysics of Morals*, Kant does not wholeheartedly embrace such feelings. In sections 34–35, he draws a distinction between two ways in which we can share in others' feelings. The first is free, based on practical reason, and he calls this

---

[51] One complication here is that, even if the goodness of reaching out in this way is categorical, it might not take the form of an *imperative*; otherwise expressed, it might be a good thing to do, regardless of what you desire, but not obligatory.

[52] Svenaeus, "Stein's Phenomenology," 757.

[53] VI: 457.23.

[54] VI: 457.22.

[55] VI: 457.3. Kant also discusses sympathy (*Sympathie*) in the *Groundwork* (see, for instance, IV: 398.28), but it gets a less sympathetic treatment there.

[56] VI: 456.23–26.

[57] VI: 456.26–28.

[58] VI: 458.2–11.

[59] In the *Critique of Practical Reason*, one special feeling will come to play a key role in Kant's thinking about morality, namely the feeling of respect. But that is another story entirely.

sympathetic (theilnehmend).[60] The second is unfree, and he calls it *communicable (mittheilend)*[61] and *compassion (Mitleidenschaft)*,[62] "since it is like receptivity to warmth or contagious diseases."[63] Kant thinks that we only have an obligation toward the first of these. This makes sense, given other commitments that Kant has, and his general emphasis on the importance of reason and freedom. However, it is not clear why we should not also look to share in others' feelings in a communicable, unfree, contagious way.

But perhaps Kant is closer to Stein here than things might initially seem. After all, Stein wants to depart from Lipps' conception of empathy as emotional contagion. As we have seen, Stein views empathy as a three step-process that involves more than just feeling what the other person feels.

Kant provides the following example, which is supposed to highlight the contrast between the two ways he conceives of sharing in others' feelings: "it was a sublime way of thinking that the Stoic ascribed to his wise men when he had him say 'I wish for a friend, not that he might help *me* in poverty, sickness, imprisonment, etc., but rather that I might stand by *him* and rescue a human being.'"[64] This seems laudable: Kant is advocating against self-interest, and for the active duty of benevolence here. He then goes on to consider the second type of feeling: "but the same wise man, when he could not rescue his friend, said to himself 'what is it to me?' In other words, he rejected compassion [Mitleidenschaft]."[65] I don't know about you, but I would not consider this person a friend, nor especially wise. "What is it to me?" seems callous, as if his friend's feelings do not reach him. He does not seem completely immoral or amoral, as he does look to actively help others when he can. But when he cannot help, he seems too cold. Imagine a close friend is an astronaut, and they are heading to the moon. Something goes wrong in space, and they are in serious trouble. The communication channels are down, but they manage to transmit a one-way broadcast of their peril. You are not an astronaut, and there is nothing you can do to help them. Nevertheless, "What is it to me?" seems like the wrong response.[66]

Kant argues against feeling with others in this way as follows: "when another suffers, and although I cannot help him, I let myself be infected by his pain (through my imagination), then two of us suffer, though the trouble really (in nature) affects only *one*. But there cannot possibly be a duty to increase the ills in the world and so to do good *from compassion*."[67] He seems to miss something importantly human here. If a close friend

---

[60] VI: 456.33.

[61] VI: 457.2.

[62] VI: 457.3.

[63] VI: 457.2.

[64] VI: 457.6–9.

[65] VI: 457.10–11.

[66] David Batho has suggested that perhaps this is not callous, but rather a way of facing up to the reality of the situation at hand, and the limits of one's agency/power; for discussion of the ethics of powerlessness, see David Batho, "The Phenomenology of Powerlessness" (Colchester: University of Essex, 2015).

[67] VI: 457.13–18.

is lost in space, even if I cannot help them, it seems callous to not worry with or about them. Without that, the world would be a colder place. I worry, echoing Kant's earlier words, that without such fellow feeling, a great moral adornment would be lost from the world.

This serves as a springboard to the next section, on Gerda Walther, where I will further consider the self and its felt relation to others. Walther offers an account of communal lived experiences, and wants to distinguish these from empathy.

4 Walther's Conception of Community

Walther is interested in the phenomenology and ontology of social communities. What is it for a social community to exist? Walther thinks that there "must be an entirely or partly similar *mental-spiritual life*, with at least *similar intentional contents* or intentions."[68] She sees this as necessary for social communities, but not sufficient. She considers the example of someone in China dedicating themselves to the same scientific problem as someone in Argentina and Norway, and notes that while their "mental-spiritual life would thus have the same intentional contents . . . as long as they do not know about each other, these people will not form a community."[69] She also adds that even if people know each other intellectually, this is not enough. A community needs *interaction*—but not merely physical interaction, as when two fishermen crash their boats![70]

Walther also wants us to take community life seriously, and not just think, for instance, of community as the outcome of its *products*: "when investigating these products of community life one must be careful not to entirely lose sight of community life and the community itself and take these products to be the only real thing in the community."[71] Rather, community life itself seems to us to be the primary and more important thing.[72] What then is a community for Walther? She has a clear answer: "a number of people who, in a certain layer of their life, relate to the *same intentional* object (in the broadest sense). These people had to *know about each other and about their relation to the same intentional object*. On the basis of this knowledge, they entered into *direct or indirect interaction with each other*, and from this interaction emerged a *communal life* (possibly with common products), which *was, in a unified sense, immediately or mediately motivated by that intention toward the same object (in the broadest sense)*."[73] There is

---

[68] Walther, *Social Communities*, 282.
[69] Walther, *Social Communities*, 283.
[70] Walther, *Social Communities*, 284.
[71] Walther notes that this assumption "causes trouble, for example, in many theories of political economy." Walther, *Social Communities*, 290n26.
[72] Walther, *Social Communities*, 290–291.
[73] Walther, *Social Communities*, 291.

a worry here, that this is slightly too intellectual; presumably one could just find oneself in, or stumble into, a community, rather than entering on the basis of knowledge. But Walther's conception of community is not overly intellectual in general. The essential feature of community for Walther, is the *feeling of belonging together*, an inner oneness (*Einigung*):[74] "only through its inner connectedness, that feeling of belonging together—however loose and limited it may be—does a social formation change into a community. . . . the essential feature of community in "that *feeling of belonging together*," that *inner oneness*."[75] And again, this does not seem overly intellectualized: "other people are always 'given,' as a more or less clear and detected 'co-presence'—even if only in a dark awareness in the background, not in attentive knowing or representing. These are the "people, who also . . ."[76] So conceived, we are not isolated individuals, but always with others, even if they are only a dark awareness in the background. There are the people who also read philosophy, or who also lived through COVID-19. It is not just that these people are there in the background though, as Walther explains:

> the subject is not only darkly aware of them, but also unified with them, in *those* strata in which the sense of community requires it. It rests in them and belongs to them, however loosely and in however limited a part of its total lived experience—and they "belong to it"—it forms a "we" with them. The subject's life, insofar as it is community life, is not just *its* life, does not only pour out from *itself*, as a single individual, but emanates from its unity with the others *within* itself. In this case, lived experience is characterized for the experiencing subject not as just "I experience like this," but as "*we* experience like this": "I *and the others*"—with whom I am united—"are experiencing *like this in me*" and we are one in this, in our lived experience.[77]

Walther goes on to distinguish these communal lived experiences from empathy.[78] She sees this distinction as crucial: "it is extremely important to clarify the difference between mere *empathizing*—as grasping any other person's lived experiences—and communal lived experiences. When I empathically grasp the lived experiences, states, person etc. of another human being, I have a totally different originary lived experience to when I experience the same lived experiences of the other myself, as communal lived

---

[74] Ezekiel makes the following note on her translation here: "the term translated here as "oneness" is *Einigung*, also frequently translated as "unification" or "union" in other translations of Walther. We decided to use the less common English word "oneness" to reflect the specific meaning that Walther gives the term in this context, including its emphasis on the importance of subjective experience—the feeling of belonging, of togetherness—for the constitution of community." Walther, *Social Communities*, 295n33.

[75] Walther, *Social Communities*, 294–295.

[76] Walther, *Social Communities*, 298.

[77] Walther, *Social Communities*, 299.

[78] Tranas and Caminada distinguish four different types of communal emotions in Walther. See Linas Tranas and Emanuele Caminada, "Gerda Walther and Hermann Schmalenbach," in *The Routledge Handbook of Phenomenology of Emotion*, ed. Thomas Szanto and Hilge Landweer (London: Routledge, 2020), 137–139.

experiences."[79] This sets up a contrast with Stein.[80] Walther's focus is not individual experience, nor individuals empathizing with one another,[81] but instead communal lived experiences, a primary lived *we*.[82]

As Anna Maria Pezzella notes, "despite her time at Freiburg, she accepts neither Husserl's not Stein's analyses of the primordiality of the I."[83] Pezzella continues: "Stein starts from I-experience to reach her understanding of community . . . whereas Walther moves from the social self and, hence, from the background of psychic interiority in which the communal we moves and lives."[84]

5 THE ETHICAL IMPLICATIONS OF COMMUNITY AND EMPATHY

Let us know turn to consider the ethical significance of Walther's conception of community, and how it differs from Stein. I began this chapter by noting that a basic theme in ethics concerns how one relates to others. Some ethical theories take as their starting point the idea that human beings are selfish individuals, and view ethics as a corrective to that. Murdoch, as we saw, contends that "so much human conduct is moved by mechanical energy of an egocentric kind."[85]

In focusing on communal lived experiences, and the formation of a primary lived *we*, Walther paints a different picture of human existence, one where we are not individuals primarily driven by mechanical energy of an egocentric kind or our own self-love. Instead, we live and experience *with others*.

Here, we can see glimpse of connections between Walther and earlier German women philosophers in the nineteenth century. Alison Stone and Giulia Valpione point out that a common theme in these thinkers involves "the rejection of Fichte's idea of the self-positing self," and note that "the women of these movements see it as inflating the self to a false position of sovereignty."[86] Stone and Valpione suggest that "the female

---

[79] Walther, *Social Communities*, 302.

[80] Stein, *Empathy*, 18, accepts that we can experience as a *we*, but contends that this occurs through empathizing and not through a feeling of oneness.

[81] Calcagno notes that "Walther has no developed account of empathy." Antonio Calcagno, "Edith Stein and Gerda Walther: The Role of Empathy in Experiencing Community," in *Women Phenomenologists on Social Ontology: We-experiences, Communal Life, and Joint Action*, ed. Sebastian Luft and Ruth Hagengruber (Cham, Switzerland: 2018), 3.

[82] For a helpful summary of Walther's account of what is required in order for emotions to be communal emotions, see Tranas and Caminada, "Walther and Schmalenbach," 135.

[83] Anna Maria Pezzella, "On Community: Edith Stein and Gerda Walther," in *Gerda Walther's Phenomenology of Sociality, Psychology, and Religion*, vol. 2, ed. Antonio Calcagno (Switzerland: Springer, 2018), 51.

[84] Pezzella, "On Community," 52.

[85] Murdoch, *Good*, 51.

[86] Chapter 17 here.

romantics and idealists take the relationality of the self further, and more emphatically give relationships priority over individual selfhood. . . . Relationships with actual concrete others, who exist outside the self, come first."[87] Alongside the importance of relationships, they also note that these romanticists emphasized the importance of feelings and affect.[88]

The gendered dimension of this is intriguing. And Stein herself contends that women are more empathetic than men and have richer emotional lives.[89] There is a risk here though, that we end up perpetuating gender stereotypes.[90] For while, as I showed earlier, Kant does emphasize the importance of reason over sensuous feelings, other men in the history of philosophy (such as Hume and Smith) do not. And it is Murdoch who insists on the ubiquity of the ego in human beings.

Murdoch does not completely miss the mark on this. Human beings can be selfish and self-absorbed in a variety of ways, and we should be on guard against this, and have correctives for it. But the worry is that we can overstate this tendency, to the detriment of other important ethical features of human life. For one, some people struggle not because they are too selfish, but because they are too selfless.[91]

It is also worth thinking about what the appropriate correctives are. For Kant, the corrective is acting for duty's sake. Murdoch draws upon Simone Weil to suggest that giving our attention to nature, for instance observing a hovering kestrel, can "clear our minds of selfish care."[92]

Weil's emphasis on attention is not exclusive to nature though. Weil thinks that paying attention to things outside oneself is key, and that can involve paying attention to a difficult problem in mathematics, or to other people. But this seems most convincing when she discusses being attentive to others: "The love of our neighbor in all its fullness simply means being able to say to him: 'What are you going through?' . . . The soul empties itself of all its own contents in order to receive into itself the being it is looking at, just as he is, in all his truth. Only he who is capable of attention can do this."[93] Weil's comments, more so than Murdoch's and Kant's, suggest that empathy could be part of the corrective against our self-absorption.[94] In order to really love our neighbor, Weil suggests, we

[87] Chapter 17 here.

[88] See chapter 17 here.

[89] See Edith Stein, *Essays on Women*, trans. Freda Mary Oben (Washington, DC: ICS, 2013), 60–72.

[90] For a fascinating discussion of some of the gendered elements of care and caring, see Tove Pettersen, "Conceptions of Care: Altruism, Feminism, and Mature Care," *Hypatia* 27, no. 2 (2012): 366–389.

[91] See Anna Bortolan, "Self-Esteem and Ethics: A Phenomenological View," *Hypatia* 33, no. 1 (2018): 62–68, for a feminist analysis of imposter syndrome and abusive relationships, and the ways in which these cases show how low self-esteem can be harmful. Else Voigtländer also offers a fascinating and thorough treatment of sense of self in Voigtländer, *Sense of Self*.

[92] Murdoch, *Good*, 82.

[93] Simone Weil, "Reflections on the Right Use of School Studies with a View to the Love of God," in Weil, *Waiting on God*, trans. Leslie A. Fielder (New York: Harper and Row, 1951), 115.

[94] See Pezzella, "On Community," 56, for a discussion of the link between the Christian elements of this, and Stein and Walther.

have to empty ourselves of all our concerns, presuppositions, and so on, ask them what they are going through, and really listen, allowing what they are going through to sink in. This facilitates empathy with other human beings.

Perhaps this misses something though. Weil asks us to empty ourselves so that we can fully pay attention and let the other in. A worry here is that not enough of the self remains. Who is it who ends up empathizing? An empty vessel, or a mere mirror? Don't we want someone to remain who they are, with their own lived experiences, thoughts, and feelings, and have that individual relate to us in their own way, rather than completely joining us in our feelings?[95] That seems to be an important part of listening, that someone else can hear you, and relate to you, but from their own different perspective.

In response to this, it helps to return to Stein's conception of empathy, with its three steps. We (1) experience someone else's emotion, (2) follow them in this, and then (3) understand what they are going through. These three steps and Stein's emphasis on the fact that it is the *other person's* emotion helps mitigate against the thought that empathy requires dissolving or completely suspending one's self.

However, we are still talking about empathy here, and not a communal lived experience. And Walther thinks that in doing so, we miss something important:

> [if . . .] I happen to have, originarily and in person, the same lived experiences as those that I grasp empathically in the other. Despite this sameness, the lived experiences stand *beside each other* as *non-united*, as *belonging to different subjects*. I experience *like this*—and the other experiences *like this*. The two may happen to be the same, and I may be immediately aware of this sameness in experiencing my own lived experiences and in empathically grasping the other's lived experiences. However, together with my lived experience *for me, closed off* in myself and *separate, I stand beside* this other, who is just as much closed off in themselves and separate. There exists, as it were, an intentional "wall," a mental "opening," an "interstice" between me and the other.[96]

Perhaps my neighbor and I have both recently lost our jobs. We might have experienced similar things, and empathize with each other, but this still would not necessarily be a communal lived experience. The difference seems to hinge on whether we are distinct individuals leading distinct lives, but capable of feeling with one another, or whether we are capable of *living together* in a deeper sense.

Walther does not draw out the ethical significance of this. But it could help overcome the supposed divide between one's self and others, if we are capable of living together in this deep sense. I might, for instance, no longer see my neighbor as someone separate from me, a potential rival for the next job, but instead think of us as going through unemployment together.

---

[95] I am grateful to Joseph Houlders for asking me these questions.
[96] Walther, *Social Communities*, 303.

One worry is that living together might end up engulfing individuals, such that they lose their distinct senses of self. Walther is aware of this,[97] but Stein is especially concerned about it.[98] As Pezzella notes:

> Stein claims the individual a great autonomy: the community cannot and must not absorb the individual because she/he has a vast personal domain that remains distinct from the community, even though she/he may be a member of a community. . . . Stein is diffident to visions that view the human being only as social beings . . . she observes: "One finds today the widespread tendency to view human beings as solely determined by their membership in a social whole, thereby denying the reality of an individual personality."[99]

> For Stein, subjects remain separate from one another: each has his or her own uniqueness or individuality, but this does not negate the possibility of subjects encountering and grasping one another as human beings.[100]

Is Stein right to be worried here? Has Walther gone too far in her emphasis on community? Once more, I think this depends upon what correctives you think human beings need. Are humans mostly self-absorbed, driven by their egos, and in need of being more aware of and attuned to others? Sometimes, and for some people, yes. But there is more to the human condition than this. Sometimes, some people do not properly value themselves as individuals. And there is evidence to suggest that this is more of a problem for women than men.[101] Some women do not need ethics to be a constant corrective against self-interest, and for them, the emphasis on community and others can be detrimental.[102]

Stein and Walther develop distinctive accounts of empathy and community. These have significant ethical implications, as they help us think through the relations between ourselves and others. In doing so, we gain understanding of what it is to be human, and to live in felt relation to, and emotional attunement with, other people. And they leave us with important questions about the human condition, how we ought to relate to others, and the ethical correctives that we need.

Speaking of others, I owe a big thanks to David Batho, Joseph Houlders, Dalia Nassar, Robert Stern, and Martin Sticker for thoughtful comments on earlier versions of this chapter. I am also grateful to Anna Ezekiel for suggesting a variety of helpful readings in this area.

---

[97] Walther, *Social Communities*, 306–308.

[98] Another interesting implication of Stein and Walther's views concerns the possibility of *communal* responsibility and guilt; see Pezzella, "On Community," 54–55.

[99] Pezzella, "On Community," 53.

[100] Pezzella, "On Community," 56.

[101] See, for instance, Sen and Nussbaum's work on women in developing countries and adaptive preferences; Nussbaum, "Commentary," in *The Quality of Life*, ed. Martha Nussbaum and Amartya Sen (Oxford: Oxford University Press, 1993), 368–369; and Amartya Sen, *Commodities and Capabilities* (New Delhi: Oxford University Press, 1999), 52–69

[102] Presumably, this also applies to men, but less so than it does to women.

BIBLIOGRAPHY

Aaltola, Elisa. "Varieties of Empathy and Moral Agency." *Topio* 33 (2014): 243–253.

Ales Bello, Angela. "The Role of Psychology According to Edith Stein." In *The Oxford Handbook of Phenomenological Psychopathology*, edited by Giovanni Stanghellini, Matthew Broome, Andrea Raballo, Anthony Vincent Fernandez, Paolo Fusar-Poli, and René Rosfort, 42–48. Oxford: Oxford University Press, 2019.

Allison, Henry. *Kant's Groundwork for the Metaphysics of Morals: A Commentary*. Oxford: Oxford University Press, 2011.

Batho, David. "The Phenomenology of Powerlessness." Colchester: University of Essex, 2015.

Baxter, Jim. *Moral Responsibility and the Psychopath: The Value of Others*. Cambridge: Cambridge University Press, 2021.

Beiser, Frederick C. *After Hegel: German Philosophy 1840–1900*. Princeton: Princeton University Press, 2014.

Bortolan, Anna. "Self-Esteem and Ethics: A Phenomenological View." *Hypatia* 33, no. 1 (2018): 56–72.

Burns, Timothy. "From I to You to We: Empathy and Community in Edith Stein's Phenomenology." In *Empathy, Sociality, and Personhood: Essays on Edith Stein's Phenomenological Investigations*, edited by Elisa Magrì and Dermot Moran, 127–142. Cham: Springer, 2017.

Calcagno, Antonio. "Edith Stein." In *The Routledge Handbook of the Phenomenology of Emotions*, edited by Thomas Szanto and Landweer Hilge, 123–132. London: Routledge, 2020.

Calcagno, Antonio. "Edith Stein and Gerda Walther: The Role of Empathy in Experiencing Community." In *Women Phenomenologists on Social Ontology: We-experiences, Communal Life, and Joint Action*, edited by Sebastian Luft and Ruth Hagengruber, 3–18. Springer: 2018.

Calcagno, Antonio, ed. *Gerda Walther's Phenomenology of Sociality, Psychology, and Religion*. Vol. 2. Switzerland: Springer, 2018.

Clarke, James, and Gabriel Gottlieb, eds. *Practical Philosophy from Kant to Hegel: Freedom, Right, and Revolution*. Cambridge: Cambridge University Press, 2021.

Cuff, Benjamin M. P., Sarah J. Brown, Laura Taylor, and Douglas J. Howat. "Empathy: Review of the Concept." *Emotion Review* 8, no. 2 (2016): 144–153.

Debes, Remy. "From Einfühlung to Empathy: Sympathy in Early Phenomenology and Psychology." In *Sympathy: A History*, edited by Eric Schliesser, 286–322. Oxford: Oxford University Press, 2015.

Kant, Immanuel. *Critique of Practical Reason*. Translated by Mary Gregor. Cambridge:Cambridge University Press, 1996.

Kant, Immanuel. *Groundwork for the Metaphysics of Morals*. Translated by Christopher Bennett, Joe Saunders, and Robert Stern. Oxford: Oxford University Press, 2019.

Kant, Immanuel. *The Metaphysics of Morals*. Translated by Mary Gregor. Cambridge: Cambridge University Press, 1996.

Landweer, Hilge, and Thomas Szanto, eds. *The Routledge Handbook of Phenomenology of Emotion*. London: Routledge, 2020.

Luft, Sebastian, and Ruth Hagengruber, eds. *Women Phenomenologists on Social Ontology:We-experiences, Communal Life, and Joint Action*. Switzerland: Springer, 2018.

MacIntyre, Alasdair. *Edith Stein: A Philosophical Prologue, 1913–1922*. Plymouth: Rowman and Littlefield, 2006.

Magrì, Elisa, and Dermot Moran, eds. *Empathy, Sociality, and Personhood: Essays on Edith Stein's Phenomenological Investigations*. Switzerland: Springer, 2017.

Murdoch, Iris. *The Sovereignty of the Good*. London: Routledge, 1970.

Nussbaum, Martha. "Commentary." In *The Quality of Life*, edited by Martha Nussbaum and Amartya Sen, 368–382. Oxford: Oxford University Press, 1993.

Pezzella, Anna Maria. "On Community: Edith Stein and Gerda Walther." In *Gerda Walther's Phenomenology of Sociality, Psychology, and Religion*, edited by Antonio Calcagno, 47–56. Switzerland: Springer, 2018.

Pettersen, Tove. "Conceptions of Care: Altruism, Feminism, and Mature Care." *Hypatia* 27, no. 2 (2012): 366–389.

Sen, Amartya. *Commodities and Capabilities*. New Delhi: Oxford University Press, 1999.

Stein, Edith. *Essays on Women*. Translated by Freda Mary Oben, Washington, DC: ICS, 2013.

Stein, Edith. *Life in a Jewish Family*. Translated by Josephine Koeppel. Washington, DC: ICS, 1986.

Stein, Edith. *On the Problem of Empathy*. Translated by Waltraut Stein. Washington, DC: ICS, 1989.

Stern, Robert. *Understanding Moral Obligation: Kant, Hegel, Kierkegaard*. Cambridge: Cambridge University Press, 2012.

Stern, Robert. "Luther's Influence on Philosophy." In *The Stanford Encyclopedia of Philosophy Archive*. Fall 2020 ed. Stanford University, 1997–. Article published July 22, 2020. https://plato.stanford.edu/archives/fall2020/entries/luther-influence/.

Sticker, Martin, and Joe Saunders. "Why We Go Wrong: Beyond Kant's Dichotomy between Duty and Self-Love." *Inquiry* (2022).

Svenaeus, Fredrik. "Edith Stein's Phenomenology of Empathy and Medical Ethics." In *Empathy, Sociality, and Personhood: Essays on Edith Stein's Phenomenological Investigations*, edited by Elisa Magrì and Dermot Moran, 161–175. Switzerland: Springer, 2017.

Svenaeus, Fredrik. "Edith Stein's Phenomenology of Sensual and Emotional Empathy." *Phenomenology and the Cognitive Sciences* 17, no. 4 (2018): 741–760.

Titchener, Edward. *Lectures on the Experimental Psychology of Thought-Processes*. New York: Macmillan, 1909.

Tranas, Linas, and Emanuele Caminada. "Gerda Walther and Hermann Schmalenbach." In *The Routledge Handbook of Phenomenology of Emotion*, edited by Thomas Szanto and Landweer Hilge, 133–143. London: Routledge, 2020.

Voigtländer, Else. *On Sense of Self (Über die Typen des Selbstgefühls)* Leipzig: R. Voigtländers Verlag, 1910.

Walther, Gerda. "Selections from *A Contribution to the Ontology of Social Communities*." Translated by Anna Ezekiel. In *Women Philosophers in the Long Nineteenth Century: The German Tradition*, edited by Dalia Nassar and Kristin Gjesdal, 281–309. New York: Oxford University Press, 2021.

Weil, Simone. *Waiting on God*. Translated by Leslie A. Fielder. New York: Harper and Row, 1951.

Winegar, Reed. "Elise Reimarus on Freedom and Rebellion." In *Practical Philosophy from Kant to Hegel: Freedom, Right, and Revolution*, edited by James Clarke, and Gabriel Gottlieb, 99–117. Cambridge: Cambridge University Press, 2021.

Zahavi, Dan. "Empathy and Direct Social Perception: A Phenomenological Proposal." *Review of Philosophy and Psychology* 2, no. 3 (2011): 541–558.

CHAPTER 28

SOCIAL AND POLITICAL PHILOSOPHY

KRISTIN GJESDAL

THE contributions of women philosophers in the long nineteenth century—the period between German idealism and romanticism, on the one hand, and early phenomenology, on the other—span a range of topics and areas. In this period, women contribute to epistemology, aesthetics, ethics, philosophy of science, philosophy of nature, philosophy of anthropology, feminism, philosophy of the human, and other areas. Yet, if one were to try and offer a lens through which these contributions are connected—not an umbrella concept under which they can be subsumed, but a looser commitment around which constellations gather with variation in distance and overlap—it would be this: social and political philosophy.

Women philosophers in this period had been raised (and raised themselves) to be intellectuals. Yet a position within academia—where campus architecture, book collections, and student communities mark a concrete commitment to the life of the mind—was denied them. They were excluded from the discourse they wanted to make their own. If they were to be philosophers, they would have to carve out space outside of the academy.

As a consequence, women philosophers in this period had to find their own, distinctive voices. They did not have the backing of powerful institutions and mentors, nor did they write for an exclusive academic readership. Instead they discuss, analyze, and deal with the concrete social and political world in which they live. And, moreover, they often write for the wider groups of people with whom they share this world rather than a select collection of peers and colleagues. In this way, women philosophers managed to turn their marginalized position into an advantage. In a time when women were not thought to be capable of rational thought and philosophy (as Rousseau, Kant, Fichte, Hegel, Schopenhauer, and Nietzsche would all indicate)[1] or were associated with the

---

[1] See Jean-Jacques Rousseau, *Emile or On Education*, trans. Allan Bloom (New York: Basic Books, 1979), 386–387; Immanuel Kant, *Anthropology from a Pragmatic Point of View*, ed. and trans. Robert

private sphere and its entertaining literature (as prescribed by others), they did indeed break both of these barriers and contribute actively and unapologetically to social and political thought. The point is not that all women in the period were social and political philosophers, but that the contributions of women philosophers are often marked by a distinct social and political engagement.[2]

This chapter explores the contributions of nineteenth-century women to social and political thought by making visible the philosophical arc from early romanticism to late nineteenth-century socialism. It covers the works of Germaine de Staël, Karoline von Günderrode, Bettina Brentano von Arnim, Hedwig Dohm, Clara Zetkin, and Rosa Luxemburg, but also, when relevant, makes references to other philosophers of the period. The chapter concludes with some brief reflections on the legacy of these movements and how they helped shape phenomenology and later twentieth-century thought. It is key to the chapter to track and demonstrate the underappreciated contributions that romantic women philosophers make to social and political philosophy, thus highlighting what I take to be a significant lineage from romanticism to midcentury socialism. However, with today's climate crisis in mind, my discussion of the social and political contributions of the early romantic philosophers will also cover their pathbreaking and radical views of nature—views that were not, in the same way, part of mid-nineteenth-century social and political thought.

1 GERMAINE DE STAËL

Born to Swiss parents and raised in Paris, Germaine de Stäel developed her thought in interaction with German philosophers. Through the many translations of her works and her contact with German intellectuals, she left a significant mark on German-speaking culture.

B. Louden (Cambridge: Cambridge University Press, 2010), 209; J. G. Fichte, *Foundations of Natural Right According to the Principles of the Wissenschaftslehre*, ed. Frederick Neuhouser, trans. Michael Baur (Cambridge: Cambridge University Press, 2000), 299, but also 266–270, 298–307; G. W. F. Hegel, *Elements of the Philosophy of Right*, ed. Allen Wood, trans. H. B. Nisbet (Cambridge: Cambridge University Press, 1991), 207; Arthur Schopenhauer, "On Women," in *Parerga and Paralipomena*, trans. Adrian del Caro and Christopher Janaway (Cambridge: Cambridge University Press, 2014), vol. 2, 555–556; Friedrich Nietzsche, *Beyond Good and Evil: Prelude to a Philosophy of the Future*, ed. Rolf-Peter Horstman and Judith Norman, trans. Judith Norman (Cambridge: Cambridge University Press, 2002), §§232–239. In this context, Nietzsche also lauds Napoleon for his rebuking of Germaine de Staël (Napoleon's reaction to her work is discussed below).

[2] Such an orientation can also be found among earlier women philosophers, e.g., of the Renaissance. However, what sets the nineteenth century apart is the increasing professionalization of philosophy, thus also an increasing awareness of marginalization among the groups who were barred from participation. Moreover, this is the century in which we see women organize politically in order to gain suffrage and access to higher education.

Staël's philosophical career ran parallel with her successful development as a novelist and her extraordinary achievements as a political agent and influencer during the French Revolution and in Napoleonic and post-Napoleonic Europe—the latter leading to her reputation as a political superpower along with Russia and England.[3] Starting with the publication of *Letters on the Character and Writings of J.-J. Rousseau* (1788),[4] Staël crafted herself as a philosophical force to be reckoned with. The book was published anonymously, but it did not take long for her fellow Parisians to figure out that the author was none other than the twenty-two-year-old daughter of Jacques Necker, the French minister of finance, and Suzanne Curchod, a well-known writer and salonnière. Following the many women philosophers whose interest in education had led them to Rousseau's *Emile*,[5] Staël offers a somewhat hagiographic recapitulation of Rousseau's work, though the very fact that *Letters* was written by a woman did itself undermine his claims about the passivity of women's intellects and the notion that their interests should be but to please their male companions.[6] Moreover, Staël denounces women's domestic slavery. Later in her life, and after the study was praised but also critiqued by Mary Wollstonecraft,[7] Staël added a new and slightly more critical introduction to the work.

Stäel's early political writings emphasize civic duty and the need for shared social values. At this point, she, like Rousseau, was even open to the idea of a state religion.[8] In *On the Current Circumstances that Can End the Revolution and the Principles that must Found the Republic in France* (1798–99),[9] she offers one of the first republican readings of the French Revolution.[10] She sees republicanism as the only real alternative to the outdated institution of absolute monarchy, on the one hand, and an unstable revolutionary

---

[3] For a discussion of her political achievements, see Glenda Sluga, "Madame de Staël and the Transformation of European Politics, 1812–17," *International History Review* 37, no. 1 (2015): 142–166.

[4] Published the following year in an English version by an unnamed translator as Germaine de Staël, *Letters on the Works and Character of J. J. Rousseau* (London: G. G. J. and J. Robinson, 1789).

[5] See Mary Seidman Trouille, *Sexual Politics in the Enlightenment: Women Writers Read Rousseau* (Albany: State University of New York Press, 1997), and Jennifer J. Popiel, *Rousseau's Daughters: Domesticity, Education, and Autonomy in Modern France* (Durham, NH: University of New Hampshire Press, 2008).

[6] Rousseau, *Emile*, 386–387.

[7] See Mary Wollstonecraft, review of *Letters on the Works and Character of J. J. Rousseau*, by Germaine de Staël, *Analytical Review* 4 (August 1789): 360–362. See also Trouille, *Sexual Politics*, 221–235.

[8] See Gérard Gengembre and Jean Goldzink, "Madame de Staël ou pour une religion politique," *Annales Benjamin Constant* 8–9 (1988): 207–222. Staël at this point leans on Rousseau's understanding of religion as a remedy against social fragmentation. Unlike Enlightenment thinkers such as Voltaire, she also sees religion as a halfway cure against political fanaticism.

[9] The full text was only published in 1979. See Aurelian Craiutu, introduction to *Considerations on the Principal Events of the French Revolution*, ed. Aurelian Craiutu [based on the 1818 translation by an unnamed translator] (Indianapolis: Liberty Fund, 2008), x.

[10] Mauro Barberis describes Staël's *On the Current Circumstances* as the most representative text of republican constitutionalism. Mauro Barberis, "Constant, Mme de Staël et la constitution républicaine. Un essay d'interprétation," in *Le groupe de Coppet et le monde modern. Conceptions-images-débats*, ed. Françoise Tilkin (Geneva: Droz, 1998), 193.

rule of the people, on the other.[11] In works such as *Germany* (1810/1813) and the posthumously published *Considerations on the Principal Events of the French Revolution* (1818), she defends a liberal point of view. It is here that she, in interaction with German political thinkers (Kant and others), comes to emphasize toleration, religious freedom, individual rights, and the rule of law.[12]

In *A Treatise on the Influence of the Passions Upon the Happiness of Individuals and of Nations* (1796),[13] Staël discusses how the passions—especially when combined with passive groupthink—inhibit judgment and action (TIP 178). Moreover, she asks what makes human beings, regardless of their political affiliations, go to the extremes of fanaticism and political violence.[14] Staël was initially a supporter of the French Revolution but, as the terror escalated, withheld her support for its present form (without thereby giving up her support of the revolution as such). She argues that in acting on raw passions, the opposing fractions had a lot in common (TIP 178). Extremes, as she put it, are not in things, but in the human perceptions of things (TIP 194). Thus, passions need to be modified by philosophical reflection, studies, and, eventually, compassion and pity. Her fight against political fanaticism, or political extremism as we today would call it, remained a key aspect of her thought right up to *Considerations on the Principal Events of the French Revolution* and thus unifies her early and late work.[15]

Throughout her work, Staël extols the virtues of tolerance and impartiality *and* seeks actively to foster it in her readers by exposing them to cultures and ways of thinking of which they had typically been suspicious (for example, this is an explicit goal in *Germany*). For Staël, philosophy, when conducted in this manner, involves a process of self-perfection. The perfection of individuals will lead to a better society *and* the other way around.

A Treatise also touches on the situation of women. Staël describes how women are barred from realizing personal ambitions and made dependent on men in terms of finances, social standing, and recognition (TIP 111). Even a learned woman, she laconically points out, has been brought up with a wish to be loved (TIP 112)—yet far too often love is denied her.

In *The Influence of Literature on Society* (1800), Staël discusses the social and political importance of literature broadly defined. She challenges a Kantian notion of aesthetic

---

[11] Her antimonarchical sentiments distinguish her work from that of Bettina Brentano von Arnim, who defended the idea of a people's king.

[12] For a discussion of Staël's transition from republicanism to liberalism, see Andreas Kalyvas and Ira Katznelson, *Liberal Beginnings: Making a Republic for the Moderns* (Cambridge: Cambridge University Press, 2008), chap. 5. The authors, however, overemphasize Kant's influence and downplay the influence of thinkers like Herder and Schleiermacher.

[13] Germaine de Staël, *A Treatise on the Influence of the Passions Upon the Happiness of Individuals and of Nations*, trans. unknown (London: Cawthorn, British Library, 1798) (henceforth abbreviated TIP; the translation is old and should be read with caution and in junction with the French original).

[14] This point was already developed in Staël's *Des Circonstances*, see, e.g., 327–330.

[15] For a systematic discussion of Staël's analysis of political fanaticism, see my "Politics and Passions: Staël on Fanaticism," in *The History and Philosophy of Fanaticism*, ed. Paul Katsafanas (London: Routledge, 2023), 143–160.

autonomy and argues, as she did in *A Treatise*, that literature (and philosophy) should serve to educate and offer moral edification (that is, she builds on Kant's analysis of the impure rather than the pure aesthetic judgment). Literature, she further argues, must be understood within its social and political context. She elaborates on the predicament of women who seek glory through their written work. Needless to say, this was a situation that Staël knew firsthand. She notes how men will forgive women who overlook household duties, but be hostile toward women with intellectual aspirations: "Women are forgiven if they sacrifice their household occupations for the sake of worldly amusements, but if they take their study seriously, they are accused of *pedantry*" (WP 32; later Dohm makes the same observation).[16] Further, Staël observes how women with intellectual ambitions are treated as outcasts (WP 32). She also discusses the situation of women under different political systems. In a monarchy, exceptional (and learned) women are ridiculed; in a republic they are despised, even though they actualize the very idea of education and excellence on which the republic builds. At this point, Staël overlooks the actual achievements of women in history (their achievements are not mapped as they are in, say, the work of Theodor von Hippel[17]). She further assumes that women intellectuals, like herself, are geniuses whose accomplishments hover above the reach of ordinary women (rather than being a privilege that comes in the wake of private tutors, libraries, etc.).

While it cannot be denied that Staël's celebration of the extraordinary woman is tainted by elitism, it should nonetheless be read in the context of the wider discussion of intellectual women that took place at the time. In Germany, Goethe and Schiller had launched a crusade against "women dilettantes."[18] In his *Foundations of Natural Right* (1796/97) Fichte, likewise, had stated that "vanity and the thirst for glory are contemptible in a man, but in a woman they are corrupting."[19] He also argues that women cannot make discoveries and should therefore stick to "popular writings for women, writings about women's upbringing, [and] moral teaching for the female sex in particular."[20] Responding to misrecognition of this kind can hardly be labeled arrogance, though the *form* of the response can clearly be discussed.[21]

---

[16] Germaine de Staël, "On Women Writers" (from *The Influence of Literature on Society*), trans. Dalia Nassar and Stephen Gaukroger, in *Women Philosophers in the Long Nineteenth Century*, ed. Dalia Nassar and Kristin Gjesdal (Oxford: Oxford University Press, 2021), 32. Henceforth abbreviated as WP. Except for the texts by Staël, all the translations are by Anna Ezekiel.

[17] See Theodor Gottlieb von Hippel, *The Status of Women: Collected Writings*, ed. and trans. Timothy F. Sellner (Middletown, DE: Xlibris, 2009), e.g., 251–252.

[18] See Helen Fronius, *Women and Literature in the Goethe Era 1770–1820* (Oxford: Oxford University Press, 2007), 62–67.

[19] J. G. Fichte, *Foundations of Natural Right*, trans. Michael Baur (Cambridge: Cambridge University Press, 2000), 300.

[20] Fichte, *Foundations of Natural Right*, 305.

[21] It should be noted that Fichte's classes were audited by Sophie Mereau and Rahel Levin Varnhagen (Mereau in 1791, Varnhagen in 1807–1808). Fichte later met with Staël, who chided him for his idealist position.

Staël's best-selling philosophical novels *Delphine* (1802) and *Corinne* (1807) further address the treatment of women that was discussed in *A Treatise* and *The Influence of Literature*.[22] The protagonist in *Delphine* is described as a philosopher herself. In this novel, Staël defends the ideals of the Enlightenment and have the characters discuss the situation of women (from a host of different points of view). In *Corinne*, she takes one step further and develops a sophisticated analysis of bias that women encounter even in a presumably enlightened society, and the social price they have to pay if they reject or fail to subject themselves to traditional gender roles. Social sanctions are issued by men, but also reproduced by women who, subject to implicit bias, uphold patriarchal values. *Corinne* offers a brutally honest picture of a (step)mother's attempt to clip the wings of the free-spirited protagonist, thus bolstering repressing social patterns and barring change (this topic is later discussed by Dohm and, in the twentieth century, Simone de Beauvoir[23]). The novel, whose discussion of romantic philosophy is accompanied by references and notes, juxtaposes the stepmother's provincial small-mindedness with Enlightenment cosmopolitanism and tolerance.

A call for tolerance and humanity is also issued in Staël's abolitionist writings. *Mirza*, Staël's 1795 novella, delivers a piercing criticism of slavery and colonialism. Staël traces slavery and colonialism back to a fundamental misrecognition of others (in this case a well-educated and high-minded Senegalese woman). We also find her criticizing American slavery in her letters to Thomas Jefferson,[24] and in her reflections on the work of the British abolitionist William Wilberforce.[25] In both cases, she offers an acute analysis of the price paid for narrow-minded conceptions of European supremacy and for a deficient commitment to developing a shared humanity. In an 1816 letter to Jefferson, she makes it clear that if Americans "manage to abolish slavery in the South, at least there would be in the world one government as perfect as human reason can imagine it."[26] In the same letter, she lets Jefferson know that nothing could make her side with Napoleon. It is important to realize that Staël's abolitionism goes hand in hand with her

---

[22] Germaine de Staël, *Corinne, or Italy*, trans. and ed. Sylvia Raphael (Oxford: Oxford University Press, 2008).

[23] See Hedwig Dohm, "The New Mother," WP 139–145, and Simone de Beauvoir, *The Second Sex*, trans. Constance Borde and Sheila Malovany-Chevallier (New York: Vintage Books, 2011), esp. 524–571.

[24] See especially Germaine de Staël to Thomas Jefferson, January 6, 1816, in *Madame de Staël: Selected Correspondence*, ed. Georges Solovieff and Kathleen Jameson-Cemper, trans. Kathleen Jameson-Cemper (Dordrecht: Springer, 2000), 367–369.

[25] See Staël, "Préface pour la traduction d'un ouvrage de M. Wilberforce" and "Appel aux Souverains" (both 1814). For a discussion of this aspect of Staël's philosophy, see Karen de Bruin, "Romantic Aesthetics and Abolitionist Activism: African Beauty in Germaine de Staël's *Mirza ou Lettre d'un voyageur*," *Symposium: A Quarterly Journal in Modern Literatures* 67, no. 3 (2013): 135–147, and Françoise Massardier-Kenney, "Staël, Translation, and Race," in *Translating Slavery: Gender and Race in French Women's Writings, 1783-1823*, ed. Doris Y. Kadish and Françoise Massardier-Kenney (Kent, OH: Kent State University Press, 1994), 135–146.

[26] Staël to Jefferson, 368. See also Richmond Laurin Hawkins, *Madame de Staël and the United States* (Cambridge, MA: Harvard University Press, 1930), 5; and Biancamaria Fontana, *Germaine de Staël: A Political Portrait* (Princeton: Princeton University Press, 2016).

critique of cultural bias and the sense of cultural superiority, ultimately also with her cosmopolitan hermeneutics.[27]

After the publication of *Delphine*, Napoleon had branded Staël an enemy of the state and exiled her from Paris. While banned from Paris, she shifted her focus from the French constitution to that of European politics. It was in this period that she traveled in the German-speaking lands and, from 1804, hired August Wilhelm Schlegel as a travel companion and tutor for her children. Staël documents her personal experiences from this period in *Ten Years of Exile* (posthumously published in 1821). The philosophical outcomes of her travels are gathered in *Germany* (1810/1813).

Germany is a major philosophical contribution. The book was positively received, especially in the United Kingdom, where at least one reviewer welcomes the "novelty" of a metaphysical treatise written by a woman.[28] In *Germany*, Staël extolls (and exemplifies) the virtues of tolerance and cosmopolitanism. While the philosophical reception of this work has sometimes been governed by a focus on whether or not Staël gets figures such as Kant, Fichte, and Schelling "right,"[29] it is more important to ask how she develops the positions held in her early work and, in doing so, interacts with the anthropological lineage of thought that reaches back to Herder and Schleiermacher, whose contributions are discussed both in the section on philosophy and in the final section on religion and enthusiasm. Staël's conception of enthusiasm, developed in her early work, represents a "disinterested," but still passionate, appreciation of nature and the universe (defined, with Schleiermacher, as "all there is"). In her early work, she had recommended this kind of healthy, contemplative self-loss as an antidote to the destructive self-loss of political fanaticism.

Germany also presents an ambitious metaphilosophical statement. What sets this statement apart from Kant and the German Idealists is how Staël, developing her position from *The Influence of Literature*, commits to situating philosophy within a concrete social and political reality. Moreover, she hones a methodology that is bottom-up, that is, that begins with the concrete experiential and historical level, and, from there, adds increasing layers of abstractions. The philosophical arc in *Germany* begins with a description of life and manners (this is how women, men, and children live across the German lands), proceeds to a discussion of literature (Jean Paul, Lessing, Goethe,

[27] See my "Spinoza's Hermeneutic Legacy: Herder, Schleiermacher, Staël," in *Spinoza in Germany: Political and Religious Thought in the Long Nineteenth Century*, ed. Jason Yonover and Kristin Gjesdal (Oxford: Oxford University Press, forthcoming).

[28] James Mackintosh, "*De L'Allemagne*. Par Madame la Baronne de Staël-Holstein, 3 vols. London 1813," *Edinburgh Review* (October 1813): 198–239.

[29] For solid discussions of Staël's reading of Schelling and Kant, see Margaret R. Higonnet, "Madame de Staël and Schelling," *Comparative Literature* 38, no. 2 (1986): 159–180; J. Gibelin H. Champion, *L'esthétique de Schelling Et l'Allemagne de Madame de Staël* (Geneva: Slatkin Reprints, 1975); James Vigus, "A Weimar Constellation: Aesthetic Autonomy in Henry Crabb Robinson's Private Lectures (1804) and Madame de Staël's *Corinne ou l'Italie*," in *Idealismus und Romantik in Jena*, ed. Michael Forster, Johannes Korngiebel, and Klaus Vieweg (Jena: Wilhelm Fink, 2018), 287–307; Reinhard Lauth, "J. G. Fichte et Madame de Staël," *Archives de Philosophie* 47, no. 1 (1984): 63–75.

Schiller, and others), philosophy (Herder, Kant, Jacobi, Schelling, Schleiermacher, and others), and finally, analyzes the sublime feeling of belonging in nature (or the universe) that Staël finds developed in German thought. While the book has sometimes been accused of nationalism—and did indeed create romantic nationalist sentiments of kinds[30]—Staël's focus is primarily on a language area (Germany was not yet politically unified), though she also brings in examples from Danish and other literatures. Her work generated a wider understanding of and interest in romanticism as a concept and movement. In the tradition of Montesquieu and Voltaire, Staël's descriptions of German culture offer a perspective on what she takes to be a (Napoleonic) French culture in decline. This did not escape Napoleon's attention. Moreover, Staël does not mention his name in the book, and she praises Prussia, against whom Napoleon had waged an eight-year-long war. Napoleon ordered the destruction of the first 10,000 copies of Staël's book. Staël fearlessly describes this and other attacks on her in the introduction to the work and in the posthumously published *Ten Years' Exile*.[31] *Germany* was eventually (re)published in French in England in 1813; an English translation followed swiftly.

Throughout her work, Staël encourages intercultural understanding. Her planned (but never finished) work on English culture and thought would in all likelihood have clarified her productive encounters not only with German idealism but also with David Hume and Adam Smith (she had already drawn on the latter in *A Treatise*, especially the culminating discussion of pity). Staël's final work, a shorter essay on translation, explores the gains of cultural exchange.[32] Her views on cultural exchange, moreover, get a real-world exemplification through the eager reception of *Germany* in Scandinavia, Italy, Germany, Russia, and the Anglophone world (including Byron in England and Ralph Waldo Emerson, Margaret Fuller, and Lydia Maria Child in the United States).

From the early *A Treatise*, via her work on literature, German culture and philosophy, and the French Revolution, Staël advocates the principles of tolerance and liberty, but also fights, in print and in deed, against extremism, bias, and the deep-seated misrecognition of others that enables misogyny, slavery, and colonialism.

2 KAROLINE VON GÜNDERRODE

Karoline von Günderrode is the author of a philosophical work that spans discussions of free will, human agency, the relevance of poetry and art (and their ability to guide

---

[30] For a discussion of this point, see John Claiborne Isbell, *The Birth of European Romanticism: Truth and Propaganda in Staël's "De L'Allemagne"* (Cambridge: Cambridge University Press, 1994). See also Glenda Sluga, "Passions, Patriotism and Nationalism, and Germaine de Staël," *Nations and Nationalism* 15, no. 2 (2009): 299–318.

[31] Germaine de Staël, *Ten Year's Exile* [translator unnamed] (London: Centaur Press, 2005).

[32] Germaine de Staël, "The Spirit of Translation," trans. Doris Y. Kadish, in Kadish and Massardier-Kenney, *Translating Slavery*, 162–168.

us beyond the limits of reason), and our obligations to human and nonhuman nature (the totality of what she calls "the earth"). Like Staël, Günderrode writes philosophical prose, drama, poetry, and letters. Like Staël, she encourages tolerance and cultural exchange. However, unlike Staël, Günderrode focuses her social and political philosophy on our irreducible commitments to nature, and thus goes beyond, even challenges, the Enlightenment celebration of human rationality and life. Moreover, whereas Staël celebrates a sublime experience of the subject's belonging to nature (thus questioning, from within a Kant-friendly perspective, the Kantian distinction between beauty and sublimity in the *Critique of the Power of Judgment*),[33] Günderrode (leaving Kant behind) describes a union between subjectivity and nature. This union can be philosophically approximated, but is more fully expressed through poetical metaphors and tropes.[34]

Until quite recently, Günderrode's philosophy would probably have been placed within the areas of metaphysics and philosophy of art. However, with the present climate crisis, her reflections on nature and the relationship between human beings and the rest of nature take on a direct, political relevance.

Günderrode's work has been associated with the romantic quest for a new mythology, familiar from, among others, Hölderlin, the young Hegel and Schelling, Novalis, and Friedrich Creuzer.[35] Her correspondence with Creuzer, with whom she was romantically involved, reveals how he sought to direct her away from a traditional Enlightenment interest in politics and history and toward a more mythological style of writing (possibly one that he saw more fit for a woman).[36] However, Günderrode had been reading mythological romantic philosophy at least from 1796 onward. Her interest in ecology, however, indicates that she, early on, carves out her own position, one in which the individual, in her relationship to nature ("the earth"), is held responsible to the larger totality of which she is a part.

Günderrode situates herself within the landscape of post-Kantian idealism. Her mother had introduced her to Fichte's philosophy and her 1804 discussion of Fichte's *The Vocation of Humankind* (published four years earlier) initially appears to be committed to a broader, idealist position. In her notes, she starts by analyzing the freedom of the self and the idea that freedom is a condition of possibility for ethical responsibility. Complementing this idea is the notion of nature as a domain of causal relations, that is, a domain in which freedom cannot exist. Günderrode, however, does not stop

---

[33] This is clear, e.g., in pt. 4 of *Germany*.

[34] Some of these metaphors verge toward a celebration of the dissolution of subjectivity in death. However, as Barbara Becker-Cantarino points out, the term "life" is far more frequent in her work than the terms "death" and "dying." See Barbara Becker-Cantarino, "'New Mythology': Myth and Death in Karoline von Günderrode's Literary Work," in *Women and Death: Women's Representation of Death in German Culture since 1500*, ed. Clare Bielby and Anna Richards (Rochester, NY: Camden House, 2010), 51–70; 66–67 in particular.

[35] See Manfred Frank, *Der kommende Gott. Vorlesungen über die Neue Mythologie*, pt. 1 (Frankfurt am Main: Suhrkamp, 1982).

[36] See Karl Preißendanz, ed., *Die Liebe der Günderode. Friedrich Creuzers Briefe an Caroline von Günderode* (Bern: Herbert Lang, 1975), 230–231.

here. Against Fichte's dualism of nature and freedom, she argues for a holistic notion in which the I sees itself as fundamentally indebted to nature as a totality.[37] This totality is addressed by Günderrode as a larger "life principle" that "binds me together with all finite entities of my kind, that connects me with itself" (WP 74). As she explains, the intuition of such a totality involves the experience (and reality) of a fundamental belonging: "I am related to that *will* and everything around me is related to *me*. And *its* life is (as far as I can grasp) a *self*-forming and presenting willing that flows through the whole universe in manifold forms. A force that organizes itself in the plants, moves in the animal, and presents its own world in each ... all personhood emerges from the sum of the whole" (WP 74).

Unlike Kant, Fichte, and Staël, Günderrode ascribes *reality*—and not simply a regulative status—to the unity between mind and nature. Yet, in going beyond the perspective of subjective idealism, Günderrode still maintains that this unity is only articulated through the manifold of its individual parts. In this way, she maintains the appreciation of diversity that we find in Kant's discussion of nature and biology in the third *Critique*, in Herder's notion of cultural plurality (Günderrode had studied his *Ideas for a Philosophy of the History of Humanity* [1784–91]), and Schleiermacher's reflections, in his *Monologues*, on a manifold of individuals complementing each other in realizing different aspects of a shared humanity. Günderrode, though, extends this kind of thinking beyond the spheres of biology and culture to the earth as such. The fundamental bond between nature and spirit is not conceived of as being prior to individuation. Instead, it rests *with* the diversity of nature. Human beings contribute to the diversity of nature, but have no privileged position or point of view. Indeed, on Günderrode's understanding it is the fact that the individual I belongs to nature that enables it to see itself as differentiated from other human and nonhuman individuals and from the rest of nature. The I is conditioned by its belonging to a totality (the earth), but this totality is conceived of as a unity in difference that allows for, indeed does itself *rely on*, individuation.

This is an original contribution to romantic and idealist philosophy—*and* to our thinking about human responsibility vis-à-vis nonhuman nature. Günderrode advocates the view that human beings, in their relation to the totality of which they are a part, should transform themselves so as to be of service to the earth.[38] The earth is given ontological primacy and this, in turn, implies a fundamental ethical demand. In defending this position, Günderrode goes beyond Kant's emphasis on the disinterested appreciation of natural form, Fichte's call to subject (causally determined) nature to subjectivity (freedom), and Novalis's and Schelling's ideas of an undifferentiated *Ur*-being that is deserving of human reverence.

Günderrode's position also deviates from Enlightenment thinkers such as Herder and Staël who, in different ways, see human self-realization as a progressive process.

---

[37]   See Dalia Nassar, "The Human Vocation and the Question of the Earth: Karoline von Günderrode's Philosophy of Nature," *Archive für Geschichte der Philosophie* 104, no. 1 (2022): 108–130, and chapter 22 here.

[38]   For an elaboration of this argument, see Nassar, "The Human Vocation."

Although progress is not ruled out, Günderrode argues that it is, to the extent that it is achieved, not teleologically necessary but historically contingent.[39] The human point of view is, for her, not the ultimate standard.

In her work, Günderrode draws on Spinoza, or at least the Spinozist influences at the time (here she is followed by Lou Salomé). Her monism entails an ethical commitment to prioritize the harmony of nature, as a totality, over against an isolated focus on the needs of human beings. As Günderrode argues in her notes on Schelling ("Philosophy of Nature"), nature is a self-producing activity or force (WP 75; again, she anticipates Salomé). Human life evolves from a totality to which the individual, after death, returns. Arguably, this model of perpetuated renewal (or, revolution) represents a link between Günderrode's philosophy of nature and her philosophy of culture: cultures, too, participate in a cycle of birth, thriving, aging, and death that, in turn, yields new life.[40]

Later strands of naturalism and vitalism have led to an understanding of the human being as fundamentally embodied (even erotic, in the widest sense of the term, such as we find it in Salomé[41]). By reintroducing, into her monism, an idealist focus on ethical subjectivity and its obligations, Günderrode moves in a different direction. However, for her, the quest for a human vocation, for a profound ethical responsibility toward the earth, is related to our obligations to see ourselves *as* part of a larger totality. We are not citizens of a separate moral sphere (that of freedom) that exceeds that of nature (causality). If we do not recognize the ultimate limitations of the human and see ourselves as part of the earth, we fail to understand ourselves and to realize our obligations toward the larger totality of which we are a part.

In two texts from 1805, Günderrode further radicalizes the intertwining of ontology and ethics. In "The Story of a Brahmin" and the posthumously published "The Idea of the Earth," she argues not only that humans are indebted to and part of the earth but also that the earth itself must be ascribed with qualities that have traditionally been associated with the human. The earth, as she now sees it, is a unity of soul and body (WP 82). Appealing to natural forces, growth, and harmony, she argues that the material world is infused with spirit and the spiritual world is realized in nature. Being part of this larger whole—the continuum of the earth—human beings have a duty not only to tread lightly on the earth, but also actively to aid the universe in its self-realization.[42] Indeed, this, for Günderrode, is ultimately a question of justice (WP 83). It is worth noting that Günderrode, early on, connects her insights with Indian philosophy. Her turn to Eastern philosophy developed independently of, say, Friedrich Schlegel and predates Hegel's and Schopenhauer's interest in the subject (it is, though, later than Herder's).[43]

---

[39] See Anna Ezekiel, "Revolution and Revitalization: Karoline von Günderrode's Political Philosophy and Its Metaphysical Foundations," *British Journal for the History of Philosophy* 30, no. 4 (2022): 666–686.

[40] See Anna Ezekiel, "Revolution and Revitalization."

[41] See Lou Andreas-Salomé, *The Erotic*, trans. John Crisp (London: Routledge, 2013).

[42] In "The Story of a Brahmin" Günderrode uses the term "Universe," coined by Schleiermacher, as the most inclusive account of humans and nature.

[43] For example, the drama *Udohla* (1805) and "The Story of a Brahmin" elaborate Indian mythology, history, and thought. For a general discussion of the reception of Indian thought in the period, see

Günderrode's philosophical and political engagement—and her interest in world religions—also fuels her dramatic work. In *Hildgund* and *Muhammad, the Prophet*,[44] she stages literal and symbolic encounters between East and West. While we find systematic explorations of non-Western cultures in the works of Herder, Humboldt, and others in this period, Günderrode is unique in directly relating an openness toward non-Western religions to an expanded understanding of our relationship to nature (rather than simply contributing to our cultural and epistemic horizons). Moreover, Günderrode does not follow the late Herder, Hegel, and others in treating European culture as more advanced than non-European cultures.[45]

While engaging philosophers such as Spinoza, Rousseau, Herder, Kant, Fichte, Schlegel, Schleiermacher, Schelling, and others, Günderrode is aware of the unique position of women, and perhaps also of traditional philosophy's tendency to take for granted a male perspective. This is clear in her analysis of the problem of free will—an analysis that bridges her philosophical writing and her drama. While Fichte emphasizes the freedom of the self to act, Günderrode insists that freedom needs to be realized in a concrete, social context (WP 73). Especially for women, this context may well be one in which the subject is not granted freedom at all. Her dramatic protagonist Hildgund, in the work carrying her name, exemplifies a woman whose will encounters limitations in the real world (her abductor, Attila, demands that she be his wife, or else he will invade her beloved Burgundy), but also summons the agency to overcome them (she plots to kill Attila, thus freeing her country without marrying to her captor).[46]

Günderrode's exploration of women's situation receives further attention when her friend Bettina Brentano von Arnim, thirty-four years after Günderrode committed suicide, published a creative reworking of their correspondence, thus celebrating Günderrode's philosophical contributions while also developing a philosophical position of her own.[47]

Bradley L. Herling, *The German Gītā: Hermeneutics and Discipline in the German Reception of Indian Thought, 1778–1831* (London: Routledge, 2006).

[44] Both texts are translated in Karoline von Günderrode, *Poetic Fragments*, trans. Anna Ezekiel (Albany: State University of New York Press, 2016). Ezekiel's translation also includes helpful introductions to Günderrode's philosophy and the aforementioned drama in particular.

[45] Indeed, in her turn to Hinduism, she goes as far as to almost romanticize widow burning (see the poem "The Malabarian Widows," in Karoline von Günderrode, *Sämtliche Werke*, ed. Walter Morgentaler [Basel: Stromfeld, 1990–91], vol. 1, 325). Here she distinguishes her perspective from that of Herder, who strongly condemns widow burning. See Herder, *Werke in zehn Bänden*, ed. Martin Bollacher et al. (Frankfurt am Main: Deutscher Klassiker Verlag, 1985–98), vol. 6, 456.

[46] Hence, while Becker-Cantarino may be right to criticize the gender aspects of Günderrode's new mythology (a woman passively gives herself to nature if not also to death), she fails to note that this mythology, allegedly supporting "traditional submissiveness," is balanced with an awareness of agency and gender. For Becker-Cantarino's view, see " 'New Mythology,' " 68.

[47] At the point of Günderrode's suicide, she and Brentano von Arnim were no longer close. It was, apparently, Creuzer who had initiated the break. See Barbara Becker-Cantarino, "Karoline von Günderrode," in *Bettina von Arnim Handbuch*, ed. Becker-Cantarino (Berlin: de Gruyter, 2019), 160.

3 BETTINA BRENTANO VON ARNIM

Bettina Brentano von Arnim's contributions cover a wide range of topics, including philosophy of art, philosophy of history, and philosophy of language. Her uncompromising social awareness flows through and motivates much of her early work, but gets stronger over the years. She adopts a clear position in the contemporary debates of her time, including the discussion of Prussia's subjugation of the Poles and the case against the so-called Göttingen Seven, the university professors who had defended the constitution against overreach from the king. She discusses topics such as the life-conditions of the poor and the shortcoming of the prison system. It is worth noting how Brentano von Arnim's position differs from that of Kant, Staël, and others whose defense of the French Revolution was based in its republican ideals, not in solidarity with lower classes. She met with Karl Marx in 1842.

From the 1820s onward, Brentano von Arnim hosted her own salon (see chapter 6 here). Among the important groups gathering in her salon were members of the Young Germany movement, whose radical writings would be banned in Prussia. Her support of the Left Hegelians caused scandal.[48] Her emphasis on individual freedom and her critique of institutionalized religion led to accusations of antireligious attitudes.

Brentano von Arnim's literary and philosophical breakthrough came with *Goethe's Correspondence with a Child* (1835), published four years after she lost her husband (the poet Achim von Arnim), and two years after Goethe's death. The book is based on her correspondence with Goethe and his mother. The actual exchange took place between 1807 and 1811, and Brentano von Arnim fails to mention that the correspondence abruptly ended after an argument. On the face of it, Brentano von Arnim's position—the child at the feet of the great poet—confirms traditional gender roles and reflects Goethe's own wavering between supporting the work of women writers and rejecting them as mere dilettantes. However, throughout the fictionalized correspondence, she cleverly works out her position, which is then solidified in the diary notes that, toward the end of the book, conclude her philosophical reflections.

Brentano von Arnim sheds light on why she describes herself as a child in the book's title. While her self-positioning alludes to Goethe's Mignon figure (from the novel *Wilhelm Meister*) and the notion of the child as an innocent truth-teller,[49] she herself draws a philosophical parallel between the child and the place of human spirit in nature: "the spirit is a child here upon earth, therefore has love created the sweet blessed

---

[48] See von Arnim, "Bettine und die Junghegelianer," in Bettine von Arnim, *Werke und Briefe*, ed. Walter Schitz and Sibylle von Steinsdorf, vol. 3, ed. Wolfgang Bunzel et al. (Frankfurt am Main: Deutscher Klassiker Verlag, 1985), 727–742 ("Kommentar").

[49] This reading is found in Christa Wolf, "Your Next Life Begins Today: A Letter about Bettine," in *Bettina von Arnim: Gender and Politics*, ed. Elke P. Frederiksen and Katherine R. Goodman (Detroit: Wayne State University Press, 1995), 35–71 (reference is to p. 38).

child-like nature, as a language for the spirit."[50] The position of the child implies an ability to take an immediate and sensuous pleasure in natural beauty.

Where Staël had further radicalized the Kantian notion of natural beauty, and Günderrrode's philosophy of nature is metaphysical and mythological, Brentano von Arnim offers concrete and lively descriptions of the wonders of nature. It is the diversity of its forms—the abundance of different plants, the changing of the weather and the seasons, the variety of minerals and landscapes—that fascinates her. In these passages, Brentano von Arnim takes her voice beyond that of a naïve admirer of Goethe's genius (for her, every human being ought to develop their genius). Her independence from Goethe is made even more visible when she critiques the poet's lack of political engagement, for example his passive attitude toward the Tyrolean struggle for independence.[51] The child, at this point, has clearly grown up and found a language of social and political critique. For Brentano von Arnim, there is a parallel between the need to cultivate the diversity of natural forms and the need to allow for human and cultural diversity. As was the case with Günderrode, Brentano von Arnim's philosophy of nature, especially her appreciation of nature's diverse forms (and the cohabitation of humans with the rest of nature), assumes political relevance when taking into account the present climate challenges.

A similar strategy—that of developing her own philosophy through a dialogical exchange—organizes *Günderode* (1840), which is built around correspondence with Karoline von Günderrode (from whom she, again, had been estranged).[52] Through their dialogues, Bettine further evolves her philosophy of nature and develops an original philosophy of love that involves our relationship to other human beings as well as to nature. Nature, for her, speaks its own language and we, as philosophers, poets, and lovers of nature, ought to listen. She also discusses the topic of history and canon-formation. In particular she relays how she fails to relate to the past when it is presented as the deeds of great (male) figures to whom she cannot relate. While her friend emphasizes the importance of mastering the historical canon, the impatient Bettine asks for a history in which a young woman can recognize herself (see WP 98–100).[53] Shortly after the book, which

---

[50] Bettina von Arnim, *Goethe's Correspondence with a Child*, 3 vols., vol. 3 (London: Longman et al., 1839), 76. While the translator is unnamed, Brentano von Arnim had taught herself English to translate the work. See Marjanne G. Goozé, "A Language of Her Own: Bettina Brentano von Arnim's Translation Theory and Her English Translation Project," in Frederiksen and Goodman, *Bettina Brentano von Arnim*, 278–304.

[51] On the dispute around Tyrol, see Ulrike Landfester, "'Die echte Politik muß Erfinderin sein.' Überlegungen zum Umgang mit Bettine von Arnims politischem Werk," in "*Die echte Politik muß Erfinderin sein." Beitäge eines Wiepersdorfer Kolloquiums zu Bettina von Arnim*, ed. Hartwig Schutz (Berlin: Saint Albin Verlag, 1999), 1–39 (esp. 9–12).

[52] For an account of their friendship, see Barbara Becker-Cantarino, "Karoline von Günderrode," 157–164. In the work, Brentano von Arnim does not mention Günderrode's suicide, though this is indeed mentioned in *Goethe's Letter to a Child* (toward the end of the correspondence with Goethe's mother, Catharina Elisabeth, in bk. 1).

[53] For a discussion of Brentano von Arnim's political philosophy, see Giulia Valpione, "Expanding the Canon: The Political Philosophy of Bettina von Arnim," *Symphilosophie* 2 (2020): 131–156. Valpione also

was dedicated to students, was first published, the students in Berlin celebrated it with a torch parade.[54]

A third epistolary work is the exchange with her brother, Clemens, in *The Spring Wreath*, published four years after *Günderode*. Here, Bettine is ready to deepen her discussions of gender. While she does not directly engage the emerging debates about women's rights, she performatively plays it out in her exchanges with her brother, who reacts to her interest in affairs of the state and the revolution by suggesting that she knit him socks.[55] Bettine's response is both hilarious and defiant as she reminds her brother that what she needs is not more knitting but more freedom.[56]

Brentano von Arnim's late work takes an even more direct political turn. Nonetheless, her epistolary writings have prepared for this by viewing natural diversity as a model for human life (rather than the other way around) and by defending each individual's right to freely develop her inner voice and calling.[57] In 1843, Brentano von Arnim published *This Book Belongs to the King*. The title reflects the dedication to Friedrich Wilhelm IV, the young king of Prussia (who, through the interventions of Alexander von Humboldt, had given his permission for the publication of her book). Due to its radical political message—that the king ought to address problems such as socioeconomic inequality—the book was immediately banned in Austria and Bavaria. In England, it was warmly received, with one commentator enthusiastically observing how a lady of high rank gives "the king a lesson in Communism and atheism."[58]

Again, Bettina speaks through a historical figure and, again, she connects to the Goethes. Through the persona of the seventy-seven-year-old Frau Rat (Goethe's mother) and her exchanges with luminaries such as Queen Louise, Bettina offers advice in a style that mirrors Plato's *Republic*. One chapter is indeed called "Socratie der Frau Rat." The book directly and boldly calls for a solution to the growing poverty problem in Prussia. Brentano von Arnim also has Frau Rat address the penal system and argue that

helpfully compares Brentano von Arnim's views on gender and agency with those of the other (male) romantics.

[54] See Wolf, "Your Next Life Begins Today," 43.

[55] The idea of women's knitting resounds in misogynist comments throughout the century. Hedwig Dohm takes on the gendered views on knitting and morality in "Reform der Mädchenschule," in *Frauen. Ein historisches Lesebuch*, ed. Andrea van Dülmen (Munich: Verlag C. H. Beck, 1991), 39–41, 41.

[56] See Bettina Brentano von Arnim, *Werke*, vol. 2 (Weimar: Aufbau Verlag, 1989), 631. As for her needing freedom, she writes: "Ich weiß, was ich bedarf!—ich bedarf, daß ich meine Freiheit behalte." Brentano von Arnim, *Werke*, vol. 2, 692.

[57] This aspect of Brentano von Arnim's philosophy becomes central in the new Hegelian Edgar Bauer's defense of her work, and also in Tugenev's celebration of it. See Heinz Härtl, "Bettina Brentano von Arnim's Relations to the Young Hegelians," in Frederiksen and Goodman, *Bettina Brentano von Arnim*, 156–158. Further, while presented with the view that her King's Book was influenced or partly even dictated by Bruno Bauer, Brentano von Arnim responds that "the philosophy in it . . . did not come from Bruno Bauer . . . but from *Günderode*"; 165.

[58] Heinz Härtl, "Zur zeitgenössischen Publizistischen Rezeption des Königbuches," in *"Der Geist muß Freiheit genießen . . . ! Studien zu Werk und Bildungsprogramm Bettine von Arnims*, ed. Walter Schmitz and Sibylle von Steinsdorff (Berlin: FSP Saint Albin Verlag, 1992), 208–235, 220.

criminality must be understood in light of society's rejection of the poor. In this sense, "the criminal is himself the victim."[59] The state, moreover, should prioritize housing for the needy over grand museums and victory monuments.[60] Toward the end of the book, she includes a lengthy report, commissioned from Heinrich Grunholzer (a young Swiss teacher, who had come to Berlin to study for a year), on poverty in Berlin, where he had spent four weeks interviewing inhabitants. Indeed, this report was often seen as the most provocative part of the book, not only because of the desperate conditions documented, but also because poverty is not blamed on bad luck or individual flaws such as drinking or laziness, but traced back to structural, social conditions. Brentano von Arnim paid Grunholzer an honorarium for his research. In its reliance on empirical data, in its turn to structural explanations, and in its combination of the two, her work broke new methodological grounds in social and political philosophy.

Brentano von Arnim's approach to poverty and pauperism, and her criticism of religion, would resound with the Left Hegelians (Bruno and Edgar Bauer, David Strauß, Arnold Ruge, and others). However, unlike the Left Hegelians, Brentano von Arnim saw social justice as best achieved not through a revolution, but through the work of a just monarch, a people's king.[61] Further, unlike the Left Hegelians, with whom she shared her critique of institutionalized religion, she cultivated a religious spirit throughout her work, albeit one that is unconventional and adaptive to her social causes.[62]

In *Conversations with Demons* (1852) the king, again, is the addressee, this time with demons conveying political advice to the slumbering regent. At this point, Brentano von Arnim was no longer close with the king, and the book received less attention.

In the 1840s, however, Brentano von Arnim had intensified her work for the poor—which had previously included charitable outreach, with among others her sister Gunda and her friend Rahel Varnhagen, during the 1831 cholera epidemic in Berlin—by gathering first-person testimonies of the conditions of the working poor, especially the weavers in Silesia. Among the methods used were newspaper calls for firsthand accounts. Again, Brentano von Arnim's work is methodologically groundbreaking, this time because it grants a voice to the poor rather than speaking over their heads or

---

[59] Bettina Brentano von Arnim, *Werke und Briefe*. Edited by Wolfgang Bunzel et al. (Frankfurt am Main: Deutscher Klassiker Verlag, 1985), vol. 3, 200. The conclusion follows Frau Rat's reflection on the state: "What is the state to the people? A lording slave trader who barters with him." In a situation like this, the state fails to take care of the people like a loving parent; 200.

[60] *Werke und Briefe*, vol. 3, 217.

[61] Similarly, Novalis defends the notion of a *Volkskönig(in)* in *Glauben und Liebe* (1798).

[62] Indeed, David Strauß uses Brentano von Arnim's religious spirit to defend his own position against blasphemy charges and asks how long it will take "for people to see a new gospel according to John in Bettina's letters." See Härtl, "Bettina Brentano von Arnim's Relations to the Young Hegelians," 145–185, 147. Härtl also discusses the nuances in the left Hegelian responses to Brentano von Arnim, especially around the issues of religion and pantheism.

interpreting their position from the outside. The book she had planned was never finished, but her correspondence around the project and the notes for what was probably
intended as an afterword were posthumously published as *The Book of the Poor (Das
Armenbuch)*.[63] The planned afterword draws on biblical references (the blissful naked-
ness of Adam and Eve as contrasted with the lack of clothing among the poor) to clarify
the suffering inflicted on the Silesian population by poverty. She condemns the Prussian
army's brutal suppression of the protests.

Brentano von Arnim, whose circles included the Grimm brothers, also published
fairy tales, a literary form that, at least in its oral transmission, was associated with
"folk culture" and thus traversing distinctions of gender and class. "The Tale of the
Lucy Purse" focuses on a widowed grandmother who struggles to take care of her
grandchildren while grieving the loss of her sons to the war.[64] Another fairy tale, also
of the political kind, is *The Life of Countess Gritta von Ratsinourhouse*, coauthored with
her daughter Gisela and posthumously published. It tells the story of a group of run-
away girls who experience a brief semiutopian adventure as they survive in nature.[65]
Brentano von Arnim here returns to central topics of the early work (female friendship,
female freedom, the relationship between human beings and the rest of nature), thus
creating a philosophical arc throughout her works and across her different modes of
expression.

Along with Staël and Günderrode, Brentano von Arnim's work goes way beyond the
image of romantic women as (naively) infatuated with myth.[66] Her oeuvre forges an important bridge between romanticism, on the one hand, and socialism, on the other.[67]
It contains original reflections on gender and agency. And it develops new strategies in
political philosophy.

---

[63] For an overview of the editions and editorial challenges, see Becker-Cantarino, "Das *Armenbuch*-
Projekt (1844/45)," in *Bettina von Arnim Handbuch*, 430–439.

[64] For an English translation, see Bettina Brentano von Arnim, "Tale of the Lucky Purse," trans. Helen
G. Morris-Keitel, in *Marvels & Tales* 11, no. 1/2 (1997), 127–133.

[65] For an English translation, see Bettine von Arnim and Gisela von Arnim Grimm, *The Life of High
Countess Gritta von Ratsinourhouse*, trans. Lisa Ohm (Lincoln: University of Nebraska Press, 1999).

[66] See Ricarda Huch's *Die Romantik* (Leipzig: H. Haeffel Verlag, 1931), vol. 2 (for the discussion
of Brentano von Arnim, see 167–193). For a critical discussion of Huch's reading, see Barbara Becker-
Cantarino, "Zur politischen Romantik. Bettina von Arnim, die 'Frauenfrage' und der 'Feminismus,'" in
Schutz, *"Die echte Politik muß Erfinderin sein,"* 217–248. While Becker-Cantarino also discusses Huch's
antifeminism, it should be mentioned that Huch, in her work, pays attention to a number of women
romantics, including Karoline Schelling (née Michaelis), Dorothea Schlegel, and others. For a more
positive assessment of Huch's contribution, see Gesa Dane, "Women Writers and Romanticism," in *The
Cambridge Companion to Romanticism*, ed. Nicholas Saul (Cambridge: Cambridge University Press,
2009), 133–146.

[67] Brentano von Arnim's endorsement of communism was clear when she gave the Bauer brothers
the right to her husband's work and Egbert Bauer in particular the right to *The Spring Wreath* "for no
other reason than to support communism where it is not advocated senselessly but founded on a moral
sentiment." See Härtl, "Bettina Brentano von Arnim's Relations to the Young Hegelians," 169.

4 HEDWIG DOHM

In the 1830s and 1840s, the new women's movement in Germany was gaining traction. Brentano von Arnim did not take part in this movement. Indeed, she did, at times, appear to (willfully) ignore it.[68] The new women's movement saw the romantic approach to women—the focus on nature, self-realization, self-expression, love, and education—as outdated and potentially regressive. What mattered was a new emphasis on women's *rights*.

In this context, Hedwig Dohm is important: she is the first to demand suffrage for women in Germany.[69] Throughout her work, Dohm insists on women's rights being human rights.[70] She delivers a scathing critique of the biological (and the metaphysical) understanding of gender. *And* she forges an important philosophical bridge between Brentano von Arnim, on the one hand, and twentieth-century feminists, on the other. Born in 1831, Dohm lived to see the introduction of women's suffrage in 1918.

Dohm expresses the feeling that her work is untimely—that she is born either a century too early or a century too late, as she puts it.[71] In a certain sense, she has a point. On the one hand, Dohm relates gender to social and cultural (rather than biological and metaphysical) concepts, thereby anticipating a central trend in twentieth-century feminism. To be *born* a woman, that is, with a fixed identity, would be tantamount to being stillborn, as Dohm puts it.[72] She speaks, moreover, for the rights of single mothers and

---

[68] Katherine R. Goodman, "Through a Different Lens: Bettina Brentano von Arnim's Views on Gender," in Frederiksen and Goodman, *Bettina Brentano von Arnim*, 116–117.

[69] "Das Stimmrecht der Frauen" (1876), in Elke Frederiksen, *Die Frauenfrage in Deutschland 1865–1915. Texte und Dokumente* (Stuttgart: Reclam, 1981), 374. See also Birgit Mikus, *The Political Woman in Print: German Women's Writing 1845–1919* (Oxford: Peter Lang, 2014), 213.

[70] Here Dohm differs from the different-but-equal attitude that, according to Chris Weedon, characterized much of the early women's movement. See Chris Weedon, "The Struggle for Women's Emancipation in the Work of Hedwig Dohm," *German Life and Letters* 47, no. 2 (1994): 182–192; see 183 in particular.

[71] Dohm, "Kindheitserinnerungen einer alten Berlinerin," in *Hedwig Dohm. Erinnerungen und weitere Schriften von und über Hedwig Dohm*, ed. Hedda Korsch (Zurich: Ala Verlag, 1980), 70 and 78.

[72] Hedwig Dohm, "Sind Berufsthätigkeit und Mutterpflichten vereinbar?" *Die Woche. Moderne illustrierte Zeitschrift* 38, September 22, 1900: 1667–1669. In the earlier "Herrenrechte" (1886), she points out that if women's inferiority is led back to nature, we also need to ask about men's nature. Are not also men characterized by historically determined social conditions? In this context, Dohm points out how philosophers like Mill benefited from marrying educated women. See Dohm, "Herrenrechte," *Die Zukunft* 14 (1896): 508–512, 511. The same point is repeated in a 1908 essay on reform in girls' schools. Dohm demands comprehensive schooling and coeducation. Dohm, "Reform der Mädchenschule," in *Frauen. Ein historisches Lesebuch*, ed. Andrea van Dülmen (Munich: Verlag C. H. Beck, 1991), 39–41. It should be pointed out, though, that in an earlier essay (1874), she keeps open the possibility that women have a mental organization (*geistige Organisation*) that is different from men's (different, but not of lesser quality, as she specifies). For Dohm, this is an argument to grant women access to the university, because they are likely to provide new and different ideas in the sciences (*neue Formen der Erkenntnis, neue Gedankenrichtungen der Wissenschaft*). See Dohm, "Ob Frauen studieren dürfen, können, sollen?" in Frederiksen, *Die Frauenfrage*, 242–255. Here Dohm echoes a point of view defended by, among others, Louise Otto-Peters. For a rendering of Otto-Peters along these lines see Weedon, "The Struggle for

unmarried women. In this, she is clearly ahead of her time. On the other hand, Dohm positions herself in the lineage of a romantic like Brentano von Arnim.[73] She writes with humor and energy, articulates a harsh critique of institutionalized religion, and seeks to describe the concrete life-situations of women. The topics discussed in her essays include mothers and daughters, the old woman, the unrealized woman, and women's education. Like the romantics, Dohm hosted her own salon and developed her thinking in interaction with women writers and activists such as Fanny Lewald, Helene Lange, Else Lasker-Schüler, Gabriele Reuter, and Lou Salomé. Dohm's work, like that of the romantics, spans a range of genres: treatises, pamphlets, essays, novels, drama (comedy), and novellas.

Dohm only started writing in earnest after she lost her husband. While she published a study of Spanish literature in 1867, it was only in 1872 and 1873 that she published major feminist texts such as *Was die Pastoren von den Frauen Denken* and *Der Jesuisismus im Hausstande*.[74] In these works, Dohm discusses the views of John Stuart Mill.[75] She also acknowledges the importance of Friedrich Schleiermacher, Dorothea Veit, Rahel Levin, Caroline Schlegel-Schelling (WP 131), Staël, and, among the idealists, Fichte.[76]

A consistent topic in Dohm's writing is the nature and power of privilege. She points out that no one is likely to give up privileges without a fight. As far as gender privileges go, "men will not voluntarily give up the rule of their sex [*Geschlechtsherrschaft*], which they regard as their legitimate right, but which is but an ancient privilege that, over the centuries, has corrupted their sense of justice."[77]

Like Staël, Dohm argues that male privileges are often upheld by making women's quests for change seem small and petty-minded. Echoing Staël's analysis of the misrecognition of the intellectual woman, Dohm observes how men accept women's participation in politics as long as they are amusing and charming, but quickly put women down if they challenge or instruct them. Given such attitudes, the fight for

Women's Emancipation." Weedon does not acknowledge Dohm's closeness to this position in the first half of the 1870s.

[73] Dohm makes it clear that she identified with Brentano von Arnim ("als Halberwachsene identifizierte ich mich mit Bettina"). "Kindheitserinnerungen einer alten Berlinerin," 70.

[74] Hedwig Dohm, *Was Die Pastoren von den Frauen denken* (Berlin: Verlag Reinhold Schlingmann, 1972), https://www.projekt-gutenberg.org/dohm/pastoren/pastoren.html; and *Der Jesuismus im Hausstande. Ein Beitrag zur Frauenfrage* (Berlin: Verlag Reinhold Schlingmann, 1972).

[75] Throughout her work, Dohm frequently quotes from *On Liberty* as well as *The Subjection of Women*.

[76] She references Staël in *Was die Pastoren von den Frauen Denken*. In this essay, Dohm also mentions George Sand and women writers whose work was published by Goethe and Schiller (Carlotte von Kalb, Therese Huber, "the two Carolines," and others). Fichte is referenced in "Ob Fraue studieren dürfen, können, sollen?," in Frederiksen, *Die Frauenfrage*, 253.

[77] Hedwig Dohm, *Der Jesuitismus im Hausstande. Ein Beitrag zur Frauenfrage* (Berlin: Wedekind & Schwieger, 1987), 225, https://www.deutschestextarchiv.de/book/show/dohm_jesuitismus_1873. In *Women's Nature and Privilege*, she puts it as follows: "the division of labor [women staying at home or not being able to access public life] is not the Right of woman, but the Advantage of man." Dohm, *Women's Nature and Privilege*, trans. Constance Campbell (Westport, CT: Hyperion Press, 1976), 34.

women's rights amounts to nothing short of a revolution—a formidable and wonderful one (*eine gewaltige und wunderbare*), as Dohm puts it.[78] At the core of this revolution is the call for women's suffrage. Hence Dohm is critical of feminists who view women's education as a goal in itself. Indeed, as she sees it, women will not be acknowledged as worthy of education *until* they are given the right to vote (rather than education possibly leading to suffrage).

If Dohm does not see education as a final goal, it nonetheless remains a topic she deeply cares about. In her 1876 *Women's Nature and Privilege*, Dohm points out that while the issue of women's education evokes strong feelings, much greater prejudices have been overcome in the past. Just think of Copernicus, she advises her readers: If he could make people realize that the earth is not the center of the universe, a similar reconsideration must be conceivable with respect to the position of men. Yet, Dohm recognizes the power of custom: "Custom and Habit are more powerful even than the law. [And] the latter is more easily evaded than the former."[79] Leaning on Mill, Dohm further develops the point that nurture, not nature, determines our understanding of gender. And from this point of view, education is indeed needed: "Not blood but up-bringing is almost the only thing which stamps the individual with its seal," as she puts it.[80]

In her later essays, Dohm analyzes the lived experiences of oppression—and reviews a series of creative attempts to resist and overcome it. In "The New Mother" (1900), she (again like Staël) points out that patriarchy is not simply upheld by men, but also by women. Mothers play a particularly important role in this context. Mothers, she claims, should not expect their daughters simply to reproduce their own values and they should be mindful that their ideals are often rooted in the past and, to a younger generation, ir-relevant or even oppressive.

Women and aging is another topic that Dohm takes on. With her characteristic mix of wit and criticism, she describes how a society that identifies women with childbearing leads to a systematic underappreciation of the old woman. The old woman, she argues, should fight back: "Mock the mockeries with which they want to intimidate you and close the doors to joy. . . . Become old for others: but not for yourself" (WP 149).[81] A different, more melancholy portrait of the old woman is found in the earlier novella *Become Who You Are!* (1894). Here, we encounter the aging (but by our standards still relatively young) Agnes Schmidt who undergoes an existential crisis upon realizing that, once she is through her years of childbearing, society no longer has a place for her. As she reflects: "What have I ever done for myself out of love? Nothing that I knew of.

---

[78] *Der Jesuismus im Hausstande.*

[79] Dohm, *Women's Nature,* 48.

[80] Dohm, *Women's Nature,* 11. It is worth noting that already Dohm's early essays, such as this one, deploy the argumentative strategy she will later make use of in her readings of Nietzsche: that of holding their work up against their own philosophical standards.

[81] Already in *Women's Nature,* Dohm criticizes Schopenhauer's view of the old woman as "a horror." *Women's Nature,* 19.

But yet I was always satisfied? I? But I wasn't even an 'I.' . . . I have lived a life in which I wasn't even present."[82] The novella opens with a reference to Nietzsche and Pindar, but also indicates how the Nietzschean topic of self-realization remains flawed unless it considers the problems of misogyny and gender injustice.

In the 1880s, many women artists and intellectuals, including Ellen Key, Laura Marholm, and Lou Salomé, took an interest in Nietzsche.[83] Dohm criticizes what she sees as this movement's hagiographic attitudes toward Nietzsche and their apparent compliance with his antifeminism.[84] Yet Nietzsche remains a philosopher on whose work Dohm often draws.

Many of the topics from Nietzsche's philosophy, however, had earlier been developed by Dohm. Her criticism of the church, which centers on its repressive view of women, is brought to focus in the 1873 text on the pastors, that is, before Nietzsche's well-known critique of Christianity in *Beyond Good and Evil* (1886) and *The Genealogy of Morality* (1887). Likewise, Dohm's early work analyzes how religion colors secular life without us being aware of it—again a point that Nietzsche later develops in *Beyond Good and Evil*. Also, the topic of self-formation, central to Nietzsche, is present in her earlier work. Yet, it remains the case that when Dohm turns to Nietzsche, she finds a voice whose critical spirit she appreciates and whose thinking serves to strengthen her arguments. Dohm's appropriation of Nietzsche, however, is never passive. With respect to self-formation, for example, she goes beyond Nietzsche by focusing on the need for a society in which self-realization can be achieved by everyone, women as well as men (through, among other things, education),[85] and she analyzes the price that is paid for systematic, social repression.

In "Nietzsche and Women" (1898), Dohm chronicles her horror and sadness upon confronting Nietzsche's misogyny. She points to Nietzsche's limited experience with women (WP 129). Moreover, she takes his claims about women to their outermost

---

[82] Hedwig Dohm, *Become Who You Are*, trans. Elizabeth G. Ametscbichler (Albany: State University of New York Press, 2006), 33.

[83] Laura Marholm and Ellen Key enthusiastically promoted Nietzsche's work. The same applies to his friend Malwida von Meysenbug (whose essay on Staël is included in her account of the history of great women in *Individualitäten* [Malwida von Meysenbug, *Individualitäten* (Berlin: Schuster und Loeffler, 1901), esp. 182–203]). Helene Stöcker, whose initial plan for a doctoral dissertation had been to work on Brentano von Arnim, introduced Nietzschean thinking into the League for the Protection of Mothers, which she took over in 1905 (it dissolved five years later). There is also Salomé, who was part of Dohm's circle. Another important figure is Lily Brown. For the women philosophers who turned to Nietzsche (often with a social and political intent), see Carol Diethe, *Nietzsche's Women: Beyond the Whip* (Berlin: de Gruyter, 1996). Diethe does not discuss Ellen Key. For Stöcker's dissertation plans, see Annegret Stopczyk-Pfundstein, *Philosophin der Liebe. Helene Stöcker* (Stuttgart: Libri, 2003), 82–83.

[84] A summary of Dohm's criticism (with reference to Key, Marholm, and Salomé) is found in "Weib contra Weib" in the 1902 *Die Antifeministen. Ein Buch der Verteidigung* (Berlin: Holzinger, 2015), 59–99. Dohm brands Salomé "antifeminist" and is especially critical of Salomé's claim that it is the call of women to become mothers (a view Nietzsche airs in *Beyond Good and Evil*). See Hedwig Dohm, "Reaktion in der Frauenbewegung," *Die Zukunft*, November 18, 1899, 279–291. However, she also characterizes Salomé as "one of the most profound authors [she knows]" (WP 134).

[85] See Dohm, "Ob Frauen studieren dürfen, können, sollen?," in Frederiksen, *Die Frauenfrage*.

consequence, thereby demonstrating their absurdity. Nietzsche claims to detect women's slave-like nature. But how is it, asks Dohm, that the *Übermensch* needs to surround himself with slaves (WP 131, 136)? And if women, as Nietzsche suggests, exist in order to procreate, the *Übermensch* will certainly have his hands full providing for an ever-expanding family (WP 131).[86] Most important, however, in critiquing Nietzsche's attitude toward women, Dohm pursues a systematic line of arguments. She demonstrates how he, in speaking about women, passively internalizes the prejudices of the period, thus failing the critical spirit he otherwise displays. Measuring Nietzsche against his own standards, Dohm's goal is to learn from his mistakes. As good Nietzscheans, she argues, we must avoid this kind of fallacy and remain critical not only of others but also of our own points of view.[87] It could be argued, though, that Dohm herself is subject to internalized bias when, in an essay such as "On the Agitators of Feminism," she praises how some exceptional men have succeeded in portraying the suffering of women (instead of discussing the works of earlier women philosophers and writers).

During World War I, Dohm was an outspoken critic of militarization and war. In the ironically titled "Der Mißbrauch des Todes. Senile Impressionen von Hedwig Dohm" ("The Misuse of Death. Senile Impressions by Hedwig Dohm," written in 1915, published two years later), she deploys her earlier emphasis on human rights to critique the "cannibalism" of war. War, she points out, reduces human beings to brutes—often under the false auspices of religion or nationalism.[88] In her antiwar activism, Dohm sees eye to eye with, among others, Helene Stöcker, Clara Zetkin, and Rosa Luxemburg.

5   CLARA ZETKIN

For Dohm, women's rights are human rights. She recognized no special rights or nature for women. Zetkin argues along similar lines. For her, however, it is the political undoing of economic injustice, not the recognition of universal human rights, that will improve the situation of women. Indeed, for Zetkin, the very notion of human rights is a token of bourgeois idealism, that is, it is an ideological construct. Similarly, her antiwar stance is not related to human rights (as it was for Dohm), but to an awareness of how it is, predominantly, the economically oppressed who are sent to war, maimed, and killed, only to see the upper classes profit from it (through for example the industrial production of arms and other goods).

---

[86] Dohm here elaborates a point she has made earlier, namely that "only a man of a powerful personality will endure the companionship of a woman who is his equal." *Women's Nature*, 23. She attributes this point to Mill (29).

[87] While Dohm developed her particular, critical strategy in her early criticism of antifeminists (e.g., in *Was die Pastoren von den Frauen denken*), it is only in the later essay that she brings it to full philosophical maturity.

[88] For this essay, see https://www.projekt-gutenberg.org/dohm/missbrau/missbrau.html.

In 1889, Zetkin was invited to give a speech at the international workers' meeting in Paris. It was here that she first advanced a philosophical articulation of her platform. Her speech, "For the Liberation of Women," offers a radical, materialist view of women's emancipation. In a capitalist economy, Zetkin argues, women's emancipation is tied to their status as economical beings, that is, their status as workers (WP 162). Women workers financially depend on men *and* on the capitalist class. The question of women's emancipation must therefore be related to class struggle more broadly. Moreover, the interests of working-class women are constitutively different from those of the bourgeoisie, who would have few incentives to call for a radical rethinking of the economic system that had initially generated and maintained their privileges. Precisely because they do not own property and are often subdued at home, working-class women represent a point of view from which social justice can be radically rethought. And without a solution to the grave injustice of the class system, the overall situation of women cannot be improved (WP 163). In this way, Zetkin takes on a question that has also been at the center of later emancipatory movements: whether an oppressed group can be emancipated without an even more comprehensive change to an economical system that feeds off systematic injustice and oppression.

For Zetkin, the oppression of women is a genuinely modern problem. Here she disagrees with Friedrich Engels, for whom, in *The Origin of the Family* (1884), it was traced back to the overthrowing of an *ur*-communist matriarchy. Zetkin pursues a more dialectical argument. As she argues, *both* the promise of freedom *and* the oppression of women are products of industrialization, that is, products of the fact that women are turned into wageworkers. The very moment women gain financial independence they *also* face the oppression of a class-stratified labor market (WP 164). Hence, the liberation of women—with their new-won freedom as paid workers—must involve liberation from the very structure that prevents women, now as members of the working class, from realizing their freedom: "The emancipation of women, like the emancipation of the whole human race, will be exclusively the work of the emancipation of labor from capital" (WP 166). From this point of view, a feminist focus on suffrage is no goal in itself—since one could well imagine suffrage being introduced without the larger political overhaul that Zetkin deems necessary. Zetkin's position on suffrage is modified over time.[89]

While she shapes her feminist thoughts from within a Marxist platform, Zetkin acknowledges that Marx did not have much to say about women.[90] Yet Marx provided the women's movement with helpful conceptual tools. In her words, Marx's "materialist concept of history has not supplied us with any ready-made formulas concerning the women's question . . . yet it has given us the correct, unerring method to explore and comprehend that question."[91] Similarly, she selectively approaches

---

[89] See Richard J. Evans, "Theory and Practice in German Social Democracy 1880–1914: Clara Zetkin and the Socialist Theory of Women's Emancipation," *History of Political Thought* 3, no. 2 (1982): 285–304.

[90] Clara Zetkin, "What the Women Owe to Karl Marx" (1903), in *Selected Writings*, ed. Philip S. Foner, various translators (Chicago: Haymarket Books, 2015), 94.

[91] Zetkin, "What the Women Owe to Karl Marx," 94.

the arguments from Engels's *On the Origin of the Family*.[92] She draws on and further develops the analysis of the family as a social construct and a function of material (production) conditions; it is not given by God or nature, but manmade and, as such, it can be overthrown. Yet, Zetkin did not share Engels's idealization of gender relations in the working-class family, his eulogies for the "primitive" cohabitation structure of free sexual conduct, and his skeptical attitude toward suffrage (which Zetkin now approved of).[93]

Another key text for Zetkin was August Bebel's *Woman under Socialism* (1883). Here Bebel identifies the double burden of women: "The female sex as such has a double yoke to bear. First, women suffer as a result of their social dependence upon men, and the inferior position allotted to them in society; formal equality before the law alleviates this condition, but does not remedy it. Second, women suffer as a result of their economic dependence, which is the lot of women in general, and especially of the proletarian women, as it is of the proletarian men."[94] Moreover, Bebel argues that "there can be no liberation of mankind without social independence and equality of the sexes."[95] Zetkin endorses these arguments.

However, while extending Marxism to involve positions on gender and class, Engels and Bebel do not focus on practical steps toward women's liberation. This lack of fit between their theories, on the one hand, and the practical shaping of the day-to-day struggle for equality, on the other, left a challenge for Zetkin. How best to make use of critical theory and achieve real-world results? Zetkin sets out to answer this question— and, as she does so, she realizes that this is not simply a matter of applying the existing theories. Instead, the practical implementation of the theories will require a reshaping of the theoretical level.

In her work, Zetkin confronts the fear, among male workers, that the introduction of women into the workforce will lower wages across the board. Typically, women were not unionized, which made it harder to negotiate better wages and work conditions. Often, women were faced with oppression at home as well as at work. Unlike Engels's idealization of the working classes, Zetkin insists that "the male workers must stop viewing the female worker primarily as a woman to be courted if she is young, beautiful, pleasant, and cheerful (or not). They must stop . . . molesting them with crude and fresh sexual advances. The workers must rather get accustomed to treat female

---

[92] Clara Zetkin, "Friedrich Engels. Nachruf zu seinem Tode," in Clara Zetkin, *Ausgewählte Reden und Schriften*, vol. 1 (Berlin: Aufbau Verlag, 1957), 82–83.

[93] As Engels concludes his study with a quote from the anthropologist Lewis Morgan, the new society will all the same be "a revival in a higher form, of the liberty, equality and fraternity of the ancient gentes." Friedrich Engels, *The Origin of the Family, Private Property and the State* (London: Penguin, 2010), 217. For Engels's views on suffrage, see Tristam Hunt, introduction to *The Origin of the Family*, 19 and 22. Hunt also points out that even though Engels was against prostitution, he did not shy away from using prostitutes himself.

[94] August Bebel, *Woman and Socialism*, trans. Meta A. Stern (New York: Socialist Literature Company, 1910), 6.

[95] Bebel, *Woman and Socialism*, 7.

laborers primarily as female proletarians, as working-class comrades."[96] Similarly, Zetkin challenges the leaders of the social democratic party in their attitudes toward women.[97]

Given the particular situation of the working-class woman—she does not possess property and has no interest in supporting a system that reproduces oppression—Zetkin makes it clear that her struggle will not benefit from cooperation with bourgeois feminists. As she puts it, "there is a women's question for the women of the proletariat, the bourgeoisie, the intelligentsia and the Upper Ten Thousand. It assumes a different form according to the class situation of each one of these strata."[98] This point had not been addressed by Engels or Bebel.[99] Moreover, Bebel had assumed that male workers would not be likely to support the liberation of women workers.[100] Zetkin, for her part, is more optimistic and predicts that the male worker will ultimately join the struggle for women's rights precisely because he will see it as a struggle for universal workers' rights.

Throughout her writings, speeches, and activism, Zetkin senses that there is a need for political information targeting working-class women. With her pragmatic attitudes on this matter, Zetkin has been accused of being condescending toward working-class women.[101] For the modern-day reader, her lack of support for birth control, a hotly debated issue at the time, is also unsettling. Again, Zetkin prioritized a class perspective and views birth control as potentially hurting the working class.[102] Her skepticism toward birth control was something Zetkin shared with Rosa Luxemburg and other socialist leaders.

Zetkin's position on women's emancipation is brought into sharp relief through the debates with Lily Braun.[103] Paradoxical as it may sound, Braun was a Nietzschean social democrat. In 1895, she argued that working-class women must join forces with the bourgeoise women's movement. For Braun, the fundamental distinction is that between men and women, not between classes. For Zetkin, by contrast, women's rights are and must

---

[96] Clara Zetkin, "Women's Work and the Organization of Trade Unions," in *Selected Writings*, ed. Philip S. Foner (Chicago: Haymarket Books, 2015), 58.

[97] See Karen Honeycutt, "Clara Zetkin: Socialist Approach to the Problem of Woman's Oppression," *Feminist Studies* 3, no. 3/4 (1976): 131–144.

[98] Clara Zetkin, "Only in Conjunction with the Proletarian Woman Will Socialism Be Victorious," in Foner, *Selected Writings*, 74.

[99] See Jean H. Quataert, *Reluctant Feminists in German Social Democracy 1885-1917* (Princeton, NJ: Princeton University Press, 1979), 69.

[100] Bebel writes: "in fighting for their rights, women should expect as little help from the men as working men do from the capitalist class." Quoted from Quataert, *Reluctant Feminists*, 69.

[101] See for example Tânia Ünlüdag, "Bourgeois Mentality and Socialist Ideology as Exemplified by Clara Zetkin's Constructs of Femininity," *International Review of Social History* 47 (2002): 33–58. In my view, Ünlüdag, while making important points about the wider philosophical context of Zetkin's period, is too selective in her choice of texts and fails to convincingly document her claims about Zetkin falling back on traditional bourgeois values (which Ünlüdag, strangely, associates with Nietzscheanism and Christianity).

[102] See Quataert, *Reluctant Feminists*, 95–99. See also R. P. Neuman, "Working Class Birth Control in Wilhelmine Germany," in *Comparative Studies in Society and History* 20, no. 3 (1978): 408–428.

[103] Quataert, *Reluctant Feminists*, 107–137.

be social rights and, as a result, there are few shared interests between working-class and bourgeois women.

For Zetkin, a worker is never simply a worker, but a concrete somebody who comes with a particular gender, age, and background. Given her focus on social injustice (under which the oppression of women is subsumed), Zetkin's engagement extends to child labor. In an essay from 1902, she details the grueling conditions of the children and blames politicians for their complacency: "the legislative authorities have kept a deaf ear towards the screams of many hundreds of thousands of tortured human beings. Their eyes have been blind to the twitching pain of the mangled bodies and spirits."[104]

In the 1930s, Zetkin takes a clear stance against systemic racism in the United States and elsewhere. Responding to the case against the so-called Scottsboro Boys, who had been wrongly accused of rape, she situates racial oppression within a larger picture of class and white privilege: "The accusation is a deliberate lie, concocted for the most sinister purposes of landowners and factory owners. They want to have the black youths burned alive, in order to terrorize the working masses of blacks, who are rebelling against their exploitation and, by doing so, forming a united front with their white brothers and sisters against hunger, imperialist wars, and bloody white terror" (WP 174). The reduction of the people to mere onlookers is, for Zetkin, "the greatest of all evils."[105]

Zetkin also opposes the increasing militarization across Europe in the early twentieth century. Her antiwar stance continued after World War I and extended into the period when the National Socialists rose to power. In "The Toilers against War" (1933), she argues that imperialism, without which capitalism cannot survive, is but another of capitalism's injustices.[106] Slavery and oppression are, for her, global phenomena. Thus, they should be fought in the same way as the struggle against oppression of women or working-class children. In both cases, we face a call for economic redistribution and justice.

Her conflict with the social democratic party over its support of World War I led Zetkin to join the Spartacus League, later the German communist party, spearheaded by Rosa Luxemburg and Karl Liebknecht. As the National Socialists were gaining ground, Zetkin left Germany for Russia, and it was there that she died in 1933, just months after she, as the oldest member of Parliament, had given the annual opening speech at the Reichstag. As the fascists were rising to power, Zetkin analyses the internal relationship between capitalism and fascist forms of government.[107] Her speech is a veritable antifascist manifesto that retains its relevance today.

---

[104] Clara Zetkin, "Protect Our Children," in Foner, *Selected Writings*, 87.

[105] Clara Zetkin, "Fascism Must be Defeated," in Foner, *Selected Writings*, 172.

[106] Clara Zetkin, "The Toilers against War," in Foner, *Selected Writings*, 178.

[107] For a discussion of her speech, see Luise Dornemann, *Clara Zetkin. Ein Lebensbild* (Berlin: Dietz Verlag, 1962), 423–429.

6 ROSA LUXEMBURG

Rosa Luxemburg is another pioneer within the socialist movement. In her eulogy of Luxemburg, written after the brutal political murder of Luxemburg and Karl Liebknecht in 1919, Zetkin observes that Luxemburg's work "combined to a rare degree the power of logical deduction with an acute understanding of everyday life and its development."[108] It is indeed Luxemburg's commitment to the "everyday"—her focus on workers (rather than on the party elite), her rejection of top-down politics, and her critique of imperialism—that distinguishes her contributions to social and political philosophy. This put her in conflict with the leaders of the German Social Democratic Party but also caught the attention, relatively early on, of Georg Lukàcs.[109] Luxemburg's work generated important discussions, still relevant today, of reform versus revolution, the nature of capitalism, and the perils of militarization.

Luxemburg's contribution to political philosophy gets its first systematic articulation in *Social Reform or Revolution*. The material was first published as a series of articles in the fall of 1898 and spring of 1899. Here, Luxemburg critiques Eduard Bernstein's efforts to shift the focus of Marxism from revolution to reform, thereby making social democracy, rather than the end of capitalism, its goal. Bernstein was a leading voice in German socialism—and therefore, by default, in the international socialist movement. For Luxemburg, Bernstein's willingness to prioritize "the movement" (i.e., reform) over "the goal" (i.e., revolution) cannot be counted as a modification of Marxism, but involves a rejection of the socialist agenda altogether.

As Luxemburg sees it, Bernstein's move represents the first bifurcation of the socialist movement into a reformist and a revolutionary branch.[110] In her view, there can be no socialism without the goal of a postcapitalist society.[111] Hence, while pretending to write under the auspices of Marxism, Bernstein in reality undermines it (RLR 130). His is not, as he claims, a strategic question about the pace of the movement (gradual reform or a sudden revolution), but the attempt to stake out an entirely new path: an effort to merge capitalism and the principles of social justice.

Writing as a political economist (she held a PhD in political economy from the University of Zurich), Luxemburg takes Bernstein to task for his understanding of labor. He fails, she argues, to realize that true democracy requires a reorganization of the

---

[108] Clara Zetkin, "Rosa Luxemburg," *Communist International* no. 5, September 1, 1919, 5. https://www.marxists.org/archive/zetkin/1919/09/rosa.htm.

[109] See Georg Lukàcs, *History and Class Consciousness: Studies in Marxist Dialectics*, trans. Rodney Livingstone (Cambridge, MA: MIT Press, 1971), especially 1–27 and 272–295.

[110] Rosa Luxemburg, "Social Reform of Revolution," in *The Rosa Luxemburg Reader* [henceforth abbreviated RLR], ed. Peter Hudis and Kevin B. Anderson (New York: Monthly Review Press, 2004), 129.

[111] The argument, in other words, echoes Clara Zetkin's concern with respect to the right of women workers and makes it clear how both Zetkin and Luxemburg develop their arguments as a reaction to what they see as political revisionism.

ownership of the means of production, rather than simply a redistribution of financial means within an existing class system (RLR 162). In effect, Bernstein moves socialism away from its material basis, reverting it to the idealist platform it had initially sought to overcome. His is but a bourgeois course (RLR 148), a case of political "opportunism," as Luxemburg calls it.[112]

Luxemburg, however, does not only speak out against Bernstein's reformism. She also engages in a dispute with Lenin. The Lenin-Luxemburg debate addresses the relationship between the working class and its political expression in the party. Where Marx and Engels had assumed that the proletariat would itself press forward with a revolution, later socialists were left to ponder the fact that a revolution had failed to materialize. This created a need to rethink the relationship between the people (the workers) and the party. For Lenin, it was clear that the Russian proletariat would not itself develop class consciousness and that, as a result, class consciousness would need to be brought in from the party elite. In his *What Is To Be Done?* (1902), he argued that "he who wants a *broad* organization of workers, with elections, reports, universal voting &x., is simply an incorrigible Utopian."[113] Two years later, Luxemburg—neither a "he," nor an "incorrigible Utopian"—responds with "Organizational Questions Concerning Russian Social Democracy"(*Neue Zeit*, 1904).[114] As Luxemburg argues, Lenin's position requires, first, that all the branches of the party and the membership blindly submit to the centralized party power and, second, that this centralized power is distinguished from the party grassroots.[115] On her view, this centralization saps socialism of its power. It is an "over-mechanistic conception of social democratic politics" (RLR 253), one that drains the working people of the agency needed for political organization (RLR 261). As Luxemburg sums up her points: "The ultracentralism that Lenin advocates seems to us, in its whole essence, to be imbued, not with a positive creative spirit, but with the sterile spirit of the night-watchman state. His line of thought is concerned principally with the control of party activity and not with its fertilization, with *narrowing* and not with *broadening*, with *tying the movement up* and not with *drawing it together*" (RLR 256). For Luxemburg, socialism is and remains fundamentally democratic. As such, it is a system "*of* the class and not of a little leading minority in the *name of* the class" (RLR 308, emphasis added).

---

[112] As Nettl points out, "revisionism," "reformism," and "opportunism" are used in this context as interchangeable terms. J. P. Nettl, *Rosa Luxemburg: The Biography* (London: Verso, 2019), 2 vols., vol. 1, 202.

[113] V. I. Lenin, *What Is To Be Done?*, ed. S. V. Utechin, trans. S. V. and Patricia Utechin (Oxford: Clarendon Press, 1963), 140.

[114] Lenin then responded to Luxemburg's response, but Kautsky, still close with Luxemburg, did not publish the response in *Neue Zeit*. Lenin's response was only published in Russian in 1930, after the death of both Luxemburg and Lenin. See Charles F. Elliott, "Rosa Luxemburg and the Dilemma of the Non-revolutionary Proletariat," *Midwest Journal of Political Science* 9, no. 4 (1965): 327–338, esp. 336–338. It should be noted, however, that Lenin and Luxemburg cooperated after their debate, especially in the aftermath of the 1905 Revolution in Russia (the First Revolution).

[115] See Luxemburg, "Organizational Questions of Russian Social Democracy," RLR 252.

Luxemburg's commitment to the people extends to her criticism of imperialism in what is often considered her main work: *Accumulation of Capital: A Contribution to an Explanation of Imperialism* (1913). Together with *Introduction to Political Economy*, a work that Luxemburg began in 1907–1908 when teaching at the Party School in Berlin, *Accumulation of Capital* presents imperialism as the necessary corollary of capitalism. In developing her argument, Luxemburg provides a historical-anthropological analysis of various forms of protocommunism (precapitalist communities). In her view, Marx's theory of imperialism had failed to explain the necessity of capitalist appropriation of noncapitalist parts of the world.[116] Because of the need to invest the surplus gained into ever new markets, it is, in Luxemburg's view, impossible to conceive of a capitalism that is not, by nature, expansive. Moreover, capitalism is the first economic system to display this feature at its very core.[117] Natural economies will typically resist appropriation by capitalism. Thus, the process of appropriation is necessarily violent and oppressive (though the degree of violence and oppression may vary).[118] By developing this argument, Luxemburg seeks to demonstrate the violence at the heart of the capitalist system (thus bolstering her critique of reformism).

At the time, Marx's studies of precapitalist societies were not yet known. *Grundrisse*, with its section on precapitalist economical formations, was only published in 1939 and, with the exception of Engels's *The Origin of the Family*, which references Marx's anthropological notes, sparse attention was paid to Marx's writings on the non-Western world (Russia, Java, India, Indigenous North and South Americans, Indigenous Australians, etc.).[119] Luxemburg, however, draws on some of the same sources as Marx (and Engels), including ethnologists such as Henry Summer Maine and Lewis Henry Morgan. Her study of historical forms of slavery critiques Engels's claim, in *Anti-Dühring*, that the notion of foreign labor only emerged with private property.[120] In her work, Luxemburg, moreover, analyzes forms of oppression that emerge within precapitalist societies. For example, the Incas, internally a proto-communist economy, imposed on other tribes "a refined system of economic exploitation and political domination."[121] Precapitalist societies are not necessarily idyllic clusters of equality, but vary in their constitutions and developments, and encompass egalitarian as well as nonegalitarian models. In addition to her original theoretical analysis, *Accumulation of Capital* and *Introduction* provide important methodological contributions in that she pursues a (more) historically

---

[116] Rosa Luxemburg, *The Accumulation of Capital: A Contribution to the Economic Theory of Imperialism*, in *The Complete Works of Rosa Luxemburg*, vol. 2, ed. Peter Hudis and Paul Le Blanc, trans. Nicholas Gray and Georg Shriver (London: Verso, 2016), esp. chaps. 4–9.

[117] Luxemburg, *The Accumulation of Capital*, 341.

[118] Luxemburg, *The Accumulation of Capital*, 267.

[119] Karl Marx, *The Ethnological Notebooks of Karl Marx*, ed. Lawrence Krader (Assen: Van Gorcum, 1971).

[120] Rosa Luxemburg, "Slavery," in Luxemburg, *Economic Writings 1*, in *The Complete Works of Rosa Luxemburg*, vol. 1, ed. Peter Hudis, trans. Joseph Fracchia and Georg Shriver (London: Verso, 2014), 301–331.

[121] Luxemburg, *Introduction to Political Economy*, in *Economic Writings 1*, 200–201.

and anthropologically founded materialism. That Lenin would deem this part of Luxemburg's work "a shocking muddle"[122] matters less than the fact that she finds it necessary to epistemically justify her analysis with a historical and anthropological review of noncapitalist societies. Despite Luxemburg's failure to grant true political (revolutionary) agency to the inhabitants of these societies (for her, such agency can only be found within the working class of the industrial era),[123] her thinking displays an unusual degree of sensitivity toward social and cultural diversity and the intrinsic value of preindustrial lifeforms.

Luxemburg's effort to display the systematic violence inherent in the capitalist system also underpins *The Crisis in the German Social Democracy*. The work was smuggled out of the prison where Luxemburg was held on account of her antiwar activism and published in 1916 under the pseudonym Junius (and is therefore often called the Junius Pamphlet). The pamphlet delivers a veritable criticism of the social democratic party and its support for Germany's militarization.[124] As Luxemburg sees it, the social democratic movement had allowed itself to be taken off track and duped by bourgeois nationalism. The consequence of this was a compromising of international class solidarity and a splitting of the socialist movements both internally (into reformists and revolutionaries) and internationally (in that collaboration across national borders was lost). Moreover, Luxemburg suggests that the very destruction of the working-class movement was initiated by capitalist forces. These forces, she argues, tend to be one step ahead of the workers, thus manufacturing preemptive strikes once criticism gains traction and protest movements get too strong.

Beyond its immediate political relevance—and call for the internationalist working class to stand up against parochial, bourgeois interests—the Junius Pamphlet furthers Luxemburg's analysis of, and arguments against, imperialism. She sees the military escalation that would culminate in World War I as a result of European imperialism in the Middle East, Africa, and Asia.[125] Neither imperialism nor war, however, is in the interest of the working people. Instead, it is the owners of capital—of the steel industry, banks, and military manufacturers (Luxemburg takes both Deutsche Bank and Krupp to task)—who benefit at the expense of the working classes that have been recruited to

---

[122] V. I. Lenin to L. B. Kamenev, Cracow, before March 29, 1913, in *Lenin Collected Works*, vol. 35, 93–94 (Moscow: Progress Publishers, [1976]), trans. Andrew Rothstein, in Lenin Internet Archive, https://www.marxists.org/archive/lenin/works/1913/mar/oolbk.htm; the webpage has Lenin's notes to Luxemburg in English translation.

[123] See Peter Hudis, "Non-linear Pathways to Social Transformation: Rosa Luxemburg and the Postcolonial Condition," *New Formations: A Journal of Culture/Theory/Politics* 94 (2018): 62–81.

[124] This had been a significant factor when Luxemburg and Liebknecht formed the Spartacus League in 1914, initially as a group within the social democratic party, then as an independent party. The League was formally renamed the German Communist Party in December 1918. In January 1919, in the midst of the post–World War II period, the party called for a mass uprising and strike. The revolt, which was quickly crushed by the Social Democrats in power, got a further blow with the murder of Liebknecht and Luxemburg.

[125] Rosa Luxemburg, *The Crisis in the German Social Democracy*, trans. unnamed (New York: Howard Fertig, 1969), 34–35.

protect their nation. Protecting the nation through imperialism, however, is mere fiction. As Luxemburg would put it: "no nation is free whose national existence is based upon the enslavement of another people, for [to the socialist] colonial peoples, too, are human beings, and, as such, parts of the national state."[126] Similarly, the war is an affront to the international solidarity of the working people—and an attempt to divert their attention and drain them of the energy needed for the class struggle that unites them.

In her focus on economic oppression, Luxemburg has been accused of overlooking the situation of (working-class) women, that is, the cause for which Zetkin had been fighting. While there is some truth to this—Luxemburg certainly did not match Zetkin's dedication to the women's cause—it is not the full picture. In a series of speeches from the 1900s, Luxemburg confronts the sexism of the social democratic party. Moreover, her focus is global and she connects the exploitation of women with imperialism (RLR 244–245). For her, the predicament of poor women presents a particularly stark picture of the sufferings of the oppressed. Luxemburg calls for emancipation, but the emancipation recommended is that of the international working class (see for instance RLR 244–245).

Luxemburg defends the right to universal suffrage (as a woman, she herself was not allowed to vote or run for office). She emphasizes, though, that it is not the job of women alone, but of men and women together, to bring about a mass movement for suffrage (RLR 239). Moreover, she insists that suffrage is earned not simply through political education and participation, but also through work. Like Zetkin, Luxemburg has little sympathy with the bourgeois women's movement (RLR 240). Again, like Zetkin, Luxemburg argues that it is not as women but as workers (i.e., in terms of their social rather than biological position) that women will gain full rights and equality. And, with its focus on the working class, who have no particular property or interests to defend, these rights will indeed be universal: "For the property-owning bourgeois woman, her house is the world. *For the proletarian woman, the whole world is her house*" (RLR 243). In this way, Luxemburg's cry for women's rights remains tied up with her fight for global justice—her fight against all ideologies that allow some groups of people to live at the expense of others.

7 CONCLUSION

Women philosophers contribute actively and importantly to nineteenth-century social and political thought. The political and social motivation of women philosophers extends beyond the philosophers discussed in this chapter and encompasses for example

---

[126] Luxemburg, *The Crisis*, 95. Ultimately, Luxemburg's antinationalism will lead her to argue that "today the nation is but a cloak that covers imperialistic desires, a battle cry for imperialistic rivalries, the last ideological measure with which the masses can be persuaded to play the role of cannon fodder in imperialistic wars" (*The Crisis*, 98).

Gerda Walther's attempt to forge a bond between socialism and phenomenology. For the women philosophers discussed, social and political philosophy is not only a *subfield*, but an entirely central concern—the very reason why they turn to philosophy in the first place. Nonetheless, their contributions have been overlooked in discussions of social and political philosophy as well as of nineteenth-century thought more generally. This neglect leaves us with an incomplete understanding of the field, but also of the period: For example, we risk overlooking the bridge from romanticism to socialism. Moreover, we risk missing the early discussions of issues that are, today, entirely central to social and political philosophy—issues such as imperialism, cultural arrogance, racism, the climate crisis, poverty, justice, the situated nature of freedom, the social nature of gender, and the relationship between economical oppression and oppression based on gender and race. By taking into account nineteenth-century women's contribution to social and political philosophy, we make the field richer in terms of positions and sharper in terms of analytical tools and concepts. If the women discussed here were ignored in traditional accounts of the history of philosophy, they should still be included in our contemporary understanding of social and political thought.

BIBLIOGRAPHY

Barberis, Mauro. "Constant, Mme de Staël et la constitution républicaine: un essay d'interprétation." In *Le groupe de Coppet et le monde modern. Conceptions-images-débats*, edited by Françoise Tilkin, 177–205. Geneva: Droz, 1998.

Beauvoir, Simone de. *The Second Sex*. Translated by Constance Borde and Sheila Malovany-Chevallier. New York: Vintage Books, 2011.

Bebel, August. *Woman and Socialism*. Translated by Meta A. Stern. New York: Socialist Literature Company, 1910.

Becker-Cantarino, Barbara, ed. *Bettina von Arnim Handbuch*. Berlin: de Gruyter, 2019.

Becker-Cantarino, Barbara. "'New Mythology': Myth and Death in Karoline von Günderrode's Literary Work." In *Women and Death: Women's Representation of Death in German Culture since 1500*. Edited by Clare Bielby and Anna Richards, 51–70. Rochester, NY: Camden House, 2010.

Becker-Cantarino, Barbara. "Zur politischen Romantik. Bettina von Arnim, die 'Frauenfrage' und der 'Feminismus'." In Schutz, *"Die echte Politik muß Erfinderin sein,"* 217–248.

Bruin, Karen de. "Romantic Aesthetics and Abolitionist Activism: African Beauty in Germaine de Staël's *Mirza ou Lettre d'un voyageur*." *Symposium: A Quarterly Journal in Modern Literatures* 67, no. 3 (2013): 135–147.

Champion, J. Gibelin H. *L'esthétique de Schelling et l'Allemagne de Madame de Staël*. Geneva: Slatkin Reprints, 1975.

Craiutu, Aurelian. "Introduction" to *Considerations on the Principal Events of the French Revolution*, by Germaine de Staël, edited by Aurelian Craiutu, vii–xxiv. Indianapolis: Liberty Fund, 2008.

Dane, Gesa. "Women Writers and Romanticism." In *The Cambridge Companion to Romanticism*, edited by Nicholas Saul, 133–146. Cambridge: Cambridge University Press, 2009.

Diethe, Carol. *Nietzsche's Women: Beyond the Whip*. Berlin: de Gruyter, 1996.

Dohm, Hedwig. *Die Antifeministen. Ein Buch der Verteidigung*. Berlin: Holzinger, 2015.

Dohm, Hedwig. *Become Who You Are*. Translated by Elizabeth G. Ametscbichler. Albany: State University of New York Press, 2006.

Dohm, Hedwig. "Herrenrechte." *Die Zukunft*, March 14, 1896, 508–512.

Dohm, Hedwig. *Der Jesuitismus im Hausstande. Ein Beitrag zur Frauenfrage*. Berlin: Wedekind & Schwieger, 1873. https://www.deutschestextarchiv.de/book/show/dohm_jesuitism us_1873.

Dohm, Hedwig. "Der Mißbrauch des Todes. Senile Impressionen von Hedwig Dohm." Berlin-Wilmersdorf: Verlag Die Aktion, 1917. https://www.projekt-gutenberg.org/dohm/missbrau/missbrau.html.

Dohm, Hedwig. "Reaktion in der Frauenbewegung." *Die Zukunft*, November 18, 1899, 279–291.

Dohm, Hedwig. "Reform der Mädchenschule." In *Frauen. Ein historisches Lesebuch*, edited by Andrea van Dülmen, 39–41. Munich: Verlag C. H. Beck, 1991.

Dohm, Hedwig. "Sind Berufsthätigkeit und Mutterpflichten vereinbar?" *Die Woche. Moderne illustrierte Zeitschrift* 38, September 22, 1900: 1667–1669.

Dohm, Hedwig. *Was Die Pastoren von den Frauen denken*. Berlin: Verlag Reinhold Schlingmann, 1972.

Dohm, Hedwig. *Women's Nature and Privilege*. Translated by Constance Campbell. Westport, CT: Hyperion Press, 1976.

Dornemann, Luise. *Clara Zetkin. Ein Lebensbild*. Berlin: Dietz Verlag, 1962.

Dülmen, Andrea van, ed. *Frauen. Ein historisches Lesebuch*. Munich: Verlag C. H. Beck, 1991.

Elliott, Charles F. "Rosa Luxemburg and the Dilemma of the Non-revolutionary Proletariat." *Midwest Journal of Political Science* 9, no. 4 (1965): 327–338.

Engels, Friedrich. *The Origin of the Family, Private Property and the State*. London: Penguin, 2010.

Evans, Richard J. "Theory and Practice in German Social Democracy 1880–1914: Clara Zetkin and the Socialist Theory of Women's Emancipation." *History of Political Thought* 3, no. 2 (1982): 285–304.

Ezekiel, Anna C. "Revolution and Revitalization: Karoline von Günderrode's Political Philosophy and Its Metaphysical Foundations." *British Journal for the History of Philosophy* 30, no. 4 (2022): 666–686.

Fichte, J. G. *Foundations of Natural Right*. Translated by Michael Baur. Cambridge: Cambridge University Press, 2000.

Fontana, Biancamaria. *Germaine de Staël: A Political Portrait*. Princeton: Princeton University Press, 2016.

Frank, Manfred. *Der kommende Gott. Vorlesungen über die Neue Mythologie*. Pt. 1. Frankfurt am Main: Suhrkamp, 1982.

Frederiksen, Elke P., and Katherine R. Goodman, eds. *Bettina Brentano-von Arnim: Gender and Politics*. Detroit: Wayne State University, 1995.

Frederiksen, Elke P. *Die Frauenfrage in Deutschland 1865–1915. Texte und Documente*. Stuttgart: Reclam, 1981.

Fronius, Helen. *Women and Literature in the Goethe Era 1770–1820*. Oxford: Oxford University Press, 2007.

Gengembre, Gérard, and Jean Goldzink. "Madame de Staël ou pour une religion politique." *Annales Benjamin Constant* 8–9 (1988): 207–222.

Gjesdal, Kristin. "Politics and Passions: Staël on Fanaticism." In *The History and Philosophy of Fanaticism*, edited by Paul Katsafanas. London: Routledge, 2023, 143–160.

Gjesdal, Kristin. "Spinoza's Hermeneutic Legacy: Herder, Schleiermacher, Staël." In *Spinoza in Germany: Political and Religious Thought in the Long Nineteenth Century*, edited by Jason Yonover and Kristin Gjesdal. Oxford: Oxford University Press, forthcoming.

Goodman, Katherine R. "Through a Different Lens: Bettina Brentano-von Arnim's Views on Gender." In Frederiksen and Goodman, *Bettina Brentano-von Arnim*, 116–117.

Goozé, Marjanne G. "A Language of Her Own: Bettina Brentano-von Arnim's Translation Theory and Her English Translation Project." In Frederiksen and Goodman, *Bettina Brentano-von Arnim*, 278–304.

Günderrode, Karoline von. *Poetic Fragments*. Translated by Anna Ezekiel. Albany: State University of New York Press, 2016.

Günderrode, Karoline von. *Sämtliche Werke*. Edited by Walter Morgentaler. Basel: Stromfeld, 1990–91.

Härtl, Heinz. "Bettina Brentano-von Arnim's Relations to the Young Hegelians." In Frederiksen and Goodman, *Bettina Brentano-von Arnim*, 145–185.

Härtl, Heinz. "Zur zeitgenossischen Publizistischen Rezeption des Königbuches." In *"Der Geist muß Freiheit genießen . . . !" Studien zu Werk und Bildungsprogramm Bettine von Arnims*, edited by Walter Schmitz and Sibylle von Steinsdorff, 208–235. Berlin: FSP Saint Albin Verlag, 1992.

Hawkins, Richmond Laurin. *Madame de Staël and the United States*. Cambridge, MA: Harvard University Press, 1930.

Hegel, G. W. F. *Elements of the Philosophy of Right*. Edited by Allen Wood. Translated by H. B. Nisbet. Cambridge: Cambridge University Press, 1991.

Herder, Johann Gottfried. *Werke in zehn Bänden*. Edited by Martin Bollacher et al. Frankfurt am Main: Deutscher Klassiker Verlag, 1985–98.

Herling, Bradley L. *The German Gītā: Hermeneutics and Discipline in the German Reception of Indian Thought, 1778–1831*. London: Routledge, 2006.

Higonnet, Margaret R. "Madame de Staël and Schelling." *Comparative Literature* 38, no. 2 (1986): 159–180.

Honeycutt, Karen. "Clara Zetkin: Socialist Approach to the Problem of Woman's Oppression." *Feminist Studies* 3, no. 3/4 (1976): 131–144.

Huch, Ricarda. *Die Romantik*. 2 vols. Leipzig: H. Haeffel Verlag, 1931.

Hudis, Peter. "Non-linear Pathways to Social Transformation: Rosa Luxemburg and the Post-colonial Condition." *New Formations: A Journal of Culture/Theory/Politics* 94 (2018): 62–81.

Isbell, John Claiborne. *The Birth of European Romanticism: Truth and Propaganda in Staël's "De L'Allemagne."* Cambridge: Cambridge University Press, 1994.

Kalyvas, Andreas, and Ira Katznelson. *Liberal Beginnings: Making a Republic for the Moderns*. Cambridge: Cambridge University Press, 2008.

Kant, Immanuel. *Anthropology from a Pragmatic Point of View*. Edited and translated by Robert B. Louden. Cambridge: Cambridge University Press, 2010.

Korsch, Hedda, ed. *Hedwig Dohm. Erinnerungen und weitere Schriften von und über Hedwig Dohm*. Zurich: Ala Verlag, 1980.

Landfester, Ulrike. "'Die echte Politik muß Erfinderin sein.' Überlegungen zum Umgang mit Bettine von Arnims politischem Werk." In Schutz, *"Die echte Politik muß Erfinderin sein,"* 1–39.

Lauth, Reinhard. "J. G. Fichte et Madame de Staël." *Archives de Philosophie* 47, no. 1 (1984): 63–75.

Lenin, V. I. V. I. Lenin to L. B. Kamenev, Cracow, before March 29, 1913. In *Lenin Collected Works*, vol. 35, 93–94. Moscow: Progress Publishers, [1976]. Translated by Andrew Rothstein in Lenin Internet Archive, https://www.marxists.org/archive/lenin/works/1913/mar/00lbk.htm.

Lenin, Vladmir I. *What Is To Be Done?* Edited by S. V. Utechin. Translated by S. V. and Patricia Utechin. Oxford: Clarendon Press, 1963.

Lukàcs, Georg. *History and Class Consciousness: Studies in Marxist Dialectics*. Translated by Rodney Livingstone. Cambridge, MA: MIT Press, 1971.

Luxemburg, Rosa. *The Accumulation of Capital: A Contribution to the Economic Theory of Imperialism*. In *Economic Writings 2*, edited by Peter Hudis and Paul Le Blanc. Vol. 2 of *The Complete Works of Rosa Luxemburg*. London: Verso, 2016.

Luxemburg, Rosa. *The Crisis in the German Social Democracy*. New York: Howard Fertig, 1969.

Luxemburg, Rosa. *The Rosa Luxemburg Reader*. Edited by Peter Hudis and Kevin B. Anderson. New York: Monthly Review Press, 2004.

Luxemburg, Rosa. "Slavery." In *Economic Writings 1*, edited by Peter Hudis, trans. Joseph Fracchia and Georg Shriver, 301–331. Vol. 1 of *The Complete Works of Rosa Luxemburg*. London: Verso, 2014.

Mackintosh, James. "*De L'Allemagne*. Par Madame la Baronne de Staël-Holstein, 3 vols. London 1813." *Edinburgh Review* (October 1813): 198–239.

Marx, Karl. *The Ethnological Notebooks of Karl Marx*. Edited by Lawrence Krader. Assen: Van Gorcum, 1971.

Massardier-Kenney, Françoise. "Staël, Translation, and Race." In *Translating Slavery: Gender and Race in French Women's Writings, 1783–1823*, edited by Doris Y. Kadish and Françoise Massardier-Kenney, 135–146. Kent, OH: Kent State University Press, 1994.

Meysenbug, Malwida von. *Individualitäten*. Berlin: Schuster and Loeffler, 1901.

Mikus, Birgit. *The Political Woman in Print: German Women's Writing 1845–1919*. Oxford: Peter Lang, 2014.

Nassar, Dalia. "The Human Vocation and the Question of the Earth: Karoline von Günderrode's Philosophy of Nature." *Archive für Geschichte der Philosophie* 104, no.1 (2022): 108–130.

Nassar, Dalia, and Kristin Gjesdal, eds. *Women Philosophers in the Nineteenth Century: The German Tradition*. Translated by Anna Ezekiel et al. Oxford: Oxford University Press, 2021.

Nettl, J. P. *Rosa Luxemburg: The Biography*. London: Verso, 2019.

Neuman, R. P. "Working Class Birth Control in Wilhelmine Germany." *Comparative Studies in Society and History* 20, no. 3 (1978): 408–428.

Nietzsche, Friedrich. *Beyond Good and Evil: Prelude to a Philosophy of the Future*. Edited by Rolf-Peter Horstman and Judith Norman. Translated by Judith Norman. Cambridge: Cambridge University Press, 2002.

Popiel, Jennifer J. *Rousseau's Daughters: Domesticity, Education, and Autonomy in Modern France*. Durham, NH: University of New Hampshire Press, 2008.

Preißendanz, Karl, ed. *Die Liebe der Günderode. Friedrich Creuzers Briefe an Caroline von Günderode*. Bern: Herbert Lang, 1975.

Quataert, Jean H. *Reluctant Feminists in German Social Democracy 1885–1917*. Princeton: Princeton University Press, 1979.

Rousseau, Jean-Jacque. *Emile or On Education*. Translated by Allan Bloom. New York: Basic Books, 1979.

Salomé, Lou Andreas-. *The Erotic*. Translated by John Crisp. London: Routledge, 2013.

Schutz, Hartwig, ed. "*Die echte Politik muß Erfinderin sein*." *Beitäge eines Wiepersdorfer Kolloquiums zu Bettina von Arnim*. Berlin: Saint Albin Verlag, 1995.

Sluga, Glenda. "Madame de Staël and the Transformation of European Politics, 1812–17." *International History Review* 37, no. 1 (2015): 142–166.

Sluga, Glenda. "Passions, Patriotism and Nationalism, and Germaine de Staël." *Nations and Nationalism* 15, no. 2 (2009): 299–318.

Staël, Germaine de. *Corinne, or Italy*. Edited and translated by Sylvia Raphael. Oxford: Oxford University Press, 2008.

Staël, Germaine de. *Letters on the Works and Character of J. J. Rousseau*. London: G. G. J. and J. Robinson, 1789.

Staël, Germaine de. *Madame de Staël: Selected Correspondence*. Edited by Georges Solovieff and Kathleen Jameson-Cemper. Translated by Kathleen Jameson-Cemper. Dordrecht: Springer, 2000.

Staël, Germaine de. "The Spirit of Translation." Translated by Doris Y. Kadish. In *Translating Slavery: Gender and Race in French Women's Writings, 1783–1823*, edited by Doris Y. Kadish and Françoise Massardier-Kenney, 162–168. Kent, OH: Kent State University Press, 1994.

Staël, Germaine de. *Ten Year's Exile*. London: Centaur Press, 2005.

Staël, Germaine de. *A Treatise on the Influence of the Passions, Upon the Happiness of Individuals and of Nations*. London: Cawthorn, British Library, 1798.

Stopczyk-Pfundstein, Annegret. *Philosophin der Liebe. Helene Stöcker*. Stuttgart: Libri, 2003.

Trouille, Mary Seidman. *Sexual Politics in the Enlightenment: Women Writers Read Rousseau*. Albany: State University of New York Press, 1997.

Ünlüdag, Tânia. "Bourgeois Mentality and Socialist Ideology as Exemplified by Clara Zetkin's Constructs of Femininity." *International Review of Social History* 47 (2002): 33–58.

Valpione, Giulia. "Expanding the Canon: The Political Philosophy of Bettina von Arnim." *Symphilosophie* 2 (2020): 131–156.

Vigus, James. "A Weimar Constellation: Aesthetic Autonomy in Henry Crabb Robinson's Private Lectures (1804) and Madame de Staël's *Corinne ou l'Italie*." In *Idealismus und Romantik in Jena*, edited by Michael Forster, Johannes Korngiebel, and Klaus Vieweg, 287–307. Jena: Wilhelm Fink, 2018.

Weedon, Chris. "The Struggle for Women's Emancipation in the Work of Hedwig Dohm." *German Life and Letters* 47, no. 2 (1994): 182–192.

von Arnim, Bettina, and Gisela von Arnim Grimm. *The Life of High Countess Gritta von Ratsinourhouse*. Translated by Lisa Ohm. Lincoln: University of Nebraska Press, 1999.

von Arnim, Bettina. *Goethe's Correspondence with a Child*. 3 vols. London: Longman et al, 1839.

von Arnim, Bettina. "Tale of the Lucky Purse." Translated by Helen G. Morris-Keitel. *Marvels & Tales* 11, no. 1/2 (1997): 127–133.

von Arnim, Bettina. *Werke*. 2 vols. Weimar: Aufbau Verlag, 1989.

von Arnim, Bettine. *Werke und Briefe*. Edited by Wolfgang Bunzel et al. Frankfurt am Main: Deutscher Klassiker Verlag, 1985.

Wolf, Christa. "Your Next Life Begins Today: A Letter about Bettine." In *Bettina von Arnim: Gender and Politics*, edited by Elke P. Frederiksen and Katherine R. Goodman, 35–70. Detroit: Wayne State University Press, 1995.

Wollstonecraft, Mary. Review of *Letters on the Works and Character of J. J. Rousseau, by Germaine de Staël. Analytical Review* 4 (August 1789): 360–362.

Zetkin, Clara. *Ausgewählte Reden und Schriften*. Vol. 1. Berlin: Aufbau Verlag, 1957.

Zetkin, Clara. "Rosa Luxemburg." *Communist International*, September 1919. https://www.marxists.org/archive/zetkin/1919/09/rosa.htm.

Zetkin, Clara. *Selected Writings*. Edited by Philip S. Foner. Chicago: Haymarket Books, 2015.

CHAPTER 29

....

PLANTS, ANIMALS, AND
THE EARTH

....

DALIA NASSAR

THE question concerning the human relation to the more-than-human world played a central role in philosophical investigations in the long nineteenth century. This is most evident in the early part of the century, where romantic and idealist philosophers argued that nature (and not the self-intuiting I or ego) should be the starting point of philosophical speculation, and construed nature (rather than the I) as "absolute." Accordingly, and in opposition to the view espoused by Immanuel Kant and J. G. Fichte that nature is nothing but an expression of the laws of hunan human intelligence, thinkers such as J. W. von Goethe, Friedrich Schelling, Germaine de Staël, Karoline von Günderrode, and Bettina Brentano von Arnim claimed that the human being (and human intelligence) should be understood in light of—and as an expression of—the natural world.

While philosophical discussion of the natural world ebbed in the middle of the century—with the majority of philosophers focusing on questions concerning workers' rights, gender equality, and human rights—concern for the human relation to the more-than-human reemerges with the rise of phenomenology at the end of the nineteenth and beginning of the twentieth century.[1] In this instance, the women took the helm,

---

[1] It is worth noting that while women philosophers did not directly engage with such questions in the midcentury, women travelers, who wrote about their travels, did. The Austrian Ida Pfeiffer, who traveled through the Middle East, Scandinavia, South America, China, and India (among others), discusses the ways in which the natural world influenced and was reflected in the mores and languages of the cultures she visited. While her focus was not so much on plants and animals, and more on the human lives she encountered, she was an acute observer of the role that the natural world plays in the development of culture. See Ottmar Ette, "Ida Pfeiffer oder die Eroberung der Frauenreise," in Ette, *ReiseSchreiben. Potsdamer Vorlesungen zur Reiseliteratur* (Berlin: de Gruyter, 2019), 510–527. Beyond the German-speaking world, Flora Tristan (born in France, to a French mother and a Peruvian father) traveled to Peru and recorded her travels in a two-volume publication which appeared in Paris in 1837. This work, which includes descriptions of the natural world she encountered, is genre-defying in that it is at once a personal memoir, a *Bildungsroman* tracing her own disillusionment, an analysis of the social structures of the city of Arequipa, and philosophical reflections on the situation of women. Tristan

exploring the ways in which we can empathize with animals and engaging with the latest scientific understanding of plant sentience. This can be most clearly seen in the works of Edith Stein and Hedwig Conrad-Martius.

In the works of the romantics and idealists, and those of the early phenomenologists, we find women who agreed with their male colleagues, but who also departed from them in crucial ways. These points of departure, as I will argue, reveal the potential of their varying philosophical starting points and pave the way for new paths, which had been left unexplored by their male counterparts. Accordingly, although the women I am considering here cannot be described as forming a movement of their own, they share important affinities which contrast them to women thinkers in other traditions *and* to male thinkers in their own traditions. For these women push the boundaries of the movements to which they contributed (romanticism and idealism, on the one hand, and phenomenology, on the other), posing new questions about what philosophy can reveal about our relationship to the more-than-human world, and paving new paths for philosophical engagement with animals, plants and the earth.

1   STAËL ON SCIENCE, NATURE, AND EDUCATION

The tenth chapter of volume 3 of Germaine de Staël's *Germany* (1813)[2] has been described as her most influential and original.[3] Titled "The Influence of German Philosophy on the Sciences," it follows a two-chapter discussion of the influence of German philosophy on the mind (chapter 8) and its influence on literature and the arts (chapter 9). In both, Staël's claim is that German philosophy has achieved an "elevated perspective"—a perspective that can grasp the "whole," rather than isolated parts.

This perspective, Staël notes, is important for science, but it is also important for morals and for human life, more generally. For, as she elaborates in the fourth volume of *Germany* (which discusses religion), the "feeling for the infinite," in Schleiermacher's formulation, is present in metaphysics, in morals, in the arts, and in religion, and it

---

was also the grandmother of Paul Gauguin. See Ottmar Ette, "Flora Tristan oder die Wallfahrten einer Ausgestoßenen," in Ette, *ReiseSchreiben*, 543–555. For an account of non-European women travelers, including Elizabeth Cary Agassiz (wife of Louis Agassiz), see Nina Gerassi-Navarro, *Women, Travel, and Science in Nineteenth-Century Americas: The Politics of Observation* (Cham, Switzerland: Palgrave, 2017).

[2]   All references to Staël's works will be made in the body, and will be as follows:

DL: Germaine de Staël, *De l'allemagne* (Paris and Geneva: J. J. Paschoud, 1814).

WP: Nassar, Dalia and Kristin Gjesdal, eds. *Women Philosophers in the Long Nineteenth Century: The German Tradition* (New York: Oxford University Press, 2021).

[3]   See Kurt Muller-Vollmer, "Staël's *Germany* and the Beginnings of an American National Literature," in *Germaine de Staël: Crossing the Borders*, ed. M. Gutwirth, A. Goldberger, and K. Szmurlo (New Brunswick, NJ: Rutgers University Press, 1991).

is what gives human life its meaning: "it is only when we give ourselves entirely up to reflections, to images, to desires which extend beyond the limits of experience," Staël writes, "that we can breathe freely" (DL 3, 248–249). While in the *Critique of the Power of Judgment* (1790) Kant had intimated the significance of this mode of knowledge for bridging the gap between theoretical philosophy and practical philosophy, it was primarily philosophers after Kant who pushed beyond the boundaries of discursive knowledge. This, Staël contends, is the distinguishing mark of German philosophy—and it is the reason why it is worthy of serious consideration.

A key aim of Staël's four-volume work (first published in London, on account of censorship in France) is to demonstrate to the French public the significance of German culture and thought. This is also the task of the third volume, in which she considers German philosophy more specifically. Staël's goal is to convince her readers that the German approach to understanding the mind, morals, and nature is not simply superior to the French approach, but that it can play a crucial role in helping French philosophy out of its various quagmires. The elevated perspective that she outlines plays an important role in this respect: it helps to illuminate the human mind, the natural world, *and* the relation between mind and nature, thereby contributing to our understanding of the "naturalness" of the human and the "humanness" of nature.

Staël's argument for the relevance of this elevated perspective rests on two main claims. First, the elevated perspective, which allows us to grasp the whole, or unity, rather than remain tethered to isolated or separate parts, has the potential to overcome the increasing fragmentation in knowledge and thereby pave the way for an expansive science. This science is neither purely empirical nor purely speculative; it does not have either the human or human culture or nature as its sole concern. Rather, it unites empirical research with metaphysical investigations and aims to understand the human being within nature and to discern human-like characteristics ("intelligence") across the natural world.

She notes that this expansive science has a clear goal of the German idealists who, as Staël puts it, "believe that an art, a science, or any other subject, cannot be understood without universal knowledge, and that from the smallest phenomenon to the greatest, nothing can be carefully examined, or poetically described, without the elevation of the mind which sees the whole while describing the parts" (DL 3, 119).[4]

Staël notes that this capacity to see the whole *and* the parts—to see the whole *in* the parts and the parts *in* the whole—has been elaborated by a number of thinkers, including Montesquieu, Spinoza, and Herder. While Montesquieu speaks of an "esprit" that discerns similarities among differences, and differences among similarities (DL 3, 119), Spinoza discusses an "intelligence by which to identify oneself with nature and

---

[4] Similarly, in the chapter on the influence of philosophy on science, Staël writes: "literature throws light on the sciences as the sciences throw light on literature, and the connection that exists between everything in nature must have a place in the realm of ideas" (WP 52). See also the preceding chapter on literature, where Staël maintains that "in Germany, the study of antiquity, like that of the sciences and of philosophy, unites the scattered branches of the human mind" (DL 3, 121).

the divine" (DL 3, 120), and Herder invokes the "imagination" in order to undertake comparative research into cultures (DL 2, 333). It also recalls what Kant, Goethe, and Schelling variously described as "intuitive understanding," "intuitive judgment," or "intellectual intuition."

What these philosophers are pointing to is the ability to grasp relations, and to see similarity where none at first appears, without, however, collapsing similarity into identity. This is not unlike analogical reflection, which Staël considers in the next chapter on science. There she describes it as the ability to see something *as* something else, in light of something else, and thereby discern how the two are both like and unlike one another (DL 3, 137; WP 53).

This leads directly to Staël's second argument for the importance of the elevated perspective. For by achieving this perspective, she explains, one is able to grasp the relationship between "the one and the many," to see how what is "one" is also many, and how this one *only* appears as many. This is especially important for the study of nature, precisely because there are relations everywhere in nature, and the goal must be to discern them. Or, as she puts it, nature "always the same, and always varying [toujours une et toujour variée], reflected entirely in every one of her works, and gives the stamp of the universe to the blade of grass, as well as to the cedar" (DL 3, 119–120).

These two points, which she develops in chapters 8 and 9, allow Staël to arrive at the most substantial claims she wishes to make in the later chapter: the study of mind and the study of nature are mutually illuminating; there is a deep continuity between mind and nature; and it is only by taking account of the whole (via an intuitive form of cognition) that empirical research can be carried out.

Staël begins chapter 10 by distinguishing between "experimental philosophy," which she identifies with Bacon, and "speculative philosophy." This distinction, she notes, originates with Bacon himself, and although useful, it is not entirely accurate when it comes to understanding trends in Germany. For—contra Bacon—the Germans, Staël contends, do *both* experimental and speculative philosophy, and each serves to enhance the other. Nonetheless, she assumes Bacon's distinction in order to make the larger claim that experimental philosophy *on its own* cannot achieve what it aims to achieve. It has, furthermore, led to problematic worldviews. As Staël puts it, "it has turned thought into sensation, morality into self-interest, and nature into mechanism" (DL 3, 134; WP 51).

While Staël acknowledges the *need* for experience and experiment—otherwise we would have no insight into nature—she also emphasizes its limitations. The trouble is that experimental philosophy, and with it all forms of common empiricism, tends to focus on nature's parts and see them as isolated. Accordingly, experimental philosophy fails to recognize relations and continuity between the parts (e.g., similarity of forms), and discern necessity among them (e.g., that one part can only exist in relation to another).[5] Furthermore, because all that is permitted is observation, experimental

---

[5] This is also a worry expressed by Kant, when he explains the reasons why it is necessary to invoke teleological judgment. See especially the Introduction, and §61 of the *Critique of the Power of Judgment*.

philosophy proceeds without principle. Lacking principle, however, means that observation is willy-nilly, and its outcome can only be unrelated data, or data that is related in a purely subjective way—that is, in relation to the particular path that the experimentalist or observer happened to have taken. Thus, Staël writes, experimental philosophers grasp those relations that come from "the accidental course of their observations" (DL 3, 137; WP 53).

The goal, then, is to overcome the limitations of pure experimentation and common empiricism, without, however, undermining the importance of empirical observation. This means using "reflection to predict what observation must confirm" (DL 3, 137; WP 53). In other words, observation must be founded on principles of reflection, which must in turn be substantiated via observation. Staël offers two principles, which recall her discussion of interdisciplinarity and intuitive cognition in the preceding chapters: first, that nature and mind are alike, and second, that the whole (nature) exhibits the same structural integrity as an organism (DL 3, 137; WP 53).[6]

Staël is careful to note that to claim that nature and mind are *alike* is not to identify the mind-likeness of nature with the specific form of human intelligence. Thus she explains that "those who consider nature as an intelligence do not give to this word the same meaning that is customarily given to it" (DL 3, 146; WP 58). In other words, "intelligence" is expanded as a category, and no longer only applies to the human form of intelligence, which, as she points out, "consists in the faculty of turning in on itself," that is, self-reflection. Accordingly, Staël distinguishes the human form of intelligence as "thought" allowing for other forms of intelligence appear in nature (DL 3, 146; WP 58). In animals, she writes, intelligence expresses itself as instinct. Crystallization, Staël continues, is also a manifestation of intelligence, which differs from both human and animal intelligence. In this case, it concerns regularity, repetition and pattern, and has nothing to do with either thought or feeling.

If we can discern intelligence throughout nature, it follows that there is an analogy—a likeness and an unlikeness—between the human being and the natural world, or the human mind and nature. This substantiates Staël's first claim, that the study of mind and the study of nature are mutually illuminating, and provides the basis for her second claim, that there is deep continuity between mind and nature.

Staël then turns to experience to further justify these claims. She begins by describing what we might call "cognitive feelings," that is, feelings that are not wholly interior or subjective, nor personal-associative (i.e., outcomes of associations we make), but are inspired by the natural world, by an event in nature or a particular landscape, and are thus, as feelings, expressions *of* the world. Put differently, these feelings are a human way of reflecting or expressing natural phenomena, such that they do not only belong to the human being experiencing them, but also to the phenomenon of which they are an expression. For instance, the feeling of constriction, of being unable to breathe lightly,

---

[6] The view that mind and nature are analogous has been revitalized in recent philosophy of mind and philosophy of biology. See for instance, Evan Thompson, *Mind in Life* (Cambridge, MA: Harvard University Press, 2007), and Peter Godfrey-Smith, *Other Minds* (London: Collins, 2016).

which a person experiences immediately before an electric storm, is an expression of the surrounding atmosphere: the thickening air, the heavy clouds, the low horizon. This feeling does not simply (or at all) reflect a subjective state of mind, but the occurring natural event. As such, it tells us something *about* this event. And, Staël contends, this demonstrates a deep connection between the human being (the human mind) and the natural world, which she describes as a "great mystery" concerning our (mental, affective) relation to nature (WP 53).[7]

To further establish her second claim, Staël points to structural similarities among various beings, and among human beings and the natural world. By homing in on structural similarities, we begin to discern not only connections between the human mind and nature, but also between the whole-part structure of organisms and nature as a whole. In other words, we begin to see that the distinctive structure of organisms is reflected in nature at large. Stäel invokes the experiments of Ernst Chladni to demonstrate evidence of continuity of form—and relations—in the natural world. (Chladni showed that certain sound vibrations result in certain arrangements of grains of sand, revealing a connection between sound and form [WP 54].).

This directly leads to her third claim, concerning the *kind* of observation required to discern relationality and continuity in nature. As she makes clear in the preceding chapters, what is needed is a form of observation that can discern similarities among differences and differences among similarities. In other words, what is needed is the ability to "see" how intelligence manifests itself differently across the natural world—to see how the "one" reiterates itself variously in the "many."

While Staël does not explicitly state the significance of this capacity in this chapter, it is suggested throughout. In turn, in light of her assessment of experimental philosophy and its limitations, Staël's claim appears to be nothing less than normative: experimental philosophers *ought* to develop a new cognitive capacity—a capacity that German philosophers have sought to delineate and develop themselves. As she puts it in her closing remarks to the chapter: "German philosophy introduces the physical sciences into that universal sphere of ideas, where both the most minute observations and the most important results are held together in the interests of the whole" (DL 3; 153; WP 61).

But this is not the only imperative that Staël articulates. In addition, she contends that the direction taken by German philosophy is necessary for human development in general. This has to do with the need to develop a higher perspective, to see the whole—a perspective that is required not only for science, but also for morals. Here, again, we see a parallel between the human and the natural, and between the natural and moral sciences.

---

[7] The full passage is as follows: "this kind of parallel progress can be perceived between the world and the mind, and indicates a great mystery [grand mystère]" (WP 53). Interestingly, this idea—and the language of a "mysterious connection"—is also found in Alexander von Humboldt, whom Staël quotes. In his 1808 essay, "Concerning Steppes and Deserts," Humboldt speaks of a "mysterious interworking" between the human mind and the natural world, which is suggested by the fact that certain human feelings are themselves expressions of natural phenomena. The foregoing example of constriction comes from that essay. See Dalia Nassar, *Romantic Empiricism: Nature, Art, and Ecology from Herder to Humboldt* (New York: Oxford University Press, 2022), chap. 7.

Agreeing with Goethe's statement that human progress assumes a "spiral shape," Staël adds that

> this comparison is all the more appropriate in that the improvement of humanity seems to move backward in many eras, and then returns upon its path, having advanced some degrees further. There are moments when skepticism is necessary to the progress of the sciences, and there are others when, as Hemsterhuis says, "the wondrous spirit must supersede the geometrical one." When a person is swallowed up, or rather reduced to dust, by unbelief, this wondrous spirit alone is able to restore to the mind the power of admiration, without which we cannot understand nature. (DL 3, 151; WP 60)

Staël's claim here is twofold. On the one hand, she contends that wonder at nature leads to wonder at the human being who is an expression of nature. In admiring nature's sagacity, for instance, we begin to admire the human form and the distinctive human manifestation of natural intelligence. On the other hand, she maintains that developing the capacity for wonder is important. To wonder, to admire, is a power of the mind that aids in understanding, and thus has the capacity to illuminate. It is, in other words, not enough to examine and investigate in a dispassionate way. One must also be passionately involved. And this passionate involvement—in nature, in the human being—has an important role to play in moral education.[8] To recognize that we *are* passionate beings, that we are beings who are *moved* by our surroundings, is to begin to understand ourselves and nature—and our *relation* to the natural world.

This means that there is a moral imperative, and not only a scientific one, at work here. Staël, however, is under no illusions that systematic German philosophy has any hope of realizing this moral imperative. For, as she elaborates in the chapter that follows, and which concerns the influence of philosophy on character (*caractère*), the way philosophy is *written* in Germany makes it impossible for most people to understand. There is an obscurity in German philosophical writing that hinders its goal of moral education. For this reason, she notes, German philosophy has had little effect on practical life.[9]

It is here, perhaps, that we find Staël's own project comes to the fore most clearly. While her purported goal is to convincingly present German philosophy to a French audience, her lucid and engaging writing style, alongside her own original arguments on behalf of German philosophy, suggest a different goal: moral education. Her defense of the ideal of the whole, her explication of the ways in which the part and whole reflect one another, and her emphasis on the need for wonder in our examination of nature and of one another, are attempts to transform our sense of ourselves, of the world, and of our relation to the world. Staël's work can thus be seen as an attempt to help *educate* humanity

[8] Schleiermacher's understanding of religion and his emphasis on feeling thus—Staël would argue—make a crucial contribution to moral education. See DL 4, 265.

[9] In this critique, Staël is specifically focusing on systematic philosophy as practiced by Kant, Fichte, Schelling, and Hegel, and not on those thinkers who wrote in a more accessible style, and who did in fact have a wider influence in the practical sphere. Schleiermacher, again, comes to mind.

by showing the significance of the moral ideals of wholeness, unity, and relationality—within ourselves as individuals, within human societies, and also between humans and more-than-human beings.

2 GÜNDERRODE AND THE IMPERATIVE TO TRANSFORM

Like Staël, Günderrode sought to unite philosophical speculation with moral ideals and practices, and in so doing, extended the works of her contemporaries, above all, Schelling.[10] While Schelling's main goal was to show how human intelligence is itself a form of natural intelligence, Günderrode's goal was to articulate a moral account of the human relation to the natural world. She does this, above all, in her piece "Idea of the Earth," which was composed in 1805, but hindered from publication.[11] This is particularly unfortunate, given the significance and originality of this piece—something that was already noted in 1805, and has been reaffirmed in the recent rise of interest in Günderrode's work.[12]

To begin with, Günderrode notes that the earth is constantly transforming, indeed striving. As such, the earth appears to be directed toward a specific goal, which Günderrode describes as the "realization" of the "idea" of the earth (GSW 1, 446; WP 82). To speak of the earth as *striving* and as an *idea* seems strange. The first implies that the earth has some kind of orientation or direction, while the second implies that the earth is not only a material reality, but somehow also an ideal reality.

In speaking of the earth in these terms, Günderrode is drawing on an argument she develops in her notes on the philosophy of nature. In that context, Günderrode explains

---

[10] All citations to Günderrode will be made in the text, as follows:

> GSW: Karoline von Günderrode, *Sämtliche Werke und ausgewählte Schriften*, ed. Walter Morgenthaler (Frankfurt: Stroemfeld/Roter Stern, 1990–91). When an English translation is used here, it refers to WP.

[11] Günderrode intended for this piece to be published along with her collection *Melete* before her death in 1806. However, the philologist Friedrich Creuzer (her married lover) halted publication following her death for fear that his affair would become common knowledge. (He recognized himself in the figure of "Eusebio" in the play and the prose pieces accompanying it.) Creuzer not only suppressed publication of these works, but also destroyed various versions of them. See Markus Hille, *Karoline von Günderrode* (Reinbeck bei Hamburg: Rowohlt, 1999), 119–121. Today we have two versions of "Idea of the Earth," one titled "To Eusebio" (*An Eusebio*) (and is in the form of a letter to the character Eusebio), the other titled "Idea of the Earth." Both are available in GSW vol. 1. "Idea of the Earth" can be found in English translation in WP.

[12] Friedrich Creuzer was the first to read "Idea of the Earth." In a letter to Günderrode from December 1, 1805, he writes, "It's been a long time since I've liked anything as much as I like your 'Idea of the Earth.'" *Friedrich Creuzer und Karoline von Günderrode. Briefe und Dichtungen*, ed. Erwin Rohde (Heidelberg: Winter, 1896), 78. More recently, Wolfgang Westphal has argued that "Idea of the Earth" contains the "kernel" of Günderrode's "thinking about nature [Naturdenken]." Wolfgang Westphal, *Karoline von Günderrode und "Naturdenken um 1800"* (Essen: Blaue Eule, 1993), 99.

(following Schelling) that what we call "nature" cannot simply be the *products* of nature—the natural phenomena we see before us—but must also include nature's "productivity," which is not reducible to any one of nature's products, but which underlies their emergence, movement, and transformation. This productivity, as a non-object, must be a kind of force. However, original productivity, as a positive or expansive force, cannot fully explain the possibility of corporeal reality, which is not merely outwardly expanded but also limited, in that it occupies a *specific* space. This means that, in addition to the outward, expansive force, it is necessary to posit a negative, contractive or limiting force. Through the continuous opposition of these two forces, products emerge in nature. These two forces cannot, of course, be seen with the physical eye, even though they must be assumed to explain the possibility of products in nature.

By speaking of the earth as an idea, Günderrode is drawing on this perspective. As she puts it in "Idea of the Earth,"

> the earth is a realized idea, a simultaneously effecting (force [Kraft]) and an effect (appearance [Erscheinung]). [It is] thus a unity of soul and body, the latter [is one] pole of her activity in which she [the earth] turns outward and which we call existence, form, body; the former is turned inward [and we call it] intensity, essence, force, soul. (GSW 1, 446; WP 82)

In addition, Günderrode is working with the view that the ideal character of the earth—the fact that it is not merely a finished material object, but also one that strives—places a normative claim upon us. It is not only human beings that strive, have interests, and aim to maintain these interests. The earth community strives as well, and as members of this community, Günderrode maintains, we are obliged to make ourselves aware of this striving and how we can support it. For this reason she regards it as our task as human beings to help realize the idea of the earth (GSW 1, 447; WP 83).

More specifically, Günderrode explains that all members of the earth's community are involved in the activity of "giv[ing] back to the earth." This is, in fact, what it means to be members of any community—and the earth community is no exception: all members are both taking *and* giving. Now, if this giving back means realizing the idea of the earth *through* our actions, then giving back must somehow contribute to the achievement of harmony between the earth as material reality and the earth as ideal—and, in turn, between our material actions and our spiritual goals. Or, as she puts it, giving back to the earth involves becoming more alive, more attuned to the earth and one another, and more unified in mind and body (GSW 1, 447; WP 83).

As a member of the earth's community that has, through the activity of reflection, separated itself from the earth, from others, and even from itself, the human being has the special task of seeking to *consciously* reconnect with the earth. This means that the human being has to actively engage in the transformation of her cognitive capacities, such that her mode of apprehending and grasping the world does not result in seeing only division and separation, but in recognizing connection and relation. Or, as Günderrode puts it, the realization of the earth requires unity between "being (body) and thought (spirit)," to such an extent that they begin to "penetrate one another" and become "indistinguishable" (GSW 1, 448; WP 83; translation altered). It is the state in which "body [Körper] is simultaneously spirit, thought is simultaneously body [Leib]" (GSW 1, 448; WP 83; translation altered).

While this may seem highly speculative, Günderrode's ultimate claim is that moral development must involve self-transformation, which should in turn involve achieving greater harmony or unity. This is particularly the case for human beings, who—more than any other beings on earth—experience a separation between inner and outer, self and world. It is thus the human being's special task to transform herself to become more aligned, not only with herself, but also with others. And this self-transformation Günderrode describes as unity with oneself.

Other philosophers had argued that self-unity is the highest goal of human development. Fichte, for instance, conceived of self-unity as a moral goal. His conceptualization of self-unity, however, specifically implies formal unity (i.e., noncontradiction), unity with one's *pure I*, which in turn means self-determination, or as he puts it, the human being must "determine himself and not permit himself to be determined by something foreign."[13] Such an account of self-unity follows from Fichte's conception of the self as absolutely self-grounding, which entails that the self does not emerge through relation with others, but that others emerge *out of* (not prior to, or in relation with) the self.[14]

For Günderrode, by contrast, the self emerges only through being with others. These others, in turn, are not only human others, but all members of the earth's community. This means that others are not secondary to the self or are outcomes of its self-determination (as is the case for Fichte), but are at its very foundation. As such, to achieve "unity" or "harmony" with oneself is to achieve unity or harmony with others—or, to put it in terms of "Idea of the Earth," unity with and through the earth.[15]

[13] As Fichte puts it in *Some Lectures Concerning the Vocation of the Scholar*: "man is always supposed to be at one with himself; he should never contradict himself. Now the pure I cannot contradict itself, since it contains no diversity but is instead always one and the same." To this he adds that for the empirical I, which does contradict itself, the goal must be "to determine himself and not permit himself to be determined by something foreign." For this reason, Fichte concludes that the fundamental moral principle "is to act so that you could consider the maxims of your willing to be eternal laws for yourself." J. G. Fichte, "Some Lectures Concerning the Vocation of the Scholar," in *Fichte: Early Philosophical Writings*, ed. and trans. Daniel Breazeale (Ithaca: Cornell University Press, 1988), 149; J. G. Fichte, *Gesamtausgabe der Bayerischen Akademie der Wissenschaften*, ed. Reinhard Lauth et al. (Stuttgart: Frommann-Holzboog, 1962–), vol. 6, 297–298.

[14] As he puts it in *Vocation of Humanity* (1800): "the ground upon which I assume the existence of something beyond myself, does not lie outside of myself, but within me, in the limitation of my own personality." It is only via a deduction from myself, that I can go on to make an "inference" with regard to the existence of others. J. G. Fichte, *Die Bestimmung des Menschen* (Berlin: Vossische Buchhandlung, 1800), 41. In light of Fichte's understanding of the self, it follows that the goal of self-unity means *only* unity with *one's self*—not unity with *others*.

[15] While in "Idea of the Earth" Günderrode's focus is on the earth and the more-than-human community of which we are part, the view that moral vocation involves transforming one's self in order to become part of a larger community—without, however, annihilating one's individuality in order to achieve this unity—is present throughout her work. See Anna Ezekiel, "Metamorphosis, Personhood, and Power in Karoline von Günderrode," *European Romantic Review* 25 (2014): 773–791.

It is thus not surprising that Günderrode goes on to claim that the goal of human moral activity—that is, unity with oneself—is essential for the realization of the idea of the earth. Her point is not that I must be identical with myself alone, but also that I must come to identify with the earth's community, and in so doing, help realize the earth's vocation. Günderrode argues that various moral virtues, including truth, justice, beauty, love, goodness and charity are based on the ideal of unity, by which she means community or totality (*Allheit*) (GSW 1, 361). While unity-as-community might be more evident in the case of love or charity, which generally involve more than one person, the ideal of community can also be found in justice, where the goal is to realize unity in and through diversity, in truth, which can be identified as the unity of different elements, and also in beauty, which as harmony, is another word for unity in diversity. Thus, Günderrode continues, by realizing these ideals, the individual frees herself from the "bonds of personality," because achieving the ideal involves bringing oneself to harmonize with what is beyond oneself, and thereby realizing a vital connection with other human beings, animals, and the earth itself (GSW 1, 449).

Self-unity as harmony with others, Günderrode concludes, is the realized idea of the earth. Or as she puts it: "what is always one with itself, in harmony with itself, not torn into particularity . . . is that which I have referred to as the realized idea of the earth" (GSW 1, 449). The realized idea of the earth is thus the achievement of truth, justice, beauty, and goodness through unity not with oneself in the limited sense, but with oneself in an extended sense.

In this way, Günerrode reimagines the human vocation, such that what it means to be human and achieve virtue involves transforming oneself *for* and *with* the earth. The relationship between self and earth is thus reconfigured: from one in which the earth exists *for* me, to one where I exist *because of* and *for the sake of* the earth. This does not imply that the self is annihilated in its relation to the earth. After all, it is only in its striving to achieve moral virtues that the self can contribute to the earth's realization. The goal is not self-elimination but self-transformation with and through the earth, in order to help the earth achieve *its* ends.

Günderrode's depiction of the self's relation to the earth and her conceptualization of the moral vocation as one of unity with others, or community, resounds with Staël's emphasis on unity and her view that we cannot separate moral from natural-scientific ends. In important ways, both thinkers prefigure contemporary environmental perspectives, while Günderrode's claim that the earth has its own ends and the goal of human culture is to align with these needs reveals the radical implications of a relational conception of identity—implications that have long been recognized within Indigenous philosophies. From this perspective, plants, animals, and the earth no longer appear as external or foreign, but as essential parts of one's self. This conceptualization of the self leads to an expansive understanding of human responsibility: responsibility extends beyond a responsibility for one's actions and includes all those whom I regard as myself.

3 STEIN AND EMPATHY WITH
ANIMALS AND PLANTS

In a conversation with one of his translators, Dorion Cairns, Edmund Husserl hesitantly weighed in on the matter of empathy in relation to animals and plants. As Cairns recalls, Husserl distinguished between what he called "Menschen-tiere," such as dogs and elephants—animals that have a relation to humans, and that have perhaps assumed human behaviors through these relations—and "eigentliche Tiere." The suggestion is that empathy is possible with only the former. In turn, Cairns notes, Husserl was uncertain whether empathy with plants is at all possible, because he was unsure whether plants are purely physical beings or psychophysical unities.[16]

In both respects, Husserl's former student and assistant Edith Stein went beyond Husserl.[17] She articulated a position on empathy toward animals and contended that plants, as living beings, are psychophysical unities. In doing so, however, Stein also came up against the limits of empathy in relation to the more-than-human world.

In *On the Problem of Empathy* (1917), Stein sets out to explicate the feeling of empathy in contrast to the way in which it had been articulated by fellow phenomenologists—above all, by Theodor Lipps. While for Lipps, empathy involves experiencing the same feeling as someone else, Stein contends that empathy is the feeling for someone's pain or joy that does not require me to experience that pain or joy as my own. As she puts it, "empathy . . . is the experience of foreign consciousness in general" (PE, 11). To explicate the distinction, Stein notes the difference between a child, who sees another child crying and begins to cry, and what she describes as empathy, where one sees the pain of another *as belonging to the other*.[18] Precisely because empathy does not depend on identity—on the disappearance of the boundaries between self and other—it has the potential to play an important role in our relation to the more-than-human world. It does not require us to experience the pain or joy of an animal, for instance, as our own.[19]

---

[16] The conversation took place in 1932. Given Husserl's uncertainty with regard to the status of plants, Cairns concludes, "I got no clear idea whether Husserl thinks of plants as limiting cases of *Einfühlung* or not." Quoted in Michael Marder, "The Life of Plants and the Limits of Empathy," *Dialogue* 51 (2012): 259–273; here: 262.

[17] All references to Stein will be in the text and will refer to WP or PE: Edith Stein, *The Problem of Empathy*, trans. Waltraut Stein (Washington, DC: ISC, 1989).

[18] Corinne Painter puts it as follows: "the inability of the empathizing subject to become one, coincident, or identified with the foreign consciousness to which she relates empathically . . . provides the basis for her related claim that empathy should not be conceived as a feeling of oneness or as fellow feeling." Corinne Painter, "Husserl and Stein: Empathy and Animals," in *Phenomenology and the Non-human Animal: At the Limits of Experience*, ed. Corinne Painter and Christian Lotz (Dordrecht: Springer, 2007), 107.

[19] As Elisa Aaltola puts it, "when looking at a fox trapped in a cage, I can perceive that she is in a state of fear and pain, without needing to feel this fear and pain myself." Elisa Aaltola, "Empathy, Intersubjectivity, and Animal Philosophy," *Environmental Philosophy* 10 (2013): 75–96, here: 80.

Stein begins her articulation of the phenomenon of empathy by arguing that it is closely connected to the phenomenon of the living body (*Leib*). This is because empathy is the form in which embodied subjects are given to us. Such subjects, she explains, possess a "zero point of orientation of the spatial world" (WP 261). That is to say, they are beings for whom there *is* a world—and who experience themselves as an "orientation center" within this world. Accordingly, they are beings who are capable of some form of experience, which means, Stein contends, that they must be, on the one hand, "bearer[s] of fields of sensation" (WP 251), and, on the other, "freely mobile" (WP 272).[20]

This leads to two crucial conclusions. First, it implies that empathy extends only to bodies that are capable of sensation, i.e. living bodies. As Stein puts it, "what makes the connection of sensation and bodily perception particularly intimate is the fact that the living body is given *as* sensing, and the sensations are given as *in* the living body" (WP 251). Second, it implies that empathy extends only to expressive bodies. For, Stein explains, as a bearer of sensation, the living body cannot but express these sensations. This expressiveness can assume different forms: it can be an action (the sensation of hunger, for instance, moves a person to eat), or it can be an outward manifestation of a feeling (blushing when one is ashamed).

It is this expressiveness that, Stein contends, reveals "psychophysical unity," where what is experienced *internally* is expressed *externally*. This psychophysical unity differs from a physical-causal relationship between inner and outer. To explicate this, Stein notes the difference between the redness that is connected to blushing and the redness that results from rigorous physical exercise. The latter is clearly a case of physical causation: physical exertion causes a physical phenomenon. This is not what happens in the case of blushing, where what is "causing" the outward expression (the redness) is not a physical "cause" (WP 258).

The question is whether Stein's explication of empathy, the living body, sensation, and expression holds for nonhuman living beings. Stein begins to tackle this question when she considers how a hand is given to me. A hand does not appear as a mere object—an inanimate being—but as belonging to a living body. This is because it is capable of sensation and expression (movement in response to feeling, for instance). Thus when a hand resting on a table is given to me, I do not see a limp hand, but a hand that is pressing on the table underneath it (WP 263). This seeing of the hand as living—as capable of sensation and expression—is the condition of empathy. But it is only the condition, Stein explains, because it reveals the given hand as like my own hand (my own living body). As she puts it, "if I fill the tendencies that lie in this 'co-grasping,' then my hand (not really, but only 'so to speak') slides in the place of the other's hand. It slides into this hand, occupies its place and posture, and senses its sensations—not originally and not as its

---

[20] Or as Fredrik Svenaeus puts it: "according to Stein . . . all forms of empathy are put in motion by lived bodily expressions addressing themselves to the empathizer." Svenaeus goes on to argue that "all cases of empathy are basically sensual in character, meaning they are bodily felt experiences of other living bodies." Fredrik Svenaeus, "Edith Stein's Phenomenology of Sensuous and Emotional Empathy," *Phenomenology and the Cognitive Sciences* 17, no. 4 (2018): 741–760, here: 746.

own, but 'with it.'" Accordingly, empathy is conditioned on likeness between myself and that which is given to me. It involves a "projecting of oneself" ("my hand slides in the place of the other's hand"), which maintains difference between self and other, but nonetheless depends on fundamental likeness (WP 263).[21]

Empathy is thus founded on my sense that there is a living body before me—a body that is a bearer of sensations. This allows me to "project" myself into the other—and thereby feel what it is like to be the other—while also maintaining my distinctness from the other. For, Stein repeatedly emphasizes, in empathy the other is seen as an other, a living, experiencing being, a being capable of feelings that are *like* my own, but are not my own.

The question of course is: to what extent must the other be "like" me in order for me to be able to empathize? Relatedly, in what ways must the other "sense" and "express" itself? Must the other's modes of sensation and expression be exactly *like* my own in order for me to empathize? Must the other, in other words, feel pain and joy in ways that parallel my feelings of pain and joy? Or is divergence possible?

Stein moves to respond to these questions first, by considering differences among humans and then by considering differences between humans and other animals. She begins by noting that the size and shape of her hand should not hinder her from empathetic fulfillment with a man or a child because, as she explains, "my physical body and its limbs are not given as a fixed type." Rather, they are manifestations of the same "type" that we might call the "human." Thus she continues, "I can only empathize with physical bodies of this type, only grasp these as living bodies" (WP 263). This suggests that empathy with nonhumans—those beings whose "type" transgresses the human type—is impossible.

This is, again, something that Stein foresees and forestalls. For, she goes on, "there are types that have various levels of generality, and various levels of possibility for empathy correspond to these." This means that "the type 'physical human body' does not delimit the realm of possible objects of my empathy," but rather allows for various degrees of empathic fulfillment (WP 264).

This is evident, for instance, in my empathic fulfillment with a dog wagging its tail. Stein notes that "I can understand the tail wagging of a dog as an expression of joy if its appearance and its behavior otherwise disclose such feelings and its situation warrants them" (PE, 86). In other words, although I don't have a tail, I have access to the joy that is expressed in tail wagging. It is not clear, however, whether this empathic fulfilment is possible *despite* my physiological difference from the dog—and is thus evidence of empathy that does not require projection—or is possible only because I can *analogize* from my own body (the "waggling of my body") to the movement of the dog's tail and thereby reveals that empathy depends on projection.[22]

---

[21] This is how Stein puts it: "during this projecting of oneself, the other's hand is constantly perceived as part of the other's physical body, while my own hand is given as part of my own living body, so that the empathized sensations constantly contrast, as other, with my own" (WP 263).

[22] This is a debate within the literature on Stein's understanding of empathy and her specific use of the dog example. Some (such as Aatola) argue that this example affirms my ability to have empathic

Whatever the case, two things are clear: first, that empathy with (at least some) non-human animals is possible, because these animals are not mere "physical things" but "living bodies" that sense and express. Thus the injured paw of a dog is given to me as "a sensing part of a living body," and this allows me to empathize with the dog (WP 264). Second, this makes clear that empathy has the potential to enrich my experiences. As Stein explains, empathy is "not only a modification of [my worldview] on the basis of the other's different orientation, but also varies with how I conceive of the attributes of their living body" (WP 267). Accordingly, differences among living beings—and the ways in which these living beings behave in the world—can give me access to experiences that I have not (yet) had or that I cannot have.

Stein gives a few examples to explicate this point. The first is of a blind person. Although their "worldview" differs from mine, and this difference may mean that on account of my habits I cannot "obtain an empathic fulfillment of their world as it is given in empty representations," she emphasizes that "these empty representations and the lack of visual fulfillment are given to me" (PE, 115). In other words, it is *in principle* possible for me to empathically assume their perspective—that is, a world in which visual input does not exist. Accordingly, the lack of visual fulfillment is *given to me* and, as such, I can project myself into this lack. Another example is of someone who "has never looked a danger in the face himself." Through empathic fulfillment, Stein writes, he is able to "experience himself as brave or cowardly in the empathic representation of another's situation" (PE, 115).

Something similar might be possible for empathic fulfillment with animals. We see in an animal's gait or posture, "in their every movement, their 'way of feeling,' their freshness and dullness, and so on. And we fulfill this co-intended lived experience of the other when we empathically carry it out with them" (WP 277). This empathic fulfillment has the potential to enrich our experience. For instance, through the gestures and behaviors of a panther locked in a cage at the zoo, I can have empathic fulfillment that can tell me something about the panther's suffering in the cage and its way of life (outside the cage).

However, Stein emphasizes, this enrichment depends on a "worldview." Whoever I have empathic fulfillment with must possess a world view—a "zero point of orientation"—which I can empathically assume and which can thereby enrich my own worldview. In other words, enrichment through empathy depends on the other being having a world, because it is on account of its having a world that I can extend my worldview to encompass its worldview as well. But the question arises: which living beings are capable of having a world or possessing a "worldview," a "zero point of orientation"? While the extent to which animals can be said to have a world and worldview is open for debate, it is not clear that plants can be said to *have* a world, or, in turn, a

---

fulfillment with animals that are physiologically unlike me, while others (such as Sveaneus) contends that it reveals that empathy must have an element of projection because the tail wagging is an analogy to "my whole body waggling." Svenaeus, "Edith Stein's Phenomenology," 749.

worldview.[23] This, in part, has to do with the fact that plants are usually identified *as* the world, such that to speak of them as having a world is to speak of nonsense. Indeed, this appears to be the conclusion that Stein herself reaches. For, she writes, "a plant is also not an orientation center of the spatial world and is also not freely mobile, although—in contrast to everything inorganic—it is capable of living movement" (WP 272).[24]

Indeed, although one could disagree with Stein regarding plant mobility, it does appear that plants are not as easily contrastable to their worlds as animals, such that it is far more difficult to speak of plants as having a worldview, or a zero point of orientation in relation to a world.[25]

What does this tell us about empathic fulfillment with more-than-human beings, and the limits of empathy?

On the one hand, Stein was aware of these limits. For, she explains, the more we move away from the "human type," the more difficult empathic fulfillment becomes. This is because there are aspects of the animal body, of animal gestures and postures, that I cannot "sense into," and thus cannot empathize with. "The further we go from the type 'human,'" Stein writes, "the smaller are the number of possibilities for fulfillment" (WP 264). Or, to return to the matter of having a zero point of orientation: if empathy depends on the other having a zero point of orientation, empathic fulfillment is impossible when we encounter beings who do not have such a point.

On the other hand, Stein contends that empathy with plants should be *in principle* possible. Plants are, after all, living beings, and are thus given to us as psychophysical unities. Just as we see "freshness" and "dullness" in humans and animals, so we can also see it in plants. For this reason, Stein writes, "here, too, we have the possibility of empathic fulfillment."

Nonetheless, Stein continues, plants appear to be living bodies of a distinctive sort. They are alive but not in the same way that animals are alive. Although their movement differs from mechanical movement—which is not inwardly motivated and thus cannot be experienced empathetically—plants (at least on Stein's view) do not appear to be capable of sensing pain or pleasure, and, on that basis developing preferences or

---

[23] The question of what is meant by a "worldview" or "zero point of orientation" is a live question. Some philosophers would argue that *any* living being is a zero point of orientation insofar as to be alive means distinguishing one's self from the world (through a membrane, skin, or bark), maintaining oneself in contradistinction to this world and tracking this world through valuing it (i.e., determining what is good and bad in the environment). This valuation amounts to having a "perspective" on the world, and as such, would mean that all forms of life possess such a perspective—including bacteria. On the connection between life, world, and valuation, see Thompson, *Mind in Life*, chap. 5.

[24] Hans Jonas similarly argues, some fifty years after Stein, that plants are not subjects that stand in contrast to a world because the plant-environmental relation "comprises of adjacent matter and impinging forces." Hans Jonas, *The Phenomenon of Life* (Evanston, IL: Northwestern University Press, 2001), 183.

[25] This goes hand in hand with the fact that it is far more difficult to discern where the plant individual (organism) ends and its world (environment) begins. As the botanist Alexander Braun famously put it, "individuality in plants is as obscure and ambiguous as in animals it appears clear and simple." Braun, "The Vegetable Individual, in its Relation to Species," *American Journal of Science and Arts* 21 (1855): 58-79.

expressions for these preferences. For this reason Stein concludes that "admittedly, in this case I am grasping a considerable modification of my own life. The general feeling of a plant does not appear as a coloration of its acts, for there is no indication that such acts are present." While animals—especially those like me—are clearly capable of sensation and expression, it is "doubtful" that plants are. This implies, however, that empathy with plants is not self-evident. This is how she puts it: "it is at least doubtful whether a plant has sensations, and empathy is therefore unwarranted if we think we are inflicting pain on a tree that we are cutting down with an axe" (WP 272).

This makes plants *both* a limit case for empathy *and* a challenge for Stein's claim that *in principle* empathic fulfillment should be possible for plants. After all, empathic fulfillment should be possible in light of the fact that plants are living beings. However, insofar as plants are not "sensing" and "expressive" as animals, they do not appear to be "alive" in the same way as animals. This leaves open the question as to how exactly they are alive and how we should distinguish them from animals.[26] By identifying empathy with sensation and expression, Stein ends up with having to make the strange (perhaps problematic) claim that although plants are alive (insofar as they are not mere mechanisms) and are capable of "living movement," they are not "living bodies" (*Leib*), with whom empathic engagement is possible.

4 CONRAD-MARTIUS AND THE QUESTION OF PLANTS

Stein's close friend, Hedwig Conrad-Martius, is perhaps one of the few early phenomenologists who engaged with the natural sciences in a deep and continuous way. Her major philosophical works were focused on the philosophy of science. However, unlike many of her neo-Kantian contemporaries, Conrad-Martius was engaged in the philosophy of *biology*: a field that was just beginning to gain ground in the early twentieth century.[27]

---

[26] As Erika Ruonakoski notes, "there is a tension between Stein's definition of foreign experience as the object of empathy and her discussion of the sluggishness and vigour of plants as objects of empathy. It is difficult to see how the vigour of a plant can be empathised with, if the object of empathy is always in content non-primordial: empathising with the plant would presuppose that it has experiences. And that is an idea that she herself finds questionable." Erika Ruonakoski, "The Object and Limits of Empathy in Stein's Philosophy," in *Celebrating Teresa of Avila and Edith Stein* (Helsinki: OCDS Finland, 2016), 35.

[27] On the history of the philosophy of biology in this period, see Daniel Nicholson and Richard Gawne, "Neither Logical Empiricism nor Vitalism, but Organicism: What the Philosophy of Biology Was," *History and Philosophy of the Life Sciences* 37 (2015): 345–381. Nicholson and Gawne, however, exclude Conrad-Martius from their account. On Conrad-Martius's contributions to the philosophy of biology, see Alessandro Cordelli, "Hedwig Conrad-Martius' Phenomenological Approach to Life Sciences and the Question of Vitalism," *Axiomathes* 18 (2008): 503–514. Cordelli closely identifies Conrad-Martius with the vitalist approach to biology—as put forth by Hans Driesch. However, Conrad-Martius's critique of Driesch's crucial concept of an "entelechy," which is equivalent to an extrasensible

While Conrad-Martius's works cover a broad range of philosophical topics—including discussions of the nature of being as such, and of the reason why there is something instead of nothing—she is perhaps the only philosopher of her time who responded to the biological debates concerning plant sensation.[28]

In a series of books published between 1906 and 1928, Indian plant physiologist Jagadis Chandra Bose presented his experiments on plants, which showed that plants conduct stimuli through electricity (rather than through chemical reactions). Bose argued that plants possess irritability and sensation, not unlike that of animals, and are able to emit signals through electric currents.[29]

In a number of works published in the early 1930s, Conrad-Martius challenges Bose's conclusions, not by questioning his experiments, but by questioning his philosophical framework.[30] To begin with, she notes that Bose makes bad use of analogical inferences: likeness does not amount to identity. Although we can see similarities in the formations of crystals, plants, animals, and humans, we must not confuse similarity with identity. In order to discern *both* similarity *and* difference, it is necessary, Conrad-Martius contends, to grasp the internal structure of plants and animals, and, in light of this structure, to consider the possibility of sensation for each.

Contra Bose, Conrad-Martius argues that plants do not have sensations, at least nothing parallel to the sensations that we find in animals. This has to do with their different structures (*Gestaltung*; SP 48), which determine whether sensation (*Empfindung*) is possible (SP 46). As she explains, sensation is "the impression [*Eindruck*] that some inner living irritability is capable of expressing, i.e., that can bring about an inner living essence." In other words, there must be an "inner reality" in which external stimuli

---

life force, signals a significant departure from the vitalist tradition. Accordingly, a new history of biology needs to be written, which takes into account Conrad-Martius's critique of Driesch, and her claim that the "entelechy" cannot be something outside the organism, but has to do with its very structure. This, I believe, might place Conrad-Martius within the organicist tradition, which goes back to Kant, and which aims to grasp the structure of the living being, rather than explain it away via an occult force.

[28]   References to Conrad-Martius's works will be made as follows:
SP: *Die Seele der Pflanze* (Berslau: Frankes, 1934).
HP 1: "Hat die Pflanze eine Empfindende Seele?," *Natur und Kultur* 30 (1933): 370–373.
HP 2: "Hat die Pflanze eine Empfindende Seele? (Schluss)," *Natur und Kultur* 30 (1933): 403–406.

[29]   In addition to Bose, who is the most well-known proponent of the idea that plants are sensitive, Conrad-Martius notes that the German Gustav Theodor Fechner also made similar claims (HP 1, 372). She disagrees with both because, as she sees it, their conclusions rest on false analogies between plant and animal bodies (HP 2, 404). Recent work on plant physiology seems to affirm Bose's perspectives—and thus challenge Conrad-Martius. This does not, however, mean that Conrad-Martius was wrong. As a philosopher, she was not doing experiments, but engaging in the theoretical frameworks and conceptual tools that the scientists used (or assumed) and challenging their interpretation or use of these tools. Accordingly, her points concerning the use (and misuse) of analogy should be brought into the current discussion, so as to help clarify what contemporary researchers mean by plant "sensation" and plant "intelligence."

[30]   These are SP, HP 1 and HP 2. The book, which was published one year after the articles, includes the articles, as well as new essays that compare plants and animals, and discuss the nature of living organisms more generally.

become internal, and thus become *felt*. For, Conrad-Martius elaborates, "sensation is the actual penetration of the relevant stimulus into the 'inside' of a living being." Beings that do not have an "inside," then, cannot feel. Plants are such beings, in that they are entirely outwardly turned—whether to the earth, in their roots, or to the air, in their branches, leaves, and flowers.

The question that Conrad-Martius is pointing to—and which perhaps evaded Bose—concerns the structure of the plant organism and its relation to its environment. Her claim is that plants exhibit a distinctive relation to their environments; unlike animals, who are mobile, and who are enclosed from their environments, plants *are* (entirely with and of) the environment. Many plants are, in fact, extremely difficult to distinguish from their environments—whether it is because they vegetatively reproduce such that almost all other beings in their environment are clones of themselves (as in the case of the 10,000 year old Huon Pine in Tasmania, or Aspen forests) or because they form and depend on their environments to a far greater degree, and on a much larger scale, than animals (consider the fact that the trees in the Southern Amazon bring the rain cycle forward by several months).[31]

This gives us a clue about the life of plants: it is not identifiable with that of animals. Accordingly, whatever we might mean by plant "sensation," it cannot be identifiable with animal sensation. Plants do not have an inner reality (*innerlichkeit*) and thus cannot feel the world as something external (SP 62). This means that "experience"—which depends on this inner-outer (self-world) distinction—cannot be ascribed to plants.[32]

For Conrad-Martius this means that what is most important for understanding living beings is focusing on their form and morphology (SP 62; 73; 77).[33] Recalling Staël's emphasis on analogy, intuition, and imagination, Conrad-Martius argues that morphology allows us to properly grasp similarities *and* differences among living beings (and indeed among all beings), see how the one is both like and unlike the other, and thereby discern continuity without collapsing difference into identity (or overlooking similarity). Conrad-Martius's goal was to distinguish plants as living beings with a distinctive form (*Urbild*), which should not be identified with either nonliving crystals, or with the living form of animals—without, however, divesting plants of their status as living, indeed as manifestations of intelligence or, as Conrad-Martius puts it, as possessive of a "soul."

---

[31] A particular strand of Huon Pine in Tasmania has been reproducing vegetatively for 10,000 years. Branches that touch the ground form roots and are eventually detached from the original stem, making it difficult to determine whether they are individual trees. Aspen forests are composed of clones connected underground through far reaching roots. This makes it extremely difficult to determine where the plant individual begins and ends—both in terms of its life cycle and in its relation to its context. See Ellen Clarke, "Plant Individuality," in *The Major Transitions in Evolution Revisited* (Cambridge, MA: MIT Press, 2011), 227-250. See also note 29 above.

[32] See the above discussion (section 3) concerning the possibility of ascribing plants a "worldview."

[33] In many ways, Conrad-Martius's turn to morphology is reminiscent of Goethe, as she contends that the goal is to discern the *Urbild* of living beings (SP 73). She invokes Goethe in the opening pages of her book, describing him as "the greatest German observer of nature [der größte deutsche Naturanschauer]," who gave us "the science of nature as a doctrine of their 'Urphenomena,' that is, their typical, typological [urbildsinnlichen] forms of presentation" (SP 7).

This is, in fact, how Stein understood Conrad-Martius's position, and later came to assume it as her own.[34] In an important sense, then, Conrad-Martius pointed to the problems in Stein's account and helped her to move beyond them. By identifying the living body with sensation and expression, and by identifying sensation with those sensations that are most like mine, Stein arrived at the questionable conclusion that plants are alive and capable of living movement, but *not* "living bodies." Thus, although Conrad-Martius's goal at times might seem to undermine the attempt to establish the moral status of plants, which continues to revolve around the question of sentience, her intentions were (perhaps) the opposite.[35] She was convinced that to understand plants properly, it was necessary to move beyond the paradigm of empathy. This meant, in turn, that to understand life properly—a category that includes plants—it was also necessary to move beyond empathy.

Here, in Conrad-Martius's thinking about plants and her turn to morphology, and in Stein's related turn to the origin and meaning of life, we find a reiteration of the questions and concerns that motivated Staël and Günderrode. Furthermore, although Conrad-Martius does not consider the moral implications of her approach to vegetal life, and her exchange with Stein might imply that moral consideration is out of the question, the connections between her thinking and that of Staël and Günderrode suggest that the moral significance of her position can be developed in productive ways. The proximity between Conrad-Martius's (and the later Stein's) approach to that of the early romantic and idealists shows not only the connections between the two traditions, but also the ways in which they can be fruitfully brought into dialogue.

BIBLIOGRAPHY

Aaltola, Elisa. "Empathy, Intersubjectivity, and Animal Philosophy." *Environmental Philosophy* 10 (2013): 75–96.
Braun, Alexander. "The Vegetable Individual, in its Relation to Species," translated by C. F. Stone. *American Journal of Science and Arts* 21 (1855): 58–79.

---

[34] It is perhaps worth noting that in her later work, Stein agreed with Conrad-Martius's analysis of the "plant soul." In her 1936–37 *Finite and Eternal Being,* Stein writes: "in a limited sense even the plant may be said to have a soul and a body. H. Conrad-Martius calls the plant soul a 'forming soul.' The latter is distinguished from the animal and human soul by the fact that its being exhausts itself in the process of 'forming' and that all the activities of the plant serve this one purpose, while in the case of the souls of other living beings, the task of forming is but one among others." Edith Stein, *Finite and Eternal Being: An Attempt at an Ascent to the Meaning of Being,* trans. Kurt F. Reinhardt (Washington, DC: ICS, 2002), 246.

[35] Despite attempts to ground moral accounts of the more-than-human in nonutilitarian, nonhedonistic foundations, many ethicists continue to attribute moral status only to those beings that possess sentience in some forms and can thus be described as "subjects of experience"—as Tom Regan puts it—or as having the ability "to feel their existence," in the words of Christine Korsgaard. See Tom Regan, "The Case for Animal Rights," in *In Defense of Animals,* ed. Peter Singer (New York: Harper & Row, 1985), 13–26, esp. 22, and Christine Korsgaard's more recent work *Fellow Creatures: Our Obligations to Other Animals* (Oxford: Oxford University Press, 2018), esp. 31 –33.

Clarke, Ellen. "Plant Individuality." In *The Major Transitions in Evolution Revisited,* edited by Brett Calcott and Kim Sterelny, 227-250. Cambridge, MA: MIT Press, 2011.

Conrad-Martius, Hedwig. *Die Seele der Pflanze.* Berslau: Frankes, 1934.

Conrad-Martius, Hedwig. "Hat die Pflanze eine Empfindende Seele?" *Natur und Kultur* 30 (1933): 370–373, 403–406.

Cordelli, Alessandro. "Hedwig Conrad-Martius' Phenomenological Approach to Life Sciences and the Question of Vitalism." *Axiomathes* 18 (2008): 503–514.

Creuzer, Friedrich, and Karoline von Günderrode. *Friedrich Creuzer und Karoline von Günderrode: Briefe und Dichtungen.* Edited by Erwin Rohde. Heidelberg: Winter, 1896.

Ette, Ottmar. "Flora Tristan oder die Wallfahrten einer Ausgestoßenen." In Ette, *ReiseSchreiben, Potsdamer Vorlesungen zur Reiseliteratur,* 543–555. Berlin: de Gruyter, 2019.

Ette, Ottmar. "Ida Pfeiffer oder die Eroberung der Frauenreise." In Ette, *ReiseSchreiben, Potsdamer Vorlesungen zur Reiseliteratur,* 510–527. Berlin: de Gruyter, 2019.

Ezekiel, Anna. "Metamorphosis, Personhood, and Power in Karoline von Günderrode." *European Romantic Review* 25 (2014): 773–791.

Fichte, Johann Gottlieb. *Die Bestimmung des Menschen.* Berlin: Vossische Buchhandlung, 1800.

Fichte, Johann Gottlieb. *Gesamtausgabe der Bayerischen Akademie der Wissenschaften.* Vol. 6. Edited by Reinhard Lauth et al. Stuttgart: Frommann-Holzboog, 1962–.

Fichte, Johann Gottlieb. "Some Lectures Concerning the Vocation of the Scholar." In *Fichte: Early Philosophical Writings,* edited and translated by Daniel Breazeale, 144–184. Ithaca: Cornell University Press, 1988.

Gerassi-Navarro, Nina. *Women, Travel, and Science in Nineteenth-Century Americas: The Politics of Observation.* Cham, Switzerland: Palgrave, 2017.

Godfrey-Smith, Peter. *Other Minds.* London: Collins, 2016.

Günderrode, Karoline von. *Sämtliche Werke und ausgewählte Schriften.* Edited by Walter Morgenthaler. Frankfurt: Stroemfeld/Roter Stern, 1990–91.

Hille, Markus. *Karoline von Günderrode.* Reinbeck bei Hamburg: Rowohlt, 1999.

Jonas, Hans. *The Phenomenon of Life.* Evanston, IL: Northwestern University Press, 2001.

Korsgaard, Christine. *Fellow Creatures: Our Obligations to Other Animals.* Oxford: Oxford University Press, 2018.

Marder, Michael. "The Life of Plants and the Limits of Empathy." *Dialogue* 51 (2012): 259–273.

Muller-Vollmer, Kurt. "Staël's *Germany* and the Beginnings of an American National Literature." In *Germaine de Staël: Crossing the Borders,* edited by M. Gutwirth, A. Goldberger, and K. Szmurlo, 141–158. New Brunswick, NJ: Rutgers University Press, 1991.

Nassar, Dalia. *Romantic Empiricism: Nature, Art, and Ecology from Herder to Humboldt.* New York: Oxford University Press, 2022.

Nassar, Dalia, and Kristin Gjesdal, eds. *Women Philosophers in the Long Nineteenth Century: The German Tradition.* New York: Oxford University Press, 2021.

Nicholson, Daniel, and Richard Gawne. "Neither Logical Empiricism nor Vitalism, but Organicism: What the Philosophy of Biology Was." *History and Philosophy of the Life Sciences* 37 (2015): 345–381.

Painter, Corinne. "Husserl and Stein: Empathy and Animals." In *Phenomenology and the Non-human Animal: At the Limits of Experience,* edited by Corinne Painter and Christian Lotz, 97–115. Dordrecht: Springer, 2007.

Regan, Tom. "The Case for Animal Rights." In *In Defense of Animals,* edited by Peter Singer, 13–26. New York: Harper & Row, 1985.

Ruonakoski, Erika. "The Object and Limits of Empathy in Stein's Philosophy." In *Celebrating Teresa of Avila and Edith* Stein, edited by H. Tuorila-Kahanpää, 25-38. Helsinki: OCDS Finland, 2016.

Staël, Germaine de. *De l'allemagne*. Paris and Geneva: J. J. Paschoud, 1814.

Stein, Edith. *Finite and Eternal Being: An Attempt at an Ascent to the Meaning of Being*. Translated by Kurt F. Reinhardt. Washington, DC: ICS, 2002.

Stein, Edith. *The Problem of Empathy*. Translated by Waltraut Stein. Washington, DC: ISC, 1989.

Svenaeus, Fredrik. "Edith Stein's Phenomenology of Sensuous and Emotional Empathy." *Phenomenology and the Cognitive Sciences* 17, no. 4 (2018): 741–760.

Thompson, Evan. *Mind in Life*. Cambridge, MA: Harvard University Press, 2007.

Westphal, Wolfgang. *Karoline von Günderrode und "Naturdenken um 1800."* Essen: Blaue Eule, 1993.

CHAPTER 30

THE PHILOSOPHICAL LETTER AND GERMAN WOMEN WRITERS IN ROMANTICISM

RENATA FUCHS

IN recent decades, many literary scholars recognized the fact that the German men Romantics are philosophers as much as they are literary critics, writers, and artists.[1] Until now the case has not been made for the German women Romantics. Women's salons and letters provided the substance for the work of two influential philosophers: for Friedrich Daniel Ernst Schleiermacher's groundbreaking work *Essay on Theory of Sociable Behavior* (*Versuch einer Theorie des geselligen Betragens*, 1799), which he based on the workings of salons; and for various works of Friedrich Schlegel, among them *Dialogue on Poetry* (*Gespräch über die Poesie*, 1800), in which he equipped the characters with the features of his friends from the early German Romantic circle in Jena.[2] It appears women were valued above all as facilitators of conversation and within the confines of the question of what the feminine could do for men. Yet, the German women Romantics found their own space between entrenched gender stereotypes and the extent of female self-expression possible within the Berlin salons.

---

[1] See Karl Ameriks, "Hegel's Aesthetics: New Perspectives on Its Response to Kant and Romanticism," *Hegel Bulletin* 23, nos. 1–2 (2002): 72–92; Frederick Beiser, *The Romantic Imperative: The Concept of Early German Romanticism* (Cambridge, MA: Harvard University Press, 2004); Andrew Bowie, *From Romanticism to Critical Theory: The Philosophy of German Literary Theory* (London: Routledge, 1997); Richard Eldridge, *The Persistence of Romanticism: Essays in Philosophy and Literature* (Cambridge: Cambridge University Press, 2001); Michael Forster and Lina Steiner, eds., *Romanticism, Philosophy, and Literature* (London: Palgrave Macmillan, 2020); Manfred Frank, *The Philosophical Foundations of Early Romanticism*, trans. Elizabeth Millán-Zaibert (Albany: State University of New York Press, 2003); Jane Kneller, *Kant and the Power of Imagination* (Cambridge: Cambridge University Press, 2007); Elizabeth Millán-Zaibert, *Friedrich Schlegel and the Emergence of Romantic Philosophy* (Albany: State University of New York Press, 2007); Fred Rush, "The Romantic Imperative: The Concept of Early German Romanticism," *Mind* 114, no. 455 (2005): 709–713.

[2] All translations are mine.

The European *salonnières* of the seventeenth to the nineteenth centuries shared a common concern: to position themselves in an ever-changing public sphere. The essence of salon sociability was the dialogue guided by the individual hostesses. The French salons that flourished between 1740 and 1780 under the guidance of Madame de Lambert, Madame du Deffand, Julie de Lespinasse, Madame Geoffrin, and Madame Necker were based on principles of polite sociability and an equality between the sexes grounded in friendship. The *salonnières* integrated conversation into a dialogical epistolary style that differed from the previous formal letter conventions, verse epistles.[3] The ideal of the Republic of Letters in seventeenth-century and prerevolutionary France of an egalitarian sociability, conversation, and the advancement of civic virtue in eighteenth-century England and of a transformatory sociability in the early Romantic salon in Germany was explored and to some extent fictionalized in the familiar letter.[4] In contrast, the luminaries of late eighteenth-century salon culture in Berlin were predominantly Jewish women rooted in the liberal Jewish family tradition and its social network.

I read letters of German *salonnières*, Rahel Levin Varnhagen (1771–1833), Dorothea Mendelssohn Veit Schlegel (1764–1839), and Bettina Brentano von Arnim (1785–1859), as contributions to Romantic philosophy based on dialogical networks of love. Using Caroline Levine's approach of *Forms*,[5] I analyze the salon's sociability and the letter network's symphilosophy, with their multiple shapes, patterns, and arrangements, overlapping, colliding, and generating complex social landscapes, and show how the form of the salon, and the form of the letter, were initiators of a new philosophical genre, and were influenced by these women's understandings of philosophy. I examine three different types of the letter genre: personal (Levin Varnhagen), literary (Mendelssohn Veit Schlegel), and fictionalized (Brentano von Arnim) and show how the authors retheorize the Romantic notions of sociability and symphilosophy (as theorized by men) arising from love. For these women writers, love is the foundation upon which everything else is built and serves as the model for all reality because reality (as manifestation of the mundane) like love, is reciprocal, communal, and dialectical, as it overcomes division through an augmenting process of seeking togetherness. When they refashioned the concepts of friendship and romantic relationship, they forged a forward-thinking original framework for dialogical interaction deriving from the energy of love.

Throughout her correspondence, Levin Varnhagen described the connections with her addressees as love relationships. In the center of her writing is the symbol of heart, which she does not associate solely with women's emotions and subjectivity since she

[3] On women and writing in France see Erica Harth, *Cartesian Women: Versions and Subversions of Rational Discourse in the Old Regime* (Ithaca: Cornell University Press, 1992), and Joan de Jean, *Tender Geographies: Women and the Origins of the Novel in France* (New York: Columbia University Press, 1991).

[4] On the English salon and letters see Chauncey Brester Tinker, *The Salon and English Letters* (New York: Macmillan, 1915).

[5] On how *Forms* organize our lives (not only works of art but also political life) and the attempts to know it see Caroline Levine, *Forms: Whole, Rhythm, Hierarchy, Network* (Princeton: Princeton University Press, 2015).

did not subscribe to the modern male-mind-rationality and female-body-feeling dualisms,[6] but rather claims that she became masculine precisely through "the most sensitive, strongest organ [das empfindlichste, das stärkste Organ]," namely, the heart— seat of love.[7] Hence, she brings together both genders into the visualization of the most vulnerable yet powerful symbol of love. For Mendelssohn Veit Schlegel, everlasting love begins on earth and extends beyond.[8] According to Brentano von Arnim, speech acts are rooted in the divine and in universal love; consequently, we cannot separate ourselves from love since it encompasses and subsumes all aspects of life. Love is tied to dialogue and redeems the act of speaking and conversing: an exchange, a question and an answer, are manifestations of divinity, of the fullness of being. Ultimately, all three writers conceive of love and dialogue as being inseparable. These conceptualizations of love support female intellectual autonomy—the new paragon of friendship as a contrast to the exclusive male bonding—which would not have been possible without Romantic sociability. By emphasizing love as an underlying theme, I am positioning these letters as a new philosophical genre within the literary movement of Romanticism. They bring Romantic philosophy to life and reveal a complete, and thus ideal, form of communication where free individuals engage in aesthetic production incorporated into social life.

1 SALON SOCIABILITY AND THE ROMANTIC LETTER

Forms indicate an arrangement of elements, patterns of repetition and difference. Caroline Levine distinguishes four major forms: whole, rhythm, hierarchy, and network. In my analysis of the form of the salon with its sociability and the form of the letter with its symphilosophy, I focus on the whole, hierarchy, and network. Levine points out that the trouble with the whole is its embrace of unified wholeness, namely, its willingness to impose boundaries. Critics have worked relentlessly to resist and unsettle social unities and totalities, celebrating instead difference and diversity. In that sense, the salon and the letter disturb the whole. We find bounded wholes and enclosures everywhere throughout history. For instance, in 1516 the Venetian senate voted to segregate Jews in the ghetto, the gates of which were locked each night.

---

[6] At that time a widespread view that divided literary genres into female and male and was held by Goethe and Schiller, "Über epische und dramatische Dichtung"; Hegel, *Vorlesungen über die Ästhetik*; A. W. Schlegel, *Die Kunstlehre and Vorlesungen*; F. Schlegel, "Gespräch über die Poesie." See Susanne Kord, *Sich einen Namen machen: Anonymität und weibliche Autorschaft 1700–1900* (Stuttgart: Metzler, 1996), 58–61.

[7] Levin Varnhagen to Gentz, December 27, 1827, in Rahel Varnhagen, *Briefwechsel*, ed. Friedhelm Kemp (Munich: Winkler, 1979), 3.157.

[8] J. M. Raich, ed., *Dorothea V. Schlegel geb. Mendelssohn und deren Söhne Johannes und Philipp Veit. Briefwechsel im Auftrage der Familie Veit*, vols. 1 and 2 (Mainz: Franz Kirchheim), vol. 2, 445.

Unlike a bounded whole, the salon was an open and inclusive space. Levin Varnhagen, Mendelssohn Veit Schlegel, and Brentano von Arnim came from varied religious backgrounds: Levin Varnhagen was Jewish but converted to Christianity much like her contemporary Mendelssohn Veit Schlegel who also converted, first from Judaism to Protestantism and later to Catholicism; Brentano von Arnim was Catholic. Yet, they all wrote at the intersection of Enlightenment and Romanticism and did not intervene in their religious cultures, as their male counterparts did.[9] Indeed, their oeuvres exhibit tolerant, cosmopolitan attitudes and suggest a renewed spirituality. Casually fusing politics, social issues, and love, they combine the ideal of universal thinking with the preoccupations of their own lives evident in content and form.

In fact, neither advocacy for Jewish nor for women's rights accounted for the emancipatory substance of the salon as much as leaving aside the categories of religion and gender and not thinking in these categories. Perhaps this is what makes this freeing moment of the salons so attractive to this day, simply the aspiration "to discuss affairs as a human with humans [als Mensch mit Menschen zu diskutieren]."[10]

For the Jewish *salonnières* Henriette Herz (1764–1847), Dorothea Mendelssohn Veit Schlegel, and Rahel Levin Varnhagen, the French salons of the seventeenth and eighteenth centuries provided the model for their own gatherings; however, they developed a more informal and familiar sociability based on an idealized notion of the Jewish family.[11] Salons were conceived as democratic spaces where members of the aristocracy mingled with the middle class and with Jewish intellectuals, and women participated in contemporary cultural, intellectual, and political discussions. Romantic discourse was intended to maximize mutual understanding without minimizing opposing voices.

Henriette Herz founded a secret society, the Society of the Virtuous (*Tugendbund*), which accrued from a productive conversation and dialogical letter writing based on the idea of love, and which ushered in the sociability of the Jena Romantics.[12] The Tugendbund comprised Henriette Herz, Dorothea Veit, Wilhelm and Alexander von Humboldt, Wilhelm's future wife Caroline von Dacheröden, and Karl Laroche, son of the novelist Sophie Laroche, who gathered at Henriette Herz's salon and practiced "the

---

[9] Clemens Brentano, the brother of Bettina Brentano von Arnim, and her husband Achim von Arnim participated in the blatantly anti-Jewish activities of the German Christian Round-Table (1811-1834, Christlich-Deutsche Tischgesellschaft)—a politically conservative society that encouraged reforms in Prussia and excluded women and Jews from being members.

[10] Hannah Lotte Lund, *Der Berliner "jüdische Salon" um 1800* (Berlin: de Gruyter, 2012), notes that in the letter exchanges of the salon from the years 1794/95, religious concepts were approached with a certain distance and veiled in irony (354 and 542).

[11] See Ursula Isselstein, "Die Titel der Dinge sind das Fürchsterlichste! Rahel Levins 'Erster Salon,'" in *Salons der Romantik. Beiträge eines Wiepersdorfer Kolloquiums zu Theorie und Geschichte des Salons*, ed. Hartwig Schultz (Berlin: de Gruyter, 1997), 171–212, and Barbara Hahn, "'Der Mythos vom Salon. 'Rahels Dachstube' als historische Fiktion," in Schultz, *Salons der Romantik. Beiträge eines Wiepersdorfer Kolloquiums zu Theorie und Geschichte des Salons*, 213–234.

[12] See Rahel Varnhagen, *Gesammelte Werke. Rahel-Bibliothek*, ed. Konrad Feilchenfeldt, Uwe Schweickert, and Rahel E. Steiner (Munich: Matthes & Seitz, 1983).

pursuit of happiness through love" by means of an exercise in active love.[13] The Early Romantic circle centered in Jena from 1798 to 1804 included Dorothea Veit (Schlegel after her marriage to Friedrich Schlegel in 1804), Caroline Schlegel-Schelling, Friedrich and August Wilhelm Schlegel, Novalis, Ludwig Tieck, Friedrich Schelling, Friedrich Schleiermacher, Friedrich Hölderlin, and Gottlieb Fichte. Their conceptions of sociability foregrounded the resemblance to family bonds and religious togetherness. The aim of the Jena Romantics was to create a sociability that furthered individual creativity within a communal framework; hence, they conducted diverse sociable collective living and working experiments as they wrote and translated collaboratively. Indeed, the periodical *Athenaeum Fragments* and the famous Shakespeare translations came out of this cooperation. This emphasis on subjective mixing to the point of intellectual love affairs was in these cases confined to interactions with trusted companions.

Similarly to the French *salonnières*, Levin Varnhagen used her salons to contribute to society. Yet, her sense of self depended on conversation and epistolary exchanges, whereas Madame de Sévigné, with the exception of the letters to her daughter, frowned on writing letters as mere social obligation. Levin Varnhagen's salon culture was much more familiar than formal and took on new aesthetic and ethical significance by bringing in sociability according to the framework of civic sovereignty and cosmopolitics and adapting to the political demands and circumstances of the time. In her writing, the boundaries between the spoken and written word, letters and literary genres are obfuscated as she understood literature to be "living sociability in words [Lebensgeselligkeit in Worten]."[14] For instance, she used colloquialisms like "dumb like an ox [dumm wie ein Ochs]" along with diplomatic expressions.[15]

A frequent visitor to her salons was Bettina Brentano von Arnim, who herself conducted different salons in her lifetime. Whereas the early one in Landshut was structured as a teacher/pupil relationship between her and her guests, the Berlin salon that convened from the mid-1830s for a decade, was less formal and guided.[16] She moved away from the discreet hospitality of the French salon model by becoming the intellectual and social center of her circle. In fact, her politicized salon was a radical embodiment of the Habermasian public sphere since it functioned as a platform for political debates

---

[13] Rainer Schmitz, ed., *Henriette Herz in Erinnerungen, Briefen und Zeugnissen* (Frankfurt am Main: Insel, 1984), 82.

[14] Levin Varnhagen to David Veit, February 16, 1805, in Varnhagen, *Gesammelte Werke*, vol. 2, 411.

[15] The following materials come from the Varnhagen Archive at the Jagiellonian University Library in Krakow, Poland: "M. P. Vermischte Schriften. Rahel. Ein Buch des Andenkens für ihre Freunde. 1834," *Jenaische Allgemeine LiteraturZeitung*, no. 221, December 1834, Zeitungsausschnitte und Notizen aus alter Zeit, Varnhagen Collection, crate no. 205. The Varnhagen Collection was previously in the Preussische Staatsbibliothek (Prussian State Library), which was evacuated from Berlin in April 1941 and eventually transferred to Kraków after World War II. By 1911, the collection contained the papers of over 9,000 German intellectuals from the early nineteenth century, including writings by prominent literary and political figures of the era such as Varnhagen's wife, Rahel Levin Varnhagen, Goethe, Wilhelm von Humboldt, Friedrich and A. W. Schlegel, Heinrich Heine, G. W. F. Hegel, J. G. Fichte, and Karl Marx.

[16] Ingrid Leitner, "Liebe und Erkenntnis: Kommunikationsstructuren bei Bettine von Arnim: ein Vergleich fiktiven Sprechens mit Gesprä chen im Salon," in Schultz, *Salons der Romantik*, 235.

that were otherwise censored and prohibited.[17] Unlike the French salons, Brentano von Arnim's salon in Berlin addressed contemporary sociopolitical problems with hands-on charitable activities during the cholera epidemic in 1831.[18] This ideological change materialized in three books, *This Book Belongs to the King* (*Dies Buch gehört dem König*, 1843), *Conversations with Demons* (*Gespräche mit Dämonen*, 1852), and the posthumously published *Book of the Poor* (*Armenbuch*, 1844) where she discussed state censorship, the abuses of political power, early capitalism, and the increasing gap between rich and poor.

The form of the salon breaks the whole by displaying life itself while being an art form. Levin Varnhagen made sociability purposeful rather than disinterested, in hopes that it would offer guidance and insight into the state of human affairs: "sociability. Actually the most human among people! It is the embodiment and the departure point for all that is moral! Without assistants, without fellow humans of worldly existence, we ourselves wouldn't be persons and not capable of ethical actions, laws, or thinking; impossible . . . if then sociability is corrupt, I am too."[19] Unlike Levin Varnhagen, Schleiermacher, who based his work *Essay on Theory of Sociable Behavior* on his experiences in Berlin salons,[20] aestheticized sociability in the same way that Kant had done with art, as Schleiermacher postulated the "disinterested contemplation of the work of art."[21] Namely, he assigned free social interaction to a separate category of leisure under the direction of women thus detaching it from both the professional sphere and the domestic space. By locating sociability in a separate sphere, not in everyday reality, he perpetuated gender division ideology and diminished the capacity for genuine transformation and advancement. Levin Varnhagen perceived the salon as a social opportunity to display a practice of life from which she, a Jew and a woman, was banned elsewhere. She insisted that the salon brought her a true enjoyment of life, hence, life and art belonged together since they had an impact on each other: "is it not the same with life as with art?"[22] This rhetorical question posed to her friend Brinckmann indicates that she considered the salon to be an aesthetic space and practice, through which the real life displays itself and encourages art production. A substantial thesis of Hannah Arendt was that Levin Varnhagen exposed herself to life akin to the "weather without an umbrella" in order to shape her life into an art form.[23] In that sense the salon sociability in the form proposed by Levin Varnhagen is a vehicle to expose the shortcomings of social interaction on both the private and public levels, and thus offers hope for the

---

[17] Leitner, "Liebe und Erkenntnis," 236–237.

[18] See Herbert Scurla, *Begegnungen mit Rahel: Der Salon der Rahel Levin* (Berlin: Verlag der Nation, 1962).

[19] Rahel Varnhagen, *Gesammelte Werke*, vol. 2, 616.

[20] Andreas Anrdt, "Philosophie," in *Friedrich Schlegel Handbuch. Leben—Werk—Wirkung*, ed. Johannes Endres, 189–211 (Stuttgart: J. B. Metzler, 2017), 45–62.

[21] Heidi Thomann Tewarson, *Rahel Levin Varnhagen: The Life and Work of a German Jewish Intellectual* (Lincoln: University of Nebraska Press, 1998), 42.

[22] Karl Varnhagen von Ense, *Denkwürdigkeiten und vermischte Schriften*, vol. 8, 654.

[23] Lund, *Der Berliner "jüdische Salon,"* 92.

future generations, as it anticipates reformation of interpersonal forms of communication and dialogue.

The form of the salon sociability was the foundation for the form of the letter symphilosophy, which the Romantics understood as an ideal confluence of compatible creative minds whose writing and discussion were so intimately connected that unilateral individuation was virtually unfeasible. Already in the first biography of Levin Varnhagen (1857), Eduard Schmidt-Weissenfels established a connection between the salon and the letter, calling the letter "the child of the salon."[24] The salon and its brainchild, the letter, were integral elements of a conceptual framework that relied on sociability organized and put into practice by women. Hosts and guests carried on tea talks in letters, but also sent short notes, along with books and invitations to discuss them.[25] Brentano von Arnim und Hermann Fürst Pückler-Muskau first met in Levin Varnhagen's salon and then continued their conversation through their letters.[26] Both Levin Varnhagen and Brentano von Arnim spent many hours a day writing several multipaged letters that were often read aloud in the circle of family and friends. Levin Varnhagen illustrates the connection between salon conversations and letters in a comment to David Veit: "your letter is my true companion; I had a cup of chocolate made for me to go with it. (Do write whether you laughed about it; I'm laughing)."[27] The idea of sociability is connected here to the salon setting, so much so that Levin Varnhagen writes as though her interlocutor were physically present in her space and within her timeframe.

Romantic writers purposefully questioned and disrupted organic form, refusing mythical wholeness in favor of fissures, discontinuities, and dissonances, namely, fragments. The genre of letter writing is fragmentary, so it breaks the boundaries of the whole, but it resembles a living organism more than a novel because of its capacity to expand and grow. Although the Romantics of both genders showed great appreciation for the letter, women's letter writing is uniquely Romantic because of the close coupling of life and writing, of the quotidian and the poetic, of artistic creation and aesthetic reflection. In their letters, dialogue serves as a powerful building block, as it captures everyday moments, while reflecting on Romantic philosophy with its emphasis on poeticizing and potentializing so that life becomes art and art life. Brentano von Arnim foregrounds precisely this aspect, noting, for example, that a friend's letter holds "a healthy, cheerful life [ein gesundes, munteres Leben]" and comments further that "poetry is always a true

---

[24] Eduard Schmidt-Weissenfels, *Rahel und ihre Zeit* (Leipzig: F. A. Brockhaus, 1857), 45.

[25] Hannah Lotte Lund, "Prussians, Jews, Egyptians?," in *Orientalism, Gender, and the Jews: Literary and Artistic Transformations of European National Discourses,* ed. Ulrike Brunotte, Anna-Dorothea Ludewig, and Axel Strähler (Oldenbourg: de Gruyter, 2015), 40.

[26] Wolfgang Bunzel, "Der Epistolare Pakt. Zum Briefwechsel zwischen Bettine von Arnim und Hermann Fürst Pückler-Muskau," in *Briefnetzwerke um Hermann von Pückler-Muskau,* ed. Jana Kittelmann (Dresden: Thelem, 2015), 17.

[27] Karl Varnhagen von Ense, *Briefwechsel zwischen Rahel und David Veit. Aus dem Nachlaß Varnhagen's von Ense,* vol. 1, ed. Karl Varnhagen von Ense (Leipzig: F. A. Brockhaus, 1861), 253.

style."[28] Brentano von Arnim was partial to apparent formlessness as a textual means to relay quotidian reality through the prism of imagination; consequently, she poeticized life by obscuring the line between life and literature.

Levin Varnhagen, Mendelssohn Veit Schlegel, and Brentano von Arnim developed, if in different ways, the salon conversation into an epistolary art form and an anticlassical epistolary poetics; thus, contradicting Aristotle's claim that the work of literature must be whole and complete resembling a living organism in all its unity. The dialogue spaces they created differ from those fashioned by Friedrich Schlegel, who in his *Dialogue on Poetry* connected conversation and poetry. According to Schlegel all poetic fragments should be read in participatory, dialogical manner, thus modeling a perfect communication (*vollendete Mitteilung*) by incorporating a conversation among authors and readers. At first, Schlegel planned to include women's contributions in this all-encompassing dialogue, but he failed to do so.[29] In contrast, salon conversation—and by extension the letter—was essentially a complete, and thus perfect, form of communication because the participants were autonomous individuals belonging to a harmonic yet still diverse universe, where life was organized according to the rules of symphilosophy and aesthetic production was integrated into social life. Thus, salon conversations, and letter dialogues are forms of symphilosophy and sympoetry as not only the writer but also the reader takes part in this kind of communication which becomes complete in a dialogue of present, past, and future and connects life with art.

Hierarchy belongs to Levine's structure of *Forms*, and I will discuss it under the rubric of gender. Gender as mechanism and apparatus is an instrument or device that produces hierarchical distinctions. Gender operates as a particularly stark form, a blunt binary that imposes its order not only on bodies, but also on other social forms, such as public and private spaces, divisions of labor, styles of dress and speech, and authority. Women needed to reaffirm their place in society, as they faced the challenge of locating themselves in a literary and philosophical debate, among men, about the intellectual capabilities of women and a new gender order. A strong and independent a figure as Levin Varnhagen was accused of lacking femininity because of her "manly pride" manifested through the authority of her "manly voice," and was condemned for having the deeply pronounced streak of an "Israelite national egoism," demonstrating itself through the unfeminine powerful speech.[30] The problem of literary recognition, then, becomes clearly entwined with gender and race issues, as her ability and license to write for a wider audience is condemned and opposed. She reveals the exasperation regarding

---

[28] Bettina von Arnim, *Die Günderode*, in *Werke und Briefe in drei Bänden*, vol. 1, ed. Walter Schmitz and Sibylle von Steinsdorff (Frankfurt am Main: Deutscher Klassiker Verlag, 1986), 394.

[29] May Mergenthaler, "Die Frühromantik als Projekt vollendeter Mitteilung zwischen den Geschlechtern: Friedrich Schlegel und Dorothea Veit im Gespräch über Friedrich Richters Romane," *German Quarterly* 81, no. 3 (2008): 302–321; here: 21.

[30] "M. P. Vermischte Schriften. Rahel. Ein Buch des Andenkens für ihre Freunde. 1834," *Jenaische Allgemeine LiteraturZeitung*, no. 221, December 1834, Zeitungsausschnitte und Notizen aus alter Zeit, Varnhagen Collection, crate no. 205.

her Jewish origin when she calls herself "a fool and a Jewess [ein Schlemihl und eine Jüdin]."[31] In addition, the praises often cited to characterize Levin's exceptional skill as a hostess could also be used to relegate her to a stereotypical woman's position. On the one hand, the salon offered expanded access to German culture for the Jews and to education for women and thus obliterated societal borders.[32] On the other hand, the separate space of the salon and letter writing might have created a detour for female writers on the long way to "autonomy" (*Mündigkeit*).[33] By current feminist standards, the salons did not necessarily provide a satisfactory intellectual or social freedom for the women who led or attended them. Still salon participants, and especially the Romantic literati, were dedicated to both the real and ideal possibilities for increased flexibility in gender roles and relations. Especially in comparison with the life of German intellectuals a few decades earlier, the salon scene advanced the progress of women.

2 RAHEL LEVIN VARNHAGEN'S DIALOGICAL NETWORK OF LOVE

The most prolific letter writer who established a network of a heterogeneous group of people who self-consciously engaged in dialogicity as a common enterprise of Romantic philosophy was unquestionably Levin Varnhagen. As the leading Berlin *salonnière* and a great thinker of her time, Levin Varnhagen created one of the most remarkable collections of letters in eighteenth- and nineteenth-century Germany. She was in contact with more than three hundred people, and her archive consists of some 6,000 letters that are part of the Varnhagen Collection. The compilation of texts Rahel Levin started as a young woman, contains an assortment of letters from a diverse group of people, namely, from famous aristocrats, influential politicians, philosophers, acculturated emancipated Jewish women, and young gentile intellectuals as well as from unestablished writers, actresses, and her unknown cook. She and her husband collected and preserved all the letters, including those she received and those she recovered from her addressees, and some of them were published during her lifetime in various journals. After his wife's passing, K. A. Varnhagen brought to press a collection of letters: *Rahel: A Commemoration for Her Friends* (*Rahel. Ein Buch des Andenkens für ihre Freunde*, 1834).

However, Levin Varnhagen did not just create a network, but rather a network of love, as she had acted toward all her guests in an open, uncomplicated loving

---

[31] Levin Varnhagen to David Veit in Göttingen, Berlin, April 2, 1793, in Rahel Varnhagen, *Briefwechsel*, vol. 3, 20.

[32] Lund, *Der Berliner "jüdische Salon,"* 62.

[33] See Barbara Becker-Cantarino, *Der lange Weg zur Mündigkeit. Frau und Literatur (1500–1800)* (Stuttgart: J. B. Metzler, 1987).

manner, regardless of their class, rank, or profession. She tolerated their mannerisms, peculiarities, and weaknesses. After her death, Gustav von Brinckmann, (1764–1847) the Swedish diplomat who served as the ambassador in Berlin (1807), acknowledged her art of salon guidance that created harmonious environment, as she diverted the conversation from any contentious issues causing resentment.[34] The practical goal of her salon was the construction of the heterogeneous constellation of guests and of the space where love could be manifested first and cultivated through letters. She was quite aware that she possessed a special social talent and defined it in a letter to Clemens Brentano: "I love company endlessly since always, and I'm convinced that for that I have been born and from nature destined and equipped. I have perpetual presence and quickness of the spirit in order to grasp, to respond, to deal with. Great sense for natures and all relationships, understand jokes and earnestness, and no subject matter, even awkward, is alien to me."[35] Levin Varnhagen conceived of her salon as an unfolding and expanding life grounded in love, which did not have to be off-limits for her, a woman and a Jew. When Clemens Brentano accused her of having inferior motives—such as desire for attention and vanity—for leading the salon, she gave an account of her sociability by declaring her love for all people and her desire for dialogue: "I am humble and reveal myself through speaking and can keep silent for a long time and love everything human, *condone* almost all people".[36] Because she understood others on a philosophical and psychological level, she was able to build many connections through the personal approach. She simply possessed "unlimited love of fellowship."[37] The genuine and fundamental interest of the *salonnière* Levin Varnhagen was the human person.

3 DOROTHEA MENDELSSOHN VEIT SCHLEGEL'S IDEA OF ROMANTIC AND SOCIABLE LOVE

The Romantics of both genders pioneered their way by trying to erase the divide of love and fellowship between lovers and spouses. The life of Mendelssohn Veit Schlegel, as

---

[34] Rahel Levin Varnhagen to Varnhagen von Ense, in Varnhagen von Ense, *Denkwürdigkeiten*, vol. 3, 639–684 and 648–649, in Seibert, *Der literarische Salon, Literatur und Geselligkeit zwischen Aufklärung und Vormärz* (Stuttgart: Metzler, 1993), 334.

[35] Rahel Varnhagen, Prague, to Clemens Brentano, Vienna, August 1813, in Rahel Varnhagen, *Briefwechsel*, vol. 3, 358.

[36] Rahel Varnhagen, Prague, to Clemens Brentano, Vienna, August 1813, in Rahel Varnhagen, *Briefwechsel*, vol. 3, 358.

[37] Rahel Levin Varnhagen to Varnhagen von Ense, in Varnhagen von Ense, *Denkwürdigkeiten und vermischte Schriften*, vol. 8, 639–684 and 648–649.

it were, was a radical form of protest against the restrictions on women's undertakings and moved beyond the limits of late eighteenth-century gender roles. Because of her divorce and open relationship with a younger man, she was fully discredited socially. Despite that, she was free and independent and found in Schlegel an equal congenial partner. She understood love to be the complete unity of the lovers in their fusion of carnality and spirituality: "one love, evermore, evermore—already here on earth; one love, that remains young forever, renews itself always; every day new mnemonic of love, new movement, new pain and aroma! Every day tears of the inner dedication! Without jealousy because the spirits that like me are loved are equal, feel, love just as I do, are not different from me, they are one with me in love."[38] According to Mendelssohn Veit Schlegel, love is regenerated and perfected every day through new emotions, pains, delights so that both partners become forever one. The Romantics paid attention to all aspects of existence, not just the rational side; thus, love that renews itself every day points to the existence of the infinite as being present in our daily personal experience. It is only in the moment in which we become aware of our limitations (in a sense of incomprehensibility) that we encounter the idea of something unlimited, fully other,[39] and it is only through Romantic irony that we are able to confront the Absolute.[40] According to Schlegel true irony is "the irony of love" because in love we are presented with the idea of the infinite that we juxtapose against our own finitude.[41] The love of Friedrich and Dorothea shaped not only their private life as a couple—although it was made public in his novel *Lucinde*, the erotic part notwithstanding—but also provided consequential material for the theoretical framework of their works and the early Romantic movement embedded in sociability and dialogicity. However, while he looked to the ancient models of Socrates and Plato when theorizing that which he experienced in his own life, she relied on her Jewish roots and predisposition for dialogue that was lived out in the Jewish salon (a form of sociability) and maintained in the letters (a form of symphilosophy). She used these forms in her novel *Florentin*.

The productive Jena dialogues thrive in the poetic zeal in *Florentin*, which, according to some scholars, was written as a feminist response to the blatant sexist *Lucinde* that fictionalized Friedrich Schlegel's illicit relationship with Dorothea (at that time) Veit.[42] I focus on Mendelssohn Veit Schlegel's work as a rejoinder to the Romantic sociability and dialogicity, including Friedrich Schlegel's philosophy of the "reciprocity principle" (*Wechselerweis*).[43] Mendelssohn Veit Schlegel develops her own strategies of dialogue

---

[38] Raich, *Dorothea V. Schlegel*, vol. 2, 445.

[39] Jacob Burda, *Das gute Unendliche in der deutschen Frühromantik* (Stuttgart: J. B. Metzler Verlag, 2020), 140.

[40] Burda, *Das gute Unendliche*, 165.

[41] Burda, *Das gute Unendliche*, 171.

[42] Elena Pnevmonidou, "Die Absage an das romantische Ich: Dorothea Schlegels *Florentin* als Umschrift von Friedrich Schlegels *Lucinde*," *German Life and Letters* 58 (2005): 271–292.

[43] Because the novel was developed in close proximity to the salon, it serves as an example of the personal and discursive overlap between the events that took place at the salon and gender discussions (Lund, *Der Berliner "jüdische Salon,"* 187).

not derived from the ancient models like those of Friedrich Schlegel, who relied on the Socratic dialogue as a process of a collaborative search for truth. His *Dialogue on Poetry* is an essay conceived in the form of a dialogue between seven young intellectuals, Amalia, Camilla, Markus, Ludoviko, Antonio, Andrea, and Lothario. Friedrich Schlegel's claim is that the wisdom of life lies in philosohizing through dialogue and finding a coherent model of truth.[44] The bookish wisdom (*Schulweisheit*) is not the same as the "ideal of a rounded educational formation" (*Bildungsideal*), and Friedrich Schlegel, who finds fault with it, claims that the way to achieve the ideal is through love.[45]

In *Florentin* Mendelssohn Veit Schlegel develops this idea further and theorizes it according to the form of salon sociability and letter symphilosophy. At first her draft versions of *Florentin* included dialogue in the classical form, similar to that of Friedrich Schlegel, and focused on the concept of love:

> Conversation between Eleonore and Clementine.
> ELEONORE: Dear Clementine, you appear, I don't know, not satisfied enough, not
>   reconciliated ...
> CLEM(ENTINE):   And no love!
> ELEON(ORE):   How?
> CLEM(ENTINE):   I upset you so unwillingly from your joy.[46]

In the final version, however, Mendelssohn Veit did not incorporate this form of dialogue into her novel. Instead she chose to emulate a salon setting in which the most important figure is a *salonnière*, Julianne's aunt Clementine, and interlaced the dialogues with the other genres of text so that they no longer bore classical attributes of an independent literary form of dialogue. For this particular conversation between Eleonore and Clementine, the author decided on the form of the letter. Moreover, throughout the course of the novel (with the exception of the last few pages) Clementine's voice—the voice of the *salonnière*—is heard exclusively through letters. She entertains a salon despite her prevailing illness and as a result is a paragon of Romantic sociability and solitude simultaneously:

> She never seeks company . . . but her house is always open for good company, also strangers visit her; the fine relaxed tone that rules in her house causes that she is sought after by all. The amusement of the countess is light, intelligent, and through these qualities alone, one expects in society the woman of extraordinary faculties. As often as there is an opportunity, she arranges for concerts and balls, where always young people find themselves, whose amusement is not disturbed by anything what could reveal the serious disposition of the hostess. Very soon she obviously retreats

---

[44] Birgit Rehme-Iffert, *Skepsis und Enthusiasmus. Friedrich Schlegels philosophischer Grundgedanke zwischen 1796 und 1805* (Bonn: Königshausen und Neumann, 2001), 85.

[45] Rehme-Iffert, *Skepsis und Enthusiasmus*, 100.

[46] Dorothea Schlegel, "Aufzeichnungen und Entwürfe zum *Florentin*," in *Florentin*, ed. Wolfgang Nehring (Stuttgart: Reclam, 2004), 199.

to her solitary room, but without the slightest intention to interrupt the fun, just as she never allows any kind of a show for her sake.[47]

The casual tone of the gathering and the fact that the house is open to newcomers and strangers reminds the reader of the prominent Berlin salons led by Henriette Herz and Rahel Levin Varnhagen. It is in Levin Varnhagen's letters that the reader encounters the unceasing need for remaining in dialogue. In *Florentin*, that same dialogical circumstance is expressed not only through Clementine's correspondence, but also through the letter exchange between Florentin and his friend Manfredi. The regular frequency of the exchange and reassurance of friendship and mutual love secure their trust and intensify their friendship. In addition, letters take precedence over the real-life conversation: "the conversation was interrupted through the letters from the Countess Clementine to the Count and Juliane."[48] Furthermore, the parties conversing enter into the dialogue with the letters: "Juliane was sad, not to be able to await her loving aunt. She read her letter over and over."[49] The process of rereading the letter suggests a prolonged and attentive conversation with the sender, as Juliane formulates thoughts and already composes the reply mentally.

Dialogical interactions in *Florentin*—be it through letters or in a salon setting— correlate with the search for a foundation of Romantic philosophy shifting from self alone to an interaction between self and world, as developed in Friedrich Schlegel's critique of Fichte's philosophy of consciousness. Friedrich Schlegel calls the maxim the *Wechselerweis*—the reciprocity axiom or principle that attributes life, activity, and interactivity to nature as well as to the self—and develops a new type of transcendental philosophy modeled on the Platonic dialogue extending this basic dialogue, enclosed within one consciousness, into various analogous dialogues: between self and world, self and other, and between the self and the images the self constructs. Laurie Johnson points out that Mendelssohn Veit Schlegel's novel represents a particular and advanced understanding of the *Wechselerweis*—crucial to grasping the progressive nature of the earliest Romanticism—in a way that the fiction of Friedrich Schlegel and Novalis never did, that is, that the "Ich" cannot be the absolute ground of thought, excluding all else.[50] The reciprocity principle, as the free stimulator of intersubjective thoughts, bridges symphilosophy and social togetherness and contributes to enrichment and further study. Florentin wishes to be alone, yet he cannot elude encountering real people. The dynamic movement of the reciprocity principle helps him reach beyond his own fragmentation and connect to real others, although those connections are always necessarily mediated by imagery, for instance, when he first meets Clementine in the form of a portrait. *Florentin*, a fragmentary novel, employs circular representations of self-other relationships and realizes the progressive character of the early years of German

---

[47] D. Schlegel, "Aufzeichnungen und Entwürfe zum *Florentin, 177.*
[48] D. Schlegel, "Aufzeichnungen und Entwürfe zum *Florentin,*" 138.
[49] D. Schlegel, "Aufzeichnungen und Entwürfe zum *Florentin,*" 139.
[50] Laurie Johnson, "Florentin and the Early Romantic Model of Alterity," *Monatshelfte* 97, no. 1 (Spring, 2005): 33–62, here 35.

Romanticism in which the Jena authors explored Romantic reason; hence, it is "a truly symphilosophical text."[51] The *Wechselerweis* captures the spirit of humanity which reveals itself as the strife between the finite and the infinite,[52] via true irony, the irony of love. In other words, they create their lives based on the philosophy love.

4 BETTINA BRENTANO VON ARNIM'S SYNTHESIS OF SPIRITUAL AND SENSUAL LOVE

The theme of love is a programmatic statement of Brentano von Arnim's epistolary novel *Die Günderode* (1840), in which she reconstructs her letter exchange with her deceased friend Karoline von Günderrode. She proposes a dialogue to develop not only a deeper friendship, but also strategies of resistance against the rules of patriarchal society. She introduces symbiosis of the intellect and sensuousness to bring about the atmosphere of intellectual conversation, akin to what took place in salons led by women, as she recreates the "art of reciprocal communication," intimate philosophical conversation, and "aesthetic reflective dialogue" that took place in the salons of Berlin attended by the Schlegels and Schleiermacher, as well as in meetings in the home of August and Caroline Schlegel in Jena.[53] By blurring the line between fact and fiction—achieved mainly through the characters' names, which are nearly identical to the real names of the author and her friend, Bettina/Bettine and Günderrode/ Günderode—Brentano von Arnim creates a space for a new mode of interaction between independently thinking women, hence the aesthetic friendship differs from the real one. Brentano von Arnim uses the epistolary novel to represent symphilosophical dialogue with her friend in that she reinvents and retheorizes the Romantic notions of sociability and symphilosophy. Furthermore, she defies Friedrich Schlegel's claim that true friendship, "a great brotherhood of united heroes," can only exist between men,[54] and she redefines the notion of *philia* (brotherly love), as she introduces erotic and spiritual elements to her theory that constitutes a cultivation of a new lifelong intellectual form of *philia* between women. The love that is discussed in Plato's *Symposium* has homosexuality as its background,[55] and Aristotle makes friendship, rather than sexual relationships or contemplation of the Good/God/s, the supreme form of love, which he calls perfect *philia* (wishing and doing well to others for their own sake and

---

[51] Johnson, "Florentin and the Early Romantic Model of Alterity," 57.

[52] Burda, *Das gute Unendliche*, 88.

[53] Jane Kneller, "Sociability and the Conduct of Philosophy: What We Can Learn from Early German Romanticism," in *The Relevance of Romanticism: Essays on German Romantic Philosophy*, ed. Dalia Nassar (New York: Oxford University Press, 2014), 113.

[54] Irving Singer, *The Nature of Love: Plato to Luther* (Chicago: University of Chicago Press, 1987), 389.

[55] Singer, *The Nature of Love*, 49–50.

seeking deep mutual harmony),[56] while Brentano von Arnim opens up both of these categorizations for wider interpretation.

Brentano von Arnim's characters, Bettine and Karoline, featured in *Die Günderode*, subscribe to female philosophy rooted in the notion of *Schwebereligion* (hovering religion—a term coined by Brentano von Arnim) free of traditional dogmas and rules, and linked to erotic desire. For medieval Christianity, God is love; for the Romantic ideology, love is God, and Brentano von Arnim writes this new theory. It is the feeling of love that motivates and strengthens Bettine, so much so that she identifies with spiritual and military figures. Similarly, Günderode, the protagonist, emphasizes spiritual dimensions of dialogue and connects praying with thinking, as in "by thinking while praying, and praying while thinking."[57] She thus refashions the Benedictine rule *ora et labora* (pray and work) into the feminine symphilosophy developed by both women according to the new maxim of thinking while praying and vice versa. By adding the component of thinking, the author follows in the footsteps of influential monastic women—for instance, Hildegard von Bingen—who were empowered not only by prayer but also by intellectual pursuits. The act of rational thinking balances out prayer and informs the new gendered spirituality invented by Bettine, *Schwebereligion*, which is free of patriarchal supervision. This new spirituality replaces feminine silence and obedience with independent thinking and self-expression.

The author employs an innovative method of writing rooted in her own divine model of communication as performance of speaking, where love means being in dialogue with God, composed of "a question and a sweet answer."[58] For that reason, the dialogue points to love. The thought that our knowledge of any language system has its origins essentially in the human heart, where our feelings are being formed and our attitudes are being molded, finds a prominent articulation in Brentano von Arnim's *Die Günderode*. Love provides the foundation for creation and is established through words. The author relies on the biblical account of creation: "then it occurred to me that God said, 'Let there *be*,' and that the words of God were creation, and I wanted to imitate this."[59] Through the use of the expression "Let there *be* [Es *werde*]" the author makes an analogy to the creation story of the Hebrew Bible, which introduces the Book of Moses (Genesis) with the words: "then God said, 'Let there be light,' and there was light."[60] It is God's love that creates through the use of words. By placing language as the instrument of creation at the center of attention, Brentano von Arnim connects language to the inspiration of nature. It is, however, the inspiration of nature combined with the force of love and the energy and femininity of *Schwebereligion* that make Brentano von Arnim's dialogue unique.

---

[56] Singer, *The Nature of Love*, 93.
[57] Von Arnim, *Die Günderode,* 449.
[58] Von Arnim, *Die Günderode,* 511–512.
[59] Von Arnim, *Die Günderode,* 467.
[60] Gen. 1:3, *New American Standard Bible,* https://biblehub.com/nasb_/genesis/1.htm.

The verbalization of nature is not only connected to thinking, but rather it begins in human experience and feeling within the human heart:

> all that I look upon, I suddenly perceive ... all this reaches my heart by something, should I call it language? With what then does one touch the soul? Is that language not the love that touches the soul, as a human being is touched by a kiss? Perhaps it is; then that which I experience in Nature is certainly language, for it kisses my soul; what else should it be if it were not this! Now pay attention: To kiss is to receive within us the form and the spirit of the form that we touch; this is the kiss; yes, form indeed is born within us. Therefore, language is kissing, as we are kissed by each word in a poem.[61]

In the end, the author concludes that the act of speaking is achieved not only through the act of thinking[62] but also through love appearing inside one's heart.[63] She compares the spiritual act of love that is able to touch the soul to the erotic act of individual words kissing the reader. She conceptualizes a divine model of communication per se: "love I believe, is only the language of God. I am conscious of knowing everything, but I cannot always find it, and seek everything in myself, and this is a conversation with God. That is a conversation of love. . . . But love is only the language of the Deity?—But of course, what else should it be?—a question and a sweet answer."[64] In the end, love becomes linked to dialogue since the act of speaking is an oscillation between a question and an answer, and these then in turn are connected to divinity.

The author connects divine elements with the material ones, that is to say, those of bodily functions, as she associates the somatosensory system with linguistic abilities. By asking "is language not love?"[65] she equates language with an act of love that moves the spirit and the heart, the place where one receives sensation. This language perception is based on bodily contact, since Brentano von Arnim transposes the function of the eye and mouth in regard to nature, writing, "eyes, for they are the mouth Nature kisses."[66] The definition "language is kissing" is built upon the common function of both actions. When Brentano von Arnim speaks about language touching the spirit and the kiss touching a human being, she uses "touch" as an encompassing term that uses the verbs "speak" and "kiss" as synonyms. The premise for this is a broadened definition of speaking as the act of love. The synonymous and interchangeable usage of spirit with sensation as of rationality with reflection signifies that nature shares itself with people by triggering sensations and relates the spiritual world to the physical one. By saying "question is love, and answer is requited love. Where the question is just love to the demon,

---

[61] Von Arnim, *Die Günderode*, 527–228.
[62] Von Arnim, *Die Günderode*, 449.
[63] Von Arnim, *Die Günderode*, 526.
[64] Von Arnim, *Die Günderode*, 511–112.
[65] Von Arnim, *Die Günderode*, 527.
[66] Von Arnim, *Die Günderode*, 528.

then he answers, the spirit cannot resist love, just as you cannot, and I cannot," Brentano von Arnim theorizes dialogue in terms of the concept of love.[67]

5 Conclusion

What is most astonishing about the salon and letter writing discussed here is that Mendelssohn Veit Schlegel, Levin Varnhagen, and Brentano von Arnim created a new practice of writing. They suggested a new vision for an emancipated community of women that develops and creates together through reflective thinking, philosophical discourse, and poetry and in effect merges art and life and thus enacts the sociability and symphilosophy of the Romantic school. They provided a model that showed future women authors how to shape intellectual and cultural life in the modern world while objecting to fixed dichotomies of class, gender, and ethnicity. Without their pioneering efforts the literary works of writers such as Fanny Lewald and Louise Aston would have been inconceivable since both Lewald and Aston studied the style of the female Romantics and drew great inspiration from them that was informed by a tradition of women's writing and relied on the art of the dialogue and the Romantic theory of sociability and symphilosophy.[68] Both in their lives and writings, these women authors demonstrated the belief that mutual love and passion belonged to a union that was intellectually and erotically compatible. Their writing synthesized the philosophical and the aesthetic and was rooted in the novel ideas of love. For them, reciprocity of love was the basis of dialogue, which has an integral role in the idea of symphilosophy. In contrast to Friedrich Schlegel, who relied on Greek structure for dialogue (Plato's *Symposium* is essentially a dialogue on the Beautiful, whereas Schlegel's *Dialogue* is a symposium on poetry), the women writers found inspiration in the salon and its issue, the letter. Yet, the philosophical underpinning of their projects resembles Plato's *Symposium*, specifically the conversation of Socrates with the priestess Diotima, who ultimately teaches the men participating in the symposium the meaning of love. Epitomizing Diotima's words, Socrates, whom Diotima instructed in the things of love, does not identify Eros with the Beautiful as did the speakers before him, but defines it as that which lacks the Beautiful and is consequently striving for it. Eros is not what is loved, but that which loves; it is a love of the Beautiful. The conversations as they transpired in the salon can be thus perceived as installation art which involved the configuration or installation of objects in a space, such as a room. This form lets the viewer move around the configured space

---

[67] Von Arnim, *Die Günderode,* 341.
[68] See Renata Fuchs, "The Politics of the Female Body in Louise Aston's and Fanny Lewald's Works through the Prism of the Romantic Theory of Sociability and Dialogue," in *Writing the Self, Creating Community: German Women Authors and the Literary Sphere, 1750–1850,* ed. Elisabeth Krimmer and Lauren Nossett (Rochester: Camden House, 2020), 230–252.

and interact with some of its elements thus allowing for an encounter with the Beautiful and rethinking people's attitudes and values.

BIBLIOGRAPHY

Ameriks, Karl. "Hegel's Aesthetics: New Perspectives on Its Response to Kant and Romanticism." *Hegel Bulletin* 23, nos. 1–2 (2002): 72–92.

Arndt, Andreas. "Philosophie." In *Friedrich Schlegel Handbuch. Leben—Werk—Wirkung*, edited by Johannes Endres, 189–211. Stuttgart: J. B. Metzler, 2017.

Becker-Cantarino, Barbara. *Der lange Weg zur Mündigkeit. Frau und Literatur (1500–1800)*. Stuttgart: J. B. Metzler, 1987.

Beiser, Frederick C. *The Romantic Imperative: The Concept of Early German Romanticism.* Cambridge, MA: Harvard University Press, 2004.

Bowie, Andrew. *From Romanticism to Critical Theory: The Philosophy of German Literary Theory*. London: Routledge, 1997.

Bunzel, Wolfgang. "Der Epistolare Pakt. Zum Briefwechsel zwischen Bettine von Arnim und Hermann Fürst Pückler-Muskau." In *Briefnetzwerke um Hermann von Pückler-Muskau*, edited by Jana Kittelmann, 15–26. Dresden: Thelem, 2015.

Burda, Jacob. *Das gute Unendliche in der deutschen Frühromantik*. Stuttgart: J. B. Metzler Verlag, 2020.

Eldridge, Richard T. *The Persistence of Romanticism: Essays in Philosophy and Literature.* Cambridge: Cambridge University Press, 2001.

Feilchenfeldt, Konrad. "Berliner Salon- und Briefkultur um 1800." *Der Deutschuntericht: Beiträge zu seiner Praxis und wissenschaftlichen Grundlegung* 36 (1984): 77–99.

Forster, Michael N., and Lina Steiner, eds. *Romanticism, Philosophy, and Literature*. London: Palgrave Macmillan, 2020.

Frank, Manfred. *The Philosophical Foundations of Early Romanticism*. Translated by Elizabeth Millán-Zaibert. Albany: State University of New York Press, 2003.

Fuchs, Renata. "The Politics of the Female Body in Louise Aston's and Fanny Lewald's Works through the Prism of the Romantic Theory of Sociability and Dialogue." In *Writing the Self, Creating Community: German Women Authors and the Literary Sphere, 1750–1850*, edited by Elisabeth Krimmer and Lauren Nossett, 230–252. Rochester, NY: Camden House, 2020.

Hahn, Barbara. "Der Mythos vom Salon. 'Rahels Dachstube' als historische Fiktion." In *Salons der Romantik. Beiträge eines Wiepersdorfer Kolloquiums zu Theorie und Geschichte des Salons*, edited by Hartwig Schultz, 213–234. Berlin: de Gruyter, 1997.

Harth, Erica. *Cartesian Women: Versions and Subversions of Rational Discourse in the Old Regime*. Ithaca: Cornell University Press, 1992.

Isselstein, Ursula. "Die Titel der Dinge sind das Fürchsterlichste! Rahel Levins 'Erster Salon.'" In *Salons der Romantik. Beiträge eines Wiepersdorfer Kolloquiums zu Theorie und Geschichte des Salons*, edited by Hartwig Schultz, 171–212. Berlin: de Gruyter, 1997.

Jean, Joan de. *Tender Geographies: Women and the Origins of the Novel in France*. New York: Columbia University Press, 1991.

Johnson, Laurie. "Florentin and the Early Romantic Model of Alterity." *Monatshelfte* 97, no. 1 (2005): 33–62.

Kneller, Jane. *Kant and the Power of Imagination*. Cambridge: Cambridge University Press, 2007.

Kneller, Jane. "Sociability and the Conduct of Philosophy: What We Can Learn from Early German Romanticism." In *The Relevance of Romanticism. Essays on German Romantic Philosophy*, edited by Dalia Nassar, 110–126. New York: Oxford University Press, 2014.

Kord, Susanne. *Sich einen Namen machen: Anonymität und weibliche Autorschaft 1700–1900*. Stuttgart: Metzler, 1996.

Leitner, Ingrid. "Liebe und Erkenntnis: Kommunikationsstructuren bei Bettine von Arnim: ein Vergleich fiktiven Sprechens mit Gesprächen im Salon." In *Salons der Romantik. Beiträge eines Wiepersdorfer Kolloquiums zu Theorie und Geschichte des Salons*, edited by Hartwig Schultz, 235–237. Berlin: de Gruyter. 1997.

Levine, Caroline. *Forms: Whole, Rhythm, Hierarchy, Network*. Princeton: Princeton University Press, 2015.

Lundt, Hannah Lotte. *Der Berliner "jüdische Salon" um 1800*. Berlin: de Gruyter, 2012.

Lundt, Hannah Lotte. "Prussians, Jews, Egyptians?" In *Orientalism, Gender, and the Jews:Literary and Artistic Transformations of European National Discourses*, edited by Ulrike Brunotte, Anna-Dorothea Ludewig, and Axel Strähler, 33–62. Oldenbourg: de Gruyter, 2015.

Mergenthaler, May. "Die Frühromantik als Projekt vollendeter Mitteilung zwischen den Geschlechtern: Friedrich Schlegel und Dorothea Veit im Gespräch über Friedrich Richters Romane." *German Quarterly* 81, no. 3 (2008): 302–321.

Millán-Zaibert, Elizabeth. *Friedrich Schlegel and the Emergence of Romantic Philosophy*. Albany: State University of New York Press, 2007.

Pnevmonidou, Elena. "Die Absage an das romantische Ich: Dorothea Schlegels *Florentin* als Umschrift von Friedrich Schlegels *Lucinde*." *German Life and Letters* 58 (2005): 271–292.

Raich, J. M., ed. *Dorothea V. Schlegel geb. Mendelssohn und deren Söhne Johannes und Philipp Veit. Briefwechsel im Auftrage der Familie Veit*. Vols. 1 and 2. Mainz: Franz Kirchheim, 1881.

Rehmen-Iffert, Birgit. *Skepsis und Enthusiasmus. Friedrich Schlegels philosophischer Grundgedanke zwischen 1796 und 1805*. Bonn: Königshausen und Neumann, 2001.

Rush, Fred. "The Romantic Imperative: The Concept of Early German Romanticism." *Mind* 114, no. 455 (2005): 709–713.

Schlegel, Dorothea. "Aufzeichnungen und Entwürfe zum *Florentin*." In *Florentin*, edited by Wolfgang Nehring, 193–249. Stuttgart: Reclam, 2004.

Schlegel, Friedrich. *Dialogue on Poetry and Literary Aphorisms*. Translated by Ernst Behler and Roman Struc. University Park: Pennsylvania State University, 1968.

Schmidt-Weissenfels, Eduard. *Rahel und ihre Zeit*. Leipzig: F. A. Brockhaus, 1857.

Schmitz, Rainer, ed. *Henriette Herz in Erinnerungen, Briefen und Zeugnissen*. Frankfurt am Main: Insel, 1984.

Scurla, Herbert. *Begegnungen mit Rahel: Der Salon der Rahel Levin*. Berlin: Verlag der Nation, 1962.

Seibert, Peter. *Der literarische Salon, Literatur und Geselligkeit zwischen Aufklärung und Vormärz*. Stuttgart: Metzler, 1993.

Singer, Irving. *The Nature of Love: Plato to Luther*. Chicago: University of Chicago Press, 1987.

Tinker, Chauncey Brewster. *The Salon and English Letters*. New York: Macmillan, 1915.

Thomann Tewarson, Heidi. *Rahel Levin Varnhagen: The Life and Work of a German Jewish Intellectual*. Lincoln: University of Nebraska Press, 1998.

Varnhagen, Rahel. *Briefwechsel*. Edited by Friedhelm Kemp. Munich: Winkler, 1979.

Varnhagen, Rahel. *Gesammelte Werke. Rahel-Bibliothek*. Edited by Konrad Feilchenfeldt, Uwe Schweickert, and Rahel E. Steiner. Munich: Matthes & Seitz, 1983.

Varnhagen von Ense, Karl. *Briefwechsel zwischen Rahel und David Veit. Aus dem Nachlaß Varnhagen's von Ense*. Vol. 1. Edited by Karl Varnhagen von Ense. Leipzig: F. A. Brockhaus, 1861.

Varnhagen von Ense, Karl. *Denkwürdigkeiten und vermischte Schriften: Denkwürdigkeiten des eigenen Lebens. Personen. Kritiken. Rahel*. Vol. 8. Leipzig: F. A. Brockhaus, 1859.

von Arnim, Bettina. *Die Günderode*. Vol. 1. In *Werke und Briefe in drei Bänden*, edited by Walter Schmitz and Sibylle von Steinsdorff. Frankfurt am Main: Deutscher Klassiker Verlag, 1986.

CHAPTER 31

....

THE AMERICAN RECEPTION OF GERMAN WOMEN PHILOSOPHERS IN THE NINETEENTH CENTURY

....

DOROTHY ROGERS

In the early decades of the nineteenth century, the American reading public was more attuned to ideas from Britain and France than to German thought. A look at some of the century's most prominent women in the early nineteenth century makes this evident: Catharine Beecher (1800–1878) was well acquainted with the writings of thinkers in the British Isles, among them the poet Lord Byron; the educator Mary Hopkins Pilkington; and the philosophers John Locke, Thomas Reid, and Dugald Stewart.[1] At her school for girls, the prominent southern educator Margaret Mercer (1791–1846) weighted the syllabus heavily toward English writers. Some French language and literature were also required, but no German texts appear on her school's course lists.[2] Sarah Josepha Hale (1788–1879), editor of widely read women's magazines from 1828 to 1878, featured numerous English and French writers, but very few German authors before the mid-1840s.[3]

It is no surprise, then, that the majority of Americans, women in particular, first encountered German literature through translations from the United Kingdom. William and Mary (Botham) Howitt, Thomas Carlyle, Samuel Coleridge, and Sarah Austin began translating writers in the romantic movement in the 1820s. Given the long tradition of affirming the masculine voice of authority in European intellectual life, the majority of this work focused on writings by men.

---

[1] Catharine Beecher, *Educational Reminiscences and Suggestions* (New York: J. B. Ford, 1874), 51–53.

[2] See Margaret Mercer, *Popular Lectures on Ethics* (Petersburg, VA: Ruffin, 1841), 230–232.

[3] Source: index searches in *Godey's Ladies Book* as well as Martin Henry Haertel, "German Literature in American Magazines, 1846–1880" (PhD diss., University of Wisconsin, 1906), 101–104.

With a selection of writings by German thinkers essentially precurated by England's translators, Americans also initially turned to male writers. The first American translations of German literature appeared in the 1830s. George Henry Calvert published fragments from Goethe's *Faust* in *A Volume from the Life of Herbert Barclay* (1833), followed by a translation of Schiller's poem *Don Carlos* (1834). At the end of the decade, others joined the trend. John Sullivan Dwight published a collection of the writings of Goethe and Schiller in 1839, with contributions from George Bancroft, James Freeman Clark, Margaret Fuller, and others: *Select Minor Poems, Translated from the German of Goethe and Schiller.* The same year, Fuller translated *Gespräche mit Goethe in den Letzten Jahren Seines Lebens* (as *Conversations with Goethe*), by Johann Peter Eckermann (1792–1854). In the 1840s, Calvert produced a more substantial set of translations from *Faust* in *Miscellany of Verse and Prose* as well as a translation, *Correspondence between Schiller and Goethe.* In 1845, Henry Wadsworth Longfellow published biographical sketches, critical commentary, and selections from *Faust* as well as several of Goethe's poems in *Poets and Poetry of Europe.*[4] By this time, American passion for German literature and philosophy was firmly in place and would remain so throughout the century. Although a number of women contributed to the development of German thought, very few of them gained the same level of recognition as their male contemporaries in this early period—at home or abroad. This was the case whether the translators and commentators were male or female.

At this point, a consideration of the impact of gender, genre, and intellectual pedigree is in order. Intellectuals of both genders in this era exchanged ideas through a range of genres—poetry, drama, narrative, speeches, correspondence—as well as the expository essay that is common in philosophy today. Yet men were more likely to produce essays, even if they were primarily creative writers. They were also likely to publish their work, thus ensuring its wide distribution. Women were more likely to produce creative work—poetry, drama, and fiction—forms of expression that are unusual in today's philosophical discourse. In addition, women shared their ideas in less public settings: salon meetings, parlor discussions, classrooms, or correspondence. For both women and men, correspondence was a common form of intellectual exchange; some letters were meant to be shared, similar to today's "open letter" or a blog post. Yet, women often conveyed their thoughts exclusively through correspondence, which was not widely distributed or formally published.

Once German literature started gaining currency in the English-speaking world, more work by women was recognized. Margaret Fuller played a central role in this process. Both in periodicals and in her groundbreaking feminist text *Woman in the Nineteenth Century* (1843), Fuller drew attention to women thinkers—in the United States, Angelina Grimké, Lydia Maria Child, and Catharine Maria Sedgwick, and in the United Kingdom, Mary Wollstonecraft, Maria Edgeworth, Harriet Martineau, Anna

---

[4] For a discussion of early translations of German thinkers, see Arthur O. Lewis, W. LaMarr Koop, and Edward J. Danis, eds., *Anglo-German and American-German Crosscurrents*, vol. 4 (Lanham, MD: University Press of America, 1990), 7–16.

Jameson; in France, Germaine de Staël and George Sand; in Switzerland, Albertine Necker de Saussure; and in Germany, Rahel Varnhagen, Karoline von Günderrode, and Bettina Brentano von Arnim.[5]

One of America's best-known women writers, even after her early death in 1850, Fuller was an autodidact who began reading German philosophy and literature independently when she was fifteen years old. As an adult she became a leading authority on German thought. Although she devoted much of her time to applauding the literary achievements of Goethe, she was also the first American writer to bring attention to women in the romantic movement. In this sense, she initiated a progression of *women's* philosophical discussions inspired by German thought in the United States—from literary analysis, to philosophy of education, to early feminist theory.

To be clear, German influence on American women's philosophical thought in the nineteenth century took place in overlapping stages as the century progressed. Fuller's discussions provided America's reading public with new understandings of romanticism (and nascent feminism) in the 1830s and 1840s. In the next decade, women educators began to adopt German pedagogical theory, nearly in full form, thus introducing educational theories and practices, many of which remain central in the United States today. Also in the 1850s and 1860s, German feminist émigrés arrived in the United States, exchanged ideas with home-grown activists, and influenced the women's rights movement throughout the second half of the century.

1   GERMAN ROMANTICISM, WOMEN, AND AMERICAN INTELLECTUAL LIFE

The transcendentalist movement emerged in and around Boston in the 1830s and 1840s and embraced many of German romanticism's main tenets: the value of individual freedom, personal exploration, intuitive/emotive knowing, and spiritual growth, for instance. Transcendentalists also celebrated the beauty of nature and sought unity and harmony among human beings and throughout the created order. The movement inherited a rationalist streak from the Enlightenment, however, particularly in regard to religion. Several of its members accepted deism, studied German biblical criticism, and became familiar with non-Christian faith traditions. As a result, they affirmed "rational religion"—the ability of each individual to discern religious truth in a cosmos sustained

---

[5] See Margaret Fuller, *Woman in the Nineteenth Century*, in *The Portable Margaret Fuller*, ed. Mary Kelly (New York: Penguin, 1994): Wollstonecraft, 267, 70; Edgeworth, 302; Martineau, 291, 323; Jameson, 291, 302–303; Sand, 267–270, 313; Necker, 315, 319, 321; de Staël, 280, 319; Grimke, 290, 291; Child, 313; Sedgwick, 322–323. Fuller's references to Varnhagen, Günderrode, and Brentano von Arnim are provided hereafter.

by a reasonable God.[6] Commitments to racial and gender equality were also features of transcendentalism. Many members of the movement became social/political activists and inspired the next generation to do the same.[7]

The German thinkers who first fascinated the American reading public, most notably Goethe, Schiller, Fichte, and Schelling, were active in intellectual circles that included women. Yet these women's voices were often muted because they served in supporting roles within the romantic movement—as salon hostesses, editors, correspondents, translators, anonymous collaborators, or even ghost writers. As such, many of them were all but invisible to an American audience.

Brief mention of romantic-era women who received less attention than they deserved will be informative and help make amends for their previous omission. Ottilie (Pogwisch) von Goethe (1796–1872), Johann von Goethe's daughter-in-law, launched and edited the journal *Chaos* (1829–1832), soliciting contributions from other women in her network. Ottilie was close to Goethe, tended to him for several years near the end of this life, and may have influenced *Faust II*, in which the *Ewig-Weibliche* (eternal feminine) is a prominent theme.[8] Dorothea (Mendelssohn) Schlegel (1764–1849) and Sophie Tieck-Bernhardi (1775–1833) worked alongside men, but with little or no recognition. Dorothea Schlegel worked with her husband as a translator and writing partner, publishing *Florentin* under Friedrich Schlegel's name. She produced some work of her own as well, including a translation of the novel *Corinne* by Germaine de Staël.[9] Similarly, Sophie Tieck-Bernhardi was not given credit for collaborations with her brother, Ludwig Tieck, or her husband, August Bernhardi. She also published a few works under her own name in *Athenaeum*, a publication edited by the Schlegel brothers, and *Musen-Almanach*, a prominent yearbook.[10]

---

[6] Enlightenment views of religion were pronounced among the more vocal and well-published men in transcendentalist circles, namely William Henry Emerson, Ralph Waldo Emerson, and William Ellery Channing. For detailed discussions, see Elisabeth Hurth, "William and Ralph Waldo Emerson and the Problem of the Lord's Supper," *Church History* 62, no. 2 (1993): 190–206; Randy Friedman, "Religious Self-Reliance," *Pluralist* 7, no. 1 (Spring 2012): 27–53; Ulrike Wagner, "Transcendentalism and the Power of Philology: Herder, Schleiermacher, and the Transformation of Biblical Scholarship in New England," *Amerikastudien/American Studies* 57, no. 3 (2012): 419–445.

[7] Transcendentalists' commitments to social/political justice were so prevalent, it is nearly redundant to mention them. Their antislavery activism has been well documented. Theodore Parker and William Greenleaf Elliot were staunch abolitionists; Elliot engaged in a standoff with officials in St. Louis, Missouri, to help free an enslaved man. Franklin Sanborn and Samuel Gridley Howe went into hiding after John Brown's arrest for attempting to start a slave rebellion. Henry David Thoreau famously refused to pay taxes in protest of both slavery and the Mexican American war, writing "Civil Disobedience," which influenced Tolstoy, Gandhi, and Martin Luther King. Margaret Fuller and Julia Ward Howe were feminists; Fuller's book *Woman in the Nineteenth Century* is a foundational text in modern feminist theory.

[8] See Carol Diethe, *Towards Emancipation: German Women Writers of the Nineteenth Century* (New York: Berghahn Books, 1998), 61–67.

[9] Deborah Hertz, "Dorothea Mendelssohn Schlegel," Jewish Women's Encyclopedia, https://jwa.org/encyclopedia/article/schlegel-dorothea-mendelssohn.

[10] Roger Paulin, *The Life of August Wilhelm Schlegel: Cosmopolitan of Art and Poetry* (Cambridge: Open Book, 2016), 182–184.

A number of other women were active in the romantic movement. Women contributed to Friedrich Schiller's short-lived journal *Die Hören* (*The Horae*). *Universitätsmamsellen*, the daughters of university professors at Göttingen, produced intellectual work. Dorothea Margaretha Liebeskind translated novels by English women writers, as well as *The Rights of Man* by Thomas Paine, and Caroline (Michaelis) Schlegel-Schelling penned reviews under the names of her first husband, August Wilhelm Schlegel, and her second husband, Friedrich Schelling.[11] Women helped shape the German romantic movement more than the received history has shown. But, again, as all but silent contributors to intellectual life, they rarely received adequate recognition at home and thus were not brought to attention in the United States. Thankfully, other women fared better: Rahel Varnhagen, Karoline von Günderrode, and Elisabeth "Bettina" Brentano von Arnim.

1.1 German Women in Romanticism and Their American Audience

1.1.1 *Rahel (Levin) Varnhagen (1771–1833)*

Rahel Varnhagen, often compared to Germaine de Staël, was a central figure in German romanticism who hosted a salon frequented by Goethe, Schiller, Schelling, Schlegel, Schleiermacher, Heine, and no doubt the women who were associated with them.[12] She published a few essays in arts and culture periodicals, the *Morning Paper* (*Das Morgenblatt*; Stuttgart and Tubingen) and the *Partner* (*Der Gesellschafter*; Berlin). A collection of aphorisms has also been attributed to Varnhagen, *Stray Thoughts of a Berliner* (*Denkblätter einer Berlinerin*, 1830), which, according to contemporary accounts, seem to have appeared in *New German Monthly* (*Neue Deutsche Monatsschrift*). However, this collection may no longer be extant. Like many of her female peers, Varnhagen was primarily an epistolary writer. Her husband, Karl, published some of her correspondence, as well as her annotations of the mystics Angelus Silesius and Louis Claude de Saint-Martin, shortly after her death. Her niece, Ludmilla Assing (1821–1880), finished the project after Karl's death in 1858.[13] More of her correspondence was discovered in the twentieth century.

---

[11] See See Janet Besserer Holmgren, *The Women Writers in Schiller's Hören: Patrons, Petticoats, and the Promotion of Weimar Classicism* (Newark: University of Delaware Press, 2007) and Katherine R. Goodman, *Amazons and Apprentices: Women and the German Parnassus in the Early Englightenment* (Rochester, NY: Camden House, 1999), both of which feature chapters on individual women.

[12] Varnhagen's biographical information is from "Rahel," review of books about Varnehagen and her work, in *Foreign Quarterly Review*, American ed. [New York: Jemima Mason, publisher] 26 (April 1841): 30–40. "Rahel Levin and Her Times," *Eclectic Magazine of Foreign Literature, Science, and Art*, new ser., 65 [New York: Pelton Publishing] (1897): 29–37. Ellen Key, *Rahel Varnhagen: A Portrait*, trans. Arthur Chater (New York: Putnam, 1913).

[13] Barbara Hahn, "Rahel Levin Varnhagen," *Jewish Women's Archive*, https://jwa.org/encyclopedia/article/varnhagen-rahel-levin (2021).

In selections from her work, Varnhagen reveals her alignment with the romantic movement by scoffing at "pompous proofs" and "system building" in philosophy. She affirms instead each person's attempt to know their own heart and aim for personal piety. She praised independence, originality, personal integrity (which she believed was lacking in de Staël), and intellectual authenticity. Varnhagen was critical of politics and social status, in large part because they lead to deception and compromise. Political diplomats subvert their entire selfhood for the sake of accommodating others or culling information. This charge is interesting because her husband served as a diplomat for many years. Intellectuals too often compromise or lose their way when their ideas become popular, a charge she leveled at Schleiermacher, who had been "ruined" by the abundance of praise he received at Halle.[14]

Varnhagen was well known throughout Germany in her lifetime, and discussions of her life and work appeared in English-language literary publications after her death in 1833. Margaret Fuller became aware of Varnhagen when her husband published *Rahel: Ein Buch des Andenkens für ihre Freunde*, a nine-volume collection of memoir, correspondence, and scattered writings, which Thomas Carlyle discussed in the *Westminster Review*.[15] Later Fuller referred to Varnhagen as the "intellectual Queen of Berlin," and saw her as a thinker with valuable insights who lived and wrote with passion. Notably, she quotes Rahel's praise of Goethe's *Wilhelm Meister*: "our Sage know[s] how to paint the good and honest mind in perpetual toil and conflict with the world."[16] In a very real sense, Varnhagen was an exemplar for Fuller, personally and intellectually. This is not surprising, of course. Fuller was both a Germanophile and a feminist who sought ideals to emulate. Other American thinkers were also impressed with Varnhagen. Ralph Waldo Emerson recognized her influence and discussed her work with Thomas Carlyle, Lydia Maria Child discussed her in letters, and John Greenleaf Whittier referred to her in a poem.[17] Varnhagen was profiled in *Woman's Record*, edited by Sarah J. Hale, in 1853. In 1876 Kate Vaughan Jennings published a biography of Varnhagen in London, which

[14] See "Rahel Levin and Her Times," 36, 38, 39.

[15] Thomas Carlyle, "Varnhagen von Ense's Memoirs," *Westminster Review* 47 (1838), reprinted in *The Modern British Essayists, vol. 5, Critical and Miscellaneous Essays*, by Thomas Carlyle (Philadelphia: A. Hart, 1854), 535–546.

[16] See Margaret Fuller, referring to Varnhagen as the "intellectual Queen" of Berlin; "The Modern Jews," *New-York Daily Tribune*, April 21, 1845, and quoting Varnhagen as "von Ense" in "Goethe," *Dial* 2, no. 1 (July 1841): 17.

[17] Emerson referred to Varnhagen as an exemplary woman in an address in memory of his mother. See Phyllis Cole, *Mary Moody Emerson and the Origins of Transcendentalism* (New York: Oxford University Press, 1998), 3. In correspondence, Emerson refers to Carlyle's essay "Rahel," in which Carlyle's attitude toward women's work is telling. Reportedly, Carlyle referred to the piece as a "scrub article" – that is, one that lacked substance and could or should have been omitted. Germaine de Staël was similarly disparaged by Carlyle. See Ralph Waldo Emerson, letter to Charles Stearns Wheeler, March 18, 1839, in *The Letters of Ralph Waldo Emerson, vol. 7, 1807–1844*, ed. Eleanor M. Tilton (New York: Columbia University Press, 1941), 335. Child's interest in Varnhagen is cited in Lydia Moland, "Lydia Maria Child on German Philosophy and American Slavery," *British Journal for the History of Philosophy* 29, no. 2 (March 2021), 262. Whittier's poem recognizing Varnhagen, "To _____," was published in *The Poetical Works of John Greenleaf Whittier* (Boston: James R. Osgood & Company, 1873), 331-34..

would have been accessible to an American audience. She continued to appear in biographical dictionaries in the United States as late as 1900. Interest in her life and work was revived in the twentieth century, with biographies by Ellen Key (1913), Hannah Arendt (1957), and Heidi Thomann Tewarson (1998).

1.1.2 *Karoline von Günderrode (1780–1806)*

As editor of the *Dial*, a transcendentalist publication, Margaret Fuller was the first American woman to publish discussions of Karoline von Günderrode and Bettina Brentano von Arnim, two important figures in German romanticism. Little is known about Günderrode's early education, but by the age of seventeen she was living in a convent, where she appears to have had access to the writings of Schelling, Novalis, Fichte, Herder, and Kant. Despite her early death by suicide, she published a considerable volume of work, including two collections of poetry, *Poems and Fantasies* (1804), *Poetic Fragments* (1805), and *Melete* (1806); three plays, *Udohla, Magic & Destiny* (both in *Studien* in 1805) and *Nikator* (in *Taschenbuch für das Jahr*, 1806); and one piece of short fiction, "Story of a Brahmin" (in *Herbsttagen*, 1805).

Fuller translated Günderrode's poetry, which appealed to her as both a transcendentalist and a feminist.[18] Günderrode explored themes and concepts that aligned with Fuller's transcendentalist ideals. She expressed the view that metaphysical "elements" in the cosmos may disintegrate and recombine to form new entities. She had a parallel view of individuals—that each consciousness may fragment after death and recombine into new life forms. These ideas correspond with transcendentalists' sense of the unity of all reality and with their fascination with eastern thought. Historians have also identified elements of the philosophy of love in Günderrode's work, which appealed to Fuller. As a feminist, Fuller no doubt identified with Günderrode's frustration at being constrained by gender norms, which was another theme that appeared in her poetry.[19] But perhaps more valuable to Fuller was her predecessor's role as an exemplar in her friendship with Bettina Brentano von Arnim.

1.1.3 *Elisabeth Bettina Brentano von Arnim (1785–1859)*

Karoline von Günderrode was close to Bettina Brentano von Arnim and her family, who were prominent intellectuals. Brentano von Arnim's brother, Clemens Brentano (1778–1842), was active in the German romantic movement. Her grandmother, Sophie von la Roche (1730–1807), was a well-known novelist and journal editor. Günderrode and Brentano von Arnim became close as young adults, particularly in the last two years of

---

[18] Günderrode scholar Anna Ezekiel identifies Fuller's translations of Günderrode's poetry, both in her rendering of the Günderrode-Arnim correspondence and in the *Dial*: "The Wanderer's Descent," "Change and Constancy," "Immortalita," "An Apocalyptic Fragment," "The Frank in Egypt," and "The Manes." See Ezekiel, "Read Günderrode," https://acezekiel.com.

[19] See Anna Ezekiel, "The Woman at the Heart of German Romantic Philosophy," in Genealogies of Modernity, a project of the University of Pennsylvania, 2020; https://genealogiesofmodernity.org/journal/2020/11/30/gnderrode.

Günderrode's life. Many years later, Brentano von Arnim published an edited version of their correspondence, *Die Günderode* (1840). Fuller took notice of this work and wrote an article in the *Dial* about the women's relationship, "Bettine Brentano and Her Friend Günderode." She later translated Brentano von Arnim's rendition of their correspondence, thus making the women's thought accessible to the American reading public.

Fuller's decision to discuss this work is telling. In it, Brentano von Arnim casts herself and Günderrode as engaging in dialogue, an intellectual communion of sorts, in which the reader is invited to participate. Fuller elected to translate and discuss this work because it portrayed ideal forms of both femininity and feminine intellectual friendships. In her view, Günderrode and Brentano von Arnim maintained the poetic and the philosophical in tandem and engaged in inquiry within their shared intellectual space. In her discussion, Fuller casts the two as a well-matched but contrasting pair. Bettina Brentano von Arnim was a force of nature who could not be constrained. Karolina von Günderrode was a source of spiritual clarity and strength. In Fuller's own words, Bettina drew "new tides of vital energy from all, [loving nature and] . . . bounding over the fences of society as easily as over the fences of the field." Günderrode, on the other hand, was able to exude "spiritual clearness . . . harmonizing all objects into their true relations, drawing from every form of life its eternal meaning." She was able to transform her friend's "fearless bursts of friendly genius . . . to hush the wild beatings of the heart."[20]

The two women appealed to Fuller as embodiments of ideal types, who in a sense represented larger metaphysical forces. Yet she found the pair even more fascinating as the incarnation of an ideal friendship—an ideal *feminine* friendship. As Carol Strauss Sotiropolous has noted, the nature of friendship had been explored in western thought, but in this article, Fuller became one of the first thinkers to explore the nature of friendship between women. In doing so, she draws a contrast between masculine and feminine friendships:

> an intimacy between two young men is heroic. They call one another to combat with the wrongs of life . . . they encourage each other to ascend the steeps of knowledge. . . . But the relation between two young girls is essentially poetic. . . . The relation before us presents all that is lovely between woman and woman, adorned by great genius and beauty on both sides. . . . The higher culture, and greater harmony of Günderode's nature is counter-balanced, by the ready springing impulse; richness and melody of [Brentano von Arnim].[21]

Part of the allure for Fuller was the sense of complementarity and equal exchange between the two women. In *Woman in the Nineteenth Century*, she reflected further on friendship across gender, pointing to the marriages of the feminist Mary Wollstonecraft

---

[20] For characterizations of both women, see Margaret Fuller, "Bettine Brentano and Her Friend Günderode," *Dial* 2, no. 3 (1842): 4.

[21] Fuller, "Bettine Brentano and Her Friend," 5.

and William Godwin and her contemporaries in England, the writers William and Mary Howitt, as egalitarian partnerships.[22]

Brentano von Arnim published other epistolary works, *Goethe's Correspondence with a Child* (*Goethes Briefwechsel mit einem Kinde*, 1834) and a tribute to her brother Clemens Brentano after his death (1844), the veracity of which puzzled many critics, even in her lifetime. Were they original letters she saved, idealized versions, or even fictionalized renditions of her exchanges with contemporaries? Yet Fuller defended Brentano von Arnim against critics regarding both the form and the content of her work: "the poetic eye cannot even *see* a fact bare and solitary as it appears to the prose observer. For such a mind the actual only exists as representing the ideal. . . . Her book is true, and of the rarest excellence, a many-petaled flower on the bosom of nature, from which the dew shall never varnish." Fuller's peer in the transcendentalist movement, Lydia Maria Child (1802–1888), shared this view and praised Brentano von Arnim as a writer who is "bright as the sunshine [and] free as the wind."[23]

As impressed with Brentano von Arnim's passion and quick intellect as Fuller was, however, she was critical of her first work, *Goethe's Correspondence with a Child*. In this work, Brentano von Arnim presents herself as a youthful admirer who seeks Goethe's wisdom. Brentano von Arnim herself noted in a preface to an 1838 English edition that the writer Sarah Austin declined to translate it. This is likely due to the effusive quality of Brentano von Arnim's writing. The work is filled with sensual imagery and often implies that the "child" in the work is infatuated with the Great Goethe. Expressive writing of this sort concerned readers in Fuller's day, particularly in America's New England, which was still tethered to its Puritan religious traditions.

In *Goethe's Correspondence with a Child*, Brentano von Arnim characterizes love as an intuition. She sees both the natural world and sensuality as symbols of the spirit, and she describes spirit as "desirously drinking up divinity." Genius, she says, is an impulse that overcomes timidity and "incites the spirit to new energy."[24]

Today, Brentano von Arnim's work has been read afresh (e.g., see Anne Pollok in chapter six of this volume). But as a contemporary, Fuller objected to many elements of her approach in *Correspondence with a Child*. In this work, she portrays herself as a young girl of thirteen. But in fact, she was in her early twenties when she met and corresponded with Goethe. She used poetic license in this case, no doubt, to portray Goethe as a great thinker whose intellect is superior—not only to her as "a child," but to nearly everyone. Yet, in doing so, she contributed to perceptions that women are infantile, superficial, and intellectually deficient. Fuller charged that Brentano von

---

[22] For Sotiropolous's discussion of Fuller on friendship, see "Fuller, Goethe, Bettine: Cultural Transfer and Imagined German Womanhood," in *Toward a Female Genealogy of Transcendentalism*, ed. Jana L. Argersinger and Phyllis Cole (Athens: University of Georgia Press, 2014), 89–93.

[23] Fuller, "Bettine Brentano and Her Friend," 22, 23. See also Moland, "Lydia Maria Child on German Philosophy and American Slavery," 262.

[24] See Bettina von Arnim, *Diary of a Child* (Bayer: Staatsbibliothek, 1838), 8, 75, 158, 247.

Arnim's sense of deference to Goethe contributed to his ability to make "a puppet show for his private entertainment of Bettina's life."[25] She preferred less adulation and more substance. Her criticism grew out of two concerns: a longing to see models of intellectual friendship and her feminist yearning for women's equality. Brentano von Arnim undermined the ideal of egalitarian friendships that Fuller had been exploring at this time, thus doing a disservice to herself and all women.

By the 1840s, Brentano von Arnim had turned to social and political issues, publishing *This Book Belongs to the King* (*Dies Buch gehört dem König*, 1843). In it, she forcefully argued for education, prison reform, and more humane ways to address poverty. The book was reviewed in the transcendentalists' *Dial*, but by that time, Fuller had taken a position as a journalist for the *New York Tribune*. Fuller also turned to addressing social and political issues around this time, however, publishing "The Great Lawsuit," about women's rights, in 1843, and then expanding it into the book *Woman in the Nineteenth Century*, published in 1845. After her move to New York, Fuller also began to condemn poverty and harsh working conditions for the laboring classes. Although neither woman seemed to be aware of the other's new focus, their parallel shifts to activism would set the stage for development of feminist theory and activism later in the century.

2 EARLY PHILOSOPHICAL IDEALISM AND PEDAGOGICAL THEORY

In the 1830s and 1840s, interest in pedagogical theory and practice began to take hold in American intellectual life. The ideas of J. F. Herbart (1776–1841), a German theorist, influenced a number of prominent Americans, most notably Horace Mann (1796–1859). In midcentury, a second wave of influence from Germany engaged women to an unprecedented degree, and it took place in two phases. First came pedagogical theories that were informed by German philosophical idealism, which characterized young minds as full of potential, naturally active, and informed by engagement with the world. In the next phase, particularly among women of color, American thinkers embraced the social and political implications of philosophical idealism as an extension of pedagogical theory. If the world is a systematic whole that is infused with mind/spirit, as idealism claims, education can and should be used as a tool to address inequities and build a just society.

In a gendered world, pedagogy quickly became a significant domain of inquiry for women, who were considered naturally suited to nurture children and facilitate their growth. German theories of education and child development were not so much "received" in the United States as they were adopted in nearly full form and incorporated

---

[25] Thomas Wentworth Higginson, citing Fuller's letter to William Henry Channing, dated February 19, 1841, in *Margaret Fuller Ossoli* (Boston: Houghton Mifflin, 1884), 191–192.

into the fabric of American society. Women of means traveled to Germany to study new pedagogical theories and then returned to teach, open schools, and set up teacher training programs. In addition, a number of German-born women made their homes in the United States and became prominent as experts and educational innovators. In this way, the development of women's ideas took place in a process of mutual exchange.

2.1 Romanticism, Idealism, and Pedagogy

Histories of education have long recognized the significance of pedagogical theory for women's professional development in the nineteenth and twentieth centuries.[26] However, as education became a domain of inquiry in which women thrived, it also became more distant from philosophy. Or perhaps philosophy began to distance itself from education as a feminine discourse. Yet, pedagogical theory has a rich history within the traditional masculine philosophical canon. Plato theorized about the best way to facilitate education in the *Republic* and reflected on the learning process in *Meno* and *Gorgias*. Aristotle discussed education in the *Politics*. Rousseau devoted his book *Emile* to the subject, including a chapter with a distinct set of claims about girls' education.

Nineteenth-century women tapped into a time-honored tradition, then, when they began to develop their own philosophies of education. But their entry into philosophy and their forms of inquiry were distinct. For many women, pedagogy served as an entry point into philosophy. They were introduced to pedagogical theories first, philosophy second. Yet elements of philosophical inquiry emerged from their work: epistemology, ontology, and moral theory, in particular. In addition, the vast majority of female philosophers of education engaged in practice first, theory second. Therefore, most of these pedagogical theorists—in both Germany and the United States—were active as practitioners for a decade or more before committing their own ideas to writing. In this sense, *pedagogical practice in the classroom* was the primary force that moved educational philosophy forward for most of the nineteenth century.

---

[26] As early as 1872, Anna Brackett recognized that teaching had become a female-dominant profession. See proceedings of the National Education Association, 1872, cited in Dorothy Rogers, *America's First Women Philosophers: Transplanting Hegel, 1860–1925* (London: Continuum, 2005), 78–79. Brackett's contemporary Susan Blow asserted that women's supposed maternal nature made them well-suited to be early childhood educators. See Rogers, *America's First Women Philosophers*, 62–64. For book-length discussions of this phenomenon: Ann Taylor Allen, *The Transatlantic Kindergarten: Education and Women's Movements in Germany and the United States* (New York: Oxford University Press, 2017); Nancy Hoffman, *Woman's True Profession: Voices from the History of Teaching* (Cambridge, MA: Harvard University Press, 2003); Elizabeth Edwards, *Women in Teacher Training Colleges, 1900–1960: A Culture of Femininity* (New York: Routledge, 2004); Patricia A. Carter, *Everybody's Paid but the Teacher: The Teaching Profession and the Women's Movement* (New York: Teachers College Press, 2002). Barbara Miller Solomon, *In the Company of Educated Women: A History of Women and Higher Education in America* (New Haven: Yale University Press, 1986); Agnes Snyder, *Dauntless Women in Childhood Education* (Washington, DC: Association of Childhood Education, 1972).

The first step toward understanding women pedagogical theorists in both Germany and the United States in this era is to recognize that ontology and epistemology were intertwined in their discussions, largely because empirical methods in educational psychology had not yet developed. The ontology of women educators reflects the influences of both German romanticism and idealism. Drawing on G. W. F. Hegel and the educational theorist Friedrich Fröbel, they took seriously the German term *Geist* (mind/spirit) and understood a human mind to be roughly equivalent to a spirit or soul. Thus they asserted that a person is a spiritual and infinite being. In their view, learning did not simply implant knowledge into a human brain, instead it initiated children's spiritual growth and helped awaken their understanding of the infinite. In this way, learning serves to facilitate the "unfolding" (*Entfaltung*)—not just of a human mind, but of the very self or soul of an individual. The majority of women pedagogical theorists did not always overtly recognize this set of assumptions about human ontology at this stage in American intellectual history, but it underlies many of their discussions.

Women's epistemological assumptions were more often directly stated, again, among both German and American thinkers. Learning entails self-activity (*Selbstaktivität*), in which a human mind actively grasps the content of experience. Our encounter with other entities in the world (nature, objects, processes) leads naturally to our examination of them, and thus to knowledge—of natural law, physical characteristics (shape, size, figure, mass, etc.), or processes (natural, mechanical, or structural). Within this idealist framework, the mind grasps different levels of knowledge at different stages of growth, but largely through the same process. Young children learn through play, traditional games, music, activities, and fairy tales. Youth and adults learn through literature, creative activities, or scientific observation.

In this educative process – that is, during the acts of imaging, role playing, reading, or study – an individual mind/spirit identifies with another character, creature, entity, or idea, and in doing so, this individual stands removed from their ordinary self-understanding.

This leads to learners' temporary estrangement from their everyday selves or social circumstances. And here we see a moral epistemology emerging: while in this imaginative "self-estrangement," a youth enters a set of new potential realities or realms of experience. When playtime or reading has ended, students return to their day-to-day life. But now they have a new set of experiences that have expanded the possibilities open to them and transformed their sense of selfhood. In this way, education facilitates the "unfolding" of the self. Pedagogical theorists discussed epistemology in/through education more thoroughly in relation to literature than to the sciences. Yet the process of learning would be similar. Students would "lose" themselves, as such, while in the process of scientific observation. They would then "return" to their everyday experience with an enriched understanding of the world.

An element of social epistemology also deserves mention, one that grew out of American theorists' understanding of the German concept *Bildung* (education/culture). Instruction that makes use of traditional games, music, and tales immerses youth in the wealth of human achievements through history. This enriches students socially and culturally. There is a conservative element here in that many educators accepted German ideals of European superiority that were current at the time. Therefore, white educators too often used education as a tool of assimilation. In later decades, American theorists, primarily progressive women of color, began to explore the cultural value of education as a tool for social and political empowerment. They identified learning as not only an equalizing force but one that helps children cope with, or even overcome, economic, racial, or cultural disparities as they develop intellectually, grow into adults, and become active participants in democratic society.

Most often, women's discussions of pedagogy in both countries focused on early childhood education, namely the then-new theories and methods of Fröbel's "kindergarten." Aside from the fact that early childhood education is a substantive enterprise in its own right, it is important to keep in mind that women educators applied their theories and methods at all stages of learning. Their emphasis was on the youngest age groups, primarily because women were thought to have a natural affinity for instructing young children. Yet German romantic and idealist thought were folded into teaching at all grade levels, including normal schools for teacher training. As one of the first avenues to higher education for women and people of color, normal schools often became havens for progressive educators and would later become the first state colleges and universities in the United States.

2.2 German Educational Theory: Reception, Exchange, and Adaptation

As noted, a good deal of the "reception" of German thought in the United States was actually a process of mutual exchange. This is most certainly true of pedagogical theory. Some women remained in Germany, but provided classroom training, and so exerted influence from afar: Bertha von Marenholtz-Bülow, Henriette (Breymann) Schrader, and Hedwig Heyl. Others ventured to America to successfully import both German ideas and educational systems: Margarethe Schurz, Maria Kraus-Boelté, Mathilde Krieg, and Emma Marwedel. Scores of US-born women seized the opportunity for the intellectual engagement and professional development that German pedagogical theory provided—far too many to discuss here. The focus here, then, is on some of the first among them, across races and cultures: Elizabeth Palmer Peabody, Susan E. Blow, Haydee Campbell, Mary Church Terrell, Josephine Silone Yates, and Emma Johnson Goulette. Some of these American women traveled to Europe to meet and learn from their German counterparts. Others remained in the United States, where they interacted with German pedagogical theorists, studied their work, or both.

2.2.1 *Sojourners: Americans in Germany, Germans in America*

Elizabeth Peabody (1804–1894) and Susan Blow (1843–1916) were among the many women who studied pedagogical theory with experts in the field in Germany in the

1860s and 1870s. Mary Church Terrell (1863–1954), who was more than a generation younger, spent time in the country in the 1880s and gained fluency in German during her stay. The two older women helped lay the foundation for German-infused pedagogy to flourish within white-dominant culture in the United States. Terrell and a number of her colleagues extended the reach of that pedagogy to communities of color. Each of these thinkers helped build networks in which women developed philosophies of education largely through classroom observations, mentor-disciple relationships, and community discourse. Few women who gained expertise in pedagogy produced theoretical work. Therefore, theirs was a practical philosophy in action, not an abstract exercise of contemplation.

Elizabeth Palmer Peabody was a central figure in the transcendentalist movement and was also among the first American women to explore pedagogical theories at the intersection of German romanticism and philosophical idealism. She and a number of educators were intrigued by Fröbel's new theories, which wedded romanticism's sentimental notions of childhood to systematic instruction through play-based activities. Peabody was introduced to Fröbel's theories by a young émigré from Germany, Margarethe Schurz (1833–1876). She was intrigued and studied these methods independently, and then opened a short-lived kindergarten in Boston in 1859. Already in her fifties when her educational experiment ended, Peabody turned to promoting early childhood education throughout the country.

Susan Blow (1843–1916) became acquainted with early childhood pedagogy while traveling with family in Europe in the late 1860s. She then served as director of the first continuous kindergarten program in an American public school system, in St. Louis, Missouri (1873–1884). In the mid-1890s, Blow published discussions of Fröbelian theory as well as teachers' guides.

When Mary Church Terrell was coming of age in the 1880s, kindergarten pedagogy was fairly well established in white communities in well-populated regions of the United States. She devoted a good deal of her time and energy to combating harsh segregation policies and to promoting high-quality education at all levels in African American communities in the 1890s and into the twentieth century.

Women from the United States as well as Europe visited Germany to observe the classrooms of Bertha von Marenholtz-Bülow (1810–1893), one of Fröbel's disciples who became an influential theorist herself. Marenholtz-Bülow published several books: three guides to Fröbel's methods, interspersed with some of their theoretical foundations; a collection of essays on early childhood education; and a historical account of Fröbel's work and influence, published the year after her death. Her most theoretical work, *The Child, Its Nature and Relations* (*Das Kind und sein Wesen*), was published in Germany in 1868; her disciple, Mathilde Kriege, translated it into English in 1872. Marenholtz-Bülow remained in Germany, but a number of other women emigrated to the United States. Mathilde Kriege (1820–1899) moved to Boston at Peabody's behest to revive kindergarten efforts there. Emma Marwedel (1818–1893) opened schools on America's East Coast and then moved west, where she mentored American-born educators Kate Douglas Wiggins and Sarah Cooper, in San Francisco. Wiggins later became an influential pedagogical theorist herself. Marie Kraus-Boelté opened a teaching training school in New York in 1872. Five years later, she published a two-volume work, *The Kindergarten Guide*, writing it in English with her husband, John Kraus. Four editions appeared in print before the end of the century. Kraus-Boelté also published short educational guides in pamphlet form.[27]

2.2.2 *German Pedagogy: American Adaptations in Communities of Color*

The first woman of color known to gain expertise in German-infused pedagogical theories was Fanny Jackson Coppin (1837–1913).[28] Although born into slavery, after an aunt purchased her freedom Coppin lived a rich intellectual life. She studied independently before earning degrees at the Rhode Island Normal School and Oberlin College and then became the first woman principal of the Institute of Colored Youth (now Cheney University) in Philadelphia. Not incidentally, as a teenager Coppin lived and worked as a domestic servant in the home of George Henry and Elizabeth (Steuart) Calvert in Newport, Rhode Island. As noted earlier, George Henry Calvert was one of the first Americans to translate work by Goethe and Schiller. He was highly regarded as a literary scholar and served as professor of moral philosophy at a predecessor of the University of Maryland in the late 1830s.[29] Coppin spoke highly of the Calverts, saying that in their home, she was granted time to study and had "contact with people of refinement and education."[30] Although she did not provide specifics about the individuals she met, a number of intellectuals well-versed in German philosophy and literature were in the Calverts' social circle at this time, among them George Bancroft and Henry James, Sr. In addition, Coppin attended the normal school in Bristol, Rhode Island, when German pedagogy was prevalent, where she said her "eyes were first opened on the subject of teaching," exclaiming: "is it possible that teaching can be made so interesting as this!"[31] At Oberlin, she shifted to the classics as a student and then taught Greek, Latin, and higher mathematics at the college for a time before taking a position at the Institute for Colored Youth and becoming the school's principal.

Pedagogically, Coppin agreed with (white) women educators who had studied with German theorists that early childhood education provides the building blocks for more

[27] See Ann Taylor Allen, "A Transatlantic Network: American and German Women in the Kindergarten Movement," in *Forging Bonds across Borders: Transatlantic Collaborations for Women's Rights and Social Justice in the Long Nineteenth Century*, ed. Britta Waldschmidt-Nelson and Anya Schuler (Washington, DC: German Historical Institute, 2017), 150–154.

[28] Coppin's biographical information is from Fanny Jackson Coppin, *Reminiscences of School Life and Hints on Teaching* (Philadelphia: AME Books, 1913), and Linda M. Perkins, "Heed Life's Demands: The Educational Philosophy of Fanny Jackson Coppin," *Journal of Negro Education* 51, no. 3 (1982), 181–190.

[29] See Dorothy Rogers, *Women Philosophers, vol. 1, Education and Activism in Nineteenth-Century America* (London: Bloomsbury, 2020), 88–92.

[30] Coppin, *Reminiscences*, 17.

[31] Coppin, *Reminiscences*, 12.

advanced learning. She further agreed that to be effective education must be delivered systematically—in stages and with an awareness of a student's learning-readiness. Just as important, however, was the role of education in promoting social uplift—particularly in African American communities. At her retirement party, Coppin noted that she had always taught two populations: students at the Institute for Colored Youth and the Black community as a whole.[32] To achieve these ends, she introduced additional innovations into the curriculum of the Institute, such as collaborative learning, project-based inquiry, and peer review—all to ensure the needs of students of color were being met. In addition, she frequently provided adult education classes at both Oberlin and the Institute, free of charge whenever possible. The theme of racial uplift was dominant, not only in Coppin's theory and practice, but in the writings and speeches of the women educators of color featured here. In their view, pedagogical theories were empty if not infused with a quest for equality, social responsibility, and justice.

Haydee Campbell (1866–1921) studied at Oberlin before accepting an offer to teach in St. Louis, where she received instruction from Susan Blow, one of the most theoretically minded educators in the era and a devotee of Hegel's thought. Campbell did not produce written work, but served as director of the African American kindergarten in St. Louis for the majority of her career. She also trained other women educators in summer programs at Tuskegee and became a founding member of the National Association of Colored Women in the 1890s, serving as its expert on early childhood education. Her friend and colleague Mary Church Terrell was also a proponent of early childhood pedagogy who lectured widely about the value of education for African American youth. Josephine Silone Yates (1859–1912) joined the campaign to put then-new pedagogical theories into practice in communities of color. A student of Fanny Jackson Coppin at the Institute for Colored Youth, Yates followed in her mentor's footsteps, attending the state normal school in Rhode Island.

Although their views were not completely identical, Terrell and Yates agreed that Fröbelian methods awakened all children to learning and opened up new possibilities.[33] They employed the terminology used in German pedagogical theories, though usually in translation: self-activity, attention, self-discipline, and education in culture (*Bildung*). "Self-activity" was a key notion—a child's innate ability to grasp concepts and advance cognitively. Both women often linked this ability to moral will and self-discipline. Yates assigned the combination of intellectual and moral will a new term, "thought-power," the ability to focus one's attention, exercise self-control, and use sound judgment. In her view "self-activity" and "thought-power" in combination have social and ethical import within the African American community, helping to sharpen a young person's intellect and moral strengths, thereby fortifying their sense of self. This would be essential for African American youth, preparing them to face injustice and resist the oppression they

---

[32] Perkins, "Heed Life's Demands," 90.

[33] For an informative discussion of Terrell and Yates as early childhood education theorists/activists, see Jean Robbins, "Black Club Women's Purposes for Establishing Kindergartens in the Progressive Era, 1896–1906," (PhD diss., Loyola University, Chicago, 2011).

were sure to encounter in the Jim Crow era. In this sense education served as an immeasurably valuable tool, especially in disadvantaged communities.

Both Terrell and Yates agreed with Susan Blow and other theorists about the importance of mothers as teachers. Enlisting mothers to assist with their children's learning at home was essentially built into early childhood pedagogy from the start, and emphasis was placed on this aspect of education in African American communities in this era. Mothers were meant not only to be their children's "first teacher" at home. Terrell and Yates also expected them to support their children's schooling and become better educated themselves, thereby helping to uplift and ennoble "the race." The motto of the National Association of Colored Women, of which Terrell and Yates were charter members and officers, was "lifting as we climb."[34] Educating young children was part of that process; motivating mothers to be the chief promoters of culture and social advancement was another.

In the 1890s, Native American women began to earn credentials in pedagogy. The first woman on record to have studied early childhood education, Emma Johnson Goulette (1876–1960), was a member of the Potawatomi tribe who attended normal school in Philadelphia, likely at the Institute for Colored Youth.[35] Goulette adopted many of the terms and ideals of German-infused pedagogical theory, often extending their application to the secondary school level. She urged for effective education in reservation schools to ensure systematic thinking, attentiveness, and self-discipline in students.[36] She also echoed Anna Brackett, a normal school educator in St. Louis, Missouri (1863–1872), by calling for high-quality training programs to produce teachers who would be "genuine civilizers."[37] Goulette taught at reservation schools for many years while intermittently working for the Bureau of Indian Affairs. Like Campbell, Terrell, and Yates, she was also an education advisor within her cultural network, serving on the board of the Society of American Indians after the turn of the twentieth century as its chair of education.

The contributions of women of color to pedagogical theory and practice is significant, in part because they expanded the reach of innovative educational methods beyond the dominant culture. In doing so they empowered their communities. In addition, they identified injustices and addressed them outright—poverty, racism, and violence—while maintaining faith in education as a means of imparting strength to fight those injustices. Goulette went even further, identifying racist policies as a direct impediment to effective education in reservation schools: "the majority of the people of the Caucasian race . . . do not recognize the ability of the Indian," she said

---

[34] See for example, Mary Church Terrell, "The Duty of the NACW to the Race," quoted in B. W. Jones, *Quest for Equality: The Life and Writings of Mary Eliza Church Terrell, 1863–1954* (New York: Carlson, 1990), 144.

[35] See Rogers, *Women Philosophers: Education and Activism*, 50–54.

[36] Emma Johnson Goulette, "Higher Standards in Civil Service for the Indian School Employee," *Quarterly Journal of the Society of the American Indian* 3 (1915): 100.

[37] Goulette, "Higher Standards," 98–99.

bluntly.[38] Campbell, Terrell, Yates, and Goulette recognized that eliminating racist pedagogical practices was essential for society's attainment of educational and social equity. For far too long, histories of both philosophy and pedagogy have rendered women like these teachers absent. Recognizing their contributions to pedagogical discourse enriches our conceptions of knowledge, will, and social and political good.

3 FEMINISM, PROGRESSIVISM, AND PHILOSOPHY—GERMAN AND AMERICAN

Feminism in nineteenth-century America was a wide-ranging movement, one that has been examined in volume after volume of text. And even though few prominent feminists in the nineteenth century cited specific sources, the intellectual roots of the movement are not difficult to trace. Two thinkers from the English- and German-speaking worlds are largely responsible for shaping feminist thought in the nineteenth century: Mary Wollstonecraft (1759–1797) in England and Amalia Holst (1758–1829) in Germany. Both rejected the gender traditionalism Rousseau put forth in *Emile*, writing their own works on education largely to counteract its influence. Both women also rejected most elements of romanticism. Instead, each incorporated Enlightenment thought into their feminism, specifically its humanistic ideals and its focus on reason. In addition, both women were influenced by French revolutionary thought, although Holst appears to have been more cautious politically.

Wollstonecraft's most influential feminist texts are *Thoughts on the Education of Daughters*, published in 1787, and *A Vindication of the Rights of Woman*, published in 1792 and translated into German the following year. Amalia Holst wrote works that make a similarly strong case for women's education and political rights: *Commentary on the Errors of Our Modern Education* (*Bemerkungen über die Fehler unserer modernen Erziehung*) in 1791 and *On the Destiny of Women for Higher Education* (*Über die Bestimmung des Weibes zur höheren Geistesbildung*) in 1802. Romanticism did not appeal to Holst as much as Enlightenment thought. She admired Theodor Gottlieb von Hippel (1741–1796) and encouraged women to read his books on marriage and education. Interestingly enough, however, in 1895 an early American doctoral recipient, Emma Rauschenbusch (1859–1940), found evidence that Hippel may have been influenced by Wollstonecraft when he revised his well-known work, *On Marriage* (*Über die Ehe*) in 1794 and 1795. Though staunchly feminist herself and fluent in German, Rauschenbusch seems to have been unaware of Amalia Holst, whose feminist arguments were so similar to Wollstonecraft's.[39]

[38] Emma Johnson Goulette, panel discussion, in *Report of the Executive Council of the Proceedings of the First Conference of the Society of American Indians, Columbus, Ohio, October 12–17, 1911* (Washington, DC: printed by the Executive Council, 1912), 101–102.

[39] Emma Rauschenbusch, *A Study of Mary Wollstonecraft and the Rights of Woman* (New York: Longman's & Green, 1895), 202–217.

It is unclear if other American-born women were familiar with Amalia Holst or other thinkers who helped lay the foundation for feminist theory in Germany, like Betty Gleim (1781–1827), an early proponent of what would become "domestic science," or writers on education, like Christine Dorothea Gurnth (1749–1813), or the German/Danish thinker Friederike Brun (1765–1835). German feminists who emigrated to the United States would have known about their intellectual foremothers, but due in part to research and writing conventions at the time, they rarely made direct references to them. Some women may have had indirect influence in America, with notices of their work appearing in feminist periodicals, like Luise Aston (1814–1871), and Fanny Lewald (1811–1889), or Louise Dittmar (1807–1884), who produced a flurry of social and political writings in the 1840s, and then disappeared from public life. Yet, there appears to have been a dearth of philosophically oriented publications by German women in the first half of the nineteenth century. Among women, there was a fear of being identified too closely with "radical" thinkers like Mary Wollstonecraft. In addition, the aftermath of the French Revolution had a chilling effect on political progressivism across Europe. In German territories, this was followed by increased censorship in the period leading up to the Prussian Revolution in 1848.[40]

In Amalia Holst and Betty Gleim, we see a dominant pair of concerns that would continue to be debated in nineteenth-century feminism. Holst's ideas were similar to those of Mary Wollstonecraft. She asserted that women were men's intellectual equals, rejected the idea of gendered virtues, and leaned toward Enlightenment individualism. At the same time Holst did not aggressively challenge gender norms in public life. Instead, she called for expanding women's access to education, appealing to their need to educate their children. In this sense she sought to reconfigure the role women played in German society in her era. Gleim's views more nearly matched the maternal feminism of Catharine Beecher. She promoted women's education, but with an emphasis on practical skills related to homemaking and childcare. Underlying these competing views are philosophical questions—about the nature of a (female) self; individual autonomy and moral agency; the nature of home, community, and family; social and political rights and duties; and the role of the state in creating a just and equitable society. The historic figures hereafter under discussion exchanged ideas within the context of informing, organizing, and educating. Given the concrete and ideological obstacles they had to overcome, theory was necessarily embedded in practice. After all, in midcentury when their work began, simply holding a women's conference was a political act—one that sometimes erupted in jeers, shouting, and threats of violence.

---

[40] Carol Strauss Sotiropolous makes a case for the impact of politics on women's expression in this era. As an example, in the 1840s, Luise Aston was sanctioned after publishing a volume of feminist poetry and was ordered to leave the city of Berlin. For biographical information see S. Friedrichsmeyer, "Luise Aston," in Encyclopedia of Revolutions of 1848, ed. James Chastain (2005), https://www.ohio.edu/chastain/ac/aston.htm; see also Gisela Brinker-Gabler, "Lewald," Jewish Women's Archive, https://jwa.org/encyclopedia/article/lewald-fanny; Dagmar Hertzog, "Louise Dittmar," in Encyclopedia of Revolutions of 1848, ed. James Chastain (2005), https://www.ohio.edu/chastain/dh/ditt.htm.

Some of the women who engaged in the lengthy struggle for women's rights remained in Germany: Louise Otto-Peters, Auguste Schmidt, Helene Lange, Marie Calm, Anna Schepeler-Lette, Jenny Hirsch, and Helene Maria Weber. They influenced their contemporaries who emigrated to the United States, however, thereby indirectly influencing American-born feminists. Those who left German territories to settle in the United States include Mathilde Anneke, Mathilde Wendt, Clara (Loew) Neymann, and Mathilde C. Weil. Both groups of women contributed to the development of feminist thought in the United States.

3.1 Feminists in Germany: Their Ideas and Influence

At the dawn of the Prussian Revolution in the 1840s, Louise Otto-Peters (1819–1895) helped launch Germany's feminist movement in Leipzig by founding two periodicals, *Women's Times* (*Frauen-Zeitung*) and *New Paths* (*Neue Bahnen*), and a women's organization, the General Union of German Women (Allgemeiner Deutscher Frauenverein; ADF). She published two book-length discussions of women's issues: *Women's Right to Earn: Glances at Women's Life Today* (*Das Recht der Frauen auf Erwerb: Blicke auf das Frauenleben der Gegenwart*, 1866) and *Women's Life in the German Reich* (*Frauenleben im Deutschen Reich*, 1876). These works were not translated in her day; thus they reached a limited American audience.

Other early members of ADF, Auguste Schmidt, Helene Lange, Marie Calm, and Minnie Cauer, also remained in Leipzig. Several of them were educators as well as feminist activists, who endorsed women's rights in the "public sphere."[41] Helene Lange and Minnie Cauer published lengthy reports on the state of women's issues in Europe and the United States in the 1870s and 1880s to keep the German feminist community up to date. After 1900, Lange published work on women's rights and a discussion of the poetry of Friedrich Schiller, one of the more philosophical poets in the romantic movement.

In Berlin, Anna Schepeler-Lette (1829–1897) led an organization that took a comprehensive approach to women's practical concerns. The Lette Society provided courses in career fields that were considered women-friendly, like arts and crafts, cooking, sewing, printing, and teaching. The organization also launched a monthly journal, *Women's Advocate* (*Frauenanwalt*) with Jenny Hirsch serving as editor. Hirsch later published a translation of John Stuart Mill's *Subjection of Woman*. Drawing on the maternal ideals of writers like Betty Gleim, overall this branch of the feminist movement was more conservative than the Leipzig branch.

Across the Atlantic, Elizabeth Cady Stanton, Susan B. Anthony, and their colleagues solicited letters from women in Europe to be read aloud at women's rights conventions.

---

[41] Ruth-Ellen B. Joeres, "Louise Otto-Peters," in "Encyclopedia of Revolutions of 1848," https://www.ohio.edu/chastain/ip/ottopetr.htm.

Helene Marie Weber (1825–?) was one of their early correspondents. Her letter to the women's convention in 1850 focused on "dress reform" because she had gained notoriety by wearing "men's clothing." Yet, while the popular press was obsessed with the tailoring of her outfits, American feminists recognized her substantive work: "Woman's Rights and Wrongs," a series of groundbreaking pamphlets in Leipzig in the mid-1840s, which appears to be no longer extant. In this set of publications, Weber covered what became familiar feminist political demands: a woman's right to own property and maintain legal rights after marriage; the liberty to pursue the career of her choice, including "men's fields," like agriculture, mechanical work, or ministry; and women's voting rights and political participation. She also made theoretical claims about gender norms versus then-common claims about women's nature. Similar to Wollstonecraft and Holst, Weber argued that women were equal to men intellectually. Yet in her view, men had more capacity for profound thought, whereas women were more perceptive and imaginative. The source of this difference in ability, however, is education. If girls had more rigorous academic training, their minds would have the freedom to expand. Related to this: women's confinement leads them to be prudish and timid. This in turn slows women's progress in their quest for equal rights. American feminists extended an open invitation to Weber for future women's rights conventions in the United States, but she does not appear to have visited the country.

3.2 German Feminists in America: Their Ideas and Influence

A number of women who emigrated to the United States actively participated in the American feminist movement and helped shape its future. German women living in America developed a strong network, but also coordinated efforts with American-born women. In 1873, the German Women's Suffrage Association (Deutscher Frauenstimmrechtsverein) met in New York. The event featured speakers from both the German and American feminist movements: Mathilde Wendt and Mathilde Anneke, along with Lucretia Mott, Elizabeth Cady Stanton, Matilda Joslyn Gage, and Susan B. Anthony. This and similar meetings helped satisfy the desire of both German and American women to join together with a sense of universal sisterhood. A few years later, Stanton and Anthony established the International Congress of Women, providing a means for feminists to gather regularly and address issues for women around the world.

Mathilde Wendt (1828–1923) and Mathilde Anneke (1817–1884) were among the most prominent German-born feminists in the United States. Wendt arrived in America just as unrest in Prussia had begun to turn into a revolt. By the 1860s she had settled near New York City, where she became editor of *Die Neue Zeit*, a weekly German-language feminist newspaper with the motto "Equal rights for all." She contributed articles on women's rights to the paper and at least one comparative discussion of the feminist movement in the United States and Europe. Wendt was also a central figure in Deutscher

Frauenstimmrechtsverein in New York, coordinating its events and acting as a liaison to American-born feminist groups in the region.

Mathilde Anneke was a "forty-eighter" who fled political unrest related to the Prussian Revolution. Like Louise Otto-Peters in Leipzig, while still living in Germany, Anneke launched a feminist newspaper, *Die Frauen-Zeitung*, in Cologne in 1848. Her husband, Fritz Anneke, was imprisoned during political unrest, and then fought alongside Carl Schurz (educator Margaretha Schurz's husband and a future US senator) in the Prussian Revolution. After the revolution failed, the couple emigrated and settled in Milwaukee, Wisconsin, where there was a thriving German community. Mathilde then launched another feminist newspaper, *Die Deutsche Frauen-Zeitung* in 1852. Like so many talented women in this era, she worked as an educator and founded a girls' school in Milwaukee, serving as its principal until her death in 1884.

Anneke was deeply committed to the feminist movement. She spoke at the women's rights convention in Boston in 1850, although she was shouted down by agitators who were both anti-feminist and xenophobic. Despite experiencing anti-immigrant hostility in this setting, years later Anneke defended Elizabeth Cady Stanton, who had sniped that women deserved to vote more than "ignorant foreigners." Anneke's response? Stanton's emphasis was on "ignorance," not on "foreigners" as such, she said. Germans can be just as ignorant or as enlightened as any other person in the country; therefore Stanton's words were harmless.[42] Leaders of the American feminist movement embraced Anneke as an intellectual and progressive woman, and she embraced the movement in return. She was an excellent orator, lectured widely, and published a number of articles about women's rights. Like Stanton and Anthony, Anneke's main focus was on women's voting rights and political participation, although she recognized that issues like education, employment, and pay equity were part of a larger puzzle, so could not be ignored.

Wendt and Anneke were among the many women who chose sides when there was a schism in the women's rights movement in the 1860s. The division was based on disagreements about two substantive issues: (1) politicians' decision to grant voting rights to African American males after the Civil War, but not to women; (2) expanding the feminist movement to address not only voting rights, but a more progressive set of issues related to marriage and sexuality. Lucy Stone and Julia Ward Howe led the American Women's Suffrage Association, based in Boston. They wanted to accept voting rights for African American males only; women could wait their turn. Wendt gravitated toward this branch. Elizabeth Cady Stanton and Susan B. Anthony led the New York branch of the feminist movement. In 1866, they had formed the Equal Suffrage Association with Frederick Douglass and other rights advocates to campaign for the voting rights of African American males and all women. Stanton and Anthony refused to support any voting rights provision in which women were not included. They also fervently believed it necessary to address a wider range of issues, such as more rights within

---

[42] Susan Piepke, *Mathilde Franciska Anneke (1817–84): The Works and Life of a German-American Activist* (New York: Peter Lang, 2006), 82–84.

marriage, which many women considered controversial. Anneke sided with the New York branch. In a letter to her husband, she announced that she represented the state of Wisconsin in their new organization, the National Women's Suffrage Association.[43]

Overall, German-born and American-born leaders of the feminist movement agreed about their shared rights struggle—a somewhat more fully developed set of the issues that Helene Maria Weber first sent to press in 1844: equal education, employment opportunity, pay equity, voting rights, and political equality. Yet German women in America had their own cultural issues to reckon with. The traditionalist motto "Kinder, Küche, Kirche" reigned in many German homes, and women were expected to defer to their husband as head of the household. Therefore, some feminists were wary of alienating conservative women in their communities.

Yet, German women saw themselves as bringing intellectual depth to the movement, namely via the legacy of the Enlightenment. For instance, Mathilde Wendt endorsed Hippel's book *On Marriage* (*Über die Ehe*), in which he affirmed expanding women's role in public life. Notably, it does not appear that Wendt cited Amalia Holst as an influence. Mathilde Weil and others also saw themselves as more progressive than American-born women. Their arguments for women's employment and pay equity were frequently paired with a call for labor rights and socialist economic policies. Clara (Loew) Neymann (1840–1931) went further, linking the "private" realm of home and family to "public" social and political issues. Economic disparities between a husband and wife creates a power imbalance in the home, she said, which leads to inequities in both home and society.[44]

To a considerable degree, German women saw themselves as partners and contributors to the American feminist movement. With the cultural hierarchies in place in this era, women from western Europe with fluency in English often held an elite status in American middle- and upper-middle class society. This was especially true of German women, who came from the country of the Enlightenment, romanticism, philosophical idealism, and progressive pedagogical theories. German feminists were both aware of their cultural legacy and devoted to moving women's agenda forward, as members of the movement in the United States, or as international partners in Europe.

4 THE CENTURY COMES TO A CLOSE

In the last decades of the nineteenth century, intellectually minded women gained a greater range of career options. Within academic philosophy, American women began earning doctoral degrees in 1880, and German women began doing so after 1900. However, the vast majority of academic women in both countries near the turn of the

---

[43] Michaela Bank, *Women of Two Countries: German-American Women, Women's Rights, and Nativism, 1848–1890* (New York: Berghahn Books, 2012), 52.

[44] Bank, *Women of Two Countries*, 57–58.

twentieth century studied the ideas of men in western philosophy. There is no evidence they studied or were influenced by German women philosophers. Several American academic women studied in Germany near the turn of the twentieth century.[45] Yet they do not seem to have made or maintained connections with their female contemporaries in Germany; perhaps correspondence will be unearthed in the future to demonstrate German-American ties among academic women.

Some of Germany's academically minded women traveled to the United States, however. Marianne Weber (1870–1954) published *Fichte's Socialism and Its Relation to Marxist Doctrine* (*Fichtes Sozialismus und sein Verhältnis zur Marxschen Doktrin*) in 1900, followed by nearly a dozen feminist works. In the early 1900s, she and her husband, the sociologist Max Weber, traveled to the United States, where they met Jane Addams and Florence Kelley. Helene Stöcker (1869–1943) earned a doctorate at the University of Bern in 1901. She later gained prominence as a women's reproductive health advocate, establishing ties with the American birth control pioneer Margaret Sanger. Alice Salomon (1872–1948) began her career as a social reformer fighting child poverty and neglect before earning a doctorate in economics at Humboldt University in Berlin in 1908. Both Stöcker and Salomon were active in the international women's peace movement in the 1910s. Both later fled Nazi Germany and found refuge in the United States, where they spent the remainder of their lives. Women now considered influential philosophers in Germany did not gain recognition in the United States until after 1920; namely, Helene von Druskowitz (1856–1918, born in Austria), Lou Andreas-Salomé (1861–1937, born in Russia), Hedwig Conrad-Martius (1888–1966), and Edith Stein (1891–1942, born in Poland).

As women continued to overcome barriers to achievement before and after 1900, they developed global networks, meeting to confer, compare, and draw up strategies for change. As the international movement gained momentum, Mary Church Terrell, an educator, feminist, and peace activist, gave a keynote address to the International Council of Women in Berlin, "The Progress of Colored Women" ("Die Fortschritte der farbigen Frauen"). She delivered the speech in German and used the opportunity not simply to highlight African American achievement, but also to awaken her audience to parallels between racism in the United States, anti-Semitism in Europe, and oppression under British colonial rule. When she toured Germany as a young woman, Terrell had considered staying in that country. She was well aware of Germany's intellectual legacy: its Enlightenment ideals, its romantic optimism, its pedagogical innovations, and its feminist activism. Part of her aim with this speech was to appeal to her listeners' sense of humanity and to inspire their commitment to justice. Over the next decade, Terrell joined other women in the United States, in Germany, and throughout Europe to initiate a global pacifist movement and establish the Women's International League for Peace and Freedom in 1915. As we know, World War I broke out, however, and world

---

[45] See Dorothy Rogers, *Women Philosophers*, vol. 2, *cEntering Academia in Nineteenth-Century America* (London: Bloomsbury, 2021).

politics shifted dramatically. The relationship between the United States and Germany would change as well, even in intellectual life.

References

Allen, Ann Taylor. *The Transatlantic Kindergarten: Education and Women's Movements in Germany and the United States*. New York: Oxford University Press, 2017.

Anderson, Bonnie. "Frauenemancipation and Beyond: The Use of the Concept of Emancipation by Early European Feminists." Paper presented at third annual Gilder Lehrman Center International Conference, Yale University, October 2001.

Argersinger, Jana, and Phyllis Cole, eds. *Toward a Female Genealogy of Transcendentalism*. Athens: University of Georgia Press, 2014, 89–93.

Bank, Michaela. *Women of Two Countries: German-American Women, Women's Rights, and Nativism, 1848–1890*. New York: Berghahn Books, 2012.

Beecher, Catharine. *Educational Reminiscences and Suggestions*. New York: J. B. Ford, 1874.

Brentano von Arnim, Bettina. *Diary of a Child*. Translated by the author. Bayer: Staatsbibliothek, 1838.

Brentano von Arnim, Bettina. *Günderode*. Translated by Margaret Fuller. Boston: E. P. Peabody, 1842.

Brinker-Gabler, Gisela. "Fanny Lewald." Jewish Women's Archive. https://jwa.org/encyclopedia/article/lewald-fanny. December 1999.

Carlyle, Thomas. "Varnhagen von Ense's Memoirs." In *The Modern British Essayists*. Vol. 5. *Critical and Miscellaneous Essays*, 535–546. Philadelphia: A. Hart, 1854.

Carter, Patricia. *Everybody's Paid but the Teacher: The Teaching Profession and the Women's Movement*. New York: Teachers College Press, 2002.

Cole, Phyllis. *Mary Moody Emerson and the Origins of Transcendentalism*. New York: Oxford University Press, 1998.

Coppin, Fanny Jackson. *Reminiscences of School Life and Hints on Teaching*. Philadelphia: AME Books, 1913.

Diethe, Carol. *Towards Emancipation: German Women Writers of the Nineteenth Century*. New York: Berghahn Books, 1998.

Edwards, Elizabeth. *Women in Teacher Training Colleges, 1900–1960: A Culture of Femininity*. London: Routledge, 2004.

Ezekiel, Anna. "Read Günderrode." ACEzekiel. https://acezekiel.com/__bibliography/.

Ezekiel, Anna. "The Woman at the Heart of German Romantic Philosophy." December 10, 2020. Genealogies of Modernity. https://genealogiesofmodernity.org/journal/2020/11/30/gnderrode.

Foreign Quarterly Review, American edition (author unknown). "Rahel [Varnehagen]." [New York: Jemima Mason, publisher, vol. 26 (April 1841): 30–40.

Friedman, Randy. "Religious Self-Reliance." *Pluralist* 7, no. 1 (Spring 2012): 27–53.

Friedrichsmeyer, S. "Luise Aston." In Encyclopedia of Revolutions of 1848, ed. James Chastain. 2005. https://www.ohio.edu/chastain/ac/aston.htm.

Fuller, Margaret. "Bettine Brentano and Her Friend Günderode." *Dial* 2, no. 3 (January 1842): 313–357.

Fuller, Margaret. "Goethe." *Dial* 2, no. 1 (July 1841): 1–41.

Fuller, Margaret. "The Modern Jews." *New-York Daily Tribune*, April 21, 1845.

Fuller, Margaret. *Woman in the Nineteenth Century*. In *The Portable Margaret Fuller*, edited by Mary Kelly. New York: Penguin, 1994.

Goodman, Katherine R. *Amazons and Apprentices: Women and the German Parnassus in the Early Enlightenment*. Rochester, NY: Camden House, 1999.

Goulette, Emma Johnson. "Higher Standards in Civil Service for the Indian School Employee." *Quarterly Journal of the Society of American Indians* 3, no. 2 (April 1915): 99–102.

Goulette, Emma Johnson. Panel Discussion. In *Report of the Executive Council of the Proceedings of the First Conference of the Society of American Indians (SAI), Columbus, Ohio, October 12–17, 1911*, 101–102. Washington, DC: Printed by SAI Executive Council, 1912.

Günderrode, Karoline von. *Poetic Fragments*. Edited and translated by Anna Ezekiel. New York: State University of New York Press, 2016.

Haertel, Martin Henry. "German Literature in American Magazines, 1846–1880." PhD diss., University of Wisconsin, 1906.

Hahn, Barbara. "Rahel Levin Varnhagen." Jewish Women's Archive. https://jwa.org/encyclopedia/article/varnhagen-rahel-levin, June 2021.

Hertz, Deborah. "Dorothea Mendelssohn Schlegel." Jewish Women's Encyclopedia. https://jwa.org/encyclopedia/article/schlegel-dorothea-mendelssohn.

Hertzog, Dagmar. "Louise Dittmar," in "Encyclopedia of Revolutions of 1848," https://www.ohio.edu/chastain/ip/ottopetr.htm (2004).

Higginson, Thomas Wentworth. *Margaret Fuller Ossoli*. Boston: Houghton Mifflin, 1884.

Hoffman, Nancy. *Woman's True Profession: Voices from the History of Teaching*. Cambridge, MA: Harvard University Press, 2003.

Holmgren, Janet Besserer. *Women Writers in Schiller's "Hören": Patrons, Petticoats, and the Promotion of Weimar Classicism*. Newark: University of Delaware Press, 2007.

Hurth, Elisabeth. "William and Ralph Waldo Emerson and the Problem of the Lord's Supper." *Church History* 62, no. 2 (1993): 190–206.

Jones, Beverly Washington. *Quest for Equality: The Life and Writings of Mary Eliza Church Terrell*. New York: Carlson, 1990.

Joeres, Ruth-Ellen B. "Louise Otto-Peters," in "Encyclopedia of Revolutions of 1848," https://www.ohio.edu/chastain/ip/ottopetr.htm (2004).

Key, Ellen. *Rahel Varnhagen: A Portrait*, trans. Arthur Chater. New York: Putnam, 1913.

Lewis, Arthur O., W. Lamarr Kopp, and Edward J. Danis, eds. *Anglo-German and American-German Crosscurrents*. Vol 4. Lanham, MD: University Press of America, 1990.

Mercer, Margaret. *Popular Lectures on Ethics*. Petersburg, VA: Ruffin, 1841.

Moland, Lydia L. "Lydia Maria Child on German Philosophy and American Slavery." *British Journal for the History of Philosophy* 29, no. 2 (2021): 259–274.

Paulin, Roger. *The Life of August Wilhelm Schlegel: Cosmopolitan of Art and Poetry*. Cambridge: Open Book, 2016.

Perkins, Linda M. "Heed Life's Demands: The Educational Philosophy of Fanny Jackson Coppin." *Journal of Negro Education* 51, no. 3 (1982): 181–190.

Piepke, Susan. *Mathilde Franziska Anneke (1817–84): The Works and Life of a German-American Activist*. New York: Peter Lang, 2006.

"Rahel Levin and Her Times." *Eclectic Magazine* 65, no. 1 (January 1897): 2–37.

Rauschenbusch, Emma. *A Study of Mary Wollstonecraft and the Rights of Woman*. New York: Longman & Green, 1895.

Robbins, Jean. "Black Club Women's Purposes for Establishing Kindergartens in the Progressive Era, 1896–1906." PhD diss., Loyola University, 2011.

Rogers, Dorothy. *America's First Women Philosophers: Transplanting Hegel, 1860–1925*. London: Continuum, 2005.

Rogers, Dorothy. *Women Philosophers*. Vol. 1. *Education and Activism in Nineteenth-Century America*. London: Bloomsbury, 2020.

Rogers, Dorothy. *Women Philosophers*. Vol. 2. *Entering Academia in Nineteenth-Century America*. London: Bloomsbury, 2021.

Shelela, Anja. "'Meine kühnsten Wünsche und Ideen': Women, Space, Place, and Mobility in Late Eighteenth- and Nineteenth-Century Germany." PhD diss., University of Minnesota, 2014.

Snyder, Agnes. *Dauntless Women in Childhood Education*. Washington, DC: Association of Childhood Education, 1972.

Solomon, Barbara Miller. *In the Company of Educated Women: A History of Women and Higher Education in America*. New Haven: Yale University Press, 1986.

Sotiropoulos, Carol Strauss. *Early Feminists and the Education Debates*. Madison, NJ: Fairleigh Dickinson University Press, 2007.

Sotiropoulos, Carol Strauss. "Fuller, Goethe, Bettine: Cultural Transfer and Imagined German Womanhood." In *Toward a Female Genealogy of Transcendentalism*, edited by Jana Argersinger and Phyllis Cole, 80–101. Atlanta: University of Georgia Press, 2014.

Sotiropoulos, Carol Strauss. "Scandal Writ Large in the Wake of the French Revolution: The Case of Amalia Holst." *Women in German Yearbook* 20 (2004): 98–121.

Tilton, Eleanor M. ed. *The Letters of Ralph Waldo Emerson*. Vol. 7. *1807–1844*. New York: Columbia University Press, 1941.

Wagner, Ulrike. "Transcendentalism and the Power of Philology: Herder, Schleiermacher, and the Transformation of Biblical Scholarship in New England." *Amerikastudien/American Studies* 57, no. 3 (2012): 419–445.

Waldschmidt-Nelson, Britta, and Anja Schüler, eds. *Forging Bonds across Borders: Transatlantic Collaborations for Women's Rights and Social Justice in the Long Nineteenth Century*. Washington, DC: German Historical Institute, 2017.

Whittier, John Greenleaf. "To _____." In *The Poetical Works of John Greenleaf Whittier*, 331–34. Boston: James R. Osgood & Company, 1873.

Index

For the benefit of digital users, indexed terms that span two pages (e.g., 52–53) may, on occasion, appear on only one of those pages.